CALIFORNIA
HIKING

FOGHORN  OUTDOORS

CALIFORNIA HIKING

The Complete Guide to
More Than 1,000 of the Best Hikes

FIFTH EDITION

Tom Stienstra • Ann Marie Brown

AVALON
TRAVEL
publishing

FOGHORN OUTDOORS: CALIFORNIA HIKING,
The Complete Guide to More Than 1,000 of the Best Hikes

5th EDITION
Tom Stienstra • Ann Marie Brown

Published by
Avalon Travel Publishing, Inc.
5855 Beaudry St.
Emeryville, CA 94608, USA

ISBN: 1-56691-246-6
ISSN: 1531-8117

Editor: Marisa Solís
Copy Editor: Carolyn Perkins
Index: Lynne Lipkind
Graphics: Bob Race
Production: Carey Wilson, David Hurst
Map Editor: Mike Ferguson
Cartography: Mike Morgenfeld

Front cover photo: Lassen Volcanic National Park/
        Laurence Parent © 2001

Printing History
1st edition—January 1994
5th edition—January 2001
5 4 3 2 1

Please send all comments, corrections,
additions, amendments, and critiques to:
FOGHORN OUTDOORS: CALIFORNIA HIKING
Fifth Edition
AVALON TRAVEL PUBLISHING, INC.
5855 BEAUDRY ST.
EMERYVILLE, CA 94608, USA
email: info@travelmatters.com
www.foghorn.com

Printed in the U.S.A. by R.R. Donnelley
Distributed in the United States and Canada by Publishers Group West.

ABOUT THIS BOOK

California Hiking features the Golden State's best 1,000 trails, including hundreds of little-known spots in all regions of the state. It was produced with the hope that it will quickly become your hiking bible.

This new fifth edition has been revised and updated to provide the most up-to-date information available. Some 2,500 updates and upgrades have been made to the book. The authors hiked many thousands of miles to cover their respective regions of California. In addition, hundreds of rangers and field scouts helped to polish the final product by reviewing trail descriptions line by line. One major alteration to this edition is that trail directions have been reworked as precisely as possible, with mileages calculated to the nearest tenth of a mile, so that the book can be converted electronically and used with a Palm Pilot and global positioning system (GPS).

California Hiking features 350 trails within 90 minutes of San Francisco and Los Angeles, along with an additional 650 trails sprinkled across the state. The hikes detail the most beautiful regions across 20 million acres of national forest, 18.5 million acres of Bureau of Land Management property, 100 state parks, 53 federal wilderness areas, 12 national parks, and dozens of regional and county parks.

A wide variety of hikes is included, ranging from 10-minute walks to lookouts and waterfalls to week-long trips into remote California backcountry. Many of the featured hikes range in length from one to four hours, perfect for most people looking for an afternoon of peace. Every section of the Pacific Crest Trail in California is also included, covering more than 1,700 trail miles.

The book also features a hiker-friendly format and easy-to-use map grid system. Any reader will be able to find the location of a quality hike in virtually any part of the state in less than 10 seconds. Each listing includes snapshot ratings for trail beauty and difficulty, as well as the estimated length and time required for each hike. In addition, precise, easy-to-follow directions to each trailhead are provided, along with special trail rules, updated access fees, information about permits, maps, and phone contacts, and a detailed description of each hike. There are 58 detailed maps, dozens of photographs taken on the trail, and a detailed, 40-page index.

We believe that the best of California's great outdoors is now in the palm of your hands. Our best advice is to pick a trail and go for a hike.

TABLE OF CONTENTS

HOW TO USE THIS BOOK. xii

BEATING THE TIME TRAP. xvi

BEST HIKES xvii
   Waterfalls; Wildflowers; Butt-Kickers; Views/Scenic Overlooks; Meadows;
   Swimming Holes; Self-Guided Nature Walks; Redwoods/Sequoia; Short
   Backpack Trips; One-Way Hikes with Shuttle; Beach/Coast Walks; Wildlife;
   Bird-Watching; Summits; Island Walks; Wheelchair Accessible; Desert
   Terrain; For Kids; Fall Colors

NORTHERN CALIFORNIA 24

Chapter A0 24

Chapter A1 38
 PACIFIC CREST TRAIL (PCT) SECTION OVERVIEW. 53

Chapter A2 56

Chapter A3 62

Chapter A4 71

Chapter B0 75

Chapter B1 84
 PACIFIC CREST TRAIL (PCT) SECTION OVERVIEW. 98

Chapter B2 100
 PACIFIC CREST TRAIL (PCT) SECTION OVERVIEW. 122

Chapter B3 125
 PACIFIC CREST TRAIL (PCT) SECTION OVERVIEW. 138

Chapter B4 141

Chapter C0 148

Chapter C1 160

Chapter C2 170

Chapter C3 178
 PACIFIC CREST TRAIL (PCT) SECTION OVERVIEW. 195

Chapter C4 200

Chapter D0 204

Chapter D1 212

Chapter D2 220

Chapter D3 225
Chapter D4 241
PACIFIC CREST TRAIL (PCT) SECTION OVERVIEW 278

Chapter E1-Marin 283
Chapter E1-San Francisco Peninsula 322
Chapter E1-East Bay 344
Chapter E1-South Bay 373
Chapter E2 403
Chapter E3 408
Chapter E4 412
PACIFIC CREST TRAIL (PCT) SECTION OVERVIEW 458

Chapter E5 463

CENTRAL CALIFORNIA 477
Chapter F1 477
Chapter F2 497
Chapter F3 505
Chapter F4 508
Chapter F5 524
PACIFIC CREST TRAIL (PCT) SECTION OVERVIEW 564

Chapter F6 567
Chapter G1 572
Chapter G2 577
Chapter G3 587
Chapter G4 591
Chapter G5 594
PACIFIC CREST TRAIL (PCT) SECTION OVERVIEW 627

Chapter G6 630
Chapter G7 637
Chapter H2 642
Chapter H3 649
Chapter H4 661
PACIFIC CREST TRAIL (PCT) SECTION OVERVIEW 669

Chapter H5 671
PACIFIC CREST TRAIL (PCT) SECTION OVERVIEW 675

Chapter H6 680
Chapter H7 684
Chapter H8 688

SOUTHERN CALIFORNIA 693
Chapter I2 693
Chapter I3 697
Chapter I4 703
Chapter I5 719
   PACIFIC CREST TRAIL (PCT) SECTION OVERVIEW 741

Chapter I6 744
   PACIFIC CREST TRAIL (PCT) SECTION OVERVIEW 760

Chapter I7 764
Chapter J5 775
Chapter J6 780
   PACIFIC CREST TRAIL (PCT) SECTION OVERVIEW 797

Chapter J7 802
Chapter J8 810

RESOURCE GUIDE 814
   National Forests; State Parks; National Parks & Reservations; Bureau of
   Land Management; U.S. Army Corps of Engineers; State Forests; County/
   Regional Park Departments; State and Federal Offices; Information
   Services; Map Companies

INDEX 827

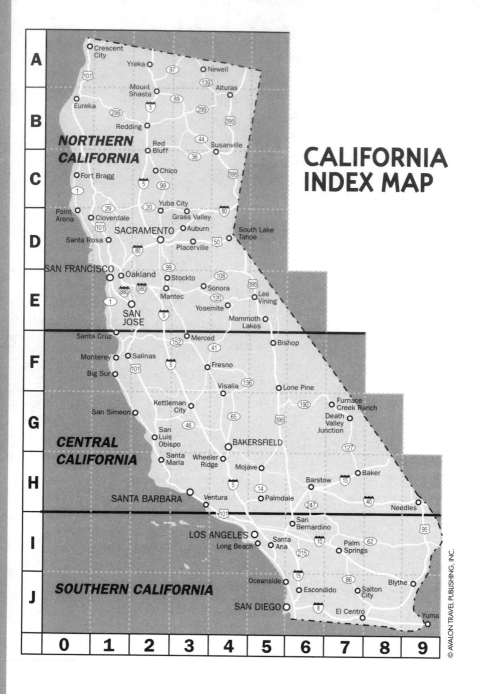

CALIFORNIA
INDEX MAP

© AVALON TRAVEL PUBLISHING, INC.

MAPS

NORTHERN CALIFORNIA

MAP A0 26
MAP A1 40
MAP A2 58
MAP A3 64
MAP A4 72
MAP B0 76
MAP B1 86
MAP B2 102
MAP B3 126
MAP B4 142
MAP C0 150
MAP C1 162
MAP C2 172
MAP C3 180
MAP C4 202
MAP D0 206
MAP D1 214
MAP D2 222
MAP D3 226
MAP D4 242
MAP E1-Marin 284
MAP E1-San Francisco 324
MAP E1-East Bay 346
MAP E1-South Bay 374
MAP E2 404
MAP E3 410
MAP E4 414
MAP E5 464

CENTRAL CALIFORNIA

MAP F1 478
MAP F2 498
MAP F3 506
MAP F4 510
MAP F5 526
MAP F6 568
MAP G1 574
MAP G2 578
MAP G3 588
MAP G4 592
MAP G5 596
MAP G6 632
MAP G7 638
MAP H2 644
MAP H3 650
MAP H4 662
MAP H5 672
MAP H6 682
MAP H7 686
MAP H8 690

SOUTHERN CALIFORNIA

MAP I2 694
MAP I3 698
MAP I4 704
MAP I5 720
MAP I6 746
MAP I7 766
MAP J5 776
MAP J6 782
MAP J7 804
MAP J8 812

HOW TO USE THIS BOOK

California Hiking is divided into three sections: Northern, Central, and Southern California. These sections are further divided into grids with maps that show where each trailhead is located.

For Northern California trails: see pages 24–476 (maps A0-E5)
For Central California trails: see pages 477–692 (maps F1-H8)
For Southern California trails: see pages 693–813 (maps I2-J8)
You can search for the perfect hike in two ways:

- If you know the name of the specific trail you'd like to hike, or the name of the surrounding geographical area (town, national park, national forest, state park, lake, river, etc.), look it up in the index beginning on page 827 and turn to the corresponding page.
- If you want to find out about hiking possibilities in a particular part of the state, use the state map on page x or in the back of this book. Find the zone where you'd like to hike (such as A0 in Northern California or I2 in Southern California), then turn to the corresponding pages.

The San Francisco Bay Area has been divided even further into four smaller maps, because of the concentration of trails in that area. You will find Marin County on pages 283–321, the San Francisco Peninsula on pages 322–343, the East Bay Area on pages 344–372, and the South Bay Area on pages 373–402.

What the Ratings Mean

Every trail in this book has been rated on a scale of 1 to 10 for its overall appeal, and on a scale of 1 to 5 for difficulty.

The overall rating is based largely on scenic beauty, but it also takes into account how crowded the trail is and whether or not you'll hear the noise of nearby civilization.

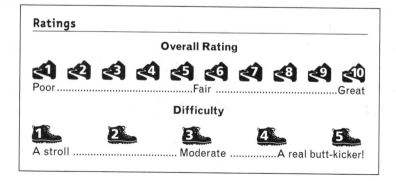

Ratings

Overall Rating

Poor...Fair...Great

Difficulty

A stroll....................................Moderate..............A real butt-kicker!

The difficulty rating is based on the steepness of the trail and how difficult it is to traverse. A flat, open, clearly marked trail is rated 🥾 , while a cross-country scramble with huge elevation gains is rated 🥾 .

Hiking the Pacific Crest Trail (PCT) and the John Muir Trail (JMT)

In addition to describing 1,000 individual hikes, this book features the entire 1,700 miles of the Pacific Crest Trail (PCT) in California and the 211-mile John Muir Trail (JMT). The PCT is split into 48 sections throughout *California Hiking* and can be found in chapters A1, B1, B2, B3, C3, D3, D4, E4, F5, G5, H4, H5, I5, I6, and J6. The JMT is broken into four sections in this book and can be found in chapters E4 and F5.

The 48 PCT sections are arranged in chapters according to the location of their major trailheads. PCT sections can be easily found on the maps, in the chapter tables of contents, and in the chapters, since they are always referred to by the initials PCT.

Because the PCT is usually hiked from south to north, you will find the first section (PCT-1) in chapter J6 and the last section (PCT-48) in chapter A1. The segments are grouped together at the end of the chapters in which they appear.

Trail Names, Distances, and Times

Each trail in this book has a number, name, and mileage listing and the approximate amount of time needed to complete the hike. The trail's number allows you to find it easily on the corresponding chapter map. The trail name is either the actual name of the trail (as listed on signposts and maps) or a name we gave to a series of connected trails or a loop trail. In these cases, the trail name is taken from the major destination or focal point of the hike. All mileages and approximate times refer to round-trip travel, unless the route is specifically noted as one way. In the case of one-way hikes, a car shuttle is advised.

Wheelchair Users

We have designated a list of user groups for each trail; under this category, we have attempted to list as much information about wheelchair facilities and access as possible. Since definitions of wheelchair accessibility and facilities vary, please call the contact number to ensure that your particular needs will be met.

Maps

For every trail in *California Hiking*, we provide the names of the U.S. Geologic Survey (USGS) topographic maps that feature the trail. These maps are sold by major sporting goods stores, outdoor retailers, and the USGS. To order maps from the USGS or to request a catalog of its maps, write to

U.S. Geologic Survey
Branch of Information Services
Box 25286, Federal Center
Denver, CO 80225

Each map listed in this book covers 7.5 minutes of longitude and latitude and costs $4, plus a $3.50 handling fee per order, no matter how many maps you order. You may order maps by phone or fax using a credit card. To reach the USGS, phone (888) 275-8747 or (303) 202-4700, or fax (303) 202-4693; website: earthexplorer.usgs.gov.

A private company called Map Link also carries a complete line of USGS topographic maps for California. While these maps cost slightly more than ordering them directly from the USGS, Map Link provides a good option if the USGS is out of stock. To reach Map Link, phone (805) 692-6777 or write to
Map Link
30 South La Patera Lane, #5
Santa Barbara, CA 93117

Our Commitment

We are committed to making *California Hiking* the most accurate, thorough, and enjoyable hiking guide to the state. With this fifth edition you can rest assured that every hiking trail in this book has been carefully reviewed and accompanied by the most up-to-date information. Be aware that with the passing of time some of the fees listed herein may have changed, and that a change in season or weather patterns may have had ill effects on a trail. With that in mind, or if you have a specific need or concern, it's best to call the location ahead of time.

If you would like to comment on the book, whether it's to suggest a trail we overlooked, or to let us know about any noteworthy experience—good or bad—that occurred while using *California Hiking* as your guide, we would appreciate hearing from you. Please address correspondence to:

Foghorn Outdoors: California Hiking, 5th edition
Avalon Travel Publishing
5855 Beaudry Street
Emeryville, CA 94608
U.S.A

email: info@travelmatters.com

ACKNOWLEDGMENTS

National Forests, Pacific Region Headquarters
Matt Mathes

Klamath National Forest
Jim Stout, Goosenest Ranger District
Pat Garrahan, Happy Camp Ranger District
Jackie Branson and Al Buckner,
    Salmon River Ranger District
Sandy Ratliff, Scott River Ranger District

Lassen National Forest
Jani Ackley, Almanor Ranger District
Tami Taylor, Hat Creek Ranger District

Mendocino National Forest
Joe Miranda, Stonyford Ranger Station

Modoc National Forest
Jamie Nield, Devils Garden Ranger District
Lorraine Worley,
    Doublehead Ranger District
Lindsay Pulliam,
    Warner Mountain Ranger District

Plumas National Forest
Sharleeen Bloom,
    Beckwourth Ranger District
Gary Rogers, Feather River Ranger District

Shasta-Trinity National Forest
Rod Duncan, Big Bar Ranger District
Pat Smith, Hayford Ranger District
Barbara Paolinetti,
    McCloud Ranger District
Don Lee, Mount Shasta Ranger District
Fay Mok and Marla Schardin,
    Weaverville Ranger District
Ken Graves, Yolla Bolla Ranger District

Smith River National Recreation Area
Phil Bono and Don Pass

Tahoe National Forest
Steve Raymond,
    Downieville Ranger District
Jan Welsh, Foresthill Ranger District
Bill Haire, Nevada City Ranger District

California State Parks
Vic Maris, Superintendent of Park
    Operations
Dick Goss, Lake Earl State Park

East Bay Regional Park District
Ned MacKay
Joe DiDonato

Bureau of Land Management
Sky Murphy, Arcata Office

Fieldscouts
Stephani Stienstra, Michael Furniss,
    Bob Stienstra, Jr., Jeffrey Patty,
Robyn Schlueter, Janet Tuttle, Eleanor
    Stienstra, Robert G. Stienstra,
    Sr., Glenn Schwarz, David Dayton, Lee
    Dittman, Rick Nelson, Don Vachini,
    Bob Simms, Pete Cafone, Phil Ford,
    Jim McDaniel

CREDITS

Senior Research Editor:
    Stephani Cruickshank

Beating the Time Trap

If the great outdoors is so great, then why don't people enjoy it more? The answer is because of the time trap, and I will tell you exactly how to beat it.

For many, the biggest problem is finding the time to go, whether it is camping, hiking, fishing, boating, backpacking, biking, or even just for a good drive in the country. The solution? Well, believe it or not, the answer is to treat your fun just as you treat your work, and I'll tell you how.

Consider how you treat your job: Always on time? Go there every day you are scheduled? Do whatever it takes to get there and get it done? Right? No foolin' that's right. Now imagine if you took the same approach to the outdoors. Suddenly your life would be a heck of a lot better.

The secret is to schedule all of your outdoor activities. For instance, I go fishing every Thursday evening, hiking every Sunday morning, and on an overnight trip every new moon (when stargazing is best). No matter what, I'm going. Just like going to work, I've scheduled it. The same approach works with longer adventures. The only reason I was able to hike from Mount Whitney to Yosemite was that I scheduled three weeks to do it. It was so much fun that I then hiked Yosemite to Tahoe a few years later. You know how I found the time? Right—I scheduled it. It's a great way to beat the time trap. It works especially well when planning trips with loved ones or best friends: Because once the dates are locked in, they can't get out of it. The reason I spend 125 to 150 days a year in the field is that I schedule them. In my top year, I had nearly 200 days where at least part of the day was enjoyed taking part in outdoor recreation.

If you get out your calendar and write in the exact dates you are going, then you'll go. If you don't, you won't. Suddenly, with only a minor change in your life plan, you can be living the life you were previously dreaming about.

See you out there.

—Tom Stienstra

BEST HIKES

TOM STIENSTRA

THE SKYLINE-TO-SEA TRAIL,
IN BIG BASIN REDWOODS STATE PARK,
IS ONE OF THE BEST HIKES IN THE STATE.

Best Hikes

Can't decide where to hike this weekend? Here are our picks for the best hikes in California in 19 different categories:

Waterfalls

Bridalveil Fall, Yosemite National Park, Chapter E4, page 449.

Lower Yosemite Fall, Yosemite National Park, Chapter E4, page 444.

Mist Trail and John Muir Loop to Nevada and Vernal Falls, Yosemite National Park, Chapter E4, page 446.

Feather Falls National Recreation Trail, Plumas National Forest, Chapter C3, page 186.

Burney Falls Trail, McArthur-Burney Falls State Park, Chapter B3, page 128.

Grouse Falls, Tahoe National Forest, Chapter D3, page 237.

Illilouette Fall, Yosemite National Park, Chapter E4, page 455.

Chilnualna Falls, Yosemite National Park, Chapter E4, page 456.

Waterwheel Falls, Yosemite National Park, Chapter E4, page 438.

Rainbow Falls Trail, Devils Postpile National Monument, Chapter E5, page 471.

Tokopah Falls, Sequoia National Park, Chapter F5, page 560.

McWay Falls Overlook, Julia Pfeiffer Burns State Park, Chapter F1, page 494.

Hetch Hetchy Reservoir, Yosemite National Park, Chapter E4, page 427.

Wildflowers

Antelope Valley Poppy Reserve Loop, Chapter H5, page 674.

Vidette Meadow (PCT-21/JMT-1), John Muir Wilderness, Chapter F5, page 564.

Lundy Lake Trailhead, Hoover Wilderness, Chapter E5, page 465.

Hites Cove, Sierra National Forest, Chapter E4, page 448.

Path of the Padres, San Luis Reservoir State Recreation Area, Chapter F2, page 500.

Alamere Falls Trail, Point Reyes National Seashore, Chapter E1-Marin, page 289.

Grass Valley Loop, Anthony Chabot Regional Park, Chapter E1-East Bay, page 359.

Montaña de Oro Bluffs Trail, Montaña de Oro State Park, Chapter G2, page 582.

Butt-Kickers

Mount Whitney Trail, John Muir Wilderness, Chapter F5, page 562.

Shasta Summit Trail, Mount Shasta Wilderness, Chapter B2, page 108.

Muir Pass (PCT-21/JMT-1), John Muir Wilderness, Chapter F5, page 564.

Half Dome, Yosemite National Park, Chapter E4, page 447.

Rooster Comb Loop, Henry W. Coe State Park, Chapter E1-South Bay, page 401.

Beacroft Trail, Tahoe National Forest, Chapter D3, page 233.

Devils Punchbowl, Siskiyou Wilderness, Chapter A1, page 42.

White Mountain Peak Trail, Inyo National Forest, Chapter E5, page 475.

Alta Peak, Sequoia National Park, Chapter F5, page 558.

Vivian Creek Trail to Mount San Gorgonio, San Gorgonio Wilderness, Chapter I6, page 755.
Mount Baldy, Angeles National Forest, Chapter I5, page 734.
Lookout Peak, Kings Canyon National Park, Chapter F5, page 539.

Views/Scenic Overlooks
Aerial Tramway to San Jacinto Peak, Mount San Jacinto State Park and Wilderness, Chapter I6, page 755.
Panorama Trail, Yosemite National Park, Chapter E4, page 454.
Mount Whitney Trail, John Muir Wilderness, Chapter F5, page 562.
Deadfall Lakes Trail (to Mount Eddy), Shasta-Trinity National Forest, Chapter B2, page 104.
High Sierra Trail to Hamilton Lake, Sequoia National Park, Chapter F5, page 554.
Moro Rock, Sequoia National Park, Chapter F5, page 553.
Upper Soda Springs Trailhead(Thousand Island Lake), Ansel Adams Wilderness, Chapter E5, page 470.
Lassen Summit Trail, Lassen Volcanic National Park, Chapter B3, page 133.
North Ridge/Sunset Trail, Angel Island State Park, Chapter E1-Marin, page 320.
Sentinel Dome, Yosemite National Park, Chapter E4, page 451.
Needles Lookout, Sequoia National Forest, Chapter G5, page 615.
Little Baldy, Sequoia National Park, Chapter F5, page 548.
Selden Pass, Whitney Portal to Lake Thomas Edison (PCT-21/JMT-1), John Muir Wilderness, Chapter F5, page 564.
Fresno Dome, Sierra National Forest, Chapter F4, page 512.
Eagle Peak, Yosemite National Park, Chapter E4, page 444.
Rubicon Trail, D.L. Bliss State Park, Chapter D4, page 252.
Mount Baldy, Angeles National Forest, Chapter I5, page 734.
Devils Slide Trail to Tahquitz Peak, San Jacinto Wilderness, Chapter I6, page 759.

Meadows
McGurk Meadow, Yosemite National Park, Chapter E4, page 450.
Vidette Meadow (PCT-21/JMT-1), John Muir Wilderness, Chapter F5, page 564.
Panther Meadows, Mount Shasta Wilderness, Chapter B2, page 109.
Grass Valley Loop, Anthony Chabot Regional Park, Chapter E1-East Bay, page 359.
Casa Vieja Meadow, Golden Trout Wilderness, Chapter G5, page 615.
Manter Meadow Loop, Dome Land Wilderness, Chapter G5, page 625.
Zumwalt Meadow Loop, Kings Canyon National Park, Chapter F5, page 541.

Swimming Holes
Toad Lake Trail, Shasta-Trinity National Forest, Chapter B2, page 113.
Lower McCloud Falls, Shasta-Trinity National Forest, Chapter B2, page 118.
Paradise Creek Trail, Sequoia National Park, Chapter F5, page 552.

(CONTINUED ON NEXT PAGE)

BEST HIKES: Swimming Holes (CONTINUED)

Green Valley Falls, Cuyamaca Rancho State Park, Chapter J6, page 793.
Santa Paula Canyon, Los Padres National Forest, Chapter H4, page 667.
Indian Pools, Sierra National Forest, Chapter F4, page 517.
Alder Creek Trail, Sequoia National Forest, Chapter G5, page 619.
Big Falls and Little Falls, Santa Lucia Wilderness, Chapter G2, page 583.
Cedar Creek and the Fishbowls, Sespe Wilderness, Chapter H4, page 664.

Self-Guided Nature Walks

McCloud Nature Trail, Shasta-Trinity National Forest, Chapter B2, page 117.
Methuselah Trail, Inyo National Forest, Chapter E5, page 476.
Unal Trail, Sequoia National Forest, Chapter G5, page 623.
Shadow of the Giants, Sierra National Forest, Chapter F4, page 512.
Trail of the Gargoyles, Stanislaus National Forest, Chapter E4, page 420.
Cottonwood Creek Botanical Trail, Tahoe National Forest, Chapter C4, page 203.
Rainbow and Lake of the Sky Trails, Lake Tahoe Basin, Chapter D4, page 256.
Piño Alto Trail, Los Padres National Forest, Chapter H3, page 652.
McGrath State Beach Nature Trail, McGrath State Beach, Chapter H3, page 659.
Inaja Memorial Trail, Cleveland National Forest, Chapter J6, page 788.
Elephant Trees, Anza-Borrego Desert State Park, Chapter J7, page 808.
Ponderosa Vista Nature Trail, San Bernardino National Forest, Chapter I6, page 751.

Redwoods/Sequoia

Tall Trees Trail, Redwood National Park, Chapter A0, page 37.
Redwood Creek Trail, Redwood National Park, Chapter A0, page 36.
Boy Scout Tree Trail, Jedediah Smith Redwoods State Park, Chapter A0, page 29.
Bull Creek Flats, Humboldt Redwoods State Park, Chapter B0, page 81.
Redwood Canyon, Kings Canyon National Park, Chapter F5, page 542.
Shadow of the Giants, Sierra National Forest, Chapter F4, page 512.
General Grant Tree, Kings Canyon National Park, Chapter F4, page 521.
Congress Trail Loop, Sequoia National Park, Chapter F5, page 556.
Trail of 100 Giants, Sequoia National Forest, Chapter G5, page 616.
Main Trail, Muir Woods National Monument, Chapter E1-Marin, page 311.

Short Backpack Trips

Ladybug Trail, Sequoia National Park, Chapter G5, page 597.
Gabrielino Trail to Bear Canyon, Angeles National Forest, Chapter I5, page 725.
Glen Aulin and Tuolumne Falls, Yosemite National Park, Chapter E4, page 439.
May Lake, Yosemite National Park, Chapter E4, page 431.
Toad Lake Trail, Shasta-Trinity National Forest, Chapter B2, page 113.
Winnemucca Lake Loop, Mokelumne Wilderness, Chapter D4, page 270.

Taylor Lake Trail, Russian Wilderness, Chapter A1, page 52.
Coast Trail, Point Reyes National Seashore, Chapter E1-Marin, page 292.

One-Way Hikes with Shuttle

John Muir Trail, begins in Chapter F5, page 564.
Panorama Trail, Yosemite National Park, Chapter E4, page 454.
Pohono Trail, Yosemite National Park, Chapter E4, page 453.
Skyline-to-Sea Trail, Big Basin Redwoods State Park, Chapter E1-South Bay, page 390.
Lost Coast Trail, Sinkyone Wilderness State Park, Chapter C0, page 154.

Beach/Coast Walks

Lost Coast Trail, Sinkyone Wilderness State Park, Chapter C0, page 154.
Lost Coast Trail, King Range National Conservation Area, Chapter B0, page 80.
Coast Trail, Point Reyes National Seashore, Chapter E1-Marin, page 292.
Old Landing Cove Trail, Wilder Ranch State Park, Chapter F1, page 481.
Razor Point and Beach Trail Loop, Torrey Pines State Reserve, Chapter J5, page 778.
Rim Loop Trail, Patrick's Point State Park, Chapter B0, page 77.
Montaña de Oro Bluffs Trail, Montaña de Oro State Park, Chapter G2, page 582.
Point Lobos Perimeter, Point Lobos State Reserve, Chapter F1, page 488.
Bayside Trail, Cabrillo National Monument, Chapter J5, page 778.
Cabrillo Tide Pools, Cabrillo National Monument, Chapter J5, page 779.

Wildlife

Note: Seeing wildlife is not guaranteed and is often seasonally influenced.
Tomales Point Trail, Point Reyes National Seashore, Chapter E1-Marin, page 285.
Año Nuevo Trail, Año Nuevo State Reserve, Chapter E1-South Bay, page 394.
Coastal Trail (Fern Canyon/Ossagon Section), Prairie Creek Redwoods State Park, Chapter A0, page 35.
Desert Tortoise Discovery Loop, Desert Tortoise Natural Area, Chapter H5, page 673.
Tule Elk State Reserve, Chapter G4, page 593.
Timber Mountain, Modoc National Forest, Chapter A3, page 69.
Spirit Lake Trail, Marble Mountain Wilderness, Chapter A1, page 50.
Captain Jack's Stronghold, Lava Beds National Monument, Chapter A3, page 65.
Pescadero Marsh, south of Pescadero, Chapter E1-South Bay, page 378.

Bird-Watching

Audubon Canyon Ranch Trail, near Bolinas Lagoon, Chapter E1-Marin, page 304.
South Tufa Trail, Mono Lake Tufa State Reserve, Chapter E5, page 467.
Arcata Marsh Trail, Arcata Marsh and Wildlife Sanctuary, Chapter B0, page 78.
Abbotts Lagoon Trail, Point Reyes National Seashore, Chapter E1-Marin, page 287.

(CONTINUED ON NEXT PAGE)

BEST HIKES: Bird-Watching (CONTINUED)

Elkhorn Slough South Marsh Loop, Elkhorn Slough National Estuarine Reserve, Chapter F1, page 484.

Chester and Winton Marsh Trails, San Luis National Wildlife Refuge, Chapter F2, page 499.

Silverwood Wildlife Sanctuary, Chapter J6, page 792.

Carrizo Plains and Painted Rock, Carrizo Plains Natural Area, Chapter G3, page 589.

Canyon Trail, Big Morongo Canyon Preserve, Chapter I7, page 767.

Arrowhead Marsh, Martin Luther King Regional Shoreline, Chapter E1-East Bay, page 356.

Summits

Shasta Summit Trail, Shasta-Trinity National Forest, Chapter B2, page 108.

Mount Whitney Trail, John Muir Wilderness, Chapter F5, page 562.

Aerial Tramway to San Jacinto Peak, Mount San Jacinto State Park, Chapter I6, page 755.

Mount Baldy, Angeles National Forest, Chapter I5, page 734.

Lassen Summit Trail, Lassen Volcanic National Park, Chapter B3, page 133.

Vivian Creek Trail to Mount San Gorgonio, San Gorgonio Wilderness, Chapter I6, page 755.

Grizzly Lake Trail (Thompson Peak), Trinity Alps Wilderness, Chapter B1, page 94.

White Mountain Peak Trail, Inyo National Forest, Chapter E5, page 475.

Preston Peak, Siskiyou Wilderness, Chapter A1, page 44.

East Peak Mount Tamalpais, Mount Tamalpais State Park, Chapter E1-Marin, page 307.

Island Walks

San Miguel Island Trail, Channel Islands National Park, Chapter I2, page 695.

East Anacapa Island Loop Trail, Channel Islands National Park, Chapter I3, page 700.

North Ridge/Sunset Trail, Angel Island State Park, Chapter E1-Marin, page 320.

Empire Landing Road Trail, Catalina Island, Chapter I4, page 717.

Two Harbors to Emerald Bay, Catalina Island, Chapter I4, page 716.

Wheelchair Accessible

South Yuba Independence Trail, near Nevada City, Chapter D3, page 228.

Kangaroo Lake Trailhead, Klamath National Forest, Chapter B2, page 103.

Taylor Lake Trail, Russian Wilderness, Chapter A1, page 52.

Abbotts Lagoon Trail, Point Reyes National Seashore, Chapter E1-Marin, page 287.

Sierra Discovery Trail, PG&E Bear Valley Recreation Area, Chapter D3, page 230.

Salt Creek Interpretive Trail, Death Valley National Park, Chapter G7, page 640.

Mc Way Falls Overlook, Julia Pfeiffer Burns State Park, Chapter F1, page 494.

Lower Yosemite Fall, Yosemite National Park, Chapter E4, page 444.
Roaring River Falls, Kings Canyon National Park, Chapter F5, page 540.
Lake Cleone Trail, MacKerricher State Park, Chapter C0, page 155.

Desert Terrain
Borrego Palm Canyon Falls, Anza-Borrego Desert State Park, Chapter J7, page 805.
Rainbow Basin, Rainbow Basin Natural Area, Chapter H6, page 683.
Afton Canyon, Afton Canyon Natural Area, Chapter H7, page 687.
Mosaic Canyon, Death Valley National Park, Chapter G6, page 633.
Wildrose Peak Trail, Death Valley National Park, Chapter G6, page 634.
Ubehebe Peak, Death Valley National Park, Chapter F6, page 570.
Ryan Mountain Trail, Joshua Tree National Park, Chapter I7, page 770.

For Kids
Angora Lakes Trail, Tahoe National Forest, Chapter D4, page 259.
Pinecrest Lake National Recreation Trail, Stanislaus National Forest, Chapter E4, page 422.
Desert Tortoise Discovery Loop, Desert Tortoise Natural Area, Chapter H5, page 673.
Rainbow and Lake of the Sky Trails, Lake Tahoe Basin, Chapter D4, page 256.
Bear Gulch Caves, Pinnacles National Monument, Chapter F2, page 503.
Rainbow Falls Trail, Devils Postpile National Monument, Chapter E5, page 471.
Tokopah Falls, Sequoia National Park, Chapter F5, page 560.
Año Nuevo Trail, Año Nuevo State Reserve, Chapter E1-South Bay, page 394.
Cabrillo Tide Pools, Cabrillo National Monument, Chapter J5, page 779.
Fitzgerald Marine Reserve, Moss Beach, Chapter E1-San Francisco Peninsula, page 336.
Tomales Point Trail, Point Reyes National Seashore, Chapter E1-Marin, page 285.

Fall Colors
Fallen Leaf Lake Trail, Tahoe National Forest, Chapter D4, page 257.
Farewell Gap Trail to Aspen Flat, Sequoia National Park, Chapter G5, page 601.
Desert View and Canyon Oak Loop, William Heise County Park, Chapter J6, page 790.
Boucher Trail and Scott's Cabin Loop, Palomar Mountain State Park, Chapter J6, page 785.
Stonewall Peak Trail, Cuyamaca Rancho State Park, Chapter J6, page 793.
Carlon Falls, Stanislaus National Forest, Chapter E4, page 427.
Lundy Lake Trailhead, Hoover Wilderness, Chapter E5, page 465.
McGee Creek to Steelhead Lake, John Muir Wilderness, Chapter F5, page 527.
Convict Lake Trailhead, Inyo National Forest, Chapter E5, page 475.

NORTHERN CALIFORNIA
CHAPTER A0

A REDWOOD GROVE: ONE OF
NORTHERN CALIFORNIA'S HALLMARKS

MAP AO

One inch equals approximately 11 miles.

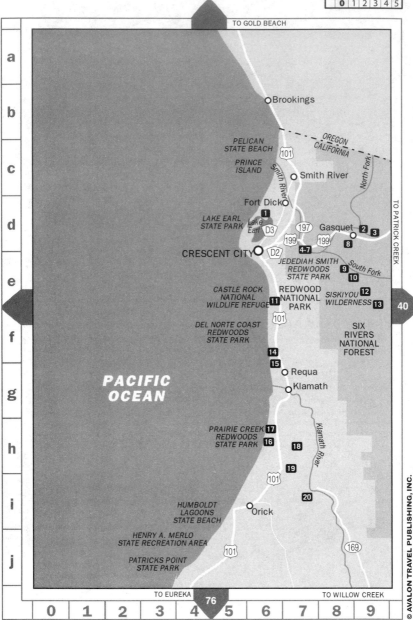

TO GOLD BEACH

O Brookings

PELICAN
STATE BEACH

OREGON
CALIFORNIA

101

PRINCE
ISLAND

Smith River

North Fork

O Smith River

Fort Dick O

1

LAKE EARL
STATE PARK

Lake
Earl

D3

197

Gasquet

2

3

TO PATRICK CREEK

199

4-7

199

8

CRESCENT CITY O

D2

JEDEDIAH SMITH
REDWOODS
STATE PARK

South Fork

9

10

CASTLE ROCK
NATIONAL
WILDLIFE REFUGE

REDWOOD
NATIONAL
PARK

11

SISKIYOU
WILDERNESS

12

13

40

DEL NORTE COAST
REDWOODS
STATE PARK

101

SIX
RIVERS
NATIONAL
FOREST

**PACIFIC
OCEAN**

14

15

O Requa

O Klamath

PRAIRIE CREEK
REDWOODS
STATE PARK

17

16

18

Klamath River

19

101

20

HUMBOLDT
LAGOONS
STATE BEACH

O Orick

HENRY A. MERLO
STATE RECREATION AREA

169

PATRICKS POINT
STATE PARK

101

TO EUREKA

76

TO WILLOW CREEK

© AVALON TRAVEL PUBLISHING, INC.

NORTHERN CALIFORNIA

CHAPTER A0

1 Wildlife Dune Area 27
2 Stony Creek Trail. 28
3 Elk Camp Ridge Trail 28
4 Stout Grove Trail 29
5 Boy Scout Tree Trail 29
6 Myrtle Creek Trail 30
7 Craig's Creek Trail 30
8 French Hill Trail. 31
9 McClendon Ford Trail. . . . 31
10 Gunbarrel Trail 32
11 Coastal Trail
(Last Chance Section) . . . 32
12 South Kelsey Trail 33

13 Summit Valley Trail 33
14 Yurok Loop 34
15 Coastal Trail
(Hidden Beach Section) . . 34
16 Coastal Trail
(Fern Canyon/
Ossagon Section) 35
17 Fern Canyon
Loop Trail 35
18 Lost Man Creek Trail 36
19 Redwood Creek Trail 36
20 Tall Trees Trail 37

1 Wildlife Dune Area

2.5 mi/1.0 hr

The Pelican Bay Sand Dunes seem to sweep on forever, spanning more than 10 miles from the mouth of the Smith River on south along the Pacific Ocean, reaching nearly all the way to Crescent City. After parking at Kellogg Beach, you can walk north or south for five minutes or five hours—take your pick. Either way, you get a walk where you feel like a solitary speck against the enormous backdrop of untouched sand dunes and ocean. Only rarely will you see other people. The area is known by several names, including Fort Dick Beach, Kellogg Beach, and Pelican Bay Sand Dunes, but by any name it's a good place to escape to nothing but wide-open beach for miles.

Location: On the coast of Del Norte County north of Crescent City; map A0, grid d6.

User groups: Hikers, dogs, and horses. Mountain bikes permitted but not recommended. No wheelchair facilities.

Permits: No permits are required. Parking and access are free.

Maps: For a free brochure and map, write to Lake Earl State Park at the address below. Ask the USGS for topographic maps of the Crescent City and Smith River areas.

Directions: On U.S. 101 in Crescent City, turn northwest on Northcrest Drive and drive 1.5 miles to Old Mill Road. Turn left on Old Mill Road and drive 1.25 miles to the end of Old Mill Road and the junction with Sand Hill Road. Turn left on Sand Hill Road (at the Department of Fish and Game office) and drive .25 mile to the parking lot and the trailhead.

For trail and walk-in beach access: On U.S. 101 in Crescent City, turn northwest on Northcrest Drive and drive six miles (it becomes Lake Earl Drive) for six miles to Lower Lake Road. Turn left on Lower Lake Road and drive 2.5 miles to Kellogg Road. Turn left and drive one-half mile to the trailhead.

Alternative access: On U.S. 101 in Crescent City, turn northwest on Northcrest Drive and drive six miles (it becomes Lake Earl Drive) for six miles to Lower Lake Road. Turn left on Lower Lake Road and drive five miles to Pala Road. Turn left and drive one-half mile to the trailhead.

Contact: Lake Earl State Park, 1375 Elk Valley Road, Crescent City, CA 95531; tel. (707) 464-6101, ext. 5151, or fax (707) 464-7722.

2 Stony Creek Trail
1.0 mi/0.75 hr

This easy walk in an unblemished river setting will take you to the mouth of Stony Creek, right where it pours into the North Fork Smith River. It's the kind of special place where you just sit and listen to the flow of moving water as it gurgles and pops its way over stones smoothed by years of river flows. The hike is easy, with a few ups and downs as it follows a bluff adjacent to the North Fork Smith, a designated Wild and Scenic River, then is routed right out to the mouth of Stony Creek. You're surrounded by woods, water, and in the spring, wildflowers. Note: For years this was spelled "Stoney" Creek, but was finally corrected and changed.

Location: In Smith River National Recreation Area northeast of Crescent City; map A0, grid d9.

User groups: Hikers and dogs. No horses or mountain bikes. No wheelchair facilities.

Permits: Campfire permits (free) are required. Parking and access are free.

Maps: For a free brochure and hiking guide, write to Smith River National Recreation Area at the address below. For a map of Six Rivers National Forest, send $6 to U.S. Forest Service, Attn: Map Sales, P.O. Box 587, Camino, CA 95709; tel. (530) 647-5390, fax (530) 647-5389, or website: www.r5.fs.fed.us/visitorcenter. Major credit cards accepted. Ask the USGS for a topographic map of the Gasquet area.

Directions: From Crescent City drive north on U.S. 101 for three miles, turn east onto U.S. 199, and drive 14 miles to Gasquet. Turn left on Middle Fork/Gasquet Road and drive about 100 feet to North Fork Road. Turn right and drive another mile. Then turn right on Stony Creek Road and drive a short distance to the trailhead.

Contact: Smith River National Recreation Area, P.O. Box 228, Gasquet, CA 95543; tel. (707) 457-3131 or fax (707) 457-3794.

3 Elk Camp Ridge Trail
7.5-16.4 mi/
3.5 hrs-2.0 days

This trail is like a walk through history. It was originally part of a pack trail between Crescent City and the gold mines in southern Oregon, and the memories of the old days can shadow your hike much of the way. The trailhead is at 1,200 feet, but the route climbs right up to the ridge, reaching more than 3,000 feet. Once you reach the ridge, you have excellent views of surrounding peaks (Preston Peak is the big one) and the Smith River Canyon. You may also notice that much of the vegetation along the trail is stunted, a result of the high mineral content in serpentine rocks. The trail keeps climbing and ends at 3,400 feet. From start to finish the trail covers 8.2 miles, although most hikers only make it half way before they return. Since most of the route traces a ridgeline, there are no suitable camping areas.

Location: In Smith River National Recreation Area northeast of Crescent City; map A0, grid d9.

User groups: Hikers, dogs, horses, and mountain bikes. No wheelchair facilities.

Permits: Campfire permits (free) are required. Parking and access are free.

Maps: For a free brochure and hiking guide, write to the Smith River National Recreation Area at the address below. For a map of Six Rivers National Forest, send $6 to U.S. Forest Service, Attn: Map Sales, P.O. Box 587, Camino, CA 95709; tel. (530) 647-5390, fax (530)

647-5389, or website: www.r5.fs.fed.us/visitorcenter. Major credit cards accepted. Ask the USGS for topographic maps of the Gasquet and High Plateau Mountain areas.

Directions: From Crescent City drive north on U.S. 101 for three miles, turn east on U.S. 199, and drive 14 miles to Gasquet. Turn left on Middle Fork/Gasquet Road and drive 100 feet; bear right as the road forks. Drive one-half mile, turn right on Old Gasquet Toll Road (County Road 314), and drive 2.3 miles. Turn left at the sign for the trailhead and drive 1.4 steep and rough miles to the trailhead.

Contact: Smith River National Recreation Area, P.O. Box 228, Gasquet, CA 95543; tel. (707) 457-3131 or fax (707) 457-3794.

4 Stout Grove Trail
0.6 mi/0.5 hr

Visiting giant old redwood trees can affect people for a long time. The Stout Tree, the largest redwood in Jedediah Smith Redwoods State Park, is the attraction on this hike. It is so old that it can make your stay on Earth seem mighty brief. The wide, level trail is a 10-minute walk that takes an easy course to the Stout Grove and then on to the Stout Tree. Most people take longer than 10 minutes, of course, because they're not used to seeing anything this size, and they take their time absorbing the surroundings. The Stout Tree is being "loved to death" by people who touch it or trample the undergrowth, and rangers make a special request that you take your picture, but leave it at that. Most everybody makes the mandatory stroll to the nearby Smith River, located a few minutes' walk beyond the Stout Tree. A trail that ran alongside the river once started here, but it was washed out by erosion from floodwaters.

Location: In Jedediah Smith Redwoods State Park northeast of Crescent City; map A0, grid e7.

User groups: Hikers and wheelchairs. No dogs, horses, or mountain bikes. Those who want closer vehicular access can call the park at (707)

464-6101, ext. 5112, to get the key to the gate.

Permits: No permits are required. Parking and access are free.

Maps: A trail map is available for $1 at Jedediah Smith Redwoods, at the address below. Ask the USGS for a topographic map of the Hiouchi area.

Directions: From Crescent City drive about three miles north on U.S. 101, then turn east on U.S. 199. Drive about 10 miles (past the formal entrance to Jedediah Smith Redwoods State Park) to Hiouchi. Just past Hiouchi turn right on South Fork Road (County Road 427) and cross two bridges. At a junction, turn right onto Howland Hill Road and drive about two miles to a small parking area on the right and the signed trailhead.

Contact: Jedediah Smith Redwoods State Park, 1375 Elk Valley Road, Crescent City, CA 95531; tel. (707) 464-6101, ext. 5112.

5 Boy Scout Tree Trail
7.0 mi/3.5 hrs

This is the kind of place where a nature lover can find religion, where the beauty is pure and untouched. The trail is a soft dirt path, often sprinkled with redwood needles, that allows hikers to penetrate deep into an old-growth redwood forest complete with a giant fern understory and high-limbed canopy. The centerpiece is the Boy Scout Tree, the largest tree in the forest here, but what you will remember the most is the pristine serenity of a forest of old redwoods.

This is an easy hike, nearly flat with only small hills, yet extremely rewarding. Just walk into the forest and a few hours later walk out. Those two hours in can change how you feel about the world. A bonus known to relatively few is Fern Falls, a 40-foot waterfall. To reach it requires a 3.5-mile hike one way, making a seven-mile round-trip hike.

Location: In Jedediah Smith Redwoods State Park northeast of Crescent City; map A0, grid e7.

User groups: Hikers only. No dogs, horses, or mountain bikes. No wheelchair facilities.

Permits: No permits are required. Parking and access are free.

Maps: A trail map is available for $1 at Jedediah Smith Redwoods State Park at the address below. Ask the USGS for a topographic map of the Hiouchi area.

Directions: From U.S. 101 in Crescent City, turn east on Elk Valley Road and drive one mile to Howland Hill Road. Turn right and drive 3.5 miles to the trailhead on the left. The last two miles are unpaved.

Note: If you are camping at Jedediah Smith Redwoods State Park, use these directions: On U.S. 199, drive east just past Hiouchi to South Fork Road. Turn right on South Fork Road (County Road 427) and cross two bridges. At a junction, turn right on Howland Hill Road and drive about five miles to a small parking area and the signed trailhead on the right side of the road.

Contact: Jedediah Smith Redwoods State Park, 1375 Elk Valley Road, Crescent City, CA 95531; tel. (707) 464-6101, ext. 5112.

6 Myrtle Creek Trail
2.0 mi/45 min.

This interpretive trail follows along year-round Myrtle Creek. The stream drainage runs along a geological boundary between typical local soils, supporting redwood and Douglas fir forest, and iron-and-magnesium-rich serpentine soil, reddish in color and dry, where rarer native species such as Bolander's and Vollmer's lily grow. It's an easy hike with a lot to look at and learn about, including the remains of an extensive hydraulic mining operation, dating back to 1853 when gold was discovered here. Hikers are asked to respect this vulnerable habitat by keeping to the trail. Collecting artifacts and plants is prohibited.

Location: In the Smith River National Recreation Area; map A0, grid e7.

User groups: Hikers and dogs. No horses or mountain bikes.

Permits: A campfire permit (free) is required for overnight use. Parking and access are free.

Maps: For a free brochure and hiking guide, write to Smith River National Recreation Area at the address below. Ask the USGS for a topographic map of the Devils Punchbowl area.

Directions: From Crescent City, drive three miles north on U.S. 101, then east on Highway 199. Drive seven miles to the parking area and trailhead. Park on the south side of Highway 199 and cross the road to access the trailhead.

Contact: Smith River National Recreation Area, P.O. Box 228, Gasquet, CA 95543; tel. (707) 457-3131 or fax (707) 457-3794.

7 Craig's Creek Trail
7.4 mi/4.25 hrs

An old miners' pack route, vintage 1800s, has been converted into this hiking trail, an obscure path that is overlooked by most visitors. It starts along the South Fork Smith River, loops up the slopes of Craig's Creek Mountain and back down to the river, ending where Craig's Creek enters the South Fork. In the process it rises above the river and passes through forest, including old-growth redwoods and Douglas fir. Because of the contour of the mountain, the hike includes a good climb. The starting and ending elevations are the same, 200 feet. Most of the time you can have the entire trail to yourself. The South Fork Smith is very pretty here, a clear, free-flowing stream that drains a huge expanse of the Siskiyou Wilderness,

Location: In Smith River National Recreation Area northeast of Crescent City; map A0, grid e7.

User groups: Hikers, dogs, horses, and mountain bikes. No wheelchair facilities.

Permits: No permits are required. For overnight use, a campfire permit (free) is required. Parking and access are free.

Maps: For a free brochure and hiking guide, write to Smith River National Recreation Area at the address below. For a map of Six Rivers National Forest, send $6 to U.S. Forest Service, Attn: Map Sales, P.O. Box 587, Camino, CA 95709; tel. (530) 647-5390, fax (530) 647-5389, or website: www.r5.fs.fed.us/visitorcenter. Major credit cards accepted. Ask the USGS for a topographic map of the Hiouchi area.

Directions: From Crescent City drive north on U.S. 101 for three miles, turn east on U.S. 199, and drive seven miles. Just past Hiouchi turn right on South Fork Road (County Road 427) and drive approximately one-third mile. Park in the boat access facility area.

Contact: Smith River National Recreation Area, P.O. Box 228, Gasquet, CA 95543; tel. (707) 457-3131 or fax (707) 457-3794.

8 French Hill Trail
5.6 mi/3.25 hrs

This trail was created originally as part of the route to transport supplies to build the Camp Six fire lookout station. It is fairly steep, and some use it for an aerobic workout. It passes through old-growth Douglas fir and sugar pines, a forest that has thrived from so much moisture. The beauty and quality of the trail are poor to fair compared to that of other nearby areas. The significance that rates making this book is that the while the lookout has long been retired, a high-tech automatic rain gauge was positioned in its place. In 1983, this rain gauge documented the most rain ever recorded in the continental U.S. for one season, 257 inches. You can drive right to this site.

Location: In Smith River National Recreation Area northeast of Crescent City; map A0, grid e8.

User groups: Hikers, dogs, horses, and mountain bikes. No wheelchair facilities.

Permits: No permits are required. Parking and access are free.

Maps: For a free brochure and hiking guide, write to Smith River National Recreation Area at the address below. For a map of Six Rivers National Forest, send $6 to U.S. Forest Service, Attn: Map Sales, P.O. Box 587, Camino,

CA 95709; tel. (530) 647-5390, fax (530) 647-5389, or website: www.r5.fs.fed.us/visitorcenter. Major credit cards accepted. Ask the USGS for a topographic map of the Gasquet area.

Directions: From Crescent City drive north on U.S. 101 for three miles, turn east on U.S. 199, and drive 14 miles to Gasquet. Park at the Gasquet Ranger Station. The trail is located directly across the highway.

Contact: Smith River National Recreation Area, P.O. Box 228, Gasquet, CA 95543; tel. (707) 457-3131 or fax (707) 457-3794.

9 McClendon Ford Trail
2.0 mi/1.5 hrs

This is a perfect trail for a hot summer day, complete with a swimming hole. It's an easy hike through a large forest of Douglas fir. The trail crosses Horse Creek, a small tributary, and then leads to a pretty beach on the South Fork Smith River. The starting elevation is 1,000 feet, and the ending elevation is 200 feet. Get the idea? Right, this trail follows an easy descent to the river, taking about 45 minutes to get there. The swimming hole on the river is secluded and out of the way of most vacationers, so most often you have the place completely to yourself. Note: This is also the trailhead for the South Kelsey Trail. If you are unfamiliar with the area, be sure to have a map of Six Rivers National Forest to reach the trailhead.

Location: In Smith River National Recreation Area east of Crescent City; map A0, grid e8.

User groups: Hikers, dogs, horses, and mountain bikes. No wheelchair facilities.

Permits: No permits are required. Parking and access are free.

Maps: For a free brochure and hiking guide, write to Smith River National Recreation Area at the address below. For a map of Six Rivers National Forest, send $6 to U.S. Forest Service, Attn: Map Sales, P.O. Box 587, Camino, CA 95709; tel. (530) 647-5390, fax (530) 647-5389, or website: www.r5.fs.fed.us/visitorcenter. Major credit cards accepted.

Ask the USGS for a topographic map of the Ship Mountain area.

Directions: From Crescent City drive north on U.S. 101 for three miles, turn east on U.S. 199, and drive seven miles. Just past Hiouchi turn right on South Fork Road (County Road 427) and drive 14 miles. Turn right on Forest Road 15 and drive 3.5 more miles to a sign indicating the South Kelsey Trailhead. Turn left and drive two miles. Hike on the South Kelsey Trail for one-half mile before connecting with the McClendon Ford Trail.

Contact: Smith River National Recreation Area, P.O. Box 228, Gasquet, CA 95543; tel. (707) 457-3131 or fax (707) 457-3794.

🔟 Gunbarrel Trail
2.6 mi/1.75 hrs

Now just a minute here. Do you really want to try this hike? If so, get your ambitions in clear focus, and if you like what you see, go for it, because your reward will be complete peace and solitude. But it comes with a price: a terrible, long, and circuitous drive to reach the trailhead two hours from the Gasquet Ranger Station. Then the hike itself demands a steep climb on the return trip, a 1,200-foot elevation gain over little more than a mile.

This trail starts at a ridgeline at 2,500 feet, then dives down the canyon all the way to the South Fork Smith River, where it junctions with the South Kelsey Trail. This is a beautiful spot; the water is pure and the people nil. Alas, the return is the killer, a demanding climb, and that is why few people make this round-trip.

Location: In Smith River National Recreation Area east of Crescent City; map A0, grid e8.

User groups: Hikers, dogs, horses, and mountain bikes. No wheelchair facilities.

Permits: No permits are required. Parking and access are free.

Maps: Write to Smith River National Recreation Area at the address below for a free brochure and hiking guide. For a map of Six Rivers National Forest, send $6 to U.S. Forest Service, Attn: Map Sales, P.O. Box 587,

Camino, CA 95709; tel. (530) 647-5390, fax (530) 647-5389, or website: www.r5.fs.fed.us/visitorcenter. Major credit cards accepted. Ask the USGS for a topographic map of the Ship Mountain area.

Directions: From Crescent City turn east on U.S. 199 and drive 25 miles. Turn right on Little Jones Creek Road (Forest Service Highway 16) and drive south 9.6 miles. When the road forks, bear right on Forest Road 16N02 for 4.8 miles, turn left onto Forest Road 16N18 (gated and closed in the wet season, October through January), and drive six miles. Bear left on Forest Road 15N34 and continue on this road for approximately two miles. Park at the end of the road. The trailhead is on the left.

Contact: Smith River National Recreation Area, P.O. Box 228, Gasquet, CA 95543; tel. (707) 457-3131 or fax (707) 457-3794.

🕠 Coastal Trail (Last Chance Section)
14 mi/8.0 hrs

You get a little bit of heaven and a little bit of hell on this hike. It's one of the feature trips on the Del Norte coast, coursing through a virgin forest and meadows with beautiful wildflowers in the spring and granting great coastal views in several spots. The trail starts along the coast, veers up sharply into coastal spruce and fir, and then dips into dense old-growth forest. That's the heaven. The hell starts when you begin the difficult and steep climb, a gain of 1,400 feet. It doesn't stop there. Ever wonder why the trees are so big? You're likely to find out that it's because they are dripping with moisture, with heavy rain in the winter and ponderous fog in summer. Like many coastal hikes, hitting good weather is the key. Note that when you're crossing meadows, ticks can be a common problem.

Location: In Del Norte Redwoods State Park south of Crescent City; map A0, grid f6.

User groups: Hikers and mountain bikes (restricted to first six miles only). No dogs or horses. No wheelchair facilities.

Permits: No permits are required. Parking and access are free.

Maps: A trail guide is available for $1.50 at Redwood National and State Park, 1111 2nd Street, Crescent City, CA 95531; tel. (707) 464-6101. Ask the USGS for a topographic map of the Sister Rocks area.

Directions: From Crescent City drive south on U.S. 101 for about 2.5 miles. At milepost 23.03 turn west onto Enderts Beach Road. Continue for 2.5 miles to the trailhead at the end of the road.

Contact: California State Parks, North Coast Redwoods District, 1375 Elk Valley Road, Crescent City, CA 95531; tel. (707) 464-6101, or fax (707) 464-7722.

12 South Kelsey Trail

34 mi/3.0 days

Back before cars, trains, and planes, the Kelsey Trail spanned 200 miles from Crescent City eastward to Fort Jones near Yreka. It was built in the mid-1800s by Chinese laborers as a mule train route. Today it has a different purpose, with different sections providing excellent backpacking circuits. The trailhead is near Horse Creek, on the South Fork Smith River, at a 1,200-foot elevation. The trail initially drops down along the South Fork and continues south for seven miles. A few camps are here along the river, including one with a makeshift roof, which is like finding heaven during a heavy rainstorm. The trail then rises above the river, climbing for six miles all the way to Baldy Peak and spectacular views. Another 3.1 miles will get you to your destination, Harrington Lake, set at 5,775 feet. With so much "up" going in, take heart that at least the return trip will be mainly downhill. The trailhead also provides access to the McClendon Ford Trail. Other maintained sections of the Kelsey Trail are noted in the Marble Mountain Wilderness (see chapter A1).

Location: In Smith River National Recreation Area east of Crescent City; map A0, grid e9.

User groups: Hikers, dogs, and horses. Moun-

tain bikes are permitted only to the wilderness boundary. No wheelchair facilities.

Permits: A campfire permit (free) is required. Parking and access are free.

Maps: For a free brochure and hiking guide, write to Smith River National Recreation Area at the address below. For a map of Six Rivers National Forest, send $6 to U.S. Forest Service, Attn: Map Sales, P.O. Box 587, Camino, CA 95709; tel. (530) 647-5390, fax (530) 647-5389, or website: www.r5.fs.fed.us/visitorcenter. Major credit cards accepted. Ask the USGS for a topographic map of the Summit Valley area.

Directions: From Crescent City drive north on U.S. 101 for three miles, turn east on U.S. 199, and drive seven miles. Just past Hiouchi turn right on South Fork Road (County Road 427) and drive 14 miles. Turn right on Forest Road 15 and drive 3.5 more miles to a sign indicating the South Kelsey Trailhead. Turn left and drive two miles.

Contact: Smith River National Recreation Area, P.O. Box 228, Gasquet, CA 95543; tel. (707) 457-3131 or fax (707) 457-3794.

13 Summit Valley Trail

16.2 mi/2.0 days

This hike is best taken in the early summer when the wildflowers are blooming, the Smith River is running with fresh, ample flows, and the temperatures are not too warm. The latter becomes a factor on the return trip, which is a killer climb. The trailhead is set on a ridge at 4,600 feet, with the first mile of the hike on an old jeep road. It then becomes a hiking path as it travels through meadows where the wildflowers are spectacular in early summer. But then the trail drops, plunging into a canyon, landing you along the South Fork Smith River at Elkhorn Bar, a beautiful spot at an elevation of 1,160 feet. Here it junctions with the South Kelsey Trail, where you'll find a few primitive campsites along the river. Well, when it comes to hiking, what goes

down must come up, and you got it: the return trip is a death march, a 3,500-foot climb over the span of eight miles. Your car waiting at the trailhead will never look so good. This trip can be lengthened easily by joining the South Kelsey Trail.

Location: In Smith River National Recreation Area east of Crescent City; map A0, grid f9.

User groups: Hikers, dogs, and horses. Mountain bikes are permitted only to the wilderness boundary. No wheelchair facilities.

Permits: A campfire permit (free) is required. Parking and access are free.

Maps: Write to Smith River National Recreation Area at the address below for a free brochure and hiking guide. For a map of Six Rivers National Forest, send $6 to U.S. Forest Service, Attn: Map Sales, P.O. Box 587, Camino, CA 95709; tel. (530) 647-5390, fax (530) 647-5389, or website: www.r5.fs.fed.us/visitorcenter. Major credit cards accepted. Ask the USGS for a topographic map of the Summit Valley area.

Directions: From Crescent City drive north on U.S. 101 for three miles, turn east on U.S. 199, and drive seven miles. Just past Hiouchi turn right on South Fork Road (County Road 427) and drive 14 miles, Turn right on Forest Road 15 and drive 15 miles to the trailhead on the left. Park on the side of the road.

Contact: Smith River National Recreation Area, P.O. Box 228, Gasquet, CA 95543; tel. (707) 457-3131 or fax (707) 457-3794.

14 Yurok Loop
1.0 mi/0.5 hr

The Yurok Loop is a great short loop hike that starts right next to pretty Lagoon Creek Pond in Redwood National and State Parks. Here's the deal: from the trailhead it's a 10-minute walk above a beautiful beach with lots of driftwood and a gentle climb to a great coastal overlook. From here you can scan miles of ocean and many rocky stacks. After enjoying the view, head south and when you reach a junction, turn left, and enter a forest where the trail burrows almost like a tunnel and heads gently downhill. It then emerges from the forest and leads back to the parking lot, a delightful and easy walk that makes a perfect break for highway drivers.

Special note: The Hidden Beach section of the Coastal Trail (see the following trail) junctions with this trail.

Location: In Redwood National and State Parks south of Crescent City; map A0, grid f6.

User groups: Hikers and partial wheelchair access. No dogs, horses, or mountain bikes.

Permits: No permits are required. Parking and access are free.

Maps: For a trail guide send $1.50 (includes tax and mailing) to Redwood National and State Parks Headquarters at the address below. Ask the USGS for a topographic map of the Requa area.

Directions: From Crescent City drive south on U.S. 101 for approximately 14 miles. Turn right at the sign for the Lagoon Creek Parking Area. The trailhead is adjacent to the parking lot (on the ocean/north side).

Contact: Redwood National and State Parks, 1111 2nd Street, Crescent City, CA 95531, tel. (707) 464-6101, or fax (707) 464-1812.

15 Coastal Trail (Hidden Beach Section)
8.0 mi/5.0 hrs

One of the greatest lookouts anywhere in the hemisphere is available at the Klamath Overlook, where you can scan the vast ocean-blue horizon and actually see the curvature of the earth. This is also an excellent place to see the spouts of passing whales in winter and early spring. After parking, enjoy the view and then head off. It's only a three-mile round trip to Hidden Beach and back. But you can continue to near False Klamath Rock, making it an eight-miler. The trail runs along coastal bluffs and rocky cliffs, with sweeping views of the ocean. Pray for a clear day.

Location: In Redwood National Park south of Crescent City; map A0, grid g6.

User groups: Hikers and partial wheelchair access. No dogs, horses, or mountain bikes.

Permits: No permits are required. Parking and access are free.

Maps: For a trail guide send $1.50 (includes tax and mailing) to Redwood National and State Parks Headquarters at the address below. Ask the USGS for a topographic map of the Requa area.

Directions: From Eureka drive north on U.S. 101 for about 60 miles to the Klamath River. Continue two miles north of the Klamath River Bridge to Requa Road. Turn west on Requa Road and drive 2.5 miles to the Klamath Overlook at the end of the road. The trailhead is at the south end of the parking area. Head north on the Coastal Trail.

Contact: Redwood National and State Parks, 1111 2nd Street, Crescent City, CA 95531, tel. (707) 464-6101, or fax (707) 464-1812.

16 Coastal Trail (Fern Canyon/Ossagon Section)

5.4 mi/3.0 hrs

This is a great hike, once one of the best coastal hikes anywhere. There is a good chance of seeing Roosevelt elk (Prairie Creek Redwoods State Park is loaded with them), Fern Canyon (see the following hike), a dense forest (quiet and pretty), and a series of hidden waterfalls, not to mention easy access to a huge spotless beach (not a single piece of litter). In addition, there is a great trail camp about three miles in. Start from the parking area by crossing a shallow stream, and then take the near-level walk on the trail north as far as your heart desires. Most visitors enjoy the waterfalls and the beach, stopping for a picnic before returning. Elk are common here, and while they are accustomed to seeing people, be sure to give them plenty of room anyway. The only downer here is the mountain bikes. This trail is often wet and soft, so bike tires damage the trail by leaving tire furrows, and bikers often go too fast for such a pristine spot.

Location: In Prairie Creek Redwoods State Park south of Klamath; map A0, grid h6.

User groups: Hikers and mountain bikes. No dogs or horses. No wheelchair facilities.

Permits: No permits are required. There is a state park day-use fee of $2 per vehicle.

Maps: Trail maps are available at the park visitor center for $1. A free state parks guide can be obtained by calling (707) 445-6547. Ask the USGS for a topographic map of the Fern Canyon area.

Directions: From Eureka, drive north on U.S. 101 for 41 miles to Orick. Continue north for 2.5 miles to Davison Road. Turn west on Davison Road and drive eight miles to the Fern Canyon Trail. No trailers or RVs are permitted.

Contact: Prairie Creek Redwoods State Park, 127011 Newton B. Drury Scenic Parkway, Orick, CA 95555; tel. (707) 464-6101, ext. 5300.

17 Fern Canyon Loop Trail

0.8 mi/0.5 hr

The Fern Canyon Loop might just be the most inspiring short hike in California. When you walk along the bottom of Fern Canyon, you'll be surrounded by 50-foot-high walls covered with giant ferns, a dramatic setting that isn't duplicated anywhere in the state. Also adding to the beauty is a small waterfall, pouring in through a chasm in the canyon wall and gushing into Home Creek. But it is Home Creek, which runs through the bottom of the canyon, that can cause the one serious problem here. In winter this creek can flood, making the trail impassable. Although bridges are provided from June through September, wear waterproof footwear—you often have to hop back and forth across the stream in order to reach the back of the canyon. At the end of the canyon, turn left and climb the trail to the canyon rim and then continue through the forest back to the trailhead. A bonus is the adjacent beach, wide open and spanning for miles. It is also common to see Roosevelt elk on the drive in. Note that this trail is recommended and well known by many, so it can get a lot of use during the summer months.

Location: In Prairie Creek Redwoods State Park south of Klamath; map A0, grid h6.

User groups: Hikers only. No dogs, horses, or mountain bikes. No wheelchair facilities.

Permits: No permits are required. There is a state park day-use fee of $2 per vehicle.

Maps: Trail maps are available at the park visitor center for $1. A free state parks guide can be obtained by calling (707) 445-6547. Ask the USGS for a topographic map of the Fern Canyon area.

Directions: From Eureka drive north on U.S. 101 for 41 miles to Orick. Continue north for 2.5 miles to Davison Road. Turn west on Davison Road and drive eight miles to the Fern Canyon Trail. No trailers or RVs are permitted.

Contact: Prairie Creek Redwoods State Park, 127011 Newton B. Drury Scenic Parkway, Orick, CA 95555; tel. (707) 464-6101, ext. 5300.

18 Lost Man Creek Trail
2.0 mi/1.0 hr

Lost Man Creek is very pretty, with many rock pools and lots of lush vegetation. It's also a destination that is easy to reach. The trail heads southeast, the first 1.5 miles nearly flat, then starts to climb moderately, and then nearly levels out along the creek. Bring your camera because it is rare to reach such a pristine setting with such a short walk. The trail is actually a wide gravel roadbed, an old logging road that the park service plans on reclaiming and turning into a more low-key setting. While the two-mile round-trip is as far as most hikers take it, the trail actually continues for 10 miles, all the way back down to Bald Hills Road. But only the deranged make the 20-mile round-trip—it's so steep that you'll be howling at the moon like a lone wolf.

Location: In Redwood National Park south of Klamath; map A0, grid h7.

User groups: Hikers and partial wheelchair access. No dogs, horses, or mountain bikes.

Permits: No permits are required. Parking and access are free.

Maps: For a trail guide send $1.50 (includes tax and mailing) to Redwood National and State Parks Headquarters at the address below. Ask the USGS for a topographic map of the Orick area.

Directions: From Eureka drive north on U.S. 101 for 41 miles to Orick. Continue north for 3.5 miles just past Davison Road to Lost Man Creek Road. Turn right and drive 0.75 mile to the parking area and trailhead. Trailers and RVs are not permitted on Lost Man Creek Road.

Contact: Redwood National and State Parks, 1111 2nd Street, Crescent City, CA 95531, tel. (707) 464-6101, for fax (707) 464-1812.

19 Redwood Creek Trail
16.0 mi/1.0 day

The Redwood Creek Trail has become a feature hike in Redwood National Park. Though most visitors cut the trip short, it still provides exceptional beauty even in short pieces, with a chance to see elk near the parking area. The trail is routed along Redwood Creek, a pretty stream that flows out to sea near Orick. As you hike into the interior, you'll notice the diversity of the forest, with spruce, alder, redwoods, and maples, and lush fern beds in some areas. Stinging nettle is also abundant here, so stay on the trail. The stream attracts a diversity of wildlife, with ducks, herons, and hawks the most common sightings, and ruffed grouse and eagles occasionally seen. In the summer the first mile or two of the trail can be quite crowded, but just keep on going. The farther you go, the fewer people you'll see. Note that during the winter the creek can flood the trail in some areas, making it impassable.

Location: In Redwood National Park south of Klamath; map A0, grid h7.

User groups: Hikers only. No dogs, horses, or mountain bikes. No wheelchair facilities.

Permits: No permits are required. Parking and access are free.

Maps: For a trail guide send $1.50 (includes tax and mailing) to Redwood National and State Parks Headquarters at the address below. Ask the USGS for a topographic map of the Orick area.

Directions: From Eureka drive north on U.S. 101 for approximately 41 miles to Orick and then about .25 mile north of Orick to Bald Hills Road. Turn right on Bald Hills Road and drive .25 mile to the access road. Turn right and drive one-half mile to the parking area and trailhead.

Contact: Redwood National and State Parks, Superintendent, 1111 2nd Street, Crescent City, CA 95531, tel. (707) 464-6101, ext. 5100, or fax (707) 464-1812; California State Parks, North Coast Redwoods District, tel. (707) 445-6547 or fax (707) 441-5737.

20 Tall Trees Trail

3.2 mi/1.5 hrs

This hike is routed into a grove of tall and ancient redwoods of cathedral-like beauty, with the trail shaded and surrounded by a lush fern understory. Your mission here is to reach Tall Trees Grove, home of a 357-foot high redwood estimated to be 600 years old. This tree has lost about 10 feet of height because of drying, according to rangers, and is no longer considered the "World's Tallest Tree." In the summer, the Tall Trees Trail is popular, with visitors from all over the U.S. arriving to see the giant old-growth redwoods. The hike to the grove is just over a mile, and if you want to extend the adventure, you can return cross-country along Redwood Creek or head off toward Emerald Ridge (more of a cross-country route, not a designated trail. Warning: There is poison oak off the trail in this area.

Location: In Redwood National Park south of Klamath; map A0, grid i7.

User groups: Hikers only. No dogs, horses, or mountain bikes. No wheelchair facilities.

Permits: A permit is required if you want to drive to the trailhead, with only a limited number of cars allowed per day. Permits are free and can be obtained at the Redwood Information Center starting at 9 a.m. (see directions below). In the summer months it's advisable to arrive as early as possible.

Maps: For a trail guide send $1.50 (includes tax and mailing) to Redwood National and State Parks Headquarters at the address below. Ask the USGS for a topographic map of the Orick area.

Directions: From Eureka drive north on U.S. 101 for 40 miles. About a mile before reaching Orick, stop at the Redwood Information Center at the west side of the highway. Here you secure a permit number, which is actually a gate combination number you'll need. Drive north on U.S. 101 through Orick. About .25 mile north of Orick, turn right on Bald Hills Road. Look for the "Tall Tree Access" sign and drive seven miles to a locked gate on the right. Open the gate, drive through, close and lock the gate, and then drive six miles down the gravel road (C-Line Road) to the trailhead. No RVs or trailers are permitted.

Contact: Redwood National and State Parks, 1111 2nd Street, Crescent City, CA 95531, tel. (707) 464-6101, or fax (707) 464-1812.

TOM STIENSTRA

LOOKING DOWN AT ISLAND LAKE
IN SIX RIVERS NATIONAL FOREST

MAP A1

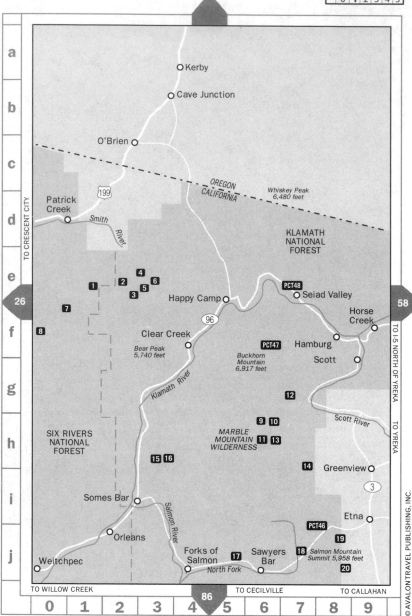

Kerby

Cave Junction

O'Brien

OREGON
CALIFORNIA

Whiskey Peak
6,480 feet

Patrick
Creek

Smith

River

199

TO CRESCENT CITY

KLAMATH
NATIONAL
FOREST

26   **58**

1

2   4

5   6

3

7

Happy Camp

PCT48

Seiad Valley

Horse
Creek

8

Clear Creek

96

Bear Peak
5,740 feet

PCT47

Hamburg

Buckhorn
Mountain
6,917 feet

Scott

Klamath River

12

SIX RIVERS
NATIONAL
FOREST

9   10

MARBLE
MOUNTAIN
WILDERNESS

11   13

Scott River

15   16

14   Greenview

3

Somes Bar

Salmon River

Etna

PCT46

Orleans

18   19

Weitchpec

Forks of
Salmon

17   Sawyers
Bar

Salmon Mountain
Summit 5,958 feet

North Fork

20

TO WILLOW CREEK   TO CECILVILLE   TO CALLAHAN

86

TO I-5 NORTH OF YREKA   TO YREKA

© AVALON TRAVEL PUBLISHING, INC.

CHAPTER A1

1 Doe Flat Trail 41
2 Buck Lake Trail 42
3 Devils Punchbowl. 42
4 Youngs Valley Trail. 43
5 Wilderness Falls. 44
6 Preston Peak 44
7 Island Lake Trail. 45
8 Baldy Peak Trail 46
9 Paradise Lake Trail. 46
10 Kings Castle Trail. 47
11 Marble Mountain Rim. . . . 47
12 Kelsey Creek Trail 48
13 Sky High Lakes. 49
14 Shackleford
Creek Trail. 49

15 Haypress Meadows
Trailhead 50
16 Spirit Lake Trail. 50
17 Little North Fork
Trailhead 51
18 Mule Bridge Trailhead . . . 52
19 Taylor Lake Trail 52
20 Statue Lake 53

**Pacific Crest Trail (PCT)
Section Overview**
PCT-46 Etna Summit
to Grider Creek 54
PCT-47 Grider Creek
to Seiad Valley. 54
PCT-48 Seiad Valley
to Oregon Border. 55

1 Doe Flat Trail

3.0 mi/1.5 hrs

Doe Flat is the best backpacking jump-off point for the Siskiyou Wilderness, and as long as you know that, you'll have all the motivation you need for the trip. There are several excellent destinations from Doe Flat, including Buck Lake, Clear Creek, and Wilderness Falls; all are detailed in the following trips. But hiking to Doe Flat is hardly inspirational. It requires a 1.5-mile jaunt on a closed road to get there, leaving Bear Basin and topping Siskiyou Pass, then cruising down to the Doe Flat Camp. The trail follows an old mining road along Doe Creek to an old mine site, reaching a good camping area at Doe Flat. The area is well wooded, with some huge Jeffrey pines and cedars. For late arrivals a bonus is the small primitive camping area at the trailhead with three campsites and a vault toilet.

Location: In Smith River National Recreation

Area east of Crescent City; map A1, grid e1.
User groups: Hikers, dogs, and horses. No mountain bikes. No wheelchair facilities.
Permits: No permits are required. A campfire permit (free) is required for overnight use. Parking and access are free.
Maps: For a free brochure and hiking guide, write to Smith River National Recreation Area at the address below. For a map of Klamath National Forest, send $6 to U.S. Forest Service, Attn: Map Sales, P.O. Box 587, Camino, CA 95709; tel. (530) 647-5390, fax (530) 647-5389, or website: www.r5.fs.fed.us/visitorcenter. Major credit cards accepted. Ask the USGS for a topographic map of the Devils Punchbowl area.
Directions: From Crescent City drive north on U.S. 101 for three miles. Turn east on U.S. 199 and drive 25 miles. Turn right on Little Jones Creek Road/Jawbone Road (Forest Road 16) and drive south 9.6 miles to a fork.

When the road forks, bear sharply left on Forest Road 16N02 and drive five miles to the trailhead at the end of the road.

Contact: Smith River National Recreation Area, P.O. Box 228, Gasquet, CA 95543; tel. (707) 457-3131 or fax (707) 457-3794.

2 Buck Lake Trail

4.5 mi/2.5 hrs

The first time we saw Buck Lake was a Memorial Day weekend as well as the opening day of trout season here, and there were so many rising brook trout that all the dimples on the lake surface looked like rain drops. Set in the heart of a wilderness forest at an elevation of 4,300 feet, Buck Lake is a little crystal lake surrounded by old-growth firs. From Doe Flat it's an easy 0.75-mile hike. There are plenty of deer and bear in the area, and the brook trout at the lake are abundant though small. From Doe Flat to Buck Lake you'll cross through beautiful meadows and forest, including Douglas, white, and red firs, along with some maples. In the fall the changing colors of the maples add a pretty touch to the trip.

Location: In the Siskiyou Wilderness east of Crescent City; map A1, grid e2.

User groups: Hikers, dogs, and horses. No mountain bikes. No wheelchair facilities.

Permits: No permits are required. A campfire permit (free) is required for overnight use. Parking and access are free.

Maps: For a free brochure and hiking guide write to Smith River National Recreation Area at the address below. For a map of Klamath National Forest send $6 to U.S. Forest Service, Attn: Map Sales, P.O. Box 587, Camino, CA 95709; tel. (530) 647-5390, fax (530) 647-5389, or website: www.r5.fs.fed.us/visitorcenter. Major credit cards accepted. Ask the USGS for a topographic map of the Devils Punchbowl area.

Directions: From Crescent City drive north on U.S. 101 for three miles. Turn east on U.S. 199 and drive 25 miles. Turn right on Little Jones Creek Road/Jawbone Road (Forest Road 16) and drive south 9.6 miles. When the road forks, bear sharply left on Forest Road 16N02 and drive five miles to the trailhead at the end of the road. Hike east on Doe Flat Trail for another mile to reach the Buck Lake Trail.

Contact: Smith River National Recreation Area, P.O. Box 228, Gasquet, CA 95543; tel. (707) 457-3131 or fax (707) 457-3794.

3 Devils Punchbowl

11.0 mi/1.5 days

You'll be wondering if you're afflicted with a hex or a charm when you take the trip to Devils Punchbowl. The hex? The trail includes a climb with about 100 switchbacks, an endless up, up, and up that'll have you wheezing like a donkey low on hay. The charm? The first sight of Devils Punchbowl is not only drop-dead gorgeous, but is a sight you will never forget. It's small but pristine, set in a mountain granite bowl, framed by an imposing back wall—a shrine. To make this trip, start by hiking past Doe Flat and continuing a short way along Doe Creek. Just after the trail passes a little dirt mound, look for a right turn across Doe Creek. The turn is signed "Devils Punchbowl," but the sign is occasionally stolen, so be alert for the trail on the right side of Doe Creek. From here you start the first of 100 switchbacks up Bear Mountain, a long, forbidding butt-kicker. When you finally top the ridge, the route crosses Devils Creek and leaves the forest behind, crossing bare granite domes, the trail marked only by small stacks of rocks. You pass a smaller lake, then cross a rise, and the beautiful gemlike lake awaits. This place is something of a legend, but is visited only by those willing to pay the price of the terrible climb to reach it.

Special note: The entire region surrounding Devils Punchbowl consists of sheets of bare granite. The few campsites here are merely small, flat sleeping spaces on rock. There is no firewood available, so bring a backpacking stove for cooking. Bring zip-lock bags to carry out waste.

Location: In the Siskiyou Wilderness east of Crescent City; map A1, grid e2.

User groups: Hikers and dogs. No horses, or mountain bikes. No wheelchair facilities.

Permits: No permits are required. A campfire permit (free) is required for overnight use. Parking and access are free.

Maps: For a free brochure and hiking guide write to Smith River National Recreation Area at the address below. For a map of Klamath National Forest, send $6 to U.S. Forest Service, Attn: Map Sales, P.O. Box 587, Camino, CA 95709; tel. (530) 647-5390, fax (530) 647-5389, or website: www.r5.fs.fed.us/visitorcenter. Major credit cards accepted. Ask the USGS for a topographic map of the Devils Punchbowl area.

Directions: From Crescent City drive north on U.S. 101 for three miles to U.S. 199. Turn east on U.S. 199 and drive 25 miles to Little Jones Creek Road/Jawbone Road (Forest Road 16). Turn right on Little Jones Creek Road (Forest Road 16) and drive south 9.6 miles. When the road forks, bear sharply left on Forest Road 16N02 and drive five miles to the trailhead at the end of the road. Hike the Doe Flat Trail for 2.5 miles to reach the trailhead for Devils Punchbowl.

Contact: Smith River National Recreation Area, P.O. Box 228, Gasquet, CA 95543; tel. (707) 457-3131 or fax (707) 457-3794. Klamath National Forest, Happy Camp Ranger District, P.O. Box 377, Happy Camp, CA 96039-0377; tel. (530) 493-2243 or fax (530) 493-2212.

🔟 Youngs Valley Trail

13.0 mi/1.0 day

The 6.5-mile trip from Youngs Valley down Clear Creek to Youngs Meadow is a beautiful and rewarding trip. Youngs Meadow, set on the western slope of Preston Peak at an elevation of 4,500 feet, is very pretty and makes an excellent picnic area and campsite.

The hike features a 600-foot descent into the canyon and to Clear Creek. From here the ambitious can take this trip farther, much farther. The Youngs Valley Trail is a great first leg of a multi-day trip, ultimately heading either farther down Clear Creek to Wilderness Falls, an awesome setting (see the following hike), or to Rattlesnake Meadows on the slopes of Preston Peak, a short but rugged climb.

Note that this trail was once much shorter, but the access road has since been gated. So when you start the hike, you will be on the old Forest Road. It eventually turns to trail, then drops down into Youngs Valley.

Location: In the Siskiyou Wilderness east of Crescent City; map A1, grid e3.

User groups: Hikers, dogs and horses. No mountain bikes. No wheelchair facilities.

Permits: No permits are required. A campfire permit (free) is required for overnight use. Parking and access are free.

Maps: For a free brochure and hiking guide write to Smith River National Recreation Area at the address below. For a map of Klamath National Forest, send $6 to U.S. Forest Service, Attn: Map Sales, P.O. Box 587, Camino, CA 95709; tel. (530) 647-5390, fax (530) 647-5389, or website: www.r5.fs.fed.us/visitorcenter. Major credit cards accepted. Ask the USGS for a topographic map of the Devils Punchbowl area.

Directions: From Crescent City drive north on U.S. 101 for three miles to U.S. 199. Bear right (east) on U.S. 199 and drive 32 miles to Forest Road 18N07. Turn right and drive five miles to Forest Road 18N07. Continue on Forest Road 18N07 for 10 miles (twisty) toward Sanger Lake. Just before Sanger Lake, bear right on Forest Road 4803 (signed Youngs Valley Trail) and drive one mile to the end of the road and the trailhead.

Contact: Smith River National Recreation Area, P.O. Box 228, Gasquet, CA 95543; tel. (707) 457-3131 or fax (707) 457-3794. Klamath National Forest, Happy Camp Ranger District, P.O. Box 377, Happy Camp, CA 96039-0377; tel. (530) 493-2243 or fax (530) 493-2212.

5 Wilderness Falls
18.0 mi/2.0 days

Wilderness Falls is one of the great secrets of northwestern California, a true hidden jewel, dramatic and pure, and not only untouched, but largely unseen. This bubbling tower of water created by Clear Creek crashes down about 35 feet into a boulder, then pounds its way down into a foaming pool 100 feet across.

Our recommended route is to start on the Clear Creek National Recreation Trail out of Youngs Valley (see Youngs Valley Trail, above). Follow the Clear Creek Trail for about nine miles to the waterfall, featuring a 600-foot descent to the stream, then a gentle descent the rest of the way. There is an excellent campsite about a quarter of a mile upstream from the falls. It's an easy hike to the waterfall, but the trip back is up all the way and is best started very early in the morning when the temperature is the coolest.

Wilderness Falls can also be accessed out of Doe Flat (see Doe Flat Trail, above), but in late May and June, this route includes a wet, cold, and slippery ford of Clear Creek. In summer, it is a much easier crossing.

Location: In the Siskiyou Wilderness east of Crescent City; map A1, grid e3.

User groups: Hikers, dogs and horses. No mountain bikes. No wheelchair facilities.

Permits: A campfire permit (free) is required for overnight use. Parking and access are free.

Maps: For a map of Klamath National Forest, send $6 to U.S. Forest Service, Attn: Map Sales, P.O. Box 587, Camino, CA 95709; tel. (530) 647-5390, fax (530) 647-5389, or website: www.r5.fs.fed.us/visitorcenter. Major credit cards accepted. Ask the USGS for a topographic map of the Devils Punchbowl area.

Directions: From Crescent City drive north on U.S. 101 for three miles to U.S. 199. Bear right (east) on U.S. 199 and drive 32 miles to Forest Road 18N07. Turn right and drive five miles to Forest Road 18N07. Continue on Forest Road 18N07 for 10 miles (twisty) toward Sanger Lake. Just before Sanger Lake, bear right on Forest Road 4803 (signed Youngs Valley Trail) and drive one mile to the end of the road and the trailhead.

Contact: Klamath National Forest, Happy Camp Ranger District, P.O. Box 377, Happy Camp, CA 96039-0377; tel. (530) 493-2243 or fax (530) 493-2212; Smith River National Recreation Area, P.O. Box 228, Gasquet, CA 95543; tel. (707) 457-3131 or fax (707) 457-3794.

6 Preston Peak
19.0 mi/2.0 days

Only mountaineers need sign up for this trip. The last mile to reach the summit of Preston Peak is steep, rough, and primitive, and with no marked trail you must have the ability to scramble cross-country and recognize a dangerous spot when you see it. That done, you'll gain the top—7,309 feet and by far the highest spot in the region—with wondrous surrounding views. Even Mount Shasta way off to the southeast comes clearly into view, along with the famous peaks in the Trinity Alps and Marble Mountain Wilderness. My favorite route to climb Preston Peak is to hike the Youngs Valley Trail to Youngs Meadow (an easy five miles), head down the Clear Creek Trail (another easy mile), and then turn east on the Rattlesnake Meadow Trail (about two very steep, rough, and primitive miles). At the end of the Rattlesnake Meadow Trail, hikers must go cross-country for another mile or so to Preston Peak. The last mile is a scramble. Pick your route very carefully and make no climbing mistakes. While this is a non-technical climb, there is one difficult spot that can be dangerous. Take your time and pick your way up one step at a time.

Special note: Always stay off this mountain in wet weather because the route is very slippery, and always avoid routes that cross through loose shale, which can be extremely dangerous. A fall here can be life threatening.

Location: In the Siskiyou Wilderness east of Crescent City; map A1, grid e3.

User groups: Hikers only. Dogs are permitted but are strongly not recommended on the non-forested slopes of Preston Peak. No horses, or mountain bikes. No wheelchair facilities.

Permits: A campfire permit is required for overnight use. Parking and access are free.

Maps: For a map of Klamath National Forest, send $6 to U.S. Forest Service, Attn: Map Sales, P.O. Box 587, Camino, CA 95709; tel. (530) 647-5390, fax (530) 647-5389, or website: www.r5.fs.fed.us/visitorcenter. Major credit cards accepted. A map of the Marble Mountain Wilderness can also be purchased for $6. Ask the USGS for a topographic map of the Devils Punchbowl area.

Directions: From Crescent City drive north on U.S. 101 for three miles to U.S. 199. Bear right (east) on U.S. 199 and drive 32 miles to Forest Road 18N07. Turn right and drive five miles to Forest Road 18N07. Continue on Forest Road 18N07 for 10 miles (twisty) toward Sanger Lake. Just before Sanger Lake, bear right on Forest Road 4803 (signed Youngs Valley Trail) and drive one mile to the end of the road and the trailhead.

Contact: Klamath National Forest, Happy Camp Ranger District, P.O. Box 377, Happy Camp, CA 96039-0377; tel. (530) 493-2243 or fax (530) 493-2212.

◪ Island Lake Trail

9.0 mi/2.0 days

Island Lake is a mountain bowl framed by the back wall of Jedediah Mountain, a wild, primitive area where threatened spotted owls are more common than hikers. The trailhead is at the Bear Basin area. The trip starts with a quick walk down to the South Fork Smith River, where you'll enter the untouched Siskiyou Wilderness. Enjoy the stream; the hike that follows is anything but enjoyable. The trail is routed up along a mountain spine, climbing up, up, and up for what seems like an endless three miles. It finally tops a ridge and turns around a bend, where little Island Lake comes into view. A great sense of relief will wash over you.

There are two excellent camps at the lake, set in trees near the lake's shore. The trout are eager to bite, but most are very small, dinker-sized brook trout. A great afternoon side trip is to hike the rim around the lake, most easily done in a counterclockwise direction, to the top of Jedediah Mountain, a perfect picnic site and a great lookout.

If you hiked to Island Lake in years prior to 2001, you will note in the directions that the trailhead has been moved to provide improved access. The access road to the previous trailhead was often impassable until mid-June.

Location: In Smith River National Recreation Area east of Crescent City; map A1, grid f0.

User groups: Hikers, dogs, and horses. No mountain bikes. No wheelchair facilities.

Permits: A campfire permit is required. Parking and access are free.

Maps: For a free brochure and hiking guide write to Smith River National Recreation Area at the address below. For a map of Klamath National Forest, send $6 to U.S. Forest Service, Attn: Map Sales, P.O. Box 587, Camino, CA 95709; tel. (530) 647-5390, fax (530) 647-5389, or website: www.r5.fs.fed.us/visitorcenter. Major credit cards accepted. Ask the USGS for a topographic map of the Devils Punchbowl area.

Directions: From Crescent City drive north on U.S. 101 for three miles to U.S. 199. Bear right (east) on U.S. 199 and drive 25 miles to Little Jones Creek Road/Jawbone Road (Forest Road 16). Turn right and drive eight miles to Forest Road 16N02. Turn left and drive 2.5 miles to Forest Road 16N10. Turn right and drive about two miles to a locked gate. This is the trailhead access point. Park and walk .25 mile to the trailhead.

Contact: Smith River National Recreation Area, P.O. Box 228, Gasquet, CA 95543; tel. (707) 457-3131 or fax (707) 457-3794. Klamath National Forest, Happy Camp Ranger District, P.O. Box 377, Happy Camp, CA 96039-0377; tel. (530) 493-2243 or fax (530) 493-2212.

8 Baldy Peak Trail
10.4 mi/2.0 days

The route to Baldy Peak is actually a section of the South Kelsey Trail (see chapter A0), the historic route that once went from Crescent City east all the way through the Marble Mountain Wilderness to Fort Jones. This part of it is an excellent trip, and if you get caught in the rain, a bonus is that the Bear Wallow Shelter (not much more than a roof) is available just beyond the summit. The trip starts on the Gunbarrel Trail (see chapter A0), which extends for 1.25 miles to the junction with the Kelsey Trail. From there, it's four miles to Baldy Peak at 5,775 feet. The views are outstanding, especially Preston Peak (at 7,309 feet) to the north, the most impressive feature in this wild landscape.

An option for those with plenty of time and endurance is to continue east on the Kelsey Trail, which extends about 12 miles farther to Red Hill (5,642 feet), Bear Peak (5,740 feet), and nearby Bear Lake. The latter has an excellent campsite.

Location: In the Siskiyou Wilderness east of Crescent City; map A1, grid f0.

User groups: Hikers, dogs, and horses. No mountain bikes. No wheelchair facilities.

Permits: A campfire permit is required. Parking and access are free.

Maps: For a free brochure and hiking guide write to Smith River National Recreation Area at the address below. For a map of Klamath National Forest, send $6 to U.S. Forest Service, Attn: Map Sales, P.O. Box 587, Camino, CA 95709; tel. (530) 647-5390, fax (530) 647-5389, or website: www.r5.fs.fed.us/visitorcenter. Major credit cards accepted. Ask the USGS for a topographic map of the Prescott Mountain area.

Directions: This recommended trailhead can be reached only by hiking the Gunbarrel Trail (see chapter A0): From Crescent City drive north on U.S. 101 for three miles to U.S. 199. Bear right (east) on U.S. 199 and drive 25 miles to Little Jones Creek Road/Jawbone Road (Forest Road 16). Turn right and drive 14.4 miles. When the road forks, bear sharply left (to stay on Forest Road 16) and continue to Forest Road 16N18. Turn left and drive five miles to Forest Road 15N34. Bear left on Forest Road 15N34 and drive 1.2 miles to the end of the road. The trailhead is on the left. Hike the Gunbarrel Trail for 1.2 miles to reach the Baldy Peak section of the South Kelsey Trail.

Note: The trailhead suggested here is fine if your planned adventure is to Baldy Peak and back. Many people have longer backpacking adventures planned and prefer the trailhead for the South Kelsey Trail (see chapter A0).

Contact: Smith River National Recreation Area, P.O. Box 228, Gasquet, CA 95543; tel. (707) 457-3131 or fax (707) 457-3794. Klamath National Forest, Happy Camp Ranger District, P.O. Box 377, Happy Camp, CA 96039-0377; tel. (530) 493-2243 or fax (530) 493-2212.

9 Paradise Lake Trail
4.0 mi/2.75 hrs

Paradise Lake, set at an elevation of 5,920 feet, is the easiest lake to reach of the 79 lakes in the Marble Mountain Wilderness. The pretty hike is short enough for a day trip, and it has good lakeside campgrounds if you want to turn your trip into an overnighter. There are also some excellent side trips, including climbing Kings Castle (see the following hike), which tops the mountain rim on the back side of the lake.

From the trailhead at 4,880 feet, the route quickly enters a designated wilderness, then climbs for nearly two miles, steeply in some areas, and switches back and forth through an old, untouched forest. It then emerges from the trees and rises to a saddle; on the other side is Paradise Lake, sitting in a mountain pocket, emerald green and peaceful. Paradise is a mostly shallow lake with few trout, but it does have one deep area. Because the hike to the lake takes only two hours, there are usually campers here all summer long.

Location: In the Marble Mountain Wilderness west of Yreka; map A1, grid h6.

User groups: Hikers, dogs, and horses. No mountain bikes. No wheelchair facilities.

Permits: No permits required. A campfire permit (free) is required for overnight use. Parking and access are free.

Maps: A trail information sheet can be obtained by contacting the Scott River Ranger District at the address below. For a map of Klamath National Forest, send $6 to U.S. Forest Service, Attn: Map Sales, P.O. Box 587, Camino, CA 95709; tel. (530) 647-5390, fax (530) 647-5389, or website: www.r5.fs.fed.us/visitorcenter. Major credit cards accepted. A map of the Marble Mountain Wilderness can also be purchased for $6. Ask the USGS for topographic maps of the Scott Bar and Marble Mountain areas.

Directions: From Interstate 5 at Yreka take the Highway 3/Fort Jones exit and drive 16.5 miles to Fort Jones. Turn right on Scott River Road and drive 16.8 miles to the turnoff for Indian Scotty Campground. Cross the concrete bridge, bear left on Forest Road 44N45 and drive about five miles. Turn right on an unmarked Forest Road and drive six miles (signed Paradise Lake) to the trailhead near the wilderness border.

Contact: Klamath National Forest, Scott River Ranger District, 11263 N. Highway 3, Fort Jones, CA 96032-9702; tel. (530) 468-5351 or fax (530) 468-1290.

🔟 Kings Castle Trail
5.5 mi/5.0 hrs

Kings Castle is the imposing perch that sits on the back side of Paradise Lake, a .5-mile climb that tops out at the summit at 7,405 feet. It's a great hike with unforgettable views, looking down at little Paradise Lake as well as far beyond to Northern California's most famous mountain peaks. From the trailhead of Paradise Lake Trail, you make the 1,040-foot climb up to Paradise Lake. From the foot of Paradise Lake, bear to the left and cross the lake's inlet on the left side. Here you will pick up the route. It climbs up out of the basin to a ridge (great views start here), and then you gain the peak

of Kings Castle by climbing up a series of switchbacks up the back side. It is a special trip every step of the way, a climb of 2,525 feet from the trailhead. While not a maintained trail, the route is worn well enough to follow.

Location: In the Marble Mountain Wilderness west of Yreka; map A1, grid h6.

User groups: Hikers only. No dogs, horses or mountain bikes. No wheelchair facilities.

Permits: No permits required. A campfire permit (free) is required for overnight use. Parking and access are free.

Maps: A trail information sheet can be obtained by contacting the Scott River Ranger District at the address below. For a map of Klamath National Forest, send $6 to U.S. Forest Service, Attn: Map Sales, P.O. Box 587, Camino, CA 95709; tel. (530) 647-5390, fax (530) 647-5389, or website: www.r5.fs.fed.us/visitorcenter. Major credit cards accepted. A map of the Marble Mountain Wilderness can also be purchased for $6. Ask the USGS for topographic maps of the Scott Bar and Marble Mountain areas.

Directions: From Interstate 5 at Yreka take the Highway 3/Fort Jones exit and drive 16.5 miles to Fort Jones. Turn right on Scott River Road and drive 16.8 miles to the turnoff for Indian Scotty Campground. Cross the concrete bridge, bear left on Forest Road 44N45 and drive about five miles. Turn right on an unmarked Forest Road and drive six miles (signed Paradise Lake) to the trailhead near the wilderness border. Hike 1.9 miles to Paradise Lake; bear right and continue another .5 mile to Kings Castle.

Contact: Klamath National Forest, Scott River Ranger District, 11263 N. Highway 3, Fort Jones, CA 96032-9702; tel. (530) 468-5351 or fax (530) 468-1290.

1️⃣1️⃣ Marble Mountain Rim
16.0 mi/2.0 days

Marble isn't usually thought of as a precious stone, but it's gemlike for hikers on this trail. With Marble Valley nearby, climbing the Marble Mountain Rim can be a perfect weekend trip, easily extended into a longer one. The trailhead at Lovers Camp is probably the most popular in the entire wilderness, especially for packers going by horse (corrals are available at the trailhead). The route heads up Canyon Creek, a moderate climb, then intersects the Pacific Crest Trail at Marble Valley. This area is very scenic, with lots of deer and wild orchids. Turn left and the trail crosses Marble Mountain itself, and once you've arrived, a side trip to the Marble Rim is mandatory. The views are stunning, sweeping in both directions, with steep drop-offs adding to the quiet drama. The rock itself is unlike anything else in Northern California, a mix of black, red, and tan marble, something you'll never forget.

Location: In the Marble Mountain Wilderness west of Yreka; map A1, grid h6.

User groups: Hikers only. No dogs, horses or mountain bikes. No wheelchair facilities.

Permits: No permits required. A campfire permit (free) is required for overnight use. Parking and access are free.

Maps: A trail information sheet can be obtained by contacting the Scott River Ranger District at the address below. For a map of Klamath National Forest, send $6 to U.S. Forest Service, Attn: Map Sales, P.O. Box 587, Camino, CA 95709; tel. (530) 647-5390, fax (530) 647-5389, or website: www.r5.fs.fed.us/visitorcenter. Major credit cards accepted. A map of the Marble Mountain Wilderness can also be purchased for $6. Ask the USGS for topographic maps of the Scott Bar and Marble Mountain areas.

Directions: From Interstate 5 at Yreka take the Highway 3/Fort Jones exit and drive 16.5 miles to Fort Jones. Turn right on Scott River Road and drive 16.8 miles to the turnoff for Indian Scotty Campground. Cross the concrete bridge, bear left on Forest Road 44N45 and drive 5.4 miles to Forest Road 43N45. Turn left and drive 1.7 miles to Lovers Camp. Bear right and drive 0.1 mile to the trailhead.

Contact: Klamath National Forest, Scott River Ranger District, 11263 N. Highway 3, Fort Jones, CA 96032-9702; tel. (530) 468-5351 or fax (530) 468-1290.

12 Kelsey Creek Trail
18.0 mi/2.0 days

The Kelsey Creek Trail offers many miles of beautiful streamside travel, with the Paradise Lake Basin as the intended destination for most hikers on this route. The trailhead is set near the confluence of Kelsey Creek and the Scott River, and from there the trail follows Kelsey Creek upstream. Wildflowers are abundant in the meadows. After four miles and two creek crossings, you'll reach Maple Falls, the prettiest waterfall in the region. The trail continues up the canyon, finally rising to intersect with the Pacific Crest Trail just below Red Rock. From this junction, you have many options. The closest lake is secluded Bear Lake, a pretty spot but, alas, with some tules and mosquitoes. To reach it from the junction requires a short but steep drop into the basin to the immediate west.

Location: In the Marble Mountain Wilderness west of Yreka; map A1, grid g7.

User groups: Hikers, dogs, and horses. No mountain bikes. No wheelchair facilities.

Permits: A campfire permit (free) is required for overnight use. Parking and access are free.

Maps: A trail information sheet can be obtained by contacting the Scott River Ranger District at the address below. For a map of Klamath National Forest, send $6 to U.S. Forest Service, Attn: Map Sales, P.O. Box 587, Camino, CA 95709; tel. (530) 647-5390, fax (530) 647-5389, or website: www.r5.fs.fed.us/visitorcenter. Major credit cards accepted. A map of the Marble Mountain Wilderness can also be purchased for $6. Ask the USGS for topographic maps of the Scott Bar and Grider Valley areas.

Directions: From Interstate 5 at Yreka take the Highway 3/Fort Jones exit and drive 16.5 miles to Fort Jones and Scott River Road. Turn right on Scott River Road and drive 16.8 miles to the Scott River Bridge. Cross it and then turn left immediately and follow the road for 0.3 mile. Bear right on another dirt road (do not continue to a second bridge) and drive .25 mile to the trailhead.

Contact: Klamath National Forest, Scott River Ranger District, 11263 N. Highway 3, Fort Jones, CA 96032-9702; tel. (530) 468-5351 or fax (530) 468-1290.

13 Sky High Lakes

14.0 mi/2.0 days

The Sky High Lakes make for a great overnighter, a seven-mile hike each day, or an inspired one-day in-and-outer. The trip starts at the Canyon Creek Trailhead near Lovers Camp. For this trip, take the Canyon Creek Trail for about a mile up to a fork, and continue straight (do not turn left and cross Canyon Creek). From here the trail continues to climb, skirting below Marble Mountain, and eventually to Lower Sky High Lake. This is your destination, set below a monster of a rock, Peak 6817. Nearby little Frying Pan Lake and Upper Sky High Lake provide side jaunts. Note that the trail continues to climb up to the rim and hooks up with the Pacific Crest Trail and makes an 18-mile loop trip possible.

Location: In the Marble Mountain Wilderness west of Yreka; map A1, grid h6.

User groups: Hikers, dogs, and horses. No mountain bikes. No wheelchair facilities.

Permits: A campfire permit is required only for hikers planning to camp in the wilderness. Parking and access are free.

Maps: A trail information sheet can be obtained by contacting the Scott River Ranger District at the address below. For a map of Klamath National Forest, send $6 to U.S. Forest Service, Attn: Map Sales, P.O. Box 587, Camino, CA 95709; tel. (530) 647-5390, fax (530) 647-5389, or website: www.r5.fs.fed.us/visitorcenter. Major credit cards accepted. A map of the Marble Mountain Wilderness can also be purchased for $6. Ask the USGS for a topographic map of the Marble Mountain area.

Directions: From Interstate 5 at Yreka take the Highway 3/Fort Jones exit and drive 16.5 miles to Fort Jones. Turn right on Scott River Road and drive 16.8 miles to the turnoff for Indian Scotty Campground. Cross the concrete bridge, bear left on Forest Road 44N45 and drive 5.4 miles to Forest Road 43N45. Turn left and drive 1.7 miles to Lovers Camp. Bear right and drive 0.1 mile to the Canyon Creek Trailhead.

Contact: Klamath National Forest, Scott River Ranger District, 11263 N. Highway 3, Fort Jones, CA 96032-9702; tel. (530) 468-5351 or fax (530) 468-1290.

14 Shackleford Creek Trail

13.0 mi/2.0 days

Campbell, Cliff, and Summit Lakes are three of the prettiest lakes in the Marble Mountain Wilderness. The ease of reaching them on the Shackleford Trail (only 5.5 miles to Campbell Lake) makes them a popular destination all summer long. The trail is routed up Shackleford Creek to a basin set just below the Pacific Crest Trail. Here you'll find a series of small mountain lakes. Note that ambitious trekkers traveling off-trail cross-country style can create routes to little Gem, Jewel, and Angel Lakes. A bonus is that the trip can be extended by hiking up the rim to the Pacific Crest Trail, then turning right and going three miles to the Sky High Lakes.

Location: In the Marble Mountain Wilderness west of Yreka; map A1, grid h7.

User groups: Hikers, dogs, and horses. No mountain bikes. No wheelchair facilities.

Permits: A campfire permit is required only for hikers planning to camp in the wilderness. Parking and access are free.

Maps: A trail information sheet can be obtained by contacting the Scott River Ranger District at the address below. For a map of Klamath National Forest, send $6 to U.S. Forest Service, Attn: Map Sales, P.O. Box 587, Camino, CA 95709; tel. (530) 647-5390, fax (530) 647-5389, or website: www.r5.fs.fed.

us/visitorcenter. Major credit cards accepted. A map of the Marble Mountain Wilderness can also be purchased for $6. Ask the USGS for a topographic map of the Boulder Peak area.

Directions: From Interstate 5 at Yreka take the Highway 3/Fort Jones exit and drive 16.5 miles to Fort Jones and Scott River Road. Turn right on Scott River Road and drive seven miles to Quartz Valley Road. Turn left on Quartz Valley Road and drive about four miles to the sign for Shackleford Trailhead and Forest Road 43N21. Turn right and drive 6.5 miles to the trailhead at the end of the road.

Contact: Klamath National Forest, Scott River Ranger District, 11263 N. Highway 3, Fort Jones, CA 96032-9702; tel. (530) 468-5351 or fax (530) 468-1290.

15 Haypress Meadows Trailhead

29.0 mi/3.0 days

The Cuddihy Lakes basin is one of the prettiest sections of the Marble Mountain Wilderness. It also is home to one of the largest concentrations of bears anywhere in California, according to the Department of Fish and Game. But this is a great trip, out to One Mile Lake and the Cuddihy Lakes. This area is perfect for backpacking, with beauty, lookouts, and good trail access. After you park at the trailhead at 4,500 feet, the first two miles of trail lead up and across a fir-covered slope of a small peak (a little butt-kicker of a climb). Then the trail descends into Haypress Meadows, a major junction. Turn right and head up Sandy Ridge, a long, steady climb; plan to top the ridge and then camp at Monument Lake, Meteor Lake, One Mile Lake, or Cuddihy Lakes. The view from Sandy Ridge is a sweeping lookout of the Marble Mountains to the east and the Siskiyous to the west, with mountaintop glimpses of Mount Shasta and the Marble Rim.

Location: In the Marble Mountain Wilderness near Somes Bar; map A1, grid h3.

User groups: Hikers, dogs, and horses. No mountain bikes. No wheelchair facilities.

Permits: A campfire permit (free) is required for overnight use. Parking and access are free.

Maps: A trail information sheet can be obtained by contacting the Orleans Ranger District at the address below. For a map, send $6 to U.S. Forest Service, Attn: Map Sales, P.O. Box 587, Camino, CA 95709; tel. (530) 647-5390, fax (530) 647-5389, or website: www.r5.fs.fed. us/visitorcenter. Major credit cards accepted. A map of the Marble Mountain Wilderness can also be purchased for $6. Ask the USGS for a topographic map of the Somes Bar area.

Directions: From Highway 299 at Willow Creek, turn north on Highway 96 and drive 42 miles to Orleans. Continue eight miles to Somes Bar and Salmon River Road. Turn right on Salmon River Road (Highway 93) and drive 100 feet to a sign "Camp 3/Haypress Trailhead" and Forest Road 15N17 (Offield Mountain Road). Turn left and drive 14.6 miles to Forest Road 15N17E. Turn left and drive 1.5 miles to the access road for Haypress Trailhead. Turn left and drive one mile to the trailhead.

Contact: Klamath National Forest, Orleans Ranger District, P.O. Box 410, Orleans, CA 95556-0410; tel. (530) 627-3291 or fax (530) 627-3401.

16 Spirit Lake Trail

34.0 mi/4.0 days

We've hiked to hundreds and hundreds of mountain lakes, and Spirit Lake is one of the prettiest we've ever seen. It sits at the bottom of a mountain bowl encircled by old-growth trees, with a few campsites set at lakeside. The Karuk tribe considers this a sacred place. The abundance of wildlife can be remarkable. The far side of the lake is a major deer migration route, an osprey makes regular trips to pluck trout out of the lake for dinner, and the fishing is quite good, especially early in the summer.

Spirit Lake can be the feature destination for a week-long backpack loop, beginning on the Haypress Meadows Trail and leading up to Sandy Ridge and then out to the lake, about

17 miles one way. Most hikers will stop for the night at One Mile or the Cuddihy Lakes on the way out, and that is why those two areas get so much use. Spirit Lake is best visited during the first week of June, when the nights are still cold, the people are few, and the area abounds with fish and deer.

Location: In the Marble Mountain Wilderness near Somes Bar; map A1, grid h3.

User groups: Hikers, dogs, and horses. No mountain bikes. No wheelchair facilities.

Permits: A campfire permit (free) is required for overnight use. Parking and access are free.

Maps: A trail information sheet can be obtained by contacting the Orleans Ranger District at the address below. For a map, send $6 to U.S. Forest Service, Attn: Map Sales, P.O. Box 587, Camino, CA 95709; tel. (530) 647-5390, fax (530) 647-5389, or website: www.r5.fs.fed. us/visitorcenter. Major credit cards accepted. A map of the Marble Mountain Wilderness can also be purchased for $6. Ask the USGS for a topographic map of the Somes Bar area.

Directions: From Highway 299 at Willow Creek, turn north on Highway 96 and drive 42 miles to Orleans. Continue eight miles to Somes Bar and Salmon River Road. Turn right on Salmon River Road (Highway 93) and drive 100 feet to a sign "Camp 3/Haypress Trailhead" and Forest Road 15N17 (Offield Mountain Road). Turn left and drive 14.6 miles to Forest Road 15N17E. Turn left and drive 1.5 miles to the access road for Haypress Trailhead. Turn left and drive one mile to the trailhead.

Contact: Klamath National Forest, Happy Camp Ranger District, P.O. Box 377, Happy Camp, CA 96039-0377; tel. (530) 493-2243, or fax (530) 493-2212.

🔟 Little North Fork Trailhead
16.0 mi/2.0 days

Your destination options from this trailhead? There are many: Chimney Rock, Clear Lake, Lily Lake, and Chimney Rock Lake. This trail provides an excellent trip, providing you don't

mind the long grind of a climb to reach the lakes. Like a lot of trails on the edge of the wilderness, this one starts with a long climb out of a river canyon. From the Little North Fork Trailhead you start by climbing out toward Chimney Rock, grunting out a rise of about 4,000 feet as you leave the river lowlands and reach the Marble Mountain Wilderness. It's about an eight-mile trip to Clear Lake, a good first day's destination, and while you can simply return the next day, most people will take several days to venture deeper into the wilderness, with 13 lakes and 20 miles of stream in the Upper Abbotts Camp (former cabin site) and English Peak areas.

Location: In the Marble Mountain Wilderness near Sawyers Bar; map A1, grid j5.

User groups: Hikers, dogs, and horses. No mountain bikes. No wheelchair facilities.

Permits: A campfire permit (free) is required for overnight use. Parking and access are free.

Maps: A trail information sheet can be obtained by contacting the Salmon Ranger District at the address below. For a map, send $6 to U.S. Forest Service, Attn: Map Sales, P.O. Box 587, Camino, CA 95709; tel. (530) 647-5390, fax (530) 647-5389, or website: www.r5.fs.fed.us/visitorcenter. Major credit cards accepted. A map of the Marble Mountain Wilderness can also be purchased for $6. Ask the USGS for a topographic map of the Sawyers Bar area.

Directions: From Interstate 5 at Yreka take the Highway 3/Fort Jones exit and drive southwest 28 miles to Etna at Sawyers Bar Road. Turn west on Sawyers Bar Road and drive about 25 miles to the town of Sawyers Bar. Continue west on the same road for four miles to Little North Fork Road (Forest Road 40N51). Turn right (north) and drive two miles to the trailhead at the end of the road.

Contact: Klamath National Forest, Salmon River Ranger District, 11263 N. Highway 3, Fort Jones, CA 96032-9702; tel. (530) 468-5351 or fax (530) 468-1290.

18 Mule Bridge Trailhead
28.0 mi/3.0 days

The trailhead at Idlewild Campground is set alongside the Salmon River, and once you've tightened your backpack, get ready for a long climb up the river drainage. The trail follows the Salmon River all the way up to its headwaters, gaining about 3,500 feet in the process. Plan on climbing for 14 or 15 miles along the river until you start reaching the higher country with many lakeside camps. The trail forks eight miles from the trailhead, with the right-hand fork leading to Shelly Meadows and the Pacific Crest Trail. The main trail continues north for access to Upper Abbotts Camp (former cabin site) and many lakes in the upper drainage. This trail ties in with the Little North Fork Trail near Hancock Lake. The prettiest glacial-formed lakes in this region are Osprey Lake (15 miles), Cabin Gulch Lake (15.5 miles), and Bug Lake (14 miles). The best way to get there is taking the Big Gulch Trail northeast from Upper Abbotts Camp and continuing to Grants Meadows Lake. From here it's up and over a ridge to the lakes. This route is the gentler way to reach this area. Once you get in this far there is a good cross-country route to nearby Wooley and Osprey Lakes. Good campsites are available at Cabin Gulch (12 miles, 6,000 feet), Grants Meadows (13.5 miles, 6,200 feet), and Shelly Meadows (15 miles, 6,300 feet).

Location: In the Marble Mountain Wilderness west of Etna; map A1, grid j7.

User groups: Hikers, dogs, and horses. No mountain bikes. No wheelchair facilities.

Permits: A campfire permit (free) is required for overnight use. Parking and access are free.

Maps: A trail information sheet can be obtained by contacting the Salmon Ranger District at the address below. For a map, send $6 to U.S. Forest Service, Attn: Map Sales, P.O. Box 587, Camino, CA 95709; tel. (530) 647-5390, fax (530) 647-5389, or website: www.r5.fs.fed.us/visitorcenter. Major credit cards accepted. A map of the Marble Mountain Wilderness can also be purchased for $6. Ask the USGS for a topographic map of the Sawyers Bar area.

Directions: From Interstate 5 at Yreka take the Highway 3/Fort Jones exit and drive southwest 28 miles to Etna. Turn west on Etna-Somes Bar Road (Main Street in town) and drive 21 miles to Idlewild Campground. As you enter the campground, take the left fork in the road and continue two miles to the trailhead.

Contact: Klamath National Forest, Salmon River Ranger District, 11263 N. Highway 3, Fort Jones, CA 96032-9702; tel. (530) 468-5351 or fax (530) 468-1290.

19 Taylor Lake Trail
1.0 mi/0.5 hr

Taylor Lake is proof that wilderness-like lakes can be accessible by wheelchair. The trail is hard-packed dirt and wheelchair accessible, though wheelchairs with wide wheels are recommended. For those with boots instead of wheels, it's about a 10-minute walk to Taylor Lake, a long, narrow lake set on the northern end of the Russian Wilderness. Trout fishing is often very good here, and the walk is short enough for you to bring along a small raft or float tube. The only downer here is that occasionally the Forest Service permits cows to graze, and they stomp the grass at the far end of the lake and sometimes even walk in the shallows. While cows are still permitted, the Forest Service has rerouted the trail so hikers won't be walking amid them at the meadow.

For a side-trip option, the Pacific Crest Trail runs east just above the lake, although the most direct access in the area for the PCT is at nearby Etna Summit.

Location: From Etna Summit into the Russian Wilderness west of Etna; map A1, grid j8.

User groups: Hikers, dogs, horses, and wheelchairs. No mountain bikes.

Permits: No permits are required for day-use. A campfire permit (free) is required for overnight use. Parking and access are free.

Maps: A trail information sheet can be obtained by contacting the Salmon Ranger District at the address below. For a map, send $6 to U.S. Forest Service, Attn: Map Sales, P.O. Box 587, Camino, CA 95709; tel. (530) 647-5390, fax (530) 647-5389, or website: www.r5.fs.fed.us/visitorcenter. Major credit cards accepted. A map of the Marble Mountain Wilderness can also be purchased for $6. Ask the USGS for a topographic map of the Eaton Peak area.

Directions: From Interstate 5 at Yreka take the Highway 3/Fort Jones exit and drive 28 miles southwest to Etna. Turn west on Etna-Somes Bar Road (Main Street in town) and drive 10.25 miles just past Etna Summit to Forest Road 41N18 (signed access road). Turn left and continue to the trailhead.

Contact: Klamath National Forest, Salmon River Ranger District, 11263 N. Highway 3, Fort Jones, CA 96032-9702; tel. (530) 468-5351 or fax (530) 468-1290.

20 Statue Lake

6.0 mi/4.0 hrs

Statue Lake earned its name from the unique granite sculptures that frame the back wall of the lake. When you first arrive at the small lake, it's a wondrous yet solemn sight, one of nature's mountain temples. Some of the granite outcrops look like fingers sculpted with a giant chisel. There is a small primitive campsite on a granite bluff, from which you can often see small brook trout in the lake rising to feed.

After parking at the Music Creek Trailhead, start the trip by hiking up a moderate grade and climbing about a mile to the Pacific Crest Trail. Turn right and hike on the PCT for about 1.5 miles, an easy walk in the forest. When you reach a small spring creek, stop and fill your canteens; then leave the trail and head uphill. It's about a 30-minute hike cross-country to the lake, the last 10 minutes over a large field of boulders.

Location: In the Russian Wilderness west of Etna; map A1, grid j8.

User groups: Hikers only. Dogs are permitted but not advised because of the route crossing a boulder field. No horses or mountain bikes. No wheelchair facilities.

Permits: No permits are required for day-use. A campfire permit (free) is required for overnight use. Parking and access are free.

Maps: A trail information sheet can be obtained by contacting the Salmon Ranger District at the address below. For a map, send $6 to U.S. Forest Service, Attn: Map Sales, P.O. Box 587, Camino, CA 95709; tel. (530) 647-5390, fax (530) 647-5389, or website: www.r5.fs.fed.us/visitorcenter. Major credit cards accepted. A map of the Marble Mountain Wilderness can also be purchased for $6. Ask the USGS for a topographic map of the Sawyers Bar area.

Directions: From Interstate 5 at Yreka take the Highway 3/Fort Jones exit and drive 28 miles southwest to Etna. Turn west on Etna-Somes Bar Road (Main Street in town) and drive over Etna Summit and continue down the other side to Forest Road 40N54 (just before the Salmon River Bridge). Turn left on Forest Road 40N54 and drive eight miles to the Music Creek Trailhead (a sign is usually posted that says Pacific Crest Trail. The sign for Music Creek Trailhead is repeatedly stolen).

Contact: Klamath National Forest, Salmon River Ranger District, 11263 N. Highway 3, Fort Jones, CA 96032-9702; tel. (530) 468-5351 or fax (530) 468-1290.

PACIFIC CREST TRAIL (PCT) SECTION OVERVIEW

92.0 mi one way/8.0 days

Trail sections extend from Etna Summit north through the Marble Mountains to Seiad Valley on Highway 96, then onward to the Rogue Wilderness in southern Oregon.

This stretch of the Pacific Crest Trail includes some of its most and least popular sections in Northern California. The Etna Trailhead is an excellent jump-off once you get past the first few miles of dry, often hot terrain. It heads directly into the Marble

Mountain Wilderness, crossing through Marble Valley, past Marble Mountain itself, then onward past Paradise Lake to the northern sections of the wilderness. Most of the trail here is above tree line, with outstanding lookouts at several points, including a great vista from Marble Rim. As you head north, the trail becomes less and less traveled, eventually leaving the Marbles and descending along Grider Creek to the Klamath River town of Seiad Valley. From here the trail is routed 34 miles north into Oregon. That section of the trail starts with a steep five-mile climb to Upper Devils Peak, which keeps most day-hikers off the route. For more specific information on major trail sections in this zone of the PCT, see the following three hikes in this chapter.

PCT-46 Etna Summit to Grider Creek

49.0 mi one way/4.0 days

The Etna Summit is one of the major access points for the Pacific Crest Trail in Northern California. There is a good, safe parking area (good views from here), and at an elevation of 5,492 feet, you don't have to start your hike with a wicked climb that is demanded at so many other wilderness trailheads. From Etna Summit the trail starts by crossing rugged, dry country that is best dealt with in the morning, reaching Shelly Lake about eight miles in. Note that there is no water available along this route until Shelly Lake. The campground at Shelly Meadows is a good first-night stopover. From there an excellent second-day destination is the Marble Valley, about another 10 miles north, with camping in the nearby Sky High Lakes Basin. The next 20 miles of trail cross through and out of the Marble Mountains. You'll pass Marble Mountain (a side trip to Marble Rim is mandatory), Paradise Lake, and Kings Castle; many visitors will make camp at Paradise Lake. From there the trail follows Big Ridge to Buckhorn Mountain (6,908 feet), continues past Huckleberry

Mountain (6,303 feet), and then drops down to the headwaters of Grider Creek, the next major trailhead access point.

Location: From Etna Summit north into the Marble Mountain Wilderness west of Etna; map A1, grid j8.

User groups: Hikers, dogs, and horses. No mountain bikes. No wheelchair facilities.

Permits: Campfire permits (free) are required. Parking and access are free.

Maps: A trail information sheet can be obtained by contacting the Salmon River Ranger District at the address below. For a map of Klamath National Forest, send $6 to U.S. Forest Service, Attn: Map Sales, P.O. Box 587, Camino, CA 95709; tel. (530) 647-5390, fax (530) 647-5389, or website: www.r5.fs.fed.us/visitorcenter. Major credit cards accepted. A map of the Marble Mountain Wilderness can also be purchased for $6. Ask the USGS for a topographic map of the Eaton Peak area.

Directions: From Interstate 5 at Yreka take the Highway 3/Fort Jones exit and drive 28 miles to Etna. Turn west on Etna-Somes Bar Road (Main Street in town) and drive 10.5 miles to Etna Summit. The parking area is along the road.

Contact: Klamath National Forest, Salmon River Ranger District, 11263 N. Highway 3, Fort Jones, CA 96032-9702; tel. (530) 468-5351 or fax (530) 468-1290.

PCT-47 Grider Creek to Seiad Valley

7.0 mi one way/1.0 day

The Pacific Crest Trail provides a good access point at the headwaters of Grider Creek, although most hikers use it to head south into the Marble Mountain Wilderness, not north. It's about a 12-mile trip north to the town of Seiad Valley on Highway 96, an excellent place for PCT hikers to pick up a food stash and dump garbage. The trail here follows Grider Creek, an easy descent northward as the stream pours toward the Klamath River. The area features magnificent stands of virgin timber, a mixed conifer forest of cedar, pine, and fir. A good Forest Service campground (Grider Creek Camp) is available about three miles before reaching Seiad Valley.

Location: In Klamath National Forest, southeast of Happy Camp to the Grider Creek Trailhead; map A1, grid f6.

User groups: Hikers, dogs, and horses. No mountain bikes. No wheelchair facilities.

Permits: A campfire permit (free) is required. Parking and access are free.

Maps: A trail information sheet can be obtained by contacting the Happy Camp Ranger District at the address below. For a map of Klamath National Forest, send $6 to U.S. Forest Service, Attn: Map Sales, P.O. Box 587, Camino, CA 95709; tel. (530) 647-5390, fax (530) 647-5389, or website: www.r5.fs.fed.us/visitorcenter. Major credit cards accepted. Ask the USGS for a topographic map of the Seiad Valley area.

Directions: From Interstate 5 north of Yreka turn west on Highway 96 and drive approximately 40 miles to Walker Creek/Grider Creek Road (Forest Road 46N64), located one mile before Seiad Valley. Turn left on Walker Creek Road and drive about 50 feet (staying to the left as it runs adjacent to the Klamath River) to Grider Creek Road. Turn right and drive two miles to the trailhead.

Contact: Klamath National Forest, Happy Camp Ranger District, P.O. Box 377, Happy Camp, CA 96039-0377; tel. (530) 493-2243 or fax (530) 493-2212.

PCT-48 Seiad Valley to Oregon Border

36.0 mi one way/3.0 days

Not many people hike this section of the Pacific Crest Trail, the northernmost segment in California. But it's a great chunk of trail, whether for a day hike or for the whole duration, all the way to Wards Fork Gap on the edge of the Rogue Wilderness in southern Oregon. The ambitious few will head up from the trailhead to the junction of the Boundary National Recreation Trail, a seven-mile trip one way. The first five miles are a steep climb out of the Klamath River Valley, rising to Upper Devils Peak, elevation 6,040 feet.

This hike marks the final steps of the 1,700-mile Pacific Crest Trail in California, south to north, an epic journey for all, but always classic, even if only sections are enjoyed.

Location: In Klamath National Forest from Seiad Valley to the Siskiyou Mountains; map A1, grid e7.

User groups: Hikers, dogs, and horses. No mountain bikes. No wheelchair facilities.

Permits: No permits are required. Parking and access are free.

Maps: A trail information sheet can be obtained by contacting the Scott River Ranger District at the address below. For a map of Klamath National Forest, send $6 to U.S. Forest Service, Attn: Map Sales, P.O. Box 587, Camino, CA 95709; tel. (530) 647-5390, fax (530) 647-5389, or website: www.r5.fs.fed.us/visitorcenter. Major credit cards accepted. Ask the USGS for a topographic map of the Seiad Valley area.

Directions: From Interstate 5 north of Yreka, turn west on Highway 96 and drive approximately 50 miles to the town of Seiad Valley. Continue another mile west on Highway 96 to the trailhead on the north (right) side. Parking is minimal; park across the highway.

Contact: Klamath National Forest, Scott River Ranger District, 11263 N. Highway 3, Fort Jones, CA 96032-9702; tel. (530) 468-5351 or fax (530) 468-1290.

HIKING BUDDIES
JEFFREY PATTY AND TOM STIENSTRA
ON ONE OF THEIR JOURNEYS

MAP A2

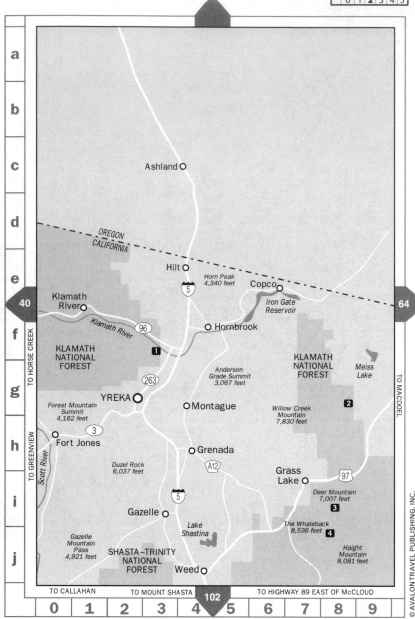

Ashland ○

OREGON
CALIFORNIA

Hilt ○

Horn Peak
4,340 feet

Copco ○

Iron Gate
Reservoir

40

Klamath
River ○

Klamath River

96

Hornbrook ○

**KLAMATH
NATIONAL
FOREST**

**KLAMATH
NATIONAL
FOREST**

Meiss
Lake

64

Anderson
Grade Summit
3,067 feet

263

Forest Mountain
Summit
4,162 feet

YREKA ○

Willow Creek
Mountain
7,830 feet

2

3

Fort Jones ○

○ Montague

Duzel Rock
6,037 feet

○ Grenada

A12

Grass
Lake ○

97

Deer Mountain
7,007 feet

3

5

Gazelle ○

Lake
Shastina

The Whaleback
8,536 feet **4**

Gazelle
Mountain
Pass
4,921 feet

**SHASTA–TRINITY
NATIONAL
FOREST**

Weed ○

Haight
Mountain
8,081 feet

TO HORSE CREEK

TO GREENVIEW

Scott River

TO MACDOEL

102

TO CALLAHAN | TO MOUNT SHASTA | TO HIGHWAY 89 EAST OF McCLOUD

0 1 2 3 4 5 6 7 8 9

a b c d e f g h i j

© AVALON TRAVEL PUBLISHING, INC.

CHAPTER A2

1 Tree of Heaven Trail 59

2 Juanita Lake Trail. 59

3 Deer Mountain 60

4 The Whaleback 60

Look for the Tree of Heaven Campground on the left. The trailhead is located at the west end of the campground.

Contact: Klamath National Forest, Scott River Ranger Station, 11263 N. Highway 3, Fort Jones, CA 96032-9702; tel. (530) 468-5351 or fax (530) 468-5654.

1 Tree of Heaven Trail
3.5 mi/2.0 hrs

The trail out of the Tree of Heaven Campground is one of the best streamside trails anywhere along the Klamath River. Heading downstream along the Klamath, it's a level path that sometimes probes through heavy vegetation and other times offers direct river access. The fall is an excellent time for berry picking. The trail ends at a good fishing access spot, but the fishing is poor during the prime camping/hiking/vacation season. Salmon start arriving in September, steelhead in November and December. The Tree of Heaven River access is also a good take-out point for rafters and drift boaters making the all-day run down from Iron Canyon Dam.

Location: On the Klamath River in Klamath National Forest northwest of Yreka; map A2, grid f3.

User groups: Hikers, dogs, horses, and mountain bikes. No wheelchair facilities.

Permits: No permits are required. Parking and access are free.

Maps: A trail guide can be obtained by contacting the Oak Knoll Ranger District at the address below. For a map of Klamath National Forest, send $6 to U.S. Forest Service, Attn: Map Sales, P.O. Box 587, Camino, CA 95709; tel. (530) 647-5390, fax (530) 647-5389, or website: www.r5.fs.fed.us/visitorcenter. Major credit cards accepted. Ask the USGS for a topographic map of the Badger Mountain area.

Directions: From Yreka drive 10 miles north on Interstate 5 to the Highway 96 exit. Turn west on Highway 96 and drive about five miles.

2 Juanita Lake Trail
1.75 mi/1.0 hr

Not many people know about Juanita Lake, including many Siskiyou County residents, but when they find out, on their first visit they often will take this easy loop trail around the lake to get a feel for the place. The lake is set in a mixed conifer forest, though few trees here are large. Wildlife in the area includes osprey and bald eagles. In the last hour of light during summer, both osprey and eagles occasionally make a fishing trip to the lake. Juanita Lake is a small lake that provides lakeside camping and fishing for brook trout—it's stocked with 2,000 per year. The small fishing piers are wheelchair accessible.

A good side trip is driving on the Forest Road up to Ball Mountain, about two miles southwest of the lake, for great views of Mount Shasta from the 7,786-foot summit.

Location: In Klamath National Forest east of Yreka; map A2, grid g8.

User groups: Hikers and dogs. No mountain bikes or horses. The fishing piers are wheelchair accessible.

Permits: No permits are required. Parking and access are free.

Maps: A trail guide can be obtained by contacting the Goosenest Ranger District at the address below. For a map of Klamath National Forest, send $6 to U.S. Forest Service, Attn: Map Sales, P.O. Box 587, Camino, CA 95709; tel. (530) 647-5390, fax (530) 647-5389, or website: www.r5.fs.fed .us/visitorcenter. Major credit cards accepted. Ask the USGS for a topographic map of the Panther Rock area.

Directions: From Interstate 5 at Weed, take the Central Weed/Klamath Falls (Highway 97) exit. Bear north through Weed to Highway 97. Turn north on Highway 97 and drive 35 miles to Ball Mountain Road. Turn left and drive two miles to a signed turnoff for Juanita Lake. Turn right and drive about three miles to the lake (well signed). The trailhead is near the boat dock at the campground.

Contact: Klamath National Forest, Goosenest Ranger District, 37805 Highway 97, Macdoel, CA 96058; tel. (530) 398-4391 or fax (530) 398-4599.

❸ Deer Mountain
4.0 mi/2.25 hrs

Deer Mountain is the second in a line of small peaks set on the north side of Mount Shasta that extend all the way to the Medicine Lake wildlands. North from Shasta the first peak is the Whaleback, at an elevation of 8,528 feet, and the second is Deer Mountain, at 7,006 feet. Starting elevation at the parking area is 6,200 feet, and from here you climb 800 feet through forest consisting of various pines and firs to gain the summit. This route gets very little use, even though it's easy to reach and the destination is a mountaintop. Most out-of-towners visiting this area are attracted to the trails on Mount Shasta instead, and most locals just plain overlook it.

Location: In Klamath National Forest north of Mount Shasta; map A2, grid i8.

User groups: Hikers, dogs, horses, and mountain bikes. No wheelchair facilities.

Permits: No permits are required. Parking and access are free.

Maps: A trail guide can be obtained by contacting the Goosenest Ranger District at the address below. For a map of Klamath National Forest, send $6 to U.S. Forest Service, Attn: Map Sales, P.O. Box 587, Camino, CA 95709; tel. (530) 647-5390, fax (530) 647-5389, or website: www.r5.fs.fed.us/visitorcenter. Major credit cards accepted. Ask the USGS for a topographic map of the Whaleback area.

Directions: From Interstate 5 at Weed, take the Central Weed/Klamath Falls (Highway 97) exit. Bear north through Weed to Highway 97. Turn north on Highway 97 and drive about 15 miles to Deer Mountain Road/Forest Road 19 (Forest Road 42N12). Turn right and drive four miles to Deer Mountain Snowmobile Park and Forest Road 44N23. Turn left on Forest Road 44N23 and drive about two miles. There is no designated trailhead; park off the road and hike cross-country to the mountaintop. Forest Road 43N69 loops around the base of the mountain; you may also hike from anywhere along that road.

Contact: Klamath National Forest, Goosenest Ranger District, 37805 Highway 97, Macdoel, CA 96058; tel. (530) 398-4391 or fax (530) 398-4599.

❹ The Whaleback
3.0 mi/2.5 hrs

Driving north on Interstate 5, you'll see a large humplike mountain that sits directly north of Shasta. It looks like a huge volcanic bump that was born when Shasta was active. This is the Whaleback, 8,528 feet high, providing an excellent hike with a surprise reward at the top. That surprise is a large crater. The Whaleback Summit is actually a volcanic cinder cone with a collapsed center. This interesting geology, along with the unsurpassed view of Mount Shasta to the south, makes this a first-rate hike. Yet almost nobody tries it, most likely because they don't realize how near you can drive to the top, or because there is no formal trail. After parking at the gate, you just hike cross-country style up to the rim, steep all the way. The 1.5-mile hike is a scramble only in a few places. In the process, you'll climb 1,100 feet, from a starting elevation of 7,400 feet to Whaleback Rim.

Location: In Klamath National Forest north of Mount Shasta; map A2, grid j8.

User groups: Hikers, dogs, horses, and mountain bikes. No wheelchair facilities.

Permits: No permits are required. Parking and access are free.

Maps: A trail guide can be obtained by contacting the Goosenest Ranger District at the address below. For a map of Klamath National Forest, send $6 to U.S. Forest Service, Attn: Map Sales, P.O. Box 587, Camino, CA 95709; tel. (530) 647-5390, fax (530) 647-5389, or website: www.r5.fs.fed.us/visitorcenter. Major credit cards accepted. Ask the USGS for a topographic map of the Whaleback area.

Directions: From Interstate 5 at Weed, take the Central Weed/Klamath Falls (Highway 97) exit. Bear north through Weed to Highway 97. Turn north on Highway 97 and drive 15 miles to Deer Mountain Road. Turn right on Deer Mountain Road and drive four miles to Deer Mountain Snowmobile Park. Drive east on Deer Mountain Road/Forest Road 19 (Forest Road 42N12) for three miles to Forest Road 42N24. Turn right on Forest Road 42N24 and drive three miles to a gate. Park and hike in. There is no designated trail; you must hike cross-country from the road. The peak is about 1.5 miles from the gate.

Contact: Klamath National Forest, Goosenest Ranger District, 37805 Highway 97, Macdoel, CA 96058; tel. (530) 398-4391 or fax (530) 398-4599.

GARY R. ZAHM

RISING DUCKS

MAP A3

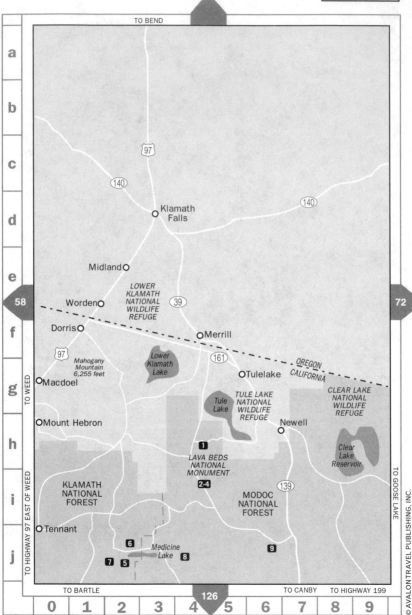

TO BEND

a

b

c

97

140

Klamath
Falls

d

Midland

e

LOWER
KLAMATH
NATIONAL
WILDLIFE
REFUGE

Worden

39

58

72

Dorris

Merrill

f

97

Mahogany
Mountain
6,255 feet

161

Lower
Klamath
Lake

Tulelake

OREGON
CALIFORNIA

Macdoel

g

Tule
Lake

TULE LAKE
NATIONAL
WILDLIFE
REFUGE

CLEAR LAKE
NATIONAL
WILDLIFE
REFUGE

Mount Hebron

Newell

h

1

Clear
Lake
Reservoir

LAVA BEDS
NATIONAL
MONUMENT

KLAMATH
NATIONAL
FOREST

2-4

MODOC
NATIONAL
FOREST

139

i

TO WEED

TO HIGHWAY 97 EAST OF WEED

TO GOOSE LAKE

Tennant

6

9

j

Medicine
Lake

8

7 **5**

TO BARTLE

126

TO CANBY

TO HIGHWAY 199

0 1 2 3 4 5 6 7 8 9

© AVALON TRAVEL PUBLISHING, INC.

CHAPTER A3

■ Captain Jack's
Stronghold 65

② Whitney Butte Trail. 65

③ Thomas Wright Trail 66

④ Schonchin Butte Trail . . . 66

⑤ Medicine Lake Loop 67

⑥ Medicine Lake
Lava Flow. 67

⑦ Little Mount Hoffman . . . 68

⑧ Glass Mountain 69

⑨ Timber Mountain. 69

■ Captain Jack's Stronghold

1.7 mi/1.5 hrs

Captain Jack was a Modoc warrior who fought U.S. troops attempting to relocate Native Americans off their historical lands and onto a reservation. In 1873 Captain Jack was finally captured and hanged, and this site was later named for him. Captain Jack's Stronghold provides a good introduction to the Lava Beds National Monument. It's an easy walk across volcanic fields, with lots of trenches, dips, and rocks. From this trailhead there are actually two loop trails available, including a shorter route that is just .5 mile long. The general terrain is level, with a trailhead elevation of 4,047 feet and a high point of 4,080 feet, but when you hike it, you'll find that the trail is anything but flat. Note that during the winter, this is an outstanding area to see mule deer. Many of the famous photographs of big bucks in California were taken in this area. The wildlife viewing is best at the onset of winter, after the first inch or two of snow has fallen. In addition, a good nearby side trip is Tule Lake, a favorite wintering area for waterfowl and bald eagles.

Location: In Lava Beds National Monument south of Klamath Wildlife Refuge; map A3, grid h4.

User groups: Hikers only. No dogs, horses, or mountain bikes. No wheelchair access.

Permits: No permits are required. A $5 park entrance fee is charged.

Maps: A free brochure is available by contacting Lava Beds National Monument at the address below. Ask the USGS for a topographic map of Captain Jack's Stronghold.

Directions: From Interstate 5 in Weed, take the Highway 97/Klamath Falls exit and drive through Central Weed to Highway 97. Turn north on Highway 97 and drive 54 miles to Highway 161. Turn right (east) on Highway 161 and drive 20 miles to Hill Road. Turn right (south) and drive 18 miles to the visitor center and look for the main monument road (unnamed). Turn north and drive 13 miles on the main monument road to the Captain Jack's Stronghold access road. Turn right and drive to the trailhead.

Contact: Lava Beds National Monument, P.O. Box 867, Tulelake, CA 96134; tel. (530) 667-2282 or fax (530) 667-2737.

② Whitney Butte Trail

6.8 mi/4.0 hrs

The Whitney Butte Trail is one of three wilderness trails in Lava Beds National Monument, and for many it's the best of the lot. From the trailhead at Merrill Cave, set at 4,880 feet, the trail heads west for 3.4 miles, skirting the northern flank of Whitney Butte (5,004 feet) and ending at the edge of the Callahan Lava Flow on the park's southwest boundary. Be sure to climb Whitney Butte. This area bears a resemblance to the surface of the moon, and skilled photographers who know how to use sunlight to their advantage can take black-and-white pictures that can fool most people into thinking they are looking at a lunar surface. Most people arrive just to see the Merrill Ice Cave at the beginning of the hike, which is actually a lava tube. For exploring the cave, bring plenty of flashlight power.

Location: In Lava Beds National Monument south of Klamath Wildlife Refuge; map A3, grid i4.

User groups: Hikers and horses. No dogs or mountain bikes. No wheelchair facilities.

Permits: No permits are required. A $5 park entrance fee is charged.

Maps: A free brochure is available by contacting Lava Beds National Monument at the address below. Ask the USGS for a topographic map of the Schonchin Butte area.

Directions: From Interstate 5 in Weed, take the Highway 97/Klamath Falls exit and drive through Central Weed to Highway 97. Turn north on Highway 97 and drive 54 miles to Highway 161. Turn right (east) on Highway 161 and drive 20 miles to Hill Road. Turn right (south) and drive 18 miles to the visitor center and look for the main monument road (unnamed). Turn north and drive two miles north on the monument main road to the turnoff for Merrill Ice Cave. Turn left and drive 0.75 mile to parking lot and trailhead at the end of the road.

Contact: Lava Beds National Monument, P.O. Box 867, Tulelake, CA 96134; tel. (530) 667-2282 or fax (530) 667-2737.

❸ Thomas Wright Trail

2.2 mi/1.0 hr

There are secrets here. One is in the first .25 mile of the hike, you can venture off-trail a short distance to reach Black Crater, a spatter cone. The other is a sense of ghosts shadowing your footsteps. Some say this area is haunted by the ghosts of Modoc Indians, who fought troops in several violent battles for custody of the land. While the Modoc warriors eventually lost that war, some say they actually won in the long run, since their spirits haunt modern-day visitors. At the end of the trail are interpretive signs that explain the Thomas Wright battlefield site. For an excellent side trip from here, continue off trail, clambering up to the Hardin Butte, a 130-foot climb, for a view. The butte sits on the western edge of the huge Schonchin Lava Flow.

Location: In Lava Beds National Monument south of Tulelake Wildlife Refuge; map A3, grid i4.

User groups: Hikers only. No dogs, horses, or mountain bikes. No wheelchair facilities.

Permits: No permits are required. A $5 park entrance fee is charged.

Maps: A free brochure is available by contacting Lava Beds National Monument at the address below. Ask the USGS for a topographic map of Captain Jack's Stronghold.

Directions: From Interstate 5 in Weed, take the Highway 97/Klamath Falls exit and drive through Central Weed to Highway 97. Turn north on Highway 97 and drive 54 miles to Highway 161. Turn right (east) on Highway 161 and drive 20 miles to Hill Road. Turn right (south) and drive five miles to the trailhead on the left (the visitor center is another five miles south).

Contact: Lava Beds National Monument, P.O. Box 867, Tulelake, CA 96134; tel. (530) 667-2282 or fax (530) 667-2737.

❹ Schonchin Butte Trail

1.8 mi/1.0 hr

This is a short hike, but for many it's a butt-kicker. A portion of it is quite steep—steep enough to get most folks wheezing like old steam locomotives. The trail climbs 600 feet, from a trailhead elevation of 4,700 feet to the lookout at 5,300 feet. There are benches along the trail in case you need to catch your breath. Schonchin Butte has an old fire lookout, and the views are spectacular, of course, especially of the Schonchin Lava Flow to the northeast. Because of the proximity to the visitor center, as well as the short distance involved, many visitors make the tromp to the top.

Location: In Lava Beds National Monument south of Tulelake Wildlife Refuge; map A3, grid i4.

User groups: Hikers only. No dogs, horses, or mountain bikes. No wheelchair facilities.

Permits: No permits are required. A $5 park entrance fee is charged.

Maps: A free brochure is available by contacting Lava Beds National Monument at the address below. Ask the USGS for a topographic map of the Schonchin Butte area.

Directions: From Interstate 5 in Weed, take the Highway 97/Klamath Falls exit and drive through Central Weed to Highway 97. Turn north on Highway 97 and drive 54 miles to Highway 161. Turn right (east) on Highway 161 and drive 20 miles to Hill Road. Turn right (south) and drive 18 miles to the visitor center and look for the main monument road (unnamed). Turn north and drive 2.3 miles to the turnoff for Schonchin Butte. Turn right at the sign for Schonchin Butte and drive about one mile on a gravel road to the trailhead.

Contact: Lava Beds National Monument, P.O. Box 867, Tulelake, CA 96134; tel. (530) 667-2282 or fax (530) 667-2737.

5 Medicine Lake Loop

4.5 mi/2.5 hrs

When you stand on the shore of Medicine Lake, it might be difficult to believe that this was once the center of a volcano. The old caldera is now filled with water and circled by conifers, and the lake is clear and crisp. Set at 6,700 feet, it's a unique and popular destination for camping, boating, and fishing. At some point in their stay, most campers will take a morning or afternoon to walk around the lake. While there is no specific trail, the route is clear enough. There is a sense of timelessness here. Although its geology is comparable to Crater Lake in Oregon, Medicine Lake is neither as deep nor as blue. But a bonus here is the good shore-fishing for large brook trout, often in the 12- to 14-inch class, buoyed by the largest stocks of trout of any lake in the region (30,000 per year). There are also many excellent nearby side trips, including ice caves (along the access road on the way in), a great mountaintop lookout from Little Mount Hoffman just west of the lake, and nearby little Bullseye and Blanche Lakes.

Location: In Modoc National Forest northeast of Mount Shasta; map A3, grid j2.

User groups: Hikers, dogs, horses, and mountain bikes. There are wheelchair facilities at the beach and the boat ramp.

Permits: No permits are required. Parking and access are free unless you're camping.

Maps: A free brochure on the Medicine Lake Highlands is available by contacting the Doublehead Ranger District at the address below. For a map of Modoc National Forest, send $6 to U.S. Forest Service, Attn: Map Sales, P.O. Box 587, Camino, CA 95709; tel. (530) 647-5390, fax (530) 647-5389, or website: www.r5.fs.fed.us/visitorcenter. Major credit cards accepted. Ask the USGS for a topographic map of the Medicine Lake area.

Directions: From Redding turn north on Interstate 5 and drive 56 miles to Highway 89/McCloud exit. Bear right on Highway 89 and drive 28 miles east to Bartle. Just past Bartle, turn left (northeast) on Powder Hill Road (Forest Road 49) and drive 31 miles (it becomes Medicine Lake Road) to the campground and lake access road. Turn left and drive .25 mile to the lake.

Contact: Modoc National Forest, Doublehead Ranger District, P.O. Box 369, Tulelake, CA 96134; tel. (530) 667-2246 or fax (530) 667-8609.

6 Medicine Lake Lava Flow

2.0 mi/2.0 hrs

The Medicine Lake Lava Flow covers 570 acres but has no designated trails. You can explore in any direction you wish, investigating the ancient, stony-gray dacite, which runs 50 to 150 feet deep. This is part of the Medicine Lake Highlands, located just a mile north of Medicine Lake, where there are "rocks that float and mountains of glass" (poetic description from Forest Service geologists). Before the first lunar landing, many originally believed this area to resemble the surface of the moon. That is why this area was selected by the Manned Spacecraft Center in 1965 for study by astronauts preparing for the

first manned trip to the moon. Most people will just poke around for an hour or two, take a few pictures, and leave saying they've never seen anything like it.

Location: In Modoc National Forest north of Medicine Lake; map A3, grid j2.

User groups: Hikers and dogs. The terrain is not suitable for mountain bikes or horses. No wheelchair facilities.

Permits: No permits are required. Parking and access are free.

Maps: A free brochure on the Medicine Lake Highlands is available by contacting the Doublehead Ranger District at the address below. For a map of Modoc National Forest, send $6 to U.S. Forest Service, Attn: Map Sales, P.O. Box 587, Camino, CA 95709; tel. (530) 647-5390, fax (530) 647-5389, or website: www.r5.fs.fed. us/visitorcenter. Major credit cards accepted. Ask the USGS for a topographic map of the Medicine Lake area.

Directions: From Redding turn north on Interstate 5 and drive 56 miles to the exit for Highway 89/McCloud. Bear right on Highway 89 and drive 28 miles to Bartle. Just past Bartle, turn left (northeast) on Powder Hill Road (Forest Road 49) and drive 31 miles (it becomes Medicine Lake Road) to the Medicine Lake turnoff. Continue ahead (do not turn) for 2.5 miles and look for the glass flow on the left side of the road. Park and go for it.

Contact: Modoc National Forest, Doublehead Ranger Station, P.O. Box 369, Tulelake, CA 96134; tel. (530) 667-2246 or fax (530) 667-8609.

⑦ Little Mount Hoffman
0.25 mi/0.25 hr

What a view! Eye-popping on clear days, yes it is. At an impressive 7,309 feet, Mount Hoffman is one of the great spots to take pictures in Northern California, and you get world-class views without a difficult hike. Looking north, you get a sweeping view of Lava Beds National Monument and beyond to Mount McLaughlin in Oregon. To the east is Big Glass Mountain, and to the south is Lassen Peak.

To the west, of course, is Mount Shasta, the most dramatic photo opportunity available here. The summit is easy to reach in the summer, with a road going eight miles right to the top, where you can walk around, enjoying the views in all directions. There is an old U.S. Forest Service lookout station, used only rarely during thunderstorms, when spotters scan the territory for lightning strikes and the start of forest fires. The lookout station is also rented out to the public by Shasta-Trinity National Forest, which operates a lookout rental service for several locations (see below).

Location: In Modoc National Forest north of Medicine Lake; map A3, grid j2.

User groups: Hikers, dogs, horses, and mountain bikes. No wheelchair facilities.

Permits: No permits are required. Parking and access are free.

Maps: A free brochure on the Medicine Lake Highlands is available by contacting the Doublehead Ranger District at the address below. For a map of Modoc National Forest, send $6 to U.S. Forest Service, Attn: Map Sales, P.O. Box 587, Camino, CA 95709; tel. (530) 647-5390, fax (530) 647-5389, or website: www.r5.fs.fed. us/visitorcenter. Major credit cards accepted. Ask the USGS for a topographic map of the Medicine Lake area.

Directions: From Redding turn north on Interstate 5 and drive 56 miles to the exit for Highway 89/McCloud. Bear right on Highway 89 and drive 28 miles to Bartle. Just past Bartle, turn left (northeast) on Powder Hill Road (Forest Road 49) and drive 31 miles (it becomes Medicine Lake Road) to the Medicine Lake and campground turnoff. Turn left on the campground road, bear right, drive past several campgrounds (on your left), and continue to Headquarters Campground. Continue straight (Headquarters Campground will be on your left) on the Mount Hoffman access road and drive three miles to the summit.

Contact: Modoc National Forest, Doublehead Ranger Station, P.O. Box 369, Tulelake, CA 96134; tel. (530) 667-2246 or fax (530) 667-8609. For information on renting the fire lookout:

McCloud Ranger District, Shasta-Trinity National Forest, tel. (530) 964-2184.

8 Glass Mountain
2.5 mi/1.5 hrs

Glass Mountain, a glass flow that covers 4,210 acres, is one of the most unusual settings in the Medicine Lake Highlands. It was created when glassy dacite and rhyolitic obsidian flowed from the same volcanic vent without mixing, creating a present-day phenomenon that exhibits no modification from weather, erosion, or vegetation. There are no designated trails on Glass Mountain, so visitors just wander about, inspecting the geologic curiosities as they go. Take care to stay clear of the obsidian, which can have arrowhead-sharp edges and be quite slippery. Don't walk on it and don't handle it. Be sure instead to stay on the gray-colored dacite.

Location: In Modoc National Forest east of Medicine Lake; map A3, grid j4.

User groups: Hikers and dogs. The terrain is not suitable for horses or mountain bikes. No wheelchair facilities.

Permits: No permits are required. Parking and access are free.

Maps: A free brochure on the Medicine Lake Highlands is available by contacting the Doublehead Ranger District at the address below. For a map of Modoc National Forest, send $6 to U.S. Forest Service, Attn: Map Sales, P.O. Box 587, Camino, CA 95709; tel. (530) 647-5390, fax (530) 647-5389, or website: www.r5.fs.fed. us/visitorcenter. Major credit cards accepted. Ask the USGS for a topographic map of the Medicine Lake area.

Directions: From Redding turn north on Interstate 5 and drive 56 miles to the exit for Highway 89/McCloud. Bear right on Highway 89 and drive 28 miles to Bartle. Just past Bartle, turn left (northeast) on Powder Hill Road (Forest Road 49) and drive about 29 miles (it becomes Medicine Lake Road) to County Road 97. Turn right on County Road 97 and drive about six miles to Forest Road 43N99.

Turn north on Forest Road 43N99 and drive to the southern border of Glass Mountain.

Contact: Modoc National Forest, Doublehead Ranger Station, P.O. Box 369, Tulelake, CA 96134; tel. (530) 667-2246 or fax (530) 667-8609.

9 Timber Mountain
0.5 mi/1.0 hr

When it comes to seeing wildlife, timing is everything. You can make this trip to Timber Mountain in the summer and wonder how it ever earned such a high rating in this book. After all, the view of the high Modoc plateau country from the lookout at 5,086 feet is quite nice, but hey, a nine? Make this trip in December and you'll see why. In three hours, we saw about 400 deer, including dozens of big mule deer bucks with giant racks. What happens, you see, is that when the cold weather starts (long after the deer season has ended), the herd migrates out of Oregon and arrives in this area for winter. In turn, what you do is make the drive to the summit, park near the U.S. Forest Service lookout, and prepare for some fun. You creep to the summit rim and peer over the side and down the mountain slope, scanning with binoculars. Small groups of 10 to 15 deer seem to be everywhere. That is how you spend your time here, creeping to the edge, peering over the tops of rocks, spotting and stalking, maybe taking a few photographs with a telephoto lens. Although some of this mountain has been burned in a forest fire, it can be the best place to see deer in California, especially as new vegetation provides a bonus food supply.

Location: In Modoc National Forest near Highway 139 California border check station; map A3, grid j6.

User groups: Hikers, dogs, horses, and mountain bikes. The lookout is partially wheelchair accessible, but the trails are not.

Permits: No permits are required. Parking and access are free.

Maps: For a map of Modoc National Forest, send $6 to U.S. Forest Service, Attn: Map Sales, P.O. Box 587, Camino, CA 95709; tel. (530) 647-5390, fax (530) 647-5389, or website: www.r5.fs.fed.us/visitorcenter. Major credit cards accepted. Ask the USGS for a topographic map of the Perez area.

Directions: From Interstate 5 at Redding take Highway 299 east for 133 miles to Canby and the junction with Highway 139. Turn left (north) on Highway 139 and drive 20 miles to County Road 97. Turn left (west) and drive about a mile 2.5 miles to Forest Road 44N19. Take Forest Road 44N19 and drive first to the base of the mountain, then continue up to the summit, where there is a Forest Service lookout (the route is well signed).

Contact: Modoc National Forest, Doublehead Ranger Station, P.O. Box 369, Tulelake, CA 96134; tel. (530) 667-2246 or fax (530) 667-8609.

CHAPTER A4

GARY R. ZAHM

SANDHILL CRANES IN FLIGHT

MAP A4

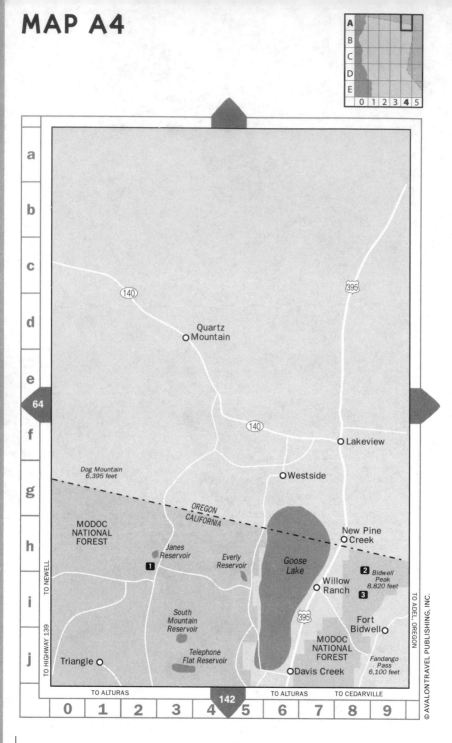

Quartz Mountain

Lakeview

Westside

Dog Mountain
6,395 feet

OREGON
CALIFORNIA

MODOC
NATIONAL
FOREST

Janes
Reservoir

Everly
Reservoir

Goose
Lake

New Pine
Creek

Bidwell
Peak
8,820 feet

Willow
Ranch

South
Mountain
Reservoir

Fort
Bidwell

MODOC
NATIONAL
FOREST

Telephone
Flat Reservoir

Fandango
Pass
6,100 feet

Triangle

Davis Creek

TO NEWELL

TO HIGHWAY 139

TO ALTURAS

TO ALTURAS

TO CEDARVILLE

TO ADEL, OREGON

142

64

CHAPTER A4

1 Janes Reservoir 73
2 Lily Lake to Cave Lake . . . 73
3 Hi Grade National
Recreation Trail 74

1 Janes Reservoir

1.0 mi/0.75 hr

A dirt road leads from the southwest corner of Janes Reservoir to Huffman Butte, about a two-mile drive. If your car can't handle the road, you can hike it. The best strategy is to park at the base of the butte and make the easy climb to the top of it. The reward is a nice view of the lake and the surrounding stark terrain.

This is sagebrush country, the high plateau land of Modoc country. You're likely to see cattle, possibly wild mustangs, and with the number of wetlands in the area, lots of waterfowl, particularly Canada geese. However, you're unlikely to see people. Even though it's very remote for a drive-to area, a bonus is that there are a number of side trips possible to other lakes. The best are the Alphabet Lakes (Reservoir C has the best trout fishing) and Big Sage Reservoir on Crowder Flat Road.

Location: In Modoc National Forest north of Alturas; map A4, grid h2.

User groups: Hikers, dogs, horses, and mountain bikes. No wheelchair facilities.

Permits: No permits are required. Parking and access are free.

Maps: For a map of Modoc National Forest, send $6 to U.S. Forest Service, Attn: Map Sales, P.O. Box 587, Camino, CA 95709; tel. (530) 647-5390, fax (530) 647-5389, or website: www.r5.fs.fed.us/visitorcenter. Major credit cards accepted. Ask the USGS for a topographic map of the South Mountain area.

Directions: From Interstate 5 at Redding turn east on Highway 299 and drive about 144 miles (17 miles past Canby). Turn left on Crowder Flat Road and continue approximately 30 miles to the reservoir.

Contact: Modoc National Forest, Devil's Garden Ranger District, 800 West 12th Street, Alturas, CA 96101; tel. (530) 233-5811, or fax (530) 233-8709.

2 Lily Lake to Cave Lake

0.5 mi/0.5 hr

While there are no designated trails, the .25-mile walk from the campground at Lily Lake over to Cave Lake is an easy and rewarding trip. The surroundings at Lily Lake are quite beautiful—mostly forest with few humans around, and pretty little flowers blooming in the lily pads along the shallow eastern shore of the lake. As you walk to Cave Lake, the surroundings quickly change. This lake is also small, but with a barren shoreline, the trees placed well back from the water. There's a great contrast between the two lakes. A bonus is decent fishing for rainbow trout at Lily Lake and brook trout at Cave Lake. A good side trip is making the short walk over to the headwaters of Pine Creek, a small, pretty stream that is overlooked by most visitors.

Location: In Modoc National Forest east of Goose Lake; map A4, grid h8.

User groups: Hikers, dogs, horses, and mountain bikes. No wheelchair facilities.

Permits: No permits are required. Parking and access are free.

Maps: For a map of Modoc National Forest, send $6 to U.S. Forest Service, Attn: Map Sales, P.O. Box 587, Camino, CA 95709; tel. (530) 647-5390, fax (530) 647-5389, or website: www.r5.fs.fed.us/visitorcenter. Major credit cards accepted. Ask the USGS for a topographic map of the Mount Bidwell area.

Directions: From Interstate 5 at Redding turn east on Highway 299 and drive approximately 146 miles to Alturas. Turn north on U.S. 395 and drive 40 miles to Forest

Road 2 (if you reach the town of New Pine Creek, you have gone one mile too far). Turn right on Forest Road 2 and drive 5.5 miles east to the lake. The access road is steep, dirt, and rough, and not recommended for trailers.

Contact: Modoc National Forest, Warner Mountain Ranger District, P.O. Box 220, Cedarville, CA 96104; tel. (530) 279-6116 or fax (530) 279-8309.

3 Hi Grade National Recreation Trail

1.1 mi/0.5 hr

The Hi Grade National Recreation Trail is actually 5.5 miles long, but only 1.1 miles are specifically designed for hiking. The remainder of this trail is designated for four-wheel-drive use, one of the only national four-wheel-drive trails in the state. Of course, you can still hike all of it, but it's better to use four-wheeling to get out there, then hike the final mile to get way out there. As you go, watch for signs of old, abandoned mining operations, because gold was discovered here. They never found enough to cause any outpouring of gold miners, though, and the result is a sparsely populated county, with this area being abandoned completely. The surrounding habitat is a mix of high desert and timber, although the trees tend to be small.

A good side trip from the nearby Buck Creek Ranger Station is to Fandango Pass, with nice views to the east of Surprise Valley and the Nevada Mountains. This is where a group of immigrants arrived, topped the ridge, looked west, saw Goose Lake, and shouted, "Aha! the Pacific Ocean! We have arrived!" So they started dancing the fandango; but alas, as lore has it, they were massacred by marauding Indians. That's how the mountain pass got its name.

Location: In Modoc National Forest east of Goose Lake; map A4, grid i8.

User groups: Hikers, dogs, horses, and mountain bikes. No wheelchair facilities.

Permits: No permits are required. Parking and access are free.

Maps: For a map of Modoc National Forest, send $6 to U.S. Forest Service, Attn: Map Sales, P.O. Box 587, Camino, CA 95709; tel. (530) 647-5390, fax (530) 647-5389, or website: www.r5.fs.fed.us/visitorcenter. Major credit cards accepted. Ask the USGS for topographic maps of the Mount Bidwell and Willow Ranch areas.

Directions: From Interstate 5 at Redding turn east on Highway 299 and drive 146 miles to Alturas. Turn north on U.S. 395 and drive about 35 miles. Turn right on Forest Road 9 and drive 4.5 miles. At the Buck Creek Ranger Station, turn left on Forest Road 47N72 and drive about six miles to the trailhead. Four-wheel-drive vehicles are required.

Contact: Modoc National Forest, Warner Mountain Ranger District, P.O. Box 220, Cedarville, CA 96104; tel. (530) 279-6116 or fax (530) 279-8309.

CHAPTER 80

PATRICK RACE

FERNS REACHING FOR SUNLIGHT

MAP BO

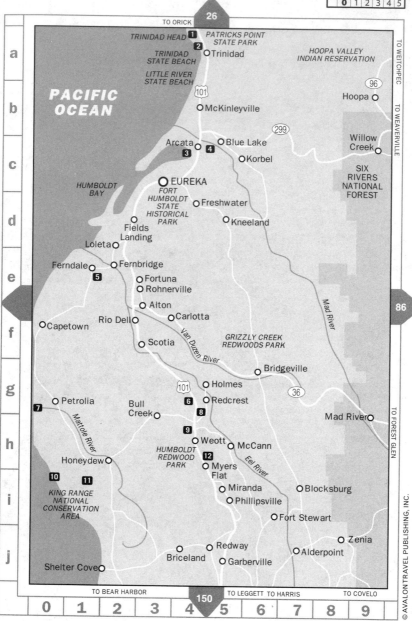

26

TRINIDAD HEAD **1**
PATRICKS POINT STATE PARK

TRINIDAD **2**
TRINIDAD STATE BEACH
○ Trinidad

LITTLE RIVER STATE BEACH

HOOPA VALLEY INDIAN RESERVATION

PACIFIC OCEAN

TO WEITCHPEC

96

○ McKinleyville

Hoopa ○

TO WEAVERVILLE

299

Arcata ○ **4** ○ Blue Lake
3
○ Korbel

Willow Creek ○

SIX RIVERS NATIONAL FOREST

○ **EUREKA**
FORT HUMBOLDT STATE HISTORICAL PARK

○ Freshwater

HUMBOLDT BAY

○ Kneeland

Fields Landing ○

Loleta ○

Ferndale ○ ○ Fernbridge

5 ○ Fortuna
○ Rohnerville

Mad River

86

○ Alton
Rio Dell ○ ○ Carlotta

Van Duzen River

GRIZZLY CREEK REDWOODS PARK

○ Capetown
○ Scotia

○ Bridgeville

○ Holmes
101

36

○ **7** ○ Petrolia
Bull Creek ○

6 ○ Redcrest
8

Mad River ○

Mattole River

9

○ Weott ○ McCann

TO FOREST GLEN

○ Honeydew

HUMBOLDT REDWOOD PARK

12
○ Myers Flat

Eel River

10 **11**

KING RANGE NATIONAL CONSERVATION AREA

○ Miranda
○ Phillipsville

○ Blocksburg

○ Fort Stewart

○ Zenia

○ Redway
○ Shelter Cove
○ Briceland
○ Garberville

○ Alderpoint

150

© AVALON TRAVEL PUBLISHING, INC.

CHAPTER B0

1 Rim Loop Trail. 77

2 Tsurai Loop. 77

3 Arcata Marsh Trail 78

4 Redwood Loop. 78

5 Russ City Park
   Double Loop 79

6 5 Allens' Trail 79

7 Lost Coast Trail. 80

8 Founders Grove
   Nature Trail 81

9 Bull Creek Flats. 81

10 Spanish Ridge Trail 82

11 King Crest Trail. 83

12 Williams Grove Trail . . . 83

1 Rim Loop Trail

5.0 mi/2.5 hrs

Patrick's Point State Park is set on a coastal headland lush with ferns, spruce, and wildflowers, and bordered by the Pacific, where you can go tidepool hopping or whale-watching. That means with this trail you get the best of two worlds. At times it tunnels through thick vegetation, and at other times it opens up to sweeping ocean views. Along the way several spur trails provide access to many feature areas, including Mussel Rocks, Wedding Rock, Agate Beach, Rocky Point, Patrick's Point, Abalone Point, and Palmer's Point. The views are sensational at every one of these spots. The spur trails, while short (they add just 1.5 miles to the hike), will make this a two- to three-hour trip, since you just won't want to rush through it. In addition, the Octopus Tree Trail offers a short hike that starts just across from the northern end of the Rim Loop Trail. This bonus trail provides a chance to see many spruce trees whose roots straddle downed logs, hence the name "Octopus Trees."

The only downers here are the fog and the heavy out-of-state tourist traffic, both common during the summer.

Special note: The best wheelchair-accessible section of the Rim Trail is from the visitor center to the Sumeg Village.

Location: At Patrick's Point State Park north of Eureka; map B0, grid a4.

User groups: Hikers only. No dogs, horses, or mountain bikes. Partial wheelchair access is available.

Permits: No permits are required. A state park day-use fee of $2 per car is charged.

Maps: For a park map and brochure, send a self-addressed stamped envelope and a check or money order for $1 to Patrick's Point State Park at the address below. Ask the USGS for a topographic map of the Trinidad area.

Directions: From Eureka drive north on U.S. 101 for 22 miles to Trinidad, and continue north for 5.5 miles. Take the Patrick's Point Drive exit. At the stop sign, turn left and drive .5 mile to the entrance station. Continue to the Agate Beach parking area.

Contact: Patrick's Point State Park, 4150 Patrick's Point Drive, Trinidad, CA 95570; tel. (707) 677-3570, fax (707) 677-9357.

2 Tsurai Loop

1.5 mi/1.0 hr

The Tsurai Loop is a great, easy walk with coastal vistas, unique terrain, and a nearby restaurant. The terrain includes the 300-foot miniature mountain at Trinidad Head, the pretty beachfront to the north of the Head area, and the Trinidad Pier. The trip is best done in a counter-clockwise loop. It starts by hiking up for beautiful views to the north, eventually reaching this perfectly situated rock lookout of the ocean. On clear days it can be an ideal spot to watch for the "puff-of-smoke" spouts on the ocean surface from migrating whales. The trail circles the mountain and then climbs to the top, a flat summit, where the views are only fair. The views are actually a lot better just 50 yards to the south, looking south towards Eureka and Humboldt Bay. As you head back down, you get more views of the rocky Trinidad Harbor and coast. The restaurant? It's called Seascape, and you can get a crab/shrimp omelet (in season) for breakfast that'll have your mouth watering every time you start driving north of Eureka on U.S. 101. If there's a waiting line at the restaurant, don't hesitate to queue up.

Location: On Trinidad Head on the Humboldt coast north of Eureka; map B0, grid a4.

User groups: Hikers and dogs. Mountain bikes are permitted but no recommended. No horses. No wheelchair facilities.

Permits: No permits are required. Parking and access are free.

Maps: Ask the USGS for a topographic map of the Trinidad area.

Directions: From Eureka drive north on U.S. 101 for 28 miles to Trinidad. Take the Trinidad exit, turn left at the stop sign, and drive under the U.S. 101 overpass to Main Street. Continue on Main Street to Trinity Street. Turn left and drive a short distance to Edwards Street. Turn right on Edwards Street and drive to the parking area at the foot of the harbor.

Contact: There is no managing agency for information.

🖪 Arcata Marsh Trail

2.0 mi/1.0 hr

The 154-acre Arcata Marsh is the most popular bird-watching area in Northern California, and it's best explored by walking the loop. It is set on a levee above the marsh; the trail is short, flat, and routed in a loop for perfect viewing possibilities. Several wooden photography blinds are available on the route, where you can hide yourself to take pictures of the birds. The setting is unique, with the coast, saltwater bay, brackish water marsh, pond, foothills, and streams all nearby. This diversity means an outstanding variety of species is attracted

to the area, with sightings often including belted kingfishers, ospreys, peregrine falcons, black phoebes, and song and Savannah sparrows. In other words, birds from nearly all habitats are represented, which explains why the Audubon Society gives guided tours every Saturday at 8:30 a.m. A lot of people drive here to eat a picnic lunch, and just like Pavlov's dog hearing the bell, tons of birds show up in the parking lot daily at noon for handouts. The rangers request that you don't feed the bears—er, the birds.

Also of interest is the Arcata Marsh Interpretive Center, located at the southwest corner of the parking area, where there are activities for children available.

Location: In Arcata Marsh and Wildlife Sanctuary on the northern edge of Humboldt Bay; map B0, grid c4.

User groups: Hikers, dogs, and mountain bikes. No horses. Part of the trail is accessible for wheelchairs.

Permits: No permits are required. Parking and access are free.

Maps: For a free, detailed trail map, contact the City of Arcata at the address below and ask for the Marsh and Wildlife Trail map. Ask the USGS for a topographic map of the Arcata South area.

Directions: From Eureka drive north on U.S. 101 for five miles to Arcata and the Somoa Boulevard exit. Take that exit and turn west on Samoa Boulevard exit and drive to I Street. Turn left (south) and continue to the parking area.

Contact: Arcata Marsh Interpretive Center, tel. (707) 826-2359. City of Arcata, Environmental Services Department, 736 F Street, Arcata, CA 95521; tel. (707) 822-8184 or fax (707) 822-8018.

🖪 Redwood Loop

6.2 mi/3.0 hrs

Arcata Redwoods Park provides a respite for students at nearby Humboldt State or for locals who want to wander amid a beautiful second-growth forest. A network of 18 trails covering about 10 miles in all is available, and the Redwood Loop is devised by connecting several of them. For newcomers a map is an absolute necessity. Mountain bikes are prohibited at about 50 percent of the trails in the Arcata redwoods, although these rules are occasionally broken.

Start at the sign noting Redwood Park Trail (mountain bikes are not allowed at this trailhead) and take the Nature Trail, which will take you by many huge stumps, a small creek, and a forest of redwoods and spruce. The complete route features a 1,200-foot elevation gain and then loss, a steep trail both on the way up and on the way down. On weekends kamikaze mountain bikers tearing downhill can turn this hike into an extremely unpleasant experience.

Location: In Arcata Redwood Park in the Arcata foothills; map B0, grid c5.

User groups: Hikers, dogs, horses, and mountain bikes. Certain sections of the trail are off-limits to horses and mountain bikes; check the trail map for details. No wheelchair facilities.

Permits: No permits are required. Parking and access are free.

Maps: For a free, detailed trail map, contact the City of Arcata at the address below and ask for the Community Forest Trail map. A free mountain bike trail map is also available. Ask the USGS for topographic maps of the Arcata North and Arcata South areas.

Directions: From Eureka drive north on U.S. 101 to Arcata and the 14th Street exit. Take the 14th Street exit and drive east for about one mile into the parking area (look for the "Redwood Park Trails" sign). No mountain bikes are permitted here. Bikers and equestrians should use the Meadow Trailhead, located where 14th Street enters the park.

Contact: City of Arcata, Environmental Services Department, 736 F Street, Arcata, CA 95521; tel. (707) 822-8184 or fax (707) 822-8018.

⑤ Russ City Park Double Loop
2.2 mi/2.0 hrs

Russ City Park is Humboldt County's backyard wilderness. Covering just 105 acres, the park has been retained in its primitive state for wildlife, birds, and hikers. Though there's no posted, official name to the route we recommend, we call the trail "Double Loop" because it's set in the shape of a figure eight, which is quite rare. The trail includes a climb up Lytel Ridge, passing Francis Creek, with sections routed through heavy fern beds and large firs and offering views of a small pond and the Eel River floodplain. While the trip is relatively short and easy enough, the terrain is steep in spots, and the trail is challenging, complete with switchbacks. Heavy fog or rain can make it slippery here. Since it's a city park, Russ is little known by outsiders and can provide quiet, secluded hiking.

Location: In Russ City Park in Ferndale south of Eureka; map B0, grid e2.

User groups: Hikers and dogs. No horses or mountain bikes. No wheelchair facilities.

Permits: No permits are required. Parking and access are free.

Maps: A free map and brochure can be obtained by contacting the City of Ferndale at the address below. Ask the USGS for a topographic map of the Ferndale area.

Directions: From Eureka drive south on U.S. 101 for 11 miles to the Ferndale/Fern Bridge exit. Take that exit and drive straight about .75 mile. Turn right and cross the Fern Bridge and drive west five miles through town to Ocean Street. Turn left on Ocean Street and drive .75 mile to the park on the right.

Contact: City of Ferndale, P.O. Box 1095, Ferndale, CA 95536; tel. (707) 786-4224 or fax (707) 786-9314.

⑥ 5 Allens' Trail
1.5 mi/1.5 hrs

The 5 Allens' Trail will provide a lasting impression of Hum-

boldt Redwoods State Park for one reason: if you're unprepared, the trail is something of a butt-kicker. Ah, but it's also very short, and well worth the effort in exchange for quiet wonders.

From the trailhead near the Eel River, walk under the highway and then start the climb. Up, up, and up it goes, ascending 1,200 feet over the course of just .75 mile. The trail passes through a forest of mixed conifers, the tree canopy providing needed shade in the summer. Even though the hike is quite short, few people make it to the end. But if you want a quiet, peaceful spot—and are willing to pay to get it—you'll find it at the end.

A great short side trip from the trailhead is to hike north instead along the Eel River to High Rock, one of the better shoreline fishing spots for steelhead during the winter migrations.

Location: In Humboldt Redwoods State Park south of Eureka; map B0, grid g4.

User groups: Hikers only. No dogs, horses, or mountain bikes. No wheelchair facilities.

Permits: No permits are required. Parking and access are free.

Maps: A map can be obtained by sending a self-addressed, stamped envelope and a check or money order for $1 to Humboldt Redwoods State Park at the address below. Ask the USGS for a topographic map of the Weott area.

Directions: From Eureka drive south on U.S. 101 to the Redcrest exit. Take that exit and turn left, drive under the overpass, and continue a short distance to Avenue of the Giants. Turn right on the Avenue of the Giants and drive south three miles (past High Rock Conservation Camp) to the 5 Allens' Trailhead parking lot on the left.

For an alternate route from Garberville, drive north on U.S. 101, to the Founders Tree/Rockefeller Forest exit. Take that exit (north), turn right, and drive about 200 yards to Avenue of the Giants. Turn left on Avenue of the Giants, cross over the South Fork Eel River, and then bear right at the intersection in order to stay on Avenue of the Giants. Drive a short distance to the 5 Allens' Trailhead parking lot on the right.

Contact: Humboldt Redwoods State Park, Box 100, Weott, CA 95571; tel. (707) 946-2409 or fax (707) 946-2326; North Coast Redwoods District, tel. (707) 445-6547 or fax (707) 441-5737.

◼ Lost Coast Trail

25.0 mi one way/3.0 days

The Lost Coast and the people who live there seem to be in a different orbit from the rest of California, and that's exactly why visitors make the trip up here. It's called the "Lost Coast" because of the way nature has isolated the area, shielded on all sides by natural boundaries. For a first visit and a great day hike, take the abandoned jeep trail from the campground at Lighthouse Road and head south three miles to the Punta Gorda Lighthouse. You'll get a glimpse of the greatness here and probably the inspiration to continue on the Lost Coast Trail, one of California's greatest weekend trips. Set primarily on bluffs and beach, the trail spans 25 miles from the mouth of the Mattole River south to Shelter Cove. Along the way it traces some of California's most remote portions of coastline. With two vehicles, one parked at each end of the trail, you can set up your own shuttle, then hike the trail one way. (A shuttle service is available; phone Shelter Cove Campground at (707-986-7474.) It's better done from north to south because of the winds out of the north; you want them at your back, not in your face. Firm-fitting waterproof boots with good gripping soles are a necessity: firm fitting because some of the walking is in soft sand, waterproof because there are several small creek crossings, and good gripping because some scrambling over wet boulders is required.

Special note: Some parts of the Lost Coast Trail are impassable during high tides. Watch for ticks and take a tide table. Be cautious, too; this is an extremely isolated area. In many parts, there is no trail, and there is a lot of boulder hopping where it is possible to twist an ankle. Also note that in the winter the beach can be angled quite steeply toward the water, making it perfect for people with legs of different length. Also note that that bears along this trail are experts at raiding food packs at night.

Location: On the Humboldt coast south of Eureka in King Range National Conservation Area; map B0, grid g0.

User groups: Hikers, dogs, horses, and mountain bikes. No wheelchair facilities.

Permits: Day-use permits are required for organized groups only. A campfire permit (free) is required for overnight use. Parking and access are free.

Maps: A detailed trail map is available for $3, and a free map and brochure can be obtained by contacting the Bureau of Land Management at the address below. Specify the King Range Conservation Area map. Ask the USGS for topographic maps of the Petrolia, Cooskie Creek, Shubrick Peak, and Shelter Cove areas.

Directions: From U.S. 101 in Garberville, drive north to the South Fork-Honeydew exit. Take that exit, drive west on Wilder Road, and continue 23 miles to Honeydew and Mattole Road. Turn right on Mattole Road and drive 14 miles (toward Petrolia). At the second bridge over the Mattole Road (one mile before Petrolia), turn left on Lighthouse Road. Drive west on Lighthouse Road to its end. The trailhead is just past Mattole Campground.

Contact: Bureau of Land Management, Arcata Field Office, 1695 Heindon Road, Arcata, CA 95521-4573; tel. (707) 825-2300 or fax (707) 825-2301.

8 Founders Grove Nature Trail

0.5 mi/0.5 hr

There's some irony on this hike. What was once the tallest redwood tree in the park is now the longest redwood tree in the park. What? That's because the Dyerville Giant fell, so this massive redwood is now in prone position. It still is

an attraction among 100 miles of trails at Humboldt Redwoods State Park, with the little .5-mile Founders Grove Nature Trail that provides the shortest and most easily accessible walk in the park. This trail also gives you the quickest payoff, which explains why it's the most popular hike in Humboldt Redwoods. The trail's location near U.S. 101 makes it easy to reach. At the trailhead you'll find a small box with brochures describing each element of the self-guided nature trail. All the while you'll be surrounded by old-growth redwoods, a great reward for such a small physical investment.

Location: In Humboldt Redwoods State Park south of Eureka; map B0, grid h4.

User groups: Hikers and wheelchairs, though the trail is a bit uneven. No dogs, horses, or mountain bikes.

Permits: No permits are required. Parking and access are free.

Maps: A map is available for $1 at Humboldt Redwoods State Park at the address below. Ask the USGS for a topographic map of the Weott area.

Directions: From Garberville drive north on U.S. 101 about 20 miles to the Founder Tree/Rockefeller Forest exit. Take that exit and drive a short distance to Avenue of the Giants. Drive 100 yards (crossing Avenue of the Giants) to the Founders Grove Parking Area/Trailhead (well signed).

Contact: Humboldt Redwoods State Park, Box 100, Weott, CA 95571; tel. (707) 946-2409 or fax (707) 946-2326; North Coast Redwoods District, tel. (707) 445-6547 or fax (707) 441-5737.

9 Bull Creek Flats

9.0 mi/5.25 hrs

This trail offers a streamside walk complete with giant redwoods and a babbling brook. Starting at the trailhead at Bull Creek Flats (a short walk to the Federation Grove), the trail heads west along Bull Creek, an easy but steady grade as you hike upstream. All the while you're surrounded by forest, both redwoods and fir in a variety of mixes. Most people cross the seasonal bridge at the Big Tree and head back towards the beginning of the trail at Bull Creek Flats to make a loop. The feature hike of the route is the Big Tree Area and the giant tree, which you'll reach after four miles of hiking. There are many redwoods here that range five to ten feet in diameter. The big attraction for years was the Flat Iron Tree, a huge leaning redwood that grew in strange dimensions in order to support itself. Well, it's not leaning anymore because it fell down and went boom. On the broad side the Flat Iron Tree measures more than 15 feet. After the trail passes the Big Tree Area, it's routed to the mouth of Albee Creek, ending at Mattole Road. The trailhead here (at Mattole Road), by the way, provides a shorter hike of about a mile to the seasonal bridge at the Big Tree Area.

Location: In Humboldt Redwoods State Park south of Eureka; map B0, grid h4.

User groups: Hikers only. No dogs, horses, or mountain bikes. No wheelchair facilities.

Permits: No permits are required. Parking and access are free.

Maps: A map is available for $1 from Humboldt Redwoods State Park at the address below. Ask the USGS for a topographic map of the Weott area.

Directions: From Garberville drive north on U.S. 101 about 20 miles to the Founder Tree/Rockefeller Forest exit. Take that exit and turn left and drive a short distance to Avenue of the Giants. Turn left and drive a short distance to Mattole Road (sign will say Rockefeller Forest/Honeydew, and not Mattole Road). Turn left and drive 1.3 miles the Lower Bull Creek Flats Trailhead.

Contact: Humboldt Redwoods State Park, Box 100, Weott, CA 95571; tel. (707) 946-2409 or fax (707) 946-2326; North Coast Redwoods District, tel. (707) 445-6547 or fax (707) 441-5737.

10 Spanish Ridge Trail
9.4 mi/4.5 hrs

In just three fast miles of walking downhill, you get access to some of the most remote sections of the California coast. Alas, there's a catch, and on the Spanish Ridge Trail it comes on the return trip. What goes down, as all hikers know, must later go up. From the trailhead the trail descends 2,000 feet in three miles en route to the coast. Know what that means? Right. Going back, you'll climb 2,000 feet in three miles, and unless you can get a helicopter ride back, you're looking at some serious grunt work. But it's worth it. The King Range is very rugged, primitive, and isolated. Thanks to that bumpy access road and the 2,000-foot climb on the return trip, it's rare to see other people here.

Location: In King Range National Conservation Area south of Eureka; map B0, grid i0.

User groups: Hikers, dogs, mountain bikes and horses. No wheelchair facilities.

Permits: No permits are required. A campfire permit (free) is required for overnight use. Parking and access are free.

Maps: A trail map is available for $3, and a free map and brochure can be obtained by contacting the Bureau of Land Management at the address below; ask for the King Range Conservation Area map. Ask the USGS for topographic maps of the Cooskie Creek and Shubrick Peak areas.

Directions: On U.S. 101 drive to the South Fork-Honeydew exit (just north of Garberville). Take that exit to Wilder Ridge Road and turn southwest. Drive one mile to Smith-Etter Road and turn west. Drive 10 miles (this is a primitive, four-wheel-drive road and is closed from November 1 to March 31) to Telegraph Ridge Road. Turn northwest on Telegraph Ridge Road and drive eight miles to the trailhead gate. In summer, continue driving two miles to the trailhead. When the gate is locked, the trailhead is accessible only by a two-mile walk.

Contact: Bureau of Land Management, Arcata Field Office, 1695 Heindon Road, Arcata, CA 95521-4573; tel. (707) 825-2300 or fax (707) 825-2301.

11 King Crest Trail
10.0 mi/6.5 hrs

King's Peak is one of the most prized destinations in the King Range. At 4,087 feet it's the highest point on the Northern California coast, and from it you get a view that can make you feel that you're perched on top of the world. The ocean seems to stretch on forever to the west, and on a perfect day you can make out the top of Mount Lassen behind the ridgeline of the Yolla Bolly Wilderness to the east.

Reaching King's Peak requires a five-mile hike from the Northslide Peak Trailhead on Smith-Etter Road, and in the process you climb some 2,200 feet. Making the trip on a clear day is an absolute necessity, since paying the price of the climb is buffered by the reward of the sweeping views. Trail signs are poor and water supplies at trail camps are from dubious sources, so it's also essential to have a good map and a double-canteen water supply. The entire King Crest Trail extends 10 miles one way, starting from the trailhead listed in this hike to Saddle Mountain Trailhead; then it descends four miles to the beach. That makes a one-way overnight trip with a shuttle vehicle at the end of the trail an ideal alternative.

Location: In King Range National Conservation Area south of Eureka; map B0, grid i1.

User groups: Hikers, dogs, horses, and mountain bikes. No wheelchair facilities.

Permits: No permits are required. A campfire permit (free) is required for overnight use. Parking and access are free.

Maps: A trail map is available for $3, and a free map and brochure can be obtained by contacting the Bureau of Land Management at the address below; ask for the King Range Conservation Area map. Ask the USGS for a topographic map of the Shubrick Peak area.

Directions: On U.S. 101 drive to the South Fork-Honeydew exit (just north of Garberville). Take that exit to Wilder Ridge Road and turn southwest. Drive one mile to Smith-Etter Road and turn west. Drive six miles to the trailhead (this is a primitive, four-wheel-drive road and is closed from November 1 to March 31).

Contact: Bureau of Land Management, Arcata Field Office, 1695 Heindon Road, Arcata, CA 95521-4573; tel. (707) 825-2300 or fax (707) 825-2301.

12 Williams Grove Trail
3.5 mi/2.0 hrs

This trail makes an ideal, easy trip for campers staying at the Hidden Springs Campground in Humboldt Redwoods State Park. The camp is set in forest just above a big bend in the South Fork Eel River, with the trailhead on the southwest side of the camp. The trail starts out nearly flat, then turns right and parallels the highway. It's easy walking all the way amid redwoods both young and old. Then the trail crosses under the highway and down the hill to Williams Grove, which has a picnic area and restrooms. Williams Grove Picnic Area can also be reached by car and then used as a trailhead to hike this route in reverse.

Location: In Humboldt Redwoods State Park south of Eureka; map B0, grid h5.

User groups: Hikers only. No dogs, horses, or mountain bikes. No wheelchair facilities.

Permits: No permits are required. A $2 parking fee is charged per vehicle, free if camping in the park.

Maps: A map is available for $1 at Humboldt Redwoods State Park at the address below. Ask the USGS for topographic maps of the Weott and Myers Flat areas.

Directions: From Garberville on U.S. 101, drive to the Myers Flat exit (north of Garberville). Take that exit to Avenue of the Giants. Turn right and drive one mile northwest to Williams Grove parking area. Note: Hidden Springs Campground (open only during summer) is located one mile south from the U.S. 101 turnoff.

Contact: Humboldt Redwoods State Park, Box 100, Weott, CA 95571; tel. (707) 946-2409 or fax (707) 946-2326; North Coast Redwoods District, tel. (707) 445-6547 or fax (707) 441-5737.

SECRET LAKE
IN TRINITY LAKES WILDERNESS

MAP B1

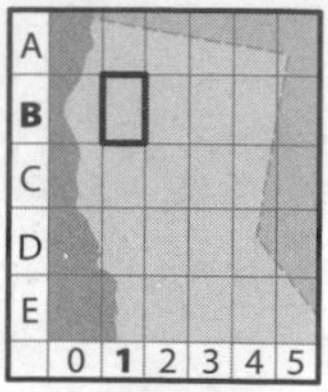

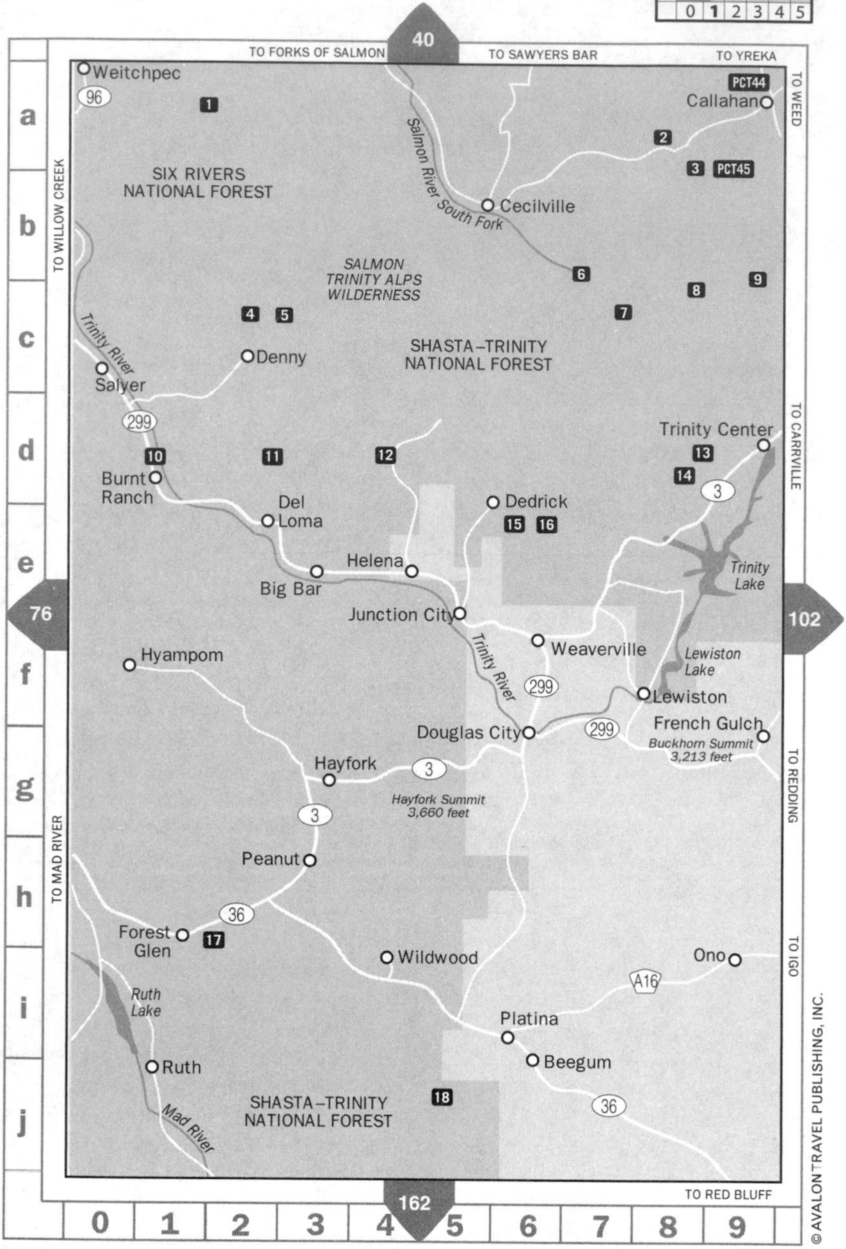

TO FORKS OF SALMON — **40** — TO SAWYERS BAR — TO YREKA

TO WEED

Weitchpec
96
1

Callahan
PCT44

SIX RIVERS
NATIONAL FOREST

2

3 PCT45

Salmon River South Fork

Cecilville

SALMON
TRINITY ALPS
WILDERNESS

6

7

8   **9**

Trinity River

4 **5**

Denny

SHASTA–TRINITY
NATIONAL FOREST

Salyer

299

TO CARRVILLE

Trinity Center

10   **11**   **12**   **13**

Burnt
Ranch

14
3

Del
Loma

Dedrick
15 **16**

Helena

Big Bar

Trinity
Lake

Junction City

76 — 76 — **102**

Hyampom

Trinity River

Weaverville

Lewiston
Lake

299

Lewiston

299

French Gulch
Buckhorn Summit
3,213 feet

TO REDDING

Douglas City

Hayfork
3

Hayfork Summit
3,660 feet

3

TO MAD RIVER

Peanut

Forest
Glen
17

36

Ono

A16

Wildwood

Ruth
Lake

TO IGO

Platina

Ruth

Beegum

Mad River

SHASTA–TRINITY
NATIONAL FOREST

18

36

TO WILLOW CREEK

TO RED BLUFF

162

0 1 2 3 4 5 6 7 8 9

© AVALON TRAVEL PUBLISHING, INC.

CHAPTER B1

1 Horse Trail Ridge National
Recreation Trail........ 87

2 Trail Creek Trail........ 88

3 Trail Gulch............ 88

4 New River Trailhead..... 89

5 East Fork Loop......... 90

6 Little South Fork
Lake Trail............. 90

7 Caribou Lakes Trail 91

8 Union Lake Trail........ 92

9 Boulder Lake Trail 92

10 Burnt Ranch Falls....... 93

11 New River Divide Trail ... 93

12 Grizzly Lake 94

13 Swift Creek Trail
to Granite Lake........ 95

14 Long Canyon
Trailhead............. 95

15 Stuart Fork
Trailhead............. 96

16 Canyon Creek
Lakes Trailhead 97

17 South Fork National
Recreation Trail........ 97

18 North Fork
Beegum Trailhead 98

**Pacific Crest Trail
(PCT) Section Overview**

PCT-44 Scott Mountain to
Cecilville Road 99

PCT-45 Cecilville Road to
Russian Wilderness... 99

1 Horse Trail Ridge National Recreation Trail

13.0 mi one way/2.0 days

This is one of the lesser-known national recreation trails in the western US, but it has many excellent features, and alas, a few negative ones as well. Leaving a shuttle vehicle at both trailheads, you can hike Horse Trail Ridge from one end to the other in a weekend, but our suggestion is to make the six-mile trip to Mill Creek Lakes, set in the least explored western sector of the Trinity Alps. Although some of the region has been burned severely by wildfire, the Mill Creek Lakes remain untouched by fire, like an island of green.

This is a good overnighter and will provide you with a feel for the area. From the trailhead at 4,800 feet, the grades are gradual with relatively easy elevation climbs and descents. A majority of the forest along the trail was burned in the 1999 Megram fire, in all, the fire affects 10 miles of this route. If you want to add to your trip, take the Devils Backbone east. Though there is no water available on this route, it peaks at Trinity Summit at about 5,800 feet, where there's a historic cabin. Other hikers are rare in this area, and most of the time you'll feel as if you have the universe to yourself.

Special note: Do not drink the water available here without first treating it with the best water filtration system you can afford.

Location: In Six Rivers National Forest on the western edge of the Trinity Alps Wilderness east of Hoopa; map B1, grid a2.

User groups: Hikers, dogs, and horses. No mountain bikes. No wheelchair facilities.

Permits: A wilderness permit is required for hikers planning on camping. Parking and access are free.

Maps: For a map of Six Rivers National Forest, send $6 to U.S. Forest Service, Attn: Map Sales, P.O. Box 587, Camino,

CA 95709; tel. (530) 647-5390, fax (530) 647-5389, or website: www.r5.fs.fed.us/visitorcenter. Major credit cards accepted. Ask the USGS for topographic maps of the Tish Tang Point and Trinity Mountain areas.

Directions: From Arcata go east on Highway 299 to Willow Creek. Turn north on Highway 96 and drive about 12 miles into Hoopa Valley to Big Hill Road. Turn right (east) on Big Hill Road and drive 11 miles to the Six Rivers National Forest border (the road becomes Forest Road 8N01). Continue for 4.5 miles (the road becomes Forest Road 10N02) to the Redcap Trailhead (once off Hoopa reservation land, stay on the chip-seal road).

Contact: Six Rivers National Forest, Lower Trinity Ranger District, P.O. Box 68, Willow Creek, CA 95573; tel. (530) 629-2118 or fax (530) 629-2102.

2 Trail Creek Trail
7.0 mi/2.0 days

The Russian Wilderness is a place so pristine and so small that it just can't handle many visitors. If you go, walk softly and treat the fragile area with care. The route into the Russian Wilderness—the Trail Creek Trail—is more of an old jeep road, involving a steep climb and drop, then a short cross-country jaunt. When you finish, you could always write the book, "My Life as a Jeep." From Trail Creek Camp to the PCT, you are unlikely to see anybody but your companions, and that's a plus.

The trailhead is located a short distance up a gravel road across from Trail Creek Campground, which is on Cecilville-Callahan Road. For the first 1.5 miles the trail heads steeply up on an old fire lane. It continues to climb, and as you near the crest, you'll junction with the Pacific Crest Trail; turn left, then just five minutes later, turn at a signed junction to Syphon Lake. This is a good first night's camp, with Russian or Waterdog Lakes good second day destinations.

Once you hit the high country, the lakes are very beautiful, especially Russian, excellent

for swimming. Because the wilderness here is small, it does not take many people hiking in to take up the campsites. Expect occasional cow sightings in midsummer.

Special note: The trailhead for the Pacific Crest Trail off the Cecilville-Callahan Road provides a much easier route into the southern portion of the Russian Wilderness, but it will add ten miles to your trip.

Location: In the Russian Wilderness west of Callahan; map B1, grid a8.

User groups: Hikers, dogs, and horses. Mountain bikes are allowed only outside of the wilderness border. No wheelchair facilities.

Permits: A wilderness permit is required for hikers planning to camp. Parking and access are free.

Maps: For a map of Klamath National Forest, send $6 to U.S. Forest Service, Attn: Map Sales, P.O. Box 587, Camino, CA 95709; tel. (530) 647-5390, fax (530) 647-5389, or website: www.r5.fs.fed.us/visitorcenter. Major credit cards accepted. Ask the USGS for topographic maps of the Deadman Peak and Eaton Peak areas.

Directions: From Redding drive north on Interstate 5 for 70 miles. Just past Weed take the Edgewood exit. At the stop sign turn left and drive through the underpass to another stop sign. Turn right on Old Highway 99 and drive six miles to Gazelle. Turn left at Gazelle on Gazelle-Callahan Road and drive about 20 miles to Callahan. From Callahan on Highway 3 turn west on County Road 402 (Cecilville Road) and drive 17 miles to Trail Creek Campground. The trail heads north from a gravel road located across from the campground.

Contact: Klamath National Forest, Scott River Ranger District, 11263 N. Highway 3, Fort Jones, CA 96032-9702; tel. (530) 468-5351 or fax (530) 468-1290.

3 Trail Gulch
4.5 mi/3.25 hrs

The Trail Gulch Trail rises along Trail Gulch Creek, steeply at times, but in just 2.25 miles arrives at Trail Gulch Lake. That makes it close enough to go in and out in a day, or better yet, you can make it a good weekend overnighter without tremendous strain. Set northeast of Deadman Peak (7,741 feet) in the Trinity Alps Wilderness, the round, pretty lake is stocked by airplane every year with small trout, a nice bonus. Another bonus is how simple it is to extend your trip either to other mountain lakes or deep into the Trinity Alps Wilderness. Long Gulch Lake is just another three miles from Trail Gulch Lake, a good side trip. If you choose to extend into the Trinity Alps instead, the trail is routed along North Fork Coffee Creek to Kickapoo Waterfall, about nine miles from Trail Gulch Lake. This trip is crowded on summer weekends. Experienced hikers may note that on many maps that Trail Gulch Lake is misidentified as Long Gulch Lake, and vice versa.

Location: In the Trinity Alps Wilderness west of Callahan; map B1, grid b8.

User groups: Hikers, dogs, and horses. No mountain bikes. No wheelchair facilities.

Permits: A wilderness permit is required for hikers planning to camp. Parking and access are free.

Maps: For a map of Klamath National Forest or the Trinity Alps Wilderness, send $6 to U.S. Forest Service, Attn: Map Sales, P.O. Box 587, Camino, CA 95709; tel. (530) 647-5390, fax (530) 647-5389, or website: www.r5.fs.fed.us/visitorcenter. Major credit cards accepted. Ask the USGS for topographic maps of the Deadman Peak and Billys Peak areas.

Directions: From Redding drive north on Interstate 5 for 70 miles. Just past Weed take the Edgewood exit. At the stop sign turn left and drive through the underpass to another stop sign. Turn right on Old Highway 99 and drive about six miles to Gazelle. Turn left on Gazelle-Callahan Road and drive about 20 miles to Callahan. From Callahan on Highway 3 turn west on County Road 402 (Cecilville Road) and drive 11 miles. Turn left on Forest Road 39N08 and drive 1.5 miles to the trailhead.

Contact: Klamath National Forest, Scott River Ranger District, 11263 N. Highway 3, Fort Jones, CA 96032-9702; tel. (530) 468-5351 or fax (530) 468-1290.

◪ New River Trailhead
18.0 mi/2.0 days

Most backpackers in the Trinity Alps Wilderness like high mountain lakes, but here is a trail that features small streams and is set in the relative vicinity of the Megram burn area of 1999. The highlights are the headwaters of the New River, a tributary to the Trinity River, and Mary Blaine Meadow. Because this is a river trail, not a lake trail, and because of the Megram fire at the headwaters of the New River, it gets very little use.

The trail starts right along the New River and immediately begins climbing. In about a mile, you'll reach Megram Cabin, the first landmark along the trail. After another mile, bear right at the fork in the trail and hike along Slide Creek. After two miles you'll arrive again at a fork, and again stay to the right. The trail passes Robbers Roost Mine, Emmons Cabin, and the Old Denny Cabin Site, all on the way to Mary Blaine Meadow, a distance of about nine miles from the trailhead. The meadow is set below Mary Blaine Mountain, and to the north, Dees Peak. The whole region is cut with small streams in crevices and canyons. From the air, you can see how the fire burned a huge area, but cut a mosaic-like swath, leaving patches of green amid blackened scars.

Location: In the Trinity Alps Wilderness east of Willow Creek; map B1, grid c2.

User groups: Hikers, dogs, and horses. No mountain bikes. No wheelchair facilities.

Permits: A wilderness permit is required for hikers planning to camp.

Maps: For a map of Shasta-Trinity National Forest or the Trinity Alps Wilderness, send $6 to U.S. Forest Service, Attn: Map Sales, P.O. Box 587, Camino, CA 95709; tel. (530) 647-5390, fax (530) 647-5389, or website: www.r5.fs.fed.us/visitorcenter. Major credit cards accepted. Ask the USGS for topographic maps of the Jim Jam Ridge, Dees Peak, and Trinity Mountain areas.

Directions: From Weaverville take Highway 299 west about 32 miles. Turn north on County Road 402 (Denny Road) and drive about 21 miles. Turn left on Forest Road 7N15 and drive four miles north to the trailhead parking area.

Contact: Shasta-Trinity National Forest, Big Bar Ranger Station, Star Route 1, Box 10, Big Bar, CA 96010; tel. (530) 623-6106 or fax (530) 623-6123.

5 East Fork Loop

20.0 mi/3.0 days

Where else can you hike 20 miles with the chance you will not see anybody? The East Fork Trailhead provides access to one of the more primitive, less-traveled regions of the Trinity Alps Wilderness. It's an area known for streams and forests in the lower reaches and bare limestone ridges in the higher reaches. It's known for some burned areas from the mosaic-like burn of the Megram fire of 1999. The trip starts at the East Fork Trailhead, adjacent to the East Fork New River. It climbs along this watershed and after two miles turns before coming to Pony Creek. In the next six miles, which include sections that are quite steep, the trail climbs to Limestone Ridge near little Rattlesnake Lake. At Limestone Ridge, turn right on the New River Divide Trail and head south for six miles, passing Cabin Peak at 6,870 feet and arriving at White Creek Lake. To complete the loop, turn right on the trail at White Creek Lake and start the trip back, descending most of the way. The trail goes past Jakes Upper Camp and Jakes Lower Camp before linking up again with the East Fork Trail for the jog back to the parking area.

Location: In the Trinity Alps Wilderness east of Willow Creek; map B1, grid c3.

User groups: Hikers, dogs, and horses. No mountain bikes. No wheelchair facilities.

Permits: A wilderness permit is required for hikers planning to camp.

Maps: For a map of Shasta-Trinity National Forest or the Trinity Alps Wilderness, send $6 to U.S. Forest Service, Attn: Map Sales, P.O. Box 587, Camino, CA 95709; tel. (530) 647-5390, fax (530) 647-5389, or website: www.r5.fs.fed.us/visitorcenter. Major credit cards accepted. Ask the USGS for a topographic map of the Jim Jam Ridge area.

Directions: From Weaverville turn west on Highway 299 and drive about 32 miles. Turn north on County Road 402 (Denny Road) and drive 22 miles (the last four miles of the road become unpaved Forest Road 7N01) to the trailhead parking area.

Contact: Shasta-Trinity National Forest, Big Bar Ranger Station, Star Route 1, Box 10, Big Bar, CA 96010; tel. (530) 623-6106 or fax (530) 623-6123.

6 Little South Fork Lake Trail

13.0 mi/2.0 days

You have to be a little bit crazy to try this trip, and that's why we signed up. A word of warning: There's just no easy way to get to Little South Fork Lake and its two idyllic campsites, excellent swimming, and large trout. It's the toughest lake to reach in Northern California. This route is largely off trail and requires skirting a big waterfall, but there's no better way in (see the special note below); we've tried three different routes.

From the South Fork Trailhead, the trip starts out easy enough with four miles along the Salmon River, then bearing up along Little South Fork Creek. For most of this route there is something of a trail. The trail dead-ends into Little South Fork Creek. (A faint route on the other—north—side of the creek climbs through brush and up the canyon and should be avoided.) From here you're on your own, heading upstream with no trail available. The best route, though still steep and very difficult, is to lateral across the slope on the right side of the stream. After leaving the trail, it's about 1.25 miles to a beautiful waterfall, divine and pristine. To get around the waterfall, loop back and circle it to the right; if you go to the left, you'll add several dreadful hours to the trip (we tried that, too). Remember, there is no trail, no marked route. It is a cross-country scramble and very slow going. If you want a trail or even a game trail, this is not the hike for you. It's another 1.25 miles to the lake, but can take hours, with very slow going all the way, scrambling up and across the wooded slope, seemingly going on forever before suddenly emerging from the forest onto granite plates. Ahead is the lake, beautifully set in a rock bowl framed by a high back wall. There are excellent campsites at each end of the lake.

Special note: We hiked into this lake once from Caribou Lakes by climbing the Sawtooth Ridge and dropping down into the basin, the entire route being off trail, a potentially hazardous proposition, with some rock climbing and descents. On another trip from Caribou Lakes, we dropped down into Little South Fork Canyon, losing thousands of feet in altitude and in the process getting caught in a brush field like bugs in a spider web. Neither of these other two routes is recommended. In fact, the suggested route is not recommended either. One ranger said we were crazy to include it in the book. He was right, of course.

Location: In the Trinity Alps Wilderness near Cecilville; map B1, grid c7.

User groups: Hikers only. Dogs are permitted but strongly advised against. No horses or mountain bikes. No wheelchair facilities.

Permits: A wilderness permit is required for hikers planning to camp.

Maps: For a map of Klamath National Forest or the Trinity Alps Wilderness, send $6 to U.S. Forest Service, Attn: Map Sales, P.O. Box 587, Camino, CA 95709; tel. (530) 647-5390, fax (530) 647-5389, or website: www.r5.fs.fed.us/visitorcenter. Major credit cards accepted. Ask the USGS for a topographic map of the Thompson Peak area.

Directions: From Redding drive north on Interstate 5 for 70 miles. Just past Weed take the Edgewood exit. At the stop sign turn left and drive through the underpass to another stop sign. Turn right on Old Highway 99 and drive about six miles to Gazelle. Turn left on Gazelle-Callahan Road and drive 27 miles to Callahan. From Callahan on Highway 3, turn west on Cecilville Road and drive 28 miles to South Fork Road/County Road 1E003 (across from East Fork Campground). Turn left (south) on South Fork Road and drive 3.5 miles to a fork. Bear right at the fork and drive 2.5 miles to the South Fork Trailhead.

Contact: Klamath National Forest, Salmon River Ranger District, 11263 N. Highway 3, Fort Jones, CA 96032-9702; tel. (530) 468-5351 or fax (530) 468-1290.

🔷 Caribou Lakes Trail
18.0 mi/2.0 days

The Caribou Lakes Basin provides the classic Trinity Alps scene: three high mountain lakes, beautiful and serene, with the back wall of the Sawtooth Ridge casting a monumental backdrop on one side, and on the other side a drop-off and great views of a series of mountain peaks and ridgelines. Sunsets are absolutely remarkable when viewed from here. The centerpiece is Caribou Lake, the largest lake in the Trinity Alps Wilderness. Because it's a nine-mile hike to the Caribou Lakes Basin, this makes an excellent first-day destination for backpackers exploring this section of the Trinity Alps Wilderness. The trail starts at the bottom of the Salmon River, however, and like all trails that start at the bottom of canyons, it means you begin the trip with a terrible climb that never seems to end. Plan on drinking a full canteen of water and be certain not to miss the natural spring that's available near the crest, just off to the right. After reaching the crest, the trail travels counterclockwise around the mountain, then drops into the Caribou Lakes Basin. Ignore your urge to stop at the first lake, because the best campsites, swimming, and views are from Caribou Lake, the last and largest lake you'll reach in this circuit. Because this is a popular destination, fishing is often poor. The lake is stocked, but these fish are very smart from the relatively large number of people making a cast over the course of a summer.

Location: In the Trinity Alps Wilderness northwest of Trinity Lake; map B1, grid c7.

User groups: Hikers and dogs. Horses are permitted but not recommended. No mountain bikes. No wheelchair facilities.

Permits: A wilderness permit is required for hikers planning to camp.

Maps: For a map of Klamath National Forest or the Trinity Alps Wilderness, send $6 to U.S. Forest Service, Attn: Map Sales, P.O. Box 587, Camino, CA 95709; tel. (530) 647-5390, fax (530) 647-5389, or website: www.r5.fs.fed.us/visitorcenter. Major credit cards accepted. Ask the USGS for a topographic map of the Caribou Lakes area.

Directions: From Weaverville drive north on Highway 3 past Trinity Lake. At the Coffee Creek Ranger Station turn west (left) on County Road 104 (Coffee Creek Road) and drive 17 miles to the trailhead at the end of the road at Big Flat Campground.

Contact: Klamath National Forest, Salmon River Ranger District, 11263 N. Highway 3, Fort Jones, CA 96032-9702; tel. (530) 468-5351 or fax (530) 468-1290.

8 Union Lake Trail
12.0 mi/2.0 days

Union Lake sits in a granite basin below Red Rock Mountain. The hike in and out is a good weekend affair, but most visitors are backpackers who are using the camp at the lake as a first-day destination for a multi-day trip. Of the trailheads on Coffee Creek Road, this one is often overlooked. The trail starts near an old sawmill along Coffee Creek, heads south (to the left), and in less than a mile starts the climb adjacent to Union Creek (on your right). Like most hikes that start at a streambed, you pay for your pleasure, going up, not down. After about two miles the trail crosses Union Creek and continues on for a

few miles, now with the stream on the left. You'll pass a trail junction for Bullards Basin, and about .5 mile later turn right on the cutoff trail to Union Lake.

Location: In the Trinity Alps Wilderness northwest of Trinity Lake; map B1, grid c8.

User groups: Hikers, dogs, and horses. No mountain bikes. No wheelchair facilities.

Permits: A wilderness permit is required for hikers planning to camp.

Maps: For a map of Shasta-Trinity National Forest or the Trinity Alps Wilderness, send $6 to U.S. Forest Service, Attn: Map Sales, P.O. Box 587, Camino, CA 95709; tel. (530) 647-5390, fax (530) 647-5389, or website: www.r5.fs.fed.us/visitorcenter. Major credit cards accepted. Ask the USGS for a topographic map of the Caribou Lakes area.

Directions: From Weaverville drive north on Highway 3 past Trinity Lake. At the Coffee Creek Ranger Station, turn west (left) on County Road 104 (Coffee Creek Road) and drive about 10 miles to the trailhead on the left.

Contact: Shasta-Trinity National Forest, Big Bar Ranger Station, Star Route 1, Box 10, Big Bar, CA 96010; tel. (530) 623-6106 or fax (530) 623-6123.

9 Boulder Lake Trail
12.0 mi/2.0 days

The hike to Boulder Lake and back makes a great weekend backpack trip. Two trails head out from the Goldfield Campground, each routed to Union Lake. Our choice is to take the trail that runs adjacent to Boulder Creek. The grade is long and steady, but the nearby cold flows of water have a way of keeping you mentally refreshed. As you near Sugar Pine Butte at 8,033 feet, the trail turns sharply to the left, loops in a clockwise direction around a butte, and then connects with the short cutoff trail that leads to Boulder Lake, a pretty lake set in a spectacular basin. This has become a very popular weekend hike and camping trip.

Location: In the Trinity Alps Wilderness northwest of Trinity Lake; map B1, grid c9.

User groups: Hikers, dogs, and horses. No mountain bikes. No wheelchair facilities.

Permits: A wilderness permit is required for hikers planning to camp.

Maps: For a map of Shasta-Trinity National Forest or the Trinity Alps Wilderness, send $6 to U.S. Forest Service, Attn: Map Sales, P.O. Box 587, Camino, CA 95709; tel. (530) 647-5390, fax (530) 647-5389, or website: www.r5.fs.fed.us/visitorcenter. Major credit cards accepted. Ask the USGS for a topographic map of the Ycatapom Peak area.

Directions: From Weaverville drive north on Highway 3 past Trinity Lake. At the Coffee Creek Ranger Station turn west (left) on County Road 104 (Coffee Creek Road) and drive about 6.5 miles to Goldfield Campground on the left and the trailhead parking area.

Contact: Shasta Trinity National Forest, Big Bar Ranger Station, Star Route 1, Box 10, Big Bar, CA 96010; tel. (530) 623-6106 or fax (530) 623-6123.

🔟 Burnt Ranch Falls
0.5 mi/0.5 hr

Burnt Ranch Falls isn't a spectacular cascade of water like other more famous waterfalls, but it is the center of a very pretty, easy-to-reach scene on the Trinity River. It's a relatively small but wide waterfall, comprised of about 10 feet of rock that in low-water conditions creates a natural barrier for migrating salmon and steelhead. Thus the highlight comes when river flows rise a bit in the fall, and you can watch the spectacular sight of salmon and steelhead jumping and sailing through the air to get over and past the falls.

The trail is a short but steep .25 mile jaunt down from the Burnt Ranch Campground. When you arrive at the river, walk out a short way on the rocky spot to watch the fish jump. The setting in an area along Highway 299 has a magnificent natural landscape. From the river the Trinity canyon walls look like they ascend into the sky. Unlike most waterfalls,

Burnt Ranch Falls is a far less compelling scene at high water. During high, turbid flows, it becomes much more difficult to see fish jumping past the falls.

Location: In Shasta-Trinity National Forest on Highway 299 east of Willow Creek; map B1, grid d1.

User groups: Hikers and dogs. No horses or mountain bikes. No wheelchair facilities.

Permits: No permits are required.

Maps: For a map of Shasta-Trinity National Forest, send $6 to U.S. Forest Service, Attn: Map Sales, P.O. Box 587, Camino, CA 95709; tel. (530) 647-5390, fax (530) 647-5389, or website: www.r5.fs.fed.us/visitorcenter. Major credit cards accepted. Ask the USGS for a topographic map of the Ironed Mountain area.

Directions: From Weaverville drive west on Highway 299 to Burnt Ranch. From Burnt Ranch drive .5 mile west on Highway 299 to the trailhead at Burnt Ranch Campground on the right.

Contact: Shasta-Trinity National Forest, Big Bar Ranger Station, Star Route 1, Box 10, Big Bar, CA 96010; tel. (530) 623-6106 or fax (530) 623-6123.

🔟🔟 New River Divide Trail
30.0 mi/3.0 days

The New River Divide Trail provides access to the Limestone Ridge of the Trinity Alps, taking a ridgeline route most of the way. This is an area known for lookouts from mountain rims, the headwaters of many small feeder streams, and few people. The trip starts at the Green Mountain Trailhead at an elevation of 5,052 feet, and in the first three miles the route skirts the southern flank of Brushy Mountain, past Panther Camp and Stove Camp, and along the eastern flank of Green Mountain. As the trail climbs toward the Limestone Ridge, you'll find yourself perched on a divide, where the streams on each side pour into different watersheds. Eventually the trail rises all the way to Cabin Peak at 6,870 feet and beyond to little Rattlesnake Lake, a one-way distance of about 15 miles. Note that the Megram fire of 1999 consumed a huge area of acreage at the headwaters of the New River off to the northwest from this ridge route.

Location: In the Trinity Alps Wilderness north of Trinity River's Big Bar; map B1, grid d3.
User groups: Hikers, dogs, and horses. No mountain bikes. No wheelchair facilities.
Permits: A wilderness permit is required. Park and access are free.
Maps: For a map of Shasta-Trinity National Forest or the Trinity Alps Wilderness, send $6 to U.S. Forest Service, Attn: Map Sales, P.O. Box 587, Camino, CA 95709; tel. (530) 647-5390, fax (530) 647-5389, or website: www.r5.fs.fed. us/visitorcenter. Major credit cards accepted. Ask the USGS for a topographic map of the Del Loam area.
Directions: From Weaverville drive west on Highway 299 for 23 miles to French Creek Road (Forest Road 5913). Turn north (right) and drive seven miles (the road becomes Forest Road 5N04). Continue straight for four miles to the trailhead at the Green Mountain parking area.
Contact: Shasta-Trinity National Forest, Big Bar Ranger Station, Star Route 1, Box 10, Big Bar, CA 96010; tel. (530) 623-6106 or fax (530) 623-6123.

12 Grizzly Lake

12 mi/two days or 38.0 mi/5.0 days

Take your pick: From the China Creek Trailhead, a butt-kicking six-mile climb with a 5,000-foot elevation gain (with a 1,500-foot canyon descent included on the way), or from the Hobo Gulch Trailhead, a moderate grade but over the course of 19 miles to make the lake. Despite this difficulty, Grizzly Lake can be crowded, because it is the preeminent destination in the Trinity Alps, set below awesome Thompson Peak (8,863 feet), along with one of the most beautiful wilderness waterfalls anywhere, 80-foot Grizzly Falls, and the lake is so pristine that you can spend hours just looking at it.

Given a choice, most people take the short, butt-kicker route, then cuss at themselves for doing so. There is almost nothing rewarding about it, and most complete the trip with head down, trying to think about something else. Before you race off to this destination, think long and hard if you really are ready to pay a terrible physical toll to get there.

Or, on the other hand, you can instead take the longer but more gradual climb. That is from the Hobo Gulch Trailhead, set deep in the national forest along Backbone Ridge. On this route, Grizzly Lake is 19 miles away. So instead of camping along lakes, hikers camp along pretty streams and flats, taking days to reach the promised land at Grizzly Lake.

The trail from Hobo Gulch starts by heading straight north about five miles along the North Fork Trinity River to Rattlesnake Camp, climbing very gently. You cross Rattlesnake Creek, pick up the Rattlesnake Creek Trail, and continue another three miles past the old Morrison Cabin (from the mining days) and on to Pfeiffer Flat. Here the North Fork Trinity is joined by Grizzly Creek, an attractive backpacking destination. From Pfeiffer Flat, the trail follows Grizzly Creek, rising high toward the Trinity Sawtooth Ridge and requiring an uphill pull to beautiful Grizzly Meadows and then to Grizzly Lake, the final mile a scramble over a clear hiking route amid rock.

For rock climbers, climbing the lake bowl in a clockwise direction makes for an exciting scramble to Thompson Peak and a perch just below the rock summit; to reach the tip-top of the mountain requires a technical climb.

Location: In the Trinity Alps Wilderness north of Junction City; map B1, grid d4.
User groups: Hikers, dogs, and horses. No mountain bikes. No wheelchair facilities.
Permits: A wilderness permit is required for hikers planning to camp.
Maps: For a map of Shasta-Trinity National Forest or the Trinity Alps Wilderness, send $6 to U.S. Forest Service, Attn: Map Sales, P.O. Box 587, Camino, CA 95709; tel. (530) 647-5390,

fax (530) 647-5389, or website: www.r5.fs.fed. us/visitorcenter. Major credit cards accepted. Ask the USGS for a topographic map of the Thurston Peaks area.

Directions to Hobo Gulch Trailhead: From Weaverville drive 13 miles west on Highway 299 to Helena and East Fork Road. Turn north on East Fork Road (County Road 421) and drive 3.9 miles to Hobo Gulch Road. Turn left on Hobo Gulch Road (Forest Road 34N07Y) and drive 12 miles to the Hobo Gulch Trailhead, located at Hobo Gulch Campground at the end of the road.

Directions to China Creek Trailhead: From Redding drive north on Interstate 5 for 70 miles. Just past Weed, take the Edgewood exit. At the stop sign turn left and drive through the underpass to another stop sign. Turn right on Old Highway 99 and drive about six miles to Gazelle. Turn left on Gazelle-Callahan Road and drive 27 miles to Callahan. From Callahan on Highway 3, turn west on Cecilville Road and drive 27 miles to Forest Road 37N24. Turn south and drive 3.8 miles to Forest Road 37N07 (well signed). Take Forest 37N07 and drive six miles to the trailhead.

Contact: Shasta-Trinity National Forest, Big Bar Ranger Station, Star Route 1, Box 10, Big Bar, CA 96010; tel. (530) 623-6106 or fax (530) 623-6123.

13 Swift Creek Trail to Granite Lake

12.0 mi/2.0 days

When hikers scan wilderness maps, they often search for trails that are routed a short distance to a beautiful lake for a first night's camp. That's exactly what you get at Granite Lake, but although the trip in is only about six miles, it's anything but easy. From the trailhead the hike starts simply enough, tracing the right side of Swift Creek. Don't be fooled. Just beyond the confluence of Swift and Granite Creeks, you must cross the stream to the left and then pick up the Granite Lake Trail. This trail runs along the right side of Granite

Creek for four miles and includes a very steep section in the final mile that will have you wondering why you ever thought this was going to be such a short, easy trip. (Two notes on the way in: 1. For the most part, the creek is not accessible as a water source, so monitor your canteen level. 2. There is a series of tumbling, churning waterfalls on Swift Creek, no great free falls, but lots of whitewater.) Finally you'll rise to Gibson Meadow and just beyond, Granite Lake, a gorgeous sight below Gibson Peak. For a natural mountain lake, it's a fair size, with good swimming during the day and trout fishing in the evening. This is a popular spot, so plan on company.

Location: In the Trinity Alps Wilderness west of Trinity Center; map B1, grid d9.

User groups: Hikers or dogs. No horses or mountain bikes. No wheelchair facilities.

Permits: A wilderness permit is required for hikers planning to camp.

Maps: For a map of Shasta-Trinity National Forest or the Trinity Alps Wilderness, send $6 to U.S. Forest Service, Attn: Map Sales, P.O. Box 587, Camino, CA 95709; tel. (530) 647-5390, fax (530) 647-5389, or website: www.r5.fs.fed. us/visitorcenter. Major credit cards accepted. Ask the USGS for topographic maps of the Covington Mill and Trinity Center areas.

Directions: From Weaverville drive north on Highway 3 for 28 miles to Trinity Center and Swift Creek Road. Turn left and drive 6.8 miles to the parking area at the wilderness border.

Contact: Shasta-Trinity National Forest, Weaverville Ranger Station, P.O. Box 1190, Weaverville, CA 96093; tel. (530) 623-2121 or fax (530) 623-6010.

14 Long Canyon Trailhead

16.0 mi/2.0 days

Your mission, should you choose to accept it, is the 6.5-mile largely uphill hike to the west side of Gibson Peak, where Deer Lake, Summit Lake, Luella Lake, Diamond Lake, and Siligo Peak can provide days of side-trip destinations. From the trailhead the trip starts by tracing along the East Fork Stuart Fork, a feeder creek to Trinity Lake. After two miles you'll arrive at a fork in the trail. Take the right fork (the left fork is routed to Bowerman Meadows and little Lake Anna), which climbs farther along the stream, then traces the southern flank of Gibson Peak. At times the trail is steep in this area, but finally you'll pass Gibson Peak, and Siligo Peak will come into view. The trail also intersects a loop trail that circles Siligo Peak and provides access to four high mountain lakes. Summit Lake is the favorite.

Location: In the Trinity Alps Wilderness northwest of Trinity Lake; map B1, grid d8.

User groups: Hikers, dogs, and horses. No mountain bikes. No wheelchair facilities.

Permits: A wilderness permit is required for hikers planning to camp.

Maps: For a map of Shasta-Trinity National Forest or the Trinity Alps Wilderness, send $6 to U.S. Forest Service, Attn: Map Sales, P.O. Box 587, Camino, CA 95709; tel. (530) 647-5390, fax (530) 647-5389, or website: www.r5.fs.fed.us/visitorcenter. Major credit cards accepted. Ask the USGS for a topographic map of the Covington Mill area.

Directions: From Weaverville drive north on Highway 3 to Covington Mill and Forest Road 115. Turn left and drive for 2.5 miles to the trailhead.

Contact: Shasta-Trinity National Forest, Weaverville Ranger Station, P.O. Box 1190, Weaverville, CA 96093; tel. (530) 623-2121 or fax (530) 623-6010.

15 Stuart Fork Trailhead

28.0 mi/4.0 days

Don't say we didn't warn you; this trail doesn't have a difficulty rating of five for nothing. The hike requires an endless climb—very steep at times, particularly as you near the Sawtooth Ridge—spanning nearly 14 miles to Emerald Lake. The first nine miles are easy, and it will have you thinking this hike is a piece of cake. But surprise: It's the last five miles from Morris Meadows that's a killer. After arriving and resting up for a night, you'll find that ecstasy follows. Emerald Lake is one of three lakes set in line in a canyon below the Sawtooth Ridge, the others being Sapphire and Mirror. The surroundings are stark and prehistoric, and the lakes are gemlike, blue and clear, with big rainbow trout and water that is perfect for refreshing swims. The trail continues a mile past Emerald Lake to Sapphire Lake, and from there it's an off-trail scramble, often across big boulders, as you climb another mile to reach Mirror Lake. The entire scene is surreal.

Special note: On the way in to Emerald Lake, you might notice a cutoff trail to the right and see on your trail map that it crosses the Sawtooth Ridge and leads into the acclaimed Caribou Lakes Basin. On the map it appears to be a short, easy trip, but in reality it involves a terrible climb with more than 100 switchbacks.

Location: In the Trinity Alps Wilderness northwest of Trinity Lake; map B1, grid e6.

User groups: Hikers, dogs, and horses. No mountain bikes. No wheelchair facilities.

Permits: A wilderness permit is required for hikers planning to camp.

Maps: For a map of Shasta-Trinity National Forest or the Trinity Alps Wilderness, send $6 to U.S. Forest Service, Attn: Map Sales, P.O. Box 587, Camino, CA 95709; tel. (530) 647-5390, fax (530) 647-5389, or website: www.r5.fs.fed.us/visitorcenter. Major credit cards accepted. Ask the USGS for a topographic map of the Covington Mill area.

Directions: From Weaverville on Highway 299 turn north onto Highway 3 and drive 15 miles to Trinity Lake. Turn left on Trinity Alps Road and drive 2.5 miles to the trailhead at Bridge Camp.

Contact: Shasta-Trinity National Forest, Weaverville Ranger Station, P.O. Box 1190, Weaverville, CA 96093; tel. (530) 623-2121 or fax (530) 623-6010.

16 Canyon Creek Lakes Trailhead

16.0 mi/2.0 days

This is the kind of place where wilderness lovers think they can find religion. But what they find, guaranteed, is tons of other people; expect about 50 other hikers on weekdays, 200 to 300 on weekends. The destination is Canyon Creek Lakes, set high in a mountain canyon, framed by Sawtooth Mountain to the east and a series of high granite rims to the north. The route in is no mystery, heading straight upstream along Bear Creek for about .25 mile, then crossing Bear Creek (a dry ford) before continuing along Canyon Creek. Four miles out you'll reach the first of four waterfalls. The first is the smallest; then they get progressively taller, and all are gorgeous. After the last waterfall, walk .5 mile to reach Lower Canyon Creek Lake, seven miles out from the trailhead. From here, now largely above tree line, cross Stonehouse Gulch to reach the first of two lakes. The trail skirts the left side of the first of the Canyon Creek Lakes, then in .5 mile arrives at the head of the larger of the two. They are like jewels set in the bottom of a gray, stark, high mountain canyon, and once you've seen them, you'll have their picture branded permanently in your mind. This has become a special weekend favorite for hikers from Eureka.

Location: In the Trinity Alps Wilderness north of Weaverville; map B1, grid e6.

User groups: Hikers and dogs. No horses or mountain bikes. No wheelchair facilities.

Permits: A wilderness permit is required for hikers planning to camp.

Maps: For a map of Shasta-Trinity National Forest or the Trinity Alps Wilderness, send $6 to U.S. Forest Service, Attn: Map Sales, P.O. Box 587, Camino, CA 95709; tel. (530) 647-5390, fax (530) 647-5389, or website: www.r5.fs.fed. us/visitorcenter. Major credit cards accepted. Ask the USGS for a topographic map of the Dedrick area.

Directions: From Weaverville, drive west on Highway 299 for eight miles to Junction City and Canyon Creek Road. Turn north on Canyon Creek Road and drive 13 miles to the trailhead at the end of the road (.75 mile past Ripstein Campground).

Contact: Shasta-Trinity National Forest, Weaverville Ranger Station, P.O. Box 1190, Weaverville, CA 96093; tel. (530) 623-2121 or fax (530) 623-6010.

17 South Fork National Recreation Trail

20.0 mi/2.0 days

This is a little-known trail for people who like walking along a stream in solitude. This is also a great early-season trail when so many others are still snowbound. It's routed along the South Fork Trinity River, heading south toward the Yolla Bolly Wilderness. There are no lakes anywhere near the trail, and for the most part the trail just meanders along, with that stream nearby providing a constant point of reference. Even the trailhead, a short drive out of the Hell Gate Campground, is remote and obscure. Immediately the trail picks up the stream, and in less than an hour you'll feel as if you've discovered your own private little universe. The temperatures can really smoke out here in the summer, and the stream is your savior. How far might you go? For many, an hour in and an hour out is plenty. You can keep going to St. Jacques Place, an abandoned camp about 10 miles farther one way, or even another five miles to the trail's end at Double Cabin Site, where you can leave a shuttle car and make this a one-way trip. Note that the trail crosses private property several times; stay on the trail, respect property rights, and help keep this trail open.

Location: In Shasta-Trinity National Forest east of Ruth Lake on Highway 36; map B1, grid h2.

User groups: Hikers and dogs. No horses or mountain bikes. No wheelchair facilities.

Permits: Campfire permits are required for overnight use. Parking and access are free.

Maps: For a map of Shasta-Trinity National Forest, send $6 to U.S. Forest Service, Attn: Map Sales, P.O. Box 587, Camino, CA 95709; tel. (530) 647-5390, fax (530) 647-5389, or website: www.r5.fs.fed.us/visitorcenter. Major credit cards accepted. Ask the USGS for a topographic map of the Forest Glen area.

Directions: From Red Bluff, drive west on Highway 36 (very twisty) past Platina to the junction with Highway 3. Continue west on Highway 36 for 10 miles to the Hell Gate campground entrance on the left. Turn left on Forest Road 1526 and drive to the trailhead.

Contact: Shasta-Trinity National Forest, South Fork Management Unit, P.O. Box 159, Hayfork, CA 96041; tel. (530) 628-5227 or (530) 352-4211, or fax (530) 628-5212.

18 North Fork Beegum Trailhead

10.0 mi/2.0 days

You want to be by yourself? This region of California gets only a scant number of visitors. While it lacks high mountains, sweeping views, and lakeside campsites, there is another benefit here that has become far more difficult to find in California: absolute peace and quiet. The trail starts out of the North Fork Beegum Campground and is routed south along Beegum Creek for the first few miles. Much of this is quite rocky and difficult, but hey, you wanted to be alone, right? It then rises to Pole Corral Gap, set at 4,360 feet and adjacent to Little Red Mountain. Pole Corral Gap can be difficult to find; the trail is not maintained and often seems to disappear and reappear. For most visitors this is plenty far enough. A good side trip is to drive for the view to Pattymocus Butte, where there's an old U.S. Forest Service lookout station (accessible by vehicle).

Special note: A portion of the trail on this route runs across posted private property, the Seeliger Ranch. So stay on the trail. Got it?

Location: In Shasta-Trinity National Forest west of Red Bluff; map B1, grid j5.

User groups: Hikers, dogs, horses, and mountain bikes. No wheelchair facilities.

Permits: No permits are required.

Maps: For a map of Shasta-Trinity National Forest, send $6 to U.S. Forest Service, Attn: Map Sales, P.O. Box 587, Camino, CA 95709; tel. (530) 647-5390, fax (530) 647-5389, or website: www.r5.fs.fed.us/visitorcenter. Major credit cards accepted. Ask the USGS for a topographic map of the Pony Buck Peak area.

Directions: From Interstate 5 at Red Bluff, turn west on Highway 36 and drive about 45 miles (west of Platina) to the Yolla Bolly Ranger Station and Stuart Gap Road. Turn south (left) on Stuart Gap Road and drive about eight miles to the trailhead at North Fork Beegum Campground on the left. If you cross North Fork Beegum Creek, you have gone too far.

Contact: Shasta-Trinity National Forest, Yolla Bolly Ranger Station, 2555 Highway 36, Platina, CA 96076; tel. (530) 352-4211.

PACIFIC CREST TRAIL (PCT) SECTION OVERVIEW

21.0 mi one way/2-3 days

Trail sections in this area extend from Scott Mountain east of Callahan to the border of the Russian Wilderness.

This segment of the Pacific Crest Trail doesn't travel north to south, but rather is routed east to west. Because it only skirts the northern edge of the Trinity Alps Wilderness, it gets less use than many of the lake-destination trails in the wilderness to the south. Regardless, this route features many excellent, short side trips to small mountain lakes in both the Trinity Alps and the Russian Wilderness, making it attractive to both weekend hikers as well as those on longer expeditions. The following provide specific information about major trail sections in this zone.

Scott Mountain to Cecilville Road

18.0 mi one way/2.0 days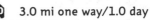

Short hikes on spur trails to a number of wilderness lakes are the highlight of this section of the Pacific Crest Trail. From the camp at Scott Mountain, the trail is routed west for five miles, where the first of a series of lakes is within .5 mile of the trail. They include Upper Boulder, East Boulder, Mid Boulder, and Telephone Lakes, all quite pretty and accessible from the main trail. After hiking past Eagle Peak, set at 7,789 feet, you'll pass additional short cutoffs that are routed to West Boulder, Mavis, and Fox Creek Lakes. Hikers often camp at one of these lakes before dropping to the South Fork Scott River and heading north into the Russian Wilderness.

Location: From Highway 3 at Scott Mountain Campground to Cecilville Road near the northern border of the Trinity Alps Wilderness; map B1, grid a9.

User groups: Hikers, dogs, and horses. No mountain bikes. No wheelchair facilities.

Permits: A wilderness permit is required for camping in the Trinity Alps Wilderness. Contact the Weaverville Ranger District at the address below for information.

Maps: Ask the USGS for topographic maps of the Scott Mountain, Tangle Blue Lake, Billys Peak, and Deadman Peak areas.

Directions: From Callahan drive south on Highway 3 about seven miles to the trailhead at Scott Mountain Campground.

Contact: Shasta-Trinity National Forest, Weaverville Ranger Station, P.O. Box 1190, Weaverville, CA 96093; tel. (530) 623-2121 or fax (530) 623-6010.

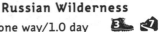 Cecilville Road to Russian Wilderness

3.0 mi one way/1.0 day

The long, steady climb up to the southern border of the Russian Wilderness starts from the bottom of the canyon at the North Fork Scott River. From the trailhead a good side trip (to the south) is the short hike to Hidden Lake or South Fork Lakes. Those venturing onward on the PCT enter a complex habitat web that includes the headwaters of the Scott, Salmon, and Trinity Rivers, along with the beautiful scenery that such diversity creates. This section of the trail is rarely used, with less than 1,000 people a year estimated to hike here. Most of them use this as a jump-off spot to the Russian Wilderness.

Location: From Cecilville Road west of Callahan to the southern border of the Russian Wilderness; map B1, grid a9.

User groups: Hikers, dogs, and horses. No mountain bikes. No wheelchair facilities.

Permits: No permits are required for this section. Parking and access are free.

Maps: Ask the USGS for topographic maps of the Deadman Peak and Eaton Peak areas.

Directions: From Callahan on Highway 3 turn west on Cecilville Road (County Road 402) and drive 11.5 miles to the Cecilville Summit. Parking is limited here; a larger parking area is located just past Cecilville Summit at the Carter Meadows Trailhead (it will add .25 mile to your hike).

Contact: Klamath National Forest, Scott River Ranger District, 11263 N. Highway 3, Fort Jones, CA 96032-9702; tel. (530) 468-5351 or fax (530) 468-1290.

PCT Continuation:

To continue hiking along the Pacific Crest Trail, see chapter A1.

TOM STIENSTRA HEADING
UP GREEN BUTTE RIDGE
ON MOUNT SHASTA

MAP B2

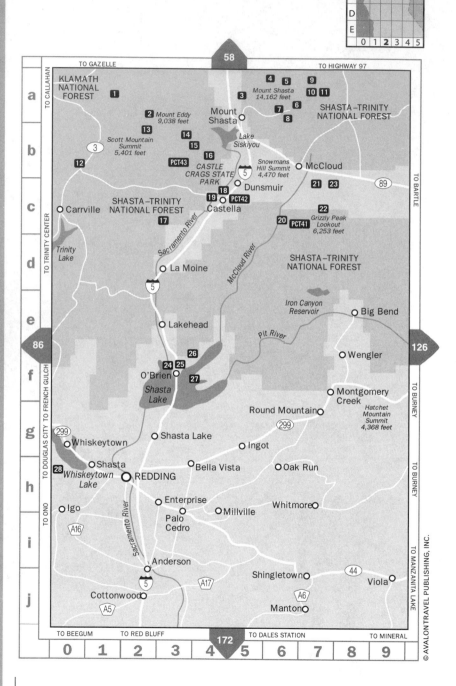

TO GAZELLE

58

TO HIGHWAY 97

KLAMATH
NATIONAL
FOREST

TO CALLAHAN

1

2 Mount Eddy
9,038 feet

13

Scott Mountain
Summit
5,401 feet

3

12

14

15

16

PCT43

4

5

3

Mount Shasta
14,162 feet

Mount
Shasta

7

8

6

9

10 **11**

SHASTA–TRINITY
NATIONAL FOREST

Lake
Siskiyou

Snowmans
Hill Summit
4,470 feet

CASTLE
CRAGS STATE
PARK

18

19 PCT42

Castella

17

SHASTA–TRINITY
NATIONAL FOREST

Carrville

Dunsmuir

McCloud

21 **23**

22
Grizzly Peak
Lookout
6,253 feet

20 PCT41

89

TO BARTLE

TO TRINITY CENTER

Trinity
Lake

Sacramento River

La Moine

5

Lakehead

McCloud River

SHASTA–TRINITY
NATIONAL FOREST

Iron Canyon
Reservoir

Big Bend

86

Pit River

126

TO BURNEY

26

24 **25**

27

O'Brien

Shasta
Lake

Wengler

Montgomery
Creek

Round Mountain

Hatchet
Mountain
Summit
4,368 feet

299

TO DOUGLAS CITY TO FRENCH GULCH

299

Whiskeytown

Shasta Lake

Ingot

28

Shasta

Whiskeytown
Lake

Bella Vista

Oak Run

TO BURNEY

REDDING

TO ONO

Igo

Enterprise

Palo
Cedro

Millville

Whitmore

A16

TO MANZANITA LAKE

Sacramento River

Anderson

5

Shingletown

44

Viola

Cottonwood

A17

A6

Manton

A5

TO BEEGUM

TO RED BLUFF

172

TO DALES STATION

TO MINERAL

0 1 2 3 4 5 6 7 8 9

© AVALON TRAVEL PUBLISHING, INC.

CHAPTER B2

1 Kangaroo Lake
Trailhead. 103

2 Deadfall Lakes Trail. . . 104

3 Black Butte Trail 105

4 Whitney Falls/Bolam
Creek Trailhead. 105

5 North Gate
Trailhead. 106

6 Sand Flat Trailhead . . . 107

7 Shasta Summit Trail . . 108

8 Panther Meadows 109

9 Brewer Creek
Trailhead. 110

10 Mud Creek Falls. 111

11 Old Ski Bowl
Trailhead. 111

12 Big Bear Lake Trail . . . 112

13 Toad Lake Trail 113

14 Sisson-Callahan. 113

15 Gumboot Lake
Trailhead. 114

16 Heart Lake Trail 115

17 Tamarack Lake
Trailhead. 116

18 Root Creek Trail 116

19 Crags Trail 116

20 McCloud
Nature Trail 117

21 Lower McCloud Falls . . 118

22 Middle Falls Trail 118

23 Grizzly Peak 119

24 Waters Gulch
Overlook. 119

25 Bailey Cove
Loop Trail 120

26 Hirz Bay Trail 120

27 Greens Creek
Boat-In Trail 121

28 Davis Gulch Trail. 121

**Pacific Crest Trail
(PCT) Section Overview**

PCT-41 Ash Camp to Castle
Crags Wilderness . . 122

PCT-42 Castle Crags to
Mumbo Basin. 123

PCT-43 Mumbo Basin to
Scott Mountain 123

1 Kangaroo Lake Trailhead

3.0 mi/2.25 hrs

A remote paved road leads right to Kangaroo Lake, set at 6,050 feet, providing one of the most easily reached pristine mountain lakes with a campground, wheelchair-accessible fishing, and a great trailhead. From the campground the trail rises steeply and connects with the Pacific Crest Trail. From the Pacific Crest Trail you can make the scramble to Cory Peak at 7,737 feet for a 360-degree view. This is a great picnic site. All of Northern Califor-

nia's prominent mountain peaks are in view here, and immediately below you to the west is Kangaroo Lake, like a large sapphire. The lake covers only 21 acres but often produces large brook trout, most of them 12- to 14-inchers. Backpackers can extend this trip eastward four miles on the Pacific Crest Trail past Robbers Meadow to Bull Lake, a small lake in a relatively sparse setting.

Location: In Klamath National Forest east of Callahan; map B2, grid a1.

User groups: Hikers, dogs, horses, and mountain bikes. The fishing is wheelchair accessible.

Permits: No permits are required. Parking and access are free.

Maps: A trail guide can be obtained by contacting Klamath National Forest at the address below. For a map of Klamath National Forest, send $6 to U.S. Forest Service, Attn: Map Sales, P.O. Box 587, Camino, CA 95709; tel. (530) 647-5390, fax (530) 647-5389, or website: www.r5.fs.fed.us/visitorcenter. Major credit cards accepted. Ask the USGS for a topographic map of the Scott Mountain area.

Directions: On Interstate 5, drive north of Weed to the Edgewood exit. Take that exit, turn left at the stop sign, and drive a short distance (under the freeway) to Old Highway 99. Turn right and drive six miles to Gazelle and Gazelle-Callahan Road. Turn left on Gazelle-Callahan Road and drive over the summit. Drive down the other side of the mountain about five miles to Rail Creek Road. Turn left on Rail Creek Road and drive seven miles to where the road dead-ends at the parking area for Kangaroo Lake. The trail starts to the right, down the road from the campground.

Contact: Klamath National Forest, Scott River Ranger District, 11263 N. Highway 3, Fort Jones, CA 96032-9702; tel. (530) 468-5351 or fax (530) 468-1290.

2 Deadfall Lakes Trail

5.0 mi/3.0 hrs

The sight of Middle Deadfall Lake is always a happy shock to newcomers. Here, secreted away on the west side of Mount Eddy, are three wilderness lakes, the prize being Middle Deadfall. At 25 acres, it's far larger than you might expect and far prettier, too. Because the parking area and trailhead are at ridgeline, the hike to this lake is much easier than to other wilderness lakes, making an excellent day hike. Start the trip by taking the Pacific Crest Trail trailhead at the south end of the parking lot. The trail is routed through a mixed conifer forest, with views of the Trinity Alps

off to the west, with a very gentle rising grade most of the way. As you near the lake, you'll have to cross a stream (a no-wading, rock-hopping prospect) and come to a junction (the Pacific Crest Trail bears to the right, the Mount Eddy Summit Trail turns to the left). Continue straight ahead (many people walk past a winter snow survey marker) up a short rise, and then suddenly below you is Middle Deadfall Lake at 7,300 feet, one of the highlights along the Pacific Crest Trail. The best and most secluded campsite here is around the back side of the lake. There are two other lakes nearby: tiny and rarely visited Upper Deadfall at 7,800 feet and even smaller Lower Deadfall at 7,150 feet, which covers five acres and is overlooked in the shadow of its nearby big brother. You should also note that a great side trip for campers at Middle Deadfall Lake is making the 3.5-mile hike to the top of Mount Eddy at 9,025 feet, a 1,700-foot climb. It's one of Northern California's greatest lookouts, with no better view anywhere of the western slopes of Mount Shasta.

Location: In Shasta-Trinity National Forest west of Mount Shasta; map B2, grid a2.

User groups: Hikers, dogs, and horses. No mountain bikes. No wheelchair facilities.

Permits: No permits are required. A campfire permit (free) is required for overnight use. Parking and access are free.

Maps: For a map of Shasta-Trinity National Forest, send $6 to U.S. Forest Service, Attn: Map Sales, P.O. Box 587, Camino, CA 95709; tel. (530) 647-5390, fax (530) 647-5389, or website: www.r5.fs.fed.us/visitorcenter. Major credit cards accepted. Ask the USGS for a topographic map of the Mount Eddy area.

Directions: On Interstate 5, drive north of Weed to the Edgewood exit. Take that exit, turn left at the stop sign and drive a short distance (under the freeway) to Old Highway 99. Turn right and drive .5 mile to Stewart Springs Road. Turn left on Stewart Springs Road and drive to the road's end at Stewart Springs Resort. Bear right on Forest Road 17 (Parks Creek Road) and drive nine miles to the Deadfall

Lakes parking area at the summit. The trailhead is at the south side of the parking area. Take the Pacific Crest Trail, heading south.

Contact: Shasta-Trinity National Forest, Mount Shasta Ranger District, 204 West Alma, Mount Shasta, CA 96067; tel. (530) 926-4511 or fax (530) 926-5120.

3 Black Butte Trail

5.0 mi/3.5 hrs

Anybody who has cruised Interstate 5 north to Oregon and gawked in astonishment at Mount Shasta has inevitably seen Black Butte right alongside the highway. That's right, it's that barren cinder cone set between the highway and Mount Shasta, and it can pique a traveler's curiosity. The trail is routed right to the top and can answer all of your questions. But you may not like all the answers. Over the course of 2.5 miles, you'll climb 1,845 feet, much of it steep, most of it rocky, and in the summer all of it hot and dry. Shade is nonexistent. There are only two rewards: one is claiming the summit at 6,325 feet, where you'll find the foundation of an old U.S. Forest Service lookout and great 360-degree views; and the other is that the hike is an excellent warmup for people who are planning to climb Mount Shasta. That is, providing you don't need a week to recover.

Location: In Shasta-Trinity National Forest between Interstate 5 and Mount Shasta; map B2, grid a5.

User groups: Hikers and dogs. No horses or mountain bikes. No wheelchair facilities.

Permits: No permits are required.

Maps: A trail information sheet is available by contacting the Mount Shasta Ranger District at the address below. For a map of Shasta-Trinity National Forest, send $6 to U.S. Forest Service, Attn: Map Sales, P.O. Box 587, Camino, CA 95709; tel. (530) 647-5390, fax (530) 647-5389, or website: www.r5.fs.fed.us/visitorcenter. Major credit cards accepted. Ask the USGS for a topographic map of the Mount Shasta city area.

Directions: From Interstate 5 at Mount Shasta City, take the Central Mount Shasta exit and drive east on Lake Street for one mile and bear left on Washington Drive. (Washington Drive becomes Everitt Memorial Highway.) Continue on Washington/Everitt Memorial Highway (past the high school) for about two miles to the first Penny Pines sign and Forest Road 41N18. Turn left on Forest Road 41N18 (Ash Flat), drive about 200 yards, and bear right, continuing on Forest Road 41N18 for 2.5 miles. After the road crosses under the overhead power line, turn left on Forest Road 41N18A (Black Butte Road) and drive .75 mile to the trailhead. Parking is very limited; be sure to park off the road.

Contact: Shasta-Trinity National Forest, Mount Shasta Ranger District, 204 West Alma, Mount Shasta, CA 96067; tel. (530) 926-4511 or fax (530) 926-5120.

4 Whitney Falls/ Bolam Creek Trailhead

3.4 mi/2.5 hrs

Mount Shasta, at 14,162 feet, is the most prominent landmark in Northern California, and it's well known for its outstanding summit routes on its southern slopes. What is less known, however, is that there are four trailheads set on Shasta's northern and eastern foothills that grant hikers choice day walks and mountaineers a starting point for difficult climbs over glaciers to the top. Those four forgotten trailheads are at Bolam Creek, North Gate, Brewer Creek, and Clear Creek. The Bolam Creek Trailhead is at about 5,600 feet, and from it the trail heads uphill, for the most part something of a nightmare. The Bolam Trailhead and first mile were buried under a flow of mud and debris from a flash flood. While interesting to geologists, it requires hikers to negotiate rocks, boulders, logs and deep erosion channels. After a mile of crisscrossing up the flow, look for the trail heading out of the drainage. The trail spans 1.6

miles to a fork at 6,400 feet, and for day-hikers the best bet is turning right, climbing partially up the treeless slope for a fantastic lookout and picnic site. Here you'll discover hidden Whitney Falls, a 250-foot waterfall, with its thin, silvery wisp tumbling through a narrow chute in a dramatic ashen gorge. It takes perfect timing to see this waterfall at anything more than a trickle. The view to the north of Shasta Valley is outstanding, highlighted by the series of hummocks, actually chunks of Shasta's former summit that were carried here like miniature hilltops in a massive lava flow in Shasta's last eruption, 600 years ago.

Special note: If you turn left at the fork instead, you'll venture through forest, then up through another gutted stream drainage. The trail ends, and mountaineers will have to pass Coquette Falls, and then near the peak at the Bolam Glacier, in order to make the summit. Safety gear and expert climbing skills are required.

Location: On the northwest slope of Mount Shasta; map B2, grid a6.

User groups: Hikers only. No dogs, horses, or mountain bikes. No wheelchair facilities.

Permits: A $5 parking fee is required per vehicle. Hikers entering Mount Shasta Wilderness must have wilderness permit (free). Climbers hiking above 10,000 feet must also have a Summit Pass, $15 per person for three days, $25 annual. All climbers are required to pack out waste and must bring a pack-out bag.

Maps: A trail map of the Mount Shasta Wilderness can be purchased for $7.51 from the Mount Shasta Ranger District at the address below. For a map of Shasta-Trinity National Forest, send $6 to U.S. Forest Service, Attn: Map Sales, P.O. Box 587, Camino, CA 95709; tel. (530) 647-5390, fax (530) 647-5389, or website: www.r5.fs.fed.us/visitorcenter. Major credit cards accepted. Ask the USGS for a topographic map of the Mount Shasta area.

Directions: From Interstate 5, drive to the Central Weed/Klamath Falls (Highway 97) exit. Take that exit and drive through Weed to Highway 97. Turn right and drive 11 miles to Bolam

Road (Forest Road 43N21), usually unsigned. If you reach County Road A12 on the left, you have gone .25 mile too far. Drive on Bolam Road for four miles toward the mountain (Mount Shasta), crossing the railroad tracks and continuing to the trailhead at the end of the road. A high-clearance vehicle is required.

Contact: Shasta-Trinity National Forest, Mount Shasta Ranger District, 204 West Alma, Mount Shasta, CA 96067; tel. (530) 926-4511 or fax (530) 926-5120.

5 North Gate Trailhead
4.0 mi/2.75 hrs

The North Gate Trailhead, set at about 7,000 feet, is one of Mount Shasta's most obscure and least-used trails. It sits on the north flank of Shasta, just below a mountain mound called North Gate. The route skirts this mound, following a small stream uphill for 1.6 miles; then farther along, the trail deteriorates and disappears as you near tree line at 8,400 feet. From here most day-hikers will climb another 400 feet to the source of the creek, a small spring, and have lunch while enjoying the view to the north.

Special note: Mountain climbers who use this route to climb to the Shasta Summit will discover the going is quite easy at first after leaving tree line. The trip then becomes very steep, difficult, and dangerous, whether via Bolam or Hotlum Glacier. This route is only for experienced mountain climbers who are aware of the extreme risks of crossing steep, sheer glaciers.

Location: On the north slope of Mount Shasta; map B2, grid a6.

User groups: Hikers only. No dogs, horses, or mountain bikes. No wheelchair facilities.

Permits: A $5 parking fee is required per vehicle. Hikers entering Mount Shasta Wilderness must have wilderness permit (free). Climbers hiking above 10,000 feet must also have a Summit Pass, $15 per person for three days, $25 annual. All climbers are required to pack out waste and must bring a pack-out bag.

Maps: A trail map of the Mount Shasta Wilderness can be purchased for $7.51 from the Mount Shasta Ranger District at the address below. For a map of Shasta-Trinity National Forest, send $6 to U.S. Forest Service, Attn: Map Sales, P.O. Box 587, Camino, CA 95709; tel. (530) 647-5390, fax (530) 647-5389, or website: www.r5.fs.fed.us/visitorcenter. Major credit cards accepted. Ask the USGS for a topographic map of the Mount Shasta area.

Directions: From Interstate 5, drive to the Central Weed/Klamath Falls (Highway 97) exit. Take that exit and drive through Weed to Highway 97. Turn right and drive 13.5 miles to Military Pass Road (Forest Road 19). Turn right drive 4.5 miles to a fork with Forest Road 42N16 (Andesite Logging Road). Bear right and drive four miles to the parking area at the end of the road.

Contact: Shasta-Trinity National Forest, Mount Shasta Ranger District, 204 West Alma, Mount Shasta, CA 96067; tel. (530) 926-4511 or fax (530) 926-5120. A 24-hour climbing report is available by phoning (530) 926-5555.

6 Sand Flat Trailhead
3.4 mi/2.75 hrs

The hike from Sand Flat to Horse Camp, a distance of 1.7 miles, will give you a good taste of the Mount Shasta experience, and you're likely to savor the flavors. Many who make this day hike are compelled to return to climb all the way to the top. We were!

Sand Flat provides a good shaded parking area to start from at a 6,800-foot elevation. The trail immediately takes off uphill, gradually at first, and then becomes quite steep. At 7,360 feet, it intersects with the Bunny Flat Trail and then continues rising through the forest. Along the way are amazing examples of how avalanches have knocked down entire sections of forest. When you reach Horse Camp at 7,800 feet, nearing timberline, you'll find many rewards. The first is spring water flowing continuously out of a piped fountain near the Sierra Hut, perhaps the best-tasting water in the world. The second is the foreboding view of Red Bank, which forms the mountain rim above Horse Camp. The third is the opportunity to hike up a short way above tree line for the sweeping views to the south of Castle Crags and Lake Siskiyou. After taking the first steps on the Summit Trail, you'll likely yearn to keep going all the way to the very top of this magic mountain. If you wish to hike the Summit Trail, see the following hike out of Bunny Flat Trailhead.

Location: On the southern slope of Mount Shasta; map B2, grid a6.

User groups: Hikers only. No dogs, horses, or mountain bikes. No wheelchair facilities.

Permits: Parking and access are free. Hikers entering Mount Shasta Wilderness must have a wilderness permit (free). Climbers hiking above 10,000 feet must also have a Summit Pass, $15 per person for three days, $25 annual. All climbers are required to pack out waste and must bring a pack-out bag.

Maps: A trail map of the Mount Shasta Wilderness can be purchased for $7.51 from the Mount Shasta Ranger District at the address below. For a map of Shasta-Trinity National Forest, send $6 to U.S. Forest Service, Attn: Map Sales, P.O. Box 587, Camino, CA 95709; tel. (530) 647-5390, fax (530) 647-5389, or website: www.r5.fs.fed.us/visitorcenter. Major credit cards accepted. Ask the USGS for a topographic map of the Mount Shasta area.

Directions: From Interstate 5 at Mount Shasta City, take the Central Mount Shasta exit and drive east on Lake Street for one mile and bear left on Washington Drive (which becomes Everitt Memorial Highway). Continue on Everitt Memorial Highway for eight miles to Sand Flat Loop (Forest Road 41N60. Turn left and drive to the trailhead.

Contact: Shasta-Trinity National Forest, Mount Shasta Ranger District, 204 West Alma, Mount Shasta, CA 96067; tel. (530) 926-4511 or fax (530) 926-5120. A 24-hour climbing report is available by phoning (530) 926-5555.

⑦ Shasta Summit Trail
14 mi/1.5 days

The hike to the top of Mount Shasta is a great challenge, an ascent of 7,000 feet over ice, snow, and rock while trying to suck what little oxygen you can out of the thin air. It may be the greatest adventure in the West that most people have an honest chance of achieving. While there are dangers, from tumbling boulders (see the special note below) to bad weather (which stops half the people who try the climb), hikers in good condition who start the trip very early and have the proper equipment can make it all the way to the top and back in a day. Early? You should depart from Bunny Flat by 3:30 a.m., or hike in a day early, set up a base camp at Horse Camp (tree line), and start no later than 4:30 a.m. Equipment? A daypack with warm clothes, a windbreaker, two canteens of water, food, and an ice ax and crampons are mandatory. Refill your canteen wherever you find a rivulet of water, occasionally possible at Red Bank; rangers recommend using a water filter.

The trip starts out of Bunny Flat at 6,900 feet, leads through a forest of Shasta red firs, climbs to where the trail intersects with the route out of Sand Flat, then turns right and rises to Horse Camp, at an elevation of 7,800 feet and a distance of 1.8 miles. It is a must to fill your canteens here. After filling your canteens at the spring, start the Summit Trail, your first steps made across a series of large stones called Olberman's Causeway. From here, the trail quickly rises above timberline, gaining 1,000 feet per mile for six miles, and after a short time becomes a faint path. Often this is where the snow and ice start, and you must stop and strap your crampons on your boots. The walking is easy with crampons, the metal spikes poking holes into the ice surface. The trail climbs up Avalanche Gulch, and some people stop to make trail camps at a flat spot called Helen Lake at 10,440 feet. Hikers not acclimated to high altitudes may begin experiencing some dizziness, but there's no

relief in sight. At this point the hike gets steeper, about a 35-degree slope, and many give up before reaching Red Bank, a huge red volcanic outcrop at about 12,500 feet. At Red Bank you'll need your ice ax, pulling your way through a narrow and steep rock/ice chute, where a slip is certain without crampons.

When you emerge atop Red Bank, you are nearly 13,000 feet high, at the foot of a glacier field and Misery Hill, named because it's a long, slow climb, through snow in spring, scree in summer, and—hey, because some people actually mistake it for the peak. Once atop Misery Hill, though, you'll see the true Shasta Summit, a massive pinnacle of lava that seems to jut straight up into the air. With a final push, follow the trail, grabbing rocks to help pull you up and sucking the thin air, and with a few last steps, you'll be on top at 14,162 feet. On clear days you can see hundreds of miles in all directions, and the sky is a deeper cobalt blue than you ever imagined. On top, you'll sign your name in a logbook in an old rusted metal box, then take in the grand wonders surrounding you. It's a remarkable trip, one that can inspire some people to keep their bodies in good enough shape to make the trip every year.

All hikers must pack out their waste. Special waste pack-out bags are available at no charge at the trailhead and at the Mount Shasta Ranger Station in Mount Shasta.

It's an absolute must to make an early start. In the hot summer months, towering cumulus clouds sometimes form on Mount Shasta during the afternoon, and by then you'll want to be making the trip down. If towering cumuli begin forming by noon, intense thunderstorms are possible by mid-afternoon.

The biggest danger and largest number of injuries on Mount Shasta come not from falling, but from being hit by tumbling boulders. In fact, our former research assistant, Robyn Schlueter, was struck in the foot by a boulder in her first attempt at climbing Shasta. She was hit so hard that it knocked her hiking boot off, breaking her foot and requiring an emergency helicopter airlift out for medical treatment. Always keep a good distance between your hiking partners, don't hike in a vertical line, and if a rock comes bouncing down, always shout, "Rock! Rock!" Some guides recommend wearing helmets. By the way, Robyn returned to Mount Shasta the following two years and made it to the top on both trips.

The mountain is best hiked when it still has a good coating of snow and ice, which provides excellent footing with crampons. When the snow and ice melt off in late fall, tromping through the small volcanic rocks is like slogging in mushy sand.

Drink lots of water. In high altitudes dehydration is a common problem and can result in early exhaustion and extreme vulnerability to mountain sickness.

Location: At Bunny Flat Trailhead on the southern slope of Mount Shasta; map B2, grid a6.

User groups: Hikers only. No dogs, horses, or mountain bikes. No wheelchair facilities.

Permits: Parking and access are free. Hikers entering Mount Shasta Wilderness must have wilderness permit (free). Climbers hiking above 10,000 feet must also have a Summit Pass, $15 per person for three days, $25 annual. All climbers are required to pack out waste and must bring a pack-out bag.

Maps: A trail map of the Mount Shasta Wilderness can be purchased for $7.51 from the Mount Shasta Ranger District at the address below. For a map of Shasta-Trinity National Forest, send $6 to U.S. Forest Service, Attn: Map Sales, P.O. Box 587, Camino, CA 95709; tel. (530) 647-5390, fax (530) 647-5389, or website: www.r5.fs.fed.us/visitorcenter. Major credit cards accepted. Ask the USGS for a topographic map of the Mount Shasta area.

Directions: From Interstate 5 at Mount Shasta City, take the Central Mount Shasta exit and drive east on Lake Street for one mile and bear left on Washington Drive (which becomes Everitt Memorial Highway). Continue on Everitt Memorial Highway for 10 miles to Bunny Flat. As you drive in, the trailhead is on the left.

Contact: Shasta-Trinity National Forest, Mount Shasta Ranger District, 204 West Alma, Mount Shasta, CA 96067; tel. (530) 926-4511 or fax (530) 926-5120. A 24-hour climbing report is available by phoning (530) 926-5555 or (530) 926-9613. Ice axes and crampons are available for rent at Fifth Season in Mount Shasta, tel. (530) 926-3606, or the House of Ski & Board, tel. (530) 926-2359. Experienced climbing guides are available at Shasta Mountain Guides, tel. (530) 926-3117, Alpine Skills, (530) 426-9108, or Sierra Wilderness, (707) 455-9358.

8 Panther Meadows
2.8 mi/1.75 hrs

Panther Meadows is considered a sacred Native American site, and even those who are unaware of it seem intuitively to realize that this is a special place and find themselves walking softly and talking quietly when visiting. The trail is easy to reach, located just off to the right of the wide, paved, two-lane Everitt Memorial Highway. This hike is a short one, from Panther Meadows to Gray Butte and back.

From the parking area the trail starts by heading east past meadow and forest, and after 0.6 mile, turns right and begins a steady climb for 0.8 mile to the top of Gray Butte at 8,119 feet. It's a perfect lookout to the south, with Castle Crags, Mount Lassen, and the drop-off in the Sacramento Valley all prominent. If you continue on for almost a mile, you'll discover a place called The Gate, which some mountain visitors consider a sacred portal to the spiritual dimension.

Location: On the southern slope of Mount Shasta; map B2, grid a6.

User groups: Hikers only. Dogs are allowed at Gray Butte, but not beyond. No horses, or mountain bikes. No wheelchair facilities.

Permits: Parking and access are free. Hikers entering Mount Shasta Wilderness must have wilderness permit (free).

Climbers hiking above 10,000 feet must also have a Summit Pass, $15 per person for three days, $25 annual. All climbers are required to pack out waste and must bring a pack-out bag. **Maps:** A trail map of the Mount Shasta Wilderness can be purchased for $7.51 from the Mount Shasta Ranger District at the address below. For a map of Shasta-Trinity National Forest, send $6 to U.S. Forest Service, Attn: Map Sales, P.O. Box 587, Camino, CA 95709; tel. (530) 647-5390, fax (530) 647-5389, or website: www.r5.fs.fed.us/visitorcenter. Major credit cards accepted. Ask the USGS for a topographic map of the Mount Shasta area.

Directions: From Interstate 5 at Mount Shasta City, take the Central Mount Shasta exit and drive east on Lake Street for one mile and bear left on Washington Drive (which becomes Everitt Memorial Highway). Continue on Everitt Memorial Highway for 13 miles (past Bunny Flat) to Panther Meadows Campground on the right. Turn right and drive to the parking area.

Contact: Shasta-Trinity National Forest, Mount Shasta Ranger District, 204 West Alma, Mount Shasta, CA 96067; tel. (530) 926-4511 or fax (530) 926-5120. A 24-hour climbing report is available by phoning (530) 926-5555 or (530) 926-9613.

⑨ Brewer Creek Trailhead
4.2 mi/3.0 hrs

It's so quiet here that you can practically hear the wildflowers bloom. We've hiked the north slope of Shasta out of the Brewer Creek Trailhead several times and have never seen another person. The trip is a perfect day hike. The trailhead is set near Brewer Creek (7,200 feet), hence the name. After a short walk through a section of forest that was selectively logged many years ago, you'll enter the Shasta Wilderness and be surrounded by old-growth firs, many quite scraggly from enduring harsh winters and the short growing season. Here the trail gets more steep, a steady climb up through forest, gradual switchbacks as it goes. When you near tree line at 7,700 feet, the trail turns to

the left and begins to lateral across the mountain. It's 2.1 miles to timberline from the trailhead, and most people hike to this point, then turn back. However, you can add an easy mile or two by climbing a wide, volcanic slope with good footing all the way and rising to 9,500 feet. This is a great spot for a picnic, providing nice views to the north, and also perhaps inspiring dreams of the day when you'll next climb all the way to the top of Shasta.

Special note: Mountaineers who try to climb Shasta from this trailhead have only one good route from the point where the trail meets tree line, which is to head to the right up and over Hotlum Glacier. This route is extremely difficult, very steep, and dangerous.

Location: On the northeast slope of Mount Shasta; map B2, grid a7.

User groups: Hikers only. No dogs, horses, or mountain bikes. No wheelchair facilities.

Permits: A parking fee of $5 is charged each vehicle. Hikers entering Mount Shasta Wilderness must have wilderness permit (free). Climbers hiking above 10,000 feet must also have a Summit Pass, $15 per person for three days, $25 annual. All climbers are required to pack out waste and must bring a pack-out bag.

Maps: A trail map of the Mount Shasta Wilderness can be purchased for $7.51 from the Mount Shasta Ranger District at the address below. For a map of Shasta-Trinity National Forest, send $6 to U.S. Forest Service, Attn: Map Sales, P.O. Box 587, Camino, CA 95709; tel. (530) 647-5390, fax (530) 647-5389, or website: www.r5.fs.fed.us/visitorcenter. Major credit cards accepted. Ask the USGS for a topographic map of the Mount Shasta area.

Directions: From Interstate 5 in Redding, drive north for 47 miles to the Highway 89/McCloud-Reno exit. Bear right on Highway 89 and drive 11 miles to McCloud, then continue for another 2.8 miles to Pilgrim Creek Road. Turn left on Pilgrim Creek Road (Forest Road 13) and drive 7.1 miles to Forest Road 19 (Sugar Pine Butte Road). Turn left and drive 0.9 mile to Forest Road 42N02. Turn left and drive two miles to Forest Road

42N10. Turn left and drive two miles to the trailhead parking area.

Contact: Shasta-Trinity National Forest, Mount Shasta Ranger District, 204 West Alma, Mount Shasta, CA 96067; tel. (530) 926-4511 or fax (530) 926-5120. A 24-hour climbing report is available by phoning (530) 926-5555 or (530) 926-9613.

🔟 Mud Creek Falls
2.0 mi/1.5 hrs

A short walk on the remote southeast flank of Mount Shasta can provide entry to a land of enchantment that features deep canyons and views of glaciers and Mount Shasta's prettiest waterfall. The drive in is circuitous but well signed, and it's a surprise to find other cars parked at the trailhead. The hike starts on an old overgrown jeep road, slowly emerging from a sparse forest of Shasta red fir and climbing to the eastern edge of the dramatic Mud Creek Canyon at about 7,000 feet elevation. From here most hikers climb on for another 15 minutes, arriving at a perfect view of the waterfall at the bottom of the canyon below. The waterfall, best viewed with binoculars, is perhaps 125 feet high, wide, and silver, but distant. This area is rich in natural history, the canyon having been carved by a glacier and still fed with water from the towering, fractured Konwakiton Glacier above, running the color of volcanic silt.

Location: On the southeast slope of Mount Shasta; map B2, grid a7.

User groups: Hikers only. No dogs, horses, or mountain bikes. No wheelchair facilities.

Permits: A parking fee of $5 is charged each vehicle. Hikers entering Mount Shasta Wilderness must have wilderness permit (free). Climbers hiking above 10,000 feet must also have a Summit Pass, $15 per person for three days, $25 annual. All climbers are required to pack out waste and must bring a pack-out bag.

Maps: A trail map of the Mount Shasta Wilderness can be purchased for $7.51 from the Mount Shasta Ranger District at the address below. For a map of Shasta-Trinity National Forest, send $6 to U.S. Forest Service, Attn: Map Sales, P.O. Box 587, Camino, CA 95709; tel. (530) 647-5390, fax (530) 647-5389, or website: www.r5.fs.fed.us/visitorcenter. Major credit cards accepted. Ask the USGS for a topographic map of the Mount Shasta area.

Directions: From Interstate 5 in Redding, drive north for 47 miles to the Highway 89/McCloud-Reno exit. Bear right on Highway 89 and drive 11 miles to McCloud, then continue for another 2.8 miles to Pilgrim Creek Road. Turn left on Pilgrim Creek Road (Forest Road 13) and drive five miles (paved) to Forest Road 41N15 (Widow Springs Road). Turn left and drive about five miles to Forest Road 31 (McKenzie Butte). Cross this road and drive straight on Forest Road 41N61 (Cold Creek Road), a dirt and gravel road, about a mile. Turn left on Forest Road 41N25Y (Clear Creek Road) and drive about three miles to the parking area for the Clear Creek Trailhead. The road is well signed.

Contact: Shasta-Trinity National Forest, Mount Shasta Ranger District, 204 West Alma, Mount Shasta, CA 96067; tel. (530) 926-4511 or fax (530) 926-5120. A 24-hour climbing report is available by phoning (530) 926-5555 or (530) 926-9613.

🔟🔟 Old Ski Bowl Trailhead
2.5 mi/2.0 hrs

One of the great hikes on Mount Shasta is climbing from the Old Ski Bowl lodge site up to Green Butte. At 7,800 feet, it's the highest drive-to trailhead on Mount Shasta, set just above timberline. That means the entire route is across a volcanic slope with great views every step of the way and a unique destination as well. Green Butte, a huge rock outcrop set at 9,193 feet, is a perfect perch.

At the parking area there's an obvious trail (though it's unsigned) that leads up toward Green Butte, which is also clearly obvious just a mile away. But while the trip is short, it's very steep, with a

1,300-foot elevation gain. Along the way a great bonus is a natural spring set about halfway up the butte; be sure to find it and fill your canteen with this sweet-tasting spring water. While Green Butte is the destination of most visitors here, the hiking route continues to 9,600 feet before disintegrating in the lava rubble and snow. The Old Ski Bowl is one of the legendary spots on Shasta. It was here that a developer desecrated Shasta wildlands by building a ski area above tree line. Well, nature gives and nature takes back. With no trees to hold snow in place, the old mountain wiped out the ski lifts with an avalanche. Ironically, in the mid-1990s, a new ski area was proposed at the same spot. The week before the decision was made, again another avalanche pounded through, clearing a giant swath of trees and wiping out an area right where the ski bowl lodge had been proposed. Now again, the Shasta Wilderness is untouched by the hand of mankind, rising like a diamond in a field of coal.

Location: On the southern slope of Mount Shasta; map B2, grid a7.

User groups: Hikers only. No dogs (permitted in old Ski Bowl, but not beyond), horses, or mountain bikes. No wheelchair facilities.

Permits: Parking and access are free. Hikers entering Mount Shasta Wilderness must have wilderness permit (free). Climbers hiking above 10,000 feet must also have a Summit Pass, $15 per person for three days, $25 annual. All climbers are required to pack out waste and must bring a pack-out bag.

Maps: A trail map of the Mount Shasta Wilderness can be purchased for $7.51 from the Mount Shasta Ranger District at the address below. For a map of Shasta-Trinity National Forest, send $6 to U.S. Forest Service, Attn: Map Sales, P.O. Box 587, Camino, CA 95709; tel. (530) 647-5390, fax (530) 647-5389, or website: www.r5.fs.fed.us/visitorcenter. Major credit cards accepted. Ask the USGS for a topographic map of the Mount Shasta area.

Directions: From Interstate 5 at Mount Shas-

ta City, take the Central Mount Shasta exit and drive east on Lake Street for one mile and bear left on Washington Drive (which becomes Everitt Memorial Highway). Continue on Everitt Memorial Highway for 13.5 miles (past Panther Meadows Campground on the right) to the parking area for the old Ski Bowl site at the end of the road.

Contact: Shasta-Trinity National Forest, Mount Shasta Ranger District, 204 West Alma, Mount Shasta, CA 96067; tel. (530) 926-4511 or fax (530) 926-5120. A 24-hour climbing report is available by phoning (530) 926-5555 or (530) 926-9613.

12 Big Bear Lake Trail
8.0 mi/2.0 days

The four-mile hike up to Big Bear Lake, a large, beautiful lake by wilderness standards, can make for a perfect weekend backpack trip. If there's a negative to this trip, it's this: the trail ends at the lake, so if the lakeside campsites are already taken when you arrive, you're out of luck for a quality place to camp for the night. The trailhead is easy to reach, just off Highway 3 north of Trinity Lake. The route is simple but not easy. It follows Bear Creek for the entire route, with one stream crossing, but climbing all the way. Once you reach the lake, a bonus is the side trip to Little Bear Lake, which takes about a mile of scrambling cross-country to reach. The trail is steep, popular, and beautiful.

Location: In the Trinity Alps Wilderness south of Callahan; map B2, grid b0.

User groups: Hikers and dogs. Horses are allowed but not recommended. No mountain bikes. No wheelchair facilities.

Permits: A wilderness permit is required for hikers planning to camp in the wilderness.

Maps: For a map of Shasta-Trinity National Forest, send $6 to U.S. Forest Service, Attn: Map Sales, P.O. Box 587, Camino, CA 95709; tel. (530) 647-5390, fax (530) 647-5389, or website: www.r5.fs.fed.us/visitorcenter. Major credit cards accepted. Ask the USGS for a

topographic map of the Tangle Blue Lake area. **Directions:** From Interstate 5 at Yreka, take the Highway 3/Fort Jones exit and drive about 40 miles to Callahan. Continue south on Highway 3 for about 13 miles to Bear Creek Loop Road. Turn right and drive a short distance (unpaved road) to the signed trailhead (located near the Bear Creek road crossing).
Contact: Shasta-Trinity National Forest, Weaverville Ranger District, P.O. Box 1190, Weaverville, CA 96093; tel. (530) 623-2121 or fax (530) 623-6010.

13 Toad Lake Trail
1.5 mi/2.0 days

What? How is this possible? Are we suffering delusions? While the latter might be true, that's not why a 1.5-mile round-trip hike, rating only a one in difficulty, is projected as a two-day trip. The reason is that the drive to the trailhead is endless, the road winding and twisting its way up the Middle Fork drainage of the Sacramento River, rising up along the west flank of Mount Eddy. No one should go up and back in a day. Keep your tongue in your mouth, because the ride is so jarring that you might bite the end of it when you hit a big pothole. But once parked, you'll immediately notice the perfect calm, and then with a 15-minute walk to the lake at a 6,950-foot elevation, you'll be furnished with a picture-perfect lakeside campsite.

The lake covers 23 acres, provides excellent swimming, fair fishing for small trout, and great side trips. The best is the one-mile hike from Toad Lake to Porcupine Lake, an idyllic spot for a picnic or a walk along the shore. To get there from Toad Lake, take the trail that's routed behind the lake up to the Pacific Crest Trail and then walk south for .25 mile on the PCT to the Porcupine Lake cutoff on the right.
Location: In Shasta-Trinity National Forest west of Mount Shasta; map B2, grid b2.
User groups: Hikers, dogs, and horses. No mountain bikes on Pacific Crest Trail. No wheelchair facilities.

Permits: No permits are required. Parking and access are free.
Maps: For a map of Shasta-Trinity National Forest, send $6 to U.S. Forest Service, Attn: Map Sales, P.O. Box 587, Camino, CA 95709; tel. (530) 647-5390, fax (530) 647-5389, or website: www.r5.fs.fed.us/visitorcenter. Major credit cards accepted. Ask the USGS for a topographic map of the Mount Eddy area.
Directions: From Interstate 5 at Mount Shasta city, take the central Mount Shasta exit. At the stop sign, turn west and drive .5 mile to Old Stage Road. Turn left on Old Stage Road and drive .25 mile to a fork with W.A. Barr Road. Stay to the right at the fork and drive two miles, cross Box Canyon Dam at Lake Siskiyou, and continue around the lake on W.A. Barr Road (which becomes Forest Road 26/South Fork Road). Continue four miles past the Lake Siskiyou Camp resort, cross an unnamed concrete bridge, and turn right at the next dirt road (signed "Toad Lake/Morgan Meadows"). Drive 0.2 mile to the first fork, bear left, and drive 11 miles to the lake trailhead parking area. The road is very rough and twisting, and for the last .5 mile, a high-clearance, four-wheel-drive vehicle is recommended. It is a .5 mile walk from the parking area to the lake.
Contact: Shasta-Trinity National Forest, Mount Shasta Ranger District, 204 West Alma, Mount Shasta, CA 96067; tel. (530) 926-4511 or fax (530) 926-5120.

14 Sisson-Callahan
14.0 mi one-way/2.0 days

The Sisson-Callahan Trail is something of a legend in the Mount Shasta area, long ago being a well-known, well-traveled route up to Mount Eddy and Deadfall Lakes. But with a much easier route now available from the Deadfall Lakes Trailhead, this trail is often passed over. Why? The route is long, steep, and hot, climbing 5,000 feet over the course of nine miles to the top of Mount

Eddy at 9,025 feet, then down nearly 2,000 feet in two miles to Deadfall Lakes for the nearest campsite. In addition, the great scenic beauty doesn't start until you've climbed several thousand feet, and by then you'll care more about how much water is left in your canteen than about the incredible sweeping view of Mount Shasta to the east. Alas, even worse are the killer switchbacks you'll have to traverse to reach the Eddy ridge. As you reach the Eddy crest, look close and you will find an old sign for a former route for the Pacific Crest Trail that must be 50 or 60 years old. From here it is mandatory to hike the switchbacks up to the Mount Eddy Summit. After that it's a 2,000-foot descent to Middle Deadfall Lake, where you make camp. Your hiking reward comes the next morning, when after lounging around at Lower Deadfall Lake, you walk out three nearly level miles to the Park Creek/PCT Trailhead, then catch your shuttle ride back to the town of Mount Shasta. All in all, this is a genuine butt-kicker of a trail.

Location: In Shasta-Trinity National Forest near Lake Siskiyou west of Mount Shasta; map B2, grid b3.

User groups: Hikers, dogs, and horses. No mountain bikes. No wheelchair facilities.

Permits: No permits are required. Parking and access are free.

Maps: For a map of Shasta-Trinity National Forest, send $6 to U.S. Forest Service, Attn: Map Sales, P.O. Box 587, Camino, CA 95709; tel. (530) 647-5390, fax (530) 647-5389, or website: www.r5.fs.fed.us/visitorcenter. Major credit cards accepted. Ask the USGS for topographic maps of the City of Mount Shasta and Mount Eddy areas.

Directions: From Interstate 5 at Mount Shasta city, take the central Mount Shasta exit. At the stop sign, turn west and drive .5 mile to Old Stage Road. Turn left on Old Stage Road and drive .25 mile to a fork with W.A. Barr Road. Stay to the right at the fork and drive two miles to North Shore Road (if you cross the dam at Lake Siskiyou, you have gone too far). Turn right on North Shore (becomes For-

est Road 40N27/Deer Creek Road) and drive four miles and across the bridge on Deer Creek and to the next major junction, Forest Road 40N27C. Turn left on Forest Road 40N27C and park along the edge of the road before the ford on the North Fork Sacramento. (The water here is sometimes deeper than it looks; don't be tempted to drive it.) The Sisson-Callahan Trail (first appears as a road) starts on the other side of the ford, on an old logging skid road that goes to the right. Within .5 mile it turns into a trail.

Contact: Shasta-Trinity National Forest, Mount Shasta Ranger District, 204 West Alma, Mount Shasta, CA 96067; tel. (530) 926-4511 or fax (530) 926-5120.

15 Gumboot Lake Trailhead
1.5 mi/1.5 hrs

If you must always have a trail to hike on, well, this trip is not for you. But if you don't mind a little cross-country scramble to a mountain rim, then a short cutoff to a peak for spectacular views of Gumboot Lake and of Mount Shasta beyond, then sign up for this hike. Starting at an elevation of 6,050 feet at Gumboot Lake, a pretty lake with good trout fishing, you circle the lake on the right side, where there's a good trail. At the back of the lake, break off the trail to the right and start climbing the slope, heading up towards the ridge that circles the back of the lake. A little less than halfway to the top, you'll pass Little Gumboot Lake and then scramble your way to the ridge, where you'll intersect with the Pacific Crest Trail. Head to the left for a short distance, then again break off the trail, this time to the left, heading on the mountain spine toward the peak that towers over Gumboot Lake, with Mount Shasta the backdrop off to the east. This peak is your destination. The world may not be perfect, but from this lookout it comes close.

Location: In Shasta-Trinity National Forest west of Mount Shasta; map B2, grid b3.

User groups: Hikers and dogs only. No horses,

or mountain bikes. No wheelchair facilities.

Permits: No permits are required. Parking and access are free.

Maps: For a map of Shasta-Trinity National Forest, send $6 to U.S. Forest Service, Attn: Map Sales, P.O. Box 587, Camino, CA 95709; tel. (530) 647-5390, fax (530) 647-5389, or website: www.r5.fs.fed.us/visitorcenter. Major credit cards accepted. Ask the USGS for a topographic map of the Mumbo Basin area.

Directions: From Interstate 5 at Mount Shasta city, take the central Mount Shasta exit. At the stop sign, turn west and drive .5 mile to Old Stage Road. Turn left on Old Stage Road and drive .25 mile to a fork with W.A. Barr Road. Stay to the right at the fork and drive two miles, cross Box Canyon Dam at Lake Siskiyou, and continue around the lake on W.A. Barr Road (which becomes Forest Road 26/South Fork Road). Continue four miles past the Lake Siskiyou Camp resort and continue up the canyon to Gumboot Lake Road (Forest Road 40N37). Bear left on Gumboot Lake Road and drive .5 mile to the parking area near the shore of the lake.

Contact: Shasta-Trinity National Forest, Mount Shasta Ranger District, 204 West Alma, Mount Shasta, CA 96067; tel. (530) 926-4511 or fax (530) 926-5120.

16 Heart Lake Trail

3.0 mi/2.25 hrs

The tale of Castle Lake, set at an elevation of 5,450 feet, is that the water is like none other in the world, which has led some people to jump into the lake for complete renewal. In reality, the water is so pure, containing few nutrients of any kind, that U.C. Davis has a water sampling station here in an ongoing comparison study with Lake Tahoe.

The trailhead is on the left side of the lake, just across the outlet stream. From there the trail rises up along the slope just left of the lake. Below is Castle Lake, a pretty sight set in a rock bowl with a high back wall. The trail rises up to a saddle at 5,900 feet. At the saddle,

bear uphill to the right on the faint trail. It's an easy scramble up over a lip at 6,050 feet, where little Heart Lake is secreted away. Because the lake is small, the water warms up by midsummer, making it great for swimming. In addition, if you scramble up the back wall of the little lake, you'll get a breathtaking view of Mount Shasta. Also note that the best drive-to spot anywhere for photographs of Mount Shasta is on Castle Lake Road at a turnout about one mile downhill from the Castle Lake parking area.

Location: At Castle Lake in Shasta-Trinity National Forest west of Mount Shasta; map B2, grid b4.

User groups: Hikers and dogs. Not suitable for horses or mountain bikes. No wheelchair facilities.

Permits: No permits required. Parking and access is free.

Maps: For a map of Shasta-Trinity National Forest, send $6 to U.S. Forest Service, Attn: Map Sales, P.O. Box 587, Camino, CA 95709; tel. (530) 647-5390, fax (530) 647-5389, or website: www.r5.fs.fed.us/visitorcenter. Major credit cards accepted. A map of Castle Crags Wilderness can also be purchased for $7.51. Ask the USGS for a topographic map of the Mount Shasta city area.

Directions: From Interstate 5 at Mount Shasta city, take the central Mount Shasta exit. At the stop sign, turn west and drive .5 mile to Old Stage Road. Turn left on Old Stage Road and drive .25 mile to a fork with W.A. Barr Road. Stay to the right at the fork and drive two miles, cross Box Canyon Dam at Lake Siskiyou, and continue .5 mile to Castle Lake Road. Turn left and drive 7.5 miles to the parking area at the end of the road at Castle Lake. The trailhead begins on the eastern end of the parking lot.

Contact: Shasta-Trinity National Forest, Mount Shasta Ranger District, 204 West Alma, Mount Shasta, CA 96067; tel. (530) 926-4511 or fax (530) 926-5120.

17 Tamarack Lake Trailhead

5.0 mi/4.0 hrs

This is sacred country for some hikers, set high in the Trinity Divide at 5,900 feet. Tamarack is a beautiful alpine lake and a place of remarkable serenity. If you can pull yourself away from it, there's a rugged, cross-country route to the north that approaches the summit of Grey Rocks, a series of dark, craggy peaks. The route is steep and difficult, but the view of Castle Crags, Mount Shasta, the ridges of the Trinity Divide, and the Sacramento River Canyon will have you thanking a higher power for the privilege of breathing the air here.

Location: In Shasta-Trinity National Forest southwest of Mount Shasta; map B2, grid c3.

User groups: Hikers and dogs. Not suitable for horses or mountain bikes. No wheelchair facilities.

Permits: No permits are required.

Maps: For a map of Shasta-Trinity National Forest, send $6 to U.S. Forest Service, Attn: Map Sales, P.O. Box 587, Camino, CA 95709; tel. (530) 647-5390, fax (530) 647-5389, or website: www.r5.fs.fed.us/visitorcenter. Major credit cards accepted. Ask the USGS for a topographic map of the Chicken Hawk Hill area.

Directions: From Interstate 5 south of Dunsmuir, take the Castella/Castle Crags State Park exit and drive west on Castle Creek Road. Continue past the park (the road becomes Forest Road 25 (Whalen Road) and continue 12.5 miles on to Forest Road 38N17 (Tamarack Road). Turn left on Forest Road 38N17 and drive about six miles to the trailhead. This road is extremely rough, with the last mile passable only to four-wheel-drive vehicles with large tires and high clearance. Just before this bad section of road, a primitive parking area is available on the right side for other vehicles to park.

Contact: Shasta-Trinity National Forest, Mount Shasta Ranger District, 204 West Alma, Mount Shasta, CA 96067; tel. (530) 926-4511 or fax (530) 926-5120.

18 Root Creek Trail

2.3 mi/1.75 hrs

Castle Crags State Park features a series of huge granite spires that tower over the Sacramento River Canyon, the kind of sight that can take your breath away the first time you see it from Interstate 5. That sight inspires a lot of people to take one of the hikes at the park, and while most don't have the time, energy, or body conditioning to complete the Crags Trail, the Root Creek Trail is a good second choice.

From the parking area, walk back down the road about 40 yards to reach the signed trailhead at 2,500 feet. Take the Kettlebelly Trail for .25 mile, then turn right on Root Creek Trail. From here the trail is routed through a thick, cool forest, an easy walk that most visitors overlook. It continues to Root Creek, a pretty, babbling stream.

Location: In Castle Crags State Park south of Mount Shasta; map B2, grid c4.

User groups: Hikers only. No dogs, horses, or mountain bikes. No wheelchair facilities.

Permits: No permits are required. A $2 state park entrance fee is charged for each vehicle.

Maps: A trail map can be obtained for a fee by contacting Castle Crags State Park at the address below. Ask the USGS for a topographic map of the Dunsmuir area.

Directions: From Interstate 5 south of Dunsmuir, take the Castella/Castle Crags State Park exit. Turn west on Castle Creek Road and drive .25 mile to the park entrance on the right. Turn right and drive to the kiosk. Just past the kiosk, bear right and drive two miles to the parking area for Vista Point. The trailhead (signed) is back down the road about 50 yards.

Contact: Castle Crags State Park, P.O. Box 80, Castella, CA 96017; tel. (530) 235-2684 or fax (530) 235-1965.

19 Crags Trail

6.2 mi/4.0 hrs

From Vista Point in Castle Crags State Park, you can gaze up at the wondrous crags and spot Castle Dome at 4,966 feet, the leading spire on the crags' ridge. This is a high, rounded, missile-shaped piece of rock, and yes, this is your destination on the Crags Trail. If you're out of shape, this climb is a butt-kicker, gaining elevation all the way.

The well-signed trailhead is located about 40 yards down the road from the parking area at an elevation of 2,500 feet. Start by taking the Kettlebelly/Crags Trail for .25 mile; when you reach a three-trail junction, take off on the Crags Trail. Here the trail rises through a thick forest, climbing steeply at times before eventually turning to the right, emerging from the forest, and winding through the lower Crags. Once above tree line, the views get better with each rising step. In spring, snow and ice fields are common this high. An excellent picnic spot is at Indian Springs at 3,600 feet, and many hikers get no farther than this point. But the trail goes onward, always climbing, then getting quite steep before finally reaching a saddle at the foot of Castle Dome, where a few trees have somehow gained toeholds. When you set foot on this divine perch and gaze north at Mount Shasta, it will be a moment you'll prize forever.

Location: In Castle Crags State Park south of Mount Shasta; map B2, grid c4.

User groups: Hikers only. No dogs, horses, or mountain bikes. No wheelchair facilities.

Permits: No permits are required. A $2 state park entrance fee is charged for each vehicle.

Maps: A trail map can be obtained for a fee by contacting Castle Crags State Park at the address below. Ask the USGS for a topographic map of the Dunsmuir area.

Directions: From Interstate 5 south of Dunsmuir, take the Castella/Castle Crags State Park exit. Turn west on Castle Creek Road and drive .25 mile to the park entrance on the right. Turn right and drive to the kiosk. Just past the kiosk, bear right and drive two miles to its end at the parking area for Vista Point. The trailhead (signed) is back down the road about 50 yards.

Contact: Castle Crags State Park, P.O. Box 80, Castella, CA 96017; tel. (530) 235-2684 or fax (530) 235-1965.

20 McCloud Nature Trail
4.5 mi/2.5 hrs

Have you ever yearned for a place where old trees are left standing, deer and bobcat roam without fear, and where a crystal-perfect river flows free in an untouched canyon? The Mc-Cloud River Preserve is such a place, and because it's managed by the Nature Conservancy, it will always remain that way. While the lower McCloud River is best known for its fly-fishing for trout, there's an excellent hiking trail that runs alongside the river, spanning more than two miles from the parking area on downstream. It's an easy yet beautiful walk among woods and water, requiring a bit of boulder hopping in a few spots. It's well worth it to hike out to the end, where the river plunges into a series of deep holes and gorges. Note that fisherman's trail also runs upstream from Ah-Di-Na Campground, but while pretty, this is not the feature walk here. The trailhead for this hike is another one-mile drive at road's end at the Nature Conservancy section of land.

Location: At Nature Conservancy on the McCloud River south of McCloud; map B2, grid c6.

User groups: Hikers only. No dogs, horses, or mountain bikes. No wheelchair facilities.

Permits: No permits are required. Parking and access are free.

Maps: For a map of Shasta-Trinity National Forest, send $6 to U.S. Forest Service, Attn: Map Sales, P.O. Box 587, Camino, CA 95709; tel. (530) 647-5390, fax (530) 647-5389, or website: www.r5.fs.fed.us/visitorcenter. Major credit cards accepted. Ask the USGS for a topographic map of the Lake McCloud area.

Directions: From Interstate 5 in Redding, drive north for 47 miles to the Highway 89/McCloud-Reno exit. Bear right on Highway 89 and drive 11 miles to McCloud at

Squaw Valley Road. Turn right on Squaw Valley Road and drive five miles (the road becomes Forest Road 11). At the McCloud boat ramp, bear right and drive on Forest Road 11 to the end of Battle Creek Cove and Forest Road 38N53/Ah-Di-Na Road (a dirt road) on the right. Turn right and drive four miles (past Ah-Di-Na Campground) to the road's end at Wheelbarrow Creek. The Nature Conservancy boundary is .5 mile down the trail.

Contact: Shasta-Trinity National Forest, McCloud Ranger District, P.O. Box 1620, McCloud, CA 96057; tel. (530) 964-2184 or fax (530) 964-2938.

21 Lower McCloud Falls

0.25 mi/0.5 hr

The Lower McCloud Falls may not be the most majestic waterfall in California, but there may be none better for swimming. On hot summer days youngsters jump off the granite rim, plunge through the air for about 15 feet, and land in the waterfall's pool like cannon balls. You can drive right to the Lower Falls and park. There are two routes upstream. The better of the two is to rock hop your way right along the river for 10 or 15 minutes, then pick a nice little spot to sit and watch the water go by. The more common trail is the paved walkway that is routed from Lower Falls to Fowler's Camp. Lower Falls is a chute-like waterfall that pours into a large pool surrounded by a granite rim. A ladder is available for swimmers and jumpers.

Location: In Shasta-Trinity National Forest east of McCloud; map B2, grid c7.

User groups: Hikers, wheelchairs, and dogs. Not suitable for horses or mountain bikes.

Permits: No permits are required. Parking and access are free.

Maps: For a map of Shasta-Trinity National Forest, send $6 to U.S. Forest Service, Attn: Map Sales, P.O. Box 587, Camino, CA 95709; tel. (530) 647-5390, fax (530) 647-5389, or website: www.r5.fs.fed.us/visitorcenter. Major credit cards accepted. Ask the USGS for a topographic map of the Lake McCloud area.

Directions: From Interstate 5 in Redding, drive north for 47 miles to the Highway 89/McCloud-Reno exit. Bear right on Highway 89 and drive 11 miles to McCloud. Continue southeast on Highway 89 for five miles to the sign for Fowler's Campground and Forest Road 39N28. Turn right and drive one mile to a fork. Bear right at the fork for Fowler's Campground and drive to the parking area for Lower Falls.

Contact: Shasta-Trinity National Forest, McCloud Ranger District, P.O. Box 1620, McCloud, CA 96057; tel. (530) 964-2184 or fax (530) 964-2938.

22 Middle Falls Trail

0.5 mi/0.5 hr

One of the prettiest waterfalls in Northern California, the Middle Falls of the McCloud River is a wide and tall cascade of water that pours over a 75-foot cliff into a deep pool in a rock bowl. The easy hike is a 10- to 15-minute walk on a trail that skirts the left side of the McCloud River. You'll round a bend, probably hearing the waterfall before you see it, and then suddenly there it is, this wide sheet of falling water. It's something like a miniature Niagara Falls. On summer weekends, teenagers climb to the rim above the falls, then plunge 100 feet into the pool like human missiles. It's a dangerous venture that we don't recommend. Because of the remarkable beauty of this waterfall, it has become extremely popular in the summer. Plans are in the works to make the trail wheelchair accessible. The one frustrating element is that some visitors litter at this pristine spot, or worse, discard their cigarette butts on the trail. We'd like to demonstrate the collective evil of small offenses by strapping the offenders into a chair, then grabbing their upper lips with a pair of pliers and stretching their lips right over the backs of their heads.

Location: At Fowler's Camp in Shasta-Trinity National Forest east of McCloud; map B2, grid c7.

User groups: Hikers and dogs. No horses or mountain bikes. No wheelchair facilities.

Permits: No permits are required. Parking and access are free.

Maps: For a map of Shasta-Trinity National Forest, send $6 to U.S. Forest Service, Attn: Map Sales, P.O. Box 587, Camino, CA 95709; tel. (530) 647-5390, fax (530) 647-5389, or website: www.r5.fs.fed.us/visitorcenter. Major credit cards accepted. Ask the USGS for a topographic map of the McCloud area.

Directions: From Interstate 5 in Redding, drive north for 47 miles to the Highway 89/McCloud-Reno exit. Bear right on Highway 89 and drive 11 miles to McCloud. Continue southeast on Highway 89 for five miles to the sign for Fowler's Campground and Forest Road 39N28. Turn right and drive one mile to a fork. Bear left at the fork for Fowler's Campground, drive through the campground to the restroom, and park. The trailhead is across the road from the restroom.

Contact: Shasta-Trinity National Forest, McCloud Ranger District, P.O. Box 1620, McCloud, CA 96057; tel. (530) 964-2184 or fax (530) 964-2938.

23 Grizzly Peak
0.25 mi/0.25 hr

At 6,252 feet Grizzly Peak provides a sweeping view to the west of the McCloud Flats—a sea of conifers—and beyond to the eastern-facing slopes of Mount Shasta at 14,162 feet. To get here requires a dusty, bumpy, and circuitous drive past Brushy Butte and Mica Gulch. Once at Grizzly Peak you'll find a fire lookout station, which is a perfect spot to scan hundreds of thousands of acres of forest. The short walk is about a 15-minute traipse to the peak, the trail routed through low-lying brush. Lightning rods are set up here, and if you look below to the east, you'll spot a little-used segment of the Pacific Crest Trail. Bring your camera: the views are eye-popping across the McCloud Flats and on to Mount Shasta.

Location: In Shasta-Trinity National Forest southeast of Mount Shasta; map B2, grid c7.

User groups: Hikers and dogs. Horses and mountain bikes are not advised. No wheelchair facilities.

Permits: No permits are required. Parking and access are free.

Maps: For a map of Shasta-Trinity National Forest, send $6 to U.S. Forest Service, Attn: Map Sales, P.O. Box 587, Camino, CA 95709; tel. (530) 647-5390, fax (530) 647-5389, or website: www.r5.fs.fed.us/visitorcenter. Major credit cards accepted. Ask the USGS for a topographic map of the Grizzly Peak area.

Directions: From Interstate 5 in Redding, drive north for 47 miles to the Highway 89/McCloud-Reno exit. Bear right on Highway 89 and drive 11 miles to McCloud and Squaw Valley Road. Turn right on Squaw Valley Road, and drive about five miles. (Squaw Valley Road becomes Forest Road 11/Hawkins Creek Road.) Continue on Forest Road 11, keeping right past the McCloud boat ramp and continue over the McCloud Dam. Turn right (still Forest Road 11) and drive down the canyon. About a mile past the Deer Creek Bridge, look for Forest Road 39N06 (Stouts Meadow Road). Turn left on Forest Road 39N06 and drive 5.8 miles to Grizzly Peak. The road is long, bumpy, and steep in places, and four-wheel-drive vehicles with good clearance are recommended.

Contact: Shasta-Trinity National Forest, McCloud Ranger District, P.O. Box 1620, McCloud, CA 96057; tel. (530) 964-2184 or fax (530) 964-2938.

24 Waters Gulch Overlook
2.8 mi/1.5 hrs

Shasta Lake is so big—the biggest reservoir in California—that it can be difficult to know where to start in your mission to explore it. A good answer is right here on the Waters Gulch Loop. It connects to the Overlook Trail, a cutoff of 0.8 mile that climbs atop a small mountain and furnishes a view of the main lake. The trailhead is at Packers Bay, easily accessible off Interstate 5. The trail heads west across a peninsula and then turns right at Waters Gulch, a cove on the main Sacramento River arm of the lake. While there are many drive-to areas where you can get lake views, here you can get a little seclusion as well.

Location: At Packers Bay on Shasta Lake north of Redding; map B2, grid f3.

User groups: Hikers only. No dogs, horses or mountain bikes. No wheelchair facilities.

Permits: No permits are required. Parking and access are free.

Maps: For a map of Shasta-Trinity National Forest, send $6 to U.S. Forest Service, Attn: Map Sales, P.O. Box 587, Camino, CA 95709; tel. (530) 647-5390, fax (530) 647-5389, or website: www.r5.fs.fed.us/visitorcenter. Major credit cards accepted. Ask the USGS for a topographic map of the O'Brien area.

Directions: From Interstate 5 at Redding, drive north to Shasta Lake and take the Packers Bay exit. Drive southwest on Packers Bay Road for one mile to the trailhead on the right (.25 mile before the boat ramp).

Contact: Shasta-Trinity National Forest, Shasta Lake Ranger District, 14225 Holiday Road, Redding, CA 96003; tel. (530) 275-1587 or fax (530) 275-1512. Shasta Lake Visitor Center, (530) 275-1589.

25 Bailey Cove Loop Trail
2.8 mi/1.5 hrs

This hike is best done when the lake is full in May and June, or you'll be looking out at a lot of red dirt. A favorite part of Shasta Lake is the McCloud arm, where the mountain canyon features limestone formations and the lake's clear emerald waters. This trail provides a great view of these phenomena, as well as a close-to-the-water loop hike on one of the lake's peninsulas. From the trailhead, start by hiking on the left fork, which takes you out along Bailey Cove. As you continue, the loop trail heads in a clockwise direction, first along the McCloud arm of the lake, then back to the parking area along John's Creek Inlet. When you reach the mouth of Bailey Cove, stop and enjoy the view. Directly across the lake are the limestone formations, featuring North Gray Rocks at 3,114 feet and topped by Horse Mountain at 4,025 feet. The famous Shasta Caverns are located just below North Gray Rocks. And hey, watch out for the poison oak; there's plenty off trail.

Location: On the McCloud arm of Shasta Lake north of Redding; map B2, grid f3.

User groups: Hikers only. No dogs, mountain bikes or horses. No wheelchair facilities.

Permits: No permits are required.

Maps: For a map of Shasta-Trinity National Forest, send $6 to U.S. Forest Service, Attn: Map Sales, P.O. Box 587, Camino, CA 95709; tel. (530) 647-5390, fax (530) 647-5389, or website: www.r5.fs.fed.us/visitorcenter. Major credit cards accepted. Ask the USGS for a topographic map of the O'Brien area.

Directions: From Interstate 5 north of Redding, take the O'Brien Road/Shasta Caverns exit. Turn east on Shasta Caverns Road and drive 0.1 mile to the sign for Bailey Cove Boat Ramp. Bear right at the sign and drive .5 mile to the day-use parking area.

Contact: Shasta-Trinity National Forest, Shasta Lake Ranger District, 14225 Holiday Road, Redding, CA 96003; tel. (530) 275-1587 or fax (530) 275-1512. Shasta Lake Visitors Center, (530) 275-1589.

26 Hirz Bay Trail
3.2 mi/1.75 hrs

Most people discover this trail by accident, usually while camping at Hirz Bay Group Camp. That is because this trail, routed along the west side of the beautiful McCloud arm of Shasta Lake, is a natural hike from that camp. The trail traces the shoreline of the lake, in and out along small coves and creek inlets. Straight across the lake are pretty views of the deep coves at Campbell Creek and Dekkas Creek, unique limestone outcrops, and Minnesota Mountain at 4,293 feet.

Location: On the McCloud arm of Shasta Lake north of Redding; map B2, grid f3.

User groups: Hikers only. No dogs, mountain bikes or horses. No wheelchair facilities.

Permits: No permits are required. Parking and access are free.

Maps: For a map of Shasta-Trinity National Forest, send $6 to U.S. Forest Service, Attn: Map Sales, P.O. Box 587, Camino, CA 95709; tel. (530) 647-5390, fax (530) 647-5389, or website: www.r5.fs.fed.us/visitorcenter. Major credit cards accepted. Ask the USGS for a topographic map of the O'Brien area.

Directions: From Interstate 5 north of Redding take the Salt Creek/Gilman Road exit. Drive east on Gilman Road/County Road 7H009 for 10 miles to Hirz Bay Campground.

Contact: Shasta-Trinity National Forest, Shasta Lake Ranger District, 14225 Holiday Road, Redding, CA 96003; tel. (530) 275-1587 or fax (530) 275-1512. Shasta Lake Visitor Center, (530) 275-1589.

27 Greens Creek Boat-In Trail
1.0-12.0 mi/0.5-7.0 hrs

Let's get a few things straight from the start: 1) almost no one hikes this entire trail, 2) almost no one hikes part of this trail, and 3) almost no one even knows about this trail. Why? Because even with two million people estimated to visit Shasta Lake every year, the only way to access this trail is from an obscure boat-in campsite at Greens Creek on the east side of the McCloud arm of the lake. At the back of the cove at Greens Creek, you'll find a small U.S. Forest Service billboard posted with recreation guide sheets, and behind it are the campground and trailhead. There are many

fascinating side trips on the steep climb up toward a saddle between Town Mountain at 4,325 feet and Horse Mountain at 4,025 feet. The trail enters an oak and madrone forest that is interspersed with limestone formations. The latter are worth exploring, and if you spend enough time hiking and investigating, you may find some small caves, a highlight of the trip. Most people are inspired to hike just high enough to get a good clear view of the lake below, but not much farther.

Location: On the McCloud arm of Shasta Lake north of Redding; map B2, grid f3.

User groups: Hikers only. No dogs, horses or mountain bikes. No wheelchair facilities.

Permits: No permits are required. Boat-in access is free.

Maps: For a map of Shasta-Trinity National Forest, send $6 to U.S. Forest Service, Attn: Map Sales, P.O. Box 587, Camino, CA 95709; tel. (530) 647-5390, fax (530) 647-5389, or website: www.r5.fs.fed.us/visitorcenter. Major credit cards accepted. Ask the USGS for a topographic map of the O'Brien area.

Directions: This trail can be accessed only by boat. Boat ramps are located to the north at Hirz Bay Campground (see the directions in the previous hike for the Hirz Bay Trail), to the south at Lakeview Marina Resort (off Shasta Caverns Road) and at Bailey Cove. The trailhead is at Greens Creek Boat-In Camp on the east side of the McCloud River arm.

Contact: Shasta-Trinity National Forest, Shasta Lake Ranger District, 14225 Holiday Road, Redding, CA 96003; tel. (530) 275-1587 or fax (530) 275-1512. Shasta Lake Visitor Center, (530) 275-1589.

28 Davis Gulch Trail
3.0 mi one-way/3.5 hrs

The Davis Gulch Trail is Whiskeytown Lake's best hike, an easy, meandering route along the southwest end of the lake. It starts out at 1,650 feet (at an information billboard along an access road) and meanders its way down to the Brandy Creek Picnic Area at 1,300 feet. It is a moderate descent on a wide, flat footpath. Most of the trees are oaks or madrones, and as you go, there are many good views of Whiskeytown Lake. The trail spans three miles and dead-ends. With two vehicles, it is possible to make it a one-way hike with a shuttle, and better yet, hike the whole route downhill.

Location: At Whiskeytown Lake National Recreation Area west of Redding; map B2, grid h0.

User groups: Hikers and dogs. No horses or mountain bikes. No wheelchair facilities.

Permits: There's a $5 per vehicle parking fee.

Maps: For a detailed trail map, contact Whiskeytown National Recreation Area at the address below. Ask the USGS for a topographic map of the Igo area.

Directions: From Interstate 5 at Redding turn west on Highway 299 and drive 10 miles to the Whiskeytown Visitor Center. Turn left at the Visitor Center and drive on J. F. Kennedy Memorial Drive for three miles to the Davis Gulch Trailhead on the right. To reach the Brandy Creek Picnic Area (and end of the trail), continue three more miles on J.F. Kennedy Memorial Drive.

Contact: Whiskeytown National Recreation Area, P.O. Box 188, Whiskeytown, CA 96095; tel. (530) 246-1225 or fax (530) 242-3400.

PACIFIC CREST TRAIL (PCT) SECTION OVERVIEW
90.0 mi one way/8-9 days

Trail sections extend from Ash Camp at the McCloud River south of McCloud Reservoir to Highway 3 at Scott Mountain.

This section of the Pacific Crest Trail traverses some of the most diverse and dynamic country in Northern California. It includes the lush and vibrant McCloud River and Sacramento River, where the trail drops as low as 2,000 feet, and it climbs to the Trinity Divide Ridge and its dozens of small, untouched lakes.

A short side trip is available to the top of Mount Eddy at 9,025 feet. The trail also runs right beneath the series of sculpted granite spires of Castle Crags, a setting that can astonish newcomers. Following is more specific information on major trail sections in this zone.

PCT-41 Ash Camp to Castle Crags Wilderness
30.0 mi one way/2.0 days

Of the hundreds of rivers along the Pacific Crest Trail, it's the McCloud River that often seems most vibrant with life. This segment of the PCT starts right alongside the McCloud River at Ash Camp, set at about 3,000 feet. The trail is then routed downstream above the McCloud for 2.5 miles, one of the most prized sections of trail in this region. At Ah-Di-Na Camp the trail starts to rise, eventually turning up Squaw Valley Creek and climbing beyond to top Girard Ridge at 4,500 feet, a long, tiring, and dry climb. But when you top the ridge, Mount Shasta, Black Butte, and Castle Crags suddenly pop into view. After traversing the ridge for a few miles, the trail suddenly drops and cascades down to the Sacramento River Canyon. Your toes will be jamming into your boots as you head downhill. At the river you might stop to soak your feet before picking up and heading west into Castle Crags State Park.

Location: From Ash Camp on the McCloud River west into Castle Crags State Park; map B2, grid c6.

User groups: Hikers, dogs, and horses. No mountain bikes. No wheelchair facilities.

Permits: Wilderness permits are required only in Castle Crags Wilderness.

Maps: Ask the USGS for topographic maps of the Shoeinhorse Mountain, Yellowjacket Mountain, and Dunsmuir areas.

Directions: From Interstate 5 in Redding, drive north for 47 miles to the Highway 89/McCloud-Reno exit. Bear right on Highway 89 and drive 11 miles to McCloud and Squaw Valley Road.

Turn right on Squaw Valley Road, and drive about five miles. (Squaw Valley Road becomes Forest Road 11/Hawkins Creek Road.) Continue on Forest Road 11, keeping right past the McCloud boat ramp and continue over the McCloud Dam. Turn right (still Forest Road 11) and drive down the canyon for one mile. At the turnoff for Ash Camp, bear right and drive a short distance to the parking area.

Contact: Shasta-Trinity National Forest, McCloud Ranger District, P.O. Box 1620, McCloud, CA 96057; tel. (530) 964-2184 or fax (530) 964-2938.

Directions: From Interstate 5 south of Dunsmuir, take the Castella/Castle Crags State Park exit. Turn west on Castle Creek Road and drive .25 mile to the park entrance on the right. Turn right and drive to the kiosk. Just past the kiosk is a special parking area for PCT hikers. For day-hikers, continue by bearing right and then drive two miles to the end of the road at the parking area for Vista Point. The trailhead (signed) is back down the road about 50 yards.

Contact: Castle Crags State Park, P.O. Box 80, Castella, CA 96017; tel. (530) 235-2684 or fax (530) 235-1965.

PCT-42 Castle Crags to Mumbo Basin

25.0 mi one way/2.0 days

This is a key juncture for the PCT, where the trail climbs out of a river canyon and back to high ridgelines. It's in a classic region, the Trinity Divide, known for sculpted lakes in granite and sweeping views of Mount Shasta. From the Sacramento River at Castle Crags at an elevation of 2,000 feet, the trail laterals up the north side of Castle Creek Canyon, rising just below the base of the awesome Crags, then finally hitting the rim at the back side of Castle Ridge. It follows the rim in a half circle to the west to the Seven Lakes Basin and beyond to the Mumbo Basin and the Gumboot Lake Trailhead. The final five miles of this segment pass by a dozen pristine mountain lakes, but most are well off the trail.

Location: From Castle Crags State Park west into Shasta-Trinity National Forest; map B2, grid c5.

User groups: Hikers only. No dogs, horses, or mountain bikes. No wheelchair facilities.

Permits: No permits are required. A $2 state park entrance fee is charged for each vehicle.

Maps: A trail map can be obtained for a fee by contacting Castle Crags State Park at the address below. Ask the USGS for topographic maps of the Dunsmuir, Seven Lakes Basin, and Mumbo Basin areas.

PCT-43 Mumbo Basin to Scott Mountain

35.0 mi one way/4.0 days

The PCT starts at a popular trailhead but quickly jumps northward into remote, beautiful country. The first highlight, only a mile up the trail, is the view below to the left of secluded Picayune Lake. The trail heads on, passing little Porcupine Lake (well below, out of reach), an idyllic setting which requires a side trip, and then over the rim and down to Deadfall Lakes, an excellent camping spot. From the ridge, an irresistible side trip is the one-mile trek to the top of Mount Eddy, 9,025 feet, with its incomparable view of Mount Shasta. From Deadfall Lakes, the trail continues down, rounds the headwaters of the Trinity River, then climbs back up Chilcoot Pass and Bull Lake. From here, it's a 10-mile pull to the Scott Mountain Summit Trailhead.

Location: In Shasta-Trinity National Forest, from Gumboot Trailhead to Scott Mountain; map B2, grid b3.

User groups: Hikers, dogs, and horses. No mountain bikes. No wheelchair facilities.

Permits: No permits are required. Parking and access are free.

Maps: Ask the USGS for topographic maps of the Mumbo Basin, South China Mountain, and Scott Mountain areas.

Directions: From Interstate 5 at Mount Shasta city, take the central Mount Shasta exit. At the stop sign, turn west and drive .5 mile to Old Stage Road. Turn left on Old Stage Road and drive .25 mile to a fork with W.A. Barr Road. Stay to the right at the fork and drive two miles, cross Box Canyon Dam at Lake Siskiyou, and continue around the lake on W.A. Barr Road (which becomes Forest Road 26/South Fork Road). Continue four miles past the Lake Siskiyou Camp resort and continue up the canyon for 12.5 miles to Gumboot Lake Road. Bear right, staying on Forest Road 26, and continue 2.5 miles to the ridge to the parking area and trailhead.

Contact: Shasta-Trinity National Forest, McCloud Ranger District, P.O. Box 1620, McCloud, CA 96057; tel. (530) 964-2184 or fax (530) 964-2938.

PCT Continuation

To continue hiking along the Pacific Crest Trail, see chapter B1.

TOM STIENSTRA

HAT CREEK NEAR BURNEY
IN SHASTA COUNTY

MAP B3

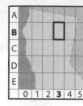

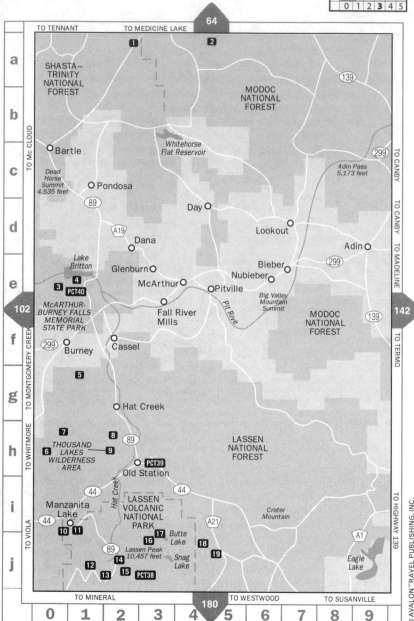

TO TENNANT   TO MEDICINE LAKE

64

TO McCLOUD

SHASTA–TRINITY NATIONAL FOREST

MODOC NATIONAL FOREST

139

Whitehorse Flat Reservoir

Bartle

299   TO CANBY

Dead Horse Summit 4,535 feet

Adin Pass 5,173 feet

Pondosa

89

Day

TO CANBY

TO MADELINE

A19

Dana

Lookout

Adin

Lake Britton

Glenburn

Bieber

Nubieber

299

102

McArthur

Pitville

3   4   PCT40

McARTHUR-BURNEY FALLS MEMORIAL STATE PARK

Fall River Mills

Pit River

Big Valley Mountain Summit

MODOC NATIONAL FOREST

139

142

TO MONTGOMERY CREEK

299   Burney

Cassel

TO TERMO

5

Hat Creek

LASSEN NATIONAL FOREST

7

TO WHITMORE

6   THOUSAND LAKES WILDERNESS AREA

8

89

9

PCT39

Old Station

44

44

Hat Creek

LASSEN VOLCANIC NATIONAL PARK

A21

Crater Mountain

TO HIGHWAY 139

Manzanita Lake

44

TO VIOLA

10   11

17   Butte Lake

A1

16

18

Lassen Peak 10,457 feet

89

14

Snag Lake

19

Eagle Lake

12

13   15   PCT38

TO MINERAL

180

TO WESTWOOD

TO SUSANVILLE

© AVALON TRAVEL PUBLISHING, INC.

126 Northern California

CHAPTER B3

1 Ice Caves Trail. 127
2 Burnt Lava Flow 128
3 Burney Falls Trail 128
4 Rim Trail. 129
5 Burney Mountain
   Summit. 129
6 Magee Trailhead 130
7 Cypress Trailhead 130
8 Tamarack Trailhead . . . 131
9 Bunchgrass Trailhead . 131
10 Manzanita Lake Trail . . 132
11 Nobles Emigrant Trail . 132
12 Lassen Summit Trail . . 133
13 Shadow Lake Trail 134
14 Summit Lake Loop . . . 134
15 Echo and Twin Lakes . . 135

16 Cinder Cone Trail 135
17 Prospect Peak Trail. . . 136
18 Cone Lake Trailhead . . 136
19 Caribou Lake
   Trailhead. 137

**Pacific Crest Trail
(PCT) Section Overview**

PCT-38 Lassen Volcanic
   National Park
   to Highway 44. 138
PCT-39 Highway 44 to
   McArthur-Burney
   Falls State Park. . . . 139
PCT-40 McArthur-Burney
   Falls State Park
   to Ash Camp. 139

1 Ice Caves Trail

0.25 mi/0.5 hr

If you're curious about the volcanic formations of the Medicine Lake area, but don't necessarily want to sign up for an expedition to explore them, the Ice Caves Trail is the perfect hike for you. The caves are located just off the road, requiring only a short walk to reach them. What you'll find here is a series of strange-looking caves, mostly shallow gouges in the volcanic rocks except for one that is deep and wide, a hollowed-out grotto in a lava flow. Call it our imagination, but on our visit here we sensed the presence of old spirits, perhaps the ghosts of the Modoc Indians that used this area. Perhaps not. Regardless, it felt strange and uncomfortable, and we left quickly.

Location: In Modoc National Forest south of Medicine Lake; map B3, grid a2.

User groups: Hikers and dogs. The terrain is not suitable for mountain bikes or horses. No wheelchair facilities.

Permits: No permits are required. Parking and access are free.

Maps: For a map of Modoc National Forest, send $6 to U.S. Forest Service, Attn: Map Sales, P.O. Box 587, Camino, CA 95709; tel. (530) 647-5390, fax (530) 647-5389, or website: www.r5.fs.fed.us/visitorcenter. Major credit cards accepted. Ask the USGS for a topographic map of the Medicine Lake area.

Directions: From Redding drive north on Interstate 5 for 56 miles to Highway 89/McCloud. Bear right on Highway 89 and drive 28 miles to Bartle. Just past Bartle, turn left on Powder Hill Road (Forest Road 49) and drive 21 miles (the road becomes Medicine Lake Road) to the ice caves (signed) on the left side of the road.

Contact: Modoc National Forest, Doublehead Ranger District, P.O. Box 369, Tulelake, CA 96134; tel. (530) 667-2246 or fax (530) 667-8609.

2 Burnt Lava Flow
2.5 mi/1.5 hrs

When you walk across the Burnt Lava Flow, a land of "rocks that float and mountains of glass," it may seem as if you're exploring some prehistoric area that resembles the moon. But get this: the lava formation is only about 200 years old, the youngest flow in the Medicine Lake Highlands. It's located south of Glass Mountain and covers some 8,760 acres, with little islands of forest amid the bare, jet-black lava flow. When we took an aerial survey of the area, the Burnt Lava Flow was one of the most fascinating portions of the entire region. On foot, it's even stranger. There is no trail, so you just pick your direction, with most visitors going from tree island to tree island. There are a few weird spots where the ground can be like quicksand when dry and like wet concrete when wet. Just walk around those spots, staying on the hard, black lava flow.

Location: In Modoc National Forest south of Medicine Lake; map B3, grid a4.

User groups: Hikers and dogs. The terrain is not suitable for mountain bikes or horses. No wheelchair facilities.

Permits: No permits are required. Parking and access are free.

Maps: For a map of Modoc National Forest, send $6 to U.S. Forest Service, Attn: Map Sales, P.O. Box 587, Camino, CA 95709; tel. (530) 647-5390, fax (530) 647-5389, or website: www.r5.fs.fed.us/visitorcenter. Major credit cards accepted. Ask the USGS for a topographic map of the Porcupine Butte area.

Directions: From Redding drive north on Interstate 5 for 56 miles to Highway 89/McCloud. Bear right on Highway 89 and drive 28 miles to Bartle. Just past Bartle, turn left on Powder Hill Road (Forest Road 49) and drive 24 miles (the road becomes Medicine Lake Road) to Forest Road 42N25. Turn right and drive (the road becomes Forest Road 56) to the Burnt

Lava Flow Geologic Area.

Contact: Modoc National Forest, Doublehead Ranger District, P.O. Box 369, Tulelake, CA 96134; tel. (530) 667-2246 or fax (530) 667-8609.

3 Burney Falls Trail
1.0 mi/0.5 hr

Visitors from across the West are attracted to this state park to see Burney Falls. It is spectacular, 129 feet high, wide, and cascading. The waterfall plunges over a cliff in two pieces, split at the rim by a small bluff where two trees have managed toeholds, although the river flows over the top of them during high water from the spring snowmelt. Underground lava tubes also transport water to the site, where it seems to ooze and drip right from the surrounding moss. From the park entrance station it's about a 50-foot walk to a rocky overlook, a perfect place for photographs of the waterfall. This spot also marks the start of the Burney Falls Trail, an easy one-mile loop around the waterfall and back. It's a self-guided nature trail, but rather than having to carry a brochure with you along the trail, you can just read the small signs that explain the featured sites. A great little side trip is to hike upstream of the falls, cross Burney Creek on the small bridge, then hike back downstream to a breathtaking overlook of the falls.

Location: In McArthur-Burney Falls State Park north of Burney; map B3, grid e0.

User groups: Hikers only. No dogs, horses, or mountain bikes. There is paved wheelchair access at the falls overlook point at the beginning of the trail.

Permits: No permits are required. A $2 state park day-use fee is charged for each vehicle.

Maps: A trail guide is available for $1 at the state park at the address below. Ask the USGS for a topographic map of the Burney Falls area.

Directions: From Interstate 5 at Redding turn east on Highway 299 and drive 50 miles to Burney. Drive five miles east on Highway 299, turn north on Highway 89, and drive 5.8 miles to the state park entrance on the left. Park at the main lot and follow the signs to the trailhead. **Contact:** McArthur-Burney Falls State Park, 24898 Highway 89, Burney, CA 96013; tel. (530) 335-2777 or fax (530) 335-5483.

4 Rim Trail

3.0 mi/1.75 hrs

The Rim Trail provides an ideal hike for campers at Burney Falls State Park. The trail starts at the campground and is routed to the rim of Lake Britton, a distance of 1.5 miles. It's an easy walk and pretty, too, heading first through forest, then emerging with a good lookout of the lake. An easy side trip is down to the beach. The lake, set in a gorge, seems to have special qualities, sometimes shimmering with effervescence. The fishing is good, too, especially for crappie, but with bass, bluegill, and trout plentiful as well.
Location: At Lake Britton in McArthur-Burney Falls State Park north of Burney; map B3, grid e1.
User groups: Hikers only. No dogs, horses, or mountain bikes. No wheelchair facilities.
Permits: No permits are required. A $2 state park day-use fee is charged for each vehicle.
Maps: A trail guide is available for $1 at the state park at the address below. Ask the USGS for a topographic map of the Burney Falls area.
Directions: From Interstate 5 at Redding turn east on Highway 299 and drive 50 miles to Burney. Go five miles east on Highway 299 to Highway 89. Turn north on Highway 89 and drive 5.8 miles to the state park entrance on the left. The trailhead is just opposite campsite number 12.
Contact: McArthur-Burney Falls State Park, 24898 Highway 89, Burney, CA 96013; tel. (530) 335-2777 or fax (530) 335-5483.

5 Burney Mountain Summit

0.25 mi/0.25 hr

The view is just so good from the top of Burney Mountain (elevation 7,863 feet) that we had to include this trip in the book. The "hike" consists of just moseying around the summit and gazing off in all directions. There is a fire lookout on top of the mountain. Occasionally, tours are available. Burney Mountain often gets lost in the shadow of its big brothers, Mount Lassen and Mount Shasta, but of the three the view just might be best from Burney. That's because a view of Lassen or Shasta offers impressive panoramas that just can't be duplicated. Note that if you show up in the winter when the access road is gated, it's a four-mile hike up the road to the top of the mountain. Almost nobody makes that trip.
Location: In Lassen National Forest south of Burney; map B3, grid g1.
User groups: Hikers, dogs, horses, and mountain bikes. No wheelchair facilities.
Permits: No permits are required. Parking and access are free.
Maps: For a map of Lassen National Forest, send $6 to U.S. Forest Service, Attn: Map Sales, P.O. Box 587, Camino, CA 95709; tel. (530) 647-5390, fax (530) 647-5389, or website: www.r5.fs.fed.us/visitorcenter. Major credit cards accepted. Ask the USGS for topographic maps of the Burney Mountain West and Burney Mountain East areas.
Directions: From Interstate 5 at Redding turn east on Highway 299 and drive 50 miles to Burney. Drive five more miles east to Highway 89. Turn south (right) on Highway 89 and drive 10.5 miles to Forest Road 26/Forest Road 34N19. Turn right on Forest Road 26 and drive 10 miles to Forest Road 34N23. Turn right and drive seven miles to the mountain summit. Note that the summit access road is blocked by a gate at 6 p.m. each day and throughout winter. You can park at the gate and hike to the top.
Contact: Lassen National Forest, Hat Creek Ranger District, P.O. Box 220, Falls River Mills, CA 96028; tel. (530) 336-5521 or fax (530) 336-5758.

6 Magee Trailhead

9.0 mi/2.0 days

Warning: You need to be at least a partially deranged soul to want to do this hike. It's very difficult, steep, and even rangers avoid it as much as possible. Vehicle access to the trailhead is also difficult on a road that is no longer maintained; many vehicles simply can't make it in. Then if they do, many bodies can't make it up the trail either. From the trailhead at 6,120 feet, you head east for 2.5 miles, then turn north toward Magee Peak, climbing all the way. The trail skirts the eastern slope of that mountain, and a possibility here is climbing .25 mile off the trail to the summit at 8,550 feet. After reaching the top of Magee Peak, you'll descend for about two miles to Magee Lake. For overnighters a mandatory side trip to Everett Lake, which is located less than .25 mile to the northeast. Note that the Thousand Lakes Wilderness is a tiny, overlooked wilderness, but it's excellent for short hikes, either for a day or a weekend. This is not one of them.
Location: On the southwest boundary of the Thousand Lakes Wilderness north of Lassen Volcanic National Park; map B3, grid h0.
User groups: Hikers, dogs, and horses (but not recommended). No mountain bikes. No wheelchair facilities.
Permits: A campfire permit (free) is required. Parking and access are free.
Maps: For a map of Lassen National Forest, send $6 to U.S. Forest Service, Attn: Map Sales, P.O. Box 587, Camino, CA 95709; tel. (530) 647-5390, fax (530) 647-5389, or website: www.r5.fs.fed.us/visitorcenter. Major credit cards accepted. A wilderness trail map is available for $6 from the Hat Creek Ranger District. Ask the USGS for topographic maps of the Thousand Lakes Valley and Jacks Backbone areas.
Directions: From Interstate 5 at Redding turn east on Highway 299 and drive 50 miles to Burney. Continue east five more miles to Highway 89. Turn south on Highway 89 and drive 31 miles to Forest Road 16 (Forest Road 33N16).

Turn right on Forest Road 16 and drive 9.5 miles to Forest Road 32N48. Turn right on Forest Road 32N48 and drive 1.5 miles to the parking area at the end of the road. That road is not maintained and can be extremely rough.
Contact: Lassen National Forest, Hat Creek Ranger District, 43225 E. Highway 299, P.O. Box 220, Falls River Mills, CA 96028; tel. (530) 336-5521 or fax (530) 336-5758.

7 Cypress Trailhead

6.0 mi/1 day

You like lakes? You came to the right place. The Cypress Trailhead at 5,400 feet is the number-one starting point for the Thousand Lakes Wilderness, with many small lakes sprinkled about in a radius of just two miles. The primary destination is Lake Eiler, a round-trip of six miles, though it is 9.9 miles if you also hike around the lake and return to the trailhead. It is the largest lake in this region, set just below Eiler Butte. But a network of trails here connects to other lakes, so an option is to keep on going for an overnighter. From the south side of Eiler Lake, the trail loops deeper into the wilderness in a clockwise arc. It passes near several other lakes, including Box and Barrett Lakes. Both of these provide good fishing for small trout.
Location: On the north boundary of the Thousand Lakes Wilderness north of Lassen Volcanic National Park; map B3, grid h0.
User groups: Hikers, dogs, and horses. No mountain bikes. No wheelchair facilities.
Permits: No permits are required. Parking and access are free.
Maps: For a map of Lassen National Forest, send $6 to U.S. Forest Service, Attn: Map Sales, P.O. Box 587, Camino, CA 95709; tel. (530) 647-5390, fax (530) 647-5389, or website: www.r5.fs.fed.us/visitorcenter. Major credit cards accepted. A wilderness trail map is available for $6 from the Hat Creek Ranger District. Ask the USGS for topographic maps of the Thousand Lakes Valley and Jacks Backbone areas.

Directions: From Interstate 5 at Redding turn east on Highway 299 and drive 50 miles to Burney. Continue east five more miles to Highway 89. Turn south on Highway 89 and drive 10.5 miles to Forest Road 26 (Forest Road 34N19). Turn west on Forest 26 (Forest Road 34N19) and drive 8.5 miles to Forest Road 34N60. Turn left and drive 2.5 miles to the parking area.

Contact: Lassen National Forest, Hat Creek Ranger District, 43225 E. Highway 299, P.O. Box 220, Falls River Mills, CA 96028; tel. (530) 336-5521 or fax (530) 336-5758.

8 Tamarack Trailhead
6.0 mi/3.5 hrs

From the Tamarack Trailhead your first destination is Lake Eiler, a three-mile hike. This is an alternative trailhead to Lake Eiler; the other is the previously listed Cypress Trailhead. The difference is that this trailhead gets far less use because the last 1.5 miles of the access road are very rough, a high-clearance, four-wheel-drive truck is required to make it in. Once in, it's on to Lake Eiler, where a variety of activities are available. Have a picnic, swim, or fish, and then return; or if you have backpacking gear, head onward to several other wilderness lakes. The trailhead elevation is 5,200 feet, and from this point the trail is routed into the northwestern interior of the Thousand Lakes Wilderness. After two miles you'll reach a fork in the trail; turn left (south) to reach Barrett Lake in just another mile of hiking. Note that there is a complex trail network in this area with many junctions, creating a situation in which backpackers can invent their own multi-day route. From Barrett Lake other attractive destinations include Durbin Lake, .5 mile to the south, and Everett and Magee Lakes, another (very challenging) 2.7 miles away.

Location: On the east boundary of the Thousand Lakes Wilderness north of Lassen Volcanic National Park; map B3, grid h2.

User groups: Hikers, dogs, and horses. No mountain bikes. No wheelchair facilities.

Permits: No permits are required. Parking and access are free.

Maps: For a map of Lassen National Forest, send $6 to U.S. Forest Service, Attn: Map Sales, P.O. Box 587, Camino, CA 95709; tel. (530) 647-5390, fax (530) 647-5389, or website: www.r5.fs.fed.us/visitorcenter. Major credit cards accepted. A wilderness trail map is available for $6 from the Hat Creek Ranger District. Ask the USGS for topographic maps of the Thousand Lakes Valley and Jacks Backbone areas.

Directions: From Interstate 5 at Redding, turn east on Highway 299 and drive 50 miles to Burney. Continue east on Highway 299 for five more miles to Highway 89. Turn south on Highway 89 and drive about 14 miles to Forest Road 33N25. Turn west on Forest Road 33N25 and drive five miles to Forest Road 33N23Y. Turn right and head to the parking area at the end of the road. The last 1.5 miles are very rough; four-wheel-drive, high-clearance trucks recommended.

Contact: Lassen National Forest, Hat Creek Ranger District, 43225 E. Highway 299, P.O. Box 220, Falls River Mills, CA 96028; tel. (530) 336-5521 or fax (530) 336-5758.

9 Bunchgrass Trailhead
8.0 mi/2.0 days

This trailhead is obscure and difficult to reach, and because of that few visitors choose it as a jump-off spot for their treks. The destination is Durbin Lake, a four-mile hike one way, making an easy weekend backpack trip. The trailhead elevation is 5,680 feet, and from there it's a fair walk in, a bit up and down, and if you're not in shape, you'll know it well before you reach the lake. You'll come to Hall Butte at 7,187 feet and then Durbin Lake. A side-trip option is to hike out on the trail for three miles, skirting the western side of Hall Butte, then going off trail for .5 mile to reach the top. This area does get frequent traffic in the fall from deer hunters.

Location: On the south boundary of the Thousand Lakes

Wilderness north of Lassen Volcanic National Park, map B3, grid h2.

User groups: Hikers, dogs, and horses. No mountain bikes. No wheelchair facilities.

Permits: A campfire permit (free) is required. Parking and access are free.

Maps: For a map of Lassen National Forest, send $6 to U.S. Forest Service, Attn: Map Sales, P.O. Box 587, Camino, CA 95709; tel. (530) 647-5390, fax (530) 647-5389, or website: www.r5.fs.fed.us/visitorcenter. Major credit cards accepted. A wilderness trail map is available for $6 from the Hat Creek Ranger District. Ask the USGS for topographic maps of the Thousand Lakes Valley and Jacks Backbone areas.

Directions: From Interstate 5 at Redding turn east on Highway 299 and drive 50 miles to Burney. Continue east five more miles to Highway 89. Turn south on Highway 89 and drive 31 miles to Forest Road 16 (Forest Road 33N16). Turn right on Forest Road 16 and drive seven miles to Forest Road 32N45. Turn right on Forest Road 32N45 and drive two miles to Forest Road 32N42Y (very steep). Turn left and head to the parking area at the end of the road.

Contact: Lassen National Forest, Hat Creek Ranger District, 43225 E. Highway 299, P.O. Box 220, Falls River Mills, CA 96028; tel. (530) 336-5521, or fax (530) 336-5758.

10 Manzanita Lake Trail
1.6 mi/1.0 hr

There's no prettier lake that you can reach by car in Lassen Park than Manzanita Lake. That is why many consider the campground here a perfect destination. It's the largest camp in the park, with 179 sites, and it's easy to reach, located just beyond the entrance station at the western boundary of the park. The trail simply traces the shoreline of this pretty lake at a 5,950-foot elevation and is easily accessible from either the parking area just beyond the entrance station or from the campground. A good side trip is across the road to Reflection Lake, a small and also very pretty lake,

which adds about .5 mile to the trip. Note that the fishing at Manzanita Lake is catch-and-release only, using artificials: no bait, and pinch down your barbs.

Location: At the western entrance to Lassen Volcanic National Park on Highway 44; map B3, grid j0.

User groups: Hikers only. No dogs, horses, or mountain bikes. No wheelchair facilities.

Permits: No permit required. A $10 entry fee is charged each vehicle.

Maps: Trail maps are available for a fee from Loomis Museum, c/o Lassen Volcanic National Park at the address below. For a map of Lassen National Forest, send $6 to U.S. Forest Service, Attn: Map Sales, P.O. Box 587, Camino, CA 95709; tel. (530) 647-5390, fax (530) 647-5389, or website: www.r5.fs.fed.us/visitorcenter. Major credit cards accepted. Ask the USGS for a topographic map of the Manzanita Lake area.

Directions: From Interstate 5 at Redding turn east on Highway 44 and drive 46 miles to the junction with Highway 89. Turn south on Highway 89 and drive one mile to the park entrance station. Continue on Lassen Park Highway .5 mile to the turnoff for Manzanita Lake Campground. Turn right and drive .5 mile to the day-use parking area.

Contact: Lassen Volcanic National Park, P.O. Box 100, Mineral, CA 96063-0100; tel. (530) 595-4444 or fax (530) 595-3262.

11 Nobles Emigrant Trail
2-10 mi/1 hr-1 day

The most difficult part of this hike is the first two steps. Why? Because the trailhead is set near the park entrance amid a number of small roads and a maintenance area, and despite a trail sign, many visitors can't find it and give up. It's worth the search because it's a great day hike for campers staying at Manzanita Lake. The trail, with its easy, moderate grade, passes first through an old forest with towering firs, cedars, and Jeffrey pines. About 2.5 miles in, however, you'll arrive at Lassen's strange "Dwarf Forest." Not only are you surrounded by stunted trees, but you also get views of Chaos Crags, a jumble of pinkish rocks constituting what's left of an old broken-down volcano. Many visitors hike to this point, then turn around and return to the campground. The trail follows part of a historical route that was originally an east-west portion of the California Trail used by emigrants in the 1850s. There is no water available on the trail, so be sure to have at least one filled canteen per hiker. Because of the moderate slope, this trail is an ideal cross-country ski route in the winter months.

Location: From the Manzanita Lake Trailhead in Lassen Volcanic National Park east of Red Bluff; map B3, grid j1.

User groups: Hikers and horses. No dogs or mountain bikes. No wheelchair facilities.

Permits: A wilderness permit (free) is required for hikers planning to camp in the backcountry. A $10 park entrance fee is charged for each vehicle.

Maps: Trail maps are available for a fee from Loomis Museum, c/o Lassen Volcanic National Park at the address below. For a map of Lassen National Forest, send $6 to U.S. Forest Service, Attn: Map Sales, P.O. Box 587, Camino, CA 95709; tel. (530) 647-5390, fax (530) 647-5389, or website: www.r5.fs.fed.us/visitorcenter. Major credit cards accepted. Ask the USGS for a topographic map of the Manzanita Lake area.

Directions: From Interstate 5 at Redding, turn east on Highway 44 and drive 46 miles to the junction with Highway 89. Turn south on Highway 89 and drive one mile to the park entrance station. Continue on Lassen Park Highway .5 mile to the turnoff for Manzanita Lake. The trailhead is across the road from Manzanita Lake, just past the visitor center.

Contact: Lassen Volcanic National Park, P.O. Box 100, Mineral, CA 96063-0100; tel. (530) 595-4444 or fax (530) 595-3262.

12 Lassen Summit Trail
5.0 mi/4.0 hrs

At 10,457 feet Mount Lassen Summit is a huge volcanic flume with hardened lava flows, craters, outcrops, and extraordinary views in all directions. Exploring Lassen Peak has become such a popular hike—perhaps the best introduction to mountain climbing a hiker could desire—that the National Park Service may enforce a trail quota in the future. The climb to the top is a 2.5-mile zigzag of a hike on a hard, flat trail, ascending just more than 2,000 feet in the process. The trailhead at 8,500 feet is adjacent to a large parking area set at the base of the summit along Highway 89 (Lassen Park Highway), which means that many visitors can spontaneously decide to try the climb. Our suggestion is to plan it instead, starting early, at least by 7:30 a.m. Bring a lunch and a canteen or two of water. In the morning, with the air still cool, it's about a two-hour walk to the top, a 15 percent grade most of the way. The views are superb, with Mount Shasta 100 miles north appearing close enough to reach out and grab. To the east are hundreds of miles of forests and lakes, and to the west, the land drops off to several small volcanic cones and the northern Sacramento Valley. This is an exceptional first climb for youngsters, providing for plenty of encouragement and rest stops.

Special note: Winds are common at Lassen Summit, especially on summer afternoons. Hikers should stash a windbreaker in their daypacks. It's always a mistake to suddenly climb the summit without planning the trip. Stay at lower elevations if there's any chance of lightning activity.

Location: In Lassen Volcanic National Park east of Red Bluff; map B3, grid j1.

User groups: Hikers only. No dogs, horses, or mountain bikes. No wheelchair facilities.

Permits: No permits required. A $10 entrance fee is charged for each vehicle.

Maps: Trail maps are available for a fee at Loomis Museum, c/o Lassen Volcanic National Park at the address below. For a map of Lassen National Forest, send $6 to U.S. Forest Service, Attn: Map Sales, P.O. Box 587, Camino, CA 95709; tel. (530) 647-5390, fax (530) 647-5389, or website: www.r5.fs.fed.us/visitorcenter. Major credit cards accepted. Ask the USGS for a topographic map of the Lassen Peak area.

Directions: From Interstate 5 at Red Bluff, turn east on Highway 36 and drive 47 miles to the junction with Highway 89. Turn north (left) on Highway 89 and continue 4.5 miles to the park entrance. Continue seven miles on Highway 89 (Lassen Park Highway) to the parking area and trailhead on the left.

Contact: Lassen Volcanic National Park, P.O. Box 100, Mineral, CA 96063-0100; tel. (530) 595-4444 or fax (530) 595-3262.

13 Shadow Lake Trail
1.6 mi/1.0 hr　　　

A hike of less than a mile on this trail will take you past little Terrace Lake and then shortly after to Shadow Lake. It's rare to reach such a pretty lake surrounded by wildlands in such a short distance. The trail involves a short, steep climb to Terrace Lake, and then .25 mile junket to skirt the southeast shoreline of Shadow Lake (at least three times the size of Terrace Lake). The lakes are set just north of Reading Peak, which reaches 8,701 feet. The trailhead is at 8,000 feet, and because of the altitude some hikers may experience shortness of breath making the climb to the lakes. But if you're still feeling good, then by all means continue .75 mile to Cliff Lake, a beautiful spot, well worth the extra hour.

Location: In Lassen Volcanic National Park east of Red Bluff; map B3, grid j2.

User groups: Hikers. No dogs, horses, or mountain bikes. No wheelchair facilities.

Permits: No permits required. A $10 park entrance fee is charged for each vehicle.

Maps: Trail maps are available for a fee at

Loomis Museum, c/o Lassen Volcanic National Park at the address below. For a map of Lassen National Forest, send $6 to U.S. Forest Service, Attn: Map Sales, P.O. Box 587, Camino, CA 95709; tel. (530) 647-5390, fax (530) 647-5389, or website: www.r5.fs.fed.us/visitorcenter. Major credit cards accepted. Ask the USGS for a topographic map of the Reading Peak area.

Directions: From Interstate 5 at Red Bluff, turn east on Highway 36 and drive 47 miles to the junction with Highway 89. Turn north (left) on Highway 89 and continue 4.5 miles to the park entrance. Continue nine miles on Highway 89 (Lassen Park Highway) to the parking area and trailhead on the left (two miles past the parking area for Lassen Summit).

Contact: Lassen Volcanic National Park, P.O. Box 100, Mineral, CA 96063-0100; tel. (530) 595-4444 or fax (530) 595-3262.

14 Summit Lake Loop
0.5 mi/0.5 hr　　　

At 7,000 feet, Summit Lake is a beautiful spot where deer visit almost every summer evening. Nearby campgrounds on both sides of the lake (north and south) are set in conifers, with a pretty meadow just south of the lake along Kings Creek. This hike is a simple walk around Summit Lake, best taken at dusk when the changing evening colors reflect a variety of tints across the lake surface. Though no lakes in Lassen Park are stocked with trout and the fishing is typically poor, you may still see a rising trout or two. The best place to see wildlife, especially deer, is in the meadow adjacent to Kings Creek, the lake's outlet stream.

Location: In Lassen Volcanic National Park east of Red Bluff; map B3, grid j2.

User groups: Hikers and horses. No dogs or mountain bikes. No wheelchair facilities.

Permits: No permits required. A $10 park entrance fee is charged for each vehicle.

Maps: Trail maps are available for a fee at Loomis Museum, c/o Lassen Volcanic National Park at the address below. For a map of

Lassen National Forest, send $6 to U.S. Forest Service, Attn: Map Sales, P.O. Box 587, Camino, CA 95709; tel. (530) 647-5390, fax (530) 647-5389, or website: www.r5.fs.fed.us/visitorcenter. Major credit cards accepted. Ask the USGS for a topographic map of the Reading Peak area.

Directions: From Interstate 5 at Redding, turn east on Highway 44 and drive 46 miles to the junction with Highway 89. Turn south on Highway 89 and drive one mile to the park entrance station. Continue on Lassen Park Highway (Highway 89) for 12 miles to the turnoff for Summit Lake North Campground. Turn left and park in the day-use area near the lake.

Contact: Lassen Volcanic National Park, P.O. Box 100, Mineral, CA 96063-0100; tel. (530) 595-4444 or fax (530) 595-3262.

15 Echo and Twin Lakes

8.0 mi/5.5 hrs

You get it all on this hike to Lower Twin Lake: beautiful lakes, forest, meadows, and wildflowers, all a prime testimonial to the beauty of the Lassen Wilderness. It makes an outstanding day hike for campers staying at Summit Lake Campground or an easy overnighter for backpackers. The trail starts on the north side of Summit Lake, rising 500 feet in the first mile. If you can endure this climb, the rest of the hike will be a breeze. You'll arrive at Echo Lake in just another mile and at Upper Twin and Lower Twin in the next two miles, dropping 500 feet on your way. It's all very pretty, and a great bonus for Summit Lake campers.

Special note: No campfires are permitted in Lassen Park.

Location: In Lassen Volcanic National Park east of Red Bluff; map B3, grid j2.

User groups: Hikers and horses. No dogs or mountain bikes. No wheelchair facilities.

Permits: No permit required. A $10 park entrance fee is charged for each vehicle.

Maps: Trail maps are available for a fee at Loomis Museum, c/o Lassen Volcanic National Park at the address below. For a map of

Lassen National Forest, send $6 to U.S. Forest Service, Attn: Map Sales, P.O. Box 587, Camino, CA 95709; tel. (530) 647-5390, fax (530) 647-5389, or website: www.r5.fs.fed.us/visitorcenter. Major credit cards accepted. Ask the USGS for a topographic map of the Reading Peak area.

Directions: From Interstate 5 at Redding turn east on Highway 44 and drive 46 miles to the junction with Highway 89. Turn south on Highway 89 and drive one mile to the park entrance station. Continue on Lassen Park Highway (Highway 89) for 12 miles to the turnoff for Summit Lake North Campground. Turn left and park in the day-use area near the lake. Look for the footbridge that leads to a trail sign, then turn left and start your hike.

Contact: Lassen Volcanic National Park, P.O. Box 100, Mineral, CA 96063; tel. (530) 595-4444 or fax (530) 595-3262.

16 Cinder Cone Trail

4.0 mi/3.0 hrs

Huge chunks of Lassen Park are overlooked by visitors simply because access is not off the park's main roadway, Highway 89. Butte Lake and the Cinder Cone Trail, set in the northeastern corner of the park, are such areas. When you arrive by car, you'll find large, attractive Butte Lake, quite a surprise for newcomers. The trailhead for the Nobles Emigrant Trail/Cinder Cone Trail (elevation 6,100 feet) is located at the northwest corner of the lake. The trail starts out easy, heading southwest through forest. But don't be fooled. After 1.5 miles, you'll reach the Cinder Cone cutoff, and there everything suddenly changes. The last .5 mile rises to the top of the Cinder Cone, a short but very intense climb of 750 feet to the summit at 6,907 feet. The views are unforgettable, especially south to the Painted Dunes and Fantastic Lava Beds, a classic volcanic landscape.

Location: From Butte Lake Trailhead in Lassen Volcanic National Park; map B3, grid j3.

User groups: Hikers only. No dogs, horses or mountain bikes. No wheelchair facilities.

Permits: No permit required. A $10 park entrance fee is charged for each vehicle.

Maps: Trail maps are available for a fee from Loomis Museum, c/o Lassen Volcanic National Park at the address below. For a map of Lassen National Forest, send $6 to U.S. Forest Service, Attn: Map Sales, P.O. Box 587, Camino, CA 95709; tel. (530) 647-5390, fax (530) 647-5389, or website: www.r5.fs.fed.us/visitor-center. Major credit cards accepted. Ask the USGS for a topographic map of the Prospect Peak area.

Directions: From Interstate 5 at Redding, turn east on Highway 44 and drive 60 miles to Highway 89/44. Turn left (north) on Highway 89/44 and drive 13 miles to Old Station. Just past Old Station, turn right (east) on Highway 44 and drive 10 miles to Forest Road 32N21. Turn right (south) on Forest Road 32N21 and drive seven miles to Butte Lake. The trailhead is located near the boat ramp.

Contact: Lassen Volcanic National Park, P.O. Box 100, Mineral, CA 96063-0100; tel. (530) 595-4444 or fax (530) 595-3262.

17 Prospect Peak Trail
6.6 mi/4.5 hrs

Hiking to the top of most mountains requires a long, grinding climb. Alas, gaining the summit of Prospect Peak is no different. Your reward is some of the best views in Lassen Park and a trail that gets little use compared to the others in the park. The trailhead (Nobles Emigrant Trail), at elevation 6,100 feet, is adjacent to Butte Lake. After less than .5 mile, you'll turn right at the junction with the Prospect Peak Trail. The trail immediately starts to climb, and get used to it because there's no respite for several hours. It climbs more than 2,200 feet over the course of just 3.3 miles, finally topping the summit at 8,338 feet. From here you can see most of the prominent peaks in the park, including Mount Lassen, Mount Hoffman, and Crater Butte, along with thousands and thousands of acres of national forest to the north. Since the snowmelt occurs earlier here than in the rest of the park, this trip makes a perfect hike in the early spring when the air is still cool. If you wait until summer, you'll find this a dry, forsaken place.

Location: At Butte Lake in Lassen Volcanic National Park; map B3, grid j3.

User groups: Hikers only. No dogs, horses or mountain bikes. No wheelchair facilities.

Permits: No permit required. A $10 park entrance fee is charged for each vehicle.

Maps: Trail maps are available for a fee from Loomis Museum, c/o Lassen Volcanic National Park at the address below. For a map of Lassen National Forest, send $6 to U.S. Forest Service, Attn: Map Sales, P.O. Box 587, Camino, CA 95709; tel. (530) 647-5390, fax (530) 647-5389, or website: www.r5.fs.fed.us/visitor-center. Major credit cards accepted. Ask the USGS for a topographic map of the Prospect Peak area.

Directions: From Interstate 5 at Redding, turn east on Highway 44 and drive 60 miles to Highway 89/44. Turn left (north) on Highway 89/44 and drive 13 miles to Old Station. Just past Old Station, turn right (east) on Highway 44 and drive 10 miles to Forest Road 32N21. Turn right (south) on Forest Road 32N21 and drive seven miles to Butte Lake and the parking area near the boat ramp. Look for the Nobles Emigrant Trailhead and hike .5 mile to the Prospect Peak Trail on the right.

Contact: Lassen Volcanic National Park, P.O. Box 100, Mineral, CA 96063-0100; tel. (530) 595-4444 or fax (530) 595-3262.

18 Cone Lake Trailhead
4.0 mi/2.5 hrs

The prize destination on this excellent day hike is Triangle Lake, a pretty spot set in the northern Caribou Wilderness near Black Butte. The trailhead is located at tiny Cone Lake, just outside the wilderness. From here you hike for nearly a mile before passing the wilderness boundary, which is clearly marked. At that point you can sense the change in features as the land becomes wild and untouched, in striking contrast to the start of the hike. You head a mile south, arriving at Triangle Lake, which provides good fishing during the evening for pan-sized trout. If you want more, you can get more. Here the trail forks. The right fork is routed right into Lassen Volcanic National Park, a distance of only 1.5 miles, from which you can access Widow Lake (a free wilderness permit is required from Lassen Volcanic National Park for overnight use). The left fork, on the other hand, leads to Twin Lakes over the course of just .5 mile.

Location: On the northern boundary of the Caribou Wilderness east of Lassen Volcanic National Park; map B3, grid j4.

User groups: Hikers, dogs and horses. No mountain bikes. No wheelchair facilities.

Permits: No permits are required. Parking and access are free.

Maps: A trail map is available for a fee from the Almanor Ranger District. For a map of Lassen National Forest, send $6 to U.S. Forest Service, Attn: Map Sales, P.O. Box 587, Camino, CA 95709; tel. (530) 647-5390, fax (530) 647-5389, or website: www.r5.fs.fed.us/visitorcenter. Major credit cards accepted. Ask the USGS for a topographic map of the Bogard Buttes area.

Directions: From Interstate 5 at Redding, turn east on Highway 44 and drive 60 miles to Highway 89/44. Turn left (north) on Highway 89/44 and drive 13 miles to Old Station. Just past Old Station, turn right (east) on Highway 44 and drive 30 miles to Bogard Work Station and nearby Forest Road 10. Turn right on Forest Road 10 and drive six miles to Forest Road 32N09. Then turn right on Forest Road 32N09 and drive three miles to the Cone Lake Trailhead. Note that the roads are unpaved from Highway 44 to the trailhead.

Contact: Lassen National Forest, Almanor Ranger District, P.O. Box 767, Chester, CA 96020; tel. (530) 258-2141 or fax (530) 258-5194.

19 Caribou Lake Trailhead

12.0 mi/2.0 days

The Caribou Lake Trailhead provides a hiking trip that is a parade past mountain lakes. Rarely are so many wilderness lakes this close to a trailhead. The trip starts at Caribou Lake, heading west, and in no time you pass all kinds of tiny lakes. The first one, Cowboy Lake, is only .25 mile down the trail. In another 15 minutes, you'll come to Jewel Lake. This procession of lakes never seems to stop—Eleanor Lake is next; then after turning left at the fork (two miles in), you pass Black Lake, North and South Divide Lakes, and farther on, Long Lake. This lake, six miles from the trailhead, should be your destination, since it makes a great two-day backpack adventure. The Caribou Wilderness is quite small, just nine miles from top to bottom, and only five miles across, with elevations ranging from 5,000 to 7,000 feet. This trip will provide a visit to the best of it.

Location: On the eastern boundary of the Caribou Wilderness east of Lassen Volcanic National Park; map B3, grid j5.

User groups: Hikers, dogs and horses (a horse corral is available at the trailhead). No mountain bikes. No wheelchair facilities.

Permits: A campfire permit (free) is required. Parking and access are free.

Maps: A trail map is available for a fee from the Almanor Ranger District. For a map of Lassen National Forest, send $6 to U.S. Forest Service, Attn: Map Sales, P.O. Box 587, Camino, CA 95709; tel. (530) 647-5390, fax (530) 647-5389, or website: www.r5.fs.fed.us/visitorcenter. Major credit cards accepted. Ask the USGS for a topographic map of the Red Cinder area.

Directions: From Interstate 5 at Red Bluff, turn east on Highway 36 and drive 83 miles to the town of Westwood (east of Lake Almanor) and County Road A21. Turn north on County Road A21 and go 14.1 miles to Silver Lake Road. Turn left on Silver Lake Road and drive five miles to a Y with Forest Road

10. Turn right on Forest Road 10 and drive .25 mile to a fork. Turn left and drive .25 mile to the trailhead.

Contact: Lassen National Forest, Almanor Ranger District, P.O. Box 767, Chester, CA 96020; tel. (530) 258-2141 or fax (530) 258-5194.

PACIFIC CREST TRAIL (PCT) SECTION OVERVIEW
114.0 mi one way/9.0 days

Trail sections extend from Lassen Volcanic National Park north to Shasta-Trinity National Forest west of McArthur-Burney Falls State Park.

You get a little bit of bliss, a little bit of paradise, then a big load of bull pucky on the 114-mile segment of the Pacific Crest Trail that crosses through this chapter's map. The bliss is in Lassen Volcanic National Park, where the trail passes by high mountain lakes circled with conifers and then goes by a strange but compelling volcanic area. The paradise comes at Burney Falls, a 129-foot waterfall that is a portrait of serenity along with nearby Lake Britton. Then it's off to no-man's-land, and here you'll be swearing your way up to Grizzly Peak in a place where water and breezes are rare and where an endless climb through brushy terrain will have you wondering why you're doing this. It gets worse when you can scarcely follow the trail because of logging roads, brush, and zero trail maintenance. Following is more specific information on major trail sections in this zone.

Lassen Volcanic National Park to Highway 44
32.0 mi one way/3.0 days ![] ![]

Every step is a pleasure in Lassen Volcanic National Park, starting from the wooded Warner Valley (at 5,680 feet) at Springs Creek and then heading north into the park's most remote terrain. The trail is routed across Grassy Swale, past Swan Lake, and on to Lower Twin Lake (seven miles in), a pretty body of water circled by conifers.

From here the trail heads north, skirting the western flank of Fairfield Peak (7,272 feet) and then onward, turning west past Soap Lake and Badger Flat, and continuing out past the park's boundary. As you hike toward Highway 44, you'll be lateraling Badger Mountain (6,973 feet) to your right, with the Hat Creek drainage off to your immediate left. In this latter stretch of trail, you'll cross no major lakes or streams (plan your water well), but just forge on through the national forest, mostly second-growth, crossing a few roads along the way. In the spring, wildflowers are exceptional on the Hat Creek rim. A small primitive U.S. Forest Service campground is located on the trail about 10 miles north of the border of Lassen Volcanic National Park.

Location: From Warner Valley Campground in Lassen Volcanic National Park to Highway 44; map B3, grid j3.

User groups: Hikers and horses. No dogs or mountain bikes are allowed in the Lassen Volcanic National Park section of the hike. No wheelchair facilities.

Permits: A wilderness permit (free) is required for hikers planning to camp in the Lassen Volcanic National Park backcountry and for equestrians. You may not camp with horses in the national park's backcountry, except a horse corral is available by reservation for overnighters at Summit Lake and Juniper Lake, and a small corral is located near the park's northern boundary for exclusive use for those on the Pacific Crest Trail. A $10 park entrance fee is charged each vehicle, or a $3 fee is charged each hiker.

Maps: Ask the USGS for topographic maps of the Reading Peak, West Prospect Peak, and Old Station areas of the route.

Directions: From Interstate 5 at Red Bluff, turn east on Highway 36 and drive 70 miles to the town of Chester and Feather River Drive. Turn left (north) and drive .75 mile to Warner Valley Road (signed Warner Valley and Drakesbad). Turn left and drive six miles to Warner Valley Road. Turn right and drive 11 miles (improved dirt) to the Warner Valley Campground and trailhead on the right.

Contact: Lassen Volcanic National Park, P.O. Box 100, Mineral, CA 96063-0100; tel. (530) 595-4444 or fax (530) 595-3262; Lassen National Forest, Hat Creek Ranger District, P.O. Box 220, Falls River Mills, CA 96028; tel. (530) 336-5521.

PCT-39 Highway 44 to McArthur-Burney Falls State Park

40.0 mi one way/3.0 days

The features of this segment of the Pacific Crest Trail are Hat Creek, Baum Lake, Crystal Lake, and the spectacular Burney Falls. From the trailhead at Highway 44, the trail passes through the wooded watershed of Hat Creek to a long, shadeless section that will have you counting the drops of water in your canteen. This is the infamous Hat Creek Rim section of the PCT, the roughest section of the entire route from Mexico to Canada, with no water available for 27 miles of trail. After departing from Hat Creek, the PCT heads past Baum and Crystal Lakes, the latter 27 miles in from the trailhead. You cross Highway 299, and from there it's an eight-mile romp to Burney Falls State Park and its breathtaking 129-foot waterfall.

Location: From the Highway 44 parking area north to McArthur-Burney Falls State Park; map B3, grid h3.

User groups: Hikers, dogs (except in the state park boundaries), and horses. No mountain bikes. No wheelchair facilities.

Permits: A campfire permit (free) is required. The state park entrance fee is $2 per vehicle.

Maps: Ask the USGS for topographic maps of the Cassel, Dana, Old Station, Murken Bench, Hogback Ridge, and Burney Falls areas of the route.

Directions: From Interstate 5 at Redding, turn east on Highway 44 and drive 60 miles to Highway 89/44. Turn left (north) on Highway 89/44 and drive 13 miles to Old Station. Just past Old Station, turn right (east) on Highway 44 and drive .25 mile beyond the Old Station Post Office to Forest Road 32N20. Turn right on Forest Road 32N20. The trail crosses the road about .5 mile from the junction of Highway 44 and Forest Road 32N20. If you have horses and need to park a horse trailer, use Mud Lake Trailhead, located three miles from the junction of Highway 89 and Highway 44.

Contact: Lassen National Forest, Hat Creek Ranger District, P.O. Box 220, Falls River Mills, CA 96028; tel. (530) 336-5521 or fax (530) 336-5758.

PCT-40 McArthur-Burney Falls State Park to Ash Camp

52.0 mi one way/4.0 days

It may be difficult to leave the woods, waters, and aura of Burney Falls, but off you go, facing dry country and some of Northern California's least-used portions of the Pacific Crest Trail. It's called Hat Creek Rim, but with no water for nearly 30 miles, most call it hell. Virtually the only hikers who complete this section are the ones hiking the entire route from Mexico to Canada; they're virtually forced to endure it, often at great hardship. This is the absolute worst section of the entire 2,700-mile PCT, where a single drop of water will be valued more than a $10,000 bill.

From Burney Falls the PCT heads west, touching the Pit River arm of Lake Britton, and then forward into Lassen Volcanic National Park, crossing into Shasta-Trinity National Forest and up to Grizzly Peak. Much of this route is across dry, hot exposed slopes, where the trail has deteriorated in many spots due to the encroachment of brush and zero trail maintenance by the U.S. Forest Service. Knowing you're smack between the lush beauty of Burney Falls (behind you) and the McCloud River (ahead of you) can make dealing with the present brush-infested landscape a frustrating encounter. Always fill your canteens with water wherever

you find it, and don't hesitate to make a camp if late in the day you find even a small flat spot with water nearby. Unfortunately, there just doesn't seem to be much water. In extremely dry years, you can go 30 miles without finding water. After the hot, beastly climb near Grizzly Peak, most hikers will want to make a lightning-fast descent to the Eden of the McCloud River at Ash Camp. But hold your horses. As long as you've come this far, make the short side trip to Grizzly Peak, and while you're looking at the incredible view of Mount Shasta and the McCloud flats, congratulate yourself for completing such a terrible hike. Considering the PCT is the feature national recreation trail in America, this stretch is an embarrassment to the U.S. Forest Service and an abomination to hikers.

Location: From McArthur-Burney Falls State Park west into Ash Camp in Shasta-Trinity National Forest; map B3, grid e1.

User groups: Hikers, dogs (except in the state park boundaries), and horses. No mountain bikes. No wheelchair facilities.

Permits: A campfire permit (free) is required. A $2 fee is charged per vehicle at the state park.

Maps: Ask the USGS for topographic maps of the Burney Falls, Skunk Ridge, and Grizzly Peak areas of the route.

Directions: From Interstate 5 at Redding, turn east on Highway 299 and drive 50 miles to Burney. Continue five miles east on Highway 299 to Highway 89. Turn north on Highway 89 and drive 5.8 miles to the state park entrance. Follow the signs to the trailhead.

Contact: McArthur-Burney Falls State Park, 24898 Highway 89, Burney, CA 96013; tel. (530) 335-2777 or fax (530) 335-5483.

PCT Continuation

To continue hiking along the Pacific Crest Trail, see chapter B2.

A GRAZING DOE

MAP B4

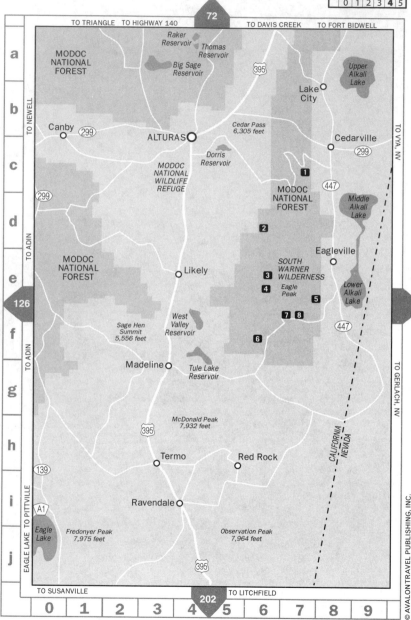

TO TRIANGLE   TO HIGHWAY 140   TO DAVIS CREEK   TO FORT BIDWELL

72

a MODOC NATIONAL FOREST — Raker Reservoir — Thomas Reservoir — Big Sage Reservoir — Upper Alkali Lake

395

b TO NEWELL — Canby (299) — ALTURAS — Cedar Pass 6,305 feet — Lake City — Cedarville (299) — TO VYA, NV

c MODOC NATIONAL WILDLIFE REFUGE — Dorris Reservoir — MODOC NATIONAL FOREST — **1** — (447)

299

Middle Alkali Lake

d **2** — Eagleville

e MODOC NATIONAL FOREST — Likely — SOUTH WARNER WILDERNESS — **3** — **4** Eagle Peak — **5** — Lower Alkali Lake

126 — TO ADIN

f Sage Hen Summit 5,556 feet — West Valley Reservoir — **7** **8** — **6** — (447)

g Madeline — Tule Lake Reservoir

h McDonald Peak 7,932 feet — 395 — Termo — Red Rock

i (139) — A1 — Ravendale

j Eagle Lake — Fredonyer Peak 7,975 feet — Observation Peak 7,964 feet

CALIFORNIA NEVADA

TO ADIN — EAGLE LAKE — TO PITTVILLE

TO GERLACH, NV

395

TO SUSANVILLE   TO LITCHFIELD

202

© AVALON TRAVEL PUBLISHING, INC.

0 1 2 3 4 5 6 7 8 9

CHAPTER B4

1 Pepperdine Trailhead. . . 143

2 Pine Creek Trailhead . . . 143

3 Soup Spring Trailhead. . 144

4 Mill Creek Falls
Trailhead. 144

5 Emerson Trailhead. 145

6 Blue Lake Loop 145

7 East Creek Loop 146

8 Summit Trail. 146

1 Pepperdine Trailhead

12.0 mi/2.0 days

The six-mile trip on the Summit Trail to Patterson Lake is the most popular hike in the South Warner Wilderness. That still doesn't mean you'll run into other people or horses, because the Warners are a remote, lonely place rarely visited by hikers from the Bay Area, Sacramento, or Los Angeles. Patterson Lake is set in a rock basin at 9,000 feet, just below Warren Peak (9,718 feet), the highest lake in the wilderness and the highlight destination for most visitors. The Pepperdine Trailhead at 6,900 feet is located just beyond Porter Reservoir, where a primitive campground and a horse corral are available. The hike is a sustained climb, gaining 2,100 feet, passing to the right of Squaw Peak (8,646 feet) and then tiny Cottonwood Lake. From Squaw Peak looking east, you'll feel as if you're looking across hundreds of miles of a stark, uninhabited landscape.

Location: On the northern boundary of the South Warner Wilderness east of Alturas; map B4, grid c7.

User groups: Hikers, dogs, and horses. No mountain bikes. No wheelchair facilities.

Permits: A campfire permit (free) is required. Parking and access are free.

Maps: For a map of the South Warner Wilder-

ness, send $6 to U.S. Forest Service, Attn: Map Sales, P.O. Box 587, Camino, CA 95709; tel. (530) 647-5390, fax (530) 647-5389, or website: www.r5.fs.fed.us/visitorcenter. Major credit cards accepted. Ask the USGS for a topographic map of the Warren Peak area.

Directions: From U.S. 395 at the south end of Alturas, turn east on County Road 56 and drive 13 miles to the Modoc National Forest boundary and Parker Creek Road. Turn left and drive six miles on Parker Creek Road and the sign for Pepperdine Campground. Turn right and drive to the trailhead.

Contact: Modoc National Forest, Warner Mountain Ranger District, P.O. Box 220, Cedarville, CA 96104; tel. (530) 279-6116 or fax (530) 279-8309.

2 Pine Creek Trailhead

4.0 mi/3.0 hrs

Modoc County is the least populated and least-known region of California, with only 10,000 residents sprinkled across a huge area. Yet there are many outstanding adventures available here, including one of the truly great short hikes available anywhere. The Pine Creek Trail is a magnificent traipse into the beautiful South Warner Wilderness.

The trail starts along the South Fork of Pine Creek, about 6,800 feet in elevation, then heads straight east into the wilderness, climbing the lush western slopes. In the course of two miles, the trail rises 1,000 feet to the Pine Creek Basin. Along the trail are several small lakes, the largest being the two set right along the trail as you enter the basin. Above you is a stark, volcanic-faced rim with few trees, where the headwaters of eight small creeks start from springs, pour down the mountain, join, and flow into several small lakes. To lengthen the hike, go on to Patterson Lake, a gorgeous mountain lake surrounded by towering rock walls; round trip is 11 miles.

Location: On the northwestern boundary of the South Warner Wilderness east of Alturas; map B4, grid d6.

User groups: Hikers, dogs, and horses. No mountain bikes. No wheelchair facilities.

Permits: No permit is required. Parking and access are free.

Maps: For a map of the South Warner Wilderness, send $6 to U.S. Forest Service, Attn: Map Sales, P.O. Box 587, Camino, CA 95709; tel. (530) 647-5390, fax (530) 647-5389, or website: www.r5.fs.fed.us/visitorcenter. Major credit cards accepted. Ask the USGS for a topographic map of the Eagle Peak area.

Directions: On U.S. 395 at the south end of Alturas, turn east on County Road 56 and drive 13 miles to the Modoc National Forest boundary. Turn south on West Warner Road and go about 10 miles to the sign for the Pine Creek Trailhead. Turn left (east) and head 1.75 miles to the parking area. The road is unpaved for the last 12 miles.

Contact: Modoc National Forest, Warner Mountain Ranger District, P.O. Box 220, Cedarville, CA 96104; tel. (530) 279-6116 or fax (530) 279-8309.

❸ Soup Spring Trailhead

3.0 mi/2.0 hrs

Mill Creek is a small, pristine trout stream that brings the lonely Warner Mountains to life. It's a short hike to get here, up a hill and then down, heading into a valley. On this valley floor you'll find Mill Creek, only a 1.5-mile walk out of the Soup Spring Trailhead. Mill Creek is a great spot for a picnic lunch or a high-finesse fishing trip. The trout are extremely sensitive, so anything clumsy, like letting your shadow hit the water or clanking your boots on the shore, will spook them off the bite. The trout are small, dark, and chunky, unlike any seen elsewhere.

Some hikers use the Soup Spring Trail as a way of climbing up near the Warner Rim and intersecting with the Summit Trail, the feature hike in the South Warner Wilderness. That makes sense, with a primitive campground and corral at the trailhead and then a four-mile romp uphill to the Summit Trail junction. It includes a 1,000-foot climb on the way, with the trail routed up the Slide Creek Canyon over the last two miles.

Location: On the western boundary of the South Warner Wilderness east of Alturas; map B4, grid e6.

User groups: Hikers, dogs, and horses. No mountain bikes. No wheelchair facilities.

Permits: No permit is required. Parking and access are free.

Maps: For a map of the South Warner Wilderness, send $6 to U.S. Forest Service, Attn: Map Sales, P.O. Box 587, Camino, CA 95709; tel. (530) 647-5390, fax (530) 647-5389, or website: www.r5.fs.fed.us/visitorcenter. Major credit cards accepted. Ask the USGS for a topographic map of the Eagle Peak area.

Directions: From Alturas, drive south on U.S. 395 for 18.5 miles to Likely and Jess Valley Road (County Road 64). Turn east on Jess Valley Road and drive nine miles to West Warner Road (Forest Road 5). Turn left on West Warner Road (Forest Road 5) and drive 4.5 miles to Soup Loop Road (Forest Road 40N24). Turn right and drive six miles (a gravel road) to the campground parking lot on the right.

Contact: Modoc National Forest, Warner Mountain Ranger District, P.O. Box 220, Cedarville, CA 96104; tel. (530) 279-6116 or fax (530) 279-8309.

❹ Mill Creek Falls Trailhead

0.5 mi/0.5 hr

The short, easy walk from the Mill Creek Falls Trailhead to Clear Lake will lead you to one of the prettiest spots in Modoc County. It's a half mile to Mill Creek Falls and another half mile to Clear Lake. At the fork, bear left for the waterfalls, bear right for the lake. Most hikers will take in both. The trail skirts along the perimeter of a pretty lake, high mountain water set at 6,000 feet. Of the lakes and streams in the Warners, it's Clear Lake that has the largest fish, with brown and rainbow trout ranging to more than 10 pounds. There just aren't many of them. Backpackers can head onward from Clear Lake on the Poison Flat Trail, but expect a very steep howler of a climb before intersecting with the Mill Creek Trail.

Location: On the southwestern boundary of the South Warner Wilderness east of Alturas; map B4, grid e6.

User groups: Hikers, dogs and horses. Some wheelchair-accessible facilities are available at nearby campgrounds. No mountain bikes.

Permits: No permit is required. Parking and access are free.

Maps: For a map of the South Warner Wilderness, send $6 to U.S. Forest Service, Attn: Map Sales, P.O. Box 587, Camino, CA 95709; tel. (530) 647-5390, fax (530) 647-5389, or website: www.r5.fs.fed.us/visitorcenter. Major credit cards accepted. Ask the USGS for a topographic map of the Eagle Peak area.

Directions: From Alturas, drive south on U.S. 395 about 18.5 miles to Likely and Jess Valley Road (County Road 64). Turn east on Jess Valley Road and drive nine miles to a fork. At the fork, bear left on Forest Road 5 and drive 2.5 miles to Forest Road 40N46. Turn right and drive two miles to the trailhead.

Contact: Modoc National Forest, Warner Mountain Ranger District, P.O. Box 220, Cedarville, CA 96104; tel. (530) 279-6116 or fax (530) 279-8309.

5 Emerson Trailhead

7.0 mi/2.0 days

Don't be yelpin' about the dreadful climb up to North Emerson Lake, because we're warning you right here, loud and clear, that it qualifies as a first-class butt-kicker. If you choose to go anyway, well, you asked for it. The trail climbs 2,000 feet in 3.5 miles, but much of that is in a hellish half-mile stretch that'll have you howling for relief. Your reward is little North Emerson Lake at 7,800 feet, a wonderland in a rock bowl with a high sheer back wall.

The Emerson Trailhead, the most remote of those providing access to the Warners, is located on the east side of the mountain rim near stark, dry country. A primitive campground is available here at the trailhead. Out of camp take the North Emerson Trail. And while you're at it, get yourself in the right frame of mind to cheerfully accept that you'll be getting your butt kicked. But rest assured that North Emerson Lake is worth every step.

Location: On the eastern boundary of the South Warner Wilderness east of Alturas; map B4, grid e7.

User groups: Hikers, dogs, and horses. No mountain bikes. No wheelchair facilities.

Permits: A campfire permit (free) is required. Parking and access are free.

Maps: For a map of the South Warner Wilderness, send $6 to U.S. Forest Service, Attn: Map Sales, P.O. Box 587, Camino, CA 95709; tel. (530) 647-5390, fax (530) 647-5389, or website: www.r5.fs.fed.us/visitorcenter. Major credit cards accepted. Ask the USGS for a topographic map of the Emerson Peak area.

Directions: From Alturas turn east on Highway 299 and drive 22 miles to Cedarville. Turn south on County Road 1 and go about 16 miles to Eagleville. Drive another 1.5 miles south on County Road 1, turn right on Emerson Road, and head three miles to the trailhead. Emerson Road is very steep and can be slippery when wet.

Contact: Modoc National Forest, Warner Mountain Ranger District, P.O. Box 220, Cedarville, CA 96104; tel. (530) 279-6116 or fax (530) 279-8309.

6 Blue Lake Loop

2.0 mi/1.25 hrs

Blue Lake, shaped like an egg and rimmed with trees, is one of the prettiest lakes you can reach by driving. That makes the easy two-mile loop hike around the lake on the Blue Lake Loop National Recreation Trail very special. With a campground at the lake, this trail makes a good side trip for overnight visitors. In addition, a fishing pier and wheelchair-accessible restroom are available. A bonus is that there are some huge trout in this lake—brown trout in the 10-pound class—and they provide quite a treasure hunt amid good numbers of foot-long rainbow trout.

Location: At Blue Lake in Modoc National Forest southeast of Alturas; map B4, grid f6.

User groups: Hikers and dogs. The fishing pier and restroom are wheelchair accessible. No horses or mountain bikes.

Permits: No permit is required. Parking and access are free.

Maps: For a map of Modoc National Forest, send $6 to U.S. Forest Service, Attn: Map Sales, P.O. Box 587, Camino, CA 95709; tel. (530) 647-5390, fax (530) 647-5389, or website: www.r5.fs.fed.us/visitorcenter. Major credit cards accepted. Ask the USGS for a topographic map of the Jess Valley area.

Directions: From Alturas drive south on U.S. 395 about 18.5 miles to Likely. Turn east on Jess Valley Road (County Road 64) and drive nine miles to a fork. When the road forks, bear right on Blue Lake Road (Forest Road 64) and drive seven miles to Forest Road 39N30 (signed for Blue Lake). Turn right and drive to the parking area.

Contact: Modoc National Forest, Warner Mountain Ranger District, P.O. Box 220, Cedarville, CA 96104; tel. (530) 279-6116 or fax (530) 279-8309.

⑦ East Creek Loop
15.0 mi/2.0 days

The East Creek Loop is our favorite loop hike in the Warner Mountains. It can be completed in a weekend, not including driving time, and provides a capsule look at the amazing contrasts of the Warners. The hike includes small, pristine streams as well as high, barren mountain rims. The East Creek Trail, elevation 7,100 feet, is routed 5.5 miles north into the wilderness. Just before the junction with Poison Flat Trail, a spring is located on the left side of the trail. Don't miss it—you'll need the water for the upcoming climb. Turn right at the junction with the Poison Flat Trail to make the 800-foot climb above tree line and turn right again on the Summit Trail.

The loop is completed by taking the Summit Trail back south, crossing high, stark country, most of it more than 8,000 feet in elevation. In the last two miles the trail drops sharply, descending 1,000 feet on the way to Patterson Campground, which marks the end of the loop trail. Reaching the parking area at East Creek Trailhead requires a half-mile walk on the Forest Road.

Location: On the southern boundary of the South Warner Wilderness east of Alturas; map B4, grid f7.

User groups: Hikers, dogs, and horses. No mountain bikes. No wheelchair facilities.

Permits: A campfire permit (free) is required. Parking and access are free.

Maps: For a map of the South Warner Wilderness, send $6 to U.S. Forest Service, Attn: Map Sales, P.O. Box 587, Camino, CA 95709; tel. (530) 647-5390, fax (530) 647-5389, or website: www.r5.fs.fed.us/visitorcenter. Major credit cards accepted. Ask the USGS for a topographic map of the Emerson Peak area.

Directions: From Alturas drive south on U.S. 395 about 18.5 miles to Likely and Jess Valley Road (County Road 64). Turn east on Jess Valley Road and drive nine miles to South Warner Road (Forest Road 64). Turn right and drive southeast (heading toward Patterson Campground) to the access road for East Creek Trail. Turn left and drive a short distance to the parking area.

Contact: Modoc National Forest, Warner Mountain Ranger District, P.O. Box 220, Cedarville, CA 96104; tel. (530) 279-6116 or fax (530) 279-8309.

⑧ Summit Trail
45.0 mi/4.0 days

The Warner Mountains have a mystique about them, a charm cultivated by the thoughts of hikers who dream of an area where the landscape is remote and untouched and the trails are empty. That is why the Summit Loop is the backpacking trek that most hikers yearn to take someday. However, only rarely do they get around to it. For most, the Warners are just too remote and too far away, and the trip requires too much time. If you are one of the lucky few to get here, you'll find this hike traverses both sides of the Warner ridge, providing an intimate look at a diverse place. The west side of the Warner Mountains is a habitat filled with small pine trees, meadows, and the headwaters of many small streams. The east side, however, is stark and rugged, with great long-distance lookouts to the east across high desert and miles of sagebrush and juniper.

Start the trip at the Patterson Camp Trailhead, elevation 7,200 feet, and from there the trail climbs quickly, rising to 8,200 feet in two miles, accessing high, barren country. Great views abound from here as you head north. To reach the north end of the wilderness, take the turn at the Owl Creek Trail and hike to Linderman Lake, set at the foot of Devils Knob (8,776 feet), and beyond past Squaw Peak (8,646 feet). To return, make the hairpin left turn at the Summit Trail and walk back on the mostly lush western slopes of the Warners. Highlights on the return loop include Patterson Lake (9,000 feet), the headwaters of Mill Creek and North Fork East Creek, and many beautiful and fragile meadows. The trail ends at the East Creek parking area, a half-mile walk from the Patterson Camp Trailhead. Savor every moment of this trip—it's one of the greatest little-known hikes anywhere in the United States.

Location: On the southern boundary of the South Warner Wilderness east of Alturas; map B4, grid f7.

User groups: Hikers, dogs, and horses. No mountain bikes. No wheelchair facilities.

Permits: A campfire permit (free) is required. Parking and access are free.

Maps: For a map of the South Warner Wilderness, send $6 to U.S. Forest Service, Attn: Map Sales, P.O. Box 587, Camino, CA 95709; tel. (530) 647-5390, fax (530) 647-5389, or website: www.r5.fs.fed.us/visitorcenter. Major credit cards accepted. Ask the USGS for a topographic map of the Emerson Peak area.

Directions: From Alturas, drive south on U.S. 395 for 18.5 miles to Likely and Jess Valley Road (County Road 64). Turn east on Jess Valley Road and drive nine miles to South Warner Road (Forest Road 64). Turn right and drive 16 miles to Patterson Campground. The trailhead is at the camp.

Contact: Modoc National Forest, Warner Mountain Ranger District, P.O. Box 220, Cedarville, CA 96104; tel. (530) 279-6116 or fax (530) 279-8309.

THE MENDOCINO COUNTY COASTLINE

MAP C0

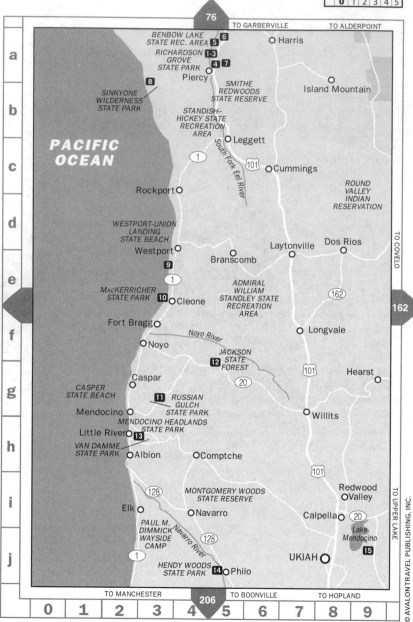

76

PACIFIC OCEAN

BENBOW LAKE STATE REC. AREA **5** **6**

Harris

RICHARDSON GROVE STATE PARK **1-3** **4** **7**

Piercy

SMITHE REDWOODS STATE RESERVE

Island Mountain

SINKYONE WILDERNESS STATE PARK **8**

STANDISH–HICKEY STATE RECREATION AREA

South Fork Eel River

Leggett

101 Cummings

ROUND VALLEY INDIAN RESERVATION

Rockport

WESTPORT-UNION LANDING STATE BEACH

Westport **9**

Branscomb

Laytonville   Dos Rios

TO COVELO

MACKERRICHER STATE PARK **10** Cleone

ADMIRAL WILLIAM STANDLEY STATE RECREATION AREA

162

162

Fort Bragg

Noyo River

Noyo

JACKSON STATE FOREST **12**

Longvale

101

Hearst

CASPER STATE BEACH

Caspar

20

RUSSIAN GULCH STATE PARK **11**

Mendocino

MENDOCINO HEADLANDS STATE PARK

Willits

Little River **13**

VAN DAMME STATE PARK

Albion   Comptche

101

MONTGOMERY WOODS STATE RESERVE

Redwood Valley

128

Elk

Navarro

Calpella **20**

TO UPPER LAKE

PAUL M. DIMMICK WAYSIDE CAMP

Navarro River

128

Lake Mendocino

UKIAH **15**

1

HENDY WOODS STATE PARK **14** Philo

206

© AVALON TRAVEL PUBLISHING, INC.

CHAPTER C0

1 Lookout Point
   Loop Trail 151
2 Durphy Creek Loop 151
3 Redwood Exhibit Trail . . 152
4 Settlers Loop Trail 152
5 Woodlands Loop Trail . . 153
6 Pioneer Trail Loop 153
7 Toumey Grove Trail 154
8 Lost Coast Trail 154

9 Bruhel Point Tide Pools . 155
10 Lake Cleone Trail 155
11 Falls Loop Trail 156
12 Chamberlain Creek
   Waterfall Trail 157
13 Fern Canyon Trail 157
14 Big Hendy
   Grove Trail 158
15 Glen Eden Trail 158

1 Lookout Point Loop Trail

1.7 mi/1.0 hr

Big woods. Big water. That's what the Lookout Point Loop Trail supplies, with a tour through giant redwoods culminating at the canyon rim over the South Fork Eel River. Giant redwoods approaching 300 feet tall and an estimated 1,000 years old are the highlight of Richardson Grove, while younger redwoods, fir, and tan oak fill out the forest. To be honest, if you look close, there's actually more tanoak and fir than redwoods. The trail passes through forest and rises to Lookout Point, where there's an excellent view of the South Fork. You can also see the Oak Flat Campground from here. As a free-flowing river, the South Fork Eel River can seem like a small trickle in late summer or a howling torrent during peak flows in winter. When looking down from Lookout Point during summer, it may seem hard to imagine how high the Eel has risen in high-water years. In 1955, 1963, 1986, 1997, and 1998, the river actually flooded its banks and wiped out several campgrounds in the state park. This is an easy and popular hike, both for daytime park visitors and for overnighters at Madrone Camp.

Location: In Richardson Grove State Park south of Garberville; map C0, grid a4.

User groups: Hikers only. No dogs, horses, or mountain bikes. No wheelchair facilities.

Permits: No permits are required. A $2 state park entrance fee is charged for each vehicle.

Maps: For a trail guide and brochure, send $1.50 to Richardson Grove State Park at the address below. Ask the USGS for a topographic map of the Garberville area.

Directions: From Santa Rosa drive north on U.S. 101 to Leggett. Continue north on U.S. 101 about 17 miles to the park entrance on the west side of the highway. Follow the signs to the Redwood Day-Use Parking Area. Access to the trailhead is at the parking area and also out of Madrone Campground.

Contact: Richardson Grove State Park, c/o California State Parks, North Coast Redwoods District, Piercy Sector, 1600 U.S. Highway 101, No. 8, Garberville, CA 95542; tel. (707) 247-3319 or fax (707) 247-3300; phone the park ranger station at (707) 247-3318.

2 Durphy Creek Loop

4.0 mi/3.0 hrs

Be ready for a good climb, have a full canteen of water, and note that no whiners are allowed. Why? Because this loop trail is the most challenging hike in Richardson

Grove State Park. It starts easily enough, routed right along the left side of Durphy Creek at a tolerable grade. But when the trail turns left and starts to climb up the canyon, all tolerance is forgotten. The trail climbs 800 feet in less than .5 mile, with a short cutoff to Tan Oak Springs, then onward to the ridge at 1,400 feet. On the way back down, the route descends through a dense forest of tan oaks and is quite steep in the last .5 mile, including some switchbacks. To complete the loop, turn left at the Lookout Point Trail and hike back toward Madrone Campground.

Location: In Richardson Grove State Park south of Garberville; map C0, grid a4.

User groups: Hikers only. No dogs, horses, or mountain bikes. No wheelchair facilities.

Permits: No permits are required. A $2 state park entrance fee is charged for each vehicle.

Maps: For a trail guide and brochure, send $1 to Richardson Grove State Park at the address below. Ask the USGS for a topographic map of the Garberville area.

Directions: From Santa Rosa drive north on U.S. 101 to Leggett. Continue north on U.S. 101 about 17 miles to the park entrance on the west side of the highway. Follow the signs to the Redwood Day-Use Parking Area. Walk .25 mile to Madrone Campground and to the trailhead.

Contact: Richardson Grove State Park, c/o California State Parks, North Coast Redwoods District, Piercy Sector, 1600 U.S. Highway 101, No. 8, Garberville, CA 95542; tel. (707) 247-3319 or fax (707) 247-3300; phone the park ranger station at (707) 247-3318.

3 Redwood Exhibit Trail
0.25 mi/0.25 hr

U.S. 101 cuts a swath right through the center of Richardson Grove State Park, and even the long-distance freeway burners slow down to 25 mph to gawk at the giant redwoods. Some even stop. If that includes you, the Redwood Exhibit Trail furnishes a short, easy stroll amid many of the park's largest and oldest trees. It is an interpretive trail with signs explaining the natural history of the area. The actual exhibit trail is only .25 mile long, but it's possible to continue on, linking up with the Lookout Point Trail (above). After walking among those old giant redwoods, you may notice that you don't have the desire to drive quite so fast on the highway anymore.

Location: In Richardson Grove State Park south of Garberville; map C0, grid a4.

User groups: Hikers and dogs. No horses or mountain bikes. No wheelchair facilities.

Permits: No permits are required. A $2 state park entrance fee is charged for each vehicle.

Maps: For a trail guide and brochure, send $1 to Richardson Grove State Park at the address below. Ask the USGS for a topographic map of the Garberville area.

Directions: From Santa Rosa drive north on U.S. 101 to Leggett. Continue north on U.S. 101 about 17 miles to the park entrance on the west side of the highway. Follow the signs to the visitor center parking area. The trailhead is located in the parking area.

Contact: Richardson Grove State Park, c/o California State Parks, North Coast Redwoods District, Piercy Sector, 1600 U.S. Highway 101, No. 8, Garberville, CA 95542; tel. (707) 247-3319 or fax (707) 247-3300; phone the park ranger station at (707) 247-3318.

4 Settlers Loop Trail
0.7 mi/0.5 hr

The Settlers Loop Trail is the most popular hike for campers staying at the Oak Flat Campground, the largest camp in Richardson Grove State Park. The trail is short and simple, set on the east side of the South Fork Eel River, and features an easy walk through Settler's Meadow. If you want to extend the hike, the Settlers Loop Trail intersects with the southern end of the Toumey Grove Trail (below). From this intersection the Toumey Trail climbs 250 feet over the course of about .5 mile to reach Panorama Point. From here you'll have a sweeping view of Richardson Grove's giant redwoods, well worth the short climb.

Location: In Richardson Grove State Park south of Garberville; map C0, grid a4.

User groups: Hikers only. No dogs, horses, or mountain bikes. No wheelchair facilities.

Permits: No permits are required. A $2 state park entrance fee is charged for each vehicle.

Maps: For a trail guide and brochure, send $1 to Richardson Grove State Park at the address below. Ask the USGS for a topographic map of the Garberville area.

Directions: From Santa Rosa drive north on U.S. 101 to Leggett. Continue north on U.S. 101 about 17 miles to the park entrance on the west side of the highway. Drive one mile to the Oak Flat Campground. The trailhead is located between campsites 123 and 126.

Contact: Richardson Grove State Park, c/o California State Parks, North Coast Redwoods District, Piercy Sector, 1600 U.S. Highway 101, No. 8, Garberville, CA 95542; tel. (707) 247-3319 or fax (707) 247-3300; phone the park ranger station at (707) 247-3318.

5 Woodlands Loop Trail
1.6 mi/1.0 hr

You want easy? You get easy. You want forest? You get forest. You want a campground trailhead? You get a campground trailhead. The Woodlands Loop, an easy, pretty trail that starts at the Huckleberry Campground, does all that and more. The trail crosses North Creek and then goes through both redwoods and tan oaks that are dense at times. It also includes a gentle uphill portion, rising about 250 feet. The trail and camp are set on the west side of U.S. 101, and with the South Fork Eel River on the east side of the highway, there's no direct river access from this trail or the nearby campground.

Location: In Richardson Grove State Park south of Garberville; map C0, grid a4.

User groups: Hikers only. No dogs, horses, or mountain bikes. No wheelchair facilities.

Permits: No permits are required. A $2 state park entrance fee is charged for each vehicle.

Maps: For a trail guide and brochure, send $1 to Richardson Grove State Park at the address below. Ask the USGS for a topographic map of the Garberville area.

Directions: From Santa Rosa drive north on U.S. 101 to Leggett. Continue north on U.S. 101 about 17 miles to the park entrance on the west side of the highway. The trailhead is accessible from the parking lot just inside the entrance.

Contact: Richardson Grove State Park, c/o California State Parks, North Coast Redwoods District, Piercy Sector, 1600 U.S. Highway 101, No. 8, Garberville, CA 95542; tel. (707) 247-3319 or fax (707) 247-3300; phone the park ranger station at (707) 247-3318.

6 Pioneer Trail Loop
2.8 mi/2.0 hrs

You can scan map after map and never find Benbow Lake. In fact, in the future you might be able to scan the landscape here and not find it either. That is because for many years Benbow Lake has been a seasonal lake, created each summer only by a temporary dam on the Eel River. Because of declines in the steelhead population, the dam was prohibited in 2000 and in 2001. The soonest the lake will reappear will be 2002. And it may never go in again if the steelhead are listed as endangered. When the Eel is dammed, Benbow Lake becomes a popular recreation site for sunbathing, swimming, non-powerboating, and camping. Hiking is a popular alternative, especially on this loop trail.

Start on the Pratt Mill Trail near campsite number 57 at an elevation of 400 feet; you can create a 3.5-mile loop by connecting to the Pioneer Trail. This route features some river frontage, a sprinkling of giant redwoods, a meadow, and a portion of trail along the Eel River drainage (Benbow Lake).

Location: In Benbow Lake State Recreation Area south of Garberville; map C0, grid a5.

User groups: Hikers only. No dogs, horses, or mountain bikes. No wheelchair facilities.

Permits: No permits are required. A $2 state park entrance fee is charged for each vehicle.

Maps: A map and brochure can be obtained by contacting Benbow Lake State Recreation Area at the address below. Ask the USGS for a topographic map of the Garberville area.

Directions: From Santa Rosa drive north on U.S. 101 to Leggett and continue for 22 miles to the Benbow exit. Take the Benbow exit, turn right on Benbow Drive, and drive one mile to the Benbow Lake State Recreation Area Campground. The trailhead is located next to campsite number 57.

Contact: Benbow Lake State Recreation Area, c/o California State Parks, North Coast Redwoods District, Piercy Sector, 1600 U.S. Highway 101, No. 8, Garberville, CA 95542; tel. (707) 247-3319 or fax (707) 247-3300; phone Benbow Lake at (707) 923-3238.

7 Toumey Grove Trail

3.8 mi/2.75 hrs

The Toumey Trail is one of Richardson Grove State Park's feature summer hikes. It includes walking over the South Fork Eel River on the summer bridge, through a majestic stand of old redwoods, up to Kauffman Springs, and beyond to the Panorama Point Lookout. The trailhead is located between campsites 123 and 126 at Oak Flat Campground. The trail crosses the river and enters the redwoods; take your time and enjoy the surroundings. The trail climbs 300 feet, rising quickly with a few switchbacks, and arrives at Panorama Point, with excellent views of the Eel River Canyon and Richardson Grove Redwoods.

Special note: This trail can be accessed only in the summer months.

Location: In Richardson Grove State Park south of Garberville; map C0, grid a5.

User groups: Hikers only. No dogs, horses, or mountain bikes. No wheelchair facilities.

Permits: No permits are required. A $2 state park entrance fee is charged for each vehicle.

Maps: For a trail guide and brochure, send $1 to Richardson Grove State Park at the address below. Ask the USGS for a topographic map of the Garberville area.

Directions: From Santa Rosa drive north on U.S. 101 to Leggett. Continue north on U.S. 101 about 17 miles to the park entrance on the west side of the highway. Follow the signs to Oak Flat Campground. The trailhead is located between campsites 123 and 126. This trail is open only in the summer months.

Contact: Richardson Grove State Park, c/o California State Parks, North Coast Redwoods District, Piercy Sector, 1600 U.S. Highway 101, No. 8, Garberville, CA 95542; tel. (707) 247-3319 or fax (707) 247-3300; phone the park ranger station at (707) 247-3318.

8 Lost Coast Trail

16.7 mi one way/2.0 days

The remote and rugged wilderness, covering more than 7,000 acres, symbolizes the Northern California coast is now protected forever in Sinkyone Wilderness State Park. Not many folks hike it or even know how to get here. There are no directional signs along roads, no highways leading here, and the park is virtually never promoted. The few people that do visit will find a primitive, steep, and unforgiving terrain that provides a rare coastal wilderness experience. The best way to get it is on the Lost Coast Trail, best hiked north to south to keep the north winds out of your face.

From the northern trailhead at Orchard Camp, we advise you to split your trip in two by camping at Little Jackass Creek Camp. That will make your first day's hike 10.2 miles, the second 6.5 miles. Following is a more detailed breakdown.

Day 1: From the trailhead at Orchard Camp, the trail starts out flat and pleasant, arcing around Bear Harbor Cove. From here the trail climbs 800 feet and then back down, passing through a redwood grove and also breaking out for sweeping coastal views. Enjoy them because the hike gets more difficult, including a steep climb up, over, and down a mountain, finally descending into Little Jackass Creek

Camp, set beside a small stream. Day 2: The closeout of a two-day hike should always be as enjoyable as possible, and so it is here, with divine views in many spots along the 6.5-mile route. Alas, there's usually payment for views, and that payment comes in several rugged climbs in the park's most remote sections. After climbing to nearly 1,000 feet, the trail ends with an 800-foot downgrade over the last mile, descending to the Usal Campground parking area.

Special note: At the northern boundary of the Sinkyone Wilderness, this trail continues north into the King Range National Conservation Area, where it's routed for another 30 miles to the mouth of the Mattole River. See chapter B0 for more hikes in this area.

Location: In Sinkyone Wilderness State Park south to Usal Campground on the Mendocino coast; map C0, grid a3.

User groups: Hikers only. Horses are allowed only on the section of trail between the trailhead at the park entrance and Wheeler Camp. No dogs or mountain bikes. No wheelchair facilities.

Permits: No permits are required. Parking and access are free unless you plan to camp.

Maps: A trail map and brochure can be obtained by sending $1.50 to Sinkyone Wilderness State Park at the address below. Ask the USGS for a topographic map of the Bear Harbor area.

Directions: From U.S. 101 north of Garberville, take the Redway exit to Briceland Road. Turn west on Briceland Road and drive 17 miles to Whitethorn. From Whitethorn, continue six miles to the Four Corners Fork. Continue straight ahead and drive six miles on a gravel road to the Needle Rock Ranger Station. Continue past the ranger station to the visitor center, and park at Orchard Camp. Be aware that the access road is unpaved, that it may close unexpectedly in the winter, and that four-wheel-drive vehicles are often required in wet weather. There are few signs pointing the way to the park. Trailers and RVs are not recommended.

Contact: Sinkyone Wilderness State Recreation Area, P.O. Box 245, Whitethorn, CA 95489; tel. (707) 986-7711; California State Parks, North Coast Redwoods District, Piercy Sector, tel. (707) 247-3319 or fax (707) 247-3300.

9 Bruhel Point Tide Pools
1.2 mi/1.0 hr

Some of the best tide pools on the Pacific Coast can be found in Mendocino, and one of the best of the best is here, located just south of Bruhel Point. When you first arrive, you'll find a CalTrans roadside vista point (no overnight parking), restrooms, and a beach access trail. This is your calling. The trail is routed north toward Bruhel Point, much of it along the edge of ocean bluffs. We don't recommend freelancing a descent down the bluff but rather urge you to take only the cutoff trails, which lead to the best tide-pool areas. Time your trip during a low tide or better yet, a minus low tide. That is when the ocean pulls back, leaving a series of holes and cuts in a rock basin that remain filled with water, providing the perfect habitat and viewing areas for all kinds of tiny marine life.

Location: On the Mendocino coast north of Fort Bragg; map C0, grid e3.

User groups: Hikers and dogs. Not suitable for mountain bikes or horses. No wheelchair facilities.

Permits: No permits are required. Parking and access are free.

Maps: Ask the USGS for a topographic map of the Inglenook area.

Directions: From Westport drive south on Highway 1 about two miles to milepost marker 74.09. The tide pools are located a short walk from the CalTrans Vista Point parking lot.

Contact: No managing agency for contact.

10 Lake Cleone Trail
1.2 mi/0.5 hr

MacKerricher State Park is filled with enticing highlights, including free day-use access and the loop trail around Lake Cleone, which is not only easy but also definitely something special. Mrs. MacKerricher aptly named the trail Cleone, which means gracious or beautiful in Greek. The route includes several sections on raised wooden walkways, which provide routes through marshy areas and which are partially wheelchair accessible. In the winter months the southern part of the trail (without the boardwalk) can be flooded. Be sure to wear your high boots in the rainy season.

The trail burrows like a tunnel through a variety of trees and lush vegetation, providing many glimpses of pretty Lake Cleone. It loops all the way around the lake, which is almost always full, with the beautiful Pacific Ocean just beyond to the west, a cypress grove to the south, and a marsh to the east. Historically the lake is stocked with trout by the Department of Fish and Game three times before Memorial Day weekend. The boardwalk is wheelchair accessible.

Special note: From the parking lot adjacent to the lake, you can walk under the built-up foundation of an old railroad line, now a bicycle trail called the Old Haul Road, and connect to the Headlands Trail. This is a must-do, an easy short walk, much of it on a raised walkway, that leads to a series of tide pools and the best seal- and whale-watching station on the coast.

Location: In MacKerricher State Park on the Mendocino coast north of Fort Bragg; map C0, grid e3.

User groups: Hikers and wheelchairs (the trail is partially wheelchair accessible). No dogs, horses, or mountain bikes. Horse trails are available elsewhere in the park.

Permits: No permits are required. Parking and access are free.

Maps: For a brochure and trail map, send $1 to MacKerricher State Park at the address below. Ask the USGS for a topographic map of the Inglenook area.

Directions: From Fort Bragg drive north on Highway 1 for three miles to the park entrance. Turn left and drive to the parking area beside the lake. The trailhead is on the east side of the parking lot.

Contact: MacKerricher State Park, c/o California State Parks, Mendocino District, P.O. Box 440, Mendocino, CA 95460; tel. (707) 937-5804 or fax (707) 937-2953.

11 Falls Loop Trail
7.0 mi/4.0 hrs

A 35-foot waterfall in deep forest makes this walk one of the prettiest on the Mendocino coast. Most of the year this waterfall is a narrow silvery stream that pours atop and across a boulder. In winter it can build into a more powerful chute and land in the rock basin with surging splashes.

The route is simple. Take the North Trail for 2.5 miles out to its junction with the Falls Loop Trail. Turn left and you'll hike less than a mile to reach the falls. Even in the summer months this is a pretty, if narrow, silver cascade, streaming 20 feet across a granite boulder and down into a pool. The entire trip has very little elevation gain—it's an easy walk out to the Falls Loop Trail, then only a 200-foot gain to reach the waterfall. As you go, you'll delve deeper and deeper into dense forest, and although a lot of the old growth was taken a long time ago, much is still divine.

Special note: A paved bicycle trail runs parallel to the North Trail and makes a great bike trip. But please note that bikes are not permitted on the dirt Falls Loop Trail. Bike racks are available at the intersection of these two trails, meaning bikers can make the trip to the falls with only a one-mile hike. In other words, ride to the Falls Loop Trail junction, park your bike, and walk one mile from there. This bike trail is also wheelchair accessible. A large number of people also walk the bike trail, a five-mile round trip.

Location: In Russian Gulch State Park on the Mendocino coast south of Fort Bragg; map C0, grid g3.

User groups: Hikers only. No mountain bikes, dogs, or horses. However, a paved trail for bicycles and wheelchairs is routed 2.5 miles to the trailhead of the Falls Loop Trail (see special note).

Permits: No permits are required. A $2 state park entrance fee is charged for each vehicle.

Maps: For a brochure and trail map, send $1 to Russian Gulch State Park at the address below. Ask the USGS for a topographic map of the Mendocino area.

Directions: From Fort Bragg drive south on Highway 1 for six miles to the Russian Gulch State Park entrance. Turn right and drive a very short distance to the state park entrance. After passing the kiosk, travel down the hill and to the bridge. Turn left and drive past the campsites to the trailhead.

Contact: Russian Gulch State Park, c/o California State Parks, Mendocino District, P.O. Box 440, Mendocino, CA 95460; tel. (707) 937-5804 or fax (707) 937-2953.

12 Chamberlain Creek Waterfall Trail

0.5 mi/0.5 hr

Hidden in Jackson State Forest is a 50-foot waterfall set in a canyon framed by redwoods, the kind of place where explorers can get religion. Set back off an old dirt logging road, the trail is short, yet steep, secluded, and beautiful. This access road (gravel/dirt), by the way, can get muddy in the winter and extremely dusty in the summer. After parking, you'll find the trail routed a short distance down the canyon to the stream, starting with a short series of steps. The trail simply heads down the canyon directly to the base of the waterfall. Despite the beauty of the area and the popularity of the Mendocino coast, Jackson State Forest is typically overlooked by most visitors, meaning you'll most likely have the place to yourself.

Location: In Jackson State Forest east of Fort Bragg; map C0, grid g5.

User groups: Hikers and dogs. No horses or mountain bikes. No wheelchair facilities.

Permits: No permits are required. Parking and access are free.

Maps: For a free trail map, contact Jackson Demonstration State Forest at the address below. Ask the USGS for a topographic map of the Northspur area.

Directions: From Willits drive west on Highway 20 for 17 miles to Forest Road 200. Turn right on Forest Road 200 and drive 1.2 miles to a fork. Bear left at forks and drive about three more miles and look for the trailhead on the left. Park on the side of the road and follow the hand railing down a steep slope to access the trail. In the heaviest rainy season, note that State Forest Road 200 is sometimes closed due to weather; call ahead for the status.

Contact: Jackson Demonstration State Forest, 802 N. Main Street, Fort Bragg, CA 95437; tel. (707) 964-5674 or fax (707) 964-0941.

13 Fern Canyon Trail

8.1 mi/5.0 hrs

This beautiful streamside walk amid coastal redwoods is one of the most popular trails on the Mendocino coast. The trail starts at the bottom of a canyon along the Little River and heads upstream, rising gently along the way, with a series of little bridges crisscrossing the water. The creek is pretty and often clear, the forest canopy is towering, and the understory of fern and sorrel is lush. Most people hike 2.3 miles (paved all the way) out to the junction of the Loop Trail and then turn around and head back. You can add on a three-mile loop, including a visit to the delightful Pygmy Forest, where an elevated wood walkway is routed amid this unusual setting. Note that heavy rains can flood out the trail and wash out the bridges. Also note that if you're a cheapskate, you can avoid paying the $2 park entrance fee by parking in the beach parking lot next to the park entrance and walking in.

Special note: Do not get this Fern Canyon Trail confused with the Fern Canyon Trail on the Humboldt County coast, which is detailed in chapter A0.

Location: In Van Damme State Park on the Mendocino coast south of Mendocino; map C0, grid h2.

User groups: Hikers only. No dogs or horses. Wheelchairs and mountain bikes are allowed only on the first 2.3 miles of the trail.

Permits: No permits are required. A $2 state park entrance fee is charged for each vehicle.

Maps: For a brochure and trail map, send $1 to Van Damme State Park at the address below. Ask the USGS for a topographic map of the Mendocino area.

Directions: From Mendocino drive south on Highway 1 for 2.5 miles to the park entrance. Turn left and drive .75 mile (well signed) to the trailhead. For campers, start near campsite number 26.

Contact: Van Damme State Park, c/o California State Parks, Mendocino District, P.O. Box 440, Mendocino, CA 95460; tel. (707) 937-5804 or fax (707) 937-2953.

14 Big Hendy Grove Trail

1.0 mi/0.5 hr

This easy and short walk through an ancient redwood forest can have visitors to Hendy Woods smiling for days. Hendy Woods is located in the redwood-filled canyon of the Navarro River, which flows to the sea on the Mendocino coast. While the park covers 845 acres, the two old-growth redwood groves, Little Hendy (20 acres) and Big Hendy (80 acres), are most compelling.

When you first arrive, you'll be stunned at the sudden interface of the foothill grasslands with redwoods. At Big Hendy start by taking the .5-mile Discovery Trail, which leaves the grasslands and enters the grove on a dirt path. Suddenly you'll be walking among towering redwoods, moss-covered stumps, and a sprinkling of giant fallen trees, all set amid ferns and sorrel. A great side trip is to walk uphill on the cutoff trail to the old hermit's hut in a hollowed-out tree stump, where one of the last of the real hermits lived for years. A newspaper clipping here details

the old hermit's strange life—kind of like that of an outdoors writer.

Location: In Hendy Woods State Park in Mendocino National Forest; map C0, grid j5.

User groups: Hikers and wheelchairs. No dogs, horses, or mountain bikes.

Permits: No permits are required. A $2 state park entrance fee is charged for each vehicle.

Maps: For a brochure and trail map, send $1 to Hendy Woods State Park at the address below. Ask the USGS for a topographic map of the Philo area.

Directions: From Mendocino drive south on Highway 1 for about five miles to Highway 128. Turn east on Highway 128 and drive about 20 miles to Philo Greenwood Road. Turn south (right) and drive .5 mile to the entrance of Hendy Woods State Park on the left. The trailhead begins just off the parking area.

Contact: Hendy Woods State Park, c/o California State Parks, Mendocino District, P.O. Box 440, Mendocino, CA 95460; tel. (707) 937-5804 or fax (707) 937-2953.

15 Glen Eden Trail

8.0 mi/5.0 hrs

This trail will have you sweating like Charles Manson's cellmate. The Glen Eden Trail is not only difficult to find (follow our directions precisely), but has several steep sections and is typically quite hot. The trail eventually crosses Mendo Rock Road (another trailhead possibility) and continues up to a series of great overlooks of Clear Lake. To return, retrace your route. The chaparral-covered slopes are peppered with pine and oak, with many miles of trails and fire roads. But it's extremely rare to see other hikers, and no off-road vehicles are allowed (unlike the southern portion of the Cow Mountain Recreation Area). In addition, the views of Clear Lake and the Mayacmas Range are outstanding.

If you do not have a high-clearance vehicle, you can access this trail from the Mayacamas Trailhead, located at the upper end of the second pond on the left side of the road. In that case, start the trip by hiking up the Mayacamas Trail, which traces first Willow Creek and then Mill Creek. In little over a mile you'll join the Glen Eden Trail. Turn right and climb out on the Glen Eden Trail.

Location: In Cow Mountain Recreation Area east of Ukiah; map C0, grid j9.

User groups: Hikers, dogs and horses. Mountain bikes are allowed on only the first 2.5 miles of trail, after which private property starts and bicycles are prohibited.

Permits: No permits are required. Parking and access are free.

Maps: For a free trail map of the Cow Mountain Recreation Area, contact the Bureau of Land Management at the address below. Ask the USGS for a topographic map of the Cow Mountain area.

Directions: From Ukiah on U.S. 101, drive east on Talmage Road to East Side Road. Turn right and drive .25 mile to Mill Creek Road (at the sign for Cow Mountain). Turn left on Mill Creek Road, drive about three miles (you'll pass two ponds), and then continue past Mill Creek County Park to Mendo Rock Road. Turn left and drive 4.5 miles to the trailhead on the right. A high-clearance vehicle is required for the last 4.5 miles. Note: If you do not have a high-clearance vehicle, you can access this trail from the Mayacmas Trailhead, located at the upper end of the second pond on the left side of the road.

Contact: Bureau of Land Management, Ukiah Field Office, 2550 N. State Street, Ukiah, CA 95482; tel. (707) 468-4000 or fax (707) 468-4027.

BLOOMING TRILLIUM
IN A REDWOOD FOREST

MAP C1

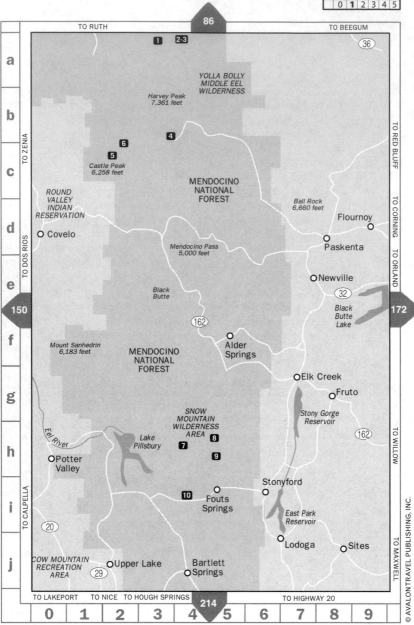

TO RUTH — **86** — TO BEEGUM

TO ZENIA

TO RED BLUFF

TO CORNING

TO ORLAND

TO DOS RIOS

150

172

TO WILLOW

TO CALPELLA

TO MAXWELL

1

2-3

36

YOLLA BOLLY
MIDDLE EEL
WILDERNESS

Harvey Peak
7,361 feet

6

5

4

Castle Peak
6,258 feet

MENDOCINO
NATIONAL
FOREST

Ball Rock
6,660 feet

Flournoy

ROUND
VALLEY
INDIAN
RESERVATION

Covelo

Mendocino Pass
5,000 feet

Paskenta

Newville

32

Black
Butte

Black
Butte
Lake

162

Mount Sanhedrin
6,183 feet

MENDOCINO
NATIONAL
FOREST

Alder
Springs

Elk Creek

Fruto

Stony Gorge
Reservoir

SNOW
MOUNTAIN
WILDERNESS
AREA

162

Eel River

Lake
Pillsbury

7

8

9

Potter
Valley

Stonyford

10

Fouts
Springs

East Park
Reservoir

20

COW MOUNTAIN
RECREATION
AREA

Upper Lake

29

Bartlett
Springs

Lodoga

Sites

TO LAKEPORT   TO NICE   TO HOUGH SPRINGS — **214** — TO HIGHWAY 20

0   1   2   3   4   5   6   7   8   9

© AVALON TRAVEL PUBLISHING, INC.

CHAPTER C1

1 Black Rock Lake Trail. . 163
2 Tomhead Saddle Loop . 163
3 Syd Cabin Ridge Trail. . 164
4 Ides Cove National
    Recreation Trail 165
5 Wrights Valley Trail . . 165
6 Soldier Ridge Trail. . . . 166
7 Waterfall Loop Trail . . 166
8 Windy Point Trailhead. 167
9 Bear Wallow Trailhead. 167
10 Overlook Loop 168

1 Black Rock Lake Trail

4.5 mi/3.0 hrs

The 2.25-mile hike from the Stuart Gap Trailhead to Black Rock Lake is one of the best day hikes in the Yolla Bolly Wilderness. One of the highlights comes in mid- to late June, when the wildflower blooms are absolutely beautiful. From the trailhead at the northern tip of the wilderness at 5,600 feet, you hike about a mile on the Pettyjohn Trail along the northwestern flank of North Yolla Bolly Mountain (7,863 feet) toward Pettyjohn Basin. You then turn right on the Stuart Gap Trail and tromp another 1.25 miles to the lake, with the trail contouring through open stands of pine and fir and some small meadows. Small Black Rock Lake is set just below Black Rock Mountain (7,755 feet), is ideal for swimming, and is stocked with trout by air every other year. There are many other excellent day hikes from this trailhead: Yolla Bolly Lake (stocked with trout every other year), Black Rock Mountain (great views), North Yolla Bolly Mountain (more sweeping vistas), and Cedar Basin (several creeks). Any of these make for classic days, remote and quiet. The trailhead can also be used as a jump-off spot for a hike straight south on the Pettyjohn Trail into the wilderness interior. Note that this trail is usually impassable prior to Memorial Day.

Location: On the northern boundary of the Yolla Bolly Wilderness west of Red Bluff; map C1, grid a3.

User groups: Hikers, dogs, and horses. No mountain bikes. No wheelchair facilities.

Permits: A campfire permit is required for hikers planning to camp.

Maps: For a map of Shasta-Trinity National Forest, send $6 to U.S. Forest Service, Attn: Map Sales, P.O. Box 587, Camino, CA 95709; tel. (530) 647-5390, fax (530) 647-5389, or website: www.r5.fs.fed.us/visitorcenter. Major credit cards accepted. Ask the USGS for a topographic map of the North Yolla Bolly area.

Directions: From Interstate 5 at Red Bluff drive west on Highway 36 for 47 miles to Platina. Continue west on Highway 36 for 11 miles to Forest Road 30 (Wildwood-Mad River Road). Turn left (south) and drive nine miles to Forest Road 35. Turn left (east) on Forest Road 35 and drive 10 miles to intersection of several roads. Take the signed fork for Stuart Gap Trailhead and drive 1.8 miles (unpaved) to the trailhead parking area. Hike on the Pettyjohn Trail for one mile to reach the Stuart Gap Trail.

Contact: Shasta-Trinity National Forest, Hayfork Ranger Station, P.O. Box 159, Hayfork, CA 96041; tel. (530) 628-5227 or fax (530) 628-5212.

2 Tomhead Saddle Loop

15.0 mi/2.0 days

Why is it that many backpacking trips with treacherous sections often start out easy, leading hikers into a misplaced sense of calm? While we don't know the answer, we do know this trail does exactly that. From the trailhead at Tomhead Saddle, elevation 5,500 feet, take the Humboldt Trail west toward East Low Gap. It's all downhill. "What, me worry?" Bear to the right down East Low Gap to get to Burnt Camp, an eight-mile first day. But get this: no water is available anywhere along the route. If your canteen is dry, Burnt Camp will seem like Eden, set along the South Fork of Cottonwood Creek. All seems right again. But it isn't, at least not if you don't like slippery stream crossings. The second day hiking out from Burnt Camp, you'll take the Cottonwood Trail to Hawk Camp, then the Syd Cabin Ridge Trail back to the parking area at Tomhead Saddle. It's uphill all the way from Hawk Camp to Tomhead Saddle, and this also includes five stream crossings, some of them across slick bedrock. We were thinking of making a video of people crossing the river and selling it as the "Yolla Bolly Guide to Ballet."

Location: Near the eastern boundary of the Yolla Bolly Wilderness west of Red Bluff; map C1, grid a4.

User groups: Hikers, dogs, and horses. No mountain bikes. No wheelchair facilities.

Permits: A campfire permit is required for hikers planning to camp.

Maps: For a map of Shasta-Trinity National Forest, send $6 to U.S. Forest Service, Attn: Map Sales, P.O. Box 587, Camino, CA 95709; tel. (530) 647-5390, fax (530) 647-5389, or website: www.r5.fs.fed.us/visitorcenter. Major credit cards accepted. Ask the USGS for a topographic map of the North Yolla Bolly area.

Directions: From Interstate 5 at Red Bluff drive west on Highway 36 about 13 miles. Turn left (south) on Cannon Road and go approximately five miles to Pettyjohn Road. Turn right (west) on Pettyjohn Road and drive to Forest Road 27N06. Turn left (south) on Forest Road 27N06 and continue three miles to the parking area at Tomhead Saddle Campground. This is a dirt road all the way in from Highway 36. A high-clearance vehicle is recommended. It can also be slippery when wet.

Contact: Shasta-Trinity National Forest, Hayfork Ranger Station, P.O. Box 159, Hayfork, CA 96041; tel. (530) 628-5227 or fax (530) 628-5212.

3 Syd Cabin Ridge Trail
8.0 mi/2.0 days

Not many people hike into the Yolla Bolly Wilderness, set up a camp, then hike back out the next day. But here is a chance to do exactly that. The trailhead is at the Tomhead Saddle, located just west of Tomhead Mountain, elevation 6,757 feet. From here you hike past Tomhead Spring on the Syd Cabin Ridge Trail, then drop down into Hawk Camp. Expect a steady climb with no water between Tomhead Spring and Hawk Camp. Set just below the confluence of three feeder streams, Hawk Camp is an ideal spot to overnight. If you plan on extending your trip for several days into the wilderness, a network of trails intersects just beyond Hawk Camp, but note that a stream crossing is required.

Location: On the eastern boundary of the Yolla Bolly Wilderness west of Red Bluff; map C1, grid a4.

User groups: Hikers, dogs, and horses. No mountain bikes. No wheelchair facilities.

Permits: A campfire permit is required for hikers planning to camp.

Maps: For a map of Shasta-Trinity National Forest, send $6 to U.S. Forest Service, Attn: Map Sales, P.O. Box 587, Camino, CA 95709; tel. (530) 647-5390, fax (530) 647-5389, or website: www.r5.fs.fed.us/visitorcenter. Major credit cards accepted. Ask the USGS for a topographic map of the North Yolla Bolly area.

Directions: From Interstate 5 at Red Bluff drive west on Highway 36 about 13 miles. Turn left (south) on Cannon Road and go approximately five miles to Pettyjohn Road. Turn right (west) on Pettyjohn Road and drive to Forest Road 27N06. Turn left (south) on Forest Road 27N06 and continue three miles to the parking area at Tomhead Saddle Campground. This is a dirt road all the way in from Highway 36. A high-clearance vehicle is recommended. It can also be slippery when wet.

Contact: Shasta-Trinity National Forest, Hayfork Ranger Station, P.O. Box 159, Hayfork, CA 96041; tel. (530) 628-5227 or fax (530) 628-5212.

4 Ides Cove National Recreation Trail

10.5 mi/5.5 hrs

At 8,092 feet, South Yolla Bolly Mountain is the highest point in this wilderness. The Ides Cove National Recreation Trail skirts this mountain as part of one of the top one-day loop trails available in the Yolla Bollys. A bonus is that a shorter loop hike (3.5 miles) is also convenient here. Another bonus is that a free campground is available at the trailhead; horse facilities are nearby, but not at the trailhead. Despite that, the trail gets only light use. From the Ides Cove Trailhead the trail drops down to the headwaters of Slide Creek and heads out to the foot of Harvey Peak at 7,361 feet, which is the halfway point and a good spot for lunch. The trail turns sharply and is routed back along the flank of the South Yolla Bolly Mountains. On the way, it passes both Long and Square Lakes, both tiny water holes stocked with brook trout.

Location: On the southeastern boundary of the Yolla Bolly Wilderness west of Red Bluff; map C1, grid b3.

User groups: Hikers, dogs, and horses. No mountain bikes. No wheelchair facilities.

Permits: A campfire permit is required for hikers planning to camp.

Maps: For a map of Mendocino National Forest, send $6 to U.S. Forest Service, Attn: Map Sales, P.O. Box 587, Camino, CA 95709; tel. (530) 647-5390, fax (530) 647-5389, or website: www.r5.fs.fed.us/visitorcenter. Major credit cards accepted. Ask the USGS for a topographic map of the South Yolla Bolly area.

Directions: From Corning on Interstate 5 take the Corning Road/Paskenta Road exit and drive west about 20 miles to Paskenta. In the town of Paskenta, Corning/Paskenta Road will split and become Round Valley Road on the left and County Road M2/Toomes Creek Road straight ahead. Continue straight on County Road M2/Toomes Creek Road for 20 miles to Cold Springs Ranger Station. Turn right on County Road M22 and drive about 15 miles to the trailhead.

For an alternate route from Red Bluff: From Red Bluff, drive west on County Road 356 (Forest Route 22) and drive about 41 miles to the signed access road from Ides Cove Trailhead. Turn right and drive to the Ides Cove Trailhead.

Contact: Mendocino National Forest, Corning Work Center, 22000 Corning Road, Corning, CA 96021; tel. (530) 824-5196 or fax (530) 824-6034.

5 Wrights Valley Trail

8.0 mi/4.5 hrs

The Rock Cabin Trail (also known as River Trail) extends north into the Yolla Bolly Wilderness and up, over, and down a short ridge before pouring into Wrights Valley. About halfway in, the River Trail jumps to Wrights Valley Trail. It's about a four-mile trip one way to your destination. Here you'll find the headwaters of the Middle Fork Eel River, one of the prettiest streams in the wilderness. The trail is well marked and includes two creek crossings. While the Yolla Bollys provide few lakes, the Middle Fork awaits you. No fishing is allowed in order to protect endangered steelhead.

Special note: Map-gazing hikers will likely notice a small lake, Henthorne Lake, complete with two wilderness cabins, set just 2.5 miles from the Rock Cabin Trailhead. Resist the urge to visit. This is maintained as private property, a nature reserve for some lucky soul. Hikers are often tempted to hike in via a very faint cowboy trail (with a river crossing) and camp here illegally.

Location: On the southern boundary of the Yolla Bolly Wilderness west of Red Bluff; map C1, grid c2.

User groups: Hikers, dogs, and horses. No mountain bikes. No wheelchair facilities.

Permits: A campfire permit is required for hikers planning to camp. Parking and access are free.

Maps: For a map of Mendocino National Forest, send $6 to U.S. Forest Service, Attn: Map Sales, P.O. Box 587, Camino, CA 95709;

tel. (530) 647-5390, fax (530) 647-5389, or website: www.r5.fs.fed.us/visitorcenter. Major credit cards accepted. Ask the USGS for a topographic map of the South Yolla Bolly area.

Directions: From Willits drive north on U.S. 101 for 13 miles to Longvale and Highway 162. Turn east on Highway 162 and drive to Covelo, the continue east on Highway 162 for 13 miles to the Eel River Bridge and Forest Road M1 (Indian Dick Road). Turn left (north) at the bridge on Forest Road M1 and drive 24 miles to Forest Road 25N15C. Turn left on Forest Road 25N15C and drive .75 mile to turnoff for the Rock Cabin Trailhead. Turn left and drive .25 mile to the trailhead at the end of the road.

Contact: Mendocino National Forest, Covelo Ranger District, 78150 Covelo Road, Covelo, CA 95428; tel. (707) 983-6118 or fax (707) 983-8004.

6 Soldier Ridge Trail
11.2 mi/2.0 days

This wilderness trail features three linked segments, Soldier Ridge Trail, Minnie Lake Trail, and Kingsley Lake Trail, a 5.5-mile walk to your destination, Kingsley Lake. The rugged climb on the Soldier Ridge Trail to get there, along with the charm of this little lake, will compel you to stay overnight. Actually, it's a long drive in the middle of nowhere just to reach the trailhead, and then when you get there, you'll face a daunting 3.5-mile climb up the spine of Soldier Ridge toward the Yolla Bolly Crest. At the crest are three mountains lined in a row, Sugarloaf Mountain (elevation 7,367 feet), Solomon Peak (7,581 feet), and Hammerhorn Mountain (7,567 feet). The trail crosses a saddle between Sugarloaf Mountain and Solomon Peak, then drops down to little Kingsley Lake, created from the headwaters of Thomes Creek. All is quiet and peaceful here.

Location: On the southern boundary of the Yolla Bolly Wilderness west of Red Bluff; map C1, grid c2.

User groups: Hikers, dogs, and horses. No mountain bikes. No wheelchair facilities.

Permits: A campfire permit is required for hikers planning to camp. Parking and access are free.

Maps: For a map of Mendocino National Forest, send $6 to U.S. Forest Service, Attn: Map Sales, P.O. Box 587, Camino, CA 95709; tel. (530) 647-5390, fax (530) 647-5389, or website: www.r5.fs.fed.us/visitorcenter. Major credit cards accepted. Ask the USGS for a topographic map of the South Yolla Bolly area.

Directions: From Willits drive north on U.S. 101 for 13 miles to Longvale and Highway 162. Turn east on Highway 162 and drive to Covelo, then continue east on Highway 162 for 13 miles to the Eel River Bridge and Forest Road M1 (Indian Dick Road). Turn left (north) at the bridge on Forest Road M1 and drive 27 miles to the trailhead at the end of the road.

Contact: Mendocino National Forest, Covelo Ranger District, 78150 Covelo Road, Covelo, CA 95428; tel. (707) 983-6118 or fax (707) 983-8004.

7 Waterfall Loop Trail
13.0 mi/1.0 day

Very few people know about the Snow Mountain Wilderness, and far fewer know about this excellent loop trail that traverses the region's most treasured areas. Double-peaked Snow Mountain itself is the big ridge located about midway between Interstate 5 at Willows and U.S. 101 at Willits. This trail starts at the northern boundary of the wilderness at the West Crockett Trailhead (just west of Crockett Peak). You hike two miles to get into Middle Fork Creek, and here it connects with the Water Loop Trail. A waterfall is located on a spur trail off the loop, (2.2 miles from the trailhead). The trail climbs much of the way, reaching a small loop set between East Snow Mountain (7,056 feet) and West Snow Mountain (7,038 feet). To return, take the North Ridge Trail, which drops down from Snow Mountain and traces the Middle Fork of Stony Creek for a good portion of the route back to the parking area. Much of this area can be quite dry and hot in midsummer, especially on the North Ridge. Two notes: Rattlesnakes are common, and hikers should always be certain to carry a lot of water here—twice as much as usual.

Location: On the northwestern boundary of the Snow Mountain Wilderness in Mendocino National Forest; map C1, grid h4.

User groups: Hikers, dogs, and horses. No mountain bikes. No wheelchair facilities.

Permits: A campfire permit is required for hikers planning to camp. Parking and access are free.

Maps: For a map of Mendocino National Forest, send $6 to U.S. Forest Service, Attn: Map Sales, P.O. Box 587, Camino, CA 95709; tel. (530) 647-5390, fax (530) 647-5389, or website: www.r5.fs.fed.us/visitorcenter. Major credit cards accepted. Ask the USGS for topographic maps of the Crockett Peak and St. John Mountain areas.

Directions: From Willows on Interstate 5 drive west on Highway 162 for 21 miles to a T junction. Turn left and drive one mile through the town of Elk Creek to Ivory Mill Road. Turn right on Ivory Mill Road (Road 308) and drive 15 miles to Forest Road M3. Turn left on Forest Road M3 and drive 15.5 miles to the signed turnoff for West Crockett Trailhead. Turn left and drive .5 mile to the trailhead.

Contact: Mendocino National Forest, Stonyford Ranger Station, 5171 Stonyford-Elk Creek Road, Stonyford, CA 95979; tel. (530) 963-3128 or fax (530) 963-3123.

8 Windy Point Trailhead

3.25 mi/1.75 hrs

Every wilderness has secret spots, and so it is here in the Snow Mountain Wilderness. On a hot summer day when every drop of water is counted as if it were liquid gold, you'll find a simple paradise on this short walk to the headwaters of a tiny fork of Bear Wallow Creek. The hike starts at Windy Point, the northernmost trailhead in the Snow Mountains. The trail heads straight east on the Bear Wallow Trail for a little more than a mile across

very dry country. About 1.5 miles in, start looking for a spur trail on the right side, and when you see it, take it. This spur drops a short distance down to the source of the North Fork of Bear Wallow Creek, a truly secret little spot. If you think there are too many people in the world, just come here and look around.

Location: On the northern boundary of the Snow Mountain Wilderness in Mendocino National Forest; map C1, grid h5.

User groups: Hikers, dogs, and horses. No mountain bikes. No wheelchair facilities.

Permits: A campfire permit is required for hikers planning to camp. Parking and access are free.

Maps: For a map of Mendocino National Forest, send $6 to U.S. Forest Service, Attn: Map Sales, P.O. Box 587, Camino, CA 95709; tel. (530) 647-5390, fax (530) 647-5389, or website: www.r5.fs.fed.us/visitorcenter. Major credit cards accepted. Ask the USGS for topographic maps of the Crockett Peak and St. John Mountain areas.

Directions: From Willows on Interstate 5 drive west on Highway 162 for 21 miles to a T junction. Turn left and drive one mile through the town of Elk Creek to Ivory Mill Road. Turn right on Ivory Mill Road (Road 308) and drive 15 miles to Forest Road M3. Turn left on Forest Road M3 and drive 13 miles to the trailhead.

Contact: Mendocino National Forest, Stonyford Ranger Station, 5171 Stonyford-Elk Creek Road, Stonyford, CA 95979; tel. (530) 963-3128 or fax (530) 963-3123.

9 Bear Wallow Trailhead

4.0 mi/2.5 hrs

Whoa, it can get hot out here. In summer a very early start for a hike is mandatory, particularly on the east-facing slopes of the Snow Mountain Wilderness. Your destination is a pretty section of Bear Wallow Creek, a small feeder stream to the Middle Fork of Stony Creek. The hike starts at the Bear Wallow Trailhead. From here the Bear Wallow Trail is routed north; after about two miles start looking for a trail junction on the left side. Be sure not to miss it. Turn left and take the .25-mile traipse down to Bear Wallow Creek, a pretty spot and a decent destination for a day's walk. Typically you'll have the place all to yourself. But of you miss the turn, the Bear Wallow Trail continues all the way to Windy Point Trailhead, and with no water available you'll be chanting, "Beam me up, Scotty."

Location: On the eastern boundary of the Snow Mountain Wilderness in Mendocino National Forest; map C1, grid h5.

User groups: Hikers, dogs, and horses. No mountain bikes. No wheelchair facilities.

Permits: A campfire permit is required for hikers planning to camp. Parking and access are free.

Maps: For a map of Mendocino National Forest, send $6 to U.S. Forest Service, Attn: Map Sales, P.O. Box 587, Camino, CA 95709; tel. (530) 647-5390, fax (530) 647-5389, or website: www.r5.fs.fed.us/visitorcenter. Major credit cards accepted. Ask the USGS for a topographic map of the Fouts Springs area.

Directions: On Interstate 5 in Maxwell, take the Maxwell exit west and to Maxwell-Sites Road. Turn west on Maxwell-Sites Road and drive to Sites and Sites-Lodoga Road. Turn left on Sites-Lodoga Road and drive to Lodoga and Lodoga-Stonyford Road. Turn left and loop around East Park Reservoir to reach Stonyford and Fouts Spring Road (Road M10). Turn west and drive eight miles to Forest Road 18N06. Turn right and drive nine miles (four-wheel-drive is necessary) to the parking area for the trailhead on the left.

Contact: Mendocino National Forest, Stonyford Ranger Station, 5171 Stonyford-Elk Creek Road, Stonyford, CA 95979; tel. (530) 963-3128 or fax (530) 963-3123.

10 Overlook Loop
8.5 mi/1.0 day

This is not a trail for the indifferent. Do you yearn for the passion of the mountain experience? Do you crave the zest of life when you have a bad case of dry mouth and discover a mountain spring? Is the price of a climb worth it for the mountaintop payoff? Are you nuts? You need to answer yes, yes, yes, and yes to be ready for this loop hike. It includes two killer climbs, a wonderful little spring along the trail, and the ascent of West Snow Mountain, 7,038 feet. Still interested? Then read on.

The trail starts at the Summit Spring Trailhead, and in the first two miles includes a no-fun clamber up to High Rock. At the trail junction here, turn right on the Box Spring Loop Trail and hike past the headwaters of Trout Creek to Box Spring, located just to the right of the trail near another trail junction. In hot weather, typically all summer, this spot is paradise. Turn left and make the three-mile climb up West Snow Mountain, sweating it out every step of the way. Enjoy this victory for a while before dropping back down for the final three miles back to the trailhead and parking area. This is an excellent loop hike, one that furnishes several rewards but makes you earn every one of them.

Location: On the southwestern boundary of the Snow Mountain Wilderness in Mendocino National Forest; map C1, grid i4.

User groups: Hikers, dogs, and horses. No mountain bikes. No wheelchair facilities.

Permits: A campfire permit is required for hikers planning to camp. Parking and access are free.

Maps: For a map of Mendocino National Forest, send $6 to U.S. Forest Service, Attn: Map Sales, P.O. Box 587, Camino, CA 95709; tel. (530) 647-5390, fax (530) 647-5389, or website: www.r5.fs.fed.us/visitorcenter. Major credit cards accepted. Ask the USGS for a topographic map of the Fouts Springs area.

Directions: On Interstate 5 in Maxwell, take the Maxwell exit west and to Maxwell-Sites Road. Turn west on Maxwell-Sites Road and drive to Sites and Sites-Lodoga Road. Turn left on Sites-Lodoga Road and drive to Lodoga and Lodoga-Stonyford Road. Turn left and loop around East Park Reservoir to reach Stonyford and Fouts Spring Road (Road M10). Turn west and drive 25 miles to a signed access road for Summit Spring Trailhead. Turn right and drive 1.5 miles to the parking area and trailhead at the end of the road.

Contact: Mendocino National Forest, Stonyford Ranger Station, 5171 Stonyford-Elk Creek Road, Stonyford, CA 95979; tel. (530) 963-3128 or fax (530) 963-3123.

A WILD PIG FEEDING IN THE
ISHI WILDERNESS FOOTHILLS

MAP C2

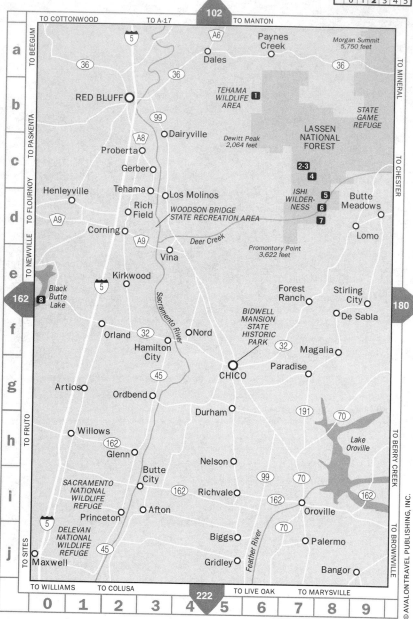

CHAPTER C2

1 McClure Trail. 173
2 Table Mountain Trail . . . 173
3 Rancheria Trail 174
4 Lower Mill Creek. 175
5 Moak Trail 175
6 Deer Creek Trail 176
7 Devils Den Trail. 176
8 Big Oak Trail 177

1 McClure Trail

9.0 mi/1.0 day

At first glance the Tehama Wildlife Area might appear to be nothing more than rolling oak woodlands. But this is a habitat managed expressly for wildlife, and it includes a beautiful stream, abundant vegetation, and plenty of animals. The area is huge, covering 44,862 acres, and is popular only in the fall during hunting season for deer and wild pigs. This trail accesses the best of the wildlife area, heading down a steep canyon to Antelope Creek, buffered by riparian vegetation. Deer are rampant in late fall (typically migrating in after the hunting season is over), and there are also lots of squirrels, hawks, and, alas, rattlesnakes. Wild pigs roam the canyons but are only occasionally seen from trails. In late winter and spring, the canyons and hillsides come alive in green, and all wildlife seems to prosper. They'd better when they have the chance, because the heat here can seem unbearable in summer. The stream is very pretty, and fishing is catch-and-release only using artificials. You can count on lots of deer hunters in October and lots of turkey hunters from late March to May 1.

Location: In the Tehama Wildlife Area east of Red Bluff; map C2, grid b6.

User groups: Hikers and dogs. Mountain bikes and horses are permitted but not recommended because of terrain. No wheelchair facilities.

Permits: No permits are required. A campfire permit (free) is required for overnight use. Parking and access are free.

Maps: For a free map, contact the Tehama Wildlife Area at the address below. For a map of Lassen National Forest, send $6 to U.S. Forest Service, Attn: Map Sales, P.O. Box 587, Camino, CA 95709; tel. (530) 647-5390, fax (530) 647-5389, or website: www.r5.fs.fed.us/visitorcenter. Major credit cards accepted. Ask the USGS for a topographic map of the Dewitt Peak area.

Directions: From Interstate 5 at Red Bluff, turn east on Highway 36 and drive 20 miles to the town of Paynes Creek. Turn south on Plum Creek Road and go to Ishi Conservation Camp. Drive about 2.5 miles south to High Trestle Road and follow it to Hogsback Road. Park across from the intersection of High Trestle and Hogsback Roads and walk about .25 mile on the dirt road to the trailhead. Access to the Tehama Wildlife Area is closed to the public from February to the first Saturday in April. Access is also restricted for a short period during deer season in late September. There are no closures on U.S. Forest Service trails.

Contact: Department of Fish and Game, Tehama Wildlife Area, P.O. Box 188, Paynes Creek, CA 96075; tel. (530) 597-2201; Redding Regional Office, tel. (530) 225-2867. Lassen National Forest, Almanor Ranger District, P.O. Box 767, Chester, CA 96020; tel. (530) 258-2141, or fax (530) 258-5194.

2 Table Mountain Trail

3.2 mi/2.5 hrs

This trail may be short, but it's anything but sweet. Except, that is, from the top of Table Mountain, elevation 2,380 feet, where you're supplied with a sweeping view of the Sacramento Valley and the surrounding land of Ishi. This is where Ishi, the last survivor of the Yahi Yana tribe, escaped from a band of white settlers who exterminated the rest of the Yahis. The Indians had lived here for 3,000 years before being killed off, another stellar moment in the history of the western frontier.

The trail starts from the northwest corner of the wilderness at the Table Mountain Trailhead and then goes 1.6 miles to the summit. It's very steep and challenging, and most hikers will be wheezing like worn-out donkeys before making the top. Because of the hot summers, it's absolutely critical either to start the trip very early in the morning or time it during cool weather and to bring plenty of water for your built-in radiator.

Special Note: A trail map is strongly advised for those hiking in the Ishi Wilderness.
Location: In the Ishi Wilderness east of Red Bluff; map C2, grid c7.
User groups: Hikers, dogs, and horses. No mountain bikes. No wheelchair facilities.
Permits: A campfire permit is required for hikers planning to camp. Parking and access are free.
Maps: A trail map is available for a fee from Almanor Ranger District. For a map of Lassen National Forest, send $6 to U.S. Forest Service, Attn: Map Sales, P.O. Box 587, Camino, CA 95709; tel. (530) 647-5390, fax (530) 647-5389, or website: www.r5.fs.fed.us/visitorcenter. Major credit cards accepted. Ask the USGS for topographic maps of the Panther Spring and Butte Meadows areas.
Directions: From Interstate 5 at Red Bluff, turn east on Highway 36 and drive to the town of Paynes Creek and continue to Little Giant Mill Road. Turn south on Little Giant Mill Road (Road 202) and drive about seven miles until you reach Ponderosa Way. Turn south at Ponderosa Way and drive about 10 miles to Forest Road 28N57. Turn west on Forest Road 28N57 and follow the Peligreen Jeep Trail for six miles to the trailhead. The last five miles of road are suitable only for four-wheel-drive vehicles.

Contact: Lassen National Forest, Almanor Ranger District, P.O. Box 767, Chester, CA 96020; tel. (530) 258-2141 or fax (530) 258-5194.

3 Rancheria Trail
4.0 mi/2.75 hrs

On a map the Rancheria Trailhead looks like the closest and easiest trailhead to reach into the Ishi Wilderness from Red Bluff. And what the heck, the trail looks pretty short, too. But when you go there, a completely different picture comes into focus. First off, the trailhead access road is quite rough, impassable for most cars, and that's just a prelude to what lies ahead. The trail starts by following an old jeep road, then leaves the road at a fence line off to the right. If it's hot, which is typical here most of the year, you'll already be reaching for your canteen. The trail then drops like a cannonball for a thousand feet into the Mill Creek Canyon, a surprising and awesome habitat with some of the prettiest areas of the Ishi. The fishing is often good; rules mandate catch-and-release with the use of artificials. Too bad you can't enjoy it more, because shadowing your every move is the knowledge that you have to climb back out of that canyon, most likely during the hottest part of the day. By the time you reach the car, your butt will be thoroughly kicked.

Special note: A trail map is strongly advised for those hiking in the Ishi Wilderness.
Location: In the Ishi Wilderness east of Red Bluff; map C2, grid c7.
User groups: Hikers, dogs, and horses. No mountain bikes. No wheelchair facilities.
Permits: No permit required. A campfire permit (free) is required for overnight use. Parking and access are free.
Maps: A trail map is available for a fee from Almanor Ranger District. For a map of Lassen National Forest, send $6 to U.S. Forest Service, Attn: Map Sales, P.O. Box 587, Camino, CA 95709; tel. (530) 647-5390, fax (530) 647-5389, or website: www.r5.fs.fed.us/visitorcenter. Major credit cards accepted. Ask the USGS

for topographic maps of the Panther Spring and Butte Meadows areas.

Directions: From Interstate 5 at Red Bluff, turn east onto Highway 36, drive to the town of Paynes Creek, and continue to Little Giant Mill Road. Turn south on Little Giant Mill Road (Road 202) and drive seven miles to Ponderosa Way. Turn south and drive about 10 miles to Forest Road 28N57. Turn west and follow the Peligreen Jeep Trail for two miles to the Rancheria Trailhead. The last two miles of road are suitable only for four-wheel-drive vehicles.

Contact: Lassen National Forest, Almanor Ranger District, P.O. Box 767, Chester, CA 96020; tel. (530) 258-2141 or fax (530) 258-5194.

4 Lower Mill Creek
13.0 mi/1.0 day

If you have time for only one trail in the Ishi Wilderness, the Mill Creek Trail is the one to pick. That goes whether you want to invest just an hour or a full day, because any length of trip can be a joy here. The trail simply parallels the creek for 6.5 miles to its headwaters at Papes Place, with magnificent scenery and many good fishing and swimming holes along the way. This is a dramatic canyon, and as you stand along the stream, the walls can seem to ascend into heaven. It's a land shaped by thousands of years of wind and water.

Directly across from the trailhead on Ponderosa Way is another trailhead, this one for a route that follows Upper Mill Creek into Lassen National Forest. While not as spectacular as Lower Mill Creek, it provides a good option for hiking, fishing, and swimming. Note that fishing is restricted to catch-and-release and the use of artificials.

Special note: A trail map is strongly advised for those hiking in the Ishi Wilderness.

Location: In the Ishi Wilderness east of Red Bluff; map C2, grid c7.

User groups: Hikers, dogs, and horses. No mountain bikes. No wheelchair facilities.

Permits: No permit required. A campfire permit (free) is required for overnight use. Parking and access are free.

Maps: A trail map is available for a fee from Almanor Ranger District. For a map of Lassen National Forest, send $6 to U.S. Forest Service, Attn: Map Sales, P.O. Box 587, Camino, CA 95709; tel. (530) 647-5390, fax (530) 647-5389, or website: www.r5.fs.fed.us/visitorcenter. Major credit cards accepted. Ask the USGS for topographic maps of the Panther Spring and Butte Meadows areas.

Directions: From Interstate 5 at Red Bluff, turn east on Highway 36, drive to the town of Paynes Creek, and continue to Little Giant Mill Road. Turn south on Little Giant Mill Road (Road 202) and drive seven miles to Ponderosa Way. Turn south at Ponderosa Way and drive about 17 miles to the Mill Creek Trailhead.

Contact: Lassen National Forest, Almanor Ranger District, P.O. Box 767, Chester, CA 96020; tel. (530) 258-2141 or fax (530) 258-5194.

5 Moak Trail
14.0 mi/1.5 days

Hit it right in the spring and the Moak Trail is likely the best overnight hike in California's foothill country. Hit it wrong in the summer and you'll wonder what you did to deserve such a terrible fate. In the spring the foothill country is loaded with wildflowers and tall, fresh grass, and the views of the Sacramento Valley are spectacular. The trail includes a poke-and-probe section over a lava rock boulder field, and there are good trail camps at Deep Hole (2,800 feet) and Drennan. It's an excellent weekend trip, including a loop route by linking the Moak Trail with the Buena Vista Trail, most of it easy walking. Alas, try this trip in the summer or fall and you'll need to have your gray matter examined at Red Bluff General. No wildflowers, no shade, 100-degree temperatures, and as for water, you're dreamin'.

Special note: A trail map is strongly advised for those hiking in the Ishi Wilderness.

Location: In the Ishi Wilderness east of Red Bluff; map C2, grid d8.

User groups: Hikers, dogs, and horses. No mountain bikes. No wheelchair facilities.

Permits: No permit required. A campfire permit (free) is required for overnight use. Parking and access are free.

Maps: A trail map is available for a fee from Almanor Ranger District. For a map of Lassen National Forest, send $6 to U.S. Forest Service, Attn: Map Sales, P.O. Box 587, Camino, CA 95709; tel. (530) 647-5390, fax (530) 647-5389, or website: www.r5.fs.fed.us/visitorcenter. Major credit cards accepted. Ask the USGS for topographic maps of the Panther Spring and Butte Meadows areas.

Directions: From Interstate 5 at Red Bluff, turn east on Highway 36, drive to the town of Paynes Creek, and continue to Little Giant Mill Road. Turn south on Little Giant Mill Road (Road 202) and drive seven miles to Ponderosa Way. Turn south at Ponderosa Way and drive about 24 miles to the Lassen Trailhead.

Contact: Lassen National Forest, Almanor Ranger District, P.O. Box 767, Chester, CA 96020; tel. (530) 258-2141 or fax (530) 258-5194.

6 Deer Creek Trail

14.0 mi/1.5 days

It's no accident the Deer Creek Trail is the most popular hike in the Ishi Wilderness. Not only are you rewarded with striking surroundings, but the hike is a pleasurable romp even if you cut the trip short to just an hour or two. That's because the trail runs midway up naked slopes, offering spectacular views of Deer Creek Canyon's basaltic cliffs and spires, and of the stream below. The trailhead is at the southeast border of the wilderness, and right from the start it's routed along the north shore of Deer Creek. Iron Mountain at 3,274 feet is located to the immediate north. The trail continues along the stream into the wilderness interior, skirting past the northern edge of what is called the Graham Pinery—a dense island of ponderosa pine growing on a moun-

tain terrace. A bonus is good bird-watching for hawks, eagles, and falcons at the rock cliffs, and looking for a large variety of wildlife, including rattlesnakes (here's your warning), wild pigs, and lots of squirrels and quail. Note that the stream is stocked with rainbow and brook trout up by Potato Patch and Alder Creek Campgrounds. Below Potato Patch Campground, fishing is catch-and-release only with the use of artificials.

Special note: A trail map is strongly advised for those hiking in the Ishi Wilderness.

Location: In the Ishi Wilderness east of Red Bluff; map C2, grid d8.

User groups: Hikers, dogs, and horses. No mountain bikes. No wheelchair facilities.

Permits: No permit required. A campfire permit (free) is required for overnight use. Parking and access are free.

Maps: A trail map is available for a fee from Almanor Ranger District. For a map of Lassen National Forest, send $6 to U.S. Forest Service, Attn: Map Sales, P.O. Box 587, Camino, CA 95709; tel. (530) 647-5390, fax (530) 647-5389, or website: www.r5.fs.fed.us/visitorcenter. Major credit cards accepted. Ask the USGS for topographic maps of the Panther Spring and Butte Meadows areas.

Directions: From Interstate 5 at Red Bluff, turn east on Highway 36, drive to the town of Paynes Creek, and continue to Little Giant Mill Road. Turn south on Little Giant Mill Road (Road 202) and drive seven miles to Ponderosa Way. Turn south at Ponderosa Way and drive about 26 miles to the Moak Trailhead.

Contact: Lassen National Forest, Almanor Ranger District, P.O. Box 767, Chester, CA 96020; tel. (530) 258-2141 or fax (530) 258-5194.

7 Devils Den Trail

9.0 mi/1.0 day

The Devils Den Trailhead is less than .5 mile from the Deer Creek Trailhead, but there the similarities between the two end. This trail includes a rough climb, beastly in summer, with no water available over the stretch where you'll need it most. The main attractions here are (1) nobody else is usually around, and (2) the trail is routed through a series of habitat zones over the course of the first 3.5 miles, providing a number of striking contrasts. The trail starts easy, following along Deer Creek for the first mile. Enjoy yourself because what follows is not exactly a picnic. Note that fishing here is restricted to catch-and-release and the use of artificials. The trail turns left, climbing up Little Pine Creek all the way to the ridge top, with the last mile on an old, hot, and chunky abandoned road. Along the way the vegetation changes from riparian along the creek to woodland on the slopes, then chaparral on the ridge. In addition, an island of conifers, the Graham Pinery, is available for viewing with a .25-mile side trip.

Special note: A trail map is strongly advised for those hiking in the Ishi Wilderness.

Location: In the Ishi Wilderness east of Red Bluff; map C2, grid d8.

User groups: Hikers, dogs, and horses. No mountain bikes. No wheelchair facilities.

Permits: No permit required. A campfire permit (free) is required for overnight use. Parking and access are free.

Maps: A trail map is available for a fee from Almanor Ranger District. For a map of Lassen National Forest, send $6 to U.S. Forest Service, Attn: Map Sales, P.O. Box 587, Camino, CA 95709; tel. (530) 647-5390, fax (530) 647-5389, or website: www.r5.fs.fed.us/visitorcenter. Major credit cards accepted. Ask the USGS for topographic maps of the Panther Spring and Butte Meadows areas.

Directions: From Interstate 5 at Red Bluff turn east on Highway 36, drive to the town of Paynes Creek, and continue to Little Giant Mill Road. Turn south on Little Giant Mill Road (Road 202) and drive seven miles to Ponderosa Way. Turn south at Ponderosa Way and drive 32.5 miles to the Devils Den Trailhead (just south of the Deer Creek Trailhead).

Contact: Lassen National Forest, Almanor Ranger District, P.O. Box 767, Chester, CA 96020; tel. (530) 258-2141 or fax (530) 258-5194.

8 Big Oak Trail
1.0 mi/0.5 hr

The Army Corps of Engineers has really screwed up some of California's once-great riverside habitat with massive rip-rap projects, but here they actually did something right: they protected Stony Creek by doing nothing but building a trail (of course, they had to build a dam here first). The route, an easy jaunt, follows the Stony Creek drainage above the head of Black Butte Reservoir. The riparian habitat here is in a protected state, providing an excellent area to see wildlife and birds in the sparse foothills of the Sacramento Valley. It has become part of California's Watchable Wildlife system. The best time for hiking is at dusk, when wildlife viewing is at its best. Alas, this hike is not without problems. First is the weather, which is close to intolerable in the summer—a real temperature tantrum—and very hot in spring and fall as well, and that's when most people have time to visit the area. Second, this was once an interpretive trail, but because a flood washed out all the signs, the Army Corps of Engineers simply decided not to replace them and stopped providing the brochure that once went with this hike.

Location: At the head of Black Butte Reservoir west of Orland; map C2, grid f0.

User groups: Hikers, dogs and mountain bikes. No horses. No wheelchair facilities.

Permits: No permits are required. Parking and access are free.

Maps: Ask the USGS for a topographic map of the Julian Rocks area.

Directions: From Interstate 5 at Orland take the Black Butte Lake exit. Drive 10 miles west on Newville Road (County Road 200) to County Road 206. Turn left on County Road 206 and drive to County Road 200A. Bear left on County Road 200A and drive to the trailhead.

Contact: U.S. Army Corps of Engineers, Black Butte Lake, 19225 Newville Road, Orland, CA 95963-8901; tel. (530) 865-4781 or fax (530) 865-5283.

ON THE BIZZ JOHNSON TRAIL, A
POPULAR RAILS-TO-TRAILS ROUTE

MAP C3

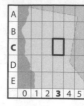

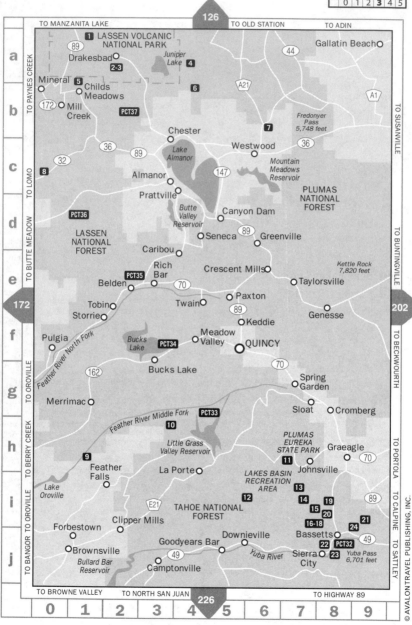

TO MANZANITA LAKE **126** TO OLD STATION TO ADIN

1 LASSEN VOLCANIC NATIONAL PARK

89 Drakesbad
2-3

Juniper Lake **4**

44

Gallatin Beach

Mineral **5**
Childs Meadows

A21

A1

172 Mill Creek

PCT37

6

Fredonyer Pass 5,748 feet

Chester

7

Westwood

36 89

Lake Almanor

147

Mountain Meadows Reservoir

TO SUSANVILLE

32

8

Almanor

Prattville

PLUMAS NATIONAL FOREST

PCT36

Butte Valley Reservoir

Canyon Dam

LASSEN NATIONAL FOREST

Caribou

Seneca 89 Greenville

Kettle Rock 7,820 feet

Rich Bar

Crescent Mills

Taylorsville

TO BUNTINGVILLE

PCT35 Belden

70

Tobin
Storrie

Twain

Paxton

89

Genesse

Keddie

172 **202**

Pulgia

Feather River North Fork

Bucks Lake

PCT34 Meadow Valley

QUINCY

TO BECKWOURTH

162

Bucks Lake

70

Spring Garden

TO OROVILLE

Merrimac

Feather River Middle Fork

PCT33

Sloat Cromberg

10

Little Grass Valley Reservoir

PLUMAS EUREKA STATE PARK

Graeagle

11 Johnsville

70

TO PORTOLA

TO BERRY CREEK

9

Feather Falls

La Porte

LAKES BASIN RECREATION AREA

13

14 **19**

89

Lake Oroville

E21

12

15 **20**

16-18

21

TO CALPINE

TO OROVILLE

Forbestown

Clipper Mills

TAHOE NATIONAL FOREST

24

Bassetts

22 **PCT32**

49

TO SATTLEY

Brownsville

Bullard Bar Reservoir

Goodyears Bar

49

Downieville

Yuba River

Sierra City **23**

Yuba Pass 6,701 feet

TO BANGOR

Camptonville

TO BROWNE VALLEY TO NORTH SAN JUAN **226** TO HIGHWAY 89

TO PAYNES CREEK
TO LOMO
TO BUTTE MEADOW

0 1 2 3 4 5 6 7 8 9

© AVALON TRAVEL PUBLISHING, INC.

CHAPTER C3

1 Bumpass Hell Trail. . . . 181
2 Devils Kitchen Trail. . . 182
3 Drake Lake Trail 182
4 Juniper Lake Loop. . . . 183
5 Spencer Meadow Trail . 184
6 Hay Meadow Trail 184
7 Bizz Johnson. 185
8 Deer Creek Trail 185
9 Feather Falls National
   Recreation Trail 186
10 Hartman Bar National
   Recreation Trail 186
11 Eureka Peak Loop 187
12 Chimney Rock Trail . . . 188
13 Upper Jamison Trail . . 188
14 Mount Elwell Trail 189
15 Bear Lakes Loop 189
16 Butcher Ranch Trail. . . 190
17 Pauley Creek Trail. . . . 191
18 Deer Lake Trail 191
19 Frazier Falls Trail 192

20 Round Lake Trailhead . 193
21 Haskell Peak Trail 193
22 Sierra Buttes Trail . . . 194
23 Wild Plum Loop/
   Haypress Creek. 194
24 Chapman Creek Trail. . 195

**Pacific Crest Trail
(PCT) Section Overview**

PCT-32 Yuba River to
   Fowler Peak. 196
PCT-33 Fowler Peak to
   Bucks Summit. 196
PCT-34 Bucks Summit to
   Feather River 197
PCT-35 Feather River to
   Humboldt Summit. . 197
PCT-36 Humboldt Summit to
   Domingo Springs . . 198
PCT-37 Domingo Springs to
   Lassen Volcanic
   National Park 198

1 Bumpass Hell Trail
3.0 mi/1.5 hrs

Bumpass Hell is like a walk into the land of perdition, complete with steam vents, boiling mud pots, and natural furnaces. It's all set amid volcanic rock and is prehistoric looking and a bit creepy, as if at any moment a dinosaur might come charging around the bend and start eating tourists. The trip to Bumpass Hell is the most popular hike in the park, and it makes sense because it's not only the park's largest thermal area but also an excellent morning walk.

The trail starts with a gradual 500-foot climb over the first mile, then descends 250 feet into the thermal area. It sits in a pocket just below Bumpass Mountain (8,753 feet), with a self-guiding leaflet available that explains the area. There are usually large numbers of tourists at Bumpass Hell, but you can get beyond them by extending your trip to Cold Boiling Lake, another 1.5 miles (one way), which includes two steep portions of trail.

Special note: For obvious reasons it's important to stay on the trail or boardwalk near hydrothermal areas.

Location: In Lassen Volcanic National Park east of Red Bluff; map C3, grid a1.

User groups: Hikers only. No dogs, horses, or mountain bikes. No wheelchair facilities.

Permits: No permits required. A $10 park entrance fee is charged for each vehicle.

Maps: Trail maps are available for a fee from Loomis Museum, c/o Lassen Volcanic National Park, at the address below. Ask the USGS for a topographic map of the Lassen Peak area.

Directions: From Interstate 5 at Red Bluff, turn east on Highway 36 and drive 47 miles to Highway 89. Turn north (left) on Highway 89 and drive 4.5 miles to the park entrance. Continue six miles on Lassen Park Highway (Highway 89) to the trailhead on the right.

Contact: Lassen Volcanic National Park, P.O. Box 100, Mineral, CA 96063-0100; tel. (530) 595-4444 or fax (530) 595-3262.

2 Devils Kitchen Trail
4.4 mi/2.5 hrs

Drakesbad is the undiscovered Lassen—beautiful, wild, and remote. It gets missed by nearly everybody because access is obscure and circuitous out of Chester. In other words, there's no way to get here when entering from either of the main Lassen Park entrances. But those who persevere will find a quiet paradise, along with this easy trip to Devils Kitchen, a unique geologic thermal area. The trail is an easy hike, heading west above Hot Springs Creek. After two miles it drops into this barren pocket of steaming vents and boiling mud pots and fumaroles, where you'll immediately see why it was tagged Devils Kitchen. It is illegal to walk off trail in this area.

Location: At Drakesbad in Lassen Volcanic National Park; map C3, grid a2.

User groups: Hikers only. Horses are allowed on a portion of the trail. No dogs or mountain bikes. No wheelchair facilities.

Permits: No permits required. A $10 park entrance fee is charged for each vehicle.

Maps: Trail maps are available for a fee from Loomis Museum, c/o Lassen Volcanic National Park at the address below. Ask the

USGS for a topographic map of the Reading Peak area.

Directions: From Interstate 5 at Red Bluff, turn east on Highway 36 and drive 47 miles to Highway 89. Do not turn. Continue east on Highway 36 toward Lake Almanor and to Chester and Feather River Drive. Turn left on Feather River Drive and drive .75 mile. Bear left for Drakesbad and Warner Valley and drive six miles to Warner Valley Road. Turn right and drive 11 miles to Warner Valley Campground. Continue .5 mile to the trailhead on the left. The last 3.5 miles is unpaved and there is one steep hill that can be difficult for trailers or RVs.

Contact: Lassen Volcanic National Park, P.O. Box 100, Mineral, CA 96063-0100; tel. (530) 595-4444 or fax (530) 595-3262.

3 Drake Lake Trail
4.5 mi/2.75 hrs

Drake is a somewhat swampy alpine lake that brightens a largely dry hillside, where deer are often more plentiful than people. Set in a remote forested pocket, it's very secluded and just difficult enough of a climb that many take a pass on the trip. From the trailhead at Drakesbad at about 5,700 feet, it's nearly an 800-foot climb over the course of two miles to Drake Lake (6,482 feet). Midway up the grade the hike becomes steep and stays that way for nearly 45 minutes.

The lake is the payoff, emerald green and circled by firs. But many are disappointed, hoping for better. After you catch your breath, you may feel like jumping in and cooling off, particularly if it's a hot summer day. Well, we've got news for you: In early summer the water is still ice cold, and just when you realize that, a battalion of mosquitoes will show up and start feasting on all your bare, sumptuous flesh. Then what? Jump in and freeze your buns? Stand there and get devoured? Heck no, you'll have your clothes back on in record time.

Location: At Drakesbad in Lassen Volcanic National Park; map C3, grid a2.

User groups: Hikers only. Horses are allowed on a portion of the trail. No dogs or mountain bikes. No wheelchair facilities.

Permits: No permits required. A $10 park entrance fee is charged for each vehicle.

Maps: Trail maps are available for a fee from Loomis Museum, c/o Lassen Volcanic National Park at the address below. Ask the USGS for a topographic map of the Reading Peak area.

Directions: From Interstate 5 at Red Bluff, turn east on Highway 36 and drive 47 miles to Highway 89. Do not turn. Continue east on Highway 36 toward Lake Almanor and to Chester and Feather River Drive. Turn left on Feather River Drive and drive .75 mile. Bear left for Drakesbad and Warner Valley and drive six miles to Warner Valley Road. Turn right and drive 11 miles to Warner Valley Campground. Continue for .5 mile to the trailhead on the left. The last 3.5 miles is unpaved and there is one steep hill that can be difficult for trailers or RVs.

Contact: Lassen Volcanic National Park, P.O. Box 100, Mineral, CA 96063-0100; tel. (530) 595-4444 or fax (530) 595-3262.

4 Juniper Lake Loop
7.5 mi/4.0 hrs

The Juniper Lake Loop explores Lassen Park's least known yet most beautiful backcountry, with many lakes, many lookouts, and the chance to turn this into an overnighter, with pretty trail camps along this route. The adventure starts at the trailhead adjacent to the Juniper Lake Ranger Station, which requires a long bumpy ride out of Chester just to reach. If you arrive late, a campground is available at the lake, elevation 6,792 feet. At the north end of Juniper Lake, the trail heads straight north, and though it has plenty of ups and downs, along with a fairly level stretch through Cameron Meadow, it's mostly down, descending 800 feet to Snag Lake, elevation 6,076 feet. The best advice is to turn south at

Snag Lake and take the trail along Grassy Creek to Horseshoe Lake. This section is the prettiest of the hike. If you want to extend your trip, options from Snag Lake including hiking out to into the backcountry to Rainbow Lake, a mile later to Lower Twin Lake (6,537 feet), and another mile farther to Swan Lake (6,628 feet). Any of these can make for a good trail camp. On the second day you'll loop back, skirt the south flank of Crater Butte (7,267 feet), head past Horseshoe Lake and then to the starting point. Alas, this trip is not flawless. The fishing is poor, mosquitoes are rampant in the early summer, and nights are very cold in the fall. Note: From the north end of Juniper Lake, the 400-foot climb to Inspiration Point doesn't provide much inspiration, with trees now blocking what was once a great view of Lassen Park's backcountry.

Location: In Lassen Volcanic National Park north of Lake Almanor; map C3, grid a4.

User groups: Hikers and horses. No dogs or mountain bikes. No wheelchair facilities.

Permits: No permits required. For overnight use, a wilderness permit (free) is required. A $10 park entrance fee is charged for each vehicle.

Maps: Trail maps are available for a fee from Loomis Museum, c/o Lassen Volcanic National Park at the address below. Ask the USGS for a topographic map of the Mount Harkness area.

Directions: From Interstate 5 at Red Bluff, turn east on Highway 36 and drive 47 miles to Highway 89. Do not turn. Continue east on Highway 36 toward Lake Almanor and to Chester and Feather River Drive. Turn left on Feather River Drive and drive .75 mile to a Y. Bear right at the Y to Juniper Lake Road and drive 13 miles to the Snag Lake trailhead near the ranger station. The access road is rough. Trailers and RVs are not recommended.

Contact: Lassen Volcanic National Park, P.O. Box 100, Mineral, CA 96063-0100; tel. (530) 595-4444 or fax (530) 595-3262.

5 Spencer Meadow Trail
10.0 mi/1.0 day

6 Hay Meadow Trail
6.0 mi/2.0 days

Spencer Meadow is a pretty mountain meadow on the southern flank of Lassen. Here explorers can discover an effervescent spring pouring forth, the source of Mill Creek and the creation of the headwaters of a Sacramento River tributary. Hiking access is easy, with the trailhead located at a parking area just off Highway 36. From here you hike straight north toward Lassen on the Spencer Meadow Trail. Over the course of five miles, the trail passes a small spring (about halfway in—look for the faint spur trail on the left), then tiny Patricia Lake (on the right, hidden), and finally Spencer Meadow and the Mill Creek Spring. Note that fishing at Mill Creek is restricted to catch-and-release and the use of artificials with single barbless hooks.

Special note: There is a trailhead closer to Spencer Meadow on Forest Road 29N40, but reaching it involves a long, rough drive.

Location: In Lassen National Forest just south of Lassen Volcanic National Park; map C3, grid b1.

User groups: Hikers, dogs, horses, and mountain bikes. No wheelchair facilities.

Permits: No permits are required. Parking and access are free.

Maps: A trail map is available for a fee from the Almanor Ranger District. For a map of Lassen National Forest, send $6 to U.S. Forest Service, Attn: Map Sales, P.O. Box 587, Camino, CA 95709; tel. (530) 647-5390, fax (530) 647-5389, or website: www.r5.fs.fed.us/visitorcenter. Major credit cards accepted. Ask the USGS for a topographic map of the Childs Meadows area.

Directions: From Interstate 5 at Red Bluff, drive east on Highway 36 for 43 miles to Mineral. Continue east on Highway 36 for about seven miles to the trailhead parking area on the left.

Contact: Lassen National Forest, Almanor Ranger District, P.O. Box 767, Chester, CA 96020; tel. (530) 258-2141 or fax (530) 258-5194.

Hidden between South Caribou Mountain and Black Cinder Rock is a little alpine pocket where dozens of small lakes are sprinkled about the southern Caribou Wilderness. It's a slice of paradise that some hikers call the "Hiking Lakes." The trail out of Hay Meadow is a loop route that crosses right through these lakes, including the area's larger and most divine settings, Beauty Lake, Long Lake, Posey Lake, and Evelyn Lake. While the trip can be made in a day, you likely won't feel like leaving, and we recommend planning an easy overnight backpacking trip. Another bonus of an overnight trip is that you can take the side trip up to Hidden Lakes, a series of several small but pretty waters, set just below South Caribou Mountain.

After arriving at the trailhead at Hay Meadow, the trip starts easily enough, first crossing Hay Meadow. In another mile you'll reach Beauty Lake, the first of five major lakes on this loop hike. They are all good for swimming, although a bit cold, and Beauty and Posey have the best trout fishing. Note that although the Caribou Wilderness abuts Lassen Volcanic National Park, it's often overlooked in the big park's shadow. That's to your benefit as long as you know about this trail.

Location: On the southern boundary of the Caribou Wilderness north of Lake Almanor; map C3, grid b4.

User groups: Hikers, dogs, and horses (a horse corral is available at the trailhead). No mountain bikes. No wheelchair facilities.

Permits: A campfire permit (free) is required. Parking and access are free.

Maps: A trail map is available for a fee from the Almanor Ranger District. For a map of Lassen National Forest, send $6 to U.S. Forest Service, Attn: Map Sales, P.O. Box 587, Camino, CA 95709; tel. (530) 647-5390, fax (530) 647-5389, or website: www.r5.fs.fed.us/visitorcenter. Major credit cards accepted. Ask the USGS for a topographic map of the Childs

Meadows area.

Directions: From Red Bluff, turn east on Highway 36 and drive to Chester. Continue east on Highway 36 for five miles to Forest Road 10. Turn north on Forest Road 10 and drive 9.5 miles to Forest Road 30N25. Turn left on Forest Road 30N25, and drive to the trailhead.

Contact: Lassen National Forest, Almanor Ranger District, P.O. Box 767, Chester, CA 96020; tel. (530) 258-2141 or fax (530)258-5194.

▉ Bizz Johnson
25 mi one way/3.0 days

In the 1960s, when Shasta legend John Reginato heard that Southern Pacific was going to abandon a rail line between Westwood and Susanville, he urged that it be converted to a hiking trail. The idea struck home, and the Bureau of Land Management worked with the U.S. Forest Service to develop and refine it. Today this trail is one of the true multiple-use routes in Northern California, with plenty of room for hikers, mountain bikers, and horseback riders. In the winter it makes a great trip on cross-country skis or on a snowmobile, with many trailheads providing different access points. The route traces the old Fernley and Lassen railroad line, following the Susan River Canyon for most of the way, basically routed from the Susanville Railroad Depot to the Mason Station Trailhead north of Westwood. The surface is a mixture of compacted dirt and small gravel. It features beautiful views in many areas, and passes through two old railroad tunnels. Yet it's raw and primitive. You won't cross any developed areas. Guess they had it right when they built that first railroad line. The one negative: Like most rails-to-trails projects, it's way too wide for a premium hiking trail.

Location: In Lassen National Forest west of Susanville; map C3, grid b6.

User groups: Hikers, dogs, horses, and mountain bikes. No wheelchair facilities.

Permits: No permits are required. Parking and access are free.

Maps: For a free brochure, contact the Bureau of Land Management at the address below. For a map of Lassen National Forest, send $6 to U.S. Forest Service, Attn: Map Sales, P.O. Box 587, Camino, CA 95709; tel. (530) 647-5390, fax (530) 647-5389, or website: www.r5.fs.fed. us/visitorcenter. Major credit cards accepted. Ask the USGS for topographic maps of the Westwood East, Fredonyer Pass, and Susanville areas.

Directions: In Susanville on Highway 36, turn south on Weatherlow Street and drive .5 mile (Weatherlow becomes Richmond Road) to the Susanville Depot and the trailhead on the right.

Alternate route: From Westwood on Highway 36, turn north on County Road A21 and drive three miles to the trailhead access road. Turn right (a dirt road) and drive .4 mile to the trailhead on the left.

Contact: Lassen National Forest, Eagle Lake Ranger District, 477-050 Eagle Lake Road, Susanville, CA 96130; tel. (530) 257-4188; Bureau of Land Management, Eagle Lake Field Office, 2950 Riverside Drive, Susanville, CA 96130; tel. (530) 257-0456 or fax (530) 257-4831.

▉ Deer Creek Trail
1-8 mi/1.0 day

The Deer Creek Trail has all the ingredients to make it ideal for a trout angler, explorer, or somebody just looking for a dunk on a hot day. The gorgeous stream runs right alongside the trail, with good access throughout and fish, often plenty of them, in the summer months. From the parking area the trail is routed downstream along the river for about 10 miles, but rarely does anybody ever walk all the way to the end. Instead they take their time, perhaps fishing or swimming along the way. In summer Deer Creek is cold and clear, tumbling its way over rocks and into pools, seemingly with trout in every one. California Department of Fish and Game rules mandate catch-and-release fishing with artificials with a single barbless hook for most of the river.

A sidelight here is that the canyon rim is made up of a series of volcanic crags, basalt spires, like something out of Jurassic Park.

Location: In Lassen National Forest along Highway 32 west of Lake Almanor; map C3, grid c0.

User groups: Hikers, dogs, and horses. Mountain bikes aren't advised. No wheelchair facilities.

Permits: No permits are required. Parking and access are free.

Maps: A trail map is available for a fee from Almanor Ranger District. For a map of Lassen National Forest, send $6 to U.S. Forest Service, Attn: Map Sales, P.O. Box 587, Camino, CA 95709; tel. (530) 647-5390, fax (530) 647-5389, or website: www.r5.fs.fed.us/visitorcenter. Major credit cards accepted. Ask the USGS for a topographic map of the Onion Butte area.

Directions: Drive north from Chico on Highway 32 for 40 miles. Just after crossing a small concrete bridge that crosses Deer Creek, park on the south side of the road where there's a dirt pullout. The trailhead is located just up from the bridge on the north side of the road.

Contact: Lassen National Forest, Almanor Ranger District, P.O. Box 767, Chester, CA 96020; tel. (530) 258-2141 or fax (530)258-5194.

9 Feather Falls National Recreation Trail

9.5 mi/4.0 hrs

Feather Falls is heaven to look at—a 640-foot silver band of water free-falling into a granite canyon, the kind of sight that can leave you feeling refreshed for weeks. In the spring, it's wide and powerful, and in years with big snowpacks in the Sierra, it stays that way well into July. But it runs all year and is beautiful even in the fall. The prime viewing area is an awesome perch, a viewing deck set on a knife ridge directly adjacent to the waterfall and seemingly hanging in midair over the Feather River Canyon. The trail is a pretty easy loop route.

From the trailhead this hike descends for a mile, crosses a stream and climbs out of the canyon, then is flat for the most part en route to the viewing area. Return on the loop, bearing left at the fork for a 4.5-mile cruise, mainly through forests and across small streams back to the parking area. Almost everybody takes the easy-graded 9.5-mile loop in a clockwise direction (an older, steeper route is two miles shorter, but takes nearly the same amount of hiking time). Note that at the waterfall some people crawl out on the brink of the falls on boulders; this is extremely dangerous. It is completely unnecessary to risk your life to get the exhilaration of this special and beautiful place.

Location: In Plumas National Forest east of Lake Oroville; map C3, grid h1.

User groups: Hikers and dogs. Horses and mountain bikes are permitted but not recommended. No wheelchair facilities.

Permits: No permits are required. Parking and access are free.

Maps: For a map of Plumas National Forest, send $6 to U.S. Forest Service, Attn: Map Sales, P.O. Box 587, Camino, CA 95709; tel. (530) 647-5390, fax (530) 647-5389, or website: www.r5.fs.fed.us/visitorcenter. Major credit cards accepted. Ask the USGS for a topographic map of the Brush Creek area.

Directions: From Oroville, drive east on Highway 162 (Oroville Dam Boulevard) about eight miles to Forbestown Road. Turn right (east) on Forbestown Road east and drive six miles to Lumpkin Road. Turn left on Lumpkin Road and drive 10.5 miles to the sign for the Feather Falls Trail. Turn left and drive 1.5 miles to the parking area at the end of the road.

Contact: Plumas National Forest, Feather River Ranger District, 875 Mitchell Avenue, Oroville, CA 95965-4699; tel. (530) 534-6500.

10 Hartman Bar National Recreation Trail

4.4 mi/3.0 hrs

Hikers often pay for their pleasure, and this hike involves two installments. The trail descends from the Hartman Ridge down the canyon to Hartman Bar Ridge on the Middle Fork Feather River. Going down will have your toes jamming into your boots, and the trip back can have your heart firing off like cannon shots. But awaiting is the Middle Fork Feather, one of the prettiest streams around, and with some of the best trout fishing as well. In fact, of the hundreds of trout streams in California, the Middle Fork Feather is clearly in the top five. If you don't like to fish but would rather explore further, a footbridge crosses the stream and climbs the other side of the canyon, meeting Catrell Creek at .5 mile. If you want to split the trip in two, the primitive Dan Beebe Camp is available along the river.

Location: In Plumas National Forest east of Lake Oroville; map C3, grid h3.

User groups: Hikers, dogs, and horses. A horse corral is available at the trailhead. Mountain bikes are not recommended. No wheelchair facilities.

Permits: No permits are required. Parking and access are free.

Maps: For a map of Plumas National Forest, send $6 to U.S. Forest Service, Attn: Map Sales, P.O. Box 587, Camino, CA 95709; tel. (530) 647-5390, fax (530) 647-5389, or website: www.r5.fs.fed.us/visitorcenter. Major credit cards accepted. Ask the USGS for topographic maps of the Cascade and Haskins Valley areas.

Directions: From Oroville drive east on Highway 162 for eight miles to Highway 174/Forbestown Road (and a junction signed Challenge/LaPorte). Turn right on Forbestown Road and drive east to Highway 120 (Quincy-LaPorte Road). Turn left and drive past LaPorte to Little Grass Valley Road. Turn left and drive a short distance to Black Rock Campground. Turn left on Forest Road 94 and drive 10 miles to Forest Road 22N42Y. Turn right and drive .25 mile to the parking area at the end of the road.

Contact: Plumas National Forest, Feather River Ranger District, 875 Mitchell Avenue, Oroville, CA 95965-4699; tel. (530) 534-6500.

11 Eureka Peak Loop
3.0 mi/2.0 hrs

The panoramic view of the southern Sierra Nevada from Eureka Peak, elevation 7,447 feet, includes all the peaks of the Gold Lakes Basin, with Mount Elwell (7,818 feet) most prominent to the south, and Plumas National Forest to the north and west, crowned by Blue Nose Mountain (7,290 feet), Stafford Mountain (7,019 feet), and Beartrap Mountain (7,232 feet). It's the vista that compels people to make the climb, a serious three-mile loop, with the first half a grunt to the top. The trailhead starts at Eureka Lake, elevation 6,300 feet. It then climbs 1,150 feet, a good, hard pull to the top. Many people start this trail by accident after seeing the trailhead sign while visiting the lake. That's a mistake. The trip should be planned; bring plenty of water and snacks to enjoy from the summit.

Location: In Plumas-Eureka State Park south of Quincy; map C3, grid h7.

User groups: Hikers only. No dogs, horses, or mountain bikes. No wheelchair facilities.

Permits: No permits are required. Parking and access are free.

Maps: For a brochure and trail map, send $.50 and a self-addressed, stamped envelope to Plumas-Eureka State Park at the address below. Ask the USGS for a topographic map of the Johnsville area.

Directions: Take Interstate 80 northeast to Truckee. Then take Highway 89 north and go past the town of Clio to County Road A14 (Graeagle-Johnsonville Road). Turn left (west) and drive six miles to the park entrance. Continue several miles to Eureka Lake (the road is rough and high-clearance vehicles are recommended). The trailhead is located at the north end of Eureka Lake.

Contact: Plumas-Eureka State Park, 310 Johnsville Road, Blairsden, CA 96103; tel. (530) 836-2380 or fax (530) 836-0498.

12 Chimney Rock Trail

5.0 mi/2.5 hrs

Chimney Rock is a huge volcanic cone that's 12 feet in diameter at its base, and rises nearly straight up for 25 feet. The great views from the top are well worth the trip. Yet brace yourself, because this little patch of land has undergone considerable change. First, the trail surface was hardened in 1999. In turn, off-highway vehicle (OHV) users started showing up in force, especially with dirt bikes. Now nearly 50 percent of the users are OHV users, 50 percent are mountain bikers, and between them they have driven out the hikers. The Downieville area in general has been taken over by mountain bikes, and often hikers looking for a natural, harmonious experience can encounter a pack of bikes. When that happens, it's adios, never to return. This trip was once a quiet spectacle, with a small climb to reach Chimney Rock, with side ventures around Needle Point and Rattlesnake Peak. Now you simply cringe when you hear the thunder of oncoming fast traffic, something like all the problems of city driving transported to a mountain trail.

Location: North of Downieville in Tahoe National Forest; map C3, grid i6.

User groups: Hikers, dogs, mountain bikes, horses, and OHV (primarily motorcycles). No wheelchair facilities.

Permits: No permits are required. Parking and access are free.

Maps: A trail map is available for a fee at the Downieville Ranger District. For a map of Tahoe National Forest, send $6 to U.S. Forest Service, Attn: Map Sales, P.O. Box 587, Camino, CA 95709; tel. (530) 647-5390, fax (530) 647-5389, or website: www.r5.fs.fed.us/visitorcenter. Major credit cards accepted. Ask the USGS for a topographic map of the Mount Fillmore area.

Directions: From Sacramento drive east on Interstate 80 to Auburn. Then take Highway 49 north to Nevada City and continue on Highway 49 (it jogs to the left in Nevada City, then narrows) for about 40 miles to an old cannon displayed on the right side of the road (.25 mile before reaching Downieville). Turn right at the cannon on an unsigned road, make a U-turn, and drive on Highway 49 westbound to Saddleback Road (do not attempt to turn left across traffic on Saddleback Road while eastbound on Highway 49 to make this turn). Turn right on Saddleback Road and drive eight miles north to a five-way intersection. Drive straight through to Road 25-23-1 and continue for 2.6 miles to Road 25-23-1-2 (look for the "Chimney Rock Trail" sign). Bear right on Road 25-23-1-2 and drive .5 mile to an intersection and head straight through. Continue another mile to a turnout on the left side of the road. Park here and hike in .6 mile to the trailhead. The total mileage from Downieville is 13 miles. Note: Sections of the road are quite rough.

Contact: Tahoe National Forest, Downieville Ranger District, 15924 Highway 49, Camptonville, CA 95922; tel. (530) 288-3231 or fax (530) 288-0727.

13 Upper Jamison Trail

8.2 mi/2.0 days

There's no reason to rush your way through this trail, which passes Grass, Jamison, and Rock Lakes, but rather take your time at it, stopping to enjoy the lakes along the way. Or take our suggestion and turn it into an overnight backpacking trip. The trail provides a glimpse of the beauty of the northern section of Lakes Basin Recreation Area, a country of alpine lakes and beveled granite mountains.

From the trailhead at the Jamison Mine building, start the trip by taking the Grass Lake Trail. It follows along Little Jamison Creek; note that a 100-foot cutoff trail provides a route to Little Jamison Falls. Back on the trail, you will climb two miles to Grass Lake, with the trail skirting the east side of the lake. For many on a day hike, this is far enough. However, we urge you to forge onward. It's another two miles to Jamison Lake, with the trail climbing more steeply, then crossing the creek twice before arriving at the outlet of Jamison Lake. Another .25 mile will route you over to Rock Lake, a pretty sight below Mount Elwell, elevation 7,818 feet. Several good trail campsites are available at Rock, Jamison, and Grass Lakes and are usually occupied on weekends.

Location: In Plumas-Eureka State Park on the northern boundary of Gold Lakes Basin, south of Quincy; map C3, grid i7.

User groups: Hikers, dogs, horses, or mountain bikes. No wheelchair facilities.

Permits: No permits are required. Parking and access are free.

Maps: For a trail map send $.50 and a self-addressed, stamped envelope to Plumas-Eureka State Park at the address below. Ask the USGS for a topographic map of the Johnsville area.

Directions: From Truckee take Highway 89 north and continue past the town of Clio to County Road A14 (Graeagle-Johnsonville Road); turn left (west) and drive 4.5 miles. Before reaching the Jamison Creek Bridge, look for a sign that reads, "Jamison Mine-Grass Lake Mine Complex." Turn left and drive on the dirt road about a mile to the Jamison Mine Complex. The trailhead starts at the far end of the parking lot.

Contact: Plumas-Eureka State Park, 310 Johnsville Road, Blairsden, CA 96103; tel. (530) 836-2380, or fax (530) 836-0498.

14 Mount Elwell Trail
6.0 mi/3.5 hrs

From atop Mount Elwell, 7,818 feet, you're surrounded by the Gold Lakes Basin, a wildland filled with alpine lakes and granite mountains. You'll find yourself dreaming of the days when you might visit them. This trail is a good way to start. It begins at the Smith Lake Trailhead and passes near Smith Lake (6,079 feet) on the Smith Lake Trail, climbing all the way— 2,018 feet over the course of three miles—to the top of Mount Elwell. It makes a great day trip for folks staying at the Gray Eagle Lodge.

Though few go onward from Mount Elwell, the trip can be extended simply enough. The trail continues past Mount Elwell, descending .75 mile to the Long Lake Trail junction, then another mile to a four-wheel-drive route. From this junction you can also make a loop back to the Smith Lake Trailhead by descending to Long Lake and continuing north three miles on the Long Lake Trail. This is one of the truly great hikes in the north Sierra.

Location: At Smith Lake in Gold Lakes Basin south of Quincy; map C3, grid i7.

User groups: Hikers, dogs, mountain bikes and horses. No wheelchair facilities.

Permits: No permits are required. Parking and access are free.

Maps: A trail map is available for a fee at the Beckwourth Ranger District. For a map of Plumas National Forest, send $6 to U.S. Forest Service, Attn: Map Sales, P.O. Box 507, Camino, CA 95709; tel. (530) 647-5390, fax (530) 647-5389, or website: www.r5.fs.fed.us/visitorcenter. Major credit cards accepted. Ask the USGS for a topographic map of the Gold Lake area.

Directions: From Sacramento drive northeast on Interstate 80 to Truckee and take Highway 89 north to the town of Clio. Continue a short distance north on Highway 89 to Forest Road 24 (Gold Lake Highway). Turn left (west) on Gold Lake Highway and drive five miles to the sign for Gray Eagle Lodge. Turn right and drive .5 mile to the Smith Lake Trailhead.

Contact: Plumas National Forest, Beckwourth Ranger District, P.O. Box 7, Blairsden, CA 96103; tel. (530) 836-2575 or fax (530) 836-0493.

15 Bear Lakes Loop
5.6 mi/3.0 hrs

Long Lake is one of the celestial settings in the heavenly Gold Lakes Basin. It's the feature destination of this hike, a good tromp that includes some steep rocky portions. The trailhead is just past the Lakes Basin Campground, elevation 6,300 feet. From here the trail is clear and well maintained but requires a huff and a puff of a mile. Here you'll see the turnoff for .25-mile spur trail to Long Lake, one mile to little Silver Lake, .75 mile to Cub Lake, and another .5 mile to Little Bear and Big Bear Lakes, and then .75 mile back to the trailhead. Long Lake is always a surprise to newcomers, since it's much larger than most high-country lakes and very pretty. The trail skirts along the southeast shoreline.

Special note: No camping is permitted at either Long or Silver Lakes.

Location: North of Sierra City; map C3, grid i7.

User groups: Hikers, dogs, mountain bikes, and horses. No wheelchair facilities.

Permits: No permits are required. Parking and access are free.

Maps: A trail map is available for a fee at the Beckwourth Ranger District. For a map of Plumas National Forest, send $6 to U.S. Forest Service, Attn: Map Sales, P.O. Box 587, Camino, CA 95709; tel. (530) 647-5390, fax (530) 647-5389, or website: www.r5.fs.fed.us/visitorcenter. Major credit cards accepted. Ask the USGS for a topographic map of the Gold Lake area.

Directions: Take Interstate 80 northeast from Sacramento to Truckee and then take Highway 89 north to the town of Clio. Continue a short distance north on Highway 89 to Forest Road 24 (Gold Lake Highway). Turn left on Gold Lake Highway and proceed about six miles until you see the sign for the Silver Lake Trailhead on the left (west) side of the road.

Contact: Plumas National Forest, Beckwourth Ranger District, P.O. Box 7, Blairsden, CA 96103; tel. (530) 836-2575 or fax (530)836-0493.

16 Butcher Ranch Trail

8.0 mi/5.0 hrs

This used to be a great hike, a picture of harmony and beauty. It still is for the few who are here at dawn and get it done before all the mountain bikes show up. The place is overrun now by mountain bikes and motorcycles, with weekends nearly intolerable. Hiker usage is down below 10 percent, having simply been driven out. This place was once a mountain canyon paradise where wildflowers were abundant, fishing was good, and a side trip would take you to a pristine stream with gorgeous deep pools, a place of peace and harmony. No more.

If you make the trip, you may wonder why it is rated a four for difficulty. After all, the trail follows the contour of Butcher Creek for 1.5 miles to the confluence of Pauley and Butcher Ranch Creeks. You then parallel Pauley Creek, with its deep and beautiful pools. On the way down you'll drop nearly 2,000 feet over the course of four miles. Try not to laugh on your way down; what goes down must come up, and on the return you'll be wondering why you ever talked yourself into this trip—especially if you run into a few motorcycles or a pack of mountain bikes heading downhill.

Location: West of Packer Lake in Tahoe National Forest; map C3, grid i7.

User groups: Off-highway vehicles, mountain bikes, hikers, dogs, and horses. No wheelchair facilities.

Permits: No permits are required. Parking and access are free.

Maps: A trail map is available for a fee at the Downieville Ranger District. For a map of Tahoe National Forest, send $6 to U.S. Forest Service, Attn: Map Sales, P.O. Box 587, Camino, CA 95709; tel. (530) 647-5390, fax (530) 647-5389, or website: www.r5.fs.fed.us/visitorcenter. Major credit cards accepted. Ask the USGS for a topographic map of the Sierra City area.

Directions: From Truckee turn north on Highway 89 and drive to Sierraville and Highway 49. Turn left on Highway 49 and drive 10 miles to Bassetts and Gold Lake Highway. Turn right (north) on Gold Lake Highway and drive 1.4 miles to Sardine Lake Road. Turn left on Sardine Lake Road and drive a short distance. Cross the Salmon Creek Bridge and continue .3 mile to Packer Lake Road. Turn right on Packer Lake Road and drive 2.5 miles to a fork (near Packer Lake). Take the left fork (Packer Saddle Road/Forest Road 93) and drive 2.1

miles and look for the sign for Sierra Buttes Lookout. Turn left and drive .5 mile and bear right; then continue .5 mile to a fork and sign for Butcher Ranch. Take the right fork (Forest Road 93-3) and drive .7 mile to a sign for the trailhead. Note: The road is quite steep and is recommended for high-clearance or four-wheel-drive vehicles only. Otherwise, park at the sign for the trailhead and hike .5 mile to the trailhead.

Contact: Tahoe National Forest, Downieville Ranger District, 15924 Highway 49, Camptonville, CA 95922; tel. (530) 288-3231 or fax (530) 288-0727.

17 Pauley Creek Trail

12.0 mi/2.0 days

The Pauley Creek Trail encompasses a land where there are streamside camps, spectacular wildflowers in early summer, and good trout fishing. Weekends are horrendous for dealing with high-speed mountain bikes and noisy motorcycles. Regardless, this is a beautiful stream and this trail is the best way to see it. Wildlife is also abundant in this watershed. The trailhead is difficult to reach, and the return hike out of the canyon back to the trailhead involves a 2,000-foot climb.

Location: West of Packer Lake in Tahoe National Forest; map C3, grid i7.

User groups: Hikers, dogs, horses, mountain bikes, and off-highway vehicles. No wheelchair facilities.

Permits: No permits are required. Parking and access are free.

Maps: A trail map is available for a fee at the Downieville Ranger District. For a map of Tahoe National Forest, send $6 to U.S. Forest Service, Attn: Map Sales, P.O. Box 587, Camino, CA 95709; tel. (530) 647-5390, fax (530) 647-5389, or website: www.r5.fs.fed.us/visitorcenter. Major credit cards accepted. Ask the USGS for topographic maps of the Downieville, Sierra City, and Gold Lake areas.

Directions: From Truckee turn north on Highway 89 and drive to Sierraville and Highway 49. Turn left on Highway 49 and drive 10 miles to Bassetts and Gold Lake Highway. Turn right (north) on Gold Lake Highway and drive 1.4 miles to Sardine Lake Road. Turn left on Sardine Lake Road and drive a short distance. Cross the Salmon Creek Bridge and continue .3 mile to Packer Lake Road. Turn right on Packer Lake Road and drive 2.5 miles to a fork (near Packer Lake). Take the left fork (Packer Saddle Road/Forest Road 93) and drive 2.1 miles and look for the sign for Sierra Buttes Lookout. Turn left, drive .5 mile, bear right, and drive .5 mile to Forest Road 93-3. Bear right and drive 2.5 miles to a sign "Gold Valley OHV Route." Turn left and drive 1.5 miles to an intersection. Bear left and cross Pauley Creek and drive .25 mile to a Y intersection. Bear left and drive .25 mile to the trailhead at the end of the road. Note: The access road is quite steep and is recommended for high-clearance or four-wheel-drive vehicles only. Otherwise, park at the sign for the trailhead and hike .5 mile to the trailhead.

Contact: Tahoe National Forest, Downieville Ranger District, 15924 Highway 49, Camptonville, CA 95922; tel. (530) 288-3231 or fax (530) 288-0727.

18 Deer Lake Trail

5.0 mi/3.5 hrs

Most lakes are green, but Deer Lake is the deepest azure blue you can imagine, and with the spectacular Sierra Buttes in the background, it's easy to understand why this trip is so popular. And popular it is, with the trail getting some of the heaviest use of any in this section of Tahoe National Forest. It's a 2.5-mile hike to the lake, climbing 1,000 feet, topping out at 7,110 feet. From the trailhead you'll climb through a basin and get a sweeping view of the massive Sierra Buttes and the surrounding forested slopes. As you head on, you'll cross a signed spur trail, a .25-mile route to Grass Lake. It's well worth the short detour, but approach quietly because

deer are common here. Then it's onward, over the ridge and down to Deer Lake. On warm evenings the brook trout leave countless circles while feeding on surface insects. This hike has it all, and, alas, that's why it often includes so many other people. Good news for hikers: Mountain bikes are few and off-highway vehicle use is prohibited.

Location: West of Packer Lake in Tahoe National Forest; map C3, grid i7.

User groups: Hikers, dogs, horses, and mountain bikes. No wheelchair facilities.

Permits: No permits are required. Parking and access are free.

Maps: A trail map is available for a fee at the Downieville Ranger District. For a map of Tahoe National Forest, send $6 to U.S. Forest Service, Attn: Map Sales, P.O. Box 587, Camino, CA 95709; tel. (530) 647-5390, fax (530) 647-5389, or website: www.r5.fs.fed.us/visitorcenter. Major credit cards accepted. Ask the USGS for a topographic map of the Sierra City area.

Directions: From Truckee turn north on Highway 89 and drive to Sierraville and Highway 49. Turn left on Highway 49 and drive 10 miles to Bassetts and Gold Lake Highway. Turn right (north) on Gold Lake Highway and drive 1.4 miles to Sardine Lake Road. Turn left on Sardine Lake Road and drive a short distance. Cross the Salmon Creek Bridge and continue .3 mile to Packer Lake Road. Turn right on Packer Lake Road and drive 2.5 miles to the trailhead. Parking is available in the Packsaddle camping area just opposite the trailhead.

Contact: Tahoe National Forest, Downieville Ranger District, 15924 Highway 49, Camptonville, CA 95922; tel. (530) 288-3231 or fax (530) 288-0727.

🔟 Frazier Falls Trail

1.0 mi/1.0 hr

Frazier Falls is a 178-foot, silver-tasseled waterfall that tumbles out of a chute into a rocky basin. It is like a miniature version of Feather Falls near Lake Oroville. The trail is a breeze, a .5-mile romp on a gentle route that leads to the scenic, fenced overlook of the falls. Starting 2001, the trail is completely accessible for wheelchairs. The best time to visit is early summer, when snowmelt from the high country is peaking, filling Frazier Falls like a huge fountain. In addition, wildflowers along the trail in early summer add a splash of color, with violet lupine the most abundant. The road to the trailhead is paved all the way, the hike is easy, the falls are beautiful, and as you might expect, thousands of people make the trip every summer.

Location: North of Sierra City; map C3, grid i8.

User groups: Hikers, dogs, horses, and wheelchairs. No mountain bikes. Wheelchair facilities are available.

Permits: No permits are required. Parking and access are free.

Maps: A trail map is available for a fee from Beckwourth Ranger District. For a map of Plumas National Forest, send $6 to U.S. Forest Service, Attn: Map Sales, P.O. Box 587, Camino, CA 95709; tel. (530) 647-5390, fax (530) 647-5389, or website: www.r5.fs.fed.us/visitorcenter. Major credit cards accepted. Ask the USGS for a topographic map of the Gold Lake area.

Directions: From Sacramento take Interstate 80 northeast to Truckee. Then take Highway 89 north to the town of Clio. Continue a short distance on Highway 89 north to Forest Road 24 (Gold Lake Highway). Turn left (west) on Forest Road 24 (Gold Lake Highway) and drive until you see the sign for Frazier Falls. Turn left and drive four miles to the trailhead on the left. Note: If you continue west on Gold Lake Highway for several miles, you will see another trailhead sign for Frazier Falls; it can also be reached on this route, but the road is rough and unpaved.

Contact: Plumas National Forest, Beckwourth Ranger District, P.O. Box 7, Blairsden, CA 96103; tel. (530) 836-2575 or fax (530) 836-0493.

20 Round Lake Trailhead

1.4 mi/1.0 hr

The .7-mile hike to Big Bear Lake is an easy, popular, and pretty walk, most commonly taken by visitors staying at Gold Lake Lodge. The trailhead is located alongside the parking lot next to the road to the lodge, and the trail itself is actually a closed road to Round Lake. It becomes trail within a few hundred yards when routed west to Big Bear Lake, the first in a series of beautiful alpine lakes in the Gold Lakes Basin. While most day users return after a picnic at Big Bear Lake, the trip can easily be extended, either west to Round Lake or Silver Lake, north to Long Lake. Most of this country is in the 6,000- to 7,000-foot elevation range and is high granite filled with alpine lakes.

Location: On the southern boundary of Gold Lakes Basin north of Sierra City; map C3, grid i8.

User groups: Hikers, dogs, mountain bikes, and horses. No wheelchair facilities.

Permits: No permits are required. Parking and access are free.

Maps: A trail map is available for a fee from Beckwourth Ranger District. For a map of Plumas National Forest, send $6 to U.S. Forest Service, Attn: Map Sales, P.O. Box 587, Camino, CA 95709; tel. (530) 647-5390, fax (530) 647-5389, or website: www.r5.fs.fed.us/visitorcenter. Major credit cards accepted. Ask the USGS for a topographic map of the Gold Lake area.

Directions: From Sacramento drive northeast on Interstate 80 to Truckee. Then take Highway 89 north to the town of Clio. Continue a short distance on Highway 89 north to Forest Road 24 (Gold Lake Highway). Turn left (west) on Forest Road 24 (Gold Lake Highway) and drive seven miles until you see the sign for Round Lake Trail. Turn right and continue to the parking area.

Contact: Plumas National Forest, Beckwourth Ranger District, P.O. Box 7, Blairsden, CA 96103; tel. (530) 836-2575 or fax (530) 836-0493.

21 Haskell Peak Trail

3.0 mi/2.0 hrs

Haskell Peak is one of the great but unknown lookouts. On clear days you can see many mountains both nearby and distant, including Mount Shasta and Mount Lassen in Northern California, Mount Rose in Nevada, and the closer Sierra Buttes. To get this view requires a 1,100-foot climb over the course of 1.5 miles, topping out at the 8,107-foot summit. The trail climbs at a decent, steady grade through heavy forest for the first mile. It then flattens and reaches an open area where Haskell Peak comes into view. From here it's only a .25-mile, but very steep, climb to the top. You'll discover that Haskell Peak is the flume of an old volcano and has many unusual volcanic rock formations. You'll also discover that just about nobody knows about this great hike. A fire lookout was once perched here, but it's gone now.

Location: North of Highway 49 in Tahoe National Forest; map C3, grid i9.

User groups: Hikers, dogs, horses, and mountain bikes. No wheelchair facilities.

Permits: No permits are required. Parking and access are free.

Maps: For a map of Tahoe National Forest, send $6 to U.S. Forest Service, Attn: Map Sales, P.O. Box 587, Camino, CA 95709; tel. (530) 647-5390, fax (530) 647-5389, or website: www.r5.fs.fed.us/visitorcenter. Major credit cards accepted. Ask the USGS for a topographic map of the Clio area.

Directions: From Truckee turn north on Highway 89 and drive to Sierraville and Highway 49. Turn left on Highway 49 and drive 10 miles to Bassetts and the Gold Lake Highway. Turn right on Gold Lake Highway and drive 3.7 miles to Forest Road 9 (Haskell Peak Road). Turn right and drive 8.4 miles. The trailhead is on the left; parking is available on either side of the road.

Contact: Tahoe National Forest, Downieville Ranger District, 15924 Highway 49, Camptonville, CA 95922; tel. (530) 288-3231 or fax (530) 288-0727.

22 Sierra Buttes Trail
5.0 mi/3.5 hrs ▨▨ ▨

The Sierra Buttes Lookout Station, sitting at 8,587 feet and with a railed stairway to its top, provides a destination for one of California's best day hikes and greatest viewpoints. Stand here one time and you'll never forget it the rest of your life. The trip starts above Packer Lake, at 6,000 feet. The trail climbs through a series of shaded switchbacks to 6,700 feet, tracing the ridge that eventually leads to the summit, crowned by a series of jagged crags. On the way you will rise to the rim of a mountain bowl that frames Sardine Lake, climbing some 1,500 feet to reach the top. The trail traces this rim to the lookout and is capped by three stairways that seem to project into wide-open space. Climbing it is an astounding sensation, almost like climbing the cable at Half Dome. The lookout itself also juts out into space, and it can seem quite eerie as you scan miles and miles of Sierra mountain country from Mount Lassen in the north all the way to the Tahoe Rim to the south, with a highlight being Union Valley Reservoir. Because the walkway around the lookout is grated, when you look straight down, you can see past your boots to a free fall, a bizarre sensation for many, that can even cause spatial disorientation.

Location: Near Packer Lake in Tahoe National Forest; map C3, grid j8.

User groups: Hikers, dogs, and horses. No mountain bikes (except on jeep trail). No wheelchair access.

Permits: No permits are required. Parking and access are free.

Maps: A trail map is available for a fee from the Downieville Ranger District. For a map of Tahoe National Forest, send $6 to U.S. Forest Service, Attn: Map Sales, P.O. Box 587, Camino, CA 95709; tel. (530) 647-5390, fax (530) 647-5389, or website: www.r5.fs.fed.us/visitorcenter. Major credit cards accepted. Ask the USGS for a topographic map of the Sierra City area.

Directions: From Truckee turn north on Highway 89 and drive to Sierraville and Highway 49. Turn left on Highway 49 and drive 10 miles to Bassetts and the Gold Lake Highway. Turn right on Gold Lake Highway and drive 1.4 miles to Sardine Lake/Packer Lake Road. Turn left, cross a small bridge, and bear right on Packer Lake Road. Continue past Packer Lake and bear left at a fork, following the signs to a trailhead for the Pacific Crest Trail (do not bear right at a jeep road). Continue to a small parking area. The trail starts as a jeep trail next to the parking area (then becomes trail on the ridge).

Contact: Tahoe National Forest, Downieville Ranger District, 15924 Highway 49, Camptonville, CA 95922; tel. (530) 288-3231 or fax (530) 288-0727.

23 Wild Plum Loop/ Haypress Creek
6.0 mi/1.0 day ▨▨ ▨

A canyon with a hidden stream and a waterfall that's surrounded by old-growth red fir make this a wonderful day hike for the properly inspired. Why properly inspired? Because the trail climbs from 4,400 feet up Haypress Creek to 5,840 feet, a 1,440-foot rise over just three miles. The trail starts out almost flat for the first .5 mile, then crosses over Haypress Creek on a footbridge. There's an excellent view of the Sierra Buttes in this area. Then you continue on the Haypress Creek Trail, rising past a rocky area and into forest, and, alas, passing some logging activity where the trail turns to road for a short spell. Don't despair. The trail soon enters an old-growth forest, contouring along Haypress Canyon, and passes by a lovely waterfall. This hike makes a great day trip with a picnic lunch, and trail use is typically quite light. Note that on the return trip, turn right on the Pacific Crest Trail to complete the loop. Walk .5 mile and turn left at the Wild Plum Loop trail sign to return.

Location: East of Sierra City in Tahoe National Forest; map C3, grid j8.

User groups: Hikers, dogs, and horses. No mountain bikes. No wheelchair facilities.

Permits: No permits are required. Parking and access are free.

Maps: For a map of Tahoe National Forest, send $6 to U.S. Forest Service, Attn: Map Sales, P.O. Box 587, Camino, CA 95709; tel. (530) 647-5390, fax (530) 647-5389, or website: www.r5.fs.fed.us/visitorcenter. Major credit cards accepted. Ask the USGS for a topographic map of the Haypress Valley area.

Directions: From Truckee drive north on Highway 89 to Sierraville and Highway 49. Turn left on Highway 49 and drive 12 miles (past Bassetts) to Wild Plum Road (near the eastern end of Sierra City) at the sign for Wild Plum Campground. Drive one mile on this road to the Wild Plum Trailhead parking area. Walk through the campground to its upper loop, walk around a locked gate, and continue up the road .25 mile to the Wild Plum Loop Trail Sign. Walk .25 mile to the intersection with the Pacific Crest Trail and turn left and cross a bridge over Haypress Creek. Continue for 200 yards to the trailhead on the right.

Contact: Tahoe National Forest, Downieville Ranger District, 15924 Highway 49, Camptonville, CA 95922; tel. (530) 288-3231 or fax (530) 288-0727.

24 Chapman Creek Trail
3.0 mi/2.0 hrs

Chapman Creek is a babbling brook where you can walk along, perhaps stopping to picnic, fish a little, or do absolutely nothing. That's right, nothing. It's that kind of place. The trailhead, elevation 5,840 feet, is set at a campground, providing easy access. Outside of campers, few others know of it. The trail winds easily along the contours of Chapman Creek under the canopy of a dense forest, rising gently along the way. It climbs to 6,400 feet, 560 feet in a span of 1.5 miles. The river is the lifeblood for a variety of birds and wildlife, but few visitors make the trip for that reason. Rather they come to stroll and let their minds wander and be free.

Location: East of Sierra City in Tahoe National Forest; map C3, grid j9.

User groups: Hikers, dogs, horses, and mountain bikes. No wheelchair facilities.

Permits: No permits are required. Parking and access are free.

Maps: For a map of Tahoe National Forest, send $6 to U.S. Forest Service, Attn: Map Sales, P.O. Box 587, Camino, CA 95709; tel. (530) 647-5390, fax (530) 647-5389, or website: www.r5.fs.fed.us/visitorcenter. Major credit cards accepted. Ask the USGS for a topographic map of the Sierra City area.

Directions: From Truckee turn north on Highway 89 and drive to Sierraville and Highway 49. Turn left on Highway 49, drive over Yuba Pass, and continue for four miles to the Chapman Creek Campground on the right. The trailhead and a parking area are located at the north end of the campground.

Contact: Tahoe National Forest, Downieville Ranger District, 15924 Highway 49, Camptonville, CA 95922; tel. (530) 288-3231 or fax (530) 288-0727.

Pacific Crest Trail (PCT) Section Overview
161.0 mi one way/2.0 weeks

Trail sections extend from the northern border of Tahoe National Forest (Yuba River) to Lassen Volcanic National Park.

If you plan on hiking only one section of the Pacific Crest Trail in this region, then make your selection with care. Highlights here include the Sierra Buttes, Gold Lakes Basin, Bucks Lake Wilderness, and Middle Fork Feather River, all world-class settings. But there are lowlights as well, including terrible chunks of trail through dry, hot country where there are too many rattlesnakes to take lightly. Much of the country ranges 5,000 to 7,000 feet in elevation, yet drops as low as 2,310 feet on the North Fork Feather River at Belden and 3,180 feet on the Middle Fork Feather. That means you'll face long, slow climbs and descents as you hike in and out of river canyons. Following is more specific information on major trail sections in this zone.

PCT-32 Yuba River to Fowler Peak

51.0 mi one way/4.0 days

Pristine alpine lakes and high mountain lookouts highlight this section of the Pacific Crest Trail. While just as beautiful as the section of trail south near Tahoe, this stretch gets far less use. It starts at the Yuba River and in the first two miles climbs an endless series of switchbacks up the back side of the Sierra Buttes—a terrible climb with a great reward. Note that the spur trail up to the Sierra Buttes Fire Lookout is an additional 1,400-foot climb, but furnishes one of the top lookouts in California. The trail then heads north, skirting past the western border of the Gold Lakes Basin, where a dozen high alpine lakes make for easy side trips and camps. With some terrible switchbacks, the PCT passes Mount Gibraltar (7,343 feet), Stafford Mountain (7,019 feet), and Mount Etna (7,163 feet), and flanks below Pilot Peak (7,457 feet). It then heads along the western slope, eventually reaching to the Fowler Peak Trailhead.

Location: In Tahoe National Forest, off Highway 49 east of Sierra City; map C3, grid j8.

User groups: Hikers, dogs, and horses. No mountain bikes. No wheelchair access.

Permits: A wilderness permit (free) is required. Parking and access are free.

Maps: For a map of Tahoe National Forest, send $6 to U.S. Forest Service, Attn: Map Sales, P.O. Box 587, Camino, CA 95709; tel. (530) 647-5390, fax (530) 647-5389, or website: www.r5.fs.fed.us/visitorcenter. Major credit cards accepted. Ask the USGS for topographic maps of the Haypress Valley, Sierra City, Mount Fillmore, and Onion Valley areas.

Directions: From Truckee turn north on Highway 89 and drive to Sierraville and Highway 49. Turn left on Highway 49 and drive 12 miles (passing Bassetts) to the eastern end of Sierra City. Look for the Pacific Crest Trail access sign and park on the right (north) side of the road.

Contact: Tahoe National Forest, Downieville Ranger District, 15924 Highway 49, Camptonville, CA 95922; tel. (530) 288-3231 or fax (530) 288-0727.

PCT-33 Fowler Peak to Bucks Summit

26.0 mi one way/3.0 days

Most PCT hikers will want to sprint through this section of trail. From Fowler Peak Trailhead, it passes through Plumas National Forest country until reaching the southern border of the Bucks Lake Wilderness. It starts quite nicely, dropping down to the Middle Fork Feather River (3,180 feet), a great trout stream, where an excellent footbridge gets you across a gorge. Enjoy it, because the rest of this route won't exactly have you writing postcards to back home. It climbs from the Middle Fork Feather to Lookout Rock, elevation 6,955 feet, and a long, dry pull, then drops down to Bucks Creek. Most of this region is dry rattlesnake country, so watch your step—and time your water stops.

Location: At Fowler Peak north of Little Grass Valley Reservoir in Plumas National Forest; map C3, grid h5.

User groups: Hikers, dogs, and horses. No mountain bikes. No wheelchair access.

Permits: A wilderness permit (free) is required. Parking and access are free.

Maps: For a map of Tahoe and Plumas National Forests, send $6 for each to U.S. Forest Service, Attn: Map Sales, P.O. Box 587, Camino, CA 95709; tel. (530) 647-5390, fax (530) 647-5389, or website: www.r5.fs.fed.us/visitorcenter. Major credit cards accepted. Ask the USGS for topographic maps of the Onion Valley, Dogwood Peak, and Bucks Lake areas.

Directions: From Oroville, drive east on Highway 162 for eight miles to Highway 174 (Forbestown Road and the junction signed Challenge/LaPorte. Turn right on Forbestown Road and drive east to Highway 120/Quincy-LaPorte Road. Turn left and drive past LaPorte to Little Grass Valley Road. Turn left on Little Grass Valley Road and drive to Black Rock Campground and Forest Road 94. Bear left on Forest Road 94 and drive three miles to Forest Road 22N27. Turn right and drive four miles to the parking area.

Contact: Plumas National Forest, Feather River Ranger District, 875 Mitchell Avenue, Oroville, CA 95965-4699; tel. (530) 534-6500 or fax (530) 532-1210.

PCT-34 Bucks Summit to Feather River

20.0 mi one way/2.0 days

It's 20 miles from Bucks Summit to Belden, all of it on the Pacific Crest Trail through the Bucks Lake Wilderness. The trail passes across a granitic-based alpine area, where forest is interspersed with glacier-smoothed rock peaks. The trailhead is at Bucks Summit, elevation 5,531 feet, and from here the route generally follows the ridgeline for many miles, climbing to the southern flank of Mount Pleasant, 6,924 feet. Along the way, a short spur trail to little Rock Lake provides a good side trip. The trail heads past Three Lakes, where another spur trail provides another option, this one to Kellogg Lake. From here the trail begins descending, then drops very sharply all the way down to 2,310 feet to the North Fork Feather River at Belden. Your big toes will be sore for days from jamming into the front of your boots.

Location: At Bucks Summit Trailhead at the southern boundary of the Bucks Lake Wilderness west of Quincy; map C3, grid f3.

User groups: Hikers, dogs, and horses. No mountain bikes. No wheelchair access.

Permits: A wilderness permit (free) is required. Parking and access are free.

Maps: For a map of Plumas National Forest, send $6 to U.S. Forest Service, Attn: Map Sales, P.O. Box 587, Camino, CA 95709; tel. (530) 647-5390, fax (530) 647-5389, or website:

www.r5.fs.fed.us/visitorcenter. Major credit cards accepted. Ask the USGS for a topographic map of the Bucks Lake area.

Directions: From Quincy turn west on Bucks Lake Road and drive about 11 miles to the trailhead at Bucks Summit.

Contact: Plumas National Forest, Mount Hough Ranger District, 39696 Highway 70, Quincy, CA 95971; tel. (530) 283-0555 or fax (530) 283-1821.

PCT-35 Feather River to Humboldt Summit

26.0 mi one way/2.0 days

The trail is not only rough from Belden to Humboldt Summit, but it's not particularly pretty, especially compared to the nearby wilderness. The climb is a mighty dry slice of life. From the North Fork Feather River at Belden, elevation 2,310 feet, the PCT climbs 4,777 feet over the course of this two-day thumper to Humboldt Summit at 7,087 feet. There are no lakes along this trail, only a few small water holes requiring short side trips. Instead, the prettiest sections are along streams, the first being Chips Creek, which runs adjacent to the trail for eight miles, then later a short crossing over the headwaters of Willow Creek. Some might prefer to take three days instead of two to hike this section, but with Lassen Volcanic National Park looming ahead, you'll put in long days to get through this area.

Location: At the Belden Trailhead on Highway 70 in Plumas National Forest; map C3, grid e2.

User groups: Hikers, dogs, and horses. No mountain bikes. No wheelchair facilities.

Permits: A wilderness permit (free) is required. Parking and access are free.

Maps: For a map of Plumas National Forest, send $6 to U.S. Forest Service, Attn: Map Sales, P.O. Box 587, Camino, CA 95709; tel. (530) 647-5390, fax (530) 647-5389, or website: www.r5.fs.fed. us/visitorcenter. Major credit cards accepted. Ask the USGS for topographic maps of the Belden and Humboldt Peak areas.

Directions: From Quincy drive west on Highway 70 about 26 miles to the trailhead, located at the roadside rest area at Belden.

Contact: Plumas National Forest, Mount Hough Ranger District, 39696 State Highway 70, Quincy, CA 95971; tel. (530) 283-0555.

PCT-36 Humboldt Summit to Domingo Springs

28.0 mi one way/2.0 days

The idea of back-to-back 14-mile days to get through this chunk of trail may not appeal to many hikers, especially while carrying full-weight expedition packs. But that's standard for most hikers on this stretch of PCT, with little here to tarry for and with Lassen Volcanic National Park beckoning ahead. The trail starts just below Humboldt Peak at 7,087 feet and heads north along the ridge line, for the most part, past Butt Mountain (7,866 feet) and down to Soldier Meadows. A spring and stream make this a delightful stop before crossing Highway 36, forging onward another three miles to the Stove Springs Campground. The trail then skirts around the western flank of North Stove Mountain and drops down to Domingo Springs, where another campground is available.

Location: At Humboldt Summit in Lassen National Forest southwest of Lake Almanor; map C3, grid d1.

User groups: Hikers, dogs, and horses. No mountain bikes. No wheelchair facilities.

Permits: A wilderness permit (free) is required. Parking and access are free.

Maps: For a map of Lassen National Forest, send $6 to U.S. Forest Service, Attn: Map Sales, P.O. Box 587, Camino, CA 95709; tel. (530) 647-5390, fax (530) 647-5389, or website: www.r5.fs.fed.us/visitorcenter. Major credit cards accepted. Ask the USGS for topographic maps of the Humboldt Peak and Stover Mountain areas.

Directions: From Chico drive north on Highway 32 to the junction with Highway 89/36. Turn right (east) and take Highway 36 toward Chester. Turn west on Highway 36 and drive two miles to the junction with Highway 89. Turn south on Highway 89 and proceed four miles; then turn right on County Road 308 (Humboldt Road) and drive 15 miles to the trailhead parking area.

Contact: Lassen National Forest, Almanor Ranger District, P.O. Box 767, Chester, CA 96020; tel. (530) 258-2141 or fax (530) 258-5194.

PCT-37 Domingo Springs to Lassen Volcanic National Park

11.0 mi one way/1.0 day

With each passing step the scenery gets better and better. Finally you leave dry, hot forest country and enter Lassen Volcanic National Park at Warner Valley. All the suffering seems over and only paradise awaits. From Domingo Springs the Pacific Crest Trail runs straight north through Lassen National Forest. The Little North Fork of the North Fork Feather River is located .25 mile to the west and is a good side trip, both for swimming and fishing for large brown trout. As you enter Lassen Volcanic National Park, you'll pass Little Willow Lake and two miles later arrive at Boiling Springs Lake and the Warner Valley Campground. This is a good layover spot, with the side trip to Devils Kitchen recommended.

Location: At the Domingo Springs Trailhead in Lassen National Forest west of Lake Almanor; map C3, grid b2.

User groups: Hikers, dogs, and horses. No mountain bikes. No wheelchair facilities.

Permits: A wilderness permit (free) is required. Parking and access are free.

Maps: For a map of Lassen National Forest, send $6 to U.S. Forest Service, Attn: Map Sales, P.O. Box 587, Camino, CA 95709; tel. (530) 647-5390, fax (530) 647-5389, or website: www.r5.fs.fed.us/visitorcenter. Major credit cards accepted. Ask the USGS for a topographic map of the Stover Mountain area.

Directions: From Chico drive north on Highway 32 to the junction with Highway 89/36. Turn right (east) and take Highway 36 toward Chester. In Chester turn north on Warner Valley Road (County Road 312) and drive about six miles. Turn left on Old Red Bluff Road (County Road 311) and go three miles to the parking area at Domingo Springs.

Contact: Lassen National Forest, Almanor Ranger District, P.O. Box 767, Chester, CA 96020; tel. (530) 258-2141 or fax (530) 258-5194.

PCT Continuation

To continue hiking along the Pacific Crest Trail, see chapter B3.

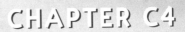

CHAPTER C4

WILLOW CREEK RUNNING
THROUGH SAGE BRUSH COUNTRY
EAST OF SUSANVILLE

MAP C4

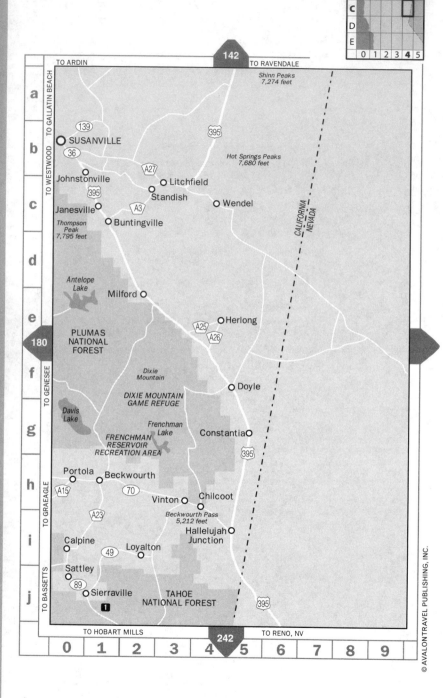

TO ARDIN

142

TO RAVENDALE

Shinn Peaks
7,274 feet

TO GALLATIN BEACH

a

139

b

SUSANVILLE

36

A27

Johnstonville

Litchfield

TO WESTWOOD

395

Standish

Hot Springs Peaks
7,680 feet

c

A3

Janesville

Wendel

Buntingville

Thompson
Peak
7,795 feet

d

Antelope
Lake

Milford

e

PLUMAS
NATIONAL
FOREST

A25

Herlong

180

A26

TO GENESEE

f

Dixie
Mountain

Doyle

DIXIE MOUNTAIN
GAME REFUGE

Davis
Lake

g

Frenchman
Lake

Constantia

FRENCHMAN
RESERVOIR
RECREATION AREA

395

Portola

h

Beckwourth

TO GRAEAGLE

A15

70

Vinton

Chilcoot

A23

Beckwourth Pass
5,212 feet

i

Hallelujah
Junction

Calpine

TO BASSETTS

Loyalton

49

j

Sattley

89

Sierraville

TAHOE
NATIONAL FOREST

395

1

TO HOBART MILLS

242

TO RENO, NV

CALIFORNIA
NEVADA

0 1 2 3 4 5 6 7 8 9

CHAPTER C4

1 Cottonwood Creek Botanical Trail

0.5 mi/0.5 hr

The Cottonwood Creek Botanical Trail is a .5-mile loop nature trail that follows along little Cottonwood Creek. The trailhead is at the Cottonwood Creek Campground, set at 5,800 feet in the Sierra Nevada. The trail leads out of camp, where a free brochure is available at the trailhead. The brochure has listings that correspond to numbered posts along the trail and explains a variety of plants and trees unique to the area. This is a short, easy trip along a refreshing stream with a little botany lesson along the way. There are several nearby side trips. Hikers can access the Fisherman's Trail and Overlook Trail from the Cottonwood Creek Botanical Trail. In addition, Sierra Hot Springs is located a very short drive west of Sierraville off Highway 49. The trailhead is between campsites 11 and 12.

Location: In Tahoe National Forest; map C4, grid j1.

User groups: Hikers and dogs. No horses or mountain bikes. No wheelchair facilities.

Permits: No permits are required. Parking and access are free.

Maps: For a map of Tahoe National Forest, send $6 to U.S. Forest Service, Attn: Map Sales, P.O. Box 587, Camino, CA 95709; tel. (530) 647-5390, fax (530) 647-5389, or website: www.r5.fs.fed.us/visitorcenter. Major credit cards accepted.

Directions: From Truckee drive north on Highway 89 about 20 miles to the Cottonwood Creek Campground entrance on the right. The trailhead is at the upper end of the campground between campsites 11 and 12. Just south of the campground entrance on the right is a large turnout providing free parking for day use. An alternate route from Sierraville is to drive four miles southeast on Highway 89 to Cottonwood Creek Campground on your left. The trail must be accessed through the campground.

Contact: Tahoe National Forest, Sierraville Ranger District, P.O. Box 95, Sierraville, CA 96126; tel. (530) 994-3401 or fax (530) 994-3143.

TRAIL THROUGH A WINDBREAK
ALONG THE COAST

MAP D0

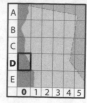

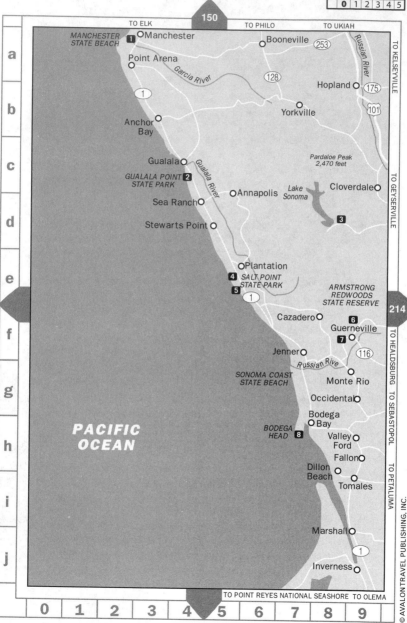

TO ELK   TO PHILO   TO UKIAH

150

MANCHESTER STATE BEACH
Manchester
Point Arena
Garcia River
Booneville (253)
(128)
Russian River
Hopland (175)
(101)
Yorkville
Anchor Bay

Gualala
GUALALA POINT STATE PARK
Gualala River
Pardaloe Peak 2,470 feet
Sea Ranch
Annapolis
Lake Sonoma
Cloverdale
Stewarts Point

Plantation
SALT POINT STATE PARK
ARMSTRONG REDWOODS STATE RESERVE
Cazadero
Guerneville
Jenner
Russian River
(116)
SONOMA COAST STATE BEACH
Monte Rio
Occidental
Bodega Bay
BODEGA HEAD
Valley Ford
Fallon
Dillon Beach
Tomales

PACIFIC OCEAN

Marshall
Inverness
(1)

TO KELSEYVILLE
TO GEYSERVILLE
TO HEALDSBURG
TO SEBASTOPOL
TO PETALUMA

214

© AVALON TRAVEL PUBLISHING, INC.

TO POINT REYES NATIONAL SEASHORE   TO OLEMA

0 1 2 3 4 5 6 7 8 9

CHAPTER D0

1 Alder Creek Trail 207
2 Headlands Loop 207
3 South Lake Trailhead . . . 208
4 Stump Beach Trail 208
5 Stockoff Creek Loop . . . 209
6 Gilliam Creek Trail 209
7 East Ridge Trail 210
8 Bodega Head Loop 210

1 Alder Creek Trail
4.0 mi/1.75 hrs

Manchester State Beach has two moods, one sweet, one foul. In late winter and fall radiant sunbeams set the Mendocino coast aglow, making for flawless beach walks. But in spring and early summer, with winds powering out of the north, it can feel as if your head would blow off if it weren't attached by the neck. The hike here starts by the park headquarters and is routed past Lake Davis to the beach, continuing north along the beach to the mouth of Alder Creek. This is an attractive coastal lagoon, known for many species of birds, including whistling swans. It's also the area where the San Andreas Fault heads off from land into the sea. Time it right here and all can seem perfect.

Location: In Manchester Beach State Park on the Mendocino coast north of Point Arena; map D0, grid a2.

User groups: Hikers and horses. No dogs. The terrain isn't suitable for mountain bikes. No wheelchair facilities.

Permits: No permits are required. A $2 state park day-use fee is charged for each vehicle.

Maps: For a brochure and trail map, send $1 to Manchester Beach State Park at the address below. Ask the USGS for a topographic map of the Point Arena area.

Directions: From Point Arena, drive north on Highway 1 for five miles to Kinney Lane. Turn left and drive one mile to the park entrance on the right.

Contact: Manchester Beach State Park, c/o California State Parks, Mendocino District, P.O. Box 440, Mendocino, CA 95460; tel. (707) 937-5804 or fax (707) 937-2953.

2 Headlands Loop
1.5 mi/0.75 hr

The Headlands to Beach Loop is an easy, short walk that furnishes coastal views (with a short cut-off on a spur trail) and a lookout over the Gualala River, not to mention a route amid giant coastal cypress trees. From the visitor center the trail is routed along the Gualala River and then turns and loops to the left. Here you can take the short cutoff trail that leads to the beach. On the way back, the trail traces the ocean bluffs for a short spell (take the spur trail), and with it comes the coastal views. Then the trail turns inland and returns to the visitor center. Bonuses here include excellent whale-watching during the winter and good wildflower blooms on the grassy hillsides in spring.

Location: In Gualala Point Regional Park on the Mendocino coast; map D0, grid c4.

User groups: Hikers and dogs. No horses. One trail is suitable for wheelchairs and mountain bikes.

Permits: No permits are required. There is a $3 parking fee.

Maps: Ask the USGS for a topographic map of the Gualala area.

Directions: From Gualala drive south on Highway 1 for .25 mile (over the Gualala River) and turn west into the park entrance. Continue to the visitor center.

Contact: Gualala Point Regional Park, P.O. Box 95, Gualala, CA 95445; tel. (707) 785-2377 or fax (707) 785-3741. Sonoma County Regional Parks Department, tel. (707) 565-2041 or fax (707) 579-8247.

3 South Lake Trailhead
5.0 mi/2.0 hrs

Lake Sonoma is one of the best examples in California of where the government folks have done something right. They not only built this lake but added a superb boat ramp, marina, and campgrounds (some boat-in) and started a good bass fishery. They also cut 43 miles of trail, enough to spend days traipsing around the hills. The South Lake Trailhead is the best starting point, though the short trail at Vista Point has the best views (and the most wind in the spring and heat in the summer).

From the trailhead the route traces along the lake, enters and exits a series of small groves, and extends along the lake's fingers. When you've had enough, just turn back. This suggested distance is routed to a boat-in campground and back. Many trails bisect the route and extend into more remote surrounding country, allowing ambitious hikers to create longer adventures. This area gets very hot in the summer. Most of the habitat is oak grasslands, and rarely you may see wild pigs, deer, or rattlesnakes.

Location: At Lake Sonoma northwest of Healdsburg; map D0, grid d8.

User groups: Hikers, dogs, and horses. No mountain bikes. No wheelchair facilities.

Permits: No permits are required. Parking and access are free.

Maps: For a free map, contact the U.S. Corps of Engineers at the address below. Ask the USGS for a topographic map of the Warm Springs Dam area.

Directions: From Santa Rosa drive 12 miles north on U.S. 101 to the town of Healdsburg and Dry Creek Road. Make a left turn at the Dry Creek Road exit and drive about 11 miles, crossing Dry Creek (Dry Creek Road becomes Skaggs Springs Road) and continuing (passing the visitor center) to Skaggs Springs-Stewart Point Road. Turn left, drive .25 mile, and then turn right and drive to the trailhead on the left.

Contact: U.S. Army Corps of Engineers, Lake Sonoma, 3333 Skaggs Springs Road, Geyserville, CA 95441; tel. (707) 433-9483.

4 Stump Beach Trail
3.5 mi/1.5 hrs

The dramatic, rocky shoreline of Salt Point State Park is memorable to anyone who has seen it. This trail provides the best look at it, including some simply awesome views from a 100-foot-high ocean bluff. The trailhead is at the parking area set near the tip of Salt Point, and from there you hike north over Warren Creek, a seasonal stream, and then across the bluffs. You can practically feel the crashing of ocean breakers below you, the spray rocketing skyward. The trail eventually winds around and down to Stump Beach Cove, a pretty, sandy beach where the calm waters are in sharp contrast to the nearby mauling ocean breakers. Salt Point State Park is known for excellent sport abalone diving in season, and also for providing one of the few marine reserves (Gerstle Cove) where no form of marine life may be taken or disturbed.

Location: In Salt Point State Park north of Jenner; map D0, grid e5.

User groups: Hikers only. Horses are allowed on designated trails only and mountain bikes are allowed only on fire roads. One trail (Gerstle Cove) is paved for wheelchairs for 100 yards out to Salt Point. No dogs.

Permits: No permits are required. A $2 state park day-use fee is charged per vehicle.

Maps: A trail map is available for $1 from Salt Point State Park at the address below. Ask the USGS for a topographic map of the Plantation area.

Directions: From U.S. 101 north of Santa Rosa, drive to the River Road exit. Take that exit and drive west for 13 miles to Highway 116 and Guerneville. Turn west on Highway 116 and drive to Highway 1 at Jenner. Turn north on Highway 1 and drive 20 miles (nine miles past Fort Ross) to the park entrance. Turn left (west) and drive to the entrance kiosk. The trailhead is at the Salt Point parking area.

Contact: Salt Point State Park, 25050 Coast Highway 1, Jenner, CA 95450; tel. (707) 847-3221 or fax (707) 847-3843.

5 Stockoff Creek Loop
1.25 mi/0.75 hr

Highway 1 is one of the top tourist drives in the United States, which explains why the coastal state parks get such heavy use in the summer months. This little regional park, however, is sometimes overlooked by out-of-state traffic. The trailhead is located at the day-use parking lot, and after starting the walk, you'll almost immediately enter a surprising forest comprised of firs and redwoods. You then come to the Loop Trail junction, where you turn right (another good idea is to take the Schoolhouse Trail, a spur trail that is routed a short distance to a historic schoolhouse, and then return). The trail is routed along the creek, crosses a few bridges, and eventually rises above the watershed and loops back through forest to the parking area. It's an easy, pretty, and secluded loop hike. A bonus is visiting Stillwater Cove, which requires crossing Highway 1 and then dropping down to the beach, a dramatic rock-strewn shore.

Location: In Stillwater Cove Regional Park north of Jenner; map D0, grid e5.

User groups: Hikers and dogs. No horses or mountain bikes. No wheelchair facilities.

Permits: No permits are required. A $3 day-use fee is charged for each vehicle.

Maps: For a free brochure, contact Stillwater Cove Regional Park at the address below. Ask the USGS for a topographic map of the Plantation area.

Directions: Just north of Santa Rosa on U.S. 101, take the River Road exit. Turn left and follow River Road past Monte Rio. Go right on Highway 116 and drive to Highway 1. Turn right and head north, past the town of Jenner for 16 miles to the park entrance on the right, at mile marker 37.01.

Contact: Stillwater Cove Regional Park, County of Sonoma, 2300 County Center Drive, Suite 120, Building A, Santa Rosa, CA 95403; tel. (707) 847-3245; Regional Parks Department; tel. (707) 565-2041 or fax (707) 579-8247.

6 Gilliam Creek Trail
8.9 mi/1.0 day

The rolling hills, open forests, and streamside riparian habitat in Austin Creek State Recreation Area can seem a million miles away from the redwood forests of Armstrong Redwoods. Yet the two parks together actually form 6,488 acres of contiguous parkland. While most tourists are walking around the redwoods at Armstrong, this trail offers a quieter, more ambitious alternative. From the trailhead at 1,100 feet, you contour across the slope, then drop down to the headwaters of Schoolhouse Creek at 400 feet. The trail then follows the stream, past the confluence with Gilliam Creek, extending 3.7 miles into the backcountry, all the way down to a 200-foot elevation. At the confluence of East Austin Creek, you turn right and hike deeper into wild, hilly country along the stream, then return on the loop on the East Austin Creek Trail, a fire road with a climb to boot. At this point, you may ask, "Are we having fun yet?" Visitors who love Armstrong Redwoods tend not to speak of the adjoining Austin Creek Recreation Area with any terms of endearment.

Location: In Austin Creek State Recreation Area north of Guerneville; map D0, grid f9.

User groups: Hikers and horses (no horses permitted during wet weather). No dogs or mountain bikes (bikes permitted on fire roads). No wheelchair facilities.

Permits: No permits are required. A $2 state park day-use fee is charged for each vehicle.

Maps: A trail map is available for $.50 from Armstrong Redwoods State Reserve at the address below. Ask the USGS for a topographic map of the Guerneville area.

Directions: From Santa Rosa drive north on U.S. 101 to the River Road exit. Take that exit and turn west on River Road and drive 13 miles to Guerneville and continue to Armstrong Woods Road. Turn right (north) on Armstrong Woods Road and drive 2.5 miles to the Armstrong Redwoods State Reserve entrance. The trailhead is about four miles past the entrance. No trailers or vehicles more than 20 feet along are permitted in Austin Creek.

Contact: Armstrong Redwoods State Reserve, 17000 Armstrong Redwoods Road, Guerneville, CA 95446; tel. (707) 869-2015 or tel. (707) 865-2391.

Directions: From Santa Rosa drive north on U.S. 101 to the River Road exit. Take that exit and turn west on River Road and drive 13 miles to Guerneville and continue to Armstrong Woods Road. Turn right (north) on Armstrong Woods Road and drive 2.5 miles to the Armstrong Redwoods State Reserve entrance. The trailhead is adjacent to the visitor center.

Contact: Armstrong Redwoods State Reserve, 17000 Armstrong Redwoods Road, Guerneville, CA 95446; tel. (707) 869-2015; Russian River District, tel. (707) 865-2391.

7 East Ridge Trail

6.8 mi/1.0 day

It's almost obligatory to hike either the Discovery Trail or Armstrong Nature Trail in Armstrong Redwoods, both very short and beautiful strolls through the park's grove of huge redwoods. But after that taste, your appetite will likely be whetted for something more inspiring. The East Ridge Trail provides it, rising 1,400 feet over the course of 3.4 miles, at times offering lookouts below into a sea of redwood tops. The trailhead is at a 200-foot elevation, adjacent to Fife Creek. The route climbs gradually at first, then in the first .5 mile rises to cross the headwaters of Fife Creek, elevation 600 feet. Your climb has only just begun, and if you're already running out of gas, you'd best head back. The trail continues climbing all the way, contouring its way up towards McCray Mountain (1,940 feet), topping out at a service road at 1,600 feet.

Location: In Armstrong Redwoods State Reserve north of Guerneville; map D0, grid f8.

User groups: Hikers and horses. No dogs or mountain bikes. No wheelchair facilities.

Permits: No permits are required. A $2 state park day-use fee is charged for each vehicle. It is possible here to park outside the entrance kiosk and walk in without paying a fee.

Maps: A trail map is available for $.50 from Armstrong Redwoods State Reserve at the address below. Ask the USGS for a topographic map of the Guerneville area.

8 Bodega Head Loop

1.5 mi/1.0 hr

A short loop hike at Bodega Head will provide an introduction to one of California's great coastal areas. The trail starts at the east parking lot, and in just 1.5 miles will take you into a wonderland with views of cliffs, untouched beaches, and southward to the sea and beyond. For a side trip take a short tromp on a spur trail to the tip-top of Bodega Head for 360-degree views. Rarely does the ocean seem so vast as it does from here. In spring and early summer the wind can really howl. In late summer, fall, or late winter, Bodega Bay gets its warmest—and often wind-free—weather.

Bonuses: The whale-watching is great in January and February, and on clear, calm evenings the sunsets are so beautiful they can break your heart.

Location: On the Sonoma coast west of Bodega Bay; map D0, grid h7.

User groups: Hikers only. No horses, dogs, or mountain bikes. No wheelchair facilities.

Permits: No permits are required. Parking and access are free.

Maps: A trail map and brochure are available for $1 from Sonoma Coast State Beach at address below.

Directions: From U.S. 101 at Petaluma, take the East Washington exit. Turn west on East Washington Street and drive through Petaluma (it becomes Bodega Avenue) for about 10 miles to Valley Ford Road. Bear right and drive 7.5 miles to Highway 1. Turn north on Highway 1 and drive nine miles to Bodega Bay and continue to East Shore Road. Turn left on East Shore Road and drive less than .5 mile to a stop sign at Bay Flat Road. Turn right and drive five miles around Bodega Bay (the road turns into West Side Road) and continue past Spud Point Marina and drive to the Bodega Head parking area.

Contact: Sonoma Coast State Beach, 3095 Highway 1, Bodega Bay, CA 94923; tel. (707) 875-3483 or fax (707) 875-3876.

PATRICK RACE

CHAPTER D1

TAKING A BREAK NEAR SPRING LAKE

MAP D1

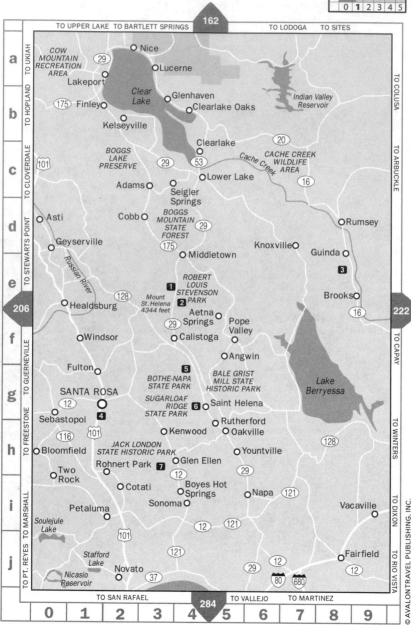

a TO UKIAH

COW MOUNTAIN RECREATION AREA
Nice
29
Lucerne
Lakeport
Clear Lake

b TO HOPLAND
175 Finley
Glenhaven
Clearlake Oaks
Kelseyville
Indian Valley Reservoir

TO COLUSA

c TO CLOVERDALE
101
BOGGS LAKE PRESERVE
29 53 Clearlake
Cache Creek
CACHE CREEK WILDLIFE AREA
20
Lower Lake
16

TO ARBUCKLE

Adams
Seigler Springs

d TO STEWARTS POINT
Asti
Cobb
BOGGS MOUNTAIN STATE FOREST
29
175
Geyserville
Middletown
Knoxville
Rumsey
Guinda
3

e 206
Russian River
128
Mount St. Helena 4344 feet
1 ROBERT LOUIS STEVENSON PARK
2
Healdsburg
Aetna Springs
Pope Valley
Brooks
16
222 TO CAPAY

f TO GUERNEVILLE
29 Calistoga
Windsor
Angwin

g Fulton
SANTA ROSA
12
5 BOTHE-NAPA STATE PARK
BALE GRIST MILL STATE HISTORIC PARK
SUGARLOAF RIDGE STATE PARK
6 Saint Helena
Sebastopol
4
Lake Berryessa

h TO FREESTONE
116 101
Kenwood
Rutherford
Oakville
Bloomfield
JACK LONDON STATE HISTORIC PARK
Glen Ellen
Yountville
128
Rohnert Park **7**
TO WINTERS

i TO MARSHALL
Two Rock
12
Cotati
Boyes Hot Springs
Sonoma
29
Napa
121
Vacaville
Petaluma
Soulejule Lake
12 121
TO DIXON

j TO PT. REYES
101
Stafford Lake
121
12
29 80 680
Fairfield
12
Nicasio Reservoir
Novato
37
TO RIO VISTA

© AVALONTRAVEL PUBLISHING, INC.

CHAPTER D1

1 Mount St. Helena Trail . . 215
2 Palisades Trail 215
3 Blue Ridge Trail 216
4 Spring Lake Trail 217
5 Coyote Peak/
Redwood Trail Loop 217
6 Bald Mountain Loop 218
7 Lake Trail 218

1 Mount St. Helena Trail

10.0 mi/4.5 hrs

Mount St. Helena is Napa County's highest mountain, the peak that strikes such a memorable silhouette when viewed from the Bay Area. This trail climbs to the summit at 4,343 feet, requiring an ascent of 2,068 feet over the course of five miles. The route follows a moderate grade for the most part, then rises above the forest and includes two steep sections, one at the very end of your climb. In the summer the hike can be pure hell, since much of the trail is actually a fire road with little shade, there's no water anywhere along the route, and the heat commonly blazes in the 90s and 100s out here. Most visitors make the trip when temperatures are more tolerable, of course, which makes the gradient feel pretty moderate. The mountain is most often visited in the winter, when the summit is commonly flecked with snow from passing storms, quite a treat for most folks in the area. In fact, when the snow level drops to 3,500 feet, the entire mountaintop can get a good pasting of a foot of snow. In spring, north winds clear the air, and visibility is best at this time, with remarkable views in all directions. A ranger pal claims that on the best days you can see Mount Shasta 192 miles away, but so far we haven't had that experience. But it is documented that in the late 1800s, surveyors sent signals back and forth between here and Mount Shasta, setting a record for longest signal distance, so hey, it must be possible. No matter when you hike, be certain to bring plenty of water, a daypack with high-energy food, a windbreaker, and a change of shirts so you won't be making the return downhill trip with a cold, wet shirt.

Location: In Robert Louis Stevenson State Park north of Calistoga; map D1, grid e3.

User groups: Hikers only. No dogs, horses, or mountain bikes. Mountain bikes are allowed on a nearby fire road .25 mile north on Highway 29. No wheelchair facilities.

Permits: No permits are required. Parking and access are free.

Maps: Ask the USGS for a topographic map of the Mount St. Helena area.

Directions: From Calistoga drive about eight miles north on Highway 29 to the signed trailhead at the edge of the parking area on the west side of the highway at Robert Louis Stevenson State Park.

Contact: Robert Louis Stevenson State Park, c/o Bothe-Napa Valley State Park, 3801 St. Helena Highway North, Calistoga, CA 94515; tel. (707) 942-4575; Silverado District, tel. (707) 938-1519.

2 Palisades Trail

10.5 mi one-way/1.0 days

A new hiking trail that overlooks the Napa Valley can make it seem as if you have gained entry into a new secret world. The key portion of the hike is routed along the base of the Palisades, from Table Rock and just below a line of unique volcanic cliffs and outcrops that are like nothing else in the region. At the same time, there are beautiful views below of the Napa Valley, as well as a sweeping long-distance panorama of the foothills to the west. It's an 10.5-mile one-way hike with a 2,000-foot descent, best completed with a shuttle car, starting at the foot of Mount St. Helena, then ending in the Napa Valley.

Ideally, you start the trip with two cars. First you leave one at the end of the trail, located at the junction of Highway 29 and Silverado Trail, just outside of Calistoga. With the other, you drive up Highway 29 about eight miles to the signed trailhead at the parking area at Robert Louis Stevenson State Park.

This parking area is set at 2,275 feet and doubles as the staging area for the five-mile trail to the top of Mount St. Helena. But instead of heading west up the mountain, which requires a climb of 2,068 feet to reach the summit, you instead discover the trailhead on the east side of the highway for the Palisades Trail, which takes you the opposite direction.

The first mile of the Palisades Trail climbs quickly, with one particularly steep portion, to Table Rock and the base of the Palisades. As you rise above forest, the landscape changes dramatically, at times nearly a moonscape amid the volcanic formations. The number of raptors gliding in the afternoon thermals can be exceptional, with turkey vultures, kestrels, red-tailed hawks and sometimes even peregrine falcons flying, hunting, and hovering.

There is a known peregrine nesting site at the Palisades, which is why the trail is routed at the base of the rocks, rather than across the top. Newcomers to the Palisades will be stunned by the stark beauty. It's a double whammy effect, the surprise of the line of volcanic cliffs and their surrounding lack of vegetation up close and the long-range views that provide a glimpse of the Napa Valley and beyond.

The views are nearly the same as offered by the summit of Mount St. Helena. The only thing you're missing is the 2,000-foot climb and views to the north.

From the Palisades, the trail eventually links up with Oat Hill Mine Road, which for years has been a relatively unknown and extremely steep climb taken by just a few deranged souls (guess who?) to get views of the valley.

But on this new route the trip is down, not up. It is still a strenuous hike. The initial climb to the Palisades is steep, and there is no drinking water available anywhere on the trail.

Location: Near Calistoga, Map D1, grid e4.

User groups: Hikers only. No dogs, horses, or mountain bikes. No wheelchair facilities.

Permits: Parking and access are free.

Maps: Ask the USGS for a topographic map of the Mount St. Helena area.

Directions: From Calistoga drive about eight miles north on Highway 29 to the signed trailhead at the edge of the parking area on the west side of the highway at Robert Louis Stevenson State Park.

Contact: For general information, phone the Land Trust, tel. (707) 252-3270; for state park information, phone tel. (707) 942-4575 or district headquarters, tel. (707) 938-1519.

3 Blue Ridge Trail
1-16 mi/1.0 day

There are relatively few trails on BLM property in Northern California, but all of them are special in one way or the other. Unfortunately, usually it's the other. The Blue Ridge Trail, for instance, includes a stretch with a 2,000-foot elevation gain in just three miles and many pieces of trail that are very steep, rocky, and dry. The trail follows the ridge for eight miles (most folks don't last anywhere near that long), and you'd better be as fit as a Tibetan Sherpa to try it. But hey, in spring this can be a sensational hike, with wildflowers ablaze and bushes and trees in full bloom. You'll see songbirds, swallows, falcons, and eagles flitting, hovering, and soaring. There are also a good share of lizards and rattlesnakes. The views are exceptional in all directions, with the Sutter Buttes and Snow Mountain most prominent, but with even Shasta and Lassen in view on clear days. In fact, the area has just about everything—everything that is, except water. You either bring at least two or three quarts per person, or you surrender, swearing never to hike here again.

Location: North of Lake Berryessa; map D1, grid e8.

User groups: Hikers and dogs. Horses and mountain bikes, while allowed, aren't recommended because of the steep, rocky terrain. No wheelchair facilities.

Permits: No permits are required. Parking and access are free.

Maps: For a free primitive trail map, contact the Bureau of Land Management at the address below. Ask the USGS for a topographic map of the Glascock area.

Directions: From Interstate 5 at Woodland drive west on Highway 16 for about 30 miles. At Lower Yolo County Park, turn left on County Road 40 (a gravel road), drive a short distance, and look for a concrete bridge (low water crossing). After crossing the bridge, look for the trailhead on the left. Park in the unpaved area near Cache Creek. Walk down the dirt road through a meadow to the trailhead. In the winter the dirt road is blocked by a locked gate; park instead at Lower Yolo County Park and walk down to the trailhead.

Contact: Bureau of Land Management, Ukiah Field Office, 2550 N. State Street, Ukiah, CA 95482; tel. (707) 468-4000.

◪ Spring Lake Trail
2.0 mi/1.0 hr

Spring Lake is Santa Rosa's backyard fishing hole, a popular place for trout fishing, an evening picnic, or a short hike. For newcomers we suggest the walk along the west shore of Spring Lake to the west dam, then turning left and heading into adjoining Howarth Park to Lake Ralphine. It's an easy, enjoyable stroll, though nothing serious. The lake is stocked with trout in winter and spring and provides a fair warm-water fishery in the summer. The lake is fun and quiet, with boats restricted to electric motors; no gas motors.

Location: In Spring Lake Regional Park in eastern Santa Rosa; map D1, grid g1.

User groups: Hikers and dogs. Horses are allowed only on designated trails. The park has 2.3 miles of trail that are paved for wheelchair and bicycle use.

Permits: No permits are required. There is a $4 parking fee per vehicle in summer season, $3 per vehicle in winter season.

Maps: A free trail map is available from Spring Lake Regional Park at the address below. Ask the USGS for a topographic map of the Santa Rosa area.

Directions: From U.S. 101 in Santa Rosa, take the Highway 12 exit and drive east. Continue on Highway 12 (it becomes Hoen Avenue) to Newanga Avenue. Turn left on Newanga Avenue and drive .5 mile to the park entrance. The various trailheads are well marked and easily accessible from the parking area at the lake.

Contact: Spring Lake Regional Park, 5390 Montgomery Drive, Santa Rosa, CA 95409; tel. (707) 539-8092. Sonoma County Regional Parks Department, tel. (707) 565-2041 or fax (707) 579-8247.

◫ Coyote Peak/ Redwood Trail Loop
4.4 mi/3.0 hrs

Who ever heard of redwoods in the Napa Valley? Who ever heard of a mountain peak there, too? Only those who also know of Bothe-Napa Valley State Park, which is like an island of wildland in a sea of winery tourist traffic. Bothe-Napa has some of the most easterly stands of coastal redwoods, plus Douglas fir and an excellent lookout from Coyote Peak, all quite a surprise for newcomers. The best way to see it is on the Coyote Peak/Redwood Trail Loop, starting just past the Ritchey Creek Campground turnoff near the picnic area. The first .5 mile is on the Ritchey Trail, a very pretty stretch of trail along beautiful Ritchey Creek. Then veer left onto the Redwood Trail, where you'll be surrounded by some of the park's highest stands of redwoods. The trail continues along Ritchey Creek for .25 mile, then connects to the Coyote Peak Trail. Take the Coyote Peak Trail, which rises quickly, skirting the northern flank of Coyote Peak. (A short spur trail will take you all the way to the top, elevation 1,170 feet.) Then the trail drops down the other side of the hill and intersects with the South Fork Trail, which heads all the way back down to Ritchey Creek. Note that temperatures can be extremely hot in the summer—as high as 105 degrees in unshaded areas—but you'll find a cool paradise along Ritchey Creek.

Location: In Bothe-Napa Valley State Park south of Calistoga; map D1, grid g4.

User groups: Hikers only. Horses are permitted on some designated trails. Mountain bikes are allowed on fire roads and designated trails, but are not permitted on most of this described loop. No dogs. No wheelchair facilities.

Permits: No permits are required. A $2 state park fee is charged per vehicle.

Maps: A brochure and trail map is available for $1 from Bothe-Napa Valley State Park at the address below. Ask the USGS for a topographic map of the Calistoga area.

Directions: From the town of St. Helena, drive north on Highway 128/29 for five miles (past Bale Grist Mill State Historic Park) to the park entrance on the left side of the road. Turn left and drive past the entrance station to just past the Ritchey Creek Campground turnoff near the picnic area, where there is trailhead parking.

Contact: Bothe-Napa Valley State Park, 3801 St. Helena Highway North, Calistoga, CA 94515; tel. (707) 942-4575, or California State Parks, Silverado District, tel. (707) 938-1519.

6 Bald Mountain Loop
8.2 mi/1.0 day

Bald Mountain, elevation 2,729 feet, overlooks the Napa Valley, with Mount St. Helena set to the north. On clear days from the summit, you can see portions of the San Francisco Bay Area, and then be thankful you're here instead of there. The old mountain is the centerpiece of Sugarloaf Ridge State Park, a 2,700-acre park featuring redwoods in Sonoma Creek watershed, open meadows peppered with oaks on the hilltops, and some chaparral on ridges. The most ambitious hike in the park is the Bald Mountain Loop, an 8.2-mile trek that starts at the parking lot, then is routed in a loop by taking the Bald Mountain, Gray Meadow, Brushy Peaks, and Meadow Trails. Many less-demanding hikes are available in the park, but this route will give you the greatest sense of the park's wildest lands. It's best hiked in the spring, when the air is still cool, the hills are green, and the wildflowers are in bloom. There's a bonus as well: when Sonoma Creek is flowing well, a 25-foot waterfall set in a wooded canyon tumbles downstream from the campground; a short trail is available from the park's entrance road, located at an unsigned turnout on the road's shoulder. A more formal route to the waterfall is on the Canyon Trail.

Location: In Sugarloaf Ridge State Park north of Sonoma; map D1, grid g4.

User groups: Hikers only. No dogs, horses, or mountain bikes. Horses and mountain bikes are allowed on fire roads only. No wheelchair facilities.

Permits: No permits are required. A $2 state park day-use fee is charged for each vehicle.

Maps: A trail map and brochure is available for $1 from Sugarloaf Ridge State Park at the address below. Ask the USGS for a topographic map of the Kenwood area.

Directions: From U.S. 101 at Santa Rosa, take the Highway 12 exit east. Drive east on Highway 12 through Kenwood to Adobe Canyon Road. Turn left and drive 3.5 miles to the main park entrance at the end of the road.

Contact: Sugarloaf Ridge State Park, 2605 Adobe Canyon Road, Kenwood, CA 95452; tel. (707) 833-5712; California State Parks, Silverado District, tel. (707) 938-1519.

7 Lake Trail
2.0 mi/0.75 hr

You'll likely feel the shadow of the ghost of Jack London as you walk in his steps on the Lake Trail. It was here that London created his dreams as one of America's truly great writers and philosophers. It was also here that those dreams were shattered, first by a fire that devoured his ranch home, then by an illness at age 40 from which he never recovered. Most visitors start the trip by touring London's cottage, winery ruins, barns, and distillery. Yearning for more? The Lake Trail easily provides it. The short walk leads to a small pond, which served as a favorite recreation area for London and his guests. The trail circles it, then returns to the parking area.

Location: In Jack London State Historic Park north of Sonoma; map D1, grid h3.

User groups: Hikers only. No dogs. Horses and mountain bikes are allowed on selected trails only. No wheelchair facilities.

Permits: No permits are required. A $3 state park day-use fee is charged for each vehicle.

Maps: For a trail map and brochure, send $1 to Jack London State Historic Park at the address below. Ask the USGS for a topographic map of the Glen Ellen area.

Directions: From U.S. 101 at Santa Rosa, take the Highway 12 exit east. Drive east to the Glen Ellen/Arnold Drive turnoff. Turn right on Arnold Drive and drive two miles to London Ranch Road. Turn right and drive one mile to the park entrance.

Contact: Jack London State Historic Park, 2400 London Ranch Road, Glen Ellen, CA 95442; tel. (707) 938-5216; California State Parks, Silverado District, tel. (707) 938-1519.

SUTTER'S FORT, IN MIDTOWN
SACRAMENTO, WAS ESTABLISHED
IN 1839.

MAP D2

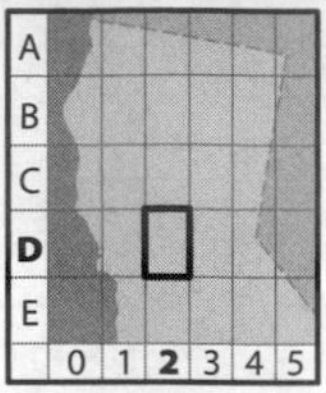

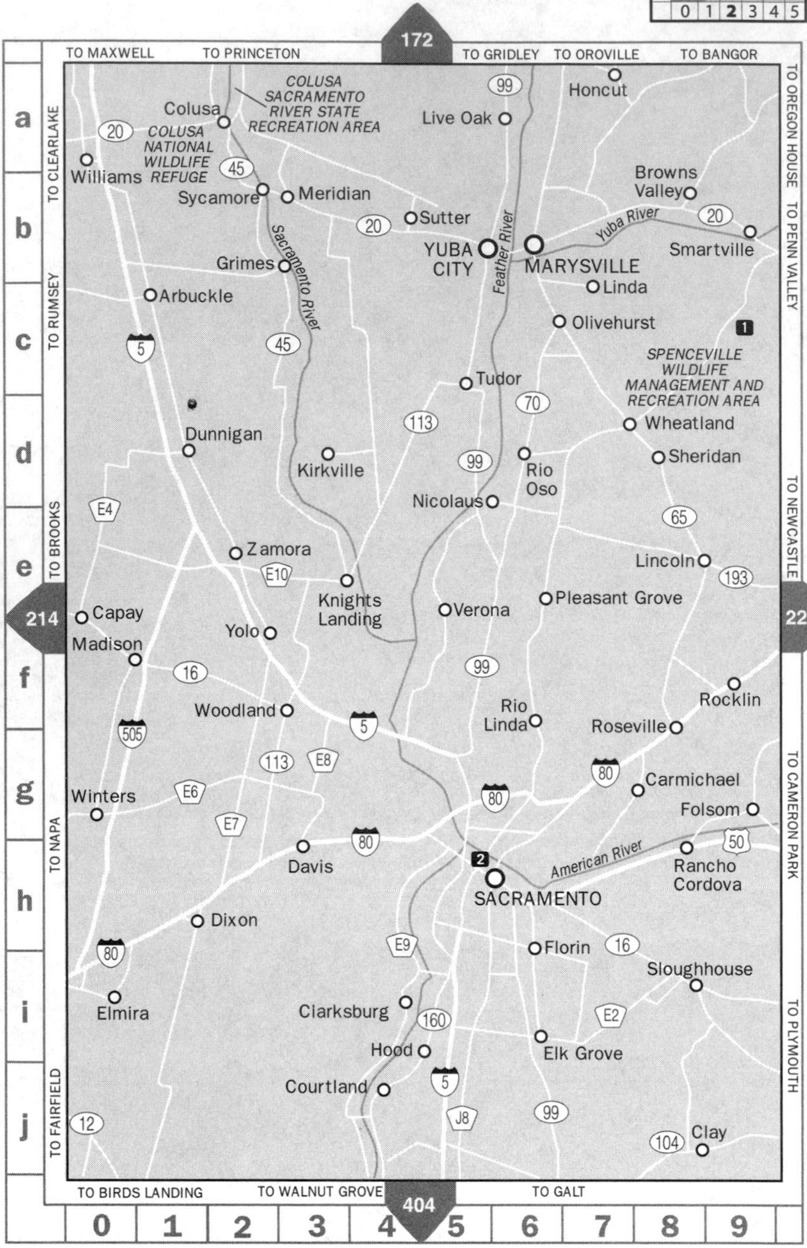

TO MAXWELL | TO PRINCETON | 172 | TO GRIDLEY | TO OROVILLE | TO BANGOR

a

TO CLEARLAKE

COLUSA SACRAMENTO RIVER STATE RECREATION AREA

Colusa
20
COLUSA NATIONAL WILDLIFE REFUGE
Williams
Live Oak
Honcut
99

b

TO RUMSEY

45
Sycamore
Meridian
Sacramento River
20
Sutter
YUBA CITY
Feather River
Yuba River
20
Browns Valley
MARYSVILLE
Smartville

Grimes
Linda
Olivehurst
1

c

5
Arbuckle
45
Tudor
70
SPENCEVILLE WILDLIFE MANAGEMENT AND RECREATION AREA

d

Dunnigan
Kirkville
113
99
Rio Oso
Nicolaus
Wheatland
Sheridan

e

TO BROOKS

E4
Zamora
E10
Knights Landing
Verona
Pleasant Grove
Lincoln
65
193
TO NEWCASTLE

214

Capay
Madison
Yolo
99
TO NAPA

f

16
Woodland
5
Rio Linda
Roseville
Rocklin
226

g

505
Winters
E6
113
E8
E7
80
80
Carmichael
Folsom
TO CAMERON PARK

h

80
Davis
80
2
American River
50
Rancho Cordova
SACRAMENTO
Dixon

i

TO FAIRFIELD

Elmira
Clarksburg
E9
Florin
16
Sloughhouse
160
E2
Hood
Elk Grove
TO PLYMOUTH

j

12
Courtland
5
99
104
Clay
J8

TO BIRDS LANDING | TO WALNUT GROVE | 404 | TO GALT

0 1 2 3 4 5 6 7 8 9

TO OREGON HOUSE
TO PENN VALLEY

© AVALON TRAVEL PUBLISHING, INC.

CHAPTER D2

1 Shingle Falls 223

2 American River
Parkway/Jedediah
Smith Memorial Trail. . . 223

1 Shingle Falls

5.0 mi/2.5 hrs

When it comes to Shingle Falls, many people call it "Dry Creek Falls." But the real name is Shingle Falls, named decades ago after a military officer from nearby Beale Air Force Base. Most of the trail here is on a gravel road, middle of arid oak-and-grassland country in the Central Valley, the stream supports a surprising variety of creekside vegetation, including various oaks, willows, and alders. Your destination is Shingle Falls, of course, easily reached by a five-mile round-trip hike. At the trailhead, cross a worn-out bridge and start hiking to your right on the fire road on the other side. After walking nearly a mile, you'll bear right and hike south on another dirt road. Keep alert, because wild turkeys are common here. At 2.5 miles from the trailhead, you'll come to the road's end, and in turn the creek, gorge, and waterfalls. The bigger one is about 60 feet, with steep cliffs walled off by a fence. If you follow use trails downstream along the creek, you'll find a smaller waterfall about 100 yards downstream. Both make fine spots for a springtime visit. Best time to hike the trail? December through April, preferably soon after a rain.

Location: In Spenceville Wildlife Area near Smartville; map D2, grid c9.

User groups: Hikers and dogs. Horses and mountain bikes are not allowed on the trail. Horses are allowed on marked trails and service roads. Mountain bikes are allowed only on service roads. No wheelchair facilities.

Permits: No permits are necessary. Parking and access are free. Organized groups must obtain a free permit.

Maps: Free maps of Spenceville Wildlife Area are available at information signposts in the refuge. Ask the USGS for a topographic map of the Camp Far West area.

Directions: From Marysville drive east on Highway 20 for 15 miles to Smartville and Smartville Road. Turn right (south) and drive 4.5 miles to Waldo Road (gravel). Turn left on Waldo Road and drive 2.1 miles to Spenceville Road. Turn left and drive two miles to the end of the road at a closed bridge. Park, walk carefully across the bridge, and begin the hike.

Contact: Spenceville Wildlife Area, c/o Oroville Wildlife Area, Department of Fish and Game, 945 Oro Dam Boulevard West, Oroville, CA 95965; tel. (530) 538-2236.

2 American River Parkway/Jedediah Smith Memorial Trail

32.0 mi one way/
0.5-hour to 2.0 days

The idea for the American River Parkway sounded good in concept, and it works even better in practice. The plan was to create a route along the American River, linking Sacramento all the way upstream past Rancho Cordova and Fair Oaks. The result was this multiuse trail that runs 32 miles from Discovery Park in Sacramento up to Folsom. There are actually two parallel trails, one paved for bicyclists only and a dirt trail for horses (note that there is no shoulder on the horse trail). Walkers and joggers should stay off the paved portion and instead use the dirt trail or the shoulder of the bike trail. The trail connects to Folsom Lake State Recreation Area off Hazel Avenue (near Nimbus Dam) and continue for another nine miles one way up to Beals Point at Folsom Lake. Virtually no one hikes, bikes, or blades the entire length, of

course; most people simply enjoy short sections, usually on evening walks, jogs, or rides.
Location: Along the American River from Sacramento to Folsom; map D2, grid h5.

User groups: Hikers, dogs, horses, and mountain bikes. Note the restrictions for mountain bikes and hikers in the trail notes above. Roller blades or roller skates are allowed only on the state park portion of trail. The state park portion is two separate trails most of the route, but a .5 mile section is shared. All nine miles of state trail is paved and wheelchairs are allowed. Elsewhere, wheelchairs are allowed on the actual trail, and wheelchair-accessible restrooms, fishing areas, and picnic grounds are available along the way.

Spring and fall are when the American River is prettiest. In spring the trees and grass are green, the water is rolling fresh, and by May, schools of shad are swimming upstream. Come autumn, the leaves of the adjacent trees turn bright colors, lighting up the river. In the intervening summer months, 100-degree temperatures keep trail use low during the day, but when evening shade emerges, so do joggers and walkers.

Permits: No permits are required. Each county park charges a $4 fee per vehicle. Folsom Lake State Recreation Area charges $3 per vehicle.

Maps: For a free trail map, contact the County Parks Department at the address below. Ask the USGS for topographic maps of the Sacramento East, Carmichael, Citrus Heights, and Folsom areas.

Directions: The trail begins at Discovery Park in Sacramento on the north side of the American River. From Interstate 5 take the Richards Boulevard exit and drive west to Jiboom Street. Turn right (north) and follow the road into the park.

Note: The trail's prettiest access point is Goethe Park in Rancho Cordova. To get to Goethe Park on the south side of the American River, drive east on U.S. 50 and take the Bradshaw North exit. Follow Bradshaw Road to Folsom Boulevard and turn right (east). Continue to Rod Beaudry Drive and turn left (north). Follow the road .5 mile into the park.

Contact: County of Sacramento, Parks and Recreation Division, Park Ranger Section 4040, Bradshaw Road, Sacramento, CA 95827; tel. (916) 875-6672 or fax (916) 875-6632. Folsom Lake State Recreation Area, tel. (916) 988-0205.

JEFFREY PATTY

TAKING A BREAK
ON THE PACIFIC CREST TRAIL

MAP D3

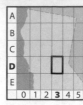

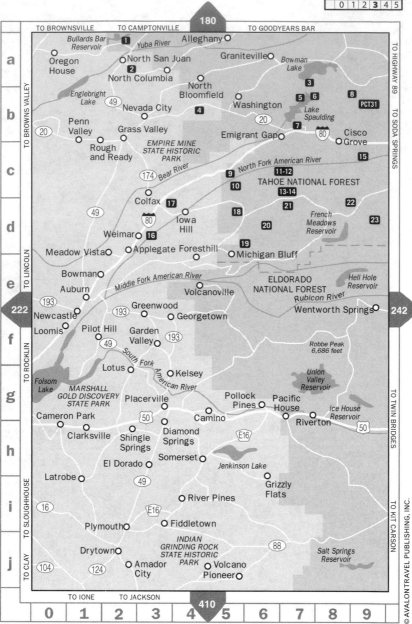

TO BROWNSVILLE   TO CAMPTONVILLE   **180**   TO GOODYEARS BAR

TO HIGHWAY 89

TO SODA SPRINGS

a

Bullards Bar Reservoir
1 *Yuba River*
Alleghany
Oregon House
North San Juan
Graniteville
Bowman Lake
2
North Columbia

b

Englebright Lake
49 Nevada City
North Bloomfield
Washington
3
5 **6**
8
PCT31
Penn Valley
Grass Valley
4
20
Lake Spaulding
Cisco Grove
20
Rough and Ready
EMPIRE MINE STATE HISTORIC PARK
Emigrant Gap
7
80

c

174 *Bear River*
Colfax
North Fork American River
9
11-12
15
10
TAHOE NATIONAL FOREST
13-14

d

49
80
17
Iowa Hill
18
21
22
Weimar
16
20
French Meadows Reservoir
23
Meadow Vista
Applegate Foresthill
19
Michigan Bluff

e

TO LINCOLN
Bowman
Auburn
Middle Fork American River
Volcanoville
ELDORADO NATIONAL FOREST
Hell Hole Reservoir
Rubicon River
222 **193**
Newcastle
193 Greenwood
Georgetown
Wentworth Springs
242

f

TO ROCKLIN
Loomis
Pilot Hill
Garden Valley
193
Robbe Peak 6,686 feet
49
Lotus
South Fork
American River
Kelsey
Union Valley Reservoir

g

Folsom Lake
MARSHALL GOLD DISCOVERY STATE PARK
Placerville
Pollock Pines
Pacific House
Ice House Reservoir
Cameron Park
50
Camino
Riverton
50

h

Clarksville
Shingle Springs
Diamond Springs
E16
El Dorado
Somerset
Jenkinson Lake

i

TO SLOUGHHOUSE
Latrobe
49
River Pines
Grizzly Flats
16
E16
Plymouth
Fiddletown

j

TO CLAY
Drytown
INDIAN GRINDING ROCK STATE HISTORIC PARK
88
Salt Springs Reservoir
104
124
Amador City
Volcano
Pioneer

TO KIT CARSON

TO TWIN BRIDGES

© AVALON TRAVEL PUBLISHING, INC.

TO IONE   TO JACKSON   **410**

0 1 2 3 4 5 6 7 8 9

CHAPTER D3

1 Bullards Bar Trail 227

2 South Yuba
Independence Trail . . . 228

3 Lindsey Lakes Trail . . . 228

4 Pioneer Trail 229

5 Penner Lake 229

6 Grouse Ridge
Trail (Sawmill to
Eagle Lakes) 230

7 Sierra Discovery Trail . 230

8 Glacier Lake 231

9 Euchre Bar Trail 231

10 Italian Bar Trail. 232

11 Mumford Bar Trail . . . 232

12 American River Trail. . 233

13 Beacroft Trail 233

14 Sailor Flat Trail 234

15 Loch Leven Lakes 235

16 Codfish Creek Trail . . . 235

17 Stevens Trail. 236

18 Green Valley Trail. . . . 236

19 Western States
Trail/Michigan Bluff . . 237

20 Grouse Falls 237

21 Forest View Trail. 238

22 Western States
Trail/McGuire 238

23 Powderhorn Trail
to Hell Hole. 239

Pacific Crest Trail
(PCT) Section Overview

PCT-31 Donner Pass to
the Yuba River 240

1 Bullards Bar Trail

1-13.5 mi/1.0 day

Don't be spooked by the seven-mile length of this trail (13.5 if you include the two loops). Most folks just saunter along for a few miles, maybe take a dunk in the water or cast out a fishing line and sit a spell, then turn back. From the trailhead at the Dark Day Picnic Area, the trail leads west and east along the shore of Bullards Bar Reservoir to Vista Point, overlooking the dam. The path is nearly flat, ranging between 2,243 and 2,250 feet in elevation. Along the way there are many good fishing and swimming spots and a sprinkling of huge ponderosa pines and Douglas firs. A bonus attraction is that the trail links up with a network of other trails that make up 23 miles of trails in this area. These include Rebel Ridge Trail, 7-Ball Trail and 8-Ball Trail, all good. Because of the summer heat, this area is best hiked in spring, and use then drops off in summer.

Location: On Bullards Bar Reservoir in Tahoe National Forest; map D3, grid a2.
User groups: Hikers, dogs, horses, and mountain bikes. No wheelchair facilities.
Permits: No permits are required. Parking and access are free.
Maps: For a map of Tahoe National Forest, send $6 to U.S. Forest Service, Attn: Map Sales, P.O. Box 587, Camino, CA 95709; tel. (530) 647-5390, fax (530) 647-5389, or website: www.r5.fs.fed. us/visitorcenter. Major credit cards accepted. Ask the USGS for topographic maps of the Camptonville and Challenge areas.
Directions: From Marysville, drive east on Highway 20 and drive 12 miles to Marysville Road. Turn left on Marysville Road (signed for Bullards Bar Reservoir) and drive 10 miles to Old Marysville Road. Turn right and drive 14 miles, over the dam, and continue four miles to Dark Day Road. Turn left and drive to the picnic area and trailhead.

Contact: Tahoe National Forest, Downieville Ranger District, 15924 Highway 49, Camptonville, CA 95922; tel. (530) 288-3231 or fax (530) 288-0727.

2 South Yuba Independence Trail

7.0 mi/2.0 hrs

This is a pretty trail, virtually flat, that is routed along Rush Creek Canyon with pretty views of the stream, a waterfall with a nearby water flume a unique sidelight. From the trailhead hike to the west (go right) to visit Rush Creek Falls and spectacular Flume 28, one mile from the trailhead. The trail is routed for nine miles through beautiful forested terrain along the Yuba River Canyon, and it's equally loved (and used) by wheelchair hikers and two-legged hikers. The path was originally a canal route, built in 1859 to carry water from the Yuba to a hydraulic mining site in Smartville. This is considered the nation's first wheelchair-accessible wilderness trail; the wheelchair-accessible portion is a seven-mile round trip. Note: Guided nature walks for groups of six or more are offered by Sequoya Challenge (see contact below).

Location: Near Nevada City; map D3, grid a3.

User groups: Hikers, dogs, and wheelchairs. No horses or mountain bikes.

Permits: No permits are necessary. Parking and access are free, but donations accepted.

Maps: Trail maps/brochures are available at the trailhead or from the Bridgeport Ranger Station. Ask the USGS for a topographic map of the Nevada City area.

Directions: From Auburn drive north on Highway 49 for 27 miles to Nevada City. Continue on Highway 49 for eight miles past Nevada City to the trailhead parking area along the highway. The parking area is a paved pullout located just before the South Yuba River bridge. If you reach the bridge, you have gone too far.

Contact: South Yuba River State Park, Bridgeport Visitor Center and Ranger Station, tel. (530) 432-2546; Sequoya Challenge (guided walks), P.O. Box 3166, Grass Valley, CA 95945; tel. (530) 477-4788.

3 Lindsey Lakes Trail

7.0 mi/3.0 hrs

The highlight of the Lindsey Lake Trail is that it intersects with other trails, including the beautiful Grouse Ridge Trail, and is set in a gorgeous landscape that features Sierra alpine landscape. But the trail itself from Lindsey Lakes to Rock Lake is a service road closed to public vehicle traffic, so you're hiking up a road. This 3.5-mile trail dead-ends after climbing past the three Lindsey Lakes and offers a great optional side trip. From the trailhead at Lower Lindsey Lake, elevation 6,160 feet, you hike up to the other lakes on a short trail that's quite steep in several places before topping out at 6,400 feet. The route gets medium use and accesses good swimming holes with cold water, but the fishing is poor. The best fishing in this basin is at nearby Culbertson Lake, where you can make a wonderful side trip by hiking out to Rock Lake and up to Bullpen Lake. The latter is one of the few lakes anywhere that has been stocked with Arctic grayling. Another side trip from the Lindsey Lakes Trail is the Crooked Lakes Trail.

Location: In Tahoe National Forest north of Emigrant Gap; map D3, grid a7.

User groups: Hikers, dogs, and horses. Mountain bikes are not advised. No wheelchair facilities.

Permits: No permits are required. Parking and access are free.

Maps: For a map of Tahoe National Forest, send $6 to U.S. Forest Service, Attn: Map Sales, P.O. Box 587, Camino, CA 95709; tel. (530) 647-5390, fax (530) 647-5389, or website: www.r5.fs.fed.us/visitorcenter. Major credit cards accepted. Ask the USGS for topographic maps of the English Mountain and Graniteville areas.

Directions: From Auburn drive east on Interstate 80 for 45 miles to Highway 20. Take the Highway 20 exit and head west, driving four miles to Bowman Lake Road (Forest Road 18). Turn right and drive 8.5 miles north until you see a sign that says "Lindsey Lake, Feely Lake, Carr Lake." Turn right and follow the signs to the parking area for Lindsey Lake. The road can be extremely rough for the last .5 mile; high-clearance vehicles are advised.

Contact: Tahoe National Forest, Nevada City Ranger District, 631 Coyote Street, Nevada City, CA 95959; tel. (530) 265-4531, or fax (530) 478-6109.

4 Pioneer Trail

24.0 mi/2.0 days

Hiking the Pioneer Trail is like taking a history lesson as you trace the route of the first wagon road opened by emigrants and gold seekers in 1850. Along the way are three campgrounds for backpackers, but the trail is better suited for mountain biking. From the trailhead at Lone Grave, elevation 3,500 feet, the trail heads east for 12 miles to Bear Valley, gaining 2,000 feet. You will pass Central House (once a stagecoach stop), White Cloud and Skillman Flat (former mill sites, one burned down), and the Omega Overlook (site of a huge hydraulic gold mining operation). From the Omega Overlook you will get dramatic views of the Yuba River and the surrounding granite cliffs. The traffic on this trail is increasing, particularly with all the mountain bikers making the one-way trip downhill from Omega Rest Area to Lone Grave. If you encounter others, demonstrate the utmost courtesy: bikers should always dismount and walk when passing hikers.

Location: East of Nevada City, off of Highway 20 in Tahoe National Forest; map D3, grid b4.

User groups: Hikers, dogs, mountain bikes, and horses. No wheelchair facilities.

Permits: A campfire permit (free) is required for overnight use. Parking and access are free.

Maps: For a map of Tahoe National Forest, send $6 to U.S. Forest Service, Attn: Map Sales, P.O. Box 587, Camino, CA 95709; tel. (530) 647-5390, fax (530) 647-5389, or website: www.r5.fs.fed.us/visitorcenter. Major credit cards accepted. Ask the USGS for a topographic map of the Washington area.

Directions: From Nevada City drive about seven miles east on Highway 20 to the trailhead, across from Lone Grave. If the parking lot there is full, additional parking and trail access are available at Skillman Flat, Upper Burlington Ridge, Harmony Ridge Market, the Omega Rest Area, and the Washington Overlook Trailhead, all located to the east of Highway 20.

Contact: Tahoe National Forest, Nevada City Ranger District, 631 Coyote Street, Nevada City, CA 95959; tel. (530) 265-4531 or fax (530) 478-6109.

5 Penner Lake

4.5 mi/3.0 hrs

The Round Lake Trail, which accesses a series of Sierra lakes, including Island Lake and Penner Lake, is extremely beautiful but also very popular, even crowded at the trailhead on weekends. From the trailhead at Feely Lake, elevation 6,720 feet, the route heads east, climbing first to Island Lake. This lake, named for the little rocky islands sprinkled about, has several good campsites. Turn left when you reach Island Lake and walk 1.5 miles on the Crooked Lakes Trail to Penner Lake. You walk through a fir forest from Island Lake to Penner Lake. The last .5 mile is uphill, but nothing serious. Penner Lake is one of the crown jewels of the Grouse Ridge area. Along with Island Lake, it has the most scenic beauty, is great for swimming, and is ideal for picnics or just gazing and taking in the mountain panorama. It is best experienced on an early weekday summer morning.

Location: At Carr Lake in Tahoe National Forest north of Emigrant Gap; map D3, grid b7.

User groups: Hikers, dogs, mountain bikes, and horses. No wheelchair facilities.

Permits: No permits are required. Parking and access are free.

Maps: For a map of Tahoe National Forest, send $6 to U.S. Forest Service, Attn: Map

Sales, P.O. Box 587, Camino, CA 95709; tel. (530) 647-5390, fax (530) 647-5389, or website: www.r5.fs.fed.us/visitorcenter. Major credit cards accepted. Ask the USGS for topographic maps of the English Mountain and Graniteville areas.

Directions: From Auburn drive east on Interstate 80 to Highway 20 exit. Take that exit and head west, driving four miles to Bowman Lake Road (Forest Road 18). Turn right and drive 8.5 miles north until you see a sign that says "Lindsey Lake, Feely Lake, Carr Lake." Turn right and follow the signs to the parking area at Carr Lake. Continue on foot to the trailhead at Feely Lake. Sections of the road can be rough; four-wheel-drive vehicles are advised.

Contact: Tahoe National Forest, Nevada City Ranger District, 631 Coyote Street, Nevada City, CA 95959; tel. (530) 265-4531 or fax (530) 478-6109.

6 Grouse Ridge Trail (Sawmill to Eagle Lakes)

6.0-16.2 mi/1-2 days

A truly gorgeous hike, the Grouse Ridge Trail weaves up and down from a mountain crest, connecting Sawmill Lake to the north with the Eagle Lakes, for a one-way distance of 8.25 miles. The beauty of this hike is that along the way are a number of short side trips you can take to make quick hits at a half dozen lakes. In fact, many people use the Grouse Ridge Trail as a jump-off point to take short and spectacular day hikes. The elevation varies from 6,160 to 6,400 feet, with the ups and downs coming in short yet serious spurts. From Sawmill Lake you climb up a timbered slope to a ridge and a turnoff for Rock Lake, itself worth a visit. You then pass Shotgun Lake (actually a wet meadow) and continue to Middle Lake, Crooked Lakes, and Milk Lake. The views are divine much of the way.

Special note: At Sawmill Lake the trail crosses the spillway of the dam, which may be impassable when high water spills into Canyon Creek.

Location: In Tahoe National Forest north of Emigrant Gap; map D3, grid b8.

User groups: Hikers, dogs, horses, and mountain bikes. No wheelchair facilities.

Permits: A campfire permit (free) is required for overnight use. No permits are required. Parking and access are free.

Maps: For a map of Tahoe National Forest, send $6 to U.S. Forest Service, Attn: Map Sales, P.O. Box 587, Camino, CA 95709; tel. (530) 647-5390, fax (530) 647-5389, or website: www.r5.fs.fed.us/visitorcenter. Major credit cards accepted. Ask the USGS for topographic maps of the Cisco Grove and English Mountain areas.

Directions: From Auburn drive east on Interstate 80 for 45 miles to the Highway 20 exit. Take that exit and head west and drive four miles to Bowman Lake Road (Forest Road 18). Turn right on Bowman Lake Road and drive 16 miles to Bowman Lake. Turn right and drive along Bowman Lake to Faucherie Lake Road. Turn right on Faucherie Lake Road and drive .5 mile to the north end of Sawmill Lake at the trailhead at the north end of the lake.

Contact: Tahoe National Forest, Nevada City Ranger District, 631 Coyote Street, Nevada City, CA 95959; tel. (530) 265-4531 or fax (530) 478-6109.

7 Sierra Discovery Trail

1.0 mi/0.5 hr

The waterfall at Bear River is your destination of an easy, short and near-flat trail that is accessible even to wheelchairs (with a bit of assistance). This is not the wilderness, with much of the trail pavement, soil cement and compressed gravel. It is designed as an interpretive loop walk, with information about ecosystems, wildlife, geology, and cultural history available as the trail winds through a forest of pines and incense cedars. Your destination, Bear River Falls, is short but wide, well framed by a forest canopy. It is an ideal mountain walk for seniors, youngsters, or those physically challenged.

Location: Off Highway 20 near Lake Spaulding; map D3, grid b7.

User groups: Hikers, dogs, and wheelchairs (with assistance). No horses or mountain bikes.

Permits: No permits are necessary. Parking and access are free.

Maps: Ask the USGS for a topographic map of the Blue Canyon area.

Directions: From Auburn drive east on Interstate 80 for 45 miles to the Highway 20 exit. Take that exit and head west and drive four miles to Bowman Lake Road. Turn right and drive .6 mile to the Sierra Discovery Trail parking lot on the left side of the road.

Contact: Pacific Gas & Electric, tel. (916) 386-5164 or (800) PGE-5000 (800-743-5000).

🎱 Glacier Lake

10 ml/1 day

In just a few hours you can be transported to heaven, though some call it Glacier Lake. It is a five-mile hike to get here, a pristine and peaceful high Sierra setting than can make you feel as if you're three days out on a backpacking expedition. The small lake is set in a rockbound bowl with the Black Buttes looming nearby. The tree cover is sparse, and the rock cover is abundant. To get there, start your hike by heading east on the Round Lake Trail at Carr Lake and hike almost three miles. You will pass a series of lakes, including Feely Lake, Island Lake, Round Lake, and Milk Lake. When the trail intersects the Sand Ridge Trail, bear right on the Glacier Lake Trail and continue through a meadow and some forest and past a small lake before entering a rocky area to the lake. Great side trips are also available. It is a one-mile hike north to the Five Lakes Basin, and a 1.5-mile hike south to Beyers Lake. The elevations here range 5,500 to 7,000 feet.

Location: In Tahoe National Forest northwest of Donner; map D3, grid b8.

Location: At Carr Lake in Tahoe National Forest north of Emigrant Gap; map D3, grid b9.

User groups: Hikers, dogs, and horses. Moun-

tain bikes are strongly discouraged. No wheelchair facilities.

Permits: No permits are required. Parking and access are free.

Maps: For a map of Tahoe National Forest, send $6 to U.S. Forest Service, Attn: Map Sales, P.O. Box 587, Camino, CA 95709; tel. (530) 647-5390, fax (530) 647-5389, or website: www.r5.fs.fed. us/visitorcenter. Major credit cards accepted. Ask the USGS for topographic maps of the Cisco Grove and English Mountain areas.

Directions: From Auburn drive east on Interstate 80 to the Highway 20 exit. Take that exit and head west, driving four miles to Bowman Lake Road (Forest Road 18). Turn right and drive 8.5 miles north until you see a sign that says "Lindsey Lake, Feely Lake, Carr Lake." Turn right and follow the signs to the parking area at Carr Lake. Continue on foot to the trailhead at Feely Lake. Sections of the road can be rough; four-wheel-drive vehicles are advised.

Contact: Tahoe National Forest, Nevada City Ranger District, 631 Coyote Street, Nevada City, CA 95959; tel. (530) 265-4531 or fax (530) 478-6109.

🎇 Euchre Bar Trail

6.0 mi/3.5 hrs

A river runs through almost every Sierra gulch and canyon, and so it is with this portion of the North Fork American River. From the trailhead the route winds steeply down to the river and Euchre Bar, where a suspension footbridge crosses the water. The trail then leads upriver for 2.4 miles, along an excellent stretch of water for fishing, camping, panning for gold, and swimming (it is cold). If you want a lesson in pain, continue hiking another five miles. You'll climb the old Dorer Ranch Road, passing mining ruins and abandoned equipment from the Gold Rush era, gaining 2,000 feet in elevation through this dry, dusty country.

Location: On the North Fork American River near Baxter in Tahoe National Forest; map D3, grid c5.

User groups: Hikers, dogs, and horses. Mountain bikes are not advised. No wheelchair facilities.

Permits: No permits are required. Parking and access are free.

Maps: For a map of Tahoe National Forest, send $6 to U.S. Forest Service, Attn: Map Sales, P.O. Box 587, Camino, CA 95709; tel. (530) 647-5390, fax (530) 647-5389, or website: www.r5.fs.fed.us/visitorcenter. Major credit cards accepted. Ask the USGS for topographic maps of the Dutch Flat and Westville areas.

Directions: From Interstate 80 east of Auburn, take the Alta exit. Turn right on Morton, then left on Casa Loma. Follow Casa Loma until you see the sign for the Rawhide Mine and then turn right. Follow the road .75 mile past the second railroad crossing to a parking area. The trailhead is .1 mile beyond the parking area.

Contact: Tahoe National Forest, Foresthill Ranger District, 22830 Foresthill Road, Foresthill, CA 95631; tel. (530) 367-2224 or fax (530) 367-2992.

🔟 Italian Bar Trail

4.5 mi/3.5 hrs

Miners in the 1850s were like mountain goats, and they knew the most direct route between two points was a straight line. As a result, this route that miners once used to reach the North Fork American River is almost straight down going in and straight up coming out, gaining 3,000 feet in elevation over the course of 2.25 miles. It's about as fun as searching for a tiny gold nugget on the beach. As you head down from the trailhead at 5,400 feet, you get little help from switchbacks. The trail ends at the river, and from there you must scramble and hop from rock to rock along the riverbanks. Eventually you end up at a secluded spot where all seems perfect—until you start the hike back. When you face the 3,000-foot climb out, you will wonder how you ever talked yourself into doing this hike.

Location: Near the North Fork American River in Tahoe National Forest; map D3, grid c5.

User groups: Hikers, dogs, and horses. Mountain bikes are not advised. No wheelchair facilities.

Permits: No permits are required. Parking and access are free.

Maps: For a map of Tahoe National Forest, send $6 to U.S. Forest Service, Attn: Map Sales, P.O. Box 587, Camino, CA 95709; tel. (530) 647-5390, fax (530) 647-5389, or website: www.r5.fs.fed.us/visitorcenter. Major credit cards accepted. Ask the USGS for a topographic map of the Westville area.

Directions: From Interstate 80 at Auburn turn east on Foresthill Road and drive 16 miles to the town of Foresthill. Continue another 13 miles northeast (the road becomes Foresthill Divide Road) to Humbug Ridge Road (Forest Road 66). Turn left and drive three miles north to the trailhead.

Contact: Tahoe National Forest, Foresthill Ranger District, 22830 Foresthill Road, Foresthill, CA 95631; tel. (530) 367-2224 or fax (530) 367-2992.

🔢 Mumford Bar Trail

6.5 mi/1.0 day

You'd have to be part mountain goat and part idiot to want to try this hike. Guess how we know? The trail leads almost straight down to the North Fork American River for more than 3.25 miles, and you know what that means. Right, it's almost straight up coming back.

From the trailhead at 5,360 feet, the first mile of trail follows an old four-wheel-drive route that deteriorates and then drops down to the river canyon at 2,640 feet. This stretch of river is designated as "wild and scenic," and is quite pretty, with good canyon views and fishing spots. We recommend that you extend your walk by taking the American River Trail and staying overnight. Otherwise you will have to climb back out of the canyon on the same day, something even most mountain goats would not choose to do.

Location: Near the North Fork American River in Tahoe National Forest; map D3, grid c7.

User groups: Hikers, dogs, and horses. Mountain bikes are not advised. No wheelchair facilities.

Permits: No permits are required. Parking and access are free.

Maps: For a map of Tahoe National Forest, send $6 to U.S. Forest Service, Attn: Map Sales, P.O. Box 587, Camino, CA 95709; tel. (530) 647-5390, fax (530) 647-5389, or website: www.r5.fs.fed.us/visitorcenter. Major credit cards accepted. Ask the USGS for topographic maps of the Duncan Peak and Westville areas.

Directions: From Interstate 80 at Auburn turn east on Foresthill Road and drive 16 miles to the town of Foresthill. Continue another 15 miles northeast (the road becomes Foresthill Divide Road) to the Mumford Trailhead on the left side of the road.

Contact: Tahoe National Forest, Foresthill Ranger District, 22830 Foresthill Road, Foresthill, CA 95631; tel. (530) 367-2224 or fax (530) 367-2992.

12 American River Trail

15.2 mi/2.0 days

A 90-minute hike from the Mumford Bar trailhead (see above) gets you down into a steep canyon and alongside the beautiful and remote North Fork American River. There you turn right and start hiking upstream on the American River Trail. This is what you came for, the chance to walk along a pristine stretch of river on a steady, easy grade. You will pass old mining sites and abandoned cabins, alternating between dense vegetation and pretty river views. This trail makes a great getaway, and hikers can enjoy exploring and trout fishing. Alas, nothing is perfect, and this hike does have some drawbacks: It crosses two creeks, Tadpole and New York, which are difficult, even dangerous, to ford when running high during the snowmelt in spring and early summer. A mile upriver of Tadpole Creek and then again at New York Creek, the trail runs adjacent to private property—check your map

and stay on the trail in these places. And the hike back out of the canyon to your car is a terrible grunt, going from 2,640 feet along the river up to 5,360 feet—a gain of 2,720 feet in just 3.25 miles.

Special note: The Mumford Trailhead is also accessible from the Sailor Flat Trail (see below).

Location: On the North Fork American River east of Foresthill in Tahoe National Forest; map D3, grid c7.

User groups: Hikers, dogs, and horses. Mountain bikes are not advised. No wheelchair facilities.

Permits: A campfire permit (free) is required for overnight use. Parking and access are free.

Maps: For a map of Tahoe National Forest, send $6 to U.S. Forest Service, Attn: Map Sales, P.O. Box 587, Camino, CA 95709; tel. (530) 647-5390, fax (530) 647-5389, or website: www.r5.fs.fed.us/visitorcenter. Major credit cards accepted. Ask the USGS for a topographic map of the Duncan Peak area.

Directions: From Interstate 80 at Auburn turn east on Foresthill Road and drive 16 miles to the town of Foresthill. Continue another 15 miles northeast (the road becomes Foresthill Divide Road) to the Mumford Trailhead on the left side of the road.

Contact: Tahoe National Forest, Foresthill Ranger District, 22830 Foresthill Road, Foresthill, CA 95631; tel. (530) 367-2224 or fax (530) 367-2992.

13 Beacroft Trail

4.5 mi/1.0 day

The Beacroft Trail is the "no-option" option to hiking down to the North Fork American River. The trailhead is located four miles beyond the Mumford Trailhead, and after having reviewed the steep descent and climb required for that hike, you might want to look elsewhere for an easier route down. That's where the Beacroft Trail comes in. Still, it isn't a much better option, requiring an even more hellacious effort, as it drops 3,240 feet in only 2.25 miles. The trip back will have you howling. How can such a short trail be so steep? Ask the people who built the darn thing; those gold miners apparently had neither an abundance of useful gray matter between their ears nor much gold to carry on the return trip. When you reach the river, you can turn left on the American River Trail, which traces some of the most beautiful, accessible portions of this stream. Alas, even here you face an obstacle. Within the first mile, you must cross New York Creek, a difficult (and sometimes dangerous) ford when full of snowmelt in early summer.

Location: Near the North Fork American River in Tahoe National Forest; map D3, grid c7.

User groups: Hikers, dogs, and horses. Mountain bikes are not advised. No wheelchair facilities.

Permits: No permits are required. Parking and access are free.

Maps: For a map of Tahoe National Forest, send $6 to U.S. Forest Service, Attn: Map Sales, P.O. Box 587, Camino, CA 95709; tel. (530) 647-5390, fax (530) 647-5389, or website: www.r5.fs.fed.us/visitorcenter. Major credit cards accepted. Ask the USGS for a topographic map of the Duncan Peak area.

Directions: From Interstate 80 at Auburn turn east on Foresthill Road and drive 16 miles to the town of Foresthill. Continue another 19 miles northeast (the road becomes Foresthill Divide Road) to the trailhead on the left side of the road (one mile past Secret House Campground).

Contact: Tahoe National Forest, Foresthill Ranger District, 22830 Foresthill Road, Foresthill, CA 95631; tel. (530) 367-2224 or fax (530) 367-2992.

14 Sailor Flat Trail

6.5 mi/1.0 day

Of the several trailheads on Foresthill Road that provide access to the North Fork American River, this is the most distant, most remote, and, yes, most difficult. The Sailor Flat

Trailhead lies at the end of the road, out in the middle of nowhere at an elevation of 6,400 feet; yet the remains of a long-abandoned gold stamp mill still stand nearby. The hike starts out easily enough, with the first 1.5 miles following an old mining road on which hikers will confront nothing serious. Don't be fooled though. The trail becomes much steeper, with switchback after switchback leading down into the canyon. When you reach the river at 3,360 feet, you will have dropped 3,040 feet in only 3.25 miles. You can explore farther by turning left on the American River Trail, which traces the most beautiful sections of this river, heading downstream past meadows, canyon views, and good spots to fish and pan for gold.

Special note: With a shuttle vehicle and a partner, you can create an excellent one-way hike covering 15.6 miles. From the Sailor Flat Trailhead, hike down to the American River Trail, turn left, hike along the river to Mumford Bar, make a left turn, and hike out to Foresthill Road (see preceding hikes).

Location: Near the North Fork American River in Tahoe National Forest; map D3, grid c7.

User groups: Hikers, dogs, and horses. Mountain bikes are not advised. No wheelchair facilities.

Permits: No permits are required. Parking and access are free.

Maps: For a map of Tahoe National Forest, send $6 to U.S. Forest Service, Attn: Map Sales, P.O. Box 587, Camino, CA 95709; tel. (530) 647-5390, fax (530) 647-5389, or website: www.r5.fs.fed.us/visitorcenter. Major credit cards accepted. Ask the USGS for topographic maps of the Royal Gorge and Duncan Peak areas.

Directions: From Interstate 80 at Auburn turn east on Foresthill Road and drive 16 miles to the town of Foresthill. Continue another 25 miles northeast (the road becomes Foresthill Divide Road) to Sailor Flat Road. Turn left and drive one mile north to the trailhead.

Contact: Tahoe National Forest, Foresthill Ranger District, 22830 Foresthill Road, Foresthill, CA 95631; tel. (530) 367-2224 or fax (530) 367-2992.

15 Loch Leven Lakes
7.0 mi/1.0 day

Most people would like to know what heaven is like, but they aren't very willing to sign up for the trip. As you get deeper into the wildlands here, the lakes become progressively more beautiful and pristine. Unfortunately this is not quite heaven on earth, because so many have discovered this place, and with access so easy off Interstate 80, it has become inundated with people, even what seems crowds, and with no trailhead quota, the numbers have just about ruined the experience.

But after all, for hikers, heaven should at least look something like this. The 3.5-mile hike to Loch Leven Lakes provides swooping vistas of ridges and valleys, gorgeous high alpine meadows, and glaciated mountain terrain with a series of pristine lakes. But this hike is not without frustration: the first hour involves a continuous climb with the roar of I-80 traffic in the background. You do not escape the noise until you top the ridge.

The trail starts at 5,680 feet, then works its way upward on a moderate grade to the southwest. Granite outcrops are numerous, and huge boulders (deposited by receding glaciers) lie sprinkled among Jeffrey pine and lodgepole pine. The trail crosses a creek and railroad tracks, climbs through a cool forest, then tops the summit and winds down to Upper Loch Leven Lake. Many people stop here, content just taking in the surroundings. But you can forge on for another mile, circling Lower Loch Leven Lake and heading east up to High Loch Leven Lake at 6,800 feet.

At Lower Loch Leven Lake you'll find the recently rebuilt Cherry Point Trail. Adventurous hikers can take that trail to the Big Granite Trail, also rebuilt, and from there continue to the North Fork American River, for a distance of about six miles. Fishing is fair during the evening bite, and there are backcountry campgrounds at each lake.

Location: South of Cisco Grove in Tahoe National Forest; map D3, grid c9.

User groups: Hikers, dogs, and horses. Mountain bikes are not advised. No wheelchair facilities.

Permits: No permits are required. Parking and access are free.

Maps: For a map of Tahoe National Forest, send $6 to U.S. Forest Service, Attn: Map Sales, P.O. Box 587, Camino, CA 95709; tel. (530) 647-5390, fax (530) 647-5389, or website: www.r5.fs.fed.us/visitorcenter. Major credit cards accepted. Ask the USGS for a topographic map of the Cisco Grove area.

Directions: From Sacramento take Interstate 80 east into the Sierra Nevada and to the Big Bend exit. Take that exit and then turn left on Hampshire Rocks Road. Follow the signs to the Big Bend Visitor Center, located adjacent to the highway. The parking area and trailhead are about .25 mile east of the visitor center. The trailhead is on the opposite side of the road.

From Reno, take Interstate 80 west to the Cisco Grove exit. Take that exit and turn right on Hampshire Rocks Road. Continue as above.

Contact: Tahoe National Forest, Nevada City Ranger District, 631 Coyote Street, Nevada City, CA 95959; tel. (530) 265-4531 or fax (530) 478-6109.

16 Codfish Creek Trail
3.0 mi/1.5 hrs

A little-known route along the North Fork American River, the Codfish Creek Trail follows an old mining route downstream along its edge, then cuts up the canyon of Codfish Creek. The highlight here is Codfish Falls and few nice swimming holes, then up for canyon views. The lowlights are hot summer temperatures, too hot on summer afternoons for enjoyment.

The trail begins at the north side of the bridge on Ponderosa Way and heads downstream on sunny and exposed slopes. The path brings you to a series of cascades on

Codfish Creek. If you can, plan your trip for March, April, or May, when you get the double bonus of a full-flowing waterfall and lots of blooming wildflowers. At 1.2 miles, the trail turns right and leads upstream along Codfish Creek, heading away from the river.

Location: In Auburn State Recreation Area; map D3, grid d3.

User groups: Hikers and dogs. No horses or mountain bikes. No wheelchair facilities.

Permits: No permits are necessary. Parking and access are free.

Maps: For a map of Tahoe National Forest, which includes Auburn State Recreation Area lands, send $6 to U.S. Forest Service, Attn: Map Sales, P.O. Box 587, Camino, CA 95709; tel. (530) 647-5390, fax (530) 647-5389, or website: www.r5.fs.fed.us/visitorcenter. Major credit cards accepted. Ask the USGS for a topographic map of the Colfax area.

Directions: Drive east from Sacramento on Interstate 80 for 40 miles to Weimar and the Weimar Crossroad exit. Take that exit and turn south on Canyon Way (it becomes Ponderosa Way after a short distance) and drive 5.5 miles (the road turns to dirt) to a bridge at the American River. Park near the bridge and look for the trailhead on the north side of the bridge, with the trail heading downstream past the beach area.

Contact: Auburn State Recreation Area, 501 El Dorado Street, Auburn, CA 95603; tel. (916) 885-4527.

17 Stevens Trail

9.0 mi/5.0 hrs

The Stevens Trail is a surprisingly lush and peaceful trail that leaves noisy Interstate 80 in Colfax and drops down into the canyon of the North Fork American River. The feature here is a gentle terrain and long-distance canyon and stream views. You can also see the railroad line that was built by Chinese laborers dangling in rope-strung baskets from the cliffs above. In the spring, you will also pass blooming wildflowers and buckeye trees. The trail is well signed, and after a short stint to pop over an easy ridge, you continue on a gentle downhill path, descending 1,200 feet over the course of 4.5 miles if you choose to head all the way to the river. The return trip is up, but well graded and not too difficult for most hikers. The biggest problem here is timing. This is no fun on a summer afternoon, with 90-degree temperatures and an afternoon climb out of a canyon. Regardless, this is a great trip for many, especially for those cruising the interstate who desire a quick getaway into a pretty setting where the highway traffic seems like a million miles away.

Location: Near Colfax; map D3, grid d4.

User groups: Hikers, dogs, horses, and mountain bikes. No wheelchair facilities.

Permits: No permits are necessary. Parking and access are free.

Maps: Ask the USGS for a topographic map of the Colfax.

Directions: From Sacramento drive east on Interstate 80 for 45 miles to Colfax and the Colfax/Grass Valley exit. Take that exit and drive a short distance to a stop sign at North Canyon Way (frontage road). Turn left at the stop sign, and drive east .7 mile to the trailhead parking area.

Contact: Bureau of Land Management, Folsom Field Office, 63 Natoma Street, Folsom, CA 95630; tel. (916) 985-4474.

18 Green Valley Trail

4.5 mi/1.0 day

It's amazing what people will go through to create a space that feels like their own. Hikers can do just that on the Green Valley Trail by finding an idyllic spot along the North Fork American River and soaking up the serenity. But the price is steep, and the return trip will put you through more punishment than is typically handed out at Folsom Prison.

The trip starts at a little-known trailhead near Sugar Pine Reservoir, at elevation 4,080 feet. From there, the Green Valley Trail is steep and often rocky, dropping 2,240 feet in 2.25

miles before reaching the river. We do not advise extending your trip from here. It is possible to continue downriver a short way, or cross the river (good luck) and hike upstream into Green Valley. However, these sections of the trail are in very poor condition, and the upstream route crosses private property owned by people who don't take kindly to visitors.

Location: On the North Fork American River near Sugar Pine Reservoir; map D3, grid d5.

User groups: Hikers, dogs, and horses. Mountain bikes are not advised. No wheelchair facilities.

Permits: No permits are required. Parking and access are free.

Maps: For a map of Tahoe National Forest, send $6 to U.S. Forest Service, Attn: Map Sales, P.O. Box 587, Camino, CA 95709; tel. (530) 647-5390, fax (530) 647-5389, or website: www.r5.fs.fed.us/visitorcenter. Major credit cards accepted. Ask the USGS for a topographic map of the Dutch Flat area.

Directions: From Interstate 80 drive to Auburn and Foresthill Road. Turn east onto Foresthill Road and drive 16 miles to the town of Foresthill. Continue northeast (it becomes Foresthill Divide Road) and drive seven miles to Forest Road 10. Turn left on Forest Road 10 (Sugar Pine Road) and drive five miles to Sugar Pine Dam. Continue one mile past the dam to Elliot Ranch Road. Turn north on Elliot Ranch Road and drive three miles to the trailhead.

Contact: Tahoe National Forest, Foresthill Ranger District, 22830 Foresthill Road, Foresthill, CA 95631; tel. (530) 367-2224 or fax (530) 367-2992.

19 Western States Trail/Michigan Bluff

4.0 mi/2.5 hrs

If only the Forest Service would ban motorcycles, or "dirt bikes" as they're called, from this trail, this hike would be just about perfect. While it is rare to run into dirt bikes here, they are legal, and it's only a matter of time until word circulates among the bikers. The attraction is beautiful Eldorado Canyon, where you can fish for trout and camp along Eldorado Creek. From the trailhead at 3,520 feet, the trail quickly drops about two miles into the canyon, with switchbacks leading to a footbridge over Eldorado Creek. Extend the trip by crossing the bridge and hiking up the other side of the canyon to scenic views of the rugged topography.

Special note: The Michigan Bluff Trail is a section of the Western States Trail, which spans from Squaw Valley to Auburn.

Location: In Tahoe National Forest east of Foresthill; map D3, grid d5.

User groups: Hikers, dogs, horses, and mountain bikes. No wheelchair facilities.

Permits: No permits are required. Parking and access are free.

Maps: For a map of Tahoe National Forest, send $6 to U.S. Forest Service, Attn: Map Sales, P.O. Box 587, Camino, CA 95709; tel. (530) 647-5390, fax (530) 647-5389, or website: www.r5.fs.fed.us/visitorcenter. Major credit cards accepted. Ask the USGS for a topographic map of the Michigan Bluff area.

Directions: From Interstate 80 drive to Auburn and Foresthill Road. Turn east onto Foresthill Road and drive 16 miles to the town of Foresthill. Continue northeast (it becomes Foresthill Divide Road) and look for the signed turnoff to Michigan Bluff. The trailhead is located about .25 mile east of Michigan Bluff.

Contact: Tahoe National Forest, Foresthill Ranger District, 22830 Foresthill Road, Foresthill, CA 95631; tel. (530) 367-2224 or fax (530) 367-2992.

20 Grouse Falls

1.0 mi/0.5 hr

Some waterfalls are simply mind-boggling in their beauty, and some provide the centerpiece of a beautiful setting. Grouse Falls is one of the latter. The hike is a 15-minute walk through old-growth forest to a viewing deck. From here you're looking out over a deep and wide canyon with absolutely no sign of human development. The waterfall is about .5 mile away across the canyon; it's several hundred feet long and when running full, can seem like a scene out of Yosemite. The overlook is a wooden platform with benches where you can sit and admire the beauty. You don't see or hear immense Grouse Falls until just before you come out to the overlook, and when you do, it's a shock to your system.

Location: In Tahoe National Forest near Foresthill; map D3, grid d6.

User groups: Hikers, dogs, horses, and mountain bikes. No wheelchair facilities.

Permits: No permits are necessary. Parking and access are free.

Maps: For a map of Tahoe National Forest, send $6 to U.S. Forest Service, Attn: Map Sales, P.O. Box 587, Camino, CA 95709; tel. (530) 647-5390, fax (530) 647-5389, or website: www.r5.fs.fed.us/visitorcenter. Major credit cards accepted. Ask the USGS for a topographic map of the Michigan Bluff area.

Directions: From Interstate 80 drive to Auburn and Foresthill Road. Turn east onto Foresthill Road and drive 16 miles to the town of Foresthill and Mosquito Ridge Road. Turn right (east) on Mosquito Ridge Road and drive 19 miles to Peavine Road (Road 33). Turn left on Peavine Road and drive 5.5 miles to the Grouse Falls turnoff on the left. Turn left and drive .5 mile to the trailhead.

Contact: Tahoe National Forest, Foresthill Ranger District, 22830 Foresthill Road, Foresthill, CA 95631; tel. (530) 367-2224 or fax (530) 367-2992.

21 Forest View Trail
1.5 mi/0.75 hr

Giant sequoias, the world's largest trees, attract many visitors to this easy, well-maintained interpretive trail that leads through California's northernmost grove of sequoias. It is set at 5,200 feet on Mosquito Ridge Road, which provides generous views of the wild

and superb landscape. The trail meanders through virgin old-growth forest, home to half a dozen truly monster-sized trees. Along the .5-mile Big Trees Interpretive Trail are 16 stops marked with numbers that coincide with numbered listings in a brochure available at the trailhead, allowing visitors to take an interesting and informative self-guided tour of the fascinating history of these massive trees. Linked with the Forest View Trail, the entire loop extends 1.5 miles. Despite the long drive to the trailhead on Mosquito Ridge, the trail gets quite a bit of use.

Location: In Tahoe National Forest east of Foresthill; map D3, grid d7.

User groups: Hikers and dogs. No horses or mountain bikes. No wheelchair facilities.

Permits: No permits are required. Parking and access are free.

Maps: Free interpretive brochures are available at the trailhead. For a map of Tahoe National Forest, send $6 to U.S. Forest Service, Attn: Map Sales, P.O. Box 587, Camino, CA 95709; tel. (530) 647-5390, fax (530) 647-5389, or website: www.r5.fs.fed.us/visitorcenter. Major credit cards accepted. Ask the USGS for a topographic map of the Greek Store area.

Directions: From Interstate 80 drive to Auburn and Foresthill Road. Turn east onto Foresthill Road and drive 16 miles to the town of Foresthill and Mosquito Ridge Road. Turn right (east) on Mosquito Ridge Road and drive 23 miles to the trailhead.

Contact: Tahoe National Forest, Foresthill Ranger District, 22830 Foresthill Road, Foresthill, CA 95631; tel. (530) 367-2224 or fax (530) 367-2992.

22 Western States Trail/McGuire
7.8 mi/4.0 hrs

The McGuire Trail has become a favorite side trip for families visiting or camping at French Meadows Reservoir (elevation 5,290 feet). The trail traces the north shore of the lake, poking in and out of timber, then goes up an easy grade to the top of Red Star Ridge (5,600 feet), offering good views of the reservoir below. French Meadows is a good-size lake, covering nearly 2,000 acres when full, and is stocked each year with more than 30,000 trout that join a healthy population of resident brown trout and holdovers from stocks of rainbow trout from prior years. Water drawdowns are a common problem in late summer, as they expose many stumps and boulders, creating a navigational hazard for boaters.

Location: At French Meadows Reservoir in Tahoe National Forest; map D3, grid d8.

User groups: Hikers, dogs, horses, and mountain bikes. No wheelchair facilities.

Permits: No permits are required. Parking and access are free.

Maps: For a map of Tahoe National Forest, send $6 to U.S. Forest Service, Attn: Map Sales, P.O. Box 587, Camino, CA 95709; tel. (530) 647-5390, fax (530) 647-5389, or website: www.r5.fs.fed.us/visitorcenter. Major credit cards accepted. Ask the USGS for a topographic map of the Bunker Hill area.

Directions: From Interstate 80 drive to Auburn and Foresthill Road. Turn east onto Foresthill Road and drive 16 miles to the town of Foresthill and Mosquito Ridge Road. Turn right (east) on Mosquito Ridge Road and drive 40 miles to the French Meadows Reservoir Dam. Cross the dam, turn left (still Mosquito Ridge Road), and drive 3.5 miles to the trailhead near McGuire Boat Ramp.

Contact: Tahoe National Forest, Foresthill Ranger District, 22830 Foresthill Road, Foresthill, CA 95631; tel. (530) 367-2224 or fax (530) 367-2992.

23 Powderhorn Trail to Hell Hole

13.0 mi one way/2.0 days

Do you yearn for a challenging trek in a very remote high-mountain wilderness setting? This is it. The Hell Hole Trail requires hikers to have wilderness skills and, worst of all, be prepared for a difficult stream crossing and traversing a landslide. Sound fun? Who said anything about fun?

Start at the remote Powderhorn Trailhead, set at 6,400 feet on the boundary of the Granite Chief Wilderness. From there you hike four miles down to Diamond Crossing (fording Powderhorn Creek), where you will meet the Hell Hole Trail. Shortly after turning left, you will have to cross Five Lakes Creek, a difficult and sometimes dangerous endeavor, especially during snowmelt. After crossing, you will descend to Little Buckskin Creeks (two more fords, both a lot easier than the first one) and into Steamboat Canyon. Approximately .5 mile from Steamboat Canyon, hikers face a slippery landslide that demands caution. The trail then drops toward the Rubicon River and Hell Hole Reservoir.

Special note I: The stream crossings required on this hike can be life threatening during periods of high snowmelt and runoff.

Special note II: For a day hike or a weekend camping trip, start the trail at the Hell Hole Dam and walk three miles to a hike-in camp set at the head of the lake.

Location: In the Granite Chief Wilderness, east of Hell Hole Reservoir in Tahoe National Forest; map D3, grid d9.

User groups: Hikers, dogs, and horses. No mountain bikes. No wheelchair facilities.

Permits: A campfire permit (free) is required for overnight use. Parking and access are free.

Maps: For a map of Tahoe National Forest, send $6 to U.S. Forest Service, Attn: Map Sales, P.O. Box 587, Camino, CA 95709; tel. (530) 647-5390, fax (530) 647-5389, or website: www.r5.fs.fed.us/visitorcenter. Major credit cards accepted. Ask the USGS for a topographic map of the Wentworth Springs area.

Directions: In Truckee turn south on Highway 89 and drive to Tahoe City. Continue four miles south on Highway 89 to the Kaspian Picnic Area. Turn west (right) on Blackwood Canyon Road and drive 2.3 miles. Cross the creek and continue for another 4.8 miles to Barker Pass.

Contact: Tahoe National Forest, Truckee Ranger District, 10342 Highway 89 North, Truckee, CA 96161; tel. (530) 587-3558 or fax (530) 587-6914.

PACIFIC CREST TRAIL (PCT) SECTION OVERVIEW

PCT-31 Donner Pass to the Yuba River

38.0 mi one way/3.0 days

Though not one of the more glamorous sections of the Pacific Crest Trail, this stretch is hardly a stinker. For the most part it follows a crest connecting a series of small mountaintops before dropping down to Jackson Meadow Reservoir and Highway 49. Some good views are to be had on the first leg of the trail, so many that some PCT hikers begin to take them for granted after awhile. Here the trail is routed past Castle Peak (elevation 9,103 feet), Basin Peak (9,015 feet), and Lacey Mountain (8,214 feet). Covering this much terrain makes for an ambitious first day, perhaps with stops at Paradise Lake or White Rock Lake. As the trail drops to Jackson Meadow Reservoir, the views end, but in time you'll catch sight of the lake; surrounded by firs, it is quite pretty. The PCT then skirts the east side of the reservoir, passes several drive-to campgrounds, heads through Bear Valley (not *the*

Bear Valley), and drops steeply to Milton Creek and four miles beyond that to Loves Falls at Highway 49.

Location: From Highway 80 to Highway 49 in Tahoe National Forest; map D3, grid b9.

User groups: Hikers, dogs, and horses. No mountain bikes. No wheelchair facilities.

Permits: A campfire permit (free) is required for overnight use. Parking and access are free.

Maps: For a map of Tahoe National Forest, send $6 to U.S. Forest Service, Attn: Map Sales, P.O. Box 587, Camino, CA 95709; tel. (530) 647-5390, fax (530) 647-5389, or website: www.r5.fs.fed.us/visitorcenter. Major credit cards accepted. Ask the USGS for topographic maps of the Norden, Soda Springs, Webber, Haypress Valley, Independence Lake, and English Mountain areas.

Directions: From Auburn drive east on Interstate 80 to Boreal/Donner Summit. Take the exit for the Pacific Crest Trailhead parking area. There is no parking in the Donner Summit rest area.

Contact: Tahoe National Forest, Sierraville Ranger District, P.O. Box 95, Highway 89, Sierraville, CA 96126; tel. (530) 994-3401 or fax (530) 994-3143.

PCT Continuation

To continue hiking along the Pacific Crest Trail, see chapter C3.

ANN MARIE BROWN

HIKER AT MOUNT ROUND TOP

MAP D4

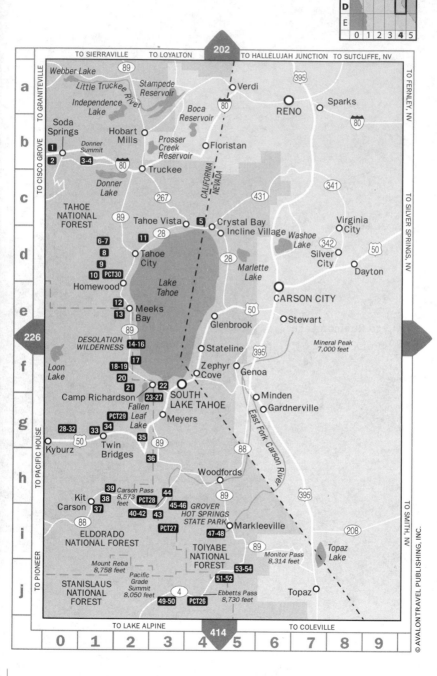

TO SIERRAVILLE TO LOYALTON **202** TO HALLELUJAH JUNCTION TO SUTCLIFFE, NV

TO GRANITEVILLE

Webber Lake 89

Little Truckee River

Independence Lake

Stampede Reservoir

Boca Reservoir

Verdi

80

395

RENO

Sparks

80

TO FERNLEY, NV

a

TO CISCO GROVE

Soda Springs

1
2

Donner Summit

3-4

Hobart Mills

Prosser Creek Reservoir

Floristan

80

Truckee

CALIFORNIA / NEVADA

341

TO SILVER SPRINGS, NV

b

Donner Lake

267

431

50

c

TAHOE NATIONAL FOREST

89

Tahoe Vista

5

Crystal Bay
Incline Village

Washoe Lake

Virginia City

342

Silver City

Dayton

50

d

6-7
8
9
10 **PCT30**

11

28

Tahoe City

Homewood

Lake Tahoe

Marlette Lake

28

CARSON CITY

e

226

12
13

Meeks Bay

DESOLATION WILDERNESS

89

14-16

Glenbrook

50

Stewart

Mineral Peak 7,000 feet

f

Loon Lake

17
18-19
20
21

22

23-27

Camp Richardson

Stateline

Zephyr Cove

Genoa

395

SOUTH LAKE TAHOE

Minden

Gardnerville

g

TO PACIFIC HOUSE

28-32 **33** **34**

PCT29

35

Fallen Leaf Lake

Meyers

89

36

Twin Bridges

50

Kyburz

East Fork Carson River

88

Woodfords

h

Kit Carson

39 Carson Pass 8,573 feet
38 **PCT28**
37

44

45-46 GROVER HOT SPRINGS STATE PARK

89

395

TO SMITH, NV

40-42 **43**

PCT27

47-48

Markleeville

208

i

88

ELDORADO NATIONAL FOREST

TOIYABE NATIONAL FOREST

89

Monitor Pass 8,314 feet

Topaz Lake

TO PIONEER

Mount Reba 8,758 feet

Pacific Grade Summit 8,050 feet

53-54

51-52

STANISLAUS NATIONAL FOREST

4

49-50 **PCT26**

Ebbetts Pass 8,730 feet

Topaz

j

TO LAKE ALPINE **414** TO COLEVILLE

© AVALON TRAVEL PUBLISHING, INC.

242 Northern California

CHAPTER D4

1 Lower Lola
Montez Lake 244

2 Palisade Creek Trail
to Heath Falls 244

3 Warren Lake 245

4 Summit Lake 246

5 Stateline Lookout 246

6 Granite Chief Trail
to Tinker Knob 247

7 Granite Chief Trail
to Emigrant Pass 247

8 Five Lakes 248

9 Ward Creek 248

10 Ellis Peak 249

11 Burton Creek Loop . . . 250

12 General Creek
to Lily Pond 250

13 Meeks Creek Trail
to Rubicon Lake 251

14 Rubicon and
Lighthouse Loop 252

15 Rubicon Trail 252

16 Balancing Rock 253

17 Vikingsholm 253

18 Eagle Falls and
Eagle Lake 254

19 Velma Lakes 254

20 Cascade Falls 255

21 Mount Tallac from
Tallac Trailhead 255

22 Rainbow and Lake
of the Sky Trails 256

23 Susie and
Heather Lakes 257

24 Fallen Leaf Lake Trail . . 257

25 Mount Tallac Loop (Glen
Alpine Trailhead) 258

26 Gilmore Lake 259

27 Angora Lakes Trail . . . 259

28 Lyons Creek Trail 260

29 Grouse, Hemlock,
and Smith Lakes 261

30 Twin and Island Lakes . 261

31 Gertrude and
Tyler Lakes 262

32 Rockbound Pass
and Lake Doris 263

33 Horsetail Falls Vista . . 264

34 Ralston Peak 265

35 Boat Taxi to
Lake Aloha 265

36 Dardanelles Lake
and Round Lake 266

37 Minkalo Trail 267

38 Emigrant Lake 268

39 Lake Margaret 268

40 Winnemucca Lake
from Woods Lake 269

41 Round Top Summit and
Winnemucca Lake
Loop 270

42 Fourth of July Lake . . . 270

43 Frog Lake 271

44 Showers Lake 272

45 Raymond Lake 272

46 Granite Lake 273

47 Hot Springs Creek
Waterfall 274

(CONTINUED ON NEXT PAGE)

(CONTINUED)

48 Burnside Lake 274

49 Heiser Lake 275

50 Bull Run Lake 275

51 Noble Lake 276

52 Kinney Lakes 277

53 Wolf Creek Trail 277

54 East Carson
River Trail 278

Pacific Crest Trail (PCT) Section Overview

PCT-26 Ebbetts Pass to
Blue Lakes Road . . . 279

PCT-27 Blue Lakes Road to
Carson Pass 279

PCT-28 Carson Pass to
Echo Lakes Resort . 280

PCT-29 Echo Lakes Resort to
Barker Pass 281

PCT-30 Barker Pass to
Donner Pass 282

1 Lower Lola Montez Lake
6.0 mi/3.0 hrs

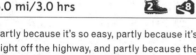

Partly because it's so easy, partly because it's right off the highway, and partly because the trail is favored by mountain bikers, the hike to Lower Lola Montez Lake is a bad choice for a July or August weekend afternoon. For hikers who enjoy peace and quiet, this is definitely an off-season trail, best left for the days of autumn when the vacationers have abandoned Lake Tahoe. The path cuts through Toll Mountain Estates, a private community, and is a mix of wide dirt roads and single-track trails. The first .25 mile is on single track; then you reach a dirt road and turn right, cross Castle Creek, and continue until the road becomes single track again. And so it goes. Luckily the route is marked all the way, and with all the people who visit here, it's unlikely you'll get lost and not be found. The good news is that the Lower Lola Montez Lake is popular for a reason; it's a beautiful alpine lake set at 7,200 feet but shallow enough to warm up for swimming. Fishing is half decent, but best early in the year.

Location: In Tahoe National Forest near Soda Springs; map D4, grid b0.

User groups: Hikers, dogs, horses, and mountain bikes. No wheelchair facilities.

Permits: No permits are required. Parking and access are free.

Maps: For a map of Tahoe National Forest, send $6 to U.S. Forest Service, Map Sales, P.O. Box 587, Camino, CA 95709; tel. (530) 647-5390 or website: www.r5.fs.fed.us/visitorcenter. Ask the USGS for a topographic map of the Soda Springs and Norden areas.

Directions: Drive east from Auburn on Interstate 80 for 55 miles to Soda Springs. Take the Soda Springs/Norden exit and cross over the overpass to the north side of the freeway. Follow the paved road east, past the fire station for .3 mile to the trailhead parking area.

Contact: Tahoe National Forest, Truckee Ranger District, 10342 Highway 89 North, Truckee, CA 96161; tel. (530) 587-3558 or fax (530) 587-6914.

2 Palisade Creek Trail to Heath Falls
10.0 mi/6.0 hrs

The hike to Heath Falls is like going on vacation on your credit card. You can have all the fun you want, but when you return home, you have to pay up. That's because the trip to the Heath Falls Overlook is downhill nearly all the way, dropping 1,700 feet over five miles, through stunning alpine scenery that will have you smiling the whole time. But the return trip is a long and steady five-mile climb back uphill, so you want to be sure you have plenty of food, water, and energy left for it. The trail begins at the dam between the two Cascade Lakes, the first of many lakes you'll see on this trip. The big hunk of imposing rock you have to walk around is 7,704-foot Devils Peak. Take the right fork signed for the North Fork American River, and get ready for a steady diet of granite, lakes, and vistas. At 2.2 miles, the trail leaves the rocks behind and enters the forest, switchbacking downhill for two miles to the Palisade Creek Bridge. Look for an unsigned junction 300 yards beyond it, where the Heath Falls Overlook Trail heads east. Follow it for .5 mile to the trail's end at a vista of the American River's Heath Falls. Camping is prohibited along this trail because much of it runs through private property, so after enjoying the falls overlook, you've got to make the long climb home. Hope you have at least one Power Bar left.

Location: In Tahoe National Forest near Soda Springs; map D4, grid b0.

User groups: Hikers, dogs, and horses. No mountain bikes. No wheelchair facilities.

Permits: No permits are required. Parking and access are free.

Maps: For a map of Tahoe National Forest, send $6 to U.S. Forest Service, Map Sales, P.O. Box 587, Camino, CA 95709; tel. (530) 647-5390 or website: www.r5.fs.fed.us/visitorcenter. Ask the USGS for a topographic map of the Soda Springs and Norden areas.

Directions: From Auburn drive east on Interstate 80 for 55 miles to Soda Springs. Take the Soda Springs/Norden exit and follow Old Highway 40 east for .8 mile to Soda Springs Road. Turn south (right) and drive for another .8 mile to Pahatsi Road. Turn right. Pahatsi Road turns to dirt in .2 mile, and its name changes to Kidd Lakes Road. At 1.5 miles, reach a fork and continue straight for 2.3 more miles, passing Kidd Lake on your left and the Royal Gorge Devils Lookout Warming Hut on your right. Take the left fork after the warming

hut and drive .5 mile farther. The trailhead, signed as Palisade Creek Trail, is on the north side of Cascade Lakes.

Contact: Tahoe National Forest, Truckee Ranger District, 10342 Highway 89 North, Truckee, CA 96161; tel. (530) 587-3558 or fax (530) 587-6914.

❸ Warren Lake
14.0 mi/2.0 days

The first 1.6 miles of this trail follow the same route as the Summit Lake Trail (see hike number five), along the PCT access trail and underneath Interstate 80, but Warren Lake hikers will take the left fork where Summit Lake hikers go right. While the Summit Lake Trail is an easy stroll in the park, the Warren Lake Trail climbs 1,500 feet and then drops 1,500 feet, which you must repeat on the return trip. The elevation change means you part company with most casual hikers. The route climbs through lodgepole pine and red fir forest to a saddle at three miles, with excellent views. (You can see where you're going to be hiking next.) Then the trail drops gently over the next 3.5 miles, into a wide valley basin that has a mix of volcanic and glaciated rocks. Wildflowers abound on the valley floor. After a brief climb to a ridge, the final mile is a steep descent, dropping 1,000 feet to Warren Lake, where you'll find many campsites on the lake's west and south sides. Note that just before you reach the top of the ridge, about 1.3 miles from Warren Lake, there is a left spur trail that leads to Devils Oven Lake. It's a good day hike for the following day.

Location: In Tahoe National Forest near Donner Summit; map D4, grid b1.

User groups: Hikers, dogs, horses, and mountain bikes. No wheelchair facilities.

Permits: No permits are required. Parking and access are free.

Maps: For a map of Tahoe National Forest, send $6 to U.S. Forest Service, Map Sales, P.O. Box 587, Camino, CA 95709; tel.

(530) 647-5390 or website: www.r5.fs.fed.us/visitorcenter. Ask the USGS for a topographic map of the Norden area.

Directions: Drive east from Auburn on Interstate 80 for 60 miles to the Castle Peak Area/Boreal Ridge Road exit just west of Donner Summit. Exit the freeway; turn right and then immediately left. Drive .4 mile to the trailhead for Donner Summit and the Pacific Crest Trail.

Contact: Tahoe National Forest, Truckee Ranger District, 10342 Highway 89 North, Truckee, CA 96161; tel. (530) 587-3558 or fax (530) 587-6914.

4 Summit Lake
4.0 mi/2.0 hrs

It's hard to believe that this much fun is accessible right off Interstate 80, but it's true. The Summit Lake Trail is a quick and easy leg-stretcher and a great hike for families, leading two miles to a pretty alpine lake at 7,400 feet. Start hiking from the PCT Trailhead, heading east and roughly paralleling the freeway. Watch carefully for an intersection at .5 mile in; there you must turn left and follow the PCT Access Trail north (signed for Castle Pass and Peter Grubb Hut), through a tunnel underneath Interstate 80. (This is not the most scenic part of the trip, but it's not as bad as it sounds.) Once you're on the north side of the freeway, you'll reach a trail fork and bear right for Summit Lake and Warren Lake, then start to climb a bit. The trail alternates through fir forest and occasional open ridges, with some excellent views to the south and east. At 1.6 miles you'll see another trail fork—Warren Lake to the left and Summit Lake to the right. Bear right and finish out your walk to the lake's edge, where you can drop in a fishing line if you wish.

Location: In Tahoe National Forest near Donner Summit; map D4, grid b1.

User groups: Hikers, dogs, horses, and mountain bikes. No wheelchair facilities.

Permits: No permits are required. Parking and access are free.

Maps: For a map of Tahoe National Forest, send $6 to U.S. Forest Service, Map Sales, P.O. Box 587, Camino, CA 95709; tel. (530) 647-5390 or website: www.r5.fs.fed.us/visitorcenter. Ask the USGS for a topographic map of the Norden area.

Directions: From Auburn drive 60 miles east on Interstate 80 to the Castle Peak Area/Boreal Ridge Road exit just west of Donner Summit. Exit the freeway, turn right, and then immediately left. Drive .4 mile to the trailhead for Donner Summit and the Pacific Crest Trail.

Contact: Tahoe National Forest, Truckee Ranger District, 10342 Highway 89 North, Truckee, CA 96161; tel. (530) 587-3558 or fax (530) 587-6914.

5 Stateline Lookout
1.0 mi/0.5 hr

For years we avoided this trail because we thought it was a dumb tourist attraction, located at the lookout tower that straddles the Nevada and California state line. It turns out that we were the dumb tourists, because this little trail is great. You can learn all about the cultural history of Lake Tahoe's north shore, which includes stories of timber, railroads, casinos, and resorts, and a little about the natural history of the area as well. After you walk the short self-guided trail, be sure to check out the views of Lake Tahoe from the telescopes located at the lookout. Or hey, forget the telescopes and just look with your own eyes. Either way, the view is unforgettable.

Location: Off Highway 28 near Tahoe Vista; map D4, grid c4.

User groups: Hikers, wheelchairs, and dogs. No horses or mountain bikes.

Permits: No permits are required. Parking and access are free.

Maps: For a map of Lake Tahoe Basin Management Unit, send $6 to U.S. Forest Service, Map Sales, P.O. Box 587, Camino, CA 95709; tel. (530) 647-5390 or website: www.r5.fs.fed.us/visitorcenter. Ask the USGS for a topographic map of the Kings Beach area.

Directions: From Tahoe City drive east on Highway 28 for six miles to Reservoir Drive, just east of the old Tahoe Biltmore Casino. Turn left (north), drive to Lakeshore Avenue, and turn right. Continue through a residential area and then turn left on Forest Service Road 1601 at an unmarked iron gate. Park in the large parking lot just below the lookout. If the gate is locked, park below it and walk up the road.

Contact: Lake Tahoe Basin Management Unit, 870 Emerald Bay Road, South Lake Tahoe, CA 96150; tel. (530) 573-2600 or fax (530) 573-2693.

6 Granite Chief Trail to Tinker Knob

14.0 mi/8.0 hrs or 2.0 days

Tinker Knob is not an easy summit to attain, but those who reach it always remember it. From the Squaw Valley fire station, it's a demanding 3.5-mile hike to the intersection of the Granite Chief Trail and the Pacific Crest Trail. The total gain is 2,000 feet; most of the climb is forested but there are occasional openings with views of Lake Tahoe and surrounding peaks. When at last you gain the PCT at 8,200 feet, turn right (north) toward Tinker Knob. Now it's another 3.5 miles, most of it on an easier, winding grade along the top of a ridge, with only one surprising, cruel stretch in which you must drop downhill and then climb up again. The last section of trail is a series of switchbacks up to the Tinker Knob Saddle, then a brief .25-mile climb to the summit of Tinker Knob at 8,950 feet. You like views? How about this one—a head-swiveling vista of Anderson Peak, Painted Rock, Silver Peak, the American River Canyon, Donner Lake, and Lake Tahoe. To cut some mileage off your trip, you can hike this trail as a shuttle trip, leaving one car at the Coldstream Trailhead near Donner Memorial State Park. (It's at the horseshoe bend in the railroad tracks at the end of Coldstream Creek access road.) The Coldstream Trail meets the PCT just below the summit of Tinker Knob, so after gaining the summit via the route described above, you can follow Coldstream Trail four miles down to its trailhead. This makes an 11-mile one-way hike with a shuttle.

Location: In Tahoe National Forest near Squaw Valley; map D4, grid d1.

User groups: Hikers, dogs, horses, and mountain bikes. No wheelchair facilities.

Permits: No permits are required. Parking and access are free.

Maps: For a map of Tahoe National Forest, send $6 to U.S. Forest Service, Map Sales, P.O. Box 587, Camino, CA 95709; tel. (530) 647-5390 or website: www.r5.fs.fed.us/visitorcenter. Ask the USGS for a topographic map of the Tahoe City and Granite Chief areas.

Directions: Drive north from Tahoe City on Highway 89 for five miles and turn west on Squaw Valley Road. Drive 2.2 miles to the Squaw Valley Fire Station, where the trail begins on its east side. You must leave your car in the large parking lot by the ski lift buildings, not by the fire station. Walk back across the bridge to the trailhead.

Contact: Tahoe National Forest, Truckee Ranger District, 10342 Highway 89 North, Truckee, CA 96161; tel. (530) 587-3558 or fax (530) 587-6914.

7 Granite Chief Trail to Emigrant Pass

12.0 mi/7.0 hrs

The Granite Chief Trail begins at the Squaw Valley fire station at 6,200 feet and climbs, climbs, and climbs some more till it reaches the Pacific Crest Trail 3.5 miles later. This is why many hikers choose to ride the tram at Squaw Valley to reach the PCT, then start hiking around from there. But not you; you like a challenge. Okay, here it is. You'll climb 2,000 feet over those 3.5 miles, roughly paralleling Squaw Creek and mostly in the woods. When you reach the PCT, turn left (south) toward Twin Peaks. What's that big blue spot down there? It's Lake Tahoe for sure. Still ascending, hike for one mile on the PCT to the eastern flank of Granite Chief Peak, elevation 9,086 feet. Finally you begin to descend, and in one more mile you reach an intersection with the Western States Trail. Turn left and take a .5-mile walk to visit the Watson Monument, a stone marker at Emigrant Pass. You probably won't stay long. Although the views are lovely, the wind is usually fierce.

Location: In Tahoe National Forest near Squaw Valley; map D4, grid d1.

User groups: Hikers, dogs, horses, and mountain bikes. No wheelchair facilities.

Permits: No permits are required. Parking and access are free.

Maps: For a map of Tahoe National Forest, send $6 to U.S. Forest Service, Map Sales, P.O. Box 587, Camino, CA 95709; tel. (530) 647-5390 or website: www.r5.fs.fed.us/visitorcenter. Ask the USGS for a topographic map of the Tahoe City and Granite Chief areas.

Directions: From Tahoe City drive north on Highway 89 for five miles and turn west on Squaw Valley Road. Drive 2.2 miles to the Squaw Valley Fire Station, where the trail begins on its east side. You must leave your car in the large parking lot by the ski lift buildings, not by the fire station. Walk back across the bridge to the trailhead.

Contact: Tahoe National Forest, Truckee Ranger District, 10342 Highway 89 North, Truckee, CA 96161; tel. (530) 587-3558 or fax (530) 587-6914.

8 Five Lakes

4.2 mi/2.0 hrs

Some say that this trek into the Granite Chief Wilderness is too easy, and they may be right. Although the trail has a moderately steep grade, it's mercifully short, which makes it incredibly popular with hikers, especially on weekends. Make your trip in the off-season or during the week, and definitely make this a day trip instead of an overnight to minimize impact at the five granite-bound lakes.

The first .5 mile is the steepest grade, whereas the next .75 mile continues uphill more gradually to the top of a ridge. Switchbacks

make it manageable, but there is almost no shade along the route as you climb 1,000 feet. At 1.8 miles, you reach the Granite Chief Wilderness boundary and enter a land of red fir, white fir, and rocks. A signed junction .25 mile farther points you to the left toward the lakes, with your trail heading directly downhill to the largest of them. From there you can follow numerous side trails to the four other lakes, all east of the big one. Most people don't go any farther than the first big lake, where the swimming is excellent. The shallow water is clear and warm. Remember: Minimize your impact in this heavily traveled area. The Five Lakes are set at 7,400 feet.

Location: In the Granite Chief Wilderness near Alpine Meadows; map D4, grid d1.

User groups: Hikers, dogs, and horses. No mountain bikes. No wheelchair facilities.

Permits: No permits are required for day hiking. Parking and access are free.

Maps: For a map of Tahoe National Forest, send $6 to U.S. Forest Service, Map Sales, P.O. Box 587, Camino, CA 95709; tel. (530) 647-5390 or website: www.r5.fs.fed.us/visitorcenter. Ask the USGS for a topographic map of the Tahoe City and Granite Chief areas.

Directions: From Tahoe City drive north on Highway 89 for 3.5 miles to Alpine Meadows Road. Turn west on Alpine Meadows Road and drive two miles to the trailhead on the right. Park alongside the road.

Contact: Tahoe National Forest, Truckee Ranger District, 10342 Highway 89 North, Truckee, CA 96161; tel. (530) 587-3558 or fax (530) 587-6914.

9 Ward Creek

6.0 mi/3.0 hrs

Compared to some of the more famous hikes at Lake Tahoe, the Ward Creek Trail is rather tame: No stellar waterfall, no drop-dead gorgeous lake views, no towering granite monoliths. But then again, there are no crowds either. For many, the trade-off is a good one. The route passes through fields of mule's ears and forests of sugar pines, with enough open sections to provide wide-open views of the surrounding mountain ridges.

The trail begins as an old dirt road, paralleling Ward Creek for 1.5 miles to a washed-out bridge and a "Road Closed" sign. You cross the creek on logs and continue hiking, now on single track. The trail climbs a little higher above Ward Creek, then enters a dense, lovely pine forest. You can go as far as you like (the trail continues to Twin Peaks, 5.3 miles from the trailhead), but for the mileage suggested above, turn around when you are about .5 mile into the trees and take an easy stroll home.

Location: In Tahoe National Forest near Tahoe City; map D4, grid d1.

User groups: Hikers, dogs, horses, and mountain bikes. No wheelchair facilities.

Permits: No permits are required. Parking and access are free.

Maps: For a map of Lake Tahoe Basin Management Unit, send $6 to U.S. Forest Service, Map Sales, P.O. Box 587, Camino, CA 95709; tel. (530) 647-5390 or website: www.r5.fs.fed.us/visitor-center. Ask the USGS for a topographic map of the Tahoe City area.

Directions: From Tahoe City drive two miles south on Highway 89 to Pineland Drive, just north of Kilner Park. Turn right on Pineland Drive and go .5 mile to Twin Peaks Drive. Turn left and drive 1.7 miles. (Twin Peaks Drive becomes Ward Creek Boulevard.) At 1.7 miles, park in the pullout on the left side of the highway and begin hiking at the gated dirt road, Forest Service Road 15N62. If the gate is open, you can drive inside and park along the dirt road.

Contact: Lake Tahoe Basin Management Unit, 870 Emerald Bay Road, South Lake Tahoe, CA 96150; tel. (530) 573-2600 or fax (530) 573-2693.

10 Ellis Peak

6.0 mi/3.5 hrs

This short but steep trek leads to the top of Ellis Peak and fabulous views of Lake Tahoe, Granite Chief and Desolation Wildernesses, and Hell Hole Reservoir. There is a total 1,300-foot elevation gain to the peak at 8,740, but the route is beautiful all the way, with close-up wildflowers rivaling the far-off views. The initial climb is a bit steep, but there is plenty of shade on this stretch. Then the route follows a sunny ridgeline for 1.5 miles with wide-open vistas. Hey, is that Lake Tahoe down there? Yes, indeed, and Hell Hole Reservoir to the west. The perspective from this ridgeline alone is worth the trip. Plus, mule's ears and other wildflowers bloom in profusion all around your ankles.

After traversing the ridgeline, you head downhill (surprise!) through the forest, dropping 400 feet in elevation. When you come to a wide dirt road, bear left to begin the trek to Ellis Peak. In .25 mile, you'll see a short left spur to tiny Ellis Lake, a worthy side trip of about 50 yards. If you ignore the spur and stay on the main trail for another 100 yards, you'll reach an old dirt road, where you turn east (left). In .25 mile you come to Knee Ridge, from which the summit of Ellis Peak is plainly visible. Go for it. Note that the only downer along this route is that some of it is accessible to off-road vehicle riders and mountain bikers, although we saw none of the former on our trip, and the latter were extremely courteous.

Location: In Tahoe National Forest near Tahoe City; map D4, grid d1.

User groups: Hikers, dogs, horses, and mountain bikes. No wheelchair facilities.

Permits: No permits are required. Parking and access are free.

Maps: For a map of Lake Tahoe Basin Management Unit, send $6 to U.S. Forest Service, Map Sales, P.O. Box 587, Camino, CA 95709; tel. (530) 647-5390 or website: www.r5.fs.fed.us/visitor-center. Ask the USGS for a topographic map of the Homewood area.

Directions: Drive four miles south from Tahoe City on Highway 89 to Forest Service Road 03 (Barker Pass Road). Turn right (west) and drive seven miles to the summit of Barker Pass. The trailhead is on the left (south) side of the road.

Contact: Lake Tahoe Basin Management Unit, 870 Emerald Bay Road, South Lake Tahoe, CA 96150; tel. (530) 573-2600 or fax (530) 573-2693.

11 Burton Creek Loop

5.0 mi/2.5 hrs

Burton Creek State Park is Lake Tahoe's second largest state park at more than 2,000 acres, so you might wonder why few people have ever heard of it. It's because the park has no visitor center, no campground, no entrance kiosk, and, unfortunately, no trail signs or official map. What really matters is that it has no crowds, a major bonus at Lake Tahoe. A five-mile loop trip is possible in the park, starting near North Tahoe High School and wandering through a mix of fir and pine forest, open meadows, and creekside riparian habitat. Although the trail is not signed at present, there are numbers painted at most intersections, which help you stay on track. (The route is frequently used for 10K races in the summer.) The loop starts .25 mile from the trailhead; you can hike it in either direction. Just make sure you remember what the spur trail looks like that leads from the loop back to the trailhead; otherwise you'll walk right past it on your return trip, like we did. Some advice: If you're visiting this park in summer, stop in at the campground at Tahoe State Recreation Area, across Highway 28 from the turnoff to Burton Creek State Park. Check with the kiosk to see if they have any updated trail information on Burton Creek.

Location: Off Highway 28 near Tahoe City; map D4, grid d2.

User groups: Hikers, dogs, horses, and mountain bikes. No wheelchair facilities.

Permits: No permits are required. Parking and access are free.

Maps: Ask the USGS for a topographic map of the Tahoe City area.

Directions: From Tahoe City drive northeast on Highway 28 for 2.3 miles to Old Mill Road. Turn left and drive .4 mile; then turn left on Polaris Road and drive .5 mile to North Tahoe

High School and the dirt road by the school parking lot. Park alongside the dirt road, being careful not to block the gate.

Contact: Tahoe State Recreation Area, P.O. Box 266, Tahoma, CA 96142; tel. (530) 525-7232, tel. (530) 583-3074, or fax (530) 525-0138.

12 General Creek to Lily Pond

7.0 mi/3.5 hrs

This trail in Sugar Pine Point State Park follows a flat open stretch of General Creek and then leads gently uphill through the forest to marshy Lily Pond, a pretty, serene spot. Most of the trail is part of a popular cross-country skiing loop in the winter, which means it's on a wide logging road. There are a couple key factors to enjoying this walk: If you're not staying in the General Creek Campground, the day-use parking area is more than .5 mile from campsite #149, where the trail begins. To make this walk to the trailhead more pleasant, be sure to take the single-track trail from the parking lot instead of walking along the paved camp road. The trail is somewhat hidden from view, so if you don't see it, ask the attendant in the entrance kiosk where it is. Next, when you finally meet up with the loop, be sure to take the north side of it, which is prettier than the south side, with lots of big sugar pines interspersed with Jeffreys and lodgepoles. The south side is mostly open meadows. If you're a history buff, it was the site of the 1960 Olympics biathlon. At 2.5 miles from the campground, at the far end of the loop, you'll see the single-track turnoff signed for Lily Pond and Lost Lake. It's a one-mile hike through a rocky, dense forest to the pond, which is indeed covered with lilies. On your return, you can always take the south side of the loop for variety, then turn left on the bridge over General Creek to return to the start of the loop.

Location: In Sugar Pine Point State Park near Lake Tahoe; map D4, grid e2.

User groups: Hikers and mountain bikes. No dogs or horses. No wheelchair facilities.

Permits: No permits are required. A $2 day-use fee is charged per vehicle.

Maps: A map of Sugar Pine Point State Park is available for $1 at the entrance station. A Lake Tahoe map is available for a fee from Tom Harrison Cartography, tel. (415) 456-7940. Ask the USGS for a topographic map of the Homewood area.

Directions: From Tahoe City drive eight miles south on Highway 89 to the General Creek Campground entrance on the right. Park in one of the day-use areas by the entrance kiosk, then walk into the campground to site #149 and the start of the trail. You can walk into the camp on the park road or take the single-track trail that leads from the parking lot.

Contact: Sugar Pine Point State Park, P.O. Box 266, Tahoma, CA 96142; tel. (530) 525-7982, tel. (530) 525-7232, or fax (530) 525-0138.

🔟🔠 Meeks Creek Trail to Rubicon Lake

15.0 mi/1–2 days

If you don't mind sharing the trail with lots of other folks, this trek into the Desolation Wilderness is a moderate backpacking trip that's loaded with alpine lakes and classic Tahoe scenery. A closed dirt road (Road 14N42) leads from the Desolation Wilderness sign near Meeks Bay for 1.3 level miles to a trail sign for Phipps Pass and Tahoe-Yosemite Trail, a popular cross-country skiing route in winter. Bear right here and begin the gradual climb to a chain of alpine lakes, beginning with Lake Genevieve at 4.5 miles and culminating with Rubicon Lake at 7.5 miles. Parallel Meeks Creek on a gently climbing trail, and pass the wilderness boundary at 2.5 miles. You're in forest most of the time, so don't expect a lot of panoramic views, but then again don't expect any brutal, sunny, exposed ascents. Cross Meeks Creek and continue straight to Lake Genevieve, a shallow, swimmable body of water. The trail then climbs up to larger Crag Lake, then continues to climb farther to small, lily-covered Shadow Lake. (A right fork be-

yond Crag Lake leads to small Hidden Lake, less than .25 mile off the main trail, a good side trip.) From Shadow Lake it's a mile farther to Stony Ridge Lake, the largest of this series of lakes, and then yet another mile to Rubicon Lake, 7.5 miles from the trailhead and with a total elevation gain of only 2,000 feet. The main steep stretch is right at the end, between Stony Ridge Lake and Rubicon Lake. Campsites can be found at most all of the lakes, but Rubicon Lake is the preferred site, since it's the most scenic of the group.

Location: In the Desolation Wilderness; map D4, grid e2.

User groups: Hikers, dogs, and horses. No mountain bikes. No wheelchair facilities.

Permits: Day-hikers must fill out a day-use permit at the wilderness trailhead. A wilderness permit is required for overnight stays. It costs $5 per person per night (first two nights only) and is available from the South Lake Tahoe Ranger Station or the Eldorado National Forest office in Camino. Quotas are in effect from June 15 to Labor Day. Reservations for this period are available in advance by phone for a $5 fee. Phone (530) 644-6048 for reservations and information.

Maps: For a map of Lake Tahoe Basin Management Unit or Desolation Wilderness, send $6 to U.S. Forest Service, Map Sales, P.O. Box 587, Camino, CA 95709; tel. (530) 647-5390 or website: www.r5.fs.fed.us/visitorcenter. A Lake Tahoe or Desolation Wilderness map is also available for a fee from Tom Harrison Cartography, tel. (415) 456-7940. Ask the USGS for a topographic map of the Homewood and Rockbound Valley areas.

Directions: From Tahoe City drive south on Highway 89 for 10 miles to Meeks Bay Resort. Look for a small dirt parking lot across from the resort on the west side of the highway, and park there. The trailhead is well marked.

Contact: Lake Tahoe Basin Management Unit, 870 Emerald Bay Road, South Lake Tahoe, CA 96150; tel. (530) 573-2600 or fax (530) 573-2693.

14 Rubicon and Lighthouse Loop

2.0 mi/1.0 hr

Not everybody is up for hiking the entire length of the Rubicon Trail, below. But if you're visiting Lake Tahoe, you should not leave the area without sampling at least a piece of this magnificent pathway that edges along the steep cliffs on the west side of the lake. An excellent short trip on the Rubicon is this loop, which starts from Calawee Cove Beach at D.L. Bliss State Park. Although the hike has very little elevation gain, it's not for those who are afraid of heights because there are 100-foot dropoffs along the trail's edge, leading straight down to Lake Tahoe. Cables are in place in some sections to keep people from falling off the trail. You hike .25 mile to a spur trail to the old lighthouse (don't bother with the spur; there's nothing to see), then continue beyond it for another .5 mile. The lake and mountain views are mind-boggling every step of the way. Bear right at the trail junction and walk to a parking lot, where you can pick up the Lighthouse Trail and loop back to Calawee Cove Beach. On the other hand, if you want to see those lake vistas one more time, forget about the loop and just head back the way you came.

Location: In D.L. Bliss State Park on the west shore of Lake Tahoe; map D4, grid f2.

User groups: Hikers only. No dogs, horses, or mountain bikes. No wheelchair facilities.

Permits: No permits are required. A $2 day-use fee is charged per vehicle.

Maps: A map of D.L. Bliss State Park is available for $1 at the entrance station. A Lake Tahoe map is available for a fee from Tom Harrison Cartography, tel. (415) 456-7940. Ask the USGS for a topographic map of the Emerald Bay area.

Directions: Drive south from Tahoe City on Highway 89 for 15 miles and turn left at the sign for D.L. Bliss State Park. Drive .5 mile to the entrance station and continue for .7 mile to a fork. Turn right and drive another .7 mile to Calawee Cove Beach and parking lot. The Ru-

bicon Trail begins on the far side of the lot. If this lot is full, you will have to use one of the other day-use parking lots in the park.

Contact: D.L. Bliss State Park, P.O. Box 266, Tahoma, CA 96142; tel. (530) 525-7277, tel. (530) 525-7232, or fax (530) 525-0138.

15 Rubicon Trail

9.0 mi/5.0 hrs

The Rubicon Trail is the premier Lake Tahoe day hike; accept no substitutes. If you want the best scenery that Lake Tahoe offers, this is the trail to hike. The only problem? Right; it's you and about a zillion other hikers. If you possibly can, walk this trail in the off-season (late September is great) and do it on a weekday. Then get ready for eye-popping, film-burning scenery as you gaze out across the surface and deep into the depths of sparkling clear, 12-mile-wide Lake Tahoe, and gawk at the rim of mountains that surrounds it. The trail stays close to the lake edge and has very little elevation change, just some mild ups and downs, holding steady near 6,300 feet. Highlights include Rubicon Point, Emerald Point, Fannette Island, and Vikingsholm Castle. If you prefer, you can start and end your Rubicon hike at Vikingsholm Castle; just leave your car in the Emerald Bay Overlook parking lot. But you'll add on nearly two miles round-trip getting from the parking lot to Vikingsholm, with a 600-foot elevation change.

Location: In D.L. Bliss State Park on the west shore of Lake Tahoe; map D4, grid f2.

User groups: Hikers only. No dogs, horses, or mountain bikes. No wheelchair facilities.

Permits: No permits are required. A $2 day-use fee is charged per vehicle.

Maps: A map of D.L. Bliss State Park is available for $1 at the entrance station. A Lake Tahoe map is available for a fee from Tom Harrison Cartography, tel. (415) 456-7940. Ask the USGS for a topographic map of the Emerald Bay area.

Directions: From Tahoe City drive south on Highway 89 for 15 miles and turn left at the sign for D.L. Bliss State Park. Drive .5 mile to the entrance station, then continue for .7 mile to a fork. Turn right and drive another .7 mile to Calawee Cove Beach and parking lot. The Rubicon Trail begins on the far side of the lot. (If this lot is full, you will have to use one of the other day-use parking lots in the park.)

Contact: D.L. Bliss State Park, P.O. Box 266, Tahoma, CA 96142; tel. (530) 525-7277, tel. (530) 525-7232, or fax (530) 525-0138.

16 Balancing Rock
1.0 mi/0.5 hr

It sounds kind of dumb, but it's quite popular and more interesting than you might expect. The Balancing Rock is a big hunk of granite that has been a curiosity at Lake Tahoe for eons. It's a 130-ton rock that sits balanced on a small rock pedestal, like a giant golf ball on an itty-bitty golf tee. The trail's interpretive brochure explains that eventually erosion will wear away the pedestal and cause the Balancing Rock to lose its balance, but Tahoe lovers have been awaiting this event forever, and it still hasn't happened. In addition to Balancing Rock, the trail shows off many of the plants and trees of the Tahoe area. It's a good learning experience for both kids and adults.

Location: In D.L. Bliss State Park on the west shore of Lake Tahoe; map D4, grid f2.

User groups: Hikers only. No dogs, horses, or mountain bikes. No wheelchair facilities.

Permits: No permits are required. A $2 day-use fee is charged per vehicle.

Maps: A map of D.L. Bliss State Park is available for $1 at the entrance station. A Lake Tahoe map is available for a fee from Tom Harrison Cartography, tel. (415) 456-7940. Ask the USGS for a topographic map of the Emerald Bay area.

Directions: From Tahoe City drive south on Highway 89 for 15 miles and turn left at the sign for D.L. Bliss State Park. Drive .5 mile to the entrance station; then continue for .7 mile to a fork. Turn left and drive .25 mile to the Balancing Rock parking lot on the left.

Contact: D.L. Bliss State Park, P.O. Box 266, Tahoma, CA 96142; tel. (530) 525-7277, tel. (530) 525-7232, or fax (530) 525-0138.

17 Vikingsholm
2.0 mi/1.0 hr

If you can take this walk very early in the morning, and preferably on a weekday, you'll experience the incredible beauty that has made Lake Tahoe the revered vacation destination that it is. If you take this walk at almost any other time—well, let's just say we hope you like a lot of company. Although the destination of this one-mile trail (really a dirt road) is Vikingsholm, a Viking castle built by an heiress in the 1930s, the beauty lies in the scenery spread out before you as you hike downhill. You see spectacular Fannette Island and the deep blue waters of Emerald Bay, and travel through an old-growth cedar and pine forest. You even gain access to some of Lake Tahoe's coveted sandy shoreline. Although you have to pay a buck to tour the inside of the castle, you can hike to it for free and add on a side trip to the base of 150-foot Eagle Falls, .25 mile from Vikingsholm. For many people, the surprise on this trail is that the return hike has a 500-foot elevation gain. What, you mean we have to breathe hard?

Special note: Be sure to arrive early. By midmorning on weekends, visitors are forced to park up to two miles away.

Location: In Emerald Bay State Park on the west shore of Lake Tahoe; map D4, grid f2.

User groups: Hikers only. No dogs, horses, or mountain bikes. No wheelchair facilities.

Permits: No permits are required. Parking and access are free, but there is a $1 fee to tour the inside of the castle.

Maps: A map of Emerald Bay and D.L. Bliss State Parks is available for $1 at the visitor center by Vikingsholm. A Lake Tahoe map is available for a fee from Tom Harrison Cartography, tel. (415) 456-7940. Ask the USGS for a topographic map of the Emerald Bay area.

Directions: From South Lake Tahoe drive northwest on Highway 89 for nine miles to the Emerald Bay Overlook parking lot on the east side of Highway 89. The trail begins from the lake side of the parking lot.

Contact: Emerald Bay State Park, P.O. Box 266, Tahoma, CA 96142; tel. (530) 525-7277, tel. (530) 525-7232, or fax (530) 525-0138.

18 Eagle Falls and Eagle Lake

2.0 mi/1.0 hr

Next to the trail to Vikingsholm, this may be the most-walked trail around Lake Tahoe. A sign by the restroom at the Eagle Falls Picnic Area points you to the Eagle Falls Trail. Unfortunately this is something of a "designer" path, with natural granite cut into flagstone-like stairs and an elaborate wooden bridge that escorts you over the top of the falls. Still it's a beautiful walk, best taken early in the morning and during the week, when the masses aren't around. The waterfall pours right under the hikers' bridge. (If you want to see the "other" Eagle Falls, the one that drops right along Highway 89, see the Vikingsholm hike, above.) Immediately after the bridge, the designer aspect of the trail ends as you enter the Desolation Wilderness and climb 400 feet in less than a mile to reach rocky Eagle Lake, surrounded by granite cliffs. People fish and picnic here; some even try to swim in the icy water.

Location: Off Highway 89 near South Lake Tahoe; map D4, grid f2.

User groups: Hikers and dogs. No horses or mountain bikes. No wheelchair facilities.

Permits: Day-hikers must fill out a permit at the wilderness trailhead. A $3 parking fee is charged per vehicle.

Maps: For a map of Lake Tahoe Basin Management Unit, send $6 to U.S. Forest Service, Map Sales, P.O. Box 587, Camino, CA 95709; tel. (530) 647-5390 or website: www.r5.fs.fed.us/visitorcenter. A Lake Tahoe map is available for a fee from Tom Harrison Cartography, tel. (415) 456-7940. Ask the USGS for a topographic map of the Emerald Bay area.

Directions: From South Lake Tahoe drive northwest on Highway 89 for 8.5 miles to the Eagle Falls Picnic Area and Trailhead. Turn left into the parking area, or park in the roadside pullout just north of the picnic area on the west side of Highway 89.

Contact: Lake Tahoe Basin Management Unit, 870 Emerald Bay Road, South Lake Tahoe, CA 96150; tel. (530) 573-2600 or fax (530) 573-2693.

19 Velma Lakes

10.0 mi/5.0 hrs

Remember to bring your sunscreen because the rocky trail to the Velma Lakes is exposed and open. The route follows the trail to Eagle Falls and Eagle Lake, above, for the first mile, then climbs through a rugged, glaciated landscape, with only occasional hardy lodgepole pines and twisted junipers providing meager shade. The lack of trees and the abundance of rock means wide-open views and plenty of granite drama; welcome to the Sierra high country. At three miles you intersect the trail heading southwest (left) to Dicks Lake, but you should head northwest (right) for Velma Lakes. Your trail heads directly to Middle Velma Lake in one mile, the most popular of the lakes. It has several granite islands and is favored for swimming. You can take a left cutoff just before Middle Velma Lake and head south to Upper Velma Lake in .5 mile, or follow a use trail north along a creek to Lower Velma Lake (on your right, also .5 mile away). Note that you can also begin the Velma Lakes hike from the trailhead at Bayview Campground, but then you miss out on seeing Eagle Lake and a world-class view of Tahoe.

Location: In the Desolation Wilderness; map D4, grid f2.

User groups: Hikers, dogs, and horses. No mountain bikes. No wheelchair facilities.

Permits: A $3 parking fee is charged per vehicle. Day-hikers must fill out a day-use permit at the wilderness trailhead. A wilderness permit is required for overnight stays. It costs $5 per person per night (first two nights only) and is available from the South Lake Tahoe Ranger Station or the Eldorado National Forest office in Camino. Quotas are in effect from June 15 to Labor Day. Reservations for this period are available in advance by phone for a $5 fee. Phone (530) 644-6048 for reservations and information.

Maps: For a map of Lake Tahoe Basin Management Unit or Desolation Wilderness, send $6 to U.S. Forest Service, Map Sales, P.O. Box 587, Camino, CA 95709; tel. (530) 647-5390 or website: www.r5.fs.fed.us/visitorcenter. A Lake Tahoe or Desolation Wilderness map is available for a fee from Tom Harrison Cartography, tel. (415) 456-7940. Ask the USGS for a topographic map of the Emerald Bay and Rockbound Valley areas.

Directions: From South Lake Tahoe drive northwest on Highway 89 for 8.5 miles to the Eagle Falls Picnic Area and Trailhead. Turn left into the parking area or park in the roadside pullout just north of the picnic area on the west side of Highway 89.

Contact: Lake Tahoe Basin Management Unit, 870 Emerald Bay Road, South Lake Tahoe, CA 96150; tel. (530) 573-2600 or fax (530) 573-2693.

20 Cascade Falls
2.0 mi/1.0 hr

We rate this trail as far and away the best easy hike at Lake Tahoe. It's short and flat enough for almost anybody to make the trip, including young children, but still feels like wilderness. The one-mile trail leads to a stunning 200-foot cascade that drops into the southwest end of Cascade Lake. Make sure you visit in spring or early summer when the fall is flowing full and wide, because by August it loses its drama. From the trailhead at Bayview Campground, take the left fork signed for Cascade Falls. In five minutes you get tremendous views of Cascade Lake, elevation 6,464 feet; then you start to hear and see the falls. The trail disintegrates as it nears the waterfall's edge, and hikers with children shouldn't get too close. But no matter; the best views

are actually farther back on the trail. Upstream of the falls are some lovely pools surrounded by wide shelves of granite.

Location: Off Highway 89 near South Lake Tahoe; map D4, grid f2.

User groups: Hikers and dogs. No horses or mountain bikes. No wheelchair facilities.

Permits: No permits are required. Parking and access are free.

Maps: For a map of Lake Tahoe Basin Management Unit, send $6 to U.S. Forest Service, Map Sales, P.O. Box 587, Camino, CA 95709; tel. (530) 647-5390 or website: www.r5.fs.fed.us/visitorcenter. A Lake Tahoe map is available for a fee from Tom Harrison Cartography, tel. (415) 456-7940. Ask the USGS for a topographic map of the Emerald Bay area.

Directions: Drive northwest on Highway 89 from South Lake Tahoe for 7.5 miles to the Bayview Campground. Turn left and drive to the far end of the campground to the trailhead parking area. If it's full, park on the shoulder of Highway 89 by the campground entrance.

Contact: Lake Tahoe Basin Management Unit, 870 Emerald Bay Road, South Lake Tahoe, CA 96150; tel. (530) 573-2600 or fax (530) 573-2693.

21 Mount Tallac from Tallac Trailhead
9.0 mi/6.0 hrs

Hikers short on time and long on energy hike to 9,735-foot Mount Tallac from the Mount Tallac Trailhead rather than from the Glen Alpine Trailhead (see hike number 26). The payment this trail extracts from you is a 2,600-foot climb over the final three miles (plus another 900 feet in the first 1.5 miles), but in exchange you get a gorgeous route that passes by Floating Island Lake and Cathedral Lake on its way to Tallac's spectacular summit. It's 1.5 miles from the trailhead to Floating Island Lake, with excellent views of Fallen Leaf Lake and Lake Tahoe along the way. Then it's another .6 mile to a trail junction just before Cathedral Lake, where a trail from Fallen Leaf

Lake joins this trail. Cathedral Lake is a good rest stop before making the final ascent to the top of Mount Tallac, a 2.4-mile butt-kicker of a climb on a rocky trail. It's made easier by a continuous and ever-changing parade of vistas, including long looks at Gilmore Lake, Susie Lake, and Lake Aloha. The trail ends .25 mile below the summit, where it meets the other Mount Tallac trail coming from Gilmore Lake. Bear right and boulder hop your way to the top. Not surprisingly, the views are wide reaching—of the Desolation Wilderness, Fallen Leaf Lake, Lake Tahoe, and even Mount Rose far off to the east. Is the vista spectacular? Yes, undeniably.

Location: In the Desolation Wilderness near Fallen Leaf Lake; map D4, grid f2.

User groups: Hikers and dogs. No horses or mountain bikes. No wheelchair facilities.

Permits: Day-hikers must fill out a day-use permit at the wilderness trailhead. A wilderness permit is required for overnight stays. It costs $5 per person per night (first two nights only) and is available from the South Lake Tahoe Ranger Station or the Eldorado National Forest office in Camino. Quotas are in effect from June 15 to Labor Day. Reservations for this period are available in advance by phone for a $5 fee. Phone (530) 644-6048 for reservations and information.

Maps: For a map of Lake Tahoe Basin Management Unit or Desolation Wilderness, send $6 to U.S. Forest Service, Map Sales, P.O. Box 587, Camino, CA 95709; tel. (530) 647-5390 or website: www.r5.fs.fed.us/visitorcenter. A Lake Tahoe or Desolation Wilderness map is also available for a fee from Tom Harrison Cartography, tel. (415) 456-7940. Ask the USGS for a topographic map of the Emerald Bay area.

Directions: From South Lake Tahoe drive northwest on Highway 89 for 3.8 miles to the signed turnoff for Mount Tallac and Camp Concord on the left, across the highway from the sign for Baldwin Beach. Drive .4 mile, turn left, and drive .6 mile to the trailhead.

Contact: Lake Tahoe Basin Management Unit, 870 Emerald Bay Road, South Lake Tahoe, CA 96150; tel. (530) 573-2600 or fax (530) 573-2693.

22 Rainbow and Lake of the Sky Trails

0.5 mi/0.5 hr

Several short interpretive walks begin at the Lake Tahoe Visitor Center, the best of which are the Rainbow Trail and Lake of the Sky Trail. You can hike them both from the same starting point at the visitor center and combine an interesting nature lesson with a walk along Lake Tahoe's shoreline for exceptional scenery and views. Start with the Rainbow Trail, which leads from the visitor center's west side and takes you to Taylor Creek and its Stream Profile Chamber. The creek is where thousands of kokanee salmon come to spawn in the fall, and you can view them through the glass walls of the profile chamber. You can also see them the ordinary way, just by peering into the creek as you walk. Then loop back to the visitor center and pick up the Lake of the Sky Trail. You'll pass by Taylor Creek Marsh on your way to Tallac Point and Tahoe's shoreline. In summer, people go swimming at this sandy stretch of beach.

Location: In Tahoe National Forest near South Lake Tahoe; map D4, grid f3.

User groups: Hikers and wheelchairs. No dogs, horses, or mountain bikes.

Permits: No permits are required. Parking and access are free.

Maps: For a map of Lake Tahoe Basin Management Unit, send $6 to U.S. Forest Service, Map Sales, P.O. Box 587, Camino, CA 95709; tel. (530) 647-5390 or website: www.r5.fs.fed.us/visitorcenter. A Lake Tahoe map is available for a fee from Tom Harrison Cartography, tel. (415) 456-7940. Ask the USGS for a topographic map of the Emerald Bay area.

Directions: From South Lake Tahoe drive northwest on Highway 89 for three miles to the Lake Tahoe Visitor Center turnoff on the right. Turn right and drive to the visitor center parking lot, where the trails begin.

Contact: Lake Tahoe Basin Management Unit, 870 Emerald Bay Road, South Lake Tahoe, CA 96150; tel. (530) 573-2600 or fax (530) 573-2693.

23 Susie and Heather Lakes
10.0 mi/5.0 hrs

Because the beautiful Desolation Wilderness is being loved to death by hordes of summer backpackers, do the area a favor and take a day hike to Susie and Heather Lakes instead. You'll minimize your impact on the land and still have a terrific outdoor experience in this area of rugged alpine beauty.

The trail to Susie and Heather Lakes begins as a rocky road and passes some summer cabins and a waterfall on Glen Alpine Creek. At 1.2 miles, the road ends near an old resort and you'll see a sign for Gilmore, Susie, and Grass Lakes. Start to climb, and shortly you'll enter the Desolation Wilderness boundary. You can take the short left cutoff to little Grass Lake (adding one mile each way to your trip) or continue straight, signed for Susie, Heather, and Aloha Lakes. At four miles, you'll reach the eastern shore of Susie Lake, then hike alongside it and around the lake's southern edge to continue another mile to Heather Lake. The granite-lined lake is deep and wide and set in a landscape of classic high Sierra scenery.

Location: In the Desolation Wilderness near Fallen Leaf Lake; map D4, grid g3.

User groups: Hikers, dogs, and horses. No mountain bikes. No wheelchair facilities.

Permits: Day-hikers must fill out a day-use permit at the wilderness trailhead. A wilderness permit is required for overnight stays. It costs $5 per person per night (first two nights only) and is available from the South Lake Tahoe Ranger Station or the Eldorado National Forest office in Camino. Quotas are in effect from June 15 to Labor Day. Reservations for this period are available in advance by phone for a $5 fee. Phone (530) 644-6048 for reservations and information.

Maps: For a map of Lake Tahoe Basin Management Unit or Desolation Wilderness, send $6 to U.S. Forest Service, Map Sales, P.O. Box 587, Camino, CA 95709; tel. (530) 647-5390 or website: www.r5.fs.fed.us/visitorcenter. A Lake Tahoe or Desolation Wilderness map is also available for a fee from Tom Harrison Cartography, tel. (415) 456-7940. Ask the USGS for a topographic map of the Emerald Bay area.

Directions: From South Lake Tahoe drive northwest on Highway 89 for 2.9 miles to Fallen Leaf Lake Road. Turn left and drive 4.8 miles on a narrow road past the Fallen Leaf Lake Marina. Take the left fork on Road 1216, signed for Lily Lake and the Desolation Wilderness. Drive .7 mile to the trailhead at road's end.

Contact: Lake Tahoe Basin Management Unit, 870 Emerald Bay Road, South Lake Tahoe, CA 96150; tel. (530) 573-2600 or fax (530) 573-2693.

24 Fallen Leaf Lake Trail
2.0 mi/1.0 hr

Fallen Leaf Lake, at 6,400 feet in elevation, is the second largest lake in the Tahoe Basin, and some say it's the prettiest. Too bad most of it is privately owned, but luckily this path allows you access to the part that is public. The short, mostly flat trail leads from the trailhead to the lake and then along its northern edge to the dam, which you can walk across. Much of the trail hugs the lake's shoreline, so you can look out across the blue water and feel that sense of peace that comes from the sight of deep, sapphire waters. You get excellent views of Glen Alpine Canyon and Mount Tallac. In the fall the shoreline of Fallen Leaf Lake is one of the best spots near Tahoe to admire the quaking aspens turning gold. Campers staying at Fallen Leaf Lake Campground can access this trail from their tents.

Location: In Tahoe National Forest near South Lake Tahoe; map D4, grid g3.

User groups: Hikers, dogs, horses, and mountain bikes. No wheelchair facilities.

Permits: No permits are required. Parking and access are free.

Maps: For a map of Lake Tahoe

Basin Management Unit, send $6 to U.S. Forest Service, Map Sales, P.O. Box 587, Camino, CA 95709; tel. (530) 647-5390 or website: www.r5.fs.fed.us/visitorcenter. A Lake Tahoe map is available for a fee from Tom Harrison Cartography, tel. (415) 456-7940. Ask the USGS for a topographic map of the Emerald Bay area.

Directions: From South Lake Tahoe drive northwest on Highway 89 for 2.9 miles to Fallen Leaf Lake Road. Turn left and drive .8 mile to the Fallen Leaf Lake Trailhead.

Contact: Lake Tahoe Basin Management Unit, 870 Emerald Bay Road, South Lake Tahoe, CA 96150; tel. (530) 573-2600 or fax (530) 573-2693.

25 Mount Tallac Loop (Glen Alpine Trailhead)
11.6 mi/7.5 hrs

You can hike to the top of 9,735-foot Mount Tallac from either of two trailheads. This trip from Glen Alpine is more gradual than the route from the Tallac Trailhead. But it's only more gradual if you hike it out and back. Many people hike this trail as a loop, in which the ascent from Glen Alpine up the back side of Mount Tallac is fairly gradual, but the descent down the front face is knee jarring and intense. Hikers who need to be gentle on their joints should consider an out-and-back trip from Glen Alpine; everyone else can follow this trail as a loop if they please.

Start at the Glen Alpine Trailhead, elevation 6,560 feet, and follow the main trail, which is lined with large cobblestone-like rock. It's a difficult walking surface for many, but luckily it ends shortly beyond the first mile (hold your whining). At the Grass Lake and Gilmore Lake junction, 1.5 miles in, bear right. Get ready for a well-graded series of switchbacks climbing out of Glen Alpine Canyon, with some, but not quite enough, shade to keep you refreshed. A good rest stop is at Gilmore Lake, 3.5 miles in, where you can stretch your hamstrings and munch a snack. From there it's just under two miles to the top of Mount Tallac, climbing

steeply up its smooth back side. This is the toughest part of the trail, and it slows down a lot of casual hikers. The official trail ends just below the summit; you must scramble over and around boulders for the last .25 mile to reach the top. The vista here is one of the finest in Northern California; you'll shoot plenty of photographs. After enjoying thoroughly tremendous views of the Desolation Wilderness, Fallen Leaf Lake, Lake Tahoe, and Mount Rose, climb back down to the trail's terminus and look for another trail heading east, toward Fallen Leaf Lake. Hikers with strong knees and ankles can take this route for a steep and fast downhill return on a loop; everyone else should retrace their steps to Glen Alpine. When loop hikers reach tiny Cathedral Lake, 2.3 miles from the summit, they should watch for a right fork shortly beyond it (it's easy to miss). Bear right and make a final knee-jarring descent to Stanford Camp, walk through the camp, and pick up the road to Glen Alpine Trailhead. A short stint on the road will deposit you back at your car.

Location: In the Desolation Wilderness near Fallen Leaf Lake; map D4, grid g3.

User groups: Hikers and dogs. No horses or mountain bikes. No wheelchair facilities.

Permits: Day-hikers must fill out a day-use permit at the wilderness trailhead. A wilderness permit is required for overnight stays. It costs $5 per person per night (first two nights only) and is available from the South Lake Tahoe Ranger Station or the Eldorado National Forest office in Camino. Quotas are in effect from June 15 to Labor Day. Reservations for this period are available in advance by phone for a $5 fee. Phone (530) 644-6048 for reservations and information.

Maps: For a map of Lake Tahoe Basin Management Unit or Desolation Wilderness, send $6 to U.S. Forest Service, Map Sales, P.O. Box 587, Camino, CA 95709; tel. (530) 647-5390 or website: www.r5.fs.fed.us/visitorcenter. A Lake Tahoe or Desolation Wilderness map is also available for a fee from Tom Harrison Cartography, tel. (415) 456-7940. Ask the USGS for a topographic map of the Echo Lake area. **Directions:** From South Lake Tahoe drive northwest on Highway 89 for 2.9 miles to Fallen Leaf Lake Road. Turn left and drive 4.8 miles on a narrow road past the Fallen Leaf Marina. Take the left fork on Road 1216, signed for Lily Lake and the Desolation Wilderness. Drive .7 mile to the trailhead at road's end. **Contact:** Lake Tahoe Basin Management Unit, 870 Emerald Bay Road, South Lake Tahoe, CA 96150; tel. (530) 573-2600 or fax (530) 573-2693.

26 Gilmore Lake

7.6 mi/4.0 hrs

If we only had time to day hike to one destination near South Lake Tahoe, Gilmore Lake would be our choice. Everything about it is a classic Lake Tahoe and Desolation Wilderness trip, a roundup of the best the area has to offer. You get to visit a scenic alpine lake, and along the way you are treated to fields of wildflowers, mountain vistas, conifer forests, and more. Of course, we're not the only ones who like this trail, so all the usual disclaimers apply about timing your trip for the off-season or during the week.

With that said, take off from the Glen Alpine Trailhead and hike down the road past the private cabins. The rocky road eventually becomes a rocky trail. This cobblestone-like stretch is by far the worst part of the hike; the rocks make rough going for hikers' ankles and knees. Bear right at the junction with the Grass Lake Trail, 1.5 miles in, where the trail surface improves dramatically. Get ready to do the majority of this trail's climbing, heading for more trail junctions at nearly three miles in, where paths lead off to the left to Susie and Heather Lakes. Bear right instead for Gilmore Lake, the largest lake in this area between Fallen Leaf Lake and Lake Aloha. You'll reach it at 3.5 miles, with a total 1,700-foot elevation gain. Despite the fact that hundreds of people cruise by Gilmore Lake each day on their way to climb Mount Tallac, few take the time to hang out for long by the lake's sapphire blue waters. The lake, ringed by grassy, flower-filled meadows, manages to stay secluded and pristine.

Location: In the Desolation Wilderness near Fallen Leaf Lake; map D4, grid g3.
User groups: Hikers and dogs. No horses or mountain bikes. No wheelchair facilities.
Permits: Day-hikers must fill out a day-use permit at the wilderness trailhead. A wilderness permit is required for overnight stays. It costs $5 per person per night (first two nights only) and is available from the South Lake Tahoe Ranger Station or the Eldorado National Forest office in Camino. Quotas are in effect from June 15 to Labor Day. Reservations for this period are available in advance by phone for a $5 fee. Phone (530) 644-6048 for reservations and information.
Maps: For a map of Lake Tahoe Basin Management Unit or Desolation Wilderness, send $6 to U.S. Forest Service, Map Sales, P.O. Box 587, Camino, CA 95709; tel. (530) 647-5390 or website: www.r5.fs.fed.us/visitorcenter. A Lake Tahoe or Desolation Wilderness map is also available for a fee from Tom Harrison Cartography, tel. (415) 456-7940. Ask the USGS for a topographic map of the Emerald Bay area.
Directions: From South Lake Tahoe drive northwest on Highway 89 for 2.9 miles to Fallen Leaf Lake Road. Turn left and drive 4.8 miles on an increasingly narrow road. Take the left fork on Road 1216, signed for Lily Lake and the Desolation Wilderness. Drive .7 mile to the trailhead.
Contact: Lake Tahoe Basin Management Unit, 870 Emerald Bay Road, South Lake Tahoe, CA 96150; tel. (530) 573-2600 or fax (530) 573-2693.

27 Angora Lakes Trail

1.0 mi/0.5 hr

First a warning: It's unwise to hike the Angora Lakes Trail unless you are accompanied by a person under the age of seven. The Angora Lakes are extremely popular with children's day camps and groups, and all summer long the little ones outnumber us old folks. Still it's a pretty hike, and the Upper Angora Lake is a sight to behold. Head uphill from the parking lot on the signed dirt road, and in 15 minutes you'll be looking at Lower Angora Lake, which has a few cabins on its far side. Continue beyond its edge another .25 mile and, voilà, you reach the upper lake and Angora Lakes Resort, built in 1917. Although the resort cabins are always rented way in advance, day users can buy a lemonade and sit at a picnic table to watch the action at the small, picturesque lake. Action? What action? Anglers fish from shore or rent rowboats for a few bucks per hour, toddlers wade around at the shallow beach area, and plenty of folks just plunk themselves down along the shoreline to stare at the bowl-shaped, glacial cirque lake. It has a high granite wall on its far side, where in early summer a waterfall of snowmelt flows down to the lake.

Location: In Tahoe National Forest near Fallen Leaf Lake; map D4, grid g3.

User groups: Hikers, dogs, horses, and mountain bikes. No wheelchair facilities.

Permits: No permits are required. Parking and access are free.

Maps: For a map of Lake Tahoe Basin Management Unit, send $6 to U.S. Forest Service, Map Sales, P.O. Box 587, Camino, CA 95709; tel. (530) 647-5390 or website: www.r5.fs.fed.us/visitorcenter. A Lake Tahoe map is available for a fee from Tom Harrison Cartography, tel. (415) 456-7940. Ask the USGS for a topographic map of the Echo Lake area.

Directions: From South Lake Tahoe drive northwest on Highway 89 for 2.9 miles to Fallen Leaf Lake Road. Turn left and drive three miles to a fork. Go left and drive .5 mile. Then turn right on Forest Service Road 12N14 and drive 2.3 miles, past the Angora Fire Lookout, to the road's end and the trailhead.

Contact: Lake Tahoe Basin Management Unit, 870 Emerald Bay Road, South Lake Tahoe, CA 96150; tel. (530) 573-2600 or fax (530) 573-2693.

28 Lyons Creek Trail
9.0 mi/4.5 hrs or 2.0 days

This may be the easiest lake hike in the entire Wrights Lake area, with only a 1,700-foot elevation gain to visit two beautiful lakes. Because this trailhead is a few miles distant from popular Wrights Lake Campground, it gets fewer visitors than the trails that start right out of camp. The trip's total mileage is long, but the grade is mellow except for the final .5 mile to Lyons Lake. If you're fond of walking along coursing waterways, following the gurgle and babble of a creek as you hike, you'll love this hike. Wildflowers proliferate in early summer, and views of Pyramid Peak (just shy of 10,000 feet in elevation) inspire you as you gently ascend. The trail keeps to the south side of Lyons Creek for four solid miles, passing through woods and meadows, then crosses the stream and reaches a junction .1 mile farther on. Lyons Lake is to the left and steeply uphill; Lake Sylvia is .5 mile to the right. Take your pick, or better yet, go see both. Lake Sylvia is shadowed by Pyramid Peak and has good campsites along its shoreline. Lyons Lake requires a nasty 450-foot climb in .5 mile, but its superior scenery makes it well worth the effort.

Location: In the Desolation Wilderness; map D4, grid g0.

User groups: Hikers, dogs, and horses. No mountain bikes. No wheelchair facilities.

Permits: Day-hikers must fill out a day-use permit at the wilderness trailhead. A wilderness permit is required for overnight stays. It costs $5 per person per night (first two nights only) and is available from the South Lake Tahoe Ranger Station or the Eldorado National Forest office in Camino. Quotas are in effect from June 15 to Labor Day. Reservations for this period are available in advance by phone for a $5 fee. Phone (530) 644-6048 for reservations and information.

Maps: For a map of Eldorado National Forest or Desolation Wilderness, send $6 to U.S. Forest Service, Map Sales, P.O. Box 587, Camino,

CA 95709; tel. (530) 647-5390 or website: www. r5.fs.fed.us/visitorcenter. A Lake Tahoe or Desolation Wilderness map is also available for a fee from Tom Harrison Cartography, tel. (415) 456-7940. Ask the USGS for a topographic map of the Pyramid Peak area.

Directions: From Placerville drive east on Highway 50 for 45 miles to the signed turnoff for Wrights Lake on the north side of the highway. It's about 15 miles west of South Lake Tahoe and five miles east of Kyburz. Drive north on Wrights Lake Road for four miles and turn right at the sign for Lyons Creek Trail.

Contact: Eldorado National Forest, 3070 Camino Heights Drive, Camino, CA 95709; tel. (530) 644-6048 or fax (530) 295-5624.

29 Grouse, Hemlock, and Smith Lakes

6.0 mi/3.0 hrs or 2.0 days

The Crystal Basin area is a magical place on the western edge of Desolation Wilderness, where the nearly 10,000-foot peaks of the Crystal Range overlook the basin and its multitude of lakes. Several excellent day hikes and backpacking trips are possible in this area, most of which begin from popular Wrights Lake Campground. Of those, the trip to Grouse, Hemlock, and Smith Lakes is one of our favorites, despite the relentless climb required to reach all three lakes. From the parking area, the Twin Lakes Trail winds past a meadow and then enters a pine and fir forest interspersed with stretches of hard granite. At a trail junction 1.2 miles out, head right for Grouse, Hemlock, and Smith Lakes. Small and pretty Grouse Lake is a one-mile, heart-pumping climb away, with many fine glances back at Wrights Lake and Icehouse Reservoir as you ascend. Many backpackers camp at Grouse Lake, but hardy types and day-hikers should head for Hemlock and Smith lakes farther uphill. The lakes get progressively prettier as you go, but the ascent gets steeper, too. Tiny Hemlock Lake is only .5 mile from Grouse Lake, and it boasts a spectacular rockslide on one shoreline and

many scrawny hemlock trees on the other. Smith Lake lies another .5 mile beyond, way up high near tree line at 8,700 feet, and it's a stunner. Don't forget your bathing suit.

Location: In the Desolation Wilderness; map D4, grid g0.

User groups: Hikers, dogs, and horses. No mountain bikes. No wheelchair facilities.

Permits: Day-hikers must fill out a day-use permit at the wilderness trailhead. A wilderness permit is required for overnight stays. It costs $5 per person per night (first two nights only) and is available from the South Lake Tahoe Ranger Station or the Eldorado National Forest office in Camino. Quotas are in effect from June 15 to Labor Day. Reservations for this period are available in advance by phone for a $5 fee. Phone (530) 644-6048 for reservations and information.

Maps: For a map of Eldorado National Forest or Desolation Wilderness, send $6 to U.S. Forest Service, Map Sales, P.O. Box 587, Camino, CA 95709; tel. (530) 647-5390 or website: www.r5.fs.fed.us/visitorcenter. A Lake Tahoe or Desolation Wilderness map is also available for a fee from Tom Harrison Cartography, tel. (415) 456-7940. Ask the USGS for a topographic map of the Pyramid Peak area.

Directions: From Placerville drive east on Highway 50 for 45 miles to the signed turnoff for Wrights Lake on the north side of the highway, about 15 miles west of South Lake Tahoe and five miles east of Kyburz. Drive north on Wrights Lake Road for eight miles to Wrights Lake Visitor Center. Turn right and continue one mile beyond the campground to the end of the road and the Twin Lakes Trailhead.

Contact: Eldorado National Forest, 3070 Camino Heights Drive, Camino, CA 95709; tel. (530) 644-6048 or fax (530) 295-5624.

30 Twin and Island Lakes

6.4 mi/4.0 hrs or 2.0 days

The only downer on the trip to Twin and Island Lakes is the sheer number of people who make this journey every day during the summer months. Of course, when you see the lakes, you'll know why they are so darn popular. Of all the hiking possibilities in the Wrights Lake area, this trip is hands-down the most scenic, with the most striking views in the entire Desolation Wilderness and miles of solid granite under your feet as you walk. The trail is extremely well marked, and its moderate grade is suitable for all types of hikers. The first 1.2 miles from the Twin Lakes trailhead have only a gentle climb to the intersection with the trail to Grouse, Hemlock, and Smith Lakes. Bear left for Twin Lakes and climb up over granite until .75 mile later you crest a ridge and start to descend. The vistas of jagged Crystal Range peaks to the northeast make an awesome backdrop. At 2.5 miles you'll reach the dam at Lower Twin Lake, then cross it and continue hiking along the lake's northwest shore to tiny Boomerang Lake at three miles. The lake is shaped like its name and is shallow enough to provide warm water for swimming. Another .25 mile on the trail brings you to the south end of Island Lake, where the vistas of the Crystal Range are the best of the trip, and most hikers burn a heck of a lot of film. If you ever wanted to sell somebody on the beauty of the Northern Sierra, this trail would be the place to do it.

Location: In the Desolation Wilderness; map D4, grid g0.

User groups: Hikers, dogs, and horses. No mountain bikes. No wheelchair facilities.

Permits: Day-hikers must fill out a day-use permit at the wilderness trailhead. A wilderness permit is required for overnight stays. It costs $5 per person per night (first two nights only) and is available from the South Lake Tahoe Ranger Station or the Eldorado National Forest office in Camino. Quotas are in effect from June 15 to Labor Day. Reservations for this period are available in advance by phone for a $5 fee. Phone (530) 644-6048 for reservations and information.

Maps: For a map of Eldorado National Forest or Desolation Wilderness, send $6 to U.S. Forest Service, Map Sales, P.O. Box 587, Camino, CA 95709; tel. (530) 647-5390 or website: www.r5.fs.fed.us/visitorcenter. A Lake Tahoe or Desolation Wilderness map is also available for a fee from Tom Harrison Cartography, tel. (415) 456-7940. Ask the USGS for a topographic map of the Pyramid Peak area.

Directions: From Placerville drive east on Highway 50 for 45 miles to the signed turnoff for Wrights Lake on the north side of the highway, about 15 miles west of South Lake Tahoe and five miles east of Kyburz. Drive north on Wrights Lake Road for eight miles to Wrights Lake Visitor Center. Turn right and continue one mile beyond the campground to the end of the road and the Twin Lakes Trailhead.

Contact: Eldorado National Forest, 3070 Camino Heights Drive, Camino, CA 95709; tel. (530) 644-6048 or fax (530) 295-5624.

31 Gertrude and Tyler Lakes
9.0 mi/5.0 hrs or 2.0 days 🥾 🎒

There's a ton of hiking to be accomplished in the Wrights Lake area, and among all the possibilities, the trip to Gertrude and Tyler Lakes stands out because it offers great scenery, a good workout, and a chance to practice your cross-country skills on the way to Tyler Lake. A clearly defined trail leads to pretty Gertrude Lake, but higher and lovelier Tyler Lake is found only by those who forge their own way. That makes for a fun little adventure if you desire. (If you don't, you can opt to visit Gertrude Lake only.) Begin on the Rockbound Pass Trail, passing pastoral Beauty Lake .5 mile out and continuing on a remarkably easy path until you see a sign for Tyler Lake at 1.9 miles. There, bear right and prepare to work a lot harder for the rest of the hike. One memorable .5-mile stretch goes straight uphill and will cause you to question your sanity. Luckily the worst part doesn't last long, and the views of the spectacular peaks of the Crystal Range will distract you. At 3.5 miles you'll reach a hard-to-spot left spur trail (100 yards long) leading to the grave of William Tyler, a rancher who died here in a blizzard in the 1920s. A half mile beyond this cutoff is Gertrude Lake at 8,000 feet. A nearly invisible right fork just past the grave cutoff is the start of an unmaintained use trail to Tyler Lake, which lies 400 feet higher than Gertrude Lake. If you miss the use trail turnoff, watch for occasional rock cairns and keep an eye on your trail map. Tyler Lake lies .5 mile southeast of Gertrude Lake. Of the two lakes, Tyler is more beautiful, set in a granite basin with a few sparse pines on its shores. Because it's slightly difficult to locate, you have an excellent chance at solitude at Tyler Lake, even on summer weekends.

Location: In the Desolation Wilderness; map D4, grid g0.

User groups: Hikers, dogs, and horses. No mountain bikes. No wheelchair facilities.

Permits: Day-hikers must fill out a day-use permit at the wilderness trailhead. A wilderness permit is required for overnight stays. It costs $5 per person per night (first two nights only) and is available from the South Lake Tahoe Ranger Station or the Eldorado National Forest office in Camino. Quotas are in effect from June 15 to Labor Day. Reservations for this period are available in advance by phone for a $5 fee. Phone (530) 644-6048 for reservations and information.

Maps: For a map of Eldorado National Forest or Desolation Wilderness, send $6 to U.S. Forest Service, Map Sales, P.O. Box 587, Camino, CA 95709; tel. (530) 647-5390 or website: www.r5.fs.fed.us/visitorcenter. A Lake Tahoe or Desolation Wilderness map is also available for a fee from Tom Harrison Cartography, tel. (415) 456-7940. Ask the USGS for a topographic map of the Pyramid Peak and Rockbound Valley areas.

Directions: From Placerville drive east on Highway 50 for 45 miles to the signed turnoff for Wrights Lake on the north side of the highway, about 15 miles west of South Lake Tahoe and five miles east of Kyburz. Drive north on Wrights Lake Road for eight miles to Wrights Lake Visitor Center. Continue straight past it

for .5 mile to the Rockbound Trailhead (on the way to Dark Lake).

Contact: Eldorado National Forest, 3070 Camino Heights Drive, Camino, CA 95709; tel. (530) 644-6048 or fax (530) 295-5624.

32 Rockbound Pass and Lake Doris

12.0 mi/6.0 hrs
or 2.0 days

To make the epic trip to 8,650-foot Rockbound Pass, follow the trail notes for hike number 32, the route to Gertrude and Tyler Lakes, for the first 1.9 miles. Bear left to stay on the Rockbound Pass Trail and hike through mixed conifers to get your first glimpse of Rockbound Pass at 2.5 miles—a distant notch in the mountains to the north. To reach it, you must descend a bit and cross the Jones Fork of Silver Creek, then parallel the stream on its course from Maud Lake. You're traveling in very rocky terrain now; the trail is blasted out of granite in places. Reach the western shores of 7,700-foot Maud Lake at 4.5 miles, where many backpackers make camp while day-hikers continue the ascent to the pass. It's not much farther; after a steady climb you gain its wide summit at 5.9 miles. The views of Desolation Wilderness open wide, including views back at Maud Lake and ahead to Lake Doris, but the howling wind often prevents you from staying long. If that's the case, descend .5 mile to Lake Doris, just to the left of the trail, where you can make camp, or if you're day hiking, just hang out and rest. The total elevation gain on this trip is 1,700 feet, plus a short descent to Lake Doris.

Location: In the Desolation Wilderness; map D4, grid g0.

User groups: Hikers, dogs, and horses. No mountain bikes. No wheelchair facilities.

Permits: Day-hikers must fill out a day-use permit at the wilderness trailhead. A wilderness permit is required for overnight stays. It costs $5 per person per night (first two nights only) and is available from the South Lake Tahoe Ranger Station or the Eldorado National Forest office in Camino. Quotas are in effect from June 15 to Labor Day. Reservations for this period are available in advance by phone for a $5 fee. Phone (530) 644-6048 for reservations and information.

Maps: For a map of Eldorado National Forest or Desolation Wilderness, send $6 to U.S. Forest Service, Map Sales, P.O. Box 587, Camino, CA 95709; tel. (530) 647-5390 or website: www.r5.fs.fed.us/visitorcenter. A Lake Tahoe or Desolation Wilderness map is also available for a fee from Tom Harrison Cartography, tel. (415) 456-7940. Ask the USGS for a topographic map of the Pyramid Peak and Rockbound Valley areas.

Directions: From Placerville drive east on Highway 50 for 45 miles to the signed turnoff for Wrights Lake on the north side of the highway, about 15 miles west of South Lake Tahoe and five miles east of Kyburz. Drive north on Wrights Lake Road for eight miles to Wrights Lake Visitor Center. Continue straight past it for .5 mile to the Rockbound Trailhead (on the way to Dark Lake).

Contact: Eldorado National Forest, 3070 Camino Heights Drive, Camino, CA 95709; tel. (530) 644-6048 or fax (530) 295-5624.

🕃🕃 Horsetail Falls Vista

2.0 mi/1.0 hr

Horsetail Falls is that plainly visible waterfall that takes your breath away as you're driving west along U.S. 50. Approximately 15,000 people each summer glimpse the falls from their cars, pull over at the giant parking lot by the trailhead, then start hiking to get closer to it. The trail has been a source of controversy for many years because the waterfall is located within the Desolation Wilderness boundary on a rough but serviceable route, but the first mile of trail is outside the wilderness boundary and easily accessible from the highway. That first easy mile has encouraged many inexperienced visitors to try to hike to the falls, resulting in numerous accidents and even deaths in the wilderness area, where the trail dissipates and follows stream banks that are rough and slippery. The Forest Service has rightfully carried out the wilderness mandate by not making mechanical alterations to the trail, such as building bridges or blasting an obvious path into the granite. We say, good for them. Instead, to decrease the frequent injuries, they built a new trail in 1999, the 1.5-mile Pyramid Creek Loop. Made specifically for day-users who just want to see Horsetail Falls and spectacular, granite-lined Pyramid Creek, the Pyramid Creek Loop takes off from the main trail about .5 mile in. Routed past a gorgeous stretch of Pyramid Creek called the Cascades, the trail stays outside of the wilderness boundary and provides a safe and easy alternative for casual visitors. Although the trail doesn't go all the way to the base of Horsetail Falls, it provides many excellent views of it, as well as of Pyramid Creek's glacier-carved canyon. This was a sensible solution to a difficult problem. The trail is a winner.

Location: In Eldorado National Forest near South Lake Tahoe; map D4, grid g1.

User groups: Hikers and dogs. No horses or mountain bikes. No wheelchair facilities.

Permits: No permits are required if you stay out of the wilderness boundary. Parking and access are free.

Maps: For a map of Eldorado National Forest, send $6 to U.S. Forest Service, Map Sales, P.O. Box 587, Camino, CA 95709; tel. (530) 647-5390 or website: www.r5.fs.fed.us/visitorcenter. A Lake Tahoe map is available for a fee from Tom Harrison Cartography, tel. (415) 456-7940. Ask the USGS for a topographic map of the Echo Lake area.

Directions: From South Lake Tahoe drive south on Highway 89 for five miles to Highway 50. Drive west on Highway 50 for about 15 miles to Twin Bridges, where there is a huge pullout on the north side of the highway just before the bridge. The pullout is .5 mile west of the turnoff for Camp Sacramento. Park in the pullout and walk across the highway bridge about 500 feet to the well-marked trailhead.

Contact: Eldorado National Forest, 3070 Camino Heights Drive, Camino, CA 95709; tel. (530) 644-6048 or fax (530) 295-5624.

34 Ralston Peak
8.0 mi/5.0 hrs

The route to Ralston Peak has a little of everything—dense forest, open manzanita-covered slopes, meadows, and granite ridges. And a lot of one thing—elevation gain. From trailhead to summit, you ascend from 6,400 feet to 9,240 feet over the course of four miles. Begin by walking northward up the paved road from the east side of the parking area for 200 yards; look for the trail leading off on the left. Climb upward through nonstop trees (and nonstop switchbacks) for a mile; then enter a more open area as you pass the wilderness boundary sign at 1.5 miles. The views start to widen. Your lungs request a lunch break, but they don't get one until 2.5 miles up, when you finally gain the ridge. A half mile later the break is over, and you climb again, this time to another ridge at 3.5 miles, covered in meadow grasses and wildflowers. Part ways with the main trail and look for a trail leading to your right to the top of Ralston Peak, .5 mile away. Scramble up over jumbled rock to gain the 9,235-foot summit, and take in the view of Lake Tahoe, Fallen Leaf Lake, Carson Pass, Echo Lakes, and below you (to the north), Ralston Lake. Wow, what a view. Wow, what a climb. Is your butt kicked?

Location: In the Desolation Wilderness near South Lake Tahoe; map D4, grid g1.

User groups: Hikers and dogs. No horses or mountain bikes. No wheelchair facilities.

Permits: Day-hikers must fill out a day-use permit at the wilderness trailhead. A wilderness permit is required for overnight stays. It costs $5 per person per night (first two nights only) and is available from the South Lake Tahoe Ranger Station or the Eldorado National Forest office in Camino. Quotas are in effect from June 15 to Labor Day. Reservations for this period are available in advance by phone for a $5 fee. Phone (530) 644-6048 for reservations and information.

Maps: For a map of Eldorado National Forest or Desolation Wilderness, send $6 to U.S. Forest Service, Map Sales, P.O. Box 587, Camino, CA 95709; tel. (530) 647-5390 or website: www.r5.fs.fed.us/visitorcenter. A Lake Tahoe or Desolation Wilderness map is also available for a fee from Tom Harrison Cartography, tel. (415) 456-7940. Ask the USGS for a topographic map of the Echo Lake area.

Directions: From South Lake Tahoe drive south on Highway 89 for five miles to Highway 50. Drive west on U.S. 50 for about 14 miles to the turnoff for Camp Sacramento. (If you reach Twin Bridges, you've gone 1.5 miles too far west.) There is a parking area off the north side of U.S. 50 and a sign for the Ralston Trail to Lake of the Woods.

Contact: Eldorado National Forest, 3070 Camino Heights Drive, Camino, CA 95709; tel. (530) 644-6048 or fax (530) 295-5624.

35 Boat Taxi to Lake Aloha
6-12.0 mi/3.5-6.0 hrs

Some people just like to take boat rides, and if you're one of them, you can have a great all-day adventure by taking the boat taxi from Echo Lakes Resort, and then hiking to Lake Aloha and its neighboring lakes in Desolation Valley. If you think it's wimpy to ride the boat instead of walking all the way (if you don't take the boat taxi it adds 2.5 miles to your hike), you're wrong. Those who ride will still end up tired at the end of the day, having completed a 10- to 14-mile hike (depending on how many side trips are taken to other lakes) with a decent amount of ups and downs. Those who take the boat will also end up a little poorer, because the ride costs seven bucks one-way.

From the hiker's parking lot, walk .25 mile downhill to the resort and the boat launch area at the edge of Echo Lake. The boat taxi leaves at frequent intervals (or whenever more than two people show up) from 8 a.m. to 6 p.m. daily all summer. The boat carries you two miles to the far end of Upper and Lower Echo Lakes, passing many lovely summer homes. From the boat taxi drop-off point, gain the main trail and head to your left. It's 3.5 miles to the eastern edge of Lake Aloha, but be forewarned: the first 1.5 miles have the worst trail surface, i.e., too many rocks. You'll pass signed junctions with numerous trails along the way, all of which lead to various lakes in very short distances. Your best bet is to stay on the main path for Lake Aloha, then take some of the cutoffs to neighboring lakes on your way back. When you reach Lake Aloha's shore, hike along its beautiful north side for a distance, admiring the rocky coves and islands of the giant, shallow lake. At one time Lake Aloha was several small lakes that were dammed to create this huge body of water. The effect is a bit surreal, although beautiful. The lake's elevation is 8,116 feet.

On the trip back, take one or more of the signed trail junctions and visit Lake of the Woods, Lake Lucille, Lake Margery, Tamarack Lake, or Ralston Lake, all less than one mile off the Lake Aloha Trail. Tamarack Lake is the best for scenery; Lake of the Woods is the best for fishing.

Location: In the Desolation Wilderness; map D4, grid g2.

User groups: Hikers only. No dogs, horses, or mountain bikes. No wheelchair facilities.

Permits: Day-hikers must fill out a day-use permit at the wilderness trailhead. A wilderness permit is required for overnight stays. It costs $5 per person per night (first two nights only) and is available from the South Lake Tahoe Ranger Station or the Eldorado National Forest office in Camino. Quotas are in effect from June 15 to Labor Day. Reservations for this period are available in advance by phone for a $5 fee. Phone (530) 644-6048 for reservations and information.

Maps: For a map of Lake Tahoe Basin Management Unit or Desolation Wilderness, send $6 to U.S. Forest Service, Map Sales, P.O. Box 587, Camino, CA 95709; tel. (530) 647-5390 or

website: www.r5.fs.fed.us/visitorcenter. A Lake Tahoe or Desolation Wilderness map is also available for a fee from Tom Harrison Cartography, tel. (415) 456-7940. Ask the USGS for a topographic map of the Echo Lake area.

Directions: From South Lake Tahoe drive south on Highway 89 for five miles to U.S. 50. Drive west on U.S. 50 for 5.5 miles to the signed turnoff for Echo Lakes on the right. (It's one mile west of Echo Summit.) Turn right and drive .5 mile on Johnson Pass Road, then turn left on Echo Lakes Road. Drive one mile to a series of parking lots .25 mile before the road ends at Echo Lakes Resort. Hikers not staying at the resort must park in one of the upper lots or alongside the road, not in the main lower lot by the resort.

Contact: Lake Tahoe Basin Management Unit, 870 Emerald Bay Road, South Lake Tahoe, CA 96150; tel. (530) 573-2600 or fax (530) 573-2693.

36 Dardanelles Lake and Round Lake
7.6 mi/4.5 hrs

The route to Dardanelles Lake and Round Lake along the Tahoe Rim Trail starts out steep but gets easier as it goes. It enters Meiss Country, that large and wonderful roadless area south of Lake Tahoe, where the forces that shaped the land were ice (glaciers) and fire (volcanic action). Both have made their presence clearly visible. The trail heads south from the parking lot, crosses Highway 89 in about 100 yards, then makes an initial climb through fir and pine forest to Big Meadow. The meadow makes lovely, level walking for .25 mile; then it's back into the trees. Follow the trail signs for Round Lake until you complete a steep, short descent at two miles out. At the bottom of the hill, turn sharply right on the Meiss Meadow Trail toward Christmas Valley. Walk less than .25 mile, then turn left and cross a creek for the final 1.2 miles to Dardanelles Lake. The 7,740-foot lake is gorgeous, with a striking granite backdrop, and it's perfect for swimming, fishing, and picnicking. If you time your trip for autumn, you'll be treated to a marvelous color display from the aspens and alders that grow along this trail's many streams.

On your return, retrace your steps to the junction at the bottom of the hill, then hike .75 mile in the opposite direction to visit Round Lake. Not quite as scenic as Dardanelles Lake, Round Lake provides a stark, fascinating contrast to its neighbor: it is surrounded by volcanic rock formations, not granite cliffs.

Note that this trail is open to mountain bikers. On a weekday trip in midsummer, we didn't see a single bike, but on weekends it's probably another story.

Location: Near Carson Pass; map D4, grid h3.

User groups: Hikers, dogs, horses, and mountain bikes. No wheelchair facilities.

Permits: No permits are required. Parking and access are free.

Maps: For a map of Lake Tahoe Basin Management Unit, send $6 to U.S. Forest Service, Map Sales, P.O. Box 587, Camino, CA 95709; tel. (530) 647-5390 or website: www.r5.fs.fed.us/visitorcenter. A Lake Tahoe map is available for a fee from Tom Harrison Cartography, tel. (415) 456-7940. Ask the USGS for a topographic map of the Echo Lake area.

Directions: From South Lake Tahoe drive south on Highway 89 for approximately 10 miles to the Big Meadow Trailhead parking area, which is five miles south of the junction of U.S. 50 and Highway 89 on the northwest side of the road. Turn left off the highway, then bear left and park near the restrooms. The trail begins from the south side of the parking lot loop and crosses Highway 89 in about 100 yards.

Contact: Lake Tahoe Basin Management Unit, 870 Emerald Bay Road, South Lake Tahoe, CA 96150; tel. (530) 573-2600 or fax (530) 573-2693.

37 Minkalo Trail

7.0 mi/3.5 hrs

Since Silver Lake has a fair number of private homes on its shore, it appears less wild than nearby Caples Lake. Still the big blue lake, at 7,300 feet in elevation, is beautiful, and if you want to hike near it, the Minkalo Trail is your best bet. The trail leads to Granite Lake in one mile and to Plasse's Resort on the south side of the lake in three miles. We say, why not hike to both, then buy a pizza or a Power Bar at Plasse's Resort Trading Post to fuel up for the hike back to the Minkalo Trailhead? The trail starts out rocky and stays that way for the first .25 mile. You cross a bridge over Squaw Creek and shortly see the right fork that leads to Plasse's Resort. Take the left fork first, heading to Granite Lake, which you'll reach in about 20 minutes after a moderate climb. It's a pretty lake and good for swimming. After you've visited, return to the trail junction and hike southward, soon coming close to the edge of Silver Lake and staying in its proximity. You'll have many pretty lake views from here on out, including long looks at Treasure Island, Silver Lake's large island. It takes about an hour to reach the campground at Plasse's, an excellent place for horse lovers (and pizza lovers).

Location: Near Silver Lake; map D4, grid i1.

User groups: Hikers, dogs, horses, and mountain bikes. No wheelchair facilities.

Permits: No permits are required. Parking and access are free.

Maps: For a map of Eldorado National Forest, send $6 to U.S. Forest Service, Map Sales, P.O. Box 587, Camino, CA 95709; tel. (530) 647-5390 or website: www.r5.fs.fed.us/visitorcenter. Ask the USGS for a topographic map of the Caples Lake area.

Directions: From Meyers at the junction of U.S. 50 and Highway 89, drive south on U.S. 89 for 11 miles to Highway 88. Turn west on Highway 88 and drive 15.5 miles to the Kit Carson Lodge turnoff on the north side of the road. It's 10.8 miles west of Carson Pass Summit, at Silver Lake. Turn north and drive past Kit Carson Lodge, go left at the first fork, go right at the second fork, and wind up at the parking for the Minkalo Trail. (It's a total 1.4 miles from Highway 88.) Walk back down the road for about 40 yards to find the start of the trail.

Contact: Eldorado National Forest, 3070 Camino Heights Drive, Camino, CA 95709; tel. (530) 644-6048 or fax (530) 295-5624; Amador Ranger District, 26820 Silver Drive, Pioneer, CA 95666; tel. (209) 295-4251 or fax (209) 295-5998.

38 Emigrant Lake

8.0 mi/4.0 hrs or 2.0 days

The trailhead at Caples Lake is often jam-packed with backpackers, so do yourself a favor—visit here midweek or in the off-season, or make your trip a day hike instead of an overnight. Why is this trail so popular? It's wonderfully scenic and surprisingly easy. The trail leads from the spillway at Caples Lake up and along the lake's south side, following an old emigrant route. The first two miles are right along the lake's edge, climbing gently above the shoreline, always in the shade of big conifers. If you enjoy hiking near water, you'll love this pathway. More climbing alongside Emigrant Creek leads you to a stream crossing at 3.5 miles, followed by another crossing. A few switchbacks carry you up to Emigrant Lake, a beautiful cirque lake set at 8,600 feet, with many fine sunbathing rocks. Covered Wagon Peak and Thimble Peak at 9,500 feet rise above the scene. The trail's total elevation gain is less than 1,000 feet, making this a surprisingly easy day hike even with its eight-mile distance. But know before you go: most of the trail's ascent is packed into the last 1.8 miles, which will leave you breathing hard.

Location: In the Mokelumne Wilderness near Caples Lake; map D4, grid h1.

User groups: Hikers, dogs, and horses. No mountain bikes. No wheelchair facilities.

Permits: No day-hiking permits are required. A free wilderness permit is required for overnight stays between April 1 and November 30; it is available from the Amador Ranger Station, the Carson Pass Information Station, or the Eldorado Information Center.

Maps: For a map of Eldorado National Forest, send $6 to U.S. Forest Service, Map Sales, P.O. Box 587, Camino, CA 95709; tel. (530) 647-5390 or website: www.r5.fs.fed.us/visitorcenter. Ask the USGS for a topographic map of the Caples Lake area.

Directions: From Meyers at the junction of U.S. 50 and Highway 89, drive south on Highway 89 for 11 miles to Highway 88. Turn west on Highway 88 and drive 14 miles to the west side of Caples Lake and the trailhead parking area, five miles west of Carson Pass Summit.

Contact: Eldorado National Forest, 3070 Camino Heights Drive, Camino, CA 95709; tel. (530) 644-6048 or fax (530) 295-5624; Amador Ranger District, 26820 Silver Drive, Pioneer, CA 95666; tel. (209) 295-4251 or fax (209) 295-5998.

39 Lake Margaret

4.6 mi/3.0 hrs

A hike to an alpine lake with only a 500-foot elevation gain? If it seems too good to be true, you need an easy-trail fix, and Lake Margaret should do the trick. The trail undulates gently, never gaining or losing more than a couple hundred feet. The first stretch is actually downhill; then the path climbs gently over a small ridge and then descends again over duck-marked granite slabs. You'll cross branches of Caples Creek twice in the first mile. At 1.5 miles, the trail passes by a couple of tiny ponds. At two miles out, after crossing another creek, you'll find yourself in a lovely grove of aspens and knee-high wildflowers. At 2.3 miles, you'll reach the granite shoreline of Lake Margaret after about an hour of walking and only a minor expenditure of energy. Swimming is excellent. A few tiny islands and many shoreline boulders make fine sunbathing spots. Figure on staying a while. The lake's elevation is 7,500 feet.

Note that although most of the trails in the Carson Pass area are famous for wildflowers, the proximity of several small streams makes the bloom especially showy on this path.

Location: Near Carson Pass and Kirkwood Lake; map D4, grid h1.

User groups: Hikers, dogs, horses, and mountain bikes. No wheelchair facilities.

Permits: No permits are required. Parking and access are free.

Maps: For a map of Eldorado National Forest, send $6 to U.S. Forest Service, Map Sales, P.O. Box 587, Camino, CA 95709; tel. (530) 647-5390 or website: www.r5.fs.fed.us/visitorcenter. Ask the USGS for a topographic map of the Caples Lake area.

Directions: From Meyers at the junction of U.S. 50 and Highway 89, drive south on Highway 89 for 11 miles to Highway 88. Turn west on Highway 88 and drive 14.5 miles to the Lake Margaret sign on the north side of the road. (It's 5.5 miles west of Carson Pass Summit, and 5.5 miles east of Silver Lake.) Turn north and park at the trailhead parking area.

Contact: Eldorado National Forest, 3070 Camino Heights Drive, Camino, CA 95709; tel. (530) 644-6048 or fax (530) 295-5624; Amador Ranger District, 26820 Silver Drive, Pioneer, CA 95666; tel. (209) 295-4251 or fax (209) 295-5998.

🔟 Winnemucca Lake from Woods Lake

3.0 mi/1.5 hrs

Woods Lake is a little magical spot where you can drive right up, walk a few feet to the water's edge, and plunk in your fishing line. It's also the trailhead for numerous great hikes into the Mokelumne Wilderness, including this easy trip to deep blue Winnemucca Lake, set at the base of fantastic-looking Mount Round Top, elevation 10,381 feet. The land here has been formed by volcanic action, so as you walk, you constantly have to remind yourself that you aren't at Mount Lassen or Mount Shasta—you're just south of Tahoe in Carson Pass.

After crossing the footbridge at the trailhead and setting off down the trail, you pass by the remains of an arrastra, a device used for crushing gold or silver ore—evidence of this area's mining past. Continue walking through big conifers until you come out to a glacial moraine where your view of Mount Round Top, a huge old volcanic vent, opens wide. Snow-capped almost all summer, imposing Round Top is a stunning sight. So are the early summer wildflowers that bloom in profusion on the open slopes surrounding the path. In 1.5 miles of gentle to moderate climbing you reach the edge of Winnemucca Lake, right at the foot of Mount Round Top, a gorgeous circle of blue. Although there are several options for hiking farther from here (see Round Top Summit and Winnemucca Lake Loop, below), for many people, this destination is perfect enough.

Note that if you're a wildflower lover, the peak bloom in this area usually occurs in mid- to late July. Don't miss it.

Location: In the Mokelumne Wilderness near Carson Pass; map D4, grid i2.

User groups: Hikers, dogs, and horses. No mountain bikes. No wheelchair facilities.

Permits: No day-hiking permits are required. A free wilderness permit is required for overnight stays between April 1 and November 30; it is available from the Amador Ranger Station, the Carson Pass Information Station, or the Eldorado Information Center.

Maps: For a map of Eldorado National Forest, send $6 to U.S. Forest Service, Map Sales, P.O. Box 587, Camino, CA 95709; tel. (530) 647-5390 or website: www.r5.fs.fed.us/visitorcenter. Ask the USGS for a topographic map of the Caples Lake and Carson Pass areas.

Directions: From Meyers at the junction of U.S. 50 and Highway 89, drive south on Highway 89 for 11 miles to Highway 88. Turn west on Highway 88 and drive 12 miles to the Woods Lake Campground turnoff on the south side of the road. It's 1.5 miles west of Carson Pass Summit. Turn left and drive 1.5 miles to the trailhead parking area at Woods Lake, by the picnic area.

Contact: Eldorado National Forest, 3070 Camino Heights Drive, Camino, CA 95709; tel. (530) 644-6048 or fax (530) 295-

5624; Amador Ranger District, 26820 Silver Drive, Pioneer, CA 95666; tel. (209) 295-4251 or fax (209) 295-5998.

41 Round Top Summit and Winnemucca Lake Loop

6.6 mi/4.0 hrs

If you want all the scenic beauty of the Winnemucca Lake Trail, but you also want a longer walk and a little more solitude, try this loop trip instead. Note that while the loop trail itself is a relatively easy hike, adding on a side trip to the summit of Mount Round Top gives this hike its resounding 4 difficulty rating. There is no real trail to Round Top's summit, and the most obvious use trail goes straight uphill at a punishing grade.

The path is the same route as the Winnemucca Lake Trail for the first 1.5 miles to Winnemucca's edge, but then you bear right and cross the stream on the west side of the lake. From there it's one mile uphill to Round Top Lake, steep enough to get you puffing. The gorgeous volcanic scenery makes it all worthwhile. Round Top Lake is set below The Sisters, two peaks that are both at 10,000 feet-plus. You also have views of Mount Round Top and Fourth of July Peak. It's incredibly dramatic. From the eastern edge of Round Top Lake, you'll see an obvious path heading up the side of Mount Round Top. If you like a little challenge and you're surefooted, go for it. The grade is brutal, but when you reach the top after a final rocky scramble, you have a stunning view of The Dardanelles, Lake Tahoe, Caples Lake, Woods Lake, Round Top Lake, Winnemucca Lake, and Frog Lake. Perhaps most impressive is deep Summit City Canyon, 3,000 feet below the south side of Round Top. At 10,380 feet, Mount Round Top is the highest peak in the Carson Pass area, and the finest place for a bird's-eye view. The summit is more like a knife-thin, rocky ridge, so watch your footing. This is not a place for children or in-experienced hikers.

After your summit visit, return downhill to Round Top Lake to finish out your loop. Follow the lake's outlet creek on the Lost Cabin Mine Trail for two miles back to Woods Lake Campground; then wind your way through the camp back to the Woods Lake Picnic Area, where you left your car.

Location: In the Mokelumne Wilderness near Carson Pass; map D4, grid i2.

User groups: Hikers, dogs, and horses. No mountain bikes. No wheelchair facilities.

Permits: No day-hiking permits are required. A free wilderness permit is required for overnight stays between April 1 and November 30; it is available from the Amador Ranger Station, the Carson Pass Information Station, or the Eldorado Information Center.

Maps: For a map of Eldorado National Forest, send $6 to U.S. Forest Service, Map Sales, P.O. Box 587, Camino, CA 95709; tel. (530) 647-5390 or website: www.r5.fs.fed.us/visitorcenter. Ask the USGS for a topographic map of the Caples Lake and Carson Pass areas.

Directions: From Meyers at the junction of U.S. 50 and Highway 89, drive south on Highway 89 for 11 miles to Highway 88. Turn west on Highway 88 and drive 12 miles to the Woods Lake Campground turnoff on the south side of the road. It's 1.5 miles west of Carson Pass Summit. Turn left and drive 1.5 miles to the trailhead parking area by the picnic area at Woods Lake.

Contact: Eldorado National Forest, 3070 Camino Heights Drive, Camino, CA 95709; tel. (530) 644-6048 or fax (530) 295-5624; Amador Ranger District, 26820 Silver Drive, Pioneer, CA 95666; tel. (209) 295-4251 or fax (209) 295-5998.

42 Fourth of July Lake

8.8 mi/4.5 hrs or 2.0 days

The biggest problem in planning a trip to Fourth of July Lake is deciding which way to go. There are so many ways from so many trailheads, including ones at Carson Pass and Upper Blue Lake. The shortest and most direct route is from Woods Lake Campground near campsite 13, and it includes a nice stopover at Round Top Lake, two miles in. Follow the dirt road from the campground for .5 mile to the start of the Lost Cabin Mine Trail. Sure enough, you pass some old mining cabins before you enter the wilderness boundary. Pass the eastern flank of 9,000-foot Black Butte, an old volcanic vent that is similar in appearance to Mount Round Top a few miles to the east. In less than an hour you arrive at Round Top Lake, a worthy destination in itself and a good spot for a snack break beneath the sturdy shoulders of the two peaks of The Sisters. It's only two miles more to Fourth of July Lake, but they are steep and downhill, which means you must climb back out on the way home. This is actually good news: it means you will leave the majority of the crowds behind. Most people give up at Fourth of July Saddle, a rocky overlook that sits 1,000 feet above the lake. In addition to the tough grade, the route is often dusty. At the lake, fishing is good for brook trout, and many campsites are found near its edge. Late in the summer, a sandy beach gets exposed, perfect for swimmers.

Location: In the Mokelumne Wilderness near Caples Lake; map D4, grid i2.

User groups: Hikers, dogs, and horses. No mountain bikes. No wheelchair facilities.

Permits: No day-hiking permits are required. A free wilderness permit is required for overnight stays between April 1 and November 30; it is available from the Amador Ranger Station, the Carson Pass Information Station, or the Eldorado Information Center.

Maps: For a map of Eldorado National Forest, send $6 to U.S. Forest Service, Map Sales, P.O. Box 587, Camino, CA 95709; tel. (530) 647-5390 or website: www.r5.fs.fed.us/visitorcenter. Ask the USGS for a topographic map of the Caples Lake area.

Directions: From Meyers at the junction of U.S. 50 and Highway 89, drive south on Highway 89 for 11 miles to Highway 88. Turn west on Highway 88 and drive 12 miles to the Woods Lake Campground turnoff on the south side of the road. It's 1.5 miles west of Carson Pass Summit. Turn left and drive one mile to the campground. Park in the day-use area and walk to site 13, where a sign reads "Lost Cabin Mine Trail—Follow this road to trailhead."

Contact: Eldorado National Forest, 3070 Camino Heights Drive, Camino, CA 95709; tel. (530) 644-6048 or fax (530) 295-5624; Amador Ranger District, 26820 Silver Drive, Pioneer, CA 95666; tel. (209) 295-4251 or fax (209) 295-5998.

43 Frog Lake
1.8 mi/1.0 hr

Any hiking trip from the Carson Pass Trailhead is going to be packed with people, but we say take this walk anyway just because it's so interesting and educational. At the trailhead and visitor center you can learn about Kit Carson, the great explorer for whom this pass was named, and you can learn about the geologic forces that shaped this region, which is called the Round Top Geologic Area. Evidence of both glacial and volcanic action can be seen with every step you take. The short walk to Frog Lake is suitable even for small children, and if you're more ambitious, you can continue another 1.5 miles to beautiful Winnemucca Lake. At Frog Lake you are provided with a fascinating look at Elephant Back, elevation 9,585 feet, which looks exactly like its name. It's a lava dome, a round mass of solid lava. The lake is a beautiful turquoise color, perfect for picnicking alongside, although because the area is rather open and exposed, the wind sometimes blows with ferocity.

A side note: plenty of people take this walk purely to see the wildflowers, especially lupine and Indian paintbrush, in late July. A huge patch of wild iris also blooms alongside Frog Lake. It's a sight to behold.

Location: In the Mokelumne Wilderness near Carson Pass; map D4, grid i3.

User groups: Hikers, dogs, and horses. No mountain bikes. No wheelchair facilities.

Permits: A $3 parking fee is charged per vehicle. A free wilderness permit is required for overnight stays between April 1 and November 30; it is available from the Amador Ranger Station, the Carson Pass Information Station, or the Eldorado Information Center.

Maps: For a map of Eldorado National Forest, send $6 to U.S. Forest Service, Map Sales, P.O. Box 587, Camino, CA 95709; tel. (530) 647-5390 or website: www.r5.fs.fed.us/visitorcenter. Ask the USGS for a topographic map of the Carson Pass area.

Directions: From Meyers at the junction of U.S. 50 and Highway 89, drive south on Highway 89 for 11 miles to Highway 88. Turn west on Highway 88 and drive 10 miles to Carson Pass Summit. The parking area and trailhead are on the left, by the Carson Pass Information Station.

Contact: Eldorado National Forest, 3070 Camino Heights Drive, Camino, CA 95709; tel. (530) 644-6048 or fax (530) 295-5624; Amador Ranger District, 26820 Silver Drive, Pioneer, CA 95666; tel. (209) 295-4251 or fax (209) 295-5998.

44 Showers Lake

10.0 mi/6.0 hrs

Here's a day hike on the Pacific Crest Trail into the land of Meiss Country, headwaters for the Upper Truckee River and home of the endangered Lahontan cutthroat trout. Although Meiss Country is not designated wilderness, it might as well be because there are no roads cutting into it, and all is peaceful and serene. The Pacific Crest Trail and a completed stretch of the Tahoe Rim Trail are the main routes through Meiss Country. For the trip to Showers Lake, head uphill from the trailhead on the PCT, climbing through Meiss Pass and then dropping into a huge valley basin. Views along the way include Mount Round Top, Elephant Back, and Red Lake Peak, expanding to include far-off Lake Tahoe to the north. It's 2.9 miles to a fork with the Tahoe Rim Trail, just beyond a crossing of the Upper Truckee River, which is little more than a stream here. The

right fork leads 2.2 miles to Round Lake, Meiss Country's largest lake and a popular destination, but stay left on the PCT and TRT, and cross the river again on your way to Showers Lake, 2.1 miles farther. The last .5 mile of trail is a 350-foot descent to Showers Lake, with 9,590-foot Little Round Top poking up above it to the west. The trail leads along the east side of the lake, where campsites can be found. The lake is set at 8,790 feet and is the highest lake in the Upper Truckee River Basin. The only downer about the place? It's popular with the horsy set. A separate trail leads to Showers Lake from Schneider Camp, a large horse camp, so weekends bring a fair amount of horse traffic.

Location: Near Caples Lake; map D4, grid h3.

User groups: Hikers, dogs, and horses. No mountain bikes. No wheelchair facilities.

Permits: A $3 parking fee is charged per vehicle. No day hiking permits are required.

Maps: For a map of Eldorado National Forest, send $6 to U.S. Forest Service, Map Sales, P.O. Box 587, Camino, CA 95709; tel. (530) 647-5390 or website: www.r5.fs.fed.us/visitorcenter. Ask the USGS for topographic maps of the Caples Lake and Carson Pass areas.

Directions: From Meyers at the junction of U.S. 50 and Highway 89, drive south on Highway 89 for 11 miles to Highway 88. Turn west on Highway 88 and drive 10 miles to Carson Pass Summit. The parking area and trailhead are on the right (north), across the highway from (and slightly west of) the Carson Pass Information Station.

Contact: Eldorado National Forest, 3070 Camino Heights Drive, Camino, CA 95709; tel. (530) 644-6048 or fax (530) 295-5624; Amador Ranger District, 26820 Silver Drive, Pioneer, CA 95666; tel. (209) 295-4251 or fax (209) 295-5998.

45 Raymond Lake

11.0 mi/1-2 days

Considering how difficult it is, we're not sure why this trip to Raymond Lake is so popular unless you figure in the gorgeous alpine scenery. The trip has become something of a rite of passage for hikers in the Carson Pass area, and the trail is busy almost as soon as it is snow free, with even not-too-fit hikers making the 3,000-foot climb to the rocky alpine lake. The trail starts near Lower Sunset Lake and heads east from the access road on the Pacific Crest Trail. Keep following the PCT trail markers for 4.5 miles; then turn right on the Raymond Lake Trail. (Most of those 4.5 miles are a moderate ascent.) The final stretch is only a mile but a butt-kicker, mostly because you're already getting tired when you begin it. The lake is about 10 acres in size and set at 9,000 feet. It's popular with people who want to catch themselves a golden trout. The best thing about the lake has nothing to do with fishing but everything to do with the fact that it is set below 10,000-foot Raymond Peak, a ruggedly beautiful mountain.

Location: In the Mokelumne Wilderness near Blue Lakes; map D4, grid i3.

User groups: Hikers, dogs, and horses. No mountain bikes. No wheelchair facilities.

Permits: No day-hiking permits are required. A free wilderness permit is required for overnight stays between April 1 and November 30; it is available from the ranger station in Markleeville or at the Carson Pass Information Station.

Maps: For a map of Humboldt-Toiyabe National Forest–Carson District, send $6 to U.S. Forest Service, Map Sales, P.O. Box 587, Camino, CA 95709; tel. (530) 647-5390 or website: www.r5.fs.fed.us/visitorcenter. Ask the USGS for topographic maps of the Pacific Valley and Ebbetts Pass areas.

Directions: From Meyers at the junction of U.S. 50 and Highway 89, drive south on Highway 89 for 11 miles to Highway 88. Turn west on Highway 88 and drive 2.5 miles to the Blue Lakes turnoff on the south side of the road. Turn south and drive 11 miles to the left turnoff for Tamarack Lake and Wet Meadows. Bear left and drive three miles to the left turnoff for Lower Sunset Lake. Turn left and drive a short distance to the trailhead.

Contact: Humboldt-Toiyabe National Forest, Carson Ranger District, 1536 South Carson Street, Carson City, NV 89701; tel. (775) 882-2766 or fax (775) 884-8199.

46 Granite Lake
4.0 mi/2.0 hrs

Campers at Middle Creek Campground can set out from their tents on this trail to Granite Lake, but everyone else must begin by the dam at Upper Blue Lake and follow a well-signed but meandering route to enter the Mokelumne Wilderness one mile in. (Don't be concerned if there are lots of cars in the dam parking lot. Most of them belong to fishermen, not hikers.) Only one mile beyond the wilderness boundary lies Granite Lake, requiring a total 550-foot climb over well-graded trail. You'll barely notice you're climbing; this is a very easy pathway. A quarter mile past the boundary sign you'll see a large pond, but don't mistake that for Granite Lake, which is another 20 minutes farther on the trail. The granite basin it's set in and the granite that lines its shores are a dead giveaway that you've made it to the proper destination. Hope you brought your swimsuit for the deep, chilly waters. If you want to hike farther, Grouse Lake is another four miles beyond.

Location: In the Mokelumne Wilderness near Blue Lakes; map D4, grid i3.

User groups: Hikers, dogs, and horses. No mountain bikes. No wheelchair facilities.

Permits: No day-hiking permits are required. A free wilderness permit is required for overnight stays between April 1 and November 30; it is available from the Amador Ranger Station, the Carson Pass Information Station, or the Eldorado Information Center.

Maps: For a map of Eldorado National Forest, send $6 to U.S. Forest Service, Map Sales, P.O. Box 587, Camino, CA 95709; tel. (530) 647-5390 or website: www.r5.fs.fed.us/visitorcenter. Ask the USGS for a topographic map of the Pacific Valley area.

Directions: From Meyers at the junction of U.S. 50 and Highway 89, drive south on Highway 89 for 11 miles to Highway 88. Turn west on Highway 88 and drive 2.5 miles to the Blue Lakes turnoff on the south side of the road. Turn south and drive 12 miles to the fork at Lower Blue Lake. Turn right and drive 1.5 miles to the dam by Upper Blue Lake, shortly past Middle Creek Campground; turn left into the parking area. The Granite Lake and Grouse Lake Trail leads from the west side of the parking area.

Contact: Eldorado National Forest, 3070 Camino Heights Drive, Camino, CA 95709; tel. (530) 644-6048 or fax (530) 295-5624; Amador Ranger District, 26820 Silver Drive, Pioneer, CA 95666; tel. (209) 295-4251 or fax (209) 295-5998.

47 Hot Springs Creek Waterfall

3.0 mi/1.5 hrs

Even without a waterfall, this would be a great trail to walk because it leads through the giant sugar pines of Hot Springs Valley, enclosed by rocky cliffs and 10,000-foot peaks. The route leaves from just beyond the campgrounds in Grover Hot Springs State Park and follows the Burnside Lake and Charity Valley Trails for .5 mile, then branches off on a left fork. The trail is well signed for the waterfall, so you'll have no chance of getting lost. There's one questionable part where the trail reaches a jumbled pile of boulders, but the correct answer is simply to go up and over them. Hot Springs Canyon gradually narrows on its way to the falls, and when you near the creek's edge, you'll see many small trout swimming in its pools. The waterfall is about 50 feet high and best seen from April to July. Technically it is outside of state parkland and in Toiyabe National Forest, so you'll see backpackers' campfire rings on the cliff above the falls.

Location: In Grover Hot Springs State Park near Markleeville; map D4, grid i4.

User groups: Hikers only. No dogs, horses, or mountain bikes. No wheelchair facilities.

Permits: No permits are required. A $2 day-

use fee is charged per vehicle.

Maps: A map of Grover Hot Springs State Park is available for $1 at the entrance station. Ask the USGS for a topographic map of the Markleeville area.

Directions: From Meyers at the junction of U.S. 50 and Highway 89, drive south on Highway 89 for 24 miles to Markleeville. At Markleeville turn right (west) on Hot Springs Road and drive 3.5 miles to the state park entrance. The signed trailhead is .25 mile beyond the entrance station and campground turnoffs at a gated dirt road.

Contact: Grover Hot Springs State Park, P.O. Box 188, Markleeville, CA 96120; tel. (530) 694-2248, tel. (530) 525-7232, or fax (530) 694-2502.

48 Burnside Lake

8.4 mi/5.0 hrs

The Burnside Lake Trail leaves Grover Hot Springs State Park at 5,900 feet in elevation and climbs west to Burnside Lake at 8,160 feet. The climb is spaced out over four miles, so it's a steady workout to the lake but not grueling. Along the way you pass tall and majestic sugar pines and rocky outcrops, with 10,023-foot Hawkins Peak and 9,417-foot Markleeville Peak towering over the scene. The lake is about 10 surface acres and popular for fishing. Although you can start hiking on the trail from Hot Springs Road shortly before the state park entrance, we recommend you start from the park's trailhead. Not only does it shave two miles off your trip, but also when you return from your hike, you can take a dip in the 102-degree hot springs and soothe those aching muscles. Note: Although you may encounter some mountain bikers on the trail at first, they will soon branch off on their way to Charity Valley.

Location: In Humboldt-Toiyabe National Forest near Markleeville; map D4, grid i4.

User groups: Hikers, dogs, horses, and mountain bikes. No wheelchair facilities.

Permits: No permits are required. A $5 day-use fee is charged per vehicle. Parking and access are free if you begin at the trailhead outside of the state park.

Maps: For a map of Humboldt-Toiyabe National Forest–Carson District, send $6 to U.S. Forest Service, Map Sales, P.O. Box 587, Camino, CA 95709; tel. (530) 647-5390 or website: www.r5.fs.fed.us/visitorcenter. A map of Grover Hot Springs State Park is available for $1 at the entrance station. Ask the USGS for a topographic map of the Markleeville area.

Directions: From Meyers at the junction of Highway 50 and Highway 89, drive south on Highway 89 for 24 miles to Markleeville. At Markleeville turn right (west) on Hot Springs Road and drive 3.5 miles to the state park entrance. The signed trailhead is .25 mile beyond the entrance station and campground turnoffs at a gated dirt road. Another trailhead is located outside the state park, on Hot Springs Road .75 mile before the state park entrance, and is signed for Charity Valley.)

Contact: Grover Hot Springs State Park, P.O. Box 188, Markleeville, CA 96120; tel. (530) 694-2248 or (530) 525-7232; Humboldt-Toiyabe National Forest, Carson Ranger District, 1536 South Carson Street, Carson City, NV 89701; tel. (775) 882-2766 or fax (775) 884-8199.

49 Heiser Lake

4.8 mi/2.5 hrs

When a trailhead is located at a spot as pretty as the Mosquito Lakes on Highway 4, you just know you're in for a good trip. The tiny little lakes are popular with fishermen from the nearby campgrounds, but this trail is popular with nature lovers, who set out on the short, moderate day hike to Heiser Lake for a few hours of peace in the Carson-Iceberg Wilderness. The trail climbs and descends, then climbs and descends some more, mostly heading in a straight-line course due south to the lake. It's one of those trails where you've got to work equally hard traveling in both directions. At a junction with the trail from Bull Run Lake two miles in, bear left and finish out the last .5 mile to Heiser Lake, set at 8,000 feet.

The lake is granite bound, with a couple of tiny islands sticking out of its shallow waters.

Location: In the Carson-Iceberg Wilderness near Ebbetts Pass; map D4, grid j3.

User groups: Hikers, dogs, and horses. No mountain bikes. No wheelchair facilities.

Permits: No day-hiking permits are required. Parking and access are free.

Maps: For a map of Stanislaus National Forest, send $6 to U.S. Forest Service, Map Sales, P.O. Box 587, Camino, CA 95709; tel. (530) 647-5390 or website: www.r5.fs.fed.us/visitorcenter. A map of the Carson-Iceberg Wilderness is also available from the Forest Service for $6. Ask the USGS for topographic maps of the Pacific Valley and Spicer Meadow Reservoir areas.

Directions: From Angels Camp at the intersection of Highways 4 and 49, go east on Highway 4 for 40 miles to Bear Valley. Set your odometer at Bear Valley and drive 10 miles farther east on Highway 4 to the Mosquito Lakes Trailhead and the Heiser Lake Trail. Park on the right (south) side of the road across from the campground; there is only enough space for a few cars.

Contact: Stanislaus National Forest, Calaveras Ranger District, P.O. Box 500, Hathaway Pines, CA 95233; tel. (209) 795-1381 or fax (209) 795-6849.

50 Bull Run Lake

7.0 mi/4.0 hrs

You might have to share the trail to Bull Run Lake with some horses (their owners like the big parking lot at the trailhead, large enough for horse trailers), but as long as you remember to pack along a few extra apples or carrots, things should turn out okay. Although longer than the nearby trail to Heiser Lake, this trip to Bull Run Lake is actually easier because the trail is well graded and the only really steep section is in the last .5 mile. The first 1.3 miles are almost level, traveling slightly downhill through a grassy meadow that is filled with wildflowers in the early summer and turns golden by September. After that you start to climb, mostly through pine forest and over duck-lined stretches of granite. Watch for a trail junction at 2.2 miles, where you should turn right for Bull Run Lake (straight ahead is Heiser Lake). After a brief flat stretch, prepare for a final mile of climbing, with the last part being the most challenging. The lake is a fine reward for your panting effort, set in a steep-walled granite bowl and with many smooth rock slabs to lie on. Note that the ambitious can add on a trip to Heiser Lake, which is two miles away from the junction. But with a steep up and down, it's better saved for backpackers or day-hikers who have gotten a very early start.

Location: In the Carson-Iceberg Wilderness near Ebbetts Pass; map D4, grid j3.

User groups: Hikers, dogs, and horses. No mountain bikes. No wheelchair facilities.

Permits: No day-hiking permits are required. Parking and access are free.

Maps: For a map of Stanislaus National Forest, send $6 to U.S. Forest Service, Map Sales, P.O. Box 587, Camino, CA 95709; tel. (530) 647-5390 or website: www.r5.fs.fed.us/visitorcenter. A map of the Carson-Iceberg Wilderness is also available from the Forest Service for $6. Ask the USGS for topographic maps of the Pacific Valley and Spicer Meadow Reservoir areas.

Directions: From Angels Camp at the intersection of Highways 4 and 49, drive east on Highway 4 for 40 miles to Bear Valley. Set your odometer at Bear Valley and drive 8.5 miles farther east on Highway 4 to the Stanislaus Meadow turnoff on the right (Road 8N13). Turn right and drive a short distance to the trailhead parking area.

Contact: Stanislaus National Forest, Calaveras Ranger District, P.O. Box 500, Hathaway Pines, CA 95233; tel. (209) 795-1381 or fax (209) 795-6849.

51 Noble Lake
9.0 mi/4.5 hrs

Noble Lake lies just outside of the Carson-Iceberg Wilderness and is reachable by a long, butt-kicking hike on the Noble Canyon Trail out of Silver Creek Campground, or a shorter, gentler route from Ebbetts Pass. Guess which one we like better? Right. From Ebbetts Pass, elevation 8,700 feet, there's a mere 1,200-foot climb to the lake at 9,440 feet (which includes some descent as well). The lake is a fine spot for camping or just spending an afternoon. The scenery is classic high Sierra—big conifers, snow-capped peaks, hard granite, and lush meadows. The hiking season is brief at this elevation, usually only about three months from July to September, but that just makes being here seem all the more special.

The lake route follows the access trail to the Pacific Crest Trail from the trailhead parking area. In .25 mile of climbing, you will join the PCT proper and head south, first climbing and then making a long descent into Noble Canyon. The trail from Silver Creek Campground joins your trail here, and some switchbacks follow. At three miles you will cross Noble Creek, then climb again to a high meadow. Soon you can see Noble Lake; the main lake is to the right of the trail, but a smaller unnamed lake is to the left, about 650 feet off the trail. Both have decent campsites and many good rocks to sit on and relax. In springtime, fishing is reportedly good at Noble Lake.

Location: In Humboldt-Toiyabe National Forest near Ebbetts Pass; map D4, grid j5.

User groups: Hikers, dogs, horses, and mountain bikes. No wheelchair facilities.

Permits: No day-hiking permits are required. Parking and access are free.

Maps: For a map of Humboldt-Toiyabe National Forest–Carson District, send $6 to U.S. Forest Service, Map Sales, P.O. Box 587, Camino, CA 95709; tel. (530) 647-5390 or website: www.r5.fs.fed.us/visitorcenter. Ask the USGS for a topographic map of the Ebbetts Pass area.

Directions: From Angels Camp at the intersection of Highways 4 and 49, go east on Highway 4 for 40 miles to Bear Valley. Set your odometer at Bear Valley and drive 15 miles farther east on Highway 4 to Ebbetts Pass and the trailhead parking area. The trail is on the south side of the road. (If you are coming from Markleeville, drive south on Highway 89/Highway 4 for 15 miles to Ebbetts Pass.)

Contact: Humboldt-Toiyabe National Forest, Carson Ranger District, 1536 South Carson Street, Carson City, NV 89701; tel. (775) 882-2766 or fax (775) 884-8199.

52 Kinney Lakes

5.0 mi/2.5 hrs

The route to Kinney Lakes follows the Pacific Crest Trail in the opposite direction of the hike to Noble Lake, heading north past minuscule Sherrold Lake on the way to large Upper Kinney Lake. You start hiking at 8,700 feet at the pass, so even though this trail has an easy to moderate grade, your lungs are getting a workout. The trail leads through a landscape of big conifers with little undergrowth, typical of the high country. When the trees thin out, your views open wide. Raymond Peak and Reynold Peak rule the skyline. At 1.6 miles you reach a signed junction for Upper and Lower Kinney Lakes, and you can take your pick as to which one to visit first. The Pacific Crest Trail leads directly to the upper lake, while the lower lake must be visited by following an eastward fork from the PCT. The upper lake, though smaller, is the prettier of the two.

Location: In Humboldt-Toiyabe National Forest near Ebbetts Pass; map D4, grid j5.

User groups: Hikers, dogs, horses, and mountain bikes. No wheelchair facilities.

Permits: No day-hiking permits are required. Parking and access are free.

Maps: For a map of Humboldt-Toiyabe National Forest–Carson District, send $6 to U.S. Forest Service, Map Sales, P.O. Box 587, Camino, CA 95709; tel. (530) 647-5390 or website: www.r5.fs.fed.us/visitorcenter. Ask the USGS for a topographic map of the Ebbetts Pass area.

Directions: From Angels Camp at the intersection of Highways 4 and 49, drive east on Highway 4 for about 40 miles to Bear Valley. Set your odometer at Bear Valley and drive 15 miles farther east on Highway 4 to Ebbetts Pass and the trailhead parking area. The trail is on the north side of the road. If you are coming from Markleeville, drive south on Highway 89/Highway 4 for 15 miles to Ebbetts Pass.

Contact: Humboldt-Toiyabe National Forest, Carson Ranger District, 1536 South Carson Street, Carson City, NV 89701; tel. (775) 882-2766 or fax (775) 884-8199.

53 Wolf Creek Trail

9.6 mi/5.0 hrs

When the temperature heats up around Markleeville, you've got two choices: Head for the mineral springs at Grover Hot Springs State Park (the cool pool, not the hot pool), or take a hike on the Wolf Creek Trail. We know, it's a tough choice. But if you pick the latter, you're in for a fine time on this easy trail along Wolf Creek, starting at 6,480 feet in elevation. The trail is wide enough to hold hands with your hiking partner (it's an old jeep road), it's almost entirely shaded, and it meanders upstream and slightly uphill for a total of nine miles one way. A perfect day hike is just to stroll along the creek for an hour or two, find a good spot along the stream to hang out for a while, then turn around and stroll back. Energetic types can hike 4.3 miles out to a fork for the steep Bull Canyon Trail to Bull Lake, then bear left and continue a half mile beyond the fork to Wolf Creek Falls. The waterfall is found just off the trail to the left, about 50 yards beyond where the trail passes through a cattle fence. It's quite impressive early in the summer as it thunders over a cliff of volcanic rock.

Location: In the Carson-Iceberg Wilderness near Markleeville; map D4, grid j5.

User groups: Hikers, dogs, and horses. No mountain bikes. No wheelchair facilities.

Permits: No day-hiking permits are required. A free wilderness permit is required for overnight stays; it is available at the trailhead. Parking and access are free.

Maps: For a map of Humboldt-Toiyabe National Forest–Carson District, send $6 to U.S. Forest Service, Map Sales, P.O. Box 587, Camino, CA 95709; tel. (530) 647-5390 or website: www.r5.fs.fed.us/visitorcenter. A map of the Carson-Iceberg Wilderness is also available from the Forest Service for $6. Ask the USGS for a topographic map of the Wolf Creek area.

Directions: From Meyers at the junction of U.S. 50 and Highway 89, drive south on Highway 89 for 24 miles to Markleeville. From Markleeville continue south on Highway 89 for four miles, then bear right (south) on Highway 4. Drive 2.5 miles on Highway 4 to the signed turnoff for Wolf Creek on the left. Turn left (south) and drive 4.9 miles to the trailhead, about 100 yards before the end of the road and a campground.

Contact: Humboldt-Toiyabe National Forest, Carson Ranger District, 1536 South Carson Street, Carson City, NV 89701; tel. (775) 882-2766 or fax (775) 884-8199.

54 East Carson River Trail

4.0 mi/2.0 hrs

If it's springtime and you're itching to go hiking but there's still too much snow around Ebbetts Pass, the East Carson River Trail can be your salvation. Trailhead elevation is only 6,240 feet at the north side of Wolf Creek Meadows, which means it's snow free before other nearby areas. Bear left at the trail junction just uphill from the trailhead. An interesting journey is 1.5 miles to Wolf Creek Lake (sometimes dry) and Railroad Canyon, the site of 19th-century logging operations. Although this trail continues onward and eventually meets up with the High Trail out of Wolf Creek Meadows, it's nearly impossible to make a loop trip

out of the two trails, especially in early season. The High Trail reaches an elevation of nearly 8,000 feet and is often covered in snow. So just hike as far as you like, then head back the way you came.

Location: In the Carson-Iceberg Wilderness near Markleeville; map D4, grid j5.

User groups: Hikers, dogs, and horses. No mountain bikes. No wheelchair facilities.

Permits: No day-hiking permits are required. A free wilderness permit is required for overnight stays; it is available at the trailhead. Parking and access are free.

Maps: For a map of Humboldt-Toiyabe National Forest–Carson District, send $6 to U.S. Forest Service, Map Sales, P.O. Box 587, Camino, CA 95709; tel. (530) 647-5390 or website: www.r5.fs.fed.us/visitorcenter. A map of the Carson-Iceberg Wilderness is also available from the Forest Service for $6. Ask the USGS for a topographic map of the Wolf Creek area.

Directions: From Meyers at the junction of U.S. 50 and Highway 89, drive south on Highway 89 for 24 miles to Markleeville. Continue south on Highway 89/Highway 4 for 7.5 miles to the signed turnoff for Wolf Creek on the left. Turn left (east) and drive 3.5 miles to the left turnoff signed for the East Carson River Trail. Turn left and drive one mile to the trailhead.

Contact: Humboldt-Toiyabe National Forest, Carson Ranger District, 1536 South Carson Street, Carson City, NV 89701; tel. (775) 882-2766 or fax (775) 884-8199.

PACIFIC CREST TRAIL (PCT) SECTION OVERVIEW

98.6 mi one way/10.0 days

Trail elevations within this section—which extends from Highway 4 near Ebbetts Pass to the trailhead parking area near Donner Pass—range from 7,000 feet to over 10,000 feet. Although the lower reaches of the PCT are open from mid-June to mid-October, several high passes within the region may remain snow covered until mid-July, making hiking difficult. Snow-covered passes are impossible to navigate with pack stock and horses. For this reason the highest usage period for the most heavily traveled section of the California PCT occurs during the month of August.

PCT-26 Ebbetts Pass to Blue Lakes Road

12.0 mi one way/1.0 day

As you leave Ebbetts Pass, you'll cross a series of fantastic volcanic formations in the Mokelumne Wilderness. The country here may look stark from a distance, but it is loaded with tiny wildflowers. The trail is quite good—a lot of hikers make great time in this area—but the lack of available water can become a concern. We suggest tanking up when you get the chance, such as at Eagle Creek below Reynold Peak (9,690 feet). The Mokelumne Wilderness is a relative breeze, and you'll find yourself approaching civilization at a series of small lakes in Tahoe National Forest. The trail rises up a stark, wind-blown, sandy ridge, with excellent views of the Blue Lakes, but again, there is no water for several miles until you drop down near Lost Lake. You'll actually cross several roads on this stretch of trail, and maybe even see a car—a moment of irony for long-distance PCT hikers.

Location: From Highway 4 near Ebbetts Pass north to Blue Lakes Road just south of Carson Pass and Highway 88; map D4, grid j4.

User groups: Hikers, dogs, and horses. No mountain bikes. No wheelchair facilities.

Permits: A backcountry permit is required for traveling through various wilderness and special-use areas that the trail traverses. In addition, a campfire permit is required for the use of portable camp stoves or the building of campfires (where permitted). To make it simple, you can contact the national forest, BLM, or national park office at your point of entry for a combined permit good for traveling through multiple-permit areas during your dates of travel.

Maps: For an overall view of the trail route in this section, send $6 for each map ordered to the U.S. Forest Service, Map Sales, P.O. Box 587, Camino, CA 95709; tel. (530) 647-5390. Ask for Lake Tahoe Basin Management Unit, Tahoe National Forest, Eldorado National Forest, and Stanislaus National Forest maps. Ask the USGS for topographic maps of the Ebbetts Pass, Pacific Valley, and Carson Pass areas of the route.

Directions: To reach the Ebbetts Pass Trailhead from Angels Camp, head east on Highway 4 to Ebbetts Pass. To reach the Blue Lakes Road Trailhead from the Highway 88/89 interchange at Hope Valley, head west on Highway 88 to Blue Lakes Road and turn left. Stay on Blue Lakes Road to the trailhead parking area, just before reaching Blue Lakes.

Contact: Eldorado National Forest, Information Center, 3070 Camino Heights Drive, Camino, CA 95709; tel. (530) 644-6048 or fax (530) 295-5624.

PCT-27 Blue Lakes Road to Carson Pass

12.0 mi one way/1.0 day

Many hikers underestimate the climb over Elephant Back to reach Carson Pass. After all, on a map it doesn't look like much, and from a distance, as you size it up, it looks easy enough. Wrong! It's a long, grueling pull. The trip out of Blue Lakes starts easily, with a dirt road often in view and adding a bit of early angst to the affair. As you go, you keep wondering when the climb will start. Well, eventually it does, and, alas, it takes a couple of hours, enough to kick the butt of anybody who's not in shape. Guess how we know? After topping the Elephant Back, the route drops down to Carson Pass at a rest stop, where you'll likely meet humanity, but believe it or not, no water. Conserve yours if you plan to go onward because it takes another hour of hiking before you'll reach the next trickle.

Location: From Blue Lakes Road north to Carson Pass and Highway 88; map D4, grid i3.

User groups: Hikers, dogs, and horses. No mountain bikes. No wheelchair access.

Permits: A backcountry permit is required for traveling through various wilderness and special-use areas that the trail traverses. In addition, a campfire permit is required for the use of portable camp stoves or the building of campfires where allowed. To make it simple, you can contact the national forest, BLM, or national park office at your point of entry for a combined permit that is good for traveling through multiple-permit areas during your dates of travel.

Maps: For an overall view of the trail route in this section, send $6 for each map ordered to the U.S. Forest Service, Map Sales, P.O. Box 587, Camino, CA 95709; tel. (530) 647-5390 or website: www.r5.fs.fed.us/visitorcenter. Ask for Lake Tahoe Basin Management Unit, Tahoe National Forest, Eldorado National Forest, and Stanislaus National Forest maps. Ask the USGS for topographic maps of the Pacific Valley and Carson Pass areas of the route.

Directions: To reach the Blue Lakes Road Trailhead from the Highway 88/89 junction at Hope Valley, go west on Highway 88 to Blue Lakes Road and turn left. Stay on Blue Lakes Road for 11 miles to the trailhead parking, just before reaching Blue Lakes. For the Carson Pass Trailhead from the Highway 88/89 junction at Hope Valley, go west on Highway 88 to Carson Pass.

Contact: Eldorado National Forest, Information Center, 3070 Camino Heights Drive, Camino, CA 95709; tel. (530) 644-6048 or fax (530) 295-5624.

PCT-28 Carson Pass to Echo Lakes Resort

15.8 mi one way/1-2 days

When you've hiked on the Pacific Crest Trail for weeks, the first glimpse of Lake Tahoe in the distance can seem like a privileged view into heaven. That view is just a few miles from Ebbetts Pass. You start by hiking over a short mountain rim (nice view to the west of Caples Lake) and then dropping into the headwaters of the Truckee River. As you look northward after making the rim, Lake Tahoe suddenly comes into view. It's like having a divine vision. And finally there is water available from several small creeks from which you can pump liquid as you walk into the Truckee headwaters. At the same time, you will be greeted by a high meadow surrounded by a light forest. All seems right with the world again. With Echo Lakes Resort within one day's hiking time, you will be amazed at how inspired you can get on this section of trail. It's very pretty, weaving through lush canyons and along creeks, eventually reaching beautiful and tiny Showers Lake. Here the trail seems to drop off to never-never land, descending very quickly and steeply in the march toward Tahoe. Contentment reigns. When you reach Little Norway, however, reality sets in. Cars are everywhere. The trail suddenly grinds down amid cabins and vacation property. There's one last hill to climb, and then the PCT drops quickly to the parking lot for Echo Lake.

Almost nobody hiking the PCT immediately heads north into the Desolation Wilderness from here. Virtually everyone stops for at least a day to get cleaned up, resupplied, and fed by something other than a Power Bar. But after a day the trail calls again. If you hear it, well, you just have to answer it.

Location: From Carson Pass at Highway 88 north to Echo Lake near U.S. 50, just south of Lake Tahoe; map D4, grid h2.

User groups: Hikers, dogs, and horses. No mountain bikes. No wheelchair facilities.

Permits: A backcountry permit is required for traveling through various wilderness and special-use areas that the trail traverses. In addition, a campfire permit is required for the use of portable camp stoves or the building of campfires where permitted. To make it simple, you can contact the national forest, BLM or national park office at your point of entry for a combined permit that is good for traveling through multiple-permit areas during your dates of travel.

Maps: For an overall view of the trail route in this section, send $6 for each map ordered to U.S. Forest Service, Map Sales, P.O. Box 587, Camino, CA 95709; tel. (530) 647-5390. Ask for Lake Tahoe Basin Management Unit, Tahoe National Forest, Eldorado National Forest, and Stanislaus National Forest maps. Ask the USGS for topographic maps of the Carson Pass, Caples Lake, and Echo Lake areas of the route.

Directions: To reach the Carson Pass Trailhead from the Highway 88/89 interchange at Hope Valley, head west on Highway 88 to Carson Pass. For the Echo Lakes Resort Trailhead, from South Lake Tahoe drive south on Highway 89 for five miles to U.S. 50. Drive west on U.S. 50 for 5.5 miles to the signed turnoff for Echo Lakes on the right (one mile west of Echo Summit). Turn right and drive .5 mile on Johnson Pass Road and then turn left on Echo Lakes Road. Drive one mile to a series of parking lots .25 mile before the road ends at Echo Lakes Resort. Park and walk downhill to the resort.

Contact: Eldorado National Forest, Information Center, 3070 Camino Heights Drive, Camino, CA 95709; tel. (530) 644-6048 or fax (530) 295-5624; Lake Tahoe Basin Management Unit, 870 Emerald Bay Road, South Lake Tahoe, CA 96150; tel. (530) 573-2600 or fax (530) 573-2693.

Echo Lakes Resort to Barker Pass

32.3 mi one way/3.0 days

Before hiking this area, we flew over it in a small airplane and understood why so many hikers are captivated with it. The Desolation Wilderness (and the neighboring Granite Chief Wilderness) are filled with sculpted granite domes and hundreds of gemlike lakes. All is pristine, yet access is also quite easy, making this the most heavily used section of the PCT all summer long. The trip starts at Echo Lake, elevation 7,400 feet, climbs through pines, past Upper Echo Lake, and then continues up and north toward Triangle Lake, one of dozens of lakes you pass on your northward route. They come and go—Lake Margery, Lake Aloha, and then Heather, Susie, Gilmore Lakes, and finally Dicks Lake (9,380 feet)—so many, in fact, that you can plan on a perfect campsite near a lake every night, providing you don't mind the company of other hikers who are drawn by classic beauty. The views are dramatic as well, across miles and miles of the glacial-carved granite, all of it marvelous high Sierra landscape. As you continue, you'll discover Upper and Middle Velma Lakes, both very pretty, with good fishing. The trail skirts the ridgeline, keeping the higher knobs to the east as it gradually descends toward Richardson Lake, just beyond the Desolation Wilderness boundary—ready now to enter the Granite Chief Wilderness.

Location: From Echo Lake near U.S. 50 south of Lake Tahoe to Forest Road 3 near Barker Pass northwest of Emerald Bay; map D4, grid g2.

User groups: Hikers, dogs, and horses. No mountain bikes. No wheelchair facilities.

Permits: A backcountry permit is required for traveling through various wilderness and special-use areas the trail traverses. In addition, a campfire permit is required for the use of portable camp stoves or the building of campfires where allowed. To make it simple, you can contact the national forest, BLM, or national park office at your point of entry for a combined permit that is good for traveling through multiple-permit areas during your dates of travel.

Maps: Ask the USGS for topographic maps of the Echo Lake, Emerald Bay, and Rockbound Valley areas of the route.

Directions: For the Echo Lakes Resort Trailhead, from South Lake Tahoe drive south on Highway 89 for five miles to U.S. 50. Drive west on U.S. 50 for 5.5 miles to the signed turnoff for Echo Lakes on the right. (It's one mile west of Echo Summit.) Turn right and drive .5 mile on Johnson Pass Road and then turn left on Echo Lakes Road. Drive one mile to a series of parking lots .25 mile before the road ends at Echo Lakes Resort. Park and walk downhill to the resort. To reach the Barker Pass Trailhead, from Tahoe Pines on Highway 89, head north for .5 mile to the Kaspian Picnic Grounds and then bear left (west) for seven miles on Forest Service Road 15N03.

Contact: Lake Tahoe Basin Management Unit, 870 Emerald Bay Road, South Lake Tahoe, CA 96150; tel. (530) 573-2600 or fax (530) 573-2693.

Barker Pass to Donner Pass

31.4 mi one way/3.0 days

The trailhead at Barker Pass, 7,650 feet, is one of the best anywhere, with direct access to the Granite Chief Wilderness to the north or the Desolation Wilderness to the south. Heading north on the PCT, the trip starts with a climb of 800 feet to enter Granite Chief, and once on the ridge you're rewarded with 360-degree views of this high-mountain landscape, a mix of volcanic rock and granite ridges, much of it above the tree line. Though hikers don't face the long, sustained climbs so common in the southern Sierra, it's enough of a roller-coaster ride to require hikers to be in excellent shape. The trail cuts the flank of Ward Peak at 8,470 feet, then switchbacks steeply down to Five Lakes and Five Lakes Creek (where there's good camping), and then continues up and down canyons all the way to Donner Pass. You can expect to see lots of hikers. One reason is that along the way you'll pass near two ski resorts, Alpine Meadows and Squaw Valley, where hikers can use the ski lifts in the summer to gain easy elevation to the ridgeline, rather than to grind out long, all-day climbs. Before making the final push to Donner Pass, a descent of more than 1,000 feet, hikers can enjoy breathtaking views of Donner Lake and miles of surrounding high country.

Location: From Forest Road 3 near Barker Pass northwest of Emerald Bay north to the trailhead parking area near Interstate 80 and old Highway 40 at Donner Pass; map D4, grid d2.

User groups: Hikers, dogs, and horses. No mountain bikes. No wheelchair facilities.

Permits: A backcountry permit is required for traveling through various wilderness and special-use areas that the trail traverses. In addition, a campfire permit is required for the use of portable camp stoves or the building of campfires where allowed. To make it simple, you can contact the national forest, BLM, or national park office at your point of entry for a combined permit that is good for traveling through multiple-permit areas during your dates of travel.

Maps: Ask the USGS for topographic maps of the Emerald Bay, Rockbound Valley, Homewood, Tahoe City, Granite Chief, and Norden areas of the route.

Directions: To reach the Barker Pass Trailhead from Tahoe Pines on Highway 89, head north for .5 mile to the Kaspian Picnic Grounds and then bear left (west) for seven miles on Forest Service Road 15N03. For the Donner Pass Trailhead from Truckee, drive west on Interstate 80 and exit at Castle Peak Area Boreal Ridge, just west of the Donner Summit roadside rest area. The sign for the Pacific Crest Trailhead is what you're looking for, and it's located on the south side of the highway.

Contact: Tahoe National Forest, Truckee Ranger District, 10342 Highway 89, North Truckee, CA 96161; tel. (530) 587-3558 or fax (530) 587-6914; Lake Tahoe Basin Management Unit, 870 Emerald Bay Road, South Lake Tahoe, CA 96150; tel. (530) 573-2600 or fax (530) 573-2693.

PCT Continuation

To continue hiking along the Pacific Crest Trail, see chapter D3.

CHAPTER E1
MARIN

TOM STIENSTRA

POINT REYES
NATIONAL SEASHORE

MAP E1 ~ MARIN

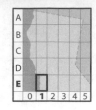

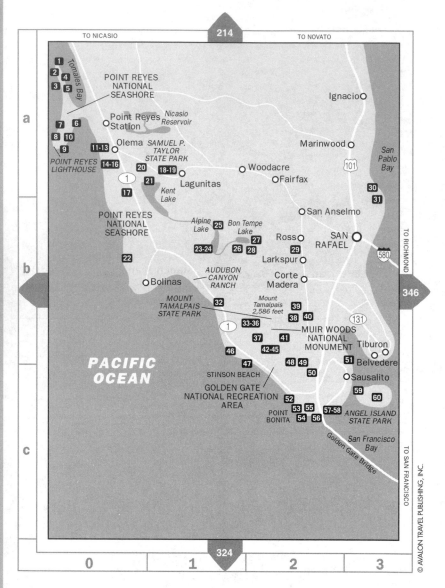

1
2 **4**
3 **5**

POINT REYES
NATIONAL
SEASHORE

Ignacio ○

Tomales Bay

a

7 **6**
8 **10**
9

Point Reyes
Station ○

Nicasio
Reservoir

Marinwood ○

San
Pablo
Bay

11-13 Olema ○

SAMUEL P.
TAYLOR
STATE PARK

101

POINT REYES
LIGHTHOUSE

14-16

20

18-19 ○

Woodacre ○

1

21

Lagunitas

○ Fairfax

17

Kent
Lake

30

31

POINT REYES
NATIONAL
SEASHORE

Alpine
Lake **25**

Bon Tempe
Lake

○ San Anselmo

23-24

26 **28**

27

Ross ○

SAN
RAFAEL ○

22

29

Larkspur ○

580

TO RICHMOND

b

○ Bolinas

AUDUBON
CANYON
RANCH

Corte
Madera ○

346

MOUNT
TAMALPAIS
STATE PARK

32

Mount
Tamalpais
2,586 feet

39

131

38 **40**

1 **33-36**

MUIR WOODS
NATIONAL
MONUMENT

Tiburon
○

PACIFIC
OCEAN

37

41

42-45

51 Belvedere
○

46

48 **49**

○ Sausalito

47

50

59

60

STINSON BEACH

GOLDEN GATE
NATIONAL RECREATION
AREA

52

Point
BONITA

53 **55**

57-58 ANGEL ISLAND
STATE PARK

54 **56**

c

Golden Gate Bridge

San Francisco
Bay

TO SAN FRANCISCO

© AVALON TRAVEL PUBLISHING, INC.

0   1   2   3

CHAPTER E1 ～ MARIN

1 Tomales Point Trail 285

2 McClures Beach Trail . . . 286

3 Abbotts Lagoon Trail . . . 287

4 Marshall Beach Trail. . . . 288

5 Johnstone Trail 288

6 Estero Trail 289

7 South Beach Trail 289

8 Point Reyes Lighthouse . 290

9 Chimney Rock Trail 290

10 Sir Francis
Drake Trail 291

11 Muddy Hollow Loop 291

12 Coast Trail. 292

13 Laguna Loop Trail 293

14 Mount Wittenberg
Loop 294

15 Bear Valley Trail 294

16 Rift Zone Trail. 295

17 Olema Valley 295

18 Barnabe Trail. 296

19 Pioneer Tree Trail 297

20 Bolinas Ridge. 297

21 Kent Dam Trail. 298

22 Alamere Falls Trail. 298

23 Alpine/Kent Lake
Pump Trail. 299

24 Cataract Falls 299

25 Pine Mountain/
Carson Falls. 300

26 Two Lakes Trail 301

27 Deer Park Trail 301

28 Phoenix Lake Trail 302

29 Dawn Falls 302

30 Shoreline Trail. 303

31 Bay View Trail 303

32 Audubon Canyon
Ranch Trail 304

33 Laurel Dell Loop 304

(CONTINUED ON NEXT PAGE)

1 Tomales Point Trail

6.0 mi/3.5 hrs

Imagine meeting up with an elk that stands five feet at the shoulders and has antlers that practically poke holes in the clouds. That is likely to happen on this trail, the best choice in California for those who want to see wildlife. Elk often wander quite close to the parking area, and in the evening the herd will usually congregate near a watering area set in a valley about three miles from the trailhead. The herd numbers over 500. We have seen as many as 75 elk in a single trip; on another, we counted 13 elk, six deer, three rabbits, and a fox—all within a two-hour span. Most people make this a five-mile round trip, hiking north to the top of a grade and a great lookout of Dillon Beach and Bodega Bay. The reason most people turn around here is because the trail descends several feet and if they continue north that means an additional climb on the way back.

The route, which has a flat walking surface and easy grades, is flanked to the west by the Pacific Ocean and to the east by Tomales Bay—both beautiful sights. By following elk paths through the low brush, you can take numerous off-trail side trips, often discovering more beautiful views and elk—always a fun surprise. For a bonus, continue hiking the extra mile all the way to Tomales Point. The only negative to this trip is that wind and fog occasionally envelop the area in midsummer.

(CONTINUED)

34 Rock Springs Trail 305
35 Barth's Retreat 306
36 Mountain Theater 306
37 Bootjack Loop 307
38 East Peak
Mount Tamalpais 307
39 Inspiration Point 308
40 Dipsea Trail 309
41 Mountain Home Trail . . . 310
42 Matt Davis Trail 310
43 Steep Ravine Trail 311
44 Main Trail 311
45 Ocean View
Trail (Panoramic
Highway Trail) 312
46 Rocky Point Trail 312
47 Owl Trail 313
48 Miwok Loop 314

49 Tennessee Valley 314
50 Morning Sun Trail 315
51 Bicentennial
Bike Path 315
52 Coastal Trail/
Fort Cronkhite 316
53 Coastal Trail/
Fort Barry 316
54 Point Bonita
Lighthouse 317
55 Hawk Hill 317
56 Upper Fisherman's
Trail 318
57 Vista Point/
East Fort Baker 318
58 Yellow Bluff Trail 319
59 Perimeter Road 319
60 North Ridge/
Sunset Trail 320

Location: In Point Reyes National Seashore in northwest Marin County; map E1-Marin, grid a0.

User groups: Hikers and horses. (Note: It is a violation of federal law to herd, chase, or otherwise harass elk.) Pierce Ranch is accessible to wheelchairs; the Tomales Point Trail is not. No dogs or mountain bikes.

Permits: No permits are required. Parking and access are free.

Maps: For a free map, write to Point Reyes National Seashore at the address below. Ask the USGS for a topographic map of the Tomales area.

Directions: From U.S. 101 in Marin, take the Sir Francis Drake Boulevard exit and drive about 20 miles west on Sir Francis Drake Boulevard to the town of Olema. Turn right on Highway 1 and drive a short distance to Bear Valley Road. Turn left on Bear Valley Road and drive two miles. Turn left on Sir Francis Drake Highway and drive 5.6 miles to Pierce Ranch Road. Bear right and drive nine miles to the Pierce Ranch parking area and the trailhead.

Contact: Superintendent, Point Reyes National Seashore, Point Reyes, CA 94956; Bear Valley Visitor Center, tel. (415) 663-1092 or fax (415) 663-8132.

2 McClures Beach Trail

1.0 mi/0.5 hr

In the divine panorama of Point Reyes, McClures Beach is one easy-to-reach spot that is often overlooked. It sits in the shadow of nearby Pierce Ranch, with its 500-strong elk herd, and many visitors never drive to the road's end, except perhaps to use the restrooms and telephone there. But an easy .5-mile walk will lead you to McClures Beach, where you'll find tide pools to the south and beachfront to the north. The best time to visit is during minus low tides so you can survey the tide pools and watch all manner of tiny marine creatures playing their war games. Beach-combing along McClures Beach and Driftwood Beach (to the immediate north) during these low tides also can unveil unusual finds. One other thing: The sunsets here can be spectacular, especially during fall and early winter, when the skies often look like a scene from *The Ten Commandments*.

Special note: Tide pooling at this beach can be dangerous, as incoming tides can cut you off, leaving no way to escape. Consult a tide table and never turn your back on the waves.

Location: In Point Reyes National Seashore in northwest Marin County; map E1-Marin, grid a0.

User groups: Hikers only. No dogs, horses, or mountain bikes. No wheelchair facilities.

Permits: No permits are required. Parking and access are free.

Maps: For a free map, write to Point Reyes National Seashore at the address below. Ask the USGS for a topographic map of the Tomales area.

Directions: From U.S. 101 in Marin, take the Sir Francis Drake Boulevard exit and drive about 20 miles west on Sir Francis Drake Boulevard to the town of Olema. Turn right on Highway 1 and drive a short distance to Bear Valley Road. Turn left on Bear Valley Road and drive two miles. Turn left on Sir Francis Drake Highway and drive 5.6 miles to Pierce Ranch Road. Bear right and drive nine miles to the Pierce Ranch parking area, then turn left and drive .5 mile to the parking area and the trailhead.

Contact: Superintendent, Point Reyes National Seashore, Point Reyes, CA 94956; Bear Valley Visitor Center, tel. (415) 663-1092 or fax (415) 663-8132.

3 Abbotts Lagoon Trail

3.2 mi/1.5 hrs

A short ridge shields Abbotts Lagoon from the sight of park visitors driving on Pierce Point Road. That is what keeps this trail se-cluded, despite being an easy walk to an excellent destination. The trail is surfaced with what is known as "soil cement" and is wheelchair accessible about halfway to the ocean bluff. From the trailhead (look for the restrooms), the trail climbs the low ridge. Just like that, below you lies Abbotts Lagoon, and beyond that, the Pacific Ocean. The lagoon is an ideal place for novice canoeists and kayakers, providing you don't mind the one-mile portage. Bird-watching is often good here, thanks to a rare mix of waterfowl that require freshwater and seabirds migrating along the coast. If you walk past the lagoon (a distance of 1.6 miles from the trailhead), you'll arrive at Point Reyes Beach, where miles and miles of sand dunes and untouched waterfront stretch to the north and south.

Location: In Point Reyes National Seashore in northwest Marin County; map E1-Marin, grid a0.

User groups: Hikers and mountain bikes (bikers on the first mile only; do not cross the bridge). Wheelchair accessible with assistance. No dogs or horses.

Permits: No permits are required. Parking and access are free.

Maps: For a free map, write to Point Reyes National Seashore at the address below. Ask the USGS for a topographic map of the Drakes Bay area.

Directions: From U.S. 101 in Marin, take the Sir Francis Drake Boulevard exit and drive about 20 miles west on Sir Francis Drake Boulevard to the town of Olema. Turn right on Highway 1 and drive a short distance to Bear Valley Road. Turn left on Bear Valley Road and drive two miles. Turn left on Sir Francis Drake Highway and drive 5.6 miles to Pierce Ranch Road. Bear right and drive 3.3 miles to a small parking area with restrooms. The trailhead is on the left side of the road.

Contact: Superintendent, Point Reyes National Seashore, Point Reyes, CA 94956; Bear Valley Visitor Center, tel. (415) 663-1092 or fax (415) 663-8132.

4 Marshall Beach Trail
2.4 mi/1.25 hrs

5 Johnstone Trail
8.0 mi/4.0 hrs

What's the most secluded beach in Marin County? Marshall Beach might just qualify. This pretty spot is set on the demure waters of Tomales Bay, sheltered from north winds by Inverness Ridge. The trailhead tends to be overlooked because there are no signs directing hikers to it until you reach the trailhead itself. In addition, the beach is overshadowed by Tomales Bay State Park, which you must drive past in order to get here—and many people don't continue driving. The hike is 1.2 miles one way, taking an elliptical route down into a gulch to a protected cove that helps shelter the beach. It's the kind of place where you can just sit and watch the water lap gently at the shore. Somehow that is plenty.

Location: In Point Reyes National Seashore in northwest Marin County; map E1-Marin, grid a0.

User groups: Hikers, horses, and mountain bikes. No dogs. No wheelchair facilities.

Permits: No permits are required. Parking and access are free.

Maps: For a free map, write to Point Reyes National Seashore at the address below. Ask the USGS for a topographic map of the Tomales area.

Directions: From U.S. 101 in Marin, take the Sir Francis Drake Boulevard exit and drive about 20 miles west on Sir Francis Drake Boulevard to the town of Olema. Turn right on Highway 1 and drive a short distance to Bear Valley Road. Turn left on Bear Valley Road and drive two miles. Turn left on Sir Francis Drake Highway and drive 5.6 miles to Pierce Ranch Road. Bear right and drive 1.3 miles (just past the entrance road to Tomales Bay State Park on the right) to Duck Cove/Marshall Beach Road. Turn right and drive 2.6 miles (bear left at the fork) to the parking area for the Marshall Beach Trail.

Contact: Superintendent, Point Reyes National Seashore, Point Reyes, CA 94956; Bear Valley Visitor Center, tel. (415) 663-1092 or fax (415) 663-8132.

The centerpiece hike of Tomales Bay State Park is the Johnstone Trail, ranging from Hearts Desire Beach to Shell Beach for a one-way trip of four miles. In the process, you will pass through a procession of different habitats, including beaches, forests, meadows, and fields. The highlight is the gentle waterfront of Tomales Bay, protected from north winds by Inverness Ridge at Point Reyes. When viewed from the ridge, the bay appears cobalt blue, beautiful, and soft, unlike most saltwater bays, which look green and harsh. Up close, its docile nature makes it perfect for wading, water play, hand-launching kayaks, or, during low tides, clamming (you must have a fishing license). For a good side trip, take the Jepson Trail cutoff to gain quick access to a dramatic grove of craggy, virgin Bishop pine. In the spring, wildflower blooms can be spectacular.

Location: In Tomales Bay State Park in northwest Marin County; map E1-Marin, grid a0.

User groups: Hikers only. The park headquarters is wheelchair accessible, but the trail is not. No dogs, horses, or mountain bikes.

Permits: A $2 day-use fee is charged at the entrance station.

Maps: A small map/brochure is available for a fee at the entrance station to Tomales Bay State Park. Ask the USGS for a topographic map of the Tomales area.

Directions: From U.S. 101 in Marin, take the Sir Francis Drake Boulevard exit and drive about 20 miles west on Sir Francis Drake Boulevard to the town of Olema. Turn right on Highway 1 and drive a short distance to Bear Valley Road. Turn left on Bear Valley Road and drive two miles. Turn left on Sir Francis Drake Highway and drive 5.6 miles to Pierce Ranch Road. Bear right and drive 1.2 miles to the entrance road to Tomales Bay State Park on the right. Turn right and drive 1.5 miles to the parking area and the trailhead at Hearts Desire Beach.

Contact: Tomales Bay State Park, Star Route, Inverness, CA 94937; tel. (415) 669-1140, tel. (415) 893-1580, or fax (415) 669-1701.

6 Estero Trail

8.8 mi/4.0 hrs

The Estero Trail crosses a valley, parallels a bay, ascends a ridge, and leads down to the waterfront, where a perfect, quiet picnic spot awaits. It's an ideal hike for newcomers to Point Reyes National Seashore, providing glimpses of a variety of settings. In addition, the round-trip is long enough for a workout yet is quite pleasant, with no gut-wrenching climbs. From the parking area you walk 2.4 miles, then turn left at the signed junction. The compensation for climbing Drakes Head is a view of Drakes Estero, an outstanding kayaking location; the walk from the turnoff to the ridge is just .6 mile. From there you turn right and walk 1.4 miles to the waterfront bordering Estero de Limantour. This is a beautiful spot, and we suggest you get an early start so you can enjoy it fully without having to rush to beat darkness on the 4.4-mile return trip. To the south is a good view of the regeneration of coastal foothills largely devoured in the wildfire of October 1995.

Location: In Point Reyes National Seashore in northwest Marin County; map E1-Marin, grid a0.

User groups: Hikers, horses, and mountain bikes (restricted at Drakes Head). The first two miles are wheelchair accessible, with assistance. No dogs.

Permits: No permits are required. Parking and access are free.

Maps: For a free map, write to Point Reyes National Seashore at the address below. Ask the USGS for a topographic map of the Drakes Bay area.

Directions: From U.S. 101 in Marin, take the Sir Francis Drake Boulevard exit and drive about 20 miles west on Sir Francis Drake Boulevard to the town of Olema. Turn right on Highway 1 and drive a short distance to Bear Valley Road. Turn left on Bear Valley Road and drive two miles. Turn left on Sir Francis Drake Highway and drive 7.5 miles to Estero Road on the left. Turn left and drive one mile to the parking area.

Contact: Superintendent, Point Reyes National Seashore, Point Reyes, CA 94956. Bear Valley Visitor Center, tel. (415) 663-1092 or fax (415) 663-8132.

7 South Beach Trail

0.1 mi/0.25 hr

If you desire miles of untouched beachfront, you've come to the right place. The Point Reyes beach extends for nearly 10 miles, all of it pristine with surf that rolls on endlessly. This short trail leads to South Beach, about three miles north of the Point Reyes Lighthouse. The beach makes a good picnic site where you can usually walk your dog on the sand (leashed, of course), and is one of the few places at Point Reyes where dogs are permitted (note that dogs may not be allowed at certain times of the year in order to protect marine mammals.) For the best stroll, walk south for about a mile to an expanse of sand dunes. It is wise to call ahead for weather conditions, as low fog is common, especially during the summer. A word of warning: Do not swim or bodysurf here. This stretch of coast is known for its treacherous undertow, the kind that can trap even the strongest swimmers, pulling people under and pushing them out to sea, despite their attempts to swim back to the beach.

Location: In Point Reyes National Seashore in northwest Marin County; map E1-Marin, grid a0.

User groups: Hikers, dogs, and horses. No mountain bikes. No wheelchair facilities.

Permits: No permits are required. Parking and access are free.

Maps: For a free map, write to Point Reyes National Seashore at the address below. Ask the USGS for a topographic map of the Drakes Bay area.

Directions: From U.S. 101 in Marin, take the Sir Francis Drake Boulevard exit and drive about 20 miles west on Sir Francis Drake Boulevard to the town of Olema. Turn right on Highway 1 and drive a short distance to Bear Valley Road. Turn left on Bear Valley Road and drive two miles. Turn left on Sir Francis Drake Highway and drive 11.6 miles to the access turnoff for the South Beach parking lot on the right. Turn right and drive to the parking lot for South Beach.

Contact: Superintendent, Point Reyes National Seashore, Point Reyes, CA 94956; Bear Valley Visitor Center, tel. (415) 663-1092 or fax (415) 663-8132.

8 Point Reyes Lighthouse
0.8 mi/0.5 hr

There may be no better place on land from which to watch migrating whales. From Point Reyes you scan the ocean, searching for what looks like a little puff of smoke on the water's surface: a whale spout. When you find one, you zoom in closer, perhaps using binoculars. If you are lucky, you might even get a tail salute. The chances are good, because 21,000 gray whales migrate past here every winter on the great whale highway just offshore of Point Reyes. The trail to the lookout is short and paved and includes a dramatic descent on a railed stairway. On the way back, of course, you face a modest climb, steep for some, so stop to pant a bit at the three rest stops. On clear weekends, particularly in winter, the place can be crowded. A fence on the edge of the cliff keeps visitors from falling overboard from one of the most dramatic coastal lookouts anywhere. Sunsets are unforgettable.

Location: In Point Reyes National Seashore in northwest Marin County; map E1-Marin, grid a0.

User groups: Hikers and mountain bikes (bikes are restricted from the stairs). Partially accessible to wheelchairs. No dogs or horses.

Permits: No permits are required. Parking and access are free. A national park day-use fee may be charged.

Maps: For a free map, write to Point Reyes National Seashore at the address below. Ask the USGS for a topographic map of the Drakes Bay area.

Directions: From U.S. 101 in Marin, take the Sir Francis Drake Boulevard exit and drive about 20 miles west on Sir Francis Drake Boulevard to the town of Olema. Turn right on Highway 1 and drive a short distance to Bear Valley Road. Turn left on Bear Valley Road and drive two miles. Turn left on Sir Francis Drake Highway and drive 17.6 miles. The road dead-ends at the parking area for the Point Reyes Lighthouse.

Contact: Superintendent, Point Reyes National Seashore, Point Reyes, CA 94956; Bear Valley Visitor Center, tel. (415) 663-1092 or fax (415) 663-8132.

9 Chimney Rock Trail
2.8 mi/1.25 hrs

A lot of visitors miss out on Chimney Rock because of its proximity to the Point Reyes Lighthouse, the feature destination of the national seashore. But the Chimney Rock lookout is easy to reach (it's about a half-hour hike), and the trail accesses a cutoff to a vista that is nearly the equal of that from the lighthouse. From the parking area, the trail is routed 1.4 miles to land's end. Chimney Rock, or at least what is supposed to be Chimney Rock, sits right offshore. Just beyond the halfway point to land's end, hikers can take a short cutoff trail that provides great views of the Pacific Ocean. During the winter, especially between late December and March, this is a great spot to watch for the spouts of migrating whales. Another bonus is that on the way back you can complete the last .8 mile on a loop trail, so you don't have to walk the same route you followed on the way in. One note: At the end of the trail, where a wooden guardrail keeps people from falling over the edge, you will look down at an assortment of coastal rocks and ask, "So, which one of those suckers is Chimney Rock?" Good question. Like most visitors, we never figured it out.

Location: In Point Reyes National Seashore in northwest Marin County; map E1-Marin, grid a0.

User groups: Hikers and mountain bikes. The first quarter mile of the trail is wheelchair accessible. No dogs or horses.

Permits: No permits are required. Parking and access are free.

Maps: For a free map, write to Point Reyes National Seashore at the address below. Ask the USGS for a topographic map of the Drakes Bay area.

Directions: From U.S. 101 in Marin, take the Sir Francis Drake Boulevard exit and drive about 20 miles west on Sir Francis Drake Boulevard to the town of Olema. Turn right on Highway 1 and drive a short distance to Bear Valley Road. Turn left on Bear Valley Road and drive two miles. Turn left on Sir Francis Drake Highway and drive 17.4 miles to Chimney Rock Road on the left. Turn left and drive one mile to the parking area and trailhead.

Contact: Superintendent, Point Reyes National Seashore, Point Reyes, CA 94956; Bear Valley Visitor Center, tel. (415) 663-1092 or fax (415) 663-8132.

🔟 Sir Francis Drake Trail
1.9 mi/1.0 hr

Hey, this spot is not exactly a secret. In fact, you might as well stand on the Golden Gate Bridge with a megaphone and announce its existence to the world. At the trailhead, for instance, you will discover a large parking lot and visitor center, complete with exhibits, maps, and books (maybe even this one). The trail traces the back of the arcing beaches along Drakes Bay, providing scenic lookouts onto the bay's protected waters. The trail continues to the mouth of Drakes Estero, then returns via an inland loop that includes a short climb up, then down, a waterfront bluff. This is one of the more popular hikes at Point Reyes National Seashore, and why not? It is an easy walk, provides great scenic beauty, and traces three habitats: beach frontage, the mouth of a lagoon, and hillside bluffs. Just don't expect solitude.

Location: In Point Reyes National Seashore in northwest Marin County; map E1-Marin, grid a0.

User groups: Hikers and mountain bikes. No dogs or horses. No wheelchair facilities.

Permits: No permits are required. Parking and access are free.

Maps: For a free map, write to Point Reyes National Seashore at the address below. Ask the USGS for a topographic map of the Drakes Bay area.

Directions: From U.S. 101 in Marin, take the Sir Francis Drake Boulevard exit and drive about 20 miles west on Sir Francis Drake Boulevard to the town of Olema. Turn right on Highway 1 and drive a short distance to Bear Valley Road. Turn left on Bear Valley Road and drive two miles. Turn left on Sir Francis Drake Highway and drive 11.1 miles and look for the sign indicating a left turn to a visitor center. Turn left and drive 1.2 miles to the parking lot at the Kenneth Patrick Visitor Center and the trailhead.

Contact: Superintendent, Point Reyes National Seashore, Point Reyes, CA 94956; Bear Valley Visitor Center, tel. (415) 663-1092 or fax (415) 663-8132.

🔟🔟 Muddy Hollow Loop
7.1 mi/3.25 hrs

This can be a wondrous coastal loop hike. The Muddy Hollow Loop is routed through various settings and terrain but starts and ends right on the beach. The most striking element of the hike is witnessing the regenerative powers of the land, as these coastal foothills—ravaged by the wildfire of October 1995—are now blooming and revegetating. This is also the best place in the park to see the exotic fallow deer, which look like half moose and half elk, often pure white, with strange antlers. Elk have also been transplanted here and are forming a new herd. From the trailhead at Limantour Beach, you hike north up Muddy Hollow, a shallow valley that drains rainfall into the Estero de Limantour. After 1.4 miles, turn left on Muddy Hollow "Road" and hike 2.1 miles. All of this area was devoured by the wildfire in October 1995. Here the trail crosses the coastal hills, climbing to about 300 feet, then dropping into another valley and crossing Glenbrook Creek. Seeing the remnants of fire damage being overcome by budding plant life can leave a profound and lasting impact. Turn left at the Glenbrook/Estero Trail, which leads back to the parking area over the course of 3.9 miles. The latter sector traces the shore of the Estero, a serene setting on calm, blue-sky days. From the Limantour parking area, this is also an excellent jump-off spot for canoeing and kayaking. The Estero de Limantour is protected by the narrow Limantour sand spit.

Location: In Point Reyes National Seashore at Limantour Beach in northwest Marin County; map E1-Marin, grid a0.

User groups: Hikers and horses. No dogs, mountain bikes, or wheelchair access.

Permits: No permits are required. Parking and access are free.

Maps: For a free map, write to Point Reyes National Seashore at the address below. Ask the USGS for a topographic map of the Drakes Bay area.

Directions: From U.S. 101 in Marin, take the Sir Francis Drake Boulevard exit and drive about 20 miles west on Sir Francis Drake Boulevard to the town of Olema. Turn right on Highway 1 and drive 100 yards. Turn left on Bear Valley Road and drive north for two miles (you pass the visitor center on your left) to Limantour Road. Turn left and drive 7.6 miles to Limantour Beach and the trailhead.

Contact: Superintendent, Point Reyes National Seashore, Point Reyes, CA 94956; Bear Valley Visitor Center, tel. (415) 663-1092 or fax (415) 663-8132.

12 Coast Trail
16.1 mi one way/ 2.0-plus days

Of the handful of overnight hiking trips available in the Bay Area, the Coast Trail provides the most extended tour into a land of charm. Located north of Bolinas on the remote Marin Coast, the trail offers camps at ocean bluffs, great ridge lookouts, coastal lakes, a beach with sculptured rocks and tide pools, and a rare coastal waterfall. This continuous backcountry route is 16.1 miles long, enough to allow lingering hikers to spend a weekend at it (Friday evening through Sunday) and short enough for the ambitious to tackle in a single day. There are only a few catches: You need a hiking partner who will double as a shuttle driver so you can leave a car at each end of the trail. Reservations are required for each camp, tel. (415) 663-8054, for $10 per night, four-day maximum stay. You'll need to come prepared to cook your food using a small backpack stove, not a campfire. And tents are recommended because the coastal weather is the most unpredictable in the Bay Area—clear, calm, and warm one day, then suddenly foggy, windy, moist, and clammy the next.

The best trailhead for the Coast Trail is at the Point Reyes Hostel, from where you will hike north to south, keeping the wind at your back and out of your face. The first camp, Coast Camp, is an easy 2.8 miles, ideal for those heading out on a Friday evening after work. As you hike in, you'll have a panoramic view of the reborn coastal foothills that were burned in the wildfire of October 1995, though luckily the campground and trail were untouched. The sound of ocean waves will waft you to sleep, or in some sensitive cases, keep you awake. The next day you will hike south, getting glimpses along the way of Sculptured Beach, with its magnificent rock stacks and tunnels. There are great cutoff trails along the Coast Trail to Sculptured Beach, Kelham Beach, and Arch Rock. It continues south to Wildcat Camp, set on a bluff overlooking the ocean for a 7.8-mile trip for day two. On day three, figure on a 5.5-mile closeout with plenty of sideshows. You will hike past a series of coastal lakes, including nearby Wildcat Lake and little Ocean Lake, and have the opportunity to see Alamere Falls, a drop-dead gorgeous waterfall that tumbles to the beach. After climbing to a short ridge, you will skirt above Pelican Lake and along the northern shore of Bass Lake. The trail then heads up a coastal hill, topping out at 563 feet, before lateraling down a canyon and back to ocean bluffs. Following the trail, you turn left and in a mile arrive at the Palomarin Trailhead. You will be ready to reach your shuttle car and head for the barn. If you have a shuttle partner, this is one of the Bay Area's greatest hikes.

Location: In Point Reyes National Seashore in northwest Marin County; map E1-Marin, grid a0.

User groups: Hikers and horses. Mountain bikes are permitted only from the Laguna Trailhead to the Coast Campground and are otherwise prohibited. Partially accessible to wheelchair users who have assistance. No dogs.

Permits: Parking and access are free, but camping requires a reservation, tel.(415) 663-8054, and a fee of $10 per night for one to eight people.

Maps: For a free map, write to Point Reyes National Seashore at the address below. Ask the USGS for topographic maps of the Inverness and Double Point areas.

Directions: From U.S. 101 in Marin, take the Sir Francis Drake Boulevard exit and drive about 20 miles west on Sir Francis Drake Boulevard to the town of Olema. Turn right on Highway 1 and drive about 100 yards. Turn left at Bear Valley Road and drive north for two miles (take the cutoff on the left to the Bear Valley Visitor Center to get your permits) to Limantour Road. Turn left and drive six miles. Turn left on the access road for the Point Reyes Hostel. The trailhead is on the right just before the hostel.

Contact: Superintendent, Point Reyes National Seashore, Point Reyes, CA 94956; Bear Valley Visitor Center, tel. (415) 663-1092 or (415) 663-8054, or fax (415) 663-8132.

13 Laguna Loop Trail
5.5 mi/2.5 hrs

The Laguna Loop Trail allows hikers to witness an amazing process known as the genesis effect, in which land devoured by fire is now being reborn. The trailhead is just .2 mile down the road from the Point Reyes Hostel, adjacent to the park's Environmental Education Center. From there the trail continues 1.8 miles up to Inverness Ridge, with great views of Drakes Bay on the way. At the ridge, you turn right and hike .7 mile toward Mount Wittenberg, at 1,407 feet the highest point at Point Reyes National Seashore. On the north flank of Mount Wittenberg, hikers should turn right on the Fire Lane Trail, which loops back around for three miles to the Laguna Trailhead. This excellent loop hike entails a bit of a climb and offers Pacific lookouts, yet is short enough to complete in a few hours.

Location: In Point Reyes National Seashore in northwest Marin County; map E1-Marin, grid a0.

User groups: Hikers and horses. Mountain bikes are permitted only from the Laguna Trailhead to the Coast Campground and are otherwise prohibited. No dogs. No wheelchair facilities.

Permits: No permits are required. Parking and access are free.

Maps: For a free map, write to Point Reyes National Seashore at the address below. Ask the USGS for a topographic map of the Inverness area.

Directions: From U.S. 101 in Marin, take the Sir Francis Drake Boulevard exit and drive about 20 miles west on Sir Francis Drake Boulevard to the town of Olema. Turn right on Highway 1 and drive about 100 yards. Turn left at Bear Valley Road and drive north for two miles to Limantour Road. Turn left and drive six miles. Turn left on the access road for the Point Reyes Hostel and drive .2 mile past the hostel to the trailhead on the right side of the road.

Contact: Superintendent, Point Reyes National Seashore, Point Reyes, CA 94956; Bear Valley Visitor Center, tel. (415) 663-1092 or fax (415) 663-8132.

14 Mount Wittenberg Loop
4.5 mi/2.5 hrs

This one of the best short hikes amid the entire Point Reyes National Seashore, providing a route through deep forest, a climb with a steady grade, and magnificent lookouts of Drakes Bay to the west and the Olema Valley to the east. The destination is Mount Wittenberg, the highest point in the park at 1,407 feet, but the best views are from the ridge just west of the rounded summit. After parking at Bear Valley Visitor Center, a huge parking lot, start the trip by taking the Bear Valley Trail, located at the south end of the parking area. Hike on the Bear Valley Trail for just .2 mile, and then bear right at the cutoff for the Sky Trail. From here, it is a 1.4-mile hike with a climb of 1,200 feet, but easily handled by those in decent condition with a steady grade, passing through old-growth forest, lush ravines and with occasional peephole lookouts to Olema Valley. It rises to the foot of Mount Wittenberg, and with another 100-foot climb, a cutoff trail takes you to the rounded summit. From here you return to Sky Trail and walk southwest .4 mile to Meadow Trail. In the process, there are dramatic views of Drakes Bay to the west, and some hidden meadows to the east, where white deer can often be spotted. You'll also have a panoramic shot of the coastal foothills, which are recovering from the wildfire of October 1995. From Meadow Trail it is an easy downhill tromp, 1.5 miles, back down to Bear Valley Trail. There you turn left, the trail widens and flattens, and you walk out .8 mile to the parking lot. There you have it—to paradise and back in just a few hours.

Location: In Point Reyes National Seashore near Olema in northwest Marin County; map E1-Marin, grid a0.

User groups: Hikers and horses. No dogs or mountain bikes. No wheelchair facilities.

Permits: No permits are required. Parking and access are free.

Maps: For a free map, write to Point Reyes National Seashore at the address below. Ask the USGS for a topographic map of the Inverness area.

Directions: From U.S. 101 in Marin, take the Sir Francis Drake Boulevard exit and drive about 20 miles west on Sir Francis Drake Boulevard to the town of Olema. Turn right on Highway 1 and drive about 100 yards. Turn left at Bear Valley Road and drive north .7 mile. Turn left at the Seashore Information sign and drive to the parking lot for the Bear Valley Visitor Center. The trailhead is at the south end of the parking lot.

Contact: Superintendent, Point Reyes National Seashore, Point Reyes, CA 94956; Bear Valley Visitor Center, tel. (415) 663-1092 or fax (415) 663-8132.

15 Bear Valley Trail
8.2 mi/4.0 hrs

The Bear Valley Trail has all the ingredients needed to earn a 10 rating. Starting with a pretty route through forests, it leads past Divide Meadow to Bear Valley then down along Coast Creek to the beach, Arch Rock, and the Sea Tunnel, where the views are marvelous. So, you ask, why is it rated a 7? The answer is that the trail is actually a park service road made of compressed rock, and it gets a ton of traffic, including bicycles. This is the most heavily used trail in Point Reyes National Seashore. The best element is that it is wheelchair accessible and, in fact, one of the prettiest wheelchair routes in California. Just put it in power drive, for there's a modest 215-foot climb from park headquarters to Divide Meadow. Wheelchairs and bikes are permitted to the Glen Camp Trail, 3.2 miles from park headquarters. After that, you hike down the Coast Creek drainage on a .7-mile trek to the beach.

Location: In Point Reyes National Seashore near Olema in northwest Marin County; map E1-Marin, grid a0.

User groups: Hikers, horses (weekdays only), and mountain bikes (first three miles only). The 1.5-mile trail to Divide Meadow is wheelchair accessible with a lot of assistance. No dogs.

Permits: No permits are required. Parking and access are free.

Maps: For a free map, write to Point Reyes National Seashore at the address below. Ask the USGS for a topographic map of the Inverness area.

Directions: From U.S. 101 in Marin, take the Sir Francis Drake Boulevard exit and drive about 20 miles west on Sir Francis Drake Boulevard to the town of Olema. Turn right on Highway 1 and drive about 100 yards. Turn left at Bear Valley Road and drive north .7 mile. Turn left at the Seashore Information sign and drive to the parking lot for the Bear Valley Visitor Center.

Contact: Superintendent, Point Reyes National Seashore, Point Reyes, CA 94956; Bear Valley Visitor Center, tel. (415) 663-1092 or fax (415) 663-8132.

ups and downs near its southern junction with the Five Brooks Trailhead.

Location: In Point Reyes National Seashore near Olema in northwest Marin County; map E1-Marin, grid a0.

User groups: Hikers and horses. No dogs or mountain bikes. No wheelchair facilities.

Permits: No permits are required. Parking and access are free.

Maps: For a free map, write to Point Reyes National Seashore at the address below. Ask the USGS for a topographic map of the Inverness area.

Directions: From U.S. 101 in Marin, take the Sir Francis Drake Boulevard exit and drive about 20 miles west on Sir Francis Drake Boulevard to the town of Olema. Turn right on Highway 1 and drive about 100 yards. Turn left at Bear Valley Road and drive north .7 mile. Turn left at the Seashore Information sign and drive to the parking lot for the Bear Valley Visitor Center.

Contact: Superintendent, Point Reyes National Seashore, Point Reyes, CA 94956; Bear Valley Visitor Center, tel. (415) 663-1092 or fax (415) 663-8132.

16 Rift Zone Trail

5.2 mi one way/2.25 hrs

Some of the best advice we ever got was this: Don't let school interfere with your education. Well, the Rift Zone Trail provides a lesson from the University of Nature, with one of the world's classic examples of an earthquake fault line: the San Andreas Fault. From park headquarters it's a 5.2-mile one-way hike to the Five Brooks Trailhead, best completed with a shuttle car. Along the way, the trail traces along Olema Creek, where horizontal movement of 21 feet was recorded during the 1906 earthquake. Much evidence of earthquake activity is visible on this trail, including parallel ridges, but the most obvious sign is the clear difference in vegetation types on each side of the fault. The trail gets heavy use, has no difficult grades, and requires only a few short

17 Olema Valley

5.3 mi one way/2.25 hrs

The phenomenon of two parallel creeks running in opposite directions is the featured attraction of the Olema Valley Trail, which starts at the Five Brooks Trailhead (elevation 180 feet) and runs adjacent to the San Andreas Fault rift zone. Two earth plates moving in opposite directions created the fault line, resulting in the strange marvel of Olema Creek and Pine Gulch Creek. From the trailhead it's 1.3 miles to the headwaters of Pine Gulch Creek. From there you can hike southward for four miles along the pretty creek before the trail ends at Highway 1. Most hikers turn back long before that, but with a partner and a shuttle car, it makes a great one-way hike, 5.3 miles in all.

Location: In Point Reyes National Seashore south of Olema in northwest Marin County; map E1-Marin, grid a0.
User groups: Hikers, horses, and mountain bikes. No dogs. No wheelchair facilities.
Permits: No permits are required. Parking and access are free.
Maps: For a free map, write to Point Reyes National Seashore at the address below. Ask the USGS for a topographic map of the Bolinas area.
Directions: From U.S. 101 in Marin, take the Sir Francis Drake Boulevard exit and drive about 20 miles west on Sir Francis Drake Boulevard to the town of Olema. Turn left on Highway 1 and drive 3.6 miles to the Five Brooks Trailhead, located on the west side of the road.
Contact: Superintendent, Point Reyes National Seashore, Point Reyes, CA 94956; Bear Valley Visitor Center, tel. (415) 663-1092 or fax (415) 663-8132.

18 Barnabe Trail

6.0 mi/3.5 hrs

Samuel P. Taylor State Park is a beautiful redwood retreat set along the primary access road to Point Reyes. The Barnabe Trail, a steep fire road through the park, climbs 2.5 miles and 1,300 feet up to Barnabe Peak (1,466 feet in elevation). It's a love/hate deal for hikers because the trail is steep and not all that intimate, yet the summit is a scenic viewpoint, with Inverness Ridge, Point Reyes, and the Pacific Ocean off to the west. On clear days it can be an eye-popping lookout. From the peak it is also common on warm days to see hawks and vultures floating aloft on rising thermals with nary a wing beat.

First note that the trailhead is not at park headquarters or the campground. It rather is located at Devils Gulch Horse Camp, located one mile west of the park entrance. Park in the dirt pullout on the south side of Sir Francis Drake, then walk across the road to the paved horse camp access road. The trailhead

is on the right at Devils Gulch Creek. Here your adventure begins.

The landscape of the park changes dramatically over the course of this hike. The canyon bottoms and north-facing slopes are cool and shaded, marked with coastal redwoods. Look for the sign "Bill's Trail to Barnabe Peak." As you begin your climb, note the cutoff trail to Stairstep Falls, well worth the trip, despite the debris from fallen trees near the plunge pool. As you climb out of the canyon on the 1,300-foot ascent to the summit, you will rise to open grasslands that are always lush and green by spring. Since the trail is a dirt service road, leashed dogs and bicycles are permitted, and all users are urged to share the route using the utmost courtesy. From the top, the last leg of this loop hike is a fast tromp downhill, just two miles. Whatever you do, don't do this hike in the opposite direction, forcing a hard climb and then a very gradual descent.
Location: In Samuel P. Taylor State Park west of San Rafael; map E1-Marin, grid a1.
User groups: Hikers, dogs, and mountain bikes (bikes are not permitted on spur trails). The park headquarters is wheelchair accessible, but the trail is not. No horses.
Permits: A $2 state park day-use fee is charged at the entrance station.
Maps: A small map/brochure is available for a fee at the entrance station to Samuel P. Taylor State Park. Ask the USGS for a topographic map of the San Geronimo area.
Directions: From U.S. 101 in Marin, take the Sir Francis Drake Boulevard exit. Turn west on this road and drive 14.5 miles to the park entrance on the left. To reach the trailhead, continue west for one mile to the dirt pullout on the left side of the road. Park, cross the road, and hike up the paved access road to Devils Gulch Horse Camp to the trailhead on the right.
Contact: Samuel P. Taylor State Park, P.O. Box 251, Lagunitas, CA 94938; tel. (415) 488-9897 or fax (415) 488-4315; Marin District Headquarters, tel. (415) 893-1580.

19 Pioneer Tree Trail

2.0 mi/1.0 hr

If you like big trees and a simple, quiet walk, the Pioneer Tree Trail in Samuel P. Taylor State Park will provide it. This loop circles through the park's prize grove of coastal redwoods, the species that produces the tallest trees in the world. The trailhead is at the south side of Lagunitas Creek at the Redwood Grove Picnic Area, about .25 mile from park headquarters. From there you hike up Wildcat Canyon, then across to the Irving Creek drainage, and follow that creek down near its confluence with Lagunitas Creek. The last .5 mile traces the southern edge of the creek back to the picnic area. It's a pleasant hike on a soft dirt trail, surrounded by the scent of redwoods, and includes a 400-foot climb and drop. Bicycles are prohibited on this route from all but the .5-mile service road along Lagunitas Creek.

Location: In Samuel P. Taylor State Park west of San Rafael; map E1-Marin, grid a1.

User groups: Hikers only. The park headquarters is wheelchair accessible, but the trail is not. No dogs, horses, or mountain bikes.

Permits: A $2 state park day-use fee is charged at the entrance station.

Maps: A small map/brochure is available for a fee at the entrance station to Samuel P. Taylor State Park. Ask the USGS for a topographic map of the San Geronimo area.

Directions: From U.S. 101 in Marin, take the Sir Francis Drake Boulevard exit. Turn west on this road and drive 14.5 miles to the park entrance on the left.

Contact: Samuel P. Taylor State Park, P.O. Box 251, Lagunitas, CA 94938; tel. (415) 488-9897 or fax (415) 488-4315; California State Parks, Marin District, tel. (415) 893-1580.

20 Bolinas Ridge

10.2 mi one way/4.5 hrs

Spectacular lookouts across miles of foothills as well as an excellent mountain bike route make this a premier trip. It is a perfect one-way hike if you arrange to have a shuttle car waiting for you at trail's end. The surrounding landscape offers a heavily wooded slope and Kent Lake to the east, Olema Valley and Inverness Ridge to the west, and Bolinas Lagoon and the Pacific Ocean to the south. The trail crosses atop Bolinas Ridge, through some of the most remote land in the Golden Gate National Recreation Area. The trailhead near Olema starts with a 700-foot climb in the first 2.5 miles. Many hikers call it quits here, stopping to enjoy the view, then turning around and heading home. Continue, though, and the trail keeps climbing, all the way to 1,329 feet in the first four miles. From that point on, the hike becomes much easier, with only moderate drops and ascents over the last 6.2 miles to the trail's end on Bolinas-Fairfax Road. Mountain biking is permitted, but hikers need not fear: the trail is not only wide enough for everyone, but has very few hidden turns. Note: Some people (especially bicyclists) prefer to complete this trail in the opposite direction in order to avoid the climb.

Location: In northwest Marin County west of San Rafael; map E1-Marin, grid a0.

User groups: Hikers, dogs, horses, and mountain bikes. No wheelchair facilities.

Permits: No permits are required. Parking and access are free.

Maps: This trail is included on a free map of Point Reyes National Seashore; write to Superintendent, Point Reyes National Seashore, Point Reyes, CA 94956. Ask the USGS for topographic maps of the Inverness, San Geronimo, and Bolinas areas.

Directions: From U.S. 101 in Marin, take the Sir Francis Drake Boulevard exit. Turn west on this road and drive 18 miles (3.4 miles past the entrance station to Samuel P. Taylor State Park). The trailhead is on the left side of the road. Park along the road.

Contact: Golden Gate National Recreation Area, Fort Mason, Building 201, San Francisco, CA 94123; tel. (415) 556-0560 or fax (415) 331-1428.

21 Kent Dam Trail
1.8 mi/1.0 hr

Most people are astounded the first time they see Kent Lake, for they have no idea such a huge lake is secreted away in a Marin canyon. But here it is, nearly four miles from north to south, with an additional large arm extending east into Big Carson Creek. One reason the lake remains little known to outsiders is that the parking at the trailhead is quite poor, just a few spaces along Sir Francis Drake Boulevard. From there you hike on a ranch road along Lagunitas Creek for about a mile, arriving at the east side of Peters Dam. By damming the canyon on Lagunitas Creek, the Marin Water District created this massive lake and at the same time annihilated the runs of steelhead and silver salmon by dewatering the stream and blocking the migratory path to spawning areas. No water contact is permitted, but quite a few people go swimming here anyway in the summer. Some get caught and cited when water district officials make the occasional patrol. Fishing is only fair for bass, and the Department of Fish and Game never makes stocks.

Location: In northwest Marin County west of San Rafael; map E1-Marin, grid a1.

User groups: Hikers, dogs, and mountain bikes. No horses. No wheelchair facilities.

Permits: No permits are required. Groups are limited to 19 people. Parking and access are free.

Maps: This trail is included on a free map of Point Reyes National Seashore; write to Superintendent, Point Reyes National Seashore, Point Reyes, CA 94956. Ask the USGS for topographic maps of the San Geronimo and Bolinas areas.

Directions: From U.S. 101 in Marin, take the Sir Francis Drake Boulevard exit. Turn west on this road and drive about 12 miles, just past Shafter Bridge, which spans Paper Mill Creek. Park here and look for the locked gate at the entrance to the trailhead on the left.

Contact: Sky Oaks Ranger Station, tel. (415) 945-1181; Marin Municipal Water District, 220 Nellen Avenue, Corte Madera, CA 94925; tel. (415) 945-1195.

22 Alamere Falls Trail
8.4 mi/4.0 hrs

The water from Alamere Falls tumbles down Alamere Creek and over an ocean bluff, cascading 40 feet to the beach below and into the Pacific Ocean. It is one of the few ocean bluff waterfalls anywhere, and after winter rains it is amazing how full, big, and beautiful it can become. One of my favorite things to do is to lie prone on the rock right at the brink of the falls, peering over the cliffs, watching the water droplets fall to the plunge pool below. The changing course of the water through sand on the beach provides a fast-moving mosaic. The best starting point is the Palomarin Trailhead, from which you'll hike the southern end of the Coast Trail. The trail is routed along the ocean for about a mile, then heads up in the coastal hills to an elevation of about 500 feet and back down westward for two miles to the falls' access point. In the process, you will skirt the northern end of Bass Lake, and a mile later, along the ridge overlooking larger Pelican Lake. When you reach Alamere Creek, there is an unsigned cut-off route on the southern side of the creek here. There is no sign and there is also no official trail maintained by the park. Instead, many people take this route and there is a well-worn path that leads down Alamere creek to the waterfall. It leads to a series of plunge pools and then ultimately to the cliff and brink of the falls. This is not an official park trail, and rangers urge visitors to hike instead to Wildcat Camp, drop down to the beach, and hike south on the beach to the base of Alamere Falls for the best views.

Location: In Point Reyes National Seashore northwest of Bolinas; map E1-Marin, grid b0.

User groups: Hikers and horses. No dogs or mountain bikes. No wheelchair facilities.

Permits: No permits are required. Parking and access are free.

Maps: For a free map, write to Point Reyes National Seashore at the address below. Ask the USGS for topographic maps of the Bolinas and Double Point areas.

Directions: From U.S. 101 in Marin, take the Sir Francis Drake Boulevard exit and drive about 20 miles west on Sir Francis Drake Boulevard to the town of Olema. Turn left on Highway 1 and drive 8.9 miles south to Horseshoe Hill Road (note that the Olema sign is commonly stolen or missing, allegedly by local residents who do not want out-of-towners discovering the area). Turn right and drive 2.1 miles to Mesa Road. Turn right and drive 5.8 miles (past an area known as "The Towers" from all the antennas) to the Palomarin Trailhead.

Contact: Superintendent, Point Reyes National Seashore, Point Reyes, CA 94956; Bear Valley Visitor Center, tel. (415) 663-1092 or fax (415) 663-8132.

23 Alpine/Kent Lake Pump Trail

6.0 mi/3.0 hrs

Hiking this trail can make you feel as if you're exploring a slice of Tennessee wilderness, not a location just five miles from the Marin suburbs. Tracing the ins and outs of Lagunitas Creek amid oak and madrone woodlands, the trail is quite pretty. It is actually a service road for the pump station between Alpine Dam and the headwaters of Kent Lake, following Lagunitas Creek as it pours northward. The trailhead is located at the north side of Alpine Dam; from there the route follows a gentle grade down along the stream. It's about 1.5 miles to the headwaters of Kent Lake; another .5 mile after that you will begin seeing the main lake. Most people make the lake their final destination and return to the trailhead for a total of six miles. The trails does continue 1.6 miles past the lake, however, ending at an elevation of 403 feet overlooking the lake; very few people continue this far. Throughout this area, you can take a short departure from the trail in the first mile to find an ideal setting for a picnic along Lagunitas Creek. Many trails require hikers to make a great physical investment in return for peace and solitude. Not this one.

Location: On the northwest slopes of Mount Tamalpais at Alpine Lake Dam; map E1-Marin, grid b1.

User groups: Hikers, dogs, horses, and mountain bikes. No wheelchair facilities.

Permits: No permits are required. Groups are limited to 19 people. Parking and access are free.

Maps: A hiking/biking map is available for a fee from the Marin Water District at the address below. A detailed hiking map of the area is available for a fee from Olmsted Brothers Map Company, P.O. Box 5351, Berkeley, CA 94705. Ask the USGS for a topographic map of the Bolinas area.

Directions: From U.S. 101 in Marin, take the Sir Francis Drake Boulevard exit and drive six miles west to the town of Fairfax. Look for the Fairfax sign and turn left (the road is unsigned); turn right immediately on Broadway Avenue. Drive one block to Bolinas Road. Turn left and drive west eight miles (continuing along Alpine Lake) to the Alpine Dam. Park on the right side of the road near the hairpin turn and look for the gated service road/trailhead.

Contact: Sky Oaks Ranger Station, tel. (415) 945-1181; Marin Municipal Water District, 220 Nellen Avenue, Corte Madera, CA 94925; tel. (415) 945-1195.

24 Cataract Falls

2.5 mi/1.5 hrs

Cataract Falls is not a single waterfall, but a series of cascades that rush down a beautifully wooded canyon set in the northwest slopes of Mount Tamalpais. And you pay for this one. The hike is quite challenging—er, make that steep— um, make that a real heart thumper. From the trailhead at the south end of Alpine Lake at elevation 644 feet, you face a 750-foot climb over the span of just a mile to reach the falls at 1,400 feet. That is why many hikers take the easier route from the Laurel Dell Trailhead, a 240-foot drop over .4 mile.

In late winter, especially when the skies have just cleared after heavy rains, the cascades in this canyon can look like something found in Hawaii. That is particularly true when rays of sunlight catch the droplets of water just right, making them sparkle. From top to bottom there's one cascade after another, ending with a silvery chute pouring into a plunge pool. This is the best-known fall in the region—so popular that finding a parking spot at the trailhead can be difficult on weekends. After getting your fill of this sight, return the way you came.

Location: On the northwest slopes of Mount Tamalpais at Alpine Lake Dam; map E1-Marin, grid b1.

User groups: Hikers and dogs. No horses or mountain bikes. No wheelchair facilities.

Permits: No permits are required. Groups are limited to 19 people. Parking and access are free.

Maps: A hiking/biking map is available for a fee from the Marin Water District at the address below. A detailed hiking map of the area is available for a fee from Olmsted Brothers Map Company, P.O. Box 5351, Berkeley, CA 94705. Ask the USGS for a topographic map of the Bolinas area.

Directions: From U.S. 101 in Marin, take the Sir Francis Drake Boulevard exit and drive six miles west to the town of Fairfax. Look for the Fairfax sign and turn left (the road is unsigned); turn right immediately onto Broadway Avenue. Drive one block to Bolinas Road. Turn left and drive west eight miles (continuing along Alpine Lake) to the Alpine Dam. Cross the dam and park at the pullouts along the hairpin turn. The trailhead is on the south side of the road.

Contact: Sky Oaks Ranger Station, tel. (415) 945-1181; Marin Municipal Water District, 220 Nellen Avenue, Corte Madera, CA 94925; tel. (415) 945-1195. Mount Tamalpais State Park, 801 Panoramic Highway, Mill Valley, CA 94941; tel. (415) 388-2070 or fax (415) 388-2968; California State Parks, Marin District, tel. (415) 893-1580.

25 Pine Mountain/ Carson Falls
3.0 mi/1.5 hrs

Your destination is Carson Falls, a set of small waterfalls that tumble into granite pools. The walk to this quiet, divine spot hidden on the north slopes of Mount Tamalpais is an easy stroll across hilly grasslands, often accompanied by a hawk or two floating about overhead, followed by a short jog down a canyon into the Carson Creek drainage.

The trailhead (1,078 feet) is adjacent to one of the better parking areas provided on lands administered by the Marin Water District. After parking, you cross Bolinas-Fairfax Road to reach the trailhead, Pine Mountain Road (a water district service road). The road climbs 400 feet over the course of a mile, reaching a junction with Oat Hill Road on the crest of a hill flanked on both sides by foothill grasslands. Turn left here, hike .3 mile, and turn right on the hiking trail (look for the power lines; that's where the trail is). The trail is routed .2 mile down to Carson Creek and the series of waterfalls. The lowest of the falls is a stunning, high silver stream that flows over a notch in a boulder and free-falls 30 feet into a beautiful pool. Of course, the cascades are best seen after a good rain, but there is usually at least a trickle of water into early summer. A trick here is when nearing the waterfalls at the bottom of the valley, hop across the stream and then work your way down on the far side. From here looking up, you get a perfect view of four waterfalls, chutes, and cascades, each pouring into pools through a beautiful rock canyon. The final fall is a 35-foot free fall, silver and powerful, where you can peer over its brink and look straight down, with adjacent color often added in cool months by nearby bright red toyon berries.

Location: On the northwest slopes of Mount Tamalpais west of Fairfax; map E1-Marin, grid b1.

User groups: Hikers, dogs, horses, and mountain bikes. No wheelchair facilities. Note that mountain bikes are allowed on Pine Mountain and Oat Hill Roads, but not on the hiking trail down to Carson Falls.

Permits: No permits are required. Groups are limited to 19 people. Parking and access are free.

Maps: A hiking/biking map is available for a fee from the Marin Water District at the address below. A detailed hiking map of the area is available for a fee from Olmsted Brothers Map Company, P.O. Box 5351, Berkeley, CA 94705. Ask the USGS for a topographic map of the Bolinas area.

Directions: From U.S. 101 in Marin, take the Sir Francis Drake Boulevard exit and drive six miles west to the town of Fairfax. Look for the Fairfax sign and turn left (the road is unsigned); turn right immediately on Broadway Avenue. Drive one block to Bolinas Road. Turn left and drive west for 3.8 miles (past the golf course) to the large dirt parking area on the left. The trailhead for Pine Mountain Road is across the road from the parking area.

Contact: Sky Oaks Ranger Station, tel. (415) 945-1181; Marin Municipal Water District, 220 Nellen Avenue, Corte Madera, CA 94925; tel. (415) 945-1195.

26 Two Lakes Trail

5.0 mi/2.5 hrs

There is no officially designated "Two Lakes Trail," so don't look for a sign. Enough people call this route by this name that it has become unofficially sanctioned. Instead, this loop hike—one of the Bay Area's best—is made up of a series of trails that lead past pretty Bon Tempe and Lagunitas Lakes, the focus of this adventure. No other hike in the Bay Area connects in such intimate fashion with some of the prettiest lakes around. The trailhead lies at elevation 740 feet at the Lagunitas Picnic Area, adjacent to Lagunitas Lake, the smallest of Marin County's eight lakes. From here walk around Lagunitas counterclockwise, eventu-

ally linking up with the Pilot Knob Trail. Turn left and hike past the parking area and connect with the Bon Tempe Shadyside Trail. This circles the lake, eventually leading all the way back to the parking area. A map will be very helpful, of course, so pick one up at the Sky Oaks Ranger Station.

Location: On the northwest slopes of Mount Tamalpais at Lagunitas Lake near San Anselmo; map E1-Marin, grid b1.

User groups: Hikers only. No dogs, horses, or mountain bikes. No wheelchair facilities.

Permits: A $4 day-use fee is charged per vehicle on weekends from April to October, $3 day on weekdays, and $3 on weekends from November to March. Groups are limited to 19 people.

Maps: A hiking/biking map is available for a fee from the Marin Water District at the address below. A detailed hiking map of the area is available for a fee from Olmsted Brothers Map Company, P.O. Box 5351, Berkeley, CA 94705. Ask the USGS for a topographic map of the Bolinas area.

Directions: From U.S. 101 in Marin, take the Sir Francis Drake Boulevard exit and drive six miles west to the town of Fairfax. Look for the Fairfax sign and turn left (the road is unsigned); turn right immediately on Broadway Avenue. Drive one block to Bolinas Road. Turn left and drive west for 1.5 miles to Sky Oaks Road on the left. Bear left and drive .5 mile to the entrance kiosk. After paying the day-use fee, drive .25 mile to a fork. Bear left at the fork to the Lake Lagunitas parking area and adjacent picnic area and trailhead.

Contact: Sky Oaks Ranger Station, tel. (415) 945-1181; Marin Municipal Water District, 220 Nellen Avenue, Corte Madera, CA 94925; tel. (415) 945-1195.

27 Deer Park Trail

2.0 mi/1.25 hrs

The trailhead at Deer Park is quite popular, but by taking the Deer Park Trail rather than one of the other options, you can find peace in addition to having quite a workout. You get both of these things because the trail climbs about 350 feet in less than a mile. That's steep, and this is one of those situations where you must pay for your pleasure. But pleasure you will get. As the trail rises up the slopes of Bald Hill, views open up around you, and not just of the surrounding countryside; it is common to see deer in this area, and wildflower blooms are quite good in the spring. If you want even more, you'll have an opportunity to link up with a spiderweb of other trails in the area.

Location: On the northwest slopes of Mount Tamalpais near San Anselmo; map E1-Marin, grid b2.

User groups: Hikers only. No dogs, horses, or mountain bikes. No wheelchair facilities.

Permits: No permits are required. Groups are limited to 19 people. Parking and access are free.

Maps: A hiking/biking map is available for a fee from the Marin Water District at the address below. A detailed hiking map of the area is available for a fee from Olmsted Brothers Map Company, P.O. Box 5351, Berkeley, CA 94705. Ask the USGS for a topographic map of the San Rafael area.

Directions: From U.S. 101 in Marin, take the Sir Francis Drake Boulevard exit and drive six miles west to the town of Fairfax. Look for the Fairfax sign and turn left (the road is unsigned); turn right immediately on Broadway Avenue. Drive one block to Bolinas Road, turn left, and drive west .5 mile to Porteous Avenue. Turn left on Porteous Avenue and drive to Deer County Park.

Contact: Sky Oaks Ranger Station, tel. (415) 945-1181; Marin Municipal Water District, 220 Nellen Avenue, Corte Madera, CA 94925; tel. (415) 945-1195.

28 Phoenix Lake Trail

2.7 mi/1.5 hrs

Of the eight lakes in Marin County, Phoenix is the least accessible. Not only is the parking

situation poor, but newcomers can have trouble finding the lake, an intolerable situation considering how beloved it is. The little 25-acre jewel set in a pocket just west of the town of Ross is indeed well loved. From Natalie Coffin Greene Park, it's an easy .2-mile walk to the lake. Stairs on one side of the small dam take visitors down to a trail at the water's edge. The distance around the entire lake is 2.3 miles. In the winter, the lake is stocked with trout twice a month, and in the spring, bass fishing can be decent. As at all Marin lakes, no one is permitted to make contact with the water.

Location: On the north slope of Mount Tamalpais near Ross; map E1-Marin, grid b2.

User groups: Hikers, leashed dogs, horses, and mountain bikes (restricted from the lake's southern shoreline). No wheelchair facilities.

Permits: No permits are required. Groups are limited to 19 people. Parking and access are free.

Maps: A hiking/biking map is available for a fee from the Marin Water District at the address below. A detailed hiking map of the area is available for a fee from Olmsted Brothers Map Company, P.O. Box 5351, Berkeley, CA 94705. Ask the USGS for a topographic map of the San Rafael area.

Directions: From U.S. 101 in Marin, take the Sir Francis Drake Boulevard exit and head west for 2.5 miles. Turn left on Lagunitas Road and drive 1.1 miles into Natalie Coffin Greene Park. The lake is .25 mile from the parking area. Parking is extremely limited.

Contact: Sky Oaks Ranger Station, tel. (415) 945-1181; Marin Municipal Water District, 220 Nellen Avenue, Corte Madera, CA 94925; tel. (415) 945-1195.

29 Dawn Falls

1.4 mi/0.75 hr

The Bay Area has many hidden waterfalls, but this one is both easy to reach and, in winter and spring, a beautiful and energizing sight. Dawn Falls, a 25-foot fountain of water, is best seen in the early morning, when rays of sunlight penetrate the atmosphere. Note, however, that in summer and fall, day after day of dry weather reduces the cascade to a trickle, and in drought years, it can go completely dry. At the trailhead, don't get confused and take the Baltimore Canyon Fire Road; that route is far less intimate than the Dawn Falls Trail, which probes a dense woodland, with model riparian habitat on each side of Larkspur Creek near the falls. This walk starts out easy and stays that way, even with the moderate 300-foot rise to the waterfall. On the way in, many don't expect the waterfall to be much, especially if the creek appears nothing but a tiny trickle. Surprise: In winter and early spring, it is very beautiful.

Location: On the eastern slopes of Mount Tamalpais near Larkspur; map E1-Marin, grid b2.

User groups: Hikers, dogs, horses (on the adjacent fire road), and mountain bikes. No wheelchair facilities.

Permits: No permits are required. Groups are limited to 19 people. Parking and access are free.

Maps: A hiking/biking map is available for a fee from the Marin Water District at the address below. A detailed hiking map of the area is available for a fee from Olmsted Brothers Map Company, P.O. Box 5351, Berkeley, CA 94705. Ask the USGS for a topographic map of the San Rafael area.

Directions: From U.S. 101 in Marin, take the Tamalpais Drive exit, and head west on Tamalpais Drive to Corte Madera Avenue. Turn right and drive about .5 mile; turn left on Madrone Avenue and drive to Valley Way. The trailhead is at the road's end.

Contact: Sky Oaks Ranger Station, tel. (415) 945-1181; Marin Municipal Water District, 220 Nellen Avenue, Corte Madera, CA 94925; tel. (415) 945-1195.

30 Shoreline Trail
5.0 mi/2.0 hrs

The Shoreline Trail is the best introduction to China Camp State Park a hiker could ask for. From the well-signed trailhead at the parking area, the trail meanders along the shore of San Pablo Bay, bordered by undisturbed hills on one side and waterfront on the other. The first mile provides good lookouts across the bay; the last .5 mile crosses a meadow, then runs adjacent to tidal areas, marshes, and wetlands, home to many species of waterfowl. The hike doesn't involve serious elevation gains or losses, so you won't face any surprise climbs on the way back. An option on the return trip is to take the Miwok Fire Trail, which loops back to headquarters with a 300-foot climb and drop.

Location: In China Camp State Park east of San Rafael; map E1-Marin, grid a3.

User groups: Hikers, horses, and mountain bikes. No dogs. No wheelchair facilities.

Permits: No permits are required. A $2 state park day-use fee is charged at the entrance station.

Maps: A small map/brochure is available for a fee at park headquarters or by contacting the State Parks district office at the address below. Ask the USGS for a topographic map of the San Quentin area.

Directions: From U.S. 101 in San Rafael, take the North San Pedro exit and drive east for four miles to the park entrance.

Contact: China Camp State Park, tel. (415) 456-0766; California State Parks, Marin District, 7665 Redwood Boulevard, Suite 150, Novato, CA 94945; tel. (415) 893-1580 or fax (415) 893-1583.

31 Bay View Trail
11.5 mi/4.5 hrs

The Bay View Trail is the most ambitious hike anywhere along the shore of San Pablo Bay. From China Camp Village start hiking out on the Shoreline Trail, then link the Peacock Gap Trail to the Bay View Trail to access the park's most remote reaches. The Bay View Trail climbs to about 600 feet, traversing much of China Camp in the process. To visit the highest point in the park, take the Back Ranch Fire Trail to the Ridge Fire Trail, for panoramic vistas of San Pablo Bay, San Francisco Bay, Mount St. Helena, Mount Diablo, Angel Island, and San Francisco. We recommend that you return to the trailhead by dropping down to the Back Ranch Meadows Campground and walking back on the Shoreline Trail. On our visit, a nearly tame deer bedded down in the meadow adjacent to the parking lot.

Location: In China Camp State Park east of San Rafael; map E1-Marin, grid b3.

User groups: Hikers, horses, and mountain bikes. No dogs. No wheelchair facilities.

Permits: No permits are required. A $2 day-use and parking fee is charged at China Camp Village.

Maps: A small map/brochure is available for a fee at park headquarters or by contacting the State Parks district office at the address below. Ask the USGS for a topographic map of the San Quentin area.

Directions: From U.S. 101 in San Rafael, take the North San Pedro exit and drive east for three miles to China Camp Village.

Contact: China Camp State Park, tel. (415) 456-0766; California State Parks, Marin District, 7665 Redwood Boulevard, Suite 150, Novato, CA 94945; tel. (415) 893-1580 or fax (415) 893-1583.

32 Audubon Canyon Ranch Trail

0.4 mi/0.25 hr

Here is a little slice of paradise, the premier place on the Pacific Coast to view herons and egrets, those large, graceful seabirds, as they court, mate, nest, and rear their young. From ranch headquarters the hike is short but steep, requiring about 20 minutes to reach the canyon overlook. Benches are provided for rest stops.

Scopes installed at the top can be used to peer across the valley and zero in on the giant nests in the redwoods. Bird-watchers might want to repeat this great trip again and again, tracking the mating process of the great birds. May and June are usually the best times to come. In May the eggs start hatching, and by June there can be as many as 200 hatchlings in the different nests. They eagerly await breakfast, lunch, and dinner, provided when their huge parents return from Bolinas Lagoon and vomit the goodies all over the nest. Hey, what's for dessert?

Special note: It is important to remember that Audubon Canyon Ranch is open only on weekends and holidays, 10 a.m. to 4 p.m., mid-March to mid-July through midsummer. It is closed the rest of the year.

Location: On the Marin coast near Bolinas Lagoon; map E1-Marin, grid b1.

User groups: Hikers only. No dogs, horses, or mountain bikes. No wheelchair facilities.

Permits: Entrance to the ranch is free, but donations are requested; $10 donation from families suggested. The ranch is open only on weekends and holidays from spring through midsummer.

Maps: A small trail map/brochure is available at ranch headquarters. Ask the USGS for a topographic map of the Bolinas area.

Directions: From U.S. 101 in Marin, take the Sir Francis Drake Boulevard exit and drive about 20 miles west on Sir Francis Drake Boulevard to the town of Olema. Turn left on Highway 1, drive south for 10.5 miles, and then turn left into Audubon Canyon Ranch.

Contact: Audubon Canyon Ranch, 4900 Highway 1, Stinson Beach, CA 94970; tel. (415) 868-9244.

33 Laurel Dell Loop

2.5 mi/1.5 hrs

Cataract Falls is the most adored waterfall on Mount Tamalpais, and the Laura Dell Trailhead provides the easiest route there. Instead of the gut-wrenching climb from Alpine Lake (see Cataract Falls hike from Alpine Dam, here you start high and glide down to the falls, then return via a gentle loop. The trailhead is at 1,640 feet, and from there you hike .4 mile on the Laurel Dell Trail to the Laurel Dell Picnic Area. At the edge of the picnic area, get on the Cataract Falls Trail and continue to the waterfall at 1,400 feet. When running at full strength, this cascade is a truly precious sight, especially when you realize it's so close to an urban setting. At the falls, turn right on the High Marsh Trail, hike onward, and turn right at any of the next three trail intersections to return to the Laurel Dell Trailhead. Of the three choices, the second makes the best return loop, as the short cutoff will put you within a few hundred yards of the trailhead.

Location: In Mount Tamalpais State Park; map E1-Marin, grid b2.

User groups: Hikers and dogs. No horses or mountain bikes. No wheelchair facilities.

Permits: No permits are required. Parking and access are free.

Maps: A map/brochure of Mount Tamalpais State Park is available for a small fee at the visitor center or by writing to the address below. A detailed hiking map of the area is available for a fee from Olmsted Brothers Map Company, P.O. Box 5351, Berkeley, CA 94705. Ask the USGS for topographic maps of the area, ask for Bolinas and San Rafael areas.

Directions: From U.S. 101 in Marin, take the Stinson Beach/Highway 1 exit. Drive west to the stoplight at the T intersection. Turn left and drive about 2.5 miles uphill to Panoramic Highway. Turn right on Panoramic Highway and continue up the hill for 5.5 miles (past the turnoff to Muir Woods). Turn right on Pantoll Road and drive about 1.5 miles to the T intersection. Turn left on Ridgecrest Road and drive 1.4 miles to the parking area for the Laura Dell Trailhead.

Contact: Mount Tamalpais State Park, 801 Panoramic Highway, Mill Valley, CA 94941; tel. (415) 388-2070 or fax (415) 388-2968; California State Parks, Marin District, tel. (415) 893-1580.

34 Rock Springs Trail
0.6 mi/0.5 hr

Five trails start at Rock Springs, but our favorite is the shorty to O'Rourke's Bench, where you can have a picnic while enjoying an awesome view to the west. On one trip the coast was socked in with low stratus clouds, appearing from this lookout like a sea of fog dotted with protruding mountaintops that resembled islands. On another day we caught an extraordinary sunset there. O'Rourke's Bench is quite easy to reach. After parking at Rock Springs, cross Ridgecrest Boulevard and take the O'Rourke's Bench Trail for .3 mile. After some 10 or 15 minutes, you will come upon a little bench set on a knoll at 2,071 feet. A plaque next to the bench reads: "Give me these hills and the friends I love. I ask no other heaven. To our dad O'Rourke, in joyous celebration of his 76th birthday, Feb. 25th, 1927. From the friends to whom he showed this heaven."

Location: In Marin Water District; map E1-Marin, grid b2.

User groups: Hikers only. No dogs, horses, or mountain bikes. No wheelchair facilities

Permits: No permits are required. Parking and access are free.

Maps: A hiking/biking map is available for a fee from the Marin Water District at the address below. A detailed hiking map of the area is available for a fee from Olmsted Brothers Map Company, P.O. Box 5351, Berkeley, CA 94705. Ask the USGS for a topographic map of the San Rafael area.

Directions: From U.S. 101 in Marin, take the Stinson Beach/Highway 1 exit. Drive west one mile to the stoplight at the T intersection at Highway 1/Shoreline Highway. Turn left and drive about 2.5 miles uphill to Panoramic Highway. Turn right on Panoramic Highway and continue up the hill for 5.5 miles (past the turnoff to Muir Woods). Turn right on Pantoll Road and drive 1.5 miles to a parking area across from a T intersection. This is the Rock Springs parking area and trailhead.

Contact: Sky Oaks Ranger Station, tel. (415) 945-1181; Marin Municipal Water District, 220 Nellen Avenue, Corte Madera, CA 94925; tel. (415) 945-1195. Mount Tamalpais State Park, 801 Panoramic Highway, Mill Valley, CA 94941; tel. (415) 388-2070 or fax (415) 388-2968; California State Parks, Marin District, tel. (415) 893-1580.

35 Barth's Retreat
2.0 mi/1.0 hr

Rarely can the features of the land change more quickly than on the hike to Barth's Retreat on Mount Tamalpais. In just a mile, you cross a serpentine swale, pass a small creek with riparian habitat, go through a forest, and then arrive at an open area called Barth's Retreat. Barth, by the way, was one Emil Barth, a prolific musician/hiker/trail builder who constructed a camp here in the early 1900s. This hike provides a quick glimpse of the diversity Mount Tam offers. When you link it with the short hike to O'Rourke's Bench, which also starts from Rock Springs, you can feel as if you've seen the world in a two-hour time span.

Location: In Marin Water District; map E1-Marin, grid b2.

User groups: Hikers only. No dogs, horses, or mountain bikes. No wheelchair facilities.

Permits: No permits are required. Parking and access are free.

Maps: A hiking/biking map is available for a fee from the Marin Water District at the address below. A detailed hiking map of the area is available for a fee from Olmsted Brothers Map Company, P.O. Box 5351, Berkeley, CA 94705. Ask the USGS for a topographic map of the San Rafael area.

Directions: From U.S. 101 in Marin, take the Stinson Beach/Highway 1 exit. Drive west one mile to the stoplight at the T intersection with Highway 1/Shoreline Highway. Turn left and drive about 2.5 miles uphill to Panoramic Highway. Turn right on Panoramic Highway and continue up the hill for 5.5 miles (past the turnoff to Muir Woods). Turn right on Pantoll Road and drive 1.5 miles to a parking area across from a T intersection. This is the Rock Springs Trailhead; there is a sign noting Barth's Retreat.

Contact: Sky Oaks Ranger Station, tel. (415) 945-1181; Marin Municipal Water District, 220 Nellen Avenue, Corte Madera, CA 94925; tel. (415) 945-1195. Mount Tamalpais State Park, 801 Panoramic Highway, Mill Valley, CA 94941; tel. (415) 388-2070 or fax (415) 388-2968; California State Parks, Marin District, tel. (415) 893-1580.

36 Mountain Theater
3.0 mi/1.5 hrs

The round-trip from the Mountain Theater to West Point Inn is a classic Mount Tamalpais walk—pretty, easy, and with a landmark on each end. The theater, Mount Tam's masterpiece outdoor amphitheater, is actually a very short distance from the parking area; you cross right behind it on the Rock Springs Trail en route to West Point Inn. The trail is quiet and tranquil—especially since it's off-limits to bikes—and weaves in and out of a hardwood forest, descending easily for most of the way. Over the course of 1.5 miles, you drop 295 feet, from a trailhead elevation of 2,080 feet to the trail's end at 1,785 feet. West Point Inn offers great views and a perfect spot for a picnic lunch, and lemonade is often available inside. Here's a secret: small cabins without electricity can be rented for overnight stays.

Special note: Much of this trail is on Marin Water District land; contact this agency for a detailed map.

Location: In Marin Water District; map E1-Marin, grid b2.

User groups: Hikers only. No dogs, horses, or mountain bikes. No wheelchair facilities.

Permits: No permits are required. Parking and access are free.

Maps: A hiking/biking map is available for a fee from the Marin Water District at the address below. A map/brochure of Mount Tamalpais State Park is available for a small fee at the visitor center or by writing to the address below. A detailed hiking map of the area is available for a fee from Olmsted Brothers Map Company, P.O. Box 5351, Berkeley, CA 94705. Ask the USGS for a topographic map of the San Rafael area.

Directions: From U.S. 101 in Marin, take the Stinson Beach/Highway 1 exit. Drive west one mile to the stoplight at the T intersection with Highway 1/Shoreline Highway. Turn left and drive about 2.5 miles uphill to Panoramic Highway. Turn right on Panoramic Highway and continue up the hill for 5.5 miles (past the turnoff to Muir Woods). Turn right on Pantoll Road and drive 1.5 miles to the T intersection. Turn right, drive .25 mile to the parking area on the right side of the road, and walk the short distance to the Mountain Theater Trailhead.

Contact: Sky Oaks Ranger Station, tel. (415) 945-1181; Marin Municipal Water District, 220 Nellen Avenue, Corte Madera, CA 94925; tel. (415) 945-1195. Mount Tamalpais State Park, 801 Panoramic Highway, Mill Valley, CA 94941; tel. (415) 388-2070 or fax (415) 388-2968; California State Parks, Marin District, tel. (415) 893-1580.

37 Bootjack Loop
6.2 mi/3.0 hrs

Few hikes provide glimpses of such a dynamic, diverse, and delightful habitat as the Bootjack Loop. The trail crosses a meadow, oak woodlands, and some hilly grasslands, then submerges deep into a redwood forest and climbs back out, all in the space of 6.2 miles. It entails a steady downgrade, so you face a huff-puffer climb on the return trip, but the redwoods make it worth the grunt.

Starting at the Pantoll Ranger Station and Trailhead, elevation 1,500 feet, in Mount Tamalpais State Park, you hike north .4 mile on the Alpine Trail to Van Wyck Meadow, descending 450 feet in the process. From there you turn right on the Bootjack Trail, heading downhill along a small stream. This leg leads 1.3 miles into Muir Woods National Monument, where you turn right on the Ben Johnson Trail and begin the steep return trip. Over the next

mile the trail climbs 500 feet, flanked the entire way by one of the Bay Area's richest redwood groves, home to many gigantic trees. To complete the loop, continue up, up, and up on the Ben Johnson Trail (to the Stapelveldt Trail) for the final .9 mile to the Pantoll Trailhead, a total elevation gain of 1,080 feet.

Location: In Mount Tamalpais State Park; map E1-Marin, grid b2.

User groups: Hikers only. No dogs, horses, or mountain bikes. No wheelchair facilities.

Permits: No permits are required. A $2 parking fee is charged.

Maps: A map/brochure of Mount Tamalpais State Park is available for a small fee at the visitor center or by writing to the address below. A detailed hiking map of the area is available for a fee from Olmsted Brothers Map Company, P.O. Box 5351, Berkeley, CA 94705. Ask the USGS for a topographic map of the San Rafael area.

Directions: From U.S. 101 in Marin, take the Stinson Beach/Highway 1 exit. Drive west one mile to the stoplight at the T intersection with Highway 1/Shoreline Highway. Turn left and drive about 2.5 miles uphill to Panoramic Highway. Turn right on Panoramic Highway and continue up the hill for 5.5 miles (past the turnoff to Muir Woods) to Pantoll Road. Turn left at Pantoll parking area.

Contact: Mount Tamalpais State Park, 801 Panoramic Highway, Mill Valley, CA 94941; tel. (415) 388-2070 or fax (415) 388-2968; California State Parks, Marin District, tel. (415) 893-1580.

38 East Peak Mount Tamalpais
0.2 mi/0.25 hr

There is simply no better place in the Bay Area to watch the sun set than atop Mount Tamalpais's East Peak, for the feelings this experience inspires will stay with you for many weeks. Mount Tam is one of those rare spots that projects a feeling of power, and while standing on its highest point, you can sense that power flowing right through you. The hike is very short—after all, a parking lot is set right at the foot of the summit trail—but quite steep, rising about 330 feet to the top at an elevation of 2,571 feet. An old lookout station is positioned at the summit, and hikers usually try to find a perch as close as possible to the top.

To the east, the bay resembles the Mediterranean Sea, an azure pool sprinkled with islands. And at night the lights of the bridges and the surrounding cities can give the Bay Area an almost surreal look. But the true magic happens at sunset, particularly on foggy days. The peak stands well above the fog line, and when the fiery sun dips into that low stratus to the west, orange light is refracted for hundreds of miles around. Witness this stunning sight even one time and you will gain a new perspective about what might be possible in this world. Perhaps you'll even set some new horizons for yourself.

Location: In Mount Tamalpais State Park; map E1-Marin, grid b2.

User groups: Hikers only. Dogs are permitted on the paved trail, but not on the mountaintop overlook. No horses or mountain bikes. No wheelchair access on the trail, but good views are available from the wheelchair-accessible parking lot.

Permits: No permits are required. A $2 parking fee is charged.

Maps: A map/brochure of Mount Tamalpais State Park is available for a small fee at the visitor center, located adjacent to the parking area, or by writing to the address below. A detailed hiking map of the area is available for a fee from Olmsted Brothers Map Company, P.O. Box 5351, Berkeley, CA 94705. Ask the USGS for a topographic map of the San Rafael area.

Directions: From U.S. 101 in Marin, take the Stinson Beach/Highway 1 exit. Drive west one mile to the stoplight at the T intersection with Highway 1/Shoreline Highway. Turn left and drive about 2.5 miles uphill to Panoramic Highway. Turn right on Panoramic Highway and continue up the hill 5.5 miles (past the turnoff to Muir Woods). Turn right on Pantoll Road and drive about 1.5 miles to the T intersection. Turn right on Ridgecrest Road and drive two miles to the East Peak. The road dead-ends at the parking area at the base of the summit.

Contact: Mount Tamalpais State Park, 801 Panoramic Highway, Mill Valley, CA 94941; tel. (415) 388-2070 or fax (415) 388-2968; California State Parks, Marin District, tel. (415) 893-1580.

39 Inspiration Point
2.6 mi/1.0 hr

Inspiration Point provides a nearby alternative to the East Peak, ideal if you want the same kind of magic found at that popular summit, yet without all the people. To get there, instead of heading up to the East Peak after parking, go the opposite direction and turn right on the fire road, Eldridge Grade. The trail wraps around the northern flank of the East Peak, then makes a hairpin turn to the left around North Knee, set at 2,000 feet. At this point, the bay comes into view to the east, and you start to understand the attraction. But keep on, because Inspiration Peak awaits just down the road. At the hairpin right turn, take the short but steep cutoff trail on the left and you will quickly reach the top at 2,040 feet, your vantage point for miles and miles of charmed views. All can seem enchanted. Much of this trail is on Marin Water District land.

Location: In Mount Tamalpais State Park; map E1-Marin, grid b2.

User groups: Hikers, dogs, and mountain bikes. No horses. No wheelchair access on the trail, but good views are available from the wheelchair-accessible parking lot.

Permits: No permits are required. A $2 parking fee is charged.

Maps: A map/brochure of Mount Tamalpais State Park is available for a small fee at the visitor center, located adjacent to the parking area, or by writing to the address below. A detailed hiking map of the area is available for a fee from Olmsted Brothers Map Company, P.O. Box 5351, Berkeley, CA 94705. Ask the USGS for a topographic map of the San Rafael area.

Directions: From U.S. 101 in Marin, take the Stinson Beach/Highway 1 exit. Drive west one mile to the stoplight at the T intersection with Highway 1/Shoreline Highway. Turn left and drive about 2.5 miles uphill to Panoramic Highway. Turn right on Panoramic Highway and continue up the hill 5.5 miles (past the turnoff to Muir Woods). Turn right on Pantoll Road and drive 1.5 miles to the T intersection. Turn right on Ridgecrest Road and drive two miles to the East Peak. The road dead-ends at the parking area at the base of the summit.

Contact: Mount Tamalpais State Park, 801 Panoramic Highway, Mill Valley, CA 94941; tel. (415) 388-2070 or fax (415) 388-2968; California State Parks, Marin District, tel. (415) 893-1580.

40 Dipsea Trail

6.6 mi one way/3.5 hrs

For Marin hikers, completing the Dipsea Trail is a rite of passage, an experience that offers a glimpse into both heaven and hell in a single morning. The annual Dipsea Race has turned the trail into something of a legend, and many people have developed a classic love-hate relationship with the hike. They love it because it's the perfect east-to-west crossing of Mount Tamalpais, from Mill Valley to Stinson Beach, passing through Muir Woods in the process and making a beautiful descent to the coast. Yet they hate it because it starts at an infamous set of seemingly unending staircase steps, crosses paved roads, and, just when hikers start to get tired, throws in a killer climb up Cardiac Hill. Of course, if you haven't figured it out by now, this is a one-way-only hike, shuttle partner required.

The trail starts in Mill Valley on Cascade Way at those hated steps, 671 in all. According to park rangers, the steps spawned the legend that Marin hikers never die, they just reach the 672nd step. When the trail tops the stairs and reaches pavement, look for the faint arrows painted on the street to mark the way. They will route you along Sequoia Road, Walsh Drive, then Bay View, where you cross Panoramic Highway and finally get off the pavement and start descending into Muir Woods. From there, the trail is well signed. Noted spots include Cardiac Hill, where you are handed a 480-foot climb in .4 mile. In return, you are also presented with phenomenal views of the Pacific Ocean and San Francisco, as well as the knowledge that most of the rest of the trail is downhill. Over the final 2.3 miles, you descend across the Marin hills, dip into lush Steep Ravine Canyon, and push across coastal bluffs to the parking area at Stinson Beach. Like we said, it's a rite of passage.

Location: On Mount Tamalpais from Mill Valley to Stinson Beach; map E1-Marin, grids b1 and b2.

User groups: Hikers only. No dogs, horses, or mountain bikes. No wheelchair facilities.

Permits: No permits required. A $2 parking fee is charged.

Maps: The Dipsea Trail crosses several jurisdictions. A map/brochure of Mount Tamalpais State Park is available for a small fee at the visitor center or by contacting Mount Tamalpais State Park at the address below. A detailed hiking map of the area is available for a fee from Olmsted Brothers Map Company, P.O. Box 5351, Berkeley, CA 94705. Ask the USGS for topographic maps of the San Rafael and Bolinas areas.

Directions: From U.S. 101 in Marin, take the East Blithedale/Tiburon Boulevard exit. Head west on East Blithedale (it becomes Throckmorton Street) into Mill Valley, and follow Throckmorton to Old Mill Park. The trailhead is at Old Mill Creek and the bridge, which leads to the staircase.

Contact: Mount Tamalpais State Park, 801 Panoramic Highway, Mill Valley, CA 94941; tel. (415) 388-2070 or fax (415) 388-2968; California State Parks, Marin District, tel. (415) 893-1580; Muir Woods National Monument, Mill Valley, CA 94941; tel. (415) 388-2596 or fax (415) 389-2596.

41 Mountain Home Trail
2.4 mi/1.0 hr

Want unique? You got unique: a 1.2-mile hike at Mount Tamalpais that ends at a great little inn called the Tourist Club, where you can "slake your thirst," as they say here, with your favorite elixir. This walk is short and has only one small steep portion. To reach the Tourist Club, park at the lot at Mountain Home along Panoramic Highway. From there, take the Panoramic Trail .4 mile (it parallels Panoramic Highway) to its junction with the Redwood Trail, which you then follow for .75 mile. The route laterals across the mountain slope before dropping into a pocket where the Tourist Club is perched on a slope. On weekends at this wood-framed building, not only can you get liquid refreshments, you can often drink while listening to German music. There is no other hiking destination like it in California. The Tourist Club is open on Saturdays and Sundays year-round from noon to sunset, closed Mondays, and otherwise during the week, hit-and-miss according to the availability of the caretaker.

Location: In Mount Tamalpais State Park; map E1-Marin, grid b2.

User groups: Hikers only. No dogs, horses, or mountain bikes. No wheelchair facilities.

Permits: No permits are required. Parking and access are free.

Maps: A map/brochure of Mount Tamalpais State Park is available for a small fee at the visitor center or by writing to the address below. A detailed hiking map of the area is available for a fee from Olmsted Brothers Map Company, P.O. Box 5351, Berkeley, CA 94705. Ask the USGS for a topographic map of the San Rafael area.

Directions: From U.S. 101 in Marin, take the Stinson Beach/Highway 1 exit. Drive west one mile to the stoplight at the T intersection. Turn left and drive about 2.5 miles uphill to Panoramic Highway. Turn right on Panoramic Highway and continue up the hill 5.5 miles (past the turnoff to Muir Woods). Turn right on Pantoll Road and continue to the Mountain Home Inn parking area. The trailhead (Panoramic Trail) is on the west side of the road.

Contact: Tourist Club, tel. (415) 388-9987; Mount Tamalpais State Park, 801 Panoramic Highway, Mill Valley, CA 94941; tel. (415) 388-2070 or fax (415) 388-2968; California State Parks, Marin District, tel. (415) 893-1580.

42 Matt Davis Trail
3.2 mi one way/1.5 hrs

The 3.2-mile section of the Matt Davis Trail from the Pantoll Trailhead down to Stinson Beach offers dramatic views of the Pacific Ocean. There are many places where you can stop, spread your arms wide, and feel as if the entire world were within your grasp. It is a great one-way hike—just make sure you go with a partner and have a shuttle car waiting at the trail's end at the Stinson Beach Firehouse. After parking at Pantoll, elevation 1,500 feet, cross the road and look for the sign marking the Matt Davis/Coastal Trail. Soon enough you will start descending toward the beach, but not before first entering a lush grove of fir trees. Here the trail is level for nearly a mile. When you emerge, the trail begins its steep descent across open grasslands down to Stinson Beach. Only thick fog can ruin the day. Note that the entire Matt Davis Trail is technically nearly double our suggested route, with the trailhead at Mountain Home. Also note that many people just enjoy a mile or two of the expansive sea views, then return.

Location: On the western slopes of Mount Tamalpais; map E1-Marin, grid b2.

User groups: Hikers only. No dogs, horses, or mountain bikes. No wheelchair facilities.

Permits: No permits are required. A $2 parking fee is charged.

Maps: A map/brochure of Mount Tamalpais State Park is available for a small fee at the visitor center or by writing to the address below. A detailed hiking map of the area is available for a fee from Olmsted Brothers Map

Company, P.O. Box 5351, Berkeley, CA 94705. Ask the USGS for a topographic map of the San Rafael area.

Directions: From U.S. 101 in Marin, take the Stinson Beach/Highway 1 exit. Drive west one mile to the stoplight at the T intersection. Turn left and drive about 2.5 miles uphill to Panoramic Highway. Turn right on Panoramic Highway and drive up the hill 5.5 miles (past the turnoff to Muir Woods) to Pantoll Road. Turn left at the Pantoll parking area.

Contact: Mount Tamalpais State Park, 801 Panoramic Highway, Mill Valley, CA 94941; tel. (415) 388-2070 or fax (415) 388-2968; California State Parks, Marin District, tel. (415) 893-1580.

43 Steep Ravine Trail
4.0 mi/1.5 hrs

Hiking the Steep Ravine Trail is like being baptized by the divine spirit of nature, and those who set foot on it will find a place where they can get their own brand of religion. The trail passes through remarkably beautiful terrain, including cathedral-like redwoods, lush undergrowth, and a pretty stream. Believe it or not, this is one of the few hikes that are best done during a rainstorm. In the canyon, the forest canopy protects you from a direct assault by the raindrops. Everything becomes vibrant with life as it drips with water. From the trailhead at Pantoll, the route descends 1,100 feet over the course of two miles, ending at Highway 1 near Rocky Point. After departing and heading downhill, it doesn't take long before the redwoods surround you. The trail follows Webb Creek, crossing the stream eight times in all. The junction with the Dipsea Trail is a trail landmark; from this point, it's .5 mile to the end.

Location: On the western slopes of Mount Tamalpais; map E1-Marin, grid b2.

User groups: Hikers only. No dogs, horses, or mountain bikes. No wheelchair facilities.

Permits: No permits are required. A $2 parking fee is charged.

Maps: A map/brochure of Mount Tamalpais

State Park is available for a small fee at the visitor center or by writing to the address below. A detailed hiking map of the area is available for a fee from Olmsted Brothers Map Company, P.O. Box 5351, Berkeley, CA 94705. Ask the USGS for a topographic map of the San Rafael area.

Directions: From U.S. 101 in Marin take the Stinson Beach/Highway 1 exit. Drive west to the stoplight at the T intersection. Turn left on Shoreline Highway/Highway 1, drive about 2.5 miles uphill to Panoramic Highway, and turn right on Panoramic Highway. Continue up the hill 5.5 miles (past the turnoff to Muir Woods) to Pantoll Road. Turn left at the Pantoll parking area.

Contact: Mount Tamalpais State Park, 801 Panoramic Highway, Mill Valley, CA 94941; tel. (415) 388-2070 or fax (415) 388-2968; California State Parks, Marin District, tel. (415) 893-1580.

44 Main Trail
2.0 mi/1.0 hr

This just might be the most heavily used trail in the Bay Area, yet not necessarily by Bay Area residents. You see, tourists from all over the world visiting San Francisco tend to follow the same routine: After taking the obligatory picture of the Golden Gate Bridge from Vista Point, they drive to Muir Woods to see a real redwood tree. Soon enough they find themselves on the Main Trail, a paved route set along Redwood Creek and completely encompassed by the giant trees. The trail is both very pretty and easy to walk, but more often than not it resembles a parade route. After about a mile, the trail starts to climb to the left, and just like that, most of the tourists head back to the parking lot. An option is to turn this into a loop hike by taking the Hillside Trail up the west side of the canyon and looping back to the Muir Woods headquarters. The loop trail is three miles long and includes a pleasant climb.

Location: In Muir Woods National Monument near Mill Valley; map E1-Marin, grid b2.

User groups: Hikers only. No dogs (except for seeing-eye dogs), horses, or mountain bikes. The first section of the trail is wheelchair accessible.

Permits: There is entry fee of $2 per person for visitors age 17 and over. No permits are required.

Maps: A map/brochure is available for a fee at the visitor center or by contacting Muir Woods National Monument at the address below. Ask the USGS for a topographic map of the San Rafael area.

Directions: From U.S. 101 in Marin, take the Stinson Beach/Highway 1 exit. Drive west to the stoplight at the T intersection with Highway 1/Shoreline Highway. Turn left and drive 2.5 miles uphill to Panoramic Highway. Turn right and drive .7 mile to the Muir Woods junction. Turn left and drive .8 mile to the Muir Woods parking area.

Contact: Muir Woods National Monument, Mill Valley, CA 94941; tel. (415) 388-2596 or fax (415) 389-2596.

45 Ocean View Trail (Panoramic Highway Trail)
3.0 mi/1.75 hrs

When you arrive at Muir Woods and see tour buses shooting out people like popcorn from a popping machine, you'll be glad you read this, because the Ocean View Trail provides the best chance of getting away from the crowds. After passing the information stand and starting down the paved path on the valley floor, turn right on the Ocean View Trail. In under a minute you will enter a different world, a world of solitude, beautiful redwoods, and, alas, a steep ascent.

From the valley floor, the trail heads up the east side of the canyon on a steady grade, steep enough to get you puffing. It climbs 570 feet in 1.2 miles, rising above the valley to where you can look down into a sea of redwoods. To complete the loop, turn left on the Lost Trail, elevation 750 feet, which descends quite steeply over just .4 mile back to the val-

ley floor at 300 feet. There you turn left and return to headquarters on the Fern Creek Trail. A great escape.

Special note: While this trail is listed as the Ocean View Trail, most people call it the Panoramic Highway Trail. It is listed both ways on various maps and signs. Ironically, there is no ocean view.

Location: In Muir Woods National Monument near Mill Valley; map E1-Marin, grid b2.

User groups: Hikers only. No dogs (except for seeing-eye dogs), horses, or mountain bikes. The first section of the trail is wheelchair accessible.

Permits: There is entry fee of $2 per person for visitors age 17 and over. No permits are required.

Maps: A map/brochure is available for a fee at the visitor center or by contacting Muir Woods National Monument at the address below. Ask the USGS for a topographic map of the San Rafael area.

Directions: From U.S. 101 in Marin, take the Stinson Beach/Highway 1 exit. Drive west to the stoplight at the T intersection with Highway 1/Shoreline Highway. Turn left and drive 2.5 miles uphill to Panoramic Highway. Turn right and drive .7 mile to the Muir Woods junction. Turn left and drive .8 mile to the Muir Woods parking area.

Contact: Muir Woods National Monument, Mill Valley, CA 94941; tel. (415) 388-2596 or fax (415) 389-2596.

46 Rocky Point Trail
0.2 mi/0.25 hr

One of the hidden secrets of the great outdoors is here at Rocky Point, where primitive cabins set on an ocean bluff are available for overnight rentals. It is one of the most dramatic camp settings on the Pacific coast, with views of passing whales, pelicans and murres, freighters and fishing boats. Sunsets can be exceptional. The cabins cost $15 per night and include a wood stove, picnic table, and flat wood surface for sleeping. You bring everything else, which should include good walking shoes to make the short hike down to the beach. From the cabins, you head back to the Rocky Point access road, turn right, then take the trail down to the cove, a descent of about 80 feet. Another beach trail on the north side of Rocky Point leads down to the southern end of Redrock Beach.

Location: On the Marin coast south of Stinson Beach; map E1-Marin, grid b1.

User groups: Hikers only. No dogs, horses, or mountain bikes. No wheelchair facilities.

Permits: Day-use parking and access are free. For overnight stays, a reservation is required at Steep Ravine Cabins/Environmental Campsites, tel. (800) 444-7275.

Maps: A map/brochure of Mount Tamalpais State Park is available for a small fee at the visitor center or by contacting Mount Tamalpais State Park at the address below. A detailed hiking map of the area is available for a fee from Olmsted Brothers Map Company, P.O. Box 5351, Berkeley, CA 94705. Ask the USGS for topographic maps of the Bolinas and Point Bonita areas.

Directions: From U.S. 101 in Marin, take the Stinson Beach/Highway 1 exit and drive to the coast at the Muir Beach Overlook. Continue north for about four miles to the Rocky Point access road (gated) on the left side of the highway. Directions for how to get through the access road are included in the reservation confirmation information for the Steep Ravine Environmental Cabins.

Contact: Mount Tamalpais State Park, 801 Panoramic Highway, Mill Valley, CA 94941; tel. (415) 388-2070 or fax (415) 388-2968; California State Parks, Marin District, tel. (415) 893-1580.

Owl Trail

3.5 mi/1.5 hrs

A delightful walk, this trail laterals down the coastal hillside to a secluded, rocky beach, with several sideshows along the way. The trailhead is near the Muir Beach Overlook, which alone is worth the trip for the great views of the southern Marin coast. Don't stop there like so many visitors do, but instead hike northward on the Owl Trail. From the unsigned trailhead on the north side of the parking area, the trail is routed through low-lying brush, which makes wearing shorts a sticky proposition. Starting at 440 feet, the trail descends 240 feet in .9 mile on its northward course to Slide Ranch. Slide Ranch consists of a hamlet of wood huts and a small farm with goats, sheep, chickens, and even some ducks, all favorites of youngsters. Two-feet-tall great horned owls sometimes roost in the giant cypress trees at Slide Ranch, but they can be difficult to see in their natural camouflage. From here the trip down to the beach adds another 15 minutes to your walk; the descent is slippery, and a rope has been affixed to aid hikers through the worst spot. Once down, you can explore numerous secret spots amid rocks of all sizes, stacks, and tide pools. On one visit we saw what must have been hundreds of tiny rock crabs sparring in the shallows.

Location: On the Marin coast south of Stinson Beach; map E1-Marin, grid c2.

User groups: Hikers only. No dogs, horses, or mountain bikes. The Muir Beach Overlook is wheelchair accessible, but the Owl Trail is not.

Permits: No permits are required. Parking and access are free.

Maps: A map/brochure is available at the Marin Headlands Visitor Center or by contacting the Golden Gate National Recreation Area, Marin Headlands, at the address below. A detailed hiking map of the area is available for a fee from Olmsted Brothers Map Company, P.O. Box 5351, Berkeley, CA 94705. Ask the USGS for a topographic map of the Point Bonita area.

Directions: From U.S. 101 in Marin, take the Stinson Beach/Highway 1 exit and drive to the coast. Turn left at the Muir Beach Overlook and drive a short distance to the parking area. The trailhead may at first seem hidden. It is located at the north side of the parking area.

Contact: Muir Woods National Monument, Mill Valley, CA 94941; tel. (415) 388-2596 or fax (415) 389-2596; Golden Gate National Recreation Area, Marin Headlands Visitor Center, Building 948, Fort Barry, Sausalito, CA 94965; tel. (415) 331-1540 or fax (415) 331-6963.

48 Miwok Loop

3.5 mi/2.0 hrs

The Miwok Loop is a near circular hike that traverses the pretty grasslands of the Marin Headlands, connecting a number of trails to provide a decent physical workout. Good views are found throughout, including those from a great 880-foot lookout to the west at the junction of Ridge Road and the Fox Trail. The hike starts at the Miwok Stables, elevation 200 feet, where you head north on the Miwok Trail, rising into higher country. The trail turns left, then heads west .6 mile, still climbing to the junction of the Miwok Trail and Coyote Ridge Road. At this point, to make the loop hike, turn left on Ridge Road, where the trail tops out at 1,000 feet. The next mile offers spectacular views of the ocean, and every step can be special. To return to the Miwok Stables, turn left at the Fox Trail and hike 1.1 miles; go left again on the paved Tennessee Valley Trail, and hike out the last .4 mile to the stables. Trail use is typically high on weekends, and that includes mountain bike traffic on Coyote Ridge Road.

Location: In the Marin Headlands near Sausalito; map E1-Marin, grid c2.

User groups: Hikers, dogs, horses, and mountain bikes (partial access). No wheelchair facilities.

Permits: No permits are required. Parking and access are free.

Maps: A map/brochure is available at the Marin Headlands Visitor Center or by contacting the Golden Gate National Recreation Area, Marin Headlands, at the address below. A detailed hiking map of the area is available for a fee from Olmsted Brothers Map Company, P.O. Box 5351, Berkeley, CA 94705. Ask the USGS for a topographic map of the Point Bonita area.

Directions: From U.S. 101 in Marin, take the Stinson Beach/Highway 1 exit. Drive .6 mile and turn left on Tennessee Valley Road. Drive two miles until the road dead-ends at the trailhead.

Contact: Golden Gate National Recreation Area, Marin Headlands Visitor Center, Building 948, Fort Barry, Sausalito, CA 94965; tel. (415) 331-1540 or fax (415) 331-6963.

49 Tennessee Valley

4.2 mi/2.0 hrs

This very popular, scenic trail in the Marin Headlands traces Tennessee Valley out to Tennessee Cove and the Pacific Ocean. While the area is not wooded, the views of the Pacific Ocean can be gorgeous and the sunsets memorable. The best trailhead is at the Miwok Stables, elevation 200 feet. From there, the first .8 mile is paved and attracts many mountain bikers. The route turns to gravel for the final 1.1 miles, tracing along a pretty lagoon before dropping the final .2 mile to Tennessee Cove. This trail has become a favorite for family hiking or biking trips.

Location: In the Marin Headlands near Sausalito; map E1-Marin, grid c2.

User groups: Hikers, horses, and mountain bikes. (Horses and mountain bikes must take the forked fire road.) No dogs. No wheelchair facilities.

Permits: No permits are required. Parking and access are free.

Maps: A map/brochure is available at the Marin Headlands Visitor Center or by contacting the Golden Gate National Recreation Area, Marin Headlands, at the address below. A detailed hiking map of the area is available for a fee from Olmsted Brothers Map Company, P.O. Box 5351, Berkeley, CA 94705. Ask the USGS for a topographic map of the Point Bonita area.

Directions: From U.S. 101 in Marin, take the Stinson Beach/Highway 1 exit. Drive .6 mile and turn left on Tennessee Valley Road. Drive two miles until the road dead-ends at the trailhead.

Contact: Golden Gate National Recreation Area Marin Headlands Visitor Center, Building 948, Fort Barry, Sausalito, CA 94965; tel. (415) 331-1540 or fax (415) 331-6963.

50 Morning Sun Trail
0.2 mi/0.5 hr

This trail didn't get its name by accident. After the short but steep climb to the junction with the Alta Trail, you will discover this is a magnificent location to watch the sun come up, casting varying hues of yellow and orange across San Francisco Bay. In fact, it is one of the best places in the Bay Area to catch a sunrise. There is a good parking area at the trailhead, and from there you climb about 400 feet, peaking out at 800 feet at the Alta Trail junction. From Alta, you can easily extend your trip in either direction, or create a pretty 5.2-mile loop by linking the Rodeo Valley Trail and the Bobcat Trail.

Location: In the Marin Headlands near Sausalito; map E1-Marin, grid c2.

User groups: Hikers only. No dogs, horses, or mountain bikes. No wheelchair facilities.

Permits: No permits are required. Parking and access are free.

Maps: A map/brochure is available at the Marin Headlands Visitor Center or by contacting the Golden Gate National Recreation Area, Marin Headlands, at the address below. A detailed hiking map of the area is available for a fee from Olmsted Brothers Map Company, P.O. Box 5351, Berkeley, CA 94705. Ask the USGS for a topographic map of the San Francisco North area.

Directions: From San Francisco drive north on U.S. 101 through the Waldo Tunnel. Take the Spencer Avenue exit, but keep straight on the frontage road on the east side of the freeway. (Do not turn right onto Spencer Avenue.) Drive about .5 mile, turn left, and drive under the freeway to the commuter parking area at the trailhead.

Contact: Golden Gate National Recreation Area, Marin Headlands Visitor Center, Building 948, Fort Barry, Sausalito, CA 94965; tel. (415) 331-1540 or fax (415) 331-6963.

51 Bicentennial Bike Path
4.5 mi/2.0 hrs

Can folks out for an easy stroll mix well with joggers and bikers? The Bicentennial Bike Path proves this is possible, primarily because it was designed just for that purpose. This paved byway starts in Sausalito and heads north, tracing the shoreline of Richardson Bay into Corte Madera. It is a great nature walk, easy and pleasant. From Sausalito the route passes beneath the U.S. 101 overpass, then pushes toward Bothin Marsh along the edge of Richardson Bay, crossing two exceptional little bridges that provide passage over tidelands. At low tide, hundreds of tiny sandpipers frequently poke around in the mud; in the nearby sloughs bordered by pickleweed, you can often spot egrets, night herons, and maybe even a pelican. Drop into the Richardson Bay Audubon Center for a good side trip. Bikers can continue all the way to Ross but will have to make a few connections on city streets to do so.

Location: On the San Francisco Bay shoreline from Sausalito to Corte Madera; map E1-Marin, grid c3.

User groups: Hikers, dogs, mountain bikes, and wheelchairs. No horses.

Permits: No permits are required. Parking and access are free.

Maps: A detailed hiking map of the area is available for a fee from Olmsted Brothers Map Company, P.O. Box 5351, Berkeley, CA 94705. Ask the USGS for a topographic map of the San Francisco North area.

Directions: From San Francisco drive north on U.S. 101 over the Golden Gate Bridge. In Marin, take the Sausalito exit. Follow 2nd Street/Bridgeway through Sausalito to Harbor Drive, then park. The trail starts there.

Contact: Richardson Bay Audubon Center, 376 Greenwood Road, Tiburon, CA 94920; tel. (415) 388-2524 or fax (415) 388-0717.

52 Coastal Trail/ Fort Cronkhite

5.2 mi/2.5 hrs

Fort Cronkhite, perched on an ocean bluff above Rodeo Beach, was the "support community" for the Headlands military fortifications in the 1930s and 1940s. From here a paved pathway extends north up to Wolf Ridge, climbing to a 960-foot summit at what is known as "Hill 88." The land consists primarily of coastal grasslands, so from the summit you get outstanding views of the Pacific Ocean. The entire route is paved, and you may encounter bikers who careen downhill hell-bent for leather, sending hikers scattering for the bushes. Enforcement of the speed limit has helped, as has peer pressure from more ethical riders. While the round-trip distance is 5.2 miles, you'll surely make the 2.6-mile return hike at least twice as fast as the journey up.

Location: In the Marin Headlands at the mouth of San Francisco Bay; map E1-Marin, grid c2.

User groups: Hikers, dogs, horses, and mountain bikes. Fort Cronkhite and the picnic area are partially wheelchair accessible.

Permits: No permits are required. Parking and access are free.

Maps: A map/brochure is available at the Marin Headlands Visitor Center or by contacting the Golden Gate National Recreation Area, Marin Headlands, at the address below. A detailed hiking map of the area is available for a fee from Olmsted Brothers Map Company, P.O. Box 5351, Berkeley, CA 94705. Ask the USGS for a topographic map of the Point Bonita area.

Directions: From San Francisco, drive north on U.S. 101 over the Golden Gate Bridge. In Marin, take the Alexander Avenue exit and turn left underneath the highway. Take the wide paved road to the right (Conzelman Road, but there is no sign), and look for the Marin Headlands sign. Drive one mile, make a right on McCullough Road (the downhill fork), and soon after turn left on Bunker Road. Drive about 2.5 miles to where the road dead-ends at the Fort Cronkhite/Rodeo Beach parking lot.

Contact: Golden Gate National Recreation Area, Marin Headlands Visitor Center, Building 948, Fort Barry, Sausalito, CA 94965; tel. (415) 331-1540 or fax (415) 331-6963.

53 Coastal Trail/Fort Barry

1.4 mi/0.75 hr

Fort Barry was a nerve center for military operations in an era long past. Today it's a place that can calm the nerves of frazzled hikers. After parking and exploring at Fort Barry a bit, take the unpaved road/trail that heads west from the fort. Covering just .7 mile, the trail is routed along the south side of Rodeo Lagoon and out to the bluffs overlooking the ocean. This is a great walk, and easy, with good views all around on clear days. The fort, set at the foot of Rodeo Valley, offers a living history lesson.

Location: In the Marin Headlands near Rodeo Lagoon; map E1-Marin, grid c2.

User groups: Hikers, dogs, and horses. No mountain bikes. No wheelchair facilities.

Permits: No permits are required. Parking and access are free.

Maps: A map/brochure is available at the Marin Headlands Visitor Center or by contacting the Golden Gate National Recreation Area, Marin Headlands, at the address below. A detailed hiking map of the area is available for a fee from Olmsted Brothers Map Company, P.O. Box 5351, Berkeley, CA 94705. Ask the USGS for a topographic map of the Point Bonita area.

Directions: From San Francisco, drive north on U.S. 101 over the Golden Gate Bridge. In Marin, take the Alexander Avenue exit and turn left underneath the highway. Take the wide paved road to the right (Conzelman, but there is no sign), and look for the Marin Headlands sign. Drive one mile, make a right on McCullough Road (the downhill fork), and soon after turn left on Bunker Road. Proceed a short distance to Fort Barry. After parking, walk from the visitor center across the street and up the hill to the trailhead.

Contact: Golden Gate National Recreation Area, Marin Headlands Visitor Center, Building 948, Fort Barry, Sausalito, CA 94965; tel. (415) 331-1540 or fax (415) 331-6963.

54 Point Bonita Lighthouse
1.0 mi/1.0 hrs

The walk to the Point Bonita Lighthouse is the most sensational easy hike in the Bay Area. What makes it special is crossing through a tunnel and then over a one-of-a-kind suspension bridge to reach the lighthouse and its perch on a rock at the mouth of the Bay, as well as the sweeping boat-level views. The hike starts with an easy traipse downhill; within .25 mile, you enter a 50-foot tunnel. You emerge seeing what looks like a miniature suspension bridge; some people say it looks like the Golden Gate Bridge in miniature. You cross the mini-suspension bridge, often just two people at a time (five is the maximum it can hold), and arrive at the lighthouse. It's a fantastic vantage point, looking east at the Golden Gate Bridge, as well as across the entrance to the Bay. Sound good? Is good. The only catch is that this trail is open only on weekends and Mondays, 12:30 to 3:30 p.m., though with guided walks available on those days at 12:30 p.m. Also note this trail is sometimes closed during wet or windy weather.

Location: In the Marin Headlands at the mouth of San Francisco Bay; map E1-Marin, grid c2.

User groups: Hikers only. No dogs, horses, or mountain bikes are permitted.

Permits: No permits are required. Parking and access are free.

Maps: A map/brochure is available at the Marin Headlands Visitor Center or by contacting the Golden Gate National Recreation Area, Marin Headlands, at the address below. Ask the USGS for a topographic map of the Point Bonita area.

Directions: From San Francisco drive north on U.S. 101 over the Golden Gate Bridge. In Marin take the Alexander Avenue exit and turn left underneath the highway. Take the wide paved road to the right (Conzelman Road, but there is no sign), and look for the Marin Headlands sign. Continue on Conzelman to its end at the Point Bonita Lighthouse parking lot.

Contact: Golden Gate National Recreation Area, Marin Headlands Visitor Center, Building 948, Fort Barry, Sausalito, CA 94965; tel. (415) 331-1540 or fax (415) 331-6963.

55 Hawk Hill
0.1 mi/0.25 hr

Awesome views make this a choice trip. Each year more than 10,000 hawks and other raptors fly over the Marin Headlands during their five-month migration season, peaking in September and October, and the raptors are best viewed from this lookout. In addition, there may be no better spot to see the Golden Gate Bridge, with the San Francisco skyline providing a backdrop. The hike is easy and fun, especially for youngsters. You can drive nearly to the top of Hawk Hill; after parking, hike a short distance, equivalent to a few blocks, to reach the lookout summit. As many as 2,800 hawks have been counted on a single day from this spot. The most commonly seen raptors are the red-tailed hawk, Cooper's hawk, turkey vulture, American kestrel, and northern harrier. All you need is a clear October day.

Location: In the Marin Headlands near Rodeo Lagoon; map E1-Marin, grid c2.

User groups: Hikers only. There are some wheelchair-accessible facilities. No dogs, horses, or mountain bikes.

Permits: No permits are required. Parking and access are free.

Maps: A map/brochure is available at the Marin Headlands Visitor Center or by contacting the Golden Gate National Recreation Area, Marin Headlands, at the address below. A detailed hiking map of the area is available for a fee from Olmsted Brothers Map Company, P.O. Box 5351, Berkeley, CA 94705. Ask the USGS for a topographic map of the San Francisco North area.

Directions: From San Francisco, drive north on U.S. 101 over the Golden Gate Bridge. In Marin, take the Alexander Avenue exit and turn left underneath the highway. Take the wide paved road to the right (Conzelman, but there is no sign), and look for the Marin Headlands sign. Continue on Conzelman (bearing left at the fork with McCullough Road) and drive a short distance. Just before Conzelman becomes a one-way road, park on the shoulder. Note: The Conzelman access road is closed each day at sunset.

Contact: Golden Gate National Recreation Area, Marin Headlands Visitor Center, Building 948, Fort Barry, Sausalito, CA 94965, tel. (415) 331-1540 or fax (415) 331-6963.

56 Upper Fisherman's Trail
0.6 mi/0.5 hr

A delightful beach and a sea-level view of the entrance to the bay await at Bonita Cove. If only the weather were better. . . . Instead, summer days are typically cold and foggy here. From the parking area the trail embarks on about .5-mile walk with an elevation change of some 300 feet—you'll know it when you make the return trip up—before emerging onto a beach sheltered by nearby Point Bonita and Point Diablo. The trail was named for the anglers who have used it over the years in the summer months to fish for striped bass and halibut. The cove is a good fishing spot because it's protected by Point Diablo, where baitfish often congregate during tidal transitions. Those baitfish, typically schools of anchovies, in turn attract the larger fish.

Special note: The rocky cliffs here can be dangerous; use extreme caution.

Location: In the Marin Headlands at the mouth of San Francisco Bay; map E1-Marin, grid c2.

User groups: Hikers only. No dogs, horses, or mountain bikes. No wheelchair facilities.

Permits: No permits are required. Parking and access are free.

Maps: A map/brochure is available at the Marin Headlands Visitor Center or by contacting the Golden Gate National Recreation Area, Marin Headlands, at the address below. A detailed hiking map of the area is available for a fee from Olmsted Brothers Map Company, P.O. Box 5351, Berkeley, CA 94705. Ask the USGS for a topographic map of the Point Bonita area.

Directions: From San Francisco drive north on U.S. 101 over the Golden Gate Bridge. In Marin, take the Alexander Avenue exit and turn left underneath the highway. Take the wide paved road to the right (Conzelman, but there is no sign), and look for the Marin Headlands sign. Drive one mile, make a right on McCullough Road (the downhill fork), and soon after turn left on Bunker Road. Drive a short distance and take the first left to the Upper Fisherman's parking area and the trailhead.

Contact: Golden Gate National Recreation Area, Marin Headlands Visitor Center, Building 948, Fort Barry, Sausalito, CA 94965; tel. (415) 331-1540 or fax (415) 331-6963.

57 Vista Point/ East Fort Baker
2.5 mi/1.5 hrs

Vista Point, the famous lookout at the northern end of the Golden Gate Bridge, is like a mini-United Nations, as travelers from around the world stop there to take photos. Little do they know that with a short walk, they can get even better views. A paved trail from the parking area loops under the north foot of the bridge, then works its way back and forth, descending to East Fort Baker. There you will find a bay cove; as you look up from the shoreline, the Golden Gate Bridge is even more inspiring. You can stroll along the shore and out to a fishing pier or check out the Bay Area Discovery Museum, ideal for families. A nearby large grassy area makes an excellent picnic site, and picnic tables are available near Lime Point, set below the north end of the bridge. You can also extend the trip out to Yellow Bluff, for more spectacular views and picnic sites.

Location: In the Marin Headlands at the northern foot of the Golden Gate Bridge; map E1-Marin, grid c2.

User groups: Hikers, dogs, and mountain bikes. Vista Point is wheelchair accessible, but the trail is not. No horses.

Permits: No permits are required. Parking and access are free.

Maps: A map/brochure is available at the East Fort Baker Visitor Center or by contacting the Golden Gate National Recreation Area, Marin Headlands, at the address below. A detailed hiking map of the area is available for a fee from Olmsted Brothers Map Company, P.O. Box 5351, Berkeley, CA 94705. Ask the USGS for a topographic map of the San Francisco North area.

Directions: From San Francisco drive north on U.S. 101 over the Golden Gate Bridge, get in the right lane, and take the Vista Point exit.

Contact: Golden Gate National Recreation Area, Marin Headlands Visitor Center, Building 948, Fort Barry, Sausalito, CA 94965; tel. (415) 331-1540 or fax (415) 331-6963.

58 Yellow Bluff Trail

1.5 mi/1.0 hr

This is a little piece of heaven. From your vantage point on Yellow Bluff, San Francisco looks like the land of Oz. The first major land point along the Marin shore east of the Golden Gate, Yellow Bluff provides a stunning lookout across San Francisco Bay and the surrounding landmarks. The trail is flat, short, and, best of all, unpublicized, and there are a few picnic tables nearby. From East Fort Baker, walk on the trail that heads east near the shoreline of the bay. You can turn the trip into a triangular loop hike by continuing along the shore, heading toward Sausalito, and then turning left at the trail junction and hiking back to Fort Baker. One of the great features of this

area is that it is often sunny, even when the Marin Headlands to the west lie buried in fog.

Location: In the Marin Headlands at the northern foot of the Golden Gate Bridge; map E1-Marin, grid c2.

User groups: Hikers, dogs, and mountain bikes. Fort Baker is wheelchair accessible, but the trail is not. No horses.

Permits: No permits are required. Parking and access are free.

Maps: A map/brochure is available at the East Fort Baker Visitor Center or by contacting the Golden Gate National Recreation Area, Marin Headlands, at the address below. A detailed hiking map of the area is available for a fee from Olmsted Brothers Map Company, P.O. Box 5351, Berkeley, CA 94705. Ask the USGS for a topographic map of the San Francisco North area.

Directions: From San Francisco drive north on U.S. 101 over the Golden Gate Bridge. In Marin take the Alexander Avenue exit and stay to the right at the split. Drive a very short distance, turn left, and drive a few hundred yards to a stop sign. Turn right and drive .5 mile to the parking area for Fort Baker.

Contact: Golden Gate National Recreation Area, Marin Headlands Visitor Center, Building 948, Fort Barry, Sausalito, CA 94965; tel. (415) 331-1540 or fax (415) 331-6963.

59 Perimeter Road

5.0 mi/2.5 hrs

A hike around Angel Island on the Perimeter Trail provides great views of the bay and a historical tour amid remnants of the island's military past. And it's long enough to provide a decent workout to boot. The trail winds past old barracks and abandoned military buildings, climbs through lush eucalyptus forests and across high bluffs, and looks out over San Francisco Bay and its world-class landmarks. Heavy logging of nonnative eucalyptus has dramatically changed the character of this island and the trail. When linked with the North Ridge/Sunset Trail, this is the

most scenic hike in the entire Bay Area. The only downer is that the trail is actually a road, yet somehow it still manages to inspire. From each lookout you see San Francisco Bay from a completely new angle.

Location: In Angel Island State Park in San Francisco Bay; map E1-Marin, grid c3.

User groups: Hikers and mountain bikes (helmets are required for bikers 17 years and under). The Perimeter Road is accessible to wheelchairs, but many portions are too steep for use. No dogs (except for seeing-eye dogs) or horses.

Permits: No permits are required. Ferryboat ticket fees, which include day-use fees, vary according to departure point and season; add $1 per bicycle.

Maps: You can purchase a topographic map/brochure for a fee at the park or by mail from the Angel Island Association, Box 866, Tiburon, CA 94920. Ask the USGS for a topographic map of the San Francisco North area.

Directions: Ferry service to Angel Island is available from Tiburon, San Francisco, Vallejo, and Oakland/Alameda.

To reach the Tiburon Ferry: Take U.S. 101 in Marin to Tiburon Boulevard. Head east on Tiburon Boulevard, curving along the bay's shoreline. Park at one of the pay lots in Tiburon, then walk a short distance to the Tiburon Ferry, which is well signed.

To reach the San Francisco Ferry: Take U.S. 101 to the Marina Boulevard exit near the southern foot of the Golden Gate Bridge. Follow Marina Boulevard toward Fisherman's Wharf. The ferry departs from Pier 41.

To reach the Vallejo Ferry: Take Interstate 80 to U.S. 780. Drive to Curtola Parkway (which becomes Mare Island Way), and continue to 495 Mare Island Way, where free parking is available. The docking area is directly across from the parking lot.

To reach the Oakland/Alameda Ferry: In Oakland drive south on Highway 980, take the Webster exit, and drive west to the ferry dock and parking lot at Jack London Square.

Contact: For ferry schedule information: From San Francisco, Vallejo and Oakland/Alameda, call (415) 705-5555; from Tiburon, call (415) 435-2131. Angel Island State Park, tel. (415) 435-1915; California State Parks, Marin District, tel. (415) 893-1580 or fax (415) 893-1583.

60 North Ridge/Sunset Trail
6.0 mi/3.0 hrs

When standing atop Mount Livermore, you will be surrounded by dramatic scenery in every direction. That is because at 781 feet, this is the highest point on Angel Island, the virtual center of San Francisco Bay. The views are superb even at night, when the lights of the Golden Gate Bridge and the city glow with charm. The trail is steep, with a 550-foot climb in just .5 mile, which will have even the best-conditioned hikers puffing like locomotives by the time they reach the top. The Summit Trail is actually a cutoff from the Perimeter Trail; for the ambitious, it's the highlight of a six-mile loop hike on Angel Island.

Location: In Angel Island State Park in San Francisco Bay; map E1-Marin, grid c3.

User groups: Hikers only. No dogs (except for seeing-eye dogs),horses, or mountain bikes (they may not even be walked on this trail). No wheelchair facilities.

Permits: No permits are required. Ferryboat ticket fees, which include day-use fees, vary according to departure point and season; add $1 per bicycle.

Maps: You can purchase a topographic map/brochure for a fee at the park or by mail from the Angel Island Association, Box 866, Tiburon, CA 94920. Ask the USGS for a topographic map of the San Francisco North area.

Directions: Ferry service to Angel Island is available from Tiburon, San Francisco, Vallejo, and Oakland/Alameda.

To reach the Tiburon Ferry: Take U.S. 101 in Marin to Tiburon Boulevard. Head east on Tiburon Boulevard, curving along the bay's shoreline. Park at one of the pay lots in Tiburon, then walk a short distance to the Tiburon Ferry, which is well signed.

To reach the San Francisco Ferry: Take U.S. 101 to the Marina Boulevard exit near the southern foot of the Golden Gate Bridge. Follow Marina Boulevard toward Fisherman's Wharf. The ferry departs from Pier 41.

To reach the Vallejo Ferry: Take Interstate 80 to U.S. 780. Drive to Curtola Parkway (which becomes Mare Island Way), and continue to 495 Mare Island Way, where free parking is available. The docking area is directly across from the parking lot.

To reach the Oakland/Alameda Ferry: In Oakland drive south on Highway 980, take the Webster exit, and drive west to the ferry dock at Jack London Square.

Contact: For ferry schedule information: From San Francisco, Vallejo and Oakland/Alameda, call (415) 705-5555; from Tiburon, call (415) 435-2131. Angel Island State Park, tel. (415) 435-1915; California State Parks, Marin District, tel. (415) 893-1580 or fax (415) 893-1583.

CHAPTER E1 ⌐
SAN FRANCISCO PENINSULA

VIEW OF THE GOLDEN GATE BRIDGE
FROM THE COASTAL TRAIL

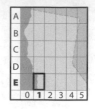

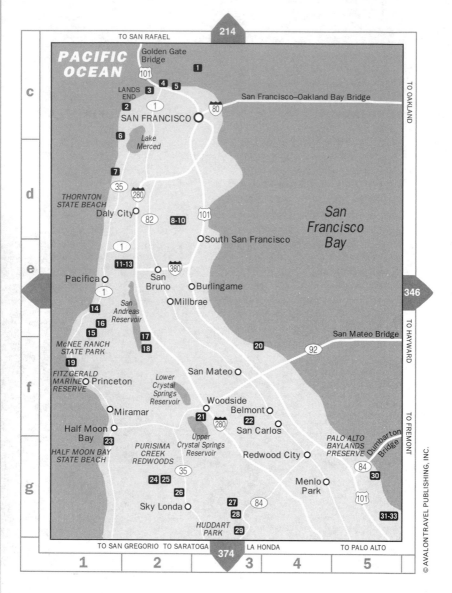

PACIFIC OCEAN

TO SAN RAFAEL

214

Golden Gate Bridge

101

1

LANDS END

3 **4** **5**

2 1

SAN FRANCISCO○

San Francisco–Oakland Bay Bridge

80

TO OAKLAND

6

Lake Merced

7

THORNTON STATE BEACH

35 280

Daly City○

82 **8-10**

101

○South San Francisco

San Francisco Bay

1

11-13

380

Pacifica○

1

San Bruno

○Burlingame

14

San Andreas Reservoir

○Millbrae

16

17

15

18

McNEE RANCH STATE PARK

San Mateo Bridge

20

92

TO HAYWARD

19

FITZGERALD MARINE RESERVE

○Princeton

○San Mateo

Lower Crystal Springs Reservoir

○Miramar

Woodside○

21 280

Belmont○

Half Moon Bay

23

HALF MOON BAY STATE BEACH

22

San Carlos○

Upper Crystal Springs Reservoir

PURISIMA CREEK REDWOODS

○Redwood City

PALO ALTO BAYLANDS PRESERVE

Dumbarton Bridge

TO FREMONT

24 **25**

35

26

Menlo○ Park

84

30

Sky Londa○

27

84

101

28

31-33

HUDDART PARK

29

TO SAN GREGORIO   TO SARATOGA

374

LA HONDA

TO PALO ALTO

346

CHAPTER E1 ~ SAN FRANCISCO PENINSULA

1 Agave Trail 325

2 Lands End Trail 326

3 Coastal Trail 327

4 Golden Gate Bridge. . . 327

5 Golden Gate
Promenade 328

6 Ocean Beach
Esplanade 328

7 Fort Funston
Sunset Trail 329

8 Summit Loop Trail . . . 329

9 Saddle Trail 330

10 Bog Trail 330

11 Milagra Ridge 331

12 Sweeney Ridge 331

13 Montara Mountain/
Brooks Creek Trail . . . 332

14 Linda Mar/Rockaway
Point Trail. 333

15 San Pedro Mountain . . 333

16 Montara Mountain/
McNee Ranch. 334

17 San Andreas Trail 334

18 Sawyer Camp Trail . . . 335

19 Fitzgerald
Marine Reserve. 336

20 Coyote Point Trail. . . . 336

21 Crystal Springs Trail. . 337

22 Waterdog Lake Trail . . 337

23 Pillar Point 337

24 Harkins Ridge Trail . . . 338

25 Whittemore Gulch . . . 339

26 Redwood Trail. 339

27 Huddart Park Loop . . . 340

28 Skyline Trail 340

29 Meadows Loop Trail. . . 341

30 Ravenswood Open
Space Preserve. 341

31 Baylands Catwalk 342

32 Baylands Trail 342

33 South Bay
Nature Trail 343

1 Agave Trail

1.5 mi/1.5 hrs

The Agave Trail at Alcatraz Island has made accessible one-third of the island that was previously closed to visitors. The catch is you must come in winter, when the trail is open from late September to February; the trail is closed from late winter on into spring and summer to protect nesting birds. The trail also provides some of the most breathtaking views found on any of the 15,000 miles of Bay Area hiking trails. The trail—named after the agave plant, which is common here—starts at the ferry landing on the east side of Alcatraz and traces the island rim to its southern tip. It is quite wide, with a few benches and cement picnic tables situated for sweeping views of both the East Bay and San Francisco.

From its southern end, the trail is routed back to the historic parade ground atop the island, where you find some sculptural masterpieces, which include 110 stone steps. The parade ground is a haven for nesting birds, and this area is closed to the public in the spring each year so the birds will not be disturbed. If you visit during a low tide, you can discover some relatively little-known tide pools at the island's southwest corner. This part of the island also has abundant bird life, including a population of night

herons; for pure cuteness, they're right up there with chipmunks and baby ducks. The old cell block is located at the center of the island, with other buildings sprinkled along the eastern shore and on the northern tip. Ranger-led park tours are available, and visitors can rent audiotapes for a self-guided cell house tour. The ghost of Al Capone is said to roam here, trying to figure out a way to pay his taxes.

Location: On Alcatraz Island; map E1-San Francisco Peninsula, grid c3.

User groups: Hikers only. No dogs, horses, or mountain bikes. No wheelchair facilities.

Permits: No permits are required. Entry tickets include the ferryboat trip to the island and cost $8.75 (plus $2.25 reservation fee) for adults, $5.50 for children 5 to 11, and are available by major credit card from Blue & Gold Fleet, tel. (415) 705-5555. A cassette tape audio tour is available for an additional fee. Evening tours cost $19.75 for adults and $10.50 for children and include audio tour and reservation fee. Ferries depart from Pier 41 in San Francisco.

Maps: A map is available at the ferry landing for a fee. Ask the USGS for a topographic map of the San Francisco North area.

Directions: From U.S. 101 at the Golden Gate Bridge in San Francisco, take the Marina Boulevard exit near the southern foot of the Golden Gate Bridge. Follow Marina Boulevard east toward Fisherman's Wharf. Park in a pay lot, walk to Pier 41 at Fisherman's Wharf, and look for the prominent sign for the Blue and Gold Fleet.

Contact: Blue & Gold Fleet, tel.(415) 705-5555; Golden Gate National Recreation Area, Fort Mason, Building 201, San Francisco, CA 94123; tel. (415) 556-0560, or fax (415) 561-4320.

◨ Lands End Trail
2.5 mi/1.0 hr

One glance from Lands End can take in the mouth of San Francisco Bay and the crashing breakers, with the Golden Gate Bridge and Marin Headlands in the foreground and the Pacific Ocean, Farallon Islands, and Point Reyes in the background. By now you've probably figured out that this is one of San Francisco's greatest lookouts. From the trailhead by the Cliff House Restaurant, you meander eastward on a dirt trail set near bluffs topped with cypress trees. You can also tromp down past the ruins of Sutro Baths, then head toward the Golden Gate Bridge atop bluffs, occasionally sighting the masts of a few sunken ships along shore, and taking in a series of beautiful views. The path is nearly flat and traces the Coastal Trail between Lands End and China Beach on a 2.5-mile round-trip course from the parking area. It is a great destination on Sunday mornings, when hikers take a brisk walk, enjoying the sea breeze on their faces, and then brunch at one of two nearby restaurants, the Cliff House or Louis'. The entire route was once a railroad track out to Sutro Baths.

Location: On the San Francisco headlands at the entrance to San Francisco Bay; map E1-San Francisco Peninsula, grid c2.

User groups: Hikers, wheelchairs, dogs, and mountain bikes (mountain bikes must be walked through narrow sections of the trail). No horses.

Permits: No permits are required. Parking and access are free.

Maps: For a free map, contact the Golden Gate National Recreation Area at the address below. Ask the USGS for a topographic map of the San Francisco North area.

Directions: From the Peninsula, take Interstate 280 to Highway 1 in San Bruno. Turn west and drive one mile to Highway 35/Skyline Boulevard. Turn right on Highway 35 and drive past Lake Merced in San Francisco, jogging left at the lake, and continue to the Cliff House Restaurant and Louis' Restaurant. Continue just past Louis' to the parking areas.

From San Francisco, take Geary Boulevard west until it reaches the ocean and Louis' and the Cliff House Restaurants. Just before Louis' look for the parking area on the right.

Contact: Golden Gate National Recreation Area, Fort Mason, Building 201, San Francisco,

CA 94123; tel. (415) 556-0560, or fax (415) 561-4320; Cliff House Visitor Center, tel. (415) 556-8642; Fort Funston, tel. (415) 239-2366.

3 Coastal Trail

2.5 mi/1.0 hr

While Vista Point at the north end of the Golden Gate Bridge may be the most popular place from which to take snapshots of the bridge, a lookout on the Coastal Trail provides even a more scenic view. This spot is just north of Baker Beach, where San Francisco Bay, the bridge, and the Marin coast all fit easily into a 35-mm frame, a postcard-like scene.

After parking, hike southwest on the Coastal Trail, passing the Fort Scott Overlook, Battery Crosby, and Battery Chamberlin en route to the south end of Baker Beach. The best strategy for photographers is to make the 30-minute walk in, scanning for photo opportunities along the way, and then capture any ideas on film on the return trip. The soft dirt pathway is set in cypress, but don't forget that this is the big, bad city: hikers should travel in pairs or go very early in the morning. For more postcard views of the bridge, take a side trip down to mile-long Baker Beach.

Location: In the Presidio on the San Francisco headlands; map E1-San Francisco Peninsula, grid c2.

User groups: Hikers and wheelchairs. Dogs are not advised. No horses or mountain bikes.

Permits: No permits are required. Parking and access are free.

Maps: For a free map, contact the Golden Gate National Recreation Area at the address below. Ask the USGS for a topographic map of the San Francisco North area.

Directions: From U.S. 101 at the southern end of the Golden Gate Bridge, take the toll plaza parking area exit. Limited parking is available directly east of the toll plaza in a paved area (after parking, you must walk through a short tunnel to reach the trailhead). There is additional unpaved parking 50 yards west of the toll plaza near the trailhead.

Contact: Presidio Visitor Center, tel. (415) 561-4323; Golden Gate National Recreation Area, Fort Mason, Building 201, San Francisco, CA 94123;, tel. (415) 556-0560, or fax (415) 561-4320.

4 Golden Gate Bridge

3.0 mi/1.25 hrs

Relatively few Bay Area residents ever get around to taking the number-one tourist walk in the world: the Golden Gate Bridge. From the center of the bridge the view is incomparable. Looking eastward, you can see Alcatraz, Angel Island, and the bay framed by the San Francisco waterfront and the East Bay hills. Parking is available at the north end of the bridge at Vista Point, and at the south end, on each side of the toll station. If you park on the west side, you walk through a short tunnel that runs under U.S. 101 and loops up to the pathway entrance. The path on the east side of the bridge is reserved for pedestrians, while the west side is for bicyclists only on weekends and evenings. From one end to the other, the bridge is 1.2 miles long (and 220 feet above the water), but most folks walk only halfway out, then return to their cars, for a round-trip of 1.5 miles.

Location: From San Francisco to Marin; map E1-San Francisco Peninsula, grid c2.

User groups: Hikers, wheelchairs, dogs, and mountain bikes (on the west side of the bridge only). No horses.

Permits: No permits are required. Parking and access are free.

Maps: For a free map, contact the Golden Gate National Recreation Area at the address below. Ask the USGS for a topographic map of the San Francisco North area.

Directions: From U.S. 101 at the southern end of the Golden Gate Bridge, take the toll plaza parking area exit. Limited parking is available directly east of the toll plaza. There is additional unpaved parking 50 yards west of the toll plaza; from there you must walk through a short tunnel to reach the foot of the bridge.

Contact: Golden Gate National Recreation Area, Fort Mason, Building 201, San Francisco, CA 94123; tel. (415) 556-0560, or fax (415) 561-4320.

5 Golden Gate Promenade
3.0 mi/1.25 hrs

This paved trail leads along the shoreline of San Francisco Bay from Marina Green to Fort Point. It is virtually flat and the views are magnificent, with a scenic backdrop of the Golden Gate Bridge, Alcatraz, Tiburon, Sausalito, and the bay itself. From the parking area at Marina Green, simply follow the paved pathway through Crissy Field, along the way out to Fort Point, and then to the southern foot of the Golden Gate Bridge. The entire trail is popular with joggers and walkers, especially in the morning. In the afternoon it can get quite windy. People looking for a workout can find one of the Bay Area's most popular par courses at Marina Green. Side trips include the old Muni Pier, the Presidio, which borders much of the route, and Fort Point and its cannons at the foot of the Golden Gate Bridge. The recent reclamation of Crissy Field as wetlands, dunes and picnic area is another highlight.

Location: On the shore of San Francisco Bay in San Francisco; map E1-San Francisco Peninsula, grid c2.

User groups: Hikers, wheelchairs, dogs, and mountain bikes. No horses.

Permits: No permits are required. Parking and access are free.

Maps: For a free map, contact the Golden Gate National Recreation Area at the address below. Ask the USGS for a topographic map of the San Francisco North area.

Directions: From U.S. 101 at the southern end of the Golden Gate Bridge in San Francisco, take the Marina Boulevard exit. Head southeast toward Fisherman's Wharf. Parking lots are available off Marina Boulevard at Fort Mason, Marina Green, Crissy Field, and near the St. Francis Yacht Club.

Contact: Golden Gate National Recreation Area, Fort Mason, Building 201, San Francisco, CA 94123; tel. (415) 556-0560, or fax (415) 561-4320; Presidio Visitor Center, tel. (415) 561-4323.

6 Ocean Beach Esplanade
6.0 mi/2.25 hrs

At Ocean Beach, located along San Francisco's coastal Great Highway, you discover a long expanse of sand, paved jogging trail, and small parks at Fort Funston and Thornton Beach. The nature of both the trail and the adjacent beach allows visitors to create trips of any length. The beach spans four miles from Seal Rock near the Cliff House south to Fort Funston, from which you can continue to explore south all the way past Center Hole to Mussel Rock at the north end of Pacifica. The huge swath of sand at Ocean Beach is popular with joggers, especially during low tides when the hard-packed sand is uncovered. A paved jogging trail is located just east of the Great Highway.

Location: On the San Francisco coast; map E1-San Francisco Peninsula, grid c1.

User groups: Hikers, dogs, and horses. Partially wheelchair accessible. No mountain bikes.

Permits: No permits are required. Parking and access are free.

Maps: For a free map, contact the Golden Gate National Recreation Area at the address below. Ask the USGS for a topographic map of the San Francisco South area.

Directions: From the Peninsula take Interstate 280 to Highway 1 in San Bruno. Turn west and drive one mile to Highway 35/Skyline Boulevard. Turn right on Highway 35 and drive five miles, bearing left to pass Lake Merced. Park on the left along the beach. Or from San Francisco take Geary Boulevard west until it dead-ends at the ocean and the Cliff House Restaurant. Turn left on the Great Highway and drive one mile to the parking area on the right.

Contact: Fort Funston Ranger Station, tel. (415) 239-2366; Golden Gate National Recreation Area, Fort Mason, Building 201, San

Francisco, CA 94123; tel. (415) 556-0560, or fax (415) 561-4320.

7 Fort Funston Sunset Trail
1.5 mi/0.5 hr

Fort Funston is perched on San Francisco's coastal bluffs, with the ocean on one side and Lake Merced on the other. The park is one of the most popular places around to take dogs. It is also the top hang gliding spot in the Bay Area, and watching those daredevils soar is the main attraction. A viewing deck is provided adjacent to the parking area, where the Sunset Trail begins. From here the trail is routed north through coastal bluffs and above sand dunes for .75 mile to the park's border. In the fall and winter the fog clears, and each evening the kinds of sunsets that can make your spine tingle put on quite a show. Those hang gliders are worth gawking at, too, especially in the spring when the north winds come up every afternoon. A few secrets: Petrified saber-toothed tiger teeth have been discovered in the veins of volcanic ore on the cliff faces, replanting of native flowers and plants and protection of the bluffs have inspired a return of burrowing owls and bank swallows, and a ton of sand dollars seem to turn up on the beach walk that leads south from Fort Funston less than a mile to Thornton Beach (collecting them is a violation of park rules).

Location: On the San Francisco coast; map E1-San Francisco Peninsula, grid d1.

User groups: Hikers, dogs, and horses. Partially wheelchair accessible. No mountain bikes.

Permits: No permits are required. Parking and access are free.

Maps: For a free map, contact the Golden Gate National Recreation Area at the address below. Ask the USGS for a topographic map of the San Francisco South area.

Directions: From the Peninsula take Interstate 280 to Highway 1 in San Bruno. Turn west and drive one mile to Highway 35/Skyline Boulevard. Turn right (north) on Highway 35 and drive five miles, bearing left to pass Lake Merced. Park on the left along the beach.

From San Francisco take Geary Boulevard west until it dead-ends at the ocean and the Cliff House Restaurant. Turn left on the Great Highway and drive four miles to the parking area on the right.

Contact: Fort Funston Ranger Station, tel. (415) 239-2366; Golden Gate National Recreation Area, Fort Mason, Building 201, San Francisco, CA 94123; tel. (415) 556-0560, or fax (415) 561-4320.

8 Summit Loop Trail
3.1 mi/1.5 hrs

People hike here for the views, often dramatic, of the South Bay and beyond. San Bruno Mountain is a unique island of open space in an urban setting. This Bay Area landmark, best known to Peninsula residents as that "big ol' hill" west of U.S. 101 near Candlestick Park, has elevations up to 1,314 feet. The summit is private and inaccessible to the public; the highest accessible point is the top parking lot at 1,225 feet. Wind and fog can be big-time downers here. If you are inspired, take the Summit Loop Trail, the most demanding and rewarding hike in the park. It starts at the parking area on the south side of Guadalupe Canyon Parkway. You can connect to the Ridge Trail and add up to five miles to your hike by walking out and back on the East Ridge, which provides beautiful vistas. On the return trip we suggest you veer right at the Dairy Ravine Trail, taking the switchback down the canyon and then heading right again at the Eucalyptus Trail (named for trees that have since been removed), which brings you to the parking area.

Location: In San Bruno Mountain State and County Park near South San Francisco; map E1-San Francisco Peninsula, grid d2.

User groups: Hikers and horses. No dogs or mountain bikes. No wheelchair facilities.

Permits: No permits are required. There is a $4 entrance fee.

Maps: For a free trail map, contact San Bruno Mountain State and County Park at the address below. Ask the USGS for a topographic map of the San Francisco South area.

Directions: From U.S. 101 north of South San Francisco, take the Brisbane/Cow Palace exit and drive two miles to Guadalupe Canyon Parkway. Turn left and follow Guadalupe Canyon Parkway for about two miles to the park entrance on the right. After passing the entrance kiosk, drive to the parking area on the south side of the road.

Contact: San Bruno Mountain State and County Park, 555 Guadalupe Canyon Parkway, Brisbane, CA 94005; tel. (650) 992-6770. County Parks, 455 County Center, 4th Floor, Redwood City, CA 94063-1646; tel. (650) 363-4020 or fax (650) 599-1721.

9 Saddle Trail

2.5 mi/1.25 hrs

Guadalupe Canyon Parkway splits San Bruno Mountain State and County Park in two, leaving hikers to decide which section to visit on a given day. The north half provides a pair of good loop hikes: the Saddle Trail, the featured hike from the parking area/trailhead on the north side, and the Bog Trail. Both are easier than the Summit Loop/Ridge Trail in the park's southern half. From the north parking area, start walking on the Old Guadalupe Trail, which junctions with the Saddle Trail after about 20 minutes. From here take the Saddle Trail and loop around the northern boundaries of the park, climbing about 150 feet in the process. The wind can absolutely howl through this area at times, so pick your hiking days with care. Most of the surrounding terrain is open hillside grasslands, so the views of the South Bay are unblocked and on clear days just spectacular.

Location: In San Bruno Mountain State and County Park; map E1-San Francisco Peninsula, grid d2.

User groups: Hikers and horses. No dogs or mountain bikes. No wheelchair facilities.

Permits: No permits are required. There is a $4 entrance fee.

Maps: For a free trail map, contact San Bruno Mountain State and County Park at the address below. Ask the USGS for a topographic map of the San Francisco South area.

Directions: From U.S. 101 north of South San Francisco, take the Brisbane/Cow Palace exit and drive two miles to Guadalupe Canyon Parkway. Turn left and follow Guadalupe Canyon Parkway for about two miles to the park entrance on the right. After passing the entrance kiosk, drive to the parking area on the north side of the road.

Contact: San Bruno Mountain State and County Park, 555 Guadalupe Canyon Parkway, Brisbane, CA 94005; tel. (650) 992-6770. County Parks, 455 County Center, 4th Floor, Redwood City, CA 94063-1646; tel. (650) 363-4020 or fax (650) 599-1721.

10 Bog Trail

0.8 mi/0.5 hr

The Bog Trail provides a good introduction to San Bruno Mountain State and County Park, although you need to hike other trails here if you desire a more passionate experience. The trail starts at the trailhead on Guadalupe Canyon Parkway's north side and is routed along the north flank of the mountain, changing only 30 feet in elevation. By turning right at the junction with the Old Guadalupe Trail, you can make this a short loop hike. Open hillsides surround the trail and are quite pretty on clear days in the spring when the grasslands turn green and are sprinkled with an explosion of wildflowers. Hikers who make this easy trip quickly get a sense of the importance of the open space buffer the park provides for the congested North Peninsula.

Location: In San Bruno Mountain State and County Park; map E1-San Francisco Peninsula, grid d2.

User groups: Hikers only. The upper part of the trail is wheelchair accessible. No dogs, horses, or mountain bikes.

Permits: No permits are required. There is a $4 entrance fee.

Maps: For a free trail map, contact San Bruno Mountain State and County Park at the address below. Ask the USGS for a topographic map of the San Francisco South area.

Directions: From U.S. 101 north of South San Francisco, take the Brisbane/Cow Palace exit and drive two miles to Guadalupe Canyon Parkway. Turn left and follow Guadalupe Canyon Parkway for about two miles to the park entrance on the right. After passing the entrance kiosk, drive to the parking area on the north side of the road.

Contact: San Bruno Mountain State and County Park, 555 Guadalupe Canyon Parkway, Brisbane, CA 94005; tel. (650) 992-6770. County Parks, 455 County Center, 4th Floor, Redwood City, CA 94063-1646; tel. (650) 363-4020 or fax (650) 599-1721.

11 Milagra Ridge

2.0 mi/0.75 hr

A mile-long paved road/trail is routed to the top of Milagra Ridge, one of the best places imaginable to fly a kite. Those coastal breezes can almost put a strong kite into orbit; some people even use saltwater fishing rods and reels filled with line, playing the kite as if it were a big fish. Kite flying is allowed only inside the gate on the hill to the left. Hikers must stay on the trail to protect the endangered mission blue butterfly.

The parking area that hikers use to gain access to Milagra Ridge is small and obscure—nobody winds up here by accident. Once you park your car, the hike up to the ridge top is an easy mile and is suitable for wheelchair users who have some assistance. The summit was flattened in the 1950s to accommodate a missile site, long since abandoned. Looking westward, visitors are surprised at the sheer drop-off from the ridge down into

Pacifica. Alas, in the summer months this can be one of the foggiest places in the world.

Location: In Pacifica near Skyline College; map E1-San Francisco Peninsula, grid e2.

User groups: Hikers and mountain bikes (allowed on only one mile of paved trail). Wheelchair accessible with assistance. No dogs or horses.

Permits: No permits are required. Parking and access are free.

Maps: For a free map, contact the Golden Gate National Recreation Area at the address below. Ask the USGS for a topographic map of the San Francisco South area.

Directions: From Interstate 280 in San Bruno, take the Westborough exit and then drive west up the hill and across Highway 35/Skyline Boulevard. Drive to College Avenue and turn right (north). Continue a very short distance to the end of the road and the trailhead. Limited parking is available.

Contact: Golden Gate National Recreation Area, Fort Mason, Building 201, San Francisco, CA 94123; tel. (415) 556-0560, or fax (415) 561-4320.

12 Sweeney Ridge

4.4 mi/2.5 hrs

Hikers usually have to pay dearly to get a 360-degree mountaintop view, but at Sweeney Ridge, payment is made via a 2.2-mile hike from the trailhead at Skyline College. This is the Bay Discovery Site, where Captain Portola became the first of the New World explorers to get a glimpse of what is now San Francisco Bay. You can make the same discovery on the steady grade up to the ridge; it takes about an hour for most people, more for some. The route traces through coastal scrub and grassland, topping out at 1,200 feet. On clear days several of the Bay Area's most impressive mountains stand in clear view: Mount Tamalpais, Mount Diablo, and nearby Montara Mountain. In 15 minutes of hiking, the views of the South Bay on one side and the Pacific Ocean on the other offer another extraordinary perspective. In another 15 minutes, you get views of the ocean as well. In the spring, when all is green, look closely and you find surprising numbers of wildflowers with their tiny blooms. The trail continues south to the border of the San Francisco Crystal Springs Watershed, including a drop-dead gorgeous meadow hidden on the west flank where deer can often be found.

Location: On the Peninsula ridgeline in San Bruno; map E1-San Francisco Peninsula, grid e2.

User groups: Hikers, dogs, horses, and mountain bikes. No wheelchair facilities.

Permits: No permits are required. Parking and access are free.

Maps: For a free map, contact the Golden Gate National Recreation Area at the address below. Ask the USGS for a topographic map of the San Francisco South area.

Directions: From Interstate 280 in San Bruno, take the Westborough exit and drive west up the hill to Highway 35/Skyline Boulevard. Turn left (south) on Highway 35 and drive a short distance to College Drive; turn right and drive to the Skyline College campus. At the stop sign turn left and drive to lot number two. The trailhead is located at the back of the parking lot. Bikes can also access the trail from Sneath Lane in San Bruno.

Contact: Golden Gate National Recreation Area, Fort Mason, Building 201, San Francisco, CA 94123; tel. (415) 556-0560, or fax (415) 561-4320; Fort Funston Visitor Center/Ranger Station, tel. (415) 239-2366.

13 Montara Mountain/ Brooks Creek Trail

7.0 mi/2.5 hrs

Just 20 minutes south of San Francisco is this secluded trail in San Pedro Valley County Park, where visitors are few, the coastal beauty divine, and hikers can carve out their own personal slice of heaven. The Montara Mountain/Brooks Creek Trail is the prize of the park, featuring the best viewing area for Brooks Falls (read on) and great lookouts to the Pacific Coast. After parking, walk about 50 yards along the Montara Mountain/Brooks Creek Trail. The trail then splits, with the Brooks Creek Trail on the left and the Montara Mountain Trail on the right; the two merge again about one mile up Brooks Creek and continue as a common route to the peak. Turn right on the well-signed Montara Mountain Trail. From here the next mile climbs several hundred feet, and suddenly Brooks Falls appears in a surprising free fall down a canyon.

The fall is connected in three narrow, silver-tasseled tiers, falling 175 feet in all. And though there never seems to be enough water in this waterfall, it still is a very pretty gorge amid a chaparral-covered mountain slope. One reason Brooks Falls is so little known is that it doesn't flow year-round. As a tributary to San Pedro Creek, Brooks Creek runs only in late winter and spring, best of course after several days of rain. Note that a great coastal lookout is available another 10 minutes up the trail on a dramatic rock outcrop. The hike continues all the way to the North Peak of Montara Mountain at 1,898 feet, 3.5 miles one way, including a final 1.1-mile push on a fire road to reach the summit. On a clear spring day, the views are absolutely stunning in all directions, highlighted by the Pacific Ocean, the Farallon Islands, and miles of the adjacent off-limits Crystal Springs Watershed.

Special note: This route is the first link in one of the few great one-way hikes (using a shuttle) in the Bay Area. From the top of Montara Mountain, you enter McNee Ranch State Park and hike 3.8 miles to Montara State Beach, descending all the way, with glorious views for the entire route. So with cars parked at each end of the trail, you can hike 7.3 miles one way from San Pedro Valley County Park, up Montara Mountain, and down to Montara State Beach.

Location: In San Pedro Valley County Park in Pacifica; map E1-San Francisco Peninsula, grid e2.

User groups: Hikers and horses (on designated trails only). Some trails and facilities are wheelchair accessible. No dogs or mountain bikes.

Permits: No permits are required. There is a $4 entrance fee.

Maps: For a free trail map, contact San Pedro Valley County Park at the address below. Ask the USGS for a topographic map of the Montara Mountain area.

Directions: From San Francisco take Highway 1 south into Pacifica. Turn east on Linda Mar Boulevard and drive until it dead-ends at Oddstad Boulevard. Turn right and drive to the park entrance, located about 50 yards on the left. The trailhead is on the southwest side of the parking lot.

Contact: San Pedro Valley County Park, 600 Oddstad Boulevard, Pacifica, CA 94044; tel. (650) 355-8280 or fax (650) 363-4020.

14 Linda Mar/ Rockaway Point Trail

2.5 mi/1.5 hrs

Sure, you could probably hike this route to the end and back in a flash. But sometimes, as you will discover here, taking the time to go slowly sure beats rushing through as quickly as possible. You just plain won't want to miss anything after you park at the Pacifica State Beach parking lot at Linda Mar and start hiking north on the beach. The northern end of this sand stretch is a great place to throw sticks to a dog (but be aware that the sand dune area provides habitat for the endangered snowy plover) and to fish for striped bass in the summer.

At the end of the beach, climb up on the dirt trail that traces around Rockaway Point. Here you find beautiful views of San Pedro Point, Montara Mountain, and of course the Pacific Ocean. Just meander along, listen to the waves, and let the beauty flow through you. Then when you feel like it, turn around and follow the same route back to your car. When you first drive up, don't get spooked if the parking lot seems crowded. Why? Because many people often prefer to spend time philosophizing about life while looking down into the mouth of a beer bottle, rather than taking this walk and experiencing the full fabric of the place.

Location: On the Pacifica shoreline near Pacifica State Beach/Linda Mar; map E1-San Francisco Peninsula, grid e1.

User groups: Hikers and dogs. No horses or mountain bikes. No wheelchair facilities.

Permits: No permits are required. Parking and access are free.

Maps: Ask the USGS for a topographic map of the Montara Mountain area.

Directions: From San Francisco head south on Interstate 280 to Daly City. Turn south on Highway 1 and drive about five miles into Pacifica. Drive to the southern end of Pacifica and turn right at the parking lot for Pacifica State Beach/Linda Mar. The trail starts at the north end of the beach.

Contact: City of Pacifica, Parks, 170 Santa Maria Avenue, Pacifica, CA 94044; tel. (650) 738-7300.

15 San Pedro Mountain

6.0 mi/2.5 hrs

For people who like dramatic coastal views, this is the ideal trail, tracing the top of coastal bluffs. Many spots along the way provide perches for flawless vistas. To get to them, take note at the entrance gate and look for the trail that is routed off to the left and up through the hilly grasslands. With those first few steps, it doesn't look like much of a trail. But as you continue, rising atop the first crest, you see how it tracks up the spine of the coastal ridgeline, eventually providing a lookout above Gray Whale Cove. From this viewpoint you may feel an odd sense of irony: below you is Highway 1, typically filled with a stream of slow-moving cars driven by people who want to get somewhere else; meanwhile, you are in a place of peace and serenity, happy right where you are. The hike includes a few short climbs across grasslands

and can be converted to a loop hike by turning right at the junction with the Montara Mountain Trail.

Location: In McNee Ranch State Park in Montara; map E1-San Francisco Peninsula, grid e1.

User groups: Hikers and dogs. No horses or mountain bikes. No wheelchair facilities.

Permits: No permits are required. Parking and access are free.

Maps: Ask the USGS for a topographic map of the Montara Mountain area.

Directions: From San Francisco, drive about 17 miles south on Highway 1. Continue through Pacifica, then through Devils Slide, and down to the base of the hill. Look for a small pullout area on the left. The access point is at a yellow gate with a state park property sign. There is room for just a few cars. Do not block the gate. If pullout area is full, drive south on Highway 1 a short distance and park at the lot on the west side of the highway at Montara State Beach.

Contact: California State Parks, Bay Area District, 250 Executive Park Boulevard, Suite 4900, San Francisco, CA 94134; tel. (415) 330-6300 or fax (415) 330-6312. Montara State Beach at tel. (650) 726-8819.

16 Montara Mountain/ McNee Ranch

7.6 mi/3.75 hrs

On a clear day from the top of Montara Mountain, the Farallon Islands to the northwest appear so close you may think you could reach out and pluck them from the ocean. To the east, it looks as if you could take a giant leap across the bay and land atop Mount Diablo. Some 10 miles to the north and south there's nothing but mountain wilderness connecting Sweeney Ridge to an off-limits state game preserve. By now you should be properly motivated for the climb, which for many is a genuine butt-kicker. From the main access gate to the top it's 3.8 miles, a rise of nearly 2,000 feet that includes three killer "ups." Follow the

ranch road up the San Pedro Mountain ridgeline to the Montara Coastal Range; at the fork, stay to the right on the dirt road as it climbs and turns. After a 20-minute wheezer of an ascent, look for a garbage can at a flat spot on the left side of the trail—30 yards down a cutoff you find a perch for a dazzling view of the Pacific Coast. After catching your breath, continue on, heading up, up, and up, eventually topping out at the summit. Only the radio transmitter here mars an otherwise pristine setting. All you need for this hike is a clear day, some water, and plenty of inspiration.

Location: In McNee Ranch State Park in Montara; map E1-San Francisco Peninsula, grid e1.

User groups: Hikers, dogs, and mountain bikes. No horses. No wheelchair facilities.

Permits: No permits are required. Parking and access are free.

Maps: Ask the USGS for a topographic map of the Montara Mountain area.

Directions: From San Francisco drive about 17 miles south on Highway 1. Continue through Pacifica, then through Devils Slide, and down to the base of the hill. Look for a small pullout area on the left. The access point is at a yellow gate with a state park property sign. There is room for just a few cars. Do not block the gate. If pullout area is full, drive south on Highway 1 a short distance and park at the lot on the west side of the highway at Montara State Beach.

Contact: California State Parks, Bay Area District, 250 Executive Park Boulevard, Suite 4900, San Francisco, CA 94134; tel. (415) 330-6300 or fax (415) 330-6312. Montara State Beach, tel. (650) 726-8819.

17 San Andreas Trail

6.0 mi/2.5 hrs

Winding its way through wooded foothills, the San Andreas Trail overlooks Upper San Andreas Lake. The only downer is that much of the route runs adjacent to Highway 35/Skyline Boulevard. Regardless, it is worth the trip, because to the west you can see the untouched slopes of Montara Mountain, a game preserve, and that sparkling lake, all off-limits to the public. The trail starts near the northern end of the lake; a signed trailhead marker is posted on Skyline Boulevard. It goes about three miles until the next access point at Hillcrest Boulevard and from there connects to the Sawyer Camp Trail. The view of Montara Mountain to the west is particularly enchanting during the summer when rolling fog banks crest the ridgeline, a spectacle.

Location: In the San Mateo County foothills southwest of San Bruno; map E1-San Francisco Peninsula, grid f2.

User groups: Hikers, horses, and mountain bikes. Note that the northern section is paved, but the southern section is not. There are some wheelchair-accessible facilities. No dogs.

Permits: No permits are required. Parking and access are free.

Maps: For a free trail map, contact San Mateo County Parks at the address below. Ask the USGS for a topographic map of the Montara Mountain area.

Directions: To access the north gate: From Interstate 280 in San Bruno, take the Westborough exit and drive west up the hill to the intersection with Highway 35/Skyline Boulevard. Turn left on Highway 35 and drive about 2.5 miles to the trailhead entrance on the right side of the road.

To access the south gate: On Highway 280 drive to the Millbrae Avenue exit. Take that exit and drive north on what appears to be a frontage road/Skyline Boulevard (on the west side of Highway 280) and continue to the parking area on the left.

Contact: San Mateo County Parks and Recreation, 455 County Center, 4th Floor, Redwood City, CA 94063-1646; tel. (650) 363-4020 or fax (650) 599-1721.

18 Sawyer Camp Trail

12.0 mi/5.0 hrs

With the Sawyer Camp Trail you get everything that there is on the connecting link to the north, the San Andreas Trail, and more. Alas, not all of it is good. On a positive note, the trail is set away from the road, so you get more peace (at least, that seems the intent). It is routed along a lake and through a forest, so you get more nature. But since this route is paved and hardly a secret, you also get more people. In fact, ever since the biking speed limit was raised to 15 miles per hour, there's been a real problem with hikers being used as flags in a slalom course. The result is that many hikers now stay away from this area rather than be put into fight-or-run showdowns with warp-speed bikers. While the listed one-way distance is six miles, at any point you can just turn around and go back, cutting the trip as short as you wish. Or better yet, bring two vehicles, leave one at each of the two trailheads along Highway 35/Skyline Boulevard, and make it a one-way walk. From north to south, the hike includes a drop of 400 feet, so if you plan on a return trip, there will be a little huff and puff on the way back. Park benches are provided at viewpoints along the lake, where you can often see trout rising and feeding on summer evenings.

Location: In the San Mateo County foothills south of San Bruno; map E1-San Francisco Peninsula, grid f2.

User groups: Hikers, horses, and mountain bikes. There are some wheelchair-accessible facilities at the south end. No dogs.

Permits: No permits are required. Parking and access are free.

Maps: For a free trail map, contact San Mateo County Parks at the address below. Ask the USGS for a topographic map of the Montara Mountain area.

Directions: From Interstate 280 in San Bruno take the Westborough exit and drive west up the hill to the intersection with Highway 35/Skyline Boulevard. Turn left on Highway 35 and drive about six miles to the trailhead entrance on the right.

Contact: San Mateo County Parks and Recreation, 455 County Center, 4th Floor, Redwood City, CA 94063-1646; tel. (650) 363-4020 or fax (650) 599-1721.

19 Fitzgerald Marine Reserve
1.0 mi/1.0 hr

The closer you look, the better it gets. When you go tide-pool hopping, there is nothing more fascinating than discovering a variety of tiny sea creatures. That is what makes the Fitzgerald Marine Reserve—a shallow 30-acre reef that exposes hundreds and hundreds of tidal pockets every time a minus low tide rolls back the ocean—so attractive. After parking, it's a short walk down to the tide pools; from here you walk on exposed rock, watching the wonders of the tidal waters. Be sure to wear boots that grip well and take care not to crush any fragile sea plants as you walk. In the tide pools you discover hermit crabs, rock crabs, sea anemones, sculpins, starfish, sea snails, and many plants and animals in various colors. An option is to continue walking south on the beach to the Moss Beach Distillery, a popular watering hole. A few notes: No dogs, no beachcombing, no shell gathering. In other words, OK looky, but no touchy. After all, this is a preserve.

Location: In Moss Beach; map E1-San Francisco Peninsula, grid f1.

User groups: Hikers only. No dogs, horses, or mountain bikes. No wheelchair facilities.

Permits: No permits are required. Parking and access are free.

Maps: Ask the USGS for a topographic map of the Montara Mountain area.

Directions: From San Francisco, take Interstate 280 to Highway 1 in Daly City and drive through Pacifica, over Devils Slide, and into Moss Beach. Turn right (west) at the signed turnoff at California Street and continue one mile to the parking area.

Alternate route: From the Peninsula, take Highway 92 into Half Moon Bay and then head north on Highway 1 for seven miles to Moss Beach. Turn left (west) at the signed turnoff at California Street and drive one mile to the parking area.

Contact: Fitzgerald Marine Reserve, P.O. Box 451, Moss Beach, CA 94038; tel. (650) 728-3584 or fax (650) 728-3621.

20 Coyote Point Trail
0.4 mi/0.5 hr

The trail is so short and flat that some hikers may question why they should bother. But give it a try and you'll see. From the lookout over the pretty South Bay on a clear day, it looks as if you could get a running start, jump, and glide across the water to the land's edge. To hike the trail, park adjacent to the boat ramp and walk out to land's end at Coyote Point. This is a good fishing area, by the way, for jacksmelt in the spring. From this point you can scan miles of open water, spotting Mount Diablo to the east, the San Mateo Bridge to the south, and on especially clear days, the Bay Bridge to the north. Many are surprised at just how big the South Bay is. An optional side trip is to hike north along the bay's shore.

Location: In Coyote Point County Park in San Mateo; map E1-San Francisco Peninsula, grid f3.

User groups: Hikers, wheelchairs, and mountain bikes. No dogs or horses.

Permits: No permits are required. There is a $4 parking fee.

Maps: For a free trail map, contact Coyote Point County Park at the address below. Ask the USGS for a topographic map of the San Mateo area.

Directions: In San Mateo on U.S. 101, take the Poplar Avenue exit and drive half a block to Humboldt Street. Turn right and drive a few blocks to Peninsula Street. Turn right and drive over, then under, U.S. 101, bearing left on the frontage road. Follow the frontage road a short distance to the Coyote Point County Park entrance.

Alternate route: In San Mateo on U.S. 101, take the Dore exit, make an immediate left turn on the frontage road, and drive a short distance to the Coyote Point County Park entrance.

Contact: Coyote Point County Park, 1701 Coyote Point Drive, San Mateo, CA 94401; tel. (650) 573-2592. San Mateo County Parks, tel. (650) 363-4020.

21 Crystal Springs Trail
6.4 mi/3.0 hrs

Crystal Springs is the forbidden paradise of the Bay Area, and this trail is as close as the bureaucrats will let you get. Enjoy the view, but don't touch and don't dare trespass or fish; they'll slam you in the pokey before you know what hit you. From the parking area the trail runs along the border of San Francisco watershed land, adjacent to Cañada Road. Beautiful Crystal Springs Reservoir is off to the west, occasionally disappearing from view behind a hill as you walk south. Deer are commonly seen in this area, a nice bonus. Your destination is 3.2 miles away, the Pulgas Water Temple (closed to the public), where waters from Hetch Hetchy in Yosemite arrive via canal and thunder into this giant bathtub-like structure surrounded by Roman pillars and a canopy. At the Pulgas Water Temple, you have the option of continuing for another 4.2 miles to Huddart Park. With a shuttle car, that makes a great one-way hike.

Location: Along Crystal Springs Reservoir in the Woodside foothills; map E1-San Francisco Peninsula, grid f3.

User groups: Hikers and mountain bikes. No dogs or horses. No wheelchair facilities.

Permits: No permits are required. Parking and access are free.

Maps: For a free trail map, contact San Mateo County Parks at the address below. Ask the USGS for a topographic map of the San Mateo area.

Directions: From Interstate 280 in San Mateo, take the Highway 92 exit and drive west to Cañada Road/Highway 95. Turn south on Cañada Road and drive .2 mile to the parking area on the right.

Contact: San Mateo County Parks and Recreation, 455 County Center, 4th Floor, Redwood City, CA 94063-1646; tel. (650) 363-4020 or fax (650) 599-1721.

22 Waterdog Lake Trail
4.0 mi/1.75 hrs

The lack of public access to a half dozen lakes on the Peninsula makes little Waterdog Lake all the more special. Out of the way and often forgotten, the lake was created by damming Belmont Creek in Diablo Canyon. While not exactly a jewel, it still makes for a unique recreation site, but it gets overlooked because the parking access is so obscure. It takes only 15 minutes to reach the lake, with the trail skirting the northern edge of the shore. Many people stop here, but if you forge on, you will be well compensated. The trail, which is more of a dirt road, rises above the lake and enters John Brooks Memorial Open Space. At the crest of the hill, reached after a climb of about 300 feet, there are pretty views of Crystal Springs Reservoir. An option is to extend your trip on the Sheep Camp Trail, a dirt road that is linked to a gravel road set adjacent to the San Francisco Fish and Game Refuge.

Location: In the Belmont foothills; map E1-San Francisco Peninsula, grid f3.

User groups: Hikers and mountain bikes. No dogs or horses. No wheelchair facilities.

Permits: No permits are required. Parking and access are free.

Maps: For a trail map, contact the City of Belmont Parks at the address below. Ask the USGS for a topographic map of the San Mateo area.

Directions: From Highway 92 in San Mateo, take the Ralston Avenue exit and turn south on Lyall Way. Drive to the corner of Lyall Way and Lake Road to find the parking entrance. Parking is available along the street.

Contact: City of Belmont, Parks, 1225 Ralston Avenue, Belmont, CA 94002; tel. (650) 595-7441 or fax (650) 595-7419.

23 Pillar Point
2.5 mi/1.5 hrs

One of the truly great coastal walks, this place is nevertheless overlooked by many visitors and locals alike. It includes a secluded beach with inshore kelp beds and sea lions playing peek-aboo, and during low tide, you can walk around the corner at Pillar Point and boulder hop in wondrous seclusion. Watch your tide book, because the Pillar Point tidal area is under water most of the time.

To start, park at the western side of Princeton Harbor, just below the radar station, then walk out along the west side of the harbor. The trail here is on hard-packed dirt above two quiet beaches where grebes, cormorants, and pelicans often cavort. During the evening the harbor lights are quite pretty here. When you reach the Princeton jetty, turn right and walk along the beach toward Pillar Point; this is where the sea lions frequently play "now-you-see-me, now-you-don't." At low tides, continue around Pillar Point and enjoy the rugged beauty, solitude, and ocean views, taking your time as you hop along from rock to rock.

Location: In Princeton at Half Moon Bay; map E1-San Francisco Peninsula, grid g1.

User groups: Hikers, dogs, and horses (not advised). No mountain bikes. No wheelchair facilities.

Permits: No permits are required. Parking and access are free.

Maps: Ask the USGS for a topographic map of the Half Moon Bay area.

Directions: From the Peninsula take Interstate 280 to San Mateo and Highway 92. Turn west on Highway 92 and drive to Half Moon Bay. Turn right on Highway 1 and drive five miles to Princeton. Turn left at the traffic signal, drive about .5 mile through Princeton Village, and turn left again, going one mile toward a radar station. There is limited parking on the left side of the road. Follow the trail on the west side of the harbor.

Contact: There is no managing agency. For general information, contact Huck Finn Sportfishing (closed November through December 26), tel. (650) 726-7133, or Capt. John's, tel. (650) 726-2913.

24 Harkins Ridge Trail
3.2 mi one way/1.5 hrs

Purisima Creek Redwoods is a magnificent 2,633-acre redwood preserve set on the western slopes of the Santa Cruz Mountains from Skyline Boulevard down to Half Moon Bay. One of the best ways to explore the area is on the Harkins Ridge Trail. We recommend making it a one-way trip by having a shuttle car waiting at the trail's end at the Higgins Purisima parking access.

The trail starts at the Skyline Access on Skyline Boulevard, elevation 2,000 feet, located at a parking area just south of a small store. From here the trail descends over the course of 3.2 miles to 400 feet; the last portion of the trail drops quite steeply in a series of switchbacks. (To turn this into a loop hike, return via the Whittemore Gulch Trail.) In the process you are routed through redwoods that many people don't even realize exist. For those who want a pristine experience, a good option is to take the Soda Gulch Trail; about a mile down the Harkins Ridge Trail, turn left at the junction. No mountain bikes are allowed on this portion of the trail, which heads past giant trees, redwood sorrel, and fern-lined creek banks.

Location: In Purisima Creek Redwoods Open Space Preserve, on Skyline Ridge near San Mateo; map E1-San Francisco Peninsula, grid g2.

User groups: Hikers, horses, and mountain bikes. No dogs. No wheelchair facilities.

Permits: No permits are required. Parking and access are free.

Maps: For a free map, contact the Midpeninsula Regional Open Space District at the address below or pick one up at the trailhead. Ask the USGS for a topographic map of the Woodside area.

Directions: From San Francisco drive south on Interstate 280 for about 15 miles to the Highway 92 cutoff. Turn west on Highway 92 and drive to Highway 35/Skyline Boulevard. Turn south (left) on Highway 35 and drive 4.5

miles to the Purisima Creek Redwoods parking area on the right (west side of the road, just past a small store). If you are planning a shuttle trip, drive a second car to the Higgins Purisima Road parking area.

Contact: Midpeninsula Regional Open Space District, 330 Distel Circle, Los Altos, CA 94022; tel. (650) 691-1200 or fax (650) 691-0485; during nonbusiness hours a Touch-Tone phone menu is available for trail events, conditions, and news.

25 Whittemore Gulch
4.3 mi/3.25 hrs

Most folks come to this popular trailhead, located just south of Half Moon Bay, to take a short stroll along Purisima Creek and then turn back. The Whittemore Gulch Trail, however, offers more of a challenge, especially near the end. It also forms the return route for a loop hike starting at Skyline Boulevard. The payoffs for hikers can be fantastic.

The trail begins innocently enough from the Higgins Purisima parking area, set in the beautiful foothills southeast of Half Moon Bay. The trail is routed right up Whittemore Gulch for a gentle climb over the first mile. This stretch is even suitable for wheelchairs and strollers. All seems well with the world as you pass through a grove of shaded redwoods and by a small stream. You cross the stream and continue up the canyon, amid a beautiful redwood forest, complete with enclosed canopy, and this beautiful little creek. At the head of the canyon, you then begin to climb. In a series of switchbacks, the trail climbs 600 feet in just over .25 mile, at about a 10 percent grade. After the switchbacks, the trail climbs another 400 feet in a more gracious fashion to reach the Whittemore Gulch parking access on Skyline Boulevard, which, at 2,000 feet, features a great lookout of Half Moon Bay and Pillar Point Harbor. The trailhead elevation is 400 feet, so that means it's a 1,600-foot climb to Skyline Boulevard.

Location: In Purisima Creek Redwoods Open Space Preserve, near Half Moon Bay; map E1-San Francisco Peninsula, grid g2.

User groups: Hikers only. Horses and mountain bikes are sometimes restricted due to wet weather, so check with a ranger beforehand. No dogs. No wheelchair facilities.

Permits: No permits are required. Parking and access are free.

Maps: For a free map, contact the Midpeninsula Regional Open Space District at the address below or pick one up at the trailhead. Ask the USGS for a topographic map of the Woodside area.

Directions: From San Francisco drive south on Interstate 280 for about 15 miles to the Highway 92 cutoff. Turn west on Highway 92 and drive to Half Moon Bay. At the stoplight turn left on Main Street and drive south through town to Higgins Purisima Road. Turn left and drive on the winding road for four miles to the trailhead parking area on the left.

Contact: Midpeninsula Regional Open Space District, 330 Distel Circle, Los Altos, CA 94022; tel. (650) 691-1200 or fax (650) 691-0485; during nonbusiness hours a Touch-Tone phone menu is available for trail events, conditions, and news.

26 Redwood Trail
0.5 mi/0.5 hr

The .25-mile-long Redwood Trail allows just about anybody to experience the grandeur of a redwood forest. Anybody? People with baby strollers, wheelchairs, or walkers, and those recovering from poor health will be able to do this trail. It starts at 2,000 feet on Skyline Boulevard and is routed north under a canopy of giant redwoods. At the end there are picnic tables and restrooms. And the return trip is just as easy. Most people don't really hike the trail, they just kind of mosey along, seeing how it feels to wander freely among ancient trees.

Location: In Purisima Creek Redwoods Open Space Preserve, on Skyline Ridge near

Woodside; map E1-San Francisco Peninsula, grid g2.

User groups: Hikers and wheelchairs. No dogs, horses, or mountain bikes.

Permits: No permits are required. Parking and access are free.

Maps: For a free map, contact the Midpeninsula Regional Open Space District at the address below or pick one up at the trailhead. Ask the USGS for a topographic map of the Woodside area.

Directions: From San Francisco drive south on Interstate 280 for approximately 15 miles to the Highway 92 cutoff. Turn west on Highway 92 and continue driving to Highway 35/Skyline Boulevard. Turn west on Highway 35 and drive to the Purisima Creek parking area, located at mile marker 16.65.

Contact: Midpeninsula Regional Open Space District, 330 Distel Circle, Los Altos, CA 94022; tel. (650) 691-1200 or fax (650) 691-0485; during nonbusiness hours a Touch-Tone telephone menu is available for trail events, conditions, and news.

27 Huddart Park Loop
5.0 mi/3.25 hrs

Huddart Park is a Peninsula treasure, covering 1,000 acres from the foothills near Woodside on up to Skyline Boulevard. Redwoods grow on much of the land, a creek runs right through the park, and when you hike high on the east slope, there are occasional views of the South Bay. While several short loop trips are available here, including the .5-mile Redwood Trail, we recommend creating a loop hike and circling the park. Some of the shorter trips here do not provide the kind of pay-off in natural beauty that many are looking for.

A map is a necessity, of course. At the Werder Picnic Area, start on the Dean Trail. To make a complete loop and return to the trailhead, connect to the Richard Road's Trail, Summit Springs Trail, and Archery Fire Trail. In the process you will get a good overview of the entire area and discover why this is one

of the best hiking parks on the Peninsula. A unique option is taking the Skyline Ridge Trail, which connects Huddart Park with Wunderlich Park.

Special note: The Chickadee Trail at Huddart Park is wheelchair accessible. Also, horses are allowed on many other park trails.

Location: In the Woodside foothills; map E1-San Francisco Peninsula, grid g3.

User groups: Hikers and horses. Mountain bikes are permitted on paved roads only. Limited wheelchair facilities. No dogs.

Permits: No permits are required. A $4 park entrance fee is charged.

Maps: For a trail map, contact Huddart Park at the address below. Ask the USGS for a topographic map of the Woodside area.

Directions: From Interstate 280 in Woodside, take the Woodside Road/Highway 84 exit and drive about nine miles west to King's Mountain Road. Turn right and drive 2.2 miles to the park entrance.

Contact: Huddart Park, 1100 Kings Mountain Road, Woodside, CA 94062; tel. (650) 851-1210, (650) 851-0326, or fax (650) 851-9558; San Mateo County Parks and Recreation, 455 County Center, 4th Floor, Redwood City, CA 94063-1646; tel. (650) 363-4020 or fax (650) 599-1721.

28 Skyline Trail
8.0 mi one way/4.5 hrs

Great ridgeline views of the South Bay, giant stumps and trees, and a good, long walk are the highlights of the Skyline Trail. This route connects Huddart Park to Wunderlich Park, for an excellent one-way-only walk with a shuttle partner. The trip includes a climb of about 700 feet followed by a descent of some 1,000 feet. For the most part, though, it traces through redwoods along the Skyline Ridge, which provides wonderful views. From Huddart Park heading south, the trail emerges from the park and crosses King's Mountain Road, then climbs gradually (it has been reconstructed to avoid a former steep grade) to the Skyline Ridge before turning south again.

Skyline Boulevard/Highway 35 may be nearby, but there are few reminders, as the trail is routed to trace ridges and laterals above canyons. Some of the old tree stumps in the area are huge; when you start spotting them, look closely for the Methuselah Tree. The centerpiece of the forest, this colossal survivor spans 15 feet in diameter. When you enter Wunderlich Park, the trail descends sharply in a series of switchbacks, then turns tightly for the last .5 mile to Skylonda.

Location: From Huddart Park to Skylonda, near the Skyline Ridge and Woodside; map E1-San Francisco Peninsula, grid g3.

User groups: Hikers and horses. No dogs or mountain bikes. No wheelchair facilities.

Permits: No permits are required. A $4 park entrance fee is charged.

Maps: For a trail map, contact Huddart Park at the address below. Ask the USGS for a topographic map of the Woodside area.

Directions: From San Francisco drive south on Interstate 280 for about 15 miles to the Highway 92 cutoff. Turn west on Highway 92 and drive to Highway 35/Skyline Boulevard. Turn south (left) on Highway 35 and drive 6.5 miles to the trailhead on the east side of the road. Look for the blue sign marking the Bay Ridge Trail.

Contact: Huddart Park, 1100 Kings Mountain Road, Woodside, CA 94062; tel. (650) 851-1210 or (650) 851-0326, or fax (650) 851-9558; San Mateo County Parks and Recreation, 455 County Center, 4th Floor, Redwood City, CA 94063-1646; tel. (650) 363-4020 or fax (650) 599-1721.

29 Meadows Loop Trail

5.5 mi/3.0 hrs

Wunderlich Park is one of the better spots on the Peninsula for clearing out the brain cobwebs. The network of trails here provides a variety of adventures, from short strolls to all-day treks. Take your pick. Ours is the Meadows Loop, which circles much of the park, crossing first through oak woodlands, rising to open grasslands, then passing a redwood forest on the way back. This hike includes an elevation gain of nearly 1,000 feet, so come prepared for a workout. Make sure you have a trail map, then take this route: Near the park office look for the signed trailhead for the Alambique Trail and hike about .5 mile. At the junction with the Meadows Trail, turn right, hike a short distance, and then turn left on the Meadows Trail and climb up to the Meadows. This is a perfect picnic site, with rolling hills, grasslands, and great views. To complete the loop, forge onward, then turn right at the Bear Gulch Trail and take it all the way back, including switchbacks, to the park entrance.

Location: In Wunderlich Park in the Woodside foothills; map E1-San Francisco Peninsula, grid g3.

User groups: Hikers and horses. No dogs or mountain bikes. No wheelchair facilities.

Permits: No permits are required. Parking and access are free.

Maps: For a free map, contact San Mateo County Parks at the address below. Ask the USGS for a topographic map of the Woodside area.

Directions: From Interstate 280 on the Peninsula in Woodside, take the Woodside/Highway 84 exit. Drive west for 2.5 miles to the park on the right.

Contact: Wunderlich Park, c/o Huddart Park, 1100 Kings Mountain Road, Woodside, CA 94062; tel. (650) 851-1210 or (650) 851-0326, or fax (650) 851-9558; San Mateo County Parks and Recreation, 455 County Center, 4th Floor, Redwood City, CA 94063-1646; tel. (650) 363-4020 or fax (650) 599-1721.

30 Ravenswood Open Space Preserve

2.0 mi/0.75 hr

This 370-acre parcel of land is rich in marshland habitat and home to many types of birds. The first trails became accessible in the 1990s, along with two excellent observation decks. From the parking area at the end of Bay Road, backtrack by walking across a bridged slough to the trailhead on the north side of the road. You will immediately come to a fork in the road. You can turn right and walk 200 feet to an observation deck with great views of the South Bay. Go left instead and you will find a hard-surface path that heads north and hooks out toward the bay to another wood observation deck. This is the primary destination for most visitors.

Location: On the shore of South San Francisco Bay at Ravenswood; map E1-San Francisco Peninsula, grid g5.

User groups: Hikers, wheelchairs, and mountain bikes. No dogs or horses.

Permits: No permits are required. Parking and access are free.

Maps: For a free map, contact the Midpeninsula Regional Open Space District at the address below. Ask the USGS for a topographic map of the Mountain View area.

Directions: From U.S. 101 in Palo Alto, take the University Avenue exit and drive east to Bay Road. Turn right on Bay Road and drive to the end of the road. The preserve entrance is adjacent to Cooley Landing.

Contact: Midpeninsula Regional Open Space District, 330 Distel Circle, Los Altos, CA 94022; tel. (650) 691-1200 or fax (650) 691-0485; during nonbusiness hours a Touch-Tone phone menu is available for trail events, conditions, and news.

31 Baylands Catwalk
0.25 mi/0.5 hr

What the heck is the Baylands Catwalk, you ask? As you will discover here, it is an old wooden walkway placed across tidal marshland and routed under giant electrical towers and out to the shoreline of South San Francisco Bay. In recent years the catwalk has been improved, with a new observation deck set on the edge of the bay waters. You start at the Baylands Interpretive Center, which houses exhibits explaining the marshland habitat.

From there you can make the short walk straight east out to the observation deck, about a 10-minute trip. The marsh supports an abundant population of bird life, especially egrets, coots, and ducks. Occasional dawn and sunset walks are led by naturalists; call the Interpretive Center for information.

Special note: The catwalk extends north and south across the marsh for a mile. This was once a great, easy walk, but access is now forbidden in order to protect an endangered mouse, and passage is blocked by a barbed-wire-edged gate.

Location: On the shore of South San Francisco Bay in Palo Alto; map E1-San Francisco Peninsula, grid g5.

User groups: Hikers only. No dogs, horses, or mountain bikes. No wheelchair facilities.

Permits: No permits are required. Parking and access are free.

Maps: Ask the USGS for a topographic map of the Mountain View area.

Directions: From U.S. 101 in Palo Alto, take the Embarcadero exit east. Drive toward the bay, bearing left past the airport. Drive past the yacht harbor until you reach a sharp right turn. Park at the lot on the right (south). The nature preserve is on the left (north). Note: A gate is closed on the access route each evening just after sunset and is opened each morning at 8 year-round; access is still available by foot or bike.

Contact: Palo Alto Baylands Interpretive Center, tel. (650) 329-2506; Recreation Division, tel. (650) 329-2261.

32 Baylands Trail
4.0 mi/1.5 hrs

The farther you go on this trail, the better it gets. The Baylands Trail starts without much fanfare, a simple hard-gravel road with an ugly slough on the left and the Palo Alto Golf Course on the right. If you keep looking ahead, you will often see ground squirrels scurrying about, along with an occasional jackrabbit. The trail then reaches a fork. Bikers should turn left, taking the outstanding Baylands bike trail; it extends all the way to the Dumbarton Bridge, which has a bike lane, and across the bay to Fremont. Hikers are better off turning right. Here the trail softens and the slough melds into the tidal waters of San Francisquito Creek. The pathway continues along past the golf course, then crosses the departure runway for the Palo Alto Airport and leads out to land's end, where the creek pours into the bay. This is a classic salt marsh habitat, with lots of birds and wildlife. The views are pretty, the walk is as flat as it gets, and hikers are always sighting squirrels, rabbits, egrets, coots, and ducks.

Location: On the shore of South San Francisco Bay in Palo Alto; map E1-San Francisco Peninsula, grid g5.

User groups: Hikers, wheelchairs, and mountain bikes. No dogs or horses.

Permits: No permits are required. Parking and access are free.

Maps: Ask the USGS for a topographic map of the Mountain View area.

Directions: From U.S. 101 in Palo Alto take the Embarcadero East exit. At the second light, across from Ming's Restaurant, turn left on Geng Street and drive to the end of the road. The trailhead is right behind the Baylands Baseball Park grandstand.

Contact: Palo Alto Baylands Interpretive Center, tel. (650) 329-2506; Recreation Division, tel. (650) 329-2261.

🥾 South Bay Nature Trail
2.0 mi/1.0 hr

Everybody knows about the South Bay Nature Trail at the San Francisco Bay National Wildlife Refuge, right? That's the big nature center located at the eastern foot of the Dumbarton Bridge, right? Very popular, right? Wrong, wrong, and wrong. A little-known portion of the wildlife refuge is set deep in the South Bay marsh near Alviso, where it receives scant attention compared to its big brother to the north. Headquarters are at the Environmental Education Center; from there, you walk on a dirt path along a wild tidal marshland. As you stroll northward, you will delve into wilder and wilder habitat, and in the process have a chance at seeing a dozen species of birds in a matter of minutes. The endangered harvest salt mouse lives in this habitat. Guided nature walks are held regularly on weekend mornings, and they are well worth attending. The sloughs and quiet waters here also make for a unique opportunity for saltwater canoeing.

Location: In San Francisco Bay National Wildlife Refuge near Alviso; map E1-San Francisco Peninsula, grid g5.

User groups: Hikers and mountain bikes. No dogs or horses. No wheelchair facilities.

Permits: No permits are required. Parking and access are free.

Maps: Ask the USGS for a topographic map of the Mountain View area.

Directions: From U.S. 101 near Sunnyvale, take Highway 237. Drive east on Highway 237 to Zanker Street. Turn left on Zanker Street and drive to the parking area at the Environmental Education Center.

Contact: Environmental Education Center, tel. (408) 832-7745; Don Edwards San Francisco Bay National Wildlife Refuge, P.O. Box 524, Newark, CA 94560; tel. (510) 792-4275 or fax (510) 792-5828.

ROLLING GRASSLANDS
AT MOUNT DIABLO STATE PARK

MAP E1 ~ EAST BAY

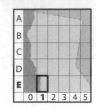

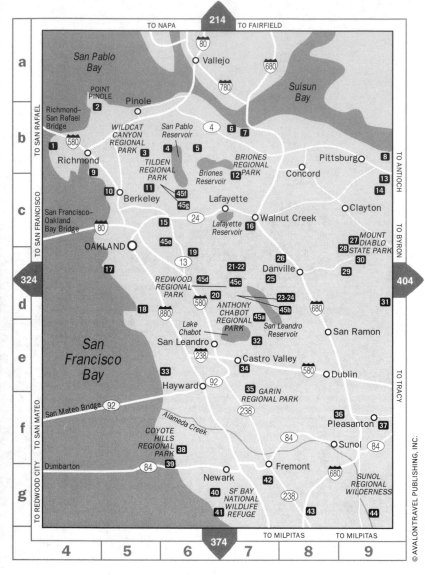

TO NAPA · **214** · TO FAIRFIELD

a

San Pablo Bay

80

Vallejo

680

780

Suisun Bay

b

TO SAN RAFAEL

POINT PINOLE

2

Pinole

Richmond–San Rafael Bridge

WILDCAT CANYON REGIONAL PARK

San Pablo Reservoir

4

6

7

580

1

Richmond

3

4

5

BRIONES REGIONAL PARK

Pittsburg

8

TO ANTIOCH

9

TILDEN REGIONAL PARK

Briones Reservoir

12

Concord

13

14

c

TO SAN FRANCISCO

10

Berkeley

11

45f

45g

Lafayette

16

Walnut Creek

Clayton

15

24

Lafayette Reservoir

27

MOUNT DIABLO STATE PARK

San Francisco–Oakland Bay Bridge

80

45e

19

28

30

OAKLAND

13

21-22

26

Danville

29

d

TO SAN FRANCISCO

17

REDWOOD REGIONAL PARK

45d

20

580

45c

25

23-24

45b

680

31

18

880

ANTHONY CHABOT REGIONAL PARK

45a

San Ramon

Lake Chabot

San Leandro Reservoir

e

San Francisco Bay

San Leandro

238

32

Castro Valley

34

580

Dublin

TO TRACY

33

Hayward

92

35

GARIN REGIONAL PARK

f

TO SAN MATEO

San Mateo Bridge

92

238

36

Pleasanton

37

Alameda Creek

84

Sunol

84

COYOTE HILLS REGIONAL PARK

38

g

TO REDWOOD CITY

Dumbarton

84

39

Newark

Fremont

42

680

SUNOL REGIONAL WILDERNESS

40

SF BAY NATIONAL WILDLIFE REFUGE

238

41

43

44

374

TO MILPITAS · TO MILPITAS

324

404

| 4 | 5 | 6 | 7 | 8 | 9 |

© AVALON TRAVEL PUBLISHING, INC.

CHAPTER E1 ~ EAST BAY

1 False Gun Vista Point . 347
2 Bay View Loop 348
3 San Pablo Ridge Loop . 348
4 Laurel Loop Trail. 349
5 Sobrante Ridge Trail . . 350
6 Franklin Ridge
Loop Trail 350
7 Martinez Shoreline. . . 350
8 Antioch Pier. 351
9 Point Isabel Shoreline. 351
10 Berkeley Pier 352
11 Nimitz Way. 352
12 Briones Crest Loop. . . 353
13 Prospect Tunnel Loop . 353
14 Contra Loma Loop. . . . 354
15 Round Top Loop Trail. . 354
16 Lafayette-
Moraga Trail 355
17 Shoreline Trail 356
18 Arrowhead Marsh. . . . 356
19 Huckleberry
Loop Path 357
20 Graham Trail Loop . . . 357
21 Stream Trail Loop. . . . 358
22 East Ridge Loop. 358
23 Grass Valley Loop 359
24 Bort Meadow. 359

25 Rocky Ridge Loop 360
26 Iron Horse
Regional Trail 360
27 Donner Falls 361
28 Giant Loop 361
29 China Wall Loop 362
30 Mount Diablo
Summit Loop 362
31 Volvon Loop Trail/
Bob Walker Ridge 363
32 Shoreline Loop Trail . . 364
33 Cogswell Marsh Loop. . 364
34 Don Castro
Lake Loop 365
35 High Ridge Loop 365
36 Ridgeline Trail. 366
37 North Arroyo Trail . . . 366
38 Bayview Trail. 367
39 Dumbarton Bridge . . . 367
40 Tidelands Trail. 368
41 Dumbarton Pier 368
42 Alameda Creek
Regional Trail 369
43 Peak Trail 369
44 Sunol Loop 370
45 East Bay Skyline
National Trail 370

1 False Gun Vista Point

1.0 mi/0.75 hr

A little-known lookout over San Francisco Bay is the highlight of Miller-Knox Regional Shoreline, and getting to it requires only a short hike and climb. This parkland covers 260 acres of hill and shoreline property at Point Richmond, where strong afternoon winds in the summer create excellent conditions for kite flying. While most people make the short stroll along Keller Beach, this hike is preferred for the view. From the parking area it leads about .5 mile up Old Country Road and the Marine View Trail, making a right turn on the Crest Trail to reach the False Gun Vista Point. In the process the trail climbs 300 feet to the lookout at 322 feet. On clear days, you get picture-perfect views of San Francisco Bay and its many surrounding landmarks.

Location: In Miller-Knox Regional Shoreline west of Richmond on the shore of San Francisco Bay; map E1-East Bay, grid b4.

User groups: Hikers and dogs. No horses or mountain bikes. No wheelchair facilities.

Permits: No permits are required. Parking and access are free.

Maps: For a free trail map, contact the East Bay Regional Parks District at the address below and ask for the Miller-Knox Regional Shoreline brochure. Ask the USGS for a topographic map of the San Quentin area.

Directions from Berkeley: From Berkeley drive north on Interstate 80 to Interstate 580 west. Take Interstate 580 west to Canal Street/Garrard Boulevard. Turn right on Canal Boulevard and drive .25 mile to Garrard Boulevard. Turn left and drive through the tunnel (the road becomes Dornan Drive). Continue on Dornan Drive for .5 mile to the parking area on the right.

Directions from Richmond: From Richmond, drive south on Interstate 80, exit west at Cutting Boulevard, and drive to Garrard Boulevard. Turn left and drive through the tunnel. The road becomes Dornan Drive; follow Dornan Drive .5 mile to the parking area on the right.

Contact: East Bay Regional Parks District, 2950 Peralta Oaks Court, P.O. Box 5381, Oakland, CA 94605-0381; tel. (510) 635-0135, ext. 2200, or fax (510) 635-3478; Miller-Knox Regional Shoreline, tel. (510) 235-1631.

🄴 Bay View Loop

3.0 mi/1.5 hrs

On the Bay View Loop, you can walk several miles along the shore of San Pablo Bay and see nothing but water, passing ships, and birds. That's because visitors to Point Pinole must park at the entrance station and catch a shuttle bus to the shoreline. There you will find a long, pretty, cobbled beach and beautiful views of San Pablo Bay, Marin, and Mount

Tamalpais. An excellent fishing pier is also available. The park covers 2,147 acres, and this loop trail is a great way to explore it. From the parking area, it is routed along the shore to Point Pinole, then swings back on the Woods Trail, which runs through a large grove of eucalyptus.

Location: In Point Pinole Regional Shoreline; map E1-East Bay, grid b4.

User groups: Hikers, dogs, horses, and mountain bikes. The trail is partially wheelchair accessible.

Permits: No permits are required. A $4 parking fee is charged when the kiosk is attended. The shuttle bus costs $1 for ages 12 through 61 and $.50 for seniors and youngsters 6 through 11. Children under six and the disabled ride free.

Maps: For a free trail map, contact the East Bay Regional Parks District at the address below and ask for the Point Pinole Regional Shoreline brochure. Ask the USGS for a topographic map of the Richmond area.

Directions: From Interstate 80 in San Pablo, take the Hilltop exit. Drive west on Hilltop to the intersection with San Pablo Avenue. Turn right on San Pablo Avenue and drive north for a short distance, then turn left on Richmond Parkway. Drive a few miles to Giant Highway. Turn right and drive .75 mile to the well-signed park entrance on the left. Take the shuttle bus to the bay.

Contact: Point Pinole Regional Park, tel. (510) 237-6896; East Bay Regional Parks District, 2950 Peralta Oaks Court, P.O. Box 5381, Oakland, CA 94605-0381; tel. (510) 635-0135, ext. 2200, or fax (510) 635-3478;

🄴 San Pablo Ridge Loop

6.2 mi/3.0 hrs

Newcomers to Wildcat Canyon Regional Park may find it hard to believe how quickly they can get to a remote land with great views. But it is true. Just east of Richmond, San Pablo Ridge rises about 1,000 feet; it takes a short grunt of a hike to get to the top, but you'll find it well worth the grunting. That's because you get great views of San Pablo Reservoir and Briones Reservoir off one side of the ridge, and of San Francisco Bay on the other. Of all the views of San Francisco, this is certainly one of the best. Start at the parking area and hike up the Belgum Trail, turning right at San Pablo Ridge and climbing about 700 feet over the course of 2.5 miles. Once on top, slow down and enjoy the cruise. To loop around, turn right on the Mezue Trail, then right again on the Wildcat Creek Trail and walk back to the parking area.

Location: In Wildcat Canyon Regional Park in the Richmond foothills; map E1-East Bay, grid b5.

User groups: Hikers, dogs, horses, and mountain bikes. No wheelchair facilities.

Permits: No permits are required. Parking and access are free.

Maps: For a free trail map, contact the East Bay Regional Parks District at the address below and ask for the Wildcat Canyon Regional Park brochure. Ask the USGS for a topographic map of the Richmond area.

Directions: In Richmond head north on Interstate 80 to the Amador/Solano exit. Take that exit, turn left on Amador, and drive three blocks to McBryde Avenue. Turn right on McBryde Avenue and head east. After passing Arlington Boulevard, drive straight (the road becomes Park Avenue) and bear left through a piped gate to the parking area.

Contact: Tilden Nature Area, tel. (510) 525-2233; Wildcat Canyon Park Office, tel. (510) 236-1262; East Bay Regional Parks District, 2950 Peralta Oaks Court, P.O. Box 5381, Oakland, CA 94605-0381; tel. (510) 635-0135, ext. 2200, or fax (510) 635-3478;

4 Laurel Loop Trail
0.7 mi/0.5 hr

Kennedy Grove is set at the base of San Pablo Dam, where visitors will discover a rich grove of eucalyptus located adjacent to a large lawn/meadow. This loop hike takes hikers through the eucalyptus and then back, skirting the lawn areas. It is best hiked in a clockwise direction, departing from the trailhead at the gate at the northeast corner of the parking area. This is the kind of park where people toss Frisbees, pass footballs, or play low-key games of softball.

A must-do: A hiking and equestrian trail is located off the Laurel Loop Trail that can extend your adventure and provide sensational views. From the other side of the grove, take the one-mile Seafoam Trail. It ascends a hill through a woodland of bay and oak trees and provides spectacular views of San Pablo Ridge, Wildcat Canyon, San Pablo Reservoir, and San Pablo Bay.

Location: In the Kennedy Grove Regional Recreation Area near the San Pablo Reservoir in El Sobrante; map E1-East Bay, grid b6.

User groups: Hikers, dogs, horses, and mountain bikes. No wheelchair facilities.

Permits: No permits are required. There is a $4 parking fee when the kiosk is attended.

Maps: For a free trail map, contact the East Bay Regional Parks District at the address below and ask for the Kennedy Grove Regional Recreation Area brochure. Ask the USGS for a topographic map of the Richmond area.

Directions from Richmond: From Interstate 80 in Richmond, take the San Pablo Dam Road exit. Turn east and drive through El Sobrante for 3.5 miles to the park entrance on the left. Follow the pavement to the northwestern parking lot.

Directions from Orinda: From Orinda on Highway 24, turn north on Camino Pablo and drive north along San Pablo Reservoir to the park entrance on the right.

Contact: East Bay Regional Parks District, 2950 Peralta Oaks Court, P.O. Box 5381, Oakland, CA 94605-0381; tel. (510) 635-0135, ext. 2200, or fax (510) 635-3478; Kennedy Grove Regional Park, tel. (510) 223-7840.

5 Sobrante Ridge Trail
1.6 mi/1.0 hr

Sobrante Ridge Park was the missing link in an East Bay corridor of open space until finally being acquired in the mid-1980s. The wild and scenic land is now protected and should remain that way forever. The park covers 277 acres of rolling hills, open ridgeline, and wooded ravines, and this hike accesses the best of it. From the trailhead at Coach Drive, take the Sobrante Ridge Trail, which rises in an elliptical half-loop to the left. After .7 mile, you will come to the junction with the Broken Oaks Trail. Turn left here and make the short loop (less than .25 mile long), and then retrace your steps on the Sobrante Ridge Trail. This walk provides an easy yet intimate look at one of the Bay Area's newest parklands.

Location: In the Sobrante Ridge Regional Preserve near El Sobrante; map E1-East Bay, grid b6.

User groups: Hikers, dogs, horses, and mountain bikes. No wheelchair facilities.

Permits: No permits are required. Parking and access are free.

Maps: For a free trail map, contact the East Bay Regional Parks District at the address below and ask for the Sobrante Ridge Regional Preserve brochure. Ask the USGS for a topographic map of the Briones Valley area.

Directions: From Interstate 80 in Richmond, take the San Pablo Dam Road exit. Drive east for three miles and turn left on Castro Ranch Road. Drive about two miles to Conestoga Way, turn left, and proceed to Carriage Drive. Turn left again and drive two blocks to Coach Way. Turn right and proceed to the park entrance and parking area at the end of the road.

Contact: East Bay Regional Parks District, 2950 Peralta Oaks Court, P.O. Box 5381, Oakland, CA 94605-0381; tel. (510) 635-0135, ext. 2200, or fax (510) 635-3478; Sobrante Ridge Regional Preserve, tel. (510) 223-7840.

6 Franklin Ridge Loop Trail
3.1 mi/1.75 hrs

Set on the hillsides overlooking Martinez, this land is the gateway to the San Joaquin Delta. The Franklin Ridge Loop Trail is the best way to explore the park, rising to 750 feet. From the ridge are spectacular views of Carquinez Strait, Mount Diablo, and Mount Tamalpais. From the parking area at the Carquinez Strait East Staging Area, the hike heads south on the California Riding and Hiking Trail toward Franklin Ridge, climbing as it goes, then connects to the Franklin Ridge Loop. When you reach the loop, note that this trail is best hiked in a clockwise direction. Most of the park consists of open, rolling grasslands, but there are some groves of eucalyptus and a few wooded ravines.

Location: At Carquinez Strait Regional Shoreline near Martinez; map E1-East Bay, grid b7.

User groups: Hikers, dogs, horses, and mountain bikes. No wheelchair facilities.

Permits: No permits are required. Parking and access are free.

Maps: For a free trail map, contact the East Bay Regional Parks District at the address below and ask for the Carquinez Strait Regional Shoreline brochure. Ask the USGS for a topographic map of the Benicia area.

Directions: From Highway 4 in Martinez, take the Alhambra Avenue exit and drive north for two miles toward the Carquinez Strait. Turn left on Escobar Street, drive three blocks, and turn right on Talbart Street, which becomes Carquinez Scenic Drive. Follow that road for about .5 mile to the parking area on the left.

Contact: East Bay Regional Parks District, 2950 Peralta Oaks Court, P.O. Box 5381, Oakland, CA 94605-0381; tel. (510) 635-0135, ext. 2200, or fax (510) 635-3478; Carquinez Strait Regional Shoreline, tel. (925) 228-0112.

7 Martinez Shoreline
2.2 mi/1.0 hr

The Shoreline Trail is the most attractive walk at Martinez Waterfront Park, a 343-acre parcel that includes marshlands and bay frontage. Start hiking from the parking area located at the foot of the Martinez Fishing Pier and walk back on North Court Street to the trailhead at Sand Beach. The hike skirts a pond, crosses Arch Bridge over Alhambra Creek, and runs along the waterfront, past an old schooner hull, to the park's western boundary. The trail is easy and flat, with the bay on one side, marshlands on the other. It is popular for bicycling, jogging, and bird-watching. An option is to walk a short distance from the parking lot to the Martinez Pier, one of the few piers in the Bay Area where striped bass, sturgeon, and steelhead are occasionally caught in the winter.

Location: At Martinez Regional Shoreline near Martinez; map E1-East Bay, grid b7.

User groups: Hikers, dogs, horses, and mountain bikes. The restrooms are wheelchair accessible, but the trail is not.

Permits: No permits are required. Parking and access are free.

Maps: For a free trail map, contact the East Bay Regional Parks District at the address below and ask for the Martinez Regional Shoreline brochure. Ask the USGS for a topographic map of the Benicia area.

Directions: From Highway 4 in Martinez, take the Alhambra Avenue exit. Drive north on Alhambra Avenue for two miles and turn right on Escobar Street. Continue for three blocks to Ferry Street and turn left. Drive across the railroad tracks and bear right onto Joe DiMaggio Drive. Turn left on North Court Street and drive to the parking area next to the fishing pier.

Contact: East Bay Regional Parks District, 2950 Peralta Oaks Court, P.O. Box 5381, Oakland, CA 94605-0381; tel. (510) 635-0135, ext. 2200, or fax (510) 635-3478; Martinez Regional Shoreline, tel. (925) 228-0112.

8 Antioch Pier
0.5 mi/0.5 hr

This is a short but scenic walk along a marshland and out to the end of a 550-foot pier, one of the best fishing piers in the Bay Area. The parkland encompasses only 7.5 acres, but it is set along the lower San Joaquin River just upstream from the Antioch Bridge. From the parking lot, the trail leads .14 mile to the foot of the pier, with a gated, wheelchair-accessible road on the right and wetlands on the left. The pier extends into the San Joaquin River, right into the pathway of migrating striped bass, sturgeon, and at other times, catfish and even salmon. If you don't catch any fish, you can still go to the end of the pier and catch views of the Antioch Bridge and the San Joaquin River at its widest point.

Location: At Antioch/Oakley Regional Shoreline near Antioch and Oakley; map E1-East Bay, grid b9.

User groups: Hikers, wheelchairs, dogs, and mountain bikes. No horses.

Permits: No permits are required. Parking and access are free. To fish from the shore or the pier, people 16 and over must obtain a fishing license.

Maps: For a free trail map, contact the East Bay Regional Parks District at the address below and ask for the Antioch Regional Shoreline brochure. Ask the USGS for a topographic map of the Antioch North area.

Directions: From Highway 4 in Antioch, take the Wilbur Avenue exit and turn right on Wilbur Avenue. Make an immediate left on Bridgehead Road; the parking area is at the end of the road.

Contact: East Bay Regional Parks District, 2950 Peralta Oaks Court, P.O. Box 5381, Oakland, CA 94605-0381; tel. (510) 635-0135, ext. 2200, or fax (510) 635-3478; Antioch/Oakley Regional Shoreline, tel. (925) 228-0112.

9 Point Isabel Shoreline
1.0 mi/0.75 hr

Beautiful bay front views of San Francisco and the Golden Gate, plus the fact that it's a popular place to walk dogs, attract visitors to the Point Isabel Regional Shoreline. The point extends into San Francisco Bay just north of Golden Gate Fields Racetrack, and the 21-acre park provides an easy shoreline walk, rich bird-watching opportunities, and those great views. From the parking area, the trail extends northward along the shore of the bay, then east along Hoffman Channel, and ends with a short loop trail around the edge of Hoffman Marsh. The best time to see birds here is in the fall, when year-round residents are joined by migratory species.

Location: At Point Isabel Regional Shoreline near Berkeley; map E1-East Bay, grid c4.

User groups: Hikers and dogs. No horses or mountain bikes. The restrooms are wheelchair accessible, but the trail is not.

Permits: No permits are required. Parking and access are free.

Maps: For a free trail map, contact the East Bay Regional Parks District at the address below and ask for the Point Isabel Regional Shoreline brochure. Ask the USGS for a topographic map of the Richmond area.

Directions: From Interstate 80 in south Richmond, take the Central Avenue exit and drive west to Isabel Street. Turn right and drive to the parking area at the end of the road.

Contact: East Bay Regional Parks District, 2950 Peralta Oaks Court, P.O. Box 5381, Oakland, CA 94605-0381; tel. (510) 635-0135, ext. 2200, or fax (510) 635-3478; Point Isabel Regional Shoreline, tel. (510) 235-1631.

10 Berkeley Pier
1.2 mi/0.75 hr

This historic structure extends 3,000 feet into San Francisco Bay amid landmarks that people come from around the world to see. The walk is easy—straight, flat, and long—and while most people can get to the end of the pier in 20 minutes, there is no reason to hurry. The Golden Gate Bridge is a classic sight from your vantage point at the end of the pier, especially during sunsets, when you will discover how the Golden Gate earned its name. Things look different here, especially if you bring a loaf of French bread to nibble on and maybe your favorite elixir to wash it down. Fishing success varies; the best time is early summer, when halibut school on the Berkeley Flats.

Location: Near Berkeley on the shore of San Francisco Bay; map E1-East Bay, grid c5.

User groups: Hikers and wheelchairs. No dogs, horses, or mountain bikes.

Permits: No permits are required. Parking and access are free.

Maps: Ask the USGS for a topographic map of the Oakland West area.

Directions: From Interstate 80 in Berkeley, take the University Avenue exit and follow the signs to the Berkeley Marina. The pier is at the foot of University Avenue, on the west side of Interstate 80, just past the bait shop and marina on the shore of San Francisco Bay.

Contact: Berkeley City Parks, tel. (510) 644-6376; Berkeley Marina, tel. (510) 849-2727.

11 Nimitz Way
10.0 mi/4.25 hrs

When you start down this trail, you might wonder why it is rated so high. The farther you go, the better it gets, and then everything explains itself. The views? Sure, the sweeping vistas of the East Bay foothills are great, but hey, the paved trail seems more appropriate for bikes, wheelchairs, and joggers than hikers. And so it is for the first four miles, until suddenly you enter a different universe. After passing a gate, the trail turns to dirt, and just like that, there's no one else around as you climb San Pablo Ridge. The views are stunning in all directions, particularly of Briones and San Pablo Reservoirs to the east, and San Francisco Bay and the city's skyline to the west. Your goal should be to climb at least to Wildcat Peak, elevation 1,250 feet, and two miles out before turning around and heading for home. This is one of the best sections of the 31-mile East Bay Skyline National Trail.

Location: In Tilden Regional Park at Inspiration Point in the Berkeley hills; map E1-East Bay, grid c5.

User groups: Hikers, dogs, horses, and mountain bikes. The trail is partially wheelchair accessible.

Permits: No permits are required. Parking and access are free.

Maps: For a free trail map, contact the East Bay Regional Parks District at the address below and ask for the Tilden Regional Park brochure. Ask the USGS for a topographic map of the Briones Valley area.

Directions: From Highway 24 in the East Bay, drive to just east of the Caldecott Tunnel and take the Fish Ranch Road exit northwest to Grizzly Peak Boulevard. Turn right, drive up the hill, and turn right again on South Park Drive. Drive one mile to Wildcat Canyon Road, bear right, and drive to the parking area at Inspiration Point on the left.

Directions in winter: Note that South Park Drive is closed each year from November through March to protect migrating newts. To avoid South Park Drive, from Highway 24 drive through the Caldecott Tunnel and exit at Orinda. Turn left on Camino Pablo. Drive north for about two miles, turn left on Wildcat Canyon Road, and follow it to Inspiration Point on the right.

Contact: East Bay Regional Parks District, 2950 Peralta Oaks Court, P.O. Box 5381, Oakland, CA 94605-0381; tel. (510) 635-0135, ext. 2200, or fax (510) 635-3478; Tilden Nature Area, tel. (510) 525-2233.

12 Briones Crest Loop

5.6 mi/3.25 hrs

Briones Regional Park is a 5,700-acre sanctuary of peace set amid several fast-growing communities. It is one of the best parks for hiking in the East Bay, with an intricate network of trails, and this is the best of the lot. There are many trail junctions on the loop, and a map will help you from making a wrong turn. From the trailhead take the Alhambra Creek Trail and the Spengler Trail (turn right) to the Briones Crest Trail and turn left. This stretch rises to Briones Peak at 1,483 feet in just 2.5

miles. It is the highest point in the park and grants a panoramic view of the East Bay's rolling hillsides, quiet and tranquil. The view includes Mount Diablo, the west Delta, Suisun Bay, and the Mothball Fleet. To complete the loop, turn left on the Spengler Trail, then right on the Diablo View Trail. The latter closes out the hike in 1.1 miles, offering great views of the slopes of Mount Diablo.

Location: In Briones Regional Park north of Lafayette; map E1-East Bay, grid c7.

User groups: Hikers, dogs, and horses. Mountain bikes are allowed on all but the last mile of the loop. No wheelchair facilities.

Permits: No permits are required. There is a $4 parking fee when the kiosk is attended.

Maps: For a free trail map, contact the East Bay Regional Parks District at the address below and ask for the Briones Regional Park brochure. Ask the USGS for a topographic map of the Briones Valley area.

Directions: From Interstate 680 north of Pleasant Hill, take Highway 4 west for three miles to the Alhambra Avenue exit. Turn south on Alhambra Avenue, drive for .5 mile, and bear right onto Alhambra Valley Road. Drive another mile to Reliez Valley Road. Turn left and follow Reliez Valley Road .5 mile to the park entrance. Turn right and drive .5 mile to the parking area. Look for the trailhead indicating the Alhambra Creek Trail.

Contact: East Bay Regional Parks District, 2950 Peralta Oaks Court, P.O. Box 5381, Oakland, CA 94605-0381; tel. (510) 635-0135, ext. 2200, or fax (510) 635-3478; Briones Regional Park, tel. (925) 370-3020.

13 Prospect Tunnel Loop

4.5 mi/2.5 hrs

Bring a flashlight with fresh batteries so you can explore 200 feet of mountain tunnel, the featured attraction of Black Diamond Mines Regional Preserve. The Prospect Tunnel, driven in the 1860s by miners in search of coal, probes 400 feet into the side of

Mount Diablo, and half of that length is now accessible to the public. To reach the tunnel, it's about a 1.5-mile hike from the trailhead, taking the Stewartville Trail (well signed) off Frederickson Lane. It is a paved road at the beginning, but then turns to dirt. Most of the surrounding area is grasslands and foothill country. After exploring the Prospect Tunnel, you can tack a loop onto your hike. Turn left on the Star Mine Trail, which loops for 1.6 miles and passes by a barred tunnel, one of the last active coal mines in the area. The Prospect Tunnel and the Star Mine are two of the most unusual spots in the preserve's 3,700 acres.

Location: In the Black Diamond Mines Regional Preserve in the Mount Diablo foothills near Antioch; map E1-East Bay, grid c9.

User groups: Hikers, dogs, horses, and mountain bikes. A short portion of the trail is accessible to hikers only. No wheelchair facilities.

Permits: No permits are required. The parking fee is $4 when the kiosk is attended.

Maps: For a free trail map, contact the East Bay Regional Parks District at the address below and ask for the Black Diamond Mines Regional Preserve brochure. Ask the USGS for a topographic map of the Antioch South area.

Directions: From Highway 4 at Antioch, take the Lone Tree Way exit and drive south to Blue Rock Drive. Turn right, drive to Frederickson Lane, bear right, and drive about one mile to the gate. There is limited parking on the left (at the corner of a right turn). Note: The signs along the way say "Contra Loma Regional Park," not "Black Diamond Mines." Once past the gate, you will be in Black Diamond Mines Regional Preserve.

Contact: East Bay Regional Parks District, 2950 Peralta Oaks Court, P.O. Box 5381, Oakland, CA 94605-0381; tel. (510) 635-0135, ext. 2200, or fax (510) 635-3478; Black Diamond Mines Regional Park, tel. (925) 757-2620.

14 Contra Loma Loop
1.6 mi/1.0 hr

Most people go to Contra Loma Regional Park to fish at Contra Loma Lake, swim and sunbathe, or picnic. This short loop trail provides an alternative to those activities, tracing along the northwest shore of the lake, then climbing up and over a short hill and looping back to the starting point. From the parking area, head out on the trail to the Cattail Cove Picnic Area. Just after that, the trail turns right and you'll follow the shore of the lake, pass a fishing pier, and then start a 10-minute climb up a small hill. To close out the loop, glide down the hill. The trail turns left and a mile later returns to the Cattail Cove Picnic Area.

Location: In Contra Loma Regional Park near Antioch; map E1-East Bay, grid c9.

User groups: Hikers, wheelchairs, dogs, horses, and mountain bikes.

Permits: No permits are required. The parking fee is $4 when the kiosk is attended; there's a $1 dog fee year-round.

Maps: For a free trail map, contact the East Bay Regional Parks District at the address below and ask for the Contra Loma Regional Park brochure. Ask the USGS for a topographic map of the Antioch South area.

Directions: From Highway 4 at Antioch, take the Lone Tree Way exit and drive south to Blue Rock Drive. Turn right, drive to Frederickson Lane, bear right, and drive to the gate. Turn right, pass the kiosk, and bear left. Drive to the parking lot by the beach.

Contact: East Bay Regional Parks District, 2950 Peralta Oaks Court, P.O. Box 5381, Oakland, CA 94605-0381; tel. (510) 635-0135, ext. 2200, or fax (510) 635-3478; Contra Loma Regional Park, tel. (925) 757-0404.

15 Round Top Loop Trail
1.7 mi/1.0 hr

The remains of the Bay Area's long-extinct volcano, Mount Round Top, can be explored at Sibley Preserve. As you walk along the exposed volcanic rock, you can take a self-guided tour using a pamphlet available at the trailhead. After the volcano blasted out its lava contents about nine million years ago, the interior of the mountain collapsed into the void left by the outburst, and blocks of volcanic stone lie scattered everywhere around the flanks of the mountain. A gated road leads to the top at elevation 1,763 feet, but the best way to see the mountain is on the Round Top Loop Trail. Hike in a clockwise direction so the numbered posts (one through nine) on the self-guided tour correspond in order with the most interesting volcanic outcrops.

Location: In the Robert Sibley Volcanic Regional Preserve in the Berkeley hills; map E1-East Bay, grid c6.

User groups: Hikers and dogs. The trail is partially accessible to wheelchairs, horses, and mountain bikes.

Permits: No permits are required. Parking and access are free.

Maps: For a free trail map, contact the East Bay Regional Parks District at the address below and ask for the Sibley Volcanic Regional Preserve brochure. Ask the USGS for a topographic map of the Briones Valley area.

Directions: From Highway 24 in the East Bay, drive to just east of the Caldecott Tunnel and take the Fish Ranch Road exit northwest to Grizzly Peak Boulevard. Turn left and drive to Skyline Boulevard. Then drive straight ahead for another .25 mile to the park entrance and parking area on the left.

Alternate route from Montclair Village: From Montclair Village, east of Highway 13 in Oakland, take Snake Road uphill to Skyline Boulevard. Turn left on Skyline Boulevard and drive .5 mile to the park entrance on the right.

Contact: East Bay Regional Parks District, 2950 Peralta Oaks Court, P.O. Box 5381, Oakland, CA 94605-0381; tel. (510) 635-0135, ext. 2200, or fax (510) 635-3478; Robert Sibley Volcanic Regional Preserve, tel. (510) 644-0436.

16 Lafayette-Moraga Trail
7.75 mi one way/4.0 hrs

The Lafayette-Moraga Trail is a 7.75-mile linear park. In other words, the trail is a park that forms a line from Lafayette to Moraga. Much of it is paved, while the rest is either dirt or compacted soil, making most of the route more popular with bikers and joggers than hikers. The hike starts at the Olympic Staging Area in Lafayette and curls to the left for the first 3.5 miles, eventually heading south along Las Trampas Creek to Bollinger Canyon. It then passes through downtown Moraga to the Valle Vista Staging Area on Canyon Road. For most this is the end of the trip, as bicycles, dogs, and horses are not allowed to continue. Hikers, however, may keep walking west on land managed by the East Bay Municipal Utility District. Permits are required on East Bay MUD lands; phone (510) 287-0469.

Location: North of the San Leandro Reservoir; map E1-East Bay, grid c7.

User groups: Hikers, wheelchairs, dogs, horses, and mountain bikes.

Permits: No permits are required. Parking and access are free.

Maps: For a free trail map, contact the East Bay Regional Parks District at the address below and ask for the Lafayette-Moraga Regional Trail brochure. Ask the USGS for topographic maps of the Walnut Creek and Las Trampas Ridge areas.

Directions: From Highway 24 near Lafayette, take the Pleasant Hill Road exit south. Drive one mile to Olympic Boulevard. Turn right and drive .25 mile to the Olympic Staging Area.

Contact: East Bay Regional Parks District, 2950 Peralta Oaks Court, P.O. Box 5381, Oakland, CA 94605-0381; tel. (510) 635-0135, ext. 2200, or fax (510) 635-3478; Lafayette-Moraga Linear Park, tel. (925) 687-3419.

17 Shoreline Trail

5.0 mi/2.25 hrs

The tide book is your bible at Crown Memorial State Beach, which is set along the shore of San Francisco Bay just south of Crab Cove. High tide is the best time to observe seabirds such as loons, grebes, and ducks. Low tide, however, is the best time to watch shorebirds such as sandpipers poking around the exposed mudflats. The trail is a paved bicycle path that follows the bay's shoreline, running 2.5 miles south to an overlook of the Elsie Roemer Bird Sanctuary. The bay views are also quite good. When the wind is down, this is one of the best swimming areas in the bay; when the wind is up, it's excellent for windsurfing.

Location: At Crown Memorial State Beach on the shore of San Francisco Bay in Alameda; map E1-East Bay, grid d5.

User groups: Hikers, wheelchairs, dogs (on the paved trail only, not the beach), and mountain bikes. No horses.

Permits: No permits are required. There is a $4 parking fee when the entrance kiosk is attended; there's a $1 dog fee year-round.

Maps: For a free trail map, contact the East Bay Regional Parks District at the address below and ask for the Crown Memorial State Beach brochure. Ask the USGS for a topographic map of the Oakland West area.

Directions: From Interstate 580 take Interstate 980 west into Oakland. Take the 12th Street/Alameda exit. Follow the road under Interstate 880 and turn left onto 5th Street. Drive to the Oakland/Alameda Tube. At the end of the tube, you will be on Webster Street, which dead-ends at Central. Turn left on Central and drive two blocks to Eighth Street. Turn right on 8th Street and drive .25 mile to the Crown Beach entrance on the right.

Contact: East Bay Regional Parks District, 2950 Peralta Oaks Court, P.O. Box 5381, Oakland, CA 94605-0381; tel. (510) 635-0135, ext. 2200, or fax (510) 635-3478; Crown Memorial State Beach, tel. (510) 521-7090.

18 Arrowhead Marsh

2.0 mi/1.0 hr

Arrowhead Marsh is one of the best bird-watching areas in the East Bay, with 30 species commonly sighted, including several pairs of blue-winged teal. At high tide this is also a top spot to see rails, typically elusive birds that are more often heard than seen. The paved trail skirts the edge of the marsh, which is set along San Leandro Bay. From the parking area the trail is routed one mile out along the Airport Channel, with the marsh on your left. If you want to extend your walk across a bridge at San Leandro Creek and continue along the shore to Garretson Point, adding 1.4 miles round-trip. This parkland covers 1,220 acres, including some of the bay's most valuable wetland habitat.

Location: At Martin Luther King Regional Shoreline on San Leandro Bay near Oakland; map E1-East Bay, grid d5.

User groups: Hikers, wheelchairs, and mountain bikes. No dogs or horses.

Permits: No permits are required. Parking and access are free.

Maps: For a free trail map, contact the East Bay Regional Parks District at the address below and ask for the Martin Luther King Regional Shoreline brochure. Ask the USGS for a topographic map of the San Leandro area.

Directions: From Interstate 880 in Oakland take the Hegenberger Road exit and follow it toward the airport and Doolittle Drive. Turn right on Doolittle Drive and proceed to Swan Way. Turn right again and drive a short distance to the park entrance. Turn left and drive to the parking area at the end of the road.

Alternate route: From Interstate 880 in Oakland, take the Hegenberger Road exit and drive .5 mile to Pardee Drive. Turn right and drive a few blocks to Swan Way. Turn left and drive one block to Gravel Access Road. Turn right on Gravel Access Road and drive .5 mile to the marsh area.

Contact: East Bay Regional Parks District, 2950 Peralta Oaks Court, P.O. Box 5381, Oakland, CA 94605-0381; tel. (510) 635-0135, ext. 2200, or fax (510) 635-3478; Martin Luther King Regional Shoreline, tel. (510) 562-1373.

19 Huckleberry Loop Path
1.7 mi/1.25 hrs

If you know what you're looking for, this is a trip into an ecological wonderland. If you don't, well, it's still a rewarding, tranquil venture. The only reason people come to Huckleberry is to hike, not to play games or fish. That is because the Huckleberry Loop is routed through a remarkable variety of rare and beautiful plants. From the parking area follow the path to the left fork, where you then descend steeply through a mature bay forest for a mile. The trail returns by turning right and climbing .7 mile out of the canyon. This last section is particularly rich in diverse plant life.

Location: In the Huckleberry Botanic Regional Preserve in the Oakland hills; map E1-East Bay, grid d6.

User groups: Hikers only. No dogs, horses, or mountain bikes. No wheelchair facilities.

Permits: No permits are required. Parking and access are free.

Maps: For a free trail map, contact the East Bay Regional Parks District at the address below and ask for the Huckleberry Botanic Regional Preserve brochure. Ask the USGS for a topographic map of the Oakland East area.

Directions: From Highway 24 in the East Bay, drive to just east of the Caldecott Tunnel and take the Fish Ranch Road exit northwest to Grizzly Peak Boulevard. Drive two miles and bear left onto Skyline Boulevard (the roads merge). Drive a short distance past Sibley Volcanic Preserve to the park entrance and parking lot on the left.

Contact: East Bay Regional Parks District, 2950 Peralta Oaks Court, P.O. Box 5381, Oakland, CA 94605-0381; tel. (510) 635-0135, ext. 2200, or fax (510) 635-3478; Huckleberry Botanic Regional Preserve, tel. (510) 644-0436.

20 Graham Trail Loop
0.75 mi/0.5 hr

Because the entrance to Roberts Regional Recreation Area lies amid redwood trees, it has proven to be a popular stop for visitors who want to see Sequoia sempervirens with a minimum effort. If you want to enter a redwood forest in the East Bay without having to walk far, this is the best bet. From the entrance of the parking area, near the swimming pool, take the short trail that is linked to the Graham Trail. Turn right and you will be routed in a short circle past a restroom to Diablo Vista; then turn right and head back to the parking area. The walk is short and sweet, just right for those who do not wish for a more challenging encounter.

Location: In the Roberts Regional Recreation Area in the Oakland hills; map E1-East Bay, grid d7.

User groups: Hikers and dogs. No horses or mountain bikes. The restroom is wheelchair accessible, but the trail is not.

Permits: No permits are required. There is a $4 parking fee on weekends and holidays.

Maps: For a free trail map, contact the East Bay Regional Parks District at the address below and ask for the Roberts Regional Recreation Area and Redwood Regional Park brochures. Ask the USGS for a topographic map of the Oakland East area.

Directions: From Highway 24 in the East Bay, drive to Highway 13 in Oakland. Turn south on Highway 13 (follow the signs carefully) and drive three miles to Joaquin Miller Road. Turn left (east) on Joaquin Miller Road and drive one mile to Skyline Boulevard. Turn left on Skyline Boulevard and drive about one mile to the park entrance on the right.

Contact: East Bay Regional Parks District, 2950 Peralta Oaks Court, P.O. Box 5381, Oakland, CA 94605-0381; tel. (510) 635-0135, ext. 2200, or fax (510) 635-3478; Roberts Regional Recreation Area, tel. (510) 482-6028.

21 Stream Trail Loop
3.5 mi/2.0 hrs

Newcomers to Redwood Regional Park are often amazed at the beauty of this trail. After all, whoever heard of redwood forests and trout streams in Oakland? But visitors to this park know you get both of these things here. For the best loop route, hike up the Stream Trail for .25 mile, then turn left on the French Trail. You will climb along the western slopes of the redwood canyon, rising to 1,000 feet. With the puffing behind you (always hike up when you're fresh), you will turn right on the Fern Trail and soon junction with the Stream Trail. The rest of the route back to the park entrance is easy and downhill, tracing along pretty Redwood Creek through the center of the redwood forest. In late winter and spring, trout swim upstream from San Leandro Reservoir to spawn in these waters (fishing is not permitted).

Location: In Redwood Regional Park in the Oakland hills; map E1-East Bay, grid d7.

User groups: Hikers, wheelchairs, dogs, and horses. No mountain bikes.

Permits: No permits are required. There is a $4 parking fee when the kiosk is attended; there's a $1 dog fee year-round.

Maps: For a free trail map, contact the East Bay Regional Parks District at the address below and ask for the Redwood Regional Park brochure. Ask the USGS for a topographic map of the Oakland East area.

Directions: From Highway 24 in Oakland turn south on Highway 13 and drive to Redwood Road. Turn left on Redwood Road and drive two miles past Skyline Boulevard to the park entrance on the left. Turn left and park at the Canyon Meadow Staging Area at the end of the road.

Alternate route: From the Oakland side of the Bay Bridge, take Highway 580 to the 35th Avenue exit. Drive east on 35th Avenue, which becomes Redwood Road, and continue as above to the parking area.

Contact: East Bay Regional Parks District, 2950 Peralta Oaks Court, P.O. Box 5381, Oak-land, CA 94605-0381; tel. (510) 635-0135, ext. 2200, or fax (510) 635-3478; Redwood Regional Park, tel. (510) 482-6024.

22 East Ridge Loop
4.0 mi/2.5 hrs

From atop the East Ridge at 1,100 feet, you can look down into a canyon that appears to be a sea of redwoods. The view is quite a treat after climbing nearly 900 feet from the trailhead. The payback comes when you turn left and loop down into that canyon, where Redwood Creek awaits under the cool canopy of a lush forest. This trip is an option to the Stream Trail Loop for ambitious hikers and mountain bikers; unlike on that trail, bikes are allowed on the East Ridge. From the parking area turn right on the Canyon Trail, climbing up to the East Ridge in .5 mile. Turn left and make the loop by hiking out on the ridge, climbing much of the way, turning left again on Prince Road, and returning on the Stream Trail.

Location: In Redwood Regional Park in the Oakland hills; map E1-East Bay, grid d7.

User groups: Hikers, dogs, and horses. Mountain bikes and wheelchairs are permitted on the paved part of the trail.

Permits: No permits are required. There is a $4 parking fee when the kiosk is attended.

Maps: For a free trail map, contact the East Bay Regional Parks District at the address below and ask for the Redwood Regional Park brochure. Ask the USGS for a topographic map of the Oakland East area.

Directions: From Highway 24 in Oakland turn south on Highway 13 and drive to Redwood Road. Turn left on Redwood Road and drive two miles past Skyline Boulevard to the park entrance on the left. Turn left and park at the Canyon Meadow Staging Area at the end of the road.

Alternate route: From the Oakland side of the Bay Bridge, take Highway 580 to the 35th Avenue exit. Drive east on 35th Avenue, which becomes Redwood Road, and continue as above to the parking area.

Contact: East Bay Regional Parks District, 2950 Peralta Oaks Court, P.O. Box 5381, Oakland, CA 94605-0381; tel. (510) 635-0135, ext. 2200, or fax (510) 635-3478; Redwood Regional Park, tel. (510) 482-6024.

23 Grass Valley Loop
2.8 mi/1.5 hrs

Grass Valley lies hidden in the East Bay hills, providing a simple paradise. This meadow lines more than a mile of a valley floor, framed on each side by the rims of miniature mountains. In the spring, the land glows with the various hues of green from wild grasses, along with wild radish, blue-eyed grass, and golden poppies. The scene is quiet and beautiful, and the Grass Valley Trail is one of the quickest routes into tranquillity. Starting at the Bort Meadow Staging Area, at a trailhead for the East Bay Skyline National Trail, hike downhill to the Bort Meadow picnic area, turn left, head south through Grass Valley and on to Stonebridge, for a distance of 1.5 miles. To get back from Stonebridge, walk north on the Brandon Trail, which is routed along the west side of Grass Valley. To crown a perfect day, end the hike with lunch at Bort Meadow.

Location: In Anthony Chabot Regional Park in the Oakland hills; map E1-East Bay, grid d7.

User groups: Hikers, dogs, horses, and mountain bikes. No wheelchair facilities.

Permits: No permits are required. Parking and access are free.

Maps: For a free trail map, contact the East Bay Regional Parks District at the address below and ask for the Anthony Chabot Regional Park brochure. Ask the USGS for a topographic map of the Las Trampas Ridge area.

Directions: From Interstate 580 in Oakland, take the 35th Avenue exit and drive east (35th Avenue becomes Redwood Road). Follow Redwood Road past Skyline Boulevard and drive three more miles to the Bort Meadow Staging Area on the right.

Contact: East Bay Regional Parks District, 2950 Peralta Oaks Court, P.O. Box 5381, Oakland, CA 94605-0381; tel. (510) 635-0135, ext. 2200, or fax (510) 635-3478; Anthony Chabot Regional Park, tel. (510) 639-4751.

24 Bort Meadow
5.4 mi/3.25 hrs

This trail has good views of a beautiful valley and, in the spring, a diverse array of pretty wildflowers. You start at the Bort Meadow Staging Area, a trailhead for the East Bay Skyline National Trail. Head out north (to the right) where the trail meanders along an old ranch road, climbing only slightly above Bort Meadow and Grass Valley. At the ridge, turn and look south for a great view of Grass Valley, a divine sight in the springtime. From the ridge the trail proceeds north, with valley and hilltop views along the way; watch closely for the hidden bench on the right side of the trail so you can sit and look out over the remote foothill country. After enjoying the views, return the way you came.

Location: In Anthony Chabot Regional Park north of Castro Valley; map E1-East Bay, grid d7.

User groups: Hikers, dogs, horses, and mountain bikes. No wheelchair facilities.

Permits: No permits are required. Parking and access are free.

Maps: For a free trail map, contact the East Bay Regional Parks District at the address below and ask for the Anthony Chabot Regional Park brochure. Ask the USGS for a topographic map of the Las Trampas Ridge area.

Directions: From Interstate 580 in Oakland, take the 35th Avenue exit and drive east (35th Avenue becomes Redwood Road). Follow Redwood Road past Skyline Boulevard and drive three more miles to the Bort Meadow Staging Area on the right.

Contact: East Bay Regional Parks District, 2950 Peralta Oaks Court, P.O. Box 5381, Oakland, CA 94605-0381; tel. (510) 635-0135, ext. 2200, or fax (510) 635-3478; Anthony Chabot Regional Park, tel. (510) 639-4751.

25 Rocky Ridge Loop
4.4 mi/2.5 hrs

Rocky Ridge is the prime destination for hikers visiting the 3,800-acre Las Trampas Regional Wilderness. The grassy rolling ridge with sandstone outcrops provides spectacular views to the east and the west. The outcrops have been beautifully sculpted by the wind and are colored by various lichen species. You can spend an entire day, if you so desire, just poking around the ridge. To reach Rocky Ridge, begin at the staging area at the end of Bollinger Road. Take the Rocky Ridge Trail, which starts out with a steep climb, rising about 800 feet over the course of 1.5 miles. Have faith, because once that climb is behind you, you'll be atop Rocky Ridge and the trail eases up. Head south down the ridge (take the Upper Trail) for a mile, enjoying the views on the way. To hike out the loop, turn left on the Elderberry Trail and walk two miles downhill to the staging area.

Special note: For an added adventure, explore the Wind Caves. To reach these hollowed openings in the sandstone outcrops from the Upper Trail, turn right on the Sycamore Trail and hike a steep .3 mile down to the caves.

Location: In Las Trampas Regional Wilderness south of Moraga; map E1-East Bay, grid d7.

User groups: Hikers, dogs, and horses. No mountain bikes. No wheelchair facilities.

Permits: No permits are required. Parking and access are free.

Maps: For a free trail map, contact the East Bay Regional Parks District at the address below and ask for the Las Trampas Regional Wilderness brochure. Ask the USGS for a topographic map of the Las Trampas Ridge area.

Directions: From Interstate 680 in San Ramon, take the Crow Canyon Road exit and head west to Bollinger Canyon Road. Turn right on Bollinger Canyon Road and drive five miles to the parking area.

Contact: East Bay Regional Parks District, 2950 Peralta Oaks Court, P.O. Box 5381, Oakland, CA 94605-0381; tel. (510) 635-0135, ext. 2200, or fax (510) 635-3478; Las Trampas Regional Wilderness, tel. (925) 687-3419.

26 Iron Horse Regional Trail
15.0 mi one way/1.0 day

The Iron Horse Regional Trail is a focal point of the national "Rails to Trails" program, which converts abandoned rail lines into hiking trails. When complete, the Iron Horse Trail will span northward from Shadow Cliffs Lake in Pleasanton all the way to Suisun Bay near Martinez. The rail route that it follows was established in 1890 and abandoned officially in 1976. It took only two years to remove all the tracks, but the trail conversion is requiring quite a bit more time.

The completed portion starts at Amador Valley Boulevard in Dublin and heads about 17 miles north to Walnut Creek. It is often hot and dry out here, with little shade (the trail is 75 feet wide in places) and no drinking water available, but the trail deserves mention anyway. When shade trees are planted, drinking water is made available, and the route is lengthened, Iron Horse will become a prominent long-distance trail for jogging, biking, and even walking.

Location: In the San Ramon Valley from San Ramon to Walnut Creek; map E1-East Bay, grid d8.

User groups: Hikers, wheelchairs, dogs, horses, and mountain bikes.

Permits: No permits are required. Parking and access are free.

Maps: For a free trail map, contact the East Bay Regional Parks District at the address below and ask for the Iron Horse Regional Trail brochure. Ask the USGS for a topographic map of the Las Trampas Ridge area.

Directions: From Interstate 680 in Walnut Creek, take the Rudgear Road exit. Turn east and park at either the park and ride lot (on the east side of the freeway) or the Staging Area (south side).

Contact: East Bay Regional Parks District, 2950 Peralta Oaks Court, P.O. Box 5381, Oakland, CA 94605-0381; tel. (510) 635-0135, ext. 2200, or fax (510) 635-3478.

27 Donner Falls

6.5 mi/2.5 hr

At Mt. Diablo, the Bay Area's grand old mountain rising above the East Bay hills, there are a series of largely secret waterfalls that can be as pretty as anything after a rain and yet well hidden. Reaching them requires a 6.5-mile hike, a good climb and something of a fortune hunt, and in return you get an experience that shows why the Bay Area is one of the most special places on earth. This is a great winter hike, best after heavy rain has brought the waterfalls to life. The trailhead for the Donner Creek Falls is at the end of Regency Drive, which is located off Clayton Road (and becomes Marsh Creek Road) out of Clayton. From here you turn left on an old ranch road, right from the start hiking along a pretty creek. You hike along the creek, set amid pretty rolling hills peppered with oaks, heading up a fair climb to Cardinet Junction. You turn left, shortly later cross the creek, then face about a 600-foot climb in five switchbacks before reaching the signed turnoff for the falls trail. Rewards feature views to the north of Clayton, Suisun Bay and the Mothball Fleet, and a good chance of seeing rabbits, deer and hawks. From here, the trail turns to single track, laterally along the left side of a canyon, and one by one, the falls start to come in view. The first is a 20-foot cascade across the other side of the canyon. Then moments later you see another, straight ahead, more of a chute. You keep on, and two more come in view, including one short but pretty free fall; then scanning across the slopes, you can see yet another, a smaller cascade. You just keep on and find that the trail will guide you right across two streams, the source of the falls. The trail loops back to the Cardinet Junction, and from here it's an easy (but often muddy in winter) traipse downhill back to the trailhead. We can't imagine Diablo any prettier than on this hike.

Location: In Mount Diablo State Park near Danville; map E1-East Bay, grid d9.

User groups: Hikers and horses. No dogs. Mountain bikes are permitted on the service road, but not the single-track trail that provides access to the waterfalls. The first half of the trail is designed for wheelchair use.

Permits: No permits are required. Parking and access are free.

Maps: For a trail map, send $5 (brochure is $1) to Mount Diablo State Park at the address below. Ask the USGS for a topographic map of the Diablo area.

Directions: From Interstate 680 in Walnut Creek, take the Ygnacio Valley Road exit. Drive east on Ygnacio Valley Road for 7.5 miles to Clayton Road. Turn right on Clayton Road and drive three miles (the road becomes Marsh Creek Road) to Regency Drive. Turn right on Regency Drive and drive .5 mile to the end of the road and the trailhead.

Contact: Mount Diablo State Park, 96 Mitchell Canyon Road, Clayton, CA 94517; tel. (925) 837-2525 or (925) 837-0904.

28 Giant Loop

8.6 mi/4.75 hrs

You face an endurance test on this hike, but it allows you to get a real feel for Mount Diablo with the least chance of meeting up with other park visitors. First, note there is no sign at the trailhead or anywhere else that says "Giant Loop Trail." That is an adopted name by people who have learned to pay the price on this loop hike and love it anyway. A trail map is essential. It set on the north side of Mount Diablo. Start in Mitchell Canyon on the Mitchell Canyon Trail and make the steady 1,800-foot climb to Meridian Ridge/Deer Flat (a good spot for lookouts). Then fork left on to Donner Canyon Trail (a fire road). Here you make a steep descent into Donner Canyon. On the way, you will pass flower-strewn grasslands (spectacular in the spring) and take in seemingly endless views of

Northern California. At the end of Donner Canyon Trail, take a left on the fire road (known as the Donner Trail). From here it's a two-mile hike to return to Mitchell Canyon Trailhead. This hike can be hot, dry, and difficult, so set aside most of a day and enjoy it slowly.

Location: In Mount Diablo State Park near Danville; map E1-East Bay, grid d9.

User groups: Hikers and horses. Mountain bikes are allowed on a portion of this route. No dogs. No wheelchair facilities.

Permits: No permits are required. A $2 state park entrance fee is charged for each vehicle.

Maps: For a trail map, send $5 (brochure is $1) to Mount Diablo State Park at the address below. Ask the USGS for a topographic map of the Diablo area.

Directions: From Interstate 680 in Walnut Creek, take the Ygnacio Valley Road exit and drive 7.5 miles on Ygnacio Valley Road into Clayton. Turn right on Clayton Road and drive one mile to Mitchell Canyon Road. Turn right and drive to the trailhead at the end of the road.

Contact: Mount Diablo State Park, 96 Mitchell Canyon Road, Clayton, CA 94517; tel. (925) 837-2525 or (925) 837-0904.

29 China Wall Loop

3.3 mi/2.0 hrs

First of all, there is no sign for the China Wall Loop at the trailhead. But after taking this hike, some call this loop hike by that name anyway, hence the unofficial recognition. So at the trailhead, look instead for Borges Ranch Trailhead and the Briones-to-Mount Diablo Trail although China Wall is your destination. The China Wall rock formation sits on the slopes of Mount Diablo. What you see on this hike is a line of rocks that looks like the Great Wall of China in miniature (well, kind of)— they are prehistoric-looking sandstone formations. In addition, on the hike out, you will get glimpses to the east of Castle Rocks and other prominent sandstone outcrops located just outside the park's boundary. Look closer and you might also see golden eagles, hawks,

and falcons, all of which nest here. Reaching China Wall requires only a 1.5-mile hike from the Borges Ranch Trailhead, heading off on the Briones-to-Mount Diablo Trail. Turn right at the junction with the Alamo Trail, which runs .5 mile along the base of China Wall. To complete the loop, turn right again on the Hanging Valley Trail and hike back to the trailhead.

Location: In Diablo Foothills Regional Park on the northwest slopes of Mount Diablo near Danville; map E1-East Bay, grid d9.

User groups: Hikers, dogs, horses, and mountain bikes. No wheelchair facilities.

Permits: No permits are required. Parking and access are free.

Maps: For a free trail map, contact the East Bay Regional Parks District at the address below and ask for the Diablo Foothills Regional Park brochure. Ask the USGS for a topographic map of the Diablo area.

Directions: Northbound on Interstate 680 in Walnut Creek, take the Ygnacio Valley Road exit. Turn right, drive several miles to Walnut Avenue, and turn right. Drive to Oak Grove Road, turn right, then turn right again on Castle Rock Road, and drive to Borges Ranch Road. Turn right and drive to the parking area at the end of Borges Ranch Road.

Alternate route: Southbound on Interstate 680, drive south to the North Main Street exit. Drive south on North Main Street to Ygnacio Valley Road. Turn left and proceed as above.

Contact: East Bay Regional Parks District, 2950 Peralta Oaks Court, P.O. Box 5381, Oakland, CA 94605-0381; tel. (510) 635-0135, ext. 2200, or fax (510) 635-3478; Diablo Foothills Regional Park, tel. (925) 837-4145.

30 Mount Diablo Summit Loop

0.7 mi/0.5 hr

One of the best lookouts in the world is at the top of Mount Diablo. No matter how fouled up things get, you can't foul up that view. This loop—called both the Fire Interpretive Trail and the Diablo Summit Loop—allows hikers to take a short, easy walk around the top of this East Bay landmark. Since you can drive nearly to the top of the mountain at 3,849 feet, it is the easiest hike in the park, yet also provides the best views.

Looking west, you can see across the bay to the Golden Gate Bridge, the Pacific Ocean, and, 25 miles out to sea, the Farallon Islands. To the north, you can see up the Central Valley. To the east, the frosted Sierra crest is often in view; using binoculars on a perfect day, it is even possible to see a piece of Half Dome sticking out from Yosemite Valley (135 miles). The view from the top of Mount Diablo is said to be second only to that of Mount Kilimanjaro in terms of the amount of visible earth surface.

Location: In Mount Diablo State Park near Danville; map E1-East Bay, grid d9.

User groups: Hikers and horses. No dogs or mountain bikes. The first half of the trail is designed for wheelchair use.

Permits: No permits are required. A $2 state park entrance fee is charged for each vehicle.

Maps: For a trail map, send $5 (brochure is $1) to Mount Diablo State Park at the address below. Ask the USGS for a topographic map of the Diablo area.

Directions: From Interstate 680 in Danville, take the Diablo Road exit and drive east (bear right after .75 mile to stay on Diablo Road) for three miles to Mount Diablo Scenic Boulevard. Turn left and drive 3.7 miles (the road becomes South Gate Road) to the park entrance station. Continue for 7.3 miles to the summit. The trailhead is just above the lower parking area just before the road becomes a one-way road.

Contact: Mount Diablo State Park, 96 Mitchell Canyon Road, Clayton, CA 94517; tel. (925) 837-2525 or (925) 837-0904.

31 Volvon Loop Trail/Bob Walker Ridge

5.7 mi/3.0 hrs

Morgan Territory Regional Preserve is located within the traditional homeland of the Volvon, one of five historical Indian nations in the Mount Diablo area. This trail, named after the first people to live here, is the preserve's featured hike. The trip is excellent, tracing along a ridge as it rises along sandstone hills to a ridgeline with terrific views. From the trailhead at about 2,000 feet, take the Volvon Trail, which is routed northward on a ranch road to a rounded mountain peak. There are beautiful views of Los Vaqueros Reservoir, as well as below to Round Valley. The trail loops around a prominent lookout at Bob Walker Ridge (1,977 feet), then returns via the Coyote Trail (hikers only) and back to the starting point. This parkland is most beautiful in the spring, and not just because the hills are greened up; one of the best wildflower displays in the Bay Area occurs here at that time. Views of Mount Diablo are also excellent. The one downer: Too many cows. But a secret: there are Native American grinding bowls carved out of bedrock mortars available for those who search out these bedrock depressions. Note while the name Volvon Loop Trail is still used, many are calling this hike "Bob Walker Ridge," as in, "Hey, let's do the Bob Walker Ridge out at Morgan Territory." The ridge was named in the 1990s for Bob Walker, a landscape photographer and open-space advocate who helped ensure that Morgan Territory was added to the East Bay Regional Park District.

Location: In the Morgan Territory Regional Preserve north of Livermore; map E1-East Bay, grid d9.

User groups: The first half of the loop is accessible to hikers, dogs, horses, and mountain bikes. The second half is for hikers and dogs only. No wheelchair facilities.

Permits: No permits are required. Parking and access are free.

Maps: For a free trail map, contact the East Bay Regional Parks District at the address below and ask for the Morgan Territory Regional Preserve brochure. Ask the USGS for a topographic map of the Tassajara area.

Directions: From Interstate 580 in Livermore, take the North

Livermore Avenue exit. Drive north to Highland Road and turn left; then drive a short distance and turn right on Morgan Territory Road. Follow Morgan Territory Road to the parking area just past the ridge summit.

Contact: East Bay Regional Parks District, 2950 Peralta Oaks Court, P.O. Box 5381, Oakland, CA 94605-0381; tel. (510) 635-0135, ext. 2200, or fax (510) 635-3478; Morgan Territory Regional Preserve, tel. (925) 757-2620.

32 Shoreline Loop Trail
1.75 mi/1.0 hr

Little Cull Canyon Reservoir, covering just 18 acres, is the backdrop for a picnic lunch in a canyon, and this short hike along the lake is popular with park visitors. From the parking area, walk over to the picnic areas and turn left along the Shoreline Trail. It skirts the western bank of the narrow lake, then loops back along a lagoon. This is a pleasant walk most of the year. However, just plain forget it on summer afternoons when the hot sun brands everything in sight. That is why this park is most famous for its swimming complex, complete with bathhouse and snack bar, not for the hiking and, heaven knows, not for the fishing.

Location: In the Cull Canyon Regional Recreation Area in the Castro Valley foothills; map E1-East Bay, grid e7.

User groups: Hikers and dogs. No horses or mountain bikes. No wheelchair facilities.

Permits: No permits are required. No entrance fee. A fee for swimming is charged.

Maps: For a free trail map, contact the East Bay Regional Parks District at the address below and ask for the Cull Canyon Regional Recreation Area brochure. Ask the USGS for a topographic map of the Hayward area.

Directions: From eastbound Interstate 580 in Castro Valley, take the Center Street exit and drive north to Heyer Avenue. Turn right on Heyer and proceed to Cull Canyon Road. Turn left and drive to the park entrance.

From westbound Interstate 580, take the

Castro Valley exit and turn left onto Castro Valley Boulevard. Drive to Crow Canyon Road, turn right, and drive .5 mile. Turn left on Cull Canyon Road and drive to the park entrance.

Contact: East Bay Regional Parks District, 2950 Peralta Oaks Court, P.O. Box 5381, Oakland, CA 94605-0381; tel. (510) 635-0135, ext. 2200, or fax (510) 635-3478; Cull Canyon Regional Recreation Area, tel. (510) 537-2240.

33 Cogswell Marsh Loop
2.8 mi/1.5 hrs

Cogswell Marsh is the heart of an 800-acre marshy wetlands, a great place to take short nature hikes and try to identify many rare birds. It's always a good choice for viewing shorebirds; as a bonus, peregrine falcons are typically seen either hovering over the marsh or perched on power pylons. As many as 200 white pelicans have been seen here, along with the occasional merlin. From the parking area, the trail starts with a .37-mile hike across landfill, then enters the marshlands, where a loop trail circles the most vital habitat. To keep feet from getting wet, two short sections are bridged. The loop is best hiked clockwise, so you face the Bay Bridge and the San Francisco skyline, an outstanding view, as you walk along the water's edge of the South Bay. Guided weekend nature walks are available.

Location: At Hayward Regional Shoreline on South San Francisco Bay in Hayward; map E1-East Bay, grid e6.

User groups: Hikers and mountain bikes. No dogs or horses. No wheelchair facilities.

Permits: No permits are required. Parking and access are free.

Maps: For a free trail map, contact the East Bay Regional Parks District at the address below and ask for the Hayward Regional Shoreline brochure. Ask the USGS for a topographic map of the San Leandro area.

Directions: From Interstate 880 in Hayward, take the West Winton Avenue exit and follow the road west toward the bay to the entrance and parking area.

Contact: East Bay Regional Parks District, 2950 Peralta Oaks Court, P.O. Box 5381, Oakland, CA 94605-0381; tel. (510) 635-0135, ext. 2200, or fax (510) 635-3478; Hayward Regional Shoreline, tel. (510) 783-1066.

34 Don Castro Lake Loop

1.7 mi/1.0 hr

Don Castro is a small (23 acres) but pretty lake that attracts swimmers to its lagoon and clear, warm, blue waters. Hiking is typically an afterthought for visitors, who come primarily to picnic or fish. The trail, actually a road, is routed completely around the lake for an easy walk or jog in a nice setting. From the parking area, walk a short distance along the West Lawn to the dam and start your hike there, circling the water in a clockwise direction. In the first .25 mile, you will pass a fishing pier, with the lake on your right and the swimming lagoon on your left. The route continues to the headwaters of the lake at San Lorenzo Creek, crosses the creek, then hems the southern shoreline all the way to the lake's spillway. After climbing a short staircase, you will be on top and can hike over the dam and back to the parking area. It's an easy circle.

Location: In the Don Castro Regional Recreation Area in the Castro Valley foothills; map E1-East Bay, grid e7.

User groups: Hikers and dogs. Portions of the trail are paved for bicycle and wheelchair use. No horses.

Permits: No permits are required. A $4 parking fee is charged when the kiosk is attended. A swimming fee is extra.

Maps: For a free trail map, contact the East Bay Regional Parks District at the address below and ask for the Don Castro Regional Recreation Area brochure. Ask the USGS for a topographic map of the Hayward area.

Directions: From eastbound Interstate 580 in Castro Valley, take the Center Street exit and turn right. Drive to Kelly Street. Turn left and drive .5 mile to Woodroe. Turn left on Woodroe and drive to the park entrance.

From westbound Interstate 580, take the Castro Valley exit and drive west on East Castro Valley Boulevard to Grove Way. Turn left and drive to Center Street. Drive .5 mile, turn left, and drive to Kelly Street. Make another left onto Kelly Street and drive to Woodroe. Turn left and drive to the park entrance.

Contact: East Bay Regional Parks District, 2950 Peralta Oaks Court, P.O. Box 5381, Oakland, CA 94605-0381; tel. (510) 635-0135, ext. 2200, or fax (510) 635-3478; Don Castro Regional Recreation Area, tel. (510) 538-1148.

35 High Ridge Loop

3.3 mi/2.0 hrs

The hilltops in Garin Regional Park render sweeping views of the East Bay foothills westward to South San Francisco Bay, the number-one attraction at this 3,000-acre parkland. The hills span for miles, and in the fall there are times late in the day when sunbeams will pour through openings between cumulus clouds, creating a divine scene. Of the 20 miles of trails in the park, the Ridge Loop Trail is the best way to see the surrounding wildlands, primarily oak grasslands amid rolling foothills. From the parking area (at 380 feet), walk .25 mile past the picnic areas to Arroyo Flats and turn left on the High Ridge Trail. In another .25 mile, it links up with the Vista Peak Loop, best hiked in a clockwise direction. You will start climbing, rising 550 feet in a mile, topping out at Vista Peak (934 feet) and shortly after, Garin Peak (948 feet). Take your time and enjoy the views.

Location: In Garin Regional Park in the Hayward foothills; map E1-East Bay, grid f7.

User groups: Hikers, dogs, horses, and mountain bikes. No wheelchair facilities.

Permits: No permits are required. There is a $4 parking fee when the kiosk is attended, and $1 dog fee.

Maps: For a free trail map, contact the East Bay Regional Parks District at the address below and ask for the Garin and Dry Creek Pioneer Regional Parks brochure.

Ask the USGS for a topographic map of the Hayward area.

Directions: From Fremont take Highway 238 (Mission Boulevard) north through Union City to Garin Avenue. Turn right onto Garin Avenue and drive one mile to the park entrance.

Contact: East Bay Regional Parks District, 2950 Peralta Oaks Court, P.O. Box 5381, Oakland, CA 94605-0381; tel. (510) 635-0135, ext. 2200, or fax (510) 635-3478; Garin Regional Park, tel. (510) 582-2206.

36 Ridgeline Trail
7.0 mi/4.0 hrs

People often overlook Pleasanton Ridge Regional Park, not knowing it offers a quiet, natural setting with excellent views from the Ridgeline Trail. Development in and around the park has purposely been limited so the surroundings could retain as natural a feel as possible. The plan has succeeded, and the best way to experience it is on this hike. The Ridgeline Trail climbs to elevations of 1,600 feet, with the northern sections giving way to sweeping views featuring miles of rolling foothills and valleys at the threshold of Mount Diablo. From the parking area, elevation 300 feet, start hiking on the Oak Tree Trail, which is routed 1.4 miles up to the Ridgeline Trail, climbing 750 feet. Turn right and hike two miles along the ridge. You can return on a loop route by turning left on the Thermalito Trail, which we recommended.

Location: In Pleasanton Ridge Regional Park west of Pleasanton; map E1-East Bay, grid f9.

User groups: Hikers, dogs, horses, and mountain bikes. No wheelchair facilities.

Permits: No permits are required. Parking and access are free.

Maps: For a free trail map, contact the East Bay Regional Parks District at the address below and ask for the Pleasanton Ridge Regional Park brochure. Ask the USGS for a topographic map of the Dublin area.

Directions: From Interstate 680 in Pleasanton, take the Bernal Road exit west and drive to Foothill Road. Turn left and drive three miles to the parking area and information center on the right.

Contact: East Bay Regional Parks District, 2950 Peralta Oaks Court, P.O. Box 5381, Oakland, CA 94605-0381; tel. (510) 635-0135, ext. 2200, or fax (510) 635-3478; Pleasanton Ridge Regional Park, tel. (925) 862-2963.

37 North Arroyo Trail
1.3 mi/0.75 hr

Though you can't walk all the way around Shadow Cliffs Lake, you can explore a series of smaller ponds in the Arroyo area. There's no place else like it in the East Bay. From the back of the first parking area, you take a trail over the top of a levee and down to the shore of the first pond. Then just follow the North Arroyo Trail along the shores of several ponds for about .5 mile. For a view of the ponds, make the short climb up the adjacent levee. These ponds are water holes left over from a gravel quarry. Shadow Cliffs Lake, the biggest pond and covering some 80 acres, has been stocked with trout and is one of the better fishing spots in the East Bay. It is also a good place to swim, as the water is often quite clear.

Location: In the Shadow Cliffs Regional Recreation Area in Pleasanton; map E1-East Bay, grid f9.

User groups: Hikers and dogs. Portions of the trail are accessible to horses and mountain bikes. No wheelchair facilities.

Permits: No permits are required. The parking fee is $5 from April through September, $4 from October through March; there is a $1 dog fee.

Maps: For a free trail map, contact the East Bay Regional Parks District at the address below and ask for the Shadow Cliffs Regional Recreation Area brochure. Ask the USGS for a topographic map of the Livermore area.

Directions: From Interstate 580 in Pleasanton take Santa Rita Road south. Drive two miles, turn left on Valley Avenue, and drive to Stanley Boulevard. Turn left and drive to the park entrance.

Contact: East Bay Regional Parks District, 2950 Peralta Oaks Court, P.O. Box 5381, Oakland, CA 94605-0381; tel. (510) 635-0135, ext. 2200, or fax (510) 635-3478; Shadow Cliffs Regional Recreation Area, tel. (925) 846-3000.

38 Bayview Trail

3.0 mi/1.5 hrs

Evidence of Coyote Hills Regional Park's rich history is visible throughout its 966 acres: four Indian shell mounds, heaps of accumulated debris from ancient living areas, can be seen. The Shoreline Trail is the favorite hike in the park, offering excellent views of the South Bay. This walk circles the park, including a 1.5-mile stretch that borders the bay and a shorter piece that runs adjacent to a marsh. The park is a wildlife sanctuary, with grassy hills and marshes that provide significant habitat for numerous migrating waterfowl. The best way to hike this loop is in a counterclockwise direction from the main parking area. For a short but enjoyable side trip from the main parking area, take the wooden boardwalk out through the North Marsh.

Location: In Coyote Hills Regional Park on the shore of the South Bay near Fremont; map E1-East Bay, grid f6.

User groups: Hikers, dogs, horses, and mountain bikes. The trail is paved and technically wheelchair accessible, but is quite steep in some sections.

Permits: No permits are required. There is a $4 parking fee when the kiosk is attended, and a $1 dog fee year-round.

Maps: For a free trail map, contact the East Bay Regional Parks District at the address below and ask for the Coyote Hills Regional Park brochure. Ask the USGS for a topographic map of the Newark area.

Directions: From Fremont drive west on Highway 84 to the Paseo Padre Parkway exit. Turn right on Paseo Padre Parkway and drive to Patterson Ranch Road. Turn left and drive to the parking area.

From Highway 880 in Fremont take the Highway 84/Decoto Road exit, and drive on Highway 84 to Paseo Padre Parkway. Proceed as above.

From the Peninsula, turn east on Highway 84, cross the Dumbarton Bridge, and take the Thornton Avenue exit. Turn left (the road becomes Paseo Padre Parkway) and drive north to Patterson Ranch Road. Turn left on Patterson Ranch Road and drive to the parking area.

Contact: East Bay Regional Parks District, 2950 Peralta Oaks Court, P.O. Box 5381, Oakland, CA 94605-0381; tel. (510) 635-0135, ext. 2200, or fax (510) 635-3478; Coyote Hills Regional Park, 8000 Patterson Ranch Road, Fremont, CA 94555; tel. (510) 795-9385.

39 Dumbarton Bridge

4.5 mi/2.5 hrs

Let this be a lesson for future bridge designers. When the Dumbarton Bridge was constructed, a biking and hiking path was added along the south side of the roadway, separated from traffic by a cement cordon. That means you can safely hike to the top of the center span for a unique view of the South Bay. This hike is best started from the Fremont side of the bridge, because it is unsafe to leave cars unattended at the western foot of the bridge in East Palo Alto.

Special note: The bridge is a link in an outstanding bicycle trip. Start at the Alameda Creek Regional Trail in Niles, head over the Dumbarton Bridge, turn left on the Baylands Trail, and ride through Palo Alto; then go farther south at Charleston Slough on the Baylands Trail to Mountain View Baylands.

Location: On the Dumbarton Bridge from Fremont to East Palo Alto; map E1-East Bay, grid g6.

User groups: Hikers, wheelchairs, and mountain bikes. No dogs or horses.

Permits: No permits are required. Parking and access are free.

Maps: Ask the USGS for a topographic map of the Newark area.

Directions: From Redwood City head east on Highway 84 and cross the Dumbarton Bridge. Take the first exit after the toll plaza, Thornton Avenue. Turn right and drive .25 mile to Marshland Road. Turn right and drive four miles to the parking area at the fishing pier.

Contact: Don Edwards San Francisco Bay National Wildlife Refuge, P.O. Box 524, Newark, CA 94560; tel. (510) 792-4275, (510) 792-0222, or fax (510) 792-5828.

40 Tidelands Trail
2.5 mi/1.5 hrs

Bird-watchers won't soon forget the diversity of bird life at the San Francisco Bay National Wildlife Refuge, with more than 250 species in a given year using this habitat for food, resting space, and nesting sites. It is not unusual to see a half dozen species of ducks, an egret, sandpiper, willet, and herons in just 15 or 20 minutes. The refuge is big, covering 23,000 acres in all, and the Tidelands Trail pours right through it. This is actually a wide dirt pathway on a levee routed amid salt marsh and bay tidewaters. Group nature tours on this trail are offered regularly on weekends. The views of the South Bay and, on clear days, the surrounding foothills are a panoramic urban backdrop. Don't forget to stop by refuge headquarters before your hike to see the exhibits and pamphlets that will help make your walk more enjoyable.

Location: In the San Francisco Bay National Wildlife Refuge at the eastern foot of the Dumbarton Bridge; map E1-East Bay, grid g6.

User groups: Hikers, dogs, and mountain bikes. There are no wheelchair facilities, but the trail can be navigated by most wheelchair users. No horses.

Permits: No permits are required. Parking and access are free.

Maps: For a free brochure, contact the refuge at the address below. Ask the USGS for a topographic map of the Newark area.

Directions: From San Francisco drive south on U.S. 101 to the Willow Road-Dumbarton exit. Drive east across the Dumbarton Bridge and take the first exit (Thornton Avenue) after the toll plaza. Turn right and drive .25 mile to Marshland Road. Turn right and drive a short distance to the visitor center.

Contact: Don Edwards San Francisco Bay National Wildlife Refuge, P.O. Box 524, Newark, CA 94560; tel. (510) 792-4275, (510) 792-0222, or fax (510) 792-5828.

41 Dumbarton Pier
1.0 mi/1.0 hr

Here is an example of how the government did something right. This pier was once the old Dumbarton Bridge, but when the new high-rise span was built in the 1980s, the roadway extending from Fremont was converted to a fishing pier and made part of the San Francisco Bay National Wildlife Refuge. The pier reaches all the way to the channel of the South Bay, a natural migratory pathway for sharks (in the summer), bat rays (winter), sturgeon (winter), perch (late fall), and jacksmelt (spring). Many seabirds and waterfowl live in this area year-round. The easy walk out to the end of the pier also renders pretty sea views of the South Bay's shoreline; looking north on a clear day, you can see the city of San Francisco as well as the San Mateo and Bay Bridges.

Location: In South San Francisco Bay in the San Francisco Bay National Wildlife Refuge in Fremont; map E1-East Bay, grid g7.

User groups: Hikers, wheelchairs, and mountain bikes. No dogs or horses.

Permits: No permits are required. Parking and access are free.

Maps: For a free brochure, contact the refuge at the address below. Ask the USGS for a topographic map of the Newark area.

Directions: From San Francisco drive south on U.S. 101 to the Willow Road-Dumbarton exit. Drive east across the Dumbarton Bridge and take the first exit (Thornton Avenue) after the toll plaza. Turn right and drive to Marshlands Road. Turn right again and drive past the San Francisco Bay National Wildlife Refuge entrance and visitor center for about three miles, following the signs to Dumbarton Pier (and the entrance to a leg of the San Francisco Bay bicycle trail).

Contact: Don Edwards San Francisco Bay National Wildlife Refuge, P.O. Box 524, Newark, CA 94560; tel. (510) 792-4275, (510) 792-0222, or fax (510) 792-5828.

42 Alameda Creek Regional Trail

11.0 mi one way/4.5 hrs

An unusual solution to the biker-versus-hiker conflict has been implemented here with the construction of a double trail. Two trails, one on each side of Alameda Creek, are routed from Niles Community Park to the shoreline of the South Bay. The trail on the north bank is designed for horseback riders and hikers. The one on the south bank is paved, perfect for bicyclists and joggers. Markers set at .25-mile intervals help joggers keep track of their exact distances. From Niles the trail goes past Shinn Pond, Alameda Creek Quarries, and Coyote Hills Regional Park. For access to Coyote Hills Regional Park and the San Francisco Bay National Wildlife Refuge, take the trail on the south side of the creek; there is no direct access to either of those areas on the northside trail.

Location: On Alameda Creek from Niles to the South Bay; map E1-East Bay, grid g7.

User groups: South Trail: Hikers, dogs, and mountain bikes. North Trail: Hikers, dogs, and horses. No wheelchair facilities.

Permits: No permits are required. Parking and access are free.

Maps: For a free trail map, contact the East Bay Regional Parks District at the address below and ask for the Alameda Creek Regional Trail brochure. Ask the USGS for a topographic map of the Niles area.

Directions: From Interstate 680 in Fremont, take the Mission Boulevard exit and drive west

to Highway 84/Niles Canyon Road. Turn right and make another immediate right on Old Canyon Road. The staging area is on the left.

Contact: East Bay Regional Parks District, 2950 Peralta Oaks Court, P.O. Box 5381, Oakland, CA 94605-0381; tel. (510) 635-0135, ext. 2200, or fax (510) 635-3478; Alameda Creek Regional Trail, tel. (510) 790-2612.

43 Peak Trail

7.0 mi/5.0 hrs

In one of the most intense climbs in the Bay Area, this trail takes you from an elevation of 400 feet at the trailhead to the summit of Mission Peak at 2,517 feet in a span of just 3.5 miles. That is why many people stay away, far away. But in the spring, it is one of the best hikes around, when the grasslands are such a bright green that the hills seem to glow, wildflowers are blooming everywhere, and there are sweeping views of San Francisco, the Santa Cruz Mountains, and on crystal clear days, the Sierra crest to the east. Two trails lead up, but the best choice is to start at the parking lot at Ohlone College, for a route that's less steep than from the other trailhead at the end of Stanford Avenue in Fremont. After parking at Ohlone College, take the Spring Valley Trail, which intersects the Peak Trail and continues along the northern flank of the mountain up to the summit. It's a good idea to bring a spare shirt for this hike, especially in the colder months. That's because you will likely sweat through whatever you are wearing on the way up, and when you stop to enjoy the views, you'll get cold and clammy. An extra shirt solves that problem.

Location: In the Mission Peak Regional Preserve near Fremont; map E1-East Bay, grid g8.

User groups: Hikers, dogs, and horses. No mountain bikes. No wheelchair facilities.

Permits: No permits are required. A parking fee is charged at the Ohlone College lot.

Maps: For a free trail map, contact the East Bay Regional

Parks District at the address below and ask for the Mission Peak Regional Preserve brochure. Ask the USGS for a topographic map of the Niles area.

Directions: From Fremont take Highway 238 (Mission Boulevard) to the Ohlone College campus. Turn into the Ohlone College Campus and park at Lot D or H. Go through the gate at the back of the campus to access the trail.

Contact: East Bay Regional Parks District, 2950 Peralta Oaks Court, P.O. Box 5381, Oakland, CA 94605-0381; tel. (510) 635-0135, ext. 2200, or fax (510) 635-3478; Mission Peak Regional Preserve, tel. (925) 862-2244.

Sunol Loop
4.75 mi/3.5 hrs

There are hidden places around the Bay Area that make you feel as if only you know about them. This is one such place. Sunol Regional Wilderness is a 6,400-acre wilderness, and this loop trail leads past many of the most striking spots: Little Yosemite, a miniature canyon with a pretty stream; Cerro Este, at 1,720 feet, one of the higher points in the park; Cave Rocks, a series of natural, gouged-out rock forms; and Indian Joe Creek, a little brook that runs along the start of the trail. From the parking area, begin your loop hike by heading north on the Indian Joe Creek Trail, then climbing one mile to Cave Rocks. Turn right on Rocks Road/Cerro Este Trail and climb up over the summit and down the other side all the way to the Canyon View Trail. Turn right and return to the parking area. A great option on the Canyon View Trail is to take the short gated cutoff trail that drops down to the floor of Little Yosemite. In the winter, the creek at the bottom of the valley has many tiny pool-and-drop waterfalls. This park is a habitat center for the largest number of nesting gold eagles in the world. In recent years peregrine falcons are also nesting on the edges of cliffs.

Location: In the Sunol Regional Wilderness near Sunol; map E1-East Bay, grid g9.

User groups: Hikers, dogs, horses, and mountain bikes. The Indian Joe Creek section of the loop is limited to hikers. No wheelchair facilities.

Permits: No permits are required for day use. A wilderness permit and camping reservation is required for overnight backpackers. A $4 access fee is charged with the kiosk is attended; there is a fee of $1 for dogs.

Maps: For a free trail map, contact the East Bay Regional Parks District at the address below and ask for the Sunol-Ohlone Regional Wilderness brochure. Ask the USGS for a topographic map of La Costa Valley area.

Directions: From Interstate 680 in the East Bay, take the Calaveras Road exit in Sunol. Turn south on Calaveras Road to Geary Road. Turn left on Geary Road and continue into the park.

Contact: East Bay Regional Parks District, 2950 Peralta Oaks Court, P.O. Box 5381, Oakland, CA 94605-0381; tel. (510) 635-0135, ext. 2200, or fax (510) 635-3478; Sunol Regional Wilderness, tel. (925) 862-2244.

45 East Bay Skyline National Trail
31.0 mi one way/2.5 days

A 31-mile trail along the East Bay's skyline offers a unique opportunity for a long-distance hike that can be chopped into many short segments over the course of days or even weeks. The trail spans from the Castro Valley foothills northward to the ridgeline behind Richmond, crossing six regional parks for a view into the area's prettiest and wildest lands. Called the East Bay Skyline National Trail, it is the Bay Area's longest single continuous trail. The trail can be hiked from south to north in two days, but it can be divided into seven sections from the different access points available at parking areas. Bicycles and horses are permitted on the 65 percent of the trail that is wide enough to accommodate them.

It is a great trip, whether you do it all in one weekend or cover a bit at a time over several weeks. No permits are needed, leashed dogs are permitted, and access is free. The only drawbacks are the lack of campgrounds along the way, which makes backpacking and overnights impossible, and the absence of piped drinking water. Water is available at only four points over the 31 miles, at Lomas Cantadas, Sibley Preserve, Skyline Gate, and Bort Meadow. So come prepared with a full canteen or two of water per person, along with a hat and sunscreen. Following is a detailed description of the trail from south to north.

Location: In the East Bay Regional Parks District, from Chabot Regional Park near Castro Valley to Wildcat Canyon Regional Park in the Richmond hills; map E1-East Bay, grids c6, d6, d7, d8.

User groups: Hikers, dogs, horses, and mountain bikes. Horses and mountain bikes are restricted in some sections.

Permits: No permits are required. A parking fee may be charged at some trailheads.

Maps: For a brochure and map of the East Bay Skyline National Trail or individual maps on each regional park, contact the East Bay Regional Parks District at the address below.

Directions: See individual trailhead listings below for specific directions.

Contact: East Bay Regional Parks District, 2950 Peralta Oaks Court, P.O. Box 5381, Oakland, CA 94605-0381; tel. (510) 635-0135, ext. 2200, or fax (510) 635-3478.

• 45a. Proctor Gate to Bort Meadow, Chabot Regional Park

The trail starts adjacent to a golf course, is routed up a ridge, then meanders on a ranch road in Chabot Regional Park. At Stonebridge (don't turn left at the trail junction!), the trail leads into Grass Valley and on to Bort Meadow. Distance: 6.5 miles; climbs 600 feet, then drops 320 feet.

Directions: From Interstate 580 in Oakland, take the 35th Avenue exit and drive east (35th Avenue becomes Redwood Road). Drive on Redwood Road to the Proctor Gate Staging Area, located on the east border of the park, next to a golf course.

• 45b. Bort Meadow to MacDonald Gate, Chabot Regional Park

If you are hiking the entire East Bay National Skyline Trail, the trail climbs steeply out of Bort Meadow. If you are starting at the parking area, however, no such climb is needed. The trail becomes a service road, from which you can turn and look south for the great view of Grass Valley. Hikers are completely exposed on the ascent; it's hot and dry in the afternoon, so it's best to go early in the morning. Once on top, it's an easy hike with many wildflowers in spring and lush green as well. It then descends into a canyon, crosses Redwood Road, and puts you at the entrance to Redwood Regional Park. Distance: 2.7 miles; climbs 300 feet, then drops 500 feet.

Directions: From Interstate 580 in Oakland, take the 35th Avenue exit and drive east (35th Avenue becomes Redwood Road). Drive on Redwood Road, three miles past Skyline Boulevard to the Bort Meadow Staging Area on the right.

• 45c. MacDonald Gate to Skyline Gate, Redwood Regional Park

Hikers have two options here, and our preference is to split off at the French Trail to hike up the canyon bottom on the Stream Trail, enveloped by redwoods. Note that bikes are banned from this section. The alternative, a must for bikers, is to take the West Ridge Trail for a steep climb to the canyon rim, then drop to the junction at Skyline Gate. Distance: five miles; the French Trail drops 200 feet, then climbs 400 feet; the West Ridge Trail climbs 900 feet, then drops 200 feet.

Directions: From Interstate 580 to the west or Interstate 680 to the east, drive to Highway 24, then to Highway 13 and go south. Drive to Redwood Road and turn left. Drive to the park entrance, turn south, and park at the Mac-Donald Gate Staging Area.

- **45d. Skyline Gate through Huckleberry Preserve to Sibley Preserve**

This section of trail is a choice hike for nature lovers, who will see an abundance of bird life and other animals, especially in the early morning and late evening. The trail passes through a deciduous woodland habitat, with a short but quite steep climb after entering Huckleberry Preserve. Distance: three miles; drops 200 feet, then climbs 480 feet.

Directions: From Highway 24 in Oakland, drive east to Highway 13. Go south and drive to Joaquin Miller Road, then head east until you hit Skyline Boulevard. Turn left on Skyline Boulevard and drive to the Skyline Gate Staging Area.

- **45e. Sibley Preserve to Lomas Cantadas, Tilden Regional Park**

A unique section of trail, this part crosses over the Caldecott Tunnel in a relatively unpeopled area. Many hawks are seen here, a nice bonus. Sibley is best known for its volcanic past, and hikers can take a side trip to Mount Round Top, a one-time volcano that blew its top off. No bicycles are permitted. Distance: 3.4 miles; drops 300 feet, then climbs 600 feet.

Directions: From Interstate 580 to the west or Interstate 680 to the east, drive to Highway 24. Continue to just east of the Caldecott Tunnel and take the Fish Ranch Road exit northwest to Grizzly Peak Boulevard. Turn left and drive to Skyline Boulevard. The park entrance and parking area are on the left.

- **45f. Lomas Cantadas to Inspiration Point, Tilden Regional Park**

This section of trail starts at a major access area off Grizzly Peak Boulevard, with an adjacent side trip available to Vollmer Peak, the highest point on the East Bay Skyline National Trail. The trail is then routed north to Inspiration Point at Wildcat Canyon Road, another well-known access point, losing elevation most of the way. Many sweeping views of the East Bay's untouched foothills are found on this hike. Distance: three miles; drops 860 feet.

Directions: From Interstate 580 to the west or Interstate 680 to the east, drive to Highway 24. Drive to just east of the Caldecott Tunnel and take the Fish Ranch Road exit to Grizzly Peak Boulevard. At the stop sign turn right and drive on Grizzly Peak Boulevard to Lomas Cantadas Road. Turn right, then immediately turn left, following the signs for the Steam Train to the parking area.

- **45g. Inspiration Point (Tilden Regional Park) to Wildcat Canyon Regional Park**

The last stretch starts at the most heavily used section of the entire route, then crosses its most dramatic and unpeopled terrain. From Inspiration Point the trail is actually paved for four miles, ideal for bicycles and wheelchairs. Beyond that, the trail turns to dirt and traces San Pablo Ridge, with inspiring views in all directions, before dropping steeply into Wildcat Canyon Regional Park in the Richmond foothills. Distance: 7.2 miles; drops 800 feet.

Directions: From Interstate 580 to the west or Interstate 680 to the east, drive to Highway 24. Continue to just east of the Caldecott Tunnel and take the Fish Ranch Road exit northwest to Grizzly Peak Boulevard. Turn right, drive up the hill, and turn right on South Park Drive. Drive one mile to Wildcat Canyon Road, bear right, and drive to the parking area at Inspiration Point on the left.

Alternate Route: To avoid South Park Drive, which is sometimes closed in the winter due to newt migrations, from Highway 24 go through the Caldecott Tunnel and exit at Orinda. Turn left on Camino Pablo. Drive north for about two miles, then turn left on Wildcat Canyon Road. Follow the road to Inspiration Point on the right.

TOM STIENSTRA

THE SKYLINE-TO-SEA TRAIL
IS A FAVORITE AMONG BACKPACKERS.

MAP E1 ⌒
SOUTH BAY

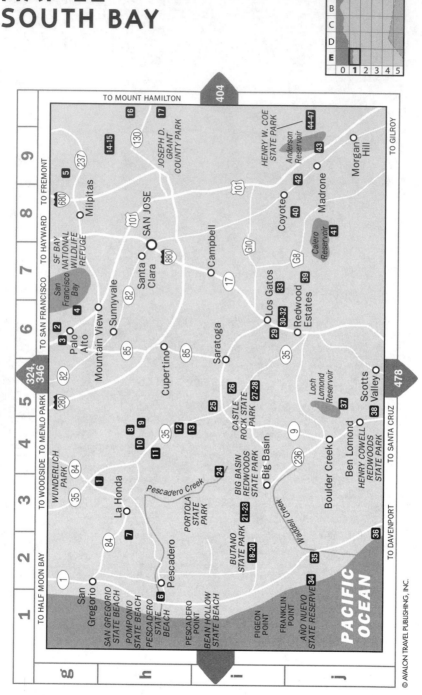

TO MOUNT HAMILTON

404

16   17

14-15

130

JOSEPH D. GRANT COUNTY PARK

HENRY W. COE STATE PARK   44-47

Anderson Reservoir   43

Morgan Hill

TO GILROY

237

5

680

Milpitas

101

SAN JOSE

101

Santa Clara

880

Campbell

G10

Coyote   42

40

Madrone   41

Calero Reservoir

TO FREMONT

TO HAYWARD

TO SAN FRANCISCO

SF BAY NATIONAL WILDLIFE REFUGE

San Francisco Bay

4   Mountain View

Sunnyvale

82

17   Los Gatos   33

G8   39

Redwood Estates

2

3   Palo Alto

85

Cupertino

85   Saratoga

35   30-32

29

Loch Lomond Reservoir

Scotts Valley

TO SANTA CRUZ

324, 346

280   82

TO WOODSIDE   TO MENLO PARK

WUNDERLICH PARK

8   9

12   13

10   35

11

26   CASTLE ROCK STATE PARK   27-28

25

37

38   Ben Lomond

35

1

35

84

La Honda

Pescadero Creek

24   BIG BASIN REDWOODS STATE PARK

Big Basin

9

236   Boulder Creek

HENRY COWELL REDWOODS STATE PARK

TO DAVENPORT

478

TO HALF MOON BAY

84

7

PORTOLA STATE PARK

21-23

Waddell Creek

San Gregorio

SAN GREGORIO STATE BEACH

POMPONIO STATE BEACH

PESCADERO STATE BEACH

6   Pescadero

BUTANO STATE PARK   18-20

PESCADERO POINT

BEAN HOLLOW STATE BEACH

PIGEON POINT

FRANKLIN POINT

AÑO NUEVO STATE RESERVE   34

35

36

PACIFIC OCEAN

© AVALON TRAVEL PUBLISHING, INC.

CHAPTER E1 ~ SOUTH BAY

1 Windy Hill Loop 375

2 Charleston Slough 376

3 Shoreline
Regional Park 376

4 Sunnyvale Baylands 377

5 Monument Peak Trail . . . 377

6 Pescadero Marsh 378

7 McDonald Loop 378

8 San Andreas
Fault Trail 379

9 Stevens Creek
Nature Trail 379

10 Coal Creek
Open Space 380

11 Borel Hill Trail 380

12 Skyline Ridge Trail 381

13 Long Ridge Loop 382

14 Eagle Rock Loop 382

15 Penitencia Creek 383

16 Halls Valley Loop 383

17 Hotel Trail 384

18 Año Nuevo Lookout 384

19 Mill Ox Loop 385

20 Butano Loop 385

21 Redwood Loop 386

22 Berry Creek Falls 387

23 Meteor Trail 387

24 Sequoia Trail 388

25 Saratoga Gap Loop 389

26 Summit Rock Loop 389

27 Trail Camp Loop 390

28 Skyline-to-Sea Trail 390

29 Ridge Trail 391

30 St. Joseph's Hill Trail . . . 392

31 Lexington Dam Trail 392

32 Priest Rock Trail 393

33 Bald Mountain Trail 393

34 Año Nuevo Trail 394

35 Waddell Creek Trail 394

36 Davenport Beach 395

37 Loch Lomond Loop 395

38 Eagle Creek Trail 396

39 Mine Hill Trail 396

40 Coyote Peak Loop 397

41 Juan Crespi Loop 398

42 Del Coyote
Nature Trail 398

43 Serpentine Trail 398

44 Frog Pond Loop 399

45 Coit Lake 399

46 Mississippi Lake Trail . . . 400

47 Rooster Comb Loop 401

1 Windy Hill Loop

8.2 mi/4.0 hrs

Windy Hill may be known for the north winds that blow through on spring afternoons, but it is even better known among hikers for offering remarkable views on clear days in any season. From the 1,900-foot summit, a grass-covered hilltop west of Portola Valley, hikers can see San Francisco Bay on one side and the Pacific Ocean on the other. If views are all you want, the .7-mile Anniversary Trail, which is routed from the parking area to the summit, provides them. If you want more, you can get more by taking an excellent loop hike that drops down into forests and climbs back out to grasslands. To do this, take the Hamms Gulch Trail, dropping 1,000 feet in elevation through a remote, pristine, wooded environment. Loop back on the Razorback Ridge Trail, hiking an extended series of switchbacks to make the return climb. The trail emerges from the woodlands and turns right on the Lost Trail. The last 2.1 miles to the parking area offer great views and a refreshing end to the hike.

Location: In the Windy Hill Open Space Preserve in the Portola Valley foothills; map E1-South Bay, grid g3.

User groups: Hikers, dogs (allowed on Hamms Gulch Trail, Eagle Trail, and Anniversary Trail, prohibited on others), and horses. No mountain bikes (except on the preserve's Spring Ridge Trail). There are wheelchair facilities in the picnic area adjacent to the parking area.

Permits: No permits are required. Parking and access are free.

Maps: For a free trail map and brochure, contact the Midpeninsula Regional Open Space District at the address below. Ask the USGS for a topographic map of the Mindego Hill area.

Directions: From Interstate 280 or U.S. 101 on the Peninsula, take Highway 84 west to Highway 35 (Skyline Boulevard). Turn left on Highway 35 and drive 2.3 miles to the parking area on the left.

Contact: Midpeninsula Regional Open Space District, 330 Distel Circle, Los Altos, CA 94022; tel. (650) 691-1200 or fax (650) 691-0485; during nonbusiness hours a Touch-Tone phone menu is available for trail news, conditions, and events.

2 Charleston Slough

4.0 mi/1.5 hrs

This trail is actually an old levee road that borders Charleston Slough, providing access to an expanse of wetlands and marsh habitat. It connects to a similar levee road that connects to Shoreline Regional Park in Mountain View—a great bike route and also good for hikes. From this trailhead the best option is to head straight out the levee along the slough. Within 10 or 15 minutes, with each step you will gain access to marshland that has been preserved in its natural state. From afar the surroundings may appear to be nothing more than pickleweed and mud, but look closer and you will begin to see the huge diversity of birds and wildlife that thrive in this very rich ecosystem. Egrets seem particularly plentiful. Way back in the 1950s, striped bass used to enter the mouth of Charleston Slough here and provide some excellent fishing. While the stripers are long gone, the serene atmosphere and the variety of birds remain, making this a favorite destination for many people. The trail/road extends out near the shore of the South Bay, near the mouth of San Francisquito Creek. A bonus is a large pit with mounds of dirt that are great for mountain bike jumping, known by locals as "the Moguls."

Location: In a South Bay marshland in Palo Alto; map E1-South Bay, grid g6.

User groups: Hikers and mountain bikes. No dogs or horses. No wheelchair facilities.

Permits: No permits are required. Parking and access are free.

Maps: Ask the USGS for a topographic map of the Mountain View area.

Directions: From U.S. 101 in south Palo Alto, take the San Antonio exit and turn east toward the bay. After a short distance, turn left on Bayshore Frontage Road and drive about a mile (curving) to Charleston Slough. The parking area is on the right side of the road.

Contact: Palo Alto Baylands Interpretive Center, tel. (650) 329-2506; Recreation Division, tel. (650) 329-2261.

3 Shoreline Regional Park

2.0 mi/1.0 hr

An ideal family destination, Shoreline Regional Park offers a wide variety of activities, including pleasant walks and bike rides on wide, crushed-gravel byways. There is also a small lake that makes an excellent spot for windsurfing, and many good kite-flying areas on tiny hills. The best trail at the park is routed along the east side of the lake and then northward on a levee through marshlands. It is quite popular with bird-watchers, who can spot everything from egrets to LBJs (Little Brown Jobs). A concession stand near the lake gets a lot of use from the corn dog-and-Coke crowd, which kind of puts everything in perspective.

Location: Along South San Francisco Bay in Mountain View; map E1-South Bay, grid g6.

User groups: Hikers, wheelchairs, and mountain bikes. No dogs or horses.

Permits: No permits are required. Parking and access are free.

Maps: Ask the USGS for a topographic map of the Mountain View area.

Directions: From U.S. 101 in Mountain View, take Shoreline Boulevard east and drive past the Shoreline Amphitheater to the park entrance station.

Contact: Shoreline Regional Park, City of Mountain View, 3070 N. Shoreline Boulevard, Mountain View, CA 94043; tel. (650) 903-6392 or fax (650) 903-6099.

4 Sunnyvale Baylands
2.0 mi/1.0 hr

Sunnyvale Baylands County Park really isn't much of a park at all, but rather a wildlife preserve surrounded by a levee that makes a good trail for hiking and jogging. It covers 177 acres of South Bay marshland, home to blue herons, great egrets, avocets, black-necked stilts, mallards, pintails, and burrowing owls. On nearly every trip you will also see a jackrabbit or two. In fact, these rabbits have a way of scaring the bejesus out of hikers. They hide in the weeds until you get close, then suddenly pop up and take off at warp speed, shocking you every time.

From the parking area adjacent to Highway 237, hike along the levee, turning left as it parallels Calabazas Creek. To your left is a seasonal wetland preserve. The trail continues along the creek, then turns left again and runs alongside Guadalupe Slough. An open-water bird preserve lies to the left.

Location: On South San Francisco Bay in Sunnyvale; map E1-South Bay, grid g6.

User groups: Hikers only. No dogs, horses, or mountain bikes. No wheelchair facilities.

Permits: No permits are required. A $3.50 parking fee is charged from May to October, no parking fee from November to April. No fees for walk-in or bike-in traffic.

Maps: For a free map, write to Sunnyvale Baylands County Park at the address below. Ask the USGS for a topographic map of the Mountain View area.

Directions: From Highway 237 in Sunnyvale, take the Caribbean exit. The park is immediately on your right hand side at 999 Caribbean (well signed, located next to Twin Creeks baseball facility).

Contact: Sunnyvale Baylands County Park, P.O. Box 3707, Sunnyvale, CA 94088; tel. (408) 730-7709 or fax (408) 745-7116.

5 Monument Peak Trail
7.5 mi/4.0 hrs

At 2,594 feet, Monument Peak offers views that nearly rival those on Mount Hamilton, with far-ranging vistas over the Santa Clara Valley. Yet the peak gets bypassed by many people, including regular visitors to Ed R. Levin County Park. Of the 13 trails in the park, the summit hike is clearly the longest, steepest, and most difficult. And most park visitors do not come for a challenge, but to play golf at Spring Valley, go fishing at Sandy Wool Lake, or just enjoy a picnic. Those who do want a challenge will find one on this climb. There are two routes to the top: The Monument Peak Trail is actually a road, and you may run head-on into mountain bikers ripping downhill on it. We suggest you take the Tularcitos/Agua Caliente Trail for a more gentle climb without having to contend with bikes.

It junctions with the Monument Peak Road near the top, where you turn left for the final push

to the summit. With the trailhead at 300 feet at Sandy Wool Lake, figure on a 2,300-foot climb over the course of about 3.75 miles.

Location: In Ed R. Levin County Park in the Milpitas foothills; map E1-South Bay, grid g9.

User groups: Hikers and horses. No dogs or mountain bikes. No wheelchair facilities.

Permits: No permits are required. A $4 day-use fee is charged. Hikers are encouraged to wait two days after a rain before hiking in order to prevent trail damage.

Maps: For a free trail map, contact Ed R. Levin County Park at the address below. Ask the USGS for topographic maps of the Milpitas and Calaveras Reservoir area.

Directions: From San Jose take Interstate 680 north to Milpitas. Take the Calaveras Boulevard East exit and drive about 3.5 miles to Downing Street. Turn left on Downing Street and drive .5 mile to the park entrance (straight ahead). Proceed to the parking area near Sandy Wool Lake.

Contact: Ed R. Levin County Park, 3100 Calaveras Road, Milpitas, CA 95035; tel. (408) 262-4527 or (408) 262-6980 or fax (408) 946-7610.

6 Pescadero Marsh
3.0 mi/1.5 hrs

Here is one of the few remaining natural marshlands on the entire Central California coast, a 600-acre parcel that is home to more than 250 species of birds. The most spectacular is the blue heron, which often grows nearly four feet tall and can have a wingspan of seven feet. A classic experience at any wetland is watching these huge birds lift off with labored wing beats. The trail is nearly flat, so this is an easy walk for almost anyone. It starts just northeast of the Pescadero Bridge on Highway 1, where a dirt path is routed amid pampas grass and bogs along the edge of wetland habitat. For the best route take the North Pond Trail to Audubon Marsh; then turn and head east and trace the southern edge of the marsh on the Sequoia Trail along Pescadero Creek. The marsh is bordered by the Pacific Ocean on one side and Pescadero Creek on the other, creating a unique setting that attracts birds that live in both saltwater and freshwater environments. Guided nature walks are conducted on most weekends by volunteers from the Half Moon Bay State Parks Department.

Location: In Pescadero Marsh south of Pescadero; map E1-South Bay, grid h1.

User groups: Hikers only. No dogs, horses, or mountain bikes. No wheelchair facilities.

Permits: No permits are required. Parking and access are free.

Maps: A map is available for $1 from state parks at the Bay Area District office listed below. Ask the USGS for a topographic map of the San Gregorio area.

Directions: From the Peninsula in San Mateo, take Highway 92 west to Half Moon Bay. Turn south on Highway 1 and drive 18 miles to Pescadero Marsh. Cross the Pescadero Bridge and park at the area on the west side of the highway. After parking, walk under the bridge (a trail is available) to the trailhead at the northeastern end of the bridge.

Contact: Pescadero State Beach, tel. (650) 879-2170; California State Parks, Bay Area District, 250 Executive Park Boulevard, Suite 4900, San Francisco, CA 94134; tel. (415) 330-6300 or fax (415) 330-6312.

7 McDonald Loop
3.1 mi/1.5 hrs

Though not a long trail, the McDonald Loop is long enough for many people, with a few surprise "ups" providing a challenge. The 1,000-acre park is best known for its redwoods, complete with the classic fern/sorrel understory, and is kept in a primitive state. Its trail network is linked by fire trail to Memorial County Park and Portola Redwood State Park. (The fire trails, by the way, are among the best mountain bike routes on the Peninsula.) This loop trail provides a fine introduction to the area and makes an excellent hike year-round; in the winter, especially during the week, you'll rarely encounter other hikers. For a great side trip, visit the adjacent Heritage Grove, which is accessible on Alpine Road about one mile east of the park. Several ancient redwoods grow there, and you can view them on a short, pleasant walk.

Location: In Sam McDonald County Park near La Honda; map E1-South Bay, grid h2.

User groups: Hikers only. No dogs, horses, or mountain bikes. No wheelchair facilities.

Permits: No permits are required. A $4 parking fee is charged.

Maps: A trail map is available for $1 at the ranger station. Ask the USGS for a topographic map of the La Honda area.

Directions: From Interstate 280 on the Peninsula, take the Woodside/Highway 84 exit. Drive up the hill past Skyline Boulevard and continue another 10 miles to La Honda. Turn left on La Honda/Pescadero Road and drive two miles to a Y. Bear right at the Y and drive a short distance to Sam McDonald County Park on the right.

Contact: Sam McDonald County Park, c/o San Mateo County Parks and Recreation Department, 455 County Center, 4th Floor, Redwood City, CA 94063-1646; tel. (650) 363-4020 or fax (650) 599-1721. Memorial Park Visitor Center, tel. (650) 879-0212.

8 San Andreas Fault Trail
0.6 mi/0.5 hr

The air at Los Trancos Open Space Preserve is always fresh, scented with bay leaves and damp woods. There are only seven miles of trails at the preserve, but one of the Peninsula's prize hikes is found here: the San Andreas Fault Trail. This is a self-guided tour of an earthquake trail and includes several examples of fault movement. The 13 numbered signposts along the way correspond with numbered explanations in the park brochure. If you don't want a geology lesson, you may be content with the good views of the Peninsula from the 2,000-foot ridgeline. Most hikers connect the San Andreas Fault Trail to the Lost Creek

Loop Trail, a pleasant and easy bonus leg that is routed into secluded spots along a pretty creek. With the Monte Bello Open Space Preserve just on the other side of Page Mill Road, there are nearly 3,000 contiguous acres of public open space here.

Location: In Los Trancos Open Space Preserve in the Palo Alto foothills; map E1-South Bay, grid h4.

User groups: Hikers only. The trail is not wheelchair accessible, but the parking lot is and offers a nice view. No dogs, horses, or mountain bikes.

Permits: No permits are required. Parking and access are free.

Maps: For a free trail map, contact the Midpeninsula Regional Open Space District at the address below. A map and trail guide are also available at the parking area. Ask the USGS for a topographic map of the Mindego Hill area.

Directions: From Interstate 280 in Palo Alto, turn west on Page Mill Road and drive seven twisty miles to the signed parking area on the right. The Monte Bello Open Space Preserve is directly across the street (on the left/south).

Contact: Midpeninsula Regional Open Space District, 330 Distel Circle, Los Altos, CA 94022; tel. (650) 691-1200 or fax (650) 691-0485; during nonbusiness hours a Touch-Tone phone menu is available for trail news, conditions, and events.

9 Stevens Creek Nature Trail
3.5 mi/2.0 hrs

The Monte Bello Open Space Preserve encompasses more than 2,700 acres of the most natural and scenic lands on the Peninsula. It includes 2,800-foot Black Mountain, the headwaters of Stevens Creek, and this pretty nature trail. The hike starts by lateraling across a grasslands bluff; then it drops 450 feet into the creek's wooded headwaters. As you descend through the forest, you will smell spicy bay leaves, feel the cool dampness on your skin, and see moss growing on many trees. The trail emerges from the forest and is routed back along the San Andreas Fault, evidenced by two starkly contrasting images: dense woodlands stand to the west, while grasslands and chaparral lie off to the east. The two habitats are the product of the differences in soil composition created by fault movement. The nature trail has signed points of interest, with explanations for each in the brochure. Longer hikes are available in the park, the most ambitious being the 7.6-mile (one-way) Canyon Trail to Saratoga Gap.

Location: In the Monte Bello Open Space Preserve in the Palo Alto foothills; map E1-South Bay, grid h4.

User groups: Hikers, horses, and mountain bikes (restricted from some trails). This trail is not open to wheelchairs, but the parking lot and a short side trail are wheelchair accessible and offer a good view. No dogs.

Permits: No permits are required unless you plan to use the preserve's backpack camp. In the winter, hikers are encouraged to phone for condition of the trail; it may be too wet to hike.

Maps: For a free trail map, contact the Midpeninsula Regional Open Space District at the address below. A map and trail guide are also available at the trailhead. Ask the USGS for a topographic map of the Mindego Hill area.

Directions: From Interstate 280 in Palo Alto, turn west on Page Mill Road and drive seven twisty miles to the signed parking area on the left (south). Los Trancos Open Space Preserve is directly across the street to the right (north).

Contact: Midpeninsula Regional Open Space District, 330 Distel Circle, Los Altos, CA 94022; tel. (650) 691-1200 or fax (650) 691-0485; during nonbusiness hours a Touch-Tone phone menu is available for trail news, conditions, and events.

10 Coal Creek Open Space
4.0 mi/2.0 hrs

Most residents of the Peninsula have never heard of the Coal Creek Open Space Preserve. That makes sense, as this is one of the lesser-developed parklands in the Bay Area. Yet it is worth making a trip to the 490-acre parcel of land set just east of Skyline Ridge, with its rolling meadows, open grasslands, and the forested headwaters of two creeks. The park's trails—actually old ranch roads—cover only four miles as they traverse the grasslands past a classic-looking barn and down along a small creek. Plan on enjoying nothing more than a short walk and a picnic. A bonus is that the parking area is adjacent to the CalTrans Vista Point, one of the best lookouts on the Peninsula.

Location: In the Coal Creek Open Space Preserve on the Peninsula's Skyline Ridge; map E1-South Bay, grid h4.

User groups: Hikers, dogs, horses, and mountain bikes. No wheelchair facilities.

Permits: No permits are required. Parking and access are free.

Maps: For a free trail map, contact the Midpeninsula Regional Open Space District at the address below. Ask the USGS for a topographic map of the Mindego Hill area.

Directions: From Highway 280 in Palo Alto, take the Page Mill Road exit and drive west on a winding two-lane road up the mountain to Skyline Boulevard. Turn right on Skyline Boulevard and drive one mile to the parking area, located on the right at the CalTrans Vista Point.

Contact: Midpeninsula Regional Open Space District, 330 Distel Circle, Los Altos, CA 94022; tel. (650) 691-1200 or fax (650) 691-0485; during nonbusiness hours a Touch-Tone phone menu is available for trail news, conditions, and events.

11 Borel Hill Trail
1.4 mi/1.0 hr

Borel Hill is one of the great lookouts on the San Francisco Peninsula, topping out at 2,572 feet and surrounded by grasslands so hikers get unobstructed, 360-degree views. Yet the hill is not well known and remains a favorite destination of only a few hikers who visit the Russian Ridge Open Space Preserve. Russian Ridge is that big grassy ridge near the intersection of Alpine Road and Skyline Boulevard above Palo Alto. From the parking area, hike southeast on the Ridge Trail, climbing about 250 feet over the course of .7 mile to Borel Hill. You'll see it just southwest of the trail: the hill is the highest spot around, bordered by grasslands and no trees. From the summit, with just a turn of the head you can see Monterey Bay one moment, Mount Diablo and the South Bay the next. There are several other trails at the preserve, the best being the 2.6-mile (one-way) hike out to the Mindego Ridge Trail, which is routed through an oak woodland forest. A return loop trail was completed in 1995.

Location: In the Russian Ridge Open Space Preserve on the Peninsula's Skyline Ridge; map E1-South Bay, grid h4.

User groups: Hikers, horses, and mountain bikes. A wheelchair-accessible trail starting at the parking area leads to Alpine Pond in the Skyline Ridge Open Space Preserve. No dogs.

Permits: No permits are required. Parking and access are free.

Maps: For a free trail map, contact the Midpeninsula Regional Open Space District at the address below. Maps are usually available at the trailhead. Ask the USGS for a topographic map of the Mindego Hill area.

Directions: From Interstate 280 in Palo Alto, take the Page Mill Road exit and drive west on a winding two-lane road up the mountain to Skyline Boulevard. Cross Skyline Boulevard, drive a short distance, and then turn right into the parking lot at the northwest corner of the intersection.

Contact: Midpeninsula Regional Open Space District, 330 Distel Circle, Los Altos, CA 94022; tel. (650) 691-1200 or fax (650) 691-0485; during nonbusiness hours a Touch-Tone phone menu is available for trail news, conditions, and events.

12 Skyline Ridge Trail

3.0 mi/1.5 hrs

Most people discover this park by accident in December, when they come up Skyline Boulevard (Highway 35) to the choose-and-cut Christmas tree farm. They see the parking area and maybe a trailhead and become a little curious. At some point many return to satisfy their curiosity with a hike, and most leave feeling well compensated for the effort. From the parking area on the west side of Skyline Boulevard, the Skyline Ridge Trail is routed around Horseshoe Lake, a pretty little farm pond (incredibly, no fishing is permitted). From there the trail pushes into the interior of the parkland, skirting the flank of the highest mountain in park boundaries (2,493 feet), and loops back to Skyline Boulevard. You play peekaboo here, heading in and out of woodlands and gaining occasional views of plunging canyons to the west. You can create a loop hike, but that requires going back on a fire road; most people return to the parking area via the same route they walked on the way in.

Location: In the Skyline Ridge Open Space Preserve on the Peninsula's Skyline Ridge; map E1-South Bay, grid h4.

User groups: Hikers, horses, and mountain bikes. A wheelchair-accessible trail leads to Horseshoe Lake. No dogs.

Permits: No permits are required. Parking and access are free.

Maps: For a free trail map, contact the Midpeninsula Regional Open Space District at the address below. Ask the USGS for a topographic map of the Mindego Hill area.

Directions: From Highway 280 in Palo Alto, take the Page Mill Road exit and drive west on a winding two-lane road up the mountain to Skyline Boulevard. Turn left on Skyline Boulevard and drive .8 mile to the main entrance and parking area on the right.

Contact: Midpeninsula Regional Open Space District, 330 Distel Circle, Los Altos, CA 94022; tel. (650) 691-1200 or fax (650) 691-0485; during nonbusiness hours a Touch-Tone phone menu is available for trail news, conditions, and events.

13 Long Ridge Loop
4.6 mi/2.0 hrs

When you walk the ridgeline here, you are rewarded with gorgeous views of the western slopes of the Santa Cruz Mountains, highlighted by Big Basin Redwoods and Butano State Parks. From the southern part of the park on a clear day, the Pacific Coast comes into view as well. The Long Ridge Open Space Preserve covers more than 1,000 acres and offers a scenic loop hike that peaks out at 2,400 feet, climbing the ridge and ducking down into pretty, wooded canyons in the process. After departing from the trailhead, you cross a small creek, then turn right to start the looping hike up Long Ridge. The trail climbs up to Long Ridge Road, turns, and is routed south across the grassy hilltops. From here the views of the coastal foothills and the ocean beyond can be wondrous. At the four-corners trail junction, turn left for the steep, switchback route down the canyon. At the end of the switchbacks, the trail passes the beautiful Jikoji Retreat, a private Zen center set along a surprising little pond, and then turns left and loops back to the parking area. You wind up near a pretty oak woodland, with an apple orchard in one area. This is one of the very best hikes on the Peninsula.

Location: In the Long Ridge Open Space Preserve in the Santa Cruz Mountains; map E1-South Bay, grid h4.

User groups: Hikers, horses, and mountain bikes (restricted from some trails, signed). No dogs. No wheelchair facilities.

Permits: No permits are required. Parking and access are free.

Maps: For a free trail map, contact the Midpeninsula Regional Open Space District at the address below. Maps are usually available at the trailhead. Ask the USGS for a topographic map of the Mindego Hill area.

Directions: From Highway 280 in Palo Alto, take the Page Mill Road exit and drive west on a winding two-lane road up the mountain to Skyline Boulevard. Turn left on Skyline Boulevard and drive three miles to a dirt parking area along the shoulder on the right side of the road.

Contact: Midpeninsula Regional Open Space District, 330 Distel Circle, Los Altos, CA 94022; tel. (650) 691-1200 or fax (650) 691-0485; during nonbusiness hours a Touch-Tone phone menu is available for trail news, conditions, and events.

14 Eagle Rock Loop
2.2 mi/1.0 hr

Eagle Rock is pretty short as far as mountains go, only 795 feet. But at Alum Rock City Park, it's the best perch in the vicinity for a picnic site and a view of the Santa Clara Valley. In the winter, after rain has cleared the air, it becomes a choice spot. For this hike, park at the lot at the road's end at the eastern end of the park, where you'll find a major trailhead for several routes. Take the one on the left, the North Rim Trail, to reach Eagle Rock. The hike climbs 300 feet to a canyon rim overlooking the valley cut by Penitencia Creek, before a short, signed cutoff trail takes you to Eagle Rock. To complete the loop, return to the North Rim Trail and continue on, working your way back down the valley floor. Turn left on the Creek Trail (more like a road), which is routed along Penitencia Creek to the parking area. Thirteen miles of trails provide access to the park's 700 acres, but this hike is our favorite.

Location: In Alum Rock City Park in the San Jose foothills; map E1-South Bay, grid h9.

User groups: Hikers, mountain bikes and horses. No dogs. No wheelchair facilities.

Permits: No permits are required. A $4 parking fee is charged.

Maps: For a free trail map, contact Alum Rock City Park at the address below. Ask the USGS for a topographic map of the Calaveras Reservoir area.

Directions: From Interstate 680 in San Jose, take the Alum Rock Avenue exit. Turn east on Alum Rock Avenue and drive 3.5 miles to the park entrance.

Contact: Alum Rock City Park, 16240 Alum Rock Avenue, San Jose, CA 95127; tel. (408) 277-4539 or (408) 259-5477.

15 Penitencia Creek

4.0 mi/1.75 hrs

To be honest, this isn't much of a hiking trail and is really more of a bike path. But with the stream running alongside, it makes a pleasant route for a leisurely stroll, jog, or bicycle ride. Two more bonuses make it worth a trip: The park's eastern boundary abuts Alum Rock City Park, providing access to an additional 13 miles of trails. And near Piedmont Road, behind the fire station, you'll find an additional 40 acres called Creek Park, which is linked to this trail, providing an optional loop hike. The Penitencia Creek Trail traces the stream for four miles, adjacent to Penitencia Creek Road, so joggers making the round-trip can have an easy eight-miler. Most hikers do about half that or extend their walks into Creek Park or Alum Rock City Park.

Location: In Penitencia Creek County Park in east San Jose; map E1-South Bay, grid h9.

User groups: Hikers and mountain bikes. No dogs or horses. No wheelchair facilities.

Permits: No permits are required. Parking and access are free.

Maps: For a free trail map, contact Penitencia Creek County Park at the address below. Ask the USGS for a topographic map of the Calaveras Reservoir area.

Directions: From Interstate 680 in San Jose, take the Berryessa Road exit. Drive east on Berryessa Road to Capitol Avenue. Turn right on Capitol Avenue and drive to Penitencia Creek Road. Turn left and drive to the parking area on the left.

Contact: Penitencia Creek County Park, San Jose City Park, (408) 277-2757, or c/o Ed R. Levin County Park, tel. (408) 262-6980.

16 Halls Valley Loop

5.5 mi/3.0 hrs

Grant County Park is the Bay Area's great undiscovered playland. The wild area covers 9,000 acres in the foothills of Mount Hamilton and can be the perfect setting for hiking and mountain biking. There is plenty of room for both endeavors, with nearly 40 miles of hiking trails (horses permitted) and 20 miles of old ranch roads for both mountain biking and hiking. The Halls Valley Loop provides the best introduction to what many call Grant Ranch. From the parking area along Mount Hamilton Road, take the main trail/road out past Grant Lake and bear left at the junction on the Halls Valley Trail. This route skirts Halls Valley to the left, an open landscape of foothills and grasslands sprinkled with oaks, a quiet and pretty scene. The trail heads out 2.5 miles, climbing east toward Mount Hamilton until it meets the Cañada de Pala Trail. Turn right, hike up .4 mile, and turn right again on the Los Huecos Trail to complete the loop. From here, it's a 1.8-mile trip back to the parking area, descending steeply most of the way.

Special note: There are many great side trips on this route. After a rain, one of the best is searching out the little creek at the bottom of Halls Valley, then following it upstream to discover a procession of little waterfalls. For the ambitious, another is climbing 2.2 miles and 500 feet up the ridge on the Pala Seca Trail above Halls Valley to the park's highest point; from Antler Point at 2,995 feet, you can look out over the Santa Clara Valley.

Location: In Joseph D. Grant County Park in the Mount Hamilton foothills east of San Jose; map E1-South Bay, grid h9.

User groups: Hikers, horses, and mountain bikes. No dogs. No wheelchair facilities.

Permits: No permits are required. A $4 entrance fee is charged year-round.

Maps: For a free trail map, contact Joseph D. Grant County Park at the address below. Ask the USGS for a topographic map of the Lick Observatory area.

Directions: From Interstate 680 in San Jose, take the Alum Rock Avenue East exit and drive to Mount Hamilton Road. Turn right on Mount Hamilton Road and drive eight miles east to the parking area on the left.

Contact: Joseph D. Grant County Park, 18405 Mount Hamilton Road, San Jose, CA 95140; tel. (408) 274-6121.

17 Hotel Trail

7.0 mi/3.25 hrs

People? What people? The remote landscape around Eagle Lake in Grant County Park provides visitors with precious tranquillity as well as good chances of seeing wildlife. Eagle Lake, set in the southernmost reaches of the park's 9,000 acres, is the prime destination of the Hotel Trail. After parking at the lot along Mount Hamilton Road, cross the road and look for the trailhead on the south side. Start hiking southeast on the ranch road (the Hotel Trail), scanning your surroundings for the wild turkeys that are commonly seen in this area. As you head deeper into the interior, you will be hiking through foothill country; bovines are the most frequently encountered animal (keep your distance from the bulls, of course), but you might see a herd of wild pigs, too. These pigs tend to sprint off when they see or hear people, so don't worry about playing out the fearless-hiker-meets-ferocious-boar scene. The route to Eagle Lake is a direct shot of 3.5 miles, climbing a couple of hundred feet in the process. There are several options for side trips along the way: the best is to turn right on the Cañada de Pala Trail and drop down about .5 mile to San Felipe Creek, the prettiest stream in the park.

Location: In Joseph D. Grant County Park in the Mount Hamilton foothills east of San Jose; map E1-South Bay, grid h9.

User groups: Hikers, horses, and mountain bikes. No dogs. No wheelchair facilities.

Permits: No permits are required. A $4 entrance fee is charged year-round.

Maps: For a free trail map, contact Joseph D. Grant County Park at the address below. Ask the USGS for a topographic map of the Lick Observatory area.

Directions: From Interstate 680 in San Jose, take the Alum Rock Avenue East exit and drive to Mount Hamilton Road. Turn right on Mount Hamilton Road and drive eight miles east to the parking area on the left. The Hotel Trail starts on the south side of the road, opposite the parking area.

Contact: Joseph D. Grant County Park, 18405 Mount Hamilton Road, San Jose, CA 95140; tel. (408) 274-6121.

18 Año Nuevo Lookout

2.75 mi/1.5 hrs

Tighten your boots and this trail will reward you with a fairly steep climb and a return trip through redwoods. It was once a premier hike to a lookout of Año Nuevo Island. No more. The trees have grown and blocked the view. But it still is a decent hike, not the best at Butano, but decent just the same. Park at the entrance station and start down the trailhead directly to the right. The trail climbs 730 feet in less than a mile to the lookout. There's a little bench here, and when you arrive and take a seat, you may wonder just what the heck the bench is here for. To rest? To look at the trees? Well, you see, 10 years ago there was a clear view of Año Nuevo Island to the south. Now that the conifers are in the way, the bench is just to catch your breath. We advise continuing on the Año Nuevo Trail, then returning on the Goat Hill Trail to complete the loop. Although short, this loop hike provides a good climb, and a chance to walk through redwoods on the return descent. Note: The name of this park is pronounced "BUTE-uh-no" and not, we repeat, not "Bew-TAH-no."

Location: In Butano State Park near Pescadero; map E1-South Bay, grid i2.

User groups: Hikers only. No dogs, horses, or mountain bikes. No wheelchair facilities.

Permits: No permits are required. A $2 day-use fee is charged per vehicle.

Maps: For a free trail map, contact Butano State Park at the address below. Ask the USGS for a topographic map of the Franklin Point area.

Directions: In Half Moon Bay, at the junction of Highway 1 and Highway 92, drive south on Highway 1 for 18 miles to the Pescadero Road exit. Turn left on Pescadero Road and drive past the town of Pescadero to Cloverdale Road. Turn right and drive 4.5 miles to the park entrance on the left.

Contact: Butano State Park, tel. (650) 879-2040; California State Parks, Bay Area District, tel. (415) 330-6300 or fax (415) 330-6312.

Location: In Butano State Park near Pescadero; map E1-South Bay, grid i2.

User groups: Hikers only. No dogs, horses, or mountain bikes. No wheelchair facilities.

Permits: No permits are required. A $2-per-vehicle state park entrance fee is charged.

Maps: For a free trail map, contact Butano State Park at the address below. Ask the USGS for a topographic map of the Franklin Point area.

Directions: In Half Moon Bay, at the junction of Highway 1 and Highway 92, drive south on Highway 1 for 18 miles to the Pescadero Road exit. Turn left on Pescadero Road and drive past the town of Pescadero to Cloverdale Road. Turn right and drive 4.5 miles to the park entrance on the left.

Contact: Butano State Park, tel. (650) 879-2040; California State Parks, Bay Area District, tel. (415) 330-6300 or fax (415) 330-6312.

19 Mill Ox Loop

5.0 mi/2.75 hrs

If you love redwoods and ferns but are also partial to sun and warm afternoons, the Mill Ox Loop at Butano State Park may be the ideal hike for you. Why? Because you get all these things in good doses. The trail starts by crossing a small creek in a dense redwood forest, then heads up a very steep grade on switchbacks, emerging at the top of the canyon on the Butano Fire Road. Here you turn right and climb more gradually as you head toward the park's interior. The fire road gets plenty of sun, and plenty of shirts come off en route to 1,138 feet. Views of the Pacific Ocean are to be had along the way if you turn and look back to the west. When you reach a junction with the Jackson Flats Trail, turn right; the trail descends quite steeply over a bare rock facing for .25 mile, then drops into Butano Canyon and the surrounding redwood forest. The rest of the hike is beautiful and pleasant, a meandering walk past ferns, trillium, redwoods, and rarely in the spring, blooming wild orchids. This is one of our favorites.

20 Butano Loop

11.0 mi/2.0 days

A trail camp makes this one of the few loop hikes in the Bay Area that can be turned into an overnight backpack trip. Note that water for drinking and cooking is usually not available at the camp, so campers must pack in their own. In addition, most of the route is on fire roads, and with the boom in mountain bike use, fewer and fewer people are making the trip on foot. Regardless, you can still arrange it so that almost half of the trip follows trails, not roads, and enjoy a mix of redwood-filled canyons and sunny lookouts from ridgelines. By following our suggested route, the first day of your hike will be spent primarily in the sun, and you'll walk through redwoods for most of the second day.

Start at the Mill Ox Trailhead at elevation 200 feet; then hike up the steep grade, turning right on the Butano Fire Road (700 feet). From here you trace the rim of Butano Canyon, enjoying views of the redwood-filled valley below and the Pacific Ocean

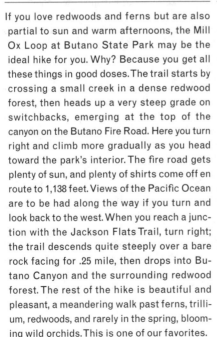

(behind you, off to the west). The trail climbs steadily before reaching 1,713 feet, crosses an old abandoned airstrip on the ridgeline, then drops down to the Butano Trail Camp at 1,550 feet for a first-day total of 5.5 miles. Reservations are required, and since this is an environmental camp, only lightweight camp stoves are permitted for cooking. On day two, you return by turning right on the Olmo Fire Trail, then taking the Doe Ridge/Goat Hill Trails back to the starting point. Much of this route laterals and descends into the south side of Butano Canyon on a soft dirt trail amid redwoods. During the winter, when the Sierra Nevada is entombed in snow and ice, this loop provides an answer for those looking for an overnight backpack trip.

Location: In Butano State Park near Pescadero; map E1-South Bay, grid i2.

User groups: Hikers only. No dogs, horses, or mountain bikes. No wheelchair facilities.

Permits: No permits are required. A $2-per-vehicle state park entrance fee is charged. For overnight use, camping reservations are required and a small camp fee is charged.

Maps: For a free trail map, contact Butano State Park at the address below. Ask the USGS for a topographic map of the Franklin Point area.

Directions: In Half Moon Bay at the junction of Highway 1 and Highway 92, drive south on Highway 1 for 18 miles to the Pescadero Road exit. Turn left on Pescadero Road and drive past the town of Pescadero to Cloverdale Road. Turn right and drive 4.5 miles to the park entrance on the left.

Contact: Butano State Park, tel. (650) 879-2040; California State Parks, Bay Area District, tel. (415) 330-6300 or fax (415) 330-6312.

21 Redwood Loop

0.6 mi/0.5 hr

Most people come to Big Basin Redwoods State Park to see giant redwoods, and the Redwood Loop is a short, easy path that meanders around many of these giants. This trail gets a lot of use, which is why we knocked the rating down a few notches. By using the numbered posts along the way and a trail brochure, you can take a self-guided nature walk. The sights include pretty Opal Creek, the Chimney Tree (which has survived many fires), and several other ancient redwoods. The Santa Clara Tree, located across Opal Creek at signpost three, is 17 feet in diameter; the Father-of-the-Forest is about 2,000 years old and stands at signpost eight; and the Mother-of-the-Forest, the tallest tree in the park at 329 feet, is at signpost nine. Many people take as much as an hour to complete the loop. There is no reason to rush.

Location: In Big Basin Redwoods State Park in the Santa Cruz Mountains near Boulder Creek; map E1-South Bay, grid i3.

User groups: Hikers only. Partially wheelchair accessible. No dogs, horses, or mountain bikes.

Permits: No permits are required. A $2-per-vehicle state park entrance fee is charged.

Maps: Detailed trail maps of Big Basin Redwoods State Park are available for a fee from Mountain Parks Foundation, 525 N. Big Trees Road, Felton, CA 95018; phone at (831) 335-3174. Ask the USGS for topographic maps of the Castle Rock Ridge and Big Basin area.

Directions: From the San Francisco Peninsula take Interstate 280 to Sunnyvale/Saratoga Road. Turn south and drive five miles to Saratoga. Turn right at Highway 9 and drive up the hill for about seven miles to Skyline Ridge. Continue over the other side of Highway 9 about seven more miles to Highway 236. Turn right and drive about 10 miles to Big Basin Redwoods State Park. Note: Highway 236 is extremely twisty and not recommended for motor homes or trailers.

Alternate route: From San Francisco take Highway 1 south to Santa Cruz. Go north on Highway 9 and drive about 12 miles. At the traffic light in Boulder Creek, turn left on Highway 236. Drive about 10 miles to park headquarters.

Contact: Big Basin Redwoods State Park,

21600 Big Basin Way, Boulder Creek, CA 95006; tel. (831) 338-8860; district headquarters, tel. (831) 429-2851; or fax (831) 429-2876.

22 Berry Creek Falls
12.0 mi/5.5 hrs

The prettiest sight in the Bay Area just might be Berry Creek Falls, a 70-foot waterfall framed by a canyon, complete with ferns, redwoods, and the sound of rushing water. It is the number-one hike in the Bay Area, one worth repeating over and over again. Getting an early start really helps you have a carefree trip with no pressure to complete the loop by a certain time. You start at park headquarters, taking the Skyline-to-Sea Trail amid the giant redwoods up to the Big Basin rim, then head down the other side, hiking west toward to the coast. After topping the rim at 1,200 feet, the hike descends 600 feet over the course of about four miles to Berry Creek Falls (4.7 miles from the trailhead). You round a bend and suddenly, there it is, this divine waterfall. A small bench is perfectly situated for viewing the scene while eating a picnic lunch.

To return, we recommend going the long way, up the staircase and past the Cascade Falls—both Silver Falls and Golden Falls—then returning on the Sunset Trail. At Silver Falls, it is possible to dunk your head into the streaming water without getting the rest of your body wet, a real thrill. Golden Falls is like no other waterfall, a beautiful cascade of water over golden sandstone, like a giant water slide. Once you pass Golden Falls, the trail climbs out to a service road near Sunset Camp. Do not miss the right turn off the service road to the Sunset Trail. From here the Sunset Trail takes you to the most remote sections of the park, in and out of chaparral and forest, then loops back into redwoods, and leads back to park headquarters. However, you can trim the hiking time down to about 4.5 hours if you double back on the same trail you came in on. But in such a beautiful place, why cut the experience short?

Location: In Big Basin Redwoods State Park in the Santa Cruz Mountains near Boulder Creek; map E1-South Bay, grid i3.

User groups: Hikers only. No dogs, horses, or mountain bikes. No wheelchair facilities.

Permits: No permits are required. A $3-per-vehicle state park entrance fee is charged.

Maps: Detailed trail maps of Big Basin Redwoods State Park are available for a fee from Mountain Parks Foundation, 525 N. Big Trees Road, Felton, CA 95018; phone at (831) 335-3174. Ask the USGS for topographic maps of the Castle Rock Ridge and Big Basin area.

Directions: From the San Francisco Peninsula take Interstate 280 to Sunnyvale/Saratoga Road. Turn south and drive five miles to Saratoga. Turn right at Highway 9 and drive up the hill for about seven miles to Skyline Ridge. Continue over the other side of Highway 9 about seven more miles to Highway 236. Turn right and drive about 10 miles to Big Basin Redwoods State Park. Note: Highway 236 is extremely twisty and not recommended for motor homes or trailers.

Alternate route: From San Francisco take Highway 1 south to Santa Cruz. Go north on Highway 9 and drive about 12 miles. At the traffic light in Boulder Creek, turn left on Highway 236. Drive about 10 miles to park headquarters.

Contact: Big Basin Redwoods State Park, 21600 Big Basin Way, Boulder Creek, CA 95006; tel. (831) 338-8860; district headquarters, tel. (831) 429-2851; or fax (831) 429-2876.

23 Meteor Trail
5.2 mi/2.5 hrs

Under the heavy redwood canopy of Big Basin, most hikers don't worry about whether or not it's foggy on the coast. But on this hike there's a unique reason to worry, as the park's best coastal lookout is at trail's end. The Meteor Trail starts at park headquarters on the Skyline-to-Sea Trail and heads northeast. (If you see a sign for Berry Creek

Falls, you're going in the wrong direction.)

For much of the route you hike along Opal Creek, a pretty stream in the spring, surrounded by redwoods. Two miles out, you will arrive at the intersection with the Meteor Trail, where you turn left and climb 400 feet over the space of a mile to the Middle Ridge Fire Road. The Ocean View Summit (1,600 feet) is only a couple hundred yards off, featuring a glimpse to the west of the Waddell Creek watershed and the Pacific Coast—though the view is largely eclipsed now by trees. Return by doubling back the way you came. If you visit Big Basin and don't have time for the Berry Creek Falls hike, this is the next best option.

Location: In Big Basin Redwoods State Park in the Santa Cruz Mountains near Boulder Creek; map E1-South Bay, grid i3.

User groups: Hikers only. No dogs, horses, or mountain bikes. No wheelchair facilities.

Permits: No permits are required. A $3-per-vehicle state park entrance fee is charged.

Maps: Detailed trail maps of Big Basin Redwoods State Park are available for a fee from Mountain Parks Foundation, 525 N. Big Trees Road, Felton, CA 95018; tel. (831) 335-3174. Ask the USGS for topographic maps of the Castle Rock Ridge and Big Basin area.

Directions: From the San Francisco Peninsula take Interstate 280 to Sunnyvale/Saratoga Road. Turn south and drive five miles to Saratoga. Turn right at Highway 9 and drive up the hill for about seven miles to Skyline Ridge. Continue over the other side of Highway 9 about seven more miles to Highway 236. Turn right and drive about 10 miles to Big Basin Redwoods State Park. Note: Highway 236 is extremely twisty and not recommended for motor homes or trailers.

Alternate route: From San Francisco take Highway 1 south to Santa Cruz. Go north on Highway 9 and drive about 12 miles. At the traffic light in Boulder Creek, turn left on Highway 236. Drive about 10 miles to park headquarters.

Contact: Big Basin Redwoods State Park, 21600 Big Basin Way, Boulder Creek, CA 95006;

tel. (831) 338-8860; district headquarters, tel. (831) 429-2851; or fax (831) 429-2876.

24 Sequoia Trail
1.0 mi/0.5 hr

The Shell Tree is one of the most unusual forest specimens on the Peninsula. This giant redwood is a strange-looking creature that has been ravaged by fire yet still lives and now measures some 17 feet in diameter. We suggest you hike the Sequoia Trail, a short, easy loop, just to see this tree. Even on such a short hike, the surrounding forest, much of it redwood and Douglas fir, can provide a sense of remoteness. If you want more of a workout, the Sequoia Trail is linked to the Summit Trail (across from the group camping area), which ventures into remote lands on the eastern border of the park. Portola Redwood State Park covers about 1,000 acres, primarily second-growth redwoods, though a few ancient monsters remain. The park has only 14 miles of trails, but the Iverson Trail connects to Memorial County Park and an additional trail network.

Location: In Portola Redwood State Park in the Santa Cruz Mountains; map E1-South Bay, grid i4.

User groups: Hikers only. No dogs, horses, or mountain bikes. No wheelchair facilities.

Permits: No permits are required. A $3-per-vehicle state park entrance fee is charged; pay at the visitor center.

Maps: A trail map is available for $1 at the visitor center. Ask the USGS for a topographic map of the Mindego Hill area.

Directions from the Peninsula: From Interstate 280 in Palo Alto, take the Page Mill Road exit. Turn west and drive nine miles to Highway 35 (Skyline Boulevard). Cross Highway 35 and continue on Alpine Road for three miles to Portola State Park Road. Turn left at Portola State Park Road and drive three miles to the park. The trailhead is just south of park headquarters.

Contact: Portola Redwood State Park, 9000

Portola State Park Road, La Honda, CA 94020; tel. (650) 948-9098 or fax (650) 948-0137.

25 Saratoga Gap Loop
9.0 mi/5.0 hrs

Saratoga Gap serves as a trailhead center for hikers exploring the Peninsula's Skyline Ridge. Trails from here lead to five other parklands, making it possible for hikers to create trips of any length. The best is the nine-mile Saratoga Gap Loop. The trail starts off northward, adjacent to Highway 35 on the Skyline Ridge. After one mile, turn right on Charcoal Road, which is routed down the slope (bikes are permitted here!) and into Upper Stevens Creek County Park. The trail descends to the headwaters of Stevens Creek, a quiet, wooded spot. Cross the creek and soon you will reach a trail junction, where you turn left (west) on the Canyon Trail; after crossing a small creek, turn left on the Grizzly Flat Trail. That trail climbs back to Skyline Boulevard, where you cross the road, enter the Long Ridge Open Space Preserve, and hike south to where the trail crosses Skyline Boulevard once again. Return on the Saratoga Gap Trail to the parking area. The hills here are grassy knobs sprinkled with oaks and madrones, while the canyons are heavily wooded, most prominently with Douglas firs.

Location: In the Saratoga Gap Open Space Preserve on Skyline Ridge in the Santa Cruz Mountains; map E1-South Bay, grid i5.

User groups: Hikers, horses, and mountain bikes. No dogs. No wheelchair facilities.

Permits: No permits are required. Parking and access are free.

Maps: For a free trail map, contact the Midpeninsula Regional Open Space District at the address below. Maps are usually available at the trailhead. Ask the USGS for topographic maps of the Mindego Hill and Cupertino area.

Directions: From Interstate 280 near Santa Clara, turn west on Saratoga Avenue and drive to Highway 9. Take Highway 9 up to the ridge to the junction of Highway 9 and Highway 35. At the junction, look for the CalTrans parking area on the left (southeast) corner. Park there. The preserve is on the northeast corner of this junction, across the road from the parking lot.

Contact: Midpeninsula Regional Open Space District, 330 Distel Circle, Los Altos, CA 94022; tel. (650) 691-1200 or fax (650) 691-0485; during nonbusiness hours a Touch-Tone phone menu is available for trail news, conditions, and events.

26 Summit Rock Loop
2.0 mi/1.0 hr

The Santa Clara Valley never looks prettier than it does from Summit Rock, set just east of the Skyline Ridge. This is the ideal perch for a lookout to the valley below, and getting there is not difficult when you take the featured hike at Sanborn-Skyline County Park. The park is so named because it connects Sanborn Creek with the Skyline Ridge, covering some 2,850 acres of mountain terrain in between. From the trailhead across Highway 35 from Castle Rock State Park, hikers start on the Skyline Trail and head north, adjacent to the road. The Skyline Trail leads right into the Summit Rock Loop, providing easy access to this great lookout. For people who like their views to come even easier, a popular option at the Skyline Trailhead is the .25-mile hike that leads to Indian Rock. Note that park headquarters are not located at this trailhead, but rather off Sanborn Road, where full facilities and other trails are available.

Location: In Sanborn-Skyline County Park on Skyline Ridge in the Santa Cruz Mountains; map E1-South Bay, grid i5.

User groups: Hikers and horses. No dogs or mountain bikes. No wheelchair facilities.

Permits: No permits are required. A $4 day-use fee is charged per vehicle.

Maps: For a free trail map, contact Sanborn-Skyline County Park at the address below. Ask the USGS for a topographic map of the Castle Rock Ridge area.

Directions: From Interstate 280 near Santa Clara, turn west on Saratoga Avenue and drive to Highway 9. Drive west on Highway 9 to the junction with Highway 35 (Skyline Boulevard). Turn south and drive 2.5 miles to Sanborn-Skyline County Park on the left. The trailhead is located roughly across from Castle Rock State Park on Skyline Boulevard.

Contact: Sanborn-Skyline County Park, 16055 Sanborn Road, Saratoga, CA 95070; tel. (408) 867-9959.

27 Trail Camp Loop

5.3 mi/2.5 hrs

Castle Rock State Park is well known to rock climbers, who practice their art here on Castle Rock and Goat Rock, two honeycombed sandstone formations. But hikers, too, are attracted to the park, a 3,600-acre semi-wilderness with 32 miles of hiking trails. The park is located on the west side of Skyline Ridge at an elevation of 3,000 feet, high enough to be above the smog, receive light snowfall in the winter, and provide scenic views to the west of Big Basin and Monterey Bay. The Trail Camp Loop offers the best introduction to the park. From the parking lot take the Saratoga Gap Trail. It drops into a gorgeous canyon, then passes a beautiful waterfall with a railed platform lookout. The trail then breaks out of forest, crosses a sandstone rock face with excellent views to the west of Big Basin, and in 2.6 miles, connects to the Ridge Trail. To complete the loop, turn right on the Ridge Trail and head back another 2.7 miles to the parking area. As you go, be on the lookout for the cutoff to the top of Goat Rock Lookout, and take that cutoff for a sensational view and picnic spot amid sandstone formations.

Location: In Castle Rock State Park on Skyline Ridge in the Santa Cruz Mountains; map E1-South Bay, grid i5.

User groups: Hikers and horses. No dogs or mountain bikes. No wheelchair facilities.

Permits: No permits are required, but you must self-register at the park entrance. A $2 day-use fee is charged.

Maps: For a free brochure, contact Castle Rock State Park at the address below. Ask the USGS for a topographic map of the Castle Rock Ridge area.

Directions: From Interstate 280 near Santa Clara, turn west on Saratoga Avenue and drive to Highway 9. Drive west on Highway 9 to the junction with Highway 35 (Skyline Boulevard). Turn south and drive 2.5 miles to the entrance to Castle Rock State Park on the right.

Contact: Castle Rock State Park, 15000 Skyline Boulevard, Los Gatos, CA 95020; tel. (408) 867-2952 or (831) 429-2851.

28 Skyline-to-Sea Trail

34 mi one way/2.5 days

What began as a good idea has been transformed into one of the most worshipped trails in the Bay Area. Years ago someone had a vision to create a trail that connected Castle Rock State Park on Skyline Ridge to Big Basin and then to Waddell Creek on the coast. The result, much of it built by volunteers, is this 34-mile backpack route, complete with primitive trail camps. It is ideal in many ways, including the fact that the hike is generally downhill, starting at 3,000 feet at Castle Rock and dropping all the way down to sea level. Fantastic views, redwood forests, waterfalls, and the backpack camps are among the rewards. Only in extremely rare conditions will you come across a discarded cigarette butt or a piece of litter; after all, most people won't trash a piece of heaven. The trail is best hiked in three days, but most do it in two. Of course, it is a must that you have a shuttle car waiting at the end of the trail at Waddell Creek on Highway 1.

From the trailhead at Castle Rock State Park, head out to the Waterman Gap trail camp (water is available) for a first-day hike of 9.6 miles. This portion includes crossing an open rock facing with fantastic views of Big Basin and the Pacific Coast to the west, which will help you envision the upcoming route. Other highlights include the headwaters of the San Lorenzo River, an old homestead and mixed forest. The logical plan for the second day is to hike 9.5 miles to Jay Camp at Big Basin headquarters. Once you cross Highway 9, you enter the state park and for a few miles, the route roughly parallels the park's access road. Then it breaks off, passes an open sandstone face with great westerly views, traces a narrow ridge, and drops down into a lush redwood canyon with a stream. Eventually it emerges at the bottom of Big Basin, and you camp relatively near park headquarters. While this camp is not a backcountry experience, the convenience of restrooms, coin showers, drinking water, and a small store are usually well received. On the last day you face hiking 12.5 miles out, up, and over the Big Basin rim, then down a wooded canyon, passing beautiful 70-foot Berry Creek Falls, crossing Waddell Creek, and finishing up at the coast. It is a fantastic trip, highlighted by the gigantic old-growth redwoods and the series of spectacular waterfalls. At Berry Creek Falls be sure to hike up the stairs to the brink of the waterfall, then head up the canyon to see Silver Falls (a gorgeous free fall, perfect for photographs), and then above that, Golden Falls, where clear water cascades over golden sandstone like a gigantic water slide. From Berry Creek Falls to the coast is a breeze, crossing over the stream with a make-shift bridge, then making the sea-level walk to Rancho del Oso and the parking area. It's a shortcut to hike out on the service road and bike path, but in the spring, take the longer, official route that loops around the valley and down to the parking area to see 20 or 30 species of wildflowers, including occasional rafts of forget-me-nots.

Location: From Castle Rock State Park via Big Basin to Waddell Creek on the Pacific coast; map E1-South Bay, grid i5.

User groups: Hikers and horses. No dogs or mountain bikes. No wheelchair facilities.

Permits: Trail camp reservations are required with a $5 reservation fee, plus a $10 camping fee per night, plus $3 per extra vehicle at the trailheads. Phone (831) 338-8861.

Maps: Detailed trail maps of Castle Rock State Park and Big Basin Redwoods State Park are available for a fee from Mountain Parks Foundation, 525 N. Big Trees Road, Felton, CA 95018; tel. (831) 335-3174. A free information sheet and a mileage chart between trail camps are available by phoning (831) 338-8861, or writing Big Basin Redwoods State Park at the address below. Ask the USGS for topographic maps of the Castle Rock Ridge and Big Basin area.

Directions: From Interstate 280 near Santa Clara, turn west on Saratoga Avenue and drive to Highway 9. Drive west on Highway 9 to the junction with Highway 35 (Skyline Boulevard). Turn south and drive 2.5 miles to the entrance to Castle Rock State Park on the right. For a one-way shuttle trip, leave a car at Waddell Creek/Rancho del Oso (see Waddell Creek Trail, below).

Contact: Big Basin Redwoods State Park, 21600 Big Basin Way, Boulder Creek, CA 95006; tel. (831) 338-8860; district headquarters, tel. (831) 429-2851, or fax (831) 429-2876. Castle Rock State Park, 15000 Skyline Boulevard, Los Gatos, CA 95020; tel. (408) 867-2952 or (831) 429-2851.

29 Ridge Trail
6.0 mi/2.75 hrs

El Sereno Open Space is one of the lesser-used parklands in the Bay Area. Why? Not only is it remote, but there's room at the trailhead for only two vehicles to park. The preserve covers 1,112 acres and is named for Mount El Sereno, a prominent peak on the adjacent ridge. From the trailhead at the pullout on Montevina Road, hike on the jeep trail, which traces a ridgeline. Though the trail bobs and weaves, you will generally head east, topping out on a rim and then descending toward Los Gatos for a distance of three miles to the end of the trail. This is where you'll find panoramic views of Lyndon Canyon, Lexington Reservoir, and the South Bay. After taking time to enjoy the vistas, return via the same route.

Location: In El Sereno Open Space Preserve in the Saratoga foothills; map E1-South Bay, grid i6.

User groups: Hikers, horses, and mountain bikes. No dogs. No wheelchair facilities.

Permits: No permits are required. Parking and access are free.

Maps: For a free trail map, contact the Midpeninsula Regional Open Space District at the address below. Ask the USGS for a topographic map of the Castle Rock Ridge area.

Directions: From the intersection of Interstate 280 and Highway 17 in San Jose, turn south on Highway 17 and drive about eight miles to Los Gatos. Continue south for about three miles to Montevina Road. Turn right and park at the roadside turnout at the end of the road. There is space for only a few cars.

Contact: Midpeninsula Regional Open Space District, 330 Distel Circle, Los Altos, CA 94022; tel. (650) 691-1200 or fax (650) 691-0485; during nonbusiness hours a Touch-Tone phone menu is available for trail news, conditions, and events.

30 St. Joseph's Hill Trail
2.7 mi/1.75 hrs

For most people to be willing to hike up, there had better be considerable compensation waiting at the trail's end. And so there is on this hike, which climbs 600 feet in the space of about 1.5 miles to a perch on top of St. Joseph's Hill, with views of Lexington Reservoir, the Santa Clara Valley, and the adjacent Sierra Azul Range. From the parking area just east of the dam at elevation 645 feet, you hike north adjacent to Los Gatos Creek for about .5 mile. At the trail junction, turn right and begin the climb up St. Joseph's Hill; a loop route is available near the top. Lexington Reservoir never looked so good.

Location: In the St. Joseph's Hill Open Space Preserve near Lexington Reservoir; map E1-South Bay, grid i6.

User groups: Hikers, dogs, and mountain bikes. No horses. No wheelchair facilities.

Permits: No permits are required. Parking at Lexington County Park is $4 per vehicle.

Maps: For a free trail map, contact the Midpeninsula Regional Open Space District at the address below. Ask the USGS for a topographic map of the Los Gatos area.

Directions: From Los Gatos, drive about four miles south on Highway 17 to the Alma Bridge Road exit at Lexington Reservoir. Turn east and drive 1.5 miles across the dam. Parking is available just east of the dam in Lexington Reservoir County Park. The trail starts opposite the boat launching area beyond the dam.

Contact: Midpeninsula Regional Open Space District, 330 Distel Circle, Los Altos, CA 94022; tel. (650) 691-1200 or fax (650) 691-0485; during nonbusiness hours a Touch-Tone phone menu is available for trail news, conditions, and events.

31 Lexington Dam Trail
1.0 mi/0.5 hr

Lexington Reservoir can be one of the prettiest places in Santa Clara County, as well as one of the ugliest. The lake might be full of water one year, then drained down to nothing the next. And after a hot summer it can resemble a dust bowl. But when it is full, some people show up in the spring just to stare at all the water. Well, you can take it literally the extra mile for a nice bonus. Park at the lot just east of the dam, then walk across the dam and turn right on the "Pedway." That's as far as many people get, as most come for the view of the lake from the dam. Keep walking, though, and you will be surprised, as the trail drops down along Los Gatos Creek. After 1.5 miles, it links up with the Los Gatos Creek Trail, which you can follow all the way into town; it's a popular bike route. Note: Alma Bridge Road circles the reservoir, and for more ambitious walks, there are several parklands nearby.

Location: In Lexington Reservoir County Park in the Saratoga foothills; map E1-South Bay, grid i6.

User groups: Hikers and limited mountain bikes. No dogs or horses. No wheelchair facilities.

Permits: No permits are required. A $4 day-use fee is charged.

Maps: For a free trail map, contact Lexington Reservoir County Park at the address below. Ask the USGS for a topographic map of the Los Gatos area.

Directions: From Los Gatos, drive about four miles south on Highway 17 to the Alma Bridge Road exit at Lexington Reservoir. Turn east and drive 1.5 miles across the dam. Parking is available just east of the dam.

Contact: Lexington Reservoir County Park, c/o Vasona Lake County Park, 298 Garden Hill Drive, Los Gatos, CA 95030; tel. (408) 356-2729.

32 Priest Rock Trail

6.1 mi/4.5 hrs

Many people find it difficult to believe these wildlands could exist so close to so many homes. But they do, and you can explore them on the Sierra Azul Loop, a strenuous hike that climbs, climbs, and climbs as it probes the Sierra Azul Range.

At the entrance to the Sierra Azul Open Space Preserve, the trail rises in the first mile to 1,762 feet at Priest Rock. There it nearly levels out for about a mile, until you reach the loop junction. Bear to the left; the trail starts climbing again and climbs another thousand feet or so in the next 1.5 miles to reach the ridgeline at 2,628 feet. Turn right at the ridge and enjoy finally being on top, cruising over the 1.6-mile stretch on the mountain rim. Turn right at the next ridge junction and take the trail back (three miles to the loop junction), relaxing on the downhill cruise.

Location: In the Sierra Azul Open Space Preserve near Lexington Reservoir; map E1-South Bay, grid i6.

User groups: Hikers, horses, and mountain bikes. No dogs. No wheelchair facilities.

Permits: No permits are required. No fee.

Maps: For a free trail map, contact the Midpeninsula Regional Open Space District at the address below. Ask the USGS for a topographic map of the Santa Teresa Hills area.

Directions: From Los Gatos, drive about four miles south on Highway 17 to the Alma Bridge Road exit at Lexington Reservoir. Turn east and drive 1.5 miles across the dam. When you reach the parking area for county parks ($4), continue on Alma Bridge Road to another parking area (free) on the right.

Contact: Midpeninsula Regional Open Space District, 330 Distel Circle, Los Altos, CA 94022; tel. (650) 691-1200 or fax (650) 691-0485; during nonbusiness hours a Touch-Tone phone menu is available for trail news, conditions, and events.

33 Bald Mountain Trail

1.0 mi/1.0 hr

It's hard to beat standing atop a mountain, especially when you're near Mount Umunhum, at 3,486 feet, the highest point in the Sierra Azul Range. From anywhere in the Santa Clara Valley, Mount Umunhum is the most prominent landmark on the western horizon—it's that mountain with the big abandoned radar station on top. Alas, the public is not permitted to hike to the summit of Umunhum due to toxic contaminates and restrictions related to private property. But the trip to adjacent Bald Mountain is the next best thing. The trail here is a .5-mile route on Mount Umunhum Road to Bald Mountain, a hilltop knoll with views of the Almaden Valley and across San Jose to Mount Hamilton, then south to San Benito County. As we said, public access to Mount Umunhum is prohibited, and the Midpeninsula Regional Open Space District requests that you call prior to visiting Bald Mountain. By the way, guess what "Umunhum" means in the Ohlone Indian language: 1. Eagle? 2. Bear? 3. Hummingbird? The answer: hummingbird.

Location: In the Sierra Azul Range south of Los Gatos; map E1-South Bay, grid i7.

User groups: Hikers, horses, and mountain bikes. No dogs. No wheelchair facilities.

Permits: No permits required. Parking and access are free.

Maps: For a free trail map, contact the Mid-peninsula Regional Open Space District at the address below. Ask the USGS for a topographic map of the Santa Teresa Hills area.

Directions: From San Jose drive south on the Almaden Expressway. Turn west on Camden Avenue and drive to the intersection with Hicks Road. Go south, drive to Mount Umunhum Road, then turn west and continue to the two-car parking area at district pipe gate SA-7. There is limited roadside parking only, not a designated parking area.

Contact: Midpeninsula Regional Open Space District, 330 Distel Circle, Los Altos, CA 94022; tel. (650) 691-1200 or fax (650) 691-0485; during nonbusiness hours a Touch-Tone phone menu is available for trail news, conditions, and events.

34 Año Nuevo Trail
2.5 mi/2.0 hrs

One of the more curious adventures in the Bay Area has become one of the most popular: touring Año Nuevo State Reserve to see the elephant seals. Yep, this is the place where these giant creatures arrive every winter to fight, mate, give birth, sunbathe, and make funny noises. So many people now want to watch them that you must make reservations and join a tour group, typically from December through March. Elephant seals look like giant slugs, often weighing 2,000 to 3,000 pounds—even the newborns weigh 75 pounds. The old boars reach nearly 20 feet in length and weigh as much as 5,000 pounds. As part of a tour group, you'll walk along roped-off trails, winding your way amid the animals. They will appear to have no interest in you, and if you keep your distance, that is just how it should be. With a 200 mm camera lens, you can get excellent pictures. The best times to visit are in mid-December, when the males battle for harems, and in late January, when hundreds of pups are born. The rest of the year this is a nice place to enjoy a quiet beach walk. At that time, it can be difficult to believe then that such a phenomenon takes place here in the winter.

Location: In Año Nuevo State Reserve on the San Mateo County coast south of Pescadero; map E1-South Bay, grid j2.

User groups: Hikers only. No dogs, horses, or mountain bikes. No wheelchair facilities.

Permits: From mid-December through March, access to the park is available only by accompanying a ranger on a scheduled walk. To make a reservation, phone (800) 444-7275. A $2 parking fee is charged. Seal walk tickets are $4 per person.

Maps: A map is available at the entrance station for $1. Ask the USGS for a topographic map of the Año Nuevo area.

Directions: From Interstate 280 in San Mateo, turn west on Highway 92 and drive to Half Moon Bay and Highway 1. Turn left (south) on Highway 1 and drive about 30 miles to the park entrance on the right (well signed).

Contact: Año Nuevo State Reserve, New Year's Creek Road, Pescadero, CA 94060; tel. (650) 879-2025, or district headquarters, tel. (415) 330-6300.

35 Waddell Creek Trail
7.0 mi/3.0 hrs

In the spring this is one of the best wildflower walks in the Bay Area. And if you make your trip on a weekday evening, it seems that deer sprout out of nowhere at a huge meadow on the north side of the trail; rabbits, squirrels, and quail are often seen hip-hopping around; baby steelhead swim in Waddell Creek; and ducks and herons make year-round homes in the marsh near the coast. The trailhead is located on Highway 1 just south of the Santa Cruz County line at the Rancho del Oso outpost. The trail contours along some low coastal foothills, and in the spring, there are often sensational wildflower blooms along the way, including some of the most widespread forget-me-nots available anywhere. The trail links back to the service road on the valley floor, and many take the shortcut by returning that way. The service road is nearly flat and has become very popular on weekends with mountain bikers, who typically go too fast and spook the wildlife. That's why you should hike during the week if you can, when trail users are few and tranquillity abounds. It can be an ideal setting for an evening wildlife walk.

Location: At Rancho del Oso on the Santa Cruz County coast south of Año Nuevo; map E1-South Bay, grid j2.

User groups: Hikers, horses (not permitted past the Henry Trail), and mountain bikes (not permitted past Waddell Creek Bridge). No dogs. No wheelchair facilities.

Permits: No permits are required. A $2-per-vehicle state park entrance fee is charged.

Maps: Contact Big Basin Redwoods State Park for the availability and prices of trail maps. Ask the USGS for a topographic map of the Franklin Point area.

Directions: From Interstate 280 in San Mateo, turn west on Highway 92 and drive to Half Moon Bay. Turn left (south) on Highway 1 and drive about 30 miles, past Año Nuevo State Reserve. Drive south for about three miles and look for the signs indicating Big Basin Redwoods State Park/Rancho del Oso, just past the Santa Cruz County line. Park along the right (west) side of Highway 1 at the entrance to Rancho del Oso.

Contact: Rancho del Oso, tel. (831) 427-2288; Big Basin Redwoods State Park, 21600 Big Basin Way, Boulder Creek, CA 95006; tel. (831) 338-8860; California State Parks, Santa Cruz District, tel. (831) 429-2851 or fax (831) 429-2876.

36 Davenport Beach
1.0 mi/1.0 hr

If you have a passion for wide-open ocean frontage, the beach at Davenport will certainly satisfy. It is made up of pristine, open sand dunes that are often deserted. Except, that is, for the daredevil hang gliders who use the coastal thermals to float off a cliff at the southern end of the beach and then glide

through the sky in apparent comfort. Well, it is a heck of a lot more comforting to take a stroll along the vast beach, often a haven of tranquillity. During the winter, venture off on a side trip up along the bluffs, one of the best land-based spots to the see the spouts of passing gray whales. Just look for the little puff of "smoke" out at sea. This is also one of the top windsurfing spots in California.

Location: On the Santa Cruz County coast north of Santa Cruz; map E1-South Bay, grid j2.

User groups: Hikers, dogs, and horses. No mountain bikes. No wheelchair facilities.

Permits: No permits are required. Parking and access are free.

Maps: Ask the USGS for a topographic map of the Davenport area.

Directions: From the San Francisco Peninsula, take Interstate 280 to Highway 92, turn west, and drive to Half Moon Bay. Turn south on Highway 1 and drive 30 miles, continuing past Año Nuevo State Reserve and driving another nine miles to Davenport. Park on the right side of the highway at the spacious beach area one mile north of the high ocean bluff.

Contact: There is no managing agency for this location.

37 Loch Lomond Loop
5.0 mi/3.25 hrs

There is no prettier lake in the greater Bay Area than Loch Lomond Reservoir, a jewel set in the Santa Cruz Mountains, complete with an island and circled by conifers. Newcomers are always surprised by its beauty and by the nearby hiking opportunities as well. Of the 12 miles of trails here, the best hike is the Loch Lomond Loop. You start east on the Loch Trail, a level path that extends along the lakeshore for 1.5 miles out to Deer Flat. There you turn uphill on the Highland Trail, climbing and looping to the right up the ridge on a moderate ascent. It peaks out at a remote weather station where you get a great view of the lake below. Bring your camera. To complete the loop, continue on the trail, which is routed down to the upper picnic area; or you can take the paved road back to the starting point. A bonus at Loch Lomond is good trout fishing, especially in April, and good bass and bluegill fishing in the summer. Great lake, great views, great hike. Note that the park is closed from mid-September through February.

Location: In Loch Lomond City Park in the Santa Cruz foothills near Ben Lomond; map E1-South Bay, grid j5.

User groups: Hikers only. No dogs, horses, or mountain bikes. No wheelchair facilities.

Permits: No permits are required. A $4 day-use fee is charged. The Loch Lomond Recreation Area is open only from March 1 through September 15. Rangers are on duty during the winter and will cite trespassers.

Maps: For a free trail map, contact Loch Lomond Park at the address below. Ask the USGS for a topographic map of the Felton area.

Directions: From San Jose drive south on Highway 17 for about 25 miles to Scotts Valley and the Mount Hermon Road exit. Take that exit, turn right and drive 3.5 miles to Graham Hill Road. Turn left on Graham Hill Road and drive a short distance to Zayante Road. Turn left on Zayante Road and drive three miles to Lompico Road. Turn left and drive 1.7 miles to West Drive. Turn left again and drive to Sequoia Road and the park entrance. The route is well signed. The trailhead is located adjacent to the boat ramp.

Contact: Loch Lomond City Park, 100 Loch Lomond Way, Felton, CA 95018; tel. (831) 335-7424 or fax (831) 335-1178.

38 Eagle Creek Trail

3.0 mi/1.5 hrs

There are two places you just plain shouldn't miss on a visit to Henry Cowell Redwoods State Park. The first one is the Eagle Creek Trail, the most direct hiking route to the River Trail and the San Lorenzo River. The other is the park's observation deck, offering first-

class views on clear days (we'll get to that).

The Eagle Creek Trail starts between campsites 82 and 84, crosses Eagle Creek, and continues adjacent to the stream as it heads out toward the San Lorenzo River. As you hike this portion of the trail, you are surrounded by redwoods. The trail then crosses Pipeline Road and junctions with the River Trail. Many people turn around and head back at this point. However, a great way to extend your hike is to head north on the River Trail along the river, adding an extra three miles to the trip. Another bonus is the observation deck, the highest point in the park, with great sweeping views of Santa Cruz and Monterey Bay. It's only a .3-mile hike from the campground via the Pine Trail, which starts near campsite 49.

Location: In Henry Cowell Redwoods State Park near Santa Cruz; map E1-South Bay, grid j5.

User groups: Hikers and horses. No dogs or mountain bikes. No wheelchair facilities.

Permits: No permits are required. A $3-per-vehicle state park entrance fee is charged.

Maps: Detailed trail maps are available for a fee from Mountain Parks Foundation, 525 N. Big Trees Road, Felton, CA 95018; tel. (831) 335-3174. Ask the USGS for a topographic map of the Felton area.

Directions: From San Jose drive south on Highway 17 for 25 miles to Scotts Valley and the Mount Hermon Road exit. Take that exit and drive west toward Felton. Turn left on Lockwood Lane and drive about one mile. Turn left on Graham Hill Road and continue .5 mile to the campground on the right.

Contact: Henry Cowell Redwoods State Park, 101 N. Big Trees Road, Felton, CA 95018; tel. (831) 335-4598 or tel. (831) 429-2851.

39 Mine Hill Trail

14.5 mi/7.0 hrs

Of the dozen trails at Almaden Quicksilver County Park, this is the most unusual. While Almaden covers 3,600 acres and has two lakes

(Almaden and Guadalupe), it is the evidence of historical mining operations that makes it fascinating. With a network of trails here, many routes and long trips are possible, but most people cut it short, enjoying a portion.

The Mine Hill Trail starts just inside the park entrance off of New Almaden Road. From here, the Mine Hill Trail is routed north to a junction. Turn left (staying on Mine Hill Trail) and you will pass and in the process pass the Dan Tunnel and San Cristobel Tunnel, remnants of the mining days. At that point, most people just return. Some will take the .75-mile April Trail Loop, with is a short cutoff loop off the Mine Hill Trail.

Note that some areas adjacent to the Mine Hill Trail are closed to public access because of hazardous residual materials from the mercury mines. Almaden was the site of the first quicksilver mine In North America. Mining began in 1845 and continued until 1975. There are still burnt ore dumps along the trail. A bonus is that wildflower blooms are good in this park in the spring.

Location: In Almaden Quicksilver County Park in the San Jose foothills; map E1-South Bay, grid j7.

User groups: Hikers and horses. Leashed dogs and mountain bikes are permitted on some trails; mountain bikes must enter from the Hacienda entrance. No wheelchair trail access.

Permits: No permits are required. Park entrance is free.

Maps: A trail map is also available at the trailhead. Ask the USGS for a topographic map of the Santa Teresa Hills area.

Directions: From San Jose, take Highway 85 south to the Almaden Expressway. Tale Almaden Expressway south and drive to Almaden Road. Take Almaden Road south through the historic town of New Almaden to the park entrance on the right.

Contact: Almaden Quicksilver County Park, c/o Calero Reservoir County Park, 23205 McKean Road, San Jose, CA 95120; tel. (408) 268-8220 (recorded information) or (408) 268-3883.

40 Coyote Peak Loop
3.4 mi/2.0 hrs

Golfers know Santa Teresa County Park best, but hikers are discovering that the park has something for them as well. Most notable is the walk up to Coyote Peak, the feature destination of a good loop hike that provides a surprise lookout to the southern Santa Clara Valley. This park covers 1,688 acres, but the main attractions are the golf course, driving range, bar, and restaurant. You can quickly leave development behind, however, by hiking south from the Hidden Springs Trailhead off Bernal Road. After one mile the trail junctions with the Coyote Peak Trail, which climbs up Coyote Peak, with a short loop cutoff getting you to the summit. To complete the loop, continue on the Coyote Peak Trail, then take the Ohlone Trail one mile back to the parking area. In contrast to the manicured greens of the golf course, this trail provides an insight into the park's most primitive and rugged areas and gives you a good view for your efforts.

Location: In Santa Teresa County Park south of San Jose; map E1-South Bay, grid j8.

User groups: Hikers, leashed dogs, and horses. No mountain bikes, except on the Ohlone Trail. No wheelchair facilities.

Permits: No permits are required. A $4-per-vehicle park entrance fee is charged.

Maps: For a free trail map, contact Santa Teresa County Park at the address below. Ask the USGS for a topographic map of the Santa Teresa Hills area.

Directions: From U.S. 101 between San Jose and Morgan Hill, take Bernal Road east and drive to the day-use parking area. Park in the main day-use lot.

Contact: Santa Teresa County Park, 985 Heller Avenue, San Jose, CA 95111; tel. (408) 268-3883; Santa Clara County Parks, tel. (408) 358-3741 or fax (408) 358-3245.

41 Juan Crespi Loop
4.8 mi/2.0 hrs

You'd better know the difference between horse droppings and Shinola if you plan to do this hike. Why? Because this is a very popular horseback trail, if you don't watch where you're going, well, you won't be stepping in shoe polish. And many people have trouble watching their steps because of the nice views of Calero Reservoir to the north. Start near the entrance gate and follow the Juan Crespi Trail, turning right toward Calero Reservoir. The trail runs along the southern shoreline of the lake for more than a mile before making a nearly 180-degree looping left turn. There it becomes Los Cerritos Trail and climbs the ridgeline bordering the southern end of the lake. When it tops the ridge, it connects to the Pena Trail. To complete the loop, turn left on the Pena Trail, making a descent. A great way to go is to descend the Pena Trail, turn right on the Vallecitos Trail and then left on the Figueroa Trail. It adds two miles to the trip, but is well worth it.

Location: In Calero Reservoir County Park southeast of San Jose; map E1-South Bay, grid j8.

User groups: Hikers and horses. No dogs or mountain bikes. No wheelchair facilities.

Permits: No permits are required. Park entrance is free (at this access point for hiking).

Maps: For a free map, contact Calero Reservoir County Park at the number below. Ask the USGS for a topographic map of the Santa Teresa Hills area.

Directions: From San Jose drive south on U.S. 101 for five miles to Coyote. Take the Bernal Road exit west and drive a short distance to the Monterey Highway exit. Head south a short way to Bailey Avenue and turn right. Turn left on McKean Road and drive to the sign for the horse stables. Park adjacent to the ranger office.

Contact: Calero Reservoir County Park, tel. (408) 268-3883. Santa Clara County Parks, tel. (408) 358-3741 or fax (408) 358-3245.

42 Del Coyote Nature Trail
1.2 mi/0.5 hr
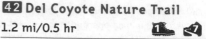

Thousands and thousands of people roar up and down U.S. 101 south of San Jose with nary a clue about the peaceful little park that sits so nearby. Yet just east of the highway is Coyote-Hellyer County Park with its small, shaded stream that is stocked with rainbow trout in the late spring and early summer. The hike starts at a picnic area, meandering along the stream from there. The flowing waters come from nearby Anderson Dam, and steady releases are made well into summer. That is what makes this park so attractive to local residents, who know this is a nice spot for a respite.

Location: In Coyote-Hellyer County Park downstream of Anderson Dam, south of San Jose; map E1-South Bay, grid j9.

User groups: Hikers only. No dogs, horses, or mountain bikes. No wheelchair facilities.

Permits: No permits are required. A $4 day-use fee is charged per vehicle.

Maps: For a free map, contact Coyote-Hellyer County Park at the address below. Ask the USGS for a topographic map of the Morgan Hill area.

Directions: From San Jose drive south on U.S. 101 and take the Hellyer Avenue exit. Turn right and drive about less than a .25 mile to the park entrance on the left.

Contact: Coyote-Hellyer County Park, 985 Hellyer Avenue, San Jose, CA 95111; tel. (408) 225-0225; Santa Clara County Parks, tel. (408) 358-3741 or fax (408) 358-3245.

43 Serpentine Trail
0.8 mi/0.5 hr

The size of Anderson Lake, nearly 1,000 acres, always shocks first-time visitors to this water-filled canyon set among the oak woodlands and foothills of the Gavilan Mountains. One of the best viewpoints at the park is the dam overlook, reached by taking a short walk on the Serpentine Trail. It starts between the Live Oak and Toyon group areas and is simply routed to the northwest corner of the dam. One major problem at Anderson Lake is the fluctuating water levels. This lake needs a lot of water to stay full, and it seems as though the water managers like to almost empty the thing every four or five years. When they do that, you might as well arrange a trip to the Grand Canyon.

Location: In Anderson Lake County Park near Morgan Hill; map E1-South Bay, grid j9.

User groups: Hikers only. No dogs, horses, or mountain bikes. No wheelchair facilities.

Permits: No permits are required. A $4 day-use fee is charged per vehicle.

Maps: For a free trail map, contact Anderson Lake County Park at the address below. Ask the USGS for topographic maps of the Mount Sizer and Morgan Hill area.

Directions: From San Jose drive south on U.S. 101 to the Cochran Road exit. Take Cochran Road east to the park entrance.

Contact: Anderson Lake County Park, 19245 Malaguerra Avenue, Morgan Hill, CA 95037; tel. (408) 779-3634; Santa Clara County Parks, tel. (408) 358-3741 or fax (408) 358-3245.

44 Frog Pond Loop

4.5 mi/3.0 hrs

A good pair of hiking boots and a reality check are your tickets to 125 square miles of wildlands that comprise Henry W. Coe State Park, a place for anyone who wants solitude and isn't averse to rugged hiking or mountain biking. The Frog Pond Loop is a short day hike that provides a glimpse of the park's primitive charms, along with a sampling of a few of the ups and downs.

You start from park headquarters by taking the Northern Heights Route over the top of Pine Ridge (elevation 3,000 feet) and then dropping 600 feet down to Little Coyote Creek, then going back up past Frog Lake and to the Middle Ridge Trail (2,800 feet). This first leg is about two miles, and most visitors will stop along the creek for a reality check and to reassess what awaits in the wilderness. Frog Pond is a pretty little spot, complete with fish-

ing line hanging from tree limbs (this lake is fished often and the catch rates are low).

Turn right on the Middle Ridge Trail, hike two miles to the junction with the Fish Trail, turn right again, and follow the trail down across Little Coyote Creek. This stream is very pretty in the spring, and though you must then walk out of the canyon, it is a tranquil and memorable setting, crowning the walk. To finish the loop, you have to climb back out of the canyon, over Pine Ridge, and back to the headquarters. This hike gives you just enough to whet your appetite for more challenging routes into the park's interior.

Location: In Henry W. Coe State Park in the Diablo Range east of Morgan Hill; map E1-South Bay, grid j9.

User groups: Hikers, horses, and mountain bikes. No dogs. No wheelchair facilities.

Permits: No permits are required unless you plan to camp in the backcountry. A $2 state park day-use fee is charged.

Maps: For a map, send $3.50 to Coe Map, Pine Ridge Association, P.O. Box 846, Morgan Hill, CA 95038. Ask the USGS for topographic maps of the Mount Sizer area.

Directions: From U.S. 101 in Morgan Hill take the East Dunne Avenue exit and drive east for 13 slow and twisty miles to the park entrance. From park headquarters take the Northern Heights Route Trailhead.

Contact: Henry W. Coe State Park, P.O. Box 846, Morgan Hill, CA 95038; tel. (408) 779-2728, (408) 848-4006 (Gilroy office), or fax (408) 848-4030.

45 Coit Lake

19.5 mi/2.0 days

The canyons and ridges at Henry W. Coe State Park seem to stretch to infinity. All of it is networked by more than 100 miles of ranch roads and 250 miles of hiking trails—providing access to 140 ponds and small lakes, hidden streams and a habitat that is paradise for fish, wildlife and wild flora. But the reality for many turns into an endurance test: you go up one canyon, then down the next, over and over. Some people get so worn down, hot and exhausted that they are practically reduced to nothing more than a little pile of hair lying in the dirt.

The best first trip into the back country at Coe is to Kelly Cabin Lake, usually by mountain bike; for hikers, continue on another mile to Coit Lake, where there is a backcountry campground, and a chance for swimming and bass fishing. We suggest starting this trip at the Coyote Creek gate, located past Coyote Reservoir.

From the Coyote Creek gate, the trip starts with a steady climb on a former ranch road, climbing past Coit Camp. From here, detour east on single track up to Mahoney Ridge. Then turn right, and the trail drops quickly down to Kelly Cabin Lake, a beautiful spot, though it is fished hard and often yields little. From Kelly Cabin Lake, the trail (well signed to Coit Lake) is another two miles to the camp, most of it a climb, out to Coit Lake, making for a nine-mile hike for the day.

Over this entire route, stay alert for wildlife. It is common to see wild turkey, coyotes, deer, wild pigs, and hawks. In the spring, wildflowers are also sensational all through here, with yarrow (clusters of white blooms), columbine (like bells), and poppies and large spreads of blue-eyed grass the most common. The park is one of the best in Northern California for wildflower blooms, with more than 60 species common and many more than that documented.

At one time at Coit Lake, you could catch nearly a bass per cast just by flipping out a one-inch floating Rapala lure. That is no longer true, but it does offer a rare chance for pond-style fishing in the greater Bay Area. For the best fishing, longer trips are required (see next listing) to more remote lakes that are only occasionally fished.

Unfortunately, the vision of great fishing inspires many excited people to start hiking off to the lake without first taking a litmus test of the quest they are about to undertake. Venturing here requires long hikes with difficult climbs both ways, particularly if the weather is hot and dry, as is common out here. Many get busted by the heat before reaching the lake and return frustrated without making a cast.

Special note: Overnight users are required to obtain a camping/wilderness permit. Hikers who choose to enter by the Coyote Creek access point must have a trail map.

Location: In Henry W. Coe State Park in the Diablo Range east of Morgan Hill; map E1-South Bay, grid j9.

User groups: Hikers, horses, and mountain bikes. No dogs. No wheelchair facilities.

Permits: A trail map and camp permit are required. A self-registration area is available at the Hunting Hollow parking area, located just off the trailhead access road. A $2 state park day-use fee is charged.

Maps: For a map, send $3.50 to Coe Map, Pine Ridge Association, P.O. Box 846, Morgan Hill, CA 95038. Ask the USGS for topographic maps of the Gilroy Hot Springs and Mississippi Creek areas.

Directions: From U.S. 101 in Gilroy drive east on Leavesley Road to New Avenue. Turn left on New Avenue and drive to Roop Road. Turn right on Roop Road and drive up into the hills to the Coyote Lake County Park turnoff. Continue past that turnoff, across the cattle guard to Gilroy Hot Springs Road/Coyote Creek Road and continue five miles to the end of the road.

Contact: Henry W. Coe State Park, P.O. Box 846, Morgan Hill, CA 95038; tel. (408) 779-2728, (408) 848-4006 (Gilroy office), or fax (408) 848-4030.

46 Mississippi Lake Trail
22.0 mi/2.0 days

Mississippi Lake is set in the virtual center of Henry W. Coe State Park, borders the Orestimba Wilderness to the east, and is the largest lake and the preeminent destination for many who venture into these vast wildlands. The fishing for bass, swimming in cool waters in early summer and wildflower blooms in spring are exceptional. To get here and back, however, requires an extraordinary physical commitment that you best think long and hard about before taking off.

From park headquarters, you hike eight miles out on the Pacheco Route, and that includes a long drop followed by a significant, steady climb gaining 1,400 feet over 2.6 miles, from East Fork Coyote Creek over Willow Crest and to the junction with the Interior Route. Turn left on the Interior Route and the trail becomes a lot easier. In 3.5 miles, you will be skirting the southern shore of the lake. The nearest trail camp, Mississippi Creek Horse Camp, is about .5 mile south of the lake. This is a long, grueling hike from headquarters, and many unprepared hikers have suffered from dehydration and had to be rescued by park staff. Some hikers will try to short-cut the trip by bringing a mountain bike, but find themselves pushing the bike uphill, then speeding fast on downhill portions.

Even though Henry W. Coe State Park was opened to the public only about 20 years ago (in 1981), a few legends have already developed, and the most mysterious involves Mississippi Lake. The lake once had a one-of-a-kind ability to create huge trout. Scientists documented 26-inch wild trout that were only 18 months old. The trout are all but gone now, as low water in the feeder creek prevented spawning during the 1988-92 drought; any trout you catch should be released immediately. (Bass were planted in 1991 and have taken over the lake, providing good fishing.) Still, the legendary huge trout of Mississippi Lake have inspired many to make the trip out, often out of curiosity, to see such a unique habitat. Provided you get a very early start, you can have a one-of-a-kind trip.

Location: In Henry W. Coe State Park in the Diablo Range east of Morgan Hill; map E1-South Bay, grid j9.

User groups: Hikers, horses, and mountain bikes. No dogs. No wheelchair facilities.

Permits: A trail map and camp permit are required. A $2 state park day-use fee is charged.

Maps: For a map, send $3.50 to Coe Map, Pine Ridge Association, P.O. Box 846, Morgan Hill, CA 95038. Ask the USGS for topographic maps of the Mount Sizer and Mississippi Creek areas.

Directions: From U.S. 101 in Morgan Hill, take the East Dunne Avenue exit and drive east over Morgan Hill and Anderson Lake for 13 miles on the twisty road to park headquarters. From there, take the Pacheco Route Trailhead.

Contact: Henry W. Coe State Park, P.O. Box 846, Morgan Hill, CA 95038; tel. (408) 779-2728, (408) 848-4006 (Gilroy Office), or fax (408) 848-4030.

47 Rooster Comb Loop
70.0 mi/6.0 days

"I've always been crazy," Waylon Jennings once said, "because it's kept me from going insane." Well, you have to be something of a deranged soul to try this hike, and that's why we signed up! Not only is it just plain long, but it includes seven climbs that'll have you cussing, and yet explores the park's most remote and arid wildlands where anything over 10 inches of rain a year is considered a flood. So why do it? Because no trail on public land in the Bay Area leads to a more isolated spot, because Paradise Lake will seem like a mirage after you've walked 33 miles, and hey, you're a little deranged anyway, right? Highlights on the trek in include Kelly Cabin Lake (about 10.5 miles in), Coit Lake (12 miles), and in the remote Orestimba Drainage, Paradise Lake and Robinson Falls. A spectacular spot is the loop's namesake, the Rooster Comb, a perch overlooking the Orestimba Valley. Some of the best fishing is located in these remote settings, highlighted by little Mustang Pond, Jackrabbit Lake, as well as the climb up the Rooster Comb, a rock formation that looks something like a miniature stegosaurus-back rim.

The only thing simple is the route: You take the Pacheco Trail (16.7 miles) out to the park's southern boundary, turn left on

the Gill Trail (10.5 miles), hike the loop on the Rooster Comb Trail (10.1 miles), reconnect with the Gill Trail (five miles), and head back the way you came. Dozens of side trips are available to creeks, lookouts, hidden valleys, and small lakes. We suggest taking a week to do it, arriving and camping at park headquarters the first night so you can go through your gear and make an early getaway the next morning, then average 10 to 12 miles per day for six days. Several trail camps are situated along the way, and camping is permitted throughout the wilderness area. If the weather turns hot, physically unprepared hikers can find themselves in real danger. Regardless of your physical condition, when you return to your car at park headquarters, you won't feel so crazy anymore.

To best explore the park, the perfect approach would be to come in on horseback or with a burro, then take a day and set up a base camp in Pacheco Canyon; note that no bikes are permitted in the designated Orestimba Wilderness, and in addition, all single-track trails are closed to bikes for 48 hours after a half inch of rain.

Location: In Henry W. Coe State Park in the Diablo Range southeast of San Jose; map E1-South Bay, grid j9.

User groups: Hikers, horses, and mountain bikes. No dogs. No wheelchair facilities.

Permits: A trail map and camp permit are required. A $2 state park day-use fee is charged.

Maps: For a map, send $3.50 to Coe Map, Pine Ridge Association, P.O. Box 846, Morgan Hill, CA 95038. Ask the USGS for topographic maps of the Mount Sizer, Mississippi Creek, Mustang Peak, Wilcox Ridge, and Mt. Stakes areas.

Directions: From U.S. 101 in Morgan Hill, take the East Dunne Avenue exit and drive east over Morgan Hill and Anderson Lake for 13 miles on the twisty road to park headquarters. From there, take the Pacheco Route Trailhead.

Contact: Henry W. Coe State Park, P.O. Box 846, Morgan Hill, CA 95038; tel. (408) 779-2728, (408) 848-4006 (Gilroy office), or fax (408) 848-4030.

AERIAL VIEW OF LAKE ANDERSON
AND THE SURROUNDING HILLS
NEAR MORGAN HILL

MAP E2

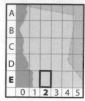

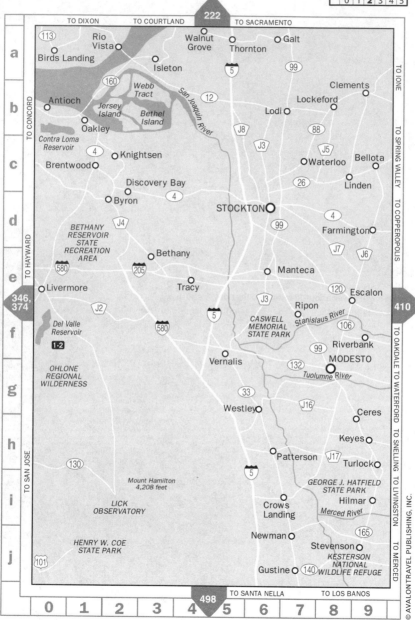

TO DIXON   TO COURTLAND   **222**   TO SACRAMENTO

a

113
Rio Vista
Birds Landing
Isleton
Walnut Grove
Thornton
Galt
5
99

TO CONCORD

b

160
Webb Tract
Antioch
Jersey Island
Bethel Island
San Joaquin River
12
Lodi
Lockeford
Clements
Oakley
Contra Loma Reservoir
J8
88

TO SPRING VALLEY   TO IONE

c

4
Knightsen
Brentwood
J3
J5
Waterloo
Bellota
Linden
26

TO COPPEROPOLIS

d

Discovery Bay
Byron
4
STOCKTON
99
Farmington
4
J4
BETHANY RESERVOIR STATE RECREATION AREA
J7
J6

e

580
205
Bethany
Tracy
Manteca
120
Escalon
Livermore
J2
J3
Ripon
Stanislaus River
106
346, 374
410

TO HAYWARD

f

Del Valle Reservoir
1-2
580
5
CASWELL MEMORIAL STATE PARK
99
Riverbank
Vernalis
132
MODESTO
Tuolumne River

TO OAKDALE   TO WATERFORD

g

OHLONE REGIONAL WILDERNESS
33
Westley
J16
Ceres

h

130
Patterson
J17
Keyes
Turlock
5

TO SAN JOSE

TO SNELLING   TO LIVINGSTON

i

Mount Hamilton 4,208 feet
LICK OBSERVATORY
Crows Landing
GEORGE J. HATFIELD STATE PARK
Hilmar
Merced River
165

j

HENRY W. COE STATE PARK
101
Newman
Stevenson
KESTERSON NATIONAL WILDLIFE REFUGE
Gustine
140

TO MERCED

498   TO SANTA NELLA   TO LOS BANOS

0   1   2   3   4   5   6   7   8   9

© AVALON TRAVEL PUBLISHING, INC.

CHAPTER E2

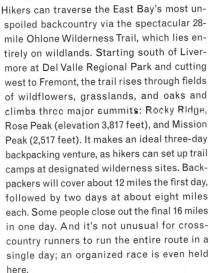

1 Ohlone
Wilderness Trail 405
2 Murietta Falls Trail 406

1 Ohlone Wilderness Trail

28.0 mi one way/3.0 days

Hikers can traverse the East Bay's most un-spoiled backcountry via the spectacular 28-mile Ohlone Wilderness Trail, which lies en-tirely on wildlands. Starting south of Liver-more at Del Valle Regional Park and cutting west to Fremont, the trail rises through fields of wildflowers, grasslands, and oaks and climbs three major summits: Rocky Ridge, Rose Peak (elevation 3,817 feet), and Mission Peak (2,517 feet). It makes an ideal three-day backpacking venture, as hikers can set up trail camps at designated wilderness sites. Back-packers will cover about 12 miles the first day, followed by two days at about eight miles each. Some people close out the final 16 miles in one day. And it's not unusual for cross-country runners to run the entire route in a single day; an organized race is even held here.

Hiking the trail east to west is the only way to fly. That way you'll face the steepest ascent right at the beginning, when you are still fresh. Starting at Del Valle Regional Park, the route first tackles Rocky Ridge for an elevation gain of 1,600 feet in just 1.5 miles. (A side trip from here, by the way, is to Murietta Falls, below.) As you crest the final ridge, Mission Peak, you'll face a moment of truth: you can actual-ly see your car waiting at the parking lot, yet it is still so far away. This last stretch drops 2,100 feet in 3.5 miles, a terrible toe jammer that will have your knees and thighs screaming for mercy. Weeks later, though, when you replay this adventure in your memory banks, the hike will suddenly seem like "fun."

Location: In the Sunol-Ohlone Regional Wild-erness, from Del Valle Regional Park south of Livermore to Mission Peak in Fremont; map E2, grid f0.

User groups: Hikers, dogs (daytime only), and horses. No mountain bikes. No wheel-chair facilities.

Permits: A trail permit/map for the Ohlone Wilderness Trail is required. You can obtain one for $2 at the park office or $2.50 by mail. To obtain a map by mail, contact the East Bay Regional Parks District at the address below. The park entrance fee is $5 from April through September, $4 from October through March; $1 dog fee.

Maps: You will receive a trail map when you purchase your permit. Ask the USGS for a topographic map of the Mendonhall Springs area.

Directions to the east trailhead: From In-terstate 580 East at Livermore, take the North Livermore Avenue exit and turn right. Drive south for 3.5 miles (the road becomes Tesla Road) to Mines Road. Turn right on Mines Road and drive 3.5 miles to Del Valle Road. Continue on Del Valle Road for three miles to the entrance to Del Valle Regional Park en-trance. Drive less than a mile to the dam at Del Valle Reservoir, cross it, then turn right and drive a half mile to the Lichen Bark Picnic Area and the trailhead for the Ohlone Trail.

Directions to the west trailhead: From High-way 680 near Fremont, take the Mission Boule-vard exit. Turn east on Stanford Avenue and drive to the parking lot and trailhead at the end of the road.

Contact: Del Valle Regional Park, tel. (925) 373-0332; East Bay Regional Parks District, 2950 Peralta Oaks Court, P.O. Box 5381, Oakland, CA 94605; tel. (510) 635-0135, ext. 2200, or fax (510) 569-4319; Sunol-Ohlone Regional Wilder-ness, tel. (925) 862-2244 or fax (925) 862-0810.

☑ Murietta Falls Trail
11.5 mi/1.0 day

Little known and only rarely seen, the Bay Area's highest waterfall lies hidden away in the southern Alameda County wilderness where few venture. Murietta Falls, named after Joaquin Murietta, a legendary outlaw of the 1800s, is set in the Sunol-Ohlone Regional Wilderness, where a free-flowing creek falls through a rocky gorge, in all a 100-foot waterfall, the longest waterfall in the Bay Area. Upstream, more small pools and cascades await, and along with Murietta Falls, they make this a destination like nowhere else in the East Bay. The key, of course, is hitting it right, when the waterfall is fountain and the view of it is breathtaking. More good news is that the trail is well signed, and a map is provided with your wilderness permit by the East Bay Regional Park District. Hit it wrong and none of that will matter long. The only thing breathtaking will be the climbs required to reach the spot and get back.

Why do so few people know about this place? Getting there requires a butt- kicker of a hike: It's 5.5 miles one way, most of which climb a terribly steep ridge. You'll first ascend 1,600 feet in just 1.5 miles, the worst stretch of the Ohlone Wilderness Trail. The route tops out at Rocky Ridge, drops 500 feet in .5 mile into Williams Gulch, then climbs again even higher, another 1,200 feet toward Wauhab Ridge. From the trailhead, you will gain as much as 3,300 feet in elevation before turning right on the Springboard Trail (signpost 35). From there it's one mile to the waterfall. Walk along a ridge about .25 mile, then turn left on the Greenside Trail, which descends into a valley and to the falls. Unfortunately, you can't get a clear view of Murietta Falls from the Greenside Trail. A cutoff route is available that leads to a good viewing area. This unsigned side road/trail off the Greenside Trail, located past the stream. Turn right on this road/trail, which drops in a looping turn down to the floor, providing a better view

of the cascade feeding through a rocky gorge into the plunge pool.

When Murietta Falls first comes into view, it stands in contrast to the East Bay hills, a grassland/oak habitat where one does not expect to find steep cliffs and waterfalls. But there it is, all 100 feet. In the springtime the rapidly greening hills frame the falls, providing a spark of freshness, relatively only a few miles from suburbia, concrete, and traffic jams. But given the difficulty of the hike, many are disappointed by how little water there can be here. It can be like a bad joke, where you stay with it all the way to the end only to be disappointed. Even in big rain years the creek is reduced to a trickle by early summer and sometimes even goes dry. In addition, it gets hot out here in the summer, really smokin', like 100 degrees. By July the hills are brown, the waterfall has disappeared, and only the ghost of Murietta remains to laugh as you struggle on the 3,300-foot climb.

Special note: If you want to stay overnight in the wilderness, a trail camp (Stewart's Camp) is available about .5 mile from Murietta Falls; reservations are required.

Location: In the Sunol-Ohlone Regional Wilderness, from Del Valle Regional Park south of Livermore to Mission Peak in Fremont; map E2, grid f0.

User groups: Hikers, dogs (daytime only), and horses. No mountain bikes. No wheelchair facilities.

Permits: A trail permit/map for the Ohlone Wilderness Trail is required. You can obtain one for $2 at the park office or $2.50 by mail. To obtain a map by mail, contact the East Bay Regional Parks District at the address below. The park entrance fee is $5 from April through September, $4 from October through March; $1 dog fee.

Maps: You will receive a trail map when you purchase your permit. Ask the USGS for a topographic map of the Mendenhall Springs area.

Directions to the east trailhead: From Interstate 580 east at Livermore, take the North

Livermore Avenue exit and turn right. Drive south for 3.5 miles (the road becomes Tesla Road) to Mines Road. Turn right on Mines Road and drive 3.5 miles to Del Valle Road. Continue on Del Valle Road for three miles to the entrance to Del Valle Regional Park entrance. Drive less than a mile to the dam at Del Valle Reservoir, cross it, and then turn right and drive .5 mile to the Lichen Bark Picnic Area and the trailhead for the Ohlone Trail. **Contact:** Del Valle Regional Park, tel. (925) 373-0332; East Bay Regional Parks District, 2950 Peralta Oaks Court, P.O. Box 5381, Oakland, CA 94605; tel. (510) 635-0135, ext. 2200, or fax (510) 569-4319; Sunol-Ohlone Regional Wilderness, tel. (925) 862-2244 or fax (925) 862-0810.

GIANT SEQUOIAS IN
CALAVERAS BIG TREES
STATE PARK

MAP E3

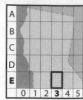

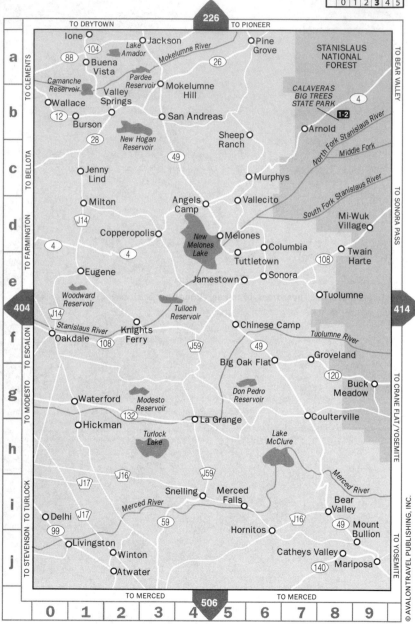

TO DRYTOWN
226
TO PIONEER

a
TO CLEMENTS
Ione ○
88
104
Lake Amador
Jackson ○
Mokelumne River
Pine Grove ○
STANISLAUS NATIONAL FOREST
TO BEAR VALLEY

Buena Vista ○
Pardee Reservoir
26
CALAVERAS BIG TREES STATE PARK
Camanche Reservoir
Valley Springs
Mokelumne Hill ○
1-2
4

b
Wallace ○
12
Burson ○
28
San Andreas ○
North Fork Stanislaus River
Arnold ○
Middle Fork

New Hogan Reservoir
Sheep Ranch ○
49
South Fork Stanislaus River

c
TO BELLOTA
Jenny Lind ○
Murphys ○

d
TO FARMINGTON
Milton ○
J14
Angels Camp ○
Vallecito ○
Mi-Wuk Village ○

Copperopolis ○
4
4
New Melones Lake
Melones ○
Columbia ○
Twain Harte ○
108

e
Eugene ○
Woodward Reservoir
Tuttletown
Jamestown ○
Sonora ○
Tuolumne ○

404
J14
Stanislaus River
Knights Ferry
Tulloch Reservoir

f
TO ESCALON
Oakdale ○
108
J59
Chinese Camp ○
Tuolumne River
49
414

g
TO MODESTO
Waterford ○
Modesto Reservoir
132
Big Oak Flat ○
Groveland ○
120
Buck Meadow ○
TO CRANE FLAT/YOSEMITE

Hickman ○
La Grange ○
Don Pedro Reservoir
Coulterville ○

h
Turlock Lake
Lake McClure

i
TO TURLOCK
J17
J16
Snelling ○
J59
Merced Falls ○
Merced River
Bear Valley ○

Delhi ○
J17
Merced River
59
Hornitos ○
J16
49
Mount Bullion ○

j
TO STEVENSON
99
Livingston ○
Winton ○
Atwater ○
Catheys Valley ○
140
Mariposa ○
TO YOSEMITE

TO MERCED
506
TO MERCED

0 1 2 3 4 5 6 7 8 9

© AVALON TRAVEL PUBLISHING, INC.

CHAPTER E3

1 North Grove Loop 411

2 South Grove Loop 411

Contact: Calaveras Big Trees State Park, P.O. Box 120, Arnold, CA 95223; tel. (209) 795-2334, or Columbia State Park, tel. (209) 532-0150.

1 North Grove Loop

1.0 mi/0.5 hr

Even though there are 150 giant sequoias at Calaveras Big Trees State Park, the highlight is actually the one known as "The Big Stump." Lore has it that the gent who first found this place wanted to prove how big the trees were, so naturally he cut one down, leaving behind the giant stump. Makes perfect sense, right? Just like you'd shoot Bigfoot. . . . Well, the state park gets a lot of visitors, and this is the most popular walk here, so you can expect other people—lots of 'em. The easy trail is routed among the giant sequoias, and the sweet fragrance of the massive trees fills the air. You will never forget that scent. These trees, of course, are known not for their height but for their tremendous diameter: it can take a few dozen people, linking hands, to encircle one.
Location: Northeast of Arnold on Highway 4; map E3, grid b8.
User groups: Hikers and wheelchairs. No dogs, horses, or mountain bikes.
Permits: No permits are required. There is a $2 state park entrance fee for each vehicle.
Maps: For a brochure and park trail map, send $1 to Calaveras Big Trees State Park at the address below. Interpretive brochures are also available at the trailhead for $.25. Ask the USGS for a topographic map of the Dorrington area.
Directions: From Angels Camp, drive east on Highway 4 for 23 miles to Arnold, and then continue east on Highway 4 for four miles to the park entrance. The trailhead is adjacent to the park entrance.

2 South Grove Loop

5.0 mi/3.0 hrs

The two largest sequoias in Calaveras Big Trees State Park are found on a spur trail of this hike, and that makes it a must-do for visitors. But so many tourists are content to just walk the little trail at the North Grove, look at the giant stump, then hit the road. Why rush? As long as you're at the park, take the South Grove Loop. The loop itself is 3.5 miles long, but the highlight is a spur trail that branches off .75 mile to the Agassiz Tree and the Palace Hotel Tree, two monster-sized specimens. For a great photograph, have someone take a picture of you standing at the base of one of these trees; you will look like a Lilliputian from *Gulliver's Travels*.
Location: Northeast of Arnold on Highway 4; map E3, grid b8.
User groups: Hikers only. No dogs, horses, or mountain bikes. No wheelchair facilities.
Permits: No permits are required. There is a $2 state park entrance fee for each vehicle.
Maps: For a brochure and complete trail map, send $1 to Calaveras Big Trees State Park at the address below. Ask the USGS for a topographic map of the Boards Crossing area.
Directions: From Angels Camp, drive east on Highway 4 for 23 miles to Arnold and then continue east on Highway 4 for four miles to the park entrance. From the park entrance, head down the parkway for nine miles to the trailhead on the right. Note: The road is closed in winter.
Contact: Calaveras Big Trees State Park, P.O. Box 120, Arnold, CA 95223; tel. (209) 795-2334, or Columbia State Park, tel. (209) 532-0150.

HIKER AT TOP OF
9,926-FOOT CLOUDS REST
IN YOSEMITE NATIONAL PARK

MAP E4

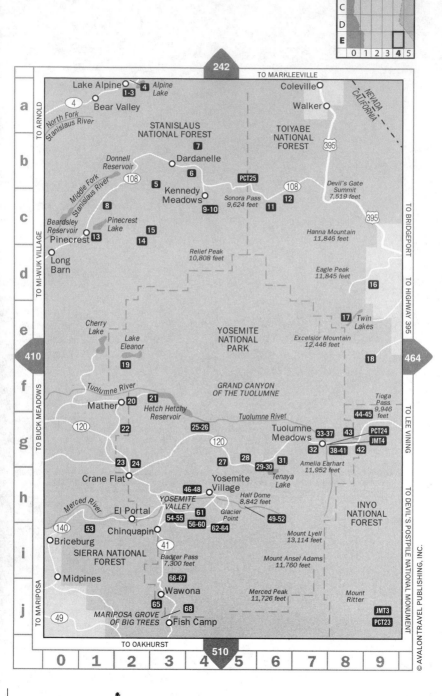

242
TO MARKLEEVILLE

Lake Alpine
Alpine Lake
1-3
4
Coleville
Bear Valley
Walker

a
TO ARNOLD
North Fork Stanislaus River
STANISLAUS NATIONAL FOREST
7
TOIYABE NATIONAL FOREST

b
Donnell Reservoir
Dardanelle
6
PCT25
Middle Fork Stanislaus River
108
5
108
395
Devil's Gate Summit 7,519 feet

c
Beardsley Reservoir
8
Kennedy Meadows
9-10
Sonora Pass 9,624 feet
11
12
395
Hanna Mountain 11,846 feet
TO BRIDGEPORT
Pinecrest Lake
15

d
TO MI-WUK VILLAGE
Pinecrest
13
14
Relief Peak 10,808 feet
Eagle Peak 11,845 feet
16
TO HIGHWAY 395
Long Barn

e
410
Cherry Lake
Lake Eleanor
YOSEMITE NATIONAL PARK
Excelsior Mountain 12,446 feet
17
Twin Lakes
18
464

f
TO BUCK MEADOWS
19
Tuolumne River
GRAND CANYON OF THE TUOLUMNE
TO LEE VINING

g
Mather
20
21
Hetch Hetchy Reservoir
25-26
Tuolumne River
Tioga Pass 9,946 feet
44-45
120
22
120
27
28
29-30
31
Tuolumne Meadows
33-37
43
PCT24
JMT4
32
38-41
42
Amelia Earhart 11,952 feet

h
23
24
Crane Flat
46-48
Yosemite Village
Tenaya Lake
49-52
INYO NATIONAL FOREST
Merced River
YOSEMITE VALLEY
61
Half Dome 8,842 feet
Glacier Point
El Portal
54-55
56-60
62-64
TO DEVIL'S POSTPILE NATIONAL MONUMENT

i
140
53
Chinquapin
Briceburg
SIERRA NATIONAL FOREST
41
Badger Pass 7,300 feet
Mount Lyell 13,114 feet
Midpines
Mount Ansel Adams 11,760 feet

j
TO MARIPOSA
66-67
Wawona
65
68
Merced Peak 11,726 feet
Mount Ritter
JMT3
49
MARIPOSA GROVE OF BIG TREES
Fish Camp
PCT23

TO OAKHURST
510

0 1 2 3 4 5 6 7 8 9

© AVALON TRAVEL PUBLISHING, INC.

CHAPTER E4

1 Osborne Hill 415

2 Lakeshore Trail and
Inspiration Point. 417

3 Duck Lake 417

4 Woodchuck Basin
to Wheeler Lake 418

5 Eagle Meadow
to Dardanelle 418

6 Columns of
the Giants. 419

7 Clark Fork and
Boulder Lake. 419

8 Trail of
the Gargoyles 420

9 Relief Reservoir 420

10 Kennedy Lake 421

11 Sardine Falls 421

12 Secret and
Poore Lakes 422

13 Pinecrest Lake National
Recreation Trail 422

14 Camp and
Bear Lakes 423

15 Burst Rock/
Powell Lake. 423

16 Buckeye Creek Trail . . 424

17 Robinson Creek Trail. . 424

18 Green, East,
and West Lakes. 425

19 Lake Eleanor 425

20 Lookout Point 426

21 Hetch Hetchy
Reservoir 427

22 Carlon Falls. 427

23 Merced Grove. 428

24 Tuolumne Grove 429

25 Lukens Lake 429

26 Ten Lakes/
Grant Lakes 430

27 North Dome 430

28 May Lake. 431

29 Clouds Rest. 432

30 Sunrise Lakes 433

31 Tenaya Lake. 433

32 Cathedral Lakes 434

33 Vogelsang Loop. 434

34 Lower Gaylor Lake . . . 435

35 Elizabeth Lake. 436

36 Lyell Canyon 436

37 Young Lakes Loop 437

(CONTINUED ON NEXT PAGE)

1 Osborne Hill

2.6 mi/1.5 hrs

We like the way Lake Alpine looks from close up on the Lakeshore Trail, but then again we like the way Lake Alpine looks from far up on Osborne Hill, also known as Osborne Point. A short, healthy climb brings you to the point, from which you can look down at the lake and beyond into the Carson-Iceberg Wilderness. The trail ends there but connects to the Emi-grant West Trail if you wish to hike farther. If you're itching for winter to be over so you can go hiking, you'll be happy to know that Highway 4 is always open as far east as Silvertip Campground but not always farther. Thus if the snow is dwindling you'll have access to this trailhead often long before you can access the others near Lake Alpine.

Location: On Highway 4 near Lake Alpine; map E4, grid a2.

(CONTINUED)

38 Waterwheel Falls..... 438

39 Glen Aulin and
Tuolumne Falls 439

40 Lembert Dome 439

41 Dog Lake........... 440

42 Mono Pass......... 441

43 Middle and Upper
Gaylor Lakes........ 441

44 Gardisky Lake....... 442

45 Saddlebag Lake Loop.. 442

46 Upper Yosemite Fall .. 443

47 Eagle Peak......... 444

48 Lower Yosemite Fall .. 444

49 Mist Trail to Top
of Vernal Fall 445

50 Mist and John Muir
Loop to Nevada Fall... 446

51 Mirror Lake/ Tenaya
Canyon Loop........ 447

52 Half Dome......... 447

53 Hites Cove 448

54 Inspiration and
Stanford Points...... 448

55 Bridalveil Fall 449

56 McGurk Meadow..... 450

57 Bridalveil Creek 450

58 Ostrander Lake...... 451

59 Sentinel Dome 451

60 Taft Point and
the Fissures 452

61 Four-Mile Trail 453

62 Pohono Trail........ 453

63 Panorama Trail 454

64 Illilouette Fall 455

65 Wawona
Meadow Loop 455

66 Chilnualna Falls...... 456

67 Alder Creek Falls..... 457

68 Mariposa Grove 457

**Pacific Crest Trail
(PCT) Section Overview**

PCT-23/
JMT-3 Agnew Meadows
to Tuolumne
Meadows........ 458

JMT-4 Tuolumne Meadows
to Yosemite Valley . 459

PCT-24 Tuolumne Meadows
to Sonora Pass.... 460

PCT-25 Sonora Pass
to Ebbetts Pass ... 461

User groups: Hikers, dogs, horses, and mountain bikes. No wheelchair facilities.

Permits: No permits are required. Parking and access are free.

Maps: For a map of Stanislaus National Forest, send $6 to U.S. Forest Service, Map Sales, P.O. Box 587, Camino, CA 95709; tel. (530) 647-5390 or website: www.r5.fs.fed.us/visitorcenter. Ask the USGS for a topographic map of the Tamarack area.

Directions: From Angels Camp at the intersection of Highways 4 and 49, drive east on Highway 4 for 40 miles to Bear Valley. Set your odometer at Bear Valley and drive three miles farther east on Highway 4 to the Osborne Ridge Trailhead just east of Silvertip Campground. Take the trail that leads from the south side of the road.

Contact: Stanislaus National Forest, Calaveras Ranger District, P.O. Box 500, Hathaway Pines, CA 95233; tel. (209) 795-1381 or fax (209) 795-6849.

2 Lakeshore Trail and Inspiration Point

4.0 mi/2.0 hrs

It's hard to say which trail is better, the Lakeshore Trail or the Inspiration Point Trail. To solve the dilemma, hike both of them together. The trip starts with a short walk down a dirt road; then you turn right onto single track. In a mere 10 minutes of hiking through a thick lodgepole pine forest littered with tiny pinecones, you're at the edge of Lake Alpine, elevation 7,350 feet. Follow the trail to your left and in another 10 minutes you reach a left fork for Inspiration Point (the Lakeshore Trail continues straight). You'll want to head out and back on both trails; it makes no difference which one you take first.

The Lakeshore Trail is flat and stays within 100 feet of the water's edge, offering many pretty lake vistas. Eventually the trail meets up with Slick Rock, a four-wheel-drive road, but there's no need to go that far. Just walk a mile or so to the dam, and then turn around and head back. The Inspiration Point Trail is more of a workout: a steep one-mile climb to the summit at Inspiration Point, from which you can see for miles. Pick a clear day and you'll be pointing out Lake Alpine, Elephant Rock, the Dardanelles, and Spicer Meadow Reservoir.

Location: On Highway 4 near Lake Alpine; map E4, grid a2.

User groups: Hikers, dogs, and horses. No mountain bikes. No wheelchair facilities.

Permits: No permits are required. Parking and access are free.

Maps: For a map of Stanislaus National Forest, send $6 to U.S. Forest Service, Map Sales, P.O. Box 587, Camino, CA 95709; tel. (530) 647-5390 or website: www.r5.fs.fed.us/visitorcenter. Ask the USGS for a topographic map of the Spicer Meadow Reservoir area.

Directions: From Angels Camp at the intersection of Highways 4 and 49, drive east on Highway 4 for 40 miles to Bear Valley. Set your odometer at Bear Valley and drive 4.3 miles farther east on Highway 4 to the Lake Alpine East Shore Trailhead turnoff on the right. Turn right, drive .25 mile, and turn right again and drive 0.1 mile past Pine Marten Campground to the signed parking area and the trailhead.

Contact: Stanislaus National Forest, Calaveras Ranger District, P.O. Box 500, Hathaway Pines, CA 95233; tel. (209) 795-1381 or fax (209) 794-6849.

3 Duck Lake

3.0 mi/1.5 hrs

The trailhead at Silver Valley Campground is the start of the route to Duck Lake, and it's also one of the busiest trailheads into the Carson-Iceberg Wilderness. The trip to Duck Lake is a perfect easy hike for families or people just in the mood for a stroll, and the more ambitious can continue past the lake on an eight-mile round-trip to Rock Lake. It's only one mile to reach Duck Lake, but once you're there, you'll want to walk the loop trail around its perimeter, adding another mile to your trip. The area is the site of a historic cow camp where animals have grazed since the late 1800s. You can examine the remains of a couple of early 20th century pioneer cabins.

Location: In the Carson-Iceberg Wilderness off Highway 4 near Lake Alpine; map E4, grid a2.

User groups: Hikers, dogs, and horses. No mountain bikes. No wheelchair facilities.

Permits: No day-use permits are required. Parking and access are free.

Maps: For a map of Stanislaus National Forest, send $6 to U.S. Forest Service, Map Sales, P.O. Box 587, Camino, CA 95709; tel. (530) 647-5390 or website: www.r5.fs.fed.us/visitorcenter. A map of the Carson-Iceberg Wilderness is also available from the U.S. Forest Service for $6. Ask the USGS for a topographic map of the Spicer Meadow Reservoir area.

Directions: From Angels Camp at the intersection of Highways 4 and 49, drive east on Highway 4 for 40 miles to Bear Valley. Set your odometer at Bear Valley and drive 4.3 miles farther east on Highway 4 to the Lake Alpine East Shore Trailhead turnoff on the right. Turn right and continue straight to Silver Valley Camp and the Silver Valley Trailhead.

Contact: Stanislaus National Forest, Calaveras Ranger District, P.O. Box 500, Hathaway Pines, CA 95233; tel. (209) 795-1381 or fax (209) 794-6849.

4 Woodchuck Basin to Wheeler Lake

6.4 mi/3.5 hrs

Located only a mile from the campgrounds at Lake Alpine, the Woodchuck Basin Trailhead at elevation 7,800 feet should have a parking lot full of cars, but it rarely does. The trail leads into the Mokelumne Wilderness, and after climbing uphill on it for 1.7 forested miles, you reach a junction where you can go left for Underwood Valley or right for tiny Wheeler Lake. Bearing right, you pass a Mokelumne Wilderness sign and in moments you are heading for a 1.5-mile steep descent to Wheeler Lake. Think it over before you go because you'll need to regain those 1,000 feet on the way home. But if you're willing to take the plunge, you're treated to a picturesque tree- and granite-lined lake where you can pass the afternoon with little fear that you'll be bugged by a busload of other hikers.

Location: In the Mokelumne Wilderness off Highway 4 near Lake Alpine; map E4, grid a2.

User groups: Hikers, dogs, and horses. No mountain bikes. No wheelchair facilities.

Permits: No day-use permits are required. Parking and access are free.

Maps: For a map of Stanislaus National Forest, send $6 to U.S. Forest Service, Map Sales, P.O. Box 587, Camino, CA 95709; tel. (530) 647-5390 or website: www.r5.fs.fed.us/visitorcenter. Ask the USGS for a topographic map of the Spicer Meadow Reservoir area.

Directions: From Angels Camp at the intersection of Highways 4 and 49, drive east on Highway 4 for 40 miles to Bear Valley. Set your odometer at Bear Valley and drive 5.5 miles farther east on Highway 4 to the Woodchuck Basin Trailhead on the left. Turn left and drive .25 mile to the parking area.

Contact: Stanislaus National Forest, Calaveras Ranger District, P.O. Box 500, Hathaway Pines, CA 95233; tel. (209) 795-1381 or fax (209) 794-6849.

5 Eagle Meadow to Dardanelle

4.0 mi one way/2.0 hrs

If you can convince someone to drop you off at Eagle Meadow and pick you up at Dardanelle Resort, or if you have two cars for a shuttle hike, you can take a scenic downhill stroll paralleling Eagle Creek. It's a trip for lovers of subalpine meadows, especially in the first mile. After it leaves the meadow the trail enters a thick and lovely conifer forest, so you get a bit of shade along the path. The route gets a little steep in sections, so make sure your knees are in good enough shape for four miles of downhill before you make the trip.

Location: Near Dardanelle; map E4, grid b3.

User groups: Hikers, dogs, horses, and mountain bikes. No wheelchair facilities.

Permits: No permits are required. Parking and access are free.

Maps: For a map of Stanislaus National Forest, send $6 to U.S. Forest Service, Map Sales, P.O. Box 587, Camino, CA 95709; tel. (530) 647-5390 or website: www.r5.fs.fed.us/visitorcenter. Ask the USGS for topographic maps of the Donnell Lake and Dardanelle areas.

Directions: From Sonora drive east on Highway 108 for 41 miles to the turnoff for Niagara Creek Campground on the right side of the highway, approximately 12 miles east of Strawberry. Turn right, then at .25 mile turn right again on Road 5N01. Follow Road 5N01 for seven miles to Eagle Meadow. This is the start of the one-way shuttle hike; the finish is at Dardanelle Resort on Highway 108, eight miles east of the Niagara Creek turnoff.

Contact: Stanislaus National Forest, Summit Ranger District, #1 Pinecrest Lake Road,

Pinecrest, CA 95364; tel. (209) 965-3434 or fax (209) 965-3372.

6 Columns of the Giants

0.5 mi/0.5 hr

This is Highway 108's answer to Devils Postpile National Monument, and take it from us, it's no cheap imitation. The rock formations at the end of the Columns of the Giants geological trail were formed 150,000 years ago when a series of volcanic eruptions occurred. The lava flow cooled rapidly, probably during cold weather, and cracked into narrow, hexagonal, basalt columns. Some of the remaining columns are 30 to 40 feet in height and three to four feet in diameter. While many are still standing tall or at least at an angle, others have shattered into thousands of pieces and created a giant pile of rubble. An interpretive trail sign explains that underneath this rock pile is evidence of the last small ice age in the Sierra—frozen remnants of ice fields that are replenished each year by winter snow and cold. All this historical information gives you plenty to think about during your very short walk. Make sure you bring your camera—it's lots of fun taking pictures of your hiking partner standing right next to the jumbled heap of rocks.

Location: Near Dardanelle; map E4, grid b4.

User groups: Hikers and dogs. No horses or mountain bikes. No wheelchair facilities.

Permits: No permits are required. Parking and access are free.

Maps: For a map of Stanislaus National Forest, send $6 to U.S. Forest Service, Map Sales, P.O. Box 587, Camino, CA 95709; tel. (530) 647-5390 or website: www.r5.fs.fed.us/visitorcenter. Ask the USGS for a topographic map of the Dardanelle area.

Directions: From Sonora drive east on Highway 108 for 50 miles to Pigeon Flat Campground, two miles east of Dardanelle and on the south side of the highway. If you're traveling west on Highway 108, the campground is 15 miles west of Sonora Pass. Park in the day-use parking lot just outside the camp.

Contact: Stanislaus National Forest, Summit Ranger District, #1 Pinecrest Lake Road, Pinecrest, CA 95364; tel. (209) 965-3434 or fax (209) 965-3372.

7 Clark Fork and Boulder Lake

8.0 mi/4.0 hrs

From this trailhead at Iceberg Meadow you immediately enter the Carson-Iceberg Wilderness at the base of imposing Iceberg Peak. Hiking upstream on the northern edge of the Clark Fork Stanislaus River, you'll enjoy good wildflowers and a lovely mixed forest of white firs and Jeffrey pines. At the water's edge the trees are more leafy, including cottonwoods and aspens. The river pools are cold but useful for cooling off on a hot day. At 2.5 miles you have a choice: bear right (really straight) and continue along the Clark Fork, or turn left and hike steeply uphill along Boulder Creek. We suggest the left fork, following Boulder Creek for 1.5 miles uphill to tiny Boulder Lake. It's a good workout to a pretty destination. But hey, if you get tired, just cut the trip short and turn around when you reach Boulder Creek. Plenty of fishing holes and picnic spots can be found along the Clark Fork.

Location: In the Carson-Iceberg Wilderness on Clark Fork Stanislaus River; map E4, grid b4.

User groups: Hikers, dogs, and horses. No mountain bikes. No wheelchair facilities.

Permits: A free wilderness permit is required for overnight stays and is available from the Summit Ranger Station. Parking and access are free.

Maps: For a map of Stanislaus National Forest, send $6 to U.S. Forest Service, Map Sales, P.O. Box 587, Camino, CA 95709; tel. (530) 647-5390 or website: www.r5.fs.fed.us/visitorcenter. A map of the Carson-Iceberg Wilderness is also available from the U.S. Forest Service for $6. Ask the USGS for a topographic map of the Donnell Lake area.

Directions: From Sonora drive east on Highway 108 for 46 miles to the left turnoff for Clark Fork Road, approximately 17 miles east of Strawberry. Turn left and follow Clark Fork Road for about seven miles to its end at the Clark Fork Trailhead at Iceberg Meadow.

Contact: Stanislaus National Forest, Summit Ranger District, #1 Pinecrest Lake Road, Pinecrest, CA 95364; tel. (209) 965-3434 or fax (209) 965-3372.

8 Trail of the Gargoyles
3.0 mi/1.5 hrs

When you park your car at the nondescript trailhead, it's hard to guess what's in store on the Trail of the Gargoyles. Sure, the odd rock formations that line the trail are fascinating to look at, but what's more significant is that they (and you) are perched at the edge of a cliff at 7,400 feet in elevation. You walk just inches away from what appears to be the edge of the world with only thin air between you and the densely forested basin several hundred feet below. It's an easy and nearly flat trail, but if you have kids with you, keep a handhold on them at all times. By the way, the rock formations don't look much like gargoyles except for the fact that they are hanging off the edge of this abrupt abyss. The trailhead is in the middle of the 1.5-mile trail, which means you'll want to walk out and back in both directions. The trail on the north rim is slightly steeper.

Location: Near Strawberry and Pinecrest Lake; map E4, grid c1.

User groups: Hikers and dogs. No horses or mountain bikes. No wheelchair facilities.

Permits: No permits are required. Parking and access are free.

Maps: For a map of Stanislaus National Forest, send $6 to U.S. Forest Service, Map Sales, P.O. Box 587, Camino, CA 95709; tel. (530) 647-5390 or website: www.r5.fs.fed.us/visitorcenter. Ask the USGS for a topographic map of the Pinecrest area.

Directions: From Sonora drive east on Highway 108 for 34 miles to Herring Creek Road (Road 4N12), 2.4 miles east of Strawberry. Turn right on Herring Creek Road and continue for 6.7 miles to an often-unsigned left turnoff. Turn left and drive 0.2 mile to the trailhead.

Contact: Stanislaus National Forest, Summit Ranger District, #1 Pinecrest Lake Road, Pinecrest, CA 95364; tel. (209) 965-3434 or fax (209) 965-3372.

9 Relief Reservoir
6.0 mi/3.0 hrs

From the mammoth trailhead and parking lot at Kennedy Meadows, you can hike to Relief Reservoir (elevation 7,200 feet), do a little fishing, then hike back out. The only downers are that pack animals have roughed up the trail and the route is seriously overused. On weekends it seems you must constantly pull off the path to let horses and other hikers go by. The route, called the Huckleberry Trail, leads along the Stanislaus River, enters the Emigrant Wilderness at one mile, then skirts its edge. Quickly you understand why this trip is so popular—the river canyon gets more and more beautiful as you head deeper into it. The trail had to be blasted into the steep and rocky hillside. Pass the left turnoff for roaring Kennedy Creek and Kennedy Lake at 2.6 miles, and then proceed straight for another .5 mile to an overlook of the reservoir. It's a steep drop down to the water's edge in the last .25 mile, which must be regained on the return trip.

Location: On the edge of the Emigrant Wilderness near Dardanelle; map E4, grid c4.

User groups: Hikers, dogs, and horses. No mountain bikes. No wheelchair facilities.

Permits: No day-use permits are required. Parking and access are free.

Maps: For a map of Stanislaus National Forest, send $6 to U.S. Forest Service, Map Sales, P.O. Box 587, Camino, CA 95709; tel. (530) 647-5390 or website: www.r5.fs.fed.us/visitorcenter. A map of the Emigrant Wilderness is also available from the U.S. Forest Service for $7. Ask the USGS for a topographic map of the Sonora Pass area.

Directions: From Sonora go east on Highway 108 for 55 miles to the Kennedy Meadows turnoff on the south side of the highway, six miles east of Dardanelle. Turn right and follow the road a mile to the well-signed parking area. Day hikers can park .5 mile farther down the road near Kennedy Meadows Resort. If you're traveling west on Highway 108, the Kennedy Meadows turnoff is 9.6 miles west of Sonora Pass.

Contact: Stanislaus National Forest, Summit Ranger District, #1 Pinecrest Lake Road, Pinecrest, CA 95364; tel. (209) 965-3434 or fax (209) 965-3372.

🔟 Kennedy Lake

14.8 mi/2.0 days

If the number of cars in the Kennedy Meadows parking lot is scaring you, take heart. Many of them belong to people day hiking to fish at Relief Reservoir. If you have the time and inclination for a longer trip to Kennedy Lake, you will leave a lot of your fellow hikers behind. Even so, don't expect solitude. You'll likely share the lake with other backpackers, horse packers, and grazing cows. Follow the trail notes to Relief Reservoir, above, but at 2.6 miles take the left fork for Kennedy Lake. The trail climbs for another 1.6 miles, then goes flat for the final 3.2 miles to the lake. It's an easy two-day backpack trip, with low mileage and only a 1,200-foot elevation gain. Note that all the campsites are downstream of the lake rather than along its shoreline.

Location: In the Emigrant Wilderness near Dardanelle; map E4, grid c4.

User groups: Hikers, dogs, and horses. No mountain bikes. No wheelchair facilities.

Permits: A free wilderness permit is required for overnight stays and is available from the Summit Ranger Station. Parking and access are free.

Maps: For a map of Stanislaus National Forest, send $6 to U.S. Forest Service, Map Sales, P.O. Box 587, Camino, CA 95709; tel. (530) 647-5390 or website: www.r5.fs.fed.us/visitorcenter.

A map of the Emigrant Wilderness is also available from the U.S. Forest Service for $7. Ask the USGS for a topographic map of the Sonora Pass area.

Directions: From Sonora drive east on Highway 108 for 55 miles to the turnoff for Kennedy Meadows, six miles east of Dardanelle and on the south side of the highway. Turn right and follow the road for another mile to the large parking area. If you're traveling west on Highway 108, the Kennedy Meadows turnoff is 9.6 miles west of Sonora Pass.

Contact: Stanislaus National Forest, Summit Ranger District, #1 Pinecrest Lake Road, Pinecrest, CA 95364; tel. (209) 965-3434 or fax (209) 965-3372.

1️⃣1️⃣ Sardine Falls

2.0 mi/1.0 hr

An easy hike through a high alpine meadow culminating at a pretty waterfall is our idea of a fine way to spend an afternoon. The trip to Sardine Falls requires a little route finding because there is no formal trail, but since you can see the falls from the road and there are several overgrown jeep routes to follow, the going is easy. From where you've left your car, head across the northwest side of the meadow. Look for a route that is signed "Route Closed" to motorized vehicles; it's the most direct path. Cross Sardine Creek, which parallels Highway 108, and walk up the right side of larger McKay Creek. After climbing uphill over a rise, you'll hear and then see Sardine Falls, gracefully framed by a few sparse lodgepole pines.

Location: Near Sonora Pass; map E4, grid c6.

User groups: Hikers and dogs. No horses or mountain bikes. No wheelchair facilities.

Permits: No permits are required. Parking and access are free.

Maps: For a map of Humboldt-Toiyabe National Forest (Bridgeport District), send $6 to U.S. Forest Service, Map Sales, P.O. Box 587, Camino, CA 95709; tel.

(530) 647-5390 or website: www.r5.fs.fed.us/visitorcenter. Ask the USGS for a topographic map of the Pickel Meadow area.

Directions: From the junction of U.S. 395 and Highway 108, drive 12.5 miles west on Highway 108. You will be 2.5 miles east of Sonora Pass Summit. Park along the road in the gravel pullouts near the overgrown jeep roads on the northwest side of the meadow.

Contact: Humboldt-Toiyabe National Forest, Bridgeport Ranger District, HCR1 Box 1000, Bridgeport, CA 93517; tel. (760) 932-7070 or fax (760) 932-1299.

12 Secret and Poore Lakes
6.5 mi/3.5 hrs

This 6.5-mile loop trip begins at a footbridge over the West Walker River at Leavitt Meadows Campground. In .25 mile take the left fork for Secret Lake (you won't be alone, most likely). Climb for nearly two miles through sage and Jeffrey pines, then descend .5 mile to Secret Lake. Much larger Poore Lake is visible over your left shoulder. Take a break at Secret Lake, then continue around the right side of the lake, hiking through sparse junipers and pines for .5 mile to the left turnoff for Poore Lake. Take the rougher, .75-mile route to the large lake. Keep your fingers crossed that there are no loud off-road vehicles racing around it. If it's quiet you can swim or fish for a few hours, then retrace your steps to the junction. From there, loop back to the campground on a lower trail that follows closer to the West Walker River through Leavitt Meadow. If Poore Lake turns out to be less than perfect, you can always hike beyond the return loop junction to little Roosevelt Lake. One caveat: As you depart the trailhead at Leavitt Meadows Camp, don't be shocked if you hear a lot of shouting and see people running through the woods across the West Walker River. It's just the U.S. Marines in training at the nearby Mountain Warfare Training Center. They scared the heck out of us.

Location: Near Sonora Pass; map E4, grid c6.

User groups: Hikers, dogs, horses, and mountain bikes. No wheelchair facilities.

Permits: No permits are required. Parking and access are free.

Maps: For a map of Humboldt-Toiyabe National Forest (Bridgeport District), send $6 to U.S. Forest Service, Map Sales, P.O. Box 587, Camino, CA 95709; tel. (530) 647-5390 or website: www.r5.fs.fed.us/visitorcenter. Ask the USGS for a topographic map of the Pickel Meadow area.

Directions: From the junction of U.S. 395 and Highway 108, drive seven miles west on Highway 108 to Leavitt Meadows Campground on the south side of the road. If you are coming from the west, the camp is eight miles east of Sonora Pass. Day hikers may park inside the campground; backpackers must park .25 mile west of the camp on Highway 108.

Contact: Humboldt-Toiyabe National Forest, Bridgeport Ranger District, HCR1 Box 1000, Bridgeport, CA 93517; tel. (760) 932-7070 or fax (760) 932-1299.

13 Pinecrest Lake National Recreation Trail
4.0 mi/2.0 hrs

Pinecrest Lake is a tremendously popular family vacation resort just off Highway 108, the kind of place that people go year after year for a week of boating, camping, and fishing. The trail that circles its banks is a lot like the lake itself—it's pretty, it's popular, and it's no place to go if you like solitude. However, the four-mile loop makes a good early morning walk or run if you're up and at it before the crowds get out of bed. In the afternoons you can hike to the east side of the lake, and take a spur trail along the South Fork Stanislaus River to some excellent swimming holes called Cleo's Bath. The main downer: the south side of the loop is littered with vacation homes. The weird part: there are pay telephones positioned right along the trail.

Location: On Pinecrest Lake near Strawberry; map E4, grid c1.

User groups: Hikers and dogs. No horses or mountain bikes. No wheelchair facilities except at the fishing ramp and day-use area.

Permits: No permits are required. Parking and access are free.

Maps: For a map of Stanislaus National Forest, send $6 to U.S. Forest Service, Map Sales, P.O. Box 587, Camino, CA 95709; tel. (530) 647-5390 or website: www.r5.fs.fed.us/visitorcenter. Ask the USGS for a topographic map of the Pinecrest area.

Directions: From Sonora drive east on Highway 108 for 31 miles to the Pinecrest turnoff. Turn right on Pinecrest Lake Road and continue for another mile to the day-use parking area on the south side of the lake. Park as close to the end of the road as possible.

Contact: Stanislaus National Forest, Summit Ranger District, #1 Pinecrest Lake Road, Pinecrest, CA 95364; tel. (209) 965-3434 or fax (209) 965-3372.

14 Camp and Bear Lakes

8.0 mi/4.0 hrs

The Crabtree Trailhead at elevation 7,180 feet is the trailhead of choice for most hikers and backpackers entering the Emigrant Wilderness. It's easy to reach and allows access to many excellent destinations with a relatively short walk. From Crabtree it's a moderate 2.5-mile hike to Camp Lake just inside the wilderness boundary. Campsites can be found on the ridge on the south side of the lake. If there are too many people there, you can go an extra 1.5 miles to Bear Lake, accessible via a one-mile-long left spur trail off the Crabtree Trail. Both lakes offer stellar granite-country scenery, good campsites, and the chance of seeing plenty of wildflowers along the route in summer. We were wowed by the wandering daisies, big blue lupine, and yellow daisies.

Location: In the Emigrant Wilderness near Pinecrest Lake; map E4, grid c2.

User groups: Hikers, dogs, and horses. No mountain bikes. No wheelchair facilities.

Permits: A free wilderness permit is required for overnight stays and is available from the Summit Ranger Station. Parking and access are free.

Maps: For a map of Stanislaus National Forest, send $6 to U.S. Forest Service, Map Sales, P.O. Box 587, Camino, CA 95709; tel. (530) 647-5390 or website: www.r5.fs.fed.us/visitorcenter. A map of the Emigrant Wilderness is also available from the U.S. Forest Service for $7. Ask the USGS for a topographic map of the Pinecrest area.

Directions: From Sonora drive east on Highway 108 for 31 miles to the Pinecrest turnoff. Turn right on Pinecrest Lake Road and continue .5 mile to the right fork for Dodge Ridge Ski Area. Bear right and drive 2.9 miles, then turn right at the sign for Aspen Meadow and Gianelli Trailhead. Drive .5 mile, turn left, and drive four miles to the turnoff for Crabtree Trailhead. Turn right and drive .25 mile to the Crabtree Trailhead. The route is well signed.

Contact: Stanislaus National Forest, Summit Ranger District, #1 Pinecrest Lake Road, Pinecrest, CA 95364; tel. (209) 965-3434 or fax (209) 965-3372.

15 Burst Rock/Powell Lake

4.0 mi/2.5 hrs

Both Burst Rock and Powell Lake are supreme day-hike destinations, but they come with a surprise for first-time visitors: neither one is located right along the trail, and since this is wilderness land, neither one is signed. This surprise results in a lot of people wandering around asking, "Which rock is Burst Rock?" The short answer is it doesn't matter. After hiking gently but steadily uphill for one mile, you'll reach an interpretive sign which details the difficulties of pioneers who tried to use this route, called the West Walker-Sonora Emigrant Trail, to cross the Sierra in the 1850s. From the wilderness boundary sign, cut off to your left for about 50 yards and you'll witness an incredible vista and drop-off to the valley below, and who knows, you might even be standing on Burst Rock. After feeling suitably humbled, retrace your steps and continue another mile on the trail until you reach an unsigned fork which leads to the left for less than .25 mile to Powell Lake, a favorite spot of young anglers. If you miss the fork, shortly you'll catch sight of the lake off to your left, and you'll know to go back and find it. If you're lucky and smart enough to be the first visitor here in the morning, you can make a wish, take off all your clothes, and dive into the lake from the peninsula of rocks in its center. The experience can feel downright religious.

Location: In the Emigrant Wilderness near Pinecrest Lake; map E4, grid c2.

User groups: Hikers, dogs, and horses. No mountain bikes. No wheelchair facilities.

Permits: A free wilderness permit is required for overnight stays and is available from the Summit Ranger Station. Parking and access are free.

Maps: For a map of Stanislaus National Forest, send $6 to U.S. Forest Service, Map Sales, P.O. Box 587, Camino, CA 95709; tel. (530) 647-5390 or website: www.r5.fs.fed.us/visitorcenter. A map of the Emigrant Wilderness is available from the U.S. Forest Service for $7. Ask the USGS for a topographic map of the Pinecrest area.

Directions: From Sonora drive east on Highway 108 for 31 miles to the Pinecrest turnoff. Turn right on Pinecrest Lake Road and continue for .5 mile to the right fork for Dodge Ridge Ski Area. Bear right, drive 2.9 miles, and turn right at the sign for Aspen Meadow and Gianelli Trailhead. Drive .5 mile, turn left, and drive 8.3 miles to the trailhead parking area. The route is well signed.

Contact: Stanislaus National Forest, Summit Ranger District, #1 Pinecrest Lake Road, Pinecrest, CA 95364; tel. (209) 965-3434 or fax (209) 965-3372.

16 Buckeye Creek Trail
5.0 mi/2.5 hrs

You can hike up to eight miles one way along Buckeye Creek since most of it is pretty level,

although few people go that far. Most hikers just take off from Buckeye Campground (7,000 feet), maybe pack along their fishing rods, and walk a couple of miles each way up and down the stream. Brook trout are planted close to the campground all summer. It's rare to hike far in the Eastern Sierra without having to climb, but that's what you get here on the bottom of Buckeye Canyon. If you don't like to fish, there's plenty of other stuff to do, like admire the wildflowers in the meadows or gape at the impressive walls of glacial summits and ridges that surround you.

Location: In Humboldt-Toiyabe National Forest west of Bridgeport and Highway 395; map E4, grid d9.

User groups: Hikers, dogs, and horses. No mountain bikes. No wheelchair facilities.

Permits: No day-use permits are required. Parking and access are free for day-hikers; backpackers must pay a $5 parking fee.

Maps: For a map of Humboldt-Toiyabe National Forest (Bridgeport District), send $6 to U.S. Forest Service, Map Sales, P.O. Box 587, Camino, CA 95709; tel. (530) 647-5390 or website: www.r5.fs.fed.us/visitorcenter. Ask the USGS for a topographic map of the Twin Lakes area.

Directions: From Bridgeport on U.S. 395, drive west on Twin Lakes Road for seven miles to the Buckeye Road turnoff. Turn right on Buckeye Road (dirt) and drive about 3.5 miles to the Buckeye Campground and trailhead.

Contact: Humboldt-Toiyabe National Forest, Bridgeport Ranger District, HCR1 Box 1000, Bridgeport, CA 93517; tel. (760) 932-7070 or fax (760) 932-1299.

17 Robinson Creek Trail
7.8 mi/5.0 hrs

Some call it the Barney Lake Trail, others the Robinson Creek Trail, but whatever you call it, you should know that this is the busiest trail into the Hoover Wilderness. Why? It's one hike that's not a butt-kicker. It gains only 1,200 feet along its four-mile length. The remedy for the crowds? Start hiking very early in the day, before the hundreds of campers in the Twin Lakes area have risen from their sleeping bags. You must park outside Mono Village Campground and then walk straight through it to reach the trailhead, which is signed for Barney Lake. The trail parallels Robinson Creek the whole way, with off-and-on views of the mammoth, jagged Sawtooth Ridge. It enters the Hoover Wilderness at 2.6 miles, then climbs a bit more steeply and reaches the lake at 3.9 miles. If you get there before everyone else, congratulate yourself and pronounce the lake your own.

Location: In the Hoover Wilderness west of Bridgeport; map E4, grid e8.

User groups: Hikers, dogs, and horses. No mountain bikes. No wheelchair facilities.

Permits: No day-use permits are required. Parking and access are free for day-hikers; backpackers must pay a $5 parking fee.

Maps: For a map of Humboldt-Toiyabe National Forest (Bridgeport District) or the Hoover Wilderness, send $6 to U.S. Forest Service, Map Sales, P.O. Box 587, Camino, CA 95709; tel. (530) 647-5390 or website: www.r5.fs.fed.us/visitorcenter. Ask the USGS for a topographic map of the Twin Lakes area.

Directions: From Bridgeport on U.S. 395, drive west on Twin Lakes Road for 13.2 miles to the signed parking area on the west end of the lakes near Mono Village Campground.

Contact: Humboldt-Toiyabe National Forest, Bridgeport Ranger District, HCR1 Box 1000, Bridgeport, CA 93517; tel. (760) 932-7070 or fax (760) 932-1299.

18 Green, East, and West Lakes

9.0 mi/5.0 hrs

All three lakes—Green, East, and West—are situated at over 9,000 feet in elevation, offer decent trout fishing, and are accessible via the Green Creek Trail. It's only five miles round-trip to Green Lake, but you can go two miles farther for a nine-mile round-trip that includes East Lake as well, or take a 1.5-mile spur off the main trail for a jaunt to West Lake. Some people make a short backpacking trip out of it and see all three lakes. The trail climbs, of course, but not so much that you'll be worn out when you reach the lakes, just enough to give you stellar valley views most of the way. Wildflowers are excellent along the trail as it closely parallels the West Fork of Green Creek. The turnoff for West Lake is on the right at 2.4 miles, and the main trail reaches Green Lake at 2.6 miles, East Lake at 4.6 miles.

Location: In the Hoover Wilderness west of Bridgeport; map E4, grid f9.

User groups: Hikers, dogs, and horses. No mountain bikes. No wheelchair facilities.

Permits: No day-use permits are required. Parking and access are free.

Maps: For a map of Humboldt-Toiyabe National Forest (Bridgeport District) or the Hoover Wilderness, send $6 to U.S. Forest Service, Map Sales, P.O. Box 587, Camino, CA 95709; tel. (530) 647-5390 or website: www.r5.fs.fed.us/visitorcenter. Ask the USGS for a topographic map of the Twin Lakes area.

Directions: From Bridgeport drive south on U.S. 395 for five miles to Green Lake Road (dirt). Turn west and drive 8.5 miles to the signed trailhead parking area shortly before Green Creek Campground.

Contact: Humboldt-Toiyabe National Forest, Bridgeport Ranger District, HCR1 Box 1000, Bridgeport, CA 93517; tel. (760) 932-7070 or fax (760) 932-1299.

19 Lake Eleanor

3.0 mi/1.5 hrs

Up here in the Hetch Hetchy region of Yosemite, elevations are low and temperatures can heat up. While that may not be good news in July and August, it's great news early in the year when the Yosemite high country is still buried in snow. You can fish all year at Lake Eleanor, elevation 4,657 feet, as long as the road is open and you can get in; and you can also hike the easy trail around the lake's edge. Swimming and canoeing are popular in summer. The access road to Lake Eleanor ends .25 mile before the lake, so you start your hike there, then cruise around the lake to find your campsite or drop a line in the water.

Special note: Check your calendar before you go. The gate at Cherry Lake is closed every year one week before deer season, which is usually sometime in September. **Location:** In northwest Yosemite National Park; map E4, grid f2.

User groups: Hikers and horses. No dogs or mountain bikes. No wheelchair facilities.

Permits: No day-hiking permits are required. Parking and access are free.

Maps: Free park maps are available at park entrance stations or by contacting Yosemite National Park at the address below. A more detailed map is available for a fee from Tom Harrison Cartography, tel. (209) 372-0200. Ask the USGS for a topographic map of the Lake Eleanor area.

Directions: From Groveland drive east on Highway 120 for 13 miles toward Yosemite National Park. Turn left on Cherry Lake Road (Road 1N03), signed for Cherry Lake and Sweetwater Camp. Follow Cherry Lake Road for 24 miles to near the edge of Cherry Lake and turn left on a dirt road that is signed for Lake Eleanor. Follow the dirt road to its end, .25 mile south of the lake.

Contact: Yosemite National Park Public Information Office, P.O. Box 577, Yosemite National Park, CA 95389; tel. (209) 372-0200 or fax (209) 372-0371.

20 Lookout Point
2.6 mi/1.2 hrs

Check your calendar. Is it springtime? Are most of the high country trails in Yosemite National Park still snowed in? Then it's time to take the easy jaunt to Lookout Point, where you can admire Hetch Hetchy Reservoir and its waterfalls from an unusual perspective and count the plentiful wildflowers along the trail as you walk.

The Lookout Point Trail begins by the Mather Ranger Station on Hetch Hetchy Road. Begin hiking at the trail sign for Cottonwood and Smith Meadows and Hetch Hetchy (it's not signed for Lookout Point). Turn left at the first junction, then follow the trail as it roughly parallels Hetch Hetchy Road for .5 mile. You turn away from the road with a brief uphill stretch, then enter a level, forested area that was severely burned in the wildfires of 1996. This is where the flowers bloom profusely in springtime. Look for a trail junction at one mile out and bear left for Lookout Point, 0.3 mile away. The path gets rather faint in places, but rock cairns mark the way. Just head for the highest point you see atop a granite knob dotted with a few Jeffrey pines. You'll know you're at Lookout Point when you can see the west end of Hetch Hetchy Reservoir, including its immense dam, and two of Hetch Hetchy's beautiful waterfalls: Wapama and Tueeulala. If you visit much later than May or June, you may see only Wapama Falls, the most robust of Hetch Hetchy's waterfalls. (Tueeulala dries up early in the year.) Although the vista is not perfect from Lookout Point—it would be better if it were 500 feet higher or perhaps farther away from the fast-growing ponderosa pines—this is still a fine spot to spread out a picnic.

Location: In northwest Yosemite National Park; map E4, grid f2.

User groups: Hikers and horses. No dogs or mountain bikes. No wheelchair facilities.

Permits: No permits are required. There is a $20 entrance fee at Yosemite National Park, good for seven days.

Maps: Free park maps are available at park entrance stations or by contacting Yosemite National Park at the address below. A more detailed map is available for a fee from Tom Harrison Cartography, tel. (415) 456-7940. Ask the USGS for a topographic map of the Lake Eleanor area.

Directions: From Groveland drive east on Highway 120 for 22.5 miles to the Evergreen Road turnoff on the left, signed for Hetch Hetchy Reservoir (it's a mile west of the Big

Oak Flat entrance to Yosemite). Drive north on Evergreen Road for 7.4 miles, then turn right on Hetch Hetchy Road. Drive 1.7 miles to the entrance kiosk by the Mather ranger station; the trail begins 100 yards past the entrance kiosk, just beyond the ranger station on the right.

Contact: Yosemite National Park Public Information Office, P.O. Box 577, Yosemite National Park, CA 95389; tel. (209) 372-0200, or fax (209) 372-0371.

21 Hetch Hetchy Reservoir
13.0 mi/1-2 days

You're hungering for a Yosemite backpacking trip, but Tuolumne Meadows is knee-deep in melting snow. There's no better time than spring to hike the northern edge of Hetch Hetchy Reservoir, elevation 3,796 feet, admiring three stunning waterfalls along the way: Tueeulala, Wapama, and Rancheria. It's a long round-trip day hike or an easy overnight backpacking trip to the eastern edge of the reservoir and Rancheria Falls, where the bears are some of the boldest in all of Yosemite. Bring a bear-proof food canister or hang your food high. While Rancheria Falls is a series of cascades, Wapama Falls on Tiltill Creek is a Bridalveil-like plume of whitewater, plunging daringly into the reservoir. In spring, Wapama Falls sometimes flows so furiously that they have to close the trail. In contrast, Tueeulala Falls is a delicate wisp of whitewater that dries up by early summer. The trail is mostly flat, with a total elevation gain of only 1,300 feet, and manageable for beginning backpackers. Fishing in the reservoir is good in spring and fall, but remember: no swimming allowed. The trail starts by crossing the giant O'Shaughnessy Dam, giving you pause to think about the San Francisco politicians who in 1908 believed that flooding Hetch Hetchy's valley, a near twin to stunning Yosemite Valley, was a good idea. It just goes to show you—the good old days were not always so good.

Location: In northwest Yosemite National Park; map E4, grid f3.

User groups: Hikers and horses. No dogs or mountain bikes. No wheelchair facilities.

Permits: There is a $20 entrance fee at Yosemite National Park, good for seven days. Free wilderness permits are required for overnight stays. They are available on a first-come, first-served basis up to one day in advance at the Yosemite Wilderness kiosk near your chosen trailhead or farther in advance by mail or phone for a $5 reservation fee; call (209) 372-0740.

Maps: Free park maps are available at park entrance stations or by contacting Yosemite National Park at the address below. A more detailed map is available for a fee from Tom Harrison Cartography, tel. (415) 456-7940. Ask the USGS for topographic maps of the Lake Eleanor and Hetch Hetchy Reservoir areas.

Directions: From Groveland drive east on Highway 120 for 22.5 miles to the Evergreen Road turnoff signed for Hetch Hetchy Reservoir on the left, a mile west of the Big Oak Flat entrance to Yosemite. Drive north on Evergreen Road for 7.4 miles and turn right on Hetch Hetchy Road. Drive 16 miles to the dam and trailhead.

Contact: Yosemite National Park Public Information Office, P.O. Box 577, Yosemite National Park, CA 95389; tel. (209) 372-0200 or fax (209) 372-0371.

22 Carlon Falls
4.5 mi/2.5 hrs

Carlon Falls is a pretty cascade on the South Fork Tuolumne River in the far western region of Yosemite. It's so far west that the trailhead is actually in Stanislaus National Forest, outside the park border. You hike into Yosemite National Park. That means no $20 entrance fee, no waiting in line at the entrance kiosk, and no crowds. The trailhead is just outside of Carlon Day-Use Area, a popular picnicking spot on the Tuolumne River. Hike along the northern bank of the river to reach the falls in just over two miles; the trail is smooth, flat, and easy to follow. The waterfall drops in two tiers over wide granite ledges, and the riverbanks surrounding it are covered with tall hardwoods and dense foliage. A bonus is that unlike most Yosemite waterfalls, Carlon Falls runs year-round, and it's great to visit in the autumn when the deciduous trees show their brilliant colors.

Location: On the border of Stanislaus National Forest and northwest Yosemite National Park; map E4, grid g2.

User groups: Hikers only. No dogs, horses, or mountain bikes. No wheelchair facilities.

Permits: No permits are required. Parking and access are free.

Maps: For a map of Stanislaus National Forest, send $6 to U.S. Forest Service, Map Sales, P.O. Box 587, Camino, CA 95709; tel. (530) 647-5390 or website: www.r5.fs.fed.us/visitorcenter. Ask the USGS for a topographic map of the Ackerson Mountain area.

Directions: From Groveland drive east on Highway 120 for 22.5 miles to the Evergreen Road turnoff signed for Hetch Hetchy Reservoir, a mile west of the Big Oak Flat entrance to Yosemite. Follow Evergreen Road north for another mile to the far side of the bridge just past Carlon Day-Use Area. Park on the right at the closed-off road on the north side of the bridge. There is room for about five cars. Begin hiking on the closed road, heading upstream. The road turns to single track after about 100 yards.

Contact: Stanislaus National Forest, Groveland Ranger District, 24545 Highway 120, Groveland, CA 95321; tel. (209) 962-7825 or fax (209) 962-7412.

23 Merced Grove
3.0 mi/1.5 hrs

There are three giant sequoia groves in Yosemite National Park—Merced, Tuolumne, and Mariposa. Because the Merced Grove is the smallest of the three groves, it is usually the least visited, which makes it the best in our opinion. Generally it only gets traffic from people who enter Yosemite at the Big Oak Flat entrance in the north and drive by it on their way to Yosemite Valley. The hiking is on a closed-off dirt road that makes good cross-country skiing in winter. The trail is level and straight for the first .5 mile; you take the left fork at a junction and head downhill through a lovely mixed forest of white firs, incense cedars, ponderosa pines, and sugar pines. You reach the small sequoia grove at 1.5 miles. The largest sequoias here are directly across the trail from a handsome old cabin. It was originally built as a retreat for the park superintendent but is no longer used. Retrace your steps from the cabin, hiking uphill for your return.

Location: In western Yosemite National Park; map E4, grid h2.

User groups: Hikers only. No dogs, horses, or mountain bikes. No wheelchair facilities.

Permits: No permits are required. There is a $20 entrance fee at Yosemite National Park, good for seven days.

Maps: Free park maps are available at park entrance stations or by contacting Yosemite National Park at the address below. A more detailed map is available for a fee from Tom Harrison Cartography, tel. (415) 456-7940. Ask the USGS for a topographic map of the Ackerson Mountain area.

Directions: From Merced drive 70 miles northeast on Highway 140 to Yosemite National Park. Follow the signs toward Yosemite Valley, entering through the Arch Rock entrance station. Continue 4.5 miles to the left turnoff for Tioga Road/Highway 120, looping back out of the valley on Big Oak Flat Road. Continue straight on Big Oak Flat Road for 13.5 miles (past the Tioga Road turnoff) to the Merced Grove parking area on the left. If you enter Yosemite from the Big Oak Flat entrance station on Highway 120, you'll drive south on Big Oak Flat Road for 4.3 miles to reach the grove on your right.

Contact: Yosemite National Park Public Information Office, P.O. Box 577, Yosemite National Park, CA 95389; tel. (209) 372-0200 or fax (209) 372-0371.

24 Tuolumne Grove

2.5 mi/1.5 hrs

What's nice about the Tuolumne Grove of giant sequoias in Yosemite National Park is that you have to walk a mile to access it, unlike the old days when motorists were allowed to drive right in. The grove is located on the old Big Oak Flat Road, which is a six-mile historic road/trail that is open to bikes and hikers. Leave your car at the parking lot near Crane Flat and hike downhill into the big trees. It's one mile to the first sequoias; you can hike farther if you like. Don't forget about the uphill return trip; save some energy for the moderate grade that climbs about 500 feet. The Tuolumne Grove's big claim to fame is that it has one of the two remaining walk-through trees in Yosemite; this one is called the Dead Giant. It's a stump that was tunneled in 1878. Go ahead, walk through it—everybody does. The grove is especially beautiful in early spring when you can take a snowshoe walk or cross-country ski through the sequoias. Of all the sights in Yosemite, there's nothing quite like the vision of those giant trees crowned with snow.

Location: In western Yosemite National Park; map E4, grid h2.

User groups: Hikers and mountain bikes. No dogs or horses. No wheelchair facilities.

Permits: No permits are required. There is a $20 entrance fee at Yosemite National Park, good for seven days.

Maps: Free park maps are available at park entrance stations or by contacting Yosemite National Park at the address below. A more detailed map is available for a fee from Tom Harrison Cartography, tel. (415) 456-7940. Ask the USGS for a topographic map of the Ackerson Mountain area.

Directions: From Merced drive 70 miles northeast on Highway 140 to Yosemite National Park. Follow the signs toward Yosemite Valley, entering through the Arch Rock entrance station. Continue 4.5 miles to the left turnoff for Tioga Road/Highway 120, looping back out of the valley on Big Oak Flat Road. In 9.3 miles turn right on Tioga Road, then drive .5 mile to the Tuolumne Grove parking lot on the left near Crane Flat.

Contact: Yosemite National Park Public Information Office, P.O. Box 577, Yosemite National Park, CA 95389; tel. (209) 372-0200 or fax (209) 372-0371.

25 Lukens Lake

1.5 mi/1.0 hr

The Lukens Lake Trail is the perfect introductory lake hike for families in Yosemite National Park. It has all the best features of a long backpacking trip to a remote alpine area without the long miles, steep climbs, and heavy weight to carry. A six-year-old could make the trip easily. A bonus is that the trailhead is on the western end of Tioga Road, so it's quickly reached from points in Yosemite Valley. The trail is .75 mile long, leading from Tioga Road up to a saddle, then dropping down to the lake. It winds through a red fir forest, then cuts across a corn lily-filled meadow to the edge of the shallow lake. It's hard to believe, but people do catch fish in this lake. Note that if you want to take a longer hike to Lukens Lake, you can start from the trailhead at White Wolf, making a 4.6 mile round-trip.

Location: Off Tioga Road in Yosemite National Park; map E4, grid g4.

User groups: Hikers only. No dogs, horses, or mountain bikes. No wheelchair facilities.

Permits: No permits are required. There is a $20 entrance fee at Yosemite National Park, good for seven days.

Maps: Free park maps are available at park entrance stations or by contacting Yosemite National Park at the address below. A more detailed map is available for a fee from Tom Harrison Cartography, tel. (415) 456-7940. Ask the USGS for a topographic map of the Tamarack Flat area.

Directions: From Merced drive 70 miles northeast on Highway 140 to Yosemite National Park. Follow the signs to Yosemite

Valley, entering through the Arch Rock entrance station. Continue 4.5 miles to the left turnoff for Tioga Road/Highway 120, looping back out of the valley on Big Oak Flat Road. In 9.3 miles turn right on Tioga Road and drive 16.2 miles to the Lukens Lake Trailhead parking area on the south side of the road. The trail begins across the road.

Contact: Yosemite National Park Public Information Office, P.O. Box 577, Yosemite National Park, CA 95389; tel. (209) 372-0200 or fax (209) 372-0371.

26 Ten Lakes/Grant Lakes
12.8 mi/1-2 days

The Ten Lakes area is incredibly popular with backpackers, so get your wilderness permit early. Or get an early-morning start and make this trip as a day hike; just be prepared for some serious climbing and long miles. From the Ten Lakes Trailhead at Tioga Road (elevation 7,500 feet), the path climbs steadily for the first four miles. There's only one brutally steep stretch, which comes between miles four and five after a pretty stroll around Half-Moon Meadow. A series of tight switchbacks pull you through an 800-foot elevation gain to the top of a ridge and the Ten Lakes/Grant Lakes junction. From there you turn right to reach Grant Lakes and head mostly downhill for a mile. To reach Ten Lakes, you continue straight, soon heading steeply downhill for 1.4 miles. The Grant Lakes offer a little more solitude (good for day-hikers), while the two larger of the Ten Lakes have the best campsites, with many trees along their shorelines offering protection from the wind. All of the lakes are sparkling, rockbound beauties. Whether you head for the Ten Lakes or the Grant Lakes, don't miss taking a side-trip to the rocky overlook above the Ten Lakes basin. It's only .5 mile from the Ten Lakes/Grant Lakes junction (continue straight for Ten Lakes, then take the unsigned trail to the left of the main trail, and head for the highest point). Four of the Ten Lakes are visible from this promontory, as well as a section of the Grand Canyon of the Tuolumne. Wow!

Location: Off Tioga Road in Yosemite National Park; map E4, grid g4.

User groups: Hikers only. No dogs, horses, or mountain bikes. No wheelchair facilities.

Permits: There is a $20 entrance fee at Yosemite National Park, good for seven days. Free wilderness permits are required for overnight stays. They are available on a first-come, first-served basis up to one day in advance at the Yosemite Wilderness kiosk near your chosen trailhead or farther in advance by mail or phone for a $5 reservation fee; call (209) 372-0740.

Maps: Free park maps are available at park entrance stations or by contacting Yosemite National Park at the address below. A more detailed map is available for a fee from Tom Harrison Cartography, tel. (415) 456-7940. Ask the USGS for topographic maps of the Yosemite Falls and Ten Lakes areas.

Directions: From Merced drive 70 miles northeast on Highway 140 to Yosemite National Park. Follow the signs toward Yosemite Valley, entering through the Arch Rock entrance station. Continue 4.5 miles to the left turnoff for Tioga Road/Highway 120, looping back out of the valley on Big Oak Flat Road. In 9.3 miles turn right on Tioga Road and drive 19.4 miles to the Yosemite Creek and Ten Lakes Trailhead parking area which is on the south side of the road. The trail begins on the north side of the road.

Contact: Yosemite National Park Public Information Office, P.O. Box 577, Yosemite National Park, CA 95389; tel. (209) 372-0200 or fax (209) 372-0371.

27 North Dome
9.0 mi/5.0 hrs

There are those who say that climbing Half Dome is a disappointment, and not just because of the crowds. When you reach the top and check out the commanding view, the panorama is not quite as awesome as you might expect, and that's because you can't see Half Dome; you're standing on it. If Half Dome is an absolute necessity in your view of Yosemite, climb North Dome instead, which offers a heart-stopping view of that big piece of granite. The route is not for the faint of heart, but when you are way up high looking down at Tenaya Canyon and across at Half Dome and Clouds Rest, well, you'll know why you came. There are two main routes to North Dome—the first is via Yosemite Valley and the Yosemite Falls Trail, but it's a long, butt-kicking trip. The better route begins at the Porcupine Creek Trailhead near Porcupine Flat Campground on Tioga Road. The dirt access road shortly brings you to a proper trail, signed as Porcupine Creek. Continue straight at two possible junctions near the 2.5-mile mark, heading due south for North Dome. After the third mile your views begin to open up, providing fine vistas of North Dome and Half Dome and increasing your anticipation. At the trail junction at 4.5 miles take the left spur for the final hike to North Dome's summit. Surprise—it's a downhill grade to reach it. Hope you brought plenty of film with you; the view from the top is sublime. Half Dome appears close enough to touch—just across the canyon. Clouds Rest is a dramatic sight to the northeast. To the southwest you can see cars crawling along the Yosemite Valley floor. On your return trip consider taking the unsigned spur trail two miles before North Dome, at an obvious saddle that leads a steep .25 mile to Indian Rock, the only natural arch on land in Yosemite. It's great fun to climb around on.

Location: Off Tioga Road in Yosemite National Park; map E4, grid h4.

User groups: Hikers only. No dogs, horses, or mountain bikes. No wheelchair facilities.

Permits: There is a $20 entrance fee at Yosemite National Park, good for seven days. Free wilderness permits are required for overnight stays. They are available on a first-come, first-served basis up to one day in advance at the Yosemite Wilderness kiosk near your chosen trailhead or farther in advance by mail or phone for a $5 reservation fee; call (209) 372-0740.

Maps: Free park maps are available at park entrance stations or by contacting Yosemite National Park at the address below. A more detailed map is available for a fee from Tom Harrison Cartography, tel. (415) 456-7940. Ask the USGS for a topographic map of the Yosemite Falls area.

Directions: From Merced drive 70 miles northeast on Highway 140 to Yosemite National Park. Follow the signs toward Yosemite Valley, entering through the Arch Rock entrance station. Continue 4.5 miles to the left turnoff for Tioga Road/Highway 120, looping back out of the valley on Big Oak Flat Road. In 9.3 miles turn right on Tioga Road and drive 24.5 miles to the Porcupine Creek Trailhead parking area on the right, a mile past Porcupine Flat Campground.

Contact: Yosemite National Park Public Information Office, P.O. Box 577, Yosemite National Park, CA 95389; tel. (209) 372-0200 or fax (209) 372-0371.

28 May Lake
2.4 mi/2.0 hrs

Here's a hike that you can take the kids on. It's an easy 1.25 miles to May Lake, tucked in below 10,850-foot Mount Hoffman. The trail's total elevation gain is only 400 feet, and better yet, it's downhill all the way home. They say May Lake is the exact geographical center of Yosemite National Park, but what matters more to most people is that it's a round, blue lake set at 9,329 feet with a spectacular mountain backdrop. The trail begins at the Snow Flat Trailhead two miles off Tioga Road, passes through a lodgepole pine forest and climbs up to granite country, then drops down to the lake's southern shore. A High Sierra Camp is located along the shore. We would recommend swimming in May Lake, but unfortunately, it's not allowed.

If you want to turn this easy walk into a butt-kicker, you can always walk around the north side of May Lake and follow the informal use trail that leads to the summit of Mount Hoffman. However, be forewarned that this is not an official park trail, and it requires scrambling skills and excellent footing to reach the summit. If you make it to the top, the view is first-class, but you won't get there without some heavy labor.

Location: Off Tioga Road in Yosemite National Park; map E4, grid g5.

User groups: Hikers and horses. No dogs or mountain bikes. No wheelchair facilities.

Permits: No permits are required. There is a $20 entrance fee at Yosemite National Park, good for seven days.

Maps: Free park maps are available at park entrance stations or by contacting Yosemite National Park at the address below. A more detailed map is available for a fee from Tom Harrison Cartography, tel. (415) 456-7940. Ask the USGS for a topographic map of the Tenaya Lake area.

Directions: From Merced drive 70 miles northeast on Highway 140 to Yosemite National Park. Follow the signs toward Yosemite Valley, entering through the Arch Rock entrance station. Continue 4.5 miles to the left turnoff for Tioga Road/Highway 120, looping back out of the valley on Big Oak Flat Road. In 9.3 miles, turn right on Tioga Road and drive 26.6 miles to the May Lake Road turnoff on the left (near road marker T-21). Drive two miles to the trailhead parking lot.

Contact: Yosemite National Park Public Information Office, P.O. Box 577, Yosemite National Park, CA 95389; tel. (209) 372-0200 or fax (209) 372-0371.

29 Clouds Rest

14.0 mi/8.0 hrs

Hiking to Clouds Rest is a trip that's as epic as climbing Half Dome, with fewer people elbowing you along the way. But with a 2,300-foot climb and 14 miles to cover, it's not for those who are out of shape. The trail ascends steadily for the first four miles, descends

steeply for .5 mile, then climbs again more moderately. Keep the faith—the first 2.5 miles from the trailhead are the toughest. The final summit ascent is a little dicey because of the terrifying drop-offs, but as with other Yosemite peaks, watch your footing on the granite slabs and you'll be fine. Overall, the route is much safer than climbing Half Dome because the final ascent is far more gradual and there are no cables to maneuver. The view from the top of Clouds Rest—of Tenaya Canyon, Half Dome, Yosemite Valley, Tenaya Lake, the Clark Range, and various peaks and ridges—will knock your socks off. Hope you brought along an extra pair. Note that if this long hike has made you hot and sweaty, you can stop at the Sunrise Lakes for a swim on the way back—the first lake is only .25 mile from the Clouds Rest/Sunrise trail junction.

Location: Off Tioga Road in Yosemite National Park; map E4, grid g6.

User groups: Hikers only. No dogs, horses, or mountain bikes. No wheelchair facilities.

Permits: No permits are required. There is a $20 entrance fee at Yosemite National Park, good for seven days.

Maps: Free park maps are available at park entrance stations or by contacting Yosemite National Park at the address below. A more detailed map is available for a fee from Tom Harrison Cartography, tel. (415) 456-7940. Ask the USGS for a topographic map of the Tenaya Lake area.

Directions: From Merced drive 70 miles northeast on Highway 140 to Yosemite National Park. Follow the signs toward Yosemite Valley, entering through the Arch Rock entrance station. Continue 4.5 miles to the left turnoff for Tioga Road/Highway 120, looping back out of the valley on Big Oak Flat Road. In 9.3 miles turn right on Tioga Road and drive 30.3 miles to the Sunrise Lakes Trailhead on the south side of Tioga Road just west of Tenaya Lake.

Contact: Yosemite National Park Public Information Office, P.O. Box 577, Yosemite National Park, CA 95389; tel. (209) 372-0200 or fax (209) 372-0371.

30 Sunrise Lakes

7.5 mi/4.5 hrs or 2.0 days

With all the people hiking to Clouds Rest, combined with all the people hiking to the Sunrise Lakes, the Sunrise Trailhead can look like a mall parking lot on a Saturday. But don't be scared off; the hike to Sunrise Lakes is a great day hike or easy backpacking trip, especially during the week or off season, with only a 1,000-foot elevation gain and a ton of stellar scenery, including great views of Clouds Rest at your back as you hike the final stretch to the lakes. You follow the trail as it climbs steeply above the edge of Tenaya Canyon. At 2.5 miles, turn left at the sign for the Sunrise High Sierra Camp. In about 10 minutes of easy walking, Lower Sunrise Lake shows up on the right, and the other lakes are shortly after it on the left. The upper lake is the largest and by far the most popular; lots of folks like to swim and picnic there on warm summer days. Backpackers can pick a site here or continue onward for two more miles to the backpackers' camp or the High Sierra Camp, depending on where they've made their plans.

Location: Off Tioga Road in Yosemite National Park; map E4, grid g6.

User groups: Hikers only. No dogs, horses, or mountain bikes. No wheelchair facilities.

Permits: There is a $20 entrance fee at Yosemite National Park, good for seven days. Free wilderness permits are required for overnight stays. They are available on a first-come, first-served basis up to one day in advance at the Yosemite Wilderness kiosk near your chosen trailhead or farther in advance by mail or phone for a $5 reservation fee; call (209) 372-0740.

Maps: Free park maps are available at park entrance stations or by contacting Yosemite National Park at the address below. A more detailed map is available for a fee from Tom Harrison Cartography, tel. (415) 456-7940. Ask the USGS for a topographic map of the Tenaya Lake area.

Directions: From Merced drive 70 miles north-east on Highway 140 to Yosemite National Park. Follow the signs toward Yosemite Valley, entering through the Arch Rock entrance station. Continue 4.5 miles to the left turnoff for Tioga Road/Highway 120, looping back out of the valley on Big Oak Flat Road. In 9.3 miles turn right on Tioga Road and drive 30.3 miles to the Sunrise Lakes trailhead on the south side of Tioga Road just west of Tenaya Lake.

Contact: Yosemite National Park Public Information Office, P.O. Box 577, Yosemite National Park, CA 95389; tel. (209) 372-0200 or fax (209) 372-0371.

31 Tenaya Lake

2.0 mi/1.0 hr

Lots of people drive east down Tioga Road in a big rush to get to Tuolumne Meadows, but when they see giant Tenaya Lake right along the road, they stop in their tire tracks. Luckily the 150-acre, sapphire-blue lake has a parking lot and picnic area at its east end where you can leave your car and take a stroll down to the lake's edge. While most people stop at the white-sand beach and picnic tables to watch the rock climbers on nearby Polly Dome, you can leave the crowds behind and stroll to the south side of the beach. Pick up the trail there that leads along the back side of Tenaya Lake, far from the road on the north side. When you get to the lake's west end, where the trail continues but the water views end, just turn around and walk back. It's a perfect, easy hike alongside one of the most beautiful lakes in Yosemite.

Location: Off Tioga Road in Yosemite National Park; map E4, grid g6.

User groups: Hikers only. No dogs, horses, or mountain bikes. No wheelchair facilities.

Permits: No permits are required. There is a $20 entrance fee at Yosemite National Park, good for seven days.

Maps: Free park maps are available at park entrance stations or by contacting Yosemite National Park at the address

below. A more detailed map is available for a fee from Tom Harrison Cartography, tel. (415) 456-7940. Ask the USGS for a topographic map of the Tenaya Lake area.

Directions: From Merced drive 70 miles northeast on Highway 140 to Yosemite National Park. Follow the signs toward Yosemite Valley, entering through the Arch Rock entrance station. Continue 4.5 miles to the left turnoff for Tioga Road/Highway 120, looping back out of the valley on Big Oak Flat Road. In 9.3 miles turn right on Tioga Road and drive 31.7 miles to the eastern Tenaya Lake picnic area (there is another Tenaya Lake picnic area .5 mile west of this one). The trail leads from the parking lot.

Contact: Yosemite National Park Public Information Office, P.O. Box 577, Yosemite National Park, CA 95389; tel. (209) 372-0200 or fax (209) 372-0371.

32 Cathedral Lakes
7.4 mi/4.0 hrs or 2.0 days

The Cathedral Lakes are a tremendously popular easy backpacking destination in Yosemite, but it's such a short hike to reach them that it also makes a great day trip. Located on a .5-mile spur off the John Muir Trail, the lakes are within a classic glacial cirque, tucked in below 10,840-foot Cathedral Peak. It's as scenic a spot as you'll find anywhere in Yosemite. Campsites are found close to the lakes but you will need to secure your wilderness permit way in advance in order to spend the night. From the trail's start at Tioga Road it's a 3.2-mile hike on the John Muir Trail with a 1,000-foot elevation gain. Much of the trail is shaded by lodgepole pines, but when the path breaks out of the trees, views of surrounding peaks (especially distinctive Cathedral Peak, which looks remarkably different from every angle) keep you oohing and ahhing the whole way. At 3.2 miles turn right on the Cathedral Lake spur to reach the lower, larger lake in .5 mile. You'll follow the lake's inlet stream through a gorgeous meadow to the water's edge, then start snapping photographs like crazy. To reach the upper lake, retrace your steps to the John Muir Trail and continue on it for another .5 mile. Fishing is often better in the upper lake, and the scenery is almost as sublime.

Location: Near Tuolumne Meadows in Yosemite National Park; map E4, grid g7.

User groups: Hikers and horses. No dogs or mountain bikes. No wheelchair facilities.

Permits: There is a $20 entrance fee at Yosemite National Park, good for seven days. Free wilderness permits are required for overnight stays. They are available on a first-come, first-served basis up to one day in advance at the Yosemite Wilderness kiosk near your chosen trailhead or farther in advance by mail or phone for a $5 reservation fee; call (209) 372-0740.

Maps: Free park maps are available at park entrance stations or by contacting Yosemite National Park at the address below. A more detailed map is available for a fee from Tom Harrison Cartography, tel. (415) 456-7940. Ask the USGS for a topographic map of the Tenaya Lake area.

Directions: From Merced drive 70 miles northeast on Highway 140 to Yosemite National Park. Follow the signs toward Yosemite Valley, entering through the Arch Rock entrance station. Continue 4.5 miles to the left turnoff for Tioga Road/Highway 120, looping back out of the valley on Big Oak Flat Road. In 9.3 miles turn right on Tioga Road and drive 37.4 miles to the Cathedral Lakes Trailhead on the right, by Tuolumne Meadows. Park your car in the pullouts on either side of Tioga Road near the trailhead; there is no formal parking lot.

Contact: Yosemite National Park Public Information Office, P.O. Box 577, Yosemite National Park, CA 95389; tel. (209) 372-0200 or fax (209) 372-0371.

33 Vogelsang Loop
19.0 mi/3-4 days

Although this loop is popular with backpackers using the Vogelsang High Sierra Camp, hikers who plan early can get a wilderness permit for their own self-designed backpacking trip.

Then they can take the loop at their leisure and spend a few peaceful days in the Yosemite backcountry. The traditional route is to head out on the western side of the loop along Rafferty Creek, then take a short spur off the loop and spend the night at Vogelsang Lake, which is without question the most visually dramatic spot seen on this trip. It's flanked by Fletcher Peak, a steep and rugged wall of glacier-carved granite. Only a few trees dare grow in this sparse high-alpine environment. The next day you rejoin the loop and continue eastward to Evelyn Lake, another favorite camping spot. When it's time to return, you hike down to Lyell Fork, a 2,000-foot descent that takes a few hours, then meet up with the John Muir Trail and follow it north through lush green and gorgeous Lyell Canyon, back to the trailhead at Tuolumne Meadows. The trailhead is at 8,600 feet, plenty high to start, and for the most part the trail undulates along, never gaining or losing more than 2,000 feet.

Location: Near Tuolumne Meadows in Yosemite National Park; map E4, grid g7.

User groups: Hikers and horses. No dogs or mountain bikes. No wheelchair facilities.

Permits: There is a $20 entrance fee at Yosemite National Park, good for seven days. Free wilderness permits are required for overnight stays. They are available on a first-come, first-served basis up to one day in advance at the Yosemite Wilderness kiosk near your chosen trailhead or farther in advance by mail or phone for a $5 reservation fee; call (209) 372-0740.

Maps: Free park maps are available at park entrance stations or by contacting Yosemite National Park at the address below. A more detailed map is available for a fee from Tom Harrison Cartography, tel. (415) 456-7940. Ask the USGS for a topographic map of the Vogelsang Peak area.

Directions: From Merced drive 70 miles northeast on Highway 140 to Yosemite National Park. Follow the signs toward Yosemite Valley, entering through the Arch Rock entrance station. Continue 4.5 miles to the left turnoff for Tioga Road/Highway 120, looping back out of the valley on Big Oak Flat Road. In 9.3 miles turn right on Tioga Road and drive 39.5 miles to the Tuolumne Lodge and Wilderness Permits turnoff on the right. Turn right and drive 0.4 mile toward Tuolumne Lodge. Park in the lot on the left signed for Dog Lake and John Muir Trail. The trail begins across the road from the parking lot. Additional parking is available in the Wilderness Permit parking lot at the turnoff from Tioga Road.

Contact: Yosemite National Park Public Information Office, P.O. Box 577, Yosemite National Park, CA 95389; tel. (209) 372-0200 or fax (209) 372-0371.

34 Lower Gaylor Lake
8.0 mi/4.0 hrs

A surprising variation on the Middle and Upper Gaylor Lakes hike, below, this route starts on the John Muir Trail near Tuolumne Lodge, then heads east along the south side of the Dana Fork Tuolumne River. After two miles the trail crosses the river and Tioga Road and heads uphill to Lower Gaylor Lake, elevation 10,049 feet. Note that if you want to get to the Upper and Middle Gaylor Lakes from the lower lake you have to go cross-country; the easier way to reach them is to drive to the Tioga Pass Trailhead and follow the trail notes in the Middle and Upper Gaylor Lakes hike. This hike, however, draws fewer crowds, which is why we prefer it. Elevation at this trailhead is 9,250 feet; the total gain is about 800 feet to Lower Gaylor Lake, a gentle climb the whole way. The lake is a deep turquoise color and hemmed in by granite, and from its edge you get wide vistas of the peaks in the Tuolumne Meadows area. This is classic high-country beauty at its finest.

Location: Near Tioga Pass in Yosemite National Park; map E4, grid g7.

User groups: Hikers only. No dogs, horses, or mountain bikes. No wheelchair facilities.

Permits: No permits are required. There is a $20 entrance fee at Yosemite National Park, good for seven days.

Maps: Free park maps are available at park entrance stations or by contacting Yosemite National Park at the address below. A more detailed map is available for a fee from Tom Harrison Cartography, tel. (415) 456-7940. Ask the USGS for topographic maps of the Vogelsang Peak and Tioga Pass areas.

Directions: From Merced drive 70 miles northeast on Highway 140 to Yosemite National Park. Follow the signs toward Yosemite Valley, entering through the Arch Rock entrance station. Continue 4.5 miles to the left turnoff for Tioga Road/Highway 120, looping back out of the valley on Big Oak Flat Road. In 9.3 miles turn right on Tioga Road and drive 39.5 miles to the Tuolumne Lodge and Wilderness Permits turnoff on the right. Turn right and drive 0.4 mile toward Tuolumne Lodge, then park in the lot on the left signed for Dog Lake and John Muir Trail. The trail begins across the road from the parking lot. Additional parking is available in the Wilderness Permit parking lot at the turnoff from Tioga Road.

Contact: Yosemite National Park Public Information Office, P.O. Box 577, Yosemite National Park, CA 95389; tel. (209) 372-0200 or fax (209) 372-0371.

35 Elizabeth Lake
4.5 mi/2.5 hrs

Starting at the trailhead elevation of 8,600 feet, you have a mere 900-foot elevation gain over 2.25 miles to get to pretty Elizabeth Lake, a day hike that is attainable for almost everybody. The only problem is that almost nobody can find the trailhead tucked into the back of Tuolumne Meadows Campground, across from the group camp restrooms. Once you locate it, be prepared to climb steeply for the first mile, then breathe easier when the trail levels out. Luckily the route is mostly shaded by lodgepole pines. Your reward is a gorgeous little lake at the base of Unicorn Peak, the kind of place to spread out a picnic, or for the brave to

take a swim provided you don't show up during the mosquito hatch, like we did. Some folks try to climb Unicorn Peak (10,900 feet) from the lake, but most are happy to sit around and admire the views of it and its neighboring peaks in the Cathedral Range.

Location: Near Tuolumne Meadows in Yosemite National Park; map E4, grid g7.

User groups: Hikers only. No dogs, horses, or mountain bikes. No wheelchair facilities.

Permits: No permits are required. There is a $20 entrance fee at Yosemite National Park, good for seven days.

Maps: Free park maps are available at park entrance stations or by contacting Yosemite National Park at the address below. A more detailed map is available for a fee from Tom Harrison Cartography, tel. (415) 456-7940. Ask the USGS for a topographic map of the Vogelsang Peak area.

Directions: From Merced drive 70 miles northeast on Highway 140 to Yosemite National Park. Follow the signs toward Yosemite Valley, entering through the Arch Rock entrance station. Continue 4.5 miles to the left turnoff for Tioga Road/Highway 120, looping back out of the valley on Big Oak Flat Road. In 9.3 miles turn right on Tioga Road and drive 39 miles to the Tuolumne Meadows Campground. Turn right and follow the signs through the main camp to the group camp. The trail begins across from the group camp restrooms near group site B49.

Contact: Yosemite National Park Public Information Office, P.O. Box 577, Yosemite National Park, CA 95389; tel. (209) 372-0200 or fax (209) 372-0371.

36 Lyell Canyon
6.0 mi/3.0 hrs

This hike is one of the easiest in the Yosemite high country, and since it is virtually flat, and also starts out beautiful and stays that way all along, you can hike it as long or as short as you like. The total trail length is eight miles one way, paralleling the Lyell Fork of the

Tuolumne River on the Pacific Crest Trail/John Muir Trail, but most people just head out for two or three miles, carrying their fishing rods, and turn back. To reach the Lyell Fork you must first cross the Dana Fork on a footbridge less than .5 mile from the parking lot. Then after .5 mile, you cross the Lyell Fork on a second footbridge, and head left along the river's south side. A third bridge takes you across Rafferty Creek and into Lyell Canyon. If you like looking at gorgeous meadows and a meandering river, this is your hike. Small trout are plentiful. A bonus is that there are backpacking sites three to four miles out on the trail, so if you get a wilderness permit you can linger for a few days in paradise.

Location: Near Tuolumne Meadows in Yosemite National Park; map E4, grid g7.

User groups: Hikers and horses. No dogs or mountain bikes. No wheelchair facilities.

Permits: No permits are required. There is a $20 entrance fee at Yosemite National Park, good for seven days.

Maps: Free park maps are available at park entrance stations or by contacting Yosemite National Park at the address below. A more detailed map is available for a fee from Tom Harrison Cartography, tel. (415) 456-7940. Ask the USGS for a topographic map of the Vogelsang Peak area.

Directions: From Merced drive 70 miles northeast on Highway 140 to Yosemite National Park. Follow the signs toward Yosemite Valley, entering through the Arch Rock entrance station. Continue 4.5 miles to the left turnoff for Tioga Road/Highway 120, looping back out of the valley on Big Oak Flat Road. In 9.3 miles turn right on Tioga Road and drive 39.5 miles to the Tuolumne Lodge and Wilderness Permits turnoff on the right. Turn right and drive 0.4 mile toward Tuolumne Lodge; park in the lot on the left signed for Dog Lake and John Muir Trail. The trail begins across the road from the parking lot. Additional parking is available in the Wilderness Permit parking lot at the turnoff from Tioga Road.

Contact: Yosemite National Park Public Information Office, P.O. Box 577, Yosemite National Park, CA 95389; tel. (209) 372-0200 or fax (209) 372-0371.

37 Young Lakes Loop
12.5 mi/1-2 days

Starting from the Lembert Dome parking lot, the Young Lakes Loop is a classic Yosemite trip that works equally well as a short backpacking trip or a long day hike. The destination is a series of lakes set in a deep and wide glacial cirque—the kind of awesome scenery that sticks in your mind months later when you're sitting at a desk somewhere staring at your computer screen. The trip starts with a walk down the wide dirt road that leads to Soda Spring, on the west side of the Lembert Dome parking lot. Pick up the trail near Parson's Lodge that leads to Glen Aulin and follow it through lodgepole pines for 1.8 miles until you see the right turnoff for Young Lakes. Follow the Young Lakes Trail for three more miles, climbing steadily. At five miles out you'll see the return leg of your loop leading off to the right (signed for Dog Lake). You'll continue straight for another 1.5 miles to Lower Young Lake and a stunning view of Mount Conness and White Mountain. Two more lakes are accessible within a mile to the east. If you have the energy, don't miss the third, upper lake, the most visually stunning of them all. When you're ready to head home, retrace your steps to the junction and take the eastern (left) fork, returning via Dog Lake and Lembert Dome. Be forewarned: if you loop back this way, it won't be an all-downhill cruise, but the scenery makes the additional climbing worthwhile. If you're exhausted from your trip to the lakes, skip the loop and return the way you came—it's downhill all the way.

Location: Near Tuolumne Meadows in Yosemite National Park; map E4, grid g7.

User groups: Hikers and horses. No dogs or mountain bikes. No wheelchair facilities.

Permits: There is a $20 entrance fee at Yosemite National Park, good for seven days. Free wilderness permits are required for overnight stays. They are available on a first-come, first-served basis up to one day in advance at the Yosemite Wilderness kiosk near your chosen trailhead or farther in advance by mail or phone for a $5 reservation fee; call (209) 372-0740.

Maps: Free park maps are available at park entrance stations or by contacting Yosemite National Park at the address below. A more detailed map is available for a fee from Tom Harrison Cartography, tel. (415) 456-7940. Ask the USGS for topographic maps of the Tioga Pass and Falls Ridge areas.

Directions: From Merced drive 70 miles northeast on Highway 140 to Yosemite National Park. Follow the signs toward Yosemite Valley, entering through the Arch Rock entrance station. Continue 4.5 miles to the left turnoff for Tioga Road/Highway 120, looping back out of the valley on Big Oak Flat Road. In 9.3 miles turn right on Tioga Road and drive 39 miles to the Lembert Dome/Soda Springs/Dog Lake/Glen Aulin Trailhead, parking on the left. Begin hiking on the western edge of the parking lot where there is a gated dirt road signed "Soda Springs, 0.5 mile."

Contact: Yosemite National Park Public Information Office, P.O. Box 577, Yosemite National Park, CA 95389; tel. (209) 372-0200 or fax (209) 372-0371.

38 Waterwheel Falls

16.0 mi/1-2 days

This hike is the Epic Waterfall Trip. If you hike the entire route, you'll see so many waterfalls and so much water along the way that you'll have enough memories to get you through a 10-year drought. The best way to do it is to arrange for a wilderness permit in advance or reserve a stay at the Glen Aulin High Sierra Camp so that you can divide the 16 miles of trail over two or more days. If you're in good enough shape, you can do the trip in one day,

because the trail is nearly flat for the first four miles (a 400-foot elevation loss), then descends some more over the next four miles (a 1,500-foot elevation loss). Unfortunately, all the climbing must be done on the way home, so you must reserve your energy and have plenty of food and water. Follow the trail notes for Glen Aulin and Tuolumne Falls, below, for the first four miles of trail; then continue downstream past Glen Aulin Camp, alternating between stretches of stunning flower- and aspen-lined meadows and stark granite slabs. Waterwheel Falls is only three miles from the camp, and two other major cascades, California and LeConte, are along the way. To see all three falls, make sure you take every spur trail you see that leads to the left off the main trail; none of the waterfalls is apparent from the main trail. People will stop you on the trail to ask if you know where the waterfalls are. While all three falls are long whitewater cascades, Waterwheel is considered Yosemite's most unusual-looking waterfall because it has sections of churning water that dip into deep holes in the granite, then shoot out with such velocity that they seem to double back on themselves. When the river level is high, they actually appear to circle around like waterwheels.

Location: Near Tuolumne Meadows in Yosemite National Park; map E4, grid g7.

User groups: Hikers and horses. No dogs or mountain bikes. No wheelchair facilities.

Permits: There is a $20 entrance fee at Yosemite National Park, good for seven days. Free wilderness permits are required for overnight stays. They are available on a first-come, first-served basis up to one day in advance at the Yosemite Wilderness kiosk near your chosen trailhead or farther in advance by mail or phone for a $5 reservation fee; call (209) 372-0740.

Maps: Free park maps are available at park entrance stations or by contacting Yosemite National Park at the address below. A more detailed map is available for a fee from Tom Harrison Cartography, tel. (415) 456-7940. Ask the USGS for topographic maps of the Tioga Pass and Falls Ridge areas.

Directions: From Merced drive 70 miles northeast on Highway 140 to Yosemite National Park. Follow the signs toward Yosemite Valley, entering through the Arch Rock entrance station. Continue 4.5 miles to the left turnoff for Tioga Road/Highway 120, looping back out of the valley on Big Oak Flat Road. In 9.3 miles turn right on Tioga Road and drive 39 miles to the Lembert Dome/Soda Springs/Dog Lake/Glen Aulin Trailhead, parking on the left. Begin hiking on the western edge of the parking lot, where there is a gated dirt road signed "Soda Springs, 0.5 mile."

Contact: Yosemite National Park Public Information Office, P.O. Box 577, Yosemite National Park, CA 95389; tel. (209) 372-0200 or fax (209) 372-0371.

39 Glen Aulin and Tuolumne Falls

9.0 mi/5.0 hrs

Those who aren't up for the Epic Waterfall Trip to Waterwheel Falls, above, can take this trip instead and maybe even sneak in a good meal at the Glen Aulin High Sierra Camp. To stay in the camp you must reserve a space a year in advance, but you can often purchase a hot meal just by showing up. Tuolumne Falls drops right by the High Sierra Camp, and reaching it requires only a 4.5-mile one-way walk with a 400-foot elevation loss. The return climb is easy, with most of the ascent being in the first mile as you head up and over the various cascades of Tuolumne Falls on granite stairs. Follow the dirt road from the Lembert Dome parking lot toward Soda Spring. When you near Parson's Lodge, veer right on the signed trail to Glen Aulin. You'll walk through forest, then move closer to the Tuolumne River and get incredible views of Cathedral and Unicorn Peaks and Fairview Dome. After three miles you'll cross the Tuolumne on a footbridge and in another .25 mile reach the first stunning drop of Tuolumne Falls, a 100-foot churning

free fall. Keep descending past more cascades to the base of the falls, where another footbridge leads back across the river and to Glen Aulin. Pick a spot downstream beside a river pool or near the bridge at the base of the waterfall, have a seat, and ponder the beauty of the world.

Location: Near Tuolumne Meadows in Yosemite National Park; map E4, grid g7.

User groups: Hikers and horses. No dogs or mountain bikes. No wheelchair facilities.

Permits: No permits are required. There is a $20 entrance fee at Yosemite National Park, good for seven days.

Maps: Free park maps are available at park entrance stations or by contacting Yosemite National Park at the address below. A more detailed map is available for a fee from Tom Harrison Cartography, tel. (415) 456-7940. Ask the USGS for topographic maps of the Tioga Pass and Falls Ridge areas.

Directions: From Merced drive 70 miles northeast on Highway 140 to Yosemite National Park. Follow the signs toward Yosemite Valley, entering through the Arch Rock entrance station. Continue 4.5 miles to the left turnoff for Tioga Road/Highway 120, looping back out of the valley on Big Oak Flat Road. In 9.3 miles turn right on Tioga Road and drive 39 miles to the Lembert Dome/Soda Springs/Dog Lake/Glen Aulin Trailhead, parking on the left. Begin hiking on the western edge of the parking lot where there is a gated dirt road signed "Soda Springs, 0.5 mile."

Contact: Yosemite National Park Public Information Office, P.O. Box 577, Yosemite National Park, CA 95389; tel. (209) 372-0200 or fax (209) 372-0371.

40 Lembert Dome

2.8 mi/1.5 hrs

Lembert Dome is a *roche moutonnée,* which is a French geologic term that means it looks something like a sheep. Well, we never saw the resemblance, but we did feel like a couple of mountain goats when we climbed Lembert Dome, elevation 9,450 feet. From the parking area at Lembert Dome's base, you can see rock climbers practicing their stuff on the steep side of the dome, but luckily the hiker's trail heads around to the more sloped back side where you can walk right up the granite—no ropes necessary. The Dog Lake and Lembert Dome Trail winds its way steeply around to the dome's north side (see Dog Lake, below); from there you pick any route along the granite that looks manageable. When you reach the top of the dome, you know that you've accomplished something. The view from its highest point—of Tuolumne Meadows and surrounding peaks and domes—is more than worth the effort.

Location: Near Tuolumne Meadows in Yosemite National Park; map E4, grid g7.

User groups: Hikers only. No dogs, horses, or mountain bikes. No wheelchair facilities.

Permits: No permits are required. There is a $20 entrance fee at Yosemite National Park, good for seven days.

Maps: Free park maps are available at park entrance stations or by contacting Yosemite National Park at the address below. A more detailed map is available for a fee from Tom Harrison Cartography, tel. (415) 456-7940. Ask the USGS for a topographic map of the Tioga Pass area.

Directions: From Merced drive 70 miles northeast on Highway 140 to Yosemite National Park. Follow the signs toward Yosemite Valley, entering through the Arch Rock entrance station. Continue 4.5 miles to the left turnoff for Tioga Road/Highway 120, looping back out of the valley on Big Oak Flat Road. In 9.3 miles turn right on Tioga Road and drive 39 miles to the Lembert Dome/Soda Springs/Dog Lake/Glen Aulin Trailhead, parking on the left. Begin hiking on the trail near the restrooms.

Contact: Yosemite National Park Public Information Office, P.O. Box 577, Yosemite National Park, CA 95389; tel. (209) 372-0200 or fax (209) 372-0371.

41 Dog Lake
3.4 mi/2.0 hrs

Dog Lake is an easy-to-reach destination from Tuolumne Meadows, a perfect place for a family to spend an afternoon in the high country. The hike begins near the base of Lembert Dome, then heads through a gorgeous meadow which offers views of snowy Cathedral and Unicorn Peaks. The trail traverses a granite slab, then splits off from the path to Lembert Dome and starts to climb steeply through a lodgepole pine and fir forest. When you reach an intersection with the Young Lakes Trail you're only .25 mile from Dog Lake. The lake is a delight to see—it's set at 9,170 feet in elevation, and it's wide, shallow, and deep blue. The colorful red peaks to the east are Mount Dana and Mount Gibbs. You can hike around its perimeter if you please, try a swim in late summer, or just sit by its peaceful shore and relax.

Location: Near Tuolumne Meadows in Yosemite National Park; map E4, grid g7.

User groups: Hikers and horses. No dogs or mountain bikes. No wheelchair facilities.

Permits: No permits are required. There is a $20 entrance fee at Yosemite National Park, good for seven days.

Maps: Free park maps are available at park entrance stations or by contacting Yosemite National Park at the address below. A more detailed map is available for a fee from Tom Harrison Cartography, tel. (415) 456-7940. Ask the USGS for a topographic map of the Tioga Pass area.

Directions: From Merced drive 70 miles northeast on Highway 140 to Yosemite National Park. Follow the signs toward Yosemite Valley, entering through the Arch Rock entrance station. Continue 4.5 miles to the left turnoff for Tioga Road/Highway 120, looping back out of the valley on Big Oak Flat Road. In 9.3 miles turn right on Tioga Road and drive 39 miles to the Lembert Dome/Soda Springs/Dog Lake/Glen Aulin Trailhead, parking on the left. Begin hiking on the trail near the restrooms.

Contact: Yosemite National Park Public Information Office, P.O. Box 577, Yosemite National Park, CA 95389; tel. (209) 372-0200 or fax (209) 372-0371.

42 Mono Pass
8.4 mi/4.5 hrs

With an elevation gain of only 900 feet spread out over four miles you'll hardly even notice you're climbing on the route to Mono Pass. That's if you're acclimated, of course, because you're starting out at 9,700 feet, where the air is mighty thin. The trail passes through barren, high-elevation lodgepole pine forests and meadows, and crosses the Dana Fork of the Tuolumne River (an easy boulder hop). Besides Mono Pass itself, the big attractions on the trail are the old mining cabins from the 19th century, some of which have been restored. Take the right spur trail at the Mono Pass sign 3.8 miles from the trailhead to see the best of them, a group of four side-by-side cabins. The hike to the pass offers great views of Mount Gibbs, Mount Dana, and the Kuna Crest. Don't stop hiking at the Mono Pass sign; continue past it for another .5 mile for the best views, looking down at Mono Lake and the surrounding desert.

Location: Near Tioga Pass in Yosemite National Park; map E4, grid g8.

User groups: Hikers and horses. No dogs or mountain bikes. No wheelchair facilities.

Permits: No permits are required. There is a $20 entrance fee at Yosemite National Park, good for seven days.

Maps: Free park maps are available at park entrance stations or by contacting Yosemite National Park at the address below. A more detailed map is available for a fee from Tom Harrison Cartography, tel. (415) 456-7940. Ask the USGS for a topographic map of the Tioga Pass area.

Directions: From Merced drive 70 miles northeast on Highway 140 to Yosemite National Park. Follow the signs toward Yosemite Valley, entering through the Arch Rock entrance station. Continue 4.5 miles to the left turnoff for Tioga Road/Highway 120, looping back out of the valley on Big Oak Flat Road. In 9.3 miles turn right on Tioga Road and drive 44.5 miles to the Mono Pass Trailhead, parking on the south side of the road near road marker T-37, 1.5 miles west of Tioga Pass.

Contact: Yosemite National Park Public Information Office, P.O. Box 577, Yosemite National Park, CA 95389; tel. (209) 372-0200 or fax (209) 372-0371.

43 Middle and Upper Gaylor Lakes
4.0 mi/2.5 hrs

The trail to Middle and Upper Gaylor Lakes is incredibly popular, which is another way of saying that it offers world-class scenery that completely wows visitors. Starting near Tioga Pass at nearly 10,000 feet, the trail climbs a ridge and then drops down to Middle Gaylor Lake. Though it's only a mile of hiking, it has a steep initial climb that makes many beg for mercy. From the middle lake you can follow the creek gently uphill to the east to reach smaller Upper Gaylor Lake in another mile. Take the trail around its north side and uphill for a few hundred yards to the site of the Great Sierra Mine and the remains of an old stone cabin. The Great Sierra Mine turned out to be not so great—no silver ore was ever refined, and the mine was eventually abandoned. The hauntingly beautiful glacial scenery is what remains. Total elevation gain on the hike to Upper Gaylor Lake is about 1,000 feet and worth every step.

Location: Near Tioga Pass in Yosemite National Park; map E4, grid g8.

User groups: Hikers only. No dogs, horses, or mountain bikes. No wheelchair facilities.

Permits: No permits are required. There is a $20 entrance fee at Yosemite National Park, good for seven days.

Maps: Free park maps are available at park entrance stations or by contacting Yosemite National Park at the address

below. A more detailed map is available for a fee from Tom Harrison Cartography, tel. (415) 456-7940. Ask the USGS for a topographic map of the Tioga Pass area.

Directions: From Merced drive miles northeast on Highway 140 to Yosemite National Park. Follow the signs toward Yosemite Valley, entering through the Arch Rock entrance station. Continue 4.5 miles to the left turnoff for Tioga Road/Highway 120, looping back out of the valley on Big Oak Flat Road. In 9.3 miles turn right on Tioga Road and drive 46 miles to the parking lot just west of the Tioga Pass Entrance Station on the north side of Tioga Road.

Contact: Yosemite National Park Public Information Office, P.O. Box 577, Yosemite National Park, CA 95389; tel. (209) 372-0200 or fax (209) 372-0371.

44 Gardisky Lake
2.0 mi/2.0 hrs

How can a two-mile round-trip hike be rated a four for difficulty? It can because it goes straight up, gaining 1,000 feet in just one mile with not nearly enough switchbacks. Although the trail distance is short, the trailhead is set at 10,000 feet, which means you don't have much oxygen for that kind of intense climbing. Hope you're acclimated. The trip offers many rewards, though, such as fewer people than nearby Saddlebag Lake and a stellar high-alpine setting. That 11,500-foot mountain you're looking at (ahead and to your right as you climb) is Tioga Peak.

Location: In Inyo National Forest just east of Tioga Pass; map E4, grid g8.

User groups: Hikers and dogs. No horses or mountain bikes. No wheelchair facilities.

Permits: No permits are required. Parking and access are free.

Maps: For a map of Inyo National Forest, send $6 to U.S. Forest Service, Map Sales, P.O. Box 587, Camino, CA 95709; tel. (530) 647-5390 or website: www.r5.fs.fed.us/visitorcenter. Ask the USGS for a topographic map of the Tioga Pass area.

Directions: From Merced drive 70 miles northeast on Highway 140 to Yosemite National Park. Follow the signs toward Yosemite Valley, entering through the Arch Rock entrance station. Continue 4.5 miles to the left turnoff for Tioga Road/Highway 120, looping back out of the valley on Big Oak Flat Road. In 9.3 miles turn right on Tioga Road and drive 48 miles (you'll exit the park) to the Saddlebag Lake turnoff on the left, two miles east of Tioga Pass. Turn left and go 1.3 miles to the trailhead parking area on the west side of the road before you reach Saddlebag Lake. The trail begins across the road.

Contact: Inyo National Forest, Mono Lake Ranger District, P.O. Box 429, Lee Vining, CA 93541; tel. (760) 647-3044 or fax (760) 647-3046.

45 Saddlebag Lake Loop
3.6 mi/2.0 hrs

Located just east of Tioga Pass and in the heart of the 20 Lakes Basin, Saddlebag Lake at 10,087 feet is a slice of paradise that's just outside the border of Yosemite National Park. The high-alpine setting is as good as anything in the park, and unfortunately on summer weekends the crowds are just as apparent. A fun aspect of hiking here is that you can make a shuttle trip by hiking one way along the length of Saddlebag Lake, then taking the boat taxi back for a fee. It cuts 1.5 miles off your total mileage and it increases the number of places you can access if you wish to go farther than this loop around the lake. You can also take the shuttle both ways and cut three miles off your trip. The only downer to the boat taxi is that because of it hikers sometimes have to contend with yahoos who bring coolers of food and drink with them, and leave their litter behind. Hopefully with increased education and awareness, this ludicrous behavior will stop; spread the word to offenders about "leaving no trace." To hike along Saddlebag Lake, you can take either of two trails, on the lake's east or west side. The trail on the west side is closest to the hiker parking area and campground, and it leads 1.5 miles to little Greenstone Lake. Look to your right and you'll see the trail coming from Saddlebag Lake's east side. To make a short 3.6-mile loop, turn right here and head back. If you continue onward instead, you'll start to climb in earnest, but your reward is the chance to visit several more lakes in the Hoover Wilderness, including Wasco, Steelhead, Shamrock, and Helen. No matter how far you go, you'll be awed by the incredibly stark scenery—just granite, water, and the occasional hardy whitebark pine.

Location: In Inyo National Forest just east of Tioga Pass; map E4, grid g9.

User groups: Hikers and dogs. No horses or mountain bikes. No wheelchair facilities.

Permits: No day-use permits are required. Parking and access are free.

Maps: For a map of Inyo National Forest, send $8 to U.S. Forest Service, Map Sales, P.O. Box 587, Camino, CA 95709; tel. (530) 647-5390 or website: www.r5.fs.fed.us/visitorcenter. Ask the USGS for a topographic map of the Tioga Pass area.

Directions: From Merced drive 70 miles northeast on Highway 140 to Yosemite National Park. Follow the signs toward Yosemite Valley, entering through the Arch Rock entrance station. Continue 4.5 miles to the left turnoff for Tioga Road/Highway 120, looping back out of the valley on Big Oak Flat Road. In 9.3 miles turn right on Tioga Road and drive 48 miles (you'll exit the park) to the Saddlebag Lake turnoff on the left, two miles east of Tioga Pass. Turn left and drive another 2.5 miles to the trailhead parking area.

Contact: Inyo National Forest, Mono Lake Ranger District, P.O. Box 429, Lee Vining, CA 93541; tel. (760) 647-3044 or fax (760) 647-3046.

46 Upper Yosemite Fall
7.2 mi/6.0 hrs

If you tucker out on this demanding climb to Upper Yosemite Fall, just remember that you always have a fallback position: you can hike only 1.2 miles one way to the Columbia Point viewpoint (also called Columbia Rock), a total gain of 1,200 feet in elevation, and call it a day. The view of Yosemite Valley from Columbia Point is a stunner, and plenty of people who planned on hiking to Upper Yosemite Fall turn around here and still leave satisfied. Those who push on are also rewarded: After a flat section of trail and then a short descent, the trail switchbacks up and up and up until, at 3.7 miles, and after gaining a total of 2,700 feet, you reach the brink of Upper Yosemite Fall. You get an incredible perspective on the fall's drop and the valley floor far below. Make sure you take the cutoff trail on your right for the best overlook point; the main trail continues on a bridge over the top of the fall. It's a great feeling to stand at the overlook and realize that you're standing on top of the tallest waterfall in North America. Still haven't had enough? You can continue another .75 mile, crossing the bridge above the falls, to Yosemite Point (6,936 feet), where you get a stunning view of the south rim of the canyon, Half Dome and North Dome, and a look at the top of Lost Arrow Spire, a single shaft of granite jutting into the sky. Believe it or not, it's a popular rock-climbing route.

Location: In Yosemite Valley; map E4, grid h4.

User groups: Hikers only. No dogs, horses, or mountain bikes. No wheelchair facilities.

Permits: No permits are required. There is a $20 entrance fee at Yosemite National Park, good for seven days.

Maps: Free park maps are available at park entrance stations or by contacting Yosemite National Park at the address below. A more detailed map is available for a fee from Tom Harrison Cartography, tel. (415) 456-7940. Ask the USGS for a topographic map of the Yosemite Falls area.

Directions: From Merced drive 70 miles northeast on Highway 140 to Yosemite National Park. Follow the signs toward Yosemite Valley, entering through the Arch Rock entrance station. Continue on Highway 140/El Portal Road, which becomes Southside

Drive, for 10.5 miles. Just beyond the Yosemite Chapel, bear left at the fork and head toward the village and visitor center, and turn left and drive west on Northside Drive .75 mile to the Yosemite Lodge parking lot. Turn left and park in the lot; then walk to the Upper Fall Trailhead across the road and .25 mile to the west, between the parking lot for Sunnyside Walk-In Campground (Camp 4) and the camp itself. You may not park in the campground lot unless you are camping there. If you are riding the free Yosemite Valley shuttle bus, take stop number 8 and walk to the trailhead.

Contact: Yosemite National Park Public Information Office, P.O. Box 577, Yosemite National Park, CA 95389; tel. (209) 372-0200 or fax (209) 372-0371.

47 Eagle Peak
13.5 mi/1–2 days

If you seek more of a challenge than the day hike to Upper Yosemite Fall, the trail to Eagle Peak gives you all of the stunning destinations of the shorter trip—Columbia Point, Lower Yosemite Fall, Upper Yosemite Fall—plus an additional three miles one way to a lookout atop of the highest rock of the Three Brothers formation. Not only can you see all of Yosemite, but also all the way to the mountains and foothills of the Coast Range. Just make sure you pick a clear day.

Follow the trail notes for the hike to Upper Yosemite Fall, above, then after taking the spur trail to the fall's brink, backtrack .25 mile to the trail junction for the Eagle Peak Trail. Take the Eagle Peak Trail northwest for 1.5 miles, then hike south for one mile through Eagle Peak Meadows. At a trail junction with the El Capitan Trail, bear left for the final .5-mile ascent to your final destination—the summit of Eagle Peak, elevation 7,779 feet. After completing this trip, you'll never view the Three Brothers the same way again.

Location: In Yosemite Valley; map E4, grid h4.
User groups: Hikers only. No dogs, horses, or mountain bikes. No wheelchair facilities.

Permits: There is a $20 entrance fee at Yosemite National Park, good for seven days. Free wilderness permits are required for overnight stays. They are available on a first-come, first-served basis up to one day in advance at the Yosemite Wilderness kiosk near your chosen trailhead or farther in advance by mail or phone for a $5 reservation fee; call (209) 372-0740.

Maps: Free park maps are available at park entrance stations or by contacting Yosemite National Park at the address below. A more detailed map is available for a fee from Tom Harrison Cartography, tel. (415) 456-7940. Ask the USGS for a topographic map of the Yosemite Falls area.

Directions: From Merced drive 70 miles northeast on Highway 140 to Yosemite National Park. Follow the signs toward Yosemite Valley and enter through the Arch Rock entrance station. Continue on Highway 140/El Portal Road, which becomes Southside Drive, for 10.5 miles. Just beyond the Yosemite Chapel, bear left at the fork and head toward the village and visitor center; then turn left and drive west on Northside Drive .75 mile to the Yosemite Lodge parking lot. Turn left and park in the lot; then walk to the Upper Yosemite Fall Trailhead, which is across the road and .25 mile to the west, between the parking lot for Sunnyside Walk-In Campground (Camp 4) and the camp itself. You may not park in the campground lot unless you are camping there. If you are riding the free Yosemite Valley shuttle bus, take stop number 8 and walk to the trailhead.

Contact: Yosemite National Park Public Information Office, P.O. Box 577, Yosemite National Park, CA 95389; tel. (209) 372-0200 or fax (209) 372-0371.

48 Lower Yosemite Fall
0.5 mi/0.5 hr

It's so short you can hardly call it a hike, and the route is paved and crawling with people nonetheless. Lower Yosemite Fall is an absolute must-do walk for visitors to Yosemite

Valley. One thing is for sure: you won't need a map for this trip. From the Lower Yosemite Fall parking lot, head up the pavement to the footbridge below the falls, where in the spring you can get soaking wet from the incredible mist and spray. It's a terrific cheap thrill. The only downer to Lower Yosemite Fall is that by late summer it and its big brother, Upper Yosemite Fall, often dry up completely. If you like water, plan your trip for sometime between April and July. The best time of day to make the trip? Check out full moon nights in the spring when you can sometimes see "moonbows" in the lower fall. And by the way, if you want to visit Upper Yosemite Fall as well, be informed that you can't hike there from here even though you can see the upper fall from the parking lot and on the first part of this walk. The only way to hike to the upper fall is from the trailhead near Sunnyside Campground/Camp 4 (see Upper Yosemite Fall, above).

Location: In Yosemite Valley; map E4, grid h4.

User groups: Hikers and wheelchairs. No dogs, horses, or mountain bikes.

Permits: No permits are required. There is a $20 entrance fee at Yosemite National Park, good for seven days.

Maps: Free park maps are available at park entrance stations or by contacting Yosemite National Park at the address below. Ask the USGS for a topographic map of the Half Dome area.

Directions: From Merced drive 70 miles northeast on Highway 140 to Yosemite National Park. Follow the signs to Yosemite Valley, entering through the Arch Rock entrance station. Continue on Highway 140/El Portal Road, which becomes Southside Drive, for 10.5 miles. Just beyond the Yosemite Chapel, bear left at the fork and head toward the village and visitor center, and turn left and drive west on Northside Drive .75 mile to the Lower Yosemite Fall parking lot on your right. If you are riding the free Yosemite Valley shuttle bus, take stop number 7.

Contact: Yosemite National Park Public Information Office, P.O. Box 577, Yosemite National Park, CA 95389; tel. (209) 372-0200 or fax (209) 372-0371.

49 Mist Trail to Top of Vernal Fall

3.0 mi/2.0 hrs

To hike to the top of Vernal Fall you have to take the free Yosemite shuttle bus to Happy Isles to start your trip or add an extra mile each way, hiking from the day-use parking area in Curry Village to Happy Isles. But once that's accomplished, prepare yourself for a stellar, world-class walk to one of the most photographed waterfalls in the world. The only minus is the hordes of people, so make your trip more enjoyable by starting early in the morning before they're out in full force. While many people hike only to the Vernal Fall footbridge, 0.8 mile from Happy Isles, it's definitely worth the extra effort to push on another .5 mile to reach the top of Vernal Fall. To do so means ascending the Mist Trail's famous granite stairway that curves around the side of Vernal Fall, so close to it that you feel as if you are practically a part of the waterfall. Actually, you are—hikers are inevitably drenched in spray and mist, particularly in springtime. Be sure to bring a rain poncho if you don't like getting wet. The route is an easy climb to the Vernal Falls bridge, then a steep tromp up the seemingly endless stairs to the top of the falls. Total elevation gain is 1,050 feet. It's a trip you have to do at least once in your life.

Location: In Yosemite Valley; map E4, grid h6.

User groups: Hikers only. No dogs, horses, or mountain bikes. No wheelchair facilities.

Permits: No permits are required. There is a $20 entrance fee at Yosemite National Park, good for seven days.

Maps: Free park maps are available at park entrance stations or by contacting Yosemite National Park at the address below. A more detailed map is available for a fee from Tom Harrison Cartography, tel. (415)

456-7940. Ask the USGS for a topographic map of the Half Dome area.

Directions: From Merced drive 70 miles northeast on Highway 140 to Yosemite National Park. Follow the signs toward Yosemite Valley, entering through the Arch Rock entrance station. Continue on Highway 140/El Portal Road, which becomes Southside Drive, for 11.6 miles to the day-use parking lot at Curry Village. Then ride the free Yosemite Valley shuttle bus to Happy Isles, stop number 16. In winter when the shuttle does not run, you must hike from the day-use parking lot in Curry Village, adding two miles to your round-trip. Trails may be closed in winter; call to check on weather conditions.

Contact: Yosemite National Park Public Information Office, P.O. Box 577, Yosemite National Park, CA 95389; tel. (209) 372-0200 or fax (209) 372-0371.

50 Mist and John Muir Loop to Nevada Fall

6.5 mi/4.0 hrs

You can hike either the John Muir Trail or the Mist Trail to reach Yosemite's classic Nevada Fall, but the best choice is to make a loop out of it by hiking up on the Mist Trail, then back down on the John Muir Trail. Both trails join above and below Nevada Fall, so you have some options. By hiking uphill rather than downhill on the Mist Trail's treacherous granite staircase you can look around at the gorgeous scenery every time you stop to catch your breath. The John Muir Trail is somewhat less scenic, especially in its lower reaches, so save it for the way back downhill.

Start at Happy Isles and follow the signed trail to the footbridge over the Merced River, below Vernal Fall. After crossing the bridge stay close along the river's edge on the Mist Trail for 1.2 miles to the top of Vernal Fall. If it's early spring make sure you bring your rain gear for this stretch. Then continue along the

river's edge, still following the Mist Trail. In .5 mile the path crosses the river again, then climbs another mile to the brink of Nevada Fall. Total elevation gain to the top of the 594-foot-tall falls is 2,600 feet, a healthy ascent. But when you get to walk this close to two world-class waterfalls, who's complaining? For your return trip, cross the footbridge above Nevada Fall and follow the John Muir Trail all the way down. As you descend, check out the great view of Nevada Fall with Liberty Cap in the background.

Location: In Yosemite Valley; map E4, grid h6.

User groups: Hikers only. No dogs or mountain bikes. Horses are allowed only on the John Muir Trail. No wheelchair facilities.

Permits: No permits are required. There is a $20 entrance fee at Yosemite National Park, good for seven days.

Maps: Free park maps are available at park entrance stations or by contacting Yosemite National Park at the address below. A more detailed map is available for a fee from Tom Harrison Cartography, tel. (415) 456-7940. Ask the USGS for a topographic map of the Half Dome area.

Directions: From Merced drive 70 miles northeast on Highway 140 to Yosemite National Park. Follow the signs toward Yosemite Valley, entering through the Arch Rock entrance station. Continue on Highway 140/El Portal Road, which becomes Southside Drive, for 11.6 miles to the day-use parking lot at Curry Village. Then ride the free Yosemite Valley shuttle bus to Happy Isles, stop number 16. In winter, when the shuttle does not run, you must hike from the day-use parking lot in Curry Village, adding two miles to your round-trip. Trails may be closed in winter; call to check on weather conditions.

Contact: Yosemite National Park Public Information Office, P.O. Box 577, Yosemite National Park, CA 95389; tel. (209) 372-0200 or fax (209) 372-0371.

51 Mirror Lake/ Tenaya Canyon Loop

4.5 mi/2.0 hrs

If you start your trip from Mirror Lake Junction by taking the shuttle bus to stop number 17 or adding an extra 1.5 miles round-trip from the Curry Village parking area, you can get away from a good chunk of the valley traffic on this easy, mostly flat loop trip into Tenaya Canyon. Walk .5 mile on pavement to Mirror Lake, follow the foot trail beyond it up Tenaya Creek for 1.5 miles, and then circle back. Check out the great views of Half Dome and Basket Dome. If you want to see Mirror Lake looking more like a lake and less like a meadow, make this trip in springtime. The lake is slowly undergoing the process of sedimentation—it's filling with sand and gravel from Tenaya Creek—and even in spring is quite shallow. The loop trail is nearly flat the whole way, and once you get past Mirror Lake and into Tenaya Canyon you may even find a little privacy.

Location: In Yosemite Valley; map E4, grid h6.

User groups: Hikers only. No dogs, horses, or mountain bikes. No wheelchair facilities.

Permits: No permits are required. There is a $20 entrance fee at Yosemite National Park, good for seven days.

Maps: Free park maps are available at park entrance stations or by contacting Yosemite National Park at the address below. A more detailed map is available for a fee from Tom Harrison Cartography, tel. (415) 456-7940. Ask the USGS for a topographic map of the Half Dome area.

Directions: From Merced drive 70 miles northeast on Highway 140 to Yosemite National Park. Follow the signs toward Yosemite Valley, entering through the Arch Rock entrance station. Continue on Highway 140/El Portal Road, which becomes Southside Drive, for 11.6 miles to the day-use parking lot at Curry Village. Then ride the free Yosemite Valley shuttle bus to Mirror Lake Junction, stop number 17.

Contact: Yosemite National Park Public Information Office, P.O. Box 577, Yosemite National Park, CA 95389; tel. (209) 372-0200 or fax (209) 372-0371.

52 Half Dome

17.0 mi/1–2 days

No argument about it, Half Dome is one of those once-in-your-life-you-gotta-do-it hikes. Just be sure you know what you're in for before you set out on this epic trail: you're looking at 17 miles round-trip, a 4,800-foot elevation gain, and an incredible amount of company. Plenty of people make the journey as a day hike, and if you do so, make sure to bring a load of water and food with you. You'll be handing it out to others who are not so well prepared, as well as gulping it down yourself. Follow either the John Muir Trail or the Mist Trail from Happy Isles to the top of Nevada Fall, above; then go left and enter Little Yosemite Valley, where backpackers can make camp. At 6.2 miles the John Muir Trail splits off from the Half Dome Trail and you head left for Half Dome. Everything usually goes smoothly until you reach the steel cables that run 200 yards up the back of the dome, at which point you'll start praying a lot and wishing there weren't so many other hikers on the cables with you. Do some soul-searching before you begin the cable ascent—turning around is not an option once you're halfway up. When you reach the top, the views are so incredible that you forget all about your tired arms and feet. During the summer about 500 people a day make this trip. To make it easier, camp at Little Yosemite Valley 4.7 miles in (wilderness permit required) and save the final ascent for the next day.

Location: In Yosemite Valley; map E4, grid h6.

User groups: Hikers only. No dogs, horses, or mountain bikes. No wheelchair facilities.

Permits: Free wilderness permits are required for overnight stays. They are available on a first-come, first-served basis up to one day in advance at the Yosemite

Wilderness kiosk near your chosen trailhead or farther in advance by mail or phone for a $5 reservation fee; call (209) 372-0740. There is a $20 entrance fee at Yosemite National Park, good for seven days.

Maps: Free park maps are available at park entrance stations or by contacting Yosemite National Park at the address below. A more detailed map is available for a fee from Tom Harrison Cartography, tel. (415) 456-7940. Ask the USGS for a topographic map of the Half Dome area.

Directions: From Merced drive 70 miles northeast on Highway 140 to Yosemite National Park. Follow the signs toward Yosemite Valley, entering through the Arch Rock entrance station. Continue on Highway 140/El Portal Road, which becomes Southside Drive, for 11.6 miles to the day-use parking lot at Curry Village. Then ride the free Yosemite Valley shuttle bus to Happy Isles, stop number 16.

Contact: Yosemite National Park Public Information Office, P.O. Box 577, Yosemite National Park, CA 95389; tel. (209) 372-0200 or fax (209) 372-0371.

53 Hites Cove

9.0 mi/5.0 hrs

The best part of the 22-mile South Fork Merced River Trail is the Hites Cove portion that begins at Savage's Trading Post on Highway 140. It runs 4.5 miles one way to Hites Cove four-wheel-drive road. Considered by many to be the premier Sierra spring wildflower trail, the Hites Cove Trail offers hikers a look at 60 flower varieties including goldfields, lupine, poppies, brodaiea, monkeyflower, shooting stars, fiesta flowers, fairy lanterns, baby blue eyes, and Indian pinks. To see them, visit from March to May before the show is over. Often this is the only time during the year when the trail is open. The only downers along the route are the hordes of people who flock here during that brief period and the fact that the first .75 mile of trail is on private property. (You start hiking on a paved driveway.) Hikers wishing

to turn this hike into an overnight can camp at Hites Cove, the site of the 1879 Hites Cove Hotel, then continue hiking to Devils Gulch, 2.5 miles farther. To do so, however, requires crossing the South Fork Merced River at Hites Cove, a difficult feat early in the year.

Special Note: Call the Mariposa Ranger District to make sure this trail is open before planning your trip. Usually the trail is only open for two or three months in the spring.

Location: On the South Fork Merced River; map E4, grid i1.

User groups: Hikers, dogs, horses, and mountain bikes. No wheelchair facilities.

Permits: All hikers must register at Savage's Trading Post. Parking and access are free.

Maps: For a map of Sierra National Forest, send $6 to U.S. Forest Service, Map Sales, P.O. Box 587, Camino, CA 95709; tel. (530) 647-5390 or website: www.r5.fs.fed.us/visitorcenter. Ask the USGS for a topographic map of the El Portal area.

Directions: From Mariposa drive 22 miles east on Highway 140 to Savage's Trading Post. The parking area is on the north side of the road but the trail actually begins on the south side, near Savage's Trading Post.

Contact: Sierra National Forest, Mariposa/Minarets Ranger District, 57003 Road 225, North Fork, CA 93643; tel. (559) 877-2218 or (559) 683-4665.

54 Inspiration and Stanford Points

7.6 mi/4.0 hrs

You need a little inspiration? You came to the right place. The view from the Wawona Tunnel Trailhead should be enough to inspire you (check out the panorama of Yosemite Valley, El Capitan, Half Dome, and Bridalveil Fall), but if it's not, just do a little climbing on the Pohono Trail to Inspiration Point and Stanford Point. The trail is uphill but well graded and just long enough to give you a good workout. The first mile of trail has numerous switchbacks with great views every time you face eastward. The trail climbs 1,000 feet over this stretch. At 1.3 miles the route reaches Inspiration Point where the view is largely obscured by trees, but keep heading upward for another 1,000-foot climb. Eventually you'll cross Meadow Brook and reach the left cutoff trail for Stanford Point. You're 3.8 miles from the trailhead and you've climbed 2,200 feet, but your reward is an eagle's-eye view of the valley floor 3,000 feet below and a vista to the east of Half Dome and all its granite neighbors.

Location: In Yosemite Valley near the Wawona Tunnel; map E4, grid i3.

User groups: Hikers only. No dogs, horses, or mountain bikes. No wheelchair facilities.

Permits: No permits are required. There is a $20 entrance fee at Yosemite National Park, good for seven days.

Maps: Free park maps are available at park entrance stations or by contacting Yosemite National Park at the address below. A more detailed map is available for a fee from Tom Harrison Cartography, tel. (415) 456-7940. Ask the USGS for a topographic map of the El Capitan area.

Directions: From Merced drive 70 miles northeast on Highway 140 to Yosemite National Park. Follow the signs to Yosemite Valley, entering through the Arch Rock entrance station. Continue 6.3 miles on Highway 140/El Portal Road, which becomes Southside Drive, and turn right at the fork for Highway 41/Wawona/Fresno. Continue 1.5 miles to the parking lots on either side of the road just before you enter the Wawona Tunnel. The trailhead is at the parking lot on the left (south) side of the road.

Contact: Yosemite National Park Public Information Office, P.O. Box 577, Yosemite National Park, CA 95389; tel. (209) 372-0200 or fax (209) 372-0371.

55 Bridalveil Fall

0.5 mi/0.5 hr

Bridalveil Fall is right up there with Lower Yosemite Fall as a must-do walk for visitors to Yosemite Valley. Like that other famous waterfall walk, the path to Bridalveil Fall is paved and crowded with people. Still, it's awesome. The best thing about this waterfall is that unlike the other falls in Yosemite Valley, Bridalveil runs year-round; it never dries up and disappoints visitors. The walk to its overlook is short and nearly level, and the small viewing area is about 70 yards from the fall. You can look straight up and see Bridalveil Creek plunging 620 feet off the edge of the south canyon wall. In high wind the fall billows and sways and if you are lucky you might see rainbows dancing in its mist. Another bonus is that in spring your position at the Bridalveil overlook is such that if you turn around you get an excellent view of Ribbon Fall flowing off the northern Yosemite Valley rim. Ribbon Fall is the highest single drop in the park at 1,612 feet.

Location: In Yosemite Valley; map F4, grid i3.

User groups: Hikers and wheelchairs. No dogs, horses, or mountain bikes.

Permits: No permits are required. There is a $20 entrance fee at Yosemite National Park, good for seven days.

Maps: Free park maps are available at park entrance stations or by contacting Yosemite National Park at the address below. Ask the USGS for a topographic map of the El Capitan area.

Directions: From Merced drive 70 miles northeast on Highway 140 to Yosemite National Park. Follow the signs toward Yosemite Valley, entering through the Arch Rock entrance station. Continue for 6.3 miles on Highway 140/El Portal Road, which becomes Southside Drive, and turn right at the fork for Highway 41/Wawona/Fresno. Turn left almost immediately into the Bridalveil Fall parking lot. The trail begins at the end of the parking lot. If you are driving into the park from the southern entrance near Wawona, watch for the Bridalveil Fall turnoff on your right as you drive into the valley on Highway 41.

Contact: Yosemite National Park Public Information Office,

P.O. Box 577, Yosemite National Park, CA 95389; tel. (209) 372-0200 or fax (209) 372-0371.

56 McGurk Meadow

2.0 mi/1.0 hr

Some hikes make you feel overjoyed to be alive, and the McGurk Meadow Trail is one of those. The trailhead is the first one you reach as you wind along Glacier Point Road to spectacular Glacier Point, and it's definitely worth stopping to take the short walk through a fir and pine forest to pristine McGurk Meadow. A quarter mile before you reach the meadow, you pass an old pioneer cabin on your left, still standing in half-decent repair. Then you come out to the mile-long meadow, and a footbridge carries you across a tiny stream that makes lazy S-turns through the grasses. You can follow the trail along the north edge of McGurk Meadow as far as you please for the route connects to the Pohono Trail, which traverses Yosemite's south rim, or do what we did: just stand there on the footbridge and be touched by the beauty.

Location: Off Glacier Point Road in Yosemite National Park; map E4, grid i4.

User groups: Hikers only. No dogs, horses, or mountain bikes. No wheelchair facilities.

Permits: No permits are required. There is a $20 entrance fee at Yosemite National Park, good for seven days.

Maps: Free park maps are available at park entrance stations or by contacting Yosemite National Park at the address below. A more detailed map is available for a fee from Tom Harrison Cartography, tel. (415) 456-7940. Ask the USGS for a topographic map of the Half Dome area.

Directions: From Merced drive 70 miles northeast on Highway 140 to Yosemite National Park. Follow the signs toward Yosemite Valley, entering through the Arch Rock entrance station. Continue 6.3 miles on Highway 140/El Portal Road, which becomes Southside Drive, and turn right at the fork for Highway 41/Wawona/Fresno. Continue for 9.2 miles and turn

left on Glacier Point Road and drive 7.5 miles to the McGurk Meadow Trailhead on the left. Park in the pullout about 75 yards farther up the road.

Contact: Yosemite National Park Public Information Office, P.O. Box 577, Yosemite National Park, CA 95389; tel. (209) 372-0200 or fax (209) 372-0371.

57 Bridalveil Creek

3.2 mi/1.5 hrs

Maybe the best time to hike to Bridalveil Creek from Glacier Point Road is to do it immediately after visiting Bridalveil Fall. After a short walk through a regenerated forest fire area, you wind up at the edge of Bridalveil Creek, a babbling brook that seems far too tame to be able to produce the giant waterfall downstream. It's a great lesson for children, as is the abundance of new growth in the burned areas of the forest. To make the trip, follow the Ostrander Lake Trail from Glacier Point Road for 1.4 miles. This stretch is almost completely flat and framed by colorful bunches of lupine. When the trail splits, take the right fork toward Bridalveil Creek. You reach it in less than .25 mile. The stream is so tame here that there is no bridge to cross—it's just an easy rock hop by midsummer. Pick a spot along its banks and spend some time counting the wildflowers or the small, darting trout.

Location: Off Glacier Point Road in Yosemite National Park; map E4, grid i4.

User groups: Hikers only. No dogs, horses, or mountain bikes. No wheelchair facilities.

Permits: No permits are required. There is a $20 entrance fee at Yosemite National Park, good for seven days.

Maps: Free park maps are available at park entrance stations or by contacting Yosemite National Park at the address below. A more detailed map is available for a fee from Tom Harrison Cartography, tel. (415) 456-7940. Ask the USGS for a topographic map of the Half Dome area.

Directions: From Merced drive 70 miles northeast on Highway 140 to Yosemite National Park. Follow the signs toward Yosemite Valley, entering through the Arch Rock entrance station. Continue for 6.3 miles on Highway 140/El Portal Road, which becomes Southside Drive, and turn right at the fork for Highway 41/Wawona/Fresno. Continue for 9.2 miles, turn left on Glacier Point Road, and drive another 8.9 miles to the Ostrander Lake Trailhead on the right.

Contact: Yosemite National Park Public Information Office, P.O. Box 577, Yosemite National Park, CA 95389; tel. (209) 372-0200 or fax (209) 372-0371.

58 Ostrander Lake

12.5 mi/1-2 days

While many people take short day hikes from Glacier Point Road, a longer 12.5-mile trip to Ostrander Lake may better suit your desires. The trail is surprisingly easy considering the long miles; the first half is quite level. You can hike out and back in a day or get a wilderness permit and camp near the lake's shores. The wide blue lake, set at 8,580 feet, is a popular destination for cross-country skiers in the winter as is evidenced by the stone Ostrander Ski Hut and the yellow markers high up on trees along the route. Although the trail (really an old road) begins in a regenerated forest fire area, it traverses a typical high country landscape of firs, pines, and as you ascend, granite. You have to gain 1,600 feet along the way, most of it in the final three miles to the lake. The culmination of the climb occurs at nearly six miles out as you reach the trail's highest point, a saddle on top of 8,700-foot Horizon Ridge. You are rewarded with excellent views of Half Dome, North Dome, Basket Dome, and Liberty Cap. This is a fine place to catch your breath. From here, the lake is less than .5 mile farther. On summer days, bring your swimsuit and a book and plan to spend a few hours on Ostrander's sand- and boulder-lined shoreline.

Location: Off Glacier Point Road in Yosemite National Park; map E4, grid i4.

User groups: Hikers only. No dogs, horses, or mountain bikes. No wheelchair facilities.

Permits: There is a $20 entrance fee at Yosemite National Park, good for seven days. Free wilderness permits are required for overnight stays. They are available on a first-come, first-served basis up to one day in advance at the Yosemite Wilderness kiosk near your chosen trailhead or farther in advance by mail or phone for a $5 reservation fee; call (209) 372-0740.

Maps: Free park maps are available at park entrance stations or by contacting Yosemite National Park at the address below. A more detailed map is available for a fee from Tom Harrison Cartography, tel. (415) 456-7940. Ask the USGS for topographic maps of the Half Dome and Mariposa Grove areas.

Directions: From Merced drive 70 miles northeast on Highway 140 to Yosemite National Park. Follow the signs toward Yosemite Valley, entering through the Arch Rock entrance station. Continue for 6.3 miles on Highway 140/El Portal Road, which becomes Southside Drive, and turn right at the fork for Highway 41/Wawona/Fresno. Continue for 9.2 miles and turn left on Glacier Point Road and drive 8.9 miles to the Ostrander Lake Trailhead on the right.

Contact: Yosemite National Park Public Information Office, P.O. Box 577, Yosemite National Park, CA 95389; tel. (209) 372-0200 or fax (209) 372-0371.

59 Sentinel Dome

2.0 mi/1.0 hr

It's hard to believe you can get so much for so little, but on the Sentinel Dome Trail you can. The granite dome is located about a mile before Glacier Point on Glacier Point Road, and its elevation is 1,000 feet higher than the point's, meaning stellar views are yours for the asking. A nearly flat one-

mile walk leads you to the base of the dome, and a 50-yard scramble up its smooth granite back side brings you to its summit. There you are greeted by stunning vistas in all directions, including an unusual perspective on Upper and Lower Yosemite Falls. Sentinel Dome is a great family hike and to make a longer day of it, you can easily combine it with the hike to Taft Point and the Fissures, which starts from the same trailhead but heads in the opposite direction.

Location: Off Glacier Point Road in Yosemite National Park; map E4, grid i4.

User groups: Hikers only. No dogs, horses, or mountain bikes. No wheelchair facilities.

Permits: No permits are required. There is a $20 entrance fee at Yosemite National Park, good for seven days.

Maps: Free park maps are available at park entrance stations or by contacting Yosemite National Park at the address below. A more detailed map is available for a fee from Tom Harrison Cartography, tel. (415) 456-7940. Ask the USGS for a topographic map of the Half Dome area.

Directions: From Merced drive 70 miles northeast on Highway 140 to Yosemite National Park. Follow the signs to Yosemite Valley, entering through the Arch Rock entrance station. Continue 6.3 miles on Highway 140/El Portal Road, which becomes Southside Drive, and turn right at the fork for Highway 41/Wawona/Fresno. Continue for 9.2 miles, turn left on Glacier Point Road, and drive 13.2 miles to the Taft Point/Sentinel Dome Trailhead parking lot on the left side of the road.

Contact: Yosemite National Park Public Information Office, P.O. Box 577, Yosemite National Park, CA 95389; tel. (209) 372-0200 or fax (209) 372-0371.

60 Taft Point and the Fissures
2.0 mi/1.0 hr

It's not so much the sweeping vista from Taft Point that you remember, although certainly you could say that the views of Yosemite's north rim and the valley floor are stunning. What you remember is the incredible sense of awe that you feel, perhaps mixed with a little fear and a lot of respect as you peer down into the fissures in Taft Point's granite—huge cracks in the rock that plunge hundreds of feet down toward the valley. One of the fissures has a couple of large boulders captured in its jaws; they're stuck there waiting for the next big earthquake or ice age to set them free. Be sure to walk to the piped railing along the edge of the cliff, where you can hold on tight and peer down at the valley far, far below. If you have kids with you or anyone who is afraid of heights, be sure to keep a tight handhold on them.

Location: Off Glacier Point Road in Yosemite National Park; map E4, grid i4.

User groups: Hikers only. No dogs, horses, or mountain bikes. No wheelchair facilities.

Permits: No permits are required. There is a $20 entrance fee at Yosemite National Park, good for seven days.

Maps: Free park maps are available at park entrance stations or by contacting Yosemite National Park at the address below. A more detailed map is available for a fee from Tom Harrison Cartography, tel. (415) 456-7940. Ask the USGS for a topographic map of the Half Dome area.

Directions: From Merced drive 70 miles northeast on Highway 140 to Yosemite National Park. Follow the signs to Yosemite Valley, entering through the Arch Rock entrance station. Continue for 6.3 miles on Highway 140/El Portal Road, which becomes Southside Drive, and turn right at the fork for Highway 41/Wawona/Fresno. Continue for 9.2 miles, turn left on Glacier Point Road, and drive 13.2 miles to the Taft Point/Sentinel Dome Trailhead parking lot on the left side of the road.

Contact: Yosemite National Park Public Information Office, P.O. Box 577, Yosemite National Park, CA 95389; tel. (209) 372-0200 or fax (209) 372-0371.

61 Four-Mile Trail
9.6 mi/6.0 hrs

Many years ago we hiked this trail on our first-ever visit to Yosemite and were shocked when we got to the top and found a giant parking lot and refreshment stand located there. What, you mean we could have driven to the high point on this trail? It's true, but your arrival at dramatic Glacier Point is somehow made all the more meaningful if you get there the hard way, which means hiking the Four-Mile Trail all the way up from the valley floor, gaining 3,220 feet in 4.8 miles and not four miles, as the name implies. The trail is partially shaded and makes for a terrific day hike with an early morning start. Then you can have a leisurely brunch or lunch from your bird's-eye perch on Glacier Point. From its promontory you get unobstructed views of just about everything, most notably Half Dome, Basket Dome, Yosemite Falls, Vernal and Nevada Falls, and the valley floor far, far below you.

Location: In Yosemite Valley; map E4, grid h4.

User groups: Hikers only. No dogs, horses, or mountain bikes. No wheelchair facilities.

Permits: No permits are required. There is a $20 entrance fee at Yosemite National Park, good for seven days.

Maps: Free park maps are available at park entrance stations or by contacting Yosemite National Park at the address below. A more detailed map is available for a fee from Tom Harrison Cartography, tel. (415) 456-7940. Ask the USGS for a topographic map of the Half Dome area.

Directions: From Merced drive 70 miles northeast on Highway 140 to Yosemite National Park. Follow the signs to Yosemite Valley, entering through the Arch Rock entrance station. Continue on Highway 140/El Portal Road, which becomes Southside Drive, for 9.5 miles. The trailhead is located next to mile marker V18 on the right side of Southside Drive. Park in the pullouts along the road.

Contact: Yosemite National Park Public Information Office, P.O. Box 577, Yosemite National Park, CA 95389; tel. (209) 372-0200 or fax (209) 372-0371.

62 Pohono Trail
13.0 mi one way/7.0 hrs

If you can arrange a shuttle trip, the Pohono Trail from Glacier Point downhill to its end at Wawona Tunnel has some incredible offerings. The two ends of the trail have the best drive-to viewpoints in all of Yosemite, and in between you are treated to dozens of other scenic spots, including Sentinel Dome at 1.5 miles, Taft Point at 3.8 miles, as well as four bird's-eye lookouts over the valley floor: Inspiration, Stanford, Dewey, and Crocker Points. Starting at Glacier Point and ending at Wawona Tunnel, you'll cover a 2,800-foot descent but there are some ups along the way, too, like at the very beginning from Glacier Point to Sentinel Dome, and between crossing Bridalveil Creek and reaching spectacular Dewey Point. The trail stays on or near Yosemite Valley's southern rim the entire way except for one major detour into the woods to access the bridge crossing of Bridalveil Creek. Remember to bring along a good map because many of the best offerings are just off the main trail, and if you don't take the short spur routes to reach them, you'll miss out on some spectacular scenery. Note: The view of Yosemite Falls from the Pohono Trail in front of Sentinel Dome is the best in all of Yosemite. For best overall vista along the trail, it's a toss-up between Glacier Point, Taft Point, and Dewey Point.

Location: Off Glacier Point Road in Yosemite National Park; map E4, grid i4.

User groups: Hikers only. No dogs, horses, or mountain bikes. No wheelchair facilities.

Permits: There is a $20 entrance fee at Yosemite National Park, good for seven days. Free wilderness permits are required for overnight stays. They are available on a first-come, first-served basis up to one day in advance at the Yosemite Wilderness kiosk near your chosen trailhead or farther in

advance by mail or phone for a $5 reservation fee; call (209) 372-0740.

Maps: Free park maps are available at park entrance stations or by contacting Yosemite National Park at the address below. A more detailed map is available for a fee from Tom Harrison Cartography, tel. (415) 456-7940. Ask the USGS for topographic maps of the Half Dome and El Capitan areas.

Directions: From Merced drive 70 miles northeast on Highway 140 to Yosemite National Park. Follow the signs to Yosemite Valley, entering through the Arch Rock entrance station. Continue for 6.3 miles on Highway 140/El Portal Road, which becomes Southside Drive, and turn right at the fork for Highway 41/Wawona/Fresno. Continue for 9.2 miles, turn left on Glacier Point Road, and drive 15.7 miles to Glacier Point. Park and walk toward the main viewing area across from the café and gift shop. Look for the Pohono Trail sign about 150 feet southeast of the café building, on your right.

Contact: Yosemite National Park Public Information Office, P.O. Box 577, Yosemite National Park, CA 95389; tel. (209) 372-0200 or fax (209) 372-0371.

63 Panorama Trail

8.5 mi one way/5.0 hrs

It's an incredibly spectacular route to walk from Glacier Point to Yosemite Valley, downhill most of the way, passing more mind-boggling scenery than you can shake a stick at, but you've got to have a shuttle car waiting at the end or it's a heck of a long climb back up. A great option is to take the Yosemite Lodge tour bus for one leg of the trip; call (209)372-1240 for rates and pickup times. The well-named Panorama Trail begins at Glacier Point, elevation 7,214 feet, the trailhead with what is probably the grandest view in the West. You switchback down from the point accompanied by ever-changing perspectives on Half Dome, Basket Dome, North Dome, Liberty Cap, and far-off Vernal and Nevada Falls. You will gape a lot. After passing Illilouette Fall and climbing

a bit for the first time on the trip, continue eastward to the Panorama Trail's end near the top of Nevada Fall. Take the short spur to the top of the fall and continue downhill (now westward) on either the John Muir Trail or the Mist Trail, passing Vernal Fall along the way. If you take the John Muir Trail, make sure you take the spur trail off it that leads to Vernal Fall. The Mist Trail goes directly by Vernal Fall. The hike ends at Happy Isles, where you can take the free valley shuttle bus to the pickup point for the Yosemite Lodge tour bus or to your shuttle car parked somewhere in the valley. Note that the entire route has a 3,200-foot elevation loss over its course, but there is also a 760-foot climb after you cross Illilouette Creek. Also be forewarned that while the starting miles of the trip are very peaceful, the final two miles by Vernal Fall can be a parade of people.

Location: Off Glacier Point Road in Yosemite National Park; map E4, grid i4.

User groups: Hikers only. No dogs, horses, or mountain bikes. No wheelchair facilities.

Permits: No permits are required. There is a $20 entrance fee at Yosemite National Park, good for seven days.

Maps: Free park maps are available at park entrance stations or by contacting Yosemite National Park at the address below. A more detailed map is available for a fee from Tom Harrison Cartography, tel. (415) 456-7940. Ask the USGS for a topographic map of the Half Dome area.

Directions: From Merced drive 70 miles northeast on Highway 140 to Yosemite National Park. Follow the signs to Yosemite Valley, entering through the Arch Rock entrance station. Continue for 6.3 miles on Highway 140/El Portal Road, which becomes Southside Drive, and turn right at the fork for Highway 41/Wawona/Fresno. Continue for 9.2 miles, turn left on Glacier Point Road, and drive 15.7 miles to Glacier Point. Park and walk toward the main viewing area across from the café and gift shop. Look for the Panorama Trail sign about 150 feet southeast of the café building, on your right.

Contact: Yosemite National Park Public Information Office, P.O. Box 577, Yosemite National Park, CA 95389; tel. (209) 372-0200 or fax (209) 372-0371.

64 Illiouette Fall
4.0 mi/2.5 hrs

Those who can't afford the time or make the car shuttle arrangements necessary to hike the entire Panorama Trail should at least take this incredible out-and-back trip on the top portion of the route. Glacier Point is your starting point and the bridge above Illilouette Fall becomes your destination, but what happens in between is sheer magic. Some say that hiking the Panorama Trail is like staring at a life-size Yosemite postcard, but we say it's more like being in the postcard. As you walk, you feel as if you've become one with the magnificent panorama of Half Dome, Basket Dome, North Dome, Liberty Cap, and far-off Vernal and Nevada Falls. The trail is downhill all the way to Illilouette Fall in two miles, which means you have a 1,200-foot elevation gain on the return trip. The path is extremely well graded though, so even children can make the climb. After viewing the waterfall from a trailside overlook, walk another .25 mile and stand on the bridge that is perched just above the 370-foot drop. For obvious reasons, don't think about swimming here.

Location: Off Glacier Point Road in Yosemite National Park; map E4, grid i4.

User groups: Hikers only. No dogs, horses, or mountain bikes. No wheelchair facilities.

Permits: No permits are required. There is a $20 entrance fee at Yosemite National Park, good for seven days.

Maps: Free park maps are available at park entrance stations or by contacting Yosemite National Park at the address below. A more detailed map is available for a fee from Tom Harrison Cartography, tel. (415) 456-7940. Ask the USGS for a topographic map of the Half Dome area.

Directions: From Merced drive 70 miles northeast on Highway 140 to Yosemite National Park. Follow the signs to Yosemite Valley, entering through the Arch Rock entrance station. Continue for 6.3 miles on Highway 140/El Portal Road, which becomes Southside Drive, and turn right at the fork for Highway 41/Wawona/Fresno. Continue for 9.2 miles, turn left on Glacier Point Road, and drive 15.7 miles to Glacier Point. Park and walk toward the main viewing area across from the café and gift shop. Look for the Panorama Trail sign on your right, about 150 feet southeast of the café building.

Contact: Yosemite National Park Public Information Office, P.O. Box 577, Yosemite National Park, CA 95389; tel. (209) 372-0200 or fax (209) 372-0371.

65 Wawona Meadow Loop
3.2 mi/1.25 hrs

Hey, sometimes you just want to take a stroll in the park and the Wawona Meadow Loop is just that. On one trip to Yosemite, we ignored this trail because of its proximity to the Wawona Golf Course, the presence of which insulted our hiking sensibilities. But on another trip, we gave the Wawona Meadow Loop a try and wound up liking it. On the easy, flat trail, you see and smell terrific wildflowers in late spring and summer, enjoy the good company of butterflies, and generally have a soothing lazy stroll around a pretty meadow. From the signed trailhead across the road from the Wawona Hotel, hike to your left on the dirt road, following the split rail fence, and then loop around the meadow. You can even bring your dog or ride your bike on this trail, a rarity in Yosemite. If you're staying at the Wawona Hotel, you can hike from there, crossing the Wawona Road on your way out and back.

Location: Off Highway 41 near Wawona, in Yosemite National Park; map E4, grid j3.

User groups: Hikers, dogs, and mountain bikes. No horses. No wheelchair facilities.

Permits: No permits are required. There is a $20 entrance fee at Yosemite National Park, good for seven days.

Maps: Free park maps are available at park entrance stations or by contacting Yosemite National Park at the address below. A more detailed map is available for a fee from Tom Harrison Cartography, tel. (415) 456-7940. Ask the USGS for a topographic map of the Wawona area.

Directions: From Merced drive 70 miles northeast on Highway 140 to Yosemite National Park. Follow the signs toward Yosemite Valley, entering through the Arch Rock entrance station. Continue for 6.3 miles on Highway 140/El Portal Road, which becomes Southside Drive, and turn right at the fork for Highway 41/Wawona/Fresno. Drive 27 miles to the trailhead, which is just south of the golf course and across the road from the Wawona Hotel.

Contact: Yosemite National Park Public Information Office, P.O. Box 577, Yosemite National Park, CA 95389; tel. (209) 372-0200 or fax (209) 372-0371.

66 Chilnualna Falls

8.2 mi/5.0 hrs

Are you ready to climb? Pick a nice, cool day since you're here in the lower-elevation part of Yosemite, and prepare for a steady four-mile uphill, gaining 2,400 feet to reach Chilnualna Falls. Your nose will be continually assaulted with the intoxicating smell of bear clover, which together with manzanita and oaks makes up the majority of the vegetation along the route. Halfway up you get a great view of Wawona Dome (elevation 6,897 feet) from a granite overlook. This is a great place to take a break and stretch your hamstrings. Shortly thereafter you begin to glimpse a section of Chilnualna Falls high up on a cliff wall, still far ahead of you. When you get closer, you see that the lower drop of the waterfall is a plunging free fall. The trail leads you on top of the free fall (unfortu-

nately not in front of it, so you never get to see it head-on) to a series of cascades. Keep walking until you reach the top cascade, consisting of five pool-and-drop tiers, which is just 100 yards to the right of the granite-lined trail. It's a great spot for a picnic before you begin the long descent back downhill.

Location: Off Highway 41 near Wawona, in Yosemite National Park; map E4, grid j3.

User groups: Hikers and horses. No dogs or mountain bikes. No wheelchair facilities.

Permits: There is a $20 entrance fee at Yosemite National Park, good for seven days. Free wilderness permits are required for overnight stays. They are available on a first-come, first-served basis up to one day in advance at the Yosemite Wilderness kiosk near your chosen trailhead or farther in advance by mail or phone for a $5 reservation fee; call (209) 372-0740.

Maps: Free park maps are available at park entrance stations or by contacting Yosemite National Park at the address below. A more detailed map is available for a fee from Tom Harrison Cartography, tel. (415) 456-7940. Ask the USGS for topographic maps of the Wawona and Mariposa Grove areas.

Directions: From Merced drive 55 miles northeast on Highway 140 to Yosemite National Park. Follow the signs to Yosemite Valley, entering through the Arch Rock entrance station. Continue for 6.3 miles on Highway 140/El Portal Road, which becomes Southside Drive, and turn right at the fork for Highway 41/Wawona/Fresno. Drive south on the Wawona Road/Highway 41 for 25 miles to Wawona, and turn left on Chilnualna Falls Road. Drive 1.7 miles east and park in the lot on the right side of the road. Walk back to Chilnualna Falls Road and pick up the single-track trail across the pavement.

Contact: Yosemite National Park Public Information Office, P.O. Box 577, Yosemite National Park, CA 95389; tel. (209) 372-0200 or fax (209) 372-0371.

67 Alder Creek Falls

8.2 mi/5.0 hrs

Maybe the best thing about Alder Creek Falls is that with all the world-famous waterfalls in Yosemite this one just plain gets overlooked. Or maybe the best thing is the fun hike to reach it, starting with the challenge of locating the trailhead along Highway 41. After you accomplish this feat, you begin with a one-mile beeline hike straight uphill through the forest, which is sure to get your heart pumping. At the top of the ridge and a trail junction, turn left and lateral through the trees for two more miles, still heading uphill but now more gently. Three miles from the trailhead the route suddenly goes flat as it joins an old railroad grade, and then it's a one-mile easy stroll to the spot where Alder Creek takes the plunge off a granite lip. The waterfall is about 250 feet tall, and the best view of it is from the trail as you stand about 100 yards in front of it. If you choose to keep hiking beyond the falls, you'll find many picnic spots among meadows and wildflowers.

Location: Off Highway 41 near Wawona, in Yosemite National Park; map E4, grid j3.

User groups: Hikers and horses. No dogs or mountain bikes. No wheelchair facilities.

Permits: There is a $20 entrance fee at Yosemite National Park, good for seven days. Free wilderness permits are required for overnight stays. They are available on a first-come, first-served basis up to one day in advance at the Yosemite Wilderness kiosk near your chosen trailhead or farther in advance by mail or phone for a $5 reservation fee; call (209) 372-0740.

Maps: Free park maps are available at park entrance stations or by contacting Yosemite National Park at the address below. A more detailed map is available for a fee from Tom Harrison Cartography, tel. (415) 456-7940. Ask the USGS for a topographic map of the Wawona area.

Directions: The easiest way to find this unmarked trailhead is to travel north from Wawona. Follow the directions to Chilnualna Falls, above, but from the turnoff for Chilnualna Falls Road, drive north on the Wawona Road/Highway 41 for 4.2 miles. You can also set your odometer at Wawona Campground; the trailhead is 3.4 miles north of the camp. The trailhead is at a hairpin turn on the east side of the Wawona Road. There is no marker except for a Yosemite Wilderness sign, which you cannot see from your car. Park in the large dirt pullout on the west side of the road.

Contact: Yosemite National Park Public Information Office, P.O. Box 577, Yosemite National Park, CA 95389; tel. (209) 372-0200 or fax (209) 372-0371.

68 Mariposa Grove

2.0 mi/1.0 hrs

The Mariposa Grove is the largest of the three groves of giant sequoias in Yosemite National Park. That's why on summer weekends the parking lot fills up and people wait in line in their cars to see the 250 or so big trees here. We hate to spill the beans, but the truth is that there are far better and more peaceful groves of sequoias just a few miles south in Sierra National Forest, such as the Nelder Grove described in Chapter F4. Still, if you're in Yosemite and you want to see the sequoias, this is the place. The star tree in the Mariposa Grove is the Grizzly Giant with a circumference of more than 100 feet. It's one of the oldest known giant sequoias, at approximately 2,700 years old, which gives you some perspective on your short time on Earth. If you want to see only the most famous trees in the grove—the Grizzly Giant, California Tunnel Tree, the Bachelor, and Three Graces—take the well-signed two-mile hike through the lower grove and turn around when you see the signs pointing to the upper grove. If you hike the entire lower and upper grove, you will cover about 6.5 miles.

Location: Off Highway 41 near Wawona, in Yosemite National Park; map E4, grid j3.

User groups: Hikers only. No dogs, horses, or mountain bikes. No wheelchair facilities.

Permits: No permits are required. There is a $20 entrance fee at Yosemite National Park, good for seven days.

Maps: Free park maps are available at park entrance stations or by contacting Yosemite National Park at the address below. A more detailed map is available for a fee from Tom Harrison Cartography, tel. (415) 456-7940. A map of the Mariposa Grove is available at the trailhead for $.50. Ask the USGS for a topographic map of the Mariposa Grove area.

Directions: From Merced drive 70 miles northeast on Highway 140 to Yosemite National Park. Follow the signs toward Yosemite Valley, entering through the Arch Rock entrance station. Continue for 6.3 miles on Highway 140/El Portal Road, which becomes Southside Drive, and turn right at the fork for Highway 41/Wawona/Fresno. Drive 32 miles to the well-signed Mariposa Grove access road by Yosemite's south entrance. Turn east and drive two miles to the parking lot. Note that this two-mile stretch of road may be closed in winter. If you enter the park on Highway 41 from the south, the Mariposa Grove is on the right just after you drive through the park entrance station.

Contact: Yosemite National Park Public Information Office, P.O. Box 577, Yosemite National Park, CA 95389; tel. (209) 372-0200 or fax (209) 372-0371.

PACIFIC CREST TRAIL (PCT) SECTION OVERVIEW
135.8 mi one way/14.0 days

Trail elevations within this section, extending from the Agnew Meadows Trailhead north to Ebbetts Pass, range from 7,000 feet to over 10,000 feet. Although the lower reaches of the PCT are open from mid-June to mid-October, several high passes within the region may remain covered with snow until mid-July, making hiking difficult. Snow-covered passes are impossible to navigate with pack stock and horses.

PCT-23 / JMT-3 Agnew Meadows to Tuolumne Meadows
28.0 mi one way/3.0 days

This section of trail features breathtaking views of the Minarets, many glacial-cut lakes, and the wondrous descent into Yosemite. The PCT starts here by leaving Reds Meadows, an excellent place to arrange a food drop and a chance to eat your first cheeseburger in weeks. The trail heads out into the most beautiful section of Inyo National Forest and the Ansel Adams Wilderness. All in a row the PCT passes Rosalie Lake, Shadow Lake, Garnet Lake, and Thousand Island Lake. If they look like Ansel Adams' pictures in real life, it's because they are. The background setting of Banner and Ritter Peaks is among the most spectacular anywhere. From Thousand Island Lake, the PCT makes a fair climb over Island Pass (10,200 feet), then drops down into the headwaters of Rush Creek where emerald green flows swirl over boulders, pouring like a wilderness fountain. From here it's a decent, steady ascent back above tree line to Donohue Pass (11,056 feet), the southern wilderness border of Yosemite National Park. It was here, while munching a trail lunch, that we saw a huge landslide on the westward canyon wall. A massive amount of rock material fell in just a few seconds—an unforgettable show of natural forces. The trail becomes quite blocky at Donohue Pass, and you rock hop your way down to the headwaters of Lyell Fork, a pretzel-like stream that meanders through the meadows. It pours all the way to Tuolumne Meadows, and following it the trail is nearly flat for more than four miles. At Tuolumne Meadows you can resupply—and get another cheeseburger.

Special Note: To continue on the Pacific Crest Trail, see PCT-24 following John Muir Trail-4.

Location: From the Agnew Meadows Trailhead north to the trailhead parking area at Tuolumne Meadows on Highway 120; map E4, grid j9.

User groups: Hikers and horses. No dogs or mountain bikes. No wheelchair facilities.

Permits: A wilderness permit is required for traveling through various wilderness and special-use areas the trail traverses. Contact either the Inyo National Forest, tel. (760) 647-3044, or Wilderness Office of the National Park Service, tel. (209) 372-0200, for a permit that is good for the length of your trip.

Maps: For an overall view of the trail route in this section, send $6 for each map ordered to U.S. Forest Service, Map Sales, P.O. Box 587, Camino, CA 95709; tel. (530) 647-5390 or website: www.r5.fs.fed.us/visitorcenter. Ask for maps of Inyo National Forest and Sierra National Forest. Ask the USGS for topographic maps of Vogelsang Peak, Mount Ritter, Koip Peak, and Mammoth Mountain.

Directions: From Lee Vining drive 26 miles south on Highway 395 to Mammoth Junction. Turn west on Highway 203/Minaret Summit Road to the town of Mammoth Lakes and drive 14 miles to the Agnew Meadows Campground and the trailhead parking area.

Contact: Public Information Office, National Park Service, P.O. Box 577, Yosemite National Park, CA 95389; tel. (209) 372-0200 or fax (209) 372-0371; Inyo National Forest, Mono Lake Ranger District, P.O. Box 429, Lee Vining, CA 93541; tel. (760) 647-3044 or fax (760) 647-3046.

JMT-4 Tuolumne Meadows to Yosemite Valley

22 mi one way / 2.0 days

The first glimpses of Yosemite Valley will seem like a privileged view into heaven after having hiked the entire John Muir Trail from Mount Whitney. For hikers making only this 22-mile section, the rewards can seem just as profound. The trip starts at Tuolumne Meadows, where backpackers can buy a good, cheap breakfast, obtain wilderness permits, and camp in a special area set aside for JMT hikers. When you take your first steps away from Tuolumne Meadows, resist the urge to rush

to the finish line in order to close out a historic expedition. Instead relax and enjoy the downhill glide, always remembering that you are in sacred land. Compared to the rest of the JMT, this leg will come with far less strain, starting with a 3.1-mile tromp past Cathedral Lakes and requiring a .5-mile walk on a signed cutoff trail. If you can time it right, this area can make a great layover camp, with deep, emerald green water and Cathedral Peak in the background. At dawn, when there isn't a breath of wind, it can seem like a mountain church. Beyond Cathedral Lakes, the trail makes a relatively short 500-foot climb over Cathedral Pass, skirts Tresidder Peak, and then descends through pristine Long Meadow. After passing Sunrise Trail Camp, a decent layover, the trail picks up little Sunrise Creek and follows it all the way down to Little Yosemite Valley, a popular trail camp. From Cathedral Lakes it's 14.5 miles to the Junction of the Half Dome Trail and another 2.2 miles to Little Yosemite.

For JMT hikers, making the climb to the top of Half Dome is a must, even though it often means putting up with a parade of people and even delays waiting for the line to move at the climbing cable. The Half Dome climb starts with a steep hike for the first mile, followed by steep switchbacks across granite on good trail to the foot of Half Dome's back wall. Here you'll find climbing cables to aid your final 300-foot ascent, and as you go, you'll discover breathtaking views of Tenaya Canyon. This is considered one of the world's glamour hikes, and while it turns hiking into an act of faith, we have seen eight-year-olds and 70-year-olds make the cable climb. By the way, if you take on Half Dome, be certain to have two canteens of water per person. Adding the Half Dome side trip to the rest of the JMT leg will add a round-trip of 5.2 miles to your hike. Because of its proximity to Half Dome, the Little Yosemite Valley Trail Camp is often crowded. From here, though, it's an easy five-mile hike downhill to Yosemite Valley. Again, try not to speed through to the end even though it's an easy tromp downhill all the way. The magic is in the moment.

From Little Yosemite, the JMT is routed along the Merced River. In a mile you'll reach Liberty Cap, and shortly later, Nevada Fall. Then down, down you go, with the trail often turning to giant granite steps, down past Emerald Pool and then to Vernal Fall, another spectacular waterfall. Since Vernal Fall is just 1.7 miles from the end of the trail you'll start meeting lots of day-hikers coming from the other direction, many gasping for breath as they make the uphill climb out of Yosemite Valley. Many will ask how far you've hiked; some may even want to take your photograph. It may feel a bit inane, but, hey, enjoy it. After all, you just finished the John Muir Trail, the greatest hiking trail in the world.

Location: From Tuolumne Meadows Campground in Yosemite, map E4, grid g9, to Happy Isles in Yosemite Valley, map E4, grid h4.

User groups: Hikers and horses. No dogs or mountain bikes. No wheelchair facilities.

Permits: A wilderness permit is required for traveling through various wilderness and special-use areas that the trail traverses. Contact the Wilderness Office of the National Park Service, tel. (209) 372-0200, for a permit that is good for the length of your trip.

Maps: Ask the USGS for topographic maps of Vogelsang Peak, Half Dome, Yosemite Falls, and Tenaya Peak. For other maps of Yosemite, free park maps are available at park entrance stations or by contacting Yosemite National Park at the address below. A more detailed map is available for a fee from Tom Harrison Cartography, tel. (209) 372-0200.

Directions: From Groveland in the Central Valley foothills, drive east on Highway 120 into Yosemite National Park and continue toward Yosemite Valley. At Crane Flat, turn left on Highway 120/Tioga Pass Road and continue for about an hour, driving past Tenaya Lake to the Tuolumne Meadows Campground. There is a signed trailhead parking area for the John Muir Trail here.

Contact: Public Information Office, National Park Service, P.O. Box 577, Yosemite National Park, CA 95389; tel. (209) 372-0200 or fax (209) 372-0371.

PCT-24 Tuolumne Meadows to Sonora Pass

77.0 mi one way/8.0 days

Yosemite National Park is well known for its crowded conditions in the valley, but you can go for days and see almost no one on this section of trail. The beauty of the deep canyons, glacial-cut peaks, untouched meadows, and abundant wildlife make it a surreal paradise.

But it's real enough. From Tuolumne Meadows the trail starts out deceptively easily as it follows the Tuolumne River towards the Grand Canyon of the Tuolumne River. It stays easy to Glen Aulin, where you get a great view of Tuolumne Falls, an excellent day trip from the Tuolumne Meadows drive-in camp. When you cross the bridge here and head up-canyon you'll be leaving most people behind. In the next three days you'll go up one canyon and down the next, one after another, with breathtaking views and long, demanding climbs. Highlights include Matterhorn Canyon (many deer, trout, and views), Benson Lake (the largest white sand beach in the Sierra Nevada), Dorothy Lake (panoramic views to the north), and many beautiful meadows, each like a wilderness church. The one serious negative is the incredible clouds of mosquitoes at the Wilmer Lake area during late spring and early summer.

When you leave Yosemite and enter Humboldt-Toiyabe National Forest the landscape changes quickly from glacial-cut granite to volcanic rock, with the trail dropping past several pretty lakes and into a river drainage. Here the trail can be difficult to follow in parts, and in others your chance of meeting grazing cows is high, particularly by the midsummer months. It will inspire you to head out to make the long climb up toward Leavitt Pass, set just below 10,800-foot Leavitt Peak, much of it a long, slow, uphill pull, almost all above tree line in gray, stark country. At Leavitt Pass the wind whistles by at high speed almost year-round, a product of the "venturi effect," in which valley winds are continually forced through the narrow saddle at the pass and must speed up to make it through. The final drop down to Sonora Pass is a one-hour descent that seems to wind all over the mountain and can be extremely dangerous and slippery when snow covered. When you reach Highway 108, cross the road and walk about 100 yards west to a large day-use parking area. The trail picks up again there.

Location: From the trailhead parking at Tuolumne Meadows on Highway 120 north to the Sonora Pass Trailhead; map E4, grid g9.

User groups: Hikers and horses. No dogs or mountain bikes. No wheelchair facilities.

Permits: A wilderness permit is required for traveling through various wilderness and special-use areas the trail traverses. Contact either the Wilderness Office of the National Park Service, tel. (209) 372-0200, or the Stanislaus National Forest, tel. (209) 795-1381, for a permit that is good for the length of your trip.

Maps: For an overall view of the trail route in this section, send $6 for each map ordered to U.S. Forest Service, Map Sales, P.O. Box 587, Camino, CA 95709; tel. (530) 647-5390 or web-site: www.r5.fs.fed.us/visitorcenter. Ask for the Stanislaus National Forest, Humboldt-Toiyabe National Forest, and the Inyo National Forest maps. Ask the USGS for topographic maps of the Pickel Meadow, Tower Peak, Piute Mountain, Matterhorn Peak, Dunderberg Peak, Vogelsang Peak, Tioga Pass, Falls Ridge, Buckeye Ridge, and Sonora Pass areas.

Directions: From Lee Vining drive west on Highway 120/Tioga Pass Road to Tuolumne Meadows and the signed trailhead parking area for the John Muir Trail/PCT and Lyell Fork.

Contact: Public Information Office, National Park Service, P.O. Box 577, Yosemite National Park, CA 95389; tel. (209) 372-0200 or fax (209) 372-0371; Stanislaus National Forest, Calaveras Ranger Station, P.O. Box 500, Hath-away Pines, CA 95233; tel. (209) 795-1381 or fax (209) 795-6849.

PCT-25 Sonora Pass to Ebbetts Pass
30.8 mi one way/3.0 days

While this section of the Pacific Crest Trail may not have the glamorous reputation of the stretch of trail in the southern Sierra, it's just as compelling for those who know it. From Sonora Pass you're forced to climb out for a good hour or two, then rise over Wolf Creek Gap (10,300 feet) and make the easy drop down the Carson Canyon. This is the start of the Carson-Iceberg Wilderness, a giant swath of land that is a rare, unpeopled paradise. The Sierra riparian zones here are lined with flowers, seemingly all kinds and all colors, often in luxuriant beds of greenness. The PCT climbs out of Carson Canyon around Boulder Peak, then down and up two more canyons. All the while you keep crossing creeks filled with natural gardens. You wind your way across and through these areas and eventually climb a ridge then head down, steeply at times, to Ebbetts Pass. Alas, there's no water here. No problem. A short half-hour climb and you can be pumping water and maybe setting up camp, too, at little Sherrold Lake, not far from the edge of the Mokelumne Wilderness.

Location: From Highway 108 at Sonora Pass north to Highway 4 near Ebbetts Pass; map E4, grid b5.

User groups: Hikers, dogs, and horses. No mountain bikes. No wheelchair facilities.

Permits: A wilderness permit is required for traveling through various wilderness and special-use areas the trail traverses. Contact the Stanislaus National Forest, tel. (209) 532-3671, to obtain a permit that is good for the length of your trip.

Maps: Ask the USGS for topographic maps of the Pickel Meadow, Disaster Peak, Dardanelles Cone, and Ebbetts Pass areas.

Directions: From Sonora head east on Highway 108 to the trailhead and parking area at Sonora Pass.

Contact: Stanislaus National Forest, Supervisor's Office, 19777 Greenley Road, Sonora, CA 95370; tel. (209) 532-3671 or fax (209) 533-1890.

PCT Continuation

To continue hiking along the Pacific Crest Trail, see chapter D4.

TUFA TOWERS AT MONO LAKE
ARE FORMED BY THE INTERACTION
OF CALCIUM-BEARING FRESHWATER
SPRINGS AND CARBONATE-RICH
ALKALINE LAKE WATER.

MAP E5

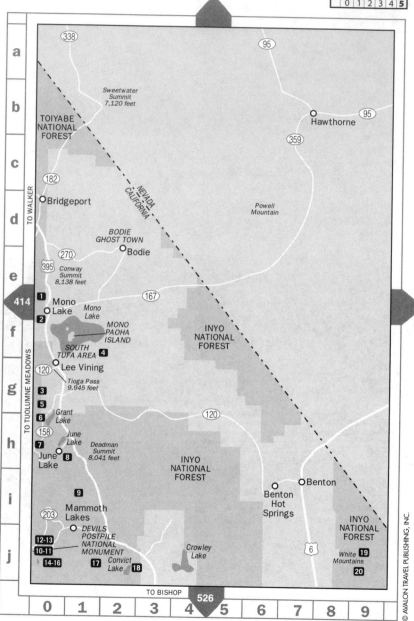

TOIYABE
NATIONAL
FOREST

Sweetwater
Summit
7,120 feet

(338)

(95)

(95)

Hawthorne

(359)

TO WALKER

(182)

Bridgeport

NEVADA
CALIFORNIA

Powell
Mountain

BODIE
GHOST TOWN

(270)

Bodie

(395)

Conway
Summit
8,138 feet

(167)

414

1

Mono
Lake

2

Mono
Lake

MONO
PAOHA
ISLAND

INYO
NATIONAL
FOREST

SOUTH
TUFA AREA **4**

Lee Vining

TO TUOLUMNE MEADOWS

(120)

Tioga Pass
9,945 feet

3

5

6

Grant
Lake

(120)

(158)

June
Lake

7

Deadman
Summit
8,041 feet

June
Lake

8

INYO
NATIONAL
FOREST

Benton

9

Benton
Hot
Springs

Mammoth
Lakes

(203)

DEVILS
POSTPILE
NATIONAL
MONUMENT

INYO
NATIONAL
FOREST

12-13

10-11

14-16

17

Convict
Lake

18

Crowley
Lake

(6)

White
Mountains

19

20

TO BISHOP

526

© AVALON TRAVEL PUBLISHING, INC.

0   1   2   3   4   5   6   7   8   9

CHAPTER E5

1 Virginia Lakes Trail . . . 465
2 Lundy Lake Trailhead. . 465
3 Gibbs Lake Trail. 466
4 Mono Lake South
   Tufa Trail. 467
5 Walker Lake Trailhead . 467
6 Parker Lake Trail. 468
7 Silver Lake Trail 468
8 Yost Lake Trail. 469
9 Inyo Craters 469
10 Upper Soda
   Springs Trailhead 470

11 Rainbow Falls Trail. . . . 471
12 Minaret Lake Trail. . . . 471
13 Fern Lake Loop 472
14 Red Cone Loop 473
15 TJ/Barrett Lake Trail. . 473
16 Emerald Lake Trail . . . 474
17 Valentine
   Lake Trailhead. 474
18 Convict Canyon. 475
19 White Mountain
   Peak Trail 475
20 Methuselah Trail 476

1 Virginia Lakes Trail

8.0 mi/2.0 days

Virginia Lakes form the gateway to a beautiful high-mountain basin that contains eight small alpine lakes within a two-mile radius. The trailhead is at the Big Virginia day-use area, set at 9,500 feet between mountain peaks that jut 12,000 feet into the sky. From here you hike west past Blue Lake to Cooney Lake and on to Frog Lakes (one mile), then start climbing seriously, continuing two more miles to Summit Lake. This lake is set just below the Sierra ridge, between Camiaca Peak (11,739 feet) to the north and Excelsior Mountain (12,446 feet) to the south. The lake makes a good first-night camp, but it can be cold and windy, and in June and early July, hikers will often encounter snow here. If you want to take a longer trip into even wilder country, you can do so from this point. The trail skirts Summit Lake's north end and then enters one of the most remote sections in Yosemite National Park, dropping down into Virginia Canyon along Return Creek.
Location: South of Bridgeport in Humboldt-Toiyabe National Forest; map E5, grid e0.
User groups: Hikers, dogs, and horses. No dogs on trail in Yosemite portion. No mountain bikes. No wheelchair facilities.
Permits: Hikers planning to camp must obtain a wilderness permit. Parking and access are free. Campfires are prohibited above 9,000 feet.
Maps: For a map of Humboldt-Toiyabe National Forest, send $6 to U.S. Forest Service, Attn: Map Sales, P.O. Box 587, Camino, CA 95709; tel. (530) 647-5390, fax (530) 647-5389, or website: www.r5.fs.fed.us/visitorcenter. Major credit cards accepted. Ask the USGS for a topographic map of the Dunderberg Peak area.
Directions: From Bridgeport, drive 13.5 miles south on U.S. 395. Turn west on Virginia Lakes Road/Forest Road 021 and drive seven miles to the trailhead at the Big Virginia day-use area.
Contact: Humboldt-Toiyabe National Forest, Bridgeport Ranger District, HCR 1, Box 1000, Bridgeport, CA 93517; tel. (760) 932-7070 or fax (760) 932-1299.

2 Lundy Lake Trailhead

6.5 mi/4.0 hrs

When you use the Lundy Lake Trailhead as a jump-off point for a backpack trip into the 20

Lakes Basin, you get a passport into the sculpted-granite high country, complete with half a dozen gemlike lakes. The trailhead lies about two miles past Lundy Lake, a long, narrow pool set at 7,800 feet. From here the trail rises along Mill Creek into the Hoover Wilderness, passes several small waterfalls, and arrives at Lake Helen after three miles. The next mile brings you to Odell Lake and little Twin Lake; take your pick. It is a 5.4-mile hike one way to the 20 Lakes Basin, though many people hike a little more than half that far, then turn around and return for an excellent day hike. This region has Yosemite-style high-country beauty, yet it's located just to the east of the park boundary. You can extend your trip quite easily, creating a great one-way hike with a shuttle. To do so, cross over the top of Lundy Pass and then drop down past Hummingbird Lake to Saddlebag Lake, which at 10,087 feet is the highest drive-to lake in California. That makes it a one-way hike of seven miles.

Location: South of Bridgeport in the Hoover Wilderness, in Inyo National Forest; map E5, grid f0.

User groups: Hikers, dogs, horses, and mountain bikes (up to the wilderness border). Note that the Lundy Canyon Trail is open to dogs, but the bordering slopes and high country bordering the trail are closed to dogs for the protection of endangered Sierra bighorn sheep. No wheelchair facilities.

Permits: Hikers planning to camp must obtain a wilderness permit.

Maps: For a map of Inyo National Forest, send $6 to U.S. Forest Service, Attn: Map Sales, P.O. Box 587, Camino, CA 95709; tel. (530) 647-5390, fax (530) 647-5389, or website: www.r5.fs.fed.us/visitorcenter. Major credit cards accepted. Ask the USGS for topographic maps of the Lundy and Dunderberg Peak areas.

Directions: From Lee Vining drive north on U.S. 395 for seven miles to the Lundy Lake Road exit. Turn west on Lundy Lake Road and drive five miles to Lundy Lake. Drive two miles west (on an unpaved road) past Lundy Lake to the trailhead at the end of the road.

Contact: Inyo National Forest, Mono Lake Visitor Center, P.O. Box 429, Lee Vining, CA 93541; tel. (760) 647-3044 or fax (760) 647-3046.

3 Gibbs Lake Trail
7.6 mi/4.75 hrs

The 3.8-mile hike from Upper Horse Meadow to Gibbs Lake truly is one of the greatest day hikes in California. Since the trailhead isn't located at a lake or other attractive setting, nobody gets here by accident. The trail starts at Upper Horse Meadow, elevation 8,000 feet, and climbs up Gibbs Canyon to Gibbs Lake, at 9,530 feet. That's about a 1,500-foot climb, and except for .5 mile of switchbacks at the beginning, most of the route rises on a steady grade along Gibbs Creek. It is a pretty spot, backed by bare granite and fronted by conifers. The trail ends at Gibbs Lake, so you do not have to compete for trail space or a lakeside picnic site with backpackers arriving from other trails.

Location: West of Lee Vining on the northern boundary of the Ansel Adams Wilderness; map E5, grid g0.

User groups: Hikers, horses, and mountain bikes (up to the wilderness border). No dogs permitted to protect endangered Sierra bighorn sheep. No wheelchair facilities.

Permits: Hikers planning to camp must obtain a wilderness permit.

Maps: For a map of Inyo National Forest, send $6 to U.S. Forest Service, Attn: Map Sales, P.O. Box 587, Camino, CA 95709; tel. (530) 647-5390, fax (530) 647-5389, or website: www.r5.fs.fed.us/visitorcenter. Major credit cards accepted. Ask the USGS for topographic maps of the Lee Vining and Mount areas.

Directions: From Lee Vining, drive about one mile south on U.S. 395 and then turn west (right) on Forest Road 1N16 (look for the sign indicating Horse Meadow). Drive about three miles to the trailhead at the end of the road. Note: Forest Road 1N16 requires a four-wheel-drive vehicle with high clearance.

Contact: Inyo National Forest, Mono Lake Visitor Center, P.O. Box 429, Lee Vining, CA 93541; tel. (760) 647-3044 or fax (760) 647-3046.

4 Mono Lake South Tufa Trail
1.0 mi/0.5 hr

The strange and remarkable tufa towers, spires, and knobs at Mono Lake embellish one of the most extraordinary landscapes in California. The terrain resembles a moonscape and has even been called "a landing pad for spaceships," but by anybody's definition it's is a peculiar place that lures thousands of people every summer who come to take a short walk. The actual loop trail is only one mile long, but there are several spurs that can add extra miles to your hike. You stroll along the southern shore of the lake, near the South Tufa Area. This is where the strange and gigantic tufa spires sit like old, untouched earth castles. Mono Lake itself is vast—covering 60 square miles—and is estimated to be more than 700,000 years old, making it one of the oldest lakes in North America. The lake's basin has become one of the world's most prolific stopover points for gulls, grebes, plovers, and phalaropes during their annual southbound flights. That's because the alkaline properties of the water create prime habitat for brine shrimp (an ideal food for these birds), and the lake's islands provide isolation from predators; 80 percent of the California gull population nests here.

Location: East of Lee Vining in the Mono Lake Tufa State Reserve, at the southern end of Mono Lake; map E5, grid f2.

User groups: Hikers, wheelchairs, and dogs. No horses or mountain bikes.

Permits: No permits are required. An entrance fee of $3 is charged adults over 17, free to those 17 and under.

Maps: For a free map of the lake, contact the Mono Lake Tufa State Reserve at the address below. Brochures are available for $1. Ask the USGS for topographic maps of the Lee Vining and Mono Mills areas.

Directions: From Lee Vining, drive five miles south on U.S. 395 and then take Highway 120 east for five miles. Turn left at the sign for South Tufa and drive (a dirt road) for .9 mile to the parking area.

Contact: Mono Lake Tufa State Reserve, P.O. Box 90, Lee Vining, CA 93541; tel. (760) 647-6331; Mono Basin National Forest Scenic Area, P.O. Box 429, Lee Vining, CA 93541; tel. (760) 525-7232 or fax (760) 647-6331.

5 Walker Lake Trailhead
8.2 mi/5.0 hrs.

Lower Sardine Lake is a jewel cradled in a high glacial bowl at 9,888 feet, the kind of lake that made the Ansel Adams Wilderness one of the most treasured places in the world. The hike in is tough and steep, with only one short, flat section to provide much of a break. At first the route is easy and beautiful, skirting the northern edge of Walker Lake to its headwaters, Walker Creek. From here you head up Bloody Canyon, climbing nearly 2,000 feet in less than two miles. The hike parallels Walker Creek, requiring two stream crossings on the way up to Lower Sardine Lake. For anyone who is either out of shape or not acclimated to the altitude, the climb can be rough going—a real wheezer. The trail usually opens by mid-June, though this varies each year depending on the snowpack. Backpackers can opt to continue hiking up and over Mono Pass and into Yosemite National Park's most remote backcountry.

Location: Southwest of Lee Vining at the northeastern boundary of the Ansel Adams Wilderness; map E5, grid g0.

User groups: Hikers, horses, and mountain bikes (up to the wilderness border). No dogs permitted to protect endangered Sierra bighorn sheep. No wheelchair facilities.

Permits: Hikers planning to camp must obtain a wilderness permit.

Maps: For a map of Inyo National Forest, send $6 to U.S. Forest Service, Attn: Map Sales, P.O. Box 587, Camino, CA 95709; tel. (530) 647-5390, fax (530) 647-5389, or website: www.r5.fs.fed.us/visitorcenter. Major credit cards accepted. Ask the USGS for topographic maps of the Mount Dana and Koip Peak areas.

Directions: From Lee Vining drive about four miles south on U.S. 395 to Walker Lake Road, located one mile north of the June Lake turnoff. Turn west on Walker Lake Road and drive 3.5 miles to a Y. Bear right and drive 2.7 miles to the trailhead (located one mile from Walker Lake). Most of the access road is unpaved.

Contact: Inyo National Forest, Mono Lake Visitor Center, P.O. Box 429, Lee Vining, CA 93541; tel. (760) 647-3044 or fax (760) 647-3046.

6 Parker Lake Trail
3.6 mi/2.0 hrs

The first 20 minutes of this hike will have you feeling as if you're on the trail to nowhere in a B-grade western flick, about to be ambushed. Hang on to your saddle horn because happy trails are ahead as you transition into a mixed forest alongside Parker Creek, complete with quaking aspens. A few minutes later you will suddenly emerge from the forest onto the lake's shore. The beauty of the lake and towering mountain just might knock your boots off, or at least socks off. The lake is surrounded by granite walls that are impassable. No trails lead out of the basin, save for the one easy route along Parker Creek. Beginning at an elevation of 8,000 feet above Parker Creek, the trail follows the creek upstream—an easy romp for most—before arriving at Parker Lake at 8,318 feet. You know, the high Sierra is known for the long killer grades that hikers must take to reach pristine high mountain lakes, but the Parker Lake Trail provides an easy alternative. Not only is the walk to the lake just 1.8 miles long, but it entails an elevation gain of a mere 300 feet. Yes, there is a God! Though the nearby June Lake Loop gets a lot of vacation traffic, this trailhead is obscure enough that most visitors pass it by. This hike makes an excellent day trip.

Location: South of Lee Vining in the Ansel Adams Wilderness, west of Grant Lake; map E5, grid h0.

User groups: Hikers, dogs, and horses. No mountain bikes. No wheelchair facilities.

Permits: Hikers planning to camp must obtain a wilderness permit.

Maps: For a map of Inyo National Forest, send $6 to U.S. Forest Service, Attn: Map Sales, P.O. Box 587, Camino, CA 95709; tel. (530) 647-5390, fax (530) 647-5389, or website: www.r5.fs.fed.us/visitorcenter. Major credit cards accepted. Ask the USGS for topographic maps of the Mount Dana and Koip Peak areas.

Directions: From Lee Vining drive about four miles south on U.S. 395 to Highway 158/June Lake Loop. Turn right, drive 1.5 miles, turn right on Parker Lake Road/Forest Road 1S25, and drive 1.8 miles. Bear left on Forest Road 1S26 and drive .6 mile until the road dead-ends at the trailhead at Parker Creek. The last 2.4 miles are unpaved.

Contact: Inyo National Forest, Mono Lake Visitor Center, P.O. Box 429, Lee Vining, CA 93541; tel. (760) 647-3044 or fax (760) 647-3046.

7 Silver Lake Trail
19.2 mi/3.0 days

Some places will never change, and people are drawn to them because they provide a sense of permanence that can't be found anywhere else. That is how it is at the Rush Creek headwaters. Created from drops of melting snow near the Sierra crest at 10,500 feet, this stream runs downhill for miles, rolling into the forest like a swirling emerald green fountain. Even a short visit requires a long drive to the trailhead, followed by a demanding backpacking trek. In the process, hikers contend with a 10-mile climb out, ice-cold stream crossings, and the possibility of afternoon thunderstorms in which lightning bolts and thunderclaps rattle off the canyon rims.

The trailhead lies at Silver Lake, elevation 7,200 feet. After departing Silver Lake, hikers follow the trail adjacent to Lower Rush Creek upstream toward the Ansel Adams Wilderness. After three miles, they arrive at beautiful Gem Lake (8,052 feet) and then at Waugh Lake (9,424 feet), at the seven-mile point. Many visitors never venture farther than these lakes, simply stopping to camp, swim, or fish. But upstream of Waugh Lake is where you find the Rush Creek headwaters, along with the flawless symmetry of the untouched high country. Getting there requires a climb of 3,300 feet over the course of 9.6 miles, but it is one of the prettiest streams anywhere and well worth the effort.

Location: On the eastern boundary of the Ansel Adams Wilderness, west of June Lake; map E5, grid h0.

User groups: Hikers, dogs, and horses. No mountain bikes. No wheelchair facilities.

Permits: Hikers planning to camp must obtain a wilderness permit.

Maps: For a map of Inyo National Forest, send $6 to U.S. Forest Service, Attn: Map Sales, P.O. Box 587, Camino, CA 95709; tel. (530) 647-5390, fax (530) 647-5389, or website: www.r5.fs.fed.us/visitorcenter. Major credit cards accepted. Ask the USGS for topographic maps of the June Lake and Koip Peak areas.

Directions: From Lee Vining drive about 11 miles south on U.S. 395 to June Lake Junction. Make a right turn on Highway 158/June Lake Road and drive seven miles to the Rush Creek trailhead across the road from the Silver Lake Campground.

Contact: Inyo National Forest, Mono Lake Visitor Center, P.O. Box 429, Lee Vining, CA 93541; tel. (760) 647-3044 or fax (760) 647-3046.

8 Yost Lake Trail
4.8-9.5 mi/1.0 day

Yost Lake is a small glacial lake hidden at 9,000 feet on the June Mountain slopes. Many people visit the June Lakes area for years without even knowing Yost exists. But it is up here, tucked away and accessible only to those willing to hike. From the trailhead (7,800 feet) at June Lake, the Yost Meadows Trail rises very steeply in the first .5 mile, climbing nearly 1,000

feet, a real butt-kicker for many. That discourages many from going farther; after all, it is 4.75 miles to the lake. Ah, but after that first grunt of a climb, the trail gets much easier, contouring across the mountain slopes. It rises gradually to the headwaters of Yost Creek and then drops into the small basin that guards the lake.

A shorter option is to begin at the Yost Creek/Fern Lake Trailhead, making it a 4.8-mile round trip. It is just as pretty, but is very steep in the first mile, and slippery for those not wearing heavy, firm-gripping hiking boots. The trailhead is located three miles west of the town of June Lake on the west (left) side of June Lake Road.

Location: On the eastern boundary of the Ansel Adams Wilderness, at June Lake; map E5, grid i0.

User groups: Hikers, dogs, and horses. No mountain bikes. No wheelchair facilities.

Permits: Hikers planning to camp must obtain a wilderness permit.

Maps: For a map of Inyo National Forest, send $6 to U.S. Forest Service, Attn: Map Sales, P.O. Box 587, Camino, CA 95709; tel. (530) 647-5390, fax (530) 647-5389, or website: www.r5.fs.fed.us/visitorcenter. Major credit cards accepted. Ask the USGS for topographic maps of the June Lake and Mammoth Mountain areas.

Directions: From Lee Vining, drive about 11 miles south on U.S. 395 to June Lake Junction. Go right on Highway 158/June Lake Road and drive two miles to the town of June Lake. The trailhead is on the west (left), across the road from the fire station.

Contact: Inyo National Forest, Mono Lake Visitor Center, P.O. Box 429, Lee Vining, CA 93541; tel. (760) 647-3044 or fax (760) 647-3046.

9 Inyo Craters
0.75 mi/1.5 hrs

A geologic phenomenon, the Inyo Craters make a great destination for an easy day hike in the Mammoth Lakes area. The craters are phreatic tips, meaning that they were created by a steam explosion. Long ago when the mountain was a smoldering volcano, melted snow poured into it, and when the cold water hit hot magma—kaboom! The hike is gentle uphill and short, less than .5 mile, but the elevation sucks the air out of some visitors from homes at sea level. The landscape through open forest sprinkled with red fir and Jeffrey pine. In each of the two craters there's a tiny pond that's filled with the collected drops of melting snow each spring.

Location: In Inyo National Forest north of Mammoth Lakes; map E5, grid i1.

User groups: Hikers, horses, and dogs. No mountain bikes. No wheelchair facilities.

Permits: No permits are required.

Maps: For a map of Inyo National Forest, send $6 to U.S. Forest Service, Attn: Map Sales, P.O. Box 587, Camino, CA 95709; tel. (530) 647-5390, fax (530) 647-5389, or website: www.r5.fs.fed.us/visitorcenter. Major credit cards accepted. Ask the USGS for a topographic map of the Mammoth Mountain area.

Directions: From Lee Vining drive about 20 miles south on U.S. 395 to the Mammoth Lakes Scenic Loop/Forest Road 3S23. Turn right and drive 3.2 miles to Forest Road 3S30. Turn right and drive .3 mile to Forest Road 3S29. Turn right and drive to the parking area for the Inyo Craters Picnic Area. The last 1.3 miles is unpaved.

Contact: Inyo National Forest, Mammoth Ranger Station, P.O. Box 148, Mammoth Lakes, CA 93546; tel. (760) 934-2505, tel. (760) 924-5500, or fax (760) 924-5537.

10 Upper Soda Springs Trailhead

2.75 mi/2.0 hrs

The Upper San Joaquin River is an angler's paradise, a beautiful stream that tumbles over rocks and into pools. There have been days in late June and July when we've caught and released 50 to 60 trout. Most of them are little guys, rarely more than 10 inches long, but they include brook, rainbow, and brown trout, and even the occasional golden trout. Things are much different just a mile or two downriver near Devils Postpile, where a small stretch of water that is easily accessible from campgrounds gets hammered day after day all summer long.

For the best fishing, hike from the Soda Springs Campground on the River Trail upstream along the San Joaquin River, heading out at least a mile before wetting a line. Along the way, enjoy the canyon views and lush streamside vegetation. The best technique is to fly-fish using a floating line, a nine-foot leader, nymphs, and a strike indicator (many of the strikes are very soft).

If you want to hike, not fish, it is a 6.9-mile trek from the trailhead to Thousand Island Lake (9,833 feet), a divine spot where huge boulders dot the surface waters, creating the appearance of miniature islands. The views of Banner and Ritter Peaks, along with the rest of the Minarets, are unsurpassed from this vantage point. In spring here, it seems that a new wildflower variety blooms every week.

Location: In the Ansel Adams Wilderness, west of Mammoth Lakes; map E5, grid j0.

User groups: Hikers, dogs, and horses. No mountain bikes. No wheelchair facilities.

Permits: Hikers planning to camp in the wilderness must obtain a wilderness permit.

Maps: For a map of Inyo National Forest, send $6 to U.S. Forest Service, Attn: Map Sales, P.O. Box 587, Camino, CA 95709; tel. (530) 647-5390, fax (530) 647-5389, or website: www.r5.fs.fed.us/visitorcenter. Major credit cards accepted. Ask the USGS for a topographic map of the Mammoth Mountain area.

Directions: On U.S. 395, drive to Mammoth Lakes Junction/Highway 203. Turn west on Highway 203 and drive four miles, through the town of Mammoth Lakes to Minaret Road (still Highway 203). Turn right and drive 4.5 miles to the entrance kiosk (adjacent to the Mammoth Mountain Ski Area). From the entry kiosk, continue nine miles to Upper Soda Springs Campground (well signed). Turn right and drive to the camping area. The trailhead is just west of here.

Access note: Noncampers arriving between 7:30 a.m. and 5:30 p.m. are required to take a shuttle bus ($5 to $9, with many price levels and exceptions) from the Mammoth Mountain Ski Area to access this area.

Contact: Inyo National Forest, Mammoth Ranger Station, P.O. Box 148, Mammoth Lakes, CA 93546; tel. (760) 924-5500 or fax (760) 924-5537.

11 Rainbow Falls Trail
1.5 mi/1.5 hrs

The first time you lay eyes on Rainbow Falls, this tall, wide, and often forceful waterfall comes as an awesome surprise. The cascade inspires as much as it astonishes, yet it is often overlooked for nearby Devils Postpile (the world's best example of columnar-jointed rock), the adjacent Ansel Adams Wilderness, and of course Mammoth Lakes and the dozens of nearby recreation destinations. But this is still one of the best short hikes in California. The trail starts just beyond the Reds Meadows Resort, which is actually more of a headquarters for horseback riders, and then is routed south down into the Middle Fork San Joaquin River canyon. Except for the first .25 mile, most of this trail is routed through burned-out forest. It's like a one-note samba, and while you will quickly tire of it, it makes Rainbow Falls seem even more beautiful. You will notice that true rainbow can be seen in the waterfall's mist from one side, but that same rainbow disappears from the other, the result of prism effect from sun rays refracting through the water. At the brink of the falls, a short cutoff trail allows hikers to loop down to the falls' base for a classic vantage point. You also can hike another .5 mile downstream to find a smaller waterfall. For such a short walk, the Rainbow Falls Trail is a classic. In addition, you can turn this hike into the Devils Postpile Waterfall "Grand Slam." This is an eight-mile circuit to see Devils Postpile, Rainbow Falls, Lower Falls and Minaret Falls. If you get up early, beat the 7:30 a.m. shuttle bus deadline, this can be an extraordinary way to spend a morning, topping it with lunch at Reds Meadows or in Mammoth Lakes.

Location: In Devils Postpile National Monument west of Mammoth Lakes; map E5, grid j0.

User groups: Hikers, dogs, and horses. No mountain bikes. No wheelchair facilities.

Permits: No permits are required.

Maps: For a map of Inyo National Forest, send $6 to U.S. Forest Service, Attn: Map Sales, P.O. Box 587, Camino, CA 95709; tel. (530) 647-5390, fax (530) 647-5389, or website: www.r5.fs.fed.us/visitorcenter. Major credit cards accepted. Ask the USGS for a topographic map of the Mammoth Mountain area.

Directions: On U.S. 395, drive to Mammoth Lakes Junction/Highway 203. Turn west on Highway 203 and drive four miles, through the town of Mammoth Lakes to Minaret Road (still Highway 203). Turn right and drive 4.5 miles to the entrance kiosk (adjacent to the Mammoth Mountain Ski Area). From the entry kiosk, continue 9.5 miles (past Reds Meadows Resort turnoff) to the parking area on the right (well signed).

Access note: Noncampers arriving between 7:30 a.m. and 5:30 p.m. are required to take a shuttle bus ($5 to $9, with many price levels and exceptions) from the Mammoth Mountain Ski Area to access this area.

Contact: Devils Postpile National Monument, tel./fax (760) 934-2289; Inyo National Forest, Mammoth Ranger Station, P.O. Box 148, Mammoth Lakes, CA 93546; tel. (760) 924-5500 or fax (760) 924-5537.

12 Minaret Lake Trail
14.8 mi/2.0 days

With an early start and a fresh head of steam, you can make the 7.4-mile, 1,800-foot climb from Devils Postpile to Minaret Lake in a good morning's effort. There's perhaps no better place to have a picnic lunch. It is enchanting, and Minaret Lake is a real prize, set just below the awesome glacial-carved Minaret Range at 9,793 feet. From the trailhead you hike north on the John Muir Trail to just beyond Johnston Lake and then take the left fork along Minaret Creek. The trail rises with the creek and in the last mile climbs steeply above tree line before skirting the Minaret Lake outlet. A high, impassable back wall frames the lake, and the trail circles around the northern shore. You've made it to the kind of place where John Muir got religion.

Location: In the Ansel Adams Wilderness, west of Mammoth Lakes; map E5, grid j0.

User groups: Hikers, dogs, and horses. Dogs must be leashed in the national monument. No mountain bikes. No wheelchair facilities.

Permits: Hikers planning to camp in the wilderness must obtain a wilderness permit.

Maps: For a map of Inyo National Forest, send $6 to U.S. Forest Service, Attn: Map Sales, P.O. Box 587, Camino, CA 95709; tel. (530) 647-5390, fax (530) 647-5389, or website: www.r5.fs.fed.us/visitorcenter. Major credit cards accepted. Ask the USGS for topographic maps of the Mammoth Mountain and Mount Ritter areas.

Directions: On U.S. 395, drive to Mammoth Lakes Junction/Highway 203. Turn west on Highway 203 and drive four miles, through the town of Mammoth Lakes to Minaret Road (still Highway 203). Turn right and drive 4.5 miles to the entrance kiosk (adjacent to the Mammoth Mountain Ski Area). From the entry kiosk, continue nine miles to Upper Soda Springs Campground. Turn here and park adjacent to the campground and trailhead for John Muir Trail. You must hike 1.5 miles on the John Muir Trail to reach the Minaret Lake Trailhead.

Access note: Noncampers arriving between 7:30 a.m. and 5:30 p.m. are required to take a shuttle bus ($5 to $9, with many price levels and exceptions) from the Mammoth Mountain Ski Area to access this area.

Contact: Inyo National Forest, Mammoth Ranger Station, P.O. Box 148, Mammoth Lakes, CA 93546; tel. (760) 924-5500 or fax (760) 924-5537.

13 Fern Lake Loop

13.0 mi/2.0 days

Fern Lake can be the focus of an ambitious round-trip day hike to Devils Postpile, or better, the start of a great 13-mile loop trip. Either way, this is an excellent hike, and one that has become very popular—the only drawback.

Starting at Devils Postpile, you hike five miles to Fern Lake, climbing most of the way. This small lake is set in a rock bowl at tree line, below Iron Mountain in the Minarets. From here, the trail contours north across the mountain, poking in and out of sparse forest and bare granite, to Beck Cabin (a 1.1-mile side trip takes you to Beck Lakes at 9,803 feet). The route back drops 4.8 miles down to the John Muir Trail, including a very steep .5 mile on switchbacks. To complete the loop, turn right and hike the final 1.4 miles to Devils Postpile. We strongly advise taking the side trip to Beck Lakes, set in a glacial-formed pocket just below the Minarets ridge amid celestial mountain scenery.

Location: In the Ansel Adams Wilderness, west of Mammoth Lakes; map E5, grid j0.

User groups: Hikers, dogs, and horses. Dogs must be leashed in the national monument. No mountain bikes. No wheelchair facilities.

Permits: Hikers planning to camp in the wilderness must obtain a wilderness permit.

Maps: For a map of Inyo National Forest, send $6 to U.S. Forest Service, Attn: Map Sales, P.O. Box 587, Camino, CA 95709; tel. (530) 647-5390, fax (530) 647-5389, or website: www.r5.fs.fed.us/visitorcenter. Major credit cards accepted. Ask the USGS for topographic maps of the Crystal Crag and Cattle Mountain areas.

Directions: On U.S. 395 drive to Mammoth Lakes Junction/Highway 203. Turn west on Highway 203 and drive four miles, through the town of Mammoth Lakes to Minaret Road (still Highway 203). Turn right and drive 4.5 miles to the entrance kiosk (adjacent to the Mammoth Mountain Ski Area). From the entry kiosk continue nine miles to Upper Soda Springs Campground. Turn here and park adjacent to the campground. The trailhead is just west of here.

Access note: Noncampers arriving between 7:30 a.m. and 5:30 p.m. are required to take a shuttle bus ($5 to $9, with many price levels and exceptions) from the Mammoth Mountain Ski Area to access this area.

Contact: Inyo National Forest, Mammoth Ranger Station, P.O. Box 148, Mammoth Lakes, CA 93546; tel. (760) 924-5500 or fax (760) 924-5537.

14 Red Cone Loop
6.7 mi/4.0 hrs

Horseshoe Lake, elevation 8,900 feet, lies at the end of the Mammoth Lakes road, an excellent trailhead that makes for a great day hike. The loop trail tops out near Crater Meadow, a beautiful little spot set just below Red Cones, about a five-minute walk off the main trail. This is your destination, a spot where you can have a picnic lunch in peace before enjoying the walk back down. The contrast is striking: just a short distance below there are typically many people at Twin Lakes, Lake Mary, Lake Mamie, and Lake George, yet you are separated from them by Mammoth Pass. You will be surprised at how relatively few people take this loop hike and happy that you made the choice to do so.

Location: At Horseshoe Lake in Mammoth Lakes; map E5, grid j0.

User groups: Hikers, dogs, and horses. No mountain bikes are allowed past the wilderness border. No wheelchair facilities.

Permits: Hikers planning to camp must obtain a wilderness permit.

Maps: For a map of Inyo National Forest, send $6 to U.S. Forest Service, Attn: Map Sales, P.O. Box 587, Camino, CA 95709; tel. (530) 647-5390, fax (530) 647-5389, or website: www.r5.fs.fed.us/visitorcenter. Major credit cards accepted. Ask the USGS for a topographic map of the Crystal Crag area.

Directions: On U.S. 395, drive to Mammoth Lakes Junction/Highway 203. Turn west on Highway 203 and drive four miles, through the town of Mammoth Lakes to the junction of Minaret Road/Highway 203 and Lake Mary Road. Continue straight on Lake Mary Road and drive 4.75 miles to road's end. The trailhead is on the west side of Horseshoe Lake.

Contact: Inyo National Forest, Mammoth Ranger Station, P.O. Box 148, Mammoth Lakes, CA 93546; tel. (760) 924-5500 or fax (760) 924-5537.

15 TJ/Barrett Lake Trail
1.0 mi/0.5 hr

Campers at Lake George will be pleased to find that this easy, short trail provides access to hidden TJ and Barrett Lakes. It's a revelation to many that a pretty alpine lake within easy reach can also be very secluded. The trail starts at the campground at Lake George and then leads up the inlet stream to TJ Lake. You make a left turn and walk .25 mile to Barrett Lake. Crystal Crag (10,377 feet) towers above the whole basin, adding great natural beauty to the scene.

Location: At Lake George in Mammoth Lakes; map E5, grid j0.

User groups: Hikers, horses, and dogs. Mountain bikes are not advised. No wheelchair facilities.

Permits: No permits are required.

Maps: For a map of Inyo National Forest, send $6 to U.S. Forest Service, Attn: Map Sales, P.O. Box 587, Camino, CA 95709; tel. (530) 647-5390, fax (530) 647-5389, or website: www.r5.fs.fed.us/visitorcenter. Major credit cards accepted. Ask the USGS for a topographic map of the Crystal Crag area.

Directions: On U.S. 395 drive to Mammoth Lakes Junction/Highway 203. Turn west on Highway 203 and drive four miles, through the town of Mammoth Lakes to the junction of Minaret Road/Highway 203 and Lake Mary Road. Continue straight on Lake Mary Road and drive 3.75 miles to Lake Mary Loop Drive. Turn left and drive .3 mile to Lake George

Road. Turn right and drive .5 mile to the campground. The trailhead is at the campground near the northeast shore of the lake.

Contact: Inyo National Forest, Mammoth Ranger Station, P.O. Box 148, Mammoth Lakes, CA 93546; tel. (760) 924-5500 or fax (760) 924-5537.

16 Emerald Lake Trail
2.0 mi/1.0 hrs

Nature's artwork is just about perfect here. This is short and sweet, a scenic trail to Emerald Lake. The trail starts just south of Lake Mary, at the end of the road beyond the Coldwater Campground. The hike is short and direct, starting by climbing up to Sky Meadows and to Emerald Lake. This short, scenic loop provides a glimpse of classic high Sierra country, most of it ranging between 9,000 and 9,500 feet in elevation.

Location: At Lake Mary in Mammoth Lakes; map E5, grid j0.

User groups: Hikers, dogs, and horses. No mountain bikes are allowed past the wilderness boundary. No wheelchair facilities.

Permits: Hikers planning to camp must obtain a wilderness permit.

Maps: For a map of Inyo National Forest, send $6 to U.S. Forest Service, Attn: Map Sales, P.O. Box 587, Camino, CA 95709; tel. (530) 647-5390, fax (530) 647-5389, or website: www.r5.fs.fed.us/visitorcenter. Major credit cards accepted. Ask the USGS for a topographic map of the Crystal Crag area.

Directions: On U.S. 395 drive to Mammoth Junction/Highway 203. Turn west on Highway 203 and drive four miles, through the town of Mammoth Lakes to the junction of Minaret Road/Highway 203 and Lake Mary Road. Continue straight on Lake Mary Road and drive to Coldwater Campground on the left. Turn left and drive a short distance to the campground. Turn left on the campground road and continue through the camp to the south end to the trailhead parking lot (south of Lake Mary).

Contact: Inyo National Forest, Mammoth Ranger Station, P.O. Box 148, Mammoth Lakes, CA 93546; tel. (760) 924-5500 or fax (760) 924-5537.

17 Valentine Lake Trailhead
11.2 mi/1.0 day

The Mammoth Lakes area is one of the eastern Sierra's star attractions, yet nearby Valentine Lake, though not quite lost, is largely forgotten. Perhaps the little lake is overlooked because the trailhead (7,600 feet) is not found at one of the lakes in the Mammoth Lakes Basin or at nearby Devils Postpile. Or perhaps it's because the climb required to get there is so steep. Regardless of the reason, a morning's hike—rising some 2,100 feet over 5.6 miles—gets you to the lake, which sits at 9,698 feet.

Some say the lake is shaped like a teardrop, but when we visited, we thought it looked more like a drop of sweat. The hike starts out with a very steep climb, including .5 mile of switchbacks, until you reach 8,500 feet. After that, the trail laterals Sherwin Creek, including two more sets of switchbacks, before finally taking you to the lake's outlet. Valentine Lake is surrounded by high mountain walls on three sides, making it impossible to go much farther.

Location: In Inyo National Forest south of Mammoth Lakes; map E5, grid j1.

User groups: Hikers, dogs, and horses. No mountain bikes are allowed past the wilderness boundary. No wheelchair facilities.

Permits: Hikers planning to camp must obtain a wilderness permit.

Maps: For a map of Inyo National Forest, send $6 to U.S. Forest Service, Attn: Map Sales, P.O. Box 587, Camino, CA 95709; tel. (530) 647-5390, fax (530) 647-5389, or website: www.r5.fs.fed.us/visitorcenter. Major credit cards accepted. Ask the USGS for a topographic map of the Crystal Crag area.

Directions: On U.S. 395 drive to Sherwin Creek Road (located two miles south of Mammoth Lakes Junction). Turn west and drive 2.5 miles to a spur road on the left (.2 mile past Summers Road; if you see the turnoffs for the

L.A.YMCA Camp or Sherwin Creek Campground, you have gone too far). Turn left on the spur road and drive a short distance to the trailhead. The last 2.5 miles of the road are unpaved.

Contact: Inyo National Forest, Mammoth Ranger Station, P.O. Box 148, Mammoth Lakes, CA 93546; tel. (760) 924-5500 or fax (760) 924-5537.

18 Convict Canyon

15.4 mi/2.0 days

Framed by a back wall of bare granite peaks, Convict Lake is a mountain shrine, and the trail that leads from here into the backcountry wilderness makes hikers feel as if they're ascending into heaven. But this is no easy trip. Not only is there a long, grueling climb—gaining 3,000 feet in 7.7 miles—but a tricky and sometimes dangerous stream crossing is involved. The trail starts near Convict Lake (the trailhead is well signed) at 7,621 feet, skirts along the lake's north shore, and then leads up through a canyon alongside Convict Creek. About three miles in you have to ford Convict Creek, which usually requires getting wet and can be dangerous in the early summer because of high snowmelt. (Many attempts to bridge this crossing have failed, as the bridge always gets washed out by high flows in early summer.) If you get past that crossing, you follow the trail up to a series of large, untouched lakes: Mildred Lake, Dorothy Lake (10,275 feet), Lake Genevieve (10,000 feet), Bighorn Lake, Edith Lake, and Cloverleaf Lake. Take your pick. You can spend days exploring this high-mountain paradise.

Location: On the eastern boundary of the John Muir Wilderness, south of Mammoth Lakes; map E5, grid j3.

User groups: Hikers, dogs, and horses. No mountain bikes. No wheelchair facilities.

Permits: No permits are required. Permits are required for campers.

Maps: For a map of Inyo National Forest, send $6 to U.S. Forest Service, Attn: Map Sales, P.O. Box 587, Camino, CA 95709; tel. (530) 647-5390, fax (530) 647-5389, or website: www.r5.fs.fed.us/visitorcenter. Major credit cards accepted. Ask the USGS for a topographic map of the Bloody Mountain area.

Directions: On U.S. 395, drive to Convict Lake Road (near Mammoth Lakes Airport, six miles south of Mammoth Lakes Junction). Turn west and drive 1.8 miles to a spur road on the right as you near the lake. Turn right and drive .25 mile to the parking area for the trailhead.

Contact: Inyo National Forest, Mammoth Ranger Station, P.O. Box 148, Mammoth Lakes, CA 93546; tel. (760) 924-5500 or fax (760) 924-5537.

19 White Mountain Peak Trail

7.5 mi/6.0 hrs

White Mountain Peak is the third tallest peak in California, only 249 feet lower than the highest, Mount Whitney (Mount Williamson is second in line), yet it is little known to hikers outside of the area. It's so tall that the 14,246-foot summit is the site of a University of California high-altitude research lab. This hike is a butt-kicker, following an old Navy-built road as it climbs 2,600 feet in 7.5 miles at high altitude. The trail starts at a locked gate and then leads past Mount Barcroft (13,040 feet) on a long grind. It's not intimate, but rather open and often wind-swept, and the high altitudes make the trip very difficult, even dizzying, for many. The summit constitutes an impressive granite massif with grand views. To the east you can see 200 miles into Nevada, and to the west, the Owens Valley and Volcanic Tableland. As you hike, you feel that you're entering a different world. When you reach the top, you realize that you are. Thunderstorms and lightning strikes are common here. Do not make this trip if cumulus start building, particularly on warm summer afternoons. Also note that marmots are prolific at the trailhead and will eat radiator hoses or even chew on radiators if there is any scent from

even a tiny leak. It not only will maroon you when you return from your hike, an exhausting trip, but can poison the friendly little fellows.
Location: In Inyo National Forest northeast of Bishop; map E5, grid j9.
User groups: Hikers only advised. Dogs, horses, and mountain bikes are permitted, but due to extremely high altitudes they are strongly not advised. No wheelchair facilities.
Permits: No permits are required.
Maps: For a map of Inyo National Forest, send $6 to U.S. Forest Service, Attn: Map Sales, P.O. Box 587, Camino, CA 95709; tel. (530) 647-5390, fax (530) 647-5389, or website: www.r5.fs.fed.us/ visitorcenter. Major credit cards accepted. Ask the USGS for a topographic map of the White Mountain Peak area.
Directions: From U.S. 395 at Big Pine, take Highway 168 east toward Nevada (after a few hundred yards, look for large sign indicating whether or not the road is open). Drive northeast on Highway 168 for 13 miles to White Mountain Road. Turn left on White Mountain Road and drive north for 10 miles to the Schulman Grove turnoff. Continue on White Mountain Road (it becomes unpaved at Schulman Grove turnoff) for 16 miles to the locked gate at the road's end. This is the trailhead. Park to the left side, making sure you aren't blocking the road.
Contact: Inyo National Forest, White Mountain Ranger Station, 798 N. Main Street, Bishop, CA 93514; tel. (760) 873-2500 or fax (760) 873-2563.

20 Methuselah Trail
4.25 mi/2.25 hrs

The Methuselah Tree is the prize of the Ancient Bristlecone Pine Forest. Here for more than 4,000 years, it's the oldest living tree documented in the world. But forest rangers won't tell you which one it is, out of fear that some dimwit will cut it down. So you have to be satisfied just knowing you have walked among the ancients, rather than actually seeing the grandfather of all trees. The trail starts at the Schulman Grove Picnic Area, where little birds sometimes eat right out of your hand. Schulman Grove, elevation 10,100 feet, is where you find the oldest trees in Bristlecone, and they look their age. Centuries of fire, sand, ice, and wind have sculpted them, giving them the appearance of living driftwood. The trail loops among these trees, with a few short climbs along the way. You will never forget this short, unusual hike.
Location: In Inyo National Forest northeast of Bishop; map E5, grid j9.
User groups: Hikers and leashed dogs. No horses or mountain bikes. No wheelchair facilities.
Permits: No permits are required; $2 fee per person, with a maximum of $5 per group.
Maps: For a map of Inyo National Forest, send $6 to U.S. Forest Service, Attn: Map Sales, P.O. Box 587, Camino, CA 95709; tel. (530) 647-5390, fax (530) 647-5389, or website: www.r5.fs.fed.us/ visitorcenter. Major credit cards accepted. Ask the USGS for a topographic map of the Westgard Pass area.
Directions: From U.S. 395 at Big Pine, take Highway 168 east toward Nevada (after a few hundred yards, look for large sign indicating whether or not the road is open). Drive northeast on Highway 168 for 13 miles to White Mountain Road. Turn left on White Mountain Road and drive north for 10 miles to the Schulman Grove turnoff. Turn right and drive 200 yards to the parking area and trailhead.
Contact: Inyo National Forest, White Mountain Ranger Station, 798 N. Main Street, Bishop, CA 93514; tel. (760) 873-2500 or fax (760) 873-2563.

ANN MARIE BROWN

THE BEACH ALONG
THE SPRING TRAIL AT
ANDREW MOLERA STATE PARK

MAP F1

One inch equals approximately 11 miles.

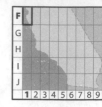

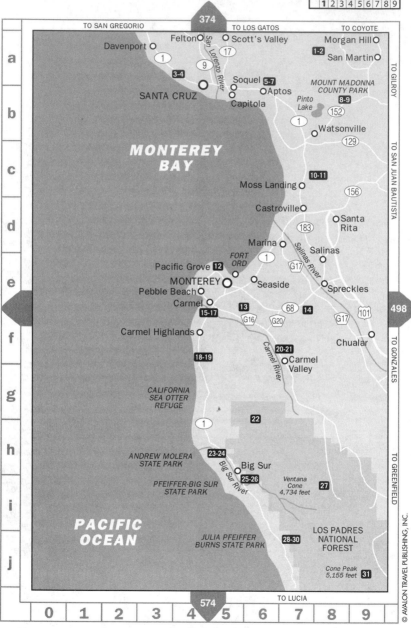

TO SAN GREGORIO   TO LOS GATOS   TO COYOTE

374

Davenport ○   Felton ○ ○ Scott's Valley   Morgan Hill ○
                                                  1-2
a   ○ 17   San Martin ○
        ① 9
      3-4   Soquel **5-7**   MOUNT MADONNA
                    ○ Aptos   COUNTY PARK
SANTA CRUZ   ○ Capitola   **8-9**
b   Pinto ① 152
                                    Lake
                              ○ Watsonville
                                          129

MONTEREY
c   *BAY*   **10-11**
                    Moss Landing ○   156

                    Castroville ○
d   183   ○ Santa
                                              Rita
                    Marina ○
                          FORT   ① 1   Salinas
        Pacific Grove **12** ORD   G17
e   MONTEREY ○   ○ Spreckles
        Pebble Beach ○ ○ Seaside
        Carmel ○   **13**   68 **14**
                    15-17 G16 G20   G17 101
f   Carmel Highlands ○   ○ Chualar
              18-19   **20-21**
                              ○ Carmel
                                Valley
        CALIFORNIA
g   SEA OTTER
        REFUGE   **22**
              ① 1
h   ANDREW MOLERA **23-24**
        STATE PARK   ○ Big Sur
                    25-26
        PFEIFFER-BIG SUR   Ventana **27**
        STATE PARK   Cone
                          4,734 feet
i
PACIFIC   LOS PADRES
OCEAN   JULIA PFEIFFER **28-30** NATIONAL
            BURNS STATE PARK   FOREST
j
                          Cone Peak **31**
                          5,155 feet

TO LUCIA
574

498 TO GONZALES
TO GREENFIELD

0 1 2 3 4 5 6 7 8 9

© AVALON TRAVEL PUBLISHING, INC.

CENTRAL CALIFORNIA

CHAPTER F1

1 Uvas Park
Waterfall Loop 479

2 Alec Canyon
and Contour Loop 480

3 Old Landing
Cove Trail 481

4 Wilder Ridge and
Zane Grey Trails 481

5 Maple Falls 482

6 Loma Prieta
Epicenter 482

7 West Ridge and
Aptos Creek Loop 483

8 White Deer Trail 483

9 Bayview Loop 484

10 Elkhorn Slough
South Marsh Loop 484

11 Moss Landing Wildlife
Area Marsh Trail 485

12 Asilomar Coast Trail . . 485

13 Skyline and
Jacks Peak Trails 486

14 Ollason Peak 486

15 Sea Lion Point Trail . . . 487

16 Whaler's Knoll and
Cypress Grove 487

17 Point Lobos
Perimeter 488

18 Rocky Ridge
and Soberanes
Canyon Loop 488

19 Soberanes Point Trail . 489

20 Lupine, Waterfall,
and Mesa Loop 490

21 Snivley's Ridge Trail . . 490

22 Skinner Ridge Trail
to Devils Peak 491

23 Molera Point Trail 491

24 Molera State
Park Loop 492

25 Pfeiffer Falls and
Valley View Loop 492

26 Buzzards Roost Trail . . 493

27 Pine Valley 493

28 McWay Falls
Overlook 494

29 Ewoldsen Loop Trail . . . 495

30 Partington Point
and Tan Bark Trails . . . 495

31 Cone Peak
Lookout Trail 496

1 Uvas Park Waterfall Loop

1.0 mi/0.5 hr

Uvas Canyon County Park is a little slice of waterfall heaven on the east side of the Santa Cruz Mountains. Although the park has only short hiking trails, it's living proof that good things come in small packages. What's the one key element to a perfect trip? Visit during the rainy season, preferably just after a good downpour. Although the park's creeks flow year-round, only immediately following a good rain can you witness the full watery spectacle. The one-mile Waterfall Loop Trail parades around Swanson Creek's canyon, crossing wooden footbridges and passing 30-foot Black Rock Falls and several smaller falls. Be sure to walk .1 mile past the far end of the loop to see Basin Falls and Upper Falls, both pretty cascades 15 to 25 feet high. The entire canyon comes alive with the sound of rushing water, and a myriad of ferns and foliage grow on every inch of ground. It's a happy place where you can hike around in your rain gear and be smiling the whole time.

Location: In Uvas Canyon County Park near Morgan Hill; map F1, grid a8.

User groups: Hikers and dogs. No horses or mountain bikes. No wheelchair facilities.

Permits: No permits are required. A $4 day-use fee is charged per vehicle.

Maps: A free map of Uvas Canyon County Park is available at the visitor center. Ask the USGS for a topographic map of the Loma Prieta area.

Directions: From San Jose take U.S. 101 south and exit at Bernal Road. At the stoplight, turn right, then right again to reach Monterey Highway. Turn left (south) on Monterey Highway. Turn right on Bailey Avenue and drive 2.8 miles to McKean Road. Turn left on McKean Road and drive six miles. McKean Road becomes Uvas Road. Turn right on Croy Road and drive 4.5 miles to the park. Continue past Svaedal, a private camp and resort. Park near the park visitor center or farther up the hill in one of the picnic area parking lots. The trailhead is the gated dirt road at Black Oak Picnic Area.

Contact: Uvas Canyon County Park, 8515 Croy Road, Morgan Hill, CA 95037; tel. (408) 779-9232 or fax (408) 779-3315.

2 Alec Canyon and Contour Loop

4.5 mi/2.5 hrs

For hikers looking for more of a workout than the Waterfall Loop in Uvas Park provides, this hike up Alec Canyon Trail will get your heart pumping. It's a good trip for a clear winter day when the views from the trail's overlook at Manzanita Point are at their best. Start hiking on the gated road at Black Oak Picnic Area and then bear left, heading up and away from the canyon and the Waterfall Loop Trail. You'll get to hike that trail on your way back down. A steep climb up the wide road brings you to Manzanita Point, where you can see far off to the north and east. Wow, there's a whole huge valley way out there. Continue .25 mile beyond the point and take the right cutoff to cascading Triple Falls, the most secluded of all the waterfalls in Uvas Park. Then retrace your steps on Alec Canyon Trail, this time bearing left on the Contour Trail less than .5 mile past Manzanita Point. Contour Trail is pure fun, winding like a snake along the hillsides, with minimal elevation change but many curves and twists. Finally it drops back down to Swanson Creek, where you can walk back to the trailhead via the Waterfall Loop.

Location: In Uvas Canyon County Park near Morgan Hill; map F1, grid a8.

User groups: Hikers and dogs. No horses or mountain bikes. No wheelchair facilities.

Permits: No permits are required. A $4 day-use fee is charged per vehicle.

Maps: A free map of Uvas Canyon County Park is available at the visitor center. Ask the USGS for a topographic map of the Loma Prieta area.

Directions: From San Jose take U.S. 101 south and exit at Bernal Road. At the stoplight turn right and then right again to reach Monterey Highway. Turn left (south) on Monterey Highway. Turn right on Bailey Avenue and drive 2.8 miles to McKean Road. Turn left on McKean Road and drive six miles (McKean Road becomes Uvas Road). Turn right on Croy Road and drive 4.5 miles to the park. Continue past Svaedal, a private camp and resort. Park near the park visitor center or farther up the hill in one of the picnic area parking lots. The trailhead is the gated dirt road at Black Oak Picnic Area.

Contact: Uvas Canyon County Park, 8515 Croy Road, Morgan Hill, CA 95037; tel. (408) 779-9232 or fax (408) 779-3315.

3 Old Landing Cove Trail

2.5 mi/1.5 hrs

When you visit Wilder Ranch, you may notice that on some maps and park signs this trail is called "Old Cove Landing," while on others it's called "Old Landing Cove." Take your pick. The Old Landing Cove Trail is a gem of a coastal hike that offers a look at a seal rookery, some spectacular pocket beaches, and a hidden fern cave. Although the trail is open to both hikers and mountain bikers, everybody seems to mind their manners and get along fine, probably because there's enough spectacular scenery to go around. The trail leads past brussels sprout fields to the coast. An odd but interesting fact is that 12 percent of our nation's brussels sprout production happens right here in this park. Once you're beyond the farming fields, turn right and walk along the tops of coastal bluffs. It's not far until you reach the trail's namesake, Old Landing Cove, where small schooners loaded lumber in the late 1800s. A little more walking brings you to the seal rookery, where you look down on huge flat rocks covered with wall-to-wall seals. Finally, near post number eight, a spur trail leads down to a small beach. If you take the spur, you find on the inland side of the beach a shallow cave filled with ferns from floor to ceiling. A quarter mile past the fern-cave beach is another excellent pocket beach perfect for picnicking or lying around.

Location: In Wilder Ranch State Park north of Santa Cruz; map F1, grid a4.

User groups: Hikers and mountain bikes. No horses or dogs. No wheelchair facilities.

Permits: No permits are required. A $3 day-use fee is charged per vehicle.

Maps: A free map of Wilder Ranch State Park is available at the entrance station. Ask the USGS for a topographic map of the Santa Cruz area.

Directions: From Santa Cruz drive north on Highway 1 for four miles. Turn left into the entrance for Wilder Ranch State Park and follow the park road to its end at the main parking area. Take the trail signed "Nature Trail" from the southwest side of the parking lot.

Contact: Wilder Ranch State Park, 1401 Old Coast Road, Santa Cruz, CA 95060; tel. (831) 423-9703 or fax (831) 423-3763.

4 Wilder Ridge and Zane Grey Trails

6.0 mi/3.0 hrs

Once you find your way to the hiker/biker tunnel underneath Highway 1 near the farm buildings at Wilder Ranch, you're on your way to a great six-mile day hike with just enough of a climb to give you a workout and a spectacular vista of Monterey Bay. Keep in mind that this side of the park is the domain of mountain bikers—hundreds of them on weekends—but the trails are wide, and there's plenty of room for everybody to enjoy. The Wilder Ridge Trail has a 500-foot climb to a gorgeous overlook, and you reach it by exiting the tunnel and heading straight and then uphill on Wilder Ridge, then bearing right on the right side of the Wilder Ridge Loop. At about 2.5 miles out, shortly after the Twin Oaks Trail forks right, you come to an obvious grassy overlook at the top of the ridge, only about 40 feet off the main trail. Enjoy the wide vista for as long as you please, then continue along the ridgetop on Wilder Ridge Loop. For an interesting loop, take the Zane Grey cut-off on the left (it's single track), and then go left again on the other side of the Wilder Ridge Loop. Altogether it's a great trip, especially in springtime when the hillside grasses are green and the summer fog is not yet visiting.

Location: In Wilder Ranch State Park north of Santa Cruz; map F1, grid a4.

User groups: Hikers, horses, and mountain bikes. No dogs. No wheelchair facilities.

Permits: No permits are required. A $3 day-use fee is charged per vehicle.

Maps: A free map of Wilder Ranch State Park is available at the entrance station. Ask the USGS for a topographic map of the Santa Cruz area.

Directions: From Santa Cruz drive north on Highway 1 for four miles. Turn left into the entrance for Wilder Ranch State Park and follow the park road to its end at the main parking area. Take the trail signed "Nature Trail" from the southwest side of the parking lot. Walk down the park road to the Wilder Ranch and Cultural Preserve, then through the cultural preserve to the picnic area and chicken coops to reach the tunnel that leads underneath Highway 1.

Contact: Wilder Ranch State Park, 1401 Old Coast Road, Santa Cruz, CA 95060; tel. (831) 423-9703 or fax (831) 423-3763.

5 Maple Falls

7-9 mi/4.5 hrs

It's either a seven- or nine-mile round-trip hike to Maple Falls, and it all depends on whether or not they've gated off the park road to Porter Picnic Area, the main trailhead. In winter and spring the road is usually closed off, which means you need to walk an extra mile in each direction in order to see the falls. Winter and spring are the best seasons to go, because that's when Maple Falls is flowing at its fullest. The trip starts out with an easy walk on Aptos Creek Fire Road, which you'll share with mountain bikers. Follow it .25 mile past Porter Picnic Area, where you cut off on the Loma Prieta Grade Trail on the left. The second-growth redwood and Douglas fir forest just keeps getting thicker, greener, and better, and the trail is now sweet single track. Where Loma Prieta Grade splits, stay to the right, heading toward Bridge Creek Historic Site, for the shortest route to the falls. You can take the other side of the Loma Prieta Grade loop on your way back if you still have the energy. When you reach Bridge Creek Historic Site, the site of a former logging camp, the maintained trail ends, and you begin a fun .5-mile stream scramble to Maple Falls, following the course of Bridge Creek. The canyon narrows as you travel through a dense green world of ferns, moss, foliage, and water, and at last you reach the back of the canyon, where 40-foot Maple Falls spills over the wall. Wow, what a great hike.

Location: Near Aptos south of Santa Cruz; map F1, grid b6.

User groups: Hikers only. No dogs or horses. Mountain bikes are allowed only on fire roads. No wheelchair facilities.

Permits: No permits are required. A $1 day-use fee is charged per vehicle.

Maps: A free map of the Forest of Nisene Marks State Park is available at the entrance kiosk. Ask the USGS for topographic maps of Laurel, Soquel, and Loma Prieta areas.

Directions: From Santa Cruz drive south on Highway 1 for six miles to the Aptos exit. Bear left at the exit, turn right on Soquel Drive, and drive .5 mile. Turn left on Aptos Creek Road. Stop at the entrance kiosk, then continue up the park road and park at Porter Picnic Area. In the winter months you must park at George's Picnic Area, a mile before Porter Picnic Area, because the park road is gated off at that point.

Contact: The Forest of Nisene Marks State Park, c/o Sunset State Beach, 201 Sunset Beach Road, Watsonville, CA 95076; tel. (831) 763-7063, (831) 429-2850, or fax (831) 763-7124.

6 Loma Prieta Epicenter

4.0 mi/2.0 hrs

The destination on this trail is the epicenter of the 1989 Loma Prieta earthquake, but the pleasure of the trip has little to do with its interesting geological focus. Instead, the joy is in the scenery, a lush second-growth redwood forest that has regenerated after a clear-cut operation at the turn of the century. The walk follows the Aptos Creek Fire Road, which you share with mountain bikers as it leads gently uphill. At 1.5 miles from the Porter Picnic Area, cross a footbridge and descend a bit on the trail until you come to the spot where a large sign once proclaimed the proximity of the earthquake epicenter (the sign was stolen). There's a small bike rack there. Cross the creek and continue up the single-track trail for .5 mile to the actual epicenter, where you will see surprisingly little evidence of anything earthshaking, but rather a lovely and peaceful redwood forest. Turn around here for a four-mile round-trip (or six miles if you had to start from George's Picnic Area instead of Porter Picnic Area).

Location: Near Aptos south of Santa Cruz; map F1, grid b6.

User groups: Hikers and mountain bikes. No dogs or horses. No wheelchair facilities.

Permits: No permits are required. A $1 day-use fee is charged per vehicle.

Maps: A free map of the Forest of Nisene Marks State Park is available at the entrance kiosk. Ask the USGS for topographic maps of the Laurel, Soquel, and Loma Prieta areas.

Directions: From Santa Cruz drive south on Highway 1 for six miles to the Aptos exit. Bear left at the exit, turn right on Soquel Drive, and drive .5 mile. Turn left on Aptos Creek Road. Stop at the entrance kiosk, continue up the park road, and park at Porter Picnic Area. In the winter months you must park at George's Picnic Area, a mile before Porter Picnic Area, because the park road is closed at that point.

Contact: The Forest of Nisene Marks State Park, c/o Sunset State Beach, 201 Sunset Beach Road, Watsonville, CA 95076; tel. (831) 763-7063, (831) 429-2850, or fax (831) 763-7124.

🄍 West Ridge and Aptos Creek Loop

**12.5 mi/
7.0 hrs or 2.0 days**

The West Ridge and Aptos Creek Loop is the grand tour of the Forest of Nisene Marks State Park, suitable only for hikers in good condition and with a lot of time on their hands. An option is to get reservations for West Ridge Trail Camp and turn this into an overnight trip; the camp is situated conveniently near spectacular Sand Point Overlook—great for sunsets. (Backpacking stoves are necessary; no campfires are allowed.) From George's Pic-

nic Area, walk up Aptos Creek Road for .25 mile to the left cutoff for West Ridge Trail and start climbing uphill along the West Ridge of Aptos Canyon. (You can also take the Loma Prieta Grade Trail if you prefer, and follow the left side of its loop and take the connector trail to West Ridge Trail.) Finally you ascend all the way to Hinckley Ridge at 1,300 feet, and meet up with the fire road that leads to West Ridge Trail Camp and Sand Point Overlook. From the overlook at 1,500 feet, you can see down into the densely forested Bridge Creek drainage and far off across sky blue Monterey Bay. Finish out the loop with a long downhill walk on Aptos Creek Fire Road, a wide path through dense redwoods and Douglas firs.

Location: Near Aptos south of Santa Cruz; map F1, grid b6.

User groups: Hikers and mountain bikes. No dogs or horses. No wheelchair facilities.

Permits: No permits are required. A $1 day-use fee is charged per vehicle. An advance reservation is necessary to stay overnight at West Ridge Trail Camp; phone the park for reservations.

Maps: A free map of the Forest of Nisene Marks State Park is available at the entrance kiosk. Ask the USGS for topographic maps of the Laurel, Soquel, and Loma Prieta areas.

Directions: From Santa Cruz drive south on Highway 1 for six miles to the Aptos exit. Bear left at the exit, turn right on Soquel Drive, and drive .5 mile. Turn left on Aptos Creek Road. Stop at the entrance kiosk, continue up the park road, and park at George's Picnic Area.

Contact: The Forest of Nisene Marks State Park, c/o Sunset State Beach, 201 Sunset Beach Road, Watsonville, CA 95076; tel. (831) 763-7063, (831) 429-2850, or fax (831) 763-7124.

🄏 White Deer Trail

0.5 mi/0.25 hr

The remainders of a rare herd of white deer are the star attraction at Mount Madonna County Park. These animals are similar to black-tailed deer, the most common deer in California, except they are larger and completely white. In late summer the bucks develop a huge set of antlers, quite a sight. They are kept in a pen about 30 feet from the parking lot next to headquarters to protect them. In the early 1990s, poachers with rifles were killing them off at night, one at a time. Justice was served when one of the gunmen accidentally shot himself and was left behind by his fellow culprits. Karma. Only three deer survived the poaching incidents, but two fawns were born in 1994, giving some cause for hope. Today the herd is rebuilding itself, and you can typically see five to 10 of these rare animals here. The "white deer" are actually white fallow deer, descendants of a pair donated in 1932 by William Randolph Hearst.

Location: In Mount Madonna County Park in the Santa Cruz Mountains west of Gilroy; map F1, grid b8.

User groups: Hikers and wheelchairs. No dogs, horses, or mountain bikes.

Permits: No permits are required. A $4 day-use fee is charged.

Maps: For a free trail map, contact Mount Madonna County Park at the address below. Ask the USGS for a topographic map of the Mount Madonna area.

Directions: From San Jose take U.S. 101 south to Gilroy. Turn west on Highway 152 and drive 10 miles; then turn right on Poleline Road and drive to the parking area.

Contact: Mount Madonna County Park, 7850 Poleline Road, Watsonville, CA 95076; tel. (408) 842-2341.

9 Bayview Loop
2.5 mi/1.75 hrs

Mount Madonna County Park provides great scenic beauty, good hiking, camping, and horseback riding. The park is set around the highest peak in the southern range of the Santa Cruz Mountains, and with 18 miles of hiking trails, the best routes are combinations of different trails. So it is with this triangular loop, starting at the park entrance station at Hecker Pass, elevation 1,270 feet. Take the Bayview Trail and hike north for 1.1 miles, scanning west to Monterey Bay along the way. Turn right on the Redwood Trail (it will cross Poleline Road), and you will walk from those coastal lookouts into forest, getting the best of both worlds. To complete the loop, take the Redwood/Rock Springs/Blackhawk/Bayview Trails as they join in sequence. Confused? This park is filled with a spiderweb of short hikes. By linking them, you can customize your adventure. Our suggested loop provides a look at some of the park's prettiest settings.

Location: In Mount Madonna County Park in the Santa Cruz Mountains west of Gilroy; map F1, grid b8.

User groups: Hikers and horses. No dogs or mountain bikes. No wheelchair facilities.

Permits: No permits are required. A $4 day-use fee is charged.

Maps: For a free trail map, contact Mount Madonna County Park at the address below. Ask the USGS for a topographic map of the Mount Madonna area.

Directions: From San Jose take U.S. 101 south to Gilroy. Turn west on Highway 152 and drive 10 miles, turn right on Poleline Road, and drive to the entrance station. The trailhead is on the left.

Contact: Mount Madonna County Park, 7850 Poleline Road, Watsonville, CA 95076; (408) 842-2341.

10 Elkhorn Slough South Marsh Loop
2.8 mi/1.5 hrs

Elkhorn Slough is 2,500 acres of marsh and tidal flats, the precious borderline between sea and land that is home to thousands of species of birds, fish, and invertebrates. It's the second largest salt marsh in California, and in the peak of the migration season, over 20,000 birds per day congregate here. Hikers with binoculars (and sometimes with just their own eyes) frequently spot golden eagles and peregrine falcons. Endangered clapper rails and least terns are also among the sanctuary's inhabitants. The South Marsh Loop Trail is a three-mile tour of this salty, marshy, bird-filled land, crossing footbridges over the slough and staying close to the water's edge and mudflats. Make sure you take all the short spurs off the loop. A highlight in the spring is walking through the heron rookery, where you may be able to spot tiny great blue heron babies. If you want to walk more, two other loop trails are available.

Special note: The reserve is open Wednesday through Sunday only. Guided tours are available on Saturday and Sunday.

Location: Near Moss Landing; map F1, grid c8.

User groups: Hikers only. No dogs, horses, or mountain bikes. Some facilities are wheelchair accessible.

Permits: No permits are required. A $2.50 entrance fee is charged per person. Children under 16 and anyone in possession of a California fishing or hunting license can enter free.

Maps: A free map of Elkhorn Slough is available at the parking lot or the visitor center. Ask the USGS for a topographic map of Moss Landing.

Directions: From Highway 1 at Moss Landing turn east on Dolan Road by the Pacific Gas and Electric Company power station. Drive three miles to Elkhorn Road, turn left (north), and drive two miles to the reserve entrance. The trail begins by the visitor center.

Contact: Elkhorn Slough National Estuarine Reserve, 1700 Elkhorn Road, Watsonville, CA 95076; tel. (831) 728-2822 or fax (831) 649-2894.

11 Moss Landing Wildlife Area Marsh Trail

3.0 mi/1.5 hrs

Located on the north bank of giant Elkhorn Slough, the Moss Landing Wildlife Area gets a little less human traffic than the more developed Elkhorn Slough Reserve, but no less bird traffic. Unlike the neighboring reserve, there's no day-use fee to visit here, and it's open

seven days a week. From the trailhead, you leave the lettuce fields and wander into the salt marsh with your camera, binoculars, and bird book or maybe just your lunch and a friend. The trail winds along the marsh for five-plus miles, but you can go just as far as you like, paying a visit to brown pelicans, egrets, herons, terns, gulls, and all their buddies. Brown pelicans summer here in large numbers. The terrain varies somewhat as you walk, moving into occasional groves of eucalyptus and oak woodlands, with a side-trip possible to some old salt harvesting ponds. Most people just walk 1.5 miles out to a picnic area situated on a bluff above the slough.

Location: In Moss Landing; map F1, grid c8.

User groups: Hikers only. No dogs, horses, or mountain bikes. No wheelchair facilities.

Permits: No permits are required. Parking and access are free.

Maps: A free map/brochure of Moss Landing Wildlife Area is available at the north entrance to Moss Landing Wildlife Area. Ask the USGS for a topographic map of Moss Landing.

Directions: From Moss Landing drive north on Highway 1 for one mile to a dirt road on the right that is signed for Moss Landing Wildlife Area. It's north of Struve Road. Turn right (east) and drive a short distance to the trailhead. If you are coming from the south, you can use the south entrance to the wildlife area. Cross the Elkhorn Slough bridge.

Contact: Department of Fish and Game, tel. (831) 728-2822. Or contact the neighboring Elkhorn Slough Reserve, tel. (831) 728-2822.

12 Asilomar Coast Trail

2.4 mi/1.5 hrs

Even if you aren't lucky enough to attend a conference at the historic Asilomar Conference Center, you can still walk its adjoining Asilomar Coast Trail, a spectacular 1.2-mile trail along coastal bluffs above rugged, windswept Asilomar Beach. There's plenty to look at and many side trails to explore.

You'll see waves crashing against jagged rocks, plentiful tide pools, tiny pocket beaches, wide sandy stretches with big white dunes, and much sea life. Be sure to take the separate boardwalk trail (on the west side of the conference center) that leads across the dunes. Kite flying is also popular along some stretches of Asilomar Beach.

Location: In Pacific Grove; map F1, grid e5.

User groups: Hikers and dogs. No horses or mountain bikes. Portions of the trail are wheelchair accessible.

Permits: No permits are required. Parking and access are free.

Maps: Ask the USGS for a topographic map of the Monterey area.

Directions: From Salinas on U.S. 101, take the Highway 68/Monterey exit and continue into Monterey and then Pacific Grove, where Highway 68 becomes Sunset Drive. Continue to Asilomar State Beach. Park alongside Sunset Drive; the trail begins opposite the conference center.

Contact: Asilomar State Beach, 804 Crocker Avenue, Pacific Grove, CA 93950; tel. (831) 372-4076 or fax (831) 372-3759.

13 Skyline and Jacks Peak Trails

1.2 mi/0.5 hr

They've got a whole park encircling Jacks Peak, the highest point on the Monterey Peninsula at 1,068 feet. Hey, it's not the Sierra, but it's high and pretty. The park and the peak are named after David Jacks, the guy who got his name on Monterey Jack cheese. The Skyline Nature Trail is an easy loop walk around the summit of Jacks Peak, set amid Monterey pines. The Jacks Peak Trail is a smaller loop inside the Skyline Nature Trail loop, and you can easily branch off the latter to join the former for a half-hour walk that provides unparalleled views of Carmel Valley, the Monterey Peninsula, Point Lobos, the Santa Lucia Mountains, and the Pacific Ocean. Even though the view is about the same on both trail loops, make sure

you walk a leg of the Jacks Peak Trail to the top of Jacks Peak, where you can sit on a bench and pull out a picnic of jack cheese sandwiches. Don't plan on watching the sun set from here, though; unfortunately the park closes before then.

Location: In Jacks Peak County Park near Monterey; map F1, grid e6.

User groups: Hikers and dogs. No horses or mountain bikes. No wheelchair facilities.

Permits: No permits are required. A $2 entrance fee is charged per vehicle on weekdays; $3 on weekends and holidays.

Maps: A free map of Jacks Peak County Park is available at the entrance station. Ask the USGS for a topographic map of the Seaside area.

Directions: From Monterey take Highway 68 east from Highway 1 for 1.7 miles to Olmsted Road. Turn right on Olmsted Road and drive 1.5 miles to Jacks Peak Drive; then follow Jacks Peak Drive to the park entrance. After passing through the entrance kiosk, turn right and drive to the parking area for Jacks Peak.

Contact: Jacks Peak County Park, 25020 Jacks Peak Road, Monterey, CA 93940; tel. (831) 372-8551.

14 Ollason Peak

7.5 mi/3.5 hrs

Pick a cool day in spring to take this inspiring jaunt to the top of Ollason Peak, elevation 1,800 feet, far from the madding crowds of popular Toro County Park. Even with a cool breeze, the Ollason Trail can be a butt-kicker, with many steep sections over a less-than-smooth route. It leads from the Quail Meadow Group Camp and climbs through wide grasslands and occasional oak groves, most of the time on wide double track. Increasingly wide views and an excellent variety of grassland wildflowers are your reward for the work. After a long stint heading southwest, the trail suddenly veers east, then resumes its southern course for the final climb to Ollason Peak, four miles from the trailhead. You get lovely views toward Monterey Bay and the Central Valley from the summit. Retrace your steps from there or continue a little farther to Coyote Spring Trail, bearing left for a 7.5-mile loop. If you're making the loop, be sure to watch for the left turnoff on Cougar Ridge from Coyote Spring, which returns you to a connector trail back to Quail Meadow Camp.

Location: In Toro County Park near Monterey; map F1, grid e7.

User groups: Hikers, dogs, and horses. No mountain bikes. No wheelchair facilities.

Permits: No permits are required. A $3 entrance fee is charged per vehicle on weekdays; $5 on weekends and holidays.

Maps: A free map of Toro County Park is available at the entrance station. Ask the USGS for a topographic map of the Spreckels area.

Directions: From Monterey take Highway 68 east from Highway 1 for 13 miles to the park entrance on the right (south) side of the road. Drive to the parking area by Quail Meadow Group Campground.

Contact: Toro County Park, 501 Monterey Highway, Salinas, CA 93908; tel. (831) 484-1108.

15 Sea Lion Point Trail
0.6 mi/0.5 hr

On summer weekends the cars are parked in a long line along the road outside Point Lobos State Reserve, Carmel's crown jewel of parks. Even on weekdays the parking lots are surprisingly full here, but the park's stunning coastal beauty and plentiful wildlife explain why. By far the biggest attraction at the park is the Sea Lion Point Trail, a round-trip loop of just over .5 mile, part of which is suitable for wheelchairs. Along the way you can look for cute little sea otters floating on their backs in the kelp and chubby harbor seals hauling out on the rocks. When the trail reaches a rocky staircase, wheelchair users will have to turn back, but other visitors can continue down to a lower trail. Rocks jut out of the breakers just offshore; these are named Sea Lion Rocks for obvious reasons. Test your hiking partner's literary knowledge with this fact: Robert Louis Stevenson used Point Lobos as the inspiration for his novel *Treasure Island.*

Location: In Point Lobos State Reserve near Carmel; map F1, grid f4.

User groups: Hikers and wheelchairs. No dogs, horses, or mountain bikes. Part of the trail is wheelchair accessible.

Permits: No permits are required. A $4 day-use fee is charged per vehicle.

Maps: A map of Point Lobos State Reserve is available for $.50 at the entrance station. Ask the USGS for a topographic map of the Monterey area.

Directions: From Carmel at Rio Road, drive south on Highway 1 for three miles to the entrance to Point Lobos State Reserve on the right. Turn right and drive through the entrance kiosk and continue straight to the information station and Sea Lion Point parking area.

Contact: Point Lobos State Reserve, Route 1, Box 62, Carmel, CA 93923; tel. (831) 624-4909 or fax (831) 624-9265.

16 Whaler's Knoll and Cypress Grove
4.0 mi/2.0 hrs

Two excellent trails lead from the north side of the Sea Lion Point parking area near the information station at Point Lobos, and you can connect them to make a stellar four-mile round-trip. Start by hiking on the Cypress Grove Trail, which shows off the park's Monterey cypress trees, one of only two remaining natural cypress groves on earth. In addition to getting a look at the marvelous windswept trees, you walk through coastal scrub to rocky cliffs with picture-perfect ocean views. The trail loops around and heads back toward the parking area, but just before you reach it, you can turn left on the North Shore Trail and climb a bit to the right turnoff for the Whaler's Knoll Trail. Whaler's Knoll Trail makes loose switchbacks uphill to the top of Whaler's Knoll, where you get the best view in the whole park. Luckily there's a bench there so you can sit down, catch your breath, and enjoy it. The knoll was where turn-of-the-century whalers would watch for whales, then hang a signal flag when they spotted them. You can continue hiking from there, heading downhill and making a loop along the coast on the North Shore Trail.

Location: In Point Lobos State Reserve near Carmel; map F1, grid f4.

User groups: Hikers only. No dogs, horses, or mountain bikes. No wheelchair facilities.

Permits: No permits are required. A $4 day-use fee is charged per vehicle.

Maps: Maps of Point Lobos State Reserve are available for $.50 each at the entrance station. Ask the USGS for a topographic map of the Monterey area.

Directions: From Carmel at Rio Road, drive south on Highway 1 for three miles to the entrance to Point Lobos State Reserve on the right. Turn right and drive through the entrance kiosk and continue straight to the information station and Sea Lion Point parking area.

Contact: Point Lobos State Reserve, Route 1, Box 62, Carmel, CA 93923; tel. (831) 624-4909 or fax (831) 624-9265.

17 Point Lobos Perimeter

6.0 mi/3.0 hrs

The perimeter hike at Point Lobos connects a number of trails to view the best highlights of the park. Make sure you get a park map at the entrance station before hiking so you can scope out the many side-trip options that are possible (and the many shortcuts if you're getting tired). Starting from the Sea Lion Point parking area, make your first destination Sea Lion Point. Then bear left on Sand Hill Trail and connect to South Shore Trail. The latter leads along the quieter south part of the park, past numerous spectacular beaches and coves, to Bird Island Trail. Make sure you take the short side path to Bird Island Overlook, then maybe walk the stairs down to the sandy beaches at China Cove and Gibson Beach.

(China Cove is one of the most beautiful spots on earth, in our opinion.) From the Bird Island Trail you connect with the South Plateau Trail, follow it northward, cross the park road to follow Carmelo Meadow Trail, and bear right for a side trip to Granite Point. Don't miss this; it's a rocky outcrop on a short loop trail with great views toward Carmel to the north. Then retrace your steps along the Granite Point Trail and finish out your loop by hiking along the park's northern shoreline, following Granite Point Trail to Cabin Trail to North Shore Trail. Possible side trips are to the Whaler's Cabin Museum or a spur trail to a lookout of Guillemot Island and its millions of birds or to the Whaler's Knoll and Cypress Grove. If you take all of the possible side trips along the route, this hike will take you almost all day, and what a fine day it will be.

Location: In Point Lobos State Reserve near Carmel; map F1, grid f4.

User groups: Hikers only. No dogs, horses, or mountain bikes. No wheelchair facilities.

Permits: No permits are required. A $4 day-use fee is charged per vehicle.

Maps: A map of Point Lobos State Reserve is available for $.50 at the entrance station. Ask the USGS for a topographic map of the Monterey area.

Directions: From Carmel at Rio Road, drive south on Highway 1 for three miles to the entrance to Point Lobos State Reserve on the right. Turn right and drive through the entrance kiosk; continue straight to the information station and Sea Lion Point parking area.

Contact: Point Lobos State Reserve, Route 1, Box 62, Carmel, CA 93923; tel. (831) 624-4909 or fax (831) 624-9265.

18 Rocky Ridge and Soberanes Canyon Loop

6.0 mi/3.0 hrs

It sounds impossible. A state park that's free on the Monterey Coast? But it's true—it won't cost you a dime to park alongside Highway 1 and hike around all day on the excellent trails of Garrapata State Park. The park is situated on both sides of Highway 1, with some trails leading to the ocean and others leading up inland canyons and hillsides. Hikers looking for a long leg-stretching walk will enjoy this loop trip on the inland side of the park, which travels through a remarkable variety of terrain. You want diversity, you get diversity. Begin hiking on the Soberanes Canyon Trail. What starts out as a ranch road through chaparral-covered hillsides quickly becomes single track through an increasingly narrow and wet canyon. The big surprise is a gorgeous stand of redwoods along Soberanes Creek, a complete contrast to the chaparral, cacti, and dry-country wildflowers at the start of the trail. The grove is a good turnaround spot for those looking for a shorter trip. If you continue on, the trail makes a substantial climb and heads north to a spur to the Peak Trail, also signed as North Ridge Trail, and an intersection with the Rocky Ridge Trail. Forget the spur and finish out your loop on Rocky Ridge Trail, where on a clear day you can look out over the ocean for miles. The trail then winds back down the hillsides and deposits you back at your car on Highway 1.

Location: In Garrapata State Park south of Carmel; map F1, grid f4.

User groups: Hikers only. No dogs, horses, or mountain bikes. No wheelchair facilities.

Permits: No permits are required. Parking and access are free.

Maps: Ask the USGS for a topographic map of Soberanes Point area.

Directions: From Carmel at Rio Road, drive south on Highway 1 for seven miles to marker 13 and the dirt pullouts along the highway at Garrapata State Park. It's four miles south of Point Lobos State Park and easy to miss; go slowly and watch for cars parked alongside the road. The Soberanes Canyon Trail begins on the east side of the road.

Contact: Garrapata State Park, c/o Pfeiffer Big Sur State Park, Big Sur, CA 93920; tel. (831) 667-2315, (831) 649-2836, or fax (831) 667-2886.

19 Soberanes Point Trail
2.0 mi/1.0 hrs

You can access the Soberanes Point Trail from three different gates along Highway 1, so if you miss marker 13, you can always stop at markers 15 or 16. Wherever you begin, you'll end up on a spectacular and easy set of trails that join in a series of loops around Soberanes Point, all basically around Whale Peak. If you time your trip at low tide, you'll have access to some excellent tide pools, and even if not, you get views of rocky shoreline bluffs and plenty of animal and bird life. Many anglers try their luck rock fishing here at the point, and it's also a popular spot for whale-watching from November to January. Note that if you start from marker 13, you can hike a short loop to your right and then a much larger loop to your left. If you start from marker 15, you're at the middle of the larger loop, so you can start hiking either right or left. Just wander as you please; the coastline and the perimeter of the point make it impossible to get lost.

Location: In Garrapata State Park south of Carmel; map F1, grid f4.

User groups: Hikers only. No dogs, horses, or mountain bikes. No wheelchair facilities.

Permits: No permits are required. Parking and access are free.

Maps: Ask the USGS for a topographic map of the Soberanes Point area.

Directions: From Carmel at Rio Road, drive south on Highway 1 for seven miles to marker 13 and the dirt pullouts along the highway at Garrapata State Park. It's four miles south of Point Lobos State Park and easy to miss; go slowly and watch for cars parked alongside the road. The Soberanes Point Trail begins on the east side of the road.

Contact: Garrapata State Park, c/o Pfeiffer Big Sur State Park, Big Sur, CA 93920; tel. (831) 667-2315, (831) 649-2836 or fax (831) 667-2886.

20 Lupine, Waterfall, and Mesa Loop

3.0 mi/1.5 hrs

Garland Ranch's excellent visitor center is the perfect place to begin your trip to the park. Take a look inside, get a trail map, and learn a few things about the area's animals, trees, and wildflowers. The center is also the trailhead for this combined loop on the Lupine, Waterfall, and Mesa Trails. Although the park's waterfall only flows during the rainy season, the trails are good to walk year-round, and they're well maintained and well signed to boot. Begin by heading to the left (northwest) from the visitor center on the Lupine Loop, which travels along the open, flat floodplains of the Carmel River. In .5 mile, leave the loop and continue straight on the Waterfall Trail, then climb through a more shady area to the rocky cliff where the waterfall sometimes falls. Beyond it, you'll ascend more seriously, following a few switchbacks to the mesa, a large high meadow with views of Carmel Valley and beyond. Follow the Mesa Trail back downhill to the other side of the Lupine Loop and take the Lupine Loop back to the visitor center. Expect an excellent wildflower show in the grasslands in springtime.

Location: In Garland Ranch Regional Park near Carmel; map F1, grid f7.

User groups: Hikers, dogs, and horses. No mountain bikes. No wheelchair facilities.

Permits: No permits are required. Parking and access are free.

Maps: A free map of Garland Ranch Regional Park is available at the visitor center. Ask the USGS for topographic maps of the Mount Carmel and Carmel Valley areas.

Directions: From Highway 1 at Carmel, turn east on Carmel Valley Road. Drive 8.6 miles on Carmel Valley Road to the Garland Ranch parking area on the right side of the road. Walk across the river bridge to get to the visitor center and trailheads.

Contact: Garland Ranch Regional Park, P.O. Box 935, Carmel Valley, CA 93924; tel. (831) 659-4488, (831) 372-3196, or (831) 659-6065.

21 Snivley's Ridge Trail

5.6 mi/3.0 hrs

If it's winter or spring, a trip to the top of Snivley's Ridge could be just what you need to keep your hiking legs in shape. It's a healthy 1,600-foot climb up to the ridge, plus a 250-foot climb to get to the ridge's highest point, so be prepared to pant a little. Much of the walk is exposed; be sure to bring water and pick a cool day to hike the trail. From the visitor center, set out on either side of the Lupine Loop (heading left is a little shorter), and continue uphill on the Mesa Trail to its junction with Fern Trail. This stretch is moist and shady, so enjoy it while you're in it. Follow Fern Trail, turn left and quickly right on Sky Trail, and begin the serious portion of the climb. Well-graded switchbacks make it easier. Many people stop where Sky Trail meets Snivley's Ridge Trail, at a bench with a panoramic view of Carmel Valley, the forested Santa Lucia Mountains, and the ocean. But those determined to go as high as possible should turn right on Snivley's Ridge, walk another .5 mile, and turn left on a spur trail that leads to the park's highest point at 2,038 feet.

Location: In Garland Ranch Regional Park near Carmel; map F1, grid f7.

User groups: Hikers, dogs, and horses. No mountain bikes. No wheelchair facilities.

Permits: No permits are required. Parking and access are free.

Maps: A free map of Garland Ranch Regional Park is available at the visitor center. Ask the USGS for topographic maps of the Mount Carmel and Carmel Valley areas.

Directions: From Highway 1 at Carmel, turn east on Carmel Valley Road. Drive 8.6 miles on Carmel Valley Road to the Garland Ranch parking area on the right side of the road. Walk across the river bridge to get to the visitor center and trailheads.

Contact: Garland Ranch Regional Park, P.O. Box 935, Carmel Valley, CA 93924; tel. (831) 659-4488, (831) 372-3196, or (831) 659-6065.

22 Skinner Ridge Trail to Devils Peak

7.6 mi/3.5 hrs

What's the best thing about this trip? The far-off ocean views in the first mile of the climb? The white marble of giant Pico Blanco to the southwest? The colors of the oak leaves in autumn? Or the huge old madrone trees that pepper Skinner Ridge? It's hard to decide; you'd better go see for yourself. Pick a cool and clear day to make the trip, preferably in autumn, or arm yourself with a ton of sunscreen and water in summer. The trailhead is at 2,000 feet, and the initial climb is through chaparral, with many open views. Then the trail enters the trees (madrones and oaks), and winds and twists its way around before making a short, steep ascent to the top of Skinner Ridge at 3,450 feet and 2.1 miles out. A wide bulldozer line runs up the ridge, left from the huge Marble Cone fire of the 1970s. From the ridge, backpackers usually continue down the other side for .75 mile to a trail junction for Turner Creek. Apple Tree Camp is a left turn and one mile away, a good place for an overnight. Day hikers should proceed straight ahead at that junction for the climb to Devils Peak, elevation 4,158 feet, and one mile farther. That final mile will get you huffing and puffing for sure, but hey, exercise is good for you, right?

Location: In the Ventana Wilderness near Carmel Valley; map F1, grid g6.

User groups: Hikers, dogs, and horses. No mountain bikes. No wheelchair facilities.

Permits: No permits are required. A national forest recreation pass is required for each vehicle; fees are $5 for one day or $30 for a year. If you don't have a recreation pass, you can pay $5 at the trailhead parking lot.

Maps: For a map of Los Padres National Forest or the Ventana Wilderness, send $6 to U.S. Forest Service, Map Sales, P.O. Box 587, Camino, CA 95709; tel. (530) 647-5390 or website: www.r5.fs.fed.us/visitorcenter. Ask the USGS for topographic maps of the Mount

Carmel and Big Sur areas.

Directions: From Carmel drive south on Highway 1 for 12 miles, past Garrapata State Park, to the left (east) turnoff for Palo Colorado Road, south of Rocky Point Restaurant. Turn left and drive eight miles to Bottcher's Gap Campground. The Skinner Ridge Trail begins at the edge of the parking lot.

Contact: Los Padres National Forest, Monterey Ranger District, 406 S. Mildred Avenue, King City, CA 93930; tel. (831) 385-5434 or fax (831) 385-0628.

23 Molera Point Trail

2.5 mi/1.5 hrs

Andrew Molera is a low-key state park without all the development and fanfare that often come with state park status. That means it's good for hikers—people who just want a good trail to walk on and not much else. An easy trail leads from the park's main parking lot to Molera Point, where you can look down on spectacular Molera Beach and count the sea lions lying on the rocks. To reach the point, take the trail from the right side of the main parking lot, which stays on the north side of the Big Sur River. The trail follows the river as it winds past the park's walk-in camp set in a wide meadow, and historic Cooper Cabin, which was built in 1861 and is the oldest structure on the Big Sur coast. At the river's mouth, a bridge leads to the beach (the bridge is in place only in summer), and a spur trail leads to the right, out to Molera Point. Take the spur trail and check out the view; then if the tide is low and the bridge is in place, go play on the beach for a while before heading back.

Location: In Andrew Molera State Park north of Big Sur; map F1, grid h5.

User groups: Hikers, dogs, horses, and mountain bikes. No wheelchair facilities.

Permits: No permits are required. A $2 day-use fee is charged per vehicle.

Maps: A map of Andrew Molera State Park is available for $.50 at this park's entrance station or at the entrance to Pfeiffer Big Sur State Park. Ask the USGS for a topographic map of the Big Sur area.

Directions: From Carmel drive 22 miles south on Highway 1 to Andrew Molera State Park's main entrance on the west side of the highway. Trails begin at the parking lot. The park is two miles north of Big Sur.

Contact: Andrew Molera State Park, c/o Pfeiffer Big Sur State Park, Big Sur, CA 93920; tel. (831) 667-2315, (831) 649-2836, or fax (831) 667-2886.

24 Molera State Park Loop
7.8 mi/4.0 hrs

This big loop around the western side of Andrew Molera State Park is easiest in summer, when the footbridge is in place over the Big Sur River. If the bridge isn't there, you must take off your shoes and socks and suffer through a very cold ford over smooth, rounded rocks. But this trail is worth any trouble you have to go to. It offers several miles of lovely ocean vistas, plus a visit to a remote beach. Start by taking the path from the west side of the parking lot and immediately crossing the river. At a junction of trails, head south (left) on River Trail, then in less than a mile turn right on Hidden Trail. Enjoy a well-graded climb through forest and meadows up to Ridge Trail, where you turn left and hike southward, paralleling the ocean. Ridge Trail is a wide fire road and rolls gently. In addition to the ocean vistas to the west, you also have fine views inland of the peaks and canyons of the Ventana Wilderness.

At 3.5 miles you meet up with Panorama Trail at a bench and overlook point. Turn right and start to switchback steeply downhill toward the ocean, enjoying wide views all the way. Spring wildflowers are lovely along the open hillsides. As you near the beach, you'll reach a junction with Spring Trail and Bluffs Trail. Take Spring Trail a few hundred feet to a lovely, driftwood-laden beach. This makes a perfect lunch stop. For your return, follow Bluffs Trail

2.5 miles back to Molera Beach. This is the most lovely stretch of the entire loop, offering long and beautiful looks at Molera Point and beach and Point Sur Light Station. Finally, take either of the trails from Molera Beach back to the main parking lot. Wow, what a perfect Big Sur day.

Location: In Andrew Molera State Park north of Big Sur; map F1, grid h5.

User groups: Hikers, dogs, horses, and mountain bikes. No wheelchair facilities.

Permits: No permits are required. A $2 dayuse fee is charged per vehicle.

Maps: A map of Andrew Molera State Park is available for $.50 at the entrance station or at the entrance to Pfeiffer Big Sur State Park. Ask the USGS for a topographic map of the Big Sur area.

Directions: From Carmel drive 22 miles south on Highway 1 to Andrew Molera State Park's main entrance, on the west side of the highway. Trails begin at the parking lot. (The park is two miles north of Big Sur.)

Contact: Andrew Molera State Park, c/o Pfeiffer Big Sur State Park, Big Sur, CA 93920; tel. (831) 667-2315, (831) 649-2836, or fax (831) 667-2886.

25 Pfeiffer Falls and Valley View Loop
1.6 mi/1.0 hr

A loop hike to a 60-foot waterfall and an overlook of the Big Sur Valley? Sounds great; let's go. And don't forget, there's a gorgeous redwood forest along the way. You get all of this when you set out on the Pfeiffer Falls Trail from the nature center at Pfeiffer Big Sur State Park and return on the Valley View Trail. After a slightly uphill walk on the Pfeiffer Falls Trail along Pfeiffer Redwood Creek (ignore all the trail junctions and stay along the creek, crossing it a couple of times on bridges), you'll wind up at the foot of tall and narrow Pfeiffer Falls, which streams down a vertical, dark rock face. You can sit for a while at the waterfall's viewing platform, then backtrack along the trail .1 mile to its junction with the Valley View Trail. Follow Valley View Trail as it climbs up and out of the canyon. You'll leave the redwoods almost immediately and hike in an oak forest for .5 mile. Look for the brilliant blooms of Douglas iris in the spring. The trail reaches an overlook of the Big Sur Valley and Point Sur. Unfortunately, the sight of Highway 1 somewhat diminishes the beauty of the view.

Head back down Valley View Trail and take the right fork (.25 mile from the overlook) to finish out your loop. This last downhill stretch is on the steep side, so wear a good pair of boots.

Location: In Pfeiffer Big Sur State Park near Big Sur; map F1, grid i6.

User groups: Hikers only. No dogs, horses, or mountain bikes. No wheelchair facilities.

Permits: No permits are required. A $3 day-use fee is charged per vehicle.

Maps: A map of Pfeiffer Big Sur State Park is available for $1 at the entrance station. Ask the USGS for a topographic map of the Big Sur area.

Directions: From Carmel drive 26 miles south on Highway 1 to Pfeiffer Big Sur State Park on the east side of the highway. It's two miles south of Big Sur. Drive through the entrance kiosk, turn left at the lodge, and then turn right, following the signs to Pfeiffer Falls Trailhead and Nature Center. Park just beyond the nature center. The trail is on the left side of the lot, signed as Oak Grove Trail, Valley View Trail, and Pfeiffer Falls Trail. If the small parking lot is full, you may have to park by the lodge and walk to the trailhead.

Contact: Pfeiffer Big Sur State Park, Big Sur, CA 93920; tel. (831) 667-2315, (831) 649-2836, or fax (831) 667-2886.

26 Buzzards Roost Trail

4.0 mi/2.0 hrs

Hikers looking for a bit of a challenge in Pfeiffer Big Sur State Park will want to try out this trail to the Buzzards Roost Overlook. Compared to the Pfeiffer Falls Trail, this trail gets surprisingly little traffic unless there are large groups camping at the nearby group campground. The trail leads along the Big Sur River through a forest of many splendid redwoods, switches back uphill onto slopes filled with oaks and bays, and finally climbs into chaparral country. You get to walk in every kind of Big Sur terrain. High up on Pfeiffer Ridge there's a 360-degree view of the Pacific Ocean, the Big Sur River gorge, and the Santa Lucia Mountains, providing a fine reward for your effort in climbing up here. The trailhead is at 200 feet in elevation, and the overlook is at nearly 1,000 feet.

Location: In Pfeiffer Big Sur State Park near Big Sur; map F1, grid i6.

User groups: Hikers only. No dogs, horses, or mountain bikes. No wheelchair facilities.

Permits: No permits are required. A $3 day-use fee is charged per vehicle.

Maps: A map of Pfeiffer Big Sur State Park is available for $1 at the entrance station. Ask the USGS for topographic maps of the Big Sur and Pfeiffer Point areas.

Directions: From Carmel drive 26 miles south on Highway 1 to Pfeiffer Big Sur State Park on the east side of the highway. It's two miles south of Big Sur. Drive through the entrance kiosk, continue past the lodge, and turn right to cross the bridge over the Big Sur River. A parking area is on the left side of the road. At the parking area the Buzzards Roost Trail is signed. You can also park at the Big Sur Lodge and walk from there.

Contact: Pfeiffer Big Sur State Park, Big Sur, CA 93920; tel. (831) 667-2315, (831) 649-2836, or fax (831) 667-2886.

27 Pine Valley

10.6 mi/
6.0 hrs or 2.0 days

The Pine Valley hike is a great one-night backpacking trip or long day hike into the Ventana Wilderness and can easily be extended into a 13-mile loop. The hike begins on the northern end of the Pine Ridge Trail at China Campground, following an up-and-down course that soon becomes more down than up. At 3.5 miles, you turn right on the Carmel River Trail and descend some more to the headwaters of the Carmel River and the beginning of fir and ponderosa pine forest. Pine Valley Camp is 5.3 miles from the trailhead, set in lush Pine Valley, a spacious high meadow lined with ferns, ponderosa pines, and rocky sandstone formations. A short side trip to Pine Falls is possible from the camp; follow a well-worn route downstream along the river for .5 mile to the waterfall. From there you can retrace your steps to the trailhead for a 10.6-mile round-trip or make camp at Pine Valley or take the trail from the upper end of camp, which meets up with the Pine Ridge Trail. Turn left on Pine Ridge Trail and hike back to the trailhead to complete a 13-mile loop.

Location: In the Ventana Wilderness near Carmel Valley; map F1, grid i8.

User groups: Hikers, dogs, and horses. No mountain bikes. No wheelchair facilities.

Permits: A free campfire permit is required for overnight stays from May through December and is available from the Monterey Ranger District or the Big Sur Station. A national forest recreation pass is required for each vehicle; fees are $5 for one day or $30 for a year.

Maps: For a map of Los Padres National Forest or the Ventana Wilderness, send $6 to U.S. Forest Service, Map Sales, P.O. Box 587, Camino, CA 95709; tel. (530) 647-5390 or website: www.r5.fs.fed.us/visitorcenter. Ask the USGS for a topographic map of the Chews Ridge area.

Directions: From Greenfield on U.S. 101 take the G-16/Monterey County Road exit and drive west for 29 miles. Turn south on Tassajara Road and drive 1.3 miles to Cachagua Road. Turn left and drive nine miles to the trailhead, located just past the turnoff for China Campground. High-clearance vehicles are recommended. The county sometimes closes the road during bad weather; phone the Monterey Ranger District before traveling.

Contact: Los Padres National Forest, Monterey Ranger District, 406 S. Mildred Avenue, King City, CA 93930; tel. (831) 385-5434 or fax (831) 385-0628.

28 McWay Falls Overlook

0.5 mi/0.5 hr

After Yosemite Falls and Bridalveil Fall, McWay Falls is probably the waterfall that appears most often on family snapshots of California vacations. Although few know its name, its image is unforgettable: an 80-foot waterfall leaping off a rugged ocean bluff and pouring gracefully into the Pacific. The walk to the waterfall's overlook is on a paved trail that leads through a tunnel underneath Highway 1 and comes out to a spectacular overlook of McWay Cove. A bench is placed along the trail, where you can sit and admire the action and maybe even catch sight of a passing gray whale. You can continue a few hundred feet beyond the bench, where the trail ends at the ruins of "Waterfall House," the home of Lathrop and Helen Hooper Brown in the 1940s. There's not much left of it now, but at one time it was obviously quite a place.

Location: In Julia Pfeiffer Burns State Park south of Big Sur; map F1, grid j7.

User groups: Hikers only. No dogs, horses, or mountain bikes. The McWay Falls Overlook Trail is wheelchair accessible via a special bridge that bypasses the stairs from the parking lot.

Permits: No permits are required. Parking and access are free.

Maps: A map of Julia Pfeiffer Burns State Park is available for $.50 at the entrance kiosk, or at the entrance kiosk for Pfeiffer Big Sur State Park. Ask the USGS for a topographic map of the Partington Ridge area.

Directions: From Carmel drive 37 miles south on Highway 1 to Julia Pfeiffer Burns State Park, located on the east side of the highway 13 miles south of Big Sur. Drive through the entrance kiosk and park near the restrooms. The Overlook Trail starts on a series of wooden stairs across the pavement from the restrooms.

Contact: Julia Pfeiffer Burns State Park, c/o Pfeiffer Big Sur State Park, Big Sur, CA 93920; tel. (831) 667-2315, (831) 649-2836, or fax (831) 667-2886.

29 Ewoldsen Loop Trail

4.3 mi/2.0 hr

Some say that the Ewoldsen Trail is the best hiking trail in all of Big Sur, and they get no argument from us. The trail begins with an easy saunter along McWay Creek and its spectacular redwood forest; then the trail splits, with Canyon Trail to the left and Ewoldsen Trail switchbacking uphill. Take the short Canyon Trail spur to its end .25 mile away and visit McWay Canyon's sweet little waterfall. It's not the big one, McWay Falls, that cascades into the ocean, but it's pretty to look at. Then retrace your steps to the junction and head uphill on the Ewoldsen Trail, which climbs steadily above the tops of the tall redwood trees below. The next fork, about 1.5 miles in, is the beginning of the loop. Hike the right side first. You'll alternate between dense redwood forest and more sparse oak woodland until at 2.5 miles you see a spur trail signed as "Overlook." Take it and climb very steeply uphill for .25 mile until you come out to a wide, grassy ridgetop with stunning views over McWay Canyon and out to the ocean. After all your time in the forest, this bald, open viewpoint comes as quite a surprise. Pull out your lunch and your camera. After a rest, retrace your steps to the junction, bear right, and take the downhill side of the loop. You're treated to more fine views of the ocean before dropping back into redwood forest. Total elevation gain along the trail is 1,600 feet.

Location: In Julia Pfeiffer Burns State Park south of Big Sur; map F1, grid j7.

User groups: Hikers only. No dogs, horses, or mountain bikes. No wheelchair facilities.

Permits: No permits are required. Parking and access are free.

Maps: A map of Julia Pfeiffer Burns State Park is available for $.50 at the entrance kiosk or at the entrance kiosk for Pfeiffer Big Sur State Park. Ask the USGS for a topographic map of the Partington Ridge area.

Directions: From Carmel drive 37 miles south on Highway 1 to Julia Pfeiffer Burns State Park on the east side of the highway. It's 13 miles south of Big Sur. Drive through the entrance kiosk and park near the restrooms. The Ewoldsen Trail starts near the picnic areas on the inland side of the parking area.

Contact: Julia Pfeiffer Burns State Park, c/o Pfeiffer Big Sur State Park, Big Sur, CA 93920; tel. (831) 667-2315, (831) 649-2836, or fax (831) 667-2886.

30 Partington Point and Tan Bark Trails

4.0 mi/2.0 hrs

If you want to hike at Julia Pfeiffer Burns State Park without the crowds, a combined out-and-back trip on the Partington Point and Tan Bark Trails could be just your cup of tea. The two trails are about as different as any trails could be except that they both start from the same point along Highway 1. The Partington Point Trail is a dirt road that leads westward and downhill to the rocky cove at Partington Point. A short, fun section goes through a tunnel in the rock. The point is home to the park's underwater playground of caves and natural bridges, but unless you're a scuba diver, you won't be able to see them. Instead, you can have a seat on a rock and look for sea otters, sea lions, and pelicans. Also keep your eyes peeled for spouting whales. Another short fork in this trail leads to the other side of the point, where there is a small, sand-and-rock beach.

When you've seen enough, hike back uphill and cross the highway to the start of the Tan Bark Trail, a thickly forested route that leads along Partington Creek, heading inland. You can hike a short .5-mile loop on the trail (a bridge carries you across Partington Creek and then back down the other side), or you can continue farther on the route, climbing steeply uphill for a mile or so until you gain some lovely views out to the coast.

Location: In Julia Pfeiffer Burns State Park south of Big Sur; map F1, grid j7.

User groups: Hikers only. No dogs, horses, or mountain bikes. No wheelchair facilities.

Permits: No permits are required. Parking and access are free.

Maps: A map of Julia Pfeiffer Burns State Park is available for $.50 at the entrance kiosk or at the entrance kiosk for Pfeiffer Big Sur State Park. Ask the USGS for a topographic map of the Partington Ridge area.

Directions: From Carmel drive 34 miles south on Highway 1 to a dirt pullout along the highway and the trailheads for the Partington Point and Tan Bark Trails. The trailheads are 10.5 miles south of Big Sur and 2.2 miles north of the main entrance to Julia Pfeiffer Burns State Park. Partington Point Trail is on the west side of the highway, Tan Bark Trail is on the east side.

Contact: Julia Pfeiffer Burns State Park, c/o Pfeiffer Big Sur State Park, Big Sur, CA 93920; tel. (831) 667-2315, (831) 649-2836, or fax (831) 667-2886.

31 Cone Peak Lookout Trail

4.0 mi/2.5 hrs

The two-mile climb to Cone Peak is a classic Ventana Wilderness adventure, and the fun begins with the drive to the trailhead. After leaving Highway 1, you get almost nonstop dramatic coastal views as your car chugs its way uphill. But that's nothing compared to the views you get at the fire lookout on Cone Peak at 5,155 feet above sea level. The hike is a re-lentless climb, and the last mile sometimes seems to go straight up, but the total elevation gain is surprisingly only 1,500 feet. Make sure you have plenty of water with you. After switchbacking upward through a mix of low brush, hardwoods, and then conifers (mostly Coulter pines), you reach a trail junction at 1.8 miles. Go east (right) and walk the final .25 mile to the fire lookout. How's the view? Well, be sure to bring a good map so you can name all the peaks and valleys in the 360-degree panorama that surrounds you.

Location: In the Ventana Wilderness north of Lucia; map F1, grid j9.

User groups: Hikers, dogs, and horses. No mountain bikes. No wheelchair facilities.

Permits: No permits are required. A national forest recreation pass is required for each vehicle; fees are $5 for one day or $30 for a year.

Maps: For a map of Los Padres National Forest or the Ventana Wilderness, send $6 to U.S. Forest Service, Map Sales, P.O. Box 587, Camino, CA 95709; tel. (530) 647-5390 or website: www.r5.fs.fed.us/visitorcenter. Ask the USGS for a topographic map of the Cone Peak area.

Directions: From Carmel drive 55 miles south on Highway 1 to Kirk Creek Campground on the west side of the highway. Continue one mile farther south on Highway 1 to the left turnoff for Nacimiento-Ferguson Road. Turn left and drive seven miles and turn left again on Cone Peak Road and drive 5.4 miles to the trailhead on the left (do not follow the road to its end).

Contact: Los Padres National Forest, Monterey Ranger District, 406 S. Mildred Avenue, King City, CA 93930; tel. (831) 385-5434 or fax (831) 385-0628.

CHAPTER F2

ANN MARIE BROWN

HIKING IN PINNACLES
NATIONAL MONUMENT

MAP F2

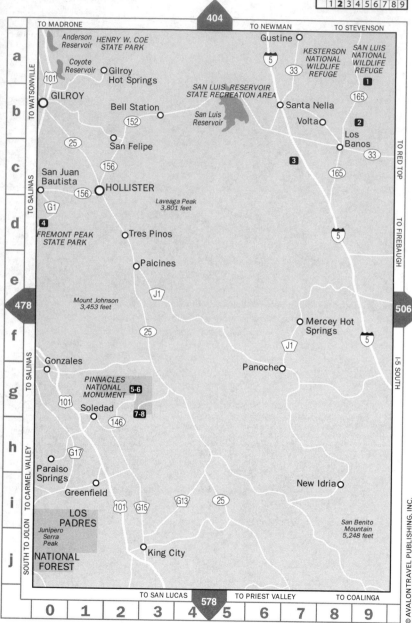

TO MADRONE   404   **TO NEWMAN**   **TO STEVENSON**

Anderson Reservoir

HENRY W. COE STATE PARK

Gustine

Coyote Reservoir

Gilroy Hot Springs

a

101

KESTERSON NATIONAL WILDLIFE REFUGE

SAN LUIS NATIONAL WILDLIFE REFUGE

5

33

165

1

GILROY

Bell Station

152

SAN LUIS RESERVOIR STATE RECREATION AREA

San Luis Reservoir

Santa Nella

Volta

Los Banos

2

b

25

San Felipe

156

165

33

San Juan Bautista

156 **HOLLISTER**

3

c

G1

Laveaga Peak 3,801 feet

4

FREMONT PEAK STATE PARK

Tres Pinos

5

d

Paicines

J1

478

Mount Johnson 3,453 feet

25

Mercey Hot Springs

506

5

e

J1

Panoche

f

Gonzales

PINNACLES NATIONAL MONUMENT

5-6

g

101

Soledad

7-8

146

Paraiso Springs

G17

New Idria

h

Greenfield

i

101 G15 G13 25

LOS PADRES

Junipero Serra Peak

San Benito Mountain 5,248 feet

NATIONAL FOREST

King City

j

TO SAN LUCAS   578   **TO PRIEST VALLEY**   **TO COALINGA**

0 1 2 3 4 5 6 7 8 9

TO WATSONVILLE

TO SALINAS

TO SALINAS

TO CARMEL VALLEY

SOUTH TO JOLON

TO RED TOP

TO FIREBAUGH

I-5 SOUTH

© AVALON TRAVEL PUBLISHING, INC.

CHAPTER F2

1 Chester and
   Winton Marsh Trails . . . 499
2 Los Banos
   Wildlife Area. 499
3 Path of the Padres. 500
4 Fremont Peak Trail 501
5 Balconies Caves. 501
6 Juniper Canyon
   and High Peaks Loop . . . 502
7 Condor Gulch and
   High Peaks Loop 502
8 Bear Gulch Caves 503

1 Chester and Winton Marsh Trails

1.8 mi/1.0 hr

While most people are taking the driving tour in San Luis National Wildlife Refuge hoping to spot a big tule elk or a flock of birds from the windows of their cars, you can take two flat and short walks through bird-filled marshes, starting from two different trailheads along the Waterfowl Tour Route. As you drive the auto route, the first trailhead you reach is for the Chester Marsh Trail on the north edge of the Waterfowl Tour Route. It's open for hiking only from February to September because the birds get the run of the place in the fall and early winter. It's a one-mile interpretive loop, and you can pick up an explanatory brochure at the trailhead. After your walk, get back in your car and continue driving along the Waterfowl Tour Route until you reach the trailhead for the Winton Marsh Trail. This trail is open year-round, is slightly shorter than the one at Chester Marsh, and has a wooden observation platform and several benches situated slightly above the marsh, so you can pull out your binoculars and peer at the feathered fowl below. What will you see? The usual

cabal: ducks, geese, moorhens, coots, pheasants, snipe, hawks, owls, egrets, herons, and even some rare types like the endangered tricolored blackbird (it's black, white, and red). Even while just driving around, we saw a coyote and about a zillion bunnies, in addition to numerous Swainson's hawks.

Location: In the San Luis National Wildlife Refuge north of Los Banos; map F2, grid a9.

User groups: Hikers and dogs. No horses or mountain bikes. No wheelchair facilities.

Permits: No permits are required. Parking and access are free.

Maps: A free map of the wildlife refuge is available by contacting the refuge headquarters at the address below. Ask the USGS for a topographic map of the Los Banos area.

Directions: From Los Banos on Highway 152/33, drive north on Highway 165 (Mercey Springs Road) for 6.4 miles to Wolfsen Road. Bear right and follow Wolfsen Road for 2.5 miles into the National Wildlife Refuge. Follow the signs for the Waterfowl Tour Route. The Chester Marsh Trail parking area will be on the left side of the road. Continue around the Waterfowl Tour Route loop to reach the Winton Marsh Trail parking area, also on the left side of the road.

Contact: San Luis National Wildlife Refuge, P.O. Box 2176, Los Banos, CA 93635; tel. (209) 826-3508, or fax (209) 826-1445.

2 Los Banos Wildlife Area

2.0 mi/1.0 hr

Los Banos Wildlife Area is like the little brother of nearby San Luis National Wildlife Refuge. It's run by the California Department of Fish and Game instead of the feds, but the birds don't care about the distinction. On our first trip here, we had barely driven past the registration kiosk when a giant sandhill crane lifted off into the air not 20 feet from our car. This was in June, which is not the sandhill crane's normal season for visiting. The two-mile loop trail near Little Buttonwillow Lake offers the best formal hiking in the preserve, although there are numerous parking areas where you can just pull off the road and wander as you please. On the loop trail you get to visit the sandhill crane viewing area, where you're almost guaranteed to see the huge, prehistoric-looking birds. Their large size, the distinctive crook in their necks, and the way they lay their feet back as they fly make them easy to identify even if you've never seen them before. In autumn, when the waterfowl migration is in full swing, up to 50,000 birds show up here—hundreds of different species. The only downer? Unlike the federal wildlife refuge, this refuge doesn't have separate areas for hunters and hikers, so hikers are discouraged from visiting during the autumn hunting season, which is also the best bird-watching season.

Location: North of Los Banos; map F2, grid b9.

User groups: Hikers and dogs. No horses or mountain bikes. No wheelchair facilities.

Permits: Visitors must register at the entrance kiosk. A $2.50 fee is charged per vehicle. If you are in possession of a valid California fishing or hunting license, entrance is free.

Maps: Ask the USGS for a topographic map of the Los Banos area.

Directions: From Los Banos on Highway 152/33, drive north on Highway 165 (Mercey Springs Road) for three miles to Henry Miller Avenue. Turn right on Henry Miller Avenue, then left into the Los Banos Wildlife Area entrance. After registering, continue down the gravel road to the parking area by Little and Big Buttonwillow Lakes.

Contact: Los Banos Wildlife Area, 18110 W. Henry Miller Avenue, Los Banos, CA 93635; tel. (209) 826-0463 or (209) 826-5188.

❸ Path of the Padres
5.0 mi/3.0 hrs

You've got to plan way in advance to take this unusual hike at Los Banos Creek Reservoir. That's because the only way to go is by boat and with a guide, and guided trips are offered only on weekends in March and April. The trip has become so popular that it usually sells out as soon as reservations are available, which is the first week of February each year. That means don't procrastinate on making your call for reservations. If you've reserved a spot, your trip begins with a boat ride down the long and narrow reservoir, set in a steep-walled canyon and popular for windsurfing and canoeing. At the reservoir's far end, everyone gets off the boat and starts hiking up the narrow canyon of Los Banos Creek, where old-growth sycamore groves and a cornucopia of spring wildflowers can be seen. The guide will teach you how to spot and identify various animal tracks along the canyon floor, and birders may thrill to see a peregrine falcon or other cliff-dwelling species. The hike ends with a climb to the top of a knoll that offers wide views of the Los Banos valley. So why is this trail called the Path of the Padres? Because the fathers at Mission San Juan Bautista came here in the early 1800s to recruit the Yokut Indians to work for them. On the trip you'll see bedrock mortars and other evidence of the Native Americans who once lived in this canyon.

Location: On Los Banos Creek, south of San Luis Reservoir; map F2, grid c7.

User groups: Hikers only. No dogs, horses, or mountain bikes. No wheelchair facilities.

Permits: Reservations are required; call to reserve a space during the first week of February. A $5 fee is charged per person for the reservation and guided tour. In addition, a $5 day-use fee is charged per vehicle.

Maps: Ask the USGS for a topographic map of the Los Banos Valley.

Directions: From Interstate 5 at the junction with Highway 152 (south of Santa Nella), turn east on Highway 152 and drive 2.5 miles. Turn right (south) on Volta Road, and drive one mile. Turn left (east) on Pioneer Road and drive .8 mile, then right on Canyon Road. Drive south on Canyon Road for five miles to Los Banos Creek Reservoir. (You will cross back to the west side of Interstate 5.) Park near the boat ramp.

Contact: San Luis Reservoir State Recreation Area, Four Rivers District, 31426 Gonzaga Road, Gustine, CA 95322; tel. (209) 826-1196.

4 Fremont Peak Trail

0.6 mi/0.5 hr

Fremont Peak State Park—it's a little tiny park with a great big view. There isn't much of a choice of hiking trails here, just a short .6-mile trail to the summit of Fremont Peak, elevation 3,169 feet. But that one little trip packs one heck of a punch. Pick a clear day in winter or spring (summer gets brutally hot and the visibility worsens), make the pretty drive from San Juan Bautista, and prepare for a panorama of Monterey Bay, Santa Cruz, Salinas, Watsonville, Hollister, and the Santa Lucia Mountains. (They say that on the clearest of days you can see the Sierra, but we've never seen it.) From the parking area, walk up the gated, paved service road for a few hundred yards and then cut off to the right on the signed Peak Trail, which winds its way up the mountain. The last .1 mile is very rocky, and the final summit climb is a bit of a scramble. Ignore the close-by transmitters and check out the far-off views. Note: Another popular activity at the park is stargazing. Fremont Peak Observatory is open to the public on some weekends and rangers hold astronomy programs here. Call for a schedule.

Location: In Fremont Peak State Park near San Juan Bautista; map F2, grid d0.

User groups: Hikers only. No dogs, horses, or mountain bikes. No wheelchair facilities.

Permits: No permits are required. A $1 day-use fee is charged per vehicle.

Maps: A free map of Fremont Peak State Park is available at the self-registration area. Ask the USGS for a topographic map of the San Juan Bautista area.

Directions: From Gilroy drive south on U.S. 101 for 10 miles to the Highway 156 East/San Juan Bautista exit. Turn east on Highway 156 and drive three miles to San Juan Bautista, then turn right (south) on San Juan Canyon Road. (It's signed for the state park.) Follow it 11 miles to its end in Fremont Peak State Park.

Contact: Fremont Peak State Park, P.O. Box 787, San Juan Bautista, CA 95045; tel. (831) 623-4255.

5 Balconies Caves

2.4 mi/1.5 hrs

If you're coming from U.S. 101 and the western edge of California, the west side of Pinnacles National Monument is a heck of a lot easier to get to than the east side. But if you're disappointed to learn that the Pinnacles' famous Bear Gulch Caves can be accessed only from the east side of the park, don't despair. The west side has its own caves, and like the east side's Bear Gulch Caves, these are a barrel of fun. Got your flashlight? Okay; then set off on the Balconies Trail, following the often dry West Fork of Chalone Creek. A mere .6 mile brings you to some huge, colorful, lichen-covered volcanic rocks, a preview of the caves to come. The sounds of the wind in the gray pines and the scurrying of squirrels keep you company. At the fork with the Balconies Cliffs Trail, go right to enter the caves. Turn on your flashlight for some good clean fun and adventure—squeezing through clefts in the rock, ducking under ledges, and climbing down rocky staircases. When you exit the caves, you can turn left and loop back on the Balconies Cliffs Trail, gaining many lovely views of the park's rocky landscape as you climb over the top of the caves.

Location: In Pinnacles National Monument near Soledad; map F2, grid g2.

User groups: Hikers only. No dogs, horses, or mountain bikes. No wheelchair facilities.

Permits: No permits are required. There is a $5 entrance fee at Pinnacles National Monument, good for seven days.

Maps: A free map of Pinnacles National Monument is available at the ranger station. Ask

the USGS for topographic maps of the Bickmore Canyon and North Chalone Peak areas.
Directions: From Salinas drive south on U.S. 101 for 22 miles to Soledad and take the Soledad/Highway 146 exit. Drive east on Highway 146 for 12 miles. (The road is signed for West Pinnacles.) Highway 146 dead-ends at the Chaparral Ranger Station and trailhead parking lot.
Contact: Pinnacles National Monument, 5000 Highway 146, Paicines, CA 95043; tel. (831) 389-4485 or fax (831) 389-4489.

⑥ Juniper Canyon and High Peaks Loop
8.4 mi/5.0 hrs

Pinnacles National Monument is a hiker's park. The first clue you get is that no road connects the east and west sides of the park, so the only way to get from one side to the other is to walk. We think that's just fine, especially since the park's first-rate trail system makes it possible to string together a loop tour around the park on the Juniper Canyon Trail, High Peaks Trail, Old Pinnacles Trail, and Balconies Trail. If you follow the trails in this order, you get almost all your climbing done in the first half of the trip and then have a fairly easy and flat homestretch. Begin hiking from the right side of the large parking lot near the Chaparral Ranger Station, following the Juniper Canyon Trail from grasslands into the rocky hills. The trail gets steeper as you go, but it's well built and has many switchbacks.

Ignore the Tunnel Trail turnoff at 1.2 miles, and keep climbing to the junction with the High Peaks Trail at 1.8 miles. Here, at a saddle, are fine views to the west and east and a bench and restroom.

The High Peaks Trail goes both north and southeast. Turn north (left) and prepare yourself for the most exciting part of the trip. This is a narrow and exciting stretch of trail with many handholds and footholds carved into the rock. Continue on the High Peaks Trail for 3.3 miles all the way to the Chalone Creek picnic

area. There you can fill up your water bottles, take a rest, and then head north on the Old Pinnacles Trail, a pleasant route that meanders along the West Fork of Chalone Creek. In winter the creek even has water in it, and spring wildflowers are tremendous. In 2.3 miles you'll reach a fork for the Balconies Trail, and if you've never been to Balconies Caves, take the left fork, which leads you through them. (The right fork climbs above the caves for some excellent views.) After ducking your head and bending your knees a lot as you wander through the caves, you'll come out to an easy and flat section of the Balconies Trail, which brings you right back to the Chaparral parking lot. If you pick a cool day and carry plenty of water, this is a stellar long-day hike in Pinnacles.

Location: In Pinnacles National Monument near Soledad; map F2, grid g2.
User groups: Hikers only. No dogs, horses, or mountain bikes. No wheelchair facilities.
Permits: No permits are required. There is a $5 entrance fee at Pinnacles National Monument, good for seven days.
Maps: A free map of Pinnacles National Monument is available at the ranger station. Ask the USGS for topographic maps of Bickmore Canyon and North Chalone Peak areas.
Directions: From Salinas drive south on U.S. 101 for 22 miles to Soledad and take the Soledad/Highway 146 exit. Drive east on Highway 146 for 12 miles. The road is signed for West Pinnacles. Highway 146 dead-ends at the Chaparral Ranger Station and trailhead parking lot.
Contact: Pinnacles National Monument, 5000 Highway 146, Paicines, CA 95043; tel. (831) 389-4485 or fax (831) 389-4489.

⑦ Condor Gulch and High Peaks Loop
5.0 mi/2.5 hr

The Condor Gulch Trail begins across the road from the Bear Gulch Ranger Station, and it's a good 30-minute climb up the hill on a smooth, switchbacked trail to an overlook of the High

Peaks. The scent of wild sage and rosemary is enticingly aromatic along the route, and your eyes are continually drawn to the colorful lichen growing on equally colorful rocks. The overlook is just a piped railing on a ledge above a huge boulder, but it's a good spot to get your bearings and look out over the trail you just climbed. It's also a good turnaround spot if you don't want to go farther. If you do, continue uphill to a junction with the High Peaks Trail at 1.7 miles and turn left. In just over .5 mile, you'll reach a junction with the Tunnel Trail. People afraid of heights should consider taking the Tunnel Trail downhill. They can then turn left on the Juniper Canyon Trail to meet up with their fellow hikers at a bench and an overlook area at the junction of Juniper Canyon Trail and High Peaks Trail. Those willing for the adventure should continue on the High Peaks Trail through narrow passageways and over and under steep rock formations. In many places the trail has been blasted into the rock, and the steep drop-offs can be dizzying. Use the handholds and guard rails. After .7 mile, you'll reach the intersection with Juniper Canyon Trail, where there is a bench, a fine view to the west, and a restroom. Take advantage of any or all of these, then turn left to stay on High Peaks Trail and head back to Bear Gulch. You'll have to walk up the Moses Spring Trail or the park road a short distance to get back to your car.

Location: In Pinnacles National Monument near Soledad; map F2, grid g2.

User groups: Hikers only. No dogs, horses, or mountain bikes. No wheelchair facilities.

Permits: No permits are required. There is a $5 entrance fee at Pinnacles National Monument, good for seven days.

Maps: A free map of Pinnacles National Monument is available at the ranger station. Ask the USGS for topographic maps of the Bickmore Canyon and North Chalone Peak areas.

Directions: From King City on U.S. 101, take the 1st Street exit and head east. First Street turns into Highway G13/Bitterwater Road. Follow it for 15 miles to Highway 25, where you turn left (north). Follow Highway 25 for 14 miles to Highway 146. Turn left on Highway 146 and drive 4.8 miles to the park visitor center. The trailhead for the Condor Gulch Trail is across the road from the visitor center.

Contact: Pinnacles National Monument, 5000 Highway 146, Paicines, CA 95043; tel. (831) 389-4485 or fax (831) 389-4489.

8 Bear Gulch Caves
2.0 mi/1.0 hr

Bear Gulch Caves is by far the most popular destination in Pinnacles National Monument, and it's easy and fun for all ages to enjoy. Make sure you've packed along a flashlight (preferably one for each person) and then set off from the Bear Gulch picnic area on the Bear Gulch Caves Trail. A quarter mile down the trail you come to a junction with the High Peaks Trail. Keep to the left to stay on Bear Gulch Caves Trail, pass through a rock tunnel, and reach another fork where you can either head into the caves directly or take the Moses Spring Trail to the right, up and over them. Stay left and consider taking the Moses Spring Trail for your return trip. Of course, most people have so much fun inside Bear Gulch Caves that they take the cave path in both directions. What kind of fun? How about this: Walk into water-sculpted volcanic caverns where only occasional beams of sunlight flash through the ceiling. Enter a circular cavern where water streams down the walls, the only sound being the constant drip. Climb up to rocky lookouts and down rocky staircases; duck through narrow passageways; stoop, twist, and turn your body, following the beam of your flashlight. It's a great adventure with no real threat of danger. Kids have a ball in the caves, but then again, so do adults.

If you care to hike a little farther before your return, continue straight ahead beyond the caves, taking the stairs uphill to Bear Gulch Reservoir. Sorry, no swimming is allowed, but it's fun to watch the rock climbers at work near its shoreline.

Special note: If you are planning to visit Pinnacles National Monument specifically to visit Bear Gulch Caves, phone ahead to be sure that the caves are open. They are frequently closed during the rainy season due to flooding, and also during certain periods of the year when endangered bats nest in the caves.

Location: In Pinnacles National Monument near Soledad; map F2, grid g2.

User groups: Hikers only. No dogs, horses, or mountain bikes. No wheelchair facilities.

Permits: No permits are required. There is a $5 entrance fee at Pinnacles National Monument, good for seven days.

Maps: A free map of Pinnacles National Monument is available at the ranger station. Ask the USGS for topographic maps of the Bickmore Canyon and North Chalone Peak areas.

Directions: From King City on U.S. 101, take the 1st Street exit and head east. First Street turns into Highway G13/Bitterwater Road. Follow it for 15 miles to Highway 25, where you turn left (north). Follow Highway 25 for 14 miles to Highway 146. Go left on Highway 146 and drive 4.8 miles to the park visitor center; continue beyond it to the parking lot at the end of the road. If this lot is full, park by the visitor center and walk down the road to the trailhead.

Contact: Pinnacles National Monument, 5000 Highway 146, Paicines, CA 95043; tel. (831) 389-4485 or fax (831) 389-4489.

ANN MARIE BROWN

MARIPOSA LILY

MAP F3

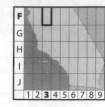

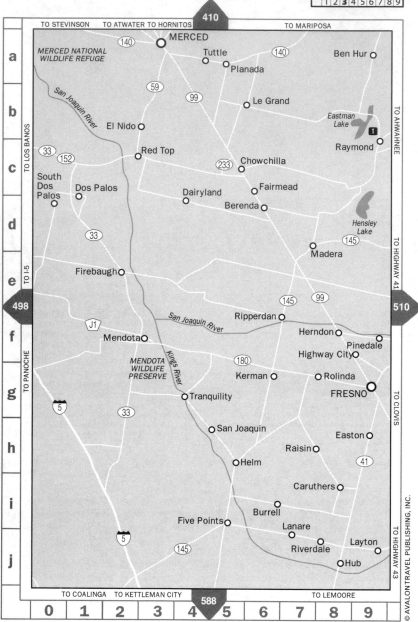

TO STEVINSON   TO ATWATER TO HORNITOS   TO MARIPOSA

MERCED NATIONAL
WILDLIFE REFUGE

140 MERCED
Tuttle
Planada   Ben Hur

59
99   Eastman
Le Grand   Lake
El Nido   TO AHWAHNEE
Raymond

33 152 Red Top
Chowchilla
233
South
Dos   Dos Palos   Fairmead
Palos   Dairyland
Berenda   Hensley
Lake
33
Madera   145   TO HIGHWAY 41

Firebaugh

498 San Joaquin River
Ripperdan   145 99
J1   Herndon
Mendota   Pinedale
MENDOTA   180 Highway City
WILDLIFE
PRESERVE   Kings River   Kerman Rolinda
5   Tranquility   FRESNO   TO CLOVIS
33
San Joaquin   Easton
Raisin   41
Helm
Caruthers
Burrell
Five Points   Lanare   Layton
5
145   Riverdale
Hub

TO COALINGA   TO KETTLEMAN CITY   TO LEMOORE

TO LOS BANOS

TO I-5

TO PANOCHE

TO HIGHWAY 43

© AVALON TRAVEL PUBLISHING, INC.

0   1   2   3   4   5   6   7   8   9

a   b   c   d   e   f   g   h   i   j

CHAPTER F3

■ Lakeview Trail
2.0 mi/1.0 hr

Let's get one thing straight: you don't want to hike here at midday in July. Got it? Good. But if it's March and the wildflowers are in bloom, you'd be wise to head out here to Eastman Lake, then hike the Lakeview Trail that leads along its south and east sides. Sure, a reservoir is a reservoir, but when the water level is high, the grasslands are green, and the flowers are blooming, this reservoir can seem like a little slice of paradise in the Central Valley. The trail leads a total of four miles one way, but unfortunately much of the route is closed from December 1 to July 15, which includes the best hiking season. But if you start hiking from the spillway, you can hike along the south side of the lake for a mile to the group campground area, and continue from there along the east side of the lake for another mile before you reach the trail closure.

The best part of the trail is this latter section, so if you're looking for a shorter trip, park in the trailhead parking lot at Codorniz Group Campground and hike north on the Lakeview Trail from there; that makes a two-mile round-trip.

Location: On the southeast shore of Eastman Lake, east of Chowchilla; map F3, grid b9.

User groups: Hikers, dogs, horses, and mountain bikes. No wheelchair facilities.

Permits: No permits are required. Parking and access are free.

Maps: A free map of Eastman Lake is available at the visitor center. Ask the USGS for a topographic map of the Raymond area.

Directions: From Merced drive south on Highway 99 for 20 miles to Chowchilla. Take the Avenue 26 exit and head east for 17 miles. Turn north on County Road 29 and drive eight miles to the lake. Turn right and park in the lot by the spillway, just beyond the visitor center and park headquarters.

Contact: U.S. Army Corps of Engineers, Eastman Lake, P.O. Box 67, Raymond, CA 93653; tel. (559) 689-3255.

CHAPTER F4

TWIN LAKES NESTLED IN
THE KAISER WILDERNESS

MAP F4

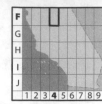

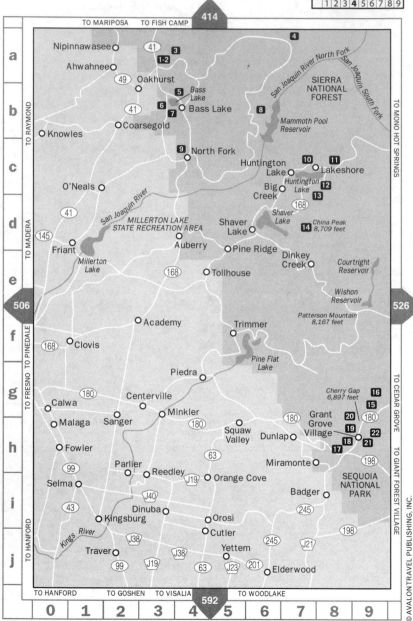

414

TO MARIPOSA   TO FISH CAMP

a

Nipinnawasee

Ahwahnee

⑷ 41

3

1-2

4

TO RAYMOND

b

⑷ 49   Oakhurst

5 Bass Lake

6

⑷ 41   **7** Bass Lake

Coarsegold

Knowles

8

San Joaquin River North Fork

San Joaquin River South Fork

SIERRA
NATIONAL
FOREST

Mammoth Pool
Reservoir

TO MONO HOT SPRINGS

c

9 North Fork

O'Neals

Huntington
Lake

10

11 Lakeshore

Big
Creek

Huntington
Lake

12

13

TO MADERA

d

⑷ 41

⑷ 145

Friant

San Joaquin River

MILLERTON LAKE
STATE RECREATION AREA

Millerton
Lake

Auberry

Shaver
Lake

Pine Ridge

Shaver
Lake

⑷ 168

China Peak
8,709 feet

14

e

506

⑷ 168   Tollhouse

Dinkey
Creek

Courtright
Reservoir

Wishon
Reservoir

526

TO PINEDALE

f

Academy

⑷ 168   Clovis

Trimmer

Patterson Mountain
8,167 feet

TO FRESNO

g

⑷ 180

Calwa

Centerville

Piedra

Pine Flat
Lake

Cherry Gap
6,897 feet

16

15

TO CEDAR GROVE

h

Malaga   Sanger

Fowler

Minkler

⑷ 180

Squaw
Valley

Dunlap

⑷ 180

Grant
Grove
Village

20

19

18

17

180

22

21

⑷ 198

TO GIANT FOREST VILLAGE

i

⑷ 99   Parlier

Selma

Reedley

J19   Orange Cove

⑷ 63

Miramonte

Badger

⑷ 245

SEQUOIA
NATIONAL
PARK

TO HANFORD

j

⑷ 43

J40

Dinuba

Kingsburg

Kings River

J38

Traver

⑷ 99   J19   J38   ⑷ 63

Orosi

Cutler

Yettem

J23   ⑷ 201   Elderwood

⑷ 245   J21   ⑷ 198

TO HANFORD   TO GOSHEN   TO VISALIA   TO WOODLAKE

592

| 0 | 1 | 2 | 3 | 4 | 5 | 6 | 7 | 8 | 9 |

CHAPTER F4

1 Lewis Creek 511
2 Shadow of the Giants . 512
3 Fresno Dome....... 512
4 The Niche and
   Cora Lakes 513
5 Willow Creek....... 513
6 Way of the Mono..... 514
7 Goat Mountain
   Lookout 514
8 French Trail at
   Mammoth Pool 515
9 Cedars Interpretive .. 515
10 Kaiser Peak........ 516
11 Twin Lakes and
   George Lake 516

12 Rancheria Falls 517
13 Indian Pools 517
14 Dinkey Lakes........ 518
15 Chicago Stump Trail .. 518
16 Boole Tree Loop 519
17 Big Stump Trail...... 520
18 Sunset Trail 520
19 North Grove and
   Dead Giant Loop..... 521
20 General Grant Tree... 521
21 Manzanita and
   Azalea Loop 522
22 Panoramic Point and
   Park Ridge Lookout... 522

1 Lewis Creek

4.0 mi/2.0 hrs

There are three trailheads that access the Lewis Creek Trail, but unless you want to hike its entire 3.5-mile one-way distance, the best place to start is at the trail's midpoint just off Highway 41. From this roadside trailhead you can take a 10-minute walk south to Corlieu Falls and walk 1.8 miles north to see Red Rock Falls. Neither waterfall is a showstopper, although both are pretty. Instead, the highlight of the trip is the hike itself, a gorgeous walk along flower-lined Lewis Creek that follows the route of the historic Madera Sugar Pine lumber flume. You'll pass many anglers along the way, as Lewis Creek is stocked with catchable trout. In addition, the white western azaleas along the stream bloom in profusion, shaded by a thick canopy of oaks, ponderosa pines, and incense cedars.

Location: Off Highway 41 north of Oakhurst; map F4, grid a3.

User groups: Hikers and dogs. No horses or mountain bikes. No wheelchair facilities.

Permits: No permits are required. Parking and access are free.

Maps: For a map of Sierra National Forest send $6 to U.S. Forest Service, Map Sales, P.O. Box 587, Camino, CA 95709; tel. (530) 647-5390 or website: www.r5.fs.fed.us/visitorcenter. Ask the USGS for a topographic map of the Ahwahnee area.

Directions: From Oakhurst drive north on Highway 41 for eight miles to the signed trailhead for the Lewis Creek Trail, on the east side of the highway. The trailhead is four miles south of Westfall Picnic Area.

Contact: Sierra National Forest, Mariposa/Minarets Ranger District, 57003 Road 225, North Fork, CA 93643; tel. (559) 877-2218 or (559) 683-4665.

2 Shadow of the Giants
1.2 mi/0.5 hr

Shadow of the Giants is a National Recreation Trail that is located within the Nelder Grove of giant sequoias. For sheer numbers of sequoias and blissful peace and quiet, it beats the heck out of the sequoia groves a few miles north in Yosemite National Park. On a Saturday afternoon in June, we walked the one-mile interpretive trail all by ourselves. The self-guided signs along the trail are interesting and informative, and the babble of Nelder Creek is a perfect accompaniment to the huge, majestic trees. In addition to the sequoias, the forest is filled with western azaleas, dogwoods, incense cedars, wild rose, sugar pines, and white firs. What's the best thing we learned on the trail? The bark of mature sequoias is so soft that squirrels use it to line their nests. The trail makes an easy loop and is set at 5,000 feet in elevation. The best redwoods are at the far end of the loop, so make sure you walk all the way.

Location: Off Highway 41 south of Yosemite National Park and north of Oakhurst; map F4, grid a3.

User groups: Hikers and dogs. No horses or mountain bikes. No wheelchair facilities.

Permits: No permits are required. Parking and access are free.

Maps: For a map of Sierra National Forest send $6 to U.S. Forest Service, Map Sales, P.O. Box 587, Camino, CA 95709; tel. (530) 647-5390 or website: www.r5.fs.fed.us/visitorcenter. Ask the USGS for a topographic map of the Bass Lake area.

Directions: From Oakhurst drive north on Highway 41 for five miles to Sky Ranch Road/Road 632. Turn east on Sky Ranch Road and drive six miles to the turnoff for Nelder Grove. Turn left, drive 1.5 miles and take the left fork, signed for Shadow of the Giants. Drive .5 mile to the trailhead.

Contact: Sierra National Forest, Mariposa/Minarets Ranger District, 57003 Road 225, North Fork, CA 93643; tel. (559) 877-2218 or (559) 683-4665.

3 Fresno Dome
2.0 mi/1.0 hr

We recommend one hour of time for this trip, but you might want to plan for more, because once you reach the top of Fresno Dome you won't want to leave. The trailhead elevation is 8,000 feet, and the trail is beautiful right from the start, where it traverses a verdant meadow filled with corn lilies, quaking aspens, and lavender shooting stars. The first .5 mile is completely flat; in the second .5 mile you climb up the sloped back side of Fresno Dome. After a moderate ascent, manageable by almost anybody, you're rewarded with 360-degree views, mostly of conifer-filled valleys. You can just make out a corner of Bass Lake, the town of Oakhurst, and the far-off snowy peaks of the John Muir Wilderness. From up on top of Fresno Dome, it all looks like heaven.

Location: Off Highway 41 south of Yosemite National Park and north of Oakhurst; map F4, grid a3.

User groups: Hikers and dogs. No horses or mountain bikes. No wheelchair facilities.

Permits: No permits are required. Parking and access are free.

Maps: For a map of Sierra National Forest send $6 to U.S. Forest Service, Map Sales, P.O. Box 587, Camino, CA 95709; tel. (530) 647-5390 or website: www.r5.fs.fed.us/visitorcenter. Ask the USGS for a topographic map of the Bass Lake area.

Directions: From Oakhurst drive north on Highway 41 for five miles to Sky Ranch Road/Road 632. Turn east on Sky Ranch Road, drive approximately 12 miles, turn left at the sign for Fresno Dome Campground and drive 4.8 miles to the trailhead (two miles past the camp).

Contact: Sierra National Forest, Mariposa/Minarets Ranger District, 57003 Road 225, North Fork, CA 93643; tel. (559) 877-2218 or (559) 683-4665.

4 The Niche and Cora Lakes

11.0 mi/
6.0 hrs or 2.0 days

Reaching the trailhead for The Niche and Cora Lakes requires a long drive on the Sierra Vista National Scenic Byway, the showpiece road of the North Fork area, and if you have the time for it, it's a great trip. The best way to make the adventure work well is to drive out and spend the night at Granite Creek Campground or nearby Clover Meadow Campground, and start hiking the next day. The trip starts with a 1.5-mile ascent to The Niche at 8,000 feet, where you enter the Ansel Adams Wilderness boundary. Follow the well-marked signs to Cora Lake at four miles. The total ascent is only about 1,200 feet. If you still have energy left, retrace your steps to The Niche, and head northeast along the ridge toward Hemlock Crossing. Go as far as you please, but at least go for a mile or two, enjoying stellar views of Mount Ritter, Mount Banner, and the Minarets.

Location: In the Ansel Adams Wilderness, southeast of Yosemite National Park; map F4, grid a7.

User groups: Hikers, dogs, and horses. No mountain bikes. No wheelchair facilities.

Permits: A free wilderness permit is required for overnight stays and is available from the Minarets Ranger Station. Quotas are in effect from June to September; reservations are available in advance by mail for this period for a $3 fee. Parking and access are free.

Maps: For a map of Sierra National Forest send $6 to U.S. Forest Service, Map Sales, P.O. Box 587, Camino, CA 95709; tel. (530) 647-5390 or website: www.r5.fs.fed.us/visitorcenter. Ask the USGS for a topographic map of the Timber Knob area.

Directions: From the town of North Fork south of Bass Lake, drive southeast on Road 225 to Minarets Road. Turn left (north) on Minarets Road/Road 81 and follow it for approximately 50 winding miles to the Clover Meadow Ranger Station/Granite Creek turnoff on the right.

Drive 4.5 miles to the Isberg trailhead just beyond Granite Creek Campground.

Contact: Sierra National Forest, Mariposa/Minarets Ranger District, 57003 Road 225, North Fork, CA 93643; tel. (559) 877-2218 or (559) 683-4665.

5 Willow Creek

4.8 mi/2.5 hrs

Most people hike the Willow Creek Trail with one of two things in mind: fishing or swimming. You can't blame them, since the trail runs alongside Willow Creek, and offers a myriad of quiet pools and fast, granite-lined cascades. The Forest Service requests that people don't swim upstream of Angel Falls, a wide cascade that looks like angel wings, because the creek is used as a domestic water supply. Downstream swimming is okay, but be wary of slippery granite all along the creek. At 2.4 miles from the trailhead, be sure to take the left spur for Devils Slide at a junction where the main trail continues to its end at McLeod Flat Road. Devils Slide is a remarkable granite water slide, with large rounded indentations in the rock. A chain-link fence keeps hikers off the dangerously slick granite. From Devils Slide, head back to the main trail and retrace your steps downhill. Expect to see some great views of bright blue Bass Lake on the return trip.

Location: On the northeast end of Bass Lake near Oakhurst; map F4, grid b4.

User groups: Hikers and dogs. No horses or mountain bikes. No wheelchair facilities.

Permits: No permits are required. Parking and access are free.

Maps: For a map of Sierra National Forest send $6 to U.S. Forest Service, Map Sales, P.O. Box 587, Camino, CA 95709; tel. (530) 647-5390 or website: www.r5.fs.fed.us/visitorcenter. Ask the USGS for a topographic map of the Bass Lake area.

Directions: From Oakhurst drive north on Highway 41 for four miles and turn right on

Road 222. Drive four miles and bear left on Road 274. Drive one mile to the trailhead parking area on the left side of the road, on the west side of the highway bridge over Willow Creek. Alternatively, you can park near Falls Beach Picnic Area on Road 222 by Bass Lake's dam and access the trail via a connector route alongside Willow Creek.

Contact: Sierra National Forest, Mariposa/Minarets Ranger District, 57003 Road 225, North Fork, CA 93643; tel. (559) 877-2218 or (559) 683-4665.

6 Way of the Mono
0.5 mi/0.5 hr

Pick up an interpretive brochure at the Bass Lake Recreation Office before you set off on this .5-mile loop trail. Brochures are supposed to be available at the trailhead, but they weren't on our trip. The Way of the Mono is an educational trail that teaches about the Western Mono Indians who once inhabited the Bass Lake area. You visit a grain-grinding place and learn about how the Monos survived through the seasonal changes. In addition to a cultural history lesson, the trail also offers beautiful vistas of Bass Lake and its surroundings. Check out the view from the large granite outcrop.

Location: On the northwest end of Bass Lake near Oakhurst; map F4, grid b3.

User groups: Hikers and dogs. No horses or mountain bikes. No wheelchair facilities.

Permits: No permits are required. Parking and access are free.

Maps: For a map of Sierra National Forest send $6 to U.S. Forest Service, Map Sales, P.O. Box 587, Camino, CA 95709; tel. (530) 647-5390 or website: www.r5.fs.fed.us/visitorcenter. Ask the USGS for a topographic map of the Blue Lakes area.

Directions: From Oakhurst drive north on Highway 41 for four miles and then turn right on Road 222. Drive four miles and bear right to stay on Road 222. The signed trailhead parking area is across from Little Denver Church Pic-

nic Area, between the Forks Resort and the California Land Management Office.

Contact: Sierra National Forest, Mariposa/Minarets Ranger District, 57003 Road 225, North Fork, CA 93643; tel. (559) 877-2218 or (559) 683-4665.

7 Goat Mountain Lookout
8.5 mi/5.0 hrs

The 4.2-mile route to Goat Mountain Fire Lookout can be hiked from trailheads at either Forks Campground or Spring Cove Campground. Both are equally good and of similar length, so take your pick. Both trails climb two miles on a moderate grade, then join and form one path for another .5 mile before meeting up with a dirt road leading to Goat Mountain Fire Lookout. As you climb up the trail, you have nearly nonstop views of Bass Lake and the forested valleys surrounding it. You'll also be breathing hard. Heading south on the fire road, you'll reach the fire lookout, at elevation 4,675 feet, in 1.7 miles. Stop in and say hello to the lookout person. If you can talk someone into driving a second car to the other trailhead and campground, you can turn this into a pleasant semi-loop trip by hiking up one trail and down the other.

Location: On the south end of Bass Lake near Oakhurst; map F4, grid b4.

User groups: Hikers and dogs. No horses or mountain bikes. No wheelchair facilities.

Permits: No permits are required. Parking and access are free.

Maps: For a map of Sierra National Forest send $6 to U.S. Forest Service, Map Sales, P.O. Box 587, Camino, CA 95709; tel. (530) 647-5390 or website: www.r5.fs.fed.us/visitorcenter. Ask the USGS for a topographic map of the Bass Lake area.

Directions: From Oakhurst drive north on Highway 41 for four miles and turn right on Road 222. Drive four miles and bear right to stay on Road 222. Continue along the western shore of Bass Lake for about five miles to Spring Cove Campground. The Spring Cove

Trail begins on the left side of the campground entrance. If there is no parking there, you can park at Rocky Point Picnic Area. You can also hike to Goat Mountain Fire Lookout from Forks Campground, three miles north on Road 222.

Contact: Sierra National Forest, Mariposa/Minarets Ranger District, 57003 Road 225, North Fork, CA 93643; tel. (559) 877-2218 or (559) 683-4665.

8 French Trail at Mammoth Pool

4.0 mi/2.0 hrs

The French Trail is a 75-mile trail that follows the route of the San Joaquin River from Redinger Lake near North Fork to south of Devils Postpile National Monument. It was surveyed in 1880 and was intended to become a wagon road, although there was never enough money or interest to make it happen. One section of the French Trail runs along the west side of Mammoth Pool Reservoir. Along this stretch, you hike through a pine and cedar forest and open chaparral hillsides with continual views of the big lake, which is a long, narrow reservoir with steep, high walls. Just remember this: if it's summertime, confine your activities at Mammoth Pool to swimming, boating, and fishing. It's too hot to hike at this 3,300-foot elevation except in spring and fall. Spring is best, because that's when the lake is full and pretty.

Location: At the Mammoth Pool Reservoir on the North Fork San Joaquin River; map F4, grid b6.

User groups: Hikers, dogs, horses, and mountain bikes. No mountain bikes are allowed on the portion of the French Trail that enters the Ansel Adams Wilderness. No wheelchair facilities.

Permits: No permits are required. Parking and access are free.

Maps: For a map of Sierra National Forest send $6 to U.S. Forest Service, Map Sales, P.O. Box 587, Camino, CA 95709; tel. (530) 647-5390 or website: www.r5.fs.fed.us/visitorcenter.

Ask the USGS for a topographic map of the Mammoth Pool Dam area.

Directions: From the town of North Fork south of Bass Lake, drive southeast on Road 225 to Minarets Road. Turn left (north) on Minarets Road/Road 81 and follow it for approximately 35 winding miles to the Mammoth Pool Road/Road 25 turnoff on the right. Turn right and drive past Wagner's Resort to the trailhead at Logan Meadow.

Contact: Sierra National Forest, Mariposa/Minarets Ranger District, 57003 Road 225, North Fork, CA 93643; tel. (559) 877-2218 or (559) 683-4665.

9 Cedars Interpretive

0.5 mi/0.5 hr

When people stop in at the North Fork Ranger Station to figure out how to spend their time in these parts, they'd be wise to take the .5-mile Cedars Interpretive Walk that begins next to the station. That way they can learn about the local flora and fauna of the area and about the people who lived on these lands long before us—the Mono Indians. A bonus is that the trail is surfaced, so wheelchair users can make the trip. Trailhead elevation is 2,600 feet.

Location: In North Fork; map F4, grid c4.

User groups: Hikers, wheelchairs, and dogs. No horses or mountain bikes.

Permits: No permits are required. Parking and access are free.

Maps: For a map of Sierra National Forest send $6 to U.S. Forest Service, Map Sales, P.O. Box 587, Camino, CA 95709; tel. (530) 647-5390 or website: www.r5.fs.fed.us/visitorcenter. Ask the USGS for a topographic map of the North Fork area.

Directions: From Oakhurst drive north on Highway 41 for four miles, and turn right on Road 222. Drive four miles and bear left on Road 274, following it approximately 10 miles to its end in North Fork. At the four-way intersection, turn right and drive .25 mile to the Minarets Ranger Station.

Contact: Sierra National Forest, Mariposa/ Minarets Ranger District, 57003 Road 225, North Fork, CA 93643; tel. (559) 877-2218 or (559) 683-4665.

10 Kaiser Peak

10.6 mi/
6.0 hrs or 2.0 days

While many visitors to Huntington Lake take the short strolls to Rancheria Falls or the Indian Pools on Big Creek, far fewer attempt the ascent of Kaiser Peak. Why? Because it's a butt-kicking 5.3-mile climb to the top, gaining 3,000 feet of elevation on the way to the 10,320-foot peak. Luckily, you get many excellent views of Huntington Lake on the way up, and at the halfway point you can scramble up for a view and a rest on huge College Rock. Then it's up, up, and up some more, for what seems like an eternity. Finally, you gain the rocky summit and at last you know why you came. You're wowed by incredible 360-degree views, which take in Mammoth Pool Reservoir, Huntington Lake, Shaver Lake, Mount Ritter, and Mount Goddard. Wow. Backpackers looking for more mileage can turn the hike into a 14-mile loop trip.

Location: In the Kaiser Wilderness north of Huntington Lake near Lakeshore; map F4, grid c7.

User groups: Hikers, dogs, and horses. No mountain bikes. No wheelchair facilities.

Permits: A free wilderness permit is required for overnight stays and is available from the Pineridge Ranger Station. Quotas are in effect from June to September; permits are available in advance by mail for this period for a $3 fee. Parking and access are free.

Maps: For a map of Sierra National Forest or Kaiser Wilderness send $6 to U.S. Forest Service, Map Sales, P.O. Box 587, Camino, CA 95709; tel. (530) 647-5390 or website: www.r5. fs.fed.us/visitorcenter. Ask the USGS for a topographic map of the Kaiser Peak area.

Directions: From Fresno drive northeast on Highway 168 through Clovis for 70 miles to Huntington Lake, turn left on Huntington Lake Road, and drive one mile. Look for the large sign for the horse stables and pack station, and turn right. Follow the pack station road (Deer Creek Road) for .5 mile to the hikers' parking area. The trailhead is signed "Kaiser Loop Trail."

Contact: Sierra National Forest, Pineridge Ranger District, P.O. Box 559, Prather, CA 93651; tel. (559) 855-5360, or fax (559) 855-5375.

11 Twin Lakes and George Lake

9.8 mi/
6.0 hrs or 2.0 days

Trails into the Kaiser Wilderness always seem to come with a climb, and the route to Twin Lakes and George Lake is no exception. But if you're willing to work your heart and lungs, your reward is a spectacular day hike or backpacking trip to three scenic alpine lakes. Along the way, you must ascend to Kaiser Ridge and cross over it through Potter Pass. You're witness to wildflower-filled meadows, dense conifer forests, and a classic Sierra view from the pass. It's a great spot to stop and catch your breath. Then it's downhill from the pass to the granite-lined Twin Lakes at three miles out, where you'll leave most of your fellow hikers behind and view the second Twin Lake, which is much prettier than the first. Then it's uphill again to George Lake, 1.3 miles from Upper Twin Lake. The final push is definitely worth it. Trailhead elevation is 8,200 feet. Another good route to these lakes is from the trailhead near Sample Meadow Campground, farther north on Kaiser Pass Road. If you're willing to drive farther, this trail has less of a climb.

Location: In the Kaiser Wilderness north of Huntington Lake near Lakeshore; map F4, grid c8.

User groups: Hikers, dogs, and horses. No mountain bikes. No wheelchair facilities.

Permits: A free wilderness permit is required for overnight stays and is available from the

Pineridge Ranger Station. Quotas are in effect from June to September; permits are available in advance by mail for this period for a $3 fee. Parking and access are free.

Maps: For a map of Sierra National Forest or Kaiser Wilderness send $6 to U.S. Forest Service, Map Sales, P.O. Box 587, Camino, CA 95709; tel. (530) 647-5390 or website: www.r5.fs.fed.us/visitorcenter. Ask the USGS for a topographic map of the Kaiser Peak area.

Directions: From Fresno drive northeast on Highway 168 through Clovis for 70 miles to Huntington Lake; turn right on Kaiser Pass Road and drive 4.8 miles. Look for a trail sign for Trail 24E03, Twin Lakes and Potter Pass. Park on the south side of the road; the trail begins on the north side of the road.

Contact: Sierra National Forest, Pineridge Ranger District, P.O. Box 559, Prather, CA 93651; tel. (559) 855-5360, or fax (559) 855-5375.

12 Rancheria Falls

2.0 mi/1.0 hr

At 7,760 feet in elevation in Sierra National Forest, the air is clean and fresh, butterflies flutter amid the wildflowers, and a 150-foot waterfall sparkles in the sunlight. Wanna go? It's an easy trip, with the trailhead located close to popular Huntington Lake. The hike to Rancheria Falls is a well-graded one mile on a National Recreation Trail, suitable for hikers of all abilities. The route leads through a fir forest with an understory of wildflowers and gooseberry, and delivers you at Rancheria Falls' base, where you watch the creek tumble over a 50-foot-wide rock ledge. On weekends the destination can be a little crowded, but you can pick a boulder downstream from the falls and call it your own. Then have a seat and watch the watery spectacle unfold.

Location: Off Highway 168 near Huntington Lake; map F4, grid c8.

User groups: Hikers, dogs, horses, and mountain bikes. No wheelchair facilities.

Permits: No permits are required. Parking and access are free.

Maps: For a map of Sierra National Forest send $6 to U.S. Forest Service, Map Sales, P.O. Box 587, Camino, CA 95709; tel. (530) 647-5390 or website: www.r5.fs.fed.us/visitorcenter. Ask the USGS for a topographic map of the Huntington Lake area.

Directions: From Fresno drive northeast on Highway 168 through Clovis for 70 miles, past Shaver Lake. A half mile before reaching Huntington Lake, take the right turnoff signed for Rancheria Falls (Road 8S31). Follow the dirt road for 1.3 miles to the signed trailhead at a sharp curve in the road. Park off the road.

Contact: Sierra National Forest, Pineridge Ranger District, P.O. Box 559, Prather, CA 93651; tel. (559) 855-5360 or fax (559) 855-5375.

13 Indian Pools

1.5 mi/1.0 hr

When campers at Huntington Lake's many campgrounds are looking for a place to cool off in the afternoon, Indian Pools is where they go. The hike is really a walk, suitable for all ages and abilities, and you can stop almost anywhere you like along Big Creek, pick a pool, and wade in. The trailhead is a bit tricky to find—it's all the way at the far end of the Sierra Summit Ski Area parking lot, near some mobile homes and trailers. Ignore the wide dirt road and instead look for the single-track trail signed for "Indian Pools." It's a smooth, dirt path that quickly meets up with Big Creek. Flowers bloom in profusion along the stream and the rocky areas of the trail. The official path ends .7 mile east of the trailhead, at a huge, clear pool that is big enough to jump into and swim across. A use trail continues farther upstream, marked by trail cairns. If you follow it, you can reach quieter, more private pools.

Location: Off Highway 168 near Huntington Lake; map F4, grid d8.

User groups: Hikers and dogs. No horses or mountain bikes. No wheelchair facilities.

Permits: No permits are required. Parking and access are free.

Maps: For a map of Sierra National Forest send $6 to U.S. Forest Service, Map Sales, P.O. Box 587, Camino, CA 95709; tel. (530) 647-5390 or website: www.r5.fs.fed.us/visitorcenter. Ask the USGS for a topographic map of the Huntington Lake area.

Directions: From Fresno drive northeast on Highway 168 through Clovis for 70 miles, past Shaver Lake. One mile before reaching Huntington Lake, turn right at the signed Sierra Summit Ski Area. Drive .5 mile to the far end of the ski area parking lot and look for the signed trailhead for Indian Pools. Occasionally the Sierra Summit parking lot is closed, and you must park on Highway 168 and walk the short distance into the ski area.

Contact: Sierra National Forest, Pineridge Ranger District, P.O. Box 559, Prather, CA 93651; tel. (559) 855-5360 or fax (559) 855-5375.

14 Dinkey Lakes
7.0 mi/4.0 hrs

We've never met anybody who doesn't love the Dinkey Lakes. What's not to love? There are dozens of lakes clustered into a small wilderness area, and most are so easily accessible that you can see them in a day hike, rather than packing along all your gear for an overnight stay. The trip begins with a stream crossing over Dinkey Creek, where you are immediately awed by the incredible array of colors in the rock streambed. Walk on flat trail through a flower-filled forest, recross the creek, and start to climb. At 1.3 miles, you reach the junction for the start of the loop. Go right and meet Mystery Lake at 1.6 miles, Swede Lake at 2.3 miles, South Lake at 3.2 miles, and finally First Dinkey Lake at 3.8 miles. First Dinkey Lake is the most beautiful of them all. After taking in the scenery, continue on the loop, now heading westward back to the parking lot. One caveat: Don't expect much solitude. The easy hiking makes this area extremely popular. Note that the loop we describe works as either a day hike or backpacking trip, but if you choose to backpack,

you can explore much farther, taking the spurs off the end of the main loop, between South Lake and First Dinkey Lake, to Second Dinkey Lake, Island Lake, Rock Lake, and so on.

Location: Off Highway 168 near Shaver Lake; map F4, grid d7.

User groups: Hikers, dogs, and horses. No mountain bikes. No wheelchair facilities.

Permits: A free wilderness permit is required for overnight stays and is available from the Pineridge Ranger Station. Quotas are in effect from June to September; permits are available in advance by mail for this period for a $3 fee. Parking and access are free.

Maps: For a map of Sierra National Forest send $6 to U.S. Forest Service, Map Sales, P.O. Box 587, Camino, CA 95709; tel. (530) 647-5390 or website: www.r5.fs.fed.us/visitorcenter. A Mono Divide High Country map, which includes Dinkey Lakes, is available for a fee from Tom Harrison Cartography, tel. (415) 456-7940. Ask the USGS for topographic maps of the Huntington Lake and Dogtooth Peak areas.

Directions: From Fresno drive northeast on Highway 168 through Clovis for 50 miles to the town of Shaver Lake. Turn right on Dinkey Creek Road and drive nine miles. Turn left on Rock Creek Road/9S09, drive six miles, turn right on 9S10, and drive 4.7 miles. Turn right at the sign for Dinkey Lakes on Road 9S62 and drive 2.2 miles to the trailhead. These last two miles are very rough road. Stay left at the fork to bypass the four-wheel-drive area and go straight to the trailhead.

Contact: Sierra National Forest, Pineridge Ranger District, P.O. Box 559, Prather, CA 93651; tel. (559) 855-5360 or fax (559) 855-5375.

15 Chicago Stump Trail
0.5 mi/0.5 hr

The Converse Basin once sheltered one of the largest and finest grove of giant sequoias in the world, before a couple of lumber companies got the bright idea to chop all the trees down. Now where the giants once stood, second-growth sequoias have taken hold. This short and easy stroll takes you through a regenerated mixed forest to the Chicago Stump, a massive stump that belonged to one of the largest trees in the world. The tree was cut down in 1883, and the lower portion of the tree was reassembled and exhibited at the Chicago World's Fair. The stump that remains is at least 10 feet high and remarkably wide. In addition to its historical interest, this easy trail provides a pleasant, peaceful change from the hustle and bustle of the neighboring national parks.

Location: In Sequoia National Forest, north of Grant Grove area of Kings Canyon National Park, map F4; grid g9.

User groups: Hikers, horses, and dogs. No mountain bikes. No wheelchair facilities.

Permits: No permits are required. There is a $10 entrance fee at Sequoia and Kings Canyon National Parks, good for seven days.

Maps: Park maps are available free at park entrance stations or by contacting Sequoia and Kings Canyon National Parks at the address below. A more detailed map is available for a fee from Tom Harrison Cartography, tel. (415) 456-7940, or Trails Illustrated, tel. (800) 962-1643. Ask the USGS for a topographic map of the Hume area.

Directions: From Fresno drive east on Highway 180 for 55 miles to the Big Stump Entrance Station at Kings Canyon National Park. Continue 1.5 miles and turn left for Grant Grove. Drive approximately 4.5 miles, passing Grant Grove Village, and turn left at the sign for Forest Service Road 13S03. Drive two miles, turn right on Road 13S65 and continue .1 mile to the Chicago Stump Trailhead.

Contact: Sequoia and Kings Canyon National Parks, Three Rivers, CA 93271-9700; tel. (559) 565-3134 or (559) 335-2856; Sequoia National Forest, Hume Lake Ranger District, 35860 East Kings Canyon Road, Dunlap, CA 93621; tel. (559) 338-2251 or fax (559) 338-2131.

16 Boole Tree Loop
2.5 mi/1.0 hr

The drive in to the Boole Tree trailhead is worth the trip by itself—you pass through a beautiful, ghostly meadow filled with giant sequoia stumps. The sight of them is so otherworldly that it will stay engrained in your memory for a long time. The Boole Tree hike is a loop, and it's a good idea to take the right side of the loop first, making the ascent more gradual. You climb 500 feet to the top of a ridge, then descend the other side, reaching the Boole Tree in one mile. (It's just off the main loop, accessible via a short, obvious spur.) At 269 feet tall and with a diameter of 35 feet, the Boole Tree is the largest tree in any of the national forests, and it's one of the largest trees in the world. Unfortunately, it is one of a very few giant sequoias left standing in the Converse Basin grove, as the rest were clear-cut at the turn of the century. Although some people go see the Boole Tree and then turn around, it's better to finish out the loop. You'll be rewarded with a stellar view of Spanish Mountain and the Kings Canyon area.

Location: In Sequoia National Forest, north of the Grant Grove area of Kings Canyon National Park, map F4; grid g9.

User groups: Hikers, horses, and dogs. No mountain bikes. No wheelchair facilities.

Permits: No permits are required. There is a $10 entrance fee at Sequoia and Kings Canyon National Parks, good for seven days.

Maps: Park maps are available free at park entrance stations or by contacting Sequoia and Kings Canyon National Parks at the address below. A more detailed map is available for a fee from Tom Harrison Cartography, tel. (415) 456-7940, or Trails Illustrated, tel. (800) 962-1643. Ask the USGS for a topographic map of the Hume area.

Directions: From Fresno drive east on Highway 180 for 55 miles to the Big Stump Entrance Station at Kings Canyon National Park. Continue 1.5 miles and turn left for Grant Grove. Drive approximately six miles, passing Grant Grove Village. Turn left at the sign for Forest Service Road 13S55, Boole Tree, Converse Basin, and Stump Meadow. Drive 2.6 miles and park in the wide parking pullout.

Contact: Sequoia and Kings Canyon National Parks, Three Rivers, CA 93271-9700; tel. (559) 565-3134 or (559) 335-2856; Sequoia National Forest, Hume Lake Ranger District, 35860 East Kings Canyon Road, Dunlap, CA 93621; tel. (559) 338-2251 or fax (559) 338-2131.

17 Big Stump Trail
1.0 mi/0.5 hr

Normally it would be hard for us to get excited about a trail called the "Big Stump Trail." In fact, this sort of thing could be quite depressing. But the Big Stump Trail at the entrance to Kings Canyon National Park is a pleasant nature walk and provides an excellent history lesson as well. The size of the mammoth trees—oops, make that stumps—just blows you away. Most of the big trees were cut for timber in the 1880s, and you'll see the remains of logging activities. Be sure to pick up a trail brochure at the Grant Grove Visitor Center or at the trailhead. It's a fun read, cleverly written in the voice of a late 1800s logger. The trail is a short loop that circles a meadow. A few sequoias still thrive along the route, including one in the first 50 feet from the parking lot. The path's highlights include the Burnt Monarch, a shell of a giant sequoia that has been ravaged by fire, but still stands, and the Mark Twain Stump. The latter belonged to a 26-foot-wide tree that took two men 13 days to cut down.

Location: In the Grant Grove area of Kings Canyon National Park, map F4; grid h8.

User groups: Hikers only. No dogs, horses, or mountain bikes. No wheelchair facilities.

Permits: No permits are required. There is a $10 entrance fee at Sequoia and Kings Canyon National Parks, good for seven days.

Maps: Park maps are available free at park entrance stations or by contacting Sequoia and Kings Canyon National Parks at the address below. A more detailed map is available for a fee from Tom Harrison Cartography, tel. (415) 456-7940, or Trails Illustrated, tel. (800) 962-1643. Ask the USGS for a topographic map of the Hume area.

Directions: From Fresno drive east on Highway 180 for 55 miles to the Big Stump Entrance Station at Kings Canyon National Park. The trail begins .5 mile past the entrance station, at the Big Stump Picnic Area.

Contact: Sequoia and Kings Canyon National Parks, Three Rivers, CA 93271-9700; tel. (559) 565-3134 or (559) 335-2856.

18 Sunset Trail
5.0 mi/2.5 hrs

The Sunset Trail leaves Sunset Campground at elevation 6,590 feet and heads gently downhill for 2.25 miles to Ella Falls, a pretty 40-foot cascade on Sequoia Creek. At 1.5 miles down the trail, you reach a junction with the South Boundary Trail and can take a short side trip to the left to Viola Falls, which isn't much of a waterfall but is a memorably scenic spot on granite-sculpted Sequoia Creek. Most people just mosey down the trail a way, enjoying the big pines and firs and flowering western azaleas, and maybe stealing a kiss on one of the wooden footbridges. If you like, you can follow the trail for its entire 2.5-mile length to Sequoia Lake. Although the lake is privately owned, hikers are allowed to walk along its edge as long as they stay out of the camp area. While you're having fun, don't forget that the return trip is all uphill with a 1,300-foot elevation gain, so save some water and energy.

Location: In the Grant Grove area of Kings Canyon National Park, map F4; grid h8.

User groups: Hikers only. No dogs, horses, or mountain bikes. No wheelchair facilities.

Permits: No permits are required. There is a $10 entrance fee at Sequoia and Kings Canyon National Parks, good for seven days.

Maps: Park maps are available free at park

entrance stations or by contacting Sequoia and Kings Canyon National Parks at the address below. A more detailed map is available for a fee from Tom Harrison Cartography, tel. (415) 456-7940, or Trails Illustrated, tel. (800) 962-1643. Ask the USGS for topographic maps of the Hume and General Grant Grove areas.

Directions: From Fresno drive east on Highway 180 for 55 miles to the Big Stump Entrance Station at Kings Canyon National Park. Continue 1.5 miles and turn left for Grant Grove. Drive 1.5 miles to Grant Grove Village and park in the large parking lot near the visitor center. Cross the road and walk on the paved trail toward Sunset Campground's amphitheater. Continue heading left through the camp to site 179, where the trail begins.

Contact: Sequoia and Kings Canyon National Parks, Three Rivers, CA 93271-9700; tel. (559) 565-3134 or (559) 335-2856.

19 North Grove and Dead Giant Loop

3.0 mi/1.5 hrs

For people who want a little more hiking than the General Grant Tree Trail, below, provides, the combined North Grove and Dead Giant Loop Trails are the answer. The walk begins on an old dirt road that leads downhill through a mixed forest of sequoia, sugar pine, white fir, and dogwood. Don't expect to see dense groves of sequoias here; the big trees are few and far between. However, the forest is pleasant, quiet, and shady.

Stay to the right at the first junction to follow the North Grove Loop. At the bottom of the hill, you'll pass an obscure junction with an old wagon road that was used to take logged sequoias to the mill. Continue to a more obvious junction at one mile out. Turn right and walk .25 mile downhill to Lion Meadow. Turn right on a single-track trail and circle around the meadow, heading for the Dead Giant. This sequoia, like some others in the park, is a nearly hollow, dead tree that somehow keeps standing. From the Dead Giant it's a short

tromp to the Sequoia Lake Overlook, a tranquil high point where you can have a snack and enjoy the view of the large, private lake in Sequoia National Forest. From the overlook, backtrack a few yards and turn right to finish out the loop, returning uphill on the wide dirt road. There is a 400-foot gain on the return.

Location: In the Grant Grove area of Kings Canyon National Park, map F4; grid h9.

User groups: Hikers only. No dogs, horses, or mountain bikes. No wheelchair facilities.

Permits: No permits are required. There is a $10 entrance fee at Sequoia and Kings Canyon National Parks, good for seven days.

Maps: Park maps are available free at park entrance stations or by contacting Sequoia and Kings Canyon National Parks at the address below. A more detailed map is available for a fee from Tom Harrison Cartography, tel. (415) 456-7940, or Trails Illustrated, tel. (800) 962-1643. Ask the USGS for topographic maps of the Hume and General Grant Grove areas.

Directions: From Fresno drive east on Highway 180 for 55 miles to the Big Stump Entrance Station at Kings Canyon National Park. Continue 1.5 miles and turn left for Grant Grove. Drive two miles, passing Grant Grove Village, to the left turnoff for General Grant Tree. Turn left and follow the access road for one mile to the parking lot. The North Grove Loop starts from the far end of the lower parking lot.

Contact: Sequoia and Kings Canyon National Parks, Three Rivers, CA 93271-9700; tel. (559) 565-3134 or (559) 335-2856.

20 General Grant Tree

0.6 mi/0.5 hr

This paved loop through a giant sequoia grove allows both wheelchair users and hikers to have a look at the General Grant Tree. Estimated at 1,800 to 2,000 years old, the General Grant is 267 feet tall and 107 feet in circumference at its base, making it the third largest tree in the world. Every year since 1926, the park has held a Christmas celebration around its base, and so the tree is dubbed "the nation's Christmas tree." Its neighbors include the Fallen Monarch, a hollow downed tree that is so wide, it was once used as a park employee camp, and a group of big sequoias named after various U.S. states. It may seem a little campy, but there are many excellent photo opportunities in the grove.

Location: In the Grant Grove area of Kings Canyon National Park, map F4; grid h9.

User groups: Hikers and wheelchairs. No dogs, horses, or mountain bikes.

Permits: No permits are required. There is a $10 entrance fee at Sequoia and Kings Canyon National Parks, good for seven days.

Maps: Park maps are available free at park entrance stations or by contacting Sequoia and Kings Canyon National Parks at the address below. A more detailed map is available for a fee from Tom Harrison Cartography, tel. (415) 456-7940, or Trails Illustrated, tel. (800) 962-1643. Ask the USGS for topographic maps of the Hume and General Grant Grove areas.

Directions: From Fresno drive east on Highway 180 for 55 miles to the Big Stump Entrance Station at Kings Canyon National Park. Continue 1.5 miles and turn left for Grant Grove. Drive two miles, passing Grant Grove Village, to the left turnoff for General Grant Tree. Turn left and follow the access road for one mile to the parking lot.

Contact: Sequoia and Kings Canyon National Parks, Three Rivers, CA 93271-9700; tel. (559) 565-3134 or (559) 335-2856.

21 Manzanita and Azalea Loop
3.3 mi/2.0 hrs

This hike is a good exercise route for vacationers staying in the cabins at Grant Grove Village or in the nearby campgrounds. It climbs 800 feet, which gives your heart and lungs a workout, and it's pretty every step of the way. From the edge of the dirt service road, the Manzanita Trail climbs a dry slope uphill to Park Ridge. Near the top, you'll parallel the dirt road that leads to the Park Ridge Fire

Lookout. Then the Manzanita Trail meets up with the Azalea Trail, and you'll descend on a much shadier, moister slope. The azaleas bloom bright white in June and July. To complete the loop, the trail skirts the boundary of Wilsonia, a private community within the national park, then crosses both the Wilsonia Road and the park road and ends across from the visitor center.

Location: In the Grant Grove area of Kings Canyon National Park, map F4; grid h9.

User groups: Hikers only. No dogs, horses, or mountain bikes. No wheelchair facilities.

Permits: No permits are required. There is a $10 entrance fee at Sequoia and Kings Canyon National Parks, good for seven days.

Maps: Park maps are available free at park entrance stations or by contacting Sequoia and Kings Canyon National Parks at the address below. A more detailed map is available for a fee from Tom Harrison Cartography, tel. (415) 456-7940, or Trails Illustrated, tel. (800) 962-1643. Ask the USGS for a topographic map of the Hume area.

Directions: From Fresno drive east on Highway 180 for 55 miles to the Big Stump Entrance Station at Kings Canyon National Park. Continue 1.5 miles and turn left for Grant Grove. Drive 1.5 miles to Grant Grove Village and park in the large parking lot near the visitor center. Walk on the service road behind the village buildings, and near the tent cabins, to reach the start of the Manzanita Trail.

Contact: Sequoia and Kings Canyon National Parks, Three Rivers, CA 93271-9700; tel. (559) 565-3134 or (559) 335-2856.

22 Panoramic Point and Park Ridge Lookout
4.7 mi/3.0 hrs

Start your trip by taking the 300-yard paved walk from the parking area to Panoramic Point, which delivers what its name implies. An interpretive display names the many peaks and valleys you can see, including the big pointy one—Mount Goddard at 13,560

feet. From Panoramic Point, take the dirt Park Ridge Trail that leads to the right along the ridge. Your views continue as you contour along the ridgeline, climbing gently uphill. The trail intersects a dirt road, which you follow for about 50 yards, then bear left onto trail again. You'll intersect this dirt road once more about 100 yards before the Park Ridge Fire Lookout. Follow the road to the lookout tower and check out the nifty outdoor shower at its base. If someone is stationed in the tower and gives you permission to come up, do so and sign the visitor register. (The lookout person rarely gets visitors on cloudy days, but he or she gets many when it's sunny and you can see for miles around.) The lookout is only operated during the fire season, which is usually May to October. For your return trip, you can walk down the trail back to Panoramic Point or take the shorter fire road, which also leads back to the parking lot. Views are far better along the trail than on the fire road.

Location: In the Grant Grove area of Kings Canyon National Park, map F4; grid h9.

User groups: Hikers only. No dogs, horses, or mountain bikes. No wheelchair facilities.

Permits: No permits are required. There is a $10 entrance fee at Sequoia and Kings Canyon National Parks, good for seven days.

Maps: Park maps are available free at park entrance stations or by contacting Sequoia and Kings Canyon National Parks at the address below. A more detailed map is available for a fee from Tom Harrison Cartography, tel. (415) 456-7940, or Trails Illustrated, tel. (800) 962-1643. Ask the USGS for a topographic map of the Hume area.

Directions: From Fresno drive east on Highway 180 for 55 miles to the Big Stump Entrance Station at Kings Canyon National Park. Continue 1.5 miles and turn left for Grant Grove. Drive 1.5 miles to Grant Grove Village and turn right by the visitor center and store. Follow the road past the cabins and take the right fork for Panoramic Point. It's 2.3 miles from the visitor center to Panoramic Point.

Contact: Sequoia and Kings Canyon National Parks, Three Rivers, CA 93271-9700; tel. (559) 565-3134 or (559) 335-2856.

HIKING ALONG THE WATCHTOWER, A GRANITE CLIFF IN SEQUOIA NATIONAL PARK.

MAP F5

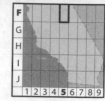

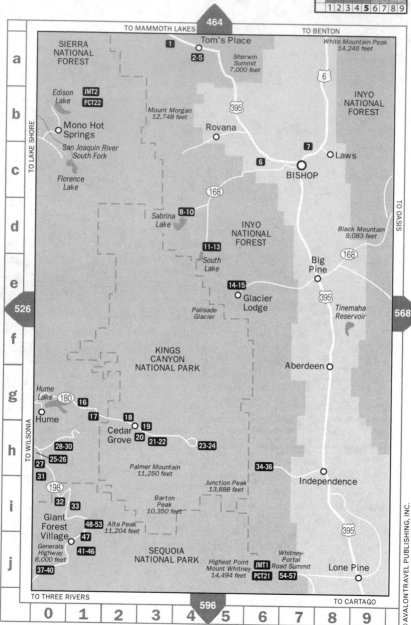

SIERRA
NATIONAL
FOREST

1

Tom's Place

2-5

Sherwin
Summit
7,000 feet

White Mountain Peak
14,246 feet

6

INYO
NATIONAL
FOREST

Edison
Lake

JMT2
PCT22

Mono Hot
Springs

Mount Morgan
12,748 feet

395

Rovana

7

Laws

San Joaquin River
South Fork

6

BISHOP

Florence
Lake

168

INYO
NATIONAL
FOREST

Sabrina
Lake

8-10

11-13

South
Lake

Big
Pine

Black Mountain
9,083 feet

168

14-15

Glacier
Lodge

395

Palisade
Glacier

Tinemaha
Reservoir

KINGS
CANYON
NATIONAL PARK

Aberdeen

Hume
Lake

180

16

17

Hume

18

Cedar
Grove

19

20

21-22

23-24

34-36

28-30

25-26

27

31

198

Palmer Mountain
11,250 feet

Junction Peak
13,888 feet

Independence

32

33

Barton
Peak
10,350 feet

Giant
Forest
Village

48-53

Alta Peak
11,204 feet

47

Generals
Highway
6,000 feet

41-46

395

37-40

SEQUOIA
NATIONAL
PARK

Highest Point
Mount Whitney
14,494 feet

Whitney-
Portal
Road Summit

JMT1

PCT21

54-57

Lone Pine

TO LAKE SHORE

TO WILSONIA

TO OASIS

© AVALON TRAVEL PUBLISHING, INC.

CHAPTER F5

1 McGee Creek to Steelhead Lake 527	**17** Windy Cliffs 538
2 Mono Pass........... 528	**18** Lewis Creek Trail...... 538
3 Little Lakes Valley..... 529	**19** Kings Canyon Overlook . 539
4 Tamarack Lakes....... 530	**20** Lookout Peak 539
5 Ruby Lake 530	**21** Roaring River Falls 540
6 Honeymoon Lake....... 531	**22** Zumwalt Meadow Loop 541
7 Fish Slough 531	**23** Mist Falls............ 541
8 Blue Lake............ 532	**24** Copper Creek Trail 542
9 Lamarck Lake 533	**25** Redwood Canyon...... 542
10 Loch Leven Lake 533	**26** Redwood Mountain Loop 543
11 Tyee Lakes........... 534	**27** Buena Vista Peak...... 544
12 Green and Brown Lakes 534	**28** Weaver Lake 544
13 Ruwau and Chocolate Lakes Loop 535	**29** Jennie Lake 545
14 First and Second Falls 536	**30** Mitchell Peak......... 546
15 First and Second Lakes......... 536	**31** Big Baldy............ 547
16 Yucca Point......... 537	**32** Muir Grove.......... 547
	33 Little Baldy 548
	34 Kearsage Pass 548

(CONTINUED ON NEXT PAGE)

1 McGee Creek to Steelhead Lake

**10.6 mi/
6.0 hrs or 2.0 days**

Unlike many trails leading into the John Muir Wilderness, the McGee Creek Trail has the benefit of starting out with a relatively flat stretch, giving your legs and lungs the opportunity for a warm-up before you start to climb. In the first two miles, you pass through plains of sage and rabbit brush, heading toward a colorful and dramatic mountain backdrop: Mount Baldwin on the right, Mount Crocker on the left, and Red and White Mountain straight ahead—all over 12,000 feet in elevation. To your left,

along McGee Creek, grows a lush garden of aspens, birches, and cottonwoods. Pass Horsetail Falls on the right at two miles out, then carefully cross and recross McGee Creek. Soon the trail enters a lodgepole pine forest and the climb steepens, and at 4.2 miles you reach a junction with the Steelhead Lake Trail heading left (east). Switchbacks carry you to a short spur to tiny Grass Lake, then to much larger Steelhead Lake (10,350 feet). The total climb over 5.3 miles is 2,300 feet.

Location: In the John Muir Wilderness; map F5, grid a3.

User groups: Hikers, dogs, and horses. No mountain bikes. No wheelchair facilities.

(CONTINUED)

35 Flower and
Matlock Lakes 549

36 Robinson Lake 550

37 Marble Falls 550

38 Potwisha to
Hospital Rock 551

39 Middle Fork Trail
to Panther Creek 551

40 Paradise Creek Trail . . . 552

41 Sunset Rock 553

42 Moro Rock 553

43 Crescent Meadow
and Tharp's Log 554

44 High Sierra Trail
and Eagle View 554

45 High Sierra Trail
to Hamilton Lake 555

46 Hazelwood and
Huckleberry Loop 556

47 Congress Trail Loop 556

48 The Lakes Trail 557

49 Heather Lake and
the Watchtower 558

50 Alta Peak 558

51 Panther Gap Loop 559

52 Tokopah Falls 560

53 Twin Lakes 560

54 Whitney Portal National
Recreation Trail 561

55 Mount Whitney Trail . . . 562

56 Lone Pine Lake 562

57 Meysan Lake 563

Pacific Crest Trail
(PCT) Section Overview

PCT-21/
JMT-1 Whitney Portal
to Lake Thomas
Edison 564

PCT-22/
JMT-2 Lake Thomas
Edison to Agnew
Meadows 565

Permits: A free wilderness permit is required for overnight stays. Quotas are in effect from the last Friday in June to September 15; permits are available in advance by mail or fax for this period for a $5 fee. Phone (760) 873-2408 for permit information, or visit website: www. r5.fs.fed.us/inyo.

Maps: For a map of Inyo National Forest, send $6 to U.S. Forest Service, Map Sales, P.O. Box 587, Camino, CA 95709; tel. (530) 647-5390 or website: www.r5.fs.fed.us/visitorcenter. Ask the USGS for a topographic map of the Convict Lake area.

Directions: From U.S. 395 in Lee Vining drive approximately 33 miles south to the McGee Creek Road turnoff on the right. It's eight miles south of the Mammoth Lakes turnoff and 30 miles north of Bishop. Drive three miles

southwest on McGee Creek Road (past the pack station) to the trailhead.

Contact: Inyo National Forest, White Mountain Ranger District, 798 N. Main Street, Bishop, CA 93514; tel. (760) 873-2500 or fax (760) 873-2563.

2 Mono Pass
7.4 mi/4.0 hrs

Since wilderness permits are hard to come by for this trail, your best bet is a day hike up to scenic, austere Mono Pass, where William Brewer and his party crossed the Sierra in 1864. Trailhead elevation is 10,300 feet, and the pass is at 12,400 feet, so get ready to climb in thin air (gasp). Also, expect it to be cold and windy at the pass, no matter how warm it is at the trailhead. Start your trip by following the trail alongside Rock Creek, with a wall of mammoth mountain peaks surrounding you. A half mile in, bear right for Mono Pass, switchbacking uphill. As you climb, you get a view of Little Lakes Valley, below, as well as continual eyefuls of classic Sierra scenery—clear blue sky, jagged mountain backdrops, and plenty of rock. When at last you gain the summit, you get a full 360-degree panoramic view, probably little different from when Brewer saw it more than a century ago.

Location: In the John Muir Wilderness; map F5, grid a4.

User groups: Hikers, dogs, and horses. No mountain bikes. No wheelchair facilities.

Permits: No day-hiking permits are required. Parking and access are free.

Maps: For a map of Inyo National Forest, send $6 to U.S. Forest Service, Map Sales, P.O. Box 587, Camino, CA 95709; tel. (530) 647-5390 or website: www.r5.fs.fed.us/visitorcenter. Ask the USGS for topographic maps of the Mount Morgan and Mount Abbot areas.

Directions: From U.S. 395 in Lee Vining drive approximately 40 miles south to Tom's Place and the Rock Creek Road turnoff on the right. It's 15 miles south of the Mammoth Lakes turnoff and 24 miles north of Bishop. Follow Rock Creek Road southwest for 10.5 miles to its end, at the Mosquito Flat parking area.

Contact: Inyo National Forest, White Mountain Ranger District, 798 N. Main Street, Bishop, CA 93514; tel. (760) 873-2500 or fax (760) 873-2563.

3 Little Lakes Valley

3-9 mi/2-5 hrs

If the mileage shown above reflects some indecision, that's because the Little Lakes Valley makes it hard to decide which lake to visit or how far to hike. It's best to decide as you go, depending on how busy the trail is and how your energy is holding up. The Little Lakes Valley is a spectacularly beautiful, glacially carved area that is littered with lakes, both

large and small, and surrounded by 13,000-foot peaks. What makes it even more special is that its trailhead is at 10,300 feet, so your car does most of the climbing instead of your feet. For this reason the trail is extremely popular, especially with beginning backpackers, day-hikers, and dog walkers.

The trail leads past Mack Lake and shallow Marsh Lake to Heart Lake, 1.5 miles in. Box Lake is .25 mile farther, and then another .25 mile farther is still larger Long Lake, both popular destinations right along the trail. Those with more stamina can continue to Chickenfoot Lake at three miles out or the Gem Lakes at 3.5 miles. Most people consider the Gem Lakes to be the most gorgeous of the lot, but frankly, it's pretty hard to choose. Those who are willing and able continue upward through 11,100-foot Morgan Pass and descend a couple hundred feet to Upper and Lower Morgan Lake, at four and 4.5 miles out respectively. There are enough hiking options along this one trail to keep most lake-lovers busy for a week.

Location: In the John Muir Wilderness; map F5, grid a4.

User groups: Hikers, dogs, and horses. No mountain bikes. No wheelchair facilities.

Permits: No day-hiking permits are required. A free wilderness permit is required for overnight stays. Quotas are in effect from the last Friday in June to September 15; permits are available in advance by mail or fax for this period for a $5 fee. Phone (760) 873-2408 for permit information, or visit website: www.r5. fs.fed.us/inyo.

Maps: For a map of Inyo National Forest, send $6 to U.S. Forest Service, Map Sales, P.O. Box 587, Camino, CA 95709; tel. (530) 647-5390 or website: www.r5.fs.fed.us/visitorcenter. Ask the USGS for topographic maps of the Mount Morgan and Mount Abbot areas.

Directions: From U.S. 395 in Lee Vining drive approximately 40 miles south to Tom's Place and the Rock Creek Road turnoff on the right, 15 miles south of the Mammoth Lakes turnoff and 24 miles north of

Bishop. Follow Rock Creek Road southwest for 10.5 miles to its end at the Mosquito Flat parking area.

Contact: Inyo National Forest, White Mountain Ranger District, 798 N. Main Street, Bishop, CA 93514; tel. (760) 873-2500 or fax (760) 873-2563.

4 Tamarack Lakes

9.4 mi/
6.0 hrs or 2.0 days

The trailhead elevation at Rock Creek Lake is nearly 10,000 feet, so the first two miles of this trail can be rather breathtaking (huff, puff) as you climb steeply to the turnoff for the Francis Lake Trail on the right, and shortly thereafter, Kenneth Lake on the left. After the initial ascent, many people decide to head for one of these two lakes instead of continuing for two more miles to the Tamarack Lakes. Another left spur trail leads to Dorothy Lake at 2.5 miles. Those who continue onward will be rewarded (after more heavy breathing) with first the smaller Tamarack Lake and then the larger one, set in a steeply sloped rocky bowl. Despite the barren look of the cliffs on the lake's edges, the larger Tamarack Lake has good fishing for golden trout. If you stop at Dorothy Lake instead, you have a chance at catching brook trout or Lahontan cutthroat trout.

Location: In the John Muir Wilderness; map F5, grid a4.

User groups: Hikers, dogs, and horses. No mountain bikes. No wheelchair facilities.

Permits: No day-hiking permits are required. A free wilderness permit is required for overnight stays. Quotas are in effect from the last Friday in June to September 15; permits are available in advance by mail or fax for this period for a $5 fee. Phone (760) 873-2408 for permit information, or visit website: www.r5.fs .fed.us/inyo.

Maps: For a map of Inyo National Forest, send $6 to U.S. Forest Service, Map Sales, P.O. Box 587, Camino, CA 95709; tel. (530) 647-5390 or website: www.r5.fs.fed.us/visitorcenter. Ask the USGS for a topographic map of the Mount Morgan area.

Directions: From U.S. 395 in Lee Vining drive approximately 40 miles south to Tom's Place and the Rock Creek Road turnoff on the right, 15 miles south of the Mammoth Lakes turnoff and 24 miles north of Bishop. Follow Rock Creek Road southwest for 8.5 miles to the east shore of Rock Creek Lake and the trailhead parking for Tamarack Lakes, on the left.

Contact: Inyo National Forest, White Mountain Ranger District, 798 N. Main Street, Bishop, CA 93514; tel. (760) 873-2500 or fax (760) 873-2563.

5 Ruby Lake

4.5 mi/2.5 hrs

For both day-hikers and backpackers, the Little Lakes Valley is the premier destination from the Rock Creek Canyon Trailhead. The only problem is the crowds, especially on the weekends, which can turn a supposedly peaceful wilderness experience into a large group encounter. A visit to Ruby Lake is a possible solution because it's off the main trail that leads into the Little Lakes Valley, situated instead on the right fork that leads to Mono Pass. Since most trail users on this fork are backpackers heading to Mono Pass and the Pioneer Basin beyond, few take the time to stop at Ruby Lake, .25 mile off the main trail. From the trailhead, hike .5 mile and bear right at the junction for Mono Pass. Grunt it out through the switchbacks as you enjoy a series of stunning vistas of the Little Lakes Valley. You'll reach the Ruby Lake spur trail on the left at two miles out. A .25-mile walk brings you to cliff-bound Ruby Lake, which is much larger than you'd expect and perfectly ringed by granite. The fishing is not great, but the picnicking is highly recommended. The lake's elevation is 11,120 feet.

Location: In the John Muir Wilderness; map F5, grid a4.

User groups: Hikers, dogs, and horses. No mountain bikes. No wheelchair facilities.

Permits: No day-hiking permits are required. Parking and access are free.

Maps: For a map of Inyo National Forest, send $6 to U.S. Forest Service, Map Sales, P.O. Box 587, Camino, CA 95709; tel. (530) 647-5390 or website: www.r5.fs.fed.us/visitorcenter. Ask the USGS for topographic maps of the Mount Abbot and Mount Morgan areas.

Directions: From U.S. 395 in Lee Vining drive approximately 40 miles south to Tom's Place and the Rock Creek Road turnoff on the right, 15 miles south of the Mammoth Lakes turnoff and 24 miles north of Bishop. Follow Rock Creek Road southwest for 10.5 miles to its end at the Mosquito Flat parking area.

Contact: Inyo National Forest, White Mountain Ranger District, 798 N. Main Street, Bishop, CA 93514; tel. (760) 873-2500 or fax (760) 873-2563.

6 Honeymoon Lake
12.2 mi/1-2 days

Since the trailhead elevation in Pine Creek Canyon is only 7,400 feet, the best destinations must be gained with a climb. That includes Honeymoon Lake, 6.1 miles and a 3,000-foot ascent away. Luckily, you pass Upper and Lower Pine Lake along the route, and there's enough spectacular scenery to keep you motivated as you huff and puff. The route begins in the trees along Pine Creek, then joins a mining road which leads to the Brownstone Mine. As you climb out of the trees, you get views of the Owens River Valley and the desert-like White Mountains. You also get sweaty and overheated, switchbacking out in the open with no shade. Above the mine the trail becomes extremely rocky and ascends more switchbacks to meet first Lower and then Upper Pine Lake at 4.7 and 5.7 miles. This section of trail is blessed with some trees and close proximity to Pine Creek. A quarter mile beyond the upper lake, you reach a trail junction and take the right fork toward Italy Pass, heading west to Honeymoon Lake in .1 mile. Many campsites are found near the granite-bound lake.

Location: In the John Muir Wilderness; map F5, grid c6.

User groups: Hikers, dogs, and horses. No mountain bikes. No wheelchair facilities.

Permits: No day-hiking permits are required. A free wilderness permit is required for overnight stays. Quotas are in effect from the last Friday in June to September 15; permits are available in advance by mail or fax for this period for a $5 fee. Phone (760) 873-2408 for permit information, or visit website: www.r5.fs.fed.us/inyo.

Maps: For a map of Inyo National Forest, send $6 to U.S. Forest Service, Map Sales, P.O. Box 587, Camino, CA 95709; tel. (530) 647-5390 or website: www.r5.fs.fed.us/visitorcenter. Ask the USGS for topographic maps of the Bishop and Tungsten Hills areas.

Directions: From Bishop drive north on U.S. 395 for seven miles and turn left (west) on Pine Creek Road. Drive 9.5 miles to the trailhead parking area near the pack station on the left side of the road.

Contact: Inyo National Forest, White Mountain Ranger District, 798 N. Main Street, Bishop, CA 93514; tel. (760) 873-2500 or fax (760) 873-2563.

7 Fish Slough
2.0 mi/1.0 hr

It's hard to believe you can see a great blue heron in the eastern Sierra, but here you can. The marshland in Fish Slough is watered by natural springs from the Owens Valley, making this area a rich riparian wetland in the middle of a giant desert and volcanic tableland. You walk in an oasis that teems with fish and wildlife while gazing out over arid desert plains and mountains. Although the area gets less than six inches of rainfall per year, the water is stored in the underlying porous volcanic rock, creating a continuous reservoir for Fish Slough. When you look into the slough's clear pools, you can see bubbles coming up from the springs below.

Because of the abundance of water, the wetlands are excellent for wildlife watching (mostly birds and bunnies) and are home to rare and endangered species of fish, like the Owens pupfish. In addition to bird-watching, you can see Native American cultural artifacts at Fish Slough, including some prehistoric petroglyphs drawn on the rocks. Remember to look but don't touch—they're protected by law.

Location: In the Fish Slough Area of Critical Environmental Concern, north of Bishop; map F5, grid c7.

User groups: Hikers and dogs. No horses or mountain bikes, except on roads. No wheelchair facilities.

Permits: No permits are required. Parking and access are free.

Maps: A free map/brochure is available from the Bureau of Land Management at the address below. Ask the USGS for a topographic map of the Fish Slough area.

Directions: From Bishop drive north on U.S. 395 to Highway 6. Drive north on Highway 6 for 2.5 miles and turn left (west) on Five Bridges Road. Drive 2.5 miles (past a gravel pit) to Fish Slough Road and turn right. Park anywhere along Fish Slough Road and begin hiking; there is no designated trail.

Contact: Bureau of Land Management, Bishop Resource Area, 785 N. Main Street, Suite E, Bishop, CA 93514; tel. (760) 872-4881.

8 Blue Lake

6.0 mi/3.0 hrs or 2 days

The Sabrina Basin Trail leads to a series of gorgeous alpine lakes set below lofty, 13,000-foot granite peaks. Of these, one of the easiest to reach is scenic Blue Lake, a popular spot for photographers, trout anglers, and cold-water swimmers. If you catch the light just right, you can take pictures of Blue Lake with towering Mount Thompson and the Thompson Ridge mirrored on its surface. It's a 1,250-foot climb to the lake, spread out gradually over three miles. Nonetheless, be prepared for the thin air at 9,000 feet, which can make the climb seem pretty strenuous if you're not acclimated. Start by hiking along the shore of Lake Sabrina, then switchback your way uphill to Blue Lake. The trail is very rocky in places; wear good boots. If you get inspired to see more of this high-alpine scenery, you can bear left from Blue Lake to Donkey Lake and the Baboon Lakes (1.5 miles farther), or bear right and hike eastward to the Emerald Lakes and Dingleberry Lake (1.8 miles farther). Any of these are likely to have fewer visitors than Blue Lake.

Location: In the John Muir Wilderness; map F5, grid d4.

User groups: Hikers, dogs, and horses. No mountain bikes. No wheelchair facilities.

Permits: No day-hiking permits are required. A free wilderness permit is required for overnight stays. Quotas are in effect from the last Friday in June to September 15; permits are available in advance by mail or fax for this period for a $5 fee. Phone (760) 873-2408 for permit information or visit website: www.r5.fs.fed.us/inyo.

Maps: For a map of Inyo National Forest, send $6 to U.S. Forest Service, Map Sales, P.O. Box 587, Camino, CA 95709; tel. (530) 647-5390 or website: www.r5.fs.fed.us/visitorcenter. A Bishop Pass map is available for a fee from Tom Harrison Cartography, tel. (415) 456-7940. Ask the USGS for topographic maps of the Mount Thompson and Mount Darwin areas.

Directions: From Bishop on U.S. 395 turn west on Line Street/Highway 168 and drive 18.5 miles to Lake Sabrina. Day-use parking is located near the end of the road, just before the boat launch area. Backpackers' parking is located at a turnout near the road to North Lake, .5 mile before the end of the road.

Contact: Inyo National Forest, White Mountain Ranger District, 798 N. Main Street, Bishop, CA 93514; tel. (760) 873-2500 or fax (760) 873-2563.

9 Lamarck Lake
8.0 mi/4.0 hrs or 2.0 days

The only downer on the Lamarck Lakes Trail is that from the trailhead parking area, you have to walk .5 mile down the road to get to the actual trailhead, which is located in North Lake Campground. With that out of the way, you're on your way for a stellar Eastern Sierra hike. The trail heads through the aspens and crosses Bishop Creek on a footbridge. You'll climb 1.7 miles to the left fork for Grass Lake, a small lake that is popular with campground anglers. Stay right and continue climbing, for what seems like forever but is actually only .75 mile farther, to the short right spur to Lower Lamarck Lake. (Although you gain only 1,500 feet in elevation on this trail, most of it is between the Grass Lake junction and Lower Lamarck Lake.) Lower Lamarck Lake is quite scenic, set in a rock-lined granite basin. Cross the lake's outlet creek and climb to the Upper Lamarck Lake, .5 mile farther and nearly double in size. Look for Mount Emerson, Mount Lamarck, and the red-colored Piute Crags in the background.

Location: In the John Muir Wilderness; map F5, grid d4.

User groups: Hikers, dogs, and horses. No mountain bikes. No wheelchair facilities.

Permits: No day-hiking permits are required. A free wilderness permit is required for overnight stays. Quotas are in effect from the last Friday in June to September 15; permits are available in advance by mail or fax for this period for a $5 fee. Phone (760) 873-2408 for permit information or visit website: www.r5.fs.fed.us/inyo.

Maps: For a map of Inyo National Forest, send $6 to U.S. Forest Service, Map Sales, P.O. Box 587, Camino, CA 95709; tel. (530) 647-5390 or website: www.r5.fs.fed.us/visitorcenter. A Bishop Pass map is available for a fee from Tom Harrison Cartography, tel. (415) 456-7940. Ask the USGS for topographic maps of the Mount Thompson and Mount Darwin areas.

Directions: From Bishop on U.S. 395 turn west on Line Street/Highway 168 and drive 18 miles toward Lake Sabrina. Just before reaching the lake, turn right at the turnoff for North Lake. Drive 1.5 miles and turn right to park in the hiker parking lot by North Lake, near the pack station. Then walk .5 mile down the road to the trailhead at the edge of North Lake Campground.

Contact: Inyo National Forest, White Mountain Ranger District, 798 N. Main Street, Bishop, CA 93514; tel. (760) 873-2500 or fax (760) 873-2563.

10 Loch Leven Lake
5.6 mi/3.0 hrs

If you're in the mood for a shorter hike in the Bishop Creek and North Lake area, Loch Leven Lake could fit the bill. After walking .5 mile from the trailhead parking area to North Lake Campground's trailhead, take the trail marked for Piute Pass. A steep climb in the first mile will leave you panting. Luckily, the route is shaded by lodgepole pines. After you leave the forest, the grade lessens. You traverse a series of switchbacks that take you to the top of a high ridge, where Loch Leven Lake is nestled at 10,740 feet. As you curve your way up the ridge, be sure to stop occasionally and look back at the incredible valley below and the reddish-colored Piute Crags towering above. You'll say "wow" a bunch of times.

Loch Leven Lake is set right alongside the trail in a rocky glacial bowl. It is very long and narrow, with little accessible shoreline. A steep talus slope, usually snow-covered, frames its back side. There are a few campsites on the far side of the lake in the whitebark pines. Ambitious hikers can continue another 1.2 miles to Piute Lake, with little additional elevation gain. A bonus on this trip: In autumn the quaking aspens along the lower reaches of the route can take your breath away.

Location: In the John Muir Wilderness; map F5, grid d4.

User groups: Hikers, dogs, and horses. No mountain bikes. No wheelchair facilities.

Permits: No day-hiking permits are required. Parking and access are free.

Maps: For a map of Inyo National Forest, send $6 to U.S. Forest Service, Map Sales, P.O. Box 587, Camino, CA 95709; tel. (530) 647-5390 or website: www.r5.fs.fed.us/visitorcenter. A Bishop Pass map is available for a fee from Tom Harrison Cartography, tel. (415) 456-7940. Ask the USGS for topographic maps of the Mount Thompson and Mount Darwin areas.

Directions: From Bishop on U.S. 395 turn west on Line Street/Highway 168 and drive 18 miles toward Lake Sabrina. Just before reaching the lake, turn right at the turnoff for North Lake. Drive 1.5 miles and turn right to park in the hiker parking lot by North Lake, near the pack station. Walk .5 mile down the road to the trailhead at the edge of North Lake Campground.

Contact: Inyo National Forest, White Mountain Ranger District, 798 N. Main Street, Bishop, CA 93514; tel. (760) 873-2500 or fax (760) 873-2563.

11 Tyee Lakes

7.0 mi/
4.0 hrs or 2.0 days

There's so much excellent hiking in the South Fork Bishop Creek Canyon, it's hard to choose where to go. Since so many backpackers opt for the Bishop Pass Trail and its many lakes, described in the Ruwau and Chocolate Lakes Loop, below, day-hikers might do well to choose this trail to the Tyee Lakes instead. Named for a brand of salmon eggs, the Tyee Lakes offer good trout fishing (what, you were expecting salmon fishing?) and plenty of classic high Sierra scenery. From the bridge over Bishop Creek, you climb through sagebrush and aspens through a few dozen switchbacks and into a lodgepole pine forest. After two miles of climbing, the trail grade eases up, and you reach one of the smaller, lower Tyee Lakes at 2.3 miles. Another .5 mile of climbing brings you to the next small lake (called Tyee Lake number two); then another .5 mile brings you to one of the larger ones (Tyee Lake num-

ber three). A total of four Tyee Lakes are reachable by following the trail for 3.5 miles, with a total elevation gain of 2,000 feet. Anglers seek out rainbow and brown trout at the two largest lakes.

Location: In the John Muir Wilderness; map F5, grid d5.

User groups: Hikers, dogs, and horses. No mountain bikes. No wheelchair facilities.

Permits: No day-hiking permits are required. A free wilderness permit is required for overnight stays. Quotas are in effect from the last Friday in June to September 15; permits are available in advance by mail or fax for this period for a $5 fee. Phone (760) 873-2408 for permit information, or visit website: www.r5.fs.fed.us/inyo.

Maps: For a map of Inyo National Forest, send $6 to U.S. Forest Service, Map Sales, P.O. Box 587, Camino, CA 95709; tel. (530) 647-5390 or website: www.r5.fs.fed.us/visitorcenter. A Bishop Pass map is available for a fee from Tom Harrison Cartography, tel. (415) 456-7940. Ask the USGS for a topographic map of the Mount Thompson areas.

Directions: From Bishop on U.S. 395 turn west on Line Street/Highway 168 and drive 14 miles to the junction for South Lake. Go left and drive 4.5 miles on South Lake Road to the footbridge that crosses Bishop Creek. It is on the right, just before Willow Campground, and it is signed as Tyee Lakes and George Lake Trailhead. Park alongside the road.

Contact: Inyo National Forest, White Mountain Ranger District, 798 N. Main Street, Bishop, CA 93514; tel. (760) 873-2500 or fax (760) 873-2563.

12 Green and Brown Lakes

6.0 mi/3.0 hrs

Brown Lake and Green Lake are two excellent day-hiking destinations from the South Lake Trailhead in Bishop Creek's South Fork Canyon. With only a 1,500-foot climb, you can visit both lakes, maybe do a little fishing for rainbow trout, and be home in time for supper. Access the trail from the pack station trailhead and follow a stock trail as it climbs along Bishop Creek through a conifer forest and joins the main Green Lake Trail at one mile. Bear left and level out to an alpine meadow at two miles, then meet Brown Lake's outlet stream and the little lake itself at 2.5 miles. If you like fishing, this is your spot, but if you like scenery, continue another .5 mile to much larger Green Lake, surrounded by wildflowers and whitebark pines.

Location: In the John Muir Wilderness; map F5, grid d5.

User groups: Hikers, dogs, and horses. No mountain bikes. No wheelchair facilities.

Permits: No day-hiking permits are required. Parking and access are free.

Maps: For a map of Inyo National Forest, send $6 to U.S. Forest Service, Map Sales, P.O. Box 587, Camino, CA 95709; tel. (530) 647-5390 or website: www.r5.fs.fed.us/visitorcenter. A Bishop Pass map is available for a fee from Tom Harrison Cartography, tel. (415) 456-7940. Ask the USGS for a topographic map of the Mount Thompson area.

Directions: From Bishop on U.S. 395 turn west on Line Street/Highway 168 and drive 14 miles to the junction for South Lake. Go left and drive six miles on South Lake Road to Parchers Resort and pack station on the left side of the road, just beyond Willow Campground.

Contact: Inyo National Forest, White Mountain Ranger District, 798 N. Main Street, Bishop, CA 93514; tel. (760) 873-2500 or fax (760) 873-2563.

13 Ruwau and Chocolate Lakes Loop

6.6 mi/
3.5 hrs or 2.0 days

Lakes, lakes, lakes everywhere. That's how it is on the Bishop Pass Trail, where in the space of only five miles you can access Long Lake, Spearhead Lake, Saddlerock Lake, Bishop Lake, and so on. But if you prefer a loop trip to an out-and-back hike, the Bishop Pass Trail provides another lake-filled option: a two-mile hike to Long Lake, then a circular route to Ruwau Lake, the Chocolate Lakes, and Bull Lake. It's the kind of trip that fills your mind with precious memories of blue-sky Sierra scenery and gem-like, rock-lined lakes. Still, the trip is not for everyone; some of the trail is an indistinct route with steep, rocky sections and not an official trail. Bring a good map with you.

The trail begins on the south side of the parking lot, and you head uphill along the eastern shore of South Lake. The views begin almost immediately, particularly of South Lake, Mount Thompson, and Mount Goode. Take the left fork at .75 mile, heading for Long Lake and Bishop Pass. Continue straight, ignoring all turnoffs as you hike up around the spectacular western shore of Long Lake, popular with anglers and backpackers. At 2.5 miles (before you reach the lake's far end), instead of continuing straight to Saddlerock Lake and Bishop Pass, take the left fork for Ruwau Lake, a steep but short .5 mile away. Skirt the edge of Ruwau Lake for about 75 yards, then look for a use trail leading uphill to your left. Make a steep uphill climb for .5 mile to the ridgetop, where you'll look down and see the Chocolate Lakes, set below Chocolate Peak. Make the steep descent to the lakes, picking your way along the rocky slope. Once you're there, the hard part is over. You'll find an easy-to-follow trail at the Chocolate Lakes, and walk downhill for .5 mile to Bull Lake, which is big, round, and beautiful. From Bull Lake you keep on hiking, and in less than .25 mile you rejoin the Bishop Pass Trail. Turn right and walk just under two miles back to the parking lot. Wow, what a day.

Location: In the John Muir Wilderness; map F5, grid d5.

User groups: Hikers, dogs, and horses. No mountain bikes. No wheelchair facilities.

Permits: No day-hiking permits are required. A free wilderness permit is required for overnight stays. Quotas are in effect from the last Friday in June to September 15; permits are available in advance by mail or fax for this period for a $5 fee. Phone (760) 873-2408 for permit information, or visit website: www.r5.fs.fed.us/inyo.

Maps: For a map of Inyo National Forest, send $6 to U.S. Forest Service, Map Sales, P.O. Box 587, Camino, CA 95709; tel. (530) 647-5390 or website: www.r5.fs.fed.us/visitorcenter. A Bishop Pass map is available for a fee from Tom Harrison Cartography, tel. (415) 456-7940. Ask the USGS for a topographic map of the Mount Thompson area.

Directions: From Bishop on U.S. 395, turn west on Line Street/Highway 168 and drive 14 miles to the junction for South Lake. Go left and drive 7.5 miles on South Lake Road to the end of the road and the trailhead parking area. This parking is for day-use only. If you are backpacking, you must park 1.5 miles from the trailhead, east of Parchers Resort.

Contact: Inyo National Forest, White Mountain Ranger District, 798 N. Main Street, Bishop, CA 93514; tel. (760) 873-2500 or fax (760) 873-2563.

14 First and Second Falls

3.0 mi/1.5 hrs

If you're camping or fishing in Big Pine Canyon, or maybe just wandering around exploring the area, there's a great walk to be taken starting from the end of the road near Glacier Lodge. Since it's just a day hike, you can park in the parking area right by the lodge and save yourself the long walk from the backpackers' parking lot.

Head west from the trailhead on the wide road, passing some private cabins, and in seconds you cross a bridge over First Falls, a noisy, 200-foot-long whitewater cascade. Bear right onto a narrower trail and start switchbacking uphill paralleling the cascade. As you climb, you get awesome views into Big Pine Canyon's South Fork. At the top of the falls, cross another bridge over the creek and take a hard left onto a dirt road, staying along the

creek. Now it's a flat stroll into the North Fork of Big Pine Canyon. Your goal is Second Falls, a larger, more impressive cascade than First Falls, less than a mile away and clearly visible from the trail. Since the route is set along the canyon bottom, you get many interesting vistas along the way, from the tall surrounding canyon walls to occasional lodgepole pines and many mountain wildflowers. When the trail starts to climb back out of the canyon, take the left spur cutoff to head closer to the waterfall, or just pick a big rock to sit on and admire the scenery.

Location: In the John Muir Wilderness; map F5, grid e5.

User groups: Hikers, dogs, and horses. No mountain bikes. No wheelchair facilities.

Permits: No day-hiking permits are required. Parking and access are free.

Maps: For a map of Inyo National Forest, send $6 to U.S. Forest Service, Map Sales, P.O. Box 587, Camino, CA 95709; tel. (530) 647-5390 or website: www.r5.fs.fed.us/visitorcenter. Ask the USGS for a topographic map of the Coyote Flat area.

Directions: From Bishop drive 15 miles south on U.S. 395 to Big Pine. Turn right (west) on Crocker Street, which becomes Glacier Lodge Road, and drive 10.5 miles to Glacier Lodge and the Big Pine Canyon Trailhead, at the end of the road. Day hikers may park in the day-use area near the lodge, but backpackers must park .5 mile east on Glacier Lodge Road in the backpackers' parking lot.

Contact: Inyo National Forest, White Mountain Ranger District, 798 N. Main Street, Bishop, CA 93514; tel. (760) 873-2500 or fax (760) 873-2563.

15 First and Second Lakes

9.6 mi/
6.0 hrs or 2.0 days

The trail to First and Second Lakes in Big Pine Canyon follows the same route as the trail to First and Second Falls, but then continues onward, climbing up and over Second Falls on the well-graded trail to Cienaga Mirth at three miles out. Here you'll see a stone cabin (now a backcountry ranger residence) built by movie star Lon Chaney. Wildflowers are excellent at the swampy, spring-fed mirth. You reach First Lake at 4.5 miles, then bear left and reach Second Lake at 4.8 miles. By Second Lake, you've climbed to over 10,000 feet, and the lake water is a stunning glacial blue green. You'll see hardy hikers with climbing equipment continuing beyond Second Lake; they're hiking a full nine miles one way to the edge of Palisade Glacier, the southernmost glacier in the Sierra. With a 5,000-foot elevation gain, the route to the glacier is not for everybody.

Location: In the John Muir Wilderness; map F5, grid e5.

User groups: Hikers, dogs, and horses. No mountain bikes. No wheelchair facilities.

Permits: No day-hiking permits are required. A free wilderness permit is required for overnight stays. Quotas are in effect from the last Friday in June to September 15; permits are available in advance by mail or fax for this period for a $5 fee. Phone (760) 873-2408 for permit information, or visit website: www.r5.fs.fed.us/inyo.

Maps: For a map of Inyo National Forest, send $6 to U.S. Forest Service, Map Sales, P.O. Box 587, Camino, CA 95709; tel. (530) 647-5390 or website: www.r5.fs.fed.us/visitorcenter. Ask the USGS for topographic maps of the Coyote Flat and Split Mountain area.

Directions: From Bishop drive 15 miles south on U.S. 395 to Big Pine. Turn right (west) on Crocker Street, which becomes Glacier Lodge Road, and drive 10.5 miles to Glacier Lodge and the Big Pine Canyon Trailhead at the end of the road. Day hikers may park in the day-use area near the lodge, but backpackers must park .5 mile east on Glacier Lodge Road in the backpackers' parking lot.

Contact: Inyo National Forest, White Mountain Ranger District, 798 N. Main Street, Bishop, CA 93514; tel. (760) 873-2500 or fax (760) 873-2563.

16 Yucca Point

4.0 mi/2.25 hrs

The Yucca Point Trail is an upside-down hike—the kind where you go down on the way in (so easy) and up on the way back (not so easy). The path descends from Highway 180 to the Kings River, dropping 1,200 feet along the way. We looked at it from the top and assumed it would be brutal on the way back, but as long as you don't climb uphill at high noon, it's not as bad as it looks. The trail is well graded; the only hardship is that the terrain is all chaparral so there's almost no shade, just the occasional tall yucca plant. The path is mostly used by anglers heading down to the wild trout section of the Kings River, but hikers like the excellent views it provides and the access to the river's cool, emerald green pools.

Location: In Sequoia National Forest, west of the Cedar Grove area of Kings Canyon National Park; map F5, grid g1.

User groups: Hikers only. No dogs, horses, or mountain bikes. No wheelchair facilities.

Permits: No permits are required. There is a $10 entrance fee for access to this section of Sequoia National Forest, payable at any of the entrance stations to Kings Canyon and Sequoia National Parks. The fee is good for seven days in both the national forest and the national parks.

Maps: For a map of Sequoia National Forest, send $6 to U.S. Forest Service, Map Sales, P.O. Box 587, Camino, CA 95709; tel. (530) 647-5390 or website: www.r5.fs.fed.us/visitorcenter. A more detailed map is available for a fee from Tom Harrison Cartography, tel. (415) 456-7940, or Trails Illustrated, tel. (800) 962-1643. Ask the USGS for a topographic map of the Wren Peak area.

Directions: From Fresno drive east on Highway 180 for 55 miles to the Big Stump entrance station at Kings Canyon National Park. Continue 1.5 miles and turn left for Grant Grove and Cedar Grove. Continue 16 miles on Highway 180, past Kings Canyon Lodge, to the Yucca Point Trailhead on the left. Park in the pullouts alongside Highway 180.

Contact: Sequoia National Forest, Hume Lake Ranger District, 35860 E. Kings Canyon Road, Dunlap, CA 93621; tel. (559) 338-2251 or fax (559) 338-2131.

17 Windy Cliffs

3.0 mi/1.5 hrs

The Forest Service concessionaire charges a fee for tours of Boyden Cave, one of many limestone caverns in the vicinity of Kings Canyon and Sequoia National Park, and the parking lot is always busy with carloads and busloads of people waiting to take the tour. But if you're low on cash, you can take this stellar hike instead and get million-dollar views of Kings Canyon free. From the cave gift shop, walk up the paved path and take the left fork near the entrance to the cave. The trail is signed as unmaintained, but never fear, it's fairly well used. It does have some steep drop-offs, however. In no time you'll climb a little higher and see a sweeping panorama of Highway 180 and the fast-flowing Kings River below. In one mile, you'll see Boulder Creek cascading down the hillside. The path ends when it reaches creekside at 1.5 miles, and you turn around and head back.

Location: In Sequoia National Forest, west of the Cedar Grove area of Kings Canyon National Park; map F5, grid g1.

User groups: Hikers only. No dogs, horses, or mountain bikes. No wheelchair facilities.

Permits: No permits are required. There is a $10 entrance fee for access to this section of Sequoia National Forest, payable at any of the entrance stations to Kings Canyon and Sequoia National Parks. The fee is good for seven days in both the national forest and the national parks.

Maps: For a map of Sequoia National Forest, send $6 to U.S. Forest Service, Map Sales, P.O. Box 587, Camino, CA 95709; tel. (530) 647-5390 or website: www.r5.fs.fed.us/visitorcenter. A more detailed map is available for a fee

from Tom Harrison Cartography, tel. (415) 456-7940, or Trails Illustrated, tel. (800) 962-1643. Ask the USGS for a topographic map of the Wren Peak area.

Directions: From Fresno drive east on Highway 180 for 55 miles to the Big Stump entrance station at Kings Canyon National Park. Continue 1.5 miles and turn left for Grant Grove and Cedar Grove. Continue 22 miles on Highway 180 to the parking area for Boyden Cave, on the right side of the road.

Contact: Sequoia National Forest, Hume Lake Ranger District, 35860 E. Kings Canyon Road, Dunlap, CA 93621; tel. (559) 338-2251 or fax (559) 338-2131.

18 Lewis Creek Trail

11.6 mi/
6.0 hrs or 2.0 days

Up, up, and up. If you're willing to climb 3,200 feet over the course of 5.5 miles, your reward is pristine Frypan Meadow, at 7,800 feet in elevation. In early summer the meadow is green and littered with wildflowers, a glorious sight after the hot, sunny climb. But there's no way to see it without first putting in some effort on the Lewis Creek Trail. The good news is that if the first mile or so proves to be too demanding, or too hot if you don't start first thing in the morning, you can always take the right fork at 1.6 miles and head back downhill on the Hotel Creek Trail, making a seven-mile loop out of the trip. If you push onward on the Lewis Creek Trail, you cross lovely Comb Creek at 3.2 miles, then Lewis Creek one mile farther. Many day-hikers make the Lewis Creek crossing their destination; there is good swimming in its pools. Backpackers continue another 1.5 miles to Frypan Meadow. If you've got your wilderness permit, campsites are available there.

Location: Off Highway 180 in the Cedar Grove area of Kings Canyon National Park; map F5, grid g2.

User groups: Hikers and horses. No dogs or mountain bikes. No wheelchair facilities.

Permits: There is a $10 entrance fee at Sequoia and Kings Canyon National Parks, good for seven days. A free wilderness permit is required for overnight stays and is available on a first-come, first-served basis at the wilderness kiosk at Roads End or in advance by mail or fax after March 1; for more information phone (559) 565-3708.

Maps: Free park maps are available at park entrance stations or by contacting Sequoia and Kings Canyon National Parks at the address below. A more detailed map is available for a fee from Tom Harrison Cartography, tel. (415) 456-7940, or Trails Illustrated, tel. (800) 962-1643. Ask the USGS for a topographic map of the Cedar Grove area.

Directions: From Fresno drive east on Highway 180 for 55 miles to the Big Stump entrance station at Kings Canyon National Park. Continue 1.5 miles and turn left for Grant Grove and Cedar Grove. Drive 31 miles on Highway 180 to the Lewis Creek Trail parking area on the north side of the road, before you reach Cedar Grove Village.

Contact: Sequoia and Kings Canyon National Parks, Three Rivers, CA 93271-9700; tel. (559) 565-3134 or (559) 335-2856.

19 Kings Canyon Overlook

5.0 mi/2.5 hrs

The destination on this trip is a stunning overlook of Kings Canyon, the deepest canyon in the continental United States. Actually, the canyon vistas are continual for most of the hike, so if you don't make it to the overlook, you'll still get an eyeful. The Hotel Creek Trail consists of dozens of switchbacks over open, sunny slopes, climbing 1,200 feet over two miles to a trail junction with the Overlook Trail. Turn left to head to the overlook, which peers down on Cedar Grove and the length of Kings Canyon. Some of the best views are of Monarch Divide's high peaks to the north. Hope you came with picnic supplies. For a five-mile round-trip, retrace your steps back to Cedar Grove. If you want to walk farther, you can continue from the overlook junction for another 1.5 miles and turn left, hiking downhill on the Lewis Creek Trail and making a seven-mile loop out of the trip. This stretch of the Lewis Creek Trail is lined with sweet-smelling ceanothus. The final 1.2 miles of the loop are a dull stretch paralleling the park road, but the rest of the hike is so good that you won't complain.

Location: Off Highway 180 in the Cedar Grove area of Kings Canyon National Park; map F5, grid h3.

User groups: Hikers and horses. No dogs or mountain bikes. No wheelchair facilities.

Permits: No permits are required. There is a $10 entrance fee at Sequoia and Kings Canyon National Parks, good for seven days.

Maps: Free park maps are available at park entrance stations or by contacting Sequoia and Kings Canyon National Parks at the address below. A more detailed map is available for a fee from Tom Harrison Cartography, tel. (415) 456-7940, or Trails Illustrated, tel. (800) 962-1643. Ask the USGS for a topographic map of the Cedar Grove area.

Directions: From Fresno drive east on Highway 180 for 55 miles to the Big Stump entrance station at Kings Canyon National Park. Continue 1.5 miles and turn left for Grant Grove and Cedar Grove. Drive 31.5 miles on Highway 180 to Cedar Grove Village. Turn left at the sign for the visitor center and Cedar Grove Lodge. Continue on the main road past the lodge for .25 mile and turn right. The Hotel Creek Trailhead is on the left in a few hundred feet.

Contact: Sequoia and Kings Canyon National Parks, Three Rivers, CA 93271-9700; tel. (559) 565-3134 or (559) 335-2856.

20 Lookout Peak

12.0 mi/7.0 hrs

Lookout Peak at 8,531 feet in elevation is a summit worth ascending, even though it's an all-day trip with a 3,900-foot elevation gain. From the top you get an unforgettable Sierra view, with Cedar Grove far below you and peaks and ridges all around. In addition, just a few hundred yards from the summit is Summit Meadow, filled with summer wildflowers. The key is to carry plenty of water and plan on an early-morning start to beat the heat. You can filter water from Sheep Creek, one mile in. Luckily, there's a decent amount of shade in the first few miles. Even though this trailhead is located right by the Cedar Grove campgrounds, few people hike all the way to the peak, so you have a chance at peace and quiet along the trail. The only downer on this hike is that when you near the summit, you see that other people have driven their cars the back way to the peak and they are reaching the summit with only a .25-mile hike. Hey, at least you earned it.

Location: Off Highway 180 in the Cedar Grove area of Kings Canyon National Park; map F5, grid h3.

User groups: Hikers and horses. No dogs or mountain bikes. No wheelchair facilities.

Permits: No permits are required. There is a $10 entrance fee at Sequoia and Kings Canyon National Parks, good for seven days.

Maps: Free park maps are available at park entrance stations or by contacting Sequoia and Kings Canyon National Parks at the address below. A more detailed map is available for a fee from Tom Harrison Cartography, tel. (415) 456-7940, or Trails Illustrated, tel. (800) 962-1643. Ask the USGS for a topographic map of the Cedar Grove area.

Directions: From Fresno drive east on Highway 180 for 55 miles to the Big Stump entrance station at Kings Canyon National Park. Continue 1.5 miles and turn left for Grant Grove and Cedar Grove. Drive 31.5 miles on Highway 180 and take the right fork for Cedar Grove. The Don Cecil Trailhead is on the right side of the road, just beyond the turnoff for Cedar Grove Village and the visitor center. If you reach Canyon View and Moraine Campgrounds, you've gone too far.

Contact: Sequoia and Kings Canyon National Parks, Three Rivers, CA 93271-9700; tel. (559) 565-3134 or (559) 335-2856.

21 Roaring River Falls

0.4 mi/0.25 hr

It's an easy stroll to Roaring River Falls, a pretty waterfall that drops through a narrow gorge into the South Fork Kings River. It's the only waterfall in Sequoia and Kings Canyon National Parks that is accessible via wheelchair. If hikers using two legs want a longer walk, they can continue downstream on the River Trail to Zumwalt Meadow in 1.6 miles or Road's End in 2.7 miles. What's extraordinary about the waterfall is not the cascade itself, but the giant rocky pool into which it falls, which is at least 50 feet wide. From where the paved trail ends at the edge of the pool, the waterfall is perfectly framed by two big conifers. About a zillion photos have been snapped here.

Location: Off Highway 180 in the Cedar Grove area of Kings Canyon National Park; map F5, grid h3.

User groups: Hikers and wheelchairs. No dogs, horses, or mountain bikes.

Permits: No permits are required. There is a $10 entrance fee at Sequoia and Kings Canyon National Parks, good for seven days.

Maps: Free park maps are available at park entrance stations or by contacting Sequoia and Kings Canyon National Parks at the address below. A more detailed map is available for a fee from Tom Harrison Cartography, tel. (415) 456-7940, or Trails Illustrated, tel. (800) 962-1643. Ask the USGS for a topographical map of the Sphinx area.

Directions: From Fresno drive east on Highway 180 for 55 miles to the Big Stump entrance station at Kings Canyon National Park. Continue 1.5 miles and turn left for Grant Grove and Cedar Grove. Continue 35 miles on Highway 180 to the sign for Roaring River Falls and the River Trail, three miles past Cedar Grove Village. The trailhead is on the right side of the road.

Contact: Sequoia and Kings Canyon National Parks, Three Rivers, CA 93271-9700; tel. (559) 565-3134 or (559) 335-2856.

22 Zumwalt Meadow Loop

1.5 mi/1.0 hr

What's the prettiest easy hike in Kings Canyon National Park? The Zumwalt Meadow Loop Trail wins hands down. A scenic 1.5-mile walk along the South Fork Kings River, the Zumwalt Meadow Loop is a delight for hikers of all abilities. Many people bring their fishing rods along to try their luck in the river, but for most, the hiking is better than the fishing. From the parking area, walk downstream along the river to an old suspension footbridge, cross it, and walk back upstream. The loop begins at an obvious fork, and you can hike it in either direction. The south side traverses a boulder field of jumbled rocks which have tumbled down from the Grand Sentinel, elevation 8,504 feet. The north side cuts through a thick, waist-high fern forest and follows a wooden walkway over a marsh. We were surprised by a deer who was up to his neck in the ferns. Views of 8,717-foot North Dome are awe inspiring. Trees, meadow, rock, stream, river, canyon walls—the Zumwalt Meadow Trail has it all.

Location: Off Highway 180 in the Cedar Grove area of Kings Canyon National Park; map F5, grid h3.

User groups: Hikers only. No dogs, horses, or mountain bikes. No wheelchair facilities.

Permits: No permits are required. There is a $10 entrance fee at Sequoia and Kings Canyon National Parks, good for seven days.

Maps: Free park maps are available at park entrance stations or by contacting Sequoia and Kings Canyon National Parks at the address below. A more detailed map is available for a fee from Tom Harrison Cartography, tel. (415) 456-7940, or Trails Illustrated, tel. (800) 962-1643. Ask the USGS for a topographical map of the Cedar Grove area.

Directions: From Fresno drive east on Highway 180 for 55 miles to the Big Stump entrance station at Kings Canyon National Park. Continue 1.5 miles and turn left for Grant Grove and Cedar Grove. Continue 36 miles on High-way 180 to the parking area for Zumwalt Meadow, on the right side of the road.

Contact: Sequoia and Kings Canyon National Parks, Three Rivers, CA 93271-9700; tel. (559) 565-3134 or (559) 335-2856.

23 Mist Falls

8.4 mi/5.0 hrs

The Mist Falls Trail is probably the most well-used pathway in Kings Canyon National Park, with good reason. It's a stellar 4.2-mile walk to an impressive cascade on the South Fork Kings River, with only 650 feet in elevation gain along the way. Many backpackers use this trail to access Paradise Valley and points beyond, while most day-hikers turn around at Mist Falls. The first two miles are a flat walk up the Kings River Valley, with canyon walls towering above you on both sides. You spend a lot of time craning your neck, looking up at the high canyon rims, where springtime waterfalls cascade down. You're in open forest much of the time. At two miles, reach a trail junction and bear left, then start to climb over granite. The farther you go, the more expansive the views become; make sure you keep turning around so you can take in the whole panorama. A highlight is the huge stone face of the Sphinx—you'll know it when you see it. At four miles, the river starts to get more waterfall-like, with crashing pools and rocky granite slides getting increasingly vertical. A quarter mile later you reach Mist Falls, which fans out over a 45-foot wide granite ledge and crashes into a boulder-lined pool. It creates a tremendous spray and mist in early summer, and mellows out as the season goes on. There are two ways to beat the crowds on this path, so listen carefully. First, start early in the morning. Second, hike part of the route on an alternate trail on the south side of the river, which runs from the Road's End parking lot to the Bailey Bridge at the trail intersection mentioned above. If you get an early start, save this alternate route for the return trip. By then, the day-hikers will be out in full force.

Location: Off Highway 180 in the Cedar Grove area of Kings Canyon National Park; map F5, grid h4.

User groups: Hikers only. No dogs, horses, or mountain bikes. No wheelchair facilities.

Permits: No permits are required. There is a $10 entrance fee at Sequoia and Kings Canyon National Parks, good for seven days.

Maps: Free park maps are available at park entrance stations or by contacting Sequoia and Kings Canyon National Parks at the address below. A more detailed map is available for a fee from Tom Harrison Cartography, tel. (415) 456-7940, or Trails Illustrated, tel. (800) 962-1643. Ask the USGS for a topographic map of the Sphinx area.

Directions: From Fresno drive east on Highway 180 for 55 miles to the Big Stump entrance station at Kings Canyon National Park. Continue 1.5 miles and turn left for Grant Grove and Cedar Grove. Continue 38 miles on Highway 180 to Road's End, six miles past Cedar Grove Village. The trailhead is at the east end of the parking lot, near the wilderness ranger station.

Contact: Sequoia and Kings Canyon National Parks, Three Rivers, CA 93271-9700; tel. (559) 565-3134 or (559) 335-2856.

24 Copper Creek Trail
21.0 mi/3-4 days

The Copper Creek Trailhead is at 5,000 feet, and Granite Lake is at 9,972 feet, so it's not hard to do the math. If you're up for a backpacking trip with a 5,000-foot elevation gain over 10 miles, the Granite Lake Basin is your ticket to happiness. But keep in mind that the route can be hot and dry as it switchbacks up manzanita-covered slopes; this trail is considered one of the most strenuous in the Cedar Grove area. Your first night's camp is at Lower Tent Meadow, four miles in and at 7,800 feet. After that, things start to get really good. With Mount Hutchings looming over

your left shoulder, the second day's six miles will go easier, bringing you to rocky, jewel-like Granite Lake in only a few hours. You must have a backpacking stove for camping by the lake or anywhere above 10,000 feet.

Location: Off Highway 180 in the Cedar Grove area of Kings Canyon National Park; map F5, grid h4.

User groups: Hikers and horses. No dogs or mountain bikes. No wheelchair facilities.

Permits: There is a $10 entrance fee at Sequoia and Kings Canyon National Parks, good for seven days. A free wilderness permit is required for overnight stays. Permits are available on a first-come, first-served basis at the wilderness kiosk at Road's End, or by mail or fax after March 1; for more information phone (559) 565-3708.

Maps: Free park maps are available at park entrance stations or by contacting Sequoia and Kings Canyon National Parks at the address below. A more detailed map is available for a fee from Tom Harrison Cartography, tel. (415) 456-7940, or Trails Illustrated, tel. (800) 962-1643. Ask the USGS for a topographic map of the Sphinx area.

Directions: From Fresno drive east on Highway 180 for 55 miles to the Big Stump entrance station at Kings Canyon National Park. Continue 1.5 miles and turn left for Grant Grove and Cedar Grove. Continue 38 miles on Highway 180 to Road's End, six miles past Cedar Grove Village. The trail begins at the long-term parking area.

Contact: Sequoia and Kings Canyon National Parks, Three Rivers, CA 93271-9700; tel. (559) 565-3134 or (559) 335-2856.

25 Redwood Canyon
4.0 mi/2.0 hrs

Several loop trips are possible in the Redwood Mountain area of Kings Canyon National Park, but one of the prettiest and simplest trips is just an out-and-back walk on the Redwood Canyon Trail, paralleling Redwood Creek. The beauty begins before you even start walking;

on the last mile of the drive to the trailhead, the road winds through giant sequoias that are so close, you can reach out your car window and touch them. The trail leads downhill from the parking area, and in just over .3 mile you reach a junction and follow the Redwood Creek Trail to the right. You'll find that this sequoia grove is far denser than many. Because they are situated by Redwood Creek, the sequoias grow amid a thriving background of dogwoods, firs, ceanothus, and mountain misery. The canyon is reminiscent of the damp, lush coastal redwood forests of northwestern California. While the standing sequoias are impressive, some of the fallen ones along the trail are really amazing, because you get a close-up look at their immense size. Make sure you hike the full two miles to the stream crossing of Redwood Creek—some of the best tree specimens are down there, and you're also near the junction with the Sugar Bowl Loop Trail. The return trip is all uphill, but easier than you'd expect.

Location: Southeast of the Grant Grove area of Kings Canyon National Park; map F5, grid h0.

User groups: Hikers only. No dogs, horses, or mountain bikes. No wheelchair facilities.

Permits: No permits are required. There is a $10 entrance fee at Sequoia and Kings Canyon National Parks, good for seven days.

Maps: Free park maps are available at park entrance stations or by contacting Sequoia and Kings Canyon National Parks at the address below. A more detailed map is available for a fee from Tom Harrison Cartography, tel. (415) 456-7940, or Trails Illustrated, tel. (800) 962-1643. Ask the USGS for a topographic map of the General Grant Grove area.

Directions: From Fresno drive east on Highway 180 for 55 miles to the Big Stump entrance station at Kings Canyon National Park. Continue 1.5 miles and turn right on the Generals Highway, heading for Sequoia National Park. Drive approximately three miles on the Generals Highway to Quail Flat, signed for Hume Lake to the left, and turn right on the dirt road

to Redwood Saddle. Drive 1.5 miles and park in the parking lot. Take the trail signed for the Hart Tree and Redwood Canyon.

Contact: Sequoia and Kings Canyon National Parks, Three Rivers, CA 93271-9700; tel. (559) 565-3134 or (559) 335-2856.

26 Redwood Mountain Loop
10.0 mi/5.0 hrs

If you've got a whole day to hike in the Redwood Mountain area of Kings Canyon National Park, you're in luck. The Redwood Mountain Loop combines all the best highlights of the area into one long trail, on which you'll wander in near solitude among the giant sequoias. If the paved, crowded trails to the General Grant Tree and the General Sherman Tree turn you off, this trail will turn you on. Start by hiking on the signed Burnt Grove/Sugar Bowl Loop Trail, which leads uphill from the parking lot. It's one mile to Burnt Grove and 2.5 miles to Sugar Bowl Grove, both very dense stands of sequoias. Beyond the groves you descend for two miles to intersect with the Redwood Canyon Trail. Head downhill and cross Redwood Creek, then proceed to the Fallen Goliath, a mammoth downed tree. One mile farther you reach the Hart Tree, the largest tree in this area. In the final three miles, you get to walk through the Tunnel Log, a hollowed sequoia, and pass by pretty Hart Meadow. Note that if you tire out halfway through this loop, you can always follow the Redwood Canyon Trail uphill back to the start, cutting three miles off your round-trip. This is one of the best day-hikes in all of Kings Canyon.

Location: Southeast of the Grant Grove area of Kings Canyon National Park; map F5, grid h0.

User groups: Hikers only. No dogs, horses, or mountain bikes. No wheelchair facilities.

Permits: No permits are required. There is a $10 entrance fee at Sequoia and Kings Canyon National Parks, good for seven days.

Maps: Free park maps are

available at park entrance stations or by contacting Sequoia and Kings Canyon National Parks at the address below. A more detailed map is available for a fee from Tom Harrison Cartography, tel. (415) 456-7940, or Trails Illustrated, tel. (800) 962-1643. Ask the USGS for a topographic map of the General Grant Grove area.

Directions: From Fresno drive east on Highway 180 for 55 miles to the Big Stump entrance station at Kings Canyon National Park. Continue 1.5 miles and turn right on the Generals Highway, heading for Sequoia National Park. Drive approximately three miles on the Generals Highway to Quail Flat, signed for Hume Lake to the left, and turn right on the dirt road to Redwood Saddle. Drive 1.5 miles and park in the parking lot. Take the trail signed as Burnt Grove/Sugar Bowl Loop.

Contact: Sequoia and Kings Canyon National Parks, Three Rivers, CA 93271-9700; tel. (559) 565-3134 or (559) 335-2856.

27 Buena Vista Peak
2.0 mi/1.0 hr

Forget driving to the Kings Canyon Overlook, because just across the road is a trailhead with an easy walk and all the same views, plus a chance at a private picnic spot. Buena Vista Peak is really a rocky dome, peaking at 7,603 feet, and one of the highest points west of Generals Highway. It offers 360-degree views: you can see a million conifers at your feet and the hazy foothills to the southwest, but the best vistas are to the east, looking out at the snow-capped peaks of the John Muir and Monarch Wildernesses. It's an easy half-hour walk up the back side of the dome, passing through pine and fir forest, manzanita and sage, and walking by some interesting rock formations—check out the giant boulder sculpture in the trail's first .25 mile. Wander all around the top of the dome, taking in many different perspectives on the vistas, before heading back to the parking lot. It's downhill all the way.

Location: Southeast of the Grant Grove area of Kings Canyon National Park; map F5, grid h0.

User groups: Hikers only. No dogs, horses, or mountain bikes. No wheelchair facilities.

Permits: No permits are required. There is a $10 entrance fee at Sequoia and Kings Canyon National Parks, good for seven days.

Maps: Free park maps are available at park entrance stations or by contacting Sequoia and Kings Canyon National Parks at the address below. A more detailed map is available for a fee from Tom Harrison Cartography, tel. (415) 456-7940, or Trails Illustrated, tel. (800) 962-1643. Ask the USGS for a topographic map of the General Grant Grove area.

Directions: From Fresno drive east on Highway 180 for 55 miles to the Big Stump entrance station at Kings Canyon National Park. Continue 1.5 miles and turn right on the Generals Highway, heading for Sequoia National Park. Drive approximately five miles on the Generals Highway to the Buena Vista Trailhead on the right, just across the road and slightly beyond the large pullout for the Kings Canyon Overlook on the left.

Contact: Sequoia and Kings Canyon National Parks, Three Rivers, CA 93271-9700; tel. (559) 565-3134 or (559) 335-2856.

28 Weaver Lake
4.2 mi/
2.0 hrs or 2.0 days

Tucked into a corner just outside the border of Kings Canyon and Sequoia National Parks, the Jennie Lakes Wilderness is a 10,500-acre wilderness area that is often overlooked by park visitors. It offers much of the same scenery as the parks—beautiful lakes, meadows, forests, and streams—but without all the fanfare. Weaver Lake is the easiest-to-reach destination in the wilderness, and it makes a perfect family backpacking trip or an equally nice day hike. The trail is well signed and passes through a mix of fir forest and meadows. At .7 mile, take the left fork for Weaver Lake, climbing uphill to the lake's basin. You'll spy the shelf-like slabs of Shell Mountain peeking out above the trees. At just over two miles, you'll reach shallow but pretty Weaver Lake at 8,700 feet, set at the base of Shell Mountain's high, rounded ridge. You can try your luck fishing, or just find a lakeside seat and gaze at the view. On warm days the brave go swimming.

Note that the road to Big Meadows and Fox Meadows is usually the last road to open in the area after snowmelt. If you're planning an early season trip, call to check on road and trail conditions.

Location: In the Jennie Lakes Wilderness; map F5, grid h0.

User groups: Hikers, dogs, and horses. No mountain bikes. No wheelchair facilities.

Permits: A free wilderness permit is required for overnight stays and is available from the Hume Lake Ranger Station. There is a $10 entrance fee for access to this section of Sequoia National Forest, payable at any of the entrance stations to Kings Canyon and Sequoia National Parks. The fee is good for seven days in both the national forest and the national parks.

Maps: For a map of Sequoia National Forest, send $6 to U.S. Forest Service, Map Sales, P.O. Box 587, Camino, CA 95709; tel. (530) 647-5390 or website: www.r5.ts.ted.us/visitorcenter. A more detailed map is available for a fee from Tom Harrison Cartography, tel. (415) 456-7940, or Trails Illustrated, tel. (800) 962-1643. Ask the USGS for a topographic map of the Muir Grove area.

Directions: From Fresno drive east on Highway 180 for 55 miles to the Big Stump entrance station at Kings Canyon National Park. Continue 1.5 miles and turn right on the Generals Highway, heading for Sequoia National Park. Drive seven miles and turn left on Forest Service Road 14S11, at the sign for Big Meadows and Horse Corral. Drive four miles, passing Big Meadows Trailhead and Big Meadows Campground, and turn right on the dirt road .5 mile beyond the camp (it's just past the bridge over Big Meadows Creek). Drive .5 mile to the fork, turn left, and turn right immediately af-

terward. Drive one more mile and park at the road's end at the Fox Meadow trailhead. Total mileage from Big Meadows Road is 1.5 miles.

Contact: Sequoia National Forest, Hume Lake Ranger District, 35860 E. Kings Canyon Road, Dunlap, CA 93621; tel. (559) 338-2251 or fax (559) 338-2131.

29 Jennie Lake

10.0 mi/
6.0 hrs or 2.0 days

This trail into the Jennie Lakes Wilderness offers more of a challenge than the route to Weaver Lake, climbing 1,500 feet over five miles with some short, steep pitches. The rewards are also greater because Jennie Lake is a beauty and receives fewer visitors than Weaver Lake. The trail is the same as the Weaver Lake Trail for .7 mile, but at the fork you bear right for Jennie Lake. The trail climbs and dips through fir, pine, and manzanita, then crosses Poop Out Pass at 3.7 miles, the highest point on this trip. At five miles you reach the outlet stream for Jennie Lake. Follow the short spur trail to the lake, set at 9,000 feet. With a white granite backdrop and some sparse trees, the shoreline looks austere and barren, but beautiful just the same. Campsites are found around the lake, and catching fish for dinner is a fair possibility. If you only came for the day, find a comfortable spot to sit and admire the scenery before you head back.

Location: In the Jennie Lakes Wilderness; map F5, grid h0.

User groups: Hikers, dogs, and horses. No mountain bikes. No wheelchair facilities.

Permits: A free wilderness permit is required for overnight stays and is available from the Hume Lake Ranger Station. There is a $10 entrance fee for access to this section of Sequoia National Forest, payable at any of the entrance stations to Kings Canyon and Sequoia National Parks. The fee is good for seven days in both the national forest and the national parks.

Maps: For a map of Sequoia National Forest, send $6 to U.S. Forest Service, Map Sales, P.O. Box 587, Camino, CA 95709; tel. (530) 647-5390 or website: www.r5.fs.fed.us/visitorcenter. A more detailed map is available for a fee from Tom Harrison Cartography, tel. (415) 456-7940, or Trails Illustrated, tel. (800) 962-1643. Ask the USGS for a topographic map of the Muir Grove area.

Directions: From Fresno drive east on Highway 180 for 55 miles to the Big Stump entrance station at Kings Canyon National Park. Continue 1.5 miles and turn right on the Generals Highway, heading for Sequoia National Park. Drive seven miles and turn left on Forest Service Road 14S11, at the sign for Big Meadows and Horse Corral. Drive four miles, passing Big Meadows Trailhead and Big Meadows Campground, and turn right on the dirt road .5 mile beyond the camp (it's just past the bridge over Big Meadows Creek). Drive .5 mile to the fork, turn left, and turn right immediately afterward. Drive one more mile and park at the road's end at the Fox Meadow trailhead. Total mileage from Big Meadows Road is 1.5 miles.

Contact: Sequoia National Forest, Hume Lake Ranger District, 35860 E. Kings Canyon Road, Dunlap, CA 93621; tel. (559) 338-2251 or fax (559) 338-2131.

🕉 Mitchell Peak

5.2 mi/3.0 hrs

If you've got the legs for a 2,000-foot climb over 2.6 miles, you can stand atop the summit of Mitchell Peak, the highest point in the Jennie Lakes Wilderness, at 10,365 feet in elevation. The peak used to have a fire lookout tower on top of it, but the Forest Service stopped using it and burned it down. What remains is the fabulous view, one of the best in this area. It's a one-mile climb from the trailhead to Marvin Pass and the boundary of the Jennie Lakes Wilderness. Bear left (east) and climb some more. At 1.6 miles you reach the next junction,

signed for Mitchell Peak. Head left (north), and in one more mile you'll make the brief climb to Mitchell's summit, which straddles the border of Kings Canyon National Park. From your rocky perch you can look out on the Great Western Divide and the Silliman Crest. It's not a bad spot to catch your breath.

Location: In the Jennie Lakes Wilderness; map F5, grid h0.

User groups: Hikers, dogs, and horses. No mountain bikes. No wheelchair facilities.

Permits: A free wilderness permit is required for overnight stays and is available from the Hume Lake Ranger Station. There is a $10 entrance fee for access to this section of Sequoia National Forest, payable at any of the entrance stations to Kings Canyon and Sequoia National Parks. The fee is good for seven days in both the national forest and the national parks.

Maps: For a map of Sequoia National Forest, send $6 to U.S. Forest Service, Map Sales, P.O. Box 587, Camino, CA 95709; tel. (530) 647-5390 or website: www.r5.fs.fed.us/visitorcenter. A more detailed map is available for a fee from Tom Harrison Cartography, tel. (415) 456-7940, or Trails Illustrated, tel. (800) 962-1643. Ask the USGS for a topographic map of the Muir Grove area.

Directions: From Fresno drive east on Highway 180 for 55 miles to the Big Stump entrance station at Kings Canyon National Park. Continue 1.5 miles and turn right on the Generals Highway, heading for Sequoia National Park. Drive seven miles and turn left on Forest Service Road 14S11, at the sign for Big Meadow and Horse Corral. Drive four miles to the Big Meadow Campground and continue six more miles to Horse Corral Meadow. Turn right on Forest Service Road 13S12 and drive 2.8 miles to the Marvin Pass Trailhead.

Contact: Sequoia National Forest, Hume Lake Ranger District, 35860 E. Kings Canyon Road, Dunlap, CA 93621; tel. (559) 338-2251 or fax (559) 338-2131.

31 Big Baldy

4.6 mi/2.5 hrs

The trip to Big Baldy comes with a million views and a little workout besides. Views? We're talking Redwood Canyon, Redwood Mountain, Buena Vista Peak, Little Baldy, Buck Rock, and the Great Western Divide. A little workout? You've got to climb 1,000 feet, but it's nicely spread out over two miles. The trail alternates between thick forest cover and open granite areas as it winds along the rim of Redwood Canyon. In the forested stretches, we were amazed at how many birds were singing in the tall firs and cedars. The trail's initial vistas are to the west, but they keep changing and getting more interesting all the way to Big Baldy's 8,209-foot summit, where your view opens up to 360 degrees. Here you get your first wide-open views of the high Sierra peaks and the Great Western Divide to the east. This trail is so fun and rewarding with so little suffering involved that you may feel as if you're getting away with something. A bonus: because the first mile of trail faces to the west, this is a great area for watching the sunset.

Location: In Sequoia National Park, southeast of the Grant Grove area of Kings Canyon National Park; map F5, grid i0.

User groups: Hikers only. No dogs, horses, or mountain bikes. No wheelchair facilities.

Permits: No permits are required. There is a $10 entrance fee at Sequoia and Kings Canyon National Parks, good for seven days.

Maps: Free park maps are available at park entrance stations or by contacting Sequoia and Kings Canyon National Parks at the address below. A more detailed map is available for a fee from Tom Harrison Cartography, tel. (415) 456-7940, or Trails Illustrated, tel. (800) 962-1643. Ask the USGS for a topographic map of the Muir Grove area.

Directions: From Fresno drive east on Highway 180 for 55 miles to the Big Stump entrance station at Kings Canyon National Park. Continue 1.5 miles and turn right on the Generals Highway, heading for Sequoia National Park. Drive approximately 6.5 miles on the Generals Highway to the Big Baldy Trailhead on the right, shortly before the turnoff for Big Meadows on the left.

Contact: Sequoia and Kings Canyon National Parks, Three Rivers, CA 93271-9700; tel. (559) 565-3134 or (559) 335-2856.

32 Muir Grove

4.0 mi/2.0 hrs

Few people hike this trail unless they happen to be staying at Dorst Campground, so you have a lot better chance of seeing big sequoias in solitude in the Muir Grove than at many places in the park. After crossing a wooden footbridge, the trail enters a mixed forest of red fir, white fir, sugar pines, and incense cedars. In early summer you can count the many varieties of wildflowers along the trail, especially where you cross tiny streams. The trail heads west and curves around a deeply carved canyon at one mile out. Just off the trail to your right is a bare granite slab with an inspiring westward view. The trail undulates, never climbing or dropping much, making this an easy and pleasant stroll. At 1.9 miles you reach the Muir Grove, a small, pristine grove of huge sequoias—the first one you come to on your left is a doozy. The grove is made even more enchanting by the thick undergrowth of blue and purple lupine blooming amid the trees.

Location: Northwest of the Lodgepole area of Sequoia National Park; map F5, grid i0.

User groups: Hikers only. No dogs, horses, or mountain bikes. No wheelchair facilities.

Permits: No permits are required. There is a $10 entrance fee at Sequoia and Kings Canyon National Parks, good for seven days.

Maps: Free park maps are available at park entrance stations or by contacting Sequoia and Kings Canyon National Parks at the address below. A more detailed map is available for a fee from Tom Harrison Cartography, tel. (415) 456-7940, or Trails Illustrated, tel. (800) 962-1643. Ask the USGS for a topographic map of the Muir Grove area.

Directions: From Fresno drive east on Highway 180 for 55 miles to the Big Stump entrance station at Kings Canyon National Park. Continue 1.5 miles and turn right on the Generals Highway, heading for Sequoia National Park. Drive approximately 17 miles on the Generals Highway to the right turnoff for Dorst Campground. Turn right and drive through the campground to the amphitheater parking lot. Park there; the trail begins at a footbridge between the amphitheater parking lot and the group campground.

Contact: Sequoia and Kings Canyon National Parks, Three Rivers, CA 93271-9700; tel. (559) 565-3134 or (559) 335-2856.

33 Little Baldy
3.5 mi/2.0 hrs

Little Baldy, Big Baldy, Buena Vista Peak—along this stretch of the Generals Highway, there are so many big rocks you can hike up that provide far-reaching views, it's hard to know where to start. Start here, on the Little Baldy Trail. It's a little more challenging than the Buena Vista Peak Trail, but it's shorter than the Big Baldy Trail, and it offers eye-popping drama for remarkably little effort. Some claim that Little Baldy's view of the Silliman Crest, the Great Western Divide, Castle Rocks, Moro Rock, the Kaweah River Canyon, and the San Joaquin foothills is the best panorama in the park.

To see for yourself, set out from the trailhead, climbing through long, tree-shaded switchbacks, heading first north, then south. Check out the unusual view of Big Baldy off to your left (far across the highway) as you climb. After 1.2 miles, the trail leaves the forest and its many wildflowers, and your views start to open up. Hike along Little Baldy's ridgeline and make the final steep summit ascent. The trail gets a little hard to discern as you near Little Baldy's wide, bare summit, but just wander around until you find the highest spot with the best view. Take a seat—you'll want to stay a while.

Special note: Be sure to pick a clear day for this hike. In summer your best bet is to hike the trail early in the morning, before the Central Valley haze rises to the mountains.

Location: Northwest of the Lodgepole area of Sequoia National Park; map F5, grid i0.

User groups: Hikers only. No dogs, horses, or mountain bikes. No wheelchair facilities.

Permits: No permits are required. There is a $10 entrance fee at Sequoia and Kings Canyon National Parks, good for seven days.

Maps: Free park maps are available at park entrance stations or by contacting Sequoia and Kings Canyon National Parks at the address below. A more detailed map is available for a fee from Tom Harrison Cartography, tel. (415) 456-7940, or Trails Illustrated, tel. (800) 962-1643. Ask the USGS for topographic maps of the Muir Grove and Giant Forest areas.

Directions: From Fresno drive east on Highway 180 for 55 miles to the Big Stump entrance station at Kings Canyon National Park. Continue 1.5 miles and turn right on the Generals Highway, heading for Sequoia National Park. Drive approximately 18 miles on the Generals Highway to the Little Baldy Trailhead on the left, a mile beyond the turnoff for Dorst Campground.

Contact: Sequoia and Kings Canyon National Parks, Three Rivers, CA 93271-9700; tel. (559) 565-3134 or (559) 335-2856.

34 Kearsage Pass
10.0 mi/
6.0 hrs or 2.0 days

The trailhead elevation for the Kearsage Pass Trail is 9,200 feet, and the elevation at Kearsage Pass is 11,823 feet. There are five miles and a good amount of climbing in between, but the route is well graded and the scenery is spectacular. The trail, which was once an Indian trading route, leads to the backcountry of Kings Canyon National Park, but most day-hikers just make the trip to the pass. Along the way, you pass several sparkling lakes and whitewater cascades, and a wealth of high-country wildflowers. Remember to bring sunglasses, sunscreen, and a jacket for the summit, which is windy and exposed. The trail climbs gradually from the trailhead, frequently nearing Independence Creek and veering away through a multitude of switchbacks. You pass Little Pothole Lake at 1.5 miles, Gilbert Lake at 2.2 miles, and Flower Lake at 2.6 miles. Continue climbing high above tree line to Kearsage Pass. You'll get a long-distance view of Heart Lake and pass the left spur trail leading to Big Pothole Lake along the way. Finally, just when you think you can climb no farther, you reach the pass at 5 miles. A wooden sign announces your arrival in Kings Canyon Park, and extraordinary Sierra views surround you. Note that if you decide to turn this into an overnight trip, food storage regulations are in effect. The bears have smartened up to the old hang-the-food-in-the-tree routine, so bear-resistant canisters are required for all backpackers. Also, you must have a backpacking stove because campfires are not permitted.

Location: In the John Muir Wilderness in Inyo National Forest; map F5, grid i6.

User groups: Hikers, dogs, and horses. Dogs are allowed to Kearsage Pass, but not beyond it. No mountain bikes. No wheelchair facilities.

Permits: No day-hiking permits are required. A free wilderness permit is required for overnight stays. Quotas are in effect from the last Friday in June to September 15; permits are available in advance by mail or fax for this period for a $5 fee. Phone (760) 873-2408 for permit information, or visit website: www.r5.fs.fed.us/inyo.

Maps: For a map of Inyo National Forest, send $6 to U.S. Forest Service, Map Sales, P.O. Box 587, Camino, CA 95709; tel. (530) 647-5390 or website: www.r5.fs.fed.us/visitorcenter. Ask the USGS for a topographic map of the Kearsage Peak area.

Directions: From Lone Pine drive 15 miles north on U.S. 395 to Independence. Turn west on Market Street, which becomes Onion Valley Road. Drive 14 miles to the end of the road

and the trailhead at the hiker parking area.

Contact: Inyo National Forest, Mount Whitney Ranger District, P.O. Box 8, Lone Pine, CA 93545; tel. (760) 876-6200 or fax (760) 876-6202.

35 Flower and Matlock Lakes
6.4 mi/3.5 hrs

If you don't have the time or the energy for the Kearsage Pass Trail, the route to Flower Lake and Matlock Lake is a close second choice. While it doesn't offer the astounding views that the pass has, it is still a stellar trip into dramatic granite country, where little grows in the harsh, exposed conditions above tree line. The beauty here can pull at your heartstrings, with both lakes being deep blue waterways that draw in all the color of the Sierra sky. The trail climbs gradually from the trailhead, switchbacking along Independence Creek. You pass Little Pothole Lake at 1.5 miles and Gilbert Lake at 2.2 miles, reaching a junction for Matlock Lake at 2.5 miles. Continue straight for .1 mile to Flower Lake, then retrace your steps to the junction and head south for .7 mile to larger Matlock Lake. Pull out your camera and a picnic and while away some time before returning to the trailhead.

Location: In the John Muir Wilderness in Inyo National Forest; map F5, grid i6.

User groups: Hikers, dogs, and horses. No mountain bikes. No wheelchair facilities.

Permits: No day-hiking permits are required. Parking and access are free.

Maps: For a map of Inyo National Forest, send $6 to U.S. Forest Service, Map Sales, P.O. Box 587, Camino, CA 95709; tel. (530) 647-5390 or website: www.r5.fs.fed.us/visitorcenter. Ask the USGS for a topographic map of the Kearsage Peak area.

Directions: From Lone Pine drive 15 miles north on U.S. 395 to Independence. Turn west on Market Street, which becomes Onion Valley Road. Drive 14 miles to the end of the road and the trailhead at the hiker parking area.

Contact: Inyo National Forest, Mount Whitney Ranger District, P.O. Box 8, Lone Pine, CA 93545; tel. (760) 876-6200 or fax (760) 876-6202.

36 Robinson Lake

3.0 mi/2.0 hrs

The Robinson Lake Trail is best described as relentlessly steep, but mercifully short. The hike is challenging in places due to the grade and relative obscurity of the trail, but the destination is superlative. In addition to beautiful Robinson Lake at 10,500 feet, you get a close and personal view of 11,744-foot Independence Peak, and an excellent wildflower display along Robinson Creek. Start by hiking up the stream just beyond campsite eight in Onion Valley Campground. Watch out for overgrown vegetation that can sometimes hide the trail. Just climb, catch your breath, and climb some more. You'll reach the shallow lake in less than an hour. Campsites and picnicking sites are found in the sand on the lake's east side, or in the pine forest on the northwest side. Plan your trip for July to September; the trail is usually free of snow to the lake by midsummer.

Location: In the John Muir Wilderness in Inyo National Forest; map F5, grid i6.

User groups: Hikers, dogs, and horses. No mountain bikes. No wheelchair facilities.

Permits: No day-hiking permits are required. A free wilderness permit is required for overnight stays. Quotas are in effect from the last Friday in June to September 15; permits are available in advance by mail or fax for this period for a $5 fee. Phone (760) 873-2408 for permit information, or visit website: www.r5.fs. fed.us/inyo.

Maps: For a map of Inyo National Forest, send $6 to U.S. Forest Service, Map Sales, P.O. Box 587, Camino, CA 95709; tel. (530) 647-5390 or website: www.r5.fs.fed.us/visitorcenter. Ask the USGS for a topographic map of the Kearsage Peak area.

Directions: From Lone Pine drive 15 miles north on U.S. 395 to Independence. Turn west on Market Street, which becomes Onion Valley Road. Drive 14 miles to the end of the road and the hiker parking area. Walk into Onion Valley Campground to find the trailhead.

Contact: Inyo National Forest, Mount Whitney Ranger District, P.O. Box 8, Lone Pine, CA 93545; tel. (760) 876-6200 or fax (760) 876-6202.

37 Marble Falls

7.0 mi/4.0 hrs

This is the waterfall to see in Sequoia and Kings Canyon in winter and spring, when there's no access to snowed-in Tokopah Falls or Mist Falls. March and April are particularly good months to visit because of high flows in the Marble Fork Kaweah River, excellent spring wildflowers in the grasslands, and chaparral that line the trail. From its rather banal start as a dirt road, this trail just keeps getting better as it follows the Marble Fork. There are no trail junctions to worry about; at 3.5 miles, the path simply dead-ends near the lower cascades of Marble Falls. Although much of the falls are hidden in the narrow, rocky river gorge, tucked out of sight, what is visible is an impressive billowing cascade of whitewater. Be very careful on the slippery granite near the river's edges; the current and cold water are even more dangerous than they look. Aside from the waterfalls and the wildflowers, the other highlights on this trail are the colorful outcroppings of marble, particularly in the last mile as you near the falls. Remember, though, that in summer this area of the park can bake like an oven. If you make the trip to the falls from late May to September, get an early morning start.

Location: Off Highway 198 in the Foothills region of Sequoia National Park; map F5, grid j0.

User groups: Hikers only. No dogs, horses, or mountain bikes. No wheelchair facilities.

Permits: No permits are required. There is a $10 entrance fee at Sequoia and Kings Canyon National Parks, good for seven days.

Maps: Free park maps are available at park

entrance stations or by contacting Sequoia and Kings Canyon National Parks at the address below. A more detailed map is available for a fee from Tom Harrison Cartography, tel. (415) 456-7940, or Trails Illustrated, tel. (800) 962-1643. Ask the USGS for a topographic map of the Giant Forest area.

Directions: From Visalia drive east on Highway 198 for 44 miles to the turnoff on the left for Potwisha Campground, 3.8 miles east of the Ash Mountain entrance station to Sequoia National Park. The trail begins next to campsite 16 in Potwisha Campground; park in the day-use parking area in the camp.

Contact: Sequoia and Kings Canyon National Parks, Three Rivers, CA 93271-9700; tel. (559) 565-3134 or (559) 335-2856.

38 Potwisha to Hospital Rock
5.0 mi/2.5 hrs

First, some advice: don't hike this trail on a hot day. If it's summertime and you want to the see the Monache Indian historical sites at Potwisha and Hospital Rock, drive to each of them and see them separately. In winter or spring, however, it's far more fun to take this five-mile hike through chaparral and oak woodlands, especially in March when the wildflowers bloom. In the first 100 yards from the trailhead, you'll see Native American grinding holes and pictographs, which look roughly like people and animals. You'll also pass many tempting pools in the Middle Fork Kaweah, which get a lot of swimmers in the summer. The trail climbs a gradual 2.5 miles from Potwisha to Hospital Rock, crossing the highway after the first mile. When you reach Hospital Rock, which is just a few feet off the road to Buckeye Flat Campground, you see a huge display of pictographs on its side. Across the campground road are more grinding holes in the boulders, and near them, a short paved path leads to deep pools and sandy beaches on the Middle Fork. Another path leads from the camp road to the underside of Hospital Rock, where there's a large,

cavelike shelter. This is where a Native American medicine man healed the sick and injured, resulting in a white man naming this place Hospital Rock.

Location: Off Highway 198 in the Foothills region of Sequoia National Park; map F5, grid j0.

User groups: Hikers only. No dogs, horses, or mountain bikes. No wheelchair facilities.

Permits: No permits are required. There is a $10 entrance fee at Sequoia and Kings Canyon National Parks, good for seven days.

Maps: Free park maps are available at park entrance stations or by contacting Sequoia and Kings Canyon National Parks at the address below. A more detailed map is available for a fee from Tom Harrison Cartography, tel. (415) 456-7940, or Trails Illustrated, tel. (800) 962-1643. Ask the USGS for a topographic map of the Giant Forest area.

Directions: From Visalia drive east on Highway 198 for 44 miles to the turnoff on the left for Potwisha Campground, 3.8 miles east of the Ash Mountain entrance station to Sequoia National Park. Don't turn left into Potwisha campground; instead, turn right on the paved road opposite the campground. Drive past the RV dumping station to the signed trailhead and parking area.

Contact: Sequoia and Kings Canyon National Parks, Three Rivers, CA 93271-9700; tel. (559) 565-3134 or (559) 335-2856.

39 Middle Fork Trail to Panther Creek
6.0 mi/3.0 hrs

You want to be alone? You don't want to see anybody else on the trail? Okay, just sign up for this trip any time between June and September, when the foothills have warmed up to their summer extremes. Don't be fooled by this path's name: the Middle Fork Trail is no streamside meander. Rather, it's a shadeless, exposed trail that leads high along the canyon of the Middle Fork Kaweah River—always at least 250 feet above it. In summer it's hot as Hades. Of course, that's what makes this trail perfect in winter and spring. While most other trails in Sequoia and Kings Canyon are still snowed under, you can take an early season day hike or backpacking trip along the Middle Fork Trail. The main destination is Panther Creek at three miles, where the trail leads across the brink of Panther Creek's 100-foot dive into the Kaweah River. But you can hike farther, if you wish. Although the Middle Fork Trail is set in grasslands and chaparral, it offers some stunning views of the area's geology, including Moro Rock, Castle Rocks, and the Great Western Divide. We hiked this trail in August, and despite the fact that we were wilting from the heat, the wide views kept our spirits up.

Location: Off Highway 198 in the Foothills region of Sequoia National Park; map F5, grid j0.

User groups: Hikers only. No dogs, horses, or mountain bikes. No wheelchair facilities.

Permits: No permits are required. There is a $10 entrance fee at Sequoia and Kings Canyon National Parks, good for seven days.

Maps: Free park maps are available at park entrance stations or by contacting Sequoia and Kings Canyon National Parks at the address below. A more detailed map is available for a fee from Tom Harrison Cartography, tel. (415) 456-7940, or Trails Illustrated, tel. (800) 962-1643. Ask the USGS for a topographic map of the Giant Forest area.

Directions: From Visalia drive east on Highway 198 for 47 miles to the turnoff on the right for Buckeye Flat Campground, across from Hospital Rock. Turn right and drive .5 mile to a left fork just before the campground. Bear left on the dirt road and drive 1.3 miles to the trailhead and parking area. In the winter, you must park at Hospital Rock and walk in to the trailhead, adding 3.6 miles to your round-trip.

Contact: Sequoia and Kings Canyon National Parks, Three Rivers, CA 93271-9700; tel. (559) 565-3134 or (559) 335-2856.

40 Paradise Creek Trail

1.2 mi/0.75 hr

From Buckeye Flat Campground, the Paradise Creek Trail meanders through oaks and buckeyes and crosses a long, picturesque footbridge over the Middle Fork Kaweah River. An inviting, Olympic-sized pool is on the right side of the bridge, where campers often go swimming on summer afternoons. Save the pool for after your hike; for now, take the signed Paradise Creek Trail at the far side of the bridge. You'll briefly visit the creek and then leave it, climbing into oak and grassland terrain. There are some high views of Moro Rock and Hanging Rock, but most of the beauty is right at your feet, in the springtime flowers that grow in the grasses and the leafy blue oaks that shade them. The maintained trail ends when it reaches Paradise Creek again, although a faint route continues along its banks.

Location: Off Highway 198 in the Foothills region of Sequoia National Park; map F5, grid j0.

User groups: Hikers only. No dogs, horses, or mountain bikes. No wheelchair facilities.

Permits: No permits are required. There is a $10 entrance fee at Sequoia and Kings Canyon National Parks, good for seven days.

Maps: Free park maps are available at park entrance stations or by contacting Sequoia and Kings Canyon National Parks at the address below. A more detailed map is available for a fee from Tom Harrison Cartography, tel. (415) 456-7940, or Trails Illustrated, tel. (800) 962-1643. Ask the USGS for a topographic map of the Giant Forest area.

Directions: From Visalia drive east on Highway 198 for 47 miles to the turnoff on the right for Buckeye Flat Campground, across from Hospital Rock. Turn right and drive .6 mile to the campground. Park in any of the dirt pullouts outside of the camp entrance; no day-use parking is allowed in the camp. You can also park at Hospital Rock and walk to the campground. The trailhead is near campsite 28.

Contact: Sequoia and Kings Canyon National Parks, Three Rivers, CA 93271-9700; tel. (559) 565-3134 or (559) 335-2856.

41 Sunset Rock

2.0 mi/1.0 hr

The trail to Sunset Rock is a first-rate easy hike, perfect at sunset, that gets much less traffic than you might expect, considering its proximity to Giant Forest. To hike to the rock, you must first park by the new Giant Forest Museum, then cross the road and pick up the signed trail. The path is lined with worn pavement and is almost completely flat. It leads through a mixed forest (with a handful of giant sequoias) and crosses Little Deer Creek on its way to Sunset Rock. The rock is a gargantuan, flat piece of granite, about the size of a football field, set at 6,412 foot in elevation. Standing on it, you get a terrific overlook of Little Baldy to your right, and a sea of conifers below in the Marble Fork Kaweah River Canyon.

Location: Off the Generals Highway in the Giant Forest area of Sequoia National Park; map F5, grid j1.

User groups: Hikers only. No dogs, horses, or mountain bikes. No wheelchair facilities.

Permits: No permits are required. There is a $10 entrance fee at Sequoia and Kings Canyon National Parks, good for seven days.

Maps: Free park maps are available at park entrance stations or by contacting Sequoia and Kings Canyon National Parks at the address below. A more detailed map is available for a fee from Tom Harrison Cartography, tel. (415) 456-7940, or Trails Illustrated, tel. (800) 962-1643. Ask the USGS for a topographic map of the Giant Forest area.

Directions: From Fresno drive east on Highway 180 for 55 miles to the Big Stump entrance station at Kings Canyon National Park. Continue 1.5 miles and turn right on the Generals Highway, heading for Sequoia National Park. Drive approximately 30 miles on the Generals Highway, past Lodgepole and Wolverton, to the

Giant Forest area of Sequoia National Park. Park near the new Giant Forest Museum.

Contact: Sequoia and Kings Canyon National Parks, Three Rivers, CA 93271-9700; tel. (559) 565-3134 or (559) 335-2856.

42 Moro Rock

0.6 mi/0.5 hr

Just about everybody has heard of Moro Rock, the prominent, pointy granite dome with the top-of-the-world sunset vistas, and if you're visiting the Giant Forest area of Sequoia National Park, well, you just have to hike to the top of it. When you climb those 380 stairs to the dome's summit and check out the view, you realize that unlike many famous attractions, Moro Rock is not overrated. It's as great as everybody says, maybe even better. If you start your trip from the Moro Rock parking area, it's only .3 mile to the top, climbing switchbacks, ramps, and granite stairs the whole way. If you want to hike more, you can start your walk from Giant Forest Village on the Moro Rock, Bear Hill, or Soldiers Trails, adding about three miles to your round-trip. Railings line the rock-blasted trail to keep you from dropping off the 6,725-foot granite dome. What's the view like? Well, on a clear day, you can see all the way to the Coast Range, 100 miles away. In closer focus is the Middle Fork Kaweah River, the Great Western Divide, Castle Rocks at 9,180 feet, Triple Divide Peak at 12,634 feet, Mount Stewart at 12,205 feet . . . and on and on. In a word, it's awesome. And even better, you don't get this view just from the top of Moro Rock—you get it all the way up, at every turn in the trail.

Our favorite tip: Check out the view from Moro Rock at sunset.

Location: Off the Generals Highway in the Giant Forest area of Sequoia National Park; map F5, grid j1.

User groups: Hikers only. No dogs, horses, or mountain bikes. No wheelchair facilities.

Permits: No permits are required. There is a $10 entrance

fee at Sequoia and Kings Canyon National Parks, good for seven days.

Maps: Free park maps are available at park entrance stations or by contacting Sequoia and Kings Canyon National Parks at the address below. A more detailed map is available for a fee from Tom Harrison Cartography, tel. (415) 456-7940, or Trails Illustrated, tel. (800) 962-1643. Ask the USGS for a topographic map of the Giant Forest area.

Directions: From Fresno drive east on Highway 180 for 55 miles to the Big Stump entrance station at Kings Canyon National Park. Continue 1.5 miles and turn right on the Generals Highway, heading for Sequoia National Park. Drive approximately 30 miles on the Generals Highway, past Lodgepole and Wolverton, to the Giant Forest area of Sequoia National Park. Just beyond the museum, turn left on Crescent Meadow Road, drive 1.5 miles, and take the right fork to the Moro Rock parking area.

Contact: Sequoia and Kings Canyon National Parks, Three Rivers, CA 93271-9700; tel. (559) 565-3134 or (559) 335-2856.

43 Crescent Meadow and Tharp's Log

1.6 mi/1.0 hr

Crescent Meadow is more than 1.5 miles long and surrounded by giant sequoias. John Muir called it "the gem of the Sierras." We don't know how Muir would feel about the pavement that lines the trail around this precious meadow, but we hope he'd like this loop hike anyhow. Follow the pavement for 200 yards from the eastern side of the parking lot, and just like that you're at the southern edge of beautiful Crescent Meadow. Take the right fork and head for Log Meadow and Tharp's Log. Log Meadow is as large and beautiful as Crescent Meadow, and Tharp's Log was the homestead of Hale Tharp, the first white man to enter this forest. He grazed cattle and horses here and built a modest home inside a fallen, fire-hollowed sequoia. You can look inside Tharp's Log and see his bed, fireplace, dining room table, and the door and windows he fashioned into the log. (Children find this incredibly thrilling.) From Tharp's Log, continue your loop back to Crescent Meadow and around its west side, where you return to the north edge of the parking lot.

Location: Off the Generals Highway in the Giant Forest area of Sequoia National Park; map F5, grid j1.

User groups: Hikers and wheelchairs (with assistance). No dogs, horses, or mountain bikes.

Permits: No permits are required. There is a $10 entrance fee at Sequoia and Kings Canyon National Parks, good for seven days.

Maps: Free park maps are available at park entrance stations or by contacting Sequoia and Kings Canyon National Parks at the address below. A more detailed map is available for a fee from Tom Harrison Cartography, tel. (415) 456-7940, or Trails Illustrated, tel. (800) 962-1643. Ask the USGS for topographic maps of the Lodgepole and Giant Forest areas.

Directions: From Fresno drive east on Highway 180 for 55 miles to the Big Stump entrance station at Kings Canyon National Park. Continue 1.5 miles and turn right on the Generals Highway, heading for Sequoia National Park. Drive approximately 30 miles on the Generals Highway, past Lodgepole and Wolverton, to the Giant Forest area of Sequoia National Park. Just beyond the museum, turn left on Crescent Meadow Road and drive 3.5 miles to the Crescent Meadow parking area.

Contact: Sequoia and Kings Canyon National Parks, Three Rivers, CA 93271-9700; tel. (559) 565-3134 or (559) 335-2856.

44 High Sierra Trail and Eagle View

1.5 mi/1.0 hr

Are you ready to be wowed? From the lower parking lot at Crescent Meadow, follow the trail that leads to the southern edge of Crescent Meadow and at .1 mile take the right fork that leads up the ridge on the High Sierra Trail toward Eagle View. The High Sierra Trail is a popular trans-Sierra route that eventually leads to Mount Whitney, the highest peak in the contiguous United States. On this trip you won't go quite that far, but you will get a taste of the visual delights of this extraordinary trail. In less than .5 mile, you'll gain the ridge and start getting wondrous, edge-of-the-world views. Numerous wildflowers line the path, which hugs the edge of this high ridge. At .7 mile, you'll reach Eagle View, an unsigned but obvious lookout from which you get a fascinating look at Moro Rock to your right, Castle Rocks straight ahead, and dozens of peaks and ridges of the Western Divide far across the canyon. The vistas are so fine and the trail is so good that you might just want to keep walking all the way to Mount Whitney.

Location: Off the Generals Highway in the Giant Forest area of Sequoia National Park; map F5, grid j1.

User groups: Hikers only. No dogs, horses, or mountain bikes. No wheelchair facilities.

Permits: No permits are required. There is a $10 entrance fee at Sequoia and Kings Canyon National Parks, good for seven days.

Maps: Free park maps are available at park entrance stations or by contacting Sequoia and Kings Canyon National Parks at the address below. A more detailed map is available for a fee from Tom Harrison Cartography, tel. (415) 456-7940, or Trails Illustrated, tel. (800) 962-1643. Ask the USGS for topographic maps of the Lodgepole and Giant Forest areas.

Directions: From Fresno drive east on Highway 180 for 55 miles to the Big Stump entrance station at Kings Canyon National Park. Continue 1.5 miles and turn right on the Generals Highway, heading for Sequoia National Park. Drive approximately 30 miles on the Generals Highway, past Lodgepole and Wolverton, to the Giant Forest area of Sequoia National Park. Just beyond the museum, turn left on Crescent Meadow Road and drive 3.5 miles to the Crescent Meadow parking area.

Contact: Sequoia and Kings Canyon National Parks, Three Rivers, CA 93271-9700; tel. (559) 565-3134 or (559) 335-2856.

45 High Sierra Trail to Hamilton Lake

30.0 mi/3.0 days

This is a classic, easy-to-moderate, three-day backpacking trip in the High Sierra, with a two-night stay at Bearpaw Meadow Camp, a shady campground that clings to the edge of a granite gorge. The route follows the High Sierra Trail from Crescent Meadow to Eagle View, then continues for 10 nearly level miles along the north rim of the Middle Fork Kaweah River Canyon. It's views, views, views all the way.

After a good night's sleep at Bearpaw Meadow, elevation 7,700 feet (reservations for a wilderness permit are definitely necessary in the summer months), you start out on an eight-mile round-trip day hike to Upper and Lower Hamilton Lake, at 8,300 feet, set in a glacially carved basin at the base of the peaks of the Great Western Divide. On the final day you hike 11 miles back to Crescent Meadow, once again witnessing 180-degree views from the sunny High Sierra Trail. By the time it's all over and you're back home, your mind is completely blown by all the high-country beauty, and you've shot about a million pictures, none of which can compare to the experience of actually being there.

Location: Off the Generals Highway in the Giant Forest area of Sequoia National Park; map F5, grid j1.

User groups: Hikers only. No dogs, horses, or mountain bikes. No wheelchair facilities.

Permits: There is a $10 entrance fee at Sequoia and Kings Canyon National Parks, good for seven days. A free wilderness permit is required for overnight stays and is available on a first-come, first-served basis at the Lodgepole Visitor Center, or in advance by mail or fax after March 1; for more information phone (559) 565-3708.

Maps: Free park maps are available at park entrance stations or by contacting Sequoia and Kings Canyon National Parks at the address below. A more detailed map is available for a fee from Tom Harrison Cartography, tel. (415) 456-7940, or Trails Illustrated, tel. (800) 962-1643. Ask the USGS for topographic maps of the Lodgepole and Giant Forest areas.

Directions: From Fresno drive east on Highway 180 for 55 miles to the Big Stump entrance station at Kings Canyon National Park. Continue 1.5 miles and turn right on the Generals Highway, heading for Sequoia National Park. Drive approximately 30 miles on the Generals Highway, past Lodgepole and Wolverton, to the Giant Forest area of Sequoia National Park. Just beyond the museum, turn left on Crescent Meadow Road and drive 3.5 miles to the Crescent Meadow parking area.

Contact: Sequoia and Kings Canyon National Parks, Three Rivers, CA 93271-9700; tel. (559) 565-3134 or (559) 335-2856.

46 Hazelwood and Huckleberry Loop

4.5 mi/2.0 hrs

This hike combines two loop trails in the Giant Forest area for an easy but excellent day hike, passing by many giant sequoias and peaceful grassy meadows. A bonus: these trails are generally less crowded than the other day hikes in the Giant Forest area.

From the Generals Highway, pick up the Hazelwood Nature Trail and take the right side of the loop to join the Alta Trail and the Huckleberry Meadow Trail Loop. Take the Alta Trail for .25 mile and bear right on the Huckleberry Meadow Trail, climbing a bit for one mile to the site of Squatter's Cabin, one of the oldest structures in Sequoia National Park, dating back to the 1880s. To stay on the loop, turn left by the cabin (don't take the trail signed for the Dead Giant). The trail skirts the edge of Huckleberry Meadow and heads north to Circle Meadow, where giant sequoias line the meadow's edges. There are several junctions, but stay on the Huckleberry Meadow Trail. A half mile farther is a short spur trail on the left heading to the Washington Tree. Follow the

spur to see the second largest tree in the world (after General Sherman)—it's 30 feet in diameter and 246.1 feet tall. The trip finishes out on the Alta Trail, where you return to the Hazelwood Nature Trail and walk the opposite side of its short loop, back to the Generals Highway.

Location: Off the Generals Highway in the Giant Forest area of Sequoia National Park; map F5, grid j1.

User groups: Hikers only. No dogs, horses, or mountain bikes. No wheelchair facilities.

Permits: No permits are required. There is a $10 entrance fee at Sequoia and Kings Canyon National Parks, good for seven days.

Maps: Free park maps are available at park entrance stations or by contacting Sequoia and Kings Canyon National Parks at the address below. A more detailed map is available for a fee from Tom Harrison Cartography, tel. (415) 456-7940, or Trails Illustrated, tel. (800) 962-1643. Ask the USGS for a topographic map of the Giant Forest area.

Directions: From Fresno drive east on Highway 180 for 55 miles to the Big Stump entrance station at Kings Canyon National Park. Continue 1.5 miles and turn right on the Generals Highway, heading for Sequoia National Park. Drive approximately 30 miles on the Generals Highway, past Lodgepole and Wolverton, to the Giant Forest area of Sequoia National Park. The Hazelwood Trailhead is on the south side of the highway .25 mile before you reach the Giant Forest Museum.

Contact: Sequoia and Kings Canyon National Parks, Three Rivers, CA 93271-9700; tel. (559) 565-3134 or (559) 335-2856.

47 Congress Trail Loop

2.1 mi/1.0 hr

The Congress Trail, a two-mile loop that starts (and ends) at the General Sherman Tree, is a much-traveled route through the Giant Forest's prize grove of sequoias. The General Sherman gets the most visitors, of course, because it is recognized as the largest living thing in the world (not by height, but by volume). After you leave its side, the crowds lessen substantially. You'll pass by many huge trees with very patriotic names, like the House and Senate clusters, the McKinley Tree, the Lincoln Tree, and—you get the idea. Every single giant tree is worth stopping to gape at. We rate the Congress Trail as the best flat, easy trail for sequoia viewing in the park. Plus, the farther you walk, the more solitude you get. Make sure you pick up an interpretive brochure at the trailhead or at the Lodgepole Visitor Center, and get away from the crowds at the Sherman Tree as fast as you can.

Location: Off the Generals Highway in the Giant Forest area of Sequoia National Park; map F5, grid j1.

User groups: Hikers only. No dogs, horses, or mountain bikes. No wheelchair facilities.

Permits: No permits are required. There is a $10 entrance fee at Sequoia and Kings Canyon National Parks, good for seven days.

Maps: Free park maps are available at park entrance stations or by contacting Sequoia and Kings Canyon National Parks at the address below. A more detailed map is available for a fee from Tom Harrison Cartography, tel. (415) 456-7940, or Trails Illustrated, tel. (800) 962-1643. Ask the USGS for a topographic map of the Giant Forest area.

Directions: From Fresno drive east on Highway 180 for 55 miles to the Big Stump entrance station at Kings Canyon National Park. Continue 1.5 miles and turn right on the Generals Highway, heading for Sequoia National Park. Drive approximately 28 miles on the Generals Highway, past Lodgepole and Wolverton, to the signed turnoff on the left for the General Sherman Tree.

Contact: Sequoia and Kings Canyon National Parks, Three Rivers, CA 93271-9700; tel. (559) 565-3134 or (559) 335-2856.

48 The Lakes Trail

13.0 mi/2-3 days

The Wolverton Trailhead is at 7,200 feet, which gives you a boost at the start for this trip into the high country. The Lakes Trail is the most popular backpacking trip in Sequoia National Park, and it's easy to see why. Wide-open views and dramatic granite walls are standard fare as you hike. Part of the route is on a loop, with one side of the loop traveling to the Watchtower, a 1,600-foot-tall granite cliff that offers incredible vistas of Tokopah Valley and beyond. The trailside scenery begins in red fir forest, then enters polished granite country, and culminates in a rocky basin with three gem-like lakes—Heather, Emerald, and Pear— as well as many sparkling creeks. The total climb to Pear Lake is a mere 2,300 feet, spread out over 6.5 miles. Backpackers take note: you may camp only at Emerald and Pear Lakes, and no campfires are allowed.

Special note: The Watchtower Trail usually isn't open until midsummer. When it is closed, you must take the alternate Hump Trail, which is not as scenic. If you're planning a trip for early in the year, check with the park to be sure the Watchtower Trail is open.

Location: Off the Generals Highway in the Wolverton area of Sequoia National Park; map F5, grid i1.

User groups: Hikers only. No dogs, horses, or mountain bikes. No wheelchair facilities.

Permits: There is a $10 entrance fee at Sequoia and Kings Canyon National Parks, good for seven days. A free wilderness permit is required for overnight stays and is available on a first-come, first-served basis at the Lodgepole Visitor Center, or in advance by mail or fax after March 1; for more information phone (559) 565-3708.

Maps: Free park maps are available at park entrance stations or by contacting Sequoia and Kings Canyon National Parks at the address below. A more detailed map is available for a fee from Tom Harrison Cartography, tel. (415) 456-7940, or Trails Illustrated, tel. (800) 962-1643. Ask the USGS for a topographic map of the Lodgepole area.

Directions: From Fresno drive east on Highway 180 for 55 miles to the Big Stump entrance station at Kings Canyon National Park. Continue 1.5 miles and turn right on the Generals Highway, heading for Sequoia National Park. Drive approximately 27 miles on the Generals Highway, past the Lodgepole Village turnoff, to the Wolverton turnoff on the left (east) side of the road. Turn left and drive to the parking area and trailhead.

Contact: Sequoia and Kings Canyon National Parks, Three Rivers, CA 93271-9700; tel. (559) 565-3134 or (559) 335-2856.

49 Heather Lake and the Watchtower

9.0 mi/5.0 hrs

There's no reason that day-hikers should be denied the incredible joys of hiking the Lakes Trail from the Wolverton area of Sequoia National Park. You don't have to carry a backpack, get a wilderness permit, or have two or more free days to hike the first part of the Lakes Trail that makes the mind-blowing ascent to the top of the 1,600-foot Watchtower and then continues to rocky Heather Lake. If you're hiking in spring or early summer, call the park first to make sure the Watchtower Trail is open. Otherwise you'll have to take the alternate Hump Trail, which is steeper and nowhere near as thrilling. The route to the Watchtower is a ledge trail, blasted into hard granite, which creeps along the high rim of Tokopah Valley. Your view is straight down, 1,500 feet. You can even see tiny people walking on the path to Tokopah Falls. It's incredible, although perhaps not a good idea for people who are afraid of heights. Walking up to the Watchtower is plenty exciting, but it's even more so when you reach the other side, where you can look back and see what you were walking on. Just .75 mile farther and you're at Heather Lake, which is designated for day-use only, so it has no campsites. It has a steep granite backdrop and a few rocky ledges to sit on. Too many people here when you arrive? No big deal. It's only another .5 mile to even prettier Emerald Lake, and the trail is nearly

level. After a rest, you get to head back and hike the Watchtower route all over again.

Location: Off the Generals Highway in the Wolverton area of Sequoia National Park; map F5, grid i1.

User groups: Hikers only. No dogs, horses, or mountain bikes. No wheelchair facilities.

Permits: No permits are required. There is a $10 entrance fee at Sequoia and Kings Canyon National Parks, good for seven days.

Maps: Free park maps are available at park entrance stations or by contacting Sequoia and Kings Canyon National Parks at the address below. A more detailed map is available for a fee from Tom Harrison Cartography, tel. (415) 456-7940, or Trails Illustrated, tel. (800) 962-1643. Ask the USGS for a topographic map of the Lodgepole area.

Directions: From Fresno drive east on Highway 180 for 55 miles to the Big Stump entrance station at Kings Canyon National Park. Continue 1.5 miles and turn right on the Generals Highway, heading for Sequoia National Park. Drive approximately 27 miles on the Generals Highway, past the Lodgepole Village turnoff, to the Wolverton turnoff on the left (east) side of the road. Turn left and drive to the parking area and trailhead.

Contact: Sequoia and Kings Canyon National Parks, Three Rivers, CA 93271-9700; tel. (559) 565-3134 or (559) 335-2856.

50 Alta Peak

13.0 mi/1-2 days

You say you like heights? You like vistas? Here's your trail, a 4,000-foot climb to the top of Alta Peak, an 11,204-foot summit in the Alta Country. Alta Peak and Mount Whitney are the only summits in Sequoia National Park that have established trails, but both of them are still butt-kickers to reach. The trail to Alta Peak and Alta Meadow starts out the same as the Lakes Trail from the Wolverton parking area, then heads south (right) to Panther Gap at 1.8 miles. After climbing through the forest to Panther Gap at 8,450 feet, you get your first set of eye-popping views—of the Middle Fork Kaweah River and the Great Western Divide. Continue on the Alta Trail to Mehrten Meadow at 3.9 miles, a popular camping spot, then reach a junction where you can go left for Alta Peak or right to Alta Meadow. You'll want to take both spurs if you have the time and energy. If you're exhausted, just walk to Alta Meadow, with its flower-filled grasses and exquisite mountain views, a flat one mile away. Alta Peak is two miles away via the left fork, with a 2,000-foot climb. These two miles are considered one of the toughest stretches of trail in Sequoia National Park due to the brutal grade and the 10,000-plus foot elevation here above tree line. The summit is at 11,204 feet, and, of course, it offers a complete panorama. Even Mount Whitney and the Coast Range are visible on a clear day.

Location: Off the Generals Highway in the Wolverton area of Sequoia National Park; map F5, grid i1.

User groups: Hikers only. No dogs, horses, or mountain bikes. No wheelchair facilities.

Permits: There is a $10 entrance fee at Sequoia and Kings Canyon National Parks, good for seven days. A free wilderness permit is required for overnight stays. They are available on a first-come, first-served basis at Lodgepole Visitor Center or in advance by mail or fax after March 1; for more information phone (559) 565-3708.

Maps: Free park maps are available at park entrance stations or by contacting Sequoia and Kings Canyon National Parks at the address below. A more detailed map is available for a fee from Tom Harrison Cartography, tel. (415) 456-7940, or Trails Illustrated, tel. (800) 962-1643. Ask the USGS for a topographic map of the Lodgepole area.

Directions: From Fresno drive east on Highway 180 for 55 miles to the Big Stump entrance station at Kings Canyon National Park. Continue 1.5 miles and turn right on the Generals Highway, heading for Sequoia National Park. Drive approximately 27 miles on the Generals Highway, past the Lodgepole Village

turnoff, to the Wolverton turnoff on the left (east) side of the road. Turn left and drive to the parking area and trailhead.

Contact: Sequoia and Kings Canyon National Parks, Three Rivers, CA 93271-9700; tel. (559) 565-3134 or (559) 335-2856.

51 Panther Gap Loop
6.0 mi/3.5 hrs

If you're not up for the marathon trip to Alta Peak, you can still get a taste of the high country on this loop from the Wolverton Trailhead. Start hiking on the Lakes Trail from the east end of the Wolverton parking lot, and at 1.8 miles bear right on the Alta Trail to parallel Wolverton Creek, following it to Panther Gap. Here at 8,450 feet you get an inspiring vista of the Middle Fork Kaweah River and the Great Western Divide. Check out 9,081-foot Castle Rocks, an obvious landmark. From the gap, turn right (west) and follow the Alta Trail to Panther Peak and Panther Meadow, then on to Red Fir Meadow. Finally, at 4.6 miles, bear right and complete the loop by descending to Long Meadow and then edging along its east side to return to the parking lot. By the way, don't get any smart ideas about hiking this loop in the opposite direction. We did and found out that it's a much steeper climb.

Location: Off the Generals Highway in the Wolverton area of Sequoia National Park; map F5, grid i1.

User groups: Hikers and horses. No dogs or mountain bikes. No wheelchair facilities.

Permits: No permits are required. There is a $10 entrance fee at Sequoia and Kings Canyon National Parks, good for seven days.

Maps: Free park maps are available at park entrance stations or by contacting Sequoia and Kings Canyon National Parks at the address below. A more detailed map is available for a fee from Tom Harrison Cartography, tel. (415) 456-7940, or Trails Illustrated, tel. (800) 962-1643. Ask the USGS for a topographic map of the Lodgepole area.

Directions: From Fresno drive east on Highway 180 for 55 miles to the Big Stump entrance station at Kings Canyon National Park. Continue 1.5 miles and turn right on the Generals Highway, heading for Sequoia National Park. Drive approximately 27 miles on the Generals Highway, past the Lodgepole Village turnoff, to the Wolverton turnoff on the left (east) side of the road. Turn left and drive to the parking area and trailhead.

Contact: Sequoia and Kings Canyon National Parks, Three Rivers, CA 93271-9700; tel. (559) 565-3134 or (559) 335-2856.

52 Tokopah Falls

3.6 mi/2.0 hrs

This is unquestionably the best waterfall day hike in Sequoia and Kings Canyon National Parks, leading to 1,200-foot-high Tokopah Falls. It's also a perfect family hike, easy on the feet and even easier on the eyes. The scenery is spectacular the whole way, from the up-close looks at wildflowers and granite boulders to the more distant views of the Watchtower, a 1,600-foot glacially carved cliff on the south side of Tokopah Valley. Then there's the valley itself, with Tokopah Falls pouring down the smooth back curve of its U-shape. Because the trail begins by the three huge Lodgepole Campgrounds, it sees a lot of foot traffic. Your best bet is to start early in the morning. Another unusual feature of the trail? Hikers see more yellow-bellied marmots on the Tokopah Falls route than anywhere else in the two parks. We saw at least 40 of the cute little blond guys sunning themselves on rocks. If you're lucky, one of them will whistle at you as you walk by.

Location: Off the Generals Highway in the Lodgepole area of Sequoia National Park; map F5, grid i1.

User groups: Hikers and horses. No dogs or mountain bikes. No wheelchair facilities.

Permits: No permits are required. There is a $10 entrance fee at Sequoia and Kings Canyon National Parks, good for seven days.

Maps: Free park maps are available at park entrance stations or by contacting Sequoia and Kings Canyon National Parks at the address below. A more detailed map is available for a fee from Tom Harrison Cartography, tel. (415) 456-7940, or Trails Illustrated, tel. (800) 962-1643. Ask the USGS for a topographic map of the Lodgepole area.

Directions: From Fresno drive east on Highway 180 for 55 miles to the Big Stump entrance station at Kings Canyon National Park. Continue 1.5 miles and turn right on the Generals Highway, heading for Sequoia National Park. Drive approximately 25 miles on the Generals Highway to the Lodgepole Campground turnoff, then drive .75 mile to the Log Bridge area of Lodgepole Camp. Park in the large lot just before the bridge over the Marble Fork Kaweah River and walk 150 yards to the trailhead, which is just after you cross the bridge.

Contact: Sequoia and Kings Canyon National Parks, Three Rivers, CA 93271-9700; tel. (559) 565-3134 or (559) 335-2856.

53 Twin Lakes

13.6 mi/1-2 days

From the Lodgepole Campground Trailhead at 6,740 feet, the Twin Lakes are a 2,800-foot elevation gain and 6.8 miles away, making this a moderate backpacking trip or a long, strenuous day hike. It's a classic Sequoia National Park trip and one that is heavily traveled each summer. The terrain is an interesting mix of dense conifer forests, glacial moraine, and open meadows. From the trailhead, you climb past Wolverton's Rock to Cahoon Meadow at three miles, .5 mile beyond a crossing of Silliman Creek. You then continue to Cahoon Gap at 4.2 miles, cross over Clover Creek at five miles (campsites are found along the creek), bear right at the J.O. Pass Trail junction at 5.5 miles, and reach the Twin Lakes at 6.8 miles. The trail leads you directly to the larger Twin Lake; the smaller one is reached by following a spur. Both are shallow and have forested banks; some hikers try their luck fishing in the larger lake. Backpackers spending the night at Twin Lakes can hike farther the next day, over rocky Silliman Pass at 10,100 feet to the less-visited Ranger Lakes, three miles farther. Note that campfires are not allowed at Twin Lakes.

Location: Off the Generals Highway in the Lodgepole area of Sequoia National Park; map F5, grid i1.

User groups: Hikers and horses. No dogs or mountain bikes. No wheelchair facilities.

Permits: There is a $10 entrance fee at Sequoia and Kings Canyon National Parks, good for seven days. A free wilderness permit is required for overnight stays and is available on a first-come, first-served basis at Lodgepole Visitor Center, or in advance by mail or fax after March 1; for more information phone (559) 565-3708.

Maps: Free park maps are available at park entrance stations or by contacting Sequoia and Kings Canyon National Parks at the address below. A more detailed map is available for a fee from Tom Harrison Cartography, tel. (415) 456-7940, or Trails Illustrated, tel. (800) 962-1643. Ask the USGS for a topographic map of the Lodgepole area.

Directions: From Fresno drive east on Highway 180 for 55 miles to the Big Stump entrance station at Kings Canyon National Park. Continue 1.5 miles and turn right on the Generals Highway, heading for Sequoia National Park. Drive approximately 25 miles on the Generals Highway to the Lodgepole Campground turnoff, and then drive .75 mile to the Log Bridge area of Lodgepole Camp. The Twin Lakes Trailhead is just beyond the Tokopah Falls Trailhead and the bridge over the Marble Fork Kaweah River.

Contact: Sequoia and Kings Canyon National Parks, Three Rivers, CA 93271-9700; tel. (559) 565-3134 or (559) 335-2856.

54 Whitney Portal National Recreation Trail

4.0 mi one way/2.0 hrs

Don't confuse this trail with the Mount Whitney Trail, because except for their nearby trailheads, they have zero in common. Although if you try to hike the Whitney Portal National Recreation Trail in both directions, instead of as a one-way downhill hike, you may find it feels darn nearly as demanding as the Mount Whitney Trail, which climbs nearly 6,000 feet to the top of Mount Whitney. (Okay, maybe not quite that demanding.) The recreation trail begins at Whitney Portal, elevation 8,360 feet, and heads downhill through conifers and granite to Lone Pine Campground, elevation 5,640. The best thing about the route is that no matter how crowded it is at Whitney Portal, this trail gets surprisingly few hikers, especially after the first .5 mile, which skirts Whitney Portal Campground. You get to leave the multitudes behind as you walk downhill along Lone Pine Creek, among the good company of granite formations and big pines. Vistas are excellent along the way, including Mount Whitney to the west and the Alabama Hills and White Mountains to the east.

Location: In Inyo National Forest near Whitney Portal; map F5, grid j7.

User groups: Hikers, dogs, and horses. No mountain bikes. No wheelchair facilities.

Permits: No day-hiking permits are required. Parking and access are free.

Maps: For a map of Inyo National Forest, send $6 to U.S. Forest Service, Map Sales, P.O. Box 587, Camino, CA 95709; tel. (530) 647-5390 or website: www.r5.fs.fed.us/visitorcenter. Ask the USGS for a topographic map of the Mount Langley area.

Directions: From Lone Pine on U.S. 395 drive west on Whitney Portal Road for 13 miles to the end of the road and the trailhead, located across from the fishing pond. You will need to leave a shuttle car or arrange a pickup at Lone Pine Campground, four

miles downhill on Whitney Portal Road.
Contact: Inyo National Forest, Mount Whitney Ranger District, P.O. Box 8, Lone Pine, CA 93545; tel. (760) 876-6200 or fax (760) 876-6202.

55 Mount Whitney Trail
22.0 mi/
15.0 hrs or 2-3 days

Mount Whitney, at 14,494 feet in elevation, is the highest peak in the contiguous United States, and also probably the most frequently climbed. It has become such a popular route that not only are quotas enforced for backpackers, but even day-hikers must obtain a wilderness permit to hike the trail. And, yes, many people do hike the entire 22-mile trail in one day, ascending and descending more than a vertical mile along the way (6,131 feet in all), but it means a pre-dawn start and a grueling march. Many people who try this suffer from altitude sickness and never make it to the top; others make it but realize they would have had a lot more fun if they had divided the trip into two or even three days. So here's the smart way to hike Mount Whitney: get your wilderness permit way in advance, and plan your trip for a weekday, not a weekend. If possible, wait to make the climb until September or early October, when the crowds have thinned considerably. (August is the month with the highest trail usage.) Spend a day or two hiking around at high elevation before you set out on the Whitney Trail, and come prepared with sunglasses, sunscreen, good boots, and warm clothes for the summit. And here's our Good Samaritan tip: bring extra food and water so you can give it out to less-fortunate hikers you meet along the trail. For more information on this spectacular but demanding trip, see the Pacific Crest Trail information at the end of this chapter.
Location: In the John Muir Wilderness; map F5, grid j7.
User groups: Hikers only. No dogs, horses, or mountain bikes. (Dogs are allowed on the first 8.5 miles of trail, but not beyond.) No wheelchair facilities.

Permits: A wilderness permit is required for both day-hikers and backpackers. Quotas are in effect for Mount Whitney from May 15 to November 1 for both day-hikers and backpackers; permits are available in advance by mail or fax for this period. Applications must be received in February for all dates during the quota period; a lottery is held in March. There is a $15 per person reservation fee. Any unreserved or cancelled permits for the quota period become available on a first-come, first-served basis. Phone (760) 876-6200 for permit information, or visit website: www.r5.fs.fed.us/inyo.
Maps: For a map of Inyo National Forest, send $6 to U.S. Forest Service, Map Sales, P.O. Box 587, Camino, CA 95709; tel. (530) 647-5390 or website: www.r5.fs.fed.us/visitorcenter. A Mount Whitney map is available for a fee from Tom Harrison Cartography, tel. (415) 456-7940. Ask the USGS for topographic maps of the Mount Whitney and Mount Langley areas.
Directions: From Lone Pine on U.S. 395 drive west on Whitney Portal Road for 13 miles to the end of the road and the trailhead.
Contact: Inyo National Forest, Mount Whitney Ranger District, P.O. Box 8, Lone Pine, CA 93545; tel. (760) 876-6200 or fax (760) 876-6202.

56 Lone Pine Lake
5.8 mi/3.0 hrs

The route to the top of Mount Whitney is so popular and so overcrowded that it has permits and quotas and regulations up the wazoo, but guess what? Sweet little Lone Pine Lake is just outside of the regulated Mount Whitney Zone, so you can hike to it anytime without dealing with any bureaucracy. It's a fun trip for people who have always dreamed of climbing Mount Whitney, because it follows the first three miles of the summit trail. While other people are trudging along carrying heavy backpacks, you're stepping lightly with only a sandwich and a bottle of water in your daypack. The trail leads through Jeffrey pines and manzanita to the John Muir Wilderness border at one mile, then switchbacks uphill and opens up to views of the Alabama Hills far below. You'll cross Lone Pine Creek at 2.8 miles, then bear left at a junction to leave the main Mount Whitney Trail and head a few hundred yards to Lone Pine Lake. It's a sweet spot, and although privacy is rare, you have a greater chance of it after Labor Day and on a weekday. Who knows, you might just get so inspired that next time you'll come back and hike all the way to the summit.

Location: In the John Muir Wilderness near Whitney Portal; map F5, grid j7.

User groups: Hikers and dogs. No horses or mountain bikes. No wheelchair facilities.

Permits: No day-hiking permits are required. Parking and access are free.

Maps: For a map of Inyo National Forest, send $6 to U.S. Forest Service, Map Sales, P.O. Box 587, Camino, CA 95709; tel. (530) 647-5390 or website: www.r5.fs.fed.us/visitorcenter. A Mount Whitney map is available for a fee from Tom Harrison Cartography, tel. (415) 456-7940. Ask the USGS for topographic maps of the Mount Langley and Mount Whitney areas.

Directions: From Lone Pine on U.S. 395 drive west on Whitney Portal Road for 13 miles to the end of the road and the Mount Whitney Trailhead.

Contact: Inyo National Forest, Mount Whitney Ranger District, P.O. Box 8, Lone Pine, CA 93545; tel. (760) 876-6200 or fax (760) 876-6202.

57 Meysan Lake

9.4 mi/
6.0 hrs or 2.0 days

The Meysan Lake Trail is less popular than the neighboring trail to the top of Mount Whitney, but still you should get your wilderness permit in advance or plan on day hiking. Better yet, plan your trip for late September and during the week. The trail to Meysan Lake is long, steep, and dry—let's just say it's grueling—but it leads to a beautiful alpine lake basin and provides spectacular views of granite walls. It also gives climbers access to climbing routes on Mount Mallory and Lone Pine Peak. The trail leads along Meysan Creek and is not well maintained, which makes it even more demanding. You pass tiny Grass Lake at 2.5 miles, where the first water is available, and then Camp Lake at 3.5 miles. The trail from Camp Lake to Meysan Lake is rather sketchy, and on a steep and rocky slope. Meysan Lake is often still frozen as late as June, even though the trail can be as hot as an oven. Trailhead elevation is 7,900 feet; Meysan Lake is at 11,460 feet. No fires are allowed at Meysan Lake, so make sure you've got your stove packed.

Location: In the John Muir Wilderness near Mount Whitney; map F5, grid j7.

User groups: Hikers and dogs. No horses or mountain bikes. No wheelchair facilities.

Permits: A free wilderness permit is required for overnight stays. Quotas are in effect from the last Friday in June to September 15; permits are available in advance by mail or fax for this period for a $5 fee. Phone (760) 873-2408 for permit information, or visit website: www.r5.fs.fed.us/inyo.

Maps: For a map of Inyo National Forest, send $6 to U.S. Forest Service, Map Sales, P.O. Box 587, Camino, CA 95709; tel. (530) 647-5390 or website: www.r5.fs.fed.us/visitorcenter. A Mount Whitney map is available for a fee from Tom Harrison Cartography, tel. (415) 456-7940. Ask the USGS for topographic maps of the Mount Whitney and Mount Langley areas.

Directions: From Lone Pine on U.S. 395 drive west on Whitney Portal Road for 12 miles to Whitney Portal Campground and the Meysan Lake Trailhead. Park on the side of Whitney Portal Road by the camp and walk through the camp to reach the trailhead.

Contact: Inyo National Forest, Mount Whitney Ranger District, P.O. Box 8, Lone Pine, CA 93545; tel. (760) 876-6200 or fax (760) 876-6202.

PACIFIC CREST TRAIL (PCT) SECTION OVERVIEW

150.0 mi one way/14.0 days

Welcome to the High Sierra, as this section, extending from the trailhead parking area at Whitney Portal north to Agnew Meadows, takes you into the heart of it. Bear precautions are at a premium now—no food in the tent and always hang your supplies. Streams may be swollen from the snowmelt and difficult to cross. Snow may still linger in the high passes as late as July. Do not attempt to cross any high-angle snowpack or icepack unless you're skilled at handling the situation with an ice ax and crampons. The trail ranges from 7,000 to over 13,000 feet along this portion of the trail.

PCT-21 / JMT-1 Whitney Portal to Lake Thomas Edison

112.0 mi one way/11.0 days 5 🥾 🎣

You can have a foothold in the sky with every step on the John Muir Trail and with this section of the PCT. The trail starts at practically the tip-top of North America, Mount Whitney, and takes you northward across a land of 12,000-foot passes and Ansel Adams-style panoramas.

From the trailhead at Whitney Portal, the hike climbs more than 6,100 feet over the course of 10 miles to reach the Whitney summit at 14,494 feet. That includes an ascent over 100 switchbacks (often snow covered) to top Wotan's Throne and reach Trail Crest (13,560 feet). Here you turn right and take the Summit Trail. In the final stretch to the top, the ridge is cut by huge notch windows in the rock; you look through and the bottom drops out more than 10,000 feet to the little town of Lone Pine below, at an elevation of 3,800 feet. Finally you make it to the top and notice how the surrounding giant blocks of rock look as if they were sculpted with a giant hammer and chisel. From here the entire Western Divide is visible, and to the north, rows of mountain peaks are lined up for miles to the horizon. Be sure to sign your name in the register, kept in a lightning-proof metal box. You may feel a bit dizzy from the altitude, but know you're someplace very special.

The journey farther north is just as captivating. The route drops into Sequoia National Park, then climbs above timberline for almost a day's worth of hiking as it nears Forester Pass, 13,180 feet. It's not only the highest point on the PCT, but the most dangerous section of trail on the entire route as well. The trail is narrow and steep, cut into a high vertical slab of rock, and is typically icy, with an iced-over snowfield near the top that's particularly treacherous. An ice ax is an absolute must—slip here and you could fall thousands of feet.

Once through Forester, the trail heads onward into the John Muir Wilderness along Bubbs Creek, with great wildflowers at nearby Vidette Meadow. Then it's up and over Kearsage Pass (10,710 feet), and after a short drop, you're back climbing again, this time over Glen Pass (11,978 feet), a spectacular, boulder-strewn ridge with great views to the north looking into Kings Canyon National Park. Just two miles from Glen Pass is Rae Lakes, a fantasy spot for camping (one-night limit), with pristine meadows, shoreline campsites, and lots of eager brook trout.

The JMT/PCT then heads through Kings Canyon National Park by following sparkling streams much of the way, finally climbing up and over Pinchot Pass (12,130 feet), then back down along the upper Kings River for a long, steady ascent over Mather Pass (12,100 feet). The wonders continue as you hike along Palisade Lakes, then down into LeConte Canyon, followed by an endless climb up to Muir Pass (11,965 feet). In early summer, snowfields are common here, and this can be the most difficult and trying section of the entire PCT, especially if your boots keep postholing through the snow. The country near Muir Pass is extremely stark—nothing but sculpted granite, ice, and a few small turquoise lakes—crowned by the stone Muir Hut at the pass, where hikers can duck in and hide for safety from sudden afternoon thunderstorms and lightning bolts.

The views astound many visitors as the trail drops into Evolution Valley. It's like a trip back to the beginning of time, where all is pure and primary, yet incredibly lush and beautiful. You finally leave Kings Canyon National Park, following the headwaters of the San Joaquin River into the Sierra National Forest. After bottoming out at 7,890 feet, the trail rises steeply in switchback after switchback as it enters the John Muir Wilderness. Finally you top Selden Pass (10,900 feet), take in an incredible view where the rows of surrounding mountaintops look like the Great Pyramids, then make the easy one-mile descent to Marie Lakes, a pretty campsite with excellent trout fishing near the lake's outlet.

The final push on this section of the PCT is climbing up Bear Mountain, then down a terrible, toe-jamming stretch to Mono Creek. Here you make a left turn and continue for two more miles until you come to Edison Lake, an excellent place to have a food stash waiting.

Special note: Crossing Mono Creek at the north fork can be dangerous in high-runoff conditions.

Location: From the trailhead parking area at Whitney Portal north, to the trailhead parking area at Lake Thomas Edison; map F5, grid j6.

User groups: Hikers and horses. No dogs or mountain bikes. No wheelchair facilities.

Permits: A wilderness permit is required for traveling through various wilderness and special-use areas the trail traverses. Contact the Inyo National Forest District Office, tel. (760) 876-6200.

Maps: For an overall view of the trail route in this section, send $6 for each map ordered to U.S. Forest Service, Map Sales, P.O. Box 587, Camino, CA 95709; tel. (530) 647-5390 or website: www.r5.fs.fed.us/visitorcenter. Ask for the Sierra National Forest, Inyo National Forest, and Sequoia National Forest maps. Ask the USGS for topographic maps of the Mount Whitney, Mount Williamson, Kearsarge Peak, Mount Clarence King, Mount Pinchot, North Palisade, Mount Goddard, Mount Darwin, Mount Henry, Ward Mountain, Florence Lake, and Graveyard Peak areas.

Directions: To reach the Mount Whitney Trailhead from Lone Pine and U.S. 395, head west on Whitney Portal Road for approximately 13 miles to Whitney Portal and the trailhead for the Mount Whitney Trail. To reach the Lake Thomas Edison Trailhead from the town of Shaver Lake, drive north on Highway 168 for approximately 21 miles to the town of Lakeshore. Turn northeast onto Kaiser Pass Road/Forest Service 4S01. Kaiser Pass Road becomes Edison Lake Road at Mono Hot Springs. Drive another five miles north past town to the Vermillion Campground and parking area for backcountry hikers. The PCT begins near the east end of the lake.

Contact: Inyo National Forest, Mount Whitney Ranger District, P.O. Box 8, Lone Pine, CA 93545; tel. (760) 876-6200 or fax (760) 876-6202; Sierra National Forest, Pineridge Ranger District, P.O. Box 559, Prather, CA 93651; tel. (559) 855-5360 or fax (559) 855-5375; Sequoia National Forest, Cannell Meadow Ranger District, P.O. Box 9, Kernville, CA 93238; tel. (760) 376-3781 or fax (760) 376-3795.

PCT-22 / JMT-2 Lake Thomas Edison to Agnew Meadows

38.0 mi one way/3.0 days 🏔️ 👟

The world is not perfect, but the scene from Silver Pass comes close. At 10,900 feet, you scan a bare, high-granite landscape sprinkled with alpine lakes. Just north of the pass are five small lakes: Chief, Papoose, Warrior, Squaw, and Lake of the Lone Indian. This is the highlight on this 38-mile section of the Pacific Crest Trail. The trip starts at Mono Creek, with a good resupply point at Edison Lake (7,650 feet), just two miles away. From the Mono Creek junction, you head north toward Silver Pass, climbing along Silver Pass Creek much of the way. Before you get to Silver Pass, there's a stream crossing that can be dangerous in high-runoff conditions. Top Silver Pass at 10,900 feet, and enjoy a five-mile descent and then a quick up to Tully Hole (9,250 feet). Climbing north, you pass Deer Creek, Purple Lake, and Lake Virginia. You head up to Red Cones and then make a steady descent toward Devils Postpile National Monument. A good resupply point is at nearby Reds Meadows Pack Station.

Special note: For food drop information, call the Vermillion Valley Resort at (559) 855-6558. It is open only in summer and fall.

Location: From Lake Thomas Edison north to Agnew Meadows; map F5, grid b1.

User groups: Hikers, dogs, and horses. No mountain bikes. No wheelchair facilities.

Permits: A wilderness permit is required for traveling through various wilderness and special-use areas the trail traverses. Contact the Inyo National Forest, tel. (760) 934-2505, or the Sierra National Forest, tel. (559) 841-3311.

Maps: For an overall view of the trail route in this section, send $6 to U.S. Forest Service, Map Sales, P.O. Box 587, Camino, CA 95709; tel. (530) 647-5390 or website: www.r5.fs.fed.us/

visitor center. Ask for the Inyo National Forest map. Ask the USGS for topographic maps of the Mammoth Mountain, Crystal Crag, Bloody Mountain, Graveyard Peak, Mount Ritter, and Coip Peak areas.

Directions: From Fresno drive northeast on Highway 168 for about 68 miles to the Lakeshore Resort Area at Huntington Lake. Turn northeast onto Kaiser Pass Road/Forest Service 4S01. Kaiser Pass Road becomes Edison Lake Road at Mono Hot Springs. Drive another five miles north past the Vermillion Resort and Campground and beyond to the parking area for backcountry hikers. The trail begins near the west end of the lake.

Contact: Inyo National Forest, Mammoth Ranger District, P.O. Box 148, Mammoth Lakes, CA 93546; tel. (760) 934-2505 or fax (760) 924-5537; Sierra National Forest, Pineridge Ranger District, P.O. Box 559, Prather, CA 93651; tel. (559) 855-5360 or fax (559) 855-5375.

PCT Continuation

To continue hiking along the Pacific Crest Trail or the John Muir Trail, see chapter E4.

ANN MARIE BROWN

EUREKA DUNES ARE THE TALLEST
SAND DUNES IN CALIFORNIA.

MAP F6

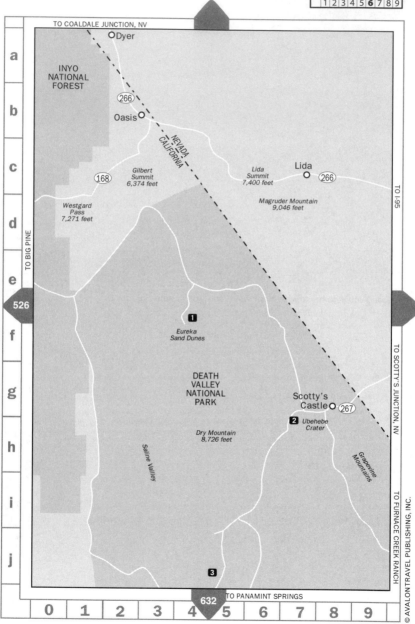

TO COALDALE JUNCTION, NV

○ Dyer

INYO NATIONAL FOREST

266

Oasis ○

NEVADA
CALIFORNIA

168

Gilbert Summit 6,374 feet

Lida Summit 7,400 feet

Lida ○

266

TO I-95

Westgard Pass 7,271 feet

Magruder Mountain 9,046 feet

TO BIG PINE

526

1

Eureka Sand Dunes

DEATH VALLEY NATIONAL PARK

Scotty's Castle ○ — 267

TO SCOTTY'S JUNCTION, NV

2 Ubehebe Crater

Dry Mountain 8,726 feet

Saline Valley

Grapevine Mountains

TO FURNACE CREEK RANCH

3

632 TO PANAMINT SPRINGS

0 1 2 3 4 5 6 7 8 9

© AVALON TRAVEL PUBLISHING, INC.

CHAPTER F6

1	Eureka Dunes	569
2	Little Hebe Crater Trail.........	569
3	Ubehebe Peak	570

1 Eureka Dunes

2.0 mi/1.0 hr

It takes a heck of a lot of time and patience to drive to Eureka Dunes, but as soon as you see those giant icons of the desert, you'll know why you came. Eureka Dunes are the tallest sand dunes in California and arguably also the tallest in North America. They rise nearly 700 feet from their base, creating a sandy, miniature mountain range that is home to several rare and endangered desert plants. Simply put, Eureka Dunes are a must-see in Death Valley. Hike to the top and snap a few pictures, and you'll go home with many weird and wonderful photographs of wind patterns on sand or your hiking partner traversing swirling dune ridge tops. From the trailhead simply start walking any which way you please, heading for the clearly visible dunes. Because of the continually shifting desert sand, there is no marked trail, so make your own. Your best bet is to climb to the top of the tallest dune you can find, then trace a ridgeline path from dune to dune. It's a strange, wonderful feeling to walk on the silky-soft sand crystals. And as you might expect, climbing the dunes is a slow proposition—take two steps forward, slide one step back, and repeat the process. Just take your time and enjoy the uniqueness of the experience.

A few tips: Prepare yourself mentally and physically for the long drive to the trailhead (especially the bumpy 44-mile section on dirt roads), and you'll be far more likely to enjoy the trip. Take plenty of water and snacks with you for a long day. And most important: At-tempt this adventure only when temperatures are cool in Death Valley.

Location: In Death Valley National Park north of Scotty's Castle; map F6, grid f4.

User groups: Hikers only. No dogs, horses, or mountain bikes. No wheelchair facilities.

Permits: No permits are required. There is a $10 entrance fee at Death Valley National Park, good for seven days.

Maps: Free park maps are available at park entrance stations or by contacting Death Valley National Park at the address below. A more detailed map is available for a fee from Tom Harrison Cartography, tel. (415) 456-7940. Ask the USGS for a topographic map of Last Chance Range Southwest.

Directions: From the Furnace Creek Visitor Center in Death Valley National Park, drive north on Highway 190 for 17 miles, then bear right on Scotty's Castle Road. In 32 miles you will pass the Grapevine entrance station. Continue northwest for three miles (keep left; don't bear right for Scotty's Castle) to the dirt road on the right signed for Eureka Dunes. (If you reach Ubehebe Crater, you've passed the dirt road.) Turn right and drive 44 miles to the Eureka Dunes parking area. A high-clearance vehicle is recommended; call to check on road conditions before heading out.

Contact: Death Valley National Park, Death Valley, CA 92328; tel. (760) 786-2331, (760) 786-3244, or fax (760) 786-3283.

2 Little Hebe Crater Trail

1.0 mi/0.5 hr

A walk along the rim of a not-so-ancient volcano is what you get on the Little Hebe Crater Trail. The trail leads along Ubehebe Crater's southwest rim to Little Hebe and several older craters. Ubehebe Crater is 500 feet deep and .5 mile across, and was formed by volcanic activity that occurred between 1,000 and 2,000 years ago. Little Hebe and the other craters are much smaller but similar in appearance—mostly black and ash colored, with eroded walls that reveal a colorful blend of orange and rust from the minerals in the rock. At .5 mile from the trailhead you reach a junction where you can continue straight ahead to Little Hebe Crater or just loop all the way around Ubehebe's rim. Take your pick—from the high rim of Ubehebe, it's easy to see where you're going, as well as down into the valley below and far off to the Last Chance Range. Note that the trail surface is a mix of gravel and cinders, and it's somewhat loose in places, so hiking boots or high-top shoes are a good idea. A side note is that most visitors to Ubehebe Crater don't even bother with this trail; instead, they just get out of their cars, make a beeline run for the bottom of the huge crater, and then moan and complain when they realize they have to make the steep climb back up. Go figure.

Location: In Death Valley National Park near Scotty's Castle; map F6, grid h7.

User groups: Hikers only. No dogs, horses, or mountain bikes. No wheelchair facilities.

Permits: No permits are required. There is a $10 entrance fee at Death Valley National Park, good for seven days.

Maps: Free park maps are available at park entrance stations or by contacting Death Valley National Park at the address below. A more detailed map is available for a fee from Tom Harrison Cartography, tel. (415) 456-7940. Ask the USGS for a topographic map of Ubehebe Crater.

Directions: From the Furnace Creek Visitor Center in Death Valley National Park, drive north on Highway 190 for 17 miles, then bear right on Scotty's Castle Road. In 32 miles you will pass the Grapevine entrance station. Continue northwest for five miles to the left turnoff to Ubehebe Crater.

Contact: Death Valley National Park, Death Valley, CA 92328; tel. (760) 786-2331, (760) 786-3244, or fax (760) 786-3283.

3 Ubehebe Peak
6.0 mi/3.0 hrs

Are you prepared for a long drive and then a difficult hike? If you are, the rewards on this trip are great. The climb to Ubehebe Peak would be strenuous enough if you just accounted for the steep grade, but add in the fact that this is Death Valley and the hike becomes a butt-kicker. The peak offers tremendous views of both the snowy Sierra Nevada and the desert-like Last Chance Range as well as Racetrack and Saline Valleys. The trail is a narrow miners' route that switchbacks up and up and up, and you can be darn sure that you won't come across any shade on the way. There is no trail for the final .5 mile to the summit; most hikers content themselves with the view from the saddle below. (If you stop here, you won't be missing out. The view is incredible, especially of the Grandstand rock formation far below, and the salt flats of the Saline Valley to the west.) Experienced climbers can make the final summit scramble. Total elevation gain is 1,900 feet; the summit is at 5,678 feet in elevation. Note: Before or after your trip, be sure to explore around the Racetrack area by the trailhead, where you can see the tracks of rocks that have slid along the surface of the mudflats, pushed by strong winds. Many a fine photograph has been shot of these fascinating rock tracks.

Location: In Death Valley National Park; map F6, grid j5.

User groups: Hikers only. No dogs, horses, or mountain bikes. No wheelchair facilities.

Permits: No permits are required. There is a $10 entrance fee at Death Valley National Park, good for seven days.

Maps: Free park maps are available at park entrance stations or by contacting Death Valley National Park at the address below. A more detailed map is available for a fee from Tom Harrison Cartography, tel. (415) 456-7940. Ask the USGS for a topographic map of the Ubehebe Peak area.

Directions: From the Furnace Creek Visitor Center in Death Valley National Park, drive north on Highway 190 for 17 miles, then bear right on Scotty's Castle Road. In 32 miles you will pass the Grapevine entrance station, then continue northwest for 5.8 miles (keep left; don't bear right for Scotty's Castle). Turn right on the dirt road signed for Racetrack. Drive 20 miles on Racetrack Road. Bear right at Teakettle Junction and drive 5.9 miles to a pullout on the right side of the road, across from the large rock formation called the Grandstand. High-clearance vehicles are necessary on Racetrack Road.

Contact: Death Valley National Park, Death Valley, CA 92328; tel. (760) 786-2331, (760) 786-3244, or fax (760) 786-3283.

These limekilns in Big Sur were used to make limestone bricks and cement in the 1880s.

MAP G1

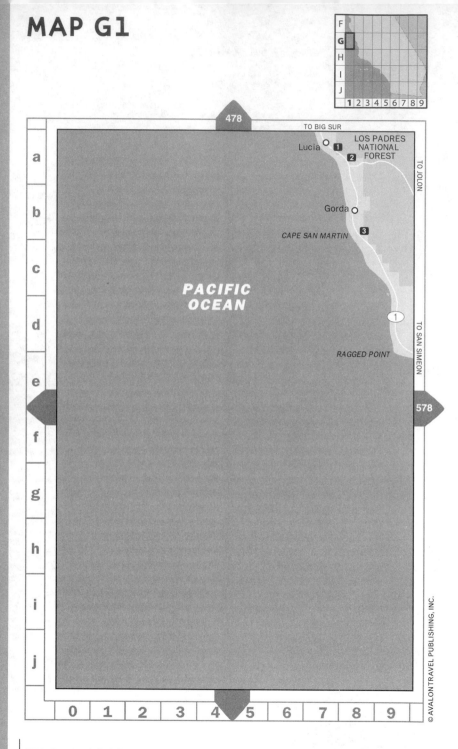

478

TO BIG SUR

LOS PADRES
NATIONAL
FOREST

Lucia ○ **1**

2

Gorda ○

CAPE SAN MARTIN **3**

PACIFIC
OCEAN

TO JOLON

TO SAN SIMEON

1

RAGGED POINT

578

© AVALON TRAVEL PUBLISHING, INC.

CHAPTER G1

1. Limekiln Trail 575
2. Kirk Creek/
   Vicente Flat Trail 575
3. Salmon Creek Trail 576

1. Limekiln Trail

1.8 mi/1.0 hr

What's Big Sur's best-kept secret? That's easy—the hiking trail at Limekiln State Park. The state park is so new and so small that it hasn't been inundated by visitors like Pfeiffer Big Sur or Julia Pfeiffer Burns State Park. The Limekiln Trail leads from the inland campground into a gorgeous redwood forest. It follows Limekiln Creek for a half mile to the park's namesake limekilns, which were used to make limestone bricks and cement in the 1880s. The four kilns look like giant smokestacks with mossy, brick bottoms; they're interesting to see and photograph, but they're not the highlight of this trail. What is? A spur trail off the main route leads to Limekiln Falls, a spectacular 100-foot waterfall that drops over a limestone face. The spur is not marked, but it comes up immediately after you cross the second bridge on your way to the limekilns. (The first bridge is right by the campground.) Getting to the waterfall requires some boulder hopping, and in spring you may end up with wet feet, but it's good fun.

Location: In Limekiln State Park south of Big Sur; map G1, grid a7.

User groups: Hikers only. No dogs, horses, or mountain bikes. No wheelchair facilities.

Permits: No permits are required. A $3 day-use fee is charged per vehicle.

Maps: A map of Limekiln State Park is available for $.50 at the entrance kiosk. Ask the USGS for a topographic map of the Lopez Point area.

Directions: From Carmel drive 52 miles south on Highway 1 to Limekiln State Park, on the east side of the highway. It's 2.5 miles south of Lucia, and 14.8 miles south of Julia Pfeiffer Burns State Park. The trailhead is at the far side of the inland campground.

Contact: Limekiln State Park, c/o Pfeiffer Big Sur State Park, Big Sur, CA 93920; tel. (831) 667-2315, (831) 649-2836, or fax (831) 667-2886.

2. Kirk Creek/Vicente Flat Trail

10.0 mi/6.0 hrs or 2.0 days

What you see at the trailhead is not exactly what you get on this popular backpacking trail. You see chaparral and no shade, but you get chaparral and no shade only part of the time; the rest of the time you're hiking in shady redwood groves or along lush ravines. The Kirk Creek Trail (also called the Vicente Flat Trail) is full of surprises. The absence of trees in some sections is actually a positive because it allows for wide-reaching views over the big blue Pacific. Your destination is Vicente Flat Camp in five miles with a 1,700-foot elevation gain, mostly on well-graded trail. The trail leads steadily northeast, passing occasional odd-looking rocks and meandering in and out of the trees. Pass small Espinoza Camp at 3.2 miles, which is seldom used because of the superiority of Vicente Flat Camp, a larger camp with a nearby stream and a beautiful setting. The final .5 mile of trail is a descent to the Stone Ridge Trail junction, where you bear left for Vicente Flat Camp. You have a choice of sites in the shade or the sun; Hare Creek provides a water source.

Location: In the Ventana Wilderness south of Lucia; map G1, grid a7.

User groups: Hikers, dogs, and horses. No mountain bikes. No wheelchair facilities.

Permits: A free campfire permit is required for overnight stays from May through December; permits are available from the Monterey Ranger District or the Big Sur Station. A national forest recreation pass is required for each vehicle; fees are $5 for one day or $30 for a year.

Maps: For a map of Los Padres National Forest or Ventana Wilderness, send $6 to U.S. Forest Service, Map Sales, P.O. Box 587, Camino, CA 95709; tel. (530) 647-5390 or website: www.r5.fs.fed.us/visitorcenter. Ask the USGS for topographic maps of the Lopez Point and Cone Peak areas.

Directions: Drive 55 miles south from Carmel on Highway 1 to Kirk Creek Campground on the west side of the highway. (It's four miles south of Lucia, and six miles north of Gorda.) The trailhead is on the east side of the highway; you must park alongside Highway 1 in the pullout and not in the campground.

Contact: Los Padres National Forest, Monterey Ranger District, 406 S. Mildred Avenue, King City, CA 93930; tel. (831) 385-5434 or fax (831) 385-0628.

🖪 Salmon Creek Trail
4.2 mi/
2.0 hrs or 2.0 days

While heading for a day hike or short backpacking trip on the Salmon Creek Trail, many people walk right by and miss seeing spectacular Salmon Creek Falls, which is just off the Salmon Creek Trail and a .25-mile walk from Highway 1. Don't be one of them; start your trip at the signed Salmon Creek Trail, but after walking a few hundred feet, cut off on any of the spur trails to your left and pay a visit to the impressive 100-foot waterfall, surrounded by cabin-sized boulders. Then return to the Salmon Creek Trail, say good-bye to the creekside shade and dampness, and start a healthy climb

to the ridge, where you can look back down at the highway and marvel at how far you've gone, and fast. From there it's still more climbing, gaining a total of 800 feet, until you start to see Douglas firs, a sure sign that you're nearing misnamed Spruce Camp at 1,325 feet. At the Spruce Creek Trail fork, stay straight (left). The final .1 mile is downhill along Spruce Creek, a beautiful stream with a myriad of pools and cascades. The camp here is in gorgeous shade from Douglas firs, and there are many good spots to stick your feet (or other body parts) into the stream. If you want to spend the night but somebody already has this spot, you can continue another 1.5 miles to Estrella Camp.

Location: In the Silver Peak Wilderness south of Gorda; map G1, grid b8.

User groups: Hikers, dogs, and horses. No mountain bikes. No wheelchair facilities.

Permits: A free campfire permit is required for overnight stays from May through December; permits are available from the Monterey Ranger District or the Big Sur Station. A national forest recreation pass is required for each vehicle; fees are $5 for one day or $30 for a year.

Maps: For a map of Los Padres National Forest, send $6 to U.S. Forest Service, Map Sales, P.O. Box 587, Camino, CA 95709; tel. (530) 647-5390 or website: www.r5.fs.fed.us/visitorcenter. Ask the USGS for a topographic map of the Villa Creek area.

Directions: From Big Sur drive 33 miles south on Highway 1 to Gorda; continue 7.6 miles south of Gorda to the trailhead for the Salmon Creek Trail on the east side of the highway at a hairpin turn. Park in the large parking pullout along the road. The Salmon Creek Trail leads from the south end of the guardrail.

Contact: Los Padres National Forest, Monterey Ranger District, 406 South Mildred Avenue, King City, CA 93930; tel. (831) 385-5434 or fax (831) 385-0628.

THE OAK TREES IN LOS OSOS OAKS RESERVE MAY BE UP TO 800 YEARS OLD.

ANN MARIE BROWN

MAP G2

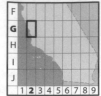

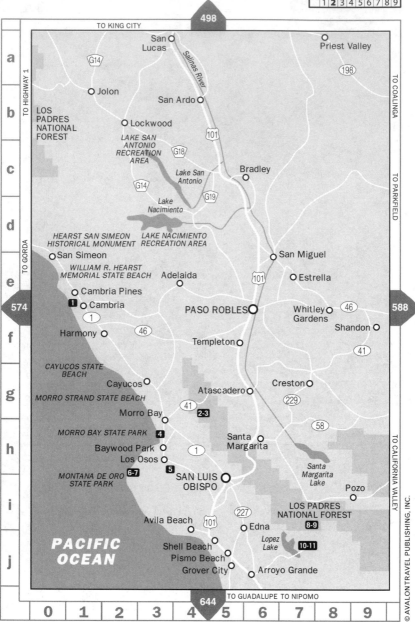

498

San Lucas

Priest Valley

G14

TO HIGHWAY 1

Jolon

San Ardo

198

TO COALINGA

LOS PADRES NATIONAL FOREST

Lockwood

101

LAKE SAN ANTONIO RECREATION AREA

G18

Lake San Antonio

Bradley

G14

Lake Nacimiento

G19

TO PARKFIELD

HEARST SAN SIMEON HISTORICAL MONUMENT

LAKE NACIMIENTO RECREATION AREA

San Miguel

TO GORDA

San Simeon

WILLIAM R. HEARST MEMORIAL STATE BEACH

Adelaida

Estrella

101

Cambria Pines

1 Cambria

PASO ROBLES

Whitley Gardens

46

574

1

Shandon

588

Harmony

46

Templeton

41

CAYUCOS STATE BEACH

Cayucos

Creston

MORRO STRAND STATE BEACH

Atascadero

229

Morro Bay

41

2-3

58

MORRO BAY STATE PARK **4**

Baywood Park

1

Santa Margarita

Los Osos

5

Santa Margarita Lake

MONTANA DE ORO STATE PARK

6-7

SAN LUIS OBISPO

Pozo

TO CALIFORNIA VALLEY

LOS PADRES NATIONAL FOREST

Avila Beach

101

227

Edna

8-9

PACIFIC OCEAN

Shell Beach

Lopez Lake

10-11

Pismo Beach

Grover City

Arroyo Grande

644

TO GUADALUPE TO NIPOMO

© AVALON TRAVEL PUBLISHING, INC.

CHAPTER G2

1 Leffingwell Landing/
   Moonstone Beach 579

2 Cerro Alto Summit... 579

3 Cerro Alto Loop 580

4 Cabrillo Peak........ 581

5 Los Osos
   Oaks Reserve 581

6 Montaña de Oro
   Bluffs Trail 582

7 Valencia and
   Oats Peaks 582

8 Big Falls 583

9 Little Falls.......... 584

10 Duna Vista and
   Two Waters Trails 584

11 Blackberry Springs
   and High Ridge 585

1 Leffingwell Landing/ Moonstone Beach

4.0 mi/2.0 hrs

What's the best time to make the trip to Cambria? That's easy—in the spring, when the rolling hills along Highway 46 on the drive to the coast are lush and green. Of course, any time of year is a good time to walk the trail that leads from Leffingwell Landing along the bluffs above Moonstone Beach. Although Moonstone Beach Drive parallels the trail all the way, the road isn't much of a bother because the vistas out to sea hold all of your attention. The parking lot at Leffingwell Landing is in the middle of this trail, which means you can walk out and back in both directions. To the south you may have a wet creek crossing at Leffingwell Creek, but you can go around it via the golf course. The bluff trail's southern terminus is at the intersection of Moonstone Beach Drive and Weymouth Street, but you can descend to the beach there and keep walking. If you head in the other direction, about .25 mile north of Leffingwell Landing the trail again descends on a wooden staircase to the beach, and you continue your walk there. In addition to the coastal vistas from the bluffs, there are many colorful patches of ice plant, cypress trees, and several benches and overlooks (accessible via short spurs off the main trail)—places where you can find a spot to call your own. We watched a winter squall come in from one of these overlooks; it was sudden, dramatic, and beautiful. Right below Leffingwell Landing are fine tide pools to be explored. Keep on the lookout for passing whales in the winter.

Location: Near Cambria; map G2, grid e1.

User groups: Hikers and dogs. No horses or mountain bikes. No wheelchair facilities.

Permits: No permits are required. Parking and access are free.

Maps: Ask the USGS for a topographic map of the Cambria area.

Directions: From north of Templeton on U.S. 101, take the Highway 46 West/Cambria/Hearst Castle exit. Drive west on Highway 46 for 22 miles to Highway 1; continue three miles north on Highway 1 past Cambria to Moonstone Beach Drive. Turn left on Moonstone Beach Drive and park at Leffingwell Landing.

Contact: San Simeon State Beach, San Simeon District, 750 Hearst Castle Road, San Simeon, CA 93452; tel. (805) 927-2020 or (805) 927-2068.

2 Cerro Alto Summit

4.0 mi/2.0 hrs

We hope you like to climb, because that's what you do on the Cerro Alto Trail to the summit of Cerro Alto, elevation 2,620 feet. The 1,600-foot climb is divided over two miles of steep terrain, much of which burned in a 1994 arson fire, but the reward for your exertion is one of the finest views of the Central Coast—a panoramic vista of the Pacific Ocean, Whale Rock Reservoir, Morro Bay, Piedras Blancas Lighthouse, and the Santa Lucia Mountains. From the trailhead along the camp road south of the parking area, you cross Morro Creek on a bridge, enter a bay and live oak forest, then leave it and head for chaparral country. After .75 mile, bear left and shortly thereafter bear right. After a series of switchbacks and some rocky sections of trail, you reach the road to the peak at 1.7 miles. Turn left and circle the peak as you climb another .25 mile to the summit.

Note that if you want to take an easier grade to the summit or if you want to turn this into a loop trip, you can begin hiking from the hiker's parking lot at campsite 19. This route takes three miles to reach Cerro Alto's summit instead of two. It joins the shorter route for the final 1.2 miles to the summit.

Location: Off Highway 41, east of Morro Bay; map G2, grid g4.

User groups: Hikers, dogs, horses, and mountain bikes. No wheelchair facilities.

Permits: No permits are required. A national forest recreation pass is required for each vehicle; fees are $5 for one day or $30 for a year.

Maps: For a map of Los Padres National Forest, send $6 to U.S. Forest Service, Map Sales, P.O. Box 587, Camino, CA 95709; tel. (530) 647-5390 or website: www.r5.fs.fed.us/visitorcenter. Ask the USGS for a topographic map of the Atascadero area.

Directions: From Atascadero on U.S. 101, take the Highway 41 West/Morro Bay exit. Drive eight miles west on Highway 41 to Cerro Alto Campground on the left, midway between Atascadero and Morro Bay. Park in the signed hikers' parking lot near the camp host's residence at the far end of the campground. Walk back down the camp road to the trailhead by the footbridge.

Contact: Los Padres National Forest, Santa Lucia Ranger District, 1616 N. Carlotti Drive, Santa Maria, CA 93454; tel. (805) 925-9538 or fax (805) 681-2781.

3 Cerro Alto Loop
2.5 mi/1.0 hr

Not everybody is up for the dry, steep hike to the top of Cerro Alto Peak, and if you're in that camp, you can take another hike that offers many of its own rewards. Since some of this area burned in a 1994 fire, you'll see much evidence of regrowth (especially spring wildflowers) as well as many blackened trees still standing. Take the trail from the far end of Cerro Alto Campground; you'll return on the trail by the bridge at the lower end of the camp. It's an up-and-down kind of deal, with not too much up or too much down. The first .5 mile is in a forest of oaks, bays, and madrones, with many ferns growing at your feet. As the trail climbs, the terrain changes to chaparral, and at one mile you reach an old road junction. Turn right, and in less than a mile the path meets the Cerro Alto Trail to the summit. Keep following the old road and switchback to the west. Then make a one-mile descent back to the camp.

Location: Off Highway 41, east of Morro Bay; map G2, grid g4.

User groups: Hikers, dogs, horses, and mountain bikes. No wheelchair facilities.

Permits: No permits are required. A national forest recreation pass is required for each vehicle; fees are $5 for one day or $30 for a year.

Maps: For a map of Los Padres National Forest, send $6 to U.S. Forest Service, Map Sales, P.O. Box 587, Camino, CA 95709; tel. (530) 647-5390 or website: www.r5.fs.fed.us/visitorcenter. Ask the USGS for a topographic map of the Atascadero area.

Directions: From Atascadero on U.S. 101, take the Highway 41 West/Morro Bay exit. Drive eight miles west on Highway 41 to Cerro Alto Campground on the left, midway between Atascadero and Morro Bay. Park in the signed hikers' parking lot near the camp host's residence at the far end of the campground. Start hiking on the signed Cerro Alto Trail from there.

Contact: Los Padres National Forest, Santa Lucia Ranger District, 1616 N. Carlotti Drive, Santa Maria, CA 93454; tel. (805) 925-9538 or fax (805) 681-2781.

4 Cabrillo Peak

3.0 mi/1.5 hrs

You hardly realize you're in a state park when you reach the trailhead for Cabrillo Peak, which is just a small dirt parking lot alongside a busy road. Where's the entrance kiosk? What about the state park entrance fee? Where are all the campgrounds and restrooms? None of that applies here at Morro Bay State Park's Cabrillo Peak, which is a quiet refuge from the hustle and bustle of Morro Bay tourism. Cabrillo Peak is one of nine "morros," small volcanic peaks that lie in a loose chain along the central coast. Morro Rock is another of these and the most famous of the group. Although no trail goes to the top of Cabrillo Peak, you can hike on the peak's lower reaches on the Quarry Trail and Park Ridge Trail. Both are accessible from two small parking areas off South Bay Boulevard; if you miss the first one, just take the second. The Park Ridge Trail goes straight up, then veers left and joins the Quarry Trail. The Cabrillo Peak area contains a variety of native plants and grasslands, including these spring bloomers: bird's eye gilia, brodiea, and mariposa lilies. On the sunniest slopes coastal sage scrub grows, including black sage and bush monkeyflower. Translation? No shade. That makes the views of Morro Bay and Morro Rock first class, but it also means you'd better carry water.

Location: In Morro Bay State Park near Morro Bay; map G2, grid h3.

User groups: Hikers, horses, and mountain bikes. No dogs. No wheelchair facilities.

Permits: No permits are required. Parking and access are free.

Maps: Ask the USGS for a topographic map of the Morro Bay South area.

Directions: From San Luis Obispo take High-way 1 northwest for 11 miles to Morro Bay. Take the Morro Bay State Park exit and continue on South Bay Boulevard. In .75 mile, take the left fork (do not head for the main part of the park) and drive another .5 mile to the Cabrillo Peak dirt parking lot on the left side of the road. The first parking lot is for the Quarry Trail; another parking lot shortly following it is for the Park Ridge Trail. Park at either; the two trails join.

Contact: Morro Bay State Park, State Park Road, Morro Bay, CA 93442; tel. (805) 772-7434; San Luis Obispo Coast State Parks, tel. (805) 549-3312.

5 Los Osos Oaks Reserve

2.0 mi/1.0 hr

It's hard to believe that a bunch of old oak trees right alongside a busy road could make for such great walking, but they do. The hike is an odd mix of elements, since you hear road noise much of the time, but the forest still seems peaceful. The venerable old oaks in Los Osos Oaks Reserve are as old as 800 years, and they can be visited by wandering on any of three short, flat trails. It's easy to walk a brief stretch on all of them. The Chumash Loop, Oak View Trail, and Los Osos Creek Trail all lead from the parking lot and split off from each other. Oak View is just a short out-and-back trip through the trees and provides the best look at the reserve's highlights; Chumash Loop is a little longer and loops around the reserve. The Los Osos Creek Trail is the least impressive of the three, showing off the fewest fine tree specimens and following a marshy stretch of creek. The oak forest is a mix of very large, old trees with moss hanging from their branches, and tiny, dwarfed ones. Some of the oaks' trunks and branches are so twisted, gnarled, and wrinkled that they look like a tangled web of elephants' trunks. If you're into photography, this is the kind of place that is best captured in black and white. And, if the coast is foggy, this hike is ideal, because all the beauty of the forest is close enough to touch.

Location: West of San Luis Obispo in Los Osos; map G2, grid h3.

User groups: Hikers only. No dogs, horses, or mountain bikes. No wheelchair facilities.

Permits: No permits are required. Parking and access are free.

Maps: Ask the USGS for a topographic map of the Morro Bay South area.

Directions: From U.S. 101 in San Luis Obispo, take the Los Osos exit and head west on Los Osos Valley Road. Drive 8.5 miles on Los Osos Valley Road to the Los Osos Oaks Reserve on the left side of the road, which is marked by a small sign. The reserve is exactly one mile east of 10th Street in Los Osos and just west of the bear statue on the road. There is a small parking area by the trailhead, just off Los Osos Valley Road.

Contact: Los Osos Oaks Reserve, c/o Morro Bay State Park, State Park Road, Morro Bay, CA 93442; tel. (805) 772-7434; San Luis Obispo Coast State Parks, tel. (805) 549-3312.

6 Montaña de Oro Bluffs Trail
3.0 mi/1.5 hrs

How can a state park this good be free of charge? We can't figure it out, but we're glad it is. The Bluffs Trail at Montaña de Oro State Park is one of the finest coast walks in Central and Southern California, blissfully free of the blight of human development and loaded with classic oceanside beauty. The flat trail winds along the top of Montaña de Oro's shale and sediment bluffs, with nonstop views of rocky offshore outcrops, colorful rock cliffs and arches, and the big blue Pacific. Wooden railings keep hikers from leaning too far over the edge of the constantly eroding bluffs. In addition to all the coastal vistas, the grasses alongside the trail explode in a display of orange poppies and other wildflowers in February, March, and April. The trail ends at a barbed wire fence and Pacific Gas and Electric Company property lined with huge cacti to keep people out. Just follow the tiny loop and retrace your steps on the trail. A good side trip is to explore the beach right across from the visitor center turnoff, near where you left your car.

Location: In Montaña de Oro State Park west of San Luis Obispo; map G2, grid i2.

User groups: Hikers and mountain bikes. No dogs or horses. No wheelchair facilities.

Permits: No permits are required. Parking and access are free.

Maps: A map of Montaña de Oro State Park is available for $1 at the visitor center or at Morro Bay State Park. Ask the USGS for a topographic map of the Morro Bay South area.

Directions: From U.S. 101 in San Luis Obispo, take the Los Osos exit and head west on Los Osos Valley Road. Drive 12 miles on Los Osos Valley Road to the Montaña de Oro entrance. Continue 2.5 miles to the small parking area on the right side of the road, 100 yards beyond the left turnoff for the visitor center. The signed Bluffs Trail begins there.

Contact: Montaña de Oro State Park, 3550 Pecho Valley Road, Los Osos, CA 93402; tel. (805) 528-0513; Morro Bay State Park, tel. (805) 772-7434; San Luis Obispo Coast State Parks, tel. (805) 549-3312.

7 Valencia and Oats Peaks
7.0 mi/3.5 hrs

With a cool ocean breeze keeping you comfortable, this seven-mile round-trip hike to two coastal peaks is a spectacular day trip. If you forget to carry water and/or hike in the heat of high noon, it can be a nightmare, so get prepared. The Valencia Peak Trail begins in Montaña de Oro State Park. The wide route heads briefly south and then turns inland for a gradual ascent through grasslands and wildflowers, chaparral and scrub. There are several junctions; all are well marked.

In two miles and with an elevation gain of 1,100 feet, you arrive at the top of Valencia Peak, elevation 1,347 feet. On a clear day you can see all the way from Point Sal in the south to Piedras Blancas in the north. From there you must descend for a mile (losing nearly 500 feet) to join a road that connects to the Oats

Peak Trail, then hike upward once again on the Oats Peak Trail. (Sorry, but there's no other way to do it from the top of Valencia Peak.)

Oats Peak is more easily gained in 1.2 miles, and a survey marker tells you when you reach its summit at 1,373 feet. From there you can walk along the ridge for a while to enjoy more of the spectacular views of the ocean, Morro Rock, and the inland mountains, or you can head back downhill. Keep to the Oats Peak Trail for your descent. If you take Oats Peak Trail all the way back, you'll have a 10-minute walk on the park road to get back to your car. One more thing to think about: If you can possibly visit from February to April, you get a good chance at crystal-clear vistas and the best chance of seeing Montaña de Oro's signature wildflower display. The park's hills are gorgeous in season.

Location: In Montaña de Oro State Park west of San Luis Obispo; map G2, grid i2.

User groups: Hikers and horses. No dogs or mountain bikes. No wheelchair facilities.

Permits: No permits are required. Parking and access are free.

Maps: A map of Montaña de Oro State Park is available for $1 at the visitor center or at Morro Bay State Park. Ask the USGS for a topographic map of the Morro Bay South area.

Directions: From U.S. 101 in San Luis Obispo, take the Los Osos exit and head west on Los Osos Valley Road. Drive 12 miles on Los Osos Valley Road to the Montaña de Oro entrance. Continue 2.5 miles to the small parking area on the right side of the road, 100 yards beyond the left turnoff for the visitor center. The Valencia Peak Tail begins on the left side of the road.

Contact: Montaña de Oro State Park, 3550 Pecho Valley Road, Los Osos, CA 93402; tel. (805) 528-0513; Morro Bay State Park, tel. (805) 772-7434; San Luis Obispo Coast State Parks, tel. (805) 549-3312.

8 Big Falls

3.0 mi/1.5 hrs

The journey to Big Falls in the Santa Lucia Wilderness is a wacky, water-filled adventure.

Even as late as June, the drive to the trailhead can require dozens of crossings of Lopez Creek. In some places the stream simply becomes the road. In comparison to the drive, the hike is surprisingly easy and fast. You walk through a fern- and flower-filled sycamore and oak forest to the first waterfall, only .5 mile in. This is not actually Big Falls; it's a smaller waterfall, although plenty of people mistake it for Big Falls. This waterfall is only about 30 feet high, with many small trout swimming in its lower pool and a much deeper pool just above its lip. People sunbathe by the rocky pools upstream. You can continue hiking beyond this cataract to the real Big Falls, another mile farther. Wildflowers are excellent all along the route and at their best in spring. The terrain gets drier and rockier as you climb up out of the canyon to Big Falls, and you'll find different types of flowers and foliage on this upper part of the trail. Big Falls is about 80 feet tall, but it's only impressive early in the year. By June it has much less flow than the smaller waterfall downstream. Note that if you want to hike more, the trail continues beyond Big Falls for another mile, making an exposed and steep ascent to Hi Mountain Road.

Location: In the Santa Lucia Wilderness near Arroyo Grande; map G2, grid i7.

User groups: Hikers, dogs, and horses. No mountain bikes. No wheelchair facilities.

Permits: No day-use permits are required. A national forest recreation pass is required for each vehicle; fees are $5 for one day or $30 for a year.

Maps: For a map of Los Padres National Forest, send $6 to U.S. Forest Service, Map Sales, P.O. Box 587, Camino, CA 95709; tel. (530) 647-5390 or website: www.r5.fs.fed.us/visitorcenter. Ask the USGS for a topographic map of the Tar Spring Ridge area.

Directions: From San Luis Obispo drive 15 miles south on U.S. 101 to Arroyo Grande and the Highway 227/Lopez Lake exit. Head east on Highway 227 and turn right on Lopez Drive, following the signs toward

Lopez Lake for 10.3 miles. Turn right on Hi Mountain Road (before Lopez Lake's entrance station). Drive .8 mile, turn left on Upper Lopez Canyon Road, and drive 6.3 miles, passing a Scout Camp, and turn right. In .1 mile the pavement ends. Continue for 3.5 miles on the dirt road, crossing Lopez Creek numerous times in the wet season, to the Big Falls Trailhead. The trailhead is not usually marked, so set your odometer and look for a small waterfall on the left side of the road. The trail leads from the right side of the road. Note: Four-wheel-drive vehicles are recommended.

Contact: Los Padres National Forest, Santa Lucia Ranger District, 1616 N. Carlotti Drive, Santa Maria, CA 93454; tel. (805) 925-9538 or fax (805) 681-2781.

9 Little Falls
1.0 mi/0.5 hr

Little Falls is just as pretty as its neighbor Big Falls in the Santa Lucia Wilderness, and getting to it requires the same wet and rugged drive, but less of it. If your car isn't up to the 3.5 miles of rocky road and stream crossings that it takes to get to Big Falls, maybe you can convince it to go only 1.6 miles to Little Falls. If even that's too much, you can always park where the pavement ends and walk to Little Falls, adding 3.2 miles round-trip to the mileage shown above. It's still a pretty easy hike and with plenty of lovely scenery. You hike from the trailhead along Little Falls Creek, a cool, shady stream that is teeming with small trout and lined with oaks, sycamores, bays, and maples. Maidenhair and giant woodwardia ferns line its rocky pools. After only 15 minutes of hiking (less than .5 mile), you'll see a spur trail heading off to the left, which you can follow upstream for a few hundred feet to Little Falls, a 50-foot limestone waterfall. The main trail continues beyond this spur to many fine, water-carved pools, perfect for wading into. The trail eventually climbs out of the canyon to Hi Mountain Road.

Location: In the Santa Lucia Wilderness near Arroyo Grande; map G2, grid i7.

User groups: Hikers, dogs, and horses. No mountain bikes. No wheelchair facilities.

Permits: No day-use permits are required. A national forest recreation pass is required for each vehicle; fees are $5 for one day or $30 for a year.

Maps: For a map of Los Padres National Forest, send $6 to U.S. Forest Service, Map Sales, P.O. Box 587, Camino, CA 95709; tel. (530) 647-5390 or website: www.r5.fs.fed.us/visitorcenter. Ask the USGS for a topographic map of the Tar Spring Ridge area.

Directions: From San Luis Obispo drive 15 miles south on U.S. 101 to Arroyo Grande and the Highway 227/Lopez Lake exit. Head east on Highway 227; turn right on Lopez Drive, following the signs toward Lopez Lake for 10.3 miles. Turn right on Hi Mountain Road (before Lopez Lake's entrance station). Drive .8 mile and turn left on Upper Lopez Canyon Road. Drive 6.3 miles, passing a Scout Camp, and then turn right. The pavement ends .1 mile farther on. Continue for 1.6 miles on the dirt road, crossing Lopez Creek numerous times in the wet season, to the Little Falls Trailhead. The trail leads from the right side of the road. Note: Four-wheel-drive vehicles are recommended.

Contact: Los Padres National Forest, Santa Lucia Ranger District, 1616 N. Carlotti Drive, Santa Maria, CA 93454; tel. (805) 925-9538 or fax (805) 681-2781.

10 Duna Vista and Two Waters Trails
2.2-6.6 mi/1-3 hrs

Most people on the Central Coast know that Lopez Lake is completely set up for water recreation—boating, waterskiing, windsurfing, fishing, you name it—but not everyone knows that the park is also great for hiking, especially in springtime. The best path in the park, Duna Vista Trail, is accessible via either a long hike or a short hike and a boat ride. The latter option works out great for people who want to go hiking while their loved ones go fishing; they can be dropped off and picked up later. Guided trips are also frequently available; check with the park for dates and times. If you're going by boat, there are two trailheads (docks) for the Two Waters Trail, one on the Lopez arm of the lake and one on the Wittenberg arm. You can start from either trailhead or arrange a shuttle pickup with a friend so you can start at one end and finish at the other. From either trailhead the Two Waters Trail runs for .6 mile to the Duna Vista Trail, which you follow uphill for .5 mile. California fuschias bloom along the trail, mixed in among the sage and chaparral. After a 600-foot climb, you're rewarded with views of the Santa Lucia Wilderness, the Pacific Ocean, and Pismo Dunes. (Oh yeah, Duna Vista—now we get it.) If you can't arrange a boat ride, you can hike to the start of the Two Waters Trail. Start walking from the end of the park road on the Wittenberg Trail, connect with the Tuouski Trail by Camp French (a Scout Camp), and follow Tuouski Trail to its junction with the east end of the Two Waters Trail. Keep in mind that this changes a 2.2-mile round-trip into a 6.6-mile round-trip.

Location: At Lopez Lake east of Arroyo Grande; map G2, grid j7.

User groups: Hikers, horses, and mountain bikes. No dogs. No wheelchair facilities.

Permits: No permits are required. A $5 day-use fee is charged per vehicle.

Maps: Ask the USGS for a topographic map of the Tar Spring Ridge area.

Directions: From San Luis Obispo drive 15 miles south on U.S. 101 to Arroyo Grande and the Highway 227/Lopez Lake exit. Head east on Highway 227 and turn right on Lopez Drive, following the signs to Lopez Lake for 10.4 miles. To reach the Two Waters Trailhead, you can take a boat ride up the Wittenberg or Lopez arms of the lake, or add four miles to your trip by hiking from the Wittenberg Trailhead. To reach the latter, drive 1.5 miles past the park entrance station to the parking area near where the park road is gated off.

Contact: Lopez Lake Recreation Area, 6800 Lopez Drive, Arroyo Grande, CA 93420; tel. (805) 788-2381.

11 Blackberry Springs and High Ridge
3.0 mi/1.5 hrs

Great views of the grassy hills and blue water of Lopez Lake are yours for the taking on the High Ridge Trail. Start from the Blackberry Springs Trailhead at Squirrel Campground, where you can pick up an interpretive brochure. Learn all about the Chumash Indians who once lived here as you follow the trail uphill through a foliage-rich creek canyon, which includes some blackberry bushes. Many of the other plants along the trail are also edible and were used by the Chumash. The trail steepens as it climbs to connect with High Ridge Trail at .75 mile, where you turn left and wander along a firebreak on Turkey Ridge, which has wide-open views. It's hot and sunny up here, so that may dictate how far you wander, but the trail leads for 1.5 miles before it drops down to the Wittenberg arm of the lake. Might as well just head out for .5 mile or so, enjoy the views of the Santa Lucia Wilderness and the coast, and then turn around and head back. Another option is to turn right instead of left on the High Ridge Trail, walk .5 mile, and connect with the Turkey Ridge Trail. Take the Turkey Ridge Trail back to the parking lot by Squirrel Campground for a nice three-mile loop trip.

Location: At Lopez Lake east of Arroyo Grande; map G2, grid j7.

User groups: Hikers, horses, and mountain bikes. No dogs. No wheelchair facilities.

Permits: No permits are required. A $5 day-use fee is charged per vehicle.

Maps: Ask the USGS for a topographic map of the Tar Spring Ridge area.

Directions: From San Luis Obispo drive 15 miles south on U.S. 101 to Arroyo Grande and the Highway 227/Lopez Lake exit. Head east on Highway 227 and turn right on Lopez Drive, following the signs to Lopez Lake for 10.4 miles. Continue past the entrance station to Squirrel Campground and the trailhead for the Blackberry Springs Trail.

Contact: Lopez Lake Recreation Area, 6800 Lopez Drive, Arroyo Grande, CA 93420; tel. (805) 788-2381.

NATIVE AMERICAN PICTOGRAPHS
ALONG THE PAINTED ROCK
INTERPRETIVE TRAIL

MAP G3

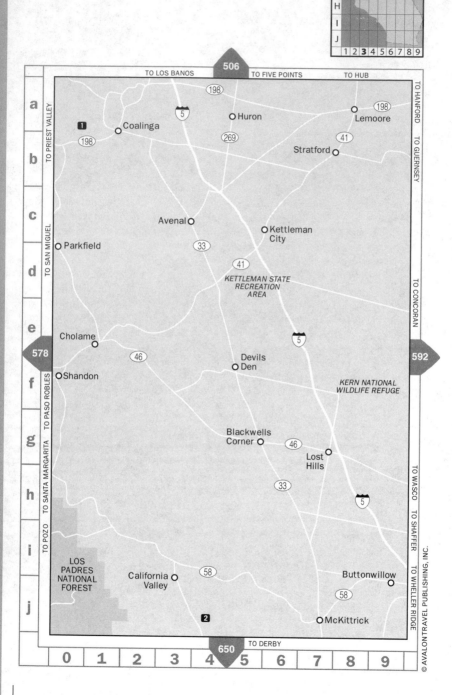

TO LOS BANOS **506** TO FIVE POINTS TO HUB

198

5 Huron

■1 Coalinga

198 269

Lemoore 198

TO HANFORD

41 Stratford

TO GUERNSEY

Avenal Kettleman City

Parkfield 33

TO SAN MIGUEL

41

KETTLEMAN STATE RECREATION AREA

TO CONCORAN

Cholame

578 46 Devils Den

5

Shandon

TO PASO ROBLES

KERN NATIONAL WILDLIFE REFUGE

592

Blackwells Corner 46 Lost Hills

TO SANTA MARGARITA

33

5

TO WASCO

TO POZO

TO SHAFFER

LOS PADRES NATIONAL FOREST

California Valley 58 Buttonwillow

58

■2 McKittrick

TO WHEELER RIDGE

650 TO DERBY

0 1 2 3 4 5 6 7 8 9

© AVALON TRAVEL PUBLISHING, INC.

CHAPTER G3

1 Kreyenhagen Peak..... 589

2 Carrizo Plains
and Painted Rock...... 589

1 Kreyenhagen Peak

4.0 mi/2.5 hrs

Most people don't realize that there's a National Recreation Trail out here near Coalinga, the town that was made famous by an earthquake, but it's true. In winter and spring, this is a first-class hike to the summit of Kreyenhagen Peak, elevation 3,558 feet, climbing through chaparral-covered hillsides. The trail begins at the far end of the picnic area and crosses a dry streambed, then begins to ascend. It's well graded all the way, with the second mile slightly steeper than the first. The vista from the peak includes the Diablo Range, the San Joaquin Valley, and miles of surrounding Bureau of Land Management land. That's a pretty wide scope considering how little effort is required to obtain the view.

Location: Northwest of Coalinga; map G3, grid a1.

User groups: Hikers, dogs, horses, and mountain bikes. No wheelchair facilities.

Permits: No permits are required. A $3 day-use fee is charged per vehicle.

Maps: Ask the USGS for a topographic map of the Curry Mountain area.

Directions: From Coalinga drive 20 miles west on Highway 198 to Coalinga Mineral Springs Road. Turn right (north) and drive four miles to Coalinga Mineral Springs County Park.

Contact: Bureau of Land Management, Hollister Resource Area, 20 Hamilton Court, Hollister, CA 95023; tel. (408) 831-5000.

2 Carrizo Plains and Painted Rock

1.5 mi/1.0 hr

Carrizo Plains is considered California's largest nature preserve, and the big draw is the number of sandhill cranes who hang around here from November to February. While thousands of migrating and resident birds can be seen in this area, it's the cranes that bring the hordes of bird-lovers and photographers to alkali Soda Lake and the surrounding plains. Since the birds don't stay in one place, most people spot them while driving around the Carrizo Plains area, or while stopping at the overlook platform near Soda Lake. The birds are unmistakable—drab gray in color but with seven-foot wing spans and three-foot-long legs. After checking out the big birds, head for the Painted Rock Interpretive Trail, where you can walk the flat dirt road that leads to 55-foot-tall Painted Rock. The interior of the rounded sandstone amphitheater has some of the best Native American pictographs in the country, although some have been eroded by time and weather. Spring wildflowers are beautiful all across the plains.

Special note: The area is closed from March 1 to July 15 to protect nesting falcons. The best time to see the sandhill cranes is December to February.

Location: In eastern San Luis Obispo County, south of California Valley; map G3, grid j4.

User groups: Hikers, dogs, horses, and mountain bikes. No wheelchair facilities.

Permits: No permits are required. Parking and access are free.

Maps: A brochure on the Carrizo Plains is available from the BLM at the address below. Ask the USGS for a topographic map of the Painted Rock area.

Directions: From San Luis Obispo on U.S. 101, drive north for 10 miles and take the Santa Margarita/Highway 58 exit.

Drive east on Highway 58 for 50 miles to the Soda Lake Road turnoff on the right. Turn right (south) and drive 13.5 miles to the Painted Rock Trail and visitor center turnoff on the right. Turn right and drive to the visitor center, then turn left and drive two miles to the Painted Rock trailhead.

Contact: Bureau of Land Management, Caliente Resource Area, 3801 Pegasus Drive, Bakersfield, CA 93308; tel. (661) 391-6000; Goodwin Education Center at Carrizo Plains, open Thursday through Sunday from December through May, tel. (805) 475-2131.

ANN MARIE BROWN

JUST OFF INTERSTATE 5 NEAR
BAKERSFIELD LIES THE TULE ELK
RESERVE; IF YOU FORGET YOUR
BINOCULARS, JUST USE THE
RESERVE'S TELESCOPES.

MAP G4

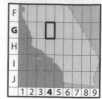

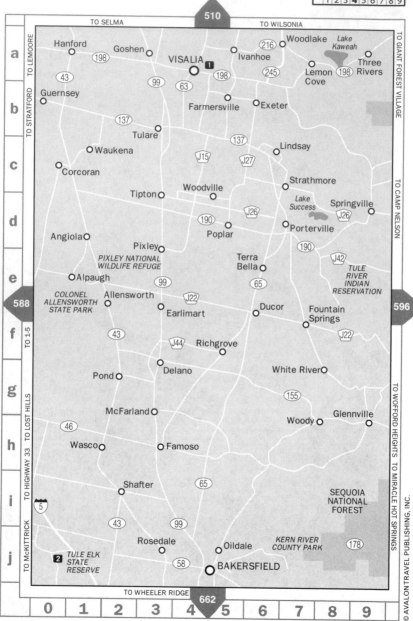

TO SELMA · 510 · TO WILSONIA

a
TO LEMOORE
TO STRATFORD
Hanford
Goshen
198
VISALIA **1**
Ivanhoe
216
Woodlake
Lake Kaweah
Lemon Cove
198
Three Rivers
TO GIANT FOREST VILLAGE

b
Guernsey
43
99
63
198
245
Farmersville
Exeter
137

c
Waukena
Tulare
J15
137
J27
Lindsay
Corcoran

d
Tipton
Woodville
Strathmore
J26
Lake Success
Springville
J26
190
Poplar
Porterville
190
TO CAMP NELSON

e
Angiola
Pixley
PIXLEY NATIONAL WILDLIFE REFUGE
Terra Bella
J42
Alpaugh
99
65
TULE RIVER INDIAN RESERVATION
COLONEL ALLENSWORTH STATE PARK
Allensworth
J22
Earlimart
Ducor
Fountain Springs

588 · **596**

f
TO I-5
43
J44
Richgrove
J22

g
TO LOST HILLS
Pond
Delano
White River
155

h
TO HIGHWAY 33
46
McFarland
Woody
Glennville
Wasco
Famoso

i
TO McKITTRICK
5
Shafter
65
SEQUOIA NATIONAL FOREST

j
2 TULE ELK STATE RESERVE
43
Rosedale
99
Oildale
58
BAKERSFIELD
KERN RIVER COUNTY PARK
178

TO WHEELER RIDGE · 662

TO WOFFORD HEIGHTS · TO MIRACLE HOT SPRINGS
© AVALON TRAVEL PUBLISHING, INC.

0 1 2 3 4 5 6 7 8 9

CHAPTER G4

1 Kaweah Oaks Preserve. . . 593
2 Tule Elk State Reserve. . . 593

1 Kaweah Oaks Preserve
2.0 mi/1.0 hr

The Kaweah Oaks Preserve is Tulare County's premier nature preserve, the slim remains of the massive oak forest that once shaded Visalia and its environs. Some big oaks still stand, as well as wild grapes growing as high as 30 feet. From the parking area, go through the cattle gate and walk down the old ranch road to the interpretive area and picnic tables on the left (about a third of a mile). Then cross the weir on the far side of the picnic area and walk the nature trail loop. You can also continue straight on the ranch road, but this is a cattle grazing area, so be sure to close all the gates behind you. As you walk, look for herons, hawks, and owls, as well as the preserve's four species of woodpeckers. In addition to the big old oaks and grapevines, you'll see some California sycamore, cottonwoods, and willows growing near the streams. This is a good walk for winter or spring, or early morning or evening in summer, when the valley is at its coolest.

Location: East of Visalia; map G4, grid a4.
User groups: Hikers and mountain bikes. No dogs or horses. No wheelchair facilities.
Permits: No permits are required. Parking and access are free.
Maps: Ask the USGS for a topographic map of the Visalia area.
Directions: From Tulare on Highway 99, drive north for 10 miles and turn east on Highway 198. Drive 13 miles on Highway 198, passing Visalia, to the left turnoff for Road 182. Turn left on Road 182 and drive .4 mile to the trailhead parking area on the left.
Contact: Kaweah Oaks Preserve, c/o Four Creeks Land Trust, tel. (559) 738-0211, website: kaweahoaks.com

2 Tule Elk State Reserve
1.0 mi/0.5 hr

Most people just plain don't know that there's a huge herd of magnificent tule elk wandering around a few miles from Interstate 5. If you didn't know, better pull off the highway and get yourself to the Tule Elk State Reserve near Tupman. There aren't a lot of trails to choose from, but if you've been driving on Interstate 5 long enough, just getting out of the car is a big deal. A dirt road runs along the east boundary of the reserve, popular with people stretching their legs and hopeful elk seekers. The animals are most active in the autumn, when their rutting season begins. Bring binoculars for your best chance at a good view, or take a stroll to the walk-up platform where you can look through a telescope at the elk. Make sure you stop in at the visitor center and check out the interesting displays on the elk and the history of the Central Valley.

Location: Off Interstate 5 west of Bakersfield; map G4, grid j0.
User groups: Hikers only. No dogs, horses, or mountain bikes. Some facilities are wheelchair accessible.
Permits: No permits are required. A $3 day-use fee is charged per vehicle.
Maps: Ask the USGS for a topographic map of the Tupman area.
Directions: From the junction of Interstate 5 and Highway 99 north of the Grapevine, drive north on Interstate 5 for 33 miles to the Stockdale Highway exit. Drive west for 1.2 miles and turn left (south) on Morris Road. Drive 1.6 miles on Morris Road and turn left into the Tule Elk State Reserve. The route is well signed.
Contact: Tule Elk State Reserve, 8653 Station Road, Buttonwillow, CA 93206; tel. (661) 764-6881.

THE TREK TO
MONARCH LAKES IS
WORTH THE CLIMB.

MAP G5

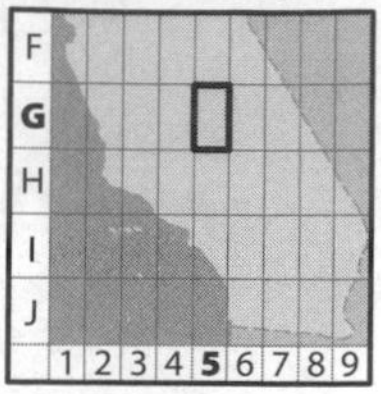

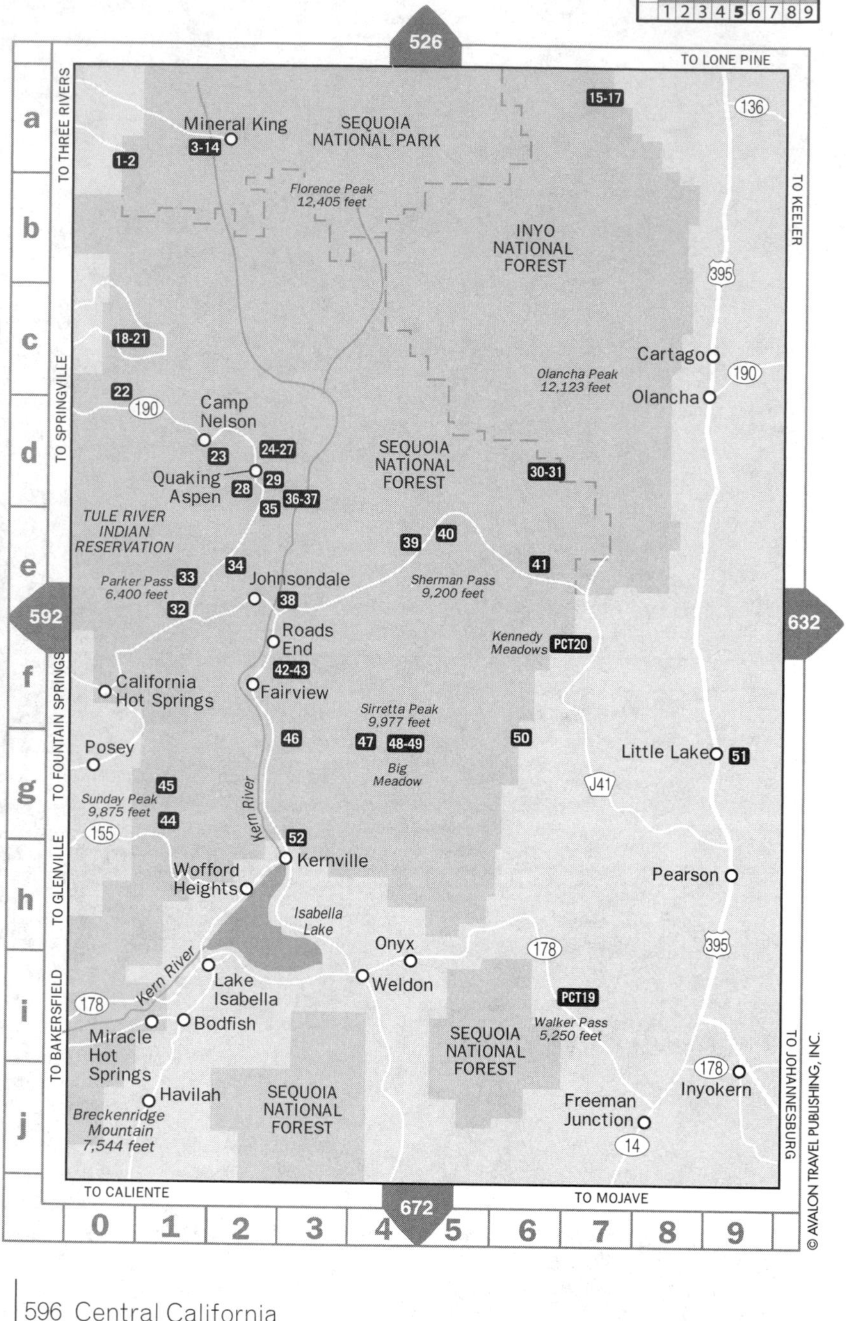

526

TO LONE PINE

TO THREE RIVERS

a

Mineral King
3-14
1-2

SEQUOIA
NATIONAL PARK

15-17

136

TO KEELER

b

Florence Peak
12,405 feet

INYO
NATIONAL
FOREST

395

c

18-21

22
190

Camp
Nelson

Olancha Peak
12,123 feet

Cartago

190

d

23
24-27
28 29
36-37
35

Quaking
Aspen

SEQUOIA
NATIONAL
FOREST

Olancha

30-31

TO SPRINGVILLE

TULE RIVER
INDIAN
RESERVATION

39 40

e

Parker Pass
6,400 feet

34
Johnsondale
33
32
38

Sherman Pass
9,200 feet

41

592

f

TO FOUNTAIN SPRINGS

California
Hot Springs

Roads
End
42-43
Fairview

Kennedy
Meadows PCT20

632

g

Posey

46

Sirretta Peak
9,977 feet

47 48-49

Big
Meadow

50

Little Lake 51

Sunday Peak
9,875 feet

45
44

155

Kern River

J41

h

TO GLENVILLE

52
Kernville

Wofford
Heights

Isabella
Lake

Pearson

i

TO BAKERSFIELD

178

Kern River

Lake
Isabella
Bodfish

Onyx
Weldon

178

PCT19
Walker Pass
5,250 feet

395

j

Miracle
Hot
Springs

Havilah

Breckenridge
Mountain
7,544 feet

SEQUOIA
NATIONAL
FOREST

SEQUOIA
NATIONAL
FOREST

Freeman
Junction

14

178 Inyokern

TO JOHANNESBURG

TO CALIENTE

672

TO MOJAVE

0 1 2 3 4 5 6 7 8 9

© AVALON TRAVEL PUBLISHING, INC.

CHAPTER G5

1 Ladybug Trail. 597

2 Garfield-Hockett Trail . . 598

3 Paradise Ridge. 599

4 Hockett Trail to
East Fork Bridge 599

5 Cold Springs
Nature Trail. 600

6 Farewell Gap Trail
to Aspen Flat 601

7 Mosquito Lakes 601

8 Eagle Lake Trail 602

9 Franklin Lakes 603

10 White Chief Mine Trail. . 604

11 Timber Gap Trail. 604

12 Monarch Lakes 605

13 Crystal Lake Trail 606

14 Black Wolf Falls 606

15 Cottonwood Lakes. 607

16 Cottonwood Pass. 608

17 Trail Pass. 608

18 Balch Park
Nature Trail 609

19 Adam and Eve
Loop Trail 609

20 Redwood Crossing. 610

21 Moses Gulch Trail 611

22 Doyle Trail. 611

23 Amos Alonzo
Stagg Tree 612

24 Jordan Peak Lookout . . . 612

25 Clicks Creek Trail 613

26 John Jordan/Hossack
Meadow Trail. 613

27 Freeman Creek Trail . . . 614

28 Summit Trail
to Slate Mountain 614

(CONTINUED ON NEXT PAGE)

1 Ladybug Trail

3.8 mi/2.0 hrs

The South Fork area is the forgotten region of Sequoia National Park. Accessible only by a 13-mile dead-end road out of Three Rivers, South Fork is the place to go when you just want to get away from it all. Solitude in a national park? You can find it here. The elevation is low—only 3,600 feet—so the area is accessible year-round, and there may be no finer winter walk than a hike on the Ladybug Trail out of South Fork. The trail leaves the far end of South Fork Campground and heads through an oak and bay forest along the South Fork Kaweah River. At 1.7 miles you reach Ladybug Camp, a primitive camping area along the river's edge, in the shade of pines and firs. A short scramble downstream of the camp gives you a look at Ladybug Falls, a 25-foot waterfall set in a rocky grotto. If you continue upstream, the trail leads another few hundred yards and then switchbacks uphill, heading for Whiskey Log Camp. A use trail leaves the main trail and continues a short distance upriver, where there are many beautiful rocky pools. And in case you haven't guessed, the trail, camp, and falls are named for the millions of ladybugs that winter near the river, then take flight in the spring to head back to the Central Valley to feed.

Location: Off Highway 198 in the South Fork region of Sequoia National Park; map G5, grid a0.

User groups: Hikers and horses. No dogs or mountain bikes. No wheelchair facilities.

Permits: No permits are required. There is a $10 entrance

(CONTINUED)

29 Needles Lookout 615
30 Casa Vieja Meadow 615
31 Jordan Hot Springs 616
32 Trail of 100 Giants 616
33 Mule Peak Lookout 617
34 Nobe Young Falls 617
35 Dome Rock 618
36 Peppermint
Creek Falls 618
37 Alder Creek Trail. 619
38 North Fork Kern
River Trail. 619
39 Sherman Peak Trail. . . . 620
40 Bald Mountain Lookout . 620
41 Jackass Creek National
Recreation Trail 621
42 Whiskey Flat Trail 621

43 Packsaddle Cave Trail . . 622
44 Unal Trail 623
45 Sunday Peak Trail 623
46 Rincon Trail. 623
47 Salmon Creek Falls 624
48 Sirretta Peak 625
49 Manter Meadow Loop . . 625
50 Rockhouse Basin 626
51 Fossil Falls. 626
52 Cannell Meadow National
Recreation Trail 627

**Pacific Crest Trail
(PCT) Section Overview**

PCT-19 Walker Pass to
Kennedy Meadows . . 628
PCT-20 Kennedy Meadows to
Mount Whitney 628

fee at Sequoia and Kings Canyon National Parks, good for seven days.

Maps: Free park maps are available at park entrance stations or by contacting Sequoia and Kings Canyon National Parks at the address below. A more detailed map is available for a fee from Tom Harrison Cartography, tel. (415) 456-7940, or Trails Illustrated, tel. (800) 962-1643. Ask the USGS for a topographic map of the Dennison Peak area.

Directions: From Visalia drive east on Highway 198 for 35 miles to one mile west of Three Rivers. Turn right on South Fork Drive and drive 12.8 miles to South Fork Campground. (At nine miles, the road turns to dirt.) Day-use parking is available just inside the camp entrance. The trailhead is at the far end of the campground loop.

Contact: Sequoia and Kings Canyon National Parks, Three Rivers, CA 93271-9700; tel. (559) 565-3134 or (559) 335-2856.

2 Garfield-Hockett Trail
5.8 mi/3.0 hrs

The trip to the magnificent Garfield Grove is only 2.9 miles from South Fork Campground, and if you don't mind a steep climb and possibly sharing the trail with horse packers, you should be sure to take this hike. The trail climbs immediately and keeps climbing, but fortunately is shaded by oaks most of the way. The ascent rewards you with a continual view of distant Homer's Nose, a granite landmark that, although prominent, looks little like anybody's nose. In just under three miles of nonstop climbing, you reach the first of many sequoias in the Garfield Grove, reported to be one of the largest groves in the national parks. By the time you reach it, you've gained 2,000 feet in elevation, so pick a big tree to lean against, pull out a snack, and take a breather.

Location: Off Highway 198 in the South Fork region of Sequoia National Park; map G5, grid a0.

User groups: Hikers and horses. No dogs or mountain bikes. No wheelchair facilities.

Permits: No permits are required. There is a $10 entrance fee at Sequoia and Kings Canyon National Parks, good for seven days.

Maps: Free park maps are available at park entrance stations or by contacting Sequoia and Kings Canyon National Parks at the address below. A more detailed map is available for a fee from Tom Harrison Cartography, tel. (415) 456-7940, or Trails Illustrated, tel. (800) 962-1643. Ask the USGS for a topographic map of the Dennison Peak area.

Directions: From Visalia drive east on Highway 198 for 35 miles to one mile west of Three Rivers. Turn right on South Fork Drive and drive 12.8 miles to South Fork Campground. (At nine miles, the road turns to dirt.) Day-use parking is available just inside the camp entrance. The trailhead is on the right side of the campground.

Contact: Sequoia and Kings Canyon National Parks, Three Rivers, CA 93271-9700; tel. (559) 565-3134 or (559) 335-2856.

3 Paradise Ridge

3.2 mi/1.5 hrs

OK, you've just driven the 20 twisting miles into Mineral King from Three Rivers. You're tired, dusty, and itching to get out of the car and move your legs. What's the first trail you can reach in Mineral King? The Paradise Ridge Trail, and it climbs right away, getting you huffing and puffing, and clearing out the road dust from your lungs. After the initial steepness of the trail, the grade becomes easier as it moves into switchbacks ascending the hill. The path is loaded with giant sequoia trees, some in clusters as large as 10 or more. At your feet are tons of ferns. As you climb, the views just keep improving—you see the East Fork Kaweah River Canyon below you and far off, the Great Western Divide. You can hike all the way to the top of the ridge at three miles, but the views aren't any better there than they are on the way up. Most people just cruise uphill a way, and turn around when they've had enough. Besides the big trees and the big views, our favorite thing about this trail was that we saw more bears than people.

Location: Off Highway 198 in the Mineral King region of Sequoia National Park; map G5, grid a1.

User groups: Hikers and horses. No dogs or mountain bikes. No wheelchair facilities.

Permits: No permits are required. There is a $10 entrance fee at Sequoia and Kings Canyon National Parks, good for seven days.

Maps: Free park maps are available at park entrance stations or by contacting Sequoia and Kings Canyon National Parks at the address below. A more detailed map is available for a fee from Tom Harrison Cartography, tel. (415) 456-7940, or Trails Illustrated, tel. (800) 962-1643. Ask the USGS for a topographic map of the Silver City area.

Directions: From Visalia drive east on Highway 198 for 38 miles to Mineral King Road, 2.5 miles east of Three Rivers. If you reach the Ash Mountain entrance station, you've gone too far. Turn right on Mineral King Road and drive 20 miles to the Hockett Trail parking area on the right, .25 mile past Atwell Mill Camp. Park there and walk back west on Mineral King Road about .3 mile to the trailhead for Paradise Ridge, on the north side of the road.

Contact: Sequoia and Kings Canyon National Parks, Three Rivers, CA 93271-9700; tel. (559) 565-3134 or (559) 335-2856.

4 Hockett Trail to East Fork Bridge

4.0 mi/2.0 hrs

The Hockett Trail makes a fine day-hiking path in Mineral King, suitable for all kinds of hikers. Families with small children can just walk a mile downhill to the footbridge over the East Fork Kaweah River, where there is a small waterfall and many sculptured granite pools, and then turn around and head back. People looking for a longer trip can continue another mile to the East Fork Grove of Sequoias and Deer Creek. Both groups get to hike through a beautiful forest of big conifers—pines, cedars, and firs—and fields of mountain misery. The trail starts in an area of sequoia stumps, near where the Atwell Mill cut lumber in the 1880s. Live sequoias still flourish farther down the path, near the river's edge; apparently they were spared because of their distance from the mill. The trail is well graded, and even the uphill return is only a moderate climb.

Location: Off Highway 198 in the Mineral King region of Sequoia National Park; map G5, grid a1.

User groups: Hikers and horses. No dogs or mountain bikes. No wheelchair facilities.

Permits: No permits are required. There is a $10 entrance fee at Sequoia and Kings Canyon National Parks, good for seven days.

Maps: Free park maps are available at park entrance stations or by contacting Sequoia and Kings Canyon National Parks at the address below. A more detailed map is available for a fee from Tom Harrison Cartography, tel. (415) 456-7940, or Trails Illustrated, tel. (800) 962-1643. Ask the USGS for a topographic map of the Mineral King area.

Directions: From Visalia drive east on Highway 198 for 38 miles to Mineral King Road, 2.5 miles east of Three Rivers. If you reach the Ash Mountain entrance station, you've gone too far. Turn right on Mineral King Road and drive 20 miles to the Hockett Trail parking area on the right, .25 mile past Atwell Mill Camp. Park there and walk into the campground to campsite 16, where the trail begins.

Contact: Sequoia and Kings Canyon National Parks, Three Rivers, CA 93271-9700; tel. (559) 565-3134 or (559) 335-2856.

5 Cold Springs Nature Trail
2.0 mi/1.0 hr

You may not expect much from a campground nature trail, but the Cold Springs Nature Trail is guaranteed to exceed your expectations. Not only is it lined with wildflowers along the East Fork Kaweah River and informative signposts that teach you to identify junipers, red and white firs, cottonwoods, and aspens, but the views of the Sawtooth Ridge are glorious. The loop is less than .5 mile, but from the far end of it, the trail continues along the East Fork Kaweah River, heading another mile into Mineral King Valley. Walk to the loop's far end and then continue at least another .25 mile along the trail. It just gets prettier as it goes. Here's the best Mineral King tip we know: take this walk right before sunset, when the valley's surrounding mountain peaks turn every imaginable shade of pink, orange, and coral, reflecting the sun setting in the west. The vistas are so beautiful that they can practically make you weep.

Location: Off Highway 198 in the Mineral King region of Sequoia National Park; map G5, grid a21.

User groups: Hikers and horses. No dogs or mountain bikes. No wheelchair facilities.

Permits: No permits are required. There is a $10 entrance fee at Sequoia and Kings Canyon National Parks, good for seven days.

Maps: Free park maps are available at park entrance stations or by contacting Sequoia and Kings Canyon National Parks at the address below. A more detailed map is available for a fee from Tom Harrison Cartography, tel. (415) 456-7940, or Trails Illustrated, tel. (800) 962-1643. Ask the USGS for a topographic map of the Mineral King area.

Directions: From Visalia drive east on Highway 198 for 38 miles to Mineral King Road, 2.5 miles east of Three Rivers. If you reach the Ash Mountain entrance station, you've gone too far. Turn right on Mineral King Road and drive 23.5 miles to Cold Springs Campground on the right. The trail begins near site six. If you aren't staying in the camp, you can park by the Mineral King Ranger Station and walk into the campground.

Contact: Sequoia and Kings Canyon National Parks, Three Rivers, CA 93271-9700; tel. (559) 565-3134 or (559) 335-2856.

6 Farewell Gap Trail to Aspen Flat

2.0 mi/1.0 hr

If ever there was a perfect family hike, this would have to be it. Actually, if ever there was a perfect hike for every two-legged person on the planet, this would have to be it. The glacial-cut Mineral King Valley, a peaceful paradise of meadows, streams, and 100-year-old cabins, has to be one of the most scenic places in the West, and possibly in the world. An easy stroll along the canyon floor leads you past waterfalls and along the headwaters of the East Fork Kaweah River, in the awesome shelter of thousand-foot cliffs. After walking to the trailhead near the pack station, you follow the Farewell Gap Trail (an old dirt road) for a mile, then cross Crystal Creek and take the right fork off the main trail. This brings you closer to the river, where you follow a narrow use trail to Aspen Flat, a lovely grove of trees, or to Soda Springs, situated right along the river's edge. There you can see mineral springs bubbling up from the ground, turning the earth around them a bright orange color. Bring a fishing rod on this trail if you like, but be absolutely certain to bring your camera.

Location: Off Highway 198 in the Mineral King region of Sequoia National Park; map G5, grid a1.

User groups: Hikers and horses. No dogs or mountain bikes. No wheelchair facilities.

Permits: No permits are required. There is a $10 entrance fee at Sequoia and Kings Canyon National Parks, good for seven days.

Maps: Free park maps are available at park entrance stations or by contacting Sequoia and Kings Canyon National Parks at the address below. A more detailed map is available for a fee from Tom Harrison Cartography, tel. (415) 456-7940, or Trails Illustrated, tel. (800) 962-1643. Ask the USGS for a topographic map of the Mineral King area.

Directions: From Visalia drive east on Highway 198 for 38 miles to Mineral King Road, 2.5 miles east of Three Rivers. If you reach the Ash Mountain entrance station, you've gone too far. Turn right on Mineral King Road and drive 25 miles to the end of the road and the Eagle/Mosquito Trailhead. Take the right fork at the end of the road to reach the parking area. Walk back out of the parking lot and follow the road to the pack station; the Farewell Gap Trail begins just beyond it.

Contact: Sequoia and Kings Canyon National Parks, Three Rivers, CA 93271-9700; tel. (559) 565-3134 or (559) 335-2856.

7 Mosquito Lakes

8.0 mi/4.0 hrs or 2.0 days

Ah, paradise. You know you're in it as soon as you park your car at the end of Mineral King Road. The Eagle/Mosquito Trailhead is at 7,830 feet, and you set out from the parking lot near one of Mineral King's adorable cabins, left from the early 20th century and privately owned. Feel jealous? Keep walking; you'll get over it. In minutes you cross a footbridge over Spring Creek's cascade, called Tufa Falls because of the calcium carbonate in Spring Creek's water. Don't expect to see much of a waterfall—most of it is hidden by brush. At one mile, you reach the junction for Eagle Lake, the Mosquito Lakes, and White Chief, and take the right fork, climbing steadily. At two miles, you reach the Mosquito Lakes junction and go right, leaving the Eagle Lake Trail for another day. Climb up and then down the other side of Miner's Ridge at 9,300 feet. The final descent covers .5 mile; you reach Mosquito Lake number one at 9,040 feet and 3.6 miles. It's considered to be the easiest lake to reach in Mineral King, with a mostly shaded trail and only a 1,500-foot gain on the way in, plus a 250-foot gain on the way out. Still, if you've visited any of the other spectacular Mineral King lakes, this lake will look a little disappointing. It's small, shallow, and greenish. But fear not: this is the first of several Mosquito Lakes, all of which are linked by Mosquito Creek. Hikers with excess energy can follow the stream uphill to four more lakes. There is no maintained trail to the upper lakes, but if you follow the use trail near the stream, the going is easier. The use trail begins on the west side of the stream at the first lake, navigates around the rocky slope behind the lake, and then crosses the stream above it. The climb from lake number one to lake number two is steep, with a 600-foot elevation gain in .5 mile, but it's worth it. Lake number two is the usual destination for day-hikers; it's a blue, deep, granite-bound beauty, and makes for an eight-mile round-trip. Backpackers can find the first campsites at Mosquito Lake number two. Mosquito Lake number five is five miles from the Eagle/Mosquito Trailhead.

Location: Off Highway 198 in the Mineral King region of Sequoia National Park; map G5, grid a1.

User groups: Hikers and horses. No dogs or mountain bikes. No wheelchair facilities.

Permits: There is a $10 entrance fee at Sequoia and Kings Canyon National Parks, good for seven days. A free wilderness permit is required for overnight stays and is available on a first-come, first-served basis at the Mineral King ranger station, or in advance by mail or fax after March 1; for more information phone (559) 565-3708.

Maps: Free park maps are available at park entrance stations or by contacting Sequoia and Kings Canyon National Parks at the address below. A more detailed map is available for a fee from Tom Harrison Cartography, tel. (415) 456-7940, or Trails Illustrated, tel. (800) 962-1643. Ask the USGS for a topographic map of the Mineral King area.

Directions: From Visalia drive east on Highway 198 for 38 miles to Mineral King Road, 2.5 miles east of Three Rivers. If you reach the Ash Mountain entrance station, you've gone too far. Turn right on Mineral King Road and drive 25 miles to the end of the road and the Eagle/Mosquito Trailhead. Take the right fork at the end of the road to reach the parking area. The trail begins at the far end of the parking lot.

Contact: Sequoia and Kings Canyon National Parks, Three Rivers, CA 93271-9700; tel. (559) 565-3134 or (559) 335-2856.

8 Eagle Lake Trail

6.8 mi/4.0 hrs or 2.0 days

Eagle Lake is the glamour destination in Mineral King, the trail to hike if you can hike only one trail in the area. Why? The blue-green lake is drop-dead gorgeous, that's why, and its trail is challenging but manageable for most day-hikers. The total elevation gain to the lake is 2,200 feet. If you can stop staring at the scenery for a minute, you might even catch a fish or two while you're there. The Eagle Lake Trail follows the same route as the Mosquito Lake Trail, above, until the two-mile point near the Eagle Sink Holes. These are small craters in the ground where Eagle Creek suddenly disappears underground. At the trail junction by the sinkholes, go left for Eagle Lake. Enjoy the brief flat stretch here, because shortly you'll gain another 1,000 feet over 1.4 miles. Much of the climb is in an exposed, rocky area—a large boulder field that gets baked by the sun on warm days. Well-graded switchbacks and beautiful scenery make it easier. Soon you arrive at Eagle Lake's dam at 10,000 feet. The big lake is surrounded by glacially carved rock and has a few rocky islands. Brook trout swim in the clear waters. The trail continues along the lake's west side to many good picnicking spots and photo opportunities. Campsites are found near the lake.

Location: Off Highway 198 in the Mineral King region of Sequoia National Park; map G5, grid a1.

User groups: Hikers and horses. No dogs or mountain bikes. No wheelchair facilities.

Permits: There is a $10 entrance fee at Sequoia and Kings Canyon National Parks, good for seven days. A free wilderness permit is required for overnight stays and is available on a first-come, first-served basis at the Mineral King ranger station, or in advance by mail or fax after March 1; for more info phone (559) 565-3708.

Maps: Free park maps are available at park entrance stations or by contacting Sequoia and Kings Canyon National Parks at the address below. A more detailed map is available for a fee from Tom Harrison Cartography, tel. (415) 456-7940, or Trails Illustrated, tel. (800) 962-1643. Ask the USGS for a topographic map of the Mineral King area.

Directions: From Visalia drive east on Highway 198 for 38 miles to Mineral King Road, 2.5 miles east of Three Rivers. If you reach the Ash Mountain entrance station, you've gone too far. Turn right on Mineral King Road and drive 25 miles to the end of the road and the Eagle/Mosquito Trailhead. Take the right fork at the end of the road to reach the parking area. The trail begins at the far end of the parking lot.

Contact: Sequoia and Kings Canyon National Parks, Three Rivers, CA 93271-9700; tel. (559) 565-3134 or (559) 335-2856.

9 Franklin Lakes

10.8 mi/
6.0 hrs or 2.0 days

Maybe the best thing about hiking to Franklin Lakes is the waterfalls you get to pass along the way, especially our favorite cascades on Franklin Creek. Or maybe it's the prolific wildflowers along the trail, or the spectacular views over Mineral King Valley that you gain as you climb. Maybe it's the big lake itself, set below Tulare Peak. Or the fact that the trail to reach it is so well graded, with a 2,500-foot elevation gain spread out over 5.4 miles. What the heck—this trail is about as close to hiking perfection as you get.

The first two miles are nearly flat, as the route winds along the bottom of Mineral King's canyon, following the Farewell Gap Trail alongside the East Fork Kaweah River. Pass Tufa Falls across the canyon at .25 mile and Crystal Creek's cascades on your side of the canyon at one mile. The trail leaves the valley floor and starts to climb moderately, reaching the bottom of Franklin Creek's cascades at 1.7 miles. After crossing Franklin Creek, you

continue south along Farewell Canyon, negotiating some switchbacks as you gain elevation. The views get better and better. One mile farther, the Franklin Lakes Trail forks left off the Farewell Gap Trail and starts climbing in earnest up the Franklin Creek Valley. At nearly 10,000 feet, the trail crosses Franklin Creek again, then parallels the creek for another mile to the largest Franklin Lake. Note that when you see the lake's dam straight ahead and an obvious campsite about 150 yards below it to the right of the trail, you should cut off the main trail. Walk to the camp and follow its use trail to the dam and the lake. The main trail switchbacks up and above the lake but doesn't go directly to its shoreline. Franklin Lake is a dramatic sight, surrounded by steep, snow-covered slopes and a few pines and junipers. Rainbow Mountain is on its northeast side; Tulare Peak is to the southwest.

Location: Off Highway 198 in the Mineral King region of Sequoia National Park; map G5, grid a1.

User groups: Hikers and horses. No dogs or mountain bikes. No wheelchair facilities.

Permits: There is a $10 entrance fee at Sequoia and Kings Canyon National Parks, good for seven days. A free wilderness permit is required for overnight stays and is available on a first-come, first-served basis at the Mineral King ranger station, or in advance by mail or fax after March 1; for more information phone (559) 565-3708.

Maps: Free park maps are available at park entrance stations or by contacting Sequoia and Kings Canyon National Parks at the address below. A more detailed map is available for a fee from Tom Harrison Cartography, tel. (415) 456-7940, or Trails Illustrated, tel. (800) 962-1643. Ask the USGS for a topographic map of the Mineral King area.

Directions: From Visalia drive east on Highway 198 for 38 miles to Mineral King Road, 2.5 miles east of Three Rivers. If you reach the Ash Mountain entrance station, you've gone too far. Turn right on Mineral

King Road and drive 25 miles to the end of the road and the Eagle/Mosquito Trailhead. Take the right fork at the end of the road to reach the parking area. Walk back out of the parking lot and follow the road to the pack station; the Farewell Gap Trail begins just beyond it.

Contact: Sequoia and Kings Canyon National Parks, Three Rivers, CA 93271-9700; tel. (559) 565-3134 or (559) 335-2856.

10 White Chief Mine Trail
5.8 mi/3.0 hrs

If you're one of those liberated hikers who doesn't need to have an alpine lake in your itinerary to be happy, the trail to White Chief Bowl is a scenic route with much to offer, including an exploration of the White Chief Mine tunnel. For years the mine was private property within the national park and off-limits to hikers until the Park Service purchased it in 1998.

The first mile of the trail is the same as the route to Eagle and Mosquito Lakes, but you'll leave most everyone behind when you continue straight at the one-mile junction, while they bear right for Eagle Lake and the Mosquito Lakes, above. The White Chief Trail continues with a hefty grade—this second mile is the toughest part of the whole trip—until it tops out at the edge of a gorgeous meadow. Just after you cross a seasonal stream (often a dry ravine by late summer), look for the ruins of Crabtree Cabin to the right of the trail. The cabin ruins are what is left of the oldest remaining structure in Mineral King. It was built by the discoverer of the White Chief Mine in the 1870s. Next comes White Chief Meadows, surrounded by high granite walls and filled with summer wildflowers in the wet areas around White Chief Creek. The meadow is also filled with dozens of downed trees, evidence of harsh winter avalanches.

Beyond the meadow the trail ascends slightly until it nears a waterfall on White Chief Creek. Shortly before the falls the trail crosses the creek and heads uphill. Look for the opening to White Chief Mine in a layer of white rock just above the trail. Scramble off the trail a few yards to reach it. The mine tunnel is tall enough to walk into and dead-ends in about 150 feet. It's a fascinating piece of history in a gorgeous, high-country location.

Location: Off Highway 198 in the Mineral King region of Sequoia National Park; map G5, grid a1.

User groups: Hikers and horses. No dogs or mountain bikes. No wheelchair facilities.

Permits: No permits are required. There is a $10 entrance fee at Sequoia and Kings Canyon National Parks, good for seven days.

Maps: Free park maps are available at park entrance stations or by contacting Sequoia and Kings Canyon National Parks at the address below. A more detailed map is available for a fee from Tom Harrison Cartography, tel. (415) 456-7940, or Trails Illustrated, tel. (800) 962-1643. Ask the USGS for a topographic map of the Mineral King area.

Directions: From Visalia drive east on Highway 198 for 38 miles to Mineral King Road, 2.5 miles east of Three Rivers. If you reach the Ash Mountain entrance station, you've gone too far. Turn right on Mineral King Road and drive 25 miles to the end of the road and the Eagle/Mosquito Trailhead. Take the right fork at the end of the road to reach the parking area. The trail begins from the far end of the parking lot.

Contact: Sequoia and Kings Canyon National Parks, Three Rivers, CA 93271-9700; tel. (559) 565-3134 or (559) 335-2856.

11 Timber Gap Trail
4.0 mi/2.0 hrs

The first thing you need to know: if you don't like horses, you'd better find another trail to hike in Mineral King because the Timber Gap Trail is popular with the folks at the pack station. If you don't mind some hoofed companions, this is an excellent and interesting route on which you can witness the mining history of Mineral King. The trail climbs steeply from the Sawtooth Trailhead on an old mining path along Monarch Creek, and forks in .25 mile. Take the left fork for Timber Gap, which climbs through a dense fir forest and then opens out to switchbacks in a wide and treeless slope—the result of continual winter avalanches. The exposed slope is home to many mountain wildflowers. The climb ends in two miles at Timber Gap, elevation 9,450 feet, a forested pass. The stumps you see among the red firs remain from early miners who cut down the trees to fuel their fires and support their mining tunnels. In addition to horses, expect to see many mule deer on this trail; the Mineral King Valley is full of them and they love to eat the young foliage along the hillsides.

Location: Off Highway 198 in the Mineral King region of Sequoia National Park; map G5, grid a1.

User groups: Hikers and horses. No dogs or mountain bikes. No wheelchair facilities.

Permits: No permits are required. There is a $10 entrance fee at Sequoia and Kings Canyon National Parks, good for seven days.

Maps: Free park maps are available at park entrance stations or by contacting Sequoia and Kings Canyon National Parks at the address below. A more detailed map is available for a fee from Tom Harrison Cartography, tel. (415) 456-7940, or Trails Illustrated, tel. (800) 962-1643. Ask the USGS for a topographic map of the Mineral King area.

Directions: From Visalia drive east on Highway 198 for 38 miles to Mineral King Road, 2.5 miles east of Three Rivers. If you reach the Ash Mountain entrance station, you've gone too far. Turn right on Mineral King Road and drive 24.5 miles to the Sawtooth parking area, .5 mile before the end of the road.

Contact: Sequoia and Kings Canyon National Parks, Three Rivers, CA 93271-9700; tel. (559) 565-3134 or (559) 335-2856.

12 Monarch Lakes
8.4 mi/5.0 hrs or 2.0 days

The Monarch Lakes Trail leads from the Sawtooth Trailhead at 8,000 feet in elevation and climbs 2,500 feet to the rocky, gemlike Monarch Lakes. The first lake is good, but the second lake is simply awesome, and the scenery along the trail is unforgettable. Walk .25 mile from the trailhead and take the right fork for Monarch and Crystal Lakes. After one steep mile, you'll reach Groundhog Meadow, named for the adorable yellow-bellied marmots that inhabit the area. (We like their blond coats and shrill whistles.) Beyond the meadow, the trail starts seriously switchbacking in and out of red fir forest, making a gut-thumping climb to the Crystal Lake trail junction. The trail forks sharply right for Crystal Lake, but you head left for one more mile—a relatively smooth mile with the easiest grade of the whole route—to Lower Monarch Lake. (This section crosses an incredible talus slope.) Snow can often be found near the lake even in late summer, and the vista is dramatic, with Sawtooth Peak dominating the skyline. If you have a wilderness permit and a backpacking stove, you can find a campsite near the lake.

While the main trail continues north to Sawtooth Pass, a use trail leads southeast from the lower lake for .5 mile to Upper Monarch Lake. Basically you head directly up the cliff that forms the back wall of the lower lake. It's worth the climb. The upper lake is wide, deep blue, and dramatic, set at the base of barren, pointy Monarch Peak. The view from the upper lake's basin, looking back down at the lower lake and various Mineral King peaks, is breathtaking. A big surprise is that the upper lake has been dammed, like many of the high lakes in Mineral King, and is operated by Southern California Edison. Note: If you're backpacking and want to take a first-rate side trip, the trail to Sawtooth Pass is a 1.3-mile, 1,200-foot climb that's not easy, but Sawtooth Pass offers one of the best views in the Southern Sierra.

Location: Off Highway 198 in the Mineral King region of Sequoia National Park; map G5, grid a1.

User groups: Hikers and horses. No dogs or mountain bikes. No wheelchair facilities.

Permits: There is a $10 entrance fee at Sequoia and Kings Canyon National Parks, good for seven days. A free wilderness permit is required for overnight stays and is available on a first-come, first-served basis at the Mineral King ranger station, or in advance by mail or fax after March 1; for more information phone (559) 565-3708.

Maps: Free park maps are available at park entrance stations or by contacting Sequoia and Kings Canyon National Parks at the address below. A more detailed map is available for a fee from Tom Harrison Cartography, tel. (415) 456-7940, or Trails Illustrated, tel. (800) 962-1643. Ask the USGS for a topographic map of the Mineral King area.

Directions: From Visalia drive east on Highway 198 for 38 miles to Mineral King Road, 2.5 miles east of Three Rivers. If you reach the Ash Mountain entrance station, you've gone too far. Turn right on Mineral King Road and drive 24.5 miles to the Sawtooth parking area, .5 mile before the end of the road.

Contact: Sequoia and Kings Canyon National Parks, Three Rivers, CA 93271-9700; tel. (559) 565-3134 or (559) 335-2856.

13 Crystal Lake Trail
9.8 mi/6.0 hrs or 2.0 days

The long and arduous path to Crystal Lake follows the same route as the trail to Monarch Lakes, above, for the first 3.2 miles. In Chihuahua Bowl, a sharp right-hand turn puts you on the trail to Crystal Lake. In .5 mile the trail leads past the ruins of the Chihuahua Mine on the right, one of Mineral King's last hopes for silver riches. Like the other mines in the area, it never produced ore to equal the miners' dreams. The trail climbs abruptly over a rocky slope to a ridge of reddish foxtail pines, where your vista opens wide. Far off you can see the Farewell Gap peaks, and down below you see the Cobalt Lakes and Crystal Creek, pouring down to the Mineral King Valley and the East Fork Kaweah River. The trail continues, following more switchbacks, to upper Crystal Creek and Crystal Lake, which has been dammed. Off to the left (north), Mineral Peak stands out at 11,500 feet, and to the right (south), Rainbow Mountain shows off its colorful rock. Views are spectacular in every direction. If you scramble .25 mile off-trail toward Mineral Peak, you will reach Little Crystal Lake, where you have a near-guarantee of solitude and a vista you won't forget.

Location: Off Highway 198 in the Mineral King region of Sequoia National Park; map G5, grid a1.

User groups: Hikers and horses. No dogs or mountain bikes. No wheelchair facilities.

Permits: There is a $10 entrance fee at Sequoia and Kings Canyon National Parks, good for seven days. A free wilderness permit is required for overnight stays and is available on a first-come, first-served basis at the Mineral King ranger station, or in advance by mail or fax after March 1; for more information phone (559) 565-3708.

Maps: Free park maps are available at park entrance stations or by contacting Sequoia and Kings Canyon National Parks at the address below. A more detailed map is available for a fee from Tom Harrison Cartography, tel. (415) 456-7940, or Trails Illustrated, tel. (800) 962-1643. Ask the USGS for a topographic map of the Mineral King area.

Directions: From Visalia drive east on Highway 198 for 38 miles to Mineral King Road, 2.5 miles east of Three Rivers. If you reach the Ash Mountain entrance station, you've gone too far. Turn right on Mineral King Road and drive 24.5 miles to the Sawtooth parking area, .5 mile before the end of the road.

Contact: Sequoia and Kings Canyon National Parks, Three Rivers, CA 93271-9700; tel. (559) 565-3134 or (559) 335-2856.

14 Black Wolf Falls
0.5 mi/0.5 hr

This hike is really just a stroll, and the destination is readily apparent from the Sawtooth

Trailhead: Black Wolf Falls, tumbling down the canyon wall in Mineral King Valley. But aside from the chance to get close to a pretty waterfall, the hike is interesting because of its historical significance. Black Wolf's name is actually an alteration of its original moniker, which was Black Wall Falls, named for the Black Wall copper mine that was located at the waterfall's base. Back in the 1870s, when miners believed that Mineral King was rich in more than just scenery, they mined the base of Monarch Creek with a modicum of success. Today you can walk right up to the falls and see the mine tunnel on its right side (it looks like a cave, but don't go inside; it's unstable). In summer, rangers lead group hikes to the waterfall and talk about Mineral King's mining history. Although the route to Black Wolf Falls isn't an official trail, the path is well used and clearly visible. If you can find its beginning across the road from the "No Parking Any Time" sign, the rest of the hike is easy.

Location: Off Highway 198 in the Mineral King region of Sequoia National Park; map G5, grid a1.

User groups: Hikers only. No dogs, horses, or mountain bikes. No wheelchair facilities.

Permits: No permits are required. There is a $10 entrance fee at Sequoia and Kings Canyon National Parks, good for seven days.

Maps: Free park maps are available at park entrance stations or by contacting Sequoia and Kings Canyon National Parks at the address below. A more detailed map is available for a fee from Tom Harrison Cartography, tel. (415) 456-7940, or Trails Illustrated, tel. (800) 962-1643. Ask the USGS for a topographic map of the Mineral King area.

Directions: From Visalia drive east on Highway 198 for 38 miles to Mineral King Road, 2.5 miles east of Three Rivers. If you reach the Ash Mountain entrance station, you've gone too far. Turn right on Mineral King Road and drive 24.5 miles to the Sawtooth parking area, .5 mile before the end of the road. Walk up the road toward Black Wolf Falls, then look for a use trail across the road from the "No Parking

Any Time" sign, just beyond where Monarch Creek flows under the road.

Contact: Sequoia and Kings Canyon National Parks, Three Rivers, CA 93271-9700; tel. (559) 565-3134 or (559) 335-2856.

15 Cottonwood Lakes
10.0 mi/
6.0 hrs or 2.0 days

Trailhead elevation is just over 10,000 feet here at Horseshoe Meadow, which makes this a wildly popular trailhead for climbing deeper into the backcountry of the John Muir Wilderness. With the trailhead situated so high, you get a jump on the ascent; your four wheels do the work instead of your two feet. An unusual feature of this hike is that it passes through two wilderness areas—first the Golden Trout Wilderness and then the John Muir Wilderness. Cottonwood Creek accompanies you for much of the trip. The trail is a straightforward climb until 3.5 miles, where you reach a junction. Take your pick as to which way to go—the trail forms a loop around Cottonwood Lakes numbers one, two, and three. If you just want to see the closest lake and head back without making the loop, go left for Cottonwood Lake number one, 1.5 miles from the junction. Your round-trip will be an even 10 miles. If you complete the whole loop, passing all three beautiful lakes, you'll travel 11.5 miles. (Lakes four and five are located .5 mile beyond the far end of the loop, if you want to see even more.) Total elevation gain is only 1,000 feet. Once at the lakes, there are a few things to remember: 1) Special fishing regulations are in effect, so get updated on the latest rules. 2) No wood fires are allowed, so bring your backpacking stove. 3) The wildflowers are spectacular, but the mosquitoes are voracious. Come prepared.

Location: In the John Muir Wilderness south of Mount Whitney; map G5, grid a7.

User groups: Hikers, dogs, and horses. No mountain bikes. No wheelchair facilities.

Permits: No day-hiking permits are required. A free wilderness permit is required for overnight stays. Quotas are in effect from the last Friday in June to September 15; permits are available in advance by mail or fax for this period for a $3 fee. Phone (760) 873-2408 for permit information or visit website: www.r5.fs.fed.us/inyo.

Maps: For a map of Inyo National Forest, send $6 to U.S. Forest Service, Map Sales, P.O. Box 587, Camino, CA 95709; tel. (530) 647-5390 or website: www.r5.fs.fed.us/visitorcenter. Ask the USGS for a topographic map of the Cirque Peak area.

Directions: From Lone Pine on U.S. 395 drive west on Whitney Portal Road for 3.3 miles and turn left (south) on Horseshoe Meadow Road. Continue 19.5 miles and bear right for the Cottonwood Lakes Trailhead parking area, near the end of Horseshoe Meadow Road.

Contact: Inyo National Forest, Mount Whitney Ranger District, P.O. Box 8, Lone Pine, CA 93545; tel. (760) 876-6200 or fax (760) 876-6202.

16 Cottonwood Pass

8.0 mi/5.0 hrs

The Cottonwood Pass Trail provides access to the Pacific Crest Trail and the Kern Plateau, a land of stark, subalpine meadows. You're entering the Golden Trout Wilderness, home of California's state fish, located at the very south end of the Sierra Nevada. This is where the steep, nearly perpendicular mountains start to mellow out into more gentle terrain, mostly in the form of rolling high-country hills and meadows. Start from wide Horseshoe Meadow and climb gently through forest for the first two miles of trail. Shortly the switchbacks begin and the views open up. After an 1,100-foot climb, you reach the pass at four miles, where you can gaze out at the Great Western Divide, Big Whitney Meadows, and the Inyo Mountains. Bring a jacket with you for the windy, 11,200-foot summit. Ambitious hikers can continue beyond the pass and take the right fork for Chicken Spring Lake, .5 mile

away on the Pacific Crest Trail (no campfires allowed).

Location: In the Golden Trout Wilderness; map G5, grid a7.

User groups: Hikers, dogs, and horses. No mountain bikes. No wheelchair facilities.

Permits: No day-hiking permits are required. A free wilderness permit is required for overnight stays. Quotas are in effect from the last Friday in June to September 15; permits are available in advance by mail or fax for this period for a $3 fee. Phone (760) 873-2408 for permit information or visit website: www.r5.fs.fed.us/inyo.

Maps: For a map of Inyo National Forest or Golden Trout Wilderness, send $6 to U.S. Forest Service, Map Sales, P.O. Box 587, Camino, CA 95709; tel. (530) 647-5390 or website: www.r5.fs.fed.us/visitorcenter. Ask the USGS for a topographic map of the Cirque Peak area.

Directions: From Lone Pine on U.S. 395 drive west on Whitney Portal Road for 3.3 miles and turn left (south) on Horseshoe Meadow Road. Continue 19.5 miles to the Horseshoe Meadow Trailhead on the left at the end of Horseshoe Meadow Road.

Contact: Inyo National Forest, Mount Whitney Ranger District, P.O. Box 8, Lone Pine, CA 93545; tel. (760) 876-6200 or fax (760) 876-6202.

17 Trail Pass

5.0 mi/3.0 hrs

Trail Pass may not be as spectacular as the other trails at Horseshoe Meadow, but it has two things going for it—far fewer people and an easier grade. It's only five miles round-trip from the trailhead to the pass, with a mere 500-foot elevation gain, unheard of in these parts. The main folks using the trail are backpackers accessing the Pacific Crest Trail and Golden Trout Wilderness, so a lot of the time you can have this gently rolling, high-country terrain all to yourself. Follow the trail from the parking area to a junction .25 mile in and bear left. In another .5 mile the trail forks, and you bear right for Trail Pass. Pass by Horseshoe Meadow and Round Valley, where you'll have the company of many packhorses. Views are good of Mount Langley and Cirque Peak. The pass is situated at 10,500 feet, just below Trail Peak at 11,600 feet.

Location: In Inyo National Forest; map G5, grid a7.

User groups: Hikers, dogs, and horses. No mountain bikes. No wheelchair facilities.

Permits: No day-hiking permits are required. A free wilderness permit is required for overnight stays. Quotas are in effect from the last Friday in June to September 15; permits are available in advance by mail or fax for this period for a $3 fee. Phone (760) 873-2408 for permit information, or visit website: www.r5.fs. fed.us/inyo.

Maps: For a map of Inyo National Forest, send $6 to U.S. Forest Service, Map Sales, P.O. Box 587, Camino, CA 95709; tel. (530) 647-5390 or website: www.r5.fs.fed.us/visitorcenter. Ask the USGS for a topographic map of the Cirque Peak area.

Directions: From Lone Pine on U.S. 395 drive west on Whitney Portal Road for 3.3 miles and turn left (south) on Horseshoe Meadow Road. Continue 19.5 miles to the Horseshoe Meadow Trailhead on the right, at the end of Horseshoe Meadow Road.

Contact: Inyo National Forest, Mount Whitney Ranger District, P.O. Box 8, Lone Pine, CA 93545; tel. (760) 876-6200 or fax (760) 876-6202.

18 Balch Park Nature Trail
1.0 mi/0.5 hr

Balch Park is the small county-run park within the borders of Mountain Home Demonstration State Park, and its easy, one-mile nature trail is a great place to take your kids for the afternoon. The trail begins next to the main entrance to Balch Park Camp, across from the museum, and your first stop is a visit to the Hollow Log, which was used as a dwelling by various pioneers, Indians, and prospectors.

You also get to see the Lady Alice Tree, which was incorrectly billed in the early 1900s as the largest tree in the world. Nonetheless, it's no slacker in the size department. Continuing along the route, you'll see and learn all about dogwoods, bracken ferns, manzanita, and gooseberry. When you're finished hiking the nature trail, you can cross the road and throw a line into one of Balch Park's two small fishing ponds, which are stocked weekly.

Location: In Mountain Home Demonstration State Forest, off Highway 190 near Springville; map G5, grid c0.

User groups: Hikers, dogs, and horses. No mountain bikes. No wheelchair facilities.

Permits: No permits are required. Parking and access are free.

Maps: A free map/brochure of Mountain Home Demonstration State Forest is available from park headquarters. Ask the USGS for a topographic map of the Camp Wishon area.

Directions: From Porterville drive east on Highway 190 for 18 miles to Springville. At Springville turn left (north) on Balch Park Road/Road 239 and drive 3.5 miles and turn right on Bear Creek Road/Road 220. Drive 14 miles to Mountain Home Demonstration State Forest Headquarters, pick up a free park map, and then continue 1.5 miles farther to the entrance to Balch Park and the nature trail.

Contact: Tulare County Parks and Recreation Department, tel. (559) 733-6291, or Mountain Home Demonstration State Forest, P.O. Box 517, Springville, CA 93265; tel. (559) 539-2321 (summer) or (559) 539-2855 (winter).

19 Adam and Eve Loop Trail
2.0 mi/1.0 hr

On the Adam and Eve Loop Trail, you can see the Adam Tree standing tall and proud, but its companion the Eve Tree is no longer thriving. It (she?) was axed during the infamous sequoia logging years, and it's strangely touching to see the gaping slash in her side. Begin your trip by taking the left side of the

loop, heading uphill to the Adam Tree, the second largest tree in this state forest at 240 feet tall and 27 feet in diameter. The Eve Tree is shortly after. The big draw on the trail is visiting the "Indian bathtubs" at Tub Flat halfway around the loop—basins formed in solid granite that were probably used by Native Americans. No one is sure if they are man-made. The basins are much larger than the traditional Indian grinding holes that are found elsewhere in the Sierra; they are truly large enough to take a bath in.

Location: In Mountain Home Demonstration State Forest, off Highway 190 near Springville; map G5, grid c0.

User groups: Hikers, dogs, and horses. No mountain bikes. No wheelchair facilities.

Permits: No permits are required. Parking and access are free.

Maps: A free map/brochure of Mountain Home Demonstration State Forest is available from park headquarters. Ask the USGS for a topographic map of the Camp Wishon area.

Directions: From Porterville drive east on Highway 190 for 18 miles to Springville. At Springville turn left (north) on Balch Park Road/Road 239 and drive 3.5 miles, and then turn right on Bear Creek Road/Road 220. Drive 14 miles to Mountain Home Demonstration State Forest Headquarters, pick up a free park map, and then continue one mile farther and turn right at the sign for Hidden Falls Recreation Area. Drive three miles to just past the pack station and before Shake Camp Campground, to the trailhead for the Adam and Eve Loop Trail on the left.

Contact: Mountain Home Demonstration State Forest, P.O. Box 517, Springville, CA 93265; tel. (559) 539-2321 (summer) or (559) 539-2855 (winter).

20 Redwood Crossing

4.0 mi/2.0 hrs

An excellent easy hike for campers and day visitors at Mountain Home Demonstration State Forest is the Long Meadow Trail from Shake Camp Campground to Redwood Crossing on the Tule River. The trail starts by the public corral at elevation 6,800 feet and leads through logged sequoia stumps to a thick mixed forest on the slopes high above the Wishon Fork Tule River. When the trail reaches clearings in the trees, the views of the Great Western Divide are excellent. At two miles out, you reach Redwood Crossing, a boulder-lined stretch of the river. Those willing to ford can cross to the other side and head into the Golden Trout Wilderness, but day-hikers should pull out a picnic at the river's edge and make an afternoon of it. Overnighters heading for the wilderness need to secure a wilderness permit from the Tule River Ranger District office.

Location: In Mountain Home Demonstration State Forest, off Highway 190 near Springville; map G5, grid c0.

User groups: Hikers, dogs, and horses. No mountain bikes. No wheelchair facilities.

Permits: No permits are required. Parking and access are free.

Maps: A free map/brochure of Mountain Home Demonstration State Forest is available from park headquarters. Ask the USGS for a topographic map of the Camp Wishon area.

Directions: From Porterville drive east on Highway 190 for 18 miles to Springville. At Springville turn left (north) on Balch Park Road/Road 239 and drive 3.5 miles and turn right on Bear Creek Road/Road 220. Drive 14 miles to Mountain Home Demonstration State Forest Headquarters, pick up a free park map, and then continue one mile farther and turn right at the sign for Hidden Falls Recreation Area. Drive 3.5 miles to Shake Camp Campground. The Long Meadow Trailhead is located by the public corral.

Contact: Mountain Home Demonstration State Forest, P.O. Box 517, Springville, CA 93265; tel. (559) 539-2321 (summer) or (559) 539-2855 (winter).

21 Moses Gulch Trail

4.0 mi/2.0 hrs

For a less-crowded alternate to the popular Redwood Crossing Trail, you can take the other trail from the public corral at Shake Flat Campground and wind your way through stands of beautiful virgin sequoias to the Wishon Fork Tule River at Moses Gulch Campground. The Moses Gulch Trail crosses park roads twice—the only downer—but it's an easy walk for families, and peaceful besides. Once you reach the river at two miles, you have the option of hiking alongside it to the north or south, adding some distance to your trip. The northern stretch leads to Hidden Falls Campground, home of many small falls and pools, and the southern stretch crosses pretty Galena and Silver Creeks and leads past a mining cabin and an old copper mine.

Location: In Mountain Home Demonstration State Forest, off Highway 190 near Springville; map G5, grid c0.

User groups: Hikers, dogs, and horses. No mountain bikes. No wheelchair facilities.

Permits: No permits are required. Parking and access are free.

Maps: A free map/brochure of Mountain Home Demonstration State Forest is available from park headquarters. Ask the USGS for a topographic map of the Camp Wishon area.

Directions: From Porterville drive east on Highway 190 for 18 miles to Springville. At Springville turn left (north) on Balch Park Road/Road 239, drive 3.5 miles, and then turn right on Bear Creek Road/Road 220. Drive 14 miles to Mountain Home Demonstration State Forest Headquarters and pick up a free park map, then continue one mile farther and turn right at the sign for Hidden Falls Recreation Area. Drive 3.5 miles to Shake Camp Campground. The Moses Gulch Trailhead is located by the public corral.

Contact: Mountain Home Demonstration State Forest, P.O. Box 517, Springville, CA 93265; tel. (559) 539-2321 (summer) or (559) 539-2855 (winter).

22 Doyle Trail

6.0 mi/3.0 hrs

The Doyle Trail is a great alternative to the heat of the Springville and Porterville Valleys. It's in the transition zone between foothills and conifers, with plenty of shade from tall manzanita, oaks, madrones, and pines. Squirrels and lizards are your primary companions on the trail, which laterals along the slopes above the Wishon Fork of the Tule River. From the gated trailhead, hike up the paved road and bear left to bypass Doyle Springs, a community of private cabins. Follow the trail that is signed "Trail to Upstream Fishing." The route climbs gently through the forest for 2.5 miles and then suddenly descends to the same level as the river, where there are some primitive campsites available. Then the trail rises again, climbing for another .5 mile to a clearing on the right, where there is an outcrop of jagged green rock alongside the river. Leave the trail and cross over the rock, where you'll find a few picture-perfect swimming holes and small waterfalls.

Location: In Sequoia National Forest near Springville; map G5, grid c0.

User groups: Hikers, dogs, horses, and mountain bikes. No wheelchair facilities.

Permits: No permits are required. Parking and access are free.

Maps: For a map of Sequoia National Forest, send $6 to U.S. Forest Service, Map Sales, P.O. Box 587, Camino, CA 95709; tel. (530) 647-5390 or website: www.r5.fs.fed.us/visitorcenter. Ask the USGS for a topographic map of the Camp Wishon area.

Directions: From Porterville drive east on Highway 190 for 18 miles to Springville. From Springville, continue east on Highway 190 for 7.5 miles to Wishon Drive/Road 208, a left fork. Turn left and drive four miles on Wishon Drive, then take the left fork which is signed for day-use parking (above the campground). Drive .25 mile and park off the road, near the gate.

Contact: Sequoia National Forest, Tule River Ranger District, 32588 Highway 190, Springville, CA 93265; tel. (559) 539-2607 or fax (559) 539-2067.

23 Amos Alonzo Stagg Tree
0.5 mi/0.5 hr

Can you name the six largest giant sequoias in the world and their general locations? Number one is the General Sherman Tree in Sequoia National Park. Number two is the Washington Tree in Sequoia National Park. Number three is the General Grant Tree in Kings Canyon National Park. Number four is the President Tree in Sequoia National Park. Number five is the Lincoln Tree in Sequoia National Park. And number six is the Stagg Tree in Sequoia National Forest, the largest tree outside of Sequoia and Kings Canyon National Parks, and the largest sequoia in the world that is under private ownership. The owner is a nice person and lets people come see his tree via an easy .5-mile hike. The Stagg Tree is 243 feet tall and 29 feet in diameter at its base, which is only about four-fifths the size of the number-one tree, the General Sherman. Here's something to ponder: the Stagg Tree weighs about 2.5 million pounds.
Location: In Sequoia National Forest near Camp Nelson; map G5, grid d2.
User groups: Hikers, dogs, horses, and mountain bikes. No wheelchair facilities.
Permits: No permits are required. Parking and access are free.
Maps: For a map of Sequoia National Forest, send $6 to U.S. Forest Service, Map Sales, P.O. Box 587, Camino, CA 95709; tel. (530) 647-5390 or website: www.r5.fs.fed.us/visitorcenter. Ask the USGS for a topographic map of the Camp Nelson area.
Directions: From Porterville drive 36 miles east on Highway 190 to 2.5 miles past Camp Nelson and turn left on Redwood Drive. Follow Redwood Drive for about five miles as it turns into Alder Drive (dirt). Follow Alder Drive to the signed parking area for the Stagg Tree and then hike down the dirt road.

Contact: Sequoia National Forest, Tule River Ranger District, 32588 Highway 190, Springville, CA 93265; tel. (559) 539-2607 or fax (559) 539-2067.

24 Jordan Peak Lookout
1.8 mi/1.0 hr

You'll see some logging activity out here by Jordan Peak, but if you can put up with it, you can climb a mere 600 feet over less than a mile to reach the summit of this 9,100-foot mountain. Few summits are so easily attained (it's a well-graded and well-maintained trail), and this one is not lacking in dramatic vistas. You can see the Wishon Fork Canyon of the Tule River, Camp Nelson, the Sequoia Crest, Slate Mountain, Maggie Mountain, and Moses Mountain close up, and the Tehachapis and the Coast Range far, far away. The peak is covered with microwave equipment, but it doesn't mar the stupendous view. Head west from the trailhead on the Jordan Lookout Trail, switchbacking up until you reach the catwalked stairs to the lookout, which was built in 1934.
Location: In Sequoia National Forest near Quaking Aspen; map G5, grid d2.
User groups: Hikers, dogs, horses, and mountain bikes. No wheelchair facilities.
Permits: No permits are required. Parking and access are free.
Maps: For a map of Sequoia National Forest, send $6 to U.S. Forest Service, Map Sales, P.O. Box 587, Camino, CA 95709; tel. (530) 647-5390 or website: www.r5.fs.fed.us/visitorcenter. Ask the USGS for a topographic map of the Sentinel Peak area.
Directions: From Porterville drive 45 miles east on Highway 190 to Forest Service Road 21S50 near Quaking Aspen Campground. Turn left on Road 21S50 and drive five miles. Bear left and continue on Road 21S50 for 2.8 miles, bearing left on Road 20S71, signed for Jordan Peak Lookout, and following it one mile to its end at the trailhead.
Contact: Sequoia National Forest, Tule River Ranger District, 32588 Highway 190, Spring-

ville, CA 93265; tel. (559) 539-2607 or fax (559) 539-2067.

25 Clicks Creek Trail
14.0 mi/2.0 days

If you like peace and quiet on your backpacking trips, the Clicks Creek Trail in the Golden Trout Wilderness may suit you just fine. The trail leads northeast from Log Cabin Meadow (elevation 7,800 feet), heading steadily downhill along Clicks Creek to the Little Kern River. The route crosses the creek several times. Shade lovers will thrill at the conifer forests that line the route, interspersed by large and grassy meadows, and anglers can bring along their gear to try their luck with the golden trout in the river. There are many possible campsites along the Little Kern, where the elevation is 6,200 feet.

Location: In the Golden Trout Wilderness near Quaking Aspen; map G5, grid d2.

User groups: Hikers, dogs, and horses. No mountain bikes. No wheelchair facilities.

Permits: A free wilderness permit is required for overnight stays and is available from the Springville or Kernville ranger stations. Parking and access are free.

Maps: For a map of Sequoia National Forest or Golden Trout Wilderness, send $6 to U.S. Forest Service, Map Sales, P.O. Box 587, Camino, CA 95709; tel. (530) 647-5390 or website: www.r5.fs.fed.us/visitorcenter. Ask the USGS for a topographic map of the Sentinel Peak area.

Directions: From Porterville drive 45 miles east on Highway 190 to Forest Service Road 21S50 near Quaking Aspen Campground. Turn left on Road 21S50 and drive five miles; bear left and continue on Road 21S50 for 1.5 miles to the Clicks Creek Trailhead at Log Cabin Meadow.

Contact: Sequoia National Forest, Tule River Ranger District, 32588 Highway 190, Springville, CA 93265; tel. (559) 539-2607 or fax (559) 539-2067.

26 John Jordan/Hossack Meadow Trail
5.0 mi/2.5 hrs

Your route on the John Jordan Trail begins with a crossing of McIntyre Creek, then traverses a level mile to an old fence, gate, and McIntyre Rock, a huge pile of granite boulders with an excellent view. Climb on top of the rock's well-graded cracking granite back side and peer over its startlingly steep front side. Surprise—it's straight down about 600 feet. The trail heads downhill through a red fir forest to Nelson Creek, the site of some logging work. Although you can walk another .5 mile to the trail's end at Hossack Meadow, most people turn around at the sight of logged trees, making for a five-mile round-trip with a 1,000-foot elevation gain on the return. So who was John Jordan, anyway? He was a trailblazer in the 1870s, who unfortunately was most famous for drowning in the Kern River on his way back to the Central Valley to tell everybody he had completed this trail, a proposed toll road.

Location: In Sequoia National Forest near Quaking Aspen; map G5, grid d2.

User groups: Hikers, dogs, horses, and mountain bikes. No wheelchair facilities.

Permits: No permits are required. Parking and access are free.

Maps: For a map of Sequoia National Forest, send $6 to U.S. Forest Service, Map Sales, P.O. Box 587, Camino, CA 95709; tel. (530) 647-5390 or website: www.r5.fs.fed.us/visitorcenter. Ask the USGS for a topographic map of the Sentinel Peak area.

Directions: From Porterville drive 45 miles east on Highway 190 to Forest Service Road 21S50 near Quaking Aspen Campground. Turn left on Road 21S50 and drive 6.6 miles, then bear left on Road 20S81. Follow Road 20S81 for 1.4 miles to the signed trailhead.

Contact: Sequoia National Forest, Tule River Ranger District, 32588 Highway 190, Springville, CA 93265; tel. (559) 539-2607 or fax (559) 539-2067.

27 Freeman Creek Trail

4.0 mi/2.0 hrs

The easternmost grove of sequoias in the world is your destination on the Freeman Creek Trail. Compared to most sequoia groves in the Sierra, the trees of the 1,700-acre Freeman Creek Grove are mere adolescents—probably not more than 1,000 years old. Among them is a tree named for former President George Bush, who visited the grove in 1992. The trail is a pleasant downhill stroll along Freeman Creek, reaching the first sequoias in about one mile, after crossing the creek. In between the big trees are large meadow areas, many of which bloom with spring and summer wildflowers, and forests of red firs. Many campsites are found along the creek. The path finally ends at Lloyd Meadows, three miles from the trailhead, but most people don't travel that far since it requires too much climbing on the way back. Two miles out and back is just about perfect.

Location: In Sequoia National Forest near Quaking Aspen; map G5, grid d2.

User groups: Hikers, dogs, horses, and mountain bikes. No wheelchair facilities.

Permits: No permits are required. Parking and access are free.

Maps: For a map of Sequoia National Forest, send $6 to U.S. Forest Service, Map Sales, P.O. Box 587, Camino, CA 95709; tel. (530) 647-5390 or website: www.r5.fs.fed.us/visitorcenter. Ask the USGS for a topographic map of the Sentinel Peak area.

Directions: From Porterville drive 45 miles east on Highway 190 to Forest Service Road 21S50 near Quaking Aspen Campground. Turn left on Road 21S50 and drive .5 mile, then turn right at the sign for the Freeman Creek Grove.

Contact: Sequoia National Forest, Tule River Ranger District, 32588 Highway 190, Springville, CA 93265; tel. (559) 539-2607 or fax (559) 539-2067.

28 Summit Trail to Slate Mountain

8.0 mi/4.0 hrs

If you're staying at Quaking Aspen Campground, you can set out on the Summit National Recreation Trail from outside your tent door, but if you're not, drive to the trailhead just south of the camp off Road 21S78. Few people hike all 12 miles of the trail, but many take this four-mile jaunt to the summit of 9,302-foot Slate Mountain, the highest peak in the area. The first two miles of trail are easy, climbing gently through meadows and forest (some logging activity can be seen); then the route climbs more steeply, ascending first the east side and then the north side of Slate Mountain. Views of the granite spires of the Needles and Olancha Peak can be seen. At 3.8 miles you reach a junction with the Bear Creek Trail, and from there it's a short scramble to your left to the top of Slate Mountain, which is a big pile of rocks with a tremendous 360-degree view. There's no trail, but a couple well-worn routes are visible.

Location: In Sequoia National Forest near Quaking Aspen; map G5, grid d2.

User groups: Hikers, dogs, horses, and mountain bikes. No wheelchair facilities.

Permits: No permits are required. Parking and access are free.

Maps: For a map of Sequoia National Forest, send $6 to U.S. Forest Service, Map Sales, P.O. Box 587, Camino, CA 95709; tel. (530) 647-5390 or website: www.r5.fs.fed.us/visitorcenter. Ask the USGS for a topographic map of the Sentinel Peak area.

Directions: From Porterville drive 46 miles east on Highway 190 to Forest Service Road 21S78, which is .5 mile south of Quaking Aspen Campground. Turn right on Road 21S78 and drive .5 mile to the Summit Trailhead.

Contact: Sequoia National Forest, Tule River Ranger District, 32588 Highway 190, Springville, CA 93265; tel. (559) 539-2607 or fax (559) 539-2067.

29 Needles Lookout

5.0 mi/2.5 hrs

Here it is, the perfect easy day hike in Sequoia National Forest. It's just long enough and undulating enough for beginning and intermediate hikers, without being too demanding, and full of visual rewards. The trail starts with a placard bearing a great old black-and-white photo that shows what the fire lookout on top of the Needles looked like early in the 20th century. Five minutes down the trail you leave the forest and come out to two wooden benches, good places to stare out at the magnificent view of the Kern River Basin before you. If you look ahead, you get a glimpse of the fire lookout, perched in what looks like a precarious fashion on top of the Needles' tall granite spires. As you continue along the trail, you lose your view of it. The trail goes up, then down, then up again, through firs, ponderosa, sugar pines, granite, and sand. The only steep section is the final set of switchbacks up the Needles, which lead to a series of stairs and catwalks that ascend to the lookout tower. When you reach the first catwalk, the rest is a cakewalk. A sign tells you if the tower is open and you may come up and visit. If it's closed, just climb up on any boulder to admire the view—it's just as fine from the base of the tower as it is from above. You look out over Lloyd Meadow and the western half of the Golden Trout Wilderness. This is a perfect place to take someone who needs to get inspired.

Location: In Sequoia National Forest near Quaking Aspen; map G5, grid d2.

User groups: Hikers, dogs, horses, and mountain bikes. No wheelchair facilities.

Permits: No permits are required. Parking and access are free.

Maps: For a map of Sequoia National Forest, send $6 to U.S. Forest Service, Map Sales, P.O. Box 587, Camino, CA 95709; tel. (530) 647-5390 or website: www.r5.fs.fed.us/visitorcenter. Ask the USGS for topographic maps of the Sentinel Peak and Durrwood Creek areas.

Directions: From Porterville drive 46 miles east on Highway 190 to Forest Service Road 21S05, which is .5 mile south of Quaking Aspen Campground. Turn left (east) on Road 21S05 and drive 2.8 miles to the trailhead.

Contact: Sequoia National Forest, Tule River Ranger District, 32588 Highway 190, Springville, CA 93265; tel. (559) 539-2607 or fax (559) 539-2067.

30 Casa Vieja Meadow

4.0 mi/2.0 hrs

The Blackrock Mountain Trailhead at elevation 8,800 feet is the jump-off point for a variety of backpacking trips into the Golden Trout Wilderness. But day-hikers can also sample the delights of this large, waterway-filled land, the home of California's state fish, the golden trout. From the end of Blackrock Road, walk for less than .25 mile to the wilderness boundary, then head gently downhill through a red fir forest to the western edge of Casa Vieja Meadow. There you'll find a snow survey cabin and a wide expanse of grass and wildflowers. Hope your day pack is full of picnic supplies. At the far end of the meadow, you must ford Ninemile Creek to continue hiking farther, so make this your turnaround point. Some people try their luck fishing here. You'll have a gradual 800-foot elevation gain on your return trip.

Location: In the Golden Trout Wilderness; map G5, grid d6.

User groups: Hikers, dogs, and horses. No mountain bikes. No wheelchair facilities.

Permits: No permits are required for day hiking. Parking and access are free.

Maps: For a map of Sequoia National Forest, Inyo National Forest, or Golden Trout Wilderness, send $6 to U.S. Forest Service, Map Sales, P.O. Box 587, Camino, CA 95709; tel. (530) 647-5390 or website: www.r5.fs.fed.us/visitorcenter. Ask the USGS for a topographic map of the Casa Vieja Meadows area.

Directions: From Kernville on the north end of Lake Isabella, drive north on Sierra Way/Road 99 for 22 miles to the turnoff for Sherman Pass Road/22S05. Turn right and drive approximately 35 miles on Sherman Pass Road to the Blackrock Information Station; continue straight on Road 21S03/Blackrock Road. Follow Road 21S03 north for eight miles to the end of the road and the Blackrock Mountain Trailhead.

Contact: Sequoia National Forest, Cannell Meadow Ranger District, P.O. Box 9, Kernville, CA 93238; tel. (760) 376-3781 or fax (760) 376-3795; Inyo National Forest, Mount Whitney Ranger District, P.O. Box 8, Lone Pine, CA 93545; tel. (760) 876-6200.

31 Jordan Hot Springs

12.0 mi/
7.0 hrs or 2.0 days

You can do it in a day if you're ambitious, or you can take a more leisurely two-day trip to Jordan Hot Springs, but however you do it, it's critical to remember that almost all the work is on the way home. The trail is a descent (sometimes knee jarring) to the grounds of an old hot springs resort, which was closed when this area became part of the Golden Trout Wilderness. The original buildings still stand, and the hot springs are still hot, which is the reason that this is one of the most popular trips in the wilderness. From the trailhead, take the Blackrock Trail for two miles to Casa Vieja Meadow, above, then cross Ninemile Creek and turn left (west) on the Jordan Hot Springs Trail. Hike another three miles downhill along Ninemile Creek, crossing it a few more times. Once you reach the old resort, have a good soak and pull your energy together, because you've got a 2,600-foot gain on the return trip.

Location: In the Golden Trout Wilderness; map G5, grid d6.

User groups: Hikers, dogs, and horses. No mountain bikes. No wheelchair facilities.

Permits: A free wilderness permit is required for overnight stays and is available from the Cannell Meadow or Lone Pine Ranger Stations. Parking and access are free.

Maps: For a map of Sequoia National Forest, Inyo National Forest, or Golden Trout Wilder-

ness, send $6 to U.S. Forest Service, Map Sales, P.O. Box 587, Camino, CA 95709; tel. (530) 647-5390 or website: www.r5.fs.fed.us/visitorcenter. Ask the USGS for a topographic map of the Casa Vieja Meadows area.

Directions: From Kernville on the north end of Lake Isabella, drive north on Sierra Way/Road 99 for 22 miles to the right turnoff for Sherman Pass Road/22S05. Turn right and drive approximately 35 miles on Sherman Pass Road to the Blackrock Information Station; continue straight on Road 21S03/Blackrock Road. Follow Road 21S03 north for eight miles to the end of the road and the Blackrock Mountain Trailhead.

Contact: Sequoia National Forest, Cannell Meadow Ranger District, P.O. Box 9, Kernville, CA 93238; tel. (760) 376-3781 or fax (760) 376-3795; Inyo National Forest, Mount Whitney Ranger District, P.O. Box 8, Lone Pine, CA 93545; tel. (760) 876-6200.

32 Trail of 100 Giants

0.5 mi/0.5 hr

The Trail of 100 Giants is as good as, maybe better than, most of the giant sequoia trails in Sequoia and Kings Canyon National Parks. Trailhead elevation is 6,400 feet, and the trail is an easy and nearly flat loop that is suitable for wheelchairs, baby strollers, and marathon runners alike. The giant sequoias are dense here, situated amid a mixed forest of cedars and pines. As you walk in from the parking lot across the road, the first sequoia tree on your right is a doozy—probably the best one on the loop. Of all the sequoia groves we've seen and admired, the Trail of 100 Giants grove stands out because it has an unusual amount of twins—two sequoias growing tightly side by side in order to share resources. In fact, this grove even has one twin that rangers call a "sequedar," a sequoia and a cedar that have grown together. If you're staying at Redwood Meadow Campground you have your own entrance to this loop, so you don't have to drive down the road to the main trailhead and parking lot.

Location: In Sequoia National Forest near Johnsondale; map G5, grid e1.

User groups: Hikers, wheelchairs (with assistance), dogs, and horses. No mountain bikes.

Permits: No permits are required. A $2 parking fee is charged per vehicle.

Maps: For a map of Sequoia National Forest, send $6 to U.S. Forest Service, Map Sales, P.O. Box 587, Camino, CA 95709; tel. (530) 647-5390 or website: www.r5.fs.fed.us/visitorcenter. Ask the USGS for a topographic map of the Johnsondale area.

Directions: From Kernville on the north end of Lake Isabella, drive north on Sierra Way/Road 99 for 27 miles to Johnsondale R-Ranch. Continue west (the road becomes Road 50) for 5.5 miles, turn right on the Western Divide Highway, and drive 2.4 miles to the trailhead parking area on the right, just before Redwood Meadow Campground. Cross the road to begin the trail.

Contact: Sequoia National Forest, Hot Springs Ranger District, Route 4, Box 548, California Hot Springs, CA 93207; tel. (661) 548-6503 or fax (661) 548-6236.

33 Mule Peak Lookout
1.2 mi/1.0 hr

While rock climbers come to Mule Peak to do their daring work, hikers can take a not-so-daring walk up the back side of Mule Peak. The area around the peak has been logged, unfortunately, but growth is coming back with moderate success. The trail follows a series of easy switchbacks up the hillside, gaining 600 feet to the summit of Mule Peak, elevation 8,142 feet. A lookout tower is positioned there, still in operation by Sequoia National Forest, and views are excellent of Onion Meadow Peak, Table Mountain, and the Tule River Valley. We have friends who took their four-year-old on this hike; it's attainable for all ages and levels of hikers.

Location: In Sequoia National Forest near Johnsondale; map G5, grid e1.

User groups: Hikers, dogs, horses, and mountain bikes. No wheelchair facilities.

Permits: No permits are required. Parking and access are free.

Maps: For a map of Sequoia National Forest, send $6 to U.S. Forest Service, Map Sales, P.O. Box 587, Camino, CA 95709; tel. (530) 647-5390 or website: www.r5.fs.fed.us/visitorcenter. Ask the USGS for a topographic map of the Sentinel Peak area.

Directions: From Kernville on the north end of Lake Isabella, drive north on Sierra Way/Road 99 for 27 miles to Johnsondale R-Ranch. Continue west (the road becomes Road 50), then in 5.5 miles, turn right on the Western Divide Highway. Drive five miles to the left turnoff signed for Mule Peak/Road 22S03. Turn left and follow Road 22S03 for five miles to the Mule Peak Trailhead.

Contact: Sequoia National Forest, Hot Springs Ranger District, Route 4, Box 548, California Hot Springs, CA 93207; tel. (661) 548-6503 or fax (661) 548-6236.

34 Nobe Young Falls
1.0 mi/1.0 hr

Nobe Young Falls is the secret waterfall of Sequoia National Forest, and now everyone is going to be mad at us for spilling the beans. There are no signs, no trail markers, and not even a trailhead to reach it. You need route-finding skills and some scrambling ability to visit the falls, but the rewards on the short path are definitely worth it. From the unmarked parking pullout, start hiking on the dirt road to your left. When it forks, bear right. Pass a makeshift camp as you draw close to Nobe Young Creek, which you will hear but not see. Listen carefully to its sound; in just a few minutes of walking beyond the trail fork, you should hear the pouring of a waterfall. Keep your eyes peeled on the left for spur trails—there are several of them—leading down to the. Take any one and carefully descend the steep and slippery dirt slope. When you reach the bottom, you're looking up at Nobe Young Falls, spilling and splashing 125 feet over three wide granite ledges. It's a great spot, with many small trout in the stream below the falls. Now don't go telling everybody.

Location: In Sequoia National Forest near Johnsondale; map G5, grid e2.

User groups: Hikers, dogs, horses, and mountain bikes. No wheelchair facilities.

Permits: No permits are required. Parking and access are free.

Maps: For a map of Sequoia National Forest, send $6 to U.S. Forest Service, Map Sales, P.O. Box 587, Camino, CA 95709; tel. (530) 647-5390 or website: www.r5.fs.fed.us/visitorcenter. Ask the USGS for a topographic map of the Sentinel Peak area.

Directions: From Kernville on the north end of Lake Isabella, drive north on Sierra Way/Road 99 for 27 miles to Johnsondale R-Ranch. Continue west (the road becomes Road 50) for 5.5 miles, turn right on the Western Divide Highway, and drive eight miles to an unsigned parking pullout on the east (right) side of the road. The pullout is exactly one mile north of the turnoff for Camp Whitsett and Lower Peppermint Camp and .25 mile south of the Crawford Road turnoff.

Contact: Sequoia National Forest, Hot Springs Ranger District, Route 4, Box 548, California Hot Springs, CA 93207; tel. (661) 548-6503 or fax (661) 548-6236.

35 Dome Rock
0.25 mi/0.5 hr

Dome Rock wins the prize for "Granite Dome with the Most Pedestrian Name." But never mind. It also wins the prize for "Shortest Walk to an Incredible View." Trailhead elevation is 7,200 feet, and the trail is really just a route leading from the left side of the parking lot. Signs at the parking lot warn you not to drop or throw anything off the top of the dome, because there are rock climbers down below, on the dome's steep side. It's a mere five-minute walk to the top of Dome Rock, a huge cap of

bare granite, where the views are incredible of Slate Mountain, Lake Isabella, and the Needles. If you look very carefully, you can just make out the fire lookout tower on top of the Needles. You'll want to hang around here for a while to ooh and aah. The only possible downer is if you show up during the few weeks of gnat season (the time varies from year to year), when little black flies hover around your face relentlessly. They don't bite, but they can be crazy-making.

Location: In Sequoia National Forest near Quaking Aspen; map G5, grid e2.

User groups: Hikers, dogs, horses, and mountain bikes. No wheelchair facilities.

Permits: No permits are required. Parking and access are free.

Maps: For a map of Sequoia National Forest, send $6 to U.S. Forest Service, Map Sales, P.O. Box 587, Camino, CA 95709; tel. (530) 647-5390 or website: www.r5.fs.fed.us/visitorcenter. Ask the USGS for a topographic map of the Sentinel Peak area.

Directions: From Kernville on the north end of Lake Isabella, drive north on Sierra Way/Road 99 for 27 miles to Johnsondale R-Ranch. Continue west (the road becomes Road 50) for 5.5 miles and turn right on the Western Divide Highway. Drive 12 miles to the Dome Rock/Road 21S69 turnoff on the right, across from Peppermint Work Center. Turn right and follow the dirt road for a few hundred yards; where it forks, bear left and continue to the trailhead, .5 mile from the Western Divide Highway. If you're traveling from the north, the turnoff is two miles south of Ponderosa Lodge.

Contact: Sequoia National Forest, Tule River Ranger District, 32588 Highway 190, Springville, CA 93265; tel. (559) 539-2607 or fax (559) 539-2067.

36 Peppermint Creek Falls
0.25 mi/0.25 hr

The trek to Peppermint Creek Falls is not so much a hike as a scramble and should not be attempted by people who don't like climbing around on rough routes. However, if you watch your footing, it's a fairly easy descent to the base of the falls, and then a breathtaking climb back up the steep slope on your return. Since you park your car practically on top of the waterfall, you need only look over the cliff edge to spot the routes going down the side. Pick any one of the dirt trails, staying off the slippery granite as you descend. When you reach the bottom, you can watch Peppermint Creek plummeting 150 feet off the edge of a rounded granite dome, dropping into a wide pool that is deep enough for wading.

Location: In Sequoia National Forest near Johnsondale; map G5, grid e3.

User groups: Hikers, dogs, horses, and mountain bikes. No wheelchair facilities.

Permits: No permits are required. Parking and access are free.

Maps: For a map of Sequoia National Forest, send $6 to U.S. Forest Service, Map Sales, P.O. Box 587, Camino, CA 95709; tel. (530) 647-5390 or website: www.r5.fs.fed.us/visitorcenter. Ask the USGS for topographic maps of the Sentinel Peak and Durrwood Creek areas.

Directions: From Kernville on the north end of Lake Isabella, drive north on Sierra Way/Road 99 for 27 miles to Johnsondale R-Ranch. Turn right on Road 22S82 and drive 11.3 miles to Road 22S82F, signed for Camping Area 6. (It's on the right, .25 mile past Lower Peppermint Camp on the left.) Turn right on 22S82F, then drive .75 mile to a large clearing near the cliff edge.

Contact: Sequoia National Forest, Hot Springs Ranger District, Route 4, Box 548, California Hot Springs, CA 93207; tel. (661) 548-6503 or fax (661) 548-6236.

37 Alder Creek Trail
1.8 mi/1.0 hr

The granite slabs and pools on Alder Creek have gotten so popular with hikers, swimmers, and picnickers that the Forest Service has installed "No Parking Any Time" signs all over the road near the trailhead. But as long as you park where you're supposed to (off the road in the day-use parking area), you can still pay a visit to the tons-of-fun pools and slides along Alder Creek. To reach them, walk up the gated dirt road (Road 22S83) and turn right on the single-track trail. The path descends to the confluence of Alder Creek and Dry Meadow Creek, where there is a long length of swimming holes and rocky slides that pour into them. Make sure you wear denim or some other heavy matrial on your backside so you can while away many happy hours pretending you are a river otter. It's exhilarating.

Location: In Sequoia National Forest near Johnsondale; map G5, grid e3.

User groups: Hikers and dogs. No horses or mountain bikes. No wheelchair facilities.

Permits: No permits are required. Parking and access are free.

Maps: For a map of Sequoia National Forest, send $6 to U.S. Forest Service, Map Sales, P.O. Box 587, Camino, CA 95709; tel. (530) 647-5390 or website: www.r5.fs.fed.us/visitorcenter. Ask the USGS for a topographic map of the Sentinel Peak area.

Directions: From Kernville on the north end of Lake Isabella, drive north on Sierra Way/Road 99 for 27 miles to .5 mile north of Johnsondale R-Ranch. Turn right on Road 22S82 and drive 5.7 miles to the day-use parking area on the right side of the road. Walk across Road 22S82 to the gated dirt road and the trailhead.

Contact: Sequoia National Forest, Hot Springs Ranger District, Route 4, Box 548, California Hot Springs, CA 93207; tel. (661) 548-6503 or fax (661) 548-6236.

38 North Fork Kern River Trail
6.0 mi/3.0 hrs or 2.0 days

Sometimes you just want to walk alongside a beautiful river, and if that's what you're in the mood for, the Wild and Scenic North Fork Kern is a first-rate choice. From the giant parking lot, you walk across the hikers' bridge (separate from but next to the highway bridge) to reach the far side of the river, and then descend on stair steps to reach the trail. The North Fork Kern River Trail winds along gently, heading deep into the dramatic Kern Canyon, sometimes under the shade of digger pines, live oaks, and incense cedars, and sometimes out in the bright sunshine. Spring wildflowers are stunning, especially in March and April. Spring river rafters are also entertaining to watch. Most people who walk this trail bring a fishing rod with them, an if you do, make sure you're up to date on the special fishing regulations. They're in effect for the first four miles of river, which is a wild trout area. Backpackers will find many campsites along the trail, even some that are under the cave-like canopy of big boulders.

Location: In Sequoia National Forest north of Kernville; map G5, grid e3.

User groups: Hikers, dogs, and mountain bikes. No horses. No wheelchair facilities.

Permits: A free wilderness permit is required for overnight stays and is available from the Springville or Kernville ranger stations. Parking and access are free.

Maps: For a map of Sequoia National Forest, send $6 to U.S. Forest Service, Map Sales, P.O. Box 587, Camino, CA 95709; tel. (530) 647-5390 or website: www.r5.fs.fed.us/visitorcenter. Ask the USGS for a topographic map of the Fairview area.

Directions: From Kernville on the north end of Lake Isabella, drive north on Sierra Way/Road 99 for 22 miles to the Johnsondale highway bridge over the Kern River. Turn right and park in the large paved parking lot by the signboard at the bridge.

Contact: Sequoia National Forest, Cannell Meadow Ranger District, P.O. Box 9, Kernville, CA 93238; tel. (760) 376-3781 or fax (760) 376-3795.

39 Sherman Peak Trail
4.0 mi/2.0 hrs

From the Sherman Pass Vista along the highway, you can look to the north to Mount Whitney and the Great Western Divide. After crossing the highway and hiking the Sherman Peak Trail to the top of Sherman Peak at 9,909 feet, you can pivot around and have a panoramic look at an even bigger chunk of the world. The trail is mostly forested with red firs and pines and is gradual enough for children to climb. If you read the interpretive display at the Vista, you'll be able to identify the myriad of mountains you're looking at from the peak, including Split Rock and Dome Rock. It's only a 700-foot climb to the summit, mostly through a series of easy switchbacks.

Location: In Sequoia National Forest near Sherman Pass; map G5, grid e4.

User groups: Hikers, dogs, horses, and mountain bikes. No wheelchair facilities.

Permits: No permits are required. Parking and access are free.

Maps: For a map of Sequoia National Forest, send $6 to U.S. Forest Service, Map Sales, P.O. Box 587, Camino, CA 95709; tel. (530) 647-5390 or website: www.r5.fs.fed.us/visitorcenter. Ask the USGS for topographic maps of the Durrwood Creek and Sirretta Peak areas.

Directions: From Kernville on the north end of Lake Isabella, drive north on Sierra Way/Road 99 for 22 miles to the right turnoff for Sherman Pass Road/22S05. Turn right and drive approximately 15 miles on Sherman Pass Road to the Sherman Pass Vista. The trailhead is across the road.

Contact: Sequoia National Forest, Cannell Meadow Ranger District, P.O. Box 9, Kernville, CA 93238; tel. (760) 376-3781 or fax (760) 376-3795.

40 Bald Mountain Lookout
0.25 mi/0.25 hr

This short hike to the summit of 9,382-foot Bald Mountain is the easiest possible introduction to the Dome Land Wilderness. It's a brief stroll to the lookout, which is perched on the very northern edge of the wilderness. This wilderness region is famous for its many granite domes and monolithic rocks, the happy hunting ground of rock climbers from all over Southern California. Of the many big hunks of rock, Church Dome is perhaps the most outstanding, and it can be seen from here directly to the south. White Dome and Black Mountain are also visible, to the east of Church Dome, as well as a sweeping vista of the Kern Plateau, the Whitney Range, and the Great Western Divide.

Location: In Sequoia National Forest on the north edge of the Dome Land Wilderness; map G5, grid e5.

User groups: Hikers, dogs, horses, and mountain bikes. No wheelchair facilities.

Permits: No permits are required. Parking and access are free.

Maps: For a map of Sequoia National Forest, send $6 to U.S. Forest Service, Map Sales, P.O. Box 587, Camino, CA 95709; tel. (530) 647-5390 or website: www.r5.fs.fed.us/visitorcenter. Ask the USGS for a topographic map of the Crag Peak area.

Directions: From Kernville on the north end of Lake Isabella, drive north on Sierra Way/Road 99 for 22 miles to the right turnoff for Sherman Pass Road/22S05. Turn right and drive approximately 25 miles on Sherman Pass Road to Forest Service Road 22S77, signed for Bald Mountain Lookout. Turn east (right) on Road 22S77 and follow it for one mile to its end.

Contact: Sequoia National Forest, Cannell Meadow Ranger District, P.O. Box 9, Kernville, CA 93238; tel. (760) 376-3781 or fax (760) 376-3795.

41 Jackass Creek National Recreation Trail

5.0 mi/2.5 hrs

The Jackass Creek Trail is way out there on the Kern Plateau. If you just want to be left alone, you have a decent chance of that here.

The trailhead is at 8,000 feet, and the trail climbs 5.5 miles to Jackass Peak (elevation 9,245 feet) on the border of the South Sierra Wilderness. Most people don't bother traveling that far; instead they follow the trail along Jackass Creek for a couple of miles through red fir forest to the western edge of Jackass Meadow. In addition to the beautiful meadow, the trail offers a look at many handsome old-growth aspens. The trail is an old dirt road, wide enough for holding hands with your hiking partner. Our recommendation? Hike this trail in late September or early October for the best of the golden aspen show.

Location: In Sequoia National Forest near the South Sierra Wilderness; map G5, grid e6.

User groups: Hikers, dogs, horses, and mountain bikes. No wheelchair facilities.

Permits: No permits are required. Parking and access are free.

Maps: For a map of Sequoia National Forest, send $6 to U.S. Forest Service, Map Sales, P.O. Box 587, Camino, CA 95709; tel. (530) 647-5390 or website: www.r5.fs.fed.us/visitorcenter. Ask the USGS for a topographic map of the Crag Peak area.

Directions: From Kernville on the north end of Lake Isabella, drive north on Sierra Way/Road 99 for 22 miles to the right turnoff for Sherman Pass Road/22S05. Turn right and drive approximately 35 miles on Sherman Pass Road to the four-way intersection with Road 21S03 near Blackrock Information Station. Turn right to continue on Road 22S05 and drive five miles to Fish Creek Campground and Road 21S01, where the trail begins.

Contact: Sequoia National Forest, Cannell Meadow Ranger District, P.O. Box 9, Kernville, CA 93238; tel. (760) 376-3781 or fax (760) 376-3795.

42 Whiskey Flat Trail

5.0 mi/2.5 hrs

The Whiskey Flat Trail is a 14.5-mile trail that parallels the Kern River from Fairview Lodge all the way south to Burlando Road in Kernville. Primarily used by anglers working the Kern River, it's also a good springtime stroll for river lovers. If you walk out and back for a few miles on the northern end of the trail by Fairview, you can end the day with a meal at Fairview Lodge's restaurant, where you can brag about the fish you did or didn't catch, like everybody else there. The Whiskey Flat Trail can be somewhat difficult to follow, especially in springtime when the numerous creeks you must cross are running full. Early in the year, the creeks can sometimes be impassable. The path begins on a suspension bridge, which is reminiscent of Huck Finn and his friends. You hike as far as you please; we suggest 2.5 miles, about an hour's walk each way. The terrain is grasslands and chaparral with occasional digger pines, which means no shade but plenty of spring wildflowers. Although the route is basically level, there are numerous steep stretches where you climb in and out of stream drainages running into the Kern. The trailhead elevation is 2,800 feet.

Location: In Sequoia National Forest near Fairview; map G5, grid f3.

User groups: Hikers, dogs, horses, and mountain bikes. No wheelchair facilities.

Permits: No permits are required. Parking and access are free.

Maps: For a map of Sequoia National Forest, send $6 to U.S. Forest Service, Map Sales, P.O. Box 587, Camino, CA 95709; tel. (530) 647-5390 or website: www.r5.fs.fed.us/visitorcenter. Ask the USGS for a topographic map of the Fairview area.

Directions: From Kernville on the north end of Lake Isabella, drive north on Sierra Way/Road 99 for 17 miles to Fairview and the Fairview Lodge on the left side of the road. To the right of the lodge is a large parking area and a trailhead for the Whiskey Flat Trail.

Contact: Sequoia National Forest, Cannell Meadow Ranger District, P.O. Box 9, Kernville, CA 93238; tel. (760) 376-3781 or fax (760) 376-3795.

43 Packsaddle Cave Trail
4.6 mi/2.3 hrs

Everybody enjoys the trip to Packsaddle Cave, even though the cave was long ago vandalized of its jewel-like stalactites and stalagmites. Nonetheless, the appeal of visiting the limestone cave keeps this trail well used and fairly well maintained. From the parking lot on Sierra Way, cross the highway and hike uphill on the path, huffing and puffing through some steep pitches. This is not a trail for summertime, because there is little shade among the manzanita, sagebrush, and deer brush, and the total climb is about 1,200 feet. At 1.8 miles, you cross Packsaddle Creek and see several campsites near it. Continue a short distance farther; the cave is off to the left, .25 mile before this trail's junction with the Rincon Trail. Don't forget your flashlight so you can take a peek inside.

Location: In Sequoia National Forest near Fairview; map G5, grid f3.

User groups: Hikers, dogs, horses, and mountain bikes. No wheelchair facilities.

Permits: No permits are required. Parking and access are free.

Maps: For a map of Sequoia National Forest, send $6 to U.S. Forest Service, Map Sales, P.O. Box 587, Camino, CA 95709; tel. (530) 647-5390 or website: www.r5.fs.fed.us/visitorcenter. Ask the USGS for a topographic map of the Fairview area.

Directions: From Kernville on the north end of Lake Isabella, drive north on Sierra Way/Road 99 for 18 miles to the Packsaddle Cave Trailhead on the right, .25 mile beyond Fairview Campground. The parking area is across the road.

Contact: Sequoia National Forest, Cannell Meadow Ranger District, P.O. Box 9, Kernville, CA 93238; tel. (760) 376-3781 or fax (760) 376-3795.

44 Unal Trail

3.0 mi/1.5 hrs

No doubt about it, this is a first-rate trail for families to hike or for anybody who wants to have a good leg-stretching walk or run around a beautiful mountain. The Unal Trail is a three-mile loop that climbs gently for two miles to Unal Peak, and then descends in one mile of switchbacks back to the trailhead. (After the first 100 yards, where the trail forks, be sure you take the left fork and hike the trail clockwise.) The trail passes a Native American cultural site on the return of the loop, the homestead of the Tubatulabal Indians. With only a 700-foot climb and an excellent grade, even mountain bikers can manage this trail, although few bother with it. You'll likely see some deer on the hillsides, and the view from the top of Unal Peak makes the whole world seem peaceful and serene. Although most of the trail is lined with conifers, the top of the loop is a little exposed and catches a strong breeze.

Location: In Sequoia National Forest near Wofford Heights; map G5, grid g1.

User groups: Hikers, dogs, horses, and mountain bikes. No wheelchair facilities.

Permits: No permits are required. Parking and access are free.

Maps: For a map of Sequoia National Forest, send $6 to U.S. Forest Service, Map Sales, P.O. Box 587, Camino, CA 95709; tel. (530) 647-5390 or website: www.r5.fs.fed.us/visitorcenter. Ask the USGS for a topographic map of the Posey area.

Directions: From Wofford Heights on the west side of Lake Isabella, turn west on Highway 155 and drive eight miles to Greenhorn Summit. Turn left at the sign for Shirley Ski Meadows and drive 100 yards to the Greenhorn Fire Station and Unal Trailhead, on the right side of the road.

Contact: Sequoia National Forest, Greenhorn Ranger District, c/o Lake Isabella Visitor Center, P.O. Box 3810, Lake Isabella, CA 93240; tel. (760) 379-5646 or fax (760) 379-8597.

45 Sunday Peak Trail

3.4 mi/2.0 hrs

From the Sunday Peak Trailhead at 7,200 feet in the Greenhorn Mountains, it's a 1,000-foot climb to the top of Sunday Peak, an excellent day hike for families. The grade is moderate and shaded by big conifers, and the destination is perfect on a day when the heat is sweltering down near Lake Isabella. From the top you can look down at the Kern River Valley and feel sorry for all those people sweating it out down there. Although the peak's fire lookout tower was abandoned and then destroyed by the Forest Service in the 1950s, the wide-angle views remain—of the Kern Valley, Kern Plateau, and far-off high Sierra peaks. There are many good picnicking spots on the summit.

Location: In Sequoia National Forest near Wofford Heights; map G5, grid g1.

User groups: Hikers, dogs, horses, and mountain bikes. No wheelchair facilities.

Permits: No permits are required. Parking and access are free.

Maps: For a map of Sequoia National Forest, send $6 to U.S. Forest Service, Map Sales, P.O. Box 587, Camino, CA 95709; tel. (530) 647-5390 or website: www.r5.fs.fed.us/visitorcenter. Ask the USGS for a topographic map of the Posey area.

Directions: From Wofford Heights on the west side of Lake Isabella, turn west on Highway 155 and drive eight miles to Greenhorn Summit. Turn right on Road 24S15/Forest Highway 90, signed for Portuguese Pass, and drive 6.5 miles north to the parking area for the Sunday Peak Trail, near the Girl Scout Camp.

Contact: Sequoia National Forest, Greenhorn Ranger District, c/o Lake Isabella Visitor Center, P.O. Box 3810, Lake Isabella, CA 93240; tel. (760) 379-5646 or fax (760) 379-8597.

46 Rincon Trail

4.0 mi/2.0 hrs

Let's say right away that this Rincon has absolutely nothing in common with the other Rincon, the classic surfing break on the Ventura coast. For one, there's no water here, and two, there's no cool ocean breeze. That means you should plan your hike for winter or spring, before the Kern Valley heats up. The trail leads first east and then steadily north along the Rincon Fault, heading for Forks of the Kern. It undulates, following the drainages of Salmon and other creeks. The destination on this trail is the long-distance view of Salmon Creek Falls, about two miles in, and the good fishing and camping prospects on the way along Salmon Creek. The trail crosses Salmon Creek on a bridge 1.7 miles in, but the waterfall view is about .25 mile farther. You might want to bring your binoculars to get a good look. If you wish to hike farther on the Rincon Trail, it intersects the route to Packsaddle Cave in another two miles, then crosses Sherman Pass Road in another 2.5 miles, and keeps going straight north all the way to Forks of the Kern. The total one-way trail length is a whopping 23 miles.

Location: In Sequoia National Forest near Fairview; map G5, grid g3.

User groups: Hikers, dogs, and mountain bikes. No horses. No wheelchair facilities.

Permits: No permits are required. Parking and access are free.

Maps: For a map of Sequoia National Forest, send $6 to U.S. Forest Service, Map Sales, P.O. Box 587, Camino, CA 95709; tel. (530) 647-5390 or website: www.r5.fs.fed.us/visitorcenter. Ask the USGS for a topographic map of the Kernville area.

Directions: From Kernville on the north end of Lake Isabella, drive north on Sierra Way/Road 99 for 13 miles to the Rincon Trailhead on the right, across from the Ant Canyon dispersed camping area.

Contact: Sequoia National Forest, Cannell Meadow Ranger District, P.O. Box 9, Kernville, CA 93238; tel. (760) 376-3781 or fax (760) 376-3795.

47 Salmon Creek Falls
9.0 mi/5.0 hrs or 2.0 days

The nine-mile round-trip to the brink of Salmon Creek Falls is a stellar walk through lodgepole pines and white fir, with a chance for fishing, skinny-dipping, and admiring a lot of beautiful scenery at 7,600 feet in elevation. Since there are campsites located along the trail, it's easy enough to turn the trip into an overnight excursion, but the trail also makes a good, long day hike. The trail is downhill all the way, dropping 600 feet over .5 mile, and follows granite-lined Salmon Creek. After skirting the edge of Horse Meadow, you simply follow the creek's meander. Trails run on both sides of the stream for the first two miles, so you can walk either side, but then they join as one. The path comes to an end above Salmon Creek Falls, where you can swim, fish, and camp, but don't expect to gaze out at the big waterfall—there's no way to get a good look at it from here, since you're perched on top of it.

Location: In Sequoia National Forest near Big Meadow; map G5, grid g4.

User groups: Hikers, dogs, horses, and mountain bikes. No wheelchair facilities.

Permits: A free wilderness permit is required for overnight stays and is available from the Springville or Kernville ranger stations. Parking and access are free.

Maps: For a map of Sequoia National Forest, send $6 to U.S. Forest Service, Map Sales, P.O. Box 587, Camino, CA 95709; tel. (530) 647-5390 or website: www.r5.fs.fed.us/visitorcenter. Ask the USGS for topographic maps of the Sirretta Peak and Fairview areas.

Directions: From Kernville on the north end of Lake Isabella, drive north on Sierra Way/Road 99 for 22 miles to the right turnoff for Sherman Pass Road/22S05. Turn right and drive 6.1 miles on Sherman Pass Road, then turn right on Road 22S12, signed for Horse Meadow Campground. Drive 6.3 miles on Road 22S12 till you reach a fork. Stay straight. At eight miles, bear left. At 9.3 miles, turn right at the Horse Meadow Campground sign (Road

23S10). You'll reach the camp at 10.7 miles, but take the right turnoff just before the camp to reach the trailhead.

Contact: Sequoia National Forest, Cannell Meadow Ranger District, P.O. Box 9, Kernville, CA 93238; tel. (760) 376-3781 or fax (760) 376-3795.

48 Sirretta Peak
8.0 mi/5.0 hrs

Hey, what's that big meadow down there? It's Big Meadow, of course—that huge expanse of green you see from the top of Sirretta Peak. From Sirretta's summit, you get an eyeful of it, as well as long, lingering glances at the many granite domes of the Dome Land Wilderness Area, Sirretta and Deadwood Meadows and the peaks of the High Sierra. The route to the peak starts at Big Meadow's northern edge, then travels north on the Cannell Trail for .5 mile. Bear right (northeast) at the fork with the Sirretta Peak Trail and climb 2.5 miles to a spur trail that leads to the summit. There are many switchbacks and plenty of fine views along the way. Take the left spur (it's obvious) for .5 mile to the rocky summit and congratulate yourself on your fine mountaineering skills. The trail has an elevation gain of 1,200 feet, and if you decide to make the final summit climb, you'll add on another 700 feet. Sirretta Peak is just shy of 10,000 feet in elevation.

Location: Near the Dome Land Wilderness; map G5, grid g4.

User groups: Hikers and dogs. No horses or mountain bikes. No wheelchair facilities.

Permits: No permits are required for day hiking. Parking and access are free.

Maps: For a map of Sequoia National Forest, send $6 to U.S. Forest Service, Map Sales, P.O. Box 587, Camino, CA 95709; tel. (530) 647-5390 or website: www.r5.fs.fed.us/visitorcenter. Ask the USGS for a topographic map of the Sirretta Peak area.

Directions: From Kernville on the north end of Lake Isabella, drive north on Sierra Way/Road 99 for 22 miles to the right turnoff for Sher-

man Pass Road/22S05. Turn right and drive 6.1 miles on Sherman Pass Road Turn right on Road 22S12, signed for Horse Meadow Campground, and drive 6.3 miles on Road 22S12 till you reach a fork. Stay straight. At eight miles, bear left, staying on Road 22S12. Continue four more miles, passing the Horse Meadow Campground turnoff, to Road 23S07 at the northern edge of Big Meadow. Turn left on Road 23S07 and drive .5 mile to the Cannell Trailhead.

Contact: Sequoia National Forest, Cannell Meadow Ranger District, P.O. Box 9, Kernville, CA 93238; tel. (760) 376-3781 or fax (760) 376-3795.

49 Manter Meadow Loop
10.0 mi/6.0 hrs

For people who love meadows, granite, and solitude, this loop trip is just about perfect. From the South Manter Trailhead at 7,800 feet, the trail goes uphill for four miles to Manter Meadow, so bring your wildflower identification book and a map to identify surrounding peaks and domes. Along the way several side trails branch off the main trail, leading to some of the granite domes of the Dome Land Wilderness, including spectacular Taylor Dome and Church Dome. A two-mile loop trail encircles the entire perimeter of the meadow, which you can add on to your trip if you wish. At the meadow's western edge, the South Manter Trail meets the North Manter Trail, and you follow the latter back to Forest Service Road 23S07 (the road you drove in on). Then it's a 1.5-mile walk on the dirt road back to your car. If you want to avoid the road, hike the South Manter Trail both ways, and take the loop walk around the meadow. The mileage is about equal to the other trip.

Location: In the Dome Land Wilderness; map G5, grid g4.

User groups: Hikers, dogs, and horses. No mountain bikes. No wheelchair facilities.

Permits: No permits are required for day hiking. Parking and access are free.

Maps: For a map of Sequoia National Forest, send $6 to U.S. Forest Service, Map Sales, P.O. Box 587, Camino, CA 95709; tel. (530) 647-5390 or website: www.r5.fs.fed.us/visitorcenter. Ask the USGS for a topographic map of the Sirretta Peak area.

Directions: From Kernville on the north end of Lake Isabella, drive north on Sierra Way/Road 99 for 22 miles to the right turnoff for Sherman Pass Road/22S05. Turn right and drive 6.1 miles on Sherman Pass Road. Turn right on Road 22S12, signed for Horse Meadow Campground, and drive 6.3 miles on Road 22S12 till you reach a fork. Stay straight. At eight miles, bear left, staying on Road 22S12. Continue four more miles, passing the Horse Meadow Campground turnoff, to Road 23S07 at the northern edge of Big Meadow. Turn left on Road 23S07 and drive three miles to the southeast edge of Big Meadow and the South Manter Trailhead.

Contact: Sequoia National Forest, Cannell Meadow Ranger District, P.O. Box 9, Kernville, CA 93238; tel. (760) 376-3781 or fax (760) 376-3795.

50 Rockhouse Basin
4.0 mi/2.0 hrs

You're driving along in no-man's-land on Highway 178 between U.S. 395 and Lake Isabella, staring at thousands of those odd-looking piñon pines. This is the transition zone between the Mojave Desert to the east and the Sierra Nevada to the west, and it doesn't look quite like either one of them. Want to see this strange land up close? This easy hike to Rockhouse Basin can take you there, and since it requires a long drive on dirt roads to reach the trailhead, you're likely to be free of the eastern Sierra hiking masses. A half mile from the trailhead, turn right and head north to Rockhouse Basin, where the noise of cicadas serenades you almost as loudly as the river. Explore the rocks, cool off in the river, and admire those piñon pines. It can be as hot as Hades out here, so plan your trip for early in the year, when you can hike along the Kern River in relative comfort.

Location: On the eastern side of the Dome Land Wilderness; map G5, grid g6.

User groups: Hikers, dogs, and horses. No mountain bikes. No wheelchair facilities.

Permits: No permits are required for day hiking. Parking and access are free.

Maps: For a map of Sequoia National Forest, send $6 to U.S. Forest Service, Map Sales, P.O. Box 587, Camino, CA 95709; tel. (530) 647-5390 or website: www.r5.fs.fed.us/visitorcenter. Ask the USGS for a topographic map of the Rockhouse Basin area.

Directions: From the junction of Highway 14 and Highway 178 north of Mojave, drive west on Highway 178 for 18 miles to the right turnoff for Chimney Peak National Backcountry Byway, or Canebrake Road. Turn right and drive approximately nine miles. Turn left (west) on Long Valley Loop Road and drive 14 miles to the gate at the start of the Rockhouse Basin Trail. You can also reach the trailhead by taking Ninemile Canyon Road west for 11 miles from the BLM administration site. Go past the BLM office, take the second dirt road on the left, and drive eight miles to the trailhead. (This road is much rougher.)

Contact: Bureau of Land Management, Ridgecrest Resource Area, 300 South Richmond Road, Ridgecrest, CA 93555; tel. (760) 384-5400 or fax (760) 384-5499; Sequoia National Forest, Cannell Meadow Ranger District, P.O. Box 9, Kernville, CA 93238; tel. (760) 376-3781 or fax (760) 376-3795.

51 Fossil Falls
1.0 mi/0.5 hr

Now don't get your hopes up and think you're going to find a waterfall way out here in the desert east of U.S. 395. There's no water to be found anywhere at Fossil Falls, but there's an excellent hike to an ancient lava field where you'll find polished and sculptured rock formations. The trail is well maintained, flat, and easy enough for children, although you don't want to hike it at high noon on a hot day. The falls look more like a giant pit or crevice in the ground, carved with beautiful wind-sculpted lava formations, which were polished in the last Ice Age. If you know what to look for, you'll also find Native American artifacts in the area, including petroglyphs and rock rings built by the Paiute Indians. If you're the kind of person who likes the weird-looking tufa formations at Mono Lake (we are), you'll enjoy this trail.

Location: Off U.S. 395 north of the Highway 178 and Highway 14 junction; map G5, grid g9.

User groups: Hikers, dogs, horses, and mountain bikes. No wheelchair facilities.

Permits: No permits are required. Parking and access are free.

Maps: Ask the USGS for a topographic map of the Little Lake area.

Directions: From the junction of Highway 14 and U.S. 395 near Inyokern, drive north on U.S. 395 for 20 miles to just north of Little Lake and turn east on Cinder Road. Drive .6 mile, bear right at the fork, and drive another .6 mile to the Fossil Falls Trailhead.

Contact: Bureau of Land Management, Ridgecrest Resource Area, 300 South Richmond Road, Ridgecrest, CA 93555; tel. (760) 384-5400 or fax (760) 384-5499.

52 Cannell Meadow National Recreation Trail

18.0 mi/3.0 days

The Cannell Meadow National Recreation Trail is the first trailhead you reach out of Kernville, and if it's summertime, you should start at the other end of this nine-mile trail. That's because the Kernville end is at 2,800 feet, set in rocky, chaparral and digger pine country, and, baby, it's hot out here. Still, if you can time your trip for late winter or spring, hiking this end of the Cannell Trail is a great adventure, watching the terrain and environment change as the elevation rises. The shadeless trail climbs right

away, through sage and occasional live oaks, affording views of the Kern River Valley. The trail gets more and more steep as you near conifer country at Pine Flat, but then you also get some blessed shade. It crosses Cannell Creek twice and reaches the Cannell Meadow Forest Service Cabin, a log cabin that was built in 1904. Cannell Meadow is a beautiful spot on the western edge of the Kern Plateau, edged by Jeffrey and lodgepole pines. Elevation is 7,500 feet, which means a total climb of 4,700 feet. Spread it out over a couple of days.

Location: In Sequoia National Forest north of Kernville; map G5, grid h3.

User groups: Hikers, dogs, horses, and mountain bikes. No wheelchair facilities.

Permits: No permits are required. Parking and access are free.

Maps: For a map of Sequoia National Forest, send $6 to U.S. Forest Service, Map Sales, P.O. Box 587, Camino, CA 95709; tel. (530) 647-5390 or website: www.r5.fs.fed.us/visitorcenter. Ask the USGS for a topographic map of the Kernville area.

Directions: From Kernville on the north end of Lake Isabella, drive north on Sierra Way/Road 99 for 1.4 miles to the Cannell Meadow Trailhead on the right. Parking is available near the horse corrals.

Contact: Sequoia National Forest, Cannell Meadow Ranger District, P.O. Box 9, Kernville, CA 93238; tel. (760) 376-3781 or fax (760) 376-3795.

PACIFIC CREST TRAIL (PCT) SECTION OVERVIEW

113.5 mi one way/11.0 days

For PCT through-hikers, this section from Walker Pass north to the flank of Mount Whitney is a baptismal rite of passage. In the space of 113 miles, you go from hell to heaven, finally passing through the last of high desert, then to the Dome Land Wilderness and onward to the Golden Trout Wilderness and Whitney. You'll get your first look at the pristine high-mountain meadows and streams, including South Fork Kern River, a gorgeous stream and memorable moment. Trail elevations within this section range from around 3,800 feet to more than 11,500 feet, and then topping out after the mandatory climb of the Whitney Summit, 14,494 feet. As you gain the higher elevations, the only downer can be heavy snow if you arrive too early in the hiking season.

PCT-19 Walker Pass to Kennedy Meadows

50.0 mi one way/5.0 days

As you take these first steps from Walker Pass, elevation 5,246 feet, you must reassess your water consumption and water store, since the first 12 miles don't have a reliable water supply. "Ha!" you may even say, since in the weeks ahead water availability will become laughable as you enter the high Sierra. These initial 12 miles climb into the Chimney Peak Wilderness, featuring long-distance views and a series of sparsely vegetated peaks. The latter include Mount Jenkins, named after the outdoors writer and PCT author, Jim Jenkins, who was hit and killed in a traffic accident on U.S. 395 when trying to assist a vehicle on the side of the road. The surrounding flora remains stark for the most part until the Dome Land Wilderness, a tromp of just over 30 miles from Walker Pass. From here the surroundings undergo stunning changes over the next 20 miles. The Dome Land Wilderness features an awesome collection of rock formations that attract rock climbers from throughout the West. The trail skirts the east side of Rockhouse Basin and is routed past a series of creeks, meadows, and, finally, high mountain forests. For long-distance hikers used to water rationing, seeing the South Fork Kern River will be like a trip into heaven. A final push will take you to the store at Kennedy Meadows, elevation 6,150 feet, where every PCT hiker will resupply.

Location: From the Walker Pass Trailhead

north to the trailhead parking area at Kennedy Meadows; map G5, grid i7.

User groups: Hikers, dogs, and horses. No mountain bikes. No wheelchair facilities.

Permits: A wilderness permit is required for traveling through various wilderness and special-use areas the trail traverses. Contact the Angeles National Forest, tel. (661) 296-9710, for a permit that is good for the length of your trip.

Maps: For an overall view of the trail route in this section, send $6 to U.S. Forest Service, Map Sales, P.O. Box 587, Camino, CA 95709; tel. (530) 647-5390 or website: www.r5.fs.fed. us/visitorcenter. Ask for the Sequoia National Forest map. Ask the USGS for topographic maps of the Walker Pass, Lamont Peak, White Dome, Rockhouse Basin, and Crag Peak areas.

Directions: To reach the Walker Pass Trailhead, from Highway 14 at Vincent head west on Highway 178 toward Lake Isabella. Drive to Mill Creek Summit. The Walker Pass Trailhead is to the right of the parking area. To reach the Kennedy Meadows Trailhead, on Highway 395 drive north to the Kennedy Meadows turnoff. Turn left on Nine Mile Canyon Road. Drive on Nine Mile Canyon Road (it becomes Kennedy Meadows Road) to Kennedy Meadows Campground and the signed PCT Trailhead.

Contact: Sequoia National Forest, Cannell Meadow Ranger District, P.O. Box 9, Kernville, CA 93238; tel. (760) 376-3781 or fax (760) 376-3795.

PCT-20 Kennedy Meadows to Mount Whitney

63.5 mi one way/6.0 days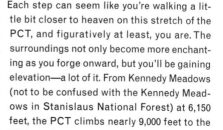

Each step can seem like you're walking a little bit closer to heaven on this stretch of the PCT, and figuratively at least, you are. The surroundings not only become more enchanting as you forge onward, but you'll be gaining elevation—a lot of it. From Kennedy Meadows (not to be confused with the Kennedy Meadows in Stanislaus National Forest) at 6,150 feet, the PCT climbs nearly 9,000 feet to the Whitney Summit, a must-do side trip. Along the way, the views and scenery are dramatic, passing through the Golden Trout and Sierra Wildernesses and arriving finally at the awesome Whitney, the highest point in the Lower 48. Often bordered by pinnacle-like granite formations, the trail is occasionally routed along the edges of meadows and forests, and sprinkled with small wildflowers, with the dramatic granite ridges always looming in the distance. The Golden Trout Wilderness has few lakes, but is better known for its small, pristine streams that are native habitat for California's state fish. When you reach Trail Pass, elevation 10,740 feet, 40 miles from Kennedy Meadows, the surrounding grandeur of the high country is astonishing. Untouched meadows, stunted pine forests, and small, pure streams become more common, a scene that draws hikers from all over the world to the high Sierra wilderness. The last 20 miles to the flank of Whitney feature unbelievable views, and it never stops, all the way to Whitney, when every mountaintop for hundreds of miles becomes visible. For PCT through-hikers, this wondrous vision makes the previous 600 miles from the Mexican border worth every step it took to get it.

Location: From the trailhead parking area at Kennedy Meadows Campground north to Mount Whitney; map G5, grid f6.

User groups: Hikers and horses. No dogs or mountain bikes. No wheelchair facilities.

Permits: A wilderness permit is required for traveling through various wilderness and special-use areas the trail traverses. Contact the Angeles National Forest, tel. (661) 296-9710, for a permit that is good for the length of your trip.

Maps: For an overall view of the trail route in this section, send $6 for each map ordered to U.S. Forest Service, Map Sales, P.O. Box 587, Camino, CA 95709; tel. (530) 647-5390 or website: www.r5.fs.fed.us/visitorcenter. Ask for the Sequoia National Forest and the Inyo National Forest maps. Ask the USGS for topographic maps of the Crag Peak, Monache Mountain, Templeton Mountain, Cirque Peak, Mount Langley, and Mount Whitney areas.

Directions: To reach the Kennedy Meadows Trailhead, drive north on U.S. 395 to the Kennedy Meadows turnoff. Turn left on Nine Mile Canyon Road. Drive on Nine Mile Canyon Road (it becomes Kennedy Meadows Road) to Kennedy Meadows Campground and the signed PCT Trailhead. To reach the Mount Whitney Trailhead, from Lone Pine and U.S. 395 head west on Whitney Portal Road for approximately 13 miles to Whitney Portal and the trailhead for the Mount Whitney Trail.

Contact: Sequoia National Forest, Cannell Meadow Ranger District, P.O. Box 9, Kernville, CA 93238; tel. (760) 376-3781 or fax (760) 376-3795; Inyo National Forest, Mount Whitney Ranger District, P.O. Box 8, Lone Pine, CA 93545; tel. (760) 876-6200 or fax (760) 876-6202.

PCT Continuation

To continue hiking along the Pacific Crest Trail, see chapter F5.

At Trona Pinnacles National Natural Landmark, some tufa spires are as high as 140 feet.

MAP G6

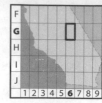

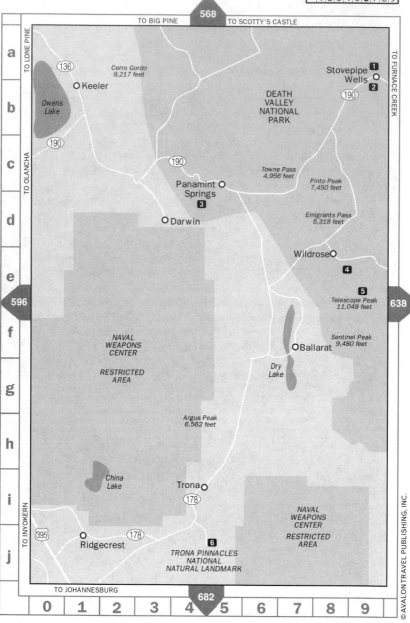

TO BIG PINE • **568** • TO SCOTTY'S CASTLE

TO LONE PINE

136

Cerro Gordo
9,217 feet

Keeler ○

Owens
Lake

190

TO OLANCHA

190

Stovepipe **1**
Wells ○ **2**

190

TO FURNACE CREEK

DEATH
VALLEY
NATIONAL
PARK

190

Towne Pass
4,956 feet

Pinto Peak
7,450 feet

Panamint ○
Springs
3

Darwin ○

Emigrants Pass
5,318 feet

Wildrose ○

4

596

5

Telescope Peak
11,049 feet

638

NAVAL
WEAPONS
CENTER

RESTRICTED
AREA

Sentinel Peak
9,480 feet

Ballarat ○

Dry
Lake

Argus Peak
6,562 feet

China
Lake

Trona ○

178

NAVAL
WEAPONS
CENTER

RESTRICTED
AREA

TO INYOKERN

395

Ridgecrest ○

178

6

TRONA PINNACLES
NATIONAL
NATURAL LANDMARK

TO JOHANNESBURG • **682**

0 1 2 3 4 5 6 7 8 9

© AVALON TRAVEL PUBLISHING, INC.

CHAPTER G6

1 Sand Dunes 633
2 Mosaic Canyon. 633
3 Darwin Falls. 634
4 Wildrose Peak Trail 634
5 Telescope Peak Trail. . . . 635
6 Trona Pinnacles. 635

1 Sand Dunes

1.5 mi/1.0 hr

The Sand Dunes Picnic Area is the start of a fun and easy cross-country walk to 80-foot-high sand dunes. No, these aren't the giant sand dunes that Death Valley is famous for; those are the Eureka Dunes. But if you've just driven into the park, this hike will convince your senses that you're really in Death Valley, a place like no place else. There's no marked trail, of course, because of the continually shifting desert sands, so you just make a bee-line from the picnic area to the dunes. How far you wander is completely up to you. Early in the morning (like 6 a.m.) or right about sunset are the best times because of the incredible show of color and light in the ghostlike dunes. Full moon nights are also popular, and it's easy to imagine why. They'll have you dreaming of Arabian nights. Note that many hikers access the tallest of these dunes by parking along Highway 190, 2.2 miles east of Stovepipe Wells, and hiking from there.

Location: In Death Valley National Park near Stovepipe Wells; map G6, grid a9.

User groups: Hikers only. No dogs, horses, or mountain bikes. No wheelchair facilities.

Permits: No permits are required. There is a $10 entrance fee at Death Valley National Park, good for seven days.

Maps: Free park maps are available at park entrance stations or by contacting Death Valley National Park at the address below. A more detailed map is available for a fee from Tom Harrison Cartography, tel. (415) 456-7940. Ask the USGS for a topographic map of Stovepipe Wells.

Directions: From Lone Pine on U.S. 395, drive east on Highway 136 for 18 miles. Continue east on Highway 190 for approximately 65 miles, passing Stovepipe Wells, to the junction of Highway 190 with Scotty's Castle Road. Turn left (north) on Scotty's Castle Road, drive three miles, and then turn left at the signed turnoff for Sand Dunes Picnic Area. Follow the dirt road to its end at the picnic area and trailhead.

Contact: Death Valley National Park, Death Valley, CA 92328; tel. (760) 786-2331, (760) 786-3244, or fax (760) 786-3283.

2 Mosaic Canyon

1.0 mi/0.5 hr

The Mosaic Canyon hike is one of the scenic highlights of Death Valley, accessible to most all kinds of hikers. The trail shows off plenty of colorful slickrock and polished marble as it winds its way up a narrow, high-walled canyon, which was formed by a fault zone. A rock formation called "mosaic breccia"—multicolored rock fragments that appear to be cemented together—can be seen embedded in the canyon walls. The best mosaics are visible in the first .25 mile, making this trip rewarding even for those who don't like to hike more than a short distance.

From the trailhead the route enters the canyon almost immediately, and the smooth marble walls close in around you. At various points, the fissure you're walking through opens wider into "rooms" lined with marble walls, then narrows again. After .3 mile, the canyon walls open out to a wide alluvial fan that is not quite as interesting as the narrows area. Many people turn around here, but if you like, you can continue walking another 1.5 miles. The path ends at a dry waterfall, too high to be scaled.

Location: In Death Valley National Park near Stovepipe Wells; map G6, grid b9.

User groups: Hikers only. No dogs, horses, or mountain bikes. No wheelchair facilities.

Permits: No permits are required. There is a $10 entrance fee at Death Valley National Park, good for seven days.

Maps: Free park maps are available at park entrance stations or by contacting Death Valley National Park at the address below. A more detailed map is available for a fee from Tom Harrison Cartography, tel. (415) 456-7940. Ask the USGS for a topographic map of Stovepipe Wells.

Directions: From Lone Pine on U.S. 395, drive east on Highway 136 for 18 miles. Continue driving east on Highway 190 for approximately 60 miles to .25 mile west of Stovepipe Wells Village. Look for the Mosaic Canyon turnoff on the right. If you reach Stovepipe Wells Village, you missed the turnoff. Turn right and drive 2.2 miles to the trailhead parking lot. The last two miles are rough dirt road but usually passable by passenger cars.

Contact: Death Valley National Park, Death Valley, CA 92328; tel. (760) 786-2331, (760) 786-3244, or fax (760) 786-3283.

🖪 Darwin Falls

1.8 mi/1.0 hr

Darwin Falls is a must-do desert hike. A waterfall in the desert is a rare and precious thing, a miracle of life in a harsh world. The trip is easy enough for young children, and although the temperatures in this area can become extreme in the summer, an early-morning start makes the short hike manageable almost year-round. Of course, be sure to carry water with you. Follow the jeep trail into the canyon, and soon you'll see a trickle of water on the ground that grows wider and more substantial the farther you walk. The path is not always clearly defined, but you simply follow the stream, crossing it a few times, for about a

mile. The canyon walls narrow, and the vegetation becomes much more lush. Just beyond a small stream-gauging station, you come to the waterfall, a 30-foot cascade tucked into a box canyon. A large cottonwood tree grows at its lip. In the spring more than 80 species of resident and migrating birds have been sighted in this canyon.

Location: In Death Valley National Park near Panamint Springs; map G6, grid d4.

User groups: Hikers only. No dogs, horses, or mountain bikes. No wheelchair facilities.

Permits: No permits are required. Parking and access are free.

Maps: Ask the USGS for a topographic map of Panamint Springs.

Directions: From Lone Pine on U.S. 395, drive east on Highway 136 for 18 miles, and then continue straight on Highway 190 for 30 miles. The right (south) turnoff for Darwin Falls is exactly one mile before you reach the Panamint Springs Resort. Look for a small "Darwin Falls" sign and a dirt road. Turn right and drive 2.5 miles on the dirt road till you reach a fork; bear right and drive .3 mile to the parking area. Alternatively, you can exit U.S. 395 at Olancha and Highway 190 and drive east on Highway 190 for 44 miles.

Contact: Death Valley National Park, Death Valley, CA 92328; tel. (760) 786-2331, (760) 786-3244, or fax (760) 786-3283.

🖪 Wildrose Peak Trail

8.4 mi/5.0 hrs

If it's boiling in Death Valley, you can always make the long drive out to Wildrose Canyon and begin your hike at a trailhead elevation of 6,800 feet. Get this: they even have trees here. Whew, what a relief—at least until you start climbing in earnest, heading for 9,064-foot Wildrose Peak. The hike begins at the 10 beehives——oops, make that 10 charcoal kilns (they look like beehives)——that were built in the 1870s to make charcoal for the local mines. Walk to the north end of the kilns to find the signed trail and start climbing through scattered piñon pines and junipers. You can see far off to the Sierra, even Mount Whitney, and then as you climb higher, you can look down at Death Valley and Panamint Valley. Well-graded switchbacks make the 2,200-foot climb manageable, and the panoramic views make the energy expenditure completely worth it. If you tire out, at least try to hike the first three miles of trail, where you'll get a good dose of vistas from a saddle below the summit. The last mile to the summit is the steepest, but no matter what, the climb is nowhere near as bad as on the Telescope Peak Trail, below.

Special note: This trail can be snowed in any time between November and May. Check with the park before making the long drive.

Location: In Death Valley National Park; map G6, grid e8.

User groups: Hikers only. No dogs, horses, or mountain bikes. No wheelchair facilities.

Permits: No permits are required. There is a $10 entrance fee at Death Valley National Park, good for seven days.

Maps: Free park maps are available at park entrance stations or by contacting Death Valley National Park at the address below. A more detailed map is available for a fee from Tom Harrison Cartography, tel. (415) 456-7940. Ask the USGS for a topographic map of Wildrose Peak.

Directions: From Stovepipe Wells drive west on Highway 190 for eight miles to Emigrant Canyon Road, then turn left (south). Drive 21 miles to a junction with Wildrose Canyon Road. Turn left (east) and drive seven miles to the parking area on the right, across from the Charcoal Kilns.

Contact: Death Valley National Park, Death Valley, CA 92328; tel. (760) 786-2331, (760) 786-3244, or fax (760) 786-3283.

5 Telescope Peak Trail
14.0 mi/9.0 hrs

The big deal about making the long hike to the summit of Telescope Peak is this: When you get there, you can pivot yourself around and in one long, sweeping glance take in Mount Whit-

ney to the west and Badwater to the east. For the uninitiated, that means you're seeing the highest point in the contiguous United States and the lowest point in the Western Hemisphere from the same spot (one is ahead of you, one to your back). The other big deal about the hike is that the trailhead is at 8,000 feet, so you don't have to worry about its being too hot in the summertime. The peak is the highest in Death Valley National Park at 11,049 feet, and the trail to reach it is well graded and well maintained. Nonetheless, the 3,000-foot climb and the long mileage take their toll, so don't try this hike unless you're in good shape. In addition to passing piñon pines and junipers, you'll also see some ancient bristlecone pine trees once you climb above 10,000 feet. To supplement the vistas of Mount Whitney and Badwater, you are also witness to Death Valley and Panamint Valley and the White Mountains to the north. It's beyond spectacular. But the climb is one heck of a workout, so be prepared.

Special note: This trail can be snowed in any time between November and May. Check with the park before making the long drive.

Location: In Death Valley National Park; map G6, grid e9.

User groups: Hikers only. No dogs, horses, or mountain bikes. No wheelchair facilities.

Permits: No permits are required. There is a $10 entrance fee at Death Valley National Park, good for seven days.

Maps: Free park maps are available at park entrance stations or by contacting Death Valley National Park at the address below. A more detailed map is available for a fee from Tom Harrison Cartography, tel. (415) 456-7940. Ask the USGS for a topographic map of Telescope Peak.

Directions: From Stovepipe Wells, drive west on Highway 190 for eight miles to Emigrant Canyon Road, then turn left (south). Drive 21 miles to a junction with Wildrose Canyon Road. Turn left (east) and drive nine miles to the end of Wildrose Canyon

Road at Mahogany Flat Campground. The road gets very rough and steep for the last two miles after the Charcoal Kilns.

Contact: Death Valley National Park, Death Valley, CA 92328; tel. (760) 786-2331, (760) 786-3244, or fax (760) 786-3283.

6 Trona Pinnacles

0.5 mi/0.5 hr

If the Trona Pinnacles were miniaturized, they'd look like little lumps of modeling clay shaped into oblongs and ready to be turned on a potter's wheel. They're actually tufa spires made of calcium carbonate, and the Trona Pinnacles National Natural Landmark features more than 500 of them, some as high as 140 feet. Like the tufa spires at Mono Lake, the Trona Pinnacles were formed underwater from calcium-rich springs in the days when giant Searles Lake still had water in it—probably 50,000 years ago. Now the lake bed is dry, so the tufa spires jut upward from a flat, dry plain. Yes, they're weird looking, but in a good way. A .5-mile loop trail leads through the pinnacles, but most people just wander around at random, gazing at the strange, giant tufa spires.

Location: East of Ridgecrest and south of Trona; map G6, grid j5.

User groups: Hikers, dogs, and horses. No mountain bikes. No wheelchair facilities.

Permits: No permits are required. Parking and access are free.

Maps: A free brochure on Trona Pinnacles is available from the Bureau of Land Management at the address below. Ask the USGS for a topographic map of the Searles Lake area.

Directions: From Ridgecrest drive east on Highway 178 for 12 miles to the right turnoff for Trona Pinnacles. Turn right on Pinnacles Road and drive seven miles to the signed trailhead. (High-clearance vehicles recommended.)

Contact: Bureau of Land Management, Ridgecrest Resource Area, 300 S. Richmond Road, Ridgecrest, CA 93555; tel. (760) 384-5400 or fax (760) 384-5499.

CHAPTER G7

LOOKING DOWN INTO
GOLDEN CANYON FROM
ZABRISKIE POINT IN DEATH VALLEY.

MAP G7

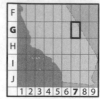

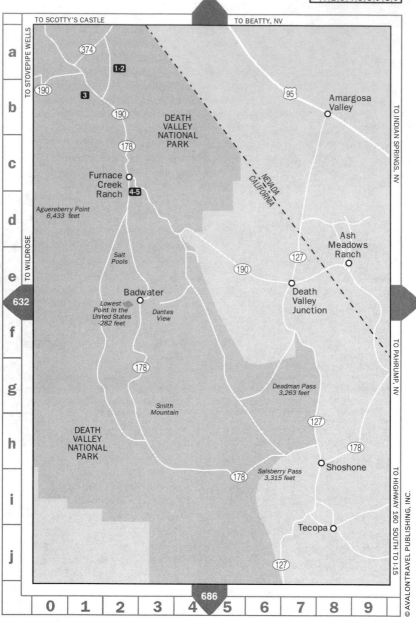

TO SCOTTY'S CASTLE   TO BEATTY, NV

TO STOVEPIPE WELLS

a

374

1-2

TO WILDROSE

190

3

b

190

190

DEATH
VALLEY
NATIONAL
PARK

95

Amargosa
Valley

TO INDIAN SPRINGS, NV

178

c

Furnace
Creek
Ranch

4-5

NEVADA
CALIFORNIA

d

Aguereberry Point
6,433 feet

Ash
Meadows
Ranch

Salt
Pools

190

127

e

Badwater

Death
Valley
Junction

632

Lowest
Point in the
United States
-282 feet

Dantes
View

f

178

TO PAHRUMP, NV

g

Deadman Pass
3,263 feet

Smith
Mountain

127

h

DEATH
VALLEY
NATIONAL
PARK

178

Shoshone

TO HIGHWAY 160 SOUTH TO I-15

i

Salsberry Pass
3,315 feet

178

Tecopa

j

127

© AVALON TRAVEL PUBLISHING, INC.

686

0   1   2   3   4   5   6   7   8   9

CHAPTER G7

1 Keane Wonder
Mine Trail 639
2 Keane Wonder Springs . . 639
3 Salt Creek
Interpretive Trail 640
4 Golden Canyon
Interpretive Trail 640
5 Zabriskie Point 641

1 Keane Wonder Mine Trail

3.2 mi/2.0 hrs

You wouldn't think a three-mile round-trip trail could be this hard. But then again, most people don't usually climb 1,600 feet in 1.5 miles, and especially not this close to sea level in the desert. The million-dollar vistas on the Keane Wonder Mine Trail are worth the trek, though, and they're sure to pay off at least as well as the Wonder gold and silver mine did in the early 1900s. The mine had such promise, in fact, that ambitious miners built an aerial tramway to carry loads of rock down the mountainside to the mill. The vein of ore ran dry in 1915, but the mine's mill and tramway ruins still exist, and you'll see them on this steep trek into the Funeral Mountains. After only .5 mile of climbing, the views of Death Valley open wide; meanwhile the path steepens as it continues straight upward. As you pass mine shafts along the trail, remember to stay out of them—there are various potential dangers. The vistas, on the other hand, are perfectly safe and yours for the taking.

Location: In Death Valley National Park; map G7, grid a2.

User groups: Hikers only. No dogs, horses, or mountain bikes. No wheelchair facilities.

Permits: No permits are required. There is a $10 entrance fee at Death Valley National Park, good for seven days.

Maps: Free park maps are available at park entrance stations or by contacting Death Valley National Park at the address below. A more detailed map is available for a fee from Tom Harrison Cartography, tel. (415) 456-7940. Ask the USGS for a topographic map of the Chloride City area.

Directions: From the Furnace Creek Visitor Center in Death Valley National Park, drive 10 miles north on Highway 190 to the Beatty Cutoff Road. Bear right (north) on Beatty Cutoff Road and drive 5.7 miles to the right turnoff for Keane Wonder Mine. Turn right and drive 2.8 miles on a rough dirt road to the parking area.

Contact: Death Valley National Park, Death Valley, CA 92328; tel. (760) 786-2331, (760) 786-3244, or fax (760) 786-3283.

2 Keane Wonder Springs

2.0 mi/1.0 hr

If you aren't up for the steep climb to the top of the tramway at Keane Wonder Mine, above, this easy and flat trail to Keane Wonder Springs provides a pleasant alternative. The mineral spring once provided water for the mining operation; now it provides a gathering place for birds and wildlife. Walk from the trailhead toward the large metal water tank to find the trail on the left side of it. Follow an old pipeline northward along the base of the mountains, cross a wash, and pass mounds of travertine, a marble-like rock formed by the sulfur-rich spring water. The spring is just slightly off the trail .75 mile from the trailhead and not worth the scramble required to access it. (It's a hole in the ground that reeks of hydrogen sulfide.) Instead, continue another .25 mile beyond the spring to the remains of an old stamp mill and cabin.

Location: In Death Valley National Park; map G7, grid a2.

User groups: Hikers only. No dogs, horses, or mountain bikes. No wheelchair facilities.

Permits: No permits are required. There is a $10 entrance fee at Death Valley National Park, good for seven days.

Maps: Free park maps are available at park entrance stations or by contacting Death Valley National Park at the address below. A more detailed map is available for a fee from Tom Harrison Cartography, tel. (415) 456-7940. Ask the USGS for a topographic map of the Chloride City area.

Directions: From the Furnace Creek Visitor Center in Death Valley National Park, drive 10 miles north on Highway 190 to the Beatty Cutoff Road. Bear right (north) on Beatty Cutoff Road and drive 5.7 miles to the turnoff for Keane Wonder Mine. Turn right and drive 2.8 miles on a rough dirt road to the parking area.

Contact: Death Valley National Park, Death Valley, CA 92328; tel. (760) 786-2331, (760) 786-3244, or fax (760) 786-3283.

❸ Salt Creek Interpretive Trail
1.0 mi/0.5 hr

Salt Creek is exactly what its name implies, a stream of saline water, and it's home to the Salt Creek pupfish, which live nowhere else. The fish underwent an incredible evolutionary change in order to live in this saline creek, once a part of a much larger freshwater lake. The biological alteration would be roughly the same as if humans decided to drink gasoline instead of water. In the right season you can look down into Salt Creek and easily spot the minnow-sized pupfish swimming about, although there is never any guarantee. Late winter and spring are the best time to view them. The plants along the stream are typical of California coastal wetlands—salt grass and pickleweed. Birds congregate by the stream, including great blue herons. Because the trail is on a wooden boardwalk, it is accessible to all hikers, including wheelchair users.

Location: In Death Valley National Park; map G7, grid b1.

User groups: Hikers and wheelchairs. No dogs, horses, or mountain bikes.

Permits: No permits are required. There is a $10 entrance fee at Death Valley National Park, good for seven days.

Maps: Interpretive trail brochures are available for 50 cents at park visitor centers or at the trailhead. Free park maps are available at park entrance stations or by contacting Death Valley National Park at the address below. A more detailed map is available for a fee from Tom Harrison Cartography, tel. (415) 456-7940. Ask the USGS for a topographic map of the Beatty Junction area.

Directions: From the Furnace Creek Visitor Center in Death Valley National Park, drive 12 miles north on Highway 190 to the turnoff for Salt Creek. Turn left and drive one mile to the Salt Creek parking area.

Contact: Death Valley National Park, Death Valley, CA 92328; tel. (760) 786-2331, (760) 786-3244, or fax (760) 786-3283.

❹ Golden Canyon Interpretive Trail
2.0 mi/1.0 hr

The Golden Canyon Interpretive Trail is a perfect path for first-timers in Death Valley National Park. Because the trail is so short, most people continue beyond the end of the self-guided trail, heading deeper into Golden Canyon to Red Cathedral, .3 mile from the last numbered trail marker. The interpretive trail follows the path of an old road through a flat alluvial fan exhibiting a colorful array of volcanic rocks, sand, and gravel. Imagine every shade of gold you can think of—from yellow to orange to apricot. That's what you'll see here in the cliffs, the layered remains of ancient lake beds. They're especially gorgeous near sunrise and sunset. At the final interpretive post, you can turn around and head back, or take the left fork of the trail and continue to Red Cathedral, the huge red cliff that looms in the background. Its lovely hue is caused by the weathering of rocks containing a large quantity of iron. A surprise is that by the time you reach Red Cathedral, you've gained some 300 feet in elevation—

enough to give you some nice views looking back the way you came.

Location: In Death Valley National Park; map G7, grid d2.

User groups: Hikers only. No dogs, horses, or mountain bikes. No wheelchair facilities.

Permits: No permits are required. There is a $10 entrance fee at Death Valley National Park, good for seven days.

Maps: Interpretive trail brochures are available for $.50 at park visitor centers or at the trailhead. Free park maps are available at park entrance stations or by contacting Death Valley National Park at the address below. A more detailed map is available for a fee from Tom Harrison Cartography, tel. (415) 456-7940. Ask the USGS for a topographic map of Furnace Creek.

Directions: From the Furnace Creek Visitor Center in Death Valley National Park, drive southeast on Highway 190 for 1.2 miles to the right turnoff for Badwater. Bear right and drive south for two miles to the Golden Canyon parking area on the east side of the road.

Contact: Death Valley National Park, Death Valley, CA 92328; tel. (760) 786-2331, (760) 786-3244, or fax (760) 786-3283.

⑤ Zabriskie Point

5.5 mi/3.0 hrs

This hike is an extension of the Golden Canyon Interpretive Trail, above, for slightly more experienced hikers. When you reach the last interpretive trail marker on the Golden Canyon Trail, take the right fork for Zabriskie Point. The path is signed with small hiker symbols; watch for them as you continue your trek into the colorful badlands—deeply creased, eroded, and barren hillsides. You'll see white outcroppings in the rock, the raison d'être for the old borax mines still found in the area. Hike across the face of Manly Beacon, a big sandstone hill and not particularly manly, but with lovely views, and continue to Zabriskie Point, which has a fine vista of the badlands and the Panamint Mountains. Be proud of yourself for walking to Zabriskie Point instead of driving like everybody else. One thing to keep in mind: Be sure to carry enough water for the few hours you'll be out on the trail. The total elevation gain is only 800 feet, but it's pretty darn hot out here.

Location: In Death Valley National Park; map G7, grid d2.

User groups: Hikers only. No dogs, horses, or mountain bikes. No wheelchair facilities.

Permits: No permits are required. There is a $10 entrance fee at Death Valley National Park, good for seven days.

Maps: Free park maps are available at park entrance stations or by contacting Death Valley National Park at the address below. A more detailed map is available for a fee from Tom Harrison Cartography, tel. (415) 456-7940. Ask the USGS for a topographic map of the Furnace Creek area.

Directions: From the Furnace Creek Visitor Center in Death Valley National Park, drive southeast on Highway 190 for 1.2 miles to the turnoff for Badwater. Turn right and drive south for two miles to the Golden Canyon parking area on the east side of the road.

Contact: Death Valley National Park, Death Valley, CA 92328; tel. (760) 786-2331, (760) 786-3244, or fax (760) 786-3283.

ANN MARIE BROWN

PISMO DUNES
AT OSO FLACO LAKE

MAP H2

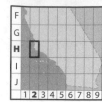

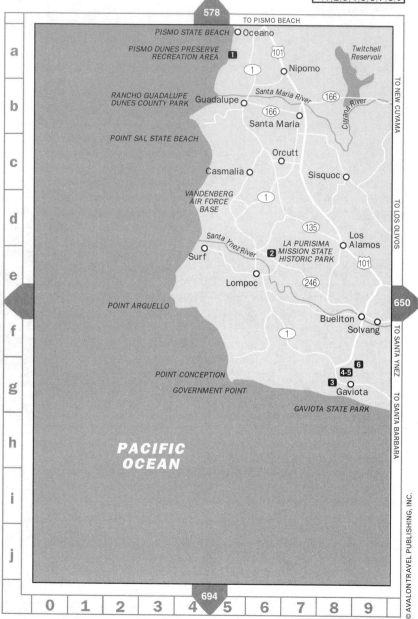

578 TO PISMO BEACH

PISMO STATE BEACH ○ Oceano

PISMO DUNES PRESERVE
RECREATION AREA **1**

○ Nipomo

101

1

RANCHO GUADALUPE
DUNES COUNTY PARK   Guadalupe ○

Santa Maria River

166

Cuyama River

Twitchell
Reservoir

166

Santa Maria

POINT SAL STATE BEACH

Orcutt ○

Casmalia ○

Sisquoc ○

VANDENBERG
AIR FORCE
BASE

1

135

Los
Alamos ○

Santa Ynez River

Surf ○

2 LA PURISIMA
MISSION STATE
HISTORIC PARK

101

Lompoc ○

246

POINT ARGUELLO

650

1

Buellton ○
Solvang ○

POINT CONCEPTION

4-5 **6**

GOVERNMENT POINT

3 Gaviota ○

GAVIOTA STATE PARK

**PACIFIC
OCEAN**

TO NEW CUYAMA

TO LOS OLIVOS

TO SANTA YNEZ

TO SANTA BARBARA

a
b
c
d
e
f
g
h
i
j

0 1 2 3 4 5 6 7 8 9

694

© AVALON TRAVEL PUBLISHING, INC.

CHAPTER H2

1 Oso Flaco Lake 645

2 Las Zanjas and
El Camino Loop 645

3 Gaviota Overlook 646

4 Gaviota Hot Springs . . . 646

5 Gaviota Peak 647

6 Nojoqui Falls 647

Location: Southwest of Arroyo Grande; map H2, grid a5.

User groups: Hikers and wheelchairs. No dogs, horses, or mountain bikes.

Permits: No permits are required. A $4 day-use fee is charged per vehicle.

Maps: Ask the USGS for a topographic map of the Oceano area.

Directions: From Santa Maria on U.S. 101, take the Highway 166/Guadalupe exit, drive nine miles west and then turn north on Highway 1 at Guadalupe. Drive 3.6 miles to Oso Flaco Lake Road, turn left, and drive three miles to the trailhead.

Contact: Pismo Dunes State Vehicular Recreation Area, c/o Oceano Dunes District, 576 Camino Mercado, Arroyo Grande, CA 93420; tel. (805) 473-7230.

1 Oso Flaco Lake
2.2 mi/1.0 hr

A nature preserve in a state vehicular recreation area? Usually the two don't go together, but that's what you get here at Oso Flaco Lake, a part of the Pismo Dunes Natural Preserve, which is a part of the larger state vehicular recreation area. The trail to Oso Flaco Lake starts out paved for .3 mile, but then cuts off to the left on a wooden walkway and footbridge that bisects the small lake. Immediately you are in the good company of shorebirds and waterfowl, including ducks that play hide-and-seek in the islands of reeds. The boardwalk extends beyond the lake's border and over a series of sand dunes. It serves the dual purpose of making the trail suitable for wheelchairs and protecting the dunes' fragile plant life. Wheelchair users note: After heavy rains, the boardwalk may be partially submerged under a few inches of water. Phone the park to check on trail conditions before planning a visit in winter or spring.

Where the boardwalk ends, you can continue walking on the dunes or head to the beach on your right. From the very end of the trail you can hear the occasional wail of off-road vehicles. Otherwise, all is peaceful here.

By the way, what does "Oso Flaco" mean? Skinny bear. But it's been a long time since they've seen one of those around here.

2 Las Zanjas and El Camino Loop
2.5 mi/1.25 hrs

If you came to La Purisima Mission seeking heavenly sanctuary but instead found a bunch of screaming school kids, you can still find your heaven in the hills surrounding the mission. There's a surprising number of good hiking trails here, considering this is a state historic park and not a recreation park. The best place to start is on a level loop trail around the mission. Set out on Las Zanjas Trail (also spelled Las Zonas on some signs), a wide ranch road that leads behind the mission buildings. If you like, take the short cutoff on the right to the large cross on the hill (the trail is signed as Vista de la Cruz). A steep climb gives you wide views of the mission area and the Pacific Coast. Then continue on Las Zanjas to the park boundary, where you can loop back on El Camino Real, an old paved park road. Along the way you'll be accompanied by cool ocean breezes, blooming buckeye trees and bush monkeyflower, and green grasslands in springtime. Be sure to take a tour of the mission before or after your hike.

Location: At La Purisima Mission north of Lompoc; map H2, grid e6.

User groups: Hikers, dogs, horses, and mountain bikes. No wheelchair facilities.

Permits: No permits are required. A $2 day-use fee is charged per vehicle.

Maps: A map of La Purisima Mission State Historic Park is available at the entrance station. Ask the USGS for a topographic map of the Los Alamos area.

Directions: From Buellton on U.S. 101, take the Solvang/Lompoc/Highway 246 exit, drive west 13.2 miles, and turn right on Purisima Road. The park entrance is one mile down the road on the right. The trailhead is at the far end of the parking lot, near the visitor center.

Contact: La Purisima Mission State Historic Park, 2295 Purisima Road, Lompoc, CA 93436; tel. (805) 733-3713.

3 Gaviota Overlook
3.0 mi/1.5 hrs

If you don't mind a little climbing to get a great coastal view, the Gaviota Overlook Trail will suit you just fine. The trail (really a ranch road) is completely out in the open as it climbs from U.S. 101 to the top of the ridge above Gaviota Beach, but as long as the weather is cool, it's an easy ascent. There are two main trail forks; bear left at both. Since this is coastal grasslands territory, wildflowers are prolific in springtime, but things get kind of arid looking by late summer. No matter; the view from the top is priceless—miles of open ocean on the one side, including the Channel Islands, and miles of grasslands and chaparral on the other side. Hey, where are all the condominiums? Just kidding. The trail ends at some microwave towers below the highest point on the ridge, but the views are just fine from where you are. The only catch on this trail is that the trailhead is darn near impossible to find, so follow directions precisely.

Location: In Gaviota State Park near Gaviota; map H2, grid g8.

User groups: Hikers, horses, and mountain bikes. No dogs. No wheelchair facilities.

Permits: No permits are required. Parking and access are free.

Maps: Ask the USGS for topographic maps of the Solvang and Gaviota areas.

Directions: Drive south from Buellton on U.S. 101 for 10 miles to just north of Gaviota Pass, to the blue sign that reads: "Rest Area 1 Mile, Tourist Information." Immediately beyond it you'll drive over a concrete bridge and must quickly turn right into the very small parking area just beyond the bridge. It's easy to miss. If you reach the rest area, you've gone past it. (Coming from Santa Barbara and points south on U.S. 101, you must exit at Highway 1/Lompoc, then get back on the freeway heading south.)

Contact: Gaviota State Park, c/o Refugio State Beach, 10 Refugio Beach Road, Goleta, CA 93117; tel. (805) 968-1033.

4 Gaviota Hot Springs
1.0 mi/0.5 hr

Gaviota State Park got smart and started charging a few bucks for people to park at this trailhead, since hot springs always draw a crowd. Still, if you show up first thing in the morning or anytime during the week, most likely you can soak all by yourself in one of the two small pools here. They're not very big or very deep or very hot either, but hey—whaddya want for a couple bucks? The pools are a quick-to-reach destination, requiring a short but steep climb from the trailhead, mostly on a fire road. The smell of sulfur and the sway of the palm tree above the upper pool will lull you into believing you're at your own private spa. The upper pool is also the hotter of the two, nearly at bathtub temperature. If you look closely, you can see little bubbles coming up from the ground under the pool—geology in action. If you want to hike more, you can combine this trip with the trek to Gaviota Peak, below.

Location: In Gaviota State Park near Gaviota; map H2, grid g8.

User groups: Hikers, horses, and mountain bikes. No dogs. No wheelchair facilities.

Permits: No permits are required. A $2 day-use fee is charged per vehicle.

Maps: Ask the USGS for a topographic map of the Gaviota area.

Directions: From Santa Barbara drive north on U.S. 101 for 35 miles, pass through the tunnel at Gaviota Pass, and take the first exit after the tunnel, which is signed as Highway 1/Lompoc/Vandenburg Air Force Base. At the stop sign turn right and head south on the frontage road that parallels the freeway. (Don't bear left on Highway 1.) The frontage road ends in .25 mile at the trailhead parking area.

Contact: Gaviota State Park, c/o Refugio State Beach, 10 Refugio Beach Road, Goleta, CA 93117; tel. (805) 968-1033.

5 Gaviota Peak

6.4 mi/3.5 hrs

The best hike for a good workout in Gaviota State Park is the trail to Gaviota Peak. Start from the Gaviota Hot Springs Trailhead, but instead of taking the short spur trail to Gaviota Hot Springs, head left on the Gaviota Peak Trail and begin your assault on Gaviota Hill—oops, that's Gaviota Peak, elevation 2,450 feet. The climb isn't too bad (2,000 feet in 3.2 miles), but, geez, it can get hot here without much shade. The trail is a dirt road (plus a few single-track sections) which climbs a series of knolls on its way to Gaviota Peak. Technically the peak is actually in Los Padres National Forest, not in the state park. Once you're there, you'll find the views are downright awesome. What can you see? Point Conception, the Pacific, the Channel Islands, Lompoc Valley, and Gaviota Pass at your feet. Hope you picked a day when the fog wasn't visiting.

Location: In Gaviota State Park near Gaviota; map H2, grid g8.

User groups: Hikers, horses, and mountain bikes. No dogs. No wheelchair facilities.

Permits: No permits are required. A $2 day-use fee is charged per vehicle.

Maps: Ask the USGS for a topographic map of the Gaviota area.

Directions: Drive north from Santa Barbara on U.S. 101 for 35 miles, pass through the tunnel at Gaviota Pass, and take the first exit after the tunnel, which is signed as Highway 1/Lompoc/Vandenburg Air Force Base. Turn right at the stop sign and head south on the frontage road that parallels the freeway. (Don't bear left on to Highway 1.) The frontage road ends in .25 mile at the trailhead parking area.

Contact: Gaviota State Park, c/o Refugio State Beach, 10 Refugio Beach Road, Goleta, CA 93117; tel. (805) 968-1033.

6 Nojoqui Falls

0.5 mi/0.5 hr

A favorite spot of Santa Barbarans cruising upcoast on U.S. 101, Nojoqui County Park has plenty of picnic areas, sports fields, and the like, but only one hiking trail. It's a great, short stroll from the parking area to impressive Nojoqui Falls, which drops 80 feet over a sandstone cliff that is almost completely covered with delicate Venus maidenhair ferns. The hike is good no matter how much or how little the falls are running—it's a flat, easy walk that everyone in the family can do, through a cooling canopy of oaks and laurels with Nojoqui Creek babbling alongside the trail. Check out the interesting rocks along the route. They're made of shale, while the waterfall cliff is made of sandstone. You'll see the difference. There's a stair-stepped rock perch right by the waterfall's pool, where you can sit in the shade of big-leaf maples and admire the scene.

Location: Near Gaviota; map H2, grid g9.

User groups: Hikers and dogs. No horses or mountain bikes. No wheelchair facilities.

Permits: No permits are required. Parking and access are free.

Maps: Ask the USGS for a topographic map of the Solvang area.

Directions: From Santa Barbara drive 40 miles north on U.S. 101 to the signed turnoff for Nojoqui Park, north of Gaviota State Beach. Drive one mile on the Old Coast Highway and turn east on Alisal Road. Drive .8 mile to the park entrance on your right. Drive .25 mile down the park access road to the parking lot and trailhead. The trail starts from the far end of the parking lot loop.

Contact: Santa Barbara County Parks and Recreation, 300 Goodwin Road, Santa Maria, CA 93455; tel. (805) 934-6123 or (805) 568-2461.

VIEWS OF THE SANTA YNEZ RIVER
CANYON AND DISTANT MOUNTAINS
CAN BE HAD FROM THE RUINS OF
KNAPP'S CASTLE.

ANN MARIE BROWN

MAP H3

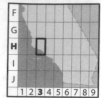

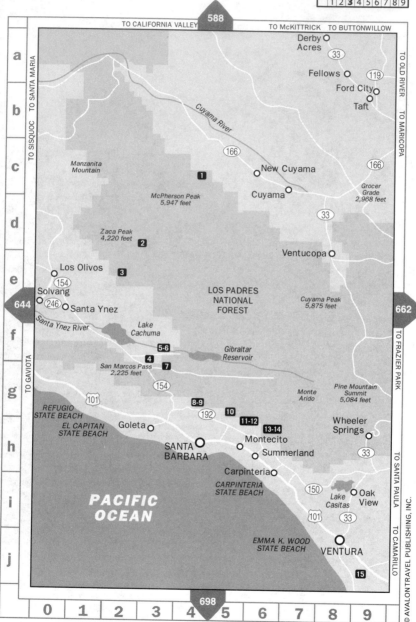

a

TO SANTA MARIA

TO SISQUOC

Derby
Acres

33

Fellows

119

Ford City

Taft

b

TO OLD RIVER

TO MARICOPA

Cuyama River

166

New Cuyama

166

Manzanita
Mountain

c

McPherson Peak
5,947 feet

Cuyama

Grocer
Grade
2,968 feet

Zaca Peak
4,220 feet

2

33

d

1

Ventucopa

Los Olivos

3

154

Solvang

246   Santa Ynez

e

644

662

Santa Ynez River

LOS PADRES
NATIONAL
FOREST

Cuyama Peak
5,875 feet

Lake
Cachuma

f

TO GAVIOTA

TO FRAZIER PARK

5-6

4

Gibraltar
Reservoir

San Marcos Pass
2,225 feet

7

154

g

REFUGIO
STATE BEACH

101

Monte
Arido

Pine Mountain
Summit
5,084 feet

8-9

192

10

EL CAPITAN
STATE BEACH

Goleta

11-12

Wheeler
Springs

13-14

h

SANTA
BARBARA

Montecito

Summerland

33

Carpinteria

CARPINTERIA
STATE BEACH

i

PACIFIC
OCEAN

150

Lake
Casitas

Oak
View

101

33

TO SANTA PAULA

TO CAMARILLO

j

EMMA K. WOOD
STATE BEACH

VENTURA

15

CHAPTER H3

1	McPherson Peak Trail . . 651	8	Seven Falls 655
2	Upper Manzana Creek Trail 651	9	Inspiration Point. 656
		10	Rattlesnake Canyon. . . . 656
3	Piño Alto Trail. 652	11	Montecito Overlook . . . 657
4	Snyder Trail 653	12	West Fork Cold Springs. 658
5	Aliso Canyon Loop Trail 653	13	San Ysidro Trail. 658
		14	McMenemy Trail. 659
6	Santa Cruz Trail 654	15	McGrath State Beach Nature Trail 659
7	Knapp's Castle. 654		

1 McPherson Peak Trail

10.0 mi/2.0 days

McPherson Peak, elevation 5,747 feet, is just on the edge of the spectacular San Rafael Wilderness, a land of condors and steep canyons. Although the trail is steep and can be hot in summer, it gives hikers outstanding views of the wilderness and the desertlike lands of Cuyama to the northeast. From Aliso Park Campground you start hiking on the dirt road that is signed for Hog Pen Spring Campground, quickly saying goodbye to the shady canyon. Reach the camp in 1.5 miles (there's a spring nearby if you need water); then pick up a trail that continues climbing, now more steeply, to Sierra Madre Road on the wilderness boundary. Turn right on the dirt road and hike another 2.5 miles through chaparral to McPherson Peak, passing McPherson Camp along the way. The camp has a spring and is an excellent place to spend the night. You can watch the sunset from McPherson Peak and then crawl into your sleeping bag and watch the stars.

Location: In the San Rafael Wilderness; map H3, grid c4.

User groups: Hikers, dogs, horses, and mountain bikes (mountain bikes may not go past the wilderness boundary). No wheelchair facilities.

Permits: No permits are required. A national forest recreation pass is required for each vehicle; fees are $5 for one day or $30 for a year.

Maps: For a map of Los Padres National Forest, send $6 to U.S. Forest Service, Map Sales, P.O. Box 587, Camino, CA 95709; tel. (530) 647-5390 or website: www.r5.fs.fed.us/visitorcenter. Ask the USGS for a topographic map of the Peak Mountain area.

Directions: From Santa Maria on U.S. 101 take Highway 166 east for 48 miles to just west of New Cuyama. Turn right (south) on Aliso Canyon Road and follow it for six miles to Aliso Park Campground. The dirt road can be very rough; high-clearance vehicles are recommended. If you are coming from Ventura or Ojai, take Highway 33 north to Highway 166; then go west past New Cuyama.

Contact: Los Padres National Forest, Santa Lucia Ranger District, 1616 N. Carlotti Drive, Santa Maria, CA 93454; tel. (805) 925-9538 or fax (805) 681-2781.

2 Upper Manzana Creek Trail

13.0 mi/1-2 days

From Nira Campground, a major entry point into the San Rafael Wilderness, you can hike east or west along Manzana Creek. In spring the creek is popular with anglers, who come here to catch the resident trout in Manzana Creek. (Some trout are stocked by the campground.) Hikers and backpackers can take the Upper Manzana Creek Trail to the east and stop at any one of several excellent campsites, including Manzana (six miles out) and Manzana Narrows (seven miles out). Both have swimming holes. The trail climbs gently from the campground, sometimes switchbacking away from the creek but always returning. There is a modicum of shade from blue oaks and gray pines, mixed in among the low-lying chaparral and manzanita. Note that the creek gets low and is less attractive by midsummer but that winter hiking can be dangerous if the stream level is too high. March through May is the best time to visit.

Location: In San Rafael Wilderness; map H3, grid d3.

User groups: Hikers, dogs, and horses. No mountain bikes. No wheelchair facilities.

Permits: No permits are required. A national forest recreation pass is required for each vehicle; fees are $5 for one day or $30 for a year.

Maps: For a map of Los Padres National Forest, send $6 to U.S. Forest Service, Map Sales, P.O. Box 587, Camino, CA 95709; tel. (530) 647-5390 or website: www.r5.fs.fed.us/visitorcenter. Ask the USGS for a topographic map of the of the Bald Mountain area.

Directions: From Santa Barbara on U.S. 101 take Highway 154 north and drive 23 miles, past Lake Cachuma, to Armour Ranch Road. Turn right and drive 1.5 miles to Happy Canyon Road (not suitable for trailers). Turn right and drive 14 miles to Cachuma Saddle and a junction with Figueroa Mountain Road; then continue straight on Sunset Valley Road and follow it for four miles to its end at Nira Campground. Park in the hikers' parking lot.

Contact: Los Padres National Forest, Santa Lucia Ranger District, 1616 N. Carlotti Drive, Santa Maria, CA 93454; tel. (805) 925-9538 or fax (805) 681-2781.

3 Piño Alto Trail
0.5 mi/0.5 hr

You just made the drive to Figueroa Mountain and you're wondering what in the heck this place is all about. The Piño Alto Interpretive Trail can spell it out for you, and besides, the vistas will knock your socks off. From one point on the trail, the Santa Ynez Valley is visible for some 20 miles from the northwest to the southeast. You can see Cuyama, Lake Cachuma, the Santa Ynez Mountains, and sometimes even the Channel Islands far off to sea. The trail is located at 4,600 feet in elevation, situated among ponderosa and Jeffrey pines and big cone spruce. Conifers? In Santa Barbara? That's right. The paved trail surface makes it suitable for wheelchairs. If you want wider vistas, make sure that you drive .5 mile uphill from the trailhead parking lot to the Figueroa lookout tower site. From there you can survey all the mountains of the San Rafael Wilderness. Note that if you like what you see on Figueroa Mountain, many longer day hikes are possible on the nearby Davy Brown/Fir Canyon Trail, starting at either Davy Brown Campground or at the trailhead on Figueroa Mountain Road.

Location: On Figueroa Mountain; map H3, grid e2.

User groups: Hikers, wheelchairs, and dogs. No horses or mountain bikes.

Permits: No permits are required. A national forest recreation pass is required for each vehicle; fees are $5 for one day or $30 for a year.

Maps: For a map of Los Padres National Forest, send $6 to U.S. Forest Service, Map Sales, P.O. Box 587, Camino, CA 95709; tel. (530) 647-5390 or website: www.r5.fs.fed.us/visitorcenter. Ask the USGS for a topographic map of the Figueroa Mountain area.

Directions: From Santa Barbara drive north on U.S. 101, through Buellton, for 45 miles to the Highway 154 East turnoff. Turn east onto Highway 154 and drive three miles to Los Olivos, then turn north (left) on Figueroa Mountain Road. Drive 13 miles to the fork for Figueroa

Mountain Lookout Road (dirt). Bear left and drive two miles to the Piño Alto Picnic Area.

Contact: Los Padres National Forest, Santa Lucia Ranger District, 1616 N. Carlotti Drive, Santa Maria, CA 93454; tel. (805) 925-9538 or fax (805) 681-2781.

4 Snyder Trail

12.0 mi/7.0 hrs

While Snyder Trail may start out looking like a plain old fire road at its lower end at Paradise Road, by the time it climbs six miles to East Camino Cielo, it becomes a lovely single-track trail that is bordered by more wildflowers than you can count and has more wide-reaching vistas than you can imagine. Don't bother twisting your neck to catch the views on your way up because on your return trip downhill they will be laid out in front of you. The nice thing about the trail is that you start gaining vistas fairly quickly, so if you're tiring of the climb, you can simply find a knoll somewhere, have a seat, and pull out your sandwiches. If you decide to go all the way up, just before the top is a popular side trip to the ruins of Knapp's Castle, below. Take the gated dirt road on the left, 5.5 miles up. If you hike the Snyder Trail's entire length, you'll be tired by the end of the day, but you'll have a whole storehouse of fine memories.

Location: Near the Santa Ynez Recreation Area; map H3, grid f3.

User groups: Hikers, dogs, horses, and mountain bikes. No wheelchair facilities.

Permits: No permits are required. A national forest recreation pass is required for each vehicle; fees are $5 for one day or $30 for a year.

Maps: For a map of Los Padres National Forest, send $6 to U.S. Forest Service, Map Sales, P.O. Box 587, Camino, CA 95709; tel. (530) 647-5390 or website: www.r5.fs.fed.us/visitorcenter. Ask the USGS for a topographic map of the San Marcos Pass area.

Directions: From U.S. 101 in Santa Barbara take the Highway 154/State Street exit and drive north for 11.5 miles. Turn right on Par-

adise Road and drive 4.2 miles to the trailhead for the Snyder Trail, which is at a locked gate on the right side of the road .25 mile west of the Los Prietos Ranger Station.

Contact: Los Padres National Forest, Santa Barbara Ranger District, 3505 Paradise Road, Santa Barbara, CA 93105; tel. (805) 967-3481 or fax (805) 967-7312.

5 Aliso Canyon Loop Trail

3.5 mi/2.0 hrs

From the east end of Sage Hill Campground you can set off on the Aliso Canyon Trail and choose between a one-mile interpretive walk or a 3.5-mile loop trail. The former is the first mile of the latter and follows Aliso Creek. Be sure to bring along a trail brochure so you can learn all about how the Chumash Indians lived in this area and what plants they used and ate. In the spring a wildflower identification book also may be a good idea, as the variety of flowers along this short route is surprising. At the end of the interpretive trail you can either turn around and hike back or continue on the longer loop trip. To do so, walk back a few feet to a trail junction and ascend for .5 mile to a meadow on a grassy plateau. From there you climb rather steeply to the top of the ridge that divides Aliso and Oso Canyons, where there are excellent views of the Santa Ynez Canyon and distant mountains. At the ridge top, turn right (often there is no trail sign), following the ridge's backbone. You'll loop around and soon head back downhill. Note that after winter rains, the sloping trails beyond the interpretive trail are often badly eroded. If you're walking the entire loop, wear some good boots.

Location: In the Santa Ynez Recreation Area; map H3, grid f3.

User groups: Hikers, dogs, horses, and mountain bikes. No wheelchair facilities.

Permits: No permits are required. A national forest recreation pass is required for each vehicle; fees are $5 for one day or $30 for a year.

Maps: For a map of Los Padres National Forest, send $6 to U.S. Forest Service, Map Sales, P.O. Box 587, Camino, CA 95709; tel. (530) 647-5390 or website: www.r5.fs.fed.us/visitorcenter. Ask the USGS for a topographic map of the San Marcos Pass area.

Directions: From U.S. 101 in Santa Barbara take the Highway 154/State Street exit and drive north for about 11.5 miles. Turn right on Paradise Road and drive 4.5 miles to the ranger station. Turn left at the ranger station and drive one mile to Sage Hill Campground. Proceed to the day-use area at the east end of the camp and the trailhead for the Aliso Canyon Trail.

Contact: Los Padres National Forest, Santa Barbara Ranger District, 3505 Paradise Road, Santa Barbara, CA 93105; tel. (805) 967-3481 or fax (805) 967-7312.

6 Santa Cruz Trail
4.0 mi/2.0 hrs

The Santa Cruz Trail is one of the most popular in the Santa Ynez Recreation Area, and it's no wonder. The hiking is easy and the swimming holes along Oso Creek are plentiful. Cooling off in the water is the number-one reason that people pay a visit to the Santa Ynez Recreation Area in summertime. The destination on this trip is Nineteen Oaks Camp, a popular picnicking spot near the base of Little Pine Mountain. The trail follows an unattractive dirt road out of Upper Oso Campground, but it becomes lovely single-track trail as it continues into the shady canyon. The sandstone-carved creek pools are lovely to see even when the water level is low, and as you climb a bit, you get views of Little Pine Mountain. A spur trail on the right at 1.9 miles leads a few hundred yards to Nineteen Oaks Camp, with shady oaks and a few campsites and picnic tables. Most day-hikers end their trip there before the trail begins its hot, exposed switchbacks to the top of Little Pine Mountain, elevation 4,506 feet. Be forewarned: You may see off-road motorcyclists at the

trailhead, but don't let them scare you off. They'll be exiting your trail in the first mile.

Location: In the Santa Ynez Recreation Area; map H3, grid f3.

User groups: Hikers, dogs, horses, and mountain bikes. No wheelchair facilities.

Permits: No permits are required. A national forest recreation pass is required for each vehicle; fees are $5 for one day or $30 for a year.

Maps: For a map of Los Padres National Forest, send $6 to U.S. Forest Service, Map Sales, P.O. Box 587, Camino, CA 95709; tel. (530) 647-5390 or website: www.r5.fs.fed.us/visitorcenter. Ask the USGS for a topographic map of the San Marcos Pass area.

Directions: From U.S. 101 in Santa Barbara take the Highway 154/State Street exit and drive north for 11.5 miles. Turn right on Paradise Road and drive 5.5 miles, past the ranger station, to the left turnoff for Upper Oso Campground. Turn left and drive one mile to the campground.

Contact: Los Padres National Forest, Santa Barbara Ranger District, 3505 Paradise Road, Santa Barbara, CA 93105; tel. (805) 967-3481 or fax (805) 967-7312.

7 Knapp's Castle
0.8 mi/0.5 hr

Some hikes are just right for all kinds of hikers, no matter what their abilities or tastes, and the trail to Knapp's Castle is one of those. The tricky part is that Knapp's Castle, or actually the remains of Knapp's Castle, is on a chunk of private property within Los Padres National Forest, and it's only by the good graces of the landowner that the public is allowed to hike there. He's a very nice gentleman, and for years he has allowed Santa Barbara hikers to visit his land, which is well known not just for the castle ruins but also for its memorable vistas. If we all mind our manners, hopefully we can keep this beautiful spot accessible for many years to come. So who was the Knapp of Knapp's Castle? George Knapp was the former chairman of the board of Union Carbide, and he built a five-bedroom sandstone mansion on this site in 1916. Although the building burned down in a canyon fire in 1940, its foundation still stands, and it offers a fine spot to sit and look out over the Santa Ynez River Canyon and distant mountains. You can even see far-off Lake Cachuma. The trail to reach Knapp's Castle is a well-graded dirt road. You hike past the gate that says "Private Property Ahead," pass through another gate, staying on the dirt road, and reach the castle remains and its fabulous lookout in less than .5 mile of walking.

Special note: Because Knapp's Castle is on private property, its accessibility to the public is subject to change at any time. Phone the Santa Barbara Ranger District office for an update before visiting.

Location: North of Santa Barbara; map H3, grid g3.

User groups: Hikers and dogs. No horses or mountain bikes. No wheelchair facilities.

Permits: No permits are required. A national forest recreation pass is required for each vehicle; fees are $5 for one day or $30 for a year.

Maps: For a map of Los Padres National Forest, send $6 to U.S. Forest Service, Map Sales, P.O. Box 587, Camino, CA 95709; tel. (530) 647-5390 or website: www.r5.fs.fed.us/visitorcenter. Ask the USGS for a topographic map of the San Marcos Pass area.

Directions: From U.S. 101 in Santa Barbara take the Highway 154/State Street exit and drive north for 10.5 miles. Turn right on East Camino Cielo and drive 2.9 miles to the parking pullout on the right, across from a locked gate and dirt road on the left. The gate is signed "Private Property Ahead."

Contact: Los Padres National Forest, Santa Barbara Ranger District, 3505 Paradise Road, Santa Barbara, CA 93105; tel. (805) 967-3481 or fax (805) 967-7312.

🎱 Seven Falls

3.0 mi/1.5 hrs

Seven Falls is a perfect springtime day trip in Santa Barbara, best visited from February to April. It has a little bit of everything: waterfalls, swimming holes, vistas, wildflowers, and good trail. The trail has a lot of unsigned junctions, however, so remember to stay left at all of them until after you cross Mission Creek for the second time. From the end of Tunnel Road, start hiking on the gated continuation of the road, passing a water tank and heading uphill on pavement for .75 mile. In a few minutes of climbing, you'll be able to see all the way out to the ocean. Cross a bridge over Mission Creek and continue hiking straight ahead on the road, which turns to dirt. In a few hundred feet you come to a junction; a sign on your left directs you to the Jesusita Trail. Follow it to the left and bear left again as the path cuts down on single track to Mission Creek, where you'll find many good swimming holes. Cross the creek, but instead of following the continuation of Jesusita Trail, head to your right, upstream, on a use trail. (Remember, this is the only right turn on the route.) In .25 mile of combined hiking and scrambling, you'll reach the first of the sandstone-carved cascades of Seven Falls. These falls flow with force only immediately after a period of rain, but the sandstone pools and canyon walls are pretty to look at even when the creek is nearly dry.

Location: North of Santa Barbara; map H3, grid g4.

User groups: Hikers, dogs, horses, and mountain bikes. No wheelchair facilities.

Permits: No permits are required. Parking and access are free.

Maps: For a map of Los Padres National Forest, send $6 to U.S. Forest Service, Map Sales, P.O. Box 587, Camino, CA 95709; tel. (530) 647-5390 or website: www.r5.fs.fed.us/visitorcenter. Ask the USGS for a topographic map of the Santa Barbara area.

Directions: From U.S. 101 in Santa Barbara take the Mission Street exit and follow it east for just over a mile, crossing State Street. When Mission Street ends, turn left on Laguna Street and drive past the Santa Barbara Mission, turning right on Los

Olivos, directly in front of the mission. Passing the mission, bear left on Mission Canyon Road for .8 mile. Turn right on Foothill Boulevard. In .1 mile, turn left onto the continuation of Mission Canyon Road. Then bear left on Tunnel Road and follow it for 1.1 miles until it ends. Park alongside the road, on the right.

Contact: Los Padres National Forest, Santa Barbara Ranger District, 3505 Paradise Road, Santa Barbara, CA 93105; tel. (805) 967-3481 or fax (805) 967-7312.

9 Inspiration Point

5.0 mi/2.5 hrs

The trail to Inspiration Point is sure to get you inspired if only because it's a great path for year-round exercise in Santa Barbara. Follow the Tunnel Road Trail to Jesusita Trail, as if you were going to Seven Falls, above, but after crossing Mission Creek, keep following the main Jesusita Trail instead. Get ready for a switchbacking climb up to Inspiration Point, which is only one mile away. The tan-colored rock outcrops you see everywhere are cold-water sandstone; often you'll see hang gliders taking off from some of the highest rocks and gliding, seemingly effortlessly, overhead. When you reach Inspiration Point at 1,750 feet, you are rewarded with sweeping views of the Pacific Coast, Santa Barbara and Goleta, and the Channel Islands.

Location: North of Santa Barbara; map H3, grid g4.

User groups: Hikers, dogs, horses, and mountain bikes. No wheelchair facilities.

Permits: No permits are required. Parking and access are free.

Maps: For a map of Los Padres National Forest, send $6 to U.S. Forest Service, Map Sales, P.O. Box 587, Camino, CA 95709; tel. (530) 647-5390 or website: www.r5.fs.fed.us/visitorcenter. Ask the USGS for a topographic map of the Santa Barbara area.

Directions: From U.S. 101 in Santa Barbara take the Mission Street exit and follow it east for just over a mile, crossing State Street.

When Mission Street ends, turn left on Laguna Street and drive past the Santa Barbara Mission, turning right on Los Olivos, directly in front of the mission. Passing the mission, bear left on Mission Canyon Road for .8 mile. Turn right on Foothill Boulevard. In .1 mile turn left onto the continuation of Mission Canyon Road. Then bear left on Tunnel Road and follow it for 1.1 miles until it ends. Park alongside the road, on the right.

Contact: Los Padres National Forest, Santa Barbara Ranger District, 3505 Paradise Road, Santa Barbara, CA 93105; tel. (805) 967-3481 or fax (805) 967-7312.

10 Rattlesnake Canyon

5.0 mi/2.5 hrs

Rattlesnake Canyon Trail is probably the most popular canyon trail in Santa Barbara and also one of the prettiest, despite its menacing name. The lower reaches of the trail can look like a parade, especially on weekends, but the higher you go, the fewer folks you see. The path is especially popular with people walking their dogs. Rattlesnake Canyon is a lush riparian environment around a year-round creek, a place where the plant life is so lavish that you may think you're in Mendocino or the North Coast. The trail starts out as a wide dirt path (an old carriage road), but soon narrows to single track. It crosses rocky Rattlesnake Creek many times, tunneling through a forest of oak, bay, and sycamore trees on the lower stretch of the trail. In the spring and summer months the wildflowers here are as good as you'll find anywhere in Santa Barbara. As you climb out of the canyon, you'll gain increasingly broad views of the Pacific Coast and Channel Islands. Watch for hang gliders soaring overhead. At an intersection with a connector trail to Tunnel Trail at 1.7 miles, bear right to finish the steep climb to Gibraltar Road. Suddenly your surroundings aren't quite so lush anymore, but the coastal views—well, on a clear day, they don't get much better than this.

Location: North of Santa Barbara; map H3, grid g5.

User groups: Hikers, dogs, and horses. No mountain bikes. No wheelchair facilities.

Permits: No permits are required. Parking and access are free.

Maps: For a map of Los Padres National Forest, send $6 to U.S. Forest Service, Map Sales, P.O. Box 587, Camino, CA 95709; tel. (530) 647-5390 or website: www.r5.fs.fed.us/visitorcenter. Ask the USGS for a topographic map of the Santa Barbara area.

Directions: From U.S. 101 in Santa Barbara take the Mission Street exit and follow it east for just over a mile, crossing State Street. When Mission Street ends, turn left on Laguna Street and drive past the Santa Barbara Mission, turning right on Los Olivos, directly in front of the mission. Passing the mission, bear left on Mission Canyon Road for .8 mile. Turn right on Foothill Boulevard. In .1 mile turn left onto the continuation of Mission Canyon Road. Drive .4 mile and turn right on Las Conoas Road. Drive 1.2 miles and park on the right side of the road across from the sign for Skofield Park and Rattlesnake Canyon Wilderness Area.

Contact: Los Padres National Forest, Santa Barbara Ranger District, 3505 Paradise Road, Santa Barbara, CA 93105; tel. (805) 967-3481 or fax (805) 967-7312.

11 Montecito Overlook

3.0 mi/1.5 hrs

The East Fork of Cold Springs is a perfect introductory hike to the Santa Barbara front country. For people who think the mountains in Santa Barbara are all chaparral-covered slopes, this trail is an eye-opener to the lush beauty of the mountain canyons. The climb to Montecito Overlook is a good aerobic workout but not a killer and affords great views of the Santa Barbara coast and Channel Islands. Many people don't go all the way to the overlook; they just hike through the shady forest to a bench that overlooks the confluence of the East Fork and Middle Fork of Cold Springs Creek and find themselves a cool pool to soak their feet. From the roadside pullout follow the path through the alders alongside Cold Springs Creek, staying on the creek's right (east) side. After the first mile you leave the creek and begin to switchback uphill to the overlook—really just a flat semi-clearing where the trail intersects a dirt road). Pick any spot amid the invading brush where the views are clear and wide. The best spot is a few hundred feet down the road to your right. Hikers looking for more trail to cover can continue another two miles to Montecito Peak, elevation 3,214 feet. The climb is steep and hot (no shade), but for many it's worth it. In addition to the views of the Santa Barbara coast, you can see all the way to the Santa Monica Mountains.

Location: In Montecito; map H3, grid h5.

User groups: Hikers, dogs, horses, and mountain bikes. No wheelchair facilities.

Permits: No permits are required. Parking and access are free.

Maps: For a map of Los Padres National Forest, send $6 to U.S. Forest Service, Map Sales, P.O. Box 587, Camino, CA 95709; tel. (530) 647-5390 or website: www.r5.fs.fed.us/visitorcenter. Ask the USGS for a topographic map of the Santa Barbara area.

Directions: From Santa Barbara drive south on U.S. 101 for four miles and exit on Hot Springs Road. Turn left on Hot Springs Road and drive 2.5 miles to Mountain Drive. Turn left and continue 1.2 miles to the Cold Springs Trailhead. Park off the road, near the sharp curve where the creek runs across the road. The trail is marked by a rusty Forest Service sign.

Contact: Los Padres National Forest, Santa Barbara Ranger District, 3505 Paradise Road, Santa Barbara, CA 93105; tel. (805) 967-3481 or fax (805) 967-7312.

12 West Fork Cold Springs
4.0 mi/2.0 hrs

If you hike the West Fork of Cold Springs from its start—where it spurs off the East Fork Trail—to its end at Gibraltar Road, you get to see the wide range of terrain that is typical in Santa Barbara. Start hiking on the East Fork Cold Springs Trail from the rusty Forest Service sign near the road. After a half-mile stretch through shady forest canopy alongside the creek, you'll reach a bench that overlooks the confluence of the East and Middle Forks of Cold Springs Creek. You'll cross the creek here; look carefully for the trail sign. Soon you leave the dense, shady, fern-laden area surrounding Cold Springs Creek, and climb out of the canyon into a drier and more exposed landscape. In early spring look for spectacular Tangerine Falls up ahead in the Middle Fork Canyon; the waterfall is clearly visible although distant from the West Fork Trail. (A use trail cuts off from the main trail to reach it, but it requires good scrambling abilities and an immunity to poison oak.) By the time you climb to the end of the West Fork Trail at Gibraltar Road, you'll be glad to turn around and head back down to the coolness below. The views are excellent from the road, however, and you'll get plenty more views as you walk back down the trail. Be careful going down—the West Fork Trail is not as well used as the East Fork Trail, and it's steep and eroded in places, especially when wet. But that's a small price to pay for the glorious vistas of the Montecito coast and the relative solitude of this trail compared to its popular neighbor, the East Fork Trail.

Location: In Montecito; map H3, grid h5.

User groups: Hikers, dogs, horses, and mountain bikes. No wheelchair facilities.

Permits: No permits are required. Parking and access are free.

Maps: For a map of Los Padres National Forest, send $6 to U.S. Forest Service, Map Sales, P.O. Box 587, Camino, CA 95709; tel. (530) 647-5390 or website: www.r5.fs.fed.us/visitorcenter.

Ask the USGS for a topographic map of the Santa Barbara area.

Directions: From Santa Barbara drive south on U.S. 101 for four miles and exit on Hot Springs Road. Turn left on Hot Springs Road and drive 2.5 miles to Mountain Drive. Turn left and continue 1.2 miles to the Cold Springs Trailhead. Park off the road, near the sharp curve where the creek crosses the road.

Contact: Los Padres National Forest, Santa Barbara Ranger District, 3505 Paradise Road, Santa Barbara, CA 93105; tel. (805) 967-3481 or fax (805) 967-7312.

13 San Ysidro Trail
8.0 mi/4.5 hrs

If you like running water, San Ysidro Canyon is your chance at seeing some, even long after the last rain. Other streams in the Santa Barbara area are often nearly dry by May, but San Ysidro keeps on flowing year-round. The trail up its canyon offers many possible destinations and stopping points; few hike all the way to its terminus at East Camino Cielo—it's four miles one way with a 3,000-foot elevation gain. The rewards are great no matter how far you go, beginning with swimming holes and waterfalls in the first two miles of trail, mostly under the shade of oaks and sycamores. After a rocky section, you climb out of the canyon into chaparral country, entering into a series of steep, exposed switchbacks. Most people give up somewhere along this stretch, but those who continue come out near Cold Spring Saddle on East Camino Cielo, elevation 3,480 feet. From there you'll feel on top of the world.

Location: In Montecito; map H3, grid h6.

User groups: Hikers, dogs, horses, and mountain bikes. No wheelchair facilities.

Permits: No permits are required. Parking and access are free.

Maps: For a map of Los Padres National Forest, send $6 to U.S. Forest Service, Map Sales, P.O. Box 587, Camino, CA 95709; tel. (530) 647-5390 or website: www.r5.fs.fed.us/visitorcenter.

Ask the USGS for a topographic map of the Carpinteria area.

Directions: From U.S. 101 in Montecito take the San Ysidro Road exit and head east for one mile to East Valley Road/Highway 192. Turn right on East Valley Road/Highway 192 and travel .9 mile. Turn left on Park Lane and drive .4 mile on Park Lane; then bear left on East Mountain Drive and drive .25 mile to the end of the road. Park alongside the road and walk to the trailhead on the right.

Contact: Los Padres National Forest, Santa Barbara Ranger District, 3505 Paradise Road, Santa Barbara, CA 93105; tel. (805) 967-3481 or fax (805) 967-7312.

14 McMenemy Trail

2.5 mi/1.0 hr

If you only have time for a short hike, this lovely trip in San Ysidro Canyon includes a stint on the McMenemy Trail, an old favorite of many Santa Barbara hikers. It has just enough of a climb to make you feel that you did your workout for the day but enough pretty views to make you forget that hiking is actually exercise. Begin your trip on the San Ysidro Trail, above, but bear left at the sign for the McMenemy Trail .5 mile in. Unfortunately, this part of the trail is routed through a construction site on private property near the San Ysidro Ranch and has looked unsightly for the last few years. Until the situation improves, just endure it, because soon a series of switchbacks brings you to the Colonel's stone bench—Colonel McMenemy, that is—where you have a fine view down into Montecito and out to the coast. It's a good place to catch your breath, read a book, or have a picnic. There is even a horse hitch available just in case you brought your horse along. If you want to keep hiking, you can make a five-mile loop by continuing on McMenemy Trail to Saddle Rock Trail. Turn right, then right again on the Edison Catwalk to return to San Ysidro Canyon Trail.

Location: In Montecito; map H3, grid h6.

User groups: Hikers, dogs, horses, and mountain bikes. No wheelchair facilities.

Permits: No permits are required. Parking and access are free.

Maps: For a map of Los Padres National Forest, send $6 to U.S. Forest Service, Map Sales, P.O. Box 587, Camino, CA 95709; tel. (530) 647-5390 or website: www.r5.fs.fed.us/visitorcenter. Ask the USGS for a topographic map of the Carpinteria area.

Directions: From U.S. 101 in Montecito take the San Ysidro Road exit and head east for one mile to East Valley Road/Highway 192. Turn right on East Valley Road/Highway 192, travel .9 mile, and turn left on Park Lane. Drive .4 mile on Park Lane and bear left on East Mountain Drive. Drive .25 mile to the end of East Mountain Drive and park alongside the road. The trailhead is on the right.

Contact: Los Padres National Forest, Santa Barbara Ranger District, 3505 Paradise Road, Santa Barbara, CA 93105; tel. (805) 967-3481 or fax (805) 967-7312.

15 McGrath State Beach Nature Trail

0.75 mi/0.5 hr

There's a great little nature trail at McGrath State Beach that offers a far different hike from a walk along the sandy public beach. The trail runs along the Santa Clara Estuary, which is designated as a natural preserve. It's the place where the Santa Clara River joins the Pacific Ocean. In that meeting space freshwater and saltwater plants and animals intermingle, which means you have the chance to see migrating birds, resident shorebirds, and fish swimming in the estuary. The trail starts out in a shaded willow thicket, a secluded and peaceful change from the hustle and bustle of the beach campground. Watch for the endangered California least tern or Belding's savannah sparrow. When you reach the beach, you can continue hiking along the shoreline or you can turn around and head back. Note that if you visit in the winter season, this trail is not maintained and can become very overgrown.

Location: In Oxnard; map H3, grid j9.

User groups: Hikers only. No dogs, horses, or mountain bikes. No wheelchair facilities.

Permits: No permits are required. A $5 day-use fee is charged per vehicle.

Maps: Ask the USGS for a topographic map of the Ventura area.

Directions: From U.S. 101 in Ventura take the Seaward Avenue exit to Harbor Boulevard. Turn south on Harbor Boulevard and drive four miles to the park entrance. The nature trail begins at the day-use parking lot, a quick right turn after the entrance kiosk. (If you are traveling north on U.S. 101, you must take the Victoria Avenue exit to reach Harbor Boulevard.)

Contact: McGrath State Beach, 901 S. San Pedro, Ventura, CA 93001; tel. (805) 654-4744 or (805) 899-1400.

THE SMOOTH SANDSTONE BOULDERS OF PIEDRA BLANCA ARE FUN TO EXPLORE.

MAP H4

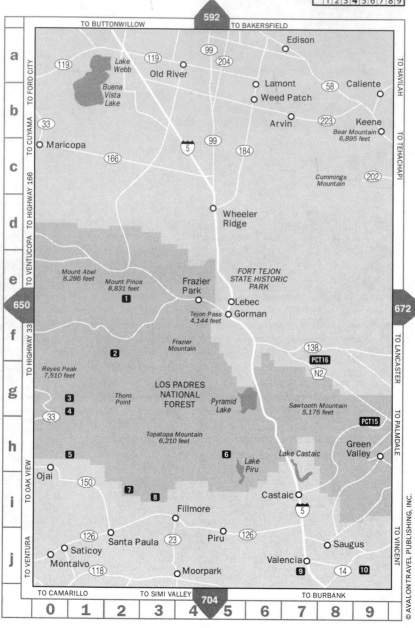

TO FORD CITY

a

Lake Webb
119   119   Old River
99
204
Buena Vista Lake
Edison
Lamont
58   Caliente
TO HAVILAH

b

TO CUYAMA
33
Weed Patch
Arvin   223   Keene
Bear Mountain 6,895 feet
TO TEHACHAPI

c

TO HIGHWAY 166
Maricopa   166
5   99   184
Cummings Mountain
202

d

TO VENTUCOPA
Wheeler Ridge

e

TO HIGHWAY 33
Mount Abel 8,286 feet   Mount Pinos 8,831 feet
Frazier Park
FORT TEJON STATE HISTORIC PARK
650   ■1
Lebec
672
Tejon Pass 4,144 feet   Gorman

f

Frazier Mountain
138
PCT16
N2

g

Reyes Peak 7,510 feet
■2
Thorn Point
LOS PADRES NATIONAL FOREST
Pyramid Lake
Sawtooth Mountain 5,175 feet
■3
33   ■4
PCT15

h

■5
Topatopa Mountain 6,210 feet
■6   Lake Piru   Lake Castaic
Green Valley

i

TO OAK VIEW
Ojai
150
■7   ■8
Castaic
5
TO PALMDALE

Fillmore

j

TO VENTURA
126   Santa Paula   23   Piru   126
Saticoy
Montalvo   118
Moorpark
Valencia   9   14   ■10   Saugus
TO VINCENT

© AVALON TRAVEL PUBLISHING, INC.

CHAPTER H4

1 Vincent
   Tumamait Trail 663
2 Cedar Creek
   and the Fishbowls 664
3 Piedra Blanca 664
4 Rose Valley Falls 665
5 Nordhoff Peak. 665
6 Pothole and
   Agua Blanca Loop 666
7 Santa Paula Canyon. . . . 667
8 Santa Paula Peak. 667

9 Canyon View Trail 668
10 Placerita Creek
   Waterfall. 668

**Pacific Crest Trail
(PCT) Section Overview**

PCT-15 San Francisquito
   Canyon Road to
   Three Points. 669
PCT-16 Three Points to
   Tehachapi/Willow
   Springs Road 670

1 Vincent Tumamait Trail

5.0 mi/2.5 hrs

A day hike in the Chumash Wilderness means the possibility of seeing a magnificent condor fly overhead and a visit to Mount Pinos, the highest point in Los Padres National Forest at 8,831 feet. This is conifer country, with the peak covered in snow a good part of the year—to the great delight of Southern California cross-country skiers. The Vincent Tumamait Trail begins on the summit of Mount Pinos and runs five miles to Mount Abel, elevation 8,286 feet (also called Mount Cerro Noroeste). If you wish, you can leave a car at Mount Abel and take a one-way shuttle trip between the two impressive peaks. Otherwise it's great fun just to check out the far-reaching views from the trailhead on Mount Pinos' summit and wander a way on the Vincent Tumamait Trail. Head out two miles, downhill at first and then up Sawmill Mountain to the North Fork Trail junction. Bear left at the junction and walk .5 mile to primitive Sheep Camp, a sweet spot in the shade of fir and pine trees to open up your day pack and have lunch. After a rest you'll be all fueled up for the uphill return trip to the summit. As you hike, keep

scanning the skies for those giant condors, many of which nest in the nearby condor sanctuary. By the way, who was Vincent Tumamait? He was a Chumash elder and beloved storyteller who lived from 1919 to 1992.

Location: In the Chumash Wilderness west of Frazier Park; map H4, grid e2.

User groups: Hikers, dogs, and horses. No mountain bikes. No wheelchair facilities.

Permits: No permits are required. A national forest recreation pass is required for each vehicle; fees are $5 for one day or $30 for a year.

Maps: For a map of Los Padres National Forest, send $6 to U.S. Forest Service, Map Sales, P.O. Box 587, Camino, CA 95709; tel. (530) 647-5390 or website: www.r5.fs.fed.us/visitorcenter. Ask the USGS for a topographic map of the Sawmill Mountain area.

Directions: From Interstate 5 near Lebec, take the Frazier Park/Mount Pinos exit and turn west. Drive 12 miles on Frazier Mountain Park Road, which will become Cuddy Valley Road. At 12 miles bear left on Mount Pinos Highway and drive nine miles to the dirt road on the left, signed for Mount Pinos Summit. Turn left and drive 1.8 miles to the summit and trailhead. Bear left at the forks.

Contact: Los Padres National Forest, Mount Pinos Ranger District, 34580 Lockwood Valley Road, Frazier Park, CA 93225; tel. (661) 245-3731 or fax (661) 245-1526.

2 Cedar Creek and the Fishbowls

9.0 mi/4.5 hrs or 2.0 days

Despite the long mileage on this trail, the Fishbowls along Piru Creek are a popular and heavily visited spot, mostly because there is little that is finer in life than a creek with good swimming holes. That and the fact that the trail has a moderate elevation gain, so even with the nine-mile round-trip, it's a manageable day hike for most people. The Cedar Creek Trail leads uphill from Thorn Meadows Campground (elevation 5,050 feet), first through oaks and then a pretty conifer forest (including the trail's namesake incense cedars). It follows the South Fork of Piru Creek much of the way. What starts out as a wide dirt road eventually narrows to a single track. At 3.5 miles in, bear right on the Fishbowls Trail, hike along a ridgeline with lovely views of the forest below, then descend to Fishbowls Camp. Walk upstream from the camp for about 300 yards to reach the Fishbowls, a series of rounded sandstone pools on Piru Creek. Now strip down to your bathing suit, jump in, and shout, "I'm alive!"

Location: In the Sespe Wilderness, southwest of Frazier Park; map H4, grid f2.

User groups: Hikers, dogs, and horses. No mountain bikes. No wheelchair facilities.

Permits: A free California campfire permit is required for building a fire or using a backpacking stove; permits are available at any Southern California Forest Service ranger station. A national forest recreation pass is required for each vehicle; fees are $5 for one day or $30 for a year.

Maps: For a map of Los Padres National Forest, send $6 to U.S. Forest Service, Map Sales, P.O. Box 587, Camino, CA 95709; tel. (530) 647-5390 or website: www.r5.fs.fed.us/visitorcenter.

A map of the Sespe Wilderness is available for a fee from Tom Harrison Cartography, tel. (415) 456-7940. Ask the USGS for a topographic map of the Lockwood Valley area.

Directions: From Interstate 5 near Lebec take the Frazier Park exit and drive three miles west to Frazier Park; continue west on Frazier Mountain Road for two miles to the Lake of the Woods fork. Bear left and drive 10.5 miles on Lockwood Valley Road. Turn left on Grade Valley Road/Road 7NO3 (dirt) and drive 7.5 miles. Turn right on Thorn Meadows Road and drive .5 mile to the Cedar Creek Trailhead.

Contact: Los Padres National Forest, Mount Pinos Ranger District, 34580 Lockwood Valley Road, Frazier Park, CA 93225; tel. (661) 245-3731 or fax (661) 245-1526.

3 Piedra Blanca

2.0 mi/1.0 hr

Sandstone lovers, this is your spot. Piedra Blanca is a series of huge, rounded sandstone boulders that are somewhat otherworldly looking. If rocks can look sensual, these are. They're set in the Rose Valley Recreation Area, just a short stretch away from Sespe Creek, in what looks a lot like the desert—plenty of sand, desert scrub, and rocks. Hike from the day-use area at Lion Campground, crossing Sespe's often dry wash and pick up the trail on the far side of the wash. The rocks of Piedra Blanca are clearly visible, so it's easy to see where you're going. Although the trail continues down the back side of the boulders and beyond, most people just climb to the top of the boulders, then spend some time wandering around and exploring. As you might guess, this is a first-class spot for watching sunsets.

Location: In the Rose Valley Recreation Area north of Ojai; map H4, grid g0.

User groups: Hikers, dogs, horses, and mountain bikes. No wheelchair facilities.

Permits: No permits are required. A national forest recreation pass is required for each vehicle; fees are $5 for one day or $30 for a year.

Maps: For a map of Los Padres National Forest, send $6 to U.S. Forest Service, Map Sales, P.O. Box 587, Camino, CA 95709; tel. (530) 647-5390 or website: www.r5.fs.fed.us/visitorcenter. Ask the USGS for a topographic map of the Lion Canyon area.

Directions: From Ojai drive north on Highway 33 for 16 miles to Rose Valley Road and the sign for Rose Valley Recreation Area. Turn right, drive 4.6 miles, and take the left fork; then drive 1.1 miles farther to Lion Campground. Park in the signed day-use area.

Contact: Los Padres National Forest, Ojai Ranger District, 1190 E. Ojai Avenue, Ojai, CA 93023; tel. (805) 646-4348 or fax (805) 646-0484.

4 Rose Valley Falls

0.6 mi/0.5 hr

The trip to Rose Valley Falls is an easy walk in the woods to the base of a stunning and unusual limestone waterfall. If you're making the drive to Rose Valley Recreation Area to camp, fish, or hike, a side trip to Rose Valley Falls is just about mandatory. Start hiking on the signed trail in Rose Valley Campground. The path is bordered on both sides by oaks and fragrant bays, and it parallels Rose Creek. Cross the creek a few times, and as you walk into the canyon, keep looking ahead (up high) for your first glimpse of the 300-foot waterfall. If it has rained lately, you'll see it for sure. In 15 minutes you reach the base of the waterfall, which is glaringly different in appearance from the falls you were just looking at. That's because this is the bottom tier of huge Rose Valley Falls, and you were seeing the upper tier. The lower tier is layered with limestone and sandstone slabs and oozing with wet moss. You can't resist touching it. Some daredevils attempt to climb up and over this lower tier to see more of the upper part of the waterfall, but this should only be attempted by experts with proper climbing equipment.

Location: In the Rose Valley Recreation Area north of Ojai; map H4, grid g0.

User groups: Hikers, dogs, horses, and mountain bikes. No wheelchair facilities.

Permits: No permits are required. A national forest recreation pass is required for each vehicle; fees are $5 for one day or $30 for a year.

Maps: For a map of Los Padres National Forest, send $6 to U.S. Forest Service, Map Sales, P.O. Box 587, Camino, CA 95709; tel. (530) 647-5390 or website: www.r5.fs.fed.us/visitorcenter. Ask the USGS for a topographic map of the Lion Canyon area.

Directions: From Ojai, drive north on Highway 33 for 16 miles to Rose Valley Road and the sign for Rose Valley Recreation Area. Turn right, drive three miles, then turn right again at the sign for Rose Valley Camp. Drive .6 mile to the campground. The trail leads from the far end of the camp near site four.

Contact: Los Padres National Forest, Ojai Ranger District, 1190 E. Ojai Avenue, Ojai, CA 93023; tel. (805) 646-4348 or fax (805) 646-0484.

5 Nordhoff Peak

11.6 mi/6.0 hrs

The hike to Nordhoff Peak is a rite of passage for Ojai hikers. After all, journalist Charles Nordhoff was the guy who made Ojai famous. In the late 1800s, he wrote various magazine articles about Ojai Valley's many charms, which encouraged people to move here and start a new life. Nordhoff's summit is at 4,425 feet, high enough to get an occasional few inches of snow, and a hike to the top is a fine way to spend an early spring day in Ojai. That's if you're up to the 5.8-mile, 3,300-foot climb, of course. Forget hiking in the heat of summer; much of the trail is on dusty, open fire roads, with no shade. From the Gridley Trailhead, hike up to Gridley Fire Road and turn right, passing by seemingly endless avocado groves. Bear left at the next junction and enter a shadier canyon and pass the primitive camp at Gridley Spring. This is almost the halfway point; take a breather. Prepare yourself for the next two miles—the steepest on the trip—then begin switchbacking your way up to Nordhoff Fire Road, where you turn left and hike one more mile to the peak. If you think that after all this climbing you ought to get some good views, you won't be disappointed. The last mile of trail offers excellent vistas, and when you reach the old Nordhoff Fire Lookout Tower, you can see all the way to the Pacific Ocean and Channel Islands, Ojai Valley and Lake Casitas closer in, and miles of Los Padres National Forest and its wilderness areas.

Location: East of Ojai; map H4, grid h1.

User groups: Hikers, dogs, horses, and mountain bikes. No wheelchair facilities.

Permits: No permits are required. A national forest recreation pass is required for each vehicle; fees are $5 for one day or $30 for a year.

Maps: For a map of Los Padres National Forest, send $6 to U.S. Forest Service, Map Sales, P.O. Box 587, Camino, CA 95709; tel. (530) 647-5390 or website: www.r5.fs.fed.us/visitorcenter. Ask the USGS for a topographic map of the Ojai area.

Directions: From Ojai at the intersection of Highways 150 and 33, drive east on Highway 150 for two miles and turn left on Gridley Road, .25 mile past the ranger station. Drive 1.5 miles north on Gridley Road until it dead-ends at a driveway. The trailhead is on the left.

Contact: Los Padres National Forest, Ojai Ranger District, 1190 E. Ojai Avenue, Ojai, CA 93023; tel. (805) 646-4348 or fax (805) 646-0484.

6 Pothole and Agua Blanca Loop

11.0 mi/1-2 days

Most people know to come to Lake Piru for waterskiing, sailing, and fishing, but not everybody knows to come here for hiking. An excellent trail begins from Blue Point Campground (beyond the north end of the lake), which can be hiked as a loop in either direction. Most people park at Blue Point Campground and hike up the Agua Blanca Trail from there, returning on the Pothole Trail, which brings you back to the road about a mile south of the campground. That makes the last mile an easy tromp on the road back to your car.

Hiking the trail in this fashion, you set out on a dirt road out of Blue Point Camp for about a mile, following Piru Creek, then bear left on Agua Blanca Trail. Climb moderately along crystal-clear Agua Blanca Creek to Devils Gateway, a rocky narrows area. The trail goes around the carved sandstone gorge, but when the water is low enough, some hikers wade through it instead, just for the fun of it. Reach Log Cabin Camp 4.5 miles in, a fine place to lay your sleeping bag. The next day is longer mileage, following the Pothole Trail for one mile to the Pothole, a huge, grassy depression in the ground. It's just off the main trail; take the .25-mile spur on your right to see it. Climb from there, more gently now, with the gain spread out over a few miles. The final two miles of the trip are a steep descent to the campground road. Views are good all the way down, especially of Lake Piru and bluish-colored Blue Point, a rock outcrop. At the road, turn left to return to Blue Point Camp.

Location: In the Sespe Wilderness near Lake Piru; map H4, grid h5.

User groups: Hikers, dogs, horses, and mountain bikes. No wheelchair facilities.

Permits: A free wilderness permit is required for overnight stays; permits are available from the Ojai Ranger District or Lake Piru Recreation Area. A national forest recreation pass is required for each vehicle; fees are $5 for one day or $30 for a year.

Maps: For a map of Los Padres National Forest, send $6 to U.S. Forest Service, Map Sales, P.O. Box 587, Camino, CA 95709; tel. (530) 647-5390 or website: www.r5.fs.fed.us/visitorcenter. A map of the Sespe Wilderness is available for a fee from Tom Harrison Cartography, tel. (415) 456-7940. Ask the USGS for a topographic map of Cobblestone Mountain.

Directions: From Fillmore take Highway 126 east for eight miles to Piru Canyon Road, signed for Lake Piru. Turn left (north) on Piru Canyon Road and follow the signs through the town of Piru to Lake Piru's entrance station; continue beyond the lake to Blue Point Campground. Continue past the camp, crossing a stream, to the day-use parking area. Total distance on Piru Canyon Road is 13.5 miles.

Contact: Los Padres National Forest, Ojai Ranger District, 1190 E. Ojai Avenue, Ojai, CA 93023; tel. (805) 646-4348 or fax (805) 646-0484; Lake Piru Recreation Area, tel. (805) 521-1500.

7 Santa Paula Canyon
6.0 mi/3.5 hrs or 2.0 days

What starts out rather pedestrian gets much, much better on the Santa Paula Canyon Trail. That's because the first mile of the route is mostly on pavement, meandering around the grounds of Thomas Aquinas College and a private ranch and oil-drilling operation, before at last you're on a real trail in the real outdoors. This slow start doesn't keep the Santa Paula Canyon Trail from being well loved and frequently used, especially by people looking for an easy overnight backpacking trip, or a place to jump in a swimming hole. You'll find a few people hiking the path even on weekdays. After following the well-signed route to the start of the "real" trail, you'll head deep into Santa Paula Canyon, following the creek and crossing it twice. The trees are dense and wildflowers are sublime. After the second creek crossing at two miles out, get ready for your first real climb on the trail as you follow a wide dirt road up and around Hill 1989. Following the ascent, the trail drops down to a lovely campground in a grassy flat, surrounded by big cone spruce. There are six sites with fire rings there at aptly named Big Cone Camp. The trail leads a short distance from the camp steeply down to Santa Paula Creek, where waterfalls and swimming holes await on a stretch of stream called the Punchbowls. Here's a tip: If you can secure the campsite on the far left side of Big Cone Camp, it has its own little overlook on one of Santa Paula Creek's nicest waterfalls.

Location: East of Ojai; map H4, grid i2.

User groups: Hikers, dogs, horses, and mountain bikes. No wheelchair facilities.

Permits: A free California campfire permit is required for building a fire or using a back-

packing stove; permits are available at the Ojai ranger station. A national forest recreation pass is required for each vehicle; fees are $5 for one day or $30 for a year.

Maps: For a map of Los Padres National Forest, send $6 to U.S. Forest Service, Map Sales, P.O. Box 587, Camino, CA 95709; tel. (530) 647-5390 or website: www.r5.fs.fed.us/visitorcenter. Ask the USGS for a topographic map of the Santa Paula Peak area.

Directions: From Ojai, at the junction of Highways 33 and 150, drive east on Highway 150 for 11.5 miles to Thomas Aquinas College on the left (look for iron gates and stone buildings). Drive 100 yards farther to the parking pullout on the right side of the road just beyond the highway bridge over Santa Paula Creek. Park there and walk back across the bridge to the paved road on the right side of the college.

Contact: Los Padres National Forest, Ojai Ranger District, 1190 E. Ojai Avenue, Ojai, CA 93023; tel. (805) 646-4348 or fax (805) 646-0484.

8 Santa Paula Peak
9.0 mi/5.0 hrs

If you're looking for a good workout but the hike to Nordhoff Peak sounds a bit too long, the trail to Santa Paula Peak is a great alternative. The climb is the same—the trail gains 3,000 feet—but it's compressed into 4.5 miles and about a million switchbacks. The peak is actually higher than Nordhoff Peak—Santa Paula's summit is just shy of 5,000 feet—but the views are somewhat different, looking down into the Santa Clarita Valley and out to the coast. There are no trail junctions to worry about until four miles up, when you reach the ridge just below the peak. Bear left (west) and finish out your climb, then pat yourself on the back for being such a fine mountaineer.

Location: East of Ojai; map H4, grid i3.

User groups: Hikers, dogs, horses, and mountain bikes. No wheelchair facilities.

Permits: No permits are required. A national forest recreation pass is required for each vehicle; fees are $5 for one day or $30 for a year.

Maps: For a map of Los Padres National Forest, send $6 to U.S. Forest Service, Map Sales, P.O. Box 587, Camino, CA 95709; tel. (530) 647-5390 or website: www.r5.fs.fed.us/visitorcenter. Ask the USGS for a topographic map of the Santa Paula Peak area.

Directions: From Fillmore take Highway 126 west for five miles. Turn right on Timber Canyon Road (dirt) and drive 4.5 miles to the gate and trailhead.

Contact: Los Padres National Forest, Ojai Ranger District, 1190 E. Ojai Avenue, Ojai, CA 93023; tel. (805) 646-4348 or fax (805) 646-0484.

🖩 Canyon View Trail
2.0 mi/1.0 hr

Little Ed Davis Park is a part of larger Towsley Canyon, which is a part of the giant Santa Monica Mountains Conservancy parcel of lands. If you visit the park any time except during the sweltering heat of summer, you can walk the two-mile Canyon View Trail and pay a visit to all of Towsley Canyon's major plant communities—grasslands, sage and scrub, riparian, oak woodlands, and just about everything except old-growth redwood forest—in one short trip. How can a park this close to Interstate 5 be this wild looking? We can't figure it out, but it is. The trail begins near the creek, east of the nature center, and ends on the Wiley Canyon Trail. (You return via the dirt entrance road.) Despite the brevity of the trail, it has a surprisingly good climb to a ridge where you have excellent views of the rock formations in Towsley Canyon and the Santa Clarita Valley.

Location: In Ed Davis Park in Towsley Canyon, south of Valencia; map H4, grid j7.

User groups: Hikers, dogs, horses, and mountain bikes. No wheelchair facilities.

Permits: No permits are required. Parking and access are free.

Maps: Ask the USGS for topographic maps of the Newhall and Oat Mountain areas.

Directions: From the San Fernando Valley

drive north on Interstate 5 to Santa Clarita (five miles north of the Interstate 5 and Highway 14 junction). Take the Calgrove exit, turn left, drive .25 mile and turn right onto the park entrance road. Park in the second parking lot. **Contact:** Santa Monica Mountains Conservancy, 5750 Ramirez Canyon Road, Malibu, CA 90265; tel. (310) 589-3200 or fax (310) 589-3207.

🔟 Placerita Creek Waterfall
5.5 mi/2.5 hrs

Placerita Canyon County Park is a perfect destination for a family outing, being just far enough out of the Los Angeles basin to feel like someplace different and with trails that are easy enough for hikers of almost any ability. Start your trip at the park nature center, where you should pay a visit to all the taxidermied animals and learn a thing or two about the flora and fauna of the area. Then start hiking on the Canyon Trail, which leads from the southeast side of the parking lot and crosses Placerita Creek. Hike through Placerita Canyon, often under the shade of sycamores and oaks, to Walker Ranch Picnic Area. At its far side look for a trail on the right signed as Waterfall Trail, and get ready for the best part of the trip. (Make sure you don't take the Los Piñetos Trail, which is just before the Waterfall Trail and doesn't go to the falls.) The canyon begins to narrow, and you twist and curve your way along the trail, crossing and recrossing the creek a few times. In the final 100 yards before the waterfall, the trail ends, and you simply hike up the streambed. Although the waterfall is only 25 feet high, it forms a lovely little grotto, a perfect place to eat a Power Bar before heading back.

Location: In Placerita Canyon County Park southeast of Valencia; map H4, grid j9.

User groups: Hikers, dogs, and horses. No mountain bikes. No wheelchair facilities.

Permits: No permits are required. Parking and access are free.

Maps: Free maps of Placerita Canyon County Park are available at the park nature center.

Ask the USGS for topographic maps of the San Fernando and Mint Canyon areas.

Directions: From the San Fernando Valley drive north on Interstate 5 to Highway 14. Follow Highway 14 northeast for four miles to Newhall; exit on Placerita Canyon Road. Turn right (east) and drive 1.5 miles to the park entrance on the right. Park in the nature center parking lot.

Contact: Placerita Canyon County Park, 19152 Placerita Canyon Road, Newhall, CA 91321; tel. (661) 259-7721.

PACIFIC CREST TRAIL (PCT) SECTION OVERVIEW
65.0 mi one way/7.0 days

While we have hiked all of the John Muir Trail and most of the Pacific Crest Trail, we took a pass on this section, which extends from the San Francisquito Canyon Road Trailhead north to the trailhead parking area on Tehachapi/Willow Springs Road. Unless you're inspired by a desire to hike the entire PCT after reaching Three Points, it makes no sense to hike beyond to Tehachapi Pass. The reason is that PCT through-hikers are forced to make a 45-mile excursion across the high-desert terrain of the Mojave Desert because the owners of megagiant Tejon Ranch wouldn't allow a true crest route to be built on their property. So hikers get dumped out on the desert, where 100-degree temperatures are common even in late spring. Water is always a critical factor here. If for some reason you decide to cross the Mojave, drink as much as possible when at a reliable source and then carry as much as possible when hiking.

PCT-15 San Francisquito Canyon Road to Three Points
34.0 mi one way/4.0 days

During this 34-mile stint from San Francisquito Road to Three Points, you'll have lots of time to contemplate the awaiting trek across the Mojave Desert. The transition from Angeles Na-

tional Forest, now well behind you, to desert is complete as you head through scrub and sparsely vegetated canyons. The views are the lone highlight. From Liebre Mountain, where off-road vehicles have ruined the experience for many hikers, you can even see a piece of Hollywood and beyond to the Pacific Ocean, along with another view of the peaks in Angeles National Forest and northeast across the Antelope Valley and the Mojave. From here it's a dry, downhill tromp to Pine Canyon, a drop of 2,000 feet, and then on to the Three Points Trailhead. Be absolutely certain to get information on water availability before heading out, and carefully plan your water stops and monitor supply and consumption.

Location: From San Francisquito Canyon Road northwest to the trailhead parking area at Three Points; map H4, grid h9.

User groups: Hikers, dogs, and horses. No mountain bikes. No wheelchair facilities.

Permits: A wilderness permit is required for traveling through various wilderness and special-use areas the trail traverses. Contact the Angeles National Forest, tel. (661) 296-9710, for a permit that is good for the length of your trip.

Maps: For an overall view of the trail route in this section, send $6 to U.S. Forest Service, Map Sales, P.O. Box 587, Camino, CA 95709; tel. (530) 647-5390 or website: www.r5.fs.fed.us/visitorcenter. Ask for the Cleveland National Forest map. Ask the USGS for topographic maps of the Lake Hughes, Burnt Peak, and Liebre Mountain areas. Two BLM surface maps cover the area as well and may be ordered from the Bureau of Land Management office listed below. Send $4 for each map ordered and ask for Tehachapi and Lancaster.

Directions: To reach the San Francisquito Canyon Trailhead from Palmdale and Highway 14, drive west on County Road N2 (Elizabeth Lake Road) and turn left onto San Francisquito Canyon Road, just before reaching Elizabeth Lake. The trailhead is located near the San Francisquito Ranger Station and the campground. To reach the Three Points Trailhead from Palmdale and Highway 14, drive west on County Road N2 (Elizabeth Lake Road) to the town of Three Points. Turn right (north) onto Oakdale Road. The PCT Trailhead is located near a small store at the junction of Oakdale Road and Pine Canyon Road. The PCT runs adjacent to Oakdale Road heading north.

Contact: Angeles National Forest, Saugus Ranger District, 30800 Bouquet Canyon Road, Saugus, CA 91350; tel. (661) 296-9710 or fax (661) 296-5847; Bureau of Land Management, Caliente Resource Area, 3801 Pegasus Drive, Bakersfield, CA 93308; tel. (661) 391-6000 or fax (661) 391-6156.

PCT-16 Three Points to Tehachapi/Willow Springs Road

31.0 mi one way/3.0 days

This is a bizarre piece of trail, one that only PCT through-hikers would take the time to hike and even then doing so only to keep intact the honor of having really hiked the entire route. After leaving Three Points, the Pacific Crest Trail follows no crest at all but is routed across the high desert up to the town of Mojave and then up into the Tehachapis. At times the trail parallels aqueducts and water pipelines, a terrible paradox, since the water is out of reach and other sources are near zero. The only features worth noting are occasional Joshua trees, and for those hiking at night with headlamps or under full moons, the chance of seeing desert wildlife that hides in shade during the day. The trail drops as low as 2,900 feet, then climbs out toward the Tehachapi Mountains, water scarce all the way. It's a rough go always. From Cottonwood Canyon, which bottoms out at 2,915 feet, it's a 30-mile hike to Tehachapi Pass at 6,280 feet, surrounded by a barren landscape. The vision of the Sierra to the north with its forests, meadows, streams, lakes, and snow-laden passes seems like a mirage. From Tehachapi Pass you descend 2,000 feet to Willow Springs Road and another PCT Trailhead.

Location: From the trailhead parking area at Three Points northeast to Tehachapi/Willow Springs Road; map H4, grid f8.

User groups: Hikers, dogs, and horses. No mountain bikes. No wheelchair facilities.

Permits: A wilderness permit is required for traveling through various wilderness and special-use areas the trail traverses. Contact the Angeles National Forest, tel. (661) 296-9710, for a permit that is good for the length of your trip.

Maps: For an overall view of the trail route in this section, send $6 to U.S. Forest Service, Map Sales, P.O. Box 587, Camino, CA 95709; tel. (530) 647-5390 or website: www.r5.fs.fed.us/visitorcenter. Ask for the Cleveland National Forest map. Ask the USGS for topographic maps of the Burnt Peak, Nenache School, Fairmont Butte, Tylerhorse Canyon, Tehachapi South, and Monolith areas. Two BLM surface maps cover the area as well and may be ordered from the Bureau of Land Management office listed below. Send $4 for each map ordered and ask for Tehachapi and Lancaster.

Directions: To reach the Three Points Trailhead from Palmdale and Highway 14, drive west on County Road N2 (Elizabeth Lake Road) to the town of Three Points. Turn right (north) onto Oakdale Road. The PCT Trailhead is located near a small store at the junction of Oakdale Road and Pine Canyon Road. The PCT runs adjacent to Oakdale Road heading north. To reach the Tehachapi/Willow Springs Road Trailhead from Mojave and Highway 14, head west on Oak Creek Road to the intersection with Tehachapi/Willow Springs Road. The trailhead is located near the intersection.

Contact: Angeles National Forest, Valyermo Ranger District, 29835 Valyermo Road, P.O. Box 15, Valyermo, CA 93563; tel. (661) 944-2187 or fax (661) 944-4698; Bureau of Land Management, Caliente Resource Area, 3801 Pegasus Drive, Bakersfield, CA 93308; tel. (661) 391-6000 or fax (661) 391-6156.

PCT Continuation

To continue hiking along the Pacific Crest Trail, see chapter G5.

ANN MARIE BROWN

A JOSHUA TREE AT SADDLEBACK
BUTTE STATE PARK

MAP H5

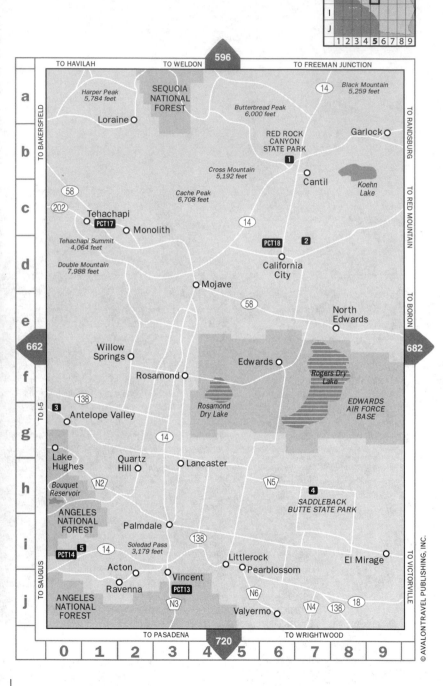

TO HAVILAH   TO WELDON   596   TO FREEMAN JUNCTION

a

TO BAKERSFIELD

Harper Peak
5,784 feet

SEQUOIA
NATIONAL
FOREST

Butterbread Peak
6,000 feet

14

Black Mountain
5,259 feet

TO RANDSBURG

Loraine ○

b

RED ROCK
CANYON
STATE PARK
1

Garlock ○

Cross Mountain
5,192 feet

Cantil ○

Koehn
Lake

TO RED MOUNTAIN

c

58
202

Cache Peak
6,708 feet

14

Tehachapi ○
PCT17
Monolith ○

PCT18   **2**

d

Tehachapi Summit
4,064 feet

California
City ○

TO BORON

Double Mountain
7,988 feet

Mojave ○

e

58

North
Edwards ○

662

Willow
Springs ○

Edwards ○

Rogers Dry
Lake

682

f

Rosamond ○

Rosamond
Dry Lake

EDWARDS
AIR FORCE
BASE

g

TO I-5

138

3

Antelope Valley ○

14

h

Lake
Hughes ○

Quartz
Hill ○

Lancaster ○

N5

Bouquet
Reservoir

N2

SADDLEBACK
BUTTE STATE PARK
4

i

ANGELES
NATIONAL
FOREST

Palmdale ○

138

TO SAUGUS

PCT14 **5**

14

Soledad Pass
3,179 feet

Littlerock ○
Pearblossom ○

El Mirage ○

TO VICTORVILLE

Acton ○

Vincent ○

j

Ravenna ○
PCT13

N6

ANGELES
NATIONAL
FOREST

N3

Valyermo ○

N4   138   18

TO PASADENA   720   TO WRIGHTWOOD

0 1 2 3 4 5 6 7 8 9

© AVALONTRAVEL PUBLISHING, INC.

CHAPTER H5

1 Red Cliffs 673
2 Desert Tortoise
   Discovery Loop 673
3 Antelope Valley Poppy
   Reserve Loop 674
4 Saddleback Butte. 674
5 Vasquez Rocks
   County Park 675

Pacific Crest Trail (PCT) Section Overview

PCT-13 Mill Creek Picnic Area
to Vasquez Rocks. . 676
PCT-14 Vasquez Rocks to|
San Francisquito
Canyon. 677
PCT-17 Tehachapi to Jawbone
Canyon Road. 677
PCT-18 Jawbone Canyon Road
to Walker Pass. . . . 678

1 Red Cliffs

2.0 mi/1.0 hr

Red Cliffs Natural Preserve is a hikers-only section of Red Rock Canyon State Park, where you can walk along and view close-up the reddish columns of 300-foot desert cliffs. The color is caused by iron oxide or rust, but the myriad creases and folds in the cliffs have been formed by a combination of fire and water—volcanic action and the course of streams and rivers. You hike on old jeep tracks, not a formal trail, passing occasional Joshua trees as you go and gaining views of El Paso Mountains. It's hard to believe that this wilderness-like desert is so close to urban Los Angeles, because when you're out here, you feel that you're really far away. At the preserve boundary .75 mile from the trailhead, you can continue on the old jeep road into the Scenic Cliffs Preserve or turn around and retrace your steps. The Scenic Cliffs area is closed each year from February to May, the nesting season for various birds of prey. If you really want to be wowed, take this hike at sunset, spend the night in the state park campground, and see the stars as you've never seen them before.

Location: In Red Rock Canyon State Park off Highway 14 north of Mojave; map H5, grid b6.

User groups: Hikers and horses. No dogs or mountain bikes. No wheelchair facilities.

Permits: No permits are required. A $3 day-use fee is charged per vehicle.

Maps: Ask the USGS for a topographic map of the Cantil area.

Directions: From Mojave, at the junction of Highways 58 and 14, drive northeast on Highway 14 for 25 miles to the Red Cliffs parking area on the right (east) side of the road.

Contact: Red Rock Canyon State Park, c/o Mojave Desert Sector Office, 43779 15th Street W, Lancaster, CA 93534; tel. (661) 942-0662.

2 Desert Tortoise Discovery Loop

2.0 mi/1.0 hr

The Desert Tortoise Natural Area features an easy interpretive trail that teaches visitors all about *Gopherus agassizi,* better known as the desert tortoise, California's state reptile. Don't get your heart set on seeing one, though, as the creatures are rather shy. You have to look for them, and you have to get lucky. At the preserve you can also learn all about other desert reptiles and desert plants. A few very short interpretive trails are worth strolling, but the two-mile Discovery Trail offers the best chance of seeing tortoises. Look for their burrows underneath creosote bushes and keep your fingers crossed that one decides to pop his or her head out. Spring is the best time for tortoise sightings, usually from early March to late May, when the wildflowers are in bloom. The tortoises like to eat them. The best tortoise fact we learned on our trip? During a sudden rainstorm, a tortoise may emerge from its burrow and drink enough water to last a full year.

Location: Off Highway 14 near California City; map H5, grid c7.

User groups: Hikers and wheelchairs. No dogs, horses, or mountain bikes.

Permits: No permits are required. Parking and access are free.

Maps: A free trail map/guide to the Desert Tortoise Natural Area is available at the trailhead. Ask the USGS for topographic maps of the California City North and Galileo Hill areas.

Directions: From Mojave, at the junction of Highways 58 and 14, drive northeast on Highway 14 for 4.5 miles to California City Boulevard. Drive east on California City Boulevard for nine miles to 20 Mule Team Parkway. Go east on the parkway and continue driving 1.3 miles to Randsburg-Mojave Road. Turn left (northeast) on Randsburg-Mojave Road and drive four miles to the signed parking area.

Contact: Bureau of Land Management, Ridgecrest Resource Area, 300 S. Richmond Road, Ridgecrest, CA 93555; tel. (760) 384-5400 or fax (760) 384-5499.

3 Antelope Valley Poppy Reserve Loop

2.0 mi/1.0 hr

Our first trip to the Antelope Valley California Poppy Reserve was a wee bit disappointing. We showed up in late March, expecting to see the hillsides completely covered in bright orange flowers, but only a few straggler poppies were left, dry and shriveled from the

desert wind. It was our own darn fault for poor planning. If you want to see the magic poppy show at Antelope Valley, you simply must time your trip perfectly. The best way to do it is to phone the park starting in late February; they'll tell you exactly when the bloom is at its best. It can be anywhere from late February to May, and it's different every year. There are several possible loop trips in the park, but the best one for poppy-watching is the North and South Poppy Loop, a combined two-mile loop that leads from the west side of the visitor center. Wheelchairs can access a short section of this trail. On either leg of the loop, be sure to take the cutoff trail that leads to the Tehachapi Vista Point, where you can get up high and take a look around.

Location: West of Lancaster and Highway 14; map H5, grid g0.

User groups: Hikers and wheelchairs. No dogs, horses, or mountain bikes.

Permits: No permits are required. A $3 day-use fee is charged per vehicle.

Maps: Ask the USGS for a topographic map of the Del Sur area.

Directions: From Lancaster on Highway 14, take the Avenue I exit and turn west on Avenue I, which becomes Lancaster Road. Drive 14 miles to the entrance to Antelope Valley California Poppy Reserve on the right. The trail begins by the visitor center.

Contact: Antelope Valley California Poppy Reserve, 15101 W. Lancaster Road, Lancaster, CA 93536; tel. (661) 724-1180 or (661) 942-0662.

4 Saddleback Butte

3.2 mi/2.0 hrs

Saddleback Butte State Park is a 3,000-acre Joshua tree woodland, but if those funny looking trees aren't enough to inspire you to make the trip, this hike to the summit of Saddleback Butte should do it. After a 1,000-foot climb to the 3,651-foot summit, you're rewarded with sweeping vistas of Antelope Valley, the San Gabriel Mountains, the Tehachapi Mountains, and the Mojave Desert. Make sure you've picked a cool day, then start hiking from the park campground through sand and plentiful Joshua trees, heading directly for the clearly visible peak. The first stretch of trail is nearly flat. At one mile out, a trail leads off to the left to Little Butte; ignore it and continue straight for granite Saddleback Butte. The last .5 mile of trail is remarkably steep and rocky. A saddle near the summit provides excellent views. Keep going to the very top, where you can fully survey the strange surrounding landscape—the meeting place of the western Mojave Desert and the high San Gabriel Mountains.

Location: East of Lancaster and Highway 14; map H5, grid h7.

User groups: Hikers only. No dogs, horses, or mountain bikes. No wheelchair facilities.

Permits: No permits are required. A $3 day-use fee is charged per vehicle.

Maps: Ask the USGS for a topographic map of the Hi Vista area.

Directions: From Lancaster on Highway 14, take the 20th Street exit. Drive north on 20th Street for less than .5 mile, then turn right (east) on Avenue J. Drive 19 miles on Avenue J to 170th Street E. Turn right, drive one mile, and turn left on Avenue K at the sign for the state park campground.

Contact: Saddleback Butte State Park, 17102 East Avenue J, Lancaster, CA 93535; (661) 942-0662.

5 Vasquez Rocks County Park
3.0 mi/1.5 hrs

In case you've started wondering whether there is any "country" left near the city of Los Angeles, the park office at Vasquez Rocks County Park should convince you. It's a barn, complete with hay and horses. After stopping by and picking up a trail map, take a walk on the Foot Trail at the park and get a close-up look at the bizarre tilted rock slabs that have made this place famous. (The park has been used in various TV and movie productions.) The largest rock slabs are nearly 150 feet high, and they are tilted at as much as 50 degrees,

jutting out at various angles toward the sky. The geologic wonders are a result of continuing earth movement along the Elkhorn Fault, which has compressed, folded, and tilted the underlying sandstone rock layers. If you think about it too much, you won't want to stand still in one place for too long. From the parking area, begin hiking on the Foot Trail through the colorful sandstone slabs, then loop back on the Pacific Crest Trail (a dirt road), which returns to the other side of the parking area. If this park interests you, pay a visit to Devils Punchbowl Natural Area, which shows off a more dramatic version of the same geologic action. See the trail notes for the Devils Punchbowl in chapter I5.

Location: In Agua Dulce; map H5, grid i0.

User groups: Hikers, dogs, horses, and mountain bikes. No wheelchair facilities.

Permits: No permits are required. Parking and access are free.

Maps: Free park trail maps are available at the visitor center. Ask the USGS for a topographic map of the Agua Dulce area.

Directions: From the junction of Interstate 5 and Highway 14, drive northeast on Highway 14 for 15 miles to Agua Dulce. Take the Vasquez Rocks/Escondido Canyon exit and drive north on Escondido Canyon Road for 2.2 miles to the park entrance. Continue down the dirt road to the large parking lot and picnic area and begin hiking on the Foot Trail.

Contact: Vasquez Rocks County Park, 10700 W. Escondido Canyon Road, Agua Dulce, CA 91350; tel. (661) 268-0840.

PACIFIC CREST TRAIL (PCT) SECTION OVERVIEW
140.0 mi one way/14.0 days

This section of the Pacific Crest Trail includes stretches from the Mill Creek Picnic Area to San Francisquito Canyon, and from Tehachapi to Walker Pass. (The stretch from San Francisquito Canyon to Tehachapi is covered in chapter H4.) Of the entire 2,700-mile PCT, this is the longest stretch of sustained hiking into a foreboding wasteland. After an initial tromp through Angeles National Forest, past Agua Dulce to Three Points, you face a 45-mile excursion across the high-desert terrain of the Mojave Desert, where 100-degree temperatures are common even in late spring. Some people time their trip here for a full moon and hike at night, wearing a headlamp to be used when necessary. Water is always a critical factor here. Drink as much as possible when at a reliable source and carry as much as possible when hiking.

PCT-13 Mill Creek Picnic Area to Vasquez Rocks

35.0 mi one way/4.0 days

Your destination on this section of the PCT is Vasquez Rocks County Park. Well, at least the ending is good; along the way, there's not much to write home about, though the views from Mount Gleason are a true highlight. First off, after departing Mill Creek Ranger Station, you won't find a reliable water source on the trail for 12 miles, and after that it's another five miles to the next water stop. The highlight of this section is the traverse near the summit of Mount Gleason at 6,502 feet. Fog often settles in the inland valleys, giving the appearance of a pearlescent sea with bald mountaintops protruding like small islands and providing a dramatic view. We once did a live remote television show from this location, during which the host's microphone disconnected and we had to carry the show on our own for several minutes. No problem, eh? What is a problem is leaving this pretty setting, tromping downhill into a dry, once-burned section of brush to Messenger Flats Campground. Try to time your stay here for midweek, when it's quiet and lonely; on weekends this campground can turn into a nightmare scene with loud drunks on a binge. From here it's 5.5 miles to Vasquez Rocks County Park, elevation 2,500

feet, a former hideout of an outlaw and now known for its unique reddish-pink rocks, a geologic wonder. Reaching the rocks requires a significant descent.

Location: From the Mill Creek Picnic Area northwest to the trailhead parking area at Vasquez Rocks; map H5, grid j3.

User groups: Hikers, dogs, and horses. No mountain bikes. No wheelchair facilities.

Permits: A wilderness permit is required for traveling through various wilderness and special-use areas that the trail traverses. Contact the Angeles National Forest, tel. (661) 296-9710, for a permit good for the length of your trip.

Maps: For an overall view of the trail route in this section, send $6 to U.S. Forest Service, Map Sales, P.O. Box 587, Camino, CA 95709; tel. (530) 647-5390 or website: www.r5.fs.fed.us/ visitorcenter. Ask for the Angeles National Forest map. Ask the USGS for topographic maps of the Mount Pacifico, Acton, and Agua Dulce areas. Two BLM surface maps cover the area as well and may be ordered from the Bureau of Land Management office listed below. Send $4 for each map ordered and ask for Tehachapi and Lancaster areas.

Directions: To reach the Mill Creek Picnic Area Trailhead from Highway 14 at Vincent, head south on the Angeles Forest Highway (Road N3) to the Mill Creek Summit and Picnic Area and the signed PCT Trailhead. To reach the Vasquez Rocks Trailhead from San Fernando Valley, drive north on Interstate 5 to the Highway 14 exit. Drive north on Highway 14 to Agua Dulce Canyon Road and exit north. Drive up Agua Dulce Canyon Road to Escondido Canyon Road and the signed park entrance. Part of the PCT runs through the park.

Contact: Angeles National Forest, Saugus Ranger District, 30800 Bouquet Canyon Road, Saugus, CA 91350; tel. (661) 296-9710 or fax (661) 296-5847; Bureau of Land Management, Caliente Resource Area, 3801 Pegasus Drive, Bakersfield, CA 93308; tel. (661) 391-6000 or fax (661) 391-6156.

Vasquez Rocks to San Francisquito Canyon

23.0 mi one way/2.0 days

This 23-mile stretch of the Pacific Crest Trail starts at impressive Vasquez Rocks County Park, above, where you can take a great day hike. But for PCT hikers it's onward you'll go, though it may be difficult to spark the inspiration for the next stretch of trail. The big highlight is the showers that are available in Agua Dulce, about a mile from Vasquez Rocks County Park. To put what awaits in perspective, the trail stretches 55 miles to Three Points, and from there you'll face a 45-mile endurance test across the high Mojave Desert to Tehachapi Pass. On this stretch, after leaving Agua Dulce, you'll march up to a saddle on the Sierra Pelona Ridge, a 2,000-foot climb, where the rewards are great views of Vasquez Rocks and the peaks of Angeles National Forest, dominated by Mount Gleason. The trail then drops more than 2,000 feet to the road in San Francisquito Canyon, where in the process you'll walk the ridge above Bouquet Canyon and view Bouquet Reservoir. Enjoy it; you'll dream of that water in the miles ahead.

Location: From the trailhead parking area at Vasquez Rocks northwest to San Francisquito Canyon Road; map H5, grid i0.

User groups: Hikers, dogs, and horses. No mountain bikes. No wheelchair facilities.

Permits: A wilderness permit is required for traveling through various wilderness and special-use areas the trail traverses. Contact the Angeles National Forest, tel. (661) 296-9710, for a permit good for the length of your trip.

Maps: For an overall view of the trail route in this section, send $6 to U.S. Forest Service, Map Sales, P.O. Box 587, Camino, CA 95709; tel. (530) 647-5390 or website: www.r5.fs.fed.us/visitorcenter. Ask for the Angeles National Forest map. Ask the USGS for topographic maps of the Agua Dulce, Sleepy Valley, Green Valley, and Lake Hughes areas. Two BLM surface maps cover the area as well and may be ordered from the Bureau of Land Management office listed below. Send $4 for each map ordered and ask for Tehachapi and Lancaster areas.

Directions: To reach the Vasquez Rocks Trailhead from San Fernando Valley, drive north on Interstate 5 to the Highway 14 exit. Drive north on Highway 14 to Agua Dulce Canyon Road and exit north. Drive on Agua Dulce Canyon Road to Escondido Canyon Road and the signed park entrance. Part of the PCT runs through the park. To reach the San Francisquito Canyon Trailhead, from Palmdale and Highway 14, drive west on County Road N2/Elizabeth Lake Road to a left turn onto San Francisquito Canyon Road, just before reaching Elizabeth Lake. The trailhead is located near the San Francisquito Ranger Station and the campground.

Contact: Angeles National Forest, Saugus Ranger District, 30800 Bouquet Canyon Road, Saugus, CA 91350; tel. (661) 296-9710 or fax (661) 296-5847; Bureau of Land Management, Caliente Resource Area, 3801 Pegasus Drive, Bakersfield, CA 93308; tel. (661) 391-6000 or fax (661) 391-6156.

PCT-17 Tehachapi to Jawbone Canyon Road

41.0 mi one way/4.0 days

PCT hikers in the midst of this scourge of a hike are acting on faith alone that somehow it will get better. Well, it doesn't, at least not for another 40 miles. The landscape is pig-ugly desert as you hike north from Tehachapi Pass, with water scarce and nobody else around. But again, remember that faith, because the first pine forest in weeks awaits relatively soon. In the meantime, the hike resembles a death march, especially if you hit it in a terrible hot spell. The positives are unobstructed views (unobstructed because there are hardly any trees anywhere) providing long-distance looks at distant ridgelines. The best view is from Cache Peak, elevation 6,698 feet, the highest mountaintop in the region, from which you can see Mount Whitney looming to the north. The trail laterals about 600 feet beneath Cache Peak; then it's 20 miles to Jawbone Canyon, with one water stop on the way at Golden Oaks Spring.

Location: From the trailhead parking area at Tehachapi northeast to Jawbone Canyon Road; map H5, grid c1.

User groups: Hikers, dogs, and horses. No mountain bikes. No wheelchair facilities.

Permits: A wilderness permit is required for traveling through various wilderness and special-use areas the trail traverses. Contact the Sequoia National Forest, tel. (760) 379-5646, for a permit good for the length of your trip.

Maps: For an overall view of the trail route in this section, send $6 to U.S. Forest Service, Map Sales, P.O. Box 587, Camino, CA 95709; tel. (530) 647-5390 or website: www.r5.fs.fed.us/visitorcenter. Ask for the Sequoia National Forest map. Ask the USGS for topographic maps of the Tehachapi South, Monolith, Tehachapi Northeast, Cache Peak, Cross Mountain, Pinon Mountain, Claraville, and Emerald Mountain areas. A BLM surface map covers the area as well and may be ordered from the Bureau of Land Management office listed below. Send $4 and ask for the Tehachapi area.

Directions: To reach the Tehachapi/Willow Springs Road Trailhead from Mojave and Highway 14, head west on Oak Creek Road to the intersection with Tehachapi/Willow Springs Road/Cameron Road. The trailhead is located near the intersection. To reach the Jawbone Canyon Road Trailhead from Highways 58/14, head north on Highway 14, past California City Boulevard to Jawbone Canyon Road. Turn left onto Jawbone Canyon Road and drive past Kelso Valley Road. Continue driving on Jawbone Canyon Road for approximately eight miles, up a series of switchbacks to the signed Pacific Crest Trail crossing and parking area.

Contact: Sequoia National Forest, Greenhorn Ranger District, Lake Isabella Visitor Center, P.O. Box 3810, Lake Isabella, CA 93240; tel.

(760) 379-5646 or fax (760) 379-8597; Bureau of Land Management, Caliente Resource Area, 3801 Pegasus Drive, Bakersfield, CA 93308; tel. (661) 391-6000 or fax (661) 391-6156.

PCT-18 Jawbone Canyon Road to Walker Pass

41.0 mi one way/4.0 days

The mind-numbing walk continues here through high desert, surrounded by low scrub and cactus and whatever thoughts you can conjure to relieve you from the present. The one redemption is knowing that the southern Sierra awaits, with Mount Whitney just a little more than 100 miles distant. This section of trail starts by crossing desert foothill-like terrain, set at about the 6,500-foot level, with Joshua trees occasionally sprinkled along the way. This is a desolate patch of life, with no shade anywhere. Another common problem here is gale-force winds out of the east, quite possible if a storm (and low barometric pressure) moves into northern Arizona and New Mexico while high barometric pressure dominates the Southern California coastal areas. The difference in barometric pressure causes horrendous winds out of the east, and it happens at least once every spring. After 30 miles of desert to Bird Spring Pass, elevation 5,355 feet, good things finally start to happen. You rise past the border of Sequoia National Forest, then shortly later, into the Kiavah Wilderness. The landscape is still desert, but after rising to nearly 7,000 feet, you start to see signs of forest, though interspersed with stretches of buckbrush. The trail rises again to nearly 7,000 feet, then descends to Walker Pass, 5,246 feet, where the Forest Service has constructed a trail for the express use of PCT hikers. Congratulations, better times are ahead.

Location: From Jawbone Canyon Road to Walker Pass; map H5, grid d6.

User groups: Hikers, dogs, and horses. No mountain bikes. No wheelchair facilities.

Permits: A wilderness permit is required for

traveling through various wilderness and special-use areas the trail traverses. Contact the Sequoia National Forest, tel. (760) 379-5646, for a permit good for the length of your trip.

Maps: For an overall view of the trail route in this section, send $6 to U.S. Forest Service, Map Sales, P.O. Box 587, Camino, CA 95709; tel. (530) 647-5390 or website: www.r5.fs.fed.us/visitorcenter. Ask for the Sequoia National Forest map. Ask the USGS for topographic maps of the Claraville, Pinon Mountain, Cane Canyon, Horse Canyon, and Walker Pass areas.

Directions: To reach the Jawbone Canyon Road Trailhead from Highways 58/14, head north on Highway 14, past California City Boulevard and to Jawbone Canyon Road. Turn left onto Jawbone Canyon Road and drive past Kelso Valley Road. Continue driving on Jawbone Canyon Road for approximately eight miles, up a series of switchbacks to the signed Pacific Crest Trail crossing and parking area. To reach the Walker Pass Trailhead from Highway 14, turn west onto Highway 178 and drive to the Walker Pass Trailhead Campground, built especially for Pacific Crest Trail hikers. The trailhead begins at the east end of the campground.

Contact: Sequoia National Forest, Cannell Meadow Ranger District, P.O. Box 9, Kernville, CA 93238; tel. (760) 376-3781 or fax (760) 376-3795.

PCT Continuation

To continue hiking along the Pacific Crest Trail, see chapters H4 and G5.

ANN MARIE BROWN

CHAPTER H6

Colorful (trust us) Owl Canyon
lies just north of Barstow.

MAP H6

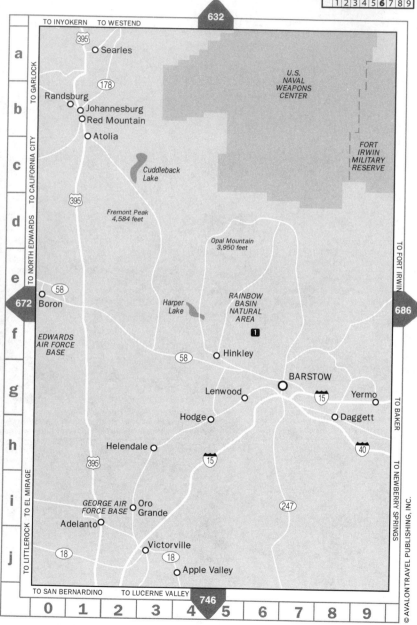

CHAPTER H6

1 Owl Canyon/
   Rainbow Basin 683

1 Owl Canyon/ Rainbow Basin
4.0 mi/2.0 hrs

You just never know what kind of good stuff you'll find when you travel around the state, and that's certainly true when you reach the Rainbow Basin area north of Barstow. From the BLM's Owl Canyon Campground, you can take a four-mile round-trip hike into some colorful desert country. The well-named Rainbow Basin is made from a cornucopia of colorful sediments—deposits that were formed in lake beds 20 million years ago. The most colorful areas can be seen by taking an auto tour around the basin, but before or after you do so, you should take this hike in Owl Canyon.

The trail begins at Owl Canyon Campground in an ordinary looking dirt-and-gravel wash. Within minutes the canyon walls get narrower and rockier, and various colorful sediments begin to show themselves in the rock. There's so much to look at and photograph, and so many boulders and obstacles to climb over and around, you won't be moving very fast. At .6 mile, look for a cave entrance on your right.

If you have a flashlight, you can tunnel through it and enter a small side canyon. If you keep traveling in the main canyon, you can hike a total of two miles out. The trail ends near the base of Velvet Peak (a granite ridge), in a colorful rock bowl.

Location: Northwest of Barstow; map H6, grid f6.

User groups: Hikers and dogs. No horses or mountain bikes. No wheelchair facilities.

Permits: No permits are required. Parking and access are free.

Maps: Ask the USGS for a topographic map of the Mud Hills area.

Directions: From Interstate 15 at Barstow, take the Barstow Road exit and drive north .8 mile. Turn left on Main Street, drive .2 mile, then turn right on First Avenue. Drive one mile and you will cross over two bridges; just after the second bridge is Irwin Road. Turn left on Irwin Road and drive 5.6 miles. Turn left on Fossil Beds Road (a gravel road) and drive 2.9 miles to the access road for Owl Canyon Campground. Turn right, drive .3 mile, then turn right again and drive 1.6 miles to the family campground (go past the group camp). The trail begins by campsite 11.

Contact: Bureau of Land Management, Barstow Resource Area, 2601 Barstow Road, Barstow, CA 92311; tel. (760) 252-6000.

CHAPTER H7

BEAVERTAIL CACTI
IN THE WESTERN MOJAVE

MAP H7

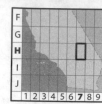

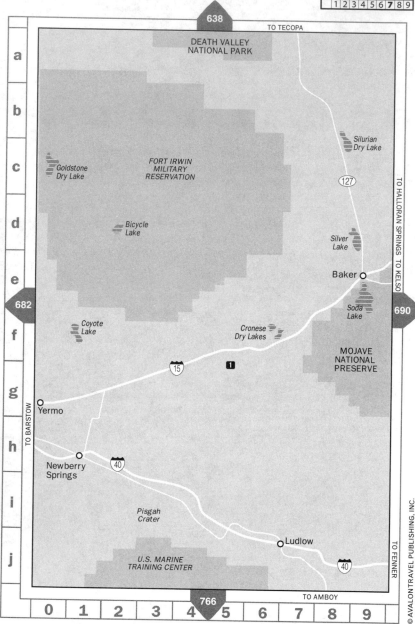

638

TO TECOPA

DEATH VALLEY
NATIONAL PARK

Silurian
Dry Lake

Goldstone
Dry Lake

FORT IRWIN
MILITARY
RESERVATION

127

TO HALLORAN SPRINGS   TO KELSO

Bicycle
Lake

Silver
Lake

Baker

682

690

Coyote
Lake

Soda
Lake

Cronese
Dry Lakes

MOJAVE
NATIONAL
PRESERVE

15

1

Yermo

TO BARSTOW

Newberry
Springs

40

Pisgah
Crater

Ludlow

TO FENNER

U.S. MARINE
TRAINING CENTER

40

766

TO AMBOY

0 1 2 3 4 5 6 7 8 9

a b c d e f g h i j

© AVALON TRAVEL PUBLISHING, INC.

CHAPTER H7

1 Afton Canyon. 687

1 Afton Canyon
3.0 mi/1.5 hrs

They call Afton Canyon "the Grand Canyon of the Mojave," and although its proportions may be smaller than the other Grand Canyon, Afton is no slacker in terms of desert drama. Sheer walls of pink and red rock rise straight up 300 feet above the Mojave River, where a thin strip of water flows almost year-round. From the campground follow the trail east along the river, amid a surprising amount of foliage considering this is the desert. Saltcedar trees thrive along the stream, as well as planted cottonwoods and willows, creating a protective habitat for birds and other wildlife. As you travel farther, the canyon gets more interesting. Its walls tower above you, beautifully carved and sculpted by the Mojave River in the days when it was a much bigger waterway—probably 50,000 years ago. Hike as far as you like into the canyon, then turn around and head back. A good side trip is a visit to Pyramid Canyon, one of Afton's side canyons. Start from the campground and cross the river under the first set of railroad trestles, then head south into Pyramid Canyon. The walls slowly narrow until it becomes a classic slot canyon. In the first .25 mile you can see why they call it "Pyramid Canyon."
Location: East of Barstow; map H7, grid g5.
User groups: Hikers, dogs, horses, and mountain bikes. No wheelchair facilities.
Permits: No permits are required. Parking and access are free.
Maps: Ask the USGS for topographic maps of the Cave Mountain and Dunn areas.
Directions: From Barstow drive 36 miles east on Interstate 15 and take the Afton Road exit. Drive 3.5 miles southwest to Afton Campground (the dirt road is well graded). Park near the railroad trestles.
Contact: Bureau of Land Management, Barstow Resource Area, 2601 Barstow Road, Barstow, CA 92311; tel. (760) 252-6000.

THE VIEW FROM
CRYSTAL SPRINGS TRAIL

MAP H8

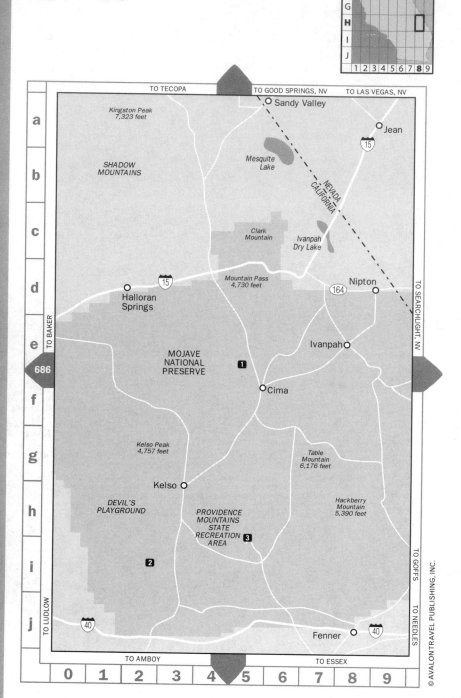

TO TECOPA · TO GOOD SPRINGS, NV · TO LAS VEGAS, NV

Sandy Valley

Jean

15

Kingston Peak
7,323 feet

SHADOW
MOUNTAINS

Mesquite
Lake

NEVADA
CALIFORNIA

Clark
Mountain

Ivanpah
Dry Lake

Mountain Pass
4,730 feet

15

Nipton

164

Halloran
Springs

TO SEARCHLIGHT, NV

TO BAKER

MOJAVE
NATIONAL
PRESERVE

Ivanpah

1

Cima

Kelso Peak
4,757 feet

Table
Mountain
6,176 feet

Kelso

DEVIL'S
PLAYGROUND

PROVIDENCE
MOUNTAINS
STATE
RECREATION
AREA

Hackberry
Mountain
5,390 feet

3

2

TO GOFFS

TO NEEDLES

TO LUDLOW

40

40

Fenner

TO AMBOY · TO ESSEX

© AVALONTRAVEL PUBLISHING, INC.

CHAPTER H8

1 Teutonia Peak. 691

2 Kelso Dunes 691

3 Crystal Springs Trail . . . 692

Maps: Maps of Mojave National Preserve are available for a fee at the park visitor center, or from Tom Harrison Cartography, tel. (415) 456-7940, or Trails Illustrated, tel. (800) 962-1643. Ask the USGS for a topographic map of the Cima Dome area.

Directions: From Barstow take Interstate 15 east for approximately 85 miles to Cima Road. (Cima Road is about 25 miles east of Baker, near the town of Valley Wells on Interstate 15.) Turn right (south) on Cima Road and drive 11 miles to the sign for the trailhead, on the right side of the road.

Contact: Mojave National Preserve, P.O. Box 241, Baker, CA 92309; tel. (760) 733-4040 or fax (760) 733-4027.

1 Teutonia Peak

4.0 mi/2.0 hrs

Teutonia Peak on Cima Dome is the perfect summit for geometry enthusiasts. Cima Dome's big claim to fame is that it's the most symmetrical dome of its type in the United States. It rises 1,500 feet above the surrounding landscape, and it's almost 70 miles square. In fact, the dome is so massive that when you're on top of it, you can't see it.

However, when you're on top of Teutonia Peak, you definitely know you're on it. The peak is at 5,755 feet, and you hike to it via a two-mile trail that leads uphill to head-swiveling desert vistas. The first mile of trail is flat and pleasant, leading through cacti, piñon pines, Joshua trees, and cattle grazing lands. Some of the Joshua trees are as tall as 25 feet. (They're a different variety from the kind found in Joshua Tree National Park.) You can clearly see your destination, Teutonia Peak, as well as the rugged-looking New York Mountains in the distance. At 1.5 miles you start your ascent up the peak. At 1.9 miles you reach a saddle just shy of Teutonia's summit, where you have panoramic desert views. Scramble the last short stretch to reach the summit and catch your breath, enjoying the far-reaching vistas. In winter you might not stay long, because the wind can howl up here. As you look around, chew on this: the flatlands below are all a part of massive Cima Dome.

Location: In the Mojave National Preserve east of Barstow; map H8, grid e5.

User groups: Hikers, dogs, and horses. No mountain bikes. No wheelchair facilities.

Permits: No permits are required. Parking and access are free.

2 Kelso Dunes

3.0 mi/1.5 hrs

What's the most popular place in Mojave National Preserve to watch the sun set? Unquestionably it's Kelso Dunes. Kelso Dunes are the second highest sand dunes in California. (Eureka Dunes in Death Valley are the highest.) The dune complex is 50 miles square, and the dunes reach a height of 500 feet. In a wet spring, desert wildflowers bloom on and around the dunes, adding brighter colors to the gold and pink sand.

Read the interesting interpretive signs at the Kelso Dunes Trailhead, walk a short distance on the old jeep road, and head any which way toward the closest dunes, which are plainly visible. Constantly moving sand makes a formal trail impossible. If you climb high enough in the sand, you are rewarded with views of the surrounding desert, including the Granite and Providence Mountains. Many people don't bother to climb to the top, though. They just plop themselves down and make sand angels or roll around on the dunes' silky surface. Another popular activity is trying to cause small sand avalanches that sometimes produce harmonic booming sounds. For this to occur, the sand must be extremely dry. Some desert lovers swear by the healing power of these vibrating noises.

Location: In the Mojave National Preserve southeast of Barstow; map H8, grid i2.

User groups: Hikers and dogs. No horses or mountain bikes. No wheelchair facilities.

Permits: No permits are required. Parking and access are free.

Maps: Maps of Mojave National Preserve are available for a fee at the park visitor center or from Tom Harrison Cartography, tel. (415) 456-7940, or Trails Illustrated, tel. (800) 962-1643. Ask the USGS for a topographic map of the Kelso Dunes area.

Directions: From Barstow take Interstate 15 east for approximately 60 miles to Baker, then turn south on Kelbaker Road and drive 42 miles, past Kelso, to the signed road on the right for Kelso Dunes. Turn right (west) and drive three miles to the dunes parking area. If you are coming from the south on Interstate 40, take the Kelso/Amboy exit and drive 14 miles north on Kelbaker Road to the signed road on the left for Kelso Dunes.

Contact: Mojave National Preserve, P.O. Box 241, Baker, CA 92309; tel. (760) 733-4040 or fax (760) 733-4027.

❸ Crystal Springs Trail
2.0 mi/1.0 hr

The big draw at Providence Mountains State Recreation Area is touring Mitchell Caverns with a park ranger, so a lot of people miss out on the excellent do-it-yourself hiking trails in the area. Crystal Springs Trail is the best of those, leading from the visitor center uphill to a rocky overlook in the Providence Mountains. Trailhead elevation is 4,300 feet. The trail is moderately steep and feels surprisingly remote, compared to the parking lot full of people waiting to tour the caverns. You hike upward through Crystal Canyon, where bighorn sheep are sometimes seen by lucky hikers.

Rocky outcrops shoot up from both sides of the trail. You'll witness a remarkable variety of high desert foliage: piñon pines, junipers, and prickly plants galore—chollas, barrel cactus, catclaw, cliff rose, and the like. As you climb, keep turning around to check out the increasingly widening vistas. The trail ends near Crystal Springs, where you get a fine view of the surrounding desert and mountains. Then just turn around and head back downhill.

A good side trip is to add a jaunt in the opposite direction from the visitor center. Follow the Niña Mora Overlook Trail from the park campground for .25 mile to an overlook of the Marble Mountains and Clipper Valley. And, of course, if you've driven all the way out here, you should sign up for a tour of Mitchell Caverns. The limestone caverns with their stalagmites, stalactites, and helictites are fascinating to see. Tours are held at 1:30 p.m. daily from September through May, and more frequently on weekends. In summer, tours are offered only on weekends.

Location: In the Providence Mountains State Recreation Area southeast of Barstow; map H8, grid i5.

User groups: Hikers only. No dogs, horses, or mountain bikes. No wheelchair facilities.

Permits: No permits are required. A $3 day-use fee is charged per vehicle. In addition, a $6 fee is charged per adult for a tour of the park's caverns.

Maps: A park map is available for $1 at the visitor center. Ask the USGS for a topographic map of the Fountain Peak area.

Directions: From Barstow take Interstate 40 east for approximately 90 miles to the exit for Essex Road, Mitchell Caverns, and Providence Mountains State Recreation Area near the town of Essex. Turn north on Essex Road and drive 15.5 miles to the Providence Mountains visitor center.

Contact: Providence Mountains State Recreation Area, P.O. Box 1, Essex, CA 92332; tel. (760) 928-2586 or (661) 942-0662.

SOUTHERN CALIFORNIA
CHAPTER 12

ANN MARIE BROWN

SAN MIGUEL ISLAND IS WHERE YOU'LL DISCOVER THE
CALICHE FOREST, CALCIUM CARBONATE SAND
CASTINGS OF DEAD PLANT ROOTS AND TRUNKS.

MAP 12

One inch equals approximately 11 miles.

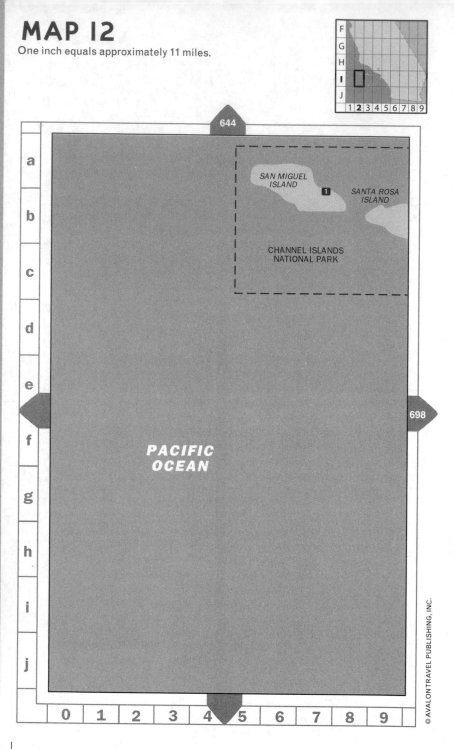

644

698

SAN MIGUEL
ISLAND

SANTA ROSA
ISLAND

CHANNEL ISLANDS
NATIONAL PARK

PACIFIC
OCEAN

© AVALON TRAVEL PUBLISHING, INC.

CHAPTER 12

1 Caliche Forest and
Point Bennett 695

1 Caliche Forest and Point Bennett

15.0 mi/2.0 days

When some people find out there's an easy way and a hard way to do something, they immediately choose the hard way. If you're in that camp, you'll choose San Miguel Island as the Channel Island you want to visit, instead of Anacapa, Santa Cruz, or any of the other islands. San Miguel is the farthest island from the mainland, requiring a much-dreaded five-hour boat ride from Ventura, or a slightly shorter four-hour boat ride from Santa Barbara. Once you finally get to San Miguel, you'll want to stay there for a couple days. To add to the challenge, strong winds and fog are nearly constant on the island, so you must plan accordingly for both hiking and camping. Of course, if you're willing, your reward is having a spectacular island practically all to yourself. No more than 30 campers are allowed on San Miguel Island at one time, and rarely do that many people show up.

From Cuyler Harbor, where you are dropped off, you hike eastward along the beach for .5 mile, then follow the path another .5 mile up Nidever Canyon. It's a steep stretch, especially if you're carrying a lot of camping gear. When you reach the ridge at the top, you can take a short spur to see a stone monument to Juan Rodriguez Cabrillo, who claimed this island for the Spaniards in 1542, and may or may not be buried here—nobody's sure. The trail continues to the campground, and then to the remains of the Lester Ranch. The Lester family lived on the island for 12 years and grazed sheep here.

Outside of the Cuyler Harbor/Lester Ranch area, you may hike only in the company of a ranger, in order to protect the island's fragile resources. If you do so, you'll find that the main wildlife on and around San Miguel Island are pinnipeds, or seals and sea lions. Up to six different species and more than 30,000 individuals can be seen at certain times of the year at Point Bennett, a 14-mile round-trip hike from the campground. An interesting feature along the way is the Caliche Forest, where the calcium carbonate sand castings of dead plant roots and trunks stand like frozen statues. They're a bit like the tufa spires at Mono Lake. Seeing the Caliche Forest requires only a seven-mile round-trip.

Special note: Truth Aquatics at Sea Landing occasionally runs day trips to San Miguel Island for those who do not wish to camp. This requires leaving Santa Barbara at 3 a.m., arriving at San Miguel Island around 7 a.m., and departing again at 1 p.m. With this schedule, day-hikers are usually led to the Caliche Forest and back with a naturalist or ranger. You can sleep on the boat the night before your 3 p.m. departure.

Location: On San Miguel Island in Channel Islands National Park; map I2, grid b7.

User groups: Hikers only. No dogs, horses, or mountain bikes. No wheelchair facilities.

Permits: A camping permit is required and can be obtained by phoning (800) 365-CAMP (800-365-2267). The camping reservation fee is $2.50. A fee is charged for boat transportation to the island. Phone the concessionaires at the numbers below for rates and departure information. The current cost is $90 per person for an overnight trip, or $75 per person for a one-day trip.

Maps: A free map of Channel Islands National Park is available from park headquarters at the address below. A more detailed map is available for a fee from Trails Illustrated, tel. (800) 962-1643. Ask the USGS for topographic maps of the San Miguel Island East and the San Miguel Island West areas.

Directions: Island Packers provides boat transportation to San Miguel Island from Ventura Harbor. Truth Aquatics at Sea Landing provides boat transportation to San Miguel Island from Santa Barbara Harbor. Reservations are required and should be obtained before you get your camping permit. Phone Island Packers, tel. (805) 642-7688 or (805) 642-1393; or Truth Aquatics at Sea Landing, tel. (805) 963-3564.

Contact: Channel Islands National Park, 1901 Spinnaker Drive, Ventura, CA 93001; tel. (805) 658-5700 or (805) 658-5730.

ANNMARIE BROWN

INSPIRATION POINT ON ANACAPA ISLAND

MAP 13

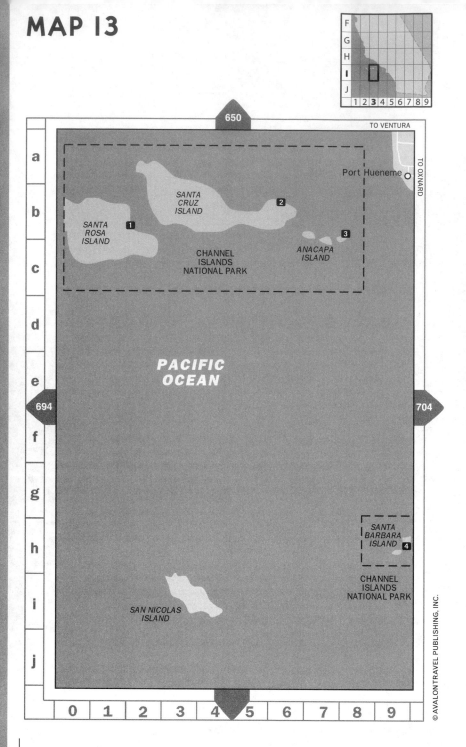

TO VENTURA

TO OXNARD

Port Hueneme

1

SANTA
ROSA
ISLAND

SANTA
CRUZ
ISLAND

2

3

ANACAPA
ISLAND

CHANNEL
ISLANDS
NATIONAL PARK

**PACIFIC
OCEAN**

650

694

704

SANTA
BARBARA
ISLAND

4

CHANNEL
ISLANDS
NATIONAL PARK

SAN NICOLAS
ISLAND

© AVALON TRAVEL PUBLISHING, INC.

CHAPTER 13

■ Torrey Pines Trail 699
■ Potato Harbor Trail 700
■ East Anacapa Island
   Loop Trail 700
■ Signal Peak Loop Trail. . . 701

■ Torrey Pines Trail

5.0 mi/2.5 hrs

One of the many charms of Santa Rosa Island is that you can fly there in about 20 minutes in a small plane instead of taking the four-hour boat ride from Ventura or Santa Barbara. The National Park Service has allowed one airplane concessionaire in addition to the two boat concessionaires, and this is the island where the plane lands. For people prone to seasickness, this makes Santa Rosa Island the Channel Island of choice. Another of the island's charms is its stand of Torrey pines— yes, the same conifers you see at Torrey Pines State Reserve in San Diego. These are the only two places in the world where those slow-growing, windswept pines are found. To see them from the boat pier or the landing strip, follow the main dirt road to the southeast, paralleling the shore. Near the far (southern) end of the landing strip on the inland side, you'll see a gate and a road that leads uphill to Water Canyon Campground. Pass this gate and continue to the next junction of roads, where you can choose to hike up above the Torrey pines or down below. You can make a loop and circle around the grove if you like, or just take the lower road to stay along the coast and avoid any further climbing. The higher you go, of course, the more outstanding the coastal views.

Note that what may be the best hike on Santa Rosa Island is in Lobos Canyon on the north side of the island. Rangers will occa-sionally drive visitors to this remote area and lead a five-mile hike through the canyon. Lobos Canyon is the only place on 84-square-mile Santa Rosa Island that harbors large quantities of native vegetation. During the island's long ranching history, stock animals were unable to access the steep canyon, and so the native vegetation survived. Other Lobos Canyon highlights include a Chumash village site and beautifully carved sandstone canyon walls.

Location: On Santa Rosa Island in Channel Islands National Park; map I3, grid b2.

User groups: Hikers only. No dogs, horses, or mountain bikes. No wheelchair facilities.

Permits: No permits are required for day hiking. A fee is charged for transportation to the island. Phone the concessionaires at the numbers below for rates and departure information. The current cost for boat travel is approximately $62 per person for a day trip or $80 per person for an overnight trip. The current cost for air travel is $85 per person for a day trip or $150 per person for an overnight trip. If you choose to stay overnight, you must get a camping permit; tel. (800) 365-CAMP (800-365-2267).

Maps: A free map of Channel Islands National Park is available from park headquarters at the address below. A more detailed map is available for a fee from Trails Illustrated, tel. (800) 962-1643. Ask the USGS for a topographic map of Santa Rosa Island North and East.

Directions: Island Packers provides boat transportation to Santa Rosa Island from Ventura Harbor. Reservations are required. Phone Island Packers at (805) 642-7688 or (805) 642-1393 for information and reservations. Truth Aquatics at Sea Landing provides boat transportation to Santa Rosa Island from Santa Barbara Harbor. Phone Truth Aquatics at Sea Landing at (805) 963-3564. Channel Islands Aviation provides air trans-

portation to Santa Rosa Island from Camarillo Airport. Phone Channel Islands Aviation at (805) 987-1301.

Contact: Channel Islands National Park, 1901 Spinnaker Drive, Ventura, CA 93001; tel. (805) 658-5700 or (805) 658-5730.

2 Potato Harbor Trail
4.4 mi/2.5 hrs

Only the very eastern tip of huge Santa Cruz Island belongs to the National Park Service; the other 90 percent of the island is managed by the Nature Conservancy. Although it's possible to visit the Nature Conservancy side of the island (phone the boat concessionaires listed above for information), you may hike on its land only with a guide. If you prefer to wander on your own or if you want to camp overnight on the island, you should visit the eastern, national park side of Santa Cruz Island. The boat ride is short enough to make this a day trip, or if you prefer a longer stay, the park service runs a campground in Scorpion Canyon. The trail to Potato Harbor begins in the campground, which is .5 mile beyond Scorpion Anchorage, where the boat drops you off. Head back into the upper end of the campground (passing the ranch and the first set of campsites) until you see a road veering off to the right, climbing above the canyon. Like almost all of the trails on eastern Santa Cruz Island, this trail is a wide dirt road, best hiked before the end of summer when it can be dry and dusty. The road climbs steeply for .5 mile, then goes mostly flat, continuing along the bluff tops almost straight west, paralleling the mainland coast. Far ahead you can see a long series of hills and canyons that eventually fade out of view in the haze, and it's easy to assume that these belong to one of the neighboring Channel Islands. Wrong—they are more of the immense bulk of this island, the largest in the chain at 96 square miles. At two miles out the trail curves to the southwest, following the line of a fence at the bluff's edge. Look for a spur trail that leads to the edge and follow it to the obvious view of Potato Harbor—a potato-shaped cove lined with rugged cliffs and filled with deep, clear water.

If you're camping on the island and have more time than the day-trippers, make sure you take the seven-mile round-trip hike to Smuggler's Cove, where there is a lovely beach. A stand of eucalyptus provides a shady picnic area at the edge of the sand.

Location: On east Santa Cruz Island in Channel Islands National Park; map I3, grid b6.

User groups: Hikers only. No dogs, horses, or mountain bikes. No wheelchair facilities.

Permits: No permits are required for day hiking. A fee is charged for boat transportation to the island. Phone the concessionaires at the numbers below for rates and departure information. The current cost is approximately $42 per person for a day trip, or $54 per person for an overnight trip. If you choose to stay overnight, you must get a camping permit; tel. (800) 365-CAMP (800-365-2267).

Maps: A free map of Channel Islands National Park is available from park headquarters at the address below. A more detailed map is available for a fee from Trails Illustrated, tel. (800) 962-1643. Ask the USGS for topographic maps of Santa Cruz Island C and D.

Directions: Island Packers provides boat transportation to Santa Cruz Island from Ventura Harbor. Reservations are required. Phone Island Packers at (805) 642-7688 or (805) 642-1393 for information and reservations. Truth Aquatics at Sea Landing provides boat transportation to Santa Cruz Island from Santa Barbara Harbor. Phone Truth Aquatics at Sea Landing at (805) 963-3564.

Contact: Channel Islands National Park, 1901 Spinnaker Drive, Ventura, CA 93001; tel. (805) 658-5700 or (805) 658-5730.

3 East Anacapa Island Loop Trail
2.0 mi/1.0 hr

Of all the Channel Islands to choose from, why

do more people go to Anacapa Island than any other? Because it's easy. It's the closest island to the mainland at only 12 miles from Port Hueneme, which means that the boat ride doesn't take forever—only about an hour and a half. As you cruise, you're likely to be entertained by dolphins, sea lions, and sometimes even flying fish. The island is actually three tiny islets, and the boat drops you off on the easternmost of the three. If you're feeling the slightest bit seasick, you'll quickly get over it when the boat pulls away and your first task is to climb up the 154 metal stair steps that cling to the island's cliffs. You'll get plenty of fresh air as you make your way to the island's visitor center, pick up some interpretive information, and set out on this trail, which tours the entire one-square-mile island. The trail's main highlights are two overlooks, at Inspiration Point and Cathedral Cove, where you can look down on seals and sea lions on the rocks below. From Inspiration Point you can also gaze at the smaller Anacapa islets and huge Santa Cruz Island beyond them. Bring your binoculars: there are millions of opportunities for bird-watching, especially brown pelicans and seagulls. Where you can see over the edge of the rocky cliffs, you'll spot some of the island's 130 sea caves, which make for great kayaking adventures.

Spring wildflowers are superb on Anacapa, including the giant coreopsis, which reportedly blooms so bright that it can sometimes be seen from the mainland. Note that beaches on East Anacapa are not accessible because the sea cliffs are hundreds of feet high, but on calm summer days you can swim at the landing cove. Bring your snorkeling gear so you can look eye-to-eye with the garibaldis and giant sea kelp.

Even though the island is small and its one hiking trail is short, this rates as one of the greatest day trips possible in California. Don't miss it.

Location: On Anacapa Island in Channel Islands National Park; map I3, grid b7.

User groups: Hikers only. No dogs, horses, or mountain bikes. No wheelchair facilities.

Permits: No permits are required for day hiking. A fee is charged for boat transportation to the island. Phone the concessionaires at the numbers below for rates and departure information. The current cost is $37 per person for a day trip, or $48 per person for an overnight trip. If you choose to stay overnight, you must get a camping permit; tel. (800) 365-CAMP (800-365-2267).

Maps: A free map of Channel Islands National Park is available from park headquarters at the address below. A more detailed map is available for a fee from Trails Illustrated, tel. (800) 962-1643. Ask the USGS for a topographic map of Anacapa Island.

Directions: Island Packers provides boat transportation to Anacapa Island from Ventura Harbor and Oxnard (Channel Island Harbor). Reservations are required. Phone Island Packers at (805) 642-7688 or (805) 642-1393 for information and reservations. Truth Aquatics at Sea Landing occasionally provides boat transportation to Anacapa Island from Santa Barbara Harbor, although the boat trip is shorter from Ventura. Phone Truth Aquatics at Sea Landing at (805) 963-3564.

Contact: Channel Islands National Park, 1901 Spinnaker Drive, Ventura, CA 93001; tel. (805) 658-5700 or (805) 658-5730.

4 Signal Peak Loop Trail
3.3 mi/1.5 hrs

Santa Barbara Island is the loneliest island in Channel Islands National Park. Located far to the south, it is geographically isolated from the other four islands that make up the national park, being closer in latitude to San Pedro than to Santa Barbara or Ventura. (But it's much farther out to sea than developed Catalina Island, which is its closest neighbor.) Getting to Santa Barbara Island requires a four-hour boat ride from Ventura, and the boat concessionaire runs only about a dozen trips to the island each year—

much less frequently than to the other islands. And Santa Barbara Island is tiny; it's the smallest of the Channel Islands at only one square mile. Similar to Anacapa Island in both its size and barren landscape, Santa Barbara Island has 5.5 miles of hiking trails, all of which are worth exploring. One of the best is the Signal Peak Trail, which makes a loop over much of the south half of the island, from the landing cove to Signal Peak, the highest point on the island at 634 feet. A great feature of this trail is its fine views of Sutil Island, an even smaller island that lies .25 mile southwest of Santa Barbara Island. (Sutil Island is an important seabird rookery; bird-watching is first-rate all over Santa Barbara Island.) The trail begins by heading inland from the landing cove. Take the left fork .5 mile out to head south and curve around the southern end of the island to Signal Peak on the southwest edge. From the peak you loop back through the center of the island over gently rolling grasslands.

If you're wondering what season to visit Santa Barbara Island, keep this in mind: as on Anacapa Island, the giant coreopsis blooms its huge yellow flowers here from late March to May.

Location: On Santa Barbara Island in Channel Islands National Park; map I3, grid h9.

User groups: Hikers only. No dogs, horses, or mountain bikes. No wheelchair facilities.

Permits: No permits are required for day hiking. A fee is charged for boat transportation to the island. Phone the boat concessionaire at the number below for rates and departure information. The current cost is approximately $49 per person for a day trip or $75 per person for an overnight trip. (If you choose to stay overnight, you must get a camping permit; tel. (800) 365-CAMP (800-365-2267).

Maps: A free map of Channel Islands National Park is available from park headquarters at the address below. A more detailed map is available for a fee from Trails Illustrated, tel. (800) 962-1643. Ask the USGS for a topographic map of Santa Barbara Island.

Directions: Island Packers provides boat transportation to Santa Barbara Island from Ventura Harbor. Reservations are required. Phone Island Packers at (805) 642-7688 or (805) 642-1393 for information and reservations.

Contact: Channel Islands National Park, 1901 Spinnaker Drive, Ventura, CA 93001; tel. (805) 658-5700 or (805) 658-5730.

SCENIC MALIBU CREEK IN—BELIEVE IT OR NOT—
GREATER LOS ANGELES

ANN MARIE BROWN

CHAPTER 14

MAP 14

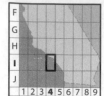

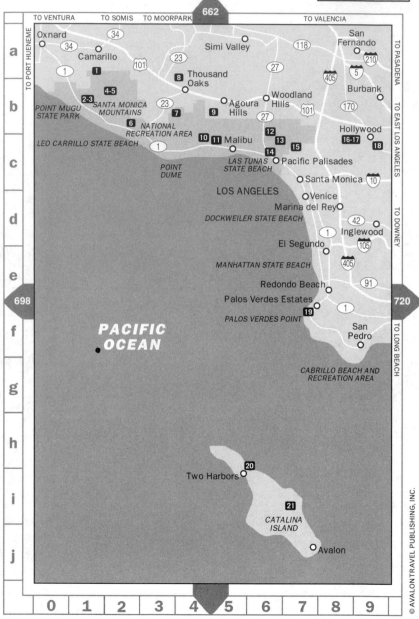

TO VENTURA   TO SOMIS   TO MOORPARK   **662**   TO VALENCIA

a
Oxnard
TO PORT HUENEME
34
Camarillo
34
Simi Valley
118
San Fernando
TO PASADENA
101
1
1
23
27
210
8 Thousand Oaks
405
5

b
POINT MUGU STATE PARK
4-5
2-3 SANTA MONICA MOUNTAINS
23
7
9 Agoura Hills
Woodland Hills
27
101
170
Burbank
TO EAST LOS ANGELES

6 NATIONAL RECREATION AREA
LEO CARRILLO STATE BEACH
1
10 **11** Malibu
12
13 **15**
14
Hollywood
16-17 **18**

c
POINT DUME
LAS TUNAS STATE BEACH
Pacific Palisades
Santa Monica
10

LOS ANGELES
Venice
Marina del Rey

d
DOCKWEILER STATE BEACH
El Segundo
1 Inglewood
42
105
405

e
MANHATTAN STATE BEACH
Redondo Beach
91
698
720
Palos Verdes Estates
1
PALOS VERDES POINT
19

f
PACIFIC OCEAN
San Pedro
TO LONG BEACH

g
CABRILLO BEACH AND RECREATION AREA

h

i
Two Harbors
20
21
CATALINA ISLAND

j
Avalon

0 1 2 3 4 5 6 7 8 9

© AVALON TRAVEL PUBLISHING, INC.

CHAPTER 14

1 Satwiwa Loop Trail and
   Waterfall. 705
2 La Jolla Valley Loop 706
3 Big Sycamore
   Canyon Loop 707
4 Grotto Trail 707
5 Mishe Mokwa and
   Backbone Loop 708
6 Nicholas Flat Trail 708
7 Meadow Trail and Ocean
   Overlook Loop 709
8 Wildwood Park Loop . . . 710
9 Rock Pool and Century
   Lake 710
10 Escondido Falls 711

11 Solstice Road and
   Rising Sun Loop Trail. . . 711
12 Eagle Rock Loop 712
13 Santa Ynez Canyon 712
14 Temescal Canyon and
   Ridge Loop 713
15 Inspiration Point Trail . . 714
16 Magic Forest Nature
   Trail 714
17 Hastain Trail 715
18 Mount Hollywood 715
19 Shipwreck Trail. 716
20 Two Harbors to
   Emerald Bay 716
21 Empire Landing Road
   Trail 717

1 Satwiwa Loop Trail and Waterfall

3.0 mi/1.5 hrs

You know the hike will be good when at the trailhead parking lot, you're greeted by two friendly roadrunners and a half dozen bunnies. That's how it is here at the Rancho Sierra Vista/Satwiwa Site, a part of the Santa Monica Mountains National Recreation Area near Newbury Park, just a couple miles off U.S. 101. The park's proximity to millions of L.A. commuters makes it a perfect place to show up after work and hike or jog on the Satwiwa Loop Trail, and in the rainy season, take a side trip to see the waterfall just inside the border of Point Mugu State Park. From the parking lot, walk up the paved Sycamore Canyon Trail for a few hundred yards, then bear left on the Satwiwa Loop Trail by the Satwiwa Native American Indian Culture Center. Be sure to take a peek at the dome-shaped stick dwelling, which was reconstructed to show traditional Native American life. Beware the sign that says "Caution—Rattlesnakes." It

stops you from crawling inside the hut. Follow the Satwiwa Loop for 1.5 miles, passing a small pond, a windmill, and grassy hillsides, then connect to the Old Boney Trail on the south side of the loop. Old Boney Trail leads downhill, and where it begins to make a sharp switchback up and out of the canyon, take the left spur up the creek that leads a few hundred feet to Sycamore Canyon Falls. The waterfall is a pretty, multi-tiered cascade over sandstone, with a surprising amount of foliage growing around it. Even when the fall is only a trickle, the big-leaf maples and ferns are a delight to visit.

Location: In the Santa Monica Mountains National Recreation Area near Newbury Park; map I4, grid a1.

User groups: Hikers and dogs. (Dogs are not allowed past the border of Point Mugu State Park, only on the Satwiwa Loop.) No horses or mountain bikes. No wheelchair facilities.

Permits: No permits are required. Parking and access are free.

Maps: A free map of the Santa

Monica Mountains National Recreation Area and a brochure on Rancho Sierra Vista/Satwiwa Site are available by contacting parking headquarters at the address below. A map of the Santa Monica Mountains is available for a fee from Tom Harrison Cartography, tel. (415) 456-7940. Ask the USGS for a topographic map of the Newbury Park area.

Directions: From U.S. 101 in Newbury Park exit on Wendy Drive and head south for 2.6 miles to Potrero Road. Turn right on Potrero Road and head west for 1.8 miles to the park entrance at the corner of West Potrero Road and Pine Hill Avenue. Turn left into the park and drive .4 mile to the main parking lot. Walk up the paved road that leads from the parking lot to a gate at the Big Sycamore Canyon Trail (also a road).

Contact: Santa Monica Mountains National Recreation Area, 401 W. Hillcrest Drive, Thousand Oaks, CA 91360; tel. (818) 597-9192, (805) 370-2300, or fax (818) 735-0778.

❷ La Jolla Valley Loop
6.8 mi/3.5 hrs or 2.0 days

We rate Point Mugu State Park as the best of all the parks in the Santa Monica Mountains, partly because of its more remote northern location, partly because of its proximity to the ocean, and partly because of its fine hiking trails. One of the best of the latter is this loop trip starting in La Jolla Canyon, which can be an excellent day hike or an easy two-day backpacking trip with an overnight at La Jolla Valley walk-in camp. Follow the La Jolla Canyon Trail from the Ray Miller Trailhead (that's the wide dirt trail on the left, not the single track on the right) gently uphill. You hike through an open valley that is continually freshened by ocean breezes blowing up the canyon. Pass a small seasonal waterfall, then climb into a rocky area, where hidden among the chaparral are rock caves that were once used by Native Americans. Go right at the first fork and take the left fork at 1.5 miles to La Jolla Valley walk-in camp, situated in a high meadow of native

grasses. It's .5 mile farther, shortly beyond a cattail-bordered pond. From the camp, bear left on the dirt road, which narrows to single track. Continue on the La Jolla Valley Loop Trail and circle around, through more native grasses, back to the La Jolla Canyon Trail. If you like, you can add on a detour around Mugu Peak on the Mugu Peak Trail, which will add two more miles to your round-trip. Turn right on La Jolla Canyon Trail to head down the canyon to your car. This trip is outstanding in winter or spring, when the hillside grasses are green and the wildflowers bloom.

Location: In Point Mugu State Park south of Oxnard; map I4, grid b1.

User groups: Hikers only. No dogs, horses, or mountain bikes. No wheelchair facilities.

Permits: No day-hiking permits are necessary. Backpacking campsites are available on a first-come, first-served basis; backpackers must register at the Sycamore Canyon Campground. A $2 day-use fee is charged per vehicle at the Ray Miller Trailhead.

Maps: A park map is available for $1 from the ranger kiosk at Sycamore Canyon Campground, one mile south on Highway 1. A map of the Santa Monica Mountains is available for a fee from Tom Harrison Cartography, tel. (415) 456-7940. Ask the USGS for a topographic map of the Point Mugu area.

Directions: From U.S. 101 in Camarillo take the Las Posas Road exit and drive south through Oxnard. Follow Las Posas Road for eight miles to Highway 1, then turn south on Highway 1. Drive five miles to the La Jolla Canyon Trailhead parking area on the left, across from Thornhill Broome State Beach.

Alternatively, from Highway 1 in Malibu, drive west on Highway 1 for 22 miles to the La Jolla Canyon Trailhead parking area on the right.

Contact: Point Mugu State Park, 9000 Pacific Coast Highway, Malibu, CA 90265; tel. (805) 488-5223 or (805) 488-1827; California State Parks, Angeles District, 1925 Los Virgenes Road, Calabasas, CA 91302; tel. (818) 880-0350.

3 Big Sycamore Canyon Loop

9.5 mi/5.5 hrs

If you don't mind hiking on fire roads and maybe sharing the trail with mountain bikers and horses, this loop trip in Point Mugu State Park offers a shady stroll in a sycamore-lined canyon, followed by miles and miles of unforgettable coastal views. Start from the gate at the far end of the campground and follow Big Sycamore Canyon Trail as it climbs very gently uphill, paralleling the creek. The sycamore trees here are large and old, and from October to February, you may spot monarch butterflies that cluster among them for the winter. At three miles, bear left on Wood Canyon Trail to reach Deer Camp Junction and picnic area. From there pick up Overlook Trail for a long, rambling walk back to the trailhead. The Overlook Trail divides Point Mugu's two canyons, Big Sycamore and La Jolla, and is a ridge-top route that offers nonstop views of the coastline to the west and the canyons on either side of you. On a clear day it's glorious. Note: When you near the end of the trail, you can take the single-track Scenic Trail to return to the trailhead. It shaves off a little distance, and it's more interesting than the final stretch of the Overlook Trail.

Location: In Point Mugu State Park south of Oxnard; map I4, grid b1.

User groups: Hikers, horses, and mountain bikes. No dogs. No wheelchair facilities.

Permits: No permits are required. A $3 day-use fee is charged per vehicle.

Maps: A park map is available for $1 from the entrance kiosk. A map of the Santa Monica Mountains is available for a fee from Tom Harrison Cartography, tel. (415) 456-7940. Ask the USGS for a topographic map of the Point Mugu area.

Directions: From U.S. 101 in Camarillo, take the Las Posas Road exit and drive south through Oxnard. Follow Las Posas Road for eight miles to Highway 1, then turn south on Highway 1. Drive seven miles to Sycamore Canyon Campground on the left.

Alternatively, from Highway 1 in Malibu drive west on Highway 1 for 20 miles to Sycamore Canyon Campground on the right.

Contact: Point Mugu State Park, 9000 Pacific Coast Highway, Malibu, CA 90265; tel. (805) 488-5223 or (805) 488-1827; California State Parks, Angeles District, 1925 Los Virgenes Road, Calabasas, CA 91302; tel. (818) 880-0350.

4 Grotto Trail

3.5 mi/2.0 hrs

If you don't mind hiking downhill to your destination and then uphill on your return, the Grotto Trail is a fine route for a little excursion in the Santa Monica Mountains. The trail roughly follows the west fork of the Arroyo Sequit on its downhill course to the Grotto, an area of jumbled volcanic boulders, many that are bigger than your average Volkswagen. Hidden among the giant rocks are small caves, pools, and waterfalls. The boulders are great fun to climb around, with millions of possible toe- and fingerholds in the porous rock. By the way, don't be bummed out when you arrive at the Grotto and see that other folks have only walked a few yards to get there; the Happy Hollow Campground is right next door and the park road leads right to it. You, on the other hand, must walk back uphill to the trailhead, covering a 600-foot elevation gain.

Location: In the Santa Monica Mountains National Recreation Area at Circle X Ranch; map I4, grid b2.

User groups: Hikers and dogs. No horses or mountain bikes. No wheelchair facilities.

Permits: No permits are required. Parking and access are free.

Maps: A free map of the Santa Monica Mountains National Recreation Area and a brochure on Circle X Ranch are available by contacting park headquarters at the address below. A map of the Santa Monica Mountains is available for a fee from Tom Harrison Cartography, tel. (415) 456-7940. Ask the USGS for a topographic map of the Triunfo Pass area.

Directions: From Malibu drive west on Highway 1 for 15 miles to Yerba Buena Road, 1.5 miles past Leo Carrillo State Beach. Turn right and drive 5.3 miles up Yerba Buena Road to the entrance to Circle X Ranch on the right. Park by the ranger station and walk down the road to the group campground, where the Grotto Trail begins.

Contact: Santa Monica Mountains National Recreation Area, 401 W. Hillcrest Drive, Thousand Oaks, CA 91360; tel. (818) 597-9192, (805) 370-2300, or fax (818) 735-0778.

5 Mishe Mokwa and Backbone Loop

6.6 mi/3.0 hrs

A great six-mile loop on the Santa Monica Mountains' Backbone Trail begins a short distance from the Circle X Ranch site on Yerba Buena Road. See all those wild-looking volcanic outcrops on the hillsides? That's where you're going. You can hike the loop in either direction, but most people start on the Mishe Mokwa Trail. From the Backbone Trailhead, hike uphill for .25 mile and take the right fork to access Mishe Mokwa's single track. Head uphill from there, gaining 1,100 feet over two miles to Split Rock, a big boulder with a cleft in the middle. It's an unspoken requirement to walk through the cleft. There's a picnic area at Split Rock among the oaks and sycamores, where you can catch some shade and your breath. From there continue on the loop to the Backbone Trail and begin to circle back. Be sure to take the short right spur to Inspiration Point, near Boney Peak, for inspiring views of the coast, and the short right spur to 3,111-foot Sandstone Peak, the highest point in the Santa Monica Mountains. Despite its name, the peak is not made of sandstone; rather it's volcanic rock. The views are outstanding—you'll think you're on top of the world. Sandstone Peak actually has another name—Mount Allen—so when you reach the top and see the Mount Allen plaque, don't think you're in the wrong place.

Location: In the Santa Monica Mountains National Recreation Area near Circle X Ranch; map I4, grid b2.

User groups: Hikers and dogs. No horses or mountain bikes. No wheelchair facilities.

Permits: No permits are required. Parking and access are free.

Maps: A free map of the Santa Monica Mountains National Recreation Area and a brochure on Circle X Ranch are available by contacting park headquarters at the address below. A map of the Santa Monica Mountains is available for a fee from Tom Harrison Cartography, tel. (415) 456-7940. Ask the USGS for a topographic map of the Triunfo Pass area.

Directions: From Malibu drive west on Highway 1 for 15 miles to Yerba Buena Road, 1.5 miles past Leo Carrillo State Beach. Turn right and drive 6.3 miles up Yerba Buena Road to the Backbone Trailhead parking area on the left side of the road, one mile beyond the entrance to Circle X Ranch on the right.

Contact: Santa Monica Mountains National Recreation Area, 401 W. Hillcrest Drive, Thousand Oaks, CA 91360; tel. (818) 597-9192, (805) 370-2300 or fax (818) 735-0778.

6 Nicholas Flat Trail

6.5 mi/3.0 hrs

Most Southern California state beaches are long stretches of sand with big campgrounds and lots of happy beach goers, but few have any hiking trails worth writing home about. Leo Carrillo State Beach is the exception to the rule, with a couple excellent trails that are far more than just a stroll along the sand. The Nicholas Flat Trail is the park's best path, a fairly steep trail that climbs to a pond at Nicholas Flat, where redwing blackbirds and other songbirds like to spend their days. Start hiking from the Willow Creek/Nicholas Flat Trailhead, and at the first junction, bear left. A short but steep climb leads to immediate ocean vistas, and at .75 mile a spur trail leads to Willow Creek Overlook, a fine viewpoint and an excellent spot to look for passing whales in winter. From the spur trail you can call it a day and hike back downhill (a short loop is possible from this point—bear right to follow it), or continue uphill to Nicholas Flat. The climb gets steeper from here, and you'll gain 1,000 feet more, but you are rewarded with two more spectacular vista points plus Nicholas Flat, with its man-made pond and high grasslands. You can loop around Nicholas Flat and choose from a myriad of good picnicking spots, then head back downhill. When you're finished hiking this trail, make sure you check out the beach across the road (take the pedestrian tunnel under the highway), where you'll find a sea-carved tunnel and many small caves and pocket beaches. Also pay a visit to the visitor center by the beach, open on weekends only, which is housed in a set of trailers painted with dolphins and whales.

Location: In Leo Carrillo State Beach near Malibu; map I4, grid b2.

User groups: Hikers and horses. No dogs or mountain bikes. No wheelchair facilities.

Permits: No permits are required. A $3 day-use fee is charged per vehicle.

Maps: A map of Leo Carrillo State Beach is available for $1 at the park entrance station. A map of the Santa Monica Mountains is available for a fee from Tom Harrison Cartography, tel. (415) 456-7940. Ask the USGS for a topographic map of the Triunfo Pass area.

Directions: From Malibu drive west on Highway 1 for 13 miles to Leo Carrillo State Beach. Turn right into the park entrance. The Nicholas Flat/Willow Creek Trail begins by the entrance kiosk, on the inland side of the highway.

Contact: Leo Carrillo State Beach, 35000 Pacific Coast Highway, Malibu, CA 90265; tel. (805) 488-5223 or (805) 488-1827; California State Parks, Angeles District, 1925 Los Virgenes Road, Calabasas, CA 91302; tel. (818) 880-0350.

7 Meadow Trail and Ocean Overlook Loop
3.0 mi/1.5 hrs

Maybe you need to change your perspective. If you've been hiking around in the lower canyons of the Santa Monica Mountains, it might be time to get up high and wander around where the wind blows and the vistas are wide. Charmlee County Park is the place to do it, located four miles up the hill from Zuma Beach. It's high enough so that you don't have to climb anywhere to gain a view; the vistas start right at the trailhead. The park's hiking trails are really fire roads, but that's okay. It just means you can hold hands with your hiking partner while you walk or carry on a serious discussion about the coastal weather. Walk through the park's picnic area and follow the dirt road as it leads downhill to a meadow, filled with wildflower blooms in February, March, and April. Follow the Meadow Trail to the Ocean Overlook, which is just one of many places where the views of the Malibu coast are excellent. From several points you have vistas in almost every direction, including up and down the Santa Monica Mountains to the east and west. When you're finished meditating on the scenery, loop back on the Meadow Trail to your starting point.

Location: In the Charmlee Natural Area near Zuma Beach; map I4, grid b4.

User groups: Hikers, dogs, horses, and mountain bikes. No wheelchair facilities.

Permits: No permits are required. A $3 day-use fee is charged per vehicle.

Maps: A map of the Santa Monica Mountains is available for a fee from Tom Harrison Cartography, tel. (415) 456-7940. Ask the USGS for topographic maps of the Triunfo and Point Dume areas.

Directions: From Highway 1 in Zuma Beach drive north on Encinal Canyon Road for four miles to the park entrance on the left. Turn left and drive .4 mile to the parking area near the park office and restrooms.

Contact: Charmlee Natural Area, City of Malibu Parks and Recreation Department, tel. (310) 457-7247 or (310) 317-1364.

8 Wildwood Park Loop
4.0 mi/2.0 hrs

Wildwood Park is one of the best-kept park secrets in Los Angeles, known mostly to the school kids who come here for outdoor field trips in the spring. From the Arboles Trailhead in Thousand Oaks, you can hike downhill into Wildwood Canyon and then stroll along its year-round stream, which produces a stunningly beautiful waterfall when the stream flow is strong. Numerous trails cross and interconnect throughout the park, so you can put together a different loop trip or out-and-back hike every time you visit. For first timers a good tour is to hike due west on the Mesa Trail .5 mile to the North Tepee Trail and turn left, dropping down into the canyon. Once there, walk to your right and then bear left at the next fork, which puts you right at the base of the 70-foot waterfall. Hey, isn't Los Angeles supposed to be a semi-arid desert? Yes, but it's full of surprises. From the falls you can continue walking downstream and then pick up the Lizard Rock Trail to loop back to the Mesa Trail. The presence of year-round water makes this canyon a haven for wildlife; look for mule deer, rabbits, coyotes, and numerous songbirds and raptors. Interpretive signs teach you to identify various plants and trees along the stream.

Location: In Wildwood Park in Thousand Oaks; map I4, grid b4.

User groups: Hikers, dogs, horses, and mountain bikes. No wheelchair facilities.

Permits: No permits are required. Parking and access are free.

Maps: Park maps are available at the park visitor center. Ask the USGS for a topographic map of the Thousand Oaks area.

Directions: From U.S. 101 in Thousand Oaks take the Lynn Road exit and head north. Drive 2.5 miles to Avenida de los Arboles, then turn

left. Drive .9 mile and make a U-turn into the Arboles parking lot on the left side of the road.

Contact: Conejo Recreation and Park District, 155 E. Wilbur Road, Thousand Oaks, CA 91360; tel. (805) 495-6471.

9 Rock Pool and Century Lake
4.4 mi/2.0 hrs

The first time you lay eyes on the Rock Pool at Malibu Creek State Park or cross the wide bridge over Malibu Creek or visit pretty blue Century Lake, you may have to ask yourself the question: where am I? Suddenly it's hard to believe you're in Los Angeles, and just a few miles off the freeway, but you are. Start hiking from the large main parking area on the flat fire road, called Crags Road, that heads for the visitor center. Continue past the visitor center on a wide bridge and take the left spur to the Rock Pool, a startlingly beautiful pool in Malibu Creek that is dammed by huge volcanic boulders. Although the pool can nearly dry up in late summer, during the rainy season and shortly thereafter it is quite dramatic. Retrace your steps to Crags Road (you'll probably pass some rock climbers practicing their craft on an outcrop along the spur trail), turn left, and continue your park tour by visiting Century Lake, dammed in 1901 and now silting up and slowly becoming a marsh. Walk another .5 mile along Crags Road to the old set of the M*A*S*H television series, where you'll find a few obvious props from the show. From there, retrace your steps through the park to the trailhead.

Location: In Malibu Creek State Park; map I4, grid b5.

User groups: Hikers, horses, and mountain bikes. No dogs. No wheelchair facilities.

Permits: No permits are required. A $3 day-use fee is charged per vehicle.

Maps: A map of Malibu Creek State Park is available for $1 at the park entrance station. A map of the Santa Monica Mountains is available for a fee from Tom Harrison Cartography, tel. (415) 456-7940. Ask the USGS for a topographic map of the Point Dume area.

Directions: From Agoura Hills on U.S. 101, take the Las Virgenes exit and drive 3.2 miles south to the entrance to Malibu Creek State Park on the right. Continue past the entrance kiosk to the day-use parking area. Or from Malibu on Highway 1, drive north on Malibu Canyon Road/Las Virgenes Road for six miles to the park entrance on the left.

Contact: Malibu Creek State Park, California State Parks, Angeles District, 1925 Los Virgenes Road, Calabasas, CA 91302; tel. (818) 880-0350.

🔟 Escondido Falls

4.2 mi/2.0 hrs

We admit it: the first mile of this trail is pretty weird. That's because of an access problem; you have to park in the lot at the start of Winding Way and then walk up the paved road for a mile, past some mammoth Malibu homes, to the actual beginning of the Escondido Canyon Trail. Just do it and don't whine; when you finally reach the canyon, you'll be glad you came. At the trailhead sign, head to the left, walking upstream. Cross the creek a few times on the flat path, which tunnels through shady sections and opens out to grassy flats. About .5 mile from the start of the "real" trail, you'll glimpse a big waterfall up ahead, and in .5 mile more you're at its base. This is the lower tier of the huge limestone waterfall; the adventurous can take the side trail that leads up and over this 50-foot tier, and climb up to a higher, larger tier. Getting there requires some careful rock scrambling, so be cautious. The upper tier is 150 feet tall, with a deep pool at its base perfect for wading.

Location: In Escondido Canyon near Malibu; map I4, grid c4.

User groups: Hikers, dogs, horses, and mountain bikes. No wheelchair facilities.

Permits: No permits are required. Parking and access are free.

Maps: A map of the Santa Monica Mountains is available for a fee from Tom Harrison Car-

tography, tel. (415) 456-7940. Ask the USGS for a topographic map of the Point Dume area.

Directions: From Malibu drive west on Highway 1 for 5.5 miles to Winding Way on the right, and the large sign for the Winding Way Trail. If you reach Kanan Dume Road, you've gone 1.5 miles too far. Turn right, then left immediately into the well-signed parking lot.

Contact: Santa Monica Mountains Conservancy, 5750 Ramirez Canyon Road, Malibu, CA 90265; tel. (310) 589-3200 or fax (310) 589-3207.

🔟🔟 Solstice Road and Rising Sun Loop Trail

2.8 mi/1.2 hrs

Solstice Canyon is one of the newest additions to the Santa Monica Mountains National Recreation Area, although it has long been a favorite hiking spot for Malibu-area locals. Previously run as a city park and then as a part of the Santa Monica Mountains Conservancy, Solstice Canyon now can brag of its national park status. Hikers will celebrate the fact that this status means no more access fees. Hurray! The park suffered from severe fire damage in the fall of 1996, but as is typical after a fire, the spring wildflowers are better than ever. This easy loop trip travels along the Old Solstice Road (also called Old Sostomo Road) to the Roberts Ranch site and returns via the winding Rising Sun Trail. Although the first mile on the Old Solstice Road is on pavement, it parallels Solstice Creek and is a pretty, pleasant stroll. Hike past the cottage by the parking lot, turn right at the T-junction with Old Solstice Road, and simply walk up the canyon, enjoying the blooming mustard and monkeyflower. Pass by the 1865 Keller house, a lovely stone house that's the oldest in Malibu, and continue to the ruins of Tropical Terrace at the Roberts Ranch. This once-beautiful home burned in a fire in 1982, but its stone terraces and foundation remain. If you walk around to the far side of the foundation, you'll discover a pretty, 30-foot waterfall that drops on Solstice Creek. Enjoy its sweet music for a while. Hike back to the end of the Old Solstice Road, picking up the Rising Sun Trail, which undulates over the hillsides for 1.7 miles to the space-age-looking TRW buildings. From there you can take the left side of the TRW Loop Trail back to the parking lot.

Location: In the Santa Monica Mountains National Recreation Area near Malibu; map I4, grid c5.

User groups: Hikers, dogs, horses, and mountain bikes. No wheelchair facilities.

Permits: No permits are required. Parking and access are free.

Maps: A free trail map is available at the parking area. A map of the Santa Monica Mountains is available for a fee from Tom Harrison Cartography, tel. (415) 456-7940. Ask the USGS for a topographic map of the Malibu Beach area.

Directions: From Malibu drive west on Highway 1 for three miles and turn right on Corral Canyon Road. Drive .2 of a mile to the park entrance on the left. Turn left and drive .5 mile to the parking area by a small cottage. Park there and walk up the paved road, past the cottage.

Contact: Santa Monica Mountains National Recreation Area, 401 W. Hillcrest Drive, Thousand Oaks, CA 91360; tel. (818) 597-9192, (805) 370-2300, or fax (818) 735-0778.

12 Eagle Rock Loop
4.5 mi/2.5 hrs

Topanga State Park's most notable feature is sandstone Eagle Rock, and a loop hike from Trippet Ranch can take you to see it. Much of the route travels on a fire road, through grasslands and oaks, with vistas increasing as you ascend. At the main trailhead, a sign announces that Eagle Rock is two miles away. Bear left in a few hundred yards and climb to a major intersection at 1.4 miles. Take the middle road, signed as North Loop Trail, and climb for .5 mile to Eagle Rock. Leave the trail to explore the tiny caves, hollows, and holes in the

smooth sandstone, and to enjoy the 360-degree views from the valley to the ocean. When you've had enough, retrace your steps to the junction, and take the single-track Musch Trail on your right for two miles back to the parking lot. You'll pass a walk-in camp along the way. Practice naming the chaparral plants as you hike: white sage, chamise, yucca, poison oak, elderberry, and chia, among others. Watch for roadrunners scurrying among them. If you're in a hurry, you can return the way you came instead, following the fire road and shaving .5 mile off the trip.

Location: At Trippet Ranch in Topanga State Park; map I4, grid c6.

User groups: Hikers, horses, and mountain bikes. No dogs. No wheelchair facilities.

Permits: No permits are required. A $3 day-use fee is charged per vehicle.

Maps: A map of Topanga State Park and/or the Santa Monica Mountains is available for a fee from Tom Harrison Cartography, tel. (415) 456-7940. Ask the USGS for a topographic map of the Topanga area.

Directions: From Santa Monica drive north on Highway 1 and turn right on Topanga Canyon Boulevard. Drive 4.7 miles to Entrada Road, then turn right and drive one mile to the park entrance at Trippet Ranch. The trailhead is at the far side of the parking lot.

Contact: Topanga State Park, 20825 Entrada Road, Topanga, CA 90290; tel. (310) 455-2465 or (818) 880-0350.

13 Santa Ynez Canyon
2.4 mi/1.2 hrs

Topanga State Park is a park with nebulous borders, a patchwork of wilderness interspersed between continually growing housing developments. The park's Santa Ynez Canyon Trail, for instance, begins in a residential neighborhood where you park your car right along the street. The surprising thing is that once you walk about 50 yards on the trail, you feel as if you've gotten away from it all, especially the sights and sounds of urban living. The canyon bottom makes for flat walking and is pleasantly shaded by oaks, willows, and sycamores. Five-foot-tall tiger lilies grow alongside the trail. At .5 mile in, cross the creek (don't take the spur trail up its right side), then shortly reach a trail junction, where you should head right. The left fork continues for several miles all the way to Trippet Ranch and the main section of Topanga State Park. A short walk and stream scramble brings you to the base of Santa Ynez Canyon's 15-foot limestone waterfall, a lovely spot that unfortunately has been defiled by graffiti. Even so, it's worth a look, and the canyon walk is pleasant whether or not the stream is flowing strong.

Location: In Topanga State Park in Pacific Palisades; map I4, grid c6.

User groups: Hikers only. No dogs, horses, or mountain bikes. No wheelchair facilities.

Permits: No permits are required. Parking and access are free.

Maps: A map of Topanga State Park and/or the Santa Monica Mountains is available for a fee from Tom Harrison Cartography, tel. (415) 456-7940. Ask the USGS for a topographic map of the Topanga area.

Directions: From Santa Monica drive north on Highway 1 and turn right on Sunset Boulevard in Pacific Palisades. Drive .5 mile and turn left on Palisades Drive. Drive 2.4 miles, and then turn left on to Vereda de la Montura. The trailhead is at the intersection of Camino de Yatasto, a private road, and Vereda de la Montura. Park alongside the road.

Contact: Topanga State Park, 20825 Entrada Road, Topanga, CA 90290; tel. (310) 455-2465 or (818) 880-0350.

14 Temescal Canyon and Ridge Loop

3.8 mi/2.0 hrs

How about a nice loop hike in Temescal Gateway Park and Topanga State Park? Hey, good idea—throw some stuff in the day pack and let's go. The signed trail leads from the parking lot (it's to the left of the kiosk where you pay your fee), and heads north through a camp and conference center. In .25 mile, you'll reach a junction of three trails. The Temescal Canyon Trail on the right is the start of the loop; the Temescal Ridge Trail in the middle is the return leg of the loop. The Temescal Canyon Trail leads you away from the camp and past a state park boundary sign; then the trail starts to climb. Although the route is bordered by rock walls and dry chaparral, leafy maples and sycamores grow along the stream beside you. At 1.2 miles you cross a footbridge over a small, seasonal waterfall, then cross over to the west side of the canyon to climb to an intersection with the Temescal Ridge Trail. If you like, you can take the right spur trail for .5 mile to Skull Rock, a somewhat spooky-looking sandstone formation, then return to the junction. Finish out the loop by heading downhill on Temescal Ridge Trail, with fine views of the coast entertaining you as you walk.

Location: In Temescal Gateway Park in Pacific Palisades; map I4, grid c6.

User groups: Hikers only. No dogs, horses, or mountain bikes. No wheelchair facilities.

Permits: No permits are required. A $6 day-use fee is charged per vehicle. Annual passes are available.

Maps: A free trail map is available at the Temescal Gateway Park kiosk. A map of the Santa Monica Mountains is available for a fee from Tom Harrison Cartography, tel. (415) 456-7940. Ask the USGS for a topographic map of the Topanga area.

Directions: From Santa Monica drive north on Highway 1 to Temescal Canyon Road in Pacific Palisades. Turn right and drive 1.1 miles to the entrance to Temescal Gateway Park. Cross Sunset Boulevard and continue up the park road for .25 mile to the park office and trail information kiosk.

Contact: Temescal Gateway Park, 15601 Sunset Boulevard, Pacific Palisades, CA 90272; tel. (310) 454-1395, (310) 589-3200, or fax (310) 454-1396.

15 Inspiration Point Trail
2.0 mi/1.0 hr

Most folks come to Will Rogers State Historic Park to visit the home of the late "Cowboy Philosopher" and humorist Will Rogers. His humble abode was a gigantic 31-room ranch/mansion. But even if you never heard of the guy and have no interest in cowboy decorating style, the two-mile loop trip to Inspiration Point makes a visit to the park worthwhile. The trail offers superb vistas of the Santa Monica Mountains and Pacific Ocean. Finding the trailhead is a bit tricky; it's behind the Rogers' mansion, at the far edge of the grassy lawn. Cross a tiny footbridge and you'll see the trailhead sign.

Ignoring all single-track cutoffs, follow the main fire road gently uphill for .75 mile to a major junction with the Backbone Trail. Turn right, leaving the fire roads, and head farther uphill for Inspiration Point, a short distance away. A few benches and a horse hitch mark the top, making this a great spot for you and Trigger to gaze out on the scene. Your view includes the Pacific Ocean, the rugged Santa Monica Mountains, the state park below you, and downtown Los Angeles to the southeast. It's hard to believe that the big city is within view of this tranquil place, but there it is. Considering the proportion of your view, it's also hard to believe you're only at 750 feet in elevation. On the clearest days you can see all the way to Catalina Island, 20-plus miles away. To finish out your hike, return to the junction with the Backbone Trail, then turn right and make a loop back downhill. You'll come out near the horse stables, not far from where you parked your car.

Location: In Will Rogers State Historic Park; map I4, grid c7.

User groups: Hikers and horses. No dogs or mountain bikes. No wheelchair facilities.

Permits: No permits are required. A $3 day-use fee is charged per vehicle.

Maps: A map of Will Rogers State Historic Park is available for $1 at the park entrance station. Ask the USGS for a topographic map of the Topanga area.

Directions: From Santa Monica drive north on Highway 1 to Sunset Boulevard in Pacific Palisades. Turn right on Sunset Boulevard and drive 4.5 miles to Will Rogers State Park Road, then turn left and drive one mile to the park entrance. The trail begins near the Rogers' mansion.

Contact: Will Rogers State Historic Park, 1501 Will Rogers State Park Road, Pacific Palisades, CA 90272; tel. (310) 454-8212 or (818) 880-0350.

16 Magic Forest Nature Trail
0.25 mi/0.25 hr

If you have kids and you're anywhere in the vicinity of Coldwater Canyon, bring them to this park for a walk on the Magic Forest Nature Trail. The trail, like Coldwater Canyon Park itself, is a complete delight and a good source of inspiration for children who are growing up in an urban world. It's the perfect place for them to learn about the importance of planting trees in urban areas, which is what TreePeople, who run this park, do in Los Angeles neighborhoods. The trail begins at a small shrine to the rainforest—a coast live oak stump that has been carved into a wood nymph—and continues in an equally charming fashion. Soft wood chips line the path. As you walk, you learn all about toyon, coast live oak, chaparral, poison oak, periwinkle, and other common flora. The park isn't exactly wilderness, but it's a great example of how good a city park can be.

Location: In Coldwater Canyon Park; map I4, grid c8.

User groups: Hikers and dogs. No horses or mountain bikes. No wheelchair facilities.

Permits: No permits are required. Parking and access are free.

Maps: A map/brochure of Coldwater Canyon Park is available for $.25 at the park kiosk. Ask the USGS for a topographic map of the Beverly Hills area.

Directions: From U.S. 101 in Studio City take the Coldwater Canyon exit and drive south for 2.3 miles, then turn left into the park entrance. The trail begins by the parking area.

Contact: Coldwater Canyon Park, c/o TreePeople, 12601 Mulholland Drive, Beverly Hills, CA 90210; tel. (818) 753-4600.

17 Hastain Trail
2.3 mi/1.5 hrs

Unlike nearby Coldwater Canyon Park (see Magic Forest Nature Trail, above), here at Franklin Canyon Park you can't hear the noise of the freeway and the city. That's because you've dropped down into a canyon that is surrounded by open space, insulating it from all urban encroachment. (We were surprised to see a coyote right by the road as we drove in.) A hike on the park's Hastain Trail is an energetic climb on a fire road to an overlook with views of Franklin Canyon and its reservoir, west Los Angeles, and all the way out to the ocean on clear days. After enjoying the view, you can return on a loop by taking the single-track trail on the right down to the Doheny House ranch and picnic area. Walk back on a trail alongside the park road. Before or after your hike, be sure to stop in at the park's Suki Goldman Nature Center, where you can learn all about the natural history of the Santa Monica Mountains. The center also features paintings of the mountains by local artists; we found them to be almost as inspiring as the hike.

Location: In Franklin Canyon in Santa Monica Mountains National Recreation Area; map I4, grid c8.

User groups: Hikers, dogs, and horses. No mountain bikes. No wheelchair facilities.

Permits: No permits are required. Parking and access are free.

Maps: A free map of the Santa Monica Mountains National Recreation Area and a brochure on Franklin Canyon are available by contacting park headquarters at the address below. Ask the USGS for a topographic map of the Beverly Hills area.

Directions: From U.S. 101 in Studio City take the Coldwater Canyon exit and drive south for 2.3 miles (the road becomes Mulholland Drive), then turn right on Franklin Canyon Drive. Drive 1.5 miles to the fork with Lake Drive and bear left on Lake Drive. Just beyond the park entrance, look for a parking area and trailhead at a fire road on the left.

Contact: Santa Monica Mountains National Recreation Area, 401 W. Hillcrest Drive, Thousand Oaks, CA 91360; tel. (818) 597-9192, (805) 370-2300, or fax (818) 735-0778.

18 Mount Hollywood
5.0 mi/2.5 hrs

Griffith Park is as much a part of Los Angeles legend as Mann's Chinese Theater or the Santa Monica Pier. In all of the park's many acres, no trail is more frequently hiked than the trail to the top of Mount Hollywood. Out-of-towners need to be told that this is not the peak that bears the famous "HOLLYWOOD" sign (that's Mount Lee), although you can see that sign from this peak. Actually, people hike to the top of Mount Hollywood for no other reason than that the view from its summit is unforgettable. To see it, start hiking across the street from the Ferndell Museum, heading uphill along the shady trail. About .5 mile out, bear right at the fork and keep climbing, soon leaving the shady, damp canyon and moving into chaparral. There are several well-signed junctions to negotiate, then all of a sudden, voilà—you're at 1,625 feet in elevation on top of Mount Hollywood, the highest point in Hollywood. Check out the view that stretches from downtown all the way out to the ocean. Oh, and just in case you need to be reminded that you're not really in the wilderness, you'll find water fountains positioned at strategic locations along the trail.

Location: In Griffith Park; map I4, grid c9.

User groups: Hikers, dogs, and horses. No mountain bikes. No wheelchair facilities.

Permits: No permits are required. Parking and access are free.

Maps: A free park map is available at the park ranger station. Ask the USGS for a topographic map of the Hollywood area.

Directions: From Interstate 5 in Hollywood take the Los Feliz Boulevard west exit and drive three miles to Ferndell Drive. Turn right and drive to the Ferndell Nature Museum. Alternately, from U.S. 101 in Hollywood take the Sunset Boulevard exit and drive east one block to Western Avenue. Turn left and go north on Western Avenue and then bear right on Los Feliz Boulevard. Turn left on Ferndell Drive and park near the Ferndell Nature Museum.

Contact: Griffith Park Ranger Station, 4730 Crystal Springs, Los Angeles, CA 90027; tel. (323) 913-4688 or (213) 485-5027.

Location: On the Palos Verdes Peninsula; map I4, grid f7.

User groups: Hikers and dogs. No horses or mountain bikes. No wheelchair facilities.

Permits: No permits are required. Parking and access are free.

Maps: Ask the USGS for a topographic map of the Redondo Beach area.

Directions: From Redondo Beach on Highway 1 drive south on Highway 1 to Palos Verdes Boulevard. Bear south on Palos Verdes Boulevard, which turns into Palos Verdes Drive W. Turn right on Via Corta and at .5 mile turn right on Via Arroyo. In another .5 mile, turn left on Paseo del Mar and drive to Flat Rock Point. If you reach Via Horcada, you've gone too far. Park along the road.

Contact: Palos Verdes Estates City Hall, Parks Department, tel. (310) 378-0383.

19 Shipwreck Trail
4.0 mi/2.5 hrs

From Flat Rock Point on Paseo del Mar, you have access to the Palos Verdes Estates Shoreline Preserve and the Shipwreck Trail, a path that's sure to stimulate the imaginations of children and adults. The trail requires some scrambling over and around boulders and running from incoming waves, but it's great fun. Note that the beach is extremely rocky, so the going is slow, but that means tide-pool viewing is good, especially near Flat Rock Point. Check your tide table to make sure you're hiking at low tide. After dropping down to the beach, hike southward past Bluff Cove, enjoying views reaching all the way to Catalina Island. At about two miles out, just before Rocky Point, you'll see the remains of the freighter *Dominator,* a Greek ship that ran aground in 1961. The ship was never salvaged, but the years of rolling waves have taken their toll; little is left of her. If you have the energy to go a little farther, just beyond the shipwreck is spectacular U-shaped Lunada Bay, with its sheer, terraced cliffs. Turn around wherever you please, and reverse your steps along the beach.

20 Two Harbors to Emerald Bay
9.0 mi/5.0 hrs

If you want to take a hiking trip to Catalina Island, but you don't want your trip to be complicated or crowded with people, there's only one key instruction to follow: take the ferry to Two Harbors, not to Avalon. This applies whether you are going for the day or staying overnight. From the ferry drop point at the Two Harbors pier, you can pick up your hiking permit and begin hiking right away on the West End Road, a dirt road that is nearly level and sticks close to the shoreline for its entire route. Head west, getting eyefuls of rocky outcrops, steep headlands, beckoning coves, and the beautiful blue Pacific, until at 1.25 miles you reach Cherry Valley and Cherry Cove. The area is named for the native Catalina cherry tree that grows there, which displays beautiful white flowers in the spring. Continue hiking on the flat dirt road, passing Howland Landing at almost four miles out. Stay far away from the plentiful Keep Out and No Trespassing signs there. Remain on the road until you see an obvious cutoff trail on your right leading to beautiful Emerald Bay at 4.5 miles. Have a picnic on the gorgeous white sand beach and ponder how lucky we are to have this fabulous island so close to Los Angeles.

Although this excursion makes a fine day-trip getaway from the mainland, your best bet is to spend the night in Two Harbors either camping or in more luxurious accommodations, then continue hiking and exploring the next day. If you're on a day trip, make sure you're back in Two Harbors in time for the boat home. Note: Outside of the summer season, ferries do not run frequently to Two Harbors, so you may have to stay overnight. Phone the ferry companies for current schedules.

Location: On Catalina Island; map I4, grid i6.

User groups: Hikers only. No dogs, horses, or mountain bikes. No wheelchair facilities.

Permits: A free Santa Catalina Island hiking permit is required and may be obtained from Visitor Services at Two Harbors; phone Santa Catalina Island Conservancy for more information. Fees are charged for the ferry from the mainland to Two Harbors. Phone the companies below for current rates and departure information. (Ferry fees are approximately $23 to $38 per adult, less for seniors and children under 12.)

Maps: A trail map of Catalina Island is available for $.50 from the Santa Catalina Island Conservancy when you pick up your hiking permit. Ask the USGS for a topographic map of the Santa Catalina West area.

Directions: Two companies provide ferry transportation to Two Harbors from San Pedro. Reservations are recommended. Phone Catalina Express at (310) 519-1212, or Catalina Cruises at (800) 228-2546. Catalina Express has the faster boat to Two Harbors.

Contact: Two Harbors Visitor Services, P.O. Box 5044, Two Harbors, CA 90704; tel. (310) 510-0303; Santa Catalina Island Conservancy, tel. (310) 510-2595.

21 Empire Landing Road Trail
8.3 mi one way/4.0 hrs

This spectacular one-way hiking trip on Catalina Island requires a bare minimum of planning in exchange for tremendous rewards. First, you have to arrange to take the ferry from the mainland to Avalon, Catalina's "big city." Then when you arrive (after about a two-hour boat ride), you must pick up your free hiking permit in town at the Santa Catalina Island Conservancy and take the shuttle bus from Avalon to Airport in the Sky. That's where your hike on the Empire Landing Road finally begins. Along its 8.3-mile length, you'll travel along the north side of the island on a curvy, up-and-down road that passes by a marble quarry, numerous coves and beaches, and fascinating rock formations. If you're lucky, you'll see Island fox, huge bison, and maybe even a wild turkey.

When the trail ends at Two Harbors, you have three choices: take the bus shuttle back to Avalon, camp or stay at the various lodgings in Two Harbors, or take the ferry from Two Harbors back to the mainland. For the latter two possibilities, you must plan in advance: phone Two Harbors Visitor Services at (310) 510-0303 for lodgings and campground information in Two Harbors. If you want to take the ferry back to the mainland, you need to alert the ferry company that you're going in to Avalon but leaving from Two Harbors. There is no extra fee for this service, but you have to make sure you finish your hike in time to catch the last boat. One more thing to consider: when is the best time of year to visit Catalina? Unquestionably, it's spring or fall, when the weather is good and the summer crowds are nonexistent.

Location: On Catalina Island; map I4, grid i7.

User groups: Hikers only. No dogs, horses, or mountain bikes. No wheelchair facilities.

Permits: A free Santa Catalina Island hiking permit is required and may be obtained from the Santa Catalina Island Conser-

vancy at 125 Clarissa Avenue in Avalon or at the Avalon airport. Fees are charged for the ferry from the mainland to Avalon, and for the shuttle bus from Avalon to Airport in the Sky. Phone the companies below for current rates and departure information. (Ferry fees are approximately $23 to $38 per adult, less for seniors and children under 12.)

Maps: A trail map of Catalina Island is available for $.50 from the Santa Catalina Island Conservancy when you pick up your hiking permit. Ask the USGS for a topographic map of the Santa Catalina area.

Directions: Several companies provide ferry transportation to Avalon from San Pedro, Long Beach, Redondo Beach, and Newport Beach. Reservations are recommended. Phone Catalina Express at (310) 519-1212, Catalina Cruises at (800) 228-2546, or Catalina Passenger Service at (949) 673-5245. Transportation is also possible by plane or helicopter; phone Island Express at (310) 510-2525. For information on shuttle bus service from Avalon to Airport in the Sky, phone (310) 510-0143.

Contact: Santa Catalina Island Conservancy; tel. (310) 510-2595; Catalina Island Chamber of Commerce and Visitors Bureau, P.O. Box 217, #1 Green Pier, Avalon, CA 90704; tel. (310) 510-1520.

MOUNT WILLIAMSON STRADDLES THE
SAN GABRIEL MOUNTAINS AND
THE MOJAVE DESERT.

ANN MARIE BROWN

MAP 15

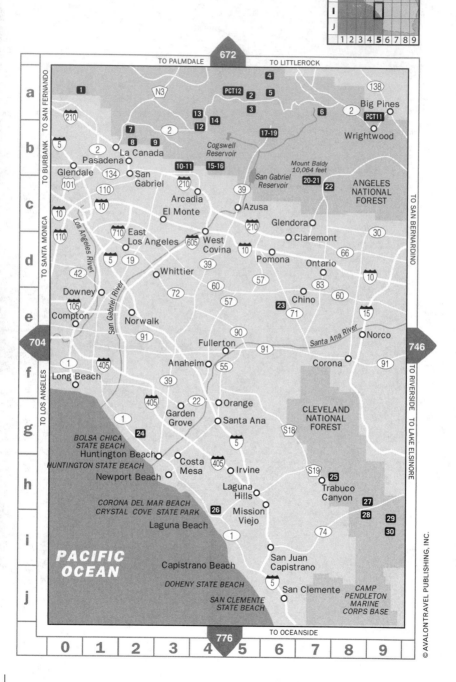

672

TO PALMDALE   TO LITTLEROCK

a

1

N3

138

PCT12 2

4

5

2

Big Pines

PCT11

TO SAN FERNANDO

210

13

14

3

6

Wrightwood

7

12

b

8   9

2

La Canada

Cogswell
Reservoir

17-19

TO BURBANK

5

Pasadena

10-11

15-16

Mount Baldy
10,064 feet

ANGELES
NATIONAL
FOREST

Glendale

134

San
Gabriel

210

San Gabriel
Reservoir

20-21

22

101

110

39

TO SAN BERNARDINO

c

10

Arcadia

Azusa

Glendora

10

El Monte

210

Claremont

30

TO SANTA MONICA

110

710

East
Los Angeles

605

West
Covina

210

Pomona

Ontario

66

d

5

19

10

83

10

42

Whittier

39

57

60

Chino

60

Los Angeles River

72

60

23

71

Downey

57

San Gabriel River

105

Norwalk

e

Compton

91

90

Santa Ana River

Norco

704

91

Fullerton

91

746

TO LOS ANGELES

1

405

Anaheim

55

Corona

91

TO RIVERSIDE

f

Long Beach

39

CLEVELAND
NATIONAL
FOREST

TO LAKE ELSINORE

g

405

22

Orange

S18

1

Garden
Grove

Santa Ana

24

BOLSA CHICA
STATE BEACH

5

Huntington Beach

Costa
Mesa

S19

25

HUNTINGTON STATE BEACH

405

Trabuco
Canyon

27

h

Newport Beach

Irvine

Laguna
Hills

28

29

CORONA DEL MAR BEACH
CRYSTAL COVE STATE PARK

26

Mission
Viejo

74

30

Laguna Beach

1

i

**PACIFIC
OCEAN**

Capistrano Beach

San Juan
Capistrano

DOHENY STATE BEACH

5

San Clemente

CAMP
PENDLETON
MARINE
CORPS BASE

j

SAN CLEMENTE
STATE BEACH

© AVALON TRAVEL PUBLISHING, INC.

776

TO OCEANSIDE

0   1   2   3   4   5   6   7   8   9

CHAPTER 15

1 Trail Canyon Trail 721

2 Cooper Canyon Falls ... 722

3 Mount Waterman 723

4 Devils Punchbowl Loop . 723

5 Mount Williamson 724

6 Vincent Gap to Mount Baden-Powell......... 725

7 Gabrielino Trail to Bear Canyon 725

8 Millard Falls.......... 726

9 Eaton Canyon 727

10 Big Santa Anita Canyon . 727

11 First Water Trail 728

12 Vetter Mountain Lookout............. 729

13 Silver Moccasin Trail to Mount Hillyer 729

14 Devils Canyon Trail 730

15 Monrovia Canyon Falls.. 730

16 Ben Overturff Trail.... 731

17 Soldier Creek/ Lewis Falls........... 732

18 Piñon Ridge Nature Trail......... 732

19 Windy Gap Trail to Mount Islip 733

20 San Antonio Falls...... 734

21 Mount Baldy 734

22 Ice House Saddle 735

23 Telegraph Canyon and South Ridge Loop 736

24 Bolsa Chica Ecological Reserve............. 737

25 Holy Jim Falls......... 737

26 El Moro Canyon and Ridge Loop........... 738

27 San Juan Loop Trail 739

28 Bear Canyon Loop Trail . 739

29 Tenaja Falls 740

30 Santa Rosa Plateau Vernal Pools 740

Pacific Crest Trail (PCT) Section Overview

PCT-11 Angeles Crest Highway to Three Points 741

PCT-12 Three Points to Mill Creek Picnic Area ... 742

1 Trail Canyon Trail

4.0 mi/2.0 hrs

Trail Canyon is located on the western side of the San Gabriel Mountains, an area that is less visited than the more celebrated eastern side. The Trail Canyon Trail (as redundant as that sounds) leads through a shady stream-carved canyon and up to open slopes, then curves its way to Trail Canyon Falls. The waterfall is so beautiful in winter and early spring that it can take your breath away. The trail begins with a ford and has several more stream crossings along the way, so be prepared for the possibility of wet feet. You walk on a dirt road past a community of cabins and wind around the canyon until, at .75 mile, you spy a single-track trail leading off on the right. Immediately you enter a densely shaded riparian area, thick with sycamores, alders, and cottonwoods. In another .5 mile, you climb out of this canyon and work your way up a slope among spring-blooming chaparral. The path is high above the creek now, and a sharp left curve suddenly reveals the waterfall up ahead about .25 mile. The trail leads to the top of it, where 50-foot Trail Canyon Falls spills over a smooth granite precipice. After admiring the falls, continue a little farther to where the trail crosses the stream. Take a look at the beautiful colors in the rocky streambed. On your return trip downhill, you have lovely canyon vistas to look forward to.

Location: In Angeles National Forest near Sunland; map I5, grid a0.

User groups: Hikers, dogs, horses, and mountain bikes. No wheelchair facilities.

Permits: No permits are required. A national forest recreation pass is required for each vehicle; fees are $5 for one day or $30 for a year.

Maps: For a map of Angeles National Forest, send $6 to U.S. Forest Service, Map Sales, P.O. Box 587, Camino, CA 95709; tel. (530) 647-5390 or website: www.r5.fs.fed.us/visitorcenter. A map of the San Gabriel Mountains is available for a fee from Tom Harrison Cartography, tel. (415) 456-7940. Ask the USGS for a topographic map of the Sunland area.

Directions: From Interstate 210 in Sunland, exit on Sunland Boulevard, which becomes Foothill Boulevard. Drive east for one mile to Mount Gleason Avenue. Turn left (north), drive 1.3 miles, and turn right on Big Tujunga Canyon Road. Drive 3.4 miles on Big Tujunga Canyon Road to a sign for Trail Canyon Trail on the left. Drive .25 mile to a fork, bear right, and drive .25 mile on rough road to a large parking lot. The trailhead is on the left side of the lot as you drive in.

Contact: Angeles National Forest, Tujunga Ranger District, 12371 N. Little Tujunga Canyon Road, San Fernando, CA 91342; tel. (818) 899-1900 or fax (818) 896-6727.

2 Cooper Canyon Falls
4.0 mi/2.0 hrs

After the snow has melted, here's a first-rate reason to make the 34-mile drive to the summit of Mount Waterman: a visit to Cooper Canyon Falls. The best thing about the waterfall, besides the fact that it's set in a gorgeous, 6,000-foot-elevation forest, is that it's just far enough away so that it doesn't get heavily visited. Start your hike at Buckhorn Campground at the trailhead for the Burkhardt Trail. Although there are small waterfalls and swimming holes along Buckhorn Creek within .25 mile of the camp, the real treasure is two miles away at Cooper Canyon. The hike is a mostly downhill trip through a dense forest of big firs, cedars, and pines. There's almost no undergrowth in these woods—just conifers and big rocks. It feels as if you're in the southern Sierra Nevada, but, no, this is the San Gabriels. The Burkhardt Trail laterals along the canyon slopes, high above Buckhorn Creek, then makes a left turn into Cooper Canyon, and traces a long switchback downhill. At 1.75 miles from the camp, you'll reach a junction with the Pacific Crest Trail and Silver Moccasin Trail. Turn right, toward Burkhardt Saddle and Eagle's Roost. It's only .1 mile to the waterfall, which drops just below the trail's edge. A rope helps you down the steep cliff to its base, where you can stand on an island of boulders and enjoy the falls' noisy, 35-foot drop. Be sure to get here early in the year, when the stream flow is still strong. Trailhead elevation is 6,300 feet.

Location: In Angeles National Forest near Mount Waterman; map I5, grid a5.

User groups: Hikers, dogs, horses, and mountain bikes. No wheelchair facilities.

Permits: No permits are required. A national forest recreation pass is required for each vehicle; fees are $5 for one day or $30 for a year.

Maps: For a map of Angeles National Forest, send $6 to U.S. Forest Service, Map Sales, P.O. Box 587, Camino, CA 95709; tel. (530) 647-5390 or website: www.r5.fs.fed.us/visitorcenter. A map of the San Gabriel Mountains is available for a fee from Tom Harrison Cartography, tel. (415) 456-7940. Ask the USGS for a topographic map of the Waterman Mountain area.

Directions: From Interstate 210 in La Cañada take Highway 2 north and drive 34 miles to Buckhorn Camp on the left. It's 1.5 miles past the Mount Waterman ski lift, just beyond Cloudburst Summit. The Burkhardt Trail starts at the far end of the camp near the restrooms (bear left at site 18).

Contact: Angeles National Forest, Arroyo Seco Ranger District, 4600 Oak Grove Drive, Flintridge, CA 91011; tel. (818) 790-1151 or fax (818) 790-5392.

3 Mount Waterman
5.8 mi/3.0 hrs

The peak of Mount Waterman at 8,038 feet is a fine destination for a moderate day hike in the San Gabriel Mountains, and the view from the summit is one you won't soon forget. The only problem that awaits is figuring out which peak is really the peak, because the top of Mount Waterman is so wide that there are three summits. From the trailhead, elevation 6,700 feet, bear left off the dirt road and head uphill on remarkably smooth, well-graded single track. The ascent is partially shaded by a mixed pine, cedar, and fir forest. At one mile out you'll reach a saddle where your views open wide. Climb some more, through long switchbacks, to a junction at two miles out, then go right for the summit. It's an easy .75 mile to the peak, with a total 1,300-foot elevation gain along the entire trail. Keep your eyes peeled for bighorn sheep, which are sometimes seen in the area. Also check out the huge sugar pine cones that are found alongside the trail. When you reach the flat top of Mount Waterman, head off-trail for .25 mile toward the southwest (to your left), where you'll find the highest of Waterman's summits atop a jumble of boulders. Here is the best possible view, looking out over the magnificent San Gabriel Mountains.

Location: In Angeles National Forest at Mount Waterman; map I5, grid a5.

User groups: Hikers, dogs, horses, and mountain bikes. No wheelchair facilities.

Permits: No permits are required. A national forest recreation pass is required for each vehicle; fees are $5 for one day or $30 for a year.

Maps: For a map of Angeles National Forest, send $6 to U.S. Forest Service, Map Sales,

P.O. Box 587, Camino, CA 95709; tel. (530) 647-5390 or website: www.r5.fs.fed.us/visitorcenter. A map of the San Gabriel Mountains is available for a fee from Tom Harrison Cartography, tel. (415) 456-7940. Ask the USGS for a topographic map of the Waterman Mountain area.

Directions: From Interstate 210 in La Cañada take Highway 2 north and drive 33 miles to a gated dirt road on the right signed as 3N03 (just west of the Buckhorn Campground sign and one mile east of Cloudburst Summit). Begin hiking on the gated dirt road and bear left in about 50 yards to the single-track Mount Waterman trail.

Contact: Angeles National Forest, Arroyo Seco Ranger District, 4600 Oak Grove Drive, Flintridge, CA 91011; tel. (818) 790-1151 or fax (818) 790-5392.

4 Devils Punchbowl Loop
1.0 mi/0.5 hr

The Devils Punchbowl is visual proof that you're in earthquake country, where faulting and erosion have made bizarre shapes out of ancient sedimentary rocks. They thrust and jut upward, creating vertical walls as high as 300 feet, and look as if they're about to topple inward on each other. From the viewpoint behind the visitor center, you look down into the land of the devil—the Punchbowl—a giant abyss that is the working of the San Andreas Fault and the result of centuries of stream carving. Juniper, piñon pine, and manzanita manage to eke out a meager living amidst all the sandstone. The park's easy, one-mile loop trail offers fine views into the depths of the Punchbowl. It switchbacks gently downhill to the canyon bottom and then climbs back up, passing by some of the taller rock slabs in the park. Here's a great tip: park rangers hold full moon hikes here once a month in the summer. Note: if you find this type of geological action fascinating, you might want to hike the park's longer trail to the dramatic Devils Chair, a breathtaking overlook above the Punchbowl. Make sure you stop in at the nature center here at Devils Punchbowl, where you can see its excellent display of wild birds.

Location: In the Devils Punchbowl Natural Area south of Pearblossom; map I5, grid a6.

User groups: Hikers, dogs, and horses. No mountain bikes are allowed on this trail, although they are allowed on other park trails. No wheelchair facilities.

Permits: No permits are required. Parking and access are free.

Maps: Park maps are available free at the nature center. Ask the USGS for a topographic map of the Valyermo area.

Directions: From Highway 14 near Palmdale take the Highway 138 exit east for 16 miles to Pearblossom. Turn right on County Road N-6 / Longview Road and drive south for eight miles to the Devils Punchbowl entrance. The trail begins behind the park nature center.

Contact: Devils Punchbowl Natural Area, 28000 Devils Punchbowl Road, Pearblossom, CA 93553; tel. (661) 944-2743.

5 Mount Williamson

5.0 mi/3.0 hrs

This summit trail feels a bit rougher and more remote than those to many other peaks in the San Gabriel Mountains, and it's famous for its steep drop-offs. But the trail's total elevation gain is only 1,600 feet, and the visual rewards are tremendous. Mount Williamson is on the north side of the Angeles Crest Highway, which means that although you're hiking in a mountain environment, you're on the desert side of the mountain. The forest on this slope is more sparse, the trail is more exposed, and many of the best vistas are of the western Mojave Desert to the north. Even if you're not in the mood to climb to the 8,214-foot summit, you can hike to a saddle at two miles out, where the Pacific Crest Trail drops down to the west. Views to the south are excellent here, with a big chunk of the San

Gabriel Mountains spread out before you. From the saddle take the summit trail on your right, heading .5 mile farther north on a remarkably steep grade. (A few switchbacks would be convenient here, but there are none.) Although the views have been excellent all along, nothing prepares you for the scene on top of Mount Williamson's narrow ridgeline, where you have dizzying views on both sides: The San Gabriels are on your left; the desert is on your right. Don't turn around at the first pointy summit you reach; follow the backbone trail a bit farther to a second and flatter summit, which is 30 feet higher. The view from here is even more extraordinary—you can look directly down into the Devils Punchbowl and the San Andreas Fault.

Location: In Angeles National Forest near Islip Saddle; map I5, grid a6.

User groups: Hikers, dogs, horses, and mountain bikes. No wheelchair facilities.

Permits: No permits are required. A national forest recreation pass is required for each vehicle; fees are $5 for one day or $30 for a year.

Maps: For a map of Angeles National Forest, send $6 to U.S. Forest Service, Map Sales, P.O. Box 587, Camino, CA 95709; tel. (530) 647-5390 or website: www.r5.fs.fed.us/visitorcenter. A map of the San Gabriel Mountains is available for a fee from Tom Harrison Cartography, tel. (415) 456-7940. Ask the USGS for a topographic map for Crystal Lake.

Directions: From Interstate 210 in La Cañada, take Highway 2 northeast and drive 42 miles to Islip Saddle (it's a mile east of the tunnels). Park in the large Pacific Crest Trail parking lot on the north side of the road; the trail begins on the northwest side. (If you are coming from Highway 138 near Phelan or Piñon Hills, take Highway 2 west for 25 miles to Islip Saddle, 16 miles west of Big Pine.)

Contact: Angeles National Forest, Arroyo Seco Ranger District, 4600 Oak Grove Drive, Flintridge, CA 91011; tel. (818) 790-1151 or fax (818) 790-5392.

6 Vincent Gap to Mount Baden-Powell

8.0 mi/4.0 hrs

Like the climb to the summit of Mount Baldy, the climb to the summit of Mount Baden-Powell is something of a requirement for Southern California hikers. Luckily, this requirement is a little easier to attain, because the trail up to Mount Baden-Powell is a mere eight-mile round-trip with a 2,800-foot elevation gain. The summit of Baden-Powell is at 9,399 feet and is directly across the San Gabriel Basin from, and slightly north of, Mount Baldy. As you might guess, the views from the summit are extraordinary. The summit area is also a botanist's delight, as 2,000-year-old limber pines can be found growing there. From the southwest edge of Vincent Gap, the trail leads through open forest—first oak, sugar pine, and Jeffrey pine, and as you climb, mostly lodgepole pine and occasional limber pines. The trail is extremely well maintained and switchbacks on a moderate grade all the way up to the peak, where you can see more than a vertical mile below you into the canyon of the East Fork San Gabriel River. In addition, your views extend north to the desert and across the canyon to Mount Baldy. In case you haven't heard, the British Lord Baden-Powell, for whom this peak is named, founded the Boy Scouts organization. The Scouts have placed a monument to him at the summit. While you're there, make a vow always to "Be Prepared," just like the Boy Scouts.

Location: In Angeles National Forest near Big Pines; map I5, grid a7.

User groups: Hikers, dogs, and horses. No mountain bikes. No wheelchair facilities.

Permits: No permits are required. A national forest recreation pass is required for each vehicle; fees are $5 for one day or $30 for a year.

Maps: For a map of Angeles National Forest, send $6 to U.S. Forest Service, Map Sales, P.O. Box 587, Camino, CA 95709; tel. (530) 647-5390 or website: www.r5.fs.fed.us/visitorcenter. A map of the San Gabriel Mountains is avail-

able for a fee from Tom Harrison Cartography, tel. (415) 456-7940. Ask the USGS for topographic maps of the Mount San Antonio and Crystal Lake areas.

Directions: From Interstate 210 in La Cañada, take Highway 2 northeast and drive 53 miles to Vincent Gap. If you are coming from Highway 138 near Phelan or Piñon Hills, take Highway 2 west for 15 miles to Vincent Gap, which is 5.5 miles west of Big Pines.

Contact: Angeles National Forest, Valyermo Ranger District, 29835 Valyermo Road, Valyermo, CA 93563; tel. (661) 944-2187 or fax (661) 944-4698.

7 Gabrielino Trail to Bear Canyon

7.0 mi/4.0 hrs or 2.0 days

The Gabrielino National Recreation Trail is your ticket to visiting the water slides, mini-cascades, and pools of spectacular Bear Canyon. Begin hiking into the canyon from the Switzer Picnic Area, which on summer weekends is usually packed with people. Head downstream on the smooth dirt trail through a shady canopy of willows, alders, oaks, and maples. A few creek crossings and one mile of trail bring you to Commodore Switzer Trail Camp, which is comprised of a few primitive sites along the creek—an excellent short and easy backpacking trip. Cross the stream by the camp and head uphill, still on the Gabrielino Trail. The trail passes 50-foot Switzer Falls, affording a decent view of it from across the canyon. The stone building ruins you see are the remains of the Switzer Chapel, where visitors at Switzer's Camp, a popular trail resort in the early 1900s, attended Sunday services above the falls. A few steps farther brings you to a junction where Gabrielino Trail heads right and uphill, and Bear Canyon Trail heads left and downhill. Bear left and descend steeply for a mile, being cautious of the steep drop-offs. When you reach the creek, continue downstream for another mile to Bear Canyon Trail Camp, passing many water slides and crystal-clear pools along the way. Big cone spruce line the cool and shady trail. Trout fishing in the creek is good, best in spring.

Location: In Angeles National Forest near La Cañada; map I5, grid b2.

User groups: Hikers, dogs, horses, and mountain bikes. No wheelchair facilities.

Permits: A free campfire permit is required only for hikers using a camp stove or building a campfire. A national forest recreation pass is required for each vehicle; fees are $5 for one day or $30 for a year.

Maps: For a map of Angeles National Forest, send $6 to U.S. Forest Service, Map Sales, P.O. Box 587, Camino, CA 95709; tel. (530) 647-5390 or website: www.r5.fs.fed.us/visitorcenter. A map of the San Gabriel Mountains is available for a fee from Tom Harrison Cartography, tel. (415) 456-7940. Ask the USGS for topographic maps of the Condor Peak and Pasadena areas.

Directions: From Interstate 210 in La Cañada, take Highway 2 north and drive 9.8 miles to Switzer Picnic Area on the right. At 9.3 miles you reach Clear Creek Information Station; bear right and reach Switzer in .5 mile.

Contact: Angeles National Forest, Arroyo Seco Ranger District, 4600 Oak Grove Drive, Flintridge, CA 91011; tel. (818) 790-1151 or fax (818) 790-5392.

🎱 Millard Falls
1.0 mi/0.5 hr

If you want to guarantee your kids (or adult friends) a good time, take them to Millard Campground for the short hike and scramble to Millard Falls. In springtime make sure you're dressed to get wet, because you may have to spend more time in the stream than on a dry trail, especially if it has rained lately. This trip is a perfect easy adventure, suitable for hikers of all abilities. The only minus on the trail is the abundance of carvings found on the smooth-barked alder trees; the carvings desecrate al-

most every tree, as high as human hands can reach. (Take this opportunity to teach your children never, ever to carve anything on trees.) The route to the falls is a .5-mile walk up the stream canyon, partly in the creek and partly on trail. Start walking at the edge of the camp just beyond the camp host's site, where the trail leads to the right and passes a couple of cabins. Simply head upstream, rock hopping where necessary, until the canyon walls come together at 60-foot Millard Falls. The stream splits in two at the fall's lip, forced to detour around two boulders which are stuck in the waterfall's notch. The two streams rejoin about two-thirds of the way down, creating a tremendous rush of water in springtime. Trailhead elevation is 1,900 feet.

Location: In Angeles National Forest near Pasadena; map I5, grid b2.

User groups: Hikers and dogs. No horses or mountain bikes. No wheelchair facilities.

Permits: No permits are required. A national forest recreation pass is required for each vehicle; fees are $5 for one day or $30 for a year.

Maps: For a map of Angeles National Forest, send $6 to U.S. Forest Service, Map Sales, P.O. Box 587, Camino, CA 95709; tel. (530) 647-5390 or website: www.r5.fs.fed.us/visitorcenter. A map of the San Gabriel Mountains is available for a fee from Tom Harrison Cartography, tel. (415) 456-7940. Ask the USGS for a topographic map of the Pasadena area.

Directions: From Interstate 210 in Pasadena, exit on Lake Avenue and drive north for 3.5 miles to Loma Alta Drive. Turn west (left) on Loma Alta Drive and drive one mile to Chaney Trail at the flashing yellow light. Turn right and drive 1.5 miles on Chaney Trail, keeping left at the fork, to Millard Campground. Park in the parking lot and follow the fire road on the right (as you drove in) that leads into the campground.

Contact: Angeles National Forest, Arroyo Seco Ranger District, 4600 Oak Grove Drive, Flintridge, CA 91011; tel. (818) 790-1151 or fax (818) 790-5392.

9 Eaton Canyon
3.0 mi/1.5 hrs

Eaton Canyon Natural Area is the kind of place where elementary school groups come in the spring. The buses unload their cargoes of children, who then set off on what may be their first real hike, through Eaton Canyon's wash. And what a fine introduction to the outdoors—a hike along Eaton Canyon in the good company of cactus, chaparral plants, willows, oaks, and occasionally bunnies and lizards. Start at the park nature center, where you can pick up a free map of the area, then walk to the far end of the parking lot and take the dirt road that leads to the right. Cross the wash and hike along the wide canyon trail, with the creek on your left. The stream attracts a large variety of wildlife, especially birds that sing all day in this canyon. When you reach a bridge where your trail intersects with the Wilson Toll Road, cross the bridge and take the steep right cutoff on its far side down to the streambed. From there hike upstream, crossing the creek several times as the canyon narrows on its way to Eaton Canyon Falls. Sadly, the waterfall's cliff has been desecrated by graffiti, but the falls remain a well-loved destination in Eaton Canyon. An odd side note: if you hear the sound of gunfire at the trailhead, don't panic as we did. The local police have a shooting range nearby. As you walk into the canyon, you'll quickly get away from the noise.

Location: In Eaton Canyon Natural Area; map I5, grid b3.

User groups: Hikers, dogs, horses, and mountain bikes. No wheelchair facilities.

Permits: No permits are required. Parking and access are free.

Maps: A free map of Eaton Canyon Natural Area is available at the nature center. Ask the USGS for topographic maps of the Pasadena and Mount Wilson areas.

Directions: Heading east from Interstate 210 in Pasadena, take the Sierra Madre Boulevard/Altadena Drive exit and drive north on Altadena Drive for 1.6 miles. Turn right into the entrance for Eaton Canyon Natural Area, which is one block north of New York Drive. If you are heading west on Interstate 210, take the Sierra Madre Boulevard exit and drive north to New York Drive, then turn right on Altadena Drive and continue to the park entrance.

Contact: Eaton Canyon Natural Area, 1750 N. Altadena Drive, Pasadena, CA 91107; tel. (626) 398-5420.

10 Big Santa Anita Canyon
6.0 mi/3.0 hrs

Big Santa Anita Canyon is probably the top easy day-hike destination in all of the Arroyo Seco District of Angeles National Forest. It's easy to reach and provides a short, simple, and sweet escape from urban life. The shady, overgrown, magical gulch is just a handful of miles from the Pasadena freeway. Day hikers can't help but covet the adorable summer cabins in the canyon, which you walk past on your way to see 60-foot Sturtevant Falls, the canyon's showpiece. The cabins are what remains of Roberts Camp, a popular weekend resort from the early 1900s. The hike begins at Chantry Flat, elevation 2,200 feet, and you follow the Gabrielino National Recreation Trail downhill. It's paved for the first .6 mile heading down into the canyon. When you reach the bottom, you cross Roberts Footbridge and head to the right on the dirt pathway. Traveling under the shade of oaks and alders and along Big Santa Anita Creek for one mile upstream leads you to Sturtevant Falls. The artificial waterfalls you see are small check dams, designed (poorly) to keep the creek from flooding. Where the Gabrielino Trail forks left and heads uphill, continue straight along the creek, admiring ferns and vines as you walk another .25 mile to Sturtevant Falls. It drops 60 feet over a granite cliff into a perfectly shaped rock bowl. Retrace your steps to the junction and follow the Gabrielino Trail uphill. Take the lower trail (the upper trail is safer for horses), which clings to the steep hillsides as it climbs above Sturtevant Falls to Cascade Picnic Area, a shady spot alongside the fern-lined creek. Take a break here before leaving Big Santa Anita Canyon and heading back uphill to the real world.

Location: In Angeles National Forest near Arcadia; map I5, grid b3.

User groups: Hikers, dogs, horses, and mountain bikes. No wheelchair facilities.

Permits: No permits are required. A national forest recreation pass is required for each vehicle; fees are $5 for one day or $30 for a year.

Maps: For a map of Angeles National Forest, send $6 to U.S. Forest Service, Map Sales, P.O. Box 587, Camino, CA 95709; tel. (530) 647-5390 or website: www.r5.fs.fed.us/visitorcenter. A map of the San Gabriel Mountains is available for a fee from Tom Harrison Cartography, tel. (415) 456-7940. Ask the USGS for a topographic map of the Mount Wilson area.

Directions: From Interstate 210 in Pasadena drive seven miles east to Arcadia. Exit on Santa Anita Avenue and drive six miles north to the road's end at Chantry Flat. The trail begins across the road from the first parking area.

Contact: Angeles National Forest, Arroyo Seco Ranger District, 4600 Oak Grove Drive, Flintridge, CA 91011; tel. (818) 790-1151 or fax (818) 790-5392.

🔟 First Water Trail
3.0 mi/1.5 hrs

You say you flat out refuse to hike on pavement? Then the trip on the Gabrielino Trail to Sturtevant Falls might not be right for you, but don't bypass beautiful Big Santa Anita Canyon because of it. An alternate trail drops down into the canyon, but this one is on gorgeous single track all the way, lined with tall oaks and alders, huge chain ferns, slender sword ferns, and half dozen other fern varieties. The First Water Trail is mostly just a path used by cabin owners in the canyon to reach their homes. That means you'll see far fewer people than on the wide, paved Gabrielino Trail, the main trail into the canyon. You begin at the same trailhead, and the first few hundred yards of the walk are the same, but then you bear off the Gabrielino Trail at the sign for the First Water Trail and Hermit Falls (on your right). The trail switchbacks gently down into the canyon and then heads south along the North Fork of Big Santa Anita Creek. The near-constant shade of the canyon, combined with the presence of a year-round stream, makes it possible for every inch of ground to spring forth plant life. As on the Gabrielino Trail, you pass many artificial waterfalls made by check dams on Santa Anita Creek, which are surprisingly beautiful. The First Water Trail crosses the creek a few times, which can be a little tricky early in the year, and follows the stream on its downstream course. The trail ends at the last cabin in the canyon, just above Hermit Falls. Pick a granite boulder, have a seat, and watch the water flow by.

Location: In Angeles National Forest near Arcadia; map I5, grid b3.

User groups: Hikers, dogs, horses, and mountain bikes. No wheelchair facilities.

Permits: No permits are required. A national forest recreation pass is required for each vehicle; fees are $5 for one day or $30 for a year.

Maps: For a map of Angeles National Forest, send $6 to U.S. Forest Service, Map Sales, P.O. Box 587, Camino, CA 95709; tel. (530) 647-5390 or website: www.r5.fs.fed.us/visitorcenter. Ask the USGS for a topographic map of the Mount Wilson area.

Directions: From Interstate 210 in Pasadena drive seven miles east to Arcadia. Exit on Santa Anita Avenue and drive six miles north to the road's end at Chantry Flat. The trail begins across the road from the first parking area.

Contact: Angeles National Forest, Arroyo Seco Ranger District, 4600 Oak Grove Drive, Flintridge, CA 91011; tel. (818) 790-1151 or fax (818) 790-5392.

12 Vetter Mountain Lookout
2.2 mi/1.0 hr

Vetter Mountain is a San Gabriel summit that even children can attain, via a trail that's only a mile long and gains just 600 feet. The peak was named for Victor Vetter, a forest ranger during the 1920s and 1930s. From the trail sign, follow the path along a small ravine, crossing the Forest Service road in .5 mile. The trail continues along the ravine, soon leaving the shade of pines and oaks and climbing into yucca and chaparral. You'll huff and puff a bit to gain the ridge top. Turn left on a dirt road and stroll 150 yards to the fire lookout tower on Vetter's summit, at elevation 5,908 feet. From the tower's perimeter deck, views are extraordinary in all directions, with more than 20 named peaks visible. Bring a map so you can identify them. A historical note: Besides being used to spot fires, the Vetter Lookout was also used to spot enemy aircraft during World War II. Trailhead elevation is 5,500 feet.
Location: In Angeles National Forest near Charlton Flat; map I5, grid b4.
User groups: Hikers, dogs, horses, and mountain bikes. No wheelchair facilities.
Permits: No permits are required. A national forest recreation pass is required for each vehicle; fees are $5 for one day or $30 for a year.
Maps: For a map of Angeles National Forest, send $6 to U.S. Forest Service, Map Sales, P.O. Box 587, Camino, CA 95709; tel. (530) 647-5390 or website: www.r5.fs.fed.us/visitorcenter. Ask the USGS for a topographic map of the Chilao Flat area.
Directions: From Interstate 210 in La Cañada take Highway 2 northeast and drive 23 miles to Charlton Flat. Turn left on the road to Charlton Flat Picnic Area and bear right at the fork. Continue through Charlton Flat for .5 mile to the gate just before the Forest Service pump house. The Vetter Mountain Trail begins on the left at the wide turnaround area before the gate.
Contact: Angeles National Forest, Arroyo Seco Ranger District, 4600 Oak Grove Drive, Flintridge, CA 91011; tel. (818) 790-1151 or fax (818) 790-5392.

13 Silver Moccasin Trail to Mount Hillyer
6.0 mi/3.0 hrs

The Silver Moccasin Trail is a whopping 53 miles long, running through the San Gabriel Mountains from the Clear Creek Trailhead to Mount Baden-Powell. Not many people hike the entire thing, except the Boy Scouts, who have been doing it since 1942. When they finish, they get the Silver Moccasin Award, which is a much bigger deal than earning a badge for building a campfire. A popular section of the Silver Moccasin Trail is the route to Mount Hillyer, an 1,100-foot climb spread out over three miles. The trail starts in chaparral and occasional gray pines, interspersed with many tall, blooming yucca plants in the spring. The trail surface is a bit sandy, but well graded. After a moderate one-mile climb, you tag the edge of Horse Flats Campground, bear left, leave the Silver Moccasin Trail, and turn left on the Mount Hillyer Trail. The path goes around the camp, then climbs through a steep, rocky area and brings you to Hillyer's summit, which some hikers describe as "just a bump on a hill." On our first trip here, we walked right past the summit without even noticing it. It's the pile of boulders just off the trail to your left. If you find yourself hiking downhill for a while, heading toward looming Mount Pacifico, you've missed the summit. Views of the surrounding mountains are only fair from the summit, but the air is clean and sweet, and the crowds are nonexistent. Mount Hillyer is surrounded by beautiful stands of Jeffrey pines and incense cedars. The sound of the wind in the pines is divine.
Location: In Angeles National Forest near the Chilao Visitor Center; map I5, grid a4.
User groups: Hikers, dogs, horses, and mountain bikes. No wheelchair facilities.
Permits: No permits are re-

quired. A national forest recreation pass is required for each vehicle; fees are $5 for one day or $30 for a year.

Maps: For a map of Angeles National Forest, send $6 to U.S. Forest Service, Map Sales, P.O. Box 587, Camino, CA 95709; tel. (530) 647-5390 or website: www.r5.fs.fed.us/visitorcenter. A map of the San Gabriel Mountains is available for a fee from Tom Harrison Cartography, tel. (415) 456-7940. Ask the USGS for a topographic map of the Chilao Flat area.

Directions: From Interstate 210 in La Cañada take Highway 2 north and drive 28 miles to the Chilao Visitor Center turnoff on the left. Turn left and drive .7 mile, past the Chilao and Upper Chilao Picnic Area turnoffs, to a small parking pullout on the right for the Silver Moccasin Trailhead.

Contact: Angeles National Forest, Arroyo Seco Ranger District, 4600 Oak Grove Drive, Flintridge, CA 91011; tel. (818) 790-1151 or fax (818) 790-5392.

🔟🔟 Devils Canyon Trail
10.0 mi/6.0 hrs or 2.0 days

When you've tired of the front country, it's time to make the trip to the rugged San Gabriel Wilderness. Just be prepared to pay for your pleasure, because this is an upside-down hike—down on the way in and up, up, up on the way out. It's a trail of extremes. There's chaparral on some slopes and tall pines and big cone spruce on others. There's sun, then shade. It's dry for the first two miles, and then you reach a tributary creek and follow its meander. The trip down to the Devils Canyon Trail Camp, 3.5 miles in, is usually pretty quick—about an hour and a half for most people. From there you can make your way downstream along Devils Creek, partly on a trail and partly rock hopping, wading, and scrambling. The canyon gets narrower as you go; willows and alders shade the stream. It's slow travel but immensely enjoyable. Fishing is surprisingly good along the creek, and the highlight of the trip is a 20-foot waterfall dropping over light-colored granite. The fall blocks any farther travel downstream, so at this point turn around and head back to camp, or back to the trailhead, when you've had enough water play. Remember to save plenty of energy, and plenty of water for the 3.5-mile trip from the camp back to the trailhead, which has a 2,000-foot elevation gain. We were convinced the miles on the way up were twice as long as they were on the trip down. Trailhead elevation is 5,200 feet.

Location: In the San Gabriel Wilderness near Mount Waterman; map I5, grid a4.

User groups: Hikers, dogs, and horses. No mountain bikes. No wheelchair facilities.

Permits: A free campfire permit is required only for hikers using a camp stove or building a campfire. A national forest recreation pass is required for each vehicle; fees are $5 for one day or $30 for a year.

Maps: For a map of Angeles National Forest, send $6 to U.S. Forest Service, Map Sales, P.O. Box 587, Camino, CA 95709; tel. (530) 647-5390 or website: www.r5.fs.fed.us/visitorcenter. A map of the San Gabriel Mountains is available for a fee from Tom Harrison Cartography, tel. (415) 456-7940. Ask the USGS for topographic maps of the Chilao Flat and Waterman Mountain areas.

Directions: From Interstate 210 in La Cañada take Highway 2 north and drive 27 miles to Chilao Campground on the left. Continue .5 mile beyond the camp on Highway 2 to a parking lot on the left (west) side of the highway. (Go past the Devils Canyon Vista Point.) Park and walk across the road to the trailhead. If you reach the Chilao Visitor Center, you've gone too far.

Contact: Angeles National Forest, Arroyo Seco Ranger District, 4600 Oak Grove Drive, Flintridge, CA 91011; tel. (818) 790-1151 or fax (818) 790-5392.

🔟🔟 Monrovia Canyon Falls
1.4 mi/1.0 hr

Everything about Monrovia Canyon Park is a great experience, including the hike to the park's showpiece: Monrovia Canyon Falls. The trail is easy enough for families with small children, yet beautiful enough to keep seasoned hikers happy. It begins at the far edge of the picnic area at the clearly signed trailhead. At the first junction, bear right and walk upstream, passing several check dams along the creek. The canyon is lush and shaded, like a smaller version of nearby Big Santa Anita Canyon, and crowded with oaks, alders, and ferns. The slightly uphill trail leads you quickly to the 50-foot waterfall. Many big rocks in front of it are perfectly situated for gazing in admiration. After visiting the falls, you can extend your hike by retracing your steps down the canyon, then continuing beyond the picnic area junction and following the trail along the creek to its end at the park road. Turn left and walk up the road to return to your car. This will increase your round-trip to two miles instead of 1.4 miles.

Special note: Check your calendar before you go. Monrovia Canyon Park is closed on Tuesdays.

Location: In Monrovia Canyon Park; map I5, grid b4.

User groups: Hikers, dogs, horses, and mountain bikes. No wheelchair facilities.

Permits: No permits are required. A $2 day-use fee is charged per vehicle.

Maps: A free park map is available at the nature center. Ask the USGS for a topographic map of the Azusa area.

Directions: From Interstate 210 in Monrovia take the Myrtle Avenue exit and drive north on Myrtle Avenue for 1.8 miles. Turn right on Scenic Drive and drive 200 yards, turning right on Encinitas Drive and turning left again immediately, back on Scenic Drive. Continue on Scenic Drive as it turns into Canyon Boulevard and turn right at the sign for Monrovia Canyon Park. Park at the far end of the park road, near the picnic area and nature center.

Contact: Monrovia Canyon Park, 1200 N. Canyon Boulevard, Monrovia, CA 91016; tel. (626) 256-8282. Or contact Monrovia Public Works at tel. (626) 932-5562.

16 Ben Overturff Trail
7.0 mi/3.5 hrs

Ben Overturff was the man who made Monrovia Canyon a popular recreation area early in this century. He ran a lodge at Deer Park from 1910 to 1945, a wilderness getaway for city dwellers. This trail to the site of Deer Park Lodge was reconstructed in the 1990s and named in his honor. Start your hike on the Sawpit Canyon Fire Road, passing Sawpit Dam almost immediately. The fire road is the trail for the first 1.25 miles to Overturff Junction, and it can feel hot and steep at midday. Just grin and bear it until at last you turn left on the single-track Ben Overturff Trail. Follow the sometimes overgrown trail as it winds its way up and above Sawpit Canyon, passing Twin Springs Junction at 2.5 miles. If you're getting tired and want to loop back, a trail on the right connects to Sawpit Canyon Fire Road from here. Continue past the junction to the Deer Park Cabin site, where you can relax and pull your lunch out of your day pack. At trail's end you have two options: retrace your steps on the Ben Overturff Trail or take the connector trail to Sawpit Canyon Fire Road and follow the fire road all the way back to the trailhead. Our choice would be the Ben Overturff Trail, but loop-lovers will probably pick the fire road.

Special note: Check your calendar before you go. Although the entire park is closed on Tuesday, the Ben Overturff Trail is closed on both Tuesday and Wednesday.

Location: In Monrovia Canyon Park; map I5, grid b4.

User groups: Hikers, dogs, and horses. No mountain bikes. No wheelchair facilities.

Permits: No permits are required. A $2 day-use fee is charged per vehicle.

Maps: A free brochure on the Ben Overturff Trail is available at the nature center. Ask the USGS for a topographic map of the Azusa area.

Directions: From Interstate 210 in Monrovia take the Myrtle Avenue exit and drive north on

Myrtle Avenue for 1.8 miles. Turn right on Scenic Drive and drive 200 yards, turning right on Encinitas Drive and turning left again immediately back onto Scenic Drive. Continue on Scenic Drive as it turns into Canyon Boulevard and turn right at the sign for Monrovia Canyon Park. Park at the first available parking lot near the entrance; the trail begins at the lower end of the park, by the park toll gate.

Contact: Monrovia Canyon Park, 1200 N. Canyon Boulevard, Monrovia, CA 91016; tel. (626) 256-8282. Or contact Monrovia Public Works at tel. (626) 932-5562.

17 Soldier Creek/ Lewis Falls
1.25 mi/1.0 hr 　　🥾 🥾

The trip to Soldier Creek Falls, also known as Lewis Falls, is the perfect kind of adventure for people who aren't really up for having an adventure. The hike is pure fun, more stream scramble than walk, especially in springtime when snowmelt and rain make Soldier Creek flow strong and full. It's a short trip to the waterfall, and the going is fairly easy. The trailhead is unmarked, so follow the directions above exactly and then walk up the canyon with the stream on your left side. The start of the trail has some graffiti and usually some litter (mutter a few curses at the perpetrators), but as you head back away from the road, conditions improve. Pass a few cabins as you wander under the shade of oaks and firs. When the trail vanishes, simply walk up the streambed, rock hopping over small boulders and climbing over big ones. Just keep going until you can't go any farther, where the canyon walls come together and Lewis Falls pours in from the left. The waterfall holds court in this narrow space, surrounded by high cliffs and verdant ferns and mosses.

Location: Near the Crystal Lake Recreation Area; map I5, grid b6.

User groups: Hikers and dogs. No horses or mountain bikes. No wheelchair facilities.

Permits: No permits are required. A national forest recreation pass is required for each vehicle; fees are $5 for one day or $30 for a year.

Maps: For a map of Angeles National Forest, send $6 to U.S. Forest Service, Map Sales, P.O. Box 587, Camino, CA 95709; tel. (530) 647-5390 or website: www.r5.fs.fed.us/visitorcenter. A map of the San Gabriel Mountains is available for a fee from Tom Harrison Cartography, tel. (415) 456-7940. Ask the USGS for a topographic map of the Crystal Lake area.

Directions: From Azusa on Interstate 210 drive north on Highway 39 for 18 miles to Coldbrook Camp on the left. From Coldbrook Camp continue 2.4 miles up Highway 39 to a dirt pullout on the right, where Soldier Creek crosses under the highway. If you reach the turnoff for Falling Springs Resort, you've gone .2 mile too far. Park in the pullout and begin hiking from the far right side, heading up the right side of the creek.

Contact: Angeles National Forest, San Gabriel River Ranger District, 110 N. Wabash Avenue, Glendora, CA 91741; tel. (626) 335-1251 or fax (626) 914-3790.

18 Piñon Ridge Nature Trail
1.0 mi/0.5 hr 　　🥾 🥾

The thing about the Crystal Lake Recreation Area is that you either know about it or you don't. Many Los Angeles families vacation here year after year, staying in the campground, hiking on the trails, and fishing in small Crystal Lake, the only natural lake in the San Gabriel Mountains. But if you take an informal poll on the streets of nearby Azusa or Glendora, at least half the people will have never heard of Crystal Lake Recreation Area. Nevertheless, it's a great outdoor destination, with high elevations, a dense forest of big cedars and pines, and clean, fresh air. The Piñon Ridge Nature Trail is a perfect introduction to the area, beginning near the park amphitheater. Follow Soldier Creek Trail a short distance, bearing left for the beginning of the Piñon Ridge loop. We went clockwise on the loop, and although it makes the numbers on the interpretive markers read in reverse order, the views are better this way. As you walk among the piñon pines, there's the remarkably steep San Gabriel Canyon on your left, and a bench on top of the ridge that looks out over the valley. You can even see the tip of the San Gabriel Reservoir, which you drove by on your way up Highway 39. If you hike this trail in the off-season or any time that the park is quiet, you're almost guaranteed to see wildlife. On our trip we saw five little black-tailed deer and dozens of chipmunks.

Location: In the Crystal Lake Recreation Area; map I5, grid b6.

User groups: Hikers, dogs, and horses. No mountain bikes. No wheelchair facilities.

Permits: No permits are required. A $5 day-use fee is charged per vehicle.

Maps: For a map of Angeles National Forest, send $6 to U.S. Forest Service, Map Sales, P.O. Box 587, Camino, CA 95709; tel. (530) 647-5390 or website: www.r5.fs.fed.us/visitorcenter. A map of the San Gabriel Mountains is available for a fee from Tom Harrison Cartography, tel. (415) 456-7940. Ask the USGS for a topographic map of the Crystal Lake area.

Directions: From Azusa on Interstate 210 drive north on Highway 39 for 25 miles to the entrance station for Crystal Lake Recreation Area. Continue one mile to the visitor center and store, then bear right and drive a short distance to the parking area for the Yerba Santa Amphitheater. The Piñon Ridge/Soldier Creek Trailhead is just to the left of the amphitheater.

Contact: Crystal Lake Recreation Area, tel. (626) 910-2848; Angeles National Forest, San Gabriel River Ranger District, 110 N. Wabash Avenue, Glendora, CA 91741; tel. (626) 335-1251 or fax (626) 914-3790.

19 Windy Gap Trail to Mount Islip

7.0 mi/3.5 hrs

There are two ways to hike to 8,250-foot Mount Islip, and although the trailheads are close together as the crow flies, they're far apart as hikers drive. If you're somewhere on Highway 2/Angeles Crest Highway, you'd hike to Mount Islip from near Islip Saddle, on the Little Jimmy Trail. But if you're spending some time in Crystal Lake Recreation Area, you'd hike to Mount Islip from this route on the Windy Gap Trail. Set off from the parking lot, leaving the busy Crystal Lake campgrounds behind. You'll cross a paved camp road about .75 mile in, then a dirt road soon afterward. On the far side of the dirt road, take the Windy Gap Trail to the right, reaching the gap at 2.5 miles out after grunting through some steep sections. Here at a low pass on the ridge between Mount Islip and Mount Hawkins, take the far left trail for one more mile to Islip's bald, pointy summit. From way up high you can see a perfect 360 degrees—miles of national forest land, the Los Angeles basin, and even north to the Mojave. That spot of blue down there is Crystal Lake. The stone foundation on the summit is left from the days when the Forest Service had a fire lookout on Mount Islip. By the way, when you get back, don't go telling everyone you climbed to the summit of "islip," or you'll get laughed at. It's pronounced "eye-slip."

Location: In the Crystal Lake Recreation Area; map I5, grid b6.

User groups: Hikers, dogs, and horses. No mountain bikes. No wheelchair facilities.

Permits: No permits are required. A $5 day-use fee is charged per vehicle.

Maps: For a map of Angeles National Forest, send $6 to U.S. Forest Service, Map Sales, P.O. Box 587, Camino, CA 95709; tel. (530) 647-5390 or website: www.r5.fs.fed.us/visitorcenter. A map of the San Gabriel Mountains is available for a fee from Tom Harrison Cartography, tel. (415) 456-7940. Ask the USGS for a topographic map of the Crystal Lake area.

Directions: From Azusa on Interstate 210 drive north on Highway 39 for 25 miles to the entrance station for Crystal Lake Recreation Area. Continue one mile to the visitor center and store, then bear left and drive .6 of a mile to the parking area for the Windy Gap Trailhead, near campground loops E and F.

Contact: Crystal Lake Recreation Area, tel. (626) 910-2848; Angeles National Forest, San Gabriel River Ranger District, 110 N. Wabash Avenue, Glendora, CA 91741; tel. (626) 335-1251 or fax (626) 914-3790.

20 San Antonio Falls
1.5 mi/1.0 hr

Mount Baldy is that big mountain that you can see from almost everywhere in the Los Angeles basin (on a clear day), and if you hike the trail to San Antonio Falls, you'll be able to see almost everywhere in the Los Angeles basin. Trailhead elevation is 6,160 feet, a fine elevation to start at if you like clean, fresh, mountain air. For the best waterfall show, you've got to time your trip carefully for the first warm days after winter, sometimes as early as March, when the snow melts off the mountain and pours into 80-foot San Antonio Falls. By early summer the waterfall show is over. The hike to the falls is easy, following the Mount Baldy ski lift maintenance road, which is paved and has only a slight uphill grade. At .7 mile you round a sharp curve and see the falls, gracefully dropping in three tiers. If you wish, you can follow a well-worn path through loose gravel and talus to the waterfall's base, but be careful on the unstable slope. One of the best parts of this trip comes on your return walk to the trailhead. You're witness to lofty views of the far away San Gabriel Basin as you stroll back down the road.

Location: On Mount Baldy; map I5, grid c7.

User groups: Hikers, dogs, horses, and mountain bikes. No wheelchair facilities.

Permits: No permits are required. A national forest recreation pass is required for each vehicle; fees are $5 for one day or $30 for a year.

Maps: For a map of Angeles National Forest, send $6 to U.S. Forest Service, Map Sales, P.O. Box 587, Camino, CA 95709; tel. (530) 647-5390 or website: www.r5.fs.fed.us/visitorcenter.

A map of the San Gabriel Mountains is available for a fee from Tom Harrison Cartography, tel. (415) 456-7940. Ask the USGS for a topographic map of the Mount San Antonio area.

Directions: From Interstate 10 at Ontario, exit on Mountain Avenue and drive north for six miles until Mountain Avenue joins Shinn Road. Bear left on Shinn Road and continue uphill to Mount Baldy Road. Bear right and drive nine miles north on Mount Baldy Road to Manker Flats Camp and continue .3 mile farther to Falls Road on the left. Park in the dirt pullouts by Falls Road and begin walking on the gated, paved road.

Contact: Angeles National Forest, San Gabriel River Ranger District, 110 N. Wabash Avenue, Glendora, CA 91741; tel. (626) 335-1251 or fax (626) 914-3790.

21 Mount Baldy
13.5 mi/8.0 hrs

You just can't call yourself a Southern California hiker until you've climbed to the top of Mount Baldy, the highest peak in the San Gabriel Mountains at 10,064 feet. The shortest and easiest route (which is neither short nor easy, with a 13.5-mile round-trip and a 3,500-foot elevation gain) starts from San Antonio Falls Road. Follow the trail to San Antonio Falls, above, but from the waterfall, continue uphill on the road for another 2.5 miles to Mount Baldy Notch. From the top of the ski lift at Baldy Notch, you'll access the infamous Devils Backbone, a sharp and jagged ridge. Prepare to act like a mountaineer because the going gets a bit dicey on the well-named Devils Backbone, with steep drop-offs on both sides. You've got three miles and a 2,200-foot elevation gain to go, and while some of it is in sparse pine and fir forest, most of it is exposed granite country. On your way you'll pass the south side of Mount Harwood at 9,552 feet. When you finally reach Baldy's summit, what can you see? Everything—desert, city, ocean, southern Sierra—it's a panoramic view like no other. Note that if you want to cut seven miles and 1,300 feet of elevation gain off your round-trip, you can ride the Mount Baldy ski lift up to Baldy Notch, rather than hiking 3.5 miles up (and then down) San Antonio Falls Road. The ski lift operates only on weekends and holidays during the hiking season, however. By the way, in case you were wondering, Mount Baldy's formal name is Mount San Antonio. "Baldy" has just been its nickname for as long as anybody can remember.

Special note: Don't try hiking to Baldy's summit in winter, as tempting as the peak looks when covered in snow, because the Devils Backbone section is too treacherous. Try to hike the trail on a spring or early summer day when there is little visible air pollution in the Los Angeles basin, so the view from the summit is at its best.

Location: In Angeles National Forest near Upland; map I5, grid c7.

User groups: Hikers and dogs. No horses or mountain bikes. No wheelchair facilities.

Permits: A free campfire permit is required only for hikers using a camp stove or building a campfire. A national forest recreation pass is required for each vehicle; fees are $5 for one day or $30 for a year.

Maps: For a map of Angeles National Forest, send $6 to U.S. Forest Service, Map Sales, P.O. Box 587, Camino, CA 95709; tel. (530) 647-5390 or website: www.r5.fs.fed.us/visitorcenter. A map of the San Gabriel Mountains and/or Mount Baldy is available for a fee from Tom Harrison Cartography, tel. (415) 456-7940. Ask the USGS for topographic maps of the Mount San Antonio and Telegraph Peak areas.

Directions: From Interstate 10 at Ontario, exit on Mountain Avenue and drive north for six miles until Mountain Avenue joins Shinn Road. Bear left on Shinn Road and continue uphill to Mount Baldy Road. Bear right and drive nine miles north on Mount Baldy Road to Manker Flats Camp and continue .3 mile farther to Falls Road on the left. Park in the dirt pullouts by Falls Road and begin walking on the gated, paved road.

Contact: Angeles National Forest, San Gabriel River Ranger District, 110 N. Wabash Avenue, Glendora, CA 91741; tel. (626) 335-1251 or fax (626) 914-3790.

22 Ice House Saddle
7.2 mi/4.0 hrs

When it's wintertime in Southern California and you get the itch to throw a few snowballs, where do you go? Ice House Canyon on Mount Baldy, of course. But Ice House Canyon is good in the summer too, especially if you want a hiking escape far from the smog of the Inland Empire. You can go for as long or as short as you like in the canyon—it's a great place to just set out from your car, climb till you're tired, then turn around and head back. If you hike only the first 1.8 miles of trail to the wilderness boundary sign, you don't even need a wilderness permit. When the stream is running in the canyon, many people just go this far and find a spot to sit by the cold, clear water.

If you're looking for a destination, Ice House Saddle at 7,580 feet is a good one, perfect for picnicking with lovely views to the east and west. The saddle is also the site of a major trail junction, where routes lead in four directions, including the famous Three Ts Trail that leads to Timber Mountain, Telegraph Peak, and Thunder Mountain. The Ice House Canyon Trail begins by passing a few summer cabins, some still in use and others in ruins. It parallels the stunningly clear stream that runs all the way through the canyon. The path is well maintained, and the forest is a lovely mix of oak, big cone spruce, pine, fir, and cedar. At one mile in, you have a choice of taking either the Ice House Canyon Trail or the Chapman Trail. Both lead to Ice House Saddle, but the Ice House Canyon Trail stays along the creek, has a steeper grade, and gets to Ice House Saddle sooner. It's 2.6 miles to the saddle, straight up the canyon, with a total 2,660-foot elevation gain. You'll be huffing and puffing for sure. If you like, you can take the longer Chapman Trail for your return trip, which will add 1.7 miles to the round-trip mileage listed above. (Or hike the loop the other way around.)

Location: In the Cucamonga Wilderness; map I5, grid c7.

User groups: Hikers, dogs, and horses. No mountain bikes. No wheelchair facilities.

Permits: A free wilderness permit is required for both day hiking and backpacking in the Cucamonga Wilderness and is available from the San Gabriel River Ranger Station in Glendora or the Mount Baldy Information Station (open weekends only). A national forest recreation pass is required for each vehicle; fees are $5 for one day or $30 for a year.

Maps: For a map of Angeles National Forest, send $6 to U.S. Forest Service, Map Sales, P.O. Box 587, Camino, CA 95709; tel. (530) 647-5390 or website: www.r5.fs.fed.us/visitorcenter. A map of the San Gabriel Mountains is available for a fee from Tom Harrison Cartography, tel. (415) 456-7940. Ask the USGS for topographic maps of the Cucamonga Peak and Telegraph Peak areas.

Directions: From Interstate 10 at Ontario, exit on Mountain Avenue and drive north for six miles until Mountain Avenue joins Shinn Road. Bear left on Shinn Road and continue uphill to Mount Baldy Road. Bear right and drive 5.5 miles north on Mount Baldy Road to Mount Baldy Village and continue straight for .25 mile to Icehouse Canyon and the unsigned parking area where the road ends at an old stone foundation. (Don't take the left fork for Mount Baldy Ski Lift.) The trail begins at the road signed as "Private Road, Authorized Vehicles Only."

Contact: Angeles National Forest, San Gabriel River Ranger District, 110 N. Wabash Avenue, Glendora, CA 91741; tel. (626) 335-1251 or fax (626) 914-3790.

23 Telegraph Canyon and South Ridge Loop

4.0 mi/2.0 hrs

If you don't mind sharing your walk with equestrians and mountain bikers, this loop trail in Chino Hills State Park may be just what you need to revive yourself from the miles of surrounding freeways and rush-hour traffic. Start walking on the wide Telegraph Canyon Trail from near park headquarters, following a seasonal creek. You'll head out for about two miles and then loop back on the South Ridge Trail. If you're in the mood for some single-track hiking, you can always take the right fork one mile out on the Hills for Everyone Trail, turning left when it ends and returning to park headquarters on the Telegraph Canyon Trail. The park is mostly grasslands and oaks, with a few wet canyon ravines providing homes for sycamore groves and wildlife. Native California walnut trees also grow here. Remember that the best time to visit the park is in winter or spring; if you come in summer, make it as early in the morning as possible. In addition to the heat, summer brings with it the infamous Inland Empire smog.

Location: In Chino Hills State Park near Pomona; map I5, grid e6.

User groups: Hikers, horses, and mountain bikes. No dogs. No wheelchair facilities.

Permits: No permits are required. A $2 day-use fee is charged per vehicle.

Maps: A map of Chino Hills State Park is available at the entrance kiosk. Ask the USGS for topographic maps of the Yorba Linda and Prado Dam areas.

Directions: From the junction of Highway 71 and Highway 91 near Corona, drive north on Highway 71 to Butterfield Ranch Road. Turn left and drive five miles on Butterfield Ranch Road. Turn left on Soquel Canyon Parkway and drive one mile to Elinvar Avenue. Turn left and drive to the end of Elinvar Avenue at its intersection with Sapphire Road. Turn left on Sapphire Road and then right immediately at the Chino Hills State Park sign. Continue down the park road to park headquarters and turn into the parking area. The Telegraph Canyon Trail begins just below park headquarters.

Contact: Chino Hills State Park, 1879 Jackson Street, Riverside, CA 92504; tel. (909) 780-6222.

24 Bolsa Chica Ecological Reserve

1.5 mi/0.75 hr

What a dichotomy. From the footbridge over the water at Bolsa Chica Ecological Reserve, you can see mussels, minnows, egrets, cordgrass, pickleweed, and huge flocks of shorebirds swirling in unison over the sparkling waters. But just a few hundred yards away, the state beach is lined with RVs, the oil-drilling grasshoppers are doing their monotonous job, and the traffic is crawling past on Highway 1. Where would you rather be? Right. The 1.5-mile loop trail at Bolsa Chica Ecological Reserve is the perfect opportunity to be reminded of what our coastline is supposed to look like and who depends on it the most—the birds on the Pacific Flyway. The 530-acre reserve is a migratory rest stop, and the birds are plentiful and fascinating to watch. The trail runs along the top of a levee, providing a vantage point that's just a few feet above the water's edge. What birds will you see on your walk? Brown pelicans, widgeons, pie-billed grebes, mergansers, pintails, and terns. If you're lucky, you may even spot a few endangered species, like the Belding's savannah sparrow (an unusual bird because it can drink sea water and process it through its kidneys) or the California least tern. Worth noting: For years private developers have been trying to pave this place over and put up pricey homes and condominiums, but so far the birds are winning. We're rooting for them.

Location: In Huntington Beach; map I5, grid g2.

User groups: Hikers only. No dogs, horses, or mountain bikes. No wheelchair facilities.

Permits: No permits are required. Parking and access are free.

Maps: Ask the USGS for a topographic map of the Seal Beach area.

Directions: From Interstate 405 in Seal Beach, exit at Seal Beach Boulevard and drive west to Highway 1. Turn south on Highway 1 and drive 4.5 miles to the Bolsa Chica Ecological Reserve entrance on the inland side of the highway, across from Bolsa Chica State Beach.

Contact: Amigos de Bolsa Chica, P.O. Box 3748, Huntington Beach, CA 92605; tel. (714) 840-1575.

25 Holy Jim Falls

2.5 mi/1.5 hrs

It seems that everybody in Orange County knows about and likes to visit Holy Jim Falls. The waterfall and its canyon were named for a beekeeper who lived here in the 1890s, James T. Smith, better known as "Cussin' Jim." Apparently he had a temper and a colorful way with language. But conservative map makers who plotted Trabuco Canyon in the early 1900s found Smith's nickname in bad taste, so they changed it to "Holy Jim," and it remains. Whether it's because of the interesting history of the area or the beauty that it still exhibits today, the trail to Holy Jim Falls is well known and frequently walked, especially in springtime. The 2.5-mile stroll is in the cool shade along Holy Jim Creek. Start by walking down the dirt road, past some leased cabins, to the signed trailhead. There the trail turns to single track. You're surrounded by a lush canyon filled with oaks, vine maples, wildflowers, and even a few bracken ferns. The trail crosses the creek several times and gently gains some elevation as it heads upstream. Where the trail steepens noticeably as you pass a large, old oak tree on your left, cross the creek one final time. Instead of following the main trail as it switchbacks uphill, you'll head to the right, continuing along the stream. An easy 300-yard stream

scramble brings you to the waterfall's base, and if there isn't a Scout troop there eating lunch (as there was on our trip), you'll be able to listen to the sweet music of the falls.

Location: In Trabuco Canyon in Cleveland National Forest; map I5, grid h8.

User groups: Hikers, dogs, horses, and mountain bikes. No wheelchair facilities.

Permits: No permits are required. A national forest recreation pass is required for each vehicle; fees are $5 for one day or $30 for a year.

Maps: For a map of Cleveland National Forest, send $6 to U.S. Forest Service, Map Sales, P.O. Box 587, Camino, CA 95709; tel. (530) 647-5390 or website: www.r5.fs.fed.us/visitorcenter. Ask the USGS for a topographic map of the Santiago Peak area.

Directions: From Laguna Hills (north of San Juan Capistrano) on Interstate 5, exit on El Toro Road and drive east for six miles. Turn right on Live Oak Canyon Road and drive about four miles (two miles past the entrance to O'Neill Regional Park). Turn left on Trabuco Canyon Road, which is an often unsigned, rocky, dirt road, just past the paved Rose Canyon Road turnoff. The road is usually suitable for passenger cars. Go five miles on the dirt road to the well-signed parking area for Holy Jim Trail. The trail leads from the left side of the parking lot.

Contact: Cleveland National Forest, Trabuco Ranger District, 1147 E. 6th Street, Corona, CA 92879; tel. (909) 736-1811 or fax (909) 736-3002.

26 El Moro Canyon and Ridge Loop

4.5 mi/2.0 hrs

El Moro Canyon is on the inland side of Crystal Cove State Park, and when you see how lush and overgrown it is, you'll have a hard time believing that only 12 inches of rain fall here each year. Although El Moro Creek flows only in the wet season, its edges are lined with oaks, sycamores, and willows, and it attracts tons of birds, small mammals, and butterflies. We managed to identify the anise swallowtail butterfly (yellow and black) and the red admiral butterfly (brown, red, and black) on our trip. Unlike the other trails on the inland side of the park, the El Moro Canyon Trail is on a gentle grade, which makes it a fine route to take into the park's backcountry. The beginning of the trail is not so great, however, as it starts on a dirt road by the park entrance kiosk and winds behind the back of a trailer park. But in 10 minutes things start to look up, as you veer left on El Moro Canyon Trail and walk up the shady, tree-lined canyon. At 1.5 miles out, turn right on East Cut Across Trail and make a switchbacking climb to El Moro Ridge. The ascent will get your heart pumping. Turn right on El Moro Ridge Trail and follow it as it rolls along the ridge top, offering many excellent ocean views. The trail leads back down to a single-track trail on the right, which in turn heads back to the trailer park. From there, proceed straight to the park entrance kiosk.

Location: In Crystal Cove State Park; map I5, grid i4.

User groups: Hikers, horses, and mountain bikes. No dogs. No wheelchair facilities.

Permits: No permits are required. A $3 dayuse fee is charged per vehicle.

Maps: A free backcountry user guide map of Crystal Cove State Park is available at the visitor center. Ask the USGS for a topographic map of the Laguna Beach area.

Directions: From Corona del Mar drive south on Highway 1 for three miles to the entrance to Crystal Cove State Park on the inland side of the highway. Park near the park headquarters building; the El Moro Canyon Trail begins down the park road by the entrance kiosk.

Contact: Crystal Cove State Park, 8471 Pacific Coast Highway, Laguna Beach, CA 92651; tel. (949) 494-3539; California State Parks, Orange Coast District; tel. (714) 848-1566.

27 San Juan Loop Trail
2.0 mi/1.0 hr

The San Juan Loop Trail is an easy and informative walk that serves as a good introduction to the Santa Ana Mountains. The only factor you must consider: don't try to hike here in summer, when these mountains can feel hotter than the desert. The trailhead features a rather negative sign, which explains in doomsday-style terms the dangers of mountain lions, rattlesnakes, poison oak, and rugged terrain. If the sign doesn't convince you to get back in the car and go to Disneyland instead, start hiking on the loop trail, which parallels the road for its first .5 mile. You'll forget about the car noise as you start examining all the plant life along the trail, which includes deep red monkeyflowers, purple nightshade, and tall, spiky yuccas with their silky, milk-white flowers. Lizards dart here and there among the foliage. The terrain is dry and exposed, but thriving nonetheless. A half mile out you'll pass a railing and overlook above a small seasonal waterfall on San Juan Creek, which has many clear, granite-lined pools. In another .5 mile you'll pass the turnoff for the Chiquito Basin Trail (it's highly recommended for those seeking a longer trip), and then pass through a lovely grove of ancient oaks. The loop trail finishes out by bringing you back to the opposite side of the parking lot.

Location: In Cleveland National Forest near Lake Elsinore; map I5, grid i8.

User groups: Hikers, dogs, horses, and mountain bikes. No wheelchair facilities.

Permits: No permits are required. A national forest recreation pass is required for each vehicle; fees are $5 for one day or $30 for a year.

Maps: For a map of Cleveland National Forest, send $6 to U.S. Forest Service, Map Sales, P.O. Box 587, Camino, CA 95709; tel. (530) 647-5390 or website: www.r5.fs.fed.us/visitorcenter. Ask the USGS for a topographic map of the Sitton Peak area.

Directions: From Interstate 5 at San Juan Capistrano, take the Ortega Highway/High-way 74 exit and drive north. In 21 miles you'll reach the Ortega Oaks store on the right, .75 mile past Upper San Juan Campground. The trailhead is across the road from the store; turn left and park in the large parking lot. Start the loop trail on the right (north) side of the parking lot.

Contact: Cleveland National Forest, Trabuco Ranger District, 1147 E. 6th Street, Corona, CA 92879; tel. (909) 736-1811 or fax (909) 736-3002.

28 Bear Canyon Loop Trail
6.7 mi/3.5 hrs

Is it winter or spring? Is the weather cool and clear? Good; this is a fine time to take a hike on the Bear Canyon Trail, either a little out-and-back trip for as far as you like, or the full 6.7-mile loop which circles a junction called Four Corners. First, we suggest you stock up on some chocolate from the candy store at the trailhead (this is why it must be a cool day; otherwise carrying chocolate is out of the question). Set off on the trail adjacent to the store, heading into the San Mateo Canyon Wilderness and climbing gently through chaparral-covered slopes. In spring, many yuccas bloom along this stretch. Take the right fork one mile in, and in another mile, you'll reach the start of the loop; take the right branch to start. The trail has a mere 700-foot elevation gain, and in places, it offers expansive views of the San Juan Canyon. Pigeon Springs is a popular resting point, where you can find some shade among the oaks. Four Corners is .5 mile beyond Pigeon Springs, and there you'll turn sharply left to loop back.

Location: In the San Mateo Canyon Wilderness near Lake Elsinore; map I5, grid i8.

User groups: Hikers, dogs, and horses. No mountain bikes. No wheelchair facilities.

Permits: No permits are required. A national forest recreation pass is required for each vehicle; fees are $5 for one day or $30 for a year.

Maps: For a map of Cleveland National Forest, send $6 to U.S. Forest Service, Map Sales, P.O. Box 587, Camino, CA 95709; tel. (530) 647-5390 or website: www.r5.fs.fed.us/visitorcenter. Ask the USGS for a topographic map of the Sitton Peak area.

Directions: From Interstate 5 at San Juan Capistrano, take the Ortega Highway/Highway 74 exit and drive north. In 21 miles, you'll reach the Ortega Oaks store on the right, .75 mile past Upper San Juan Campground. The parking area is across the road from the store; turn left and park in the large parking lot. Cross the road to begin hiking on the Bear Canyon Trail, to the right of the store.

Contact: Cleveland National Forest, Trabuco Ranger District, 1147 E. 6th Street, Corona, CA 92879; tel. (909) 736-1811 or fax (909) 736-3002.

29 Tenaja Falls
1.5 mi/1.0 hr

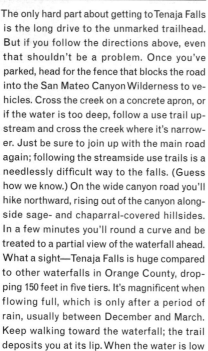

The only hard part about getting to Tenaja Falls is the long drive to the unmarked trailhead. But if you follow the directions above, even that shouldn't be a problem. Once you've parked, head for the fence that blocks the road into the San Mateo Canyon Wilderness to vehicles. Cross the creek on a concrete apron, or if the water is too deep, follow a use trail upstream and cross the creek where it's narrower. Just be sure to join up with the main road again; following the streamside use trails is a needlessly difficult way to the falls. (Guess how we know.) On the wide canyon road you'll hike northward, rising out of the canyon alongside sage- and chaparral-covered hillsides. In a few minutes you'll round a curve and be treated to a partial view of the waterfall ahead. What a sight—Tenaja Falls is huge compared to other waterfalls in Orange County, dropping 150 feet in five tiers. It's magnificent when flowing full, which is only after a period of rain, usually between December and March. Keep walking toward the waterfall; the trail deposits you at its lip. When the water is low

enough, you can cross over the top of the falls to the other side of the creek, but be extremely cautious on the slippery granite if you choose to do so.

Location: In the San Mateo Canyon Wilderness near Murrieta; map I5, grid i9.

User groups: Hikers, dogs, and horses. No mountain bikes. No wheelchair facilities.

Permits: No permits are required. A national forest recreation pass is required for each vehicle; fees are $5 for one day or $30 for a year.

Maps: For a map of Cleveland National Forest, send $6 to U.S. Forest Service, Map Sales, P.O. Box 587, Camino, CA 95709; tel. (530) 647-5390 or website: www.r5.fs.fed.us/visitorcenter. Ask the USGS for a topographic map of the Sitton Peak area.

Directions: From Lake Elsinore drive south on Interstate 15 for about 12 miles to the Clinton Keith Road exit in Murrieta. Drive south on Clinton Keith Road for five miles, which will become Tenaja Road although you won't see any signs. At a signed intersection with Tenaja Road, turn right and drive west for 4.5 miles. Turn right on Rancho California Road and drive one mile to the Tenaja Trailhead. Reset your odometer here and continue 4.4 miles on the dirt road (7S04) to a hairpin turn in the road and the parking area.

Contact: Cleveland National Forest, Trabuco Ranger District, 1147 E. 6th Street, Corona, CA 92879; tel. (909) 736-1811 or fax (909) 736-3002.

30 Santa Rosa Plateau Vernal Pools
4.8 mi/2.5 hrs

Those volcanic-looking rocky mesas you see as you drive through the foothills along Clinton Keith Road are home to some of Southern California's last vernal pools—seasonal ponds that give life to endangered plants and wildflowers and provide a resting place for wintering birds. While these pools are common in the San Joaquin Valley, here in Southern California they have all but vanished, which is one reason for the establishment of the Santa Rosa Plateau Ecological Reserve.

Another reason is the rare Engelmann oak, a semi-deciduous species of oak that only loses its leaves during times of drought. Several fine groves of Engelmann oaks are found within the reserve's border. To see them, start hiking on the Oak Tree Trail, a self-guided nature loop that is .6 mile in length. Take either side of the loop; once you've reached the far side of the loop, continue hiking on the Trans Preserve Trail, past Poppy Hill (beautiful in spring, if you time it right).

At 2.4 miles the trail intersects with the Vernal Pool Trail on top of Mesa de Colorado; turn left to see one of the preserve's vernal pools. The best time to visit, of course, is after a period of heavy rain, when the pool is filled to capacity and the grasslands are lush and green. Spring days at the preserve are often busy with docents leading school field trips.

Location: In the Santa Rosa Plateau Ecological Reserve; map I5, grid i9.

User groups: Hikers only. No dogs, horses, or mountain bikes. (Horses and mountain bikes are allowed only on special docent-led trips.) No wheelchair facilities.

Permits: No permits are required. Parking and access are free.

Maps: Ask the USGS for a topographic map of the Wildomar area.

Directions: From Lake Elsinore drive south on Interstate 15 for about 12 miles to the Clinton Keith Road exit in Murrieta. Drive south n Clinton Keith Road for six miles to the preserve entrance on the left. Park along the side of the road. The trailhead is signed for the Oak Tree Trail and Vernal Pools.

Contact: Santa Rosa Plateau Ecological Reserve, 39400 Clinton Keith Road, Murrieta, CA 92562; tel. (909) 677-6951.

PACIFIC CREST TRAIL (PCT) SECTION OVERVIEW

48.0 mi one way/5.0 days

Dramatic ridge views, deep canyons with waterfalls, and tons of ravines can make this one of the stellar sections of the PCT in Southern California, with trail sections extending from the Angeles Crest Highway to the Mill Creek Picnic Area. Highlights are the side trip to the top of Mount Baden-Powell, where you can view to the north all the way to Mount Whitney, and Cooper Canyon, where gorgeous Cooper Canyon Falls is a place you'll never want to leave. Trail elevations generally run in the 5,000- to 7,000-foot range. Water availability is decent enough, but always tank up at every opportunity.

PCT-11 Angeles Crest Highway to Three Points

32.0 mi one way/3.0 days

This particular stretch of the PCT is one of our favorites in Southern California. It starts with a great side trip to the top of Mount Baden-Powell, and with it, awesome views from the 9,399-foot summit, including all the way across the awaiting desert to the north for the first glimpse of Mount Whitney for PCT through-hikers. After this must-do trip, you'll be properly rejuvenated to forge on, and awaiting is the Sheep Mountain Wilderness, Crystal Lake Recreation Area, San Gabriel Wilderness, and several remote pieces of Angeles National Forest. The trip generally heads to the west, and after passing busy Crystal Lake, climbs up Kratka Ridge amid a sparse fir forest, providing distant views over and down canyons. Eventually, you continue to climb in and out of canyons and drop into Cooper Canyon, a favorite. This is where we found Cooper Canyon Falls, a drop-dead gorgeous waterfall, and a place we didn't want to leave, despite having run out of food (we later scored two treasured Baby Ruth candy bars before claiming dinner). From Cooper Canyon it's a butt-kicking climb out of the canyon, back up to the Angeles Crest Highway, and then to the Three Points Trailhead.

Location: From the Angeles Crest Highway to Three Points; map I5, grid a8.

User groups: Hikers, dogs, and horses. No mountain bikes. No wheelchair facilities.

Permits: A wilderness permit is required for traveling through various wilderness and special-use areas the trail traverses. Contact the Angeles National Forest for permit information. For this section of the Pacific Crest Trail, no day-use permits are required.

Maps: For an overall view of the trail route in this section, send $6 to U.S. Forest Service, Map Sales, P.O. Box 587, Camino, CA 95709; tel. (530) 647-5390 or website: www.r5.fs.fed.us/visitorcenter. Ask for the Angeles National Forest map. Ask the USGS for topographic maps of the Waterman Mountain, Crystal Lake, and Mount San Antonio areas.

Directions: To reach the Angeles Crest Trailhead from Interstate 15 near Cajon, take Highway 138 east. Turn left (west) on the Angeles Crest Highway and drive five miles to Wrightwood. Continue for three miles to Big Pines. Bear left and continue on the Angeles Crest Highway for 1.5 miles to Inspiration Point, opposite Blue Ridge Road. To reach the Three Points Trailhead from the Foothill Freeway (Interstate 210) in La Cañada, exit onto the Angeles Crest Highway/Highway 2 and drive to Three Points Junction, approximately 2.5 miles north of Chilao. The exit to Three Points is marked by a sign indicating Horse Flats. Note: Do not confuse the Three Points Trailhead with the small town of Three Points, which is located near Tejon Ranch to the north.

Contact: Angeles National Forest, 701 N. Santa Anita Avenue, Arcadia, CA 91006; tel. (626) 574-5200 or fax (626) 574-5233.

PCT-12 Three Points to Mill Creek Picnic Area

16.0 mi one way/2.0 days

This short section of the PCT features a series of ravines, draws, and short ridges, sprinkled with pines and sagebrush, with a few creeks to brighten up the trip. It's not an inspiring piece of trail work, but pleasant enough, and most PCT through-hikers make fast work of it. In the back of all minds the entire time, however, is what awaits: the butt-kicking desert tromp to the foot of the southern Sierra. This reality comes into view when you climb near the top of Mount Pacifico at 6,800 feet and enjoy the view north of the sparse Antelope Valley and beyond. All PCT hikers stop at the Mill Creek Ranger Station, typically to resupply, get water, and prepare for the more serious adventure ahead.

Location: From Three Points to Mill Creek; map I5, grid a4.

User groups: Hikers, dogs, and horses. No mountain bikes. No wheelchair facilities.

Permits: A wilderness permit is required for traveling through various wilderness and special-use areas the trail traverses. Contact the Angeles National Forest at the address below for a permit good for the length of your trip. For this section of the Pacific Crest Trail, no day-use permits are required.

Maps: For an overall view of the trail route in this section, send $6 to U.S. Forest Service, Map Sales, P.O. Box 587, Camino, CA 95709; tel. (530) 647-5390 or website: www.r5.fs.fed.us/visitorcenter. Ask for the Angeles National Forest map. Ask the USGS for topographic maps of the Waterman Mountain, Chilao Flat, and Pacifico Mountain areas.

Directions: To reach the Three Points Trailhead from the Foothill Freeway (Interstate 210) in La Cañada, exit on the Angeles Crest Highway/Highway 2 and drive to Three Points Junction, approximately 2.5 miles north of Chilao. The exit to Three Points is marked by a sign indicating Horse Flats. To reach the Mill Creek Picnic Area Trailhead from Highway 14 at Vincent, head south on the Angeles Forest Highway/County Road N3 to the Mill Creek Summit and Picnic Area and the signed PCT Trailhead.

Contact: Angeles National Forest, Saugus Ranger District, 30800 Bouquet Canyon Road, Saugus, CA 91350; tel. (661) 296-9710 or fax (661) 296-5847.

PCT Continuation

To continue hiking along the Pacific Crest Trail, see chapter H5.

DEEP CREEK FISHERMEN'S TRAIL OFFERS ACCESS TO
POOLS, WATERFALLS, AND WILD TROUT.

MAP 16

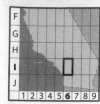

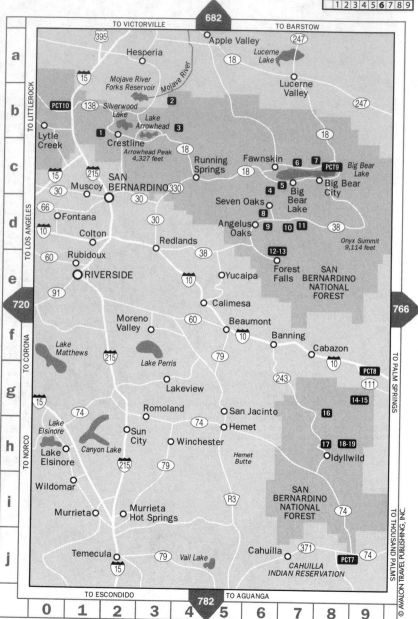

TO LITTLEROCK

395
Hesperia
15
Mojave River Forks Reservoir
Mojave River
Apple Valley
247
Lucerne Lake
18
Lucerne Valley
247

a

b
PCT10
138   Silverwood Lake
2
Mojave River
Lake Arrowhead
3
18

1
Crestline
Arrowhead Peak 4,327 feet
18
Running Springs
Fawnskin
6
7
PCT9
Big Bear Lake

c
Lytle Creek
15   215
30
Muscoy
SAN BERNARDINO
330
18
4
5
Big Bear City
Big Bear Lake

TO LOS ANGELES

d
66
Fontana
10
Colton
30
30
Seven Oaks
8
9   10   11
38
Onyx Summit 9,114 feet
Angelus Oaks

Redlands
60
Rubidoux
38
12-13

e
RIVERSIDE
91
Yucaipa
Forest Falls
SAN BERNARDINO NATIONAL FOREST

f
Moreno Valley
Lake Matthews
215
Lake Perris
60
10
Calimesa
Beaumont
Banning
Cabazon
10

g
15
74
Lakeview
Romoland
74
San Jacinto
Hemet
243
PCT8
111
14-15
16

TO NORCO

h
Lake Elsinore
Canyon Lake
Sun City
215
Winchester
79
Hemet Butte
17   18-19
Idyllwild

Lake Elsinore
Wildomar

i
Murrieta
Murrieta Hot Springs
R3
SAN BERNARDINO NATIONAL FOREST
74

j
Temecula
15
79
Vail Lake
Cahuilla
371
CAHUILLA INDIAN RESERVATION
PCT7
74

TO THOUSAND PALMS

© AVALON TRAVEL PUBLISHING, INC.

0   1   2   3   4   5   6   7   8   9

CHAPTER 16

1 Seeley Creek Trail 747
2 Deep Creek Hot
    Springs 748
3 Deep Creek
    Fishermen's Trail 748
4 Champion Lodgepole
    Pine 749
5 Castle Rock Trail 750
6 Cougar Crest Trail
    to Bertha Peak 750
7 Woodland Trail 751
8 Ponderosa Vista
    Nature Trail 751
9 Whispering Pines Trail . . 752
10 Jenks Lake 752
11 Aspen Grove Trail 753
12 Big Falls 754
13 Vivian Creek Trail to
    Mount San Gorgonio . . . 755
14 Aerial Tramway to
    Desert View Trail 755

15 Aerial Tramway to San
    Jacinto Peak 756
16 Seven Pines Trail 757
17 Deer Springs Trail to
    Suicide Rock 758
18 Ernie Maxwell Scenic
    Trail 758
19 Devils Slide Trail to
    Tahquitz Peak 759

Pacific Crest Trail
(PCT) Section Overview
PCT-7 Highway 74 to San
    Gorgonio Pass 760
PCT-8 San Gorgonio to Van
    Dusen Canyon Road . . . 761
PCT-9 Van Dusen Canyon Road
    to Cajon Pass 762
PCT-10 Cajon Pass to Angeles
    Crest Highway 763

1 Seeley Creek Trail

2.0 mi/1.0 hr

To reach the start of the Seeley Creek Trail, you have to drive through a town called Valley of Enchantment, and that should tell you just about all you need to know about the area and the trail. It's beautiful up here—no, let's say it's enchanting—and although the elevation is only 4,000 feet, the conifers grow so big you'll think you're in the southern Sierra. The Seeley Creek Trail is a short and easy walk to a destination called Heart Rock, which during periods of rain or after snowmelt becomes Heart Rock Falls. Heart Rock is a smooth giant boulder in which nature has carved a perfect, heart-shaped bowl, about three feet deep and five feet wide. When Seeley Creek is running strong, a 25-foot waterfall spills into the heart's crown, then flows out the bottom and free falls downward. The stream flows year-round, and Heart Rock is always fascinating to see, but it's most compelling when the waterfall is flowing strong. The trail begins in a rather pedestrian fashion along a road opposite the buildings of Seeley Camp, a Los Angeles Parks and Recreation camp. But once you walk beyond the camp boundary, the enchantment begins.

Location: In San Bernardino National Forest near Crestline; map I6, grid b1.

User groups: Hikers, dogs, horses, and mountain bikes. No wheelchair facilities.

Permits: No permits are required. A national forest recreation pass is required for each vehicle; fees are $5 for one day or $30 for a year.

Maps: For a map of San Bernardino National Forest, send $6 to U.S. Forest Service, Map Sales, P.O. Box 587, Camino, CA 95709; tel. (530) 647-5390 or website: www.r5.fs.fed.us/visitorcenter. Ask the USGS for a topographic map of the San Bernardino North area.

Directions: From Crestline at the junction of Highways 18 and 138, turn north on Highway 138 and drive 2.5 miles to the sign for Camp Seeley, just past the town of Valley of Enchantment. Turn left at the camp sign on Road 2N03 and take the left fork in the road (don't park in the camp parking lot). Cross the creek, which usually flows over the road, and look for the double-track trail on the right, near a sewer pipeline sign. Park alongside the road. You will be directly across the creek from the main parking lot for Camp Seeley, near the playground area.

Contact: San Bernardino National Forest, Arrowhead Ranger District, P.O. Box 350, 28104 Highway 18, Skyforest, CA 92385; tel. (909) 337-2444.

❷ Deep Creek Hot Springs
3.0 mi/1.5 hrs

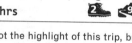

This trail is not the highlight of this trip, but its destination is. Deep Creek's hot springs are well known, well loved, and heavily visited. Although there are a few ways to hike to them, this route is the most popular simply because it's the shortest. But remember, it's called Goat Trail for a reason. This is a no-nonsense path that leads straight down from the trailhead to the creek, and straight up on the return. The total elevation change is only 700 feet, but on a hot day, it's—well, hot. Most people visit on cool days in winter and spring. The hot springs consist of three pools alongside the creek; the hottest one is the farthest from the stream's edge. Note that Goat Trail ends on the north side of Deep Creek, and you must ford the creek to reach the hot springs, then hike a short distance downstream. When Deep

Creek is running high, this ford can be difficult, so check with the Arrowhead Ranger Station before planning an early spring visit.

Location: In San Bernardino National Forest near Hesperia; map I6, grid b3.

User groups: Hikers and dogs. No horses or mountain bikes. No wheelchair facilities.

Permits: No permits are required. A toll is charged by Bowens Ranch for crossing over their private land.

Maps: For a map of San Bernardino National Forest, send $6 to U.S. Forest Service, Map Sales, P.O. Box 587, Camino, CA 95709; tel. (530) 647-5390 or website: www.r5.fs.fed.us/visitorcenter. Ask the USGS for a topographic map of the Lake Arrowhead area.

Directions: From Cajon Pass at Interstate 15 drive north for six miles and take the Hesperia exit. Drive east through the town of Hesperia on Main Street and turn left (east) on Rock Springs Road. Follow Rock Springs Road to its end. Turn left on Kiowa Road and drive .5 mile, then turn right on Roundup Way. Follow Roundup Way for 4.4 miles (it turns to dirt), then turn right on Bowens Ranch Road (dirt). Drive 2.5 miles to a fork, bear right, and drive 3.3 miles farther on Bowens Ranch Road. Stop and register at the ranch house (a toll is charged), then continue to the road's end and the parking area. The trail is signed as Goat Trail.

Contact: San Bernardino National Forest, Arrowhead Ranger District, P.O. Box 350, 28104 Highway 18, Skyforest, CA 92385; tel. (909) 337-2444.

❸ Deep Creek Fishermen's Trail
2.0 mi/1.0 hr

Deep Creek has many personalities. It's a geologically active creek sporting hot springs and pools, where warm-water lovers flock to bathe. It's a wild trout stream, filled with pockets of moss and algae, the start of a plentiful food chain for the fish. Technically it's a branch of the Mojave River, and eventually it disappears in desert sand. Here at the T-6 Crossing it's a secluded, quiet stream with many crystalline pools and small waterfalls. Few people hike this stretch, and the path here is just a fishermen's trail. You'll do a little more scrambling than walking, but the route is well worn and beautiful every step of the way. It passes granite boulders, small sandy beaches, leafy cottonwoods, and big conifers. As you walk, you'll see many small trout in the creek's pristine pools, but if you go fishing, be sure to follow the current regulations for wild trout. About one mile upstream your progress gets blocked by a rocky waterfall. At times a cable is in place here for crossing the stream and continuing your trek, but if you use it, proceed with great caution. The preferred option is to pick a smooth granite slab in the sun, or a good-sized wading pool, and spend the afternoon in streamside bliss.

Location: In San Bernardino National Forest near Lake Arrowhead; map I6, grid b4.

User groups: Hikers and dogs. No horses or mountain bikes. No wheelchair facilities.

Permits: No permits are required. A national forest recreation pass is required for each vehicle; fees are $5 for one day or $30 for a year.

Maps: For a map of San Bernardino National Forest, send $6 to U.S. Forest Service, Map Sales, P.O. Box 587, Camino, CA 95709; tel. (530) 647-5390 or website: www.r5.fs.fed.us/visitorcenter. Ask the USGS for a topographic map of the Lake Arrowhead area.

Directions: From Crestline at the junction of Highways 18 and 138, drive east on Highway 18 for 10 miles to the left turnoff for Highway 173. Drive north on Highway 173 to Lake Arrowhead and continue for 1.5 miles to Hook Creek Road. Turn right on Hook Creek Road and follow it until it turns to dirt, becoming Road 2N26Y. Continue on Road 2N26Y for one mile and bear right on Road 3N34. In .7 mile you'll reach T-6 Crossing, where the road crosses Deep Creek. Park before the crossing and begin walking upstream on the fishermen's trail. A high-clearance vehicle is recommended for the drive.

Contact: San Bernardino National Forest, Arrowhead Ranger District, P.O. Box 350, 28104 Highway 18, Skyforest, CA 92385; tel. (909) 337-2444.

4 Champion Lodgepole Pine
1.0 mi/0.5 hr

Let's see now. The biggest giant sequoia tree is the General Sherman Tree, located in Sequoia National Park. But which is the biggest lodgepole pine tree, and where do you find it? We're delighted you asked. It's the Champion Lodgepole, located only a few miles from Big Bear Lake. The big tree is growing in a grove of world champions, the largest lodgepole pines around. What's strange is that these big guys are growing at 7,500 feet in elevation, when usually in Southern California lodgepole pines won't grow at less than 8,000 feet. The Champion is about 400 years old, stands 112 feet tall, and has a circumference of 20 feet. After a long but enjoyable drive on a dirt road to the trailhead, you'll find the trail to the big tree is flat and easy. It follows a small stream to a junction. Turn right and walk the last few yards to the Champion, which is surrounded by a fence and situated at the edge of a pretty meadow.

Location: Near Big Bear Lake; map I6, grid c6.

User groups: Hikers, dogs, horses, and mountain bikes. No wheelchair facilities.

Permits: No permits are required. A national forest recreation pass is required for each vehicle; fees are $5 for one day or $30 for a year.

Maps: For a map of San Bernardino National Forest, send $6 to U.S. Forest Service, Map Sales, P.O. Box 587, Camino, CA 95709; tel. (530) 647-5390 or website: www.r5.fs.fed.us/visitorcenter. Ask the USGS for a topographic map of the Big Bear Lake area.

Directions: From the dam on the west end of Big Bear Lake, drive 3.5 miles east on Highway 18/Big Bear Boulevard to Mill Creek Road. Turn right (south) on Mill Creek

Road/Forest Service Road 2N10 and follow it for five miles, through several junctions. (The road turns to dirt.) At Forest Service Road 2N11, turn right and drive one mile to the parking area. The route is well signed for the Champion Lodgepole Pine.

Contact: San Bernardino National Forest, Big Bear Ranger District, P.O. Box 66, North Shore Drive, Highway 18, Fawnskin, CA 92333; tel. (909) 866-3437 or fax (909) 866-2867.

5 Castle Rock Trail
2.0 mi/1.0 hr

There are a couple tricky elements about this trail: There's no real parking area, just a pullout along the highway, and although the path to Castle Rock has a mere 700-foot elevation gain, it's compressed into one mile and climbs steeply right from the trailhead. The trail is smooth sand, surrounded by manzanita, big ponderosa pines, and a ton of rocks. It's located by the area of Big Bear Lake called Boulder Bay, a perfectly descriptive name. As you climb you gain tremendous views of the lake, but you'll miss them completely unless you turn around. In about 20 minutes you'll reach a rocky overlook, which is where many people stop and pull up a granite boulder to sit on. The main trail becomes a spider web of trails, as people have chosen all different routes around the rocks. If you continue upward, you'll reach a saddle and then start to descend slightly. Castle Rock, which is easily distinguishable by its shape, is just to the east, off the trail as you head downhill. If you tire out before the saddle, just pick any boulder that's easy to climb and get on top to enjoy the lovely views of the lake. When we did this in late March, we were treated to a lovely shower of snow flurries. Isn't Big Bear the greatest? Trailhead elevation is 6,700 feet.

Location: Near Big Bear Lake; map I6, grid c6.

User groups: Hikers, dogs, horses, and mountain bikes. No wheelchair facilities.

Permits: No permits are required. A national forest recreation pass is required for each vehicle; fees are $5 for one day or $30 for a year.

Maps: For a map of San Bernardino National Forest, send $6 to U.S. Forest Service, Map Sales, P.O. Box 587, Camino, CA 95709; tel. (530) 647-5390 or website: www.r5.fs.fed.us/visitorcenter. Ask the USGS for a topographic map of the Big Bear Lake area.

Directions: From the dam on the west end of Big Bear Lake, drive one mile east on Highway 18/Big Bear Boulevard to the signed Castle Rock Trailhead on the right (it's by the Big Bear City Limit sign). Park in the turnout on the lake side of Highway 18, about 50 yards farther east, and then walk across the road to the trailhead.

Contact: San Bernardino National Forest, Big Bear Ranger District, P.O. Box 66, North Shore Drive, Highway 18, Fawnskin, CA 92333; tel. (909) 866-3437 or fax (909) 866-2867.

6 Cougar Crest Trail to Bertha Peak
6.0 mi/3.0 hrs

Put on your hiking boots and prepare to climb. That's what you have to do on the Cougar Crest Trail—gain 1,300 feet over three miles to reach Bertha Peak, elevation 8,201 feet. You can see the peak, capped with electronic relay equipment, from the trailhead parking lot. Views of the Big Bear area are spectacular along the route, and the trail is well built, making this an excellent day hike. We saw several joggers using it as a running path. The first mile is on dirt roads in a forest of piñon and Jeffrey pines, but soon the path narrows to single track. The more you climb upward, the more you see; turn around every now and then to check out the lake and mountain views. Finally at two miles you reach the Pacific Crest Trail, where the grade eases considerably. Turn right and follow the PCT for .5 mile to a dirt road, then turn right again and climb steeply to reach Bertha's summit. Look for old, gnarled juniper trees along the route. The view from the peak includes Big Bear Lake, of course, plus Mount San Gorgonio and other high peaks and ridges, and green Holcomb Valley below you.

Location: Near Big Bear Lake; map I6, grid c7.

User groups: Hikers, dogs, horses, and mountain bikes. No wheelchair facilities.

Permits: No permits are required. A national forest recreation pass is required for each vehicle; fees are $5 for one day or $30 for a year.

Maps: For a map of San Bernardino National Forest, send $6 to U.S. Forest Service, Map Sales, P.O. Box 587, Camino, CA 95709; tel. (530) 647-5390 or website: www.r5.fs.fed.us/visitorcenter. Ask the USGS for a topographic map of the Fawnskin area.

Directions: From the town of Big Bear Lake on Highway 18, take the Stanfield cutoff to the north shore of the lake where it junctions with Highway 38. Turn left and drive 1.3 miles on Highway 38 (.5 mile past the Big Bear Ranger Station) to the Cougar Crest Trailhead, on the right side of the road. If you are traveling from Fawnskin, the trailhead is 2.4 miles east of Fawnskin on Highway 38, on the left side of the road.

Contact: San Bernardino National Forest, Big Bear Ranger District, P.O. Box 66, North Shore Drive, Highway 18, Fawnskin, CA 92333; tel. (909) 866-3437 or fax (909) 866-2867.

7 Woodland Trail
1.5 mi/0.75 hr

If you're spending the weekend or the week in Big Bear, you'd be well advised to pay a visit to the Forest Service Ranger Station in Fawnskin. You can get all the information you want about hiking, fishing, and exploring the area from the nice people there. Then take this terrific short walk on the Woodland Trail, which starts near the ranger station. We picked up an interpretive brochure and learned all about serviceberry, yerba santa, Jeffrey and ponderosa pines, indigo bush, and piñon pines. The only problem was that it seemed like somebody had moved the trail numbers around, because when the brochure said we

were looking at a packrat's nest, we were looking at a piñon pine tree. We're sure they'll get it all sorted out by the time you visit. A bonus is that on the return leg of the loop, you get great views of the lake, but you're far enough away from it that you don't get hit by the wind that often blows on the north side. You can see all the way across the lake to Big Bear City.

Location: Near Big Bear Lake; map I6, grid c7.

User groups: Hikers, dogs, horses, and mountain bikes. No wheelchair facilities.

Permits: No permits are required. A national forest recreation pass is required for each vehicle; fees are $5 for one day or $30 for a year.

Maps: For a map of San Bernardino National Forest, send $6 to U.S. Forest Service, Map Sales, P.O. Box 587, Camino, CA 95709; tel. (530) 647-5390 or website: www.r5.fs.fed.us/visitorcenter. Ask the USGS for a topographic map of the Fawnskin area.

Directions: From the town of Big Bear Lake on Highway 18, take the Stanfield cutoff to the north shore of the lake, where it junctions with Highway 38. Turn left on Highway 38 and drive .5 mile to the Woodland Trailhead, on the right side of the road. It's directly across the highway from the East Boat Ramp, near the ranger station.

Contact: San Bernardino National Forest, Big Bear Ranger District, P.O. Box 66, North Shore Drive, Highway 18, Fawnskin, CA 92333; tel. (909) 866-3437 or fax (909) 866-2867.

8 Ponderosa Vista Nature Trail
1.0 mi/0.5 hr

The Ponderosa Vista Nature Trail wins hands down for the trail with the most corny interpretive plaques. When you visit, you'll see what we mean. But aside from the overdone prose, everything else on this trail is first-rate, making for a great introduction to the flora and fauna of San Bernardino

National Forest. You can choose between the short loop (.3 mile) and the long loop (.6 mile), but we say, why not hike both? We learned about assorted birds of the forest, such as acorn woodpeckers, redbreasted sapsuckers, and yellow-rumped warblers, and various trees—ponderosa pine is the most common conifer in the area, but incense cedars, black oaks, white firs, and piñon pines also grow. The highlight of the trail is an overlook point with a view across the Santa Ana River Canyon. An old photograph at the overlook shows what the canyon used to look like and explains about the building of the Rim of the World Highway in 1935. That was the same year that black bears were introduced to the area. No wonder—with the new highway, they could just get in their RVs and drive in.

Location: In San Bernardino National Forest near Angelus Oaks; map I6, grid d6.

User groups: Hikers, dogs, horses, and mountain bikes. No wheelchair facilities.

Permits: No permits are required. A national forest recreation pass is required for each vehicle; fees are $5 for one day or $30 for a year.

Maps: For a map of San Bernardino National Forest, send $6 to U.S. Forest Service, Map Sales, P.O. Box 587, Camino, CA 95709; tel. (530) 647-5390 or website: www.r5.fs.fed.us/visitorcenter. Ask the USGS for a topographic map of the Big Bear Lake area.

Directions: From Interstate 10 at Redlands take the Highway 38 exit and drive northeast for 25 miles to the trailhead for Ponderosa Vista Nature Trail on the left side of the road. If you reach the Jenks Lake turnoff, you've passed it. Park in the parking lot by the trailhead.

Contact: San Bernardino National Forest, San Gorgonio Ranger District, 34701 Mill Creek Road, Mentone, CA 92359; tel. (909) 794-1123 or fax (909) 794-1125.

9 Whispering Pines Trail
0.5 mi/0.5 hr

Right across the road from the Ponderosa Vista Trail is the Whispering Pines Trail, another short, easy interpretive trail that is both fun and informative. Time to play Trivial Pursuit: This trail appeared on what television show, filmed in 1969, about a blind girl and a furry dog? If you guessed *Lassie*, you win. In the show, the girl walked this trail and read the braille interpretive displays. Anyway, this nature trail has less of a grade than the one across the highway, although it's not quite as scenic. You will see numerous pines with an incredible amount of holes drilled in them—the work of industrious acorn woodpeckers. A minus is the sound of nearby Highway 38, but the pluses are the sound of the wind in the pines and lots of squirrels and jays.

Location: In San Bernardino National Forest near Angelus Oaks; map I6, grid d6.

User groups: Hikers, dogs, horses, and mountain bikes. No wheelchair facilities.

Permits: No permits are required. A national forest recreation pass is required for each vehicle; fees are $5 for one day or $30 for a year.

Maps: For a map of San Bernardino National Forest, send $6 to U.S. Forest Service, Map Sales, P.O. Box 587, Camino, CA 95709; tel. (530) 647-5390 or website: www.r5.fs.fed.us/visitorcenter. Ask the USGS for a topographic map of the Big Bear Lake area.

Directions: From Interstate 10 at Redlands take the Highway 38 exit and drive northeast for 25 miles to the trailhead for Whispering Pines Trail on the right side of the road. If you reach the Jenks Lake turnoff, you've passed it. Park in the well-signed parking lot by the trailhead.

Contact: San Bernardino National Forest, San Gorgonio Ranger District, 34701 Mill Creek Road, Mentone, CA 92359; tel. (909) 794-1123 or fax (909) 794-1125.

10 Jenks Lake
1.0 mi/0.5 hr

If you can get to Jenks Lake on a weekday when nobody is around, you'll find it's a magical little spot of bright blue water, with Mount San Gorgonio looming in the background.

When we visited in April, the peak was crested with snow, and the wind was whipping off the surface of the small lake, creating little whitecaps. If you visit Jenks Lake on a Saturday in July, however, it's another story. The place is likely to be packed with picnicking families, kids from nearby summer camps, and people fishing for largemouth bass, bluegill, and rainbow trout in the stocked lake. No matter when you arrive, you should take the short walk around the perimeter of the lake, then head off on the nature trail that leads behind the picnic area. The south shore of the lake is the quieter side, where no swimming is permitted. After looping around the lake, walk to the back side of the picnic area, where you're likely to be surprised by the view from the trail—the canyon drops off vertically, with sheer cliffs that fall hundreds of feet. Yes, this is the Rim of the World, just like the high way of the same name. Fortunately a railing is in place to keep you from leaning too far over the edge. Note that hikers looking for a longer adventure can set off from either the South Fork or Forsee Creek Trailheads (near Jenks Lake) and head into the San Gorgonio Wilderness. If you don't have a permit, you can always walk just to the wilderness boundary and turn around.

Location: In San Bernardino National Forest near Angelus Oaks; map I6, grid d7.

User groups: Hikers, dogs, horses, and mountain bikes. No wheelchair facilities.

Permits: No permits are required. A national forest recreation pass is required for each vehicle; fees are $5 for one day or $30 for a year.

Maps: For a map of San Bernardino National Forest, send $6 to U.S. Forest Service, Map Sales, P.O. Box 587, Camino, CA 95709; tel. (530) 647-5390 or website: www.r5.fs.fed.us/visitorcenter. Ask the USGS for a topographic map of the Big Bear Lake area.

Directions: From Interstate 10 at Redlands take the Highway 38 exit and drive northeast for 27 miles to the Jenks Lake turnoff on the right. Turn right and follow Jenks Lake Road for two miles to the parking area for the lake.

Note that Jenks Lake Road continues and reconnects to Highway 38 a few miles to the east.

Contact: San Bernardino National Forest, San Gorgonio Ranger District, 34701 Mill Creek Road, Mentone, CA 92359; tel. (909) 794-1123 or fax (909) 794-1125.

11 Aspen Grove Trail
5.0 mi/2.5 hrs

From the Aspen Grove Trailhead, a short walk down a dirt road leads you into a cool and shady grove of aspen trees along Fish Creek, one of only two remaining in San Bernardino National Forest. The grove is small and is continually threatened by nonnative beavers who chew the aspens down to build dams in Fish Creek. The Department of Fish and Game introduced the beavers in the 1940s, thinking they'd be good for the ecosystem. Now they are trying to remove them, but the little guys with the big teeth are hard to catch. What a dilemma. Anyway, if you're accustomed to the aspen trees of the southern Sierra, you'll notice that these have smaller leaves—an adaptation to the dry climate. One tip: don't show up in April as we did, when the aspens have no leaves at all. Autumn is the best time to see them, when they are bright gold in color. If you want to do more than hike down the hill and wander among the aspens, you must have a wilderness permit. Once you cross Fish Creek, you're in the San Gorgonio Wilderness. The trail to the right leads to a few more aspens and then peters out. Follow the trail to your left (uphill), heading away from the creek. A pretty walk of less than two miles through a mixed conifer forest will deliver you to two meadows, first tiny Monkey Flower Flat and then, after crossing Fish Creek again, Lower Fish Creek Meadow. It's a fine place to lay out a picnic and count the wildflowers. A side note: The drive to and from the Aspen Grove Trailhead is awesome, with wide views at every turn in the road.

Location: In the San Gorgonio Wilderness near Angelus Oaks; map I6, grid d7.

User groups: Hikers, dogs, and horses. No mountain bikes. No wheelchair facilities.

Permits: A free wilderness permit is required for both day hiking and backpacking and is available from the Mill Creek Ranger Station at the address below, the Barton Flats Visitor Center on Highway 38, or the Fawnskin Ranger Station in Big Bear. A national forest recreation pass is required for each vehicle; fees are $5 for one day or $30 for a year.

Maps: For a map of San Bernardino National Forest or the San Gorgonio Wilderness, send $6 to U.S. Forest Service, Map Sales, P.O. Box 587, Camino, CA 95709; tel. (530) 647-5390 or website: www.r5.fs.fed.us/visitorcenter. A map of the San Gorgonio Wilderness is available for a fee from Tom Harrison Cartography, tel. (415) 456-7940. Ask the USGS for a topographic map of the Moonridge area.

Directions: From Interstate 10 at Redlands take the Highway 38 exit and drive northeast for 32 miles to Forest Service Road 1N02, signed for Heart Bar Campground, Coon Creek, and Fish Creek. Turn right (south) and drive 1.25 miles to Road 1N05, then bear right. Drive 1.5 miles to the Aspen Grove Trailhead on the right.

Contact: San Bernardino National Forest, San Gorgonio Ranger District, 34701 Mill Creek Road, Mentone, CA 92359; tel. (909) 794-1123 or fax (909) 794-1125.

🔟🔢 Big Falls

0.6 mi/0.5 hr

Quick—what's the largest year-round waterfall in Southern California? Big Falls, of course. At 500 feet tall, Big Falls delivers on its name, but unfortunately it's difficult to see the waterfall's full height. That's okay, though, because the Falls Recreation Area is still a great destination, and the short hike to the overlook of Big Falls is a fun and easy walk. The elevation at the trailhead is just shy of 6,000 feet, which means the air is cool and clear. Begin

hiking at the lower parking lot, below the picnic area, and set off on an unsigned path heading downstream along Mill Creek Wash. When you pass a private cabin alongside the wash, look for a good place to cross Mill Creek by rock hopping, and then do so. On the far side of the stream, pick up the trail leading uphill on the right side of Falls Creek, which is a feeder stream to Mill Creek. Hike past a small cascade on the bottom of Falls Creek and head uphill for about five minutes to the overlook area for Big Falls. What you see is the top 40 to 50 feet of a very Yosemite-like free fall, and then some cascading water below. The huge middle part of the fall is hidden in the rocky canyon. Darn. So where can you get a better view of Big Falls? Actually, the best view is from your car window as you drive past the last few houses along Valley of the Falls Drive, shortly before entering the Falls Recreation Area. Along this stretch you can see the full-length vista of Big Falls that usually appears on postcards.

Location: In the Falls Recreation Area near Forest Falls; map I6, grid e6.

User groups: Hikers, dogs, horses, and mountain bikes. No wheelchair facilities.

Permits: No permits are required. A national forest recreation pass is required for each vehicle; fees are $5 for one day or $30 for a year.

Maps: For a map of San Bernardino National Forest, send $6 to U.S. Forest Service, Map Sales, P.O. Box 587, Camino, CA 95709; tel. (530) 647-5390 or website: www.r5.fs.fed.us/visitorcenter. Ask the USGS for a topographic map of the Forest Falls area.

Directions: From Interstate 10 at Redlands take the Highway 38 exit and drive northeast for approximately 14 miles to the intersection with Forest Home Road. Bear right and continue for 4.5 miles to the Falls Recreation Area, past the town of Forest Falls. (The name of the road changes to Valley of the Falls Drive.) Park in the first parking lot on the left.

Contact: San Bernardino National Forest, San Gorgonio Ranger District, 34701 Mill Creek Road, Mentone, CA 92359; tel. (909) 794-1123 or fax (909) 794-1125.

13 Vivian Creek Trail to Mount San Gorgonio

14.0 mi/1-2 days

There are lots of ways to reach the summit of Mount San Gorgonio, the tallest mountain in Southern California, but the shortest way is on the Vivian Creek Trail. That's the good news. The bad news is that it's also the steepest way. The summit of San Gorgonio is at 11,490 feet, and the Vivian Creek Trailhead is at 6,100 feet, so you can see what you're in for. Luckily, there are several camps along the way: Vivian Creek Camp at 1.2 miles, Halfway Camp at 2.5 miles (halfway to what, we wonder), and High Creek Camp at 4.8 miles. It's a seven-mile one-way trip to the summit, and although some people hike the round-trip in a day, it's much better to take two or more days so you can enjoy yourself and not have to rush back before dark.

The trail leaves the upper end of Big Falls Picnic Area and crosses Mill Creek Wash, then starts on a steep mile-long climb to the hanging valley of Vivian Creek, where Vivian Creek Falls sometimes falls. Vivian Creek Camp is located here; it's a convenient place to camp if you've gotten a late afternoon start. The trail continues along Vivian Creek, crossing it numerous times under the shade of a mixed conifer forest, to Halfway Camp. A few more switchbacks and you cross High Creek, arriving at High Creek Camp at 9,000 feet. High Creek Camp is famous for being a cold and windy place to spend the night. At this elevation only lodgepole pines grow, and as you gain another 2,000 feet in elevation, even these stalwarts give way to granite. At the base of San Gorgonio's summit you meet up with the trail from Dollar Lake. Turn right, then left at the next junction, and climb to the 11,490-foot summit of Old Greyback, as it's called. Are you exhausted? Join the party—so is everybody else who makes it this far. But what an achievement. Hope you brought a good map so you can identify all the major landmarks of Southern California.

Location: In the San Gorgonio Wilderness near Forest Falls; map I6, grid e6.

User groups: Hikers, dogs, and horses. No mountain bikes. No wheelchair facilities.

Permits: A free wilderness permit is required for both day hiking and backpacking and is available from the Mill Creek Ranger Station at the address below, the Barton Flats Visitor Center on Highway 38, or the Fawnskin Ranger Station in Big Bear. A national forest recreation pass is required for each vehicle; fees are $5 for one day or $30 for a year.

Maps: For a map of San Bernardino National Forest or the San Gorgonio Wilderness, send $6 to U.S. Forest Service, Map Sales, P.O. Box 587, Camino, CA 95709; tel. (530) 647-5390 or website: www.r5.fs.fed.us/visitorcenter. A map of the San Gorgonio Wilderness is available for a fee from Tom Harrison Cartography, tel. (415) 456-7940. Ask the USGS for topographic maps of the Forest Falls and San Gorgonio areas.

Directions: From Interstate 10 at Redlands take the Highway 38 exit and drive northeast for about 14 miles to the intersection with Forest Home Road. Bear right and continue for 4.5 miles to the Falls Recreation Area, past the town of Forest Falls. (The name of the road changes to Valley of the Falls Drive.) Drive to the parking area at the end of the road and walk uphill through the picnic area on the dirt road to reach the trailhead.

Contact: San Bernardino National Forest, San Gorgonio Ranger District, 34701 Mill Creek Road, Mentone, CA 92359; tel. (909) 794-1123 or fax (909) 794-1125.

14 Aerial Tramway to Desert View Trail

2.0 mi/1.0 hr

The first time you ride the Palm Springs Aerial Tramway, you realize that human beings are capable of creating miracles.

In just a few minutes, which you spend gaping out the big windows at the view, you are whooshed from the desert floor at 2,643 feet in elevation to the San Jacinto State Park and Wilderness at 8,516 feet. From cacti to clouds, from palms to pines, and in our case, from desert heat to snow flurries. There are dozens of possible hikes from the top of the tramway, but the easiest of them all is on the Desert View Trail. Since the trail is in the state park, but not in the state wilderness, you don't even need a permit—just get off the tram and start hiking. Where else for so little effort can you get expansive views of the desert and high mountain country? Not too many places.

To reach the Desert View Trail, follow the park's nature trail to the left from the back of the tram station; it joins Desert View. The vistas are awesome every step of the way, especially looking out over Palm Springs and the Indian Canyons. As you walk, be on the lookout for Cooper's hawks and yellow-rumped warblers. Here's an insider's tip for planning your trip: the best deal on the Palm Springs Aerial Tramway is to buy the Ride 'n' Dine ticket (available after 2:30 p.m.) For just a couple of extra bucks you get a huge buffet dinner to go with your tram ride and day of exploring on the mountain. It's an incredible experience to spend the afternoon hiking, have dinner in the huge dining room as the sun goes down, then ride the tram back downhill in the darkness.

Location: In Mount San Jacinto State Park; map I6, grid g9.

User groups: Hikers only. No dogs, horses, or mountain bikes. No wheelchair facilities.

Permits: No permits are required. The Palm Springs Aerial Tramway charges $17.65 per adult and $11.65 per child under 12 for a round-trip ticket to Mountain Station. Phone (760) 325-1391 for more information about schedules, fees, and special programs.

Maps: A hiking trail map of the San Jacinto State Park and Wilderness is available for $1 at the state park and national forest offices listed below. For a map of San Bernardino National Forest or the San Jacinto Wilderness, send $6 to U.S. Forest Service, Map Sales, P.O. Box 587, Camino, CA 95709; tel. (530) 647-5390 or website: www.r5.fs.fed.us/visitorcenter. Ask the USGS for a topographic map of the San Jacinto Peak area.

Directions: From Banning drive 12 miles east on Interstate 10 and take the Highway 111/Palm Springs exit. Drive nine miles south on Highway 111 to Tramway Road, then turn right and drive 3.5 miles to the tramway parking area. Walk to the tram station, buy your ticket, and ride the tram to its end at Mountain Station. Walk out the back side of Mountain Station, follow the paved path downhill, and walk to your left for the Desert View Trail.

Contact: Mount San Jacinto State Park and Wilderness, P.O. Box 308, 25905 Highway 243, Idyllwild, CA 92549; tel. (909) 659-2607; San Bernardino National Forest, San Jacinto Ranger District, P.O. Box 518, 54270 Pinecrest, Idyllwild, CA 92549; tel. (909) 659-2117 or fax (909) 659-2107.

15 Aerial Tramway to San Jacinto Peak
11.6 mi/6.6 hrs

You could hike to 10,804-foot San Jacinto Peak the hard way, upward from Idyllwild on one of several possible trails, but then you'd miss out on the many delights of the Palm Springs Aerial Tramway and hiking through Long and Round Valleys. So take the tram instead, get your wilderness permit at the ranger station, and begin hiking on the Round Valley Trail. It switchbacks gently uphill through the pines and firs, most of the time following a creek laden with corn lilies, to reach beautiful Round Valley at 9,100 feet. The left fork leads to a campground and backcountry ranger station, but you'll continue straight for Wellman Divide, with a short, steep climb just before you reach it. The views to the north and east are inspiring, including jagged Tahquitz Peak and Red Tahquitz—a bit of foreshadowing of things to come.

At the divide, turn right on the Deer Springs Trail. You have 2.6 miles to go, and the views stay with you the whole way. Climb northward on the granite slopes of Miller Peak, make a sharp left switchback, and head southwest to the spur trail for San Jacinto Peak on the right. Once you're on the spur, it's only a few hundred yards to the peak, where the views are truly breathtaking. You can see just about all of Southern California, even into Mexico and Nevada, and out to the Pacific Ocean. John Muir said that the vista from San Jacinto was "one of the most sublime spectacles seen anywhere on earth," and he was a guy who saw a lot of vistas. Total elevation gain is 2,300 feet.

Location: In Mount San Jacinto State Park and Wilderness; map I6, grid g9.

User groups: Hikers only. No dogs, horses, or mountain bikes. No wheelchair facilities.

Permits: A free wilderness permit is required for day hiking or backpacking in the San Jacinto Wilderness and is available from the ranger station at Mountain Station. The Palm Springs Aerial Tramway charges $17.65 per adult and $11.65 per child under 12 for a round-trip ticket to Mountain Station. Phone (760) 325-1391 for more information about schedules, fees, and special programs.

Maps: A hiking trail map of the San Jacinto State Park and Wilderness is available for $1 at the state park and national forest offices listed below. For a map of San Bernardino National Forest or the San Jacinto Wilderness, send $6 to U.S. Forest Service, Map Sales, P.O. Box 587, Camino, CA 95709; tel. (530) 647-5390 or website: www.r5.fs.fed.us/visitorcenter. Ask the USGS for a topographic map of the San Jacinto Peak area.

Directions: From Banning drive 12 miles east on Interstate 10 and take the Highway 111/Palm Springs exit. Drive nine miles south on Highway 111 to Tramway Road, then turn right and drive 3.5 miles to the tramway parking area. Walk to the tram station, buy your ticket, and ride the tram to its end at Mountain Station. Walk out the back side of Mountain Station, follow the paved path downhill, and head right (west) for a few hundred yards to the ranger station. Get a day-hiking permit and continue hiking on the well-signed trail

heading for Round Valley.

Contact: Mount San Jacinto State Park and Wilderness, P.O. Box 308, 25905 Highway 243, Idyllwild, CA 92549; tel. (909) 659-2607; San Bernardino National Forest, San Jacinto Ranger District, P.O. Box 518, 54270 Pinecrest, Idyllwild, CA 92549; tel. (909) 659-2117 or fax (909) 659-2107.

16 Seven Pines Trail
7.4 mi/4.0 hrs

The best thing about the Seven Pines Trail is that you can just wander as far as you please and have a good time. The mileage above reflects hiking 3.7 miles, with a 2,300-foot elevation gain to the junction with Deer Springs Trail, but even a mile or two on this path is enjoyable. The first mile climbs steeply through beautiful conifers and many granite boulders and then joins the North Fork San Jacinto River. Where the path crosses the river, you enter a gorgeous forest of pines and incense cedars. Hanging out right here might suit you just fine, but if you want more exercise, continue uphill to Deer Springs Junction, which is also the headwaters for the North Fork. You'll cross the river twice more on your way. Trailhead elevation is 6,320 feet.

Location: In the San Jacinto Wilderness near Idyllwild; map I6, grid g8.

User groups: Hikers and horses. No dogs or mountain bikes. No wheelchair facilities.

Permits: A free wilderness permit is required for day hiking or backpacking and is available from the Idyllwild Ranger Station. A national forest recreation pass is required for each vehicle; fees are $5 for one day or $30 for a year.

Maps: For a map of San Bernardino National Forest or the San Jacinto Wilderness, send $6 to U.S. Forest Service, Map Sales, P.O. Box 587, Camino, CA 95709; tel. (530) 647-5390 or website: www.r5.fs.fed.us/visitorcenter. A map of the San Jacinto Wilderness is available for a fee from Tom Harrison Cartography, tel. (415) 456-7940. Ask the USGS for a

topographic map of the San Jacinto Peak area.
Directions: From Idyllwild drive northwest on Highway 243 for 5.5 miles to the right turnoff for Stone Creek, Fern Basin, Marion Mountain, and Dark Canyon Campgrounds. Turn right and drive .2 mile, then bear left, following the signs for Dark Canyon Camp. Continue through the campground and up the hill to reach the Seven Pines Trailhead.
Contact: San Bernardino National Forest, San Jacinto Ranger District, 54270 Pinecrest, Idyllwild, CA 92549; tel. (909) 659-2117 or fax (909) 659-2107.

17 Deer Springs Trail to Suicide Rock

7.0 mi/4.0 hrs

If you're wondering how to spend a morning or an afternoon in Idyllwild, the hike to Suicide Rock will turn your visit into a trip you'll never forget. Pick up a wilderness permit and head for the trailhead, but be sure to pack some snacks and water for a little celebration at the top. Most of the work is in the first 2.4 miles to Suicide Junction, as you climb up through manzanita, ceanothus, and oaks, heading into the higher country of cedars and pines. At the junction bear right and leave the Deer Springs Trail for the last mile to Suicide Rock, which contours on an easier grade. From the three-mile point onward, your views of Lily Rock and Tahquitz Peak are outstanding, and once you're on Suicide Rock at 7,528 feet in elevation, you are directly across from Lily Rock's Yosemite-like chunk of white granite. We watched a few clouds drift between us and the neighboring peaks, right at eye level. The view below is of the Idyllwild area—there's little in sight besides a few houses and water tanks tucked in among a vast sea of conifers.
Location: In the San Jacinto Wilderness near Idyllwild; map I6, grid h8.
User groups: Hikers and horses. No dogs or mountain bikes. No wheelchair facilities.
Permits: A free wilderness permit is required for both day hiking and backpacking and is

available from the Idyllwild Ranger Station. A national forest recreation pass is required for each vehicle; fees are $5 for one day or $30 for a year.
Maps: For a map of San Bernardino National Forest or the San Jacinto Wilderness, send $6 to U.S. Forest Service, Map Sales, P.O. Box 587, Camino, CA 95709; tel. (530) 647-5390 or website: www.r5.fs.fed.us/visitorcenter. A map of the San Jacinto Wilderness is available for a fee from Tom Harrison Cartography, tel. (415) 456-7940. Ask the USGS for topographic maps of the Idyllwild and San Jacinto Peak area.
Directions: From Idyllwild drive northwest on Highway 243 for one mile to the Deer Springs Trailhead on the right side of the road (across the highway from the Idyllwild County Park visitor center parking area).
Contact: San Bernardino National Forest, San Jacinto Ranger District, P.O. Box 518, 54270 Pinecrest, Idyllwild, CA 92549; tel. (909) 659-2117 or fax (909) 659-2107.

18 Ernie Maxwell Scenic Trail

5.2 mi/2.5 hrs

The Ernie Maxwell Scenic Trail is the perfect route for hikers who aren't up to the climbing that is de rigueur for most trails in the Idyllwild area. With only a 300-foot elevation change on an undulating trail, even families with small children could manage this path, which leads through a lovely conifer forest. Keep in mind, however, that since you're not climbing, you will not get the spectacular views that are granted on most other trails in the area; this is a walk that is built for enjoying the close up, rather than the far off. The trail leads downhill from the start, contouring through a forest of Jeffrey, ponderosa, and coulter pines, with scattered firs and incense cedars among them. You can practice your tree identification. The trail's end is a bit of a disappointment; it simply reaches a dirt road where you turn around and hike back. Along the way you'll see some good views of Suicide Rock and Tahquitz Peak.

Location: In San Bernardino National Forest near Idyllwild; map I6, grid h8.

User groups: Hikers, dogs, horses, and mountain bikes. No wheelchair facilities.

Permits: No permits are required. A national forest recreation pass is required for each vehicle; fees are $5 for one day or $30 for a year.

Maps: For a map of San Bernardino National Forest, send $6 to U.S. Forest Service, Map Sales, P.O. Box 587, Camino, CA 95709; tel. (530) 647-5390 or website: www.r5.fs.fed.us/visitorcenter. Ask the USGS for a topographic map of the Idyllwild area.

Directions: From Idyllwild on Highway 243 turn east on N. Circle Drive in downtown, which becomes S. Circle Drive, and then becomes Fern Valley Road. Follow Fern Valley Road to Humber Park. You will drive a total of two miles from downtown. The trailhead is on the right at the lower end of the parking lot.

Contact: San Bernardino National Forest, San Jacinto Ranger District, P.O. Box 518, 54270 Pinecrest, Idyllwild, CA 92549; tel. (909) 659-2117 or fax (909) 659-2107.

19 Devils Slide Trail to Tahquitz Peak

8.4 mi/4.0 hrs

The Devils Slide Trail is the premier hiking trail in the Idyllwild area, with 8,828-foot Tahquitz Peak as the favored destination, especially for hikers from out of town. The best solution to the crowds? Plan a trip for before Memorial Day, after Labor Day, or any time during the week. We hiked the trail in mid-May and saw almost nobody, but then again, it snowed on our trip.

The trail leads from Idyllwild's Humber Park on a steady but manageable uphill climb through the forest to Saddle Junction, 2.5 miles up. Once you reach the junction, head right for Tahquitz Peak. The next mile is loaded with far-reaching views of the desert below and San Jacinto Mountains, seen from an increasingly open lodgepole pine forest. At the next junction head right again, soon saying good-bye to the trees and hello to a stark landscape of granite. The summit is only .5 mile away. Tahquitz Peak has the only operating fire lookout in the San Jacinto Ranger District, and it's staffed by nice folks in the summertime. From the lookout, which was constructed in 1938, you're offered a panoramic view of both the San Jacinto and Santa Rosa Mountains.

Special note: If you want to hike to Tahquitz Peak via an alternate trail that sees fewer people, take the South Ridge Trail instead of Devils Slide Trail. (You still need to pick up a free wilderness permit at the Idyllwild ranger station.) It's a 7.2-mile round-trip via South Ridge Trail from the vicinity of Saunders Meadow Road. Be sure to hike early in the day in the summer months—this trail is even more exposed than Devils Slide Trail.

Location: In the San Jacinto Wilderness near Idyllwild; map I6, grid h8.

User groups: Hikers, dogs, and horses. No mountain bikes. No wheelchair facilities.

Permits: A free wilderness permit is required for both day hiking and backpacking and is available from the Idyllwild Ranger Station. A national forest recreation pass is required for each vehicle; fees are $5 for one day or $30 for a year.

Maps: For a map of San Bernardino National Forest or the San Jacinto Wilderness, send $6 to U.S. Forest Service, Map Sales, P.O. Box 587, Camino, CA 95709; tel. (530) 647-5390 or website: www.r5.fs.fed.us/visitorcenter. A map of the San Jacinto Wilderness is available for a fee from Tom Harrison Cartography, tel. (415) 456-7940. Ask the USGS for topographic maps of the Idyllwild and San Jacinto Peak areas.

Directions: From Idyllwild on Highway 243 turn east on North Circle Drive in downtown, which becomes South Circle Drive, and then becomes Fern Valley Road. Follow Fern Valley Road to Humber Park. You will drive a total of two miles from downtown. The trailhead is on the right at the upper end of the parking lot.

Contact: San Bernardino National Forest, San Jacinto Ranger District, P.O. Box 518, 54270 Pinecrest, Idyllwild, CA 92549; tel. (909) 659-2117 or fax (909) 659-2107.

PACIFIC CREST TRAIL (PCT) SECTION OVERVIEW
250.0 mi one way/25.0 days

This giant swath of land—extending all the way from the Highway 74 Trailhead north to the Angeles Crest Highway—encompasses a diverse spectrum of terrain, flora, and fauna. The trail starts near the foot of the San Gorgonios at an elevation of about 5,000 feet and climbs to nearly 9,000 feet high in the San Gorgonio Mountains, the highest the Pacific Crest Trail gets in Southern California. It then drops into semidesert lowlands, as low as 1,200 feet in elevation and the lowest the PCT gets anywhere. This represents special challenges to PCT through-hikers. The best scenario is to hike through the desert early enough in the year so that temperatures and water availability are ideal, yet not so early that you run into deep snow in the San Gorgonios. It's about a 50-50 split for hiking conditions between good years and bad. In bad years deep snow and treacherous stream crossings from high water can delay embarking on this southern portion of the route until so late in the spring that it can jeopardize the ability to complete the entire route. Why? Because you get so far behind schedule that the fall weather window in the northern portion of the route closes down before you can traverse it. For hikers not attempting to complete the entire PCT, the high country here is best hiked from late April to early May on through June. To be on schedule, however, PCT through-hikers will need to make it through the San Gorgonios well before that. Note that no campfires are permitted in most of the areas of this region.

Highway 74 to San Gorgonio Pass
60.0 mi one way/6.0 days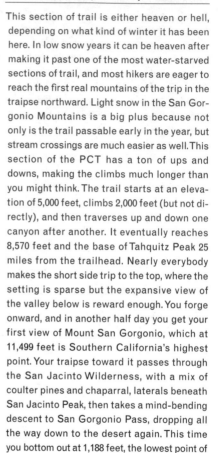

This section of trail is either heaven or hell, depending on what kind of winter it has been here. In low snow years it can be heaven after making it past one of the most water-starved sections of trail, and most hikers are eager to reach the first real mountains of the trip in the traipse northward. Light snow in the San Gorgonio Mountains is a big plus because not only is the trail passable early in the year, but stream crossings are much easier as well. This section of the PCT has a ton of ups and downs, making the climbs much longer than you might think. The trail starts at an elevation of 5,000 feet, climbs 2,000 feet (but not directly), and then traverses up and down one canyon after another. It eventually reaches 8,570 feet and the base of Tahquitz Peak 25 miles from the trailhead. Nearly everybody makes the short side trip to the top, where the setting is sparse but the expansive view of the valley below is reward enough. You forge onward, and in another half day you get your first view of Mount San Gorgonio, which at 11,499 feet is Southern California's highest point. Your traipse toward it passes through the San Jacinto Wilderness, with a mix of coulter pines and chaparral, laterals beneath San Jacinto Peak, then takes a mind-bending descent to San Gorgonio Pass, dropping all the way down to the desert again. This time you bottom out at 1,188 feet, the lowest point of the PCT in California, and a few miles later reach Interstate 10 near the pass. A strange 60 miles? You bet.

Location: From the Highway 74 Trailhead north to the trailhead parking area at Interstate 10 near San Gorgonio; map I6, grid j9.

User groups: Hikers, dogs (except in national parks), and horses. No mountain bikes. No wheelchair facilities.

Permits: A wilderness permit is required for traveling through various wilderness and special-use areas the trail traverses. Contact the

San Bernardino National Forest, tel. (909) 659-2117, for a permit good for the length of your trip.

Maps: For an overall view of the trail route in this section, send $6 to U.S. Forest Service, Map Sales, P.O. Box 587, Camino, CA 95709; tel. (530) 647-5390 or website: www.r5.fs.fed.us/visitorcenter. Ask for the San Bernardino National Forest map. Ask the USGS for topographic maps of the Butterfly Peak, Palm View Play, Idyllwild, San Jacinto Peak, and White Water areas.

Directions: To reach the Highway 74 Trailhead from the town of Hemet, head east on Highway 74 to the junction of Highways 74 and 371/Cahuilla Road. The trailhead for the PCT lies approximately one mile southeast on Highway 371, just west of the Santa Rosa Summit. To reach the Interstate 10 Trailhead from Interstate 10 near the Palm Springs exit, take the Verbania Avenue exit and drive north to Tamarack Road. Turn left onto Tamarack Road and drive approximately .25 mile to the signed PCT Trailhead, located just past Fremontia Road.

Contact: San Bernardino National Forest, San Jacinto Ranger District, P.O. Box 518, 54270 Pinecrest, Idyllwild, CA 92549; tel. (909) 659-2117 or fax (909) 659-2107.

PCT-8 San Gorgonio to Van Dusen Canyon Road

64.0 mi one way/6.0 days

When you make your first steps from the trailhead near Interstate 10, your next serious destination, just above Big Bear Lake, may seem like the impossible dream. The trip starts at just 1,400 feet and then forces you through extremely stark desert, complete with cactus and not much else, as you face a rank climb, eventually rising all the way to 8,500 feet in San Bernardino National Forest, edging the San Gorgonio Wilderness. With water hard to come by over the first 25 miles of this part of the route, most day-hikers stick exclusively to the high country, 7,000 feet and up. Admit-

tedly, that's what we did, exhilarated by the mountain air (and a shared Baby Ruth candy bar), and enjoying the deep canyon views and mixed forest, sprinkled with pines and cedars.

Once you get above the desert, passing Mission Creek, you forge northward with renewed vigor. Hikers will top out at 8,750 feet in San Bernardino National Forest and cross below Onyx Peak, after which Baldwin Lake and Big Bear Lake, come into view. The trail takes a general curving path counterclockwise and just north of Big Bear Lake, and after taking in stellar views to the south of Big Bear and the peaks of the San Gorgonio Wilderness, you are routed to the Van Dusen Forest Service Campground. Note that in the spring and early summer anything is possible here when it comes to weather. On our most recent visit it was hot, then cold, then snowed lightly, cleared, then rained, was calm, then windy, then hot again, all in just a few days.

Location: From the trailhead parking area at Interstate 10 near San Gorgonio Pass north to Van Dusen Canyon Road near Big Bear; map I6, grid g9.

User groups: Hikers, dogs (except in national parks), and horses. No mountain bikes. No wheelchair facilities.

Permits: A wilderness permit is required for traveling through various wilderness and special-use areas the trail traverses. Contact the San Bernardino National Forest, tel. (909) 794-1123, for a permit good for the length of your trip.

Maps: For an overall view of the trail route in this section, send $6 to U.S. Forest Service, Map Sales, P.O. Box 587, Camino, CA 95709; tel. (530) 647-5390 or website: www.r5.fs.fed.us/visitorcenter. Ask for the San Bernardino National Forest map. Ask the USGS for topographic maps of the White Water, Catclaw Flat, Onyx Peak, Moonridge, and Big Bear City areas.

Directions: To reach the Interstate 10 Trailhead from Interstate 10 near the Palm Springs exit, take the Verbania Avenue exit and drive north to Tamarack Road. Turn left onto Tamarack and go approximately .25 mile to the signed PCT Trailhead located just past Fremontia Road. To reach the Van Dusen Road Trailhead from Highway 18 in Big Bear City, head north on Van Dusen Canyon Road for three miles to the signed PCT Trailhead.

Contact: San Bernardino National Forest, San Gorgonio Ranger District, Mill Creek Ranger Station, 34701 Mill Creek Road, Mentone, CA 92359; tel. (909) 794-1123 or fax (909) 794-1125; Bureau of Land Management, Palm Springs-South Coast Resource Area, 690 Garnet Avenue, North Palm Springs, CA 92258; tel. (760) 251-4800 or fax (760) 251-4899.

PCT-9 Van Dusen Canyon Road to Cajon Pass

99.0 mi one way/10.0 days

The PCT traces a line along the northern rim above Big Bear Lake, and while you're walking it, our suggestion is to take your time and soak in the views of the lake. While you're at it, soak up as much drinking water as possible. In fact, you might want to pretend you're a camel, since after departing Big Bear at the Van Dusen Campground, the PCT suddenly veers off its northern course and instead heads to the west, bound eventually all the way to the San Gabriel Wilderness. Highlights of the trail from Big Bear include Holcomb Creek and Deep Creek (a favorite of ours), in the process descending about 3,000 feet over the course of a little more than 23 miles. We suggest enjoying Deep Creek to your heart's content because from here to Cajon, the trail once again becomes largely hot and dusty, even in the spring. After some 50 miles from Big Bear, Silverwood Lake provides a respite, and virtually everybody jumps in for a swim. From here it's a day's walk (13 miles) to Interstate 15 near Cajon Pass.

Location: From the trailhead parking area at Van Dusen Canyon Road near Big Bear west to the trailhead parking area at Interstate 15 near Cajon Pass; map I6, grid c8.

User groups: Hikers, dogs (except in national parks), and horses. No mountain bikes. No wheelchair facilities.

Permits: A wilderness permit is required for traveling through various wilderness and special-use areas the trail traverses. Contact the San Bernardino National Forest, tel. (909) 866-3437, for a permit good for the length of your trip.

Maps: For an overall view of the trail route in this section, send $6 for each map ordered to U.S. Forest Service, Map Sales, P.O. Box 587, Camino, CA 95709; tel. (530) 647-5390 or website: www.r5.fs.fed.us/visitorcenter. Ask for the San Bernardino National Forest and the Angeles National Forest maps. Ask the USGS for topographic maps of the Big Bear City, Fawnskin, Butler Peak, Lake Arrowhead, Silverwood Lake, and Cajon areas.

Directions: To reach the Van Dusen Road Trailhead from Highway 18 in Big Bear City, head north on Van Dusen Canyon Road for approximately three miles to the signed PCT Trailhead. To reach the Cajon Trailhead from San Bernardino, take Interstate 15 north to Cajon Junction, where Highway 138 passes over the freeway. Exit here and follow the paved road branching off Highway 138 just east of the exit, to the trailhead.

Contact: San Bernardino National Forest, Big Bear Ranger District, P.O. Box 66, Fawnskin, CA 92333; tel. (909) 866-3437 or fax (909) 866-2867.

PCT-10 Cajon Pass to Angeles Crest Highway

27.0 mi one way/3.0 days

From the trailhead at Interstate 15 and Cajon Pass, the PCT is a real butt-kicker, climbing from just under 3,000 feet in elevation to 8,200 feet over the course of 23 miles to Guffy Campground, with no reliable water source anywhere in between. It's not only a long climb, but often hot as well, so drinking all of your water early in the affair can put you in danger of dehydration. Most PCT hikers take the side trip to Wrightwood instead of making it an endurance test to Guffy Campground (a campground that can be reached by car, and where water is hard to find anyway). From Guffy Campground, the PCT runs along the Sheep Mountain Wilderness until it hits the Angeles Crest Highway. The views of the canyons here are superb on clear days, and as a trailhead it's an excellent jump-off point for those heading onward.

Location: From Interstate 15 near Cajon Pass to the Angeles Crest Highway; map I6, grid b0.

User groups: Hikers, dogs, and horses. No mountain bikes. No wheelchair facilities.

Permits: A wilderness permit is required for traveling through various wilderness and special-use areas the trail traverses. Contact the Angeles National Forest, tel. (626) 574-5200, for a permit good for the length of your trip. No day-use permits are required for this section of trail.

Maps: For an overall view of the trail route in this section, send $6 to U.S. Forest Service, Map Sales, P.O. Box 587, Camino, CA 95709; tel. (530) 647-5390 or website: www.r5.fs.fed.us/visitorcenter. Ask for the Angeles National Forest map. Ask the USGS for topographic maps of the Telegraph Peak and Cajon areas.

Directions: To reach the Cajon Trailhead from San Bernardino, take Interstate 15 north to Cajon Junction, where Highway 138 passes over the freeway. Exit here and follow a paved road branching off Highway 138, just east of the exit, to the trailhead. To reach the Angeles Crest Trailhead from Interstate 15 near Cajon, take Highway 138 east. Turn left (west) on the Angeles Crest Highway and drive five miles to Wrightwood. Continue for three miles to Big Pines. Bear left and continue on Angeles Crest Highway for 1.5 miles to Inspiration Point, opposite Blue Ridge Road.

Contact: Angeles National Forest, 701 N. Santa Anita Avenue, Arcadia, CA 91006; tel. (626) 574-5200 or fax (626) 574-5233.

PCT Continuation

To continue hiking along the Pacific Crest Trail, see chapter I5.

HIKING ALONG THE MASTODON PEAK TRAIL

MAP 17

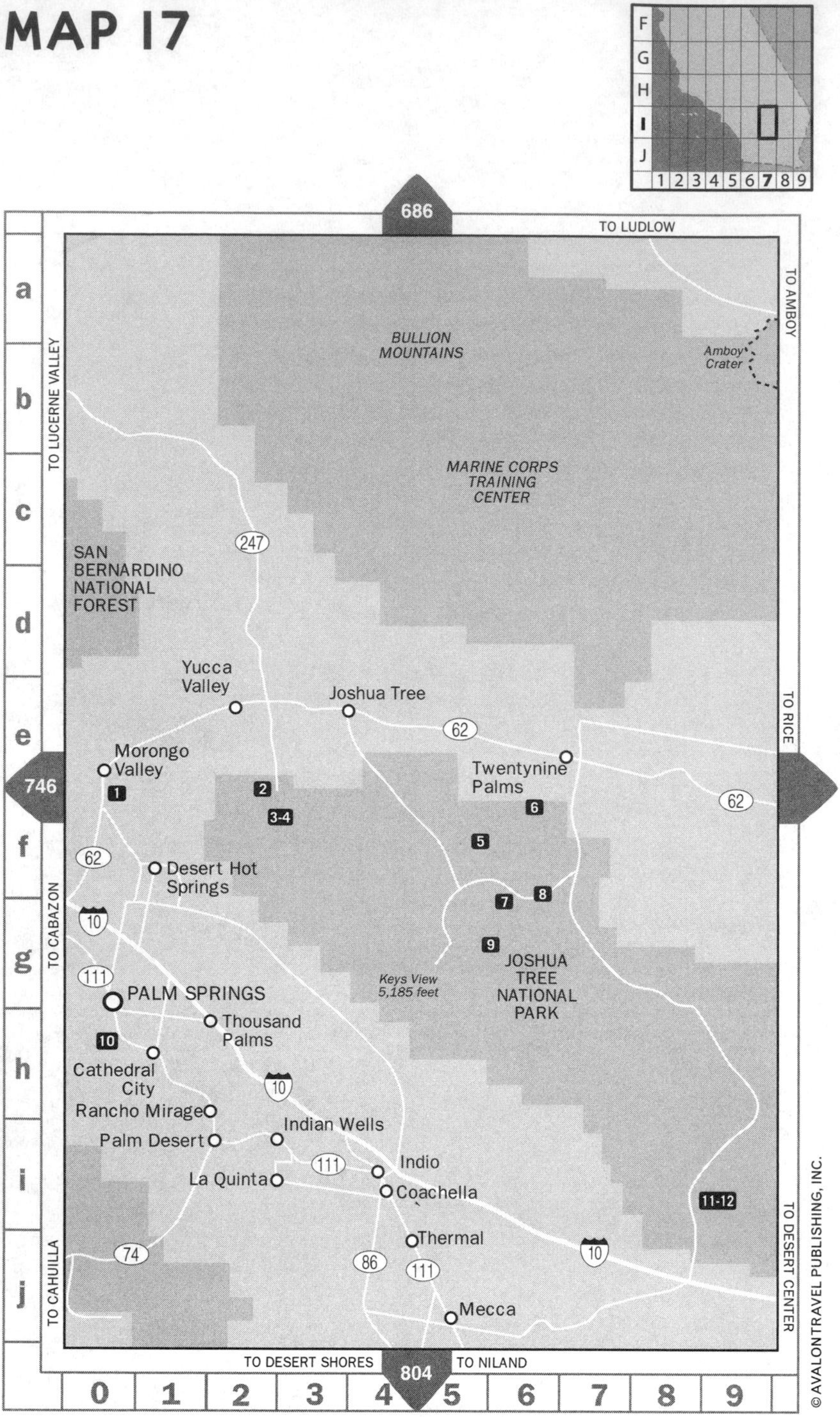

MAP 17

686

TO LUDLOW

TO AMBOY

TO LUCERNE VALLEY

BULLION
MOUNTAINS

Amboy
Crater

MARINE CORPS
TRAINING
CENTER

(247)

SAN
BERNARDINO
NATIONAL
FOREST

Yucca
Valley

Joshua Tree

62

TO RICE

62

Morongo
Valley

1

2

3-4

Twentynine
Palms

6

5

746

62

TO CABAZON

Desert Hot
Springs

10

7 **8**

9

111

Keys View
5,185 feet

JOSHUA
TREE
NATIONAL
PARK

PALM SPRINGS

Thousand
Palms

10

10

Cathedral
City

Rancho Mirage

Palm Desert

Indian Wells

111

Indio

La Quinta

Coachella

TO CAHUILLA

74

86

111

Thermal

10

TO DESERT CENTER

11-12

Mecca

TO DESERT SHORES

804

TO NILAND

© AVALON TRAVEL PUBLISHING, INC.

CHAPTER 17

1 Canyon Trail 767
2 High View Nature Trail . 767
3 Warren Peak 768
4 Eureka Peak 769
5 Barker Dam Loop 769
6 Fortynine Palms Oasis. . 770
7 Ryan Mountain Trail . . . 770
8 Skull Rock Nature Trail . 771
9 Lost Horse Mine 772
10 Murray Canyon Trail. . 772
11 Mastodon Peak 773
12 Lost Palms Oasis. 773

1 Canyon Trail
3.0 mi/1.5 hrs

The Canyon Trail at the Big Morongo Canyon Preserve is a birder's trail, plain and simple. More than 235 bird species have been identified in the preserve. In fact, if you're not carrying binoculars and a field book when you visit, you'll feel like a real outsider. Luckily, you don't have to know anything about birds to have a good time. We examined the interpretive exhibit at the trailhead kiosk, and in a few minutes of hiking we were able to spot and identify a pair of western tanagers. (And usually we can't tell a blue jay from a blue grouse.) Take the main trail out of the parking lot and bear right to follow the ranch road to the Canyon Trail. Pass a few ranch buildings, and before you know it, you're walking on a wooden boardwalk over a wet marsh, smelling the distinct scent of sulfur from underground springs. You exit the boardwalk onto a sandy trail in the canyon, where you can head back as far as you like. We startled a mule deer on this stretch, who acted as if he hadn't seen any hikers for a long, long time. On your return trip you can make a loop if you wish, by turning right on the Willow Trail just before the ranch house and following it to the Desert Wash Trail, which leads back to the parking lot.

Location: In the Big Morongo Canyon Preserve north of Palm Springs; map 17, grid f0.

User groups: Hikers only. No dogs, horses, or mountain bikes. No wheelchair facilities.

Permits: No permits are required. Parking and access are free.

Maps: Ask the USGS for a topographic map of the Morongo Valley area.

Directions: From Banning drive east on Interstate 10 for 16 miles to the Highway 62 exit. Turn north on Highway 62 and drive 11 miles to Morongo Valley. Look for a sign on the right for the Big Morongo Canyon Preserve (at East Road); turn right and drive to the preserve entrance on the left.

Contact: Big Morongo Canyon Preserve, P.O. Box 780, Morongo Valley, CA 92256; tel. (760) 363-7190 or fax (760) 363-1180.

2 High View Nature Trail
1.3 mi/1.0 hr

You're unlikely to have much company on this trail, which along with its fine vistas and easy grade is one of its best selling points. The trail is a loop that begins and ends from a parking area near Black Rock Canyon Campground. If you pick up an interpretive brochure at the Black Rock Canyon Ranger Station (you'll pass it as you drive in), you can get a brief education on desert plants and animals as you walk. The trail undulates along, climbing a total of only 350 feet, until it reaches a high point with a lovely view of Mount San Gorgonio and a less-inspiring view of the sprawling desert towns of Yucca Valley and Joshua Tree. A bench marks the spot, and there's a trail register where you can record your comments. The loop back downhill is longer and flatter than the way up.

This trail is perfect for a clear winter morning's hike. Note that the loop can also be accessed from the campground and ranger station via a .5-mile spur trail that begins just west of the ranger station.

Location: In Joshua Tree National Park near Yucca Valley; map I7, grid f2.

User groups: Hikers only. No dogs, horses, or mountain bikes. No wheelchair facilities.

Permits: No permits are required. There is a $10 entrance fee per vehicle at Joshua Tree National Park, good for seven days.

Maps: Free park maps are available at park entrance stations. A more detailed map is available for a fee from Tom Harrison Cartography, tel. (415) 456-7940, or Trails Illustrated, tel. (800) 962-1643. Ask the USGS for a topographic map of the Yucca Valley South area.

Directions: From Banning drive east on Interstate 10 for 16 miles to the Highway 62 exit. Turn north on Highway 62 and drive 24 miles to the town of Yucca Valley. Turn right on Joshua Lane (signed for Black Rock Canyon) and drive five miles to the entrance to Black Rock Canyon Campground. Just before the entrance turn right on a dirt road signed for South Park Parking Area and follow it to its end at the trailhead. The parking area is just outside of the national park boundary, but the trail is inside the park.

Contact: Joshua Tree National Park, 74485 National Park Drive, Twentynine Palms, CA 92277; tel. (760) 367-5500.

3 Warren Peak

5.6 mi/3.0 hrs

If you seek a less tame adventure than you get on many short trails in Joshua Tree National Park, the trip to Warren Peak might suit you well. Located in the far northwest corner of the park, the trail and its 5,103-foot summit destination feel surprisingly remote. The peak provides a terrific view of Southern California's tallest mountains, which are crowned with a mantle of snow in winter and early spring. The trail out of Black Rock Canyon Campground starts in a desert wash, with plenty of Joshua trees, piñon pines, and cholla cacti keeping you company. Keep your eyes on the trail signs, which funnel you into the correct forks in the canyon. (There are several critical turns to make.) The sandy wash narrows to a walled canyon, then broadens again. As you climb gently but steadily, you'll see junipers, oaks, and piñon pines replacing some of the lower desert flora. At about two miles out, you'll spy Warren Peak's pointy fractured rock ahead and to the right. The trail gets a bit hard to discern in places, but watch for trail ducks and keep your eye on Warren Peak. The last .25 mile to the summit is steep and requires some scrambling, but is easily accomplished. If it's not too windy, you'll want to stay on top of the pointy, conical peak for a while, and not just so you can read the summit register. Views of Mount San Gorgonio, Mount San Jacinto, San Gorgonio Pass, and the Mojave Desert will make your heart pound. To the southwest are Palm Springs and the Morongo and Coachella Valleys.

Location: In Joshua Tree National Park near Yucca Valley; map I7, grid f3.

User groups: Hikers only. No dogs, horses, or mountain bikes. No wheelchair facilities.

Permits: No permits are required. There is a $10 entrance fee per vehicle at Joshua Tree National Park, good for seven days.

Maps: Free park maps are available at park entrance stations. A more detailed map is available for a fee from Tom Harrison Cartography, tel. (415) 456-7940, or Trails Illustrated, tel. (800) 962-1643. Ask the USGS for a topographic map of the Yucca Valley South area.

Directions: From Banning drive east on Interstate 10 for 16 miles to the Highway 62 exit. Turn north on Highway 62 and drive 24 miles to the town of Yucca Valley. Turn right on Joshua Lane (signed for Black Rock Canyon) and drive five miles to the Black Rock Ranger Station. Park and then walk uphill to the Black Rock Canyon trailhead at the upper end of the campground.

Contact: Joshua Tree National Park, 74485 National Park Drive, Twentynine Palms, CA 92277; tel. (760) 367-5500.

4 Eureka Peak
10.8 mi/6.0 hrs

The total elevation gain on this trip is only 1,500 feet to reach the summit of Eureka Peak at 5,518 feet, but it feels more difficult than that. The problem is sand and rocks—lots of them—and the fact that the trail is hard to discern in places. However, if you're willing to put in some effort, your reward is a commanding view of the western edge of Joshua Tree National Park as well as Mount San Jacinto and Mount San Gorgonio. Sand and snow—you see it all from here. Begin hiking on the California Riding and Hiking Trail, which you'll follow for two miles until you come to a major wash. This is where things start to get tricky; keep looking for trail markers signed as "EP" (for Eureka Peak) to keep you on track. Take the right fork in the wash, leaving the California Riding and Hiking Trail. In another .5 mile take the next right fork into another wash. Hike through this wash for 1.7 miles to its end. A trail marker directs you to your left, heading up and over a ridge. At the top, turn right (south), hike up to a saddle and then on to south side of Eureka Peak, where there's a short path to the summit. When you get to the top, what's the only downer? You find that plenty of people have driven their cars up to the peak via a dirt road from Covington Flat. No fair. An option is to follow this road back downhill for one mile to the California Riding and Hiking Trail, turn left, and follow the trail back to your starting point. It makes a good loop trip and only adds one mile to your total distance.

Location: In Joshua Tree National Park near Yucca Valley; map I7, grid f3.

User groups: Hikers only. No dogs, horses, or mountain bikes. No wheelchair facilities.

Permits: No permits are required. There is a $10 entrance fee per vehicle at Joshua Tree National Park, good for seven days.

Maps: Free park maps are available at park entrance stations. A more detailed map is available for a fee from Tom Harrison Cartography, tel. (415) 456-7940, or Trails Illustrated, tel. (800) 962-1643. Ask the USGS for topographic maps of the Yucca Valley South and Joshua Tree South areas.

Directions: From Banning drive east on Interstate 10 for 16 miles to the Highway 62 exit. Turn north on Highway 62 and drive 24 miles to the town of Yucca Valley. Turn right on Joshua Lane (signed for Black Rock Canyon) and drive five miles to the Black Rock Ranger Station. Park at the ranger station and then walk uphill to the California Riding and Hiking Trail trailhead on the left (east) side of the campground entrance.

Contact: Joshua Tree National Park, 74485 National Park Drive, Twentynine Palms, CA 92277; tel. (760) 367-5500.

5 Barker Dam Loop
1.2 mi/1.0 hr

There's a lake in the desert, and it's hidden in a magical place called the Wonderland of Rocks. You can't water-ski or fish there, but you can enjoy bird-watching and photograph the reflections of odd-shaped boulders in the water's surface. The lake is formed by Barker Dam, built at the beginning of the 20th century to improve upon a natural boulder dam that captured rain runoff in this basin. This short loop trip takes you past many of the unique granite boulders of the Wonderland of Rocks and around Barker Dam's small lake. The trail loops back past some petroglyphs (take the short spur trail) and Indian grinding holes. If the petroglyphs seem remarkably visible and clear to you, it's because years ago a movie crew painted over them to make them more visible to the camera. For this tragic reason the park calls these paintings the "Disney petroglyphs."

Location: In Joshua Tree National Park near Twentynine Palms; map I7, grid f5.

User groups: Hikers only. No dogs, horses, or mountain bikes. No wheelchair facilities.

Permits: No permits are required. There is a $10 entrance fee per vehicle at Joshua Tree National Park, good for seven days.

Maps: Free park maps are available at park entrance stations. A more detailed map is available for a fee from Tom Harrison Cartography, tel. (415) 456-7940, or Trails Illustrated, tel. (800) 962-1643. Ask the USGS for a topographic map of the Indian Cove area.

Directions: From Banning drive east on Interstate 10 for 16 miles to the Highway 62 exit. Turn north on Highway 62 and drive 29 miles to the town of Joshua Tree. Turn right on Park Boulevard and drive 14 miles to Hidden Valley Campground on the left. Turn left and drive 1.8 miles, through and past the campground, to the signed trailhead for Barker Dam.

Contact: Joshua Tree National Park, 74485 National Park Drive, Twentynine Palms, CA 92277; tel. (760) 367-5500.

6 Fortynine Palms Oasis

3.0 mi/1.5 hrs

The biggest surprise on the Fortynine Palms Oasis Trail is not the large and lovely grove of palm trees at the trail's end. It's that there are no Joshua trees to be found anywhere along the trail. What? No Joshua trees in this part of Joshua Tree National Park? If you've spent a few days wandering the park's roads and trails, you've surely grown accustomed to seeing Joshuas everywhere you go. Here their absence seems strange.

The trail is an old Native American pathway, and it's well maintained and easy to follow. It winds around, climbs up and over a small ridge, and then curves around to the palm grove. Although you can see and hear Highway 62 and its sprawling suburban towns as you hike, once you reach the palm grove, all traces of civilization are left behind. The grove is pleasantly secluded. First you'll see a cluster of 10 palms, and then a larger grouping a short distance away. We counted several

times and became convinced that there truly are 49 palms in Fortynine Palms Oasis. Have a seat on a boulder to listen and watch for birds. Orioles, finches, and hummingbirds congregate here for both the trickling spring water and the palm fruits. It's a lush, green, vibrant spot. The only downer: Some of the beautiful palm trunks have people's initials carved into them.

Location: In Joshua Tree National Park near Twentynine Palms; map I7, grid f6.

User groups: Hikers only. No dogs, horses, or mountain bikes. No wheelchair facilities.

Permits: No permits are required. There is a $10 entrance fee per vehicle at Joshua Tree National Park, good for seven days.

Maps: Free park maps are available at park entrance stations. A more detailed map is available for a fee from Tom Harrison Cartography, tel. (415) 456-7940, or Trails Illustrated, tel. (800) 962-1643. Ask the USGS for a topographic map of the Queen Mountain area.

Directions: From Banning drive east on Interstate 10 for 16 miles to the Highway 62 exit. Turn north on Highway 62 and drive 29 miles to the town of Joshua Tree. Continue east on Highway 62 for 10 miles to just west of the town of Twentynine Palms. Turn right (south) on Canyon Road, located by the High Desert Animal Hospital. Drive 1.7 miles on Canyon Road; bear left where the road forks. The pavement ends at the Fortynine Palms Oasis trailhead.

Contact: Joshua Tree National Park, 74485 National Park Drive, Twentynine Palms, CA 92277; tel. (760) 367-5500.

7 Ryan Mountain Trail

3.0 mi/2.0 hrs

If you hike only one trail in Joshua Tree National Park, this should be the one. Ryan Mountain at 5,470 feet provides what many insist is the best view in the park. You can see the Queen Valley, Wonderland of Rocks, Lost Horse Valley, Pleasant Valley, and the far-off mountains, San Gorgonio and San Jacinto.

It's a complete panorama. The route travels through boulders and Joshua trees—no surprises here—on a well-maintained and easy-to-follow trail. The ascent seems a bit steep even though it's only a 700-foot elevation gain, but it's over with quickly, so just sweat it out. Be sure to sign the summit register and then have a seat on one of the rocks of Ryan Mountain to enjoy the view. The peak's boulders are estimated to be several hundred million years old, which gives you something to think about while you admire the vista.

Location: In Joshua Tree National Park near Twentynine Palms; map I7, grid g6.

User groups: Hikers only. No dogs, horses, or mountain bikes. No wheelchair facilities.

Permits: No permits are required. There is a $10 entrance fee per vehicle at Joshua Tree National Park, good for seven days.

Maps: Free park maps are available at park entrance stations. A more detailed map is available for a fee from Tom Harrison Cartography, tel. (415) 456-7940, or Trails Illustrated, tel. (800) 962-1643. Ask the USGS for a topographic map of the Keys View area.

Directions: From Banning drive east on Interstate 10 for 16 miles to the Highway 62 exit. Turn north on Highway 62 and drive 45 miles to Twentynine Palms and the park visitor center. Turn right on Utah Trail Road and drive eight miles to a Y junction. Bear right and continue for nine miles, past Sheep Pass Campground to the trailhead parking area on the south side of the road. You can also reach the trailhead via Park Boulevard out of the town of Joshua Tree, turning left at Cap Rock Junction and continuing 2.5 miles to the trailhead.

Contact: Joshua Tree National Park, 74485 National Park Drive, Twentynine Palms, CA 92277; tel. (760) 367-5500.

8 Skull Rock Nature Trail
1.7 mi/1.0 hr

Joshua Tree National Park is probably just as famous for rock formations as it is for Joshua trees. If you want a close look at some of the park's weird and wonderful hunks of quartz monzonite, the Skull Rock Trail will provide it. The trail is a loop and can be hiked in either direction, although we prefer to start on the northwest side of the park road. (Campers in Jumbo Rocks Campground can start from their tents; the loop trail goes right through the campground.) From the trail's start you get a quick education: interpretive signs point out paper-bag bush, turbinella oak, cholla cactus, and other desert flora. The path winds among giant, rounded rock formations, crosses the park road, heads through more rocks in Jumbo Rocks Campground, and leaves the camp near the entrance to Loop E. Then the trail heads for its namesake, Skull Rock. The big boulder looks loosely like what its name implies. A spiderweb of paths leads around Skull Rock in all directions; this is where everyone abandons the formal trail and starts climbing around the smooth, rounded rock surfaces. When you've had enough, just follow the short trail back to the road and your car.

Location: In Joshua Tree National Park near Twentynine Palms; map I7, grid g6.

User groups: Hikers only. No dogs, horses, or mountain bikes. No wheelchair facilities.

Permits: No permits are required. There is a $10 entrance fee per vehicle at Joshua Tree National Park, good for seven days.

Maps: Free park maps are available at park entrance stations. A more detailed map is available for a fee from Tom Harrison Cartography, tel. (415) 456-7940, or Trails Illustrated, tel. (800) 962-1643. Ask the USGS for a topographic map of the Malapai Hill area.

Directions: From Banning drive east on Interstate 10 for 16 miles to the Highway 62 exit. Turn north on Highway 62 and drive 45 miles to Twentynine Palms and the park visitor center. Turn right on Utah Trail Road and drive eight miles to a Y junction. Bear right and continue four miles to the trailhead parking area alongside the road shortly before the entrance to Jumbo Rocks Campground.

Begin hiking on the right (northwest) side of the road.

Contact: Joshua Tree National Park, 74485 National Park Drive, Twentynine Palms, CA 92277; tel. (760) 367-5500.

9 Lost Horse Mine
4.0 mi/2.0 hrs

You get the full desert experience on the Lost Horse Mine Loop, including spectacular mountain and valley vistas, high desert flora, and a visit to an old gold mine. The trail (really an old road) leads uphill for 1.8 miles to Lost Horse Mine. The mine produced a gold profit at the turn of the century—9,000 ounces of gold—and is the best preserved of all the mines in the national park. Still standing are the mine's stamp mill, old building foundations, and a few open mine shafts. Continue from the mine another .4 mile up the old road, climbing more steeply up the ridge to wide overlooks of the Queen Valley, Lost Horse Valley, Pleasant Valley, and the eastern stretch of the national park. Turn around and retrace your steps before the trail begins to descend.

Location: In Joshua Tree National Park near Twentynine Palms; map I7, grid g6.

User groups: Hikers only. No dogs, horses, or mountain bikes. No wheelchair facilities.

Permits: No permits are required. There is a $10 entrance fee per vehicle at Joshua Tree National Park, good for seven days.

Maps: Free park maps are available at park entrance stations. A more detailed map is available for a fee from Tom Harrison Cartography, tel. (415) 456-7940, or Trails Illustrated, tel. (800) 962-1643. Ask the USGS for a topographic map of the Keys View area.

Directions: From Banning drive east on Interstate 10 for 16 miles to the Highway 62 exit. Turn north on Highway 62 and drive 29 miles to the town of Joshua Tree and Park Boulevard. Turn right on Park Boulevard and drive 15.8 miles to Cap Rock junction. Bear right and drive 2.4 miles to the dirt road on the left that is signed for Lost Horse Mine. Turn left and follow the dirt road to the trailhead parking area.

Contact: Joshua Tree National Park, 74485 National Park Drive, Twentynine Palms, CA 92277; tel. (760) 367-5500.

10 Murray Canyon Trail
4.0 mi/2.0 hrs

If you think Palm Springs is all tennis courts, golf courses, and beauty parlors, you haven't been to the Indian Canyons off South Palm Canyon Drive. The Indian Canyons—Palm, Andreas, and Murray—are what's left of the old Palm Springs. They're wide open stretches of desert with red rock, fan palms, sulfur streams, barrel cactus, bighorn sheep, and broad vistas of surprising color and beauty. The Murray Canyon Trail is an excellent exploration of this area, beginning at the picnic grounds between Murray and Andreas Canyons. The trail is well-packed sand and is clearly marked along the way. After an initial wide-open desert stretch, you enter Murray Canyon, which narrows and twists and turns, so you never see where you're going until you come around the next bend. The stream you've been following slowly begins to exhibit a stronger flow, and the streamside reeds, grasses, palm trees, and wild grape intensify their growth accordingly. If you're a fan of red rock, you'll love the 100-foot-tall slanted rock outcrops and cliffs. After passing a left fork for the Kaufmann Trail, climb up and over a small waterfall in Murray Canyon, staying on the left side of the stream. In another .25 mile you'll reach a larger set of falls. These falls block any possible further progress, but provide many good pools for swimming and granite shelves for picnicking.

Location: On the Agua Caliente Indian Reservation near Palm Springs; map I7, grid h0.

User groups: Hikers, dogs, and horses. No mountain bikes. No wheelchair facilities.

Permits: No permits are required. A $10 day-use fee is charged per adult; $1 for children 6 to 12.

Maps: A free map/brochure is available at the entrance kiosk. Ask the USGS for topographic maps of the Palm Springs and Cathedral City areas.

Directions: From Palm Springs drive south through the center of town on Highway 111/Palm Canyon Drive and take the right fork signed for South Palm Canyon Drive. Drive 2.8 miles, bearing right at the sign for Palm Canyon/Andreas Canyon. Stop at the entrance kiosk, drive about 200 yards, and turn right for Murray Canyon. Drive past the Andreas Canyon Trailhead and continue to the Murray Canyon Picnic Area, a mile from the entrance kiosk.

Contact: Agua Caliente Band of Cahuilla Indians, Tribal Council Office, tel. (760) 325-5673; Indian Canyons Information, tel. (760) 325-1053.

11 Mastodon Peak
2.5 mi/1.0 hr

The Mastodon Peak Trail begins at Cottonwood Spring Oasis, a little slice of watery paradise for birds and wildlife. After a short paved section, the trail sets off in the desert sand, and after .5 mile you take the left fork for Mastodon Peak. Shortly you'll pass another trail junction with the path to Cottonwood Spring Campground; stay right. The route has almost no elevation change along its route to the base of the peak. It's a pleasant, easy stroll among tall ocotillos, yucca, and smaller cacti. At the Mastodon's base, you must choose whether or not to scramble to the top; the going is steep but short. Although it's a nice trip just to hike to the peak's base and try to imagine the Mastodon's profile, we recommend you go for the summit. The easiest route is around the back of the Mastodon on its east side. In a few minutes you are at the top, admiring the surprisingly wide view: Not only do you see a great expanse of Joshua Tree's desert and the Eagle Mountains but also snow-capped Mount San Jacinto and the mirage-like Salton Sea shim-

mering in the distance some 30 miles away. If you want to add some history to your hike, retrace your steps to the junction with the trail to Cottonwood Spring Camp. Turn right there and hike past the Mastodon Gold Mine and the Winona Mill Site. The mine was worked in the 1920s with a modicum of success. From the mill site you don't need to backtrack to the main trail; the path loops back to the Cottonwood Spring parking area.

Location: In southern Joshua Tree National Park near Cottonwood Spring; map I7, grid i9.

User groups: Hikers only. No dogs, horses, or mountain bikes. No wheelchair facilities.

Permits: No permits are required. There is a $10 entrance fee per vehicle at Joshua Tree National Park, good for seven days.

Maps: Free park maps are available at park entrance stations. A more detailed map is available for a fee from Tom Harrison Cartography, tel. (415) 456-7940, or Trails Illustrated, tel. (800) 962-1643. Ask the USGS for a topographic map of the Cottonwood Spring area.

Directions: From Indio drive east on Interstate 10 for approximately 25 miles. Turn north on Cottonwood Spring Road and drive seven miles to Cottonwood Spring ranger station. Turn right and drive another mile, passing the campground entrance, to the day-use parking area at Cottonwood Spring Oasis.

Contact: Joshua Tree National Park, 74485 National Park Drive, Twentynine Palms, CA 92277; tel. (760) 367-5500.

12 Lost Palms Oasis
7.4 mi/3.5 hrs

If the weather is cool and accommodating and you're in the mood for a longer hike in southern Joshua Tree National Park, the Lost Palms Oasis Trail comes highly recommended. Many consider Lost Palms Oasis to be the best palm grove in Joshua Tree, and the hike to reach it has little elevation change. The trail begins at Cottonwood Spring Oasis and for the first .5 mile follows the same path as the Mastodon Peak Trail. Stay straight at the junction with the trail to Mastodon Peak; continue straight through a series of washes and low ridges covered with various low-elevation desert cacti. There is no indication of the huge palm oasis until you are almost on top of it at slightly more than three miles out. The main trail brings you to an overlook point above the palms, and a steep use trail descends .25 mile into the grove. Make the rugged 200-foot descent to the canyon bottom; the remoteness of the area and the lush atmosphere of the leafy palm grove make it worth the effort. The Lost Palms Oasis grove contains more than 100 palms in its main canyon. In the upper end of the canyon is a side canyon with more palms, although these are more difficult to reach.

Location: In southern Joshua Tree National Park near Cottonwood Spring; map I7, grid i9.

User groups: Hikers only. No dogs, horses, or mountain bikes. No wheelchair facilities.

Permits: No permits are required. There is a $10 entrance fee per vehicle at Joshua Tree National Park, good for seven days.

Maps: Free park maps are available at park entrance stations. A more detailed map is available for a fee from Tom Harrison Cartography, tel. (415) 456-7940, or Trails Illustrated, tel. (800) 962-1643. Ask the USGS for a topographic map of the Cottonwood Spring area.

Directions: From Indio drive east on Interstate 10 for approximately 25 miles. Turn north on Cottonwood Spring Road and drive seven miles to Cottonwood Spring ranger station. Turn right and drive a mile, past the campground entrance, to the day-use parking area at Cottonwood Spring Oasis.

Contact: Joshua Tree National Park, 74485 National Park Drive, Twentynine Palms, CA 92277; tel. (760) 367-5500.

CHAPTER J5

ANN MARIE BROWN

TRAIL TO THE TIDE POOL AREA AT
CABRILLO NATIONAL MONUMENT

MAP J5

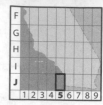

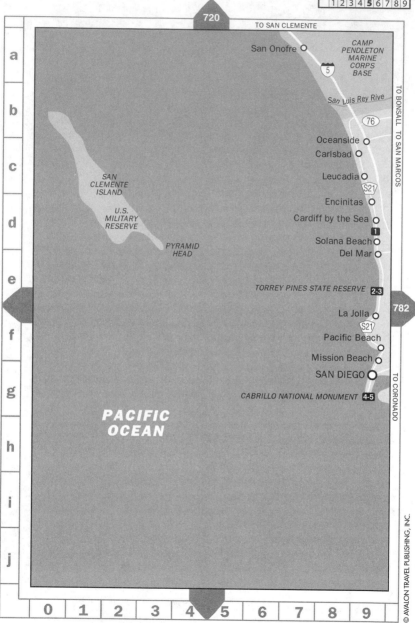

720

TO SAN CLEMENTE

San Onofre ○

CAMP
PENDLETON
MARINE
CORPS
BASE

5

TO BONSALL   TO SAN MARCOS

San Luis Rey Rive

76

Oceanside ○
Carlsbad ○

Leucadia ○
S21

Encinitas ○

Cardiff by the Sea ○
1
Solana Beach ○
Del Mar ○

*SAN
CLEMENTE
ISLAND*

*U.S.
MILITARY
RESERVE*

*PYRAMID
HEAD*

TORREY PINES STATE RESERVE **2-3**

782

La Jolla ○
S21

Pacific Beach ○

Mission Beach ○

SAN DIEGO ○

TO CORONADO

CABRILLO NATIONAL MONUMENT **4-5**

*PACIFIC
OCEAN*

© AVALON TRAVEL PUBLISHING, INC.

0   1   2   3   4   5   6   7   8   9

CHAPTER J5

1. San Elijo Lagoon 777
2. Guy Fleming Loop Trail . 777
3. Razor Point and
   Beach Trail Loop 778
4. Bayside Trail 778
5. Cabrillo Tide Pools 779

1 San Elijo Lagoon
2.5 mi/1.25 hrs

San Elijo Lagoon is bordered by Interstate 5, U.S. 101, and a whole bunch of housing developments and shopping centers; amazingly, the birds don't seem to mind. The ecological preserve is sandwiched between Lomas Santa Fe Avenue and Manchester Avenue in Solana Beach, and when you first see it, it's hard to imagine hiking so close to the freeways and roads. But suspend your disbelief for a while and pay a visit to the lagoon, which is a mixture of freshwater from inland creeks and saltwater from the ocean. The Lomas Santa Fe side is a little wilder than the Manchester Avenue side, and the trails are longer, so it's the preferred side for hiking. A gated fire road leads down to the lagoon from the end of Lomas Santa Fe, and you can hike either right or left. There are tons of white egrets to be seen, as well as stilts, gulls, and godwits. Great blue herons occasionally make an appearance, and as you wander inland, you'll see many songbirds among the chaparral. Interpretive signs explain about saltwater and freshwater marshes, coastal sage scrub, and the wildlife living in these communities. If you travel the east side of the trail, when you near Interstate 5, you'll reach a series of slot canyons in the sandstone, with cliffs that are 60 feet high. Hey, are you sure we're still in the city?

Location: In Solana Beach; map J5, grid d9.

User groups: Hikers and dogs. No horses or mountain bikes. No wheelchair facilities.

Permits: No permits are required. Parking and access are free.

Maps: Ask the USGS for a topographic map of the Encinitas area.

Directions: From Interstate 5 in Solana Beach take the Lomas Santa Fe Drive exit and drive west to North Rios Avenue. Turn right and go .8 mile to the end of the road and the trailhead. Park alongside the road.

Contact: San Elijo Lagoon Ecological Reserve, San Diego County Parks and Recreation Department, 5201 Ruffin Road, Suite P, San Diego, CA 92123; tel. (858) 694-3049; San Elijo Lagoon Conservancy, tel. (760) 436-3944.

2 Guy Fleming Loop Trail
0.75 mi/0.5 hr

Torrey Pines is one of the greatest hiking destinations in San Diego, with several short but sweet trails and enough spectacular scenery to keep you coming back for more. The Guy Fleming Loop Trail is the easiest of the trails in the park, with almost no elevation change, so it's suitable for all levels of hikers. The path has great views of the Pacific Ocean, La Jolla, Del Mar, and Los Peñasquitos Marsh. If you hike the right side of the loop first, you come to the North Overlook, where you can check out the vistas as well as San Diego's rare tree, the Torrey pine. The trail then loops around to the South Overlook, where you can sometimes see San Clemente and Catalina Islands. People frequently hold weddings at the South Overlook. If they're smart, they plan them for spring, when the wildflowers bloom along the trail.

Location: In Torrey Pines State Reserve near Del Mar; map J5, grid e9.

User groups: Hikers and wheelchairs. No dogs, horses, or mountain bikes.

Permits: No permits are required. A $2 day-use fee is charged per vehicle.

Maps: A free map of Torrey Pines State Reserve is available at the park visitor center. Ask the USGS for a topographic map of the Del Mar area.

Directions: From Interstate 5 in Del Mar take the Carmel Valley Road exit and drive west 1.5 miles. Turn south on Torrey Pines Road and drive 1.7 miles to the reserve entrance. Drive up the hill and park at the first parking area on the right, signed for the Guy Fleming Trail. If this lot is full, you can park farther up the hill at the visitor center and walk back down the road.

Contact: Torrey Pines State Reserve, c/o San Diego Coast State Parks, 9609 Waples Street, Suite 200, San Diego, CA 92121; tel. (858) 755-2063 or (858) 642-4200.

3 Razor Point and Beach Trail Loop
2.5 mi/1.5 hrs

If you can get a parking spot in the lot by the visitor center at Torrey Pines State Reserve (it's not easy on weekend afternoons), you can start hiking right away on the Razor Point Trail, cutting over to the Beach Trail from Razor Point and heading to the beach. Razor Point Trail provides dramatic views of the reserve's eroded coastal badlands, which would look like something straight out of the desert if not for the ocean beyond. There's a spiderweb of paths, only some of which are signed, but it's fine to just wander around at random and visit as many of the overlooks as possible. Windswept Torrey pines grace the bluffs, and wildflowers bloom in the sandy soil in springtime. When you're in the mood, head south from Razor Point (paralleling the ocean) until you hook up with the Beach Trail and turn right, squeezing through the narrow, steep sandstone entrance to the beach. It's great fun. A return uphill on the Beach Trail makes an excellent loop.

Location: In Torrey Pines State Reserve near Del Mar; map J5, grid e9.

User groups: Hikers only. No dogs, horses, or mountain bikes. No wheelchair facilities.

Permits: No permits are required. A $2 day-use fee is charged per vehicle.

Maps: A free map of Torrey Pines State Reserve is available at the park visitor center. Ask the USGS for a topographic map of the Del Mar area.

Directions: From Interstate 5 in Del Mar take the Carmel Valley Road exit and drive west for 1.5 miles. Turn south on Torrey Pines Road and drive 1.7 miles to the reserve entrance. Drive up the hill and park by the reserve office and visitor center. The trailhead is across the park road from the visitor center.

Contact: Torrey Pines State Reserve, c/o San Diego Coast State Parks, 9609 Waples Street, Suite 200, San Diego, CA 92121; tel. (858) 755-2063 or (858) 642-4200.

4 Bayside Trail
2.0 mi/1.0 hr

While everybody else at Cabrillo National Monument is visiting the old Point Loma Lighthouse or having their picture taken by the statue of Señor Cabrillo or checking out the wonderful view of San Diego from the visitor center buildings, you can sneak off for a hike on the Bayside Trail and find a surprising amount of solitude. Luckily, plenty of gorgeous coastal vistas come with the solitude, as well as an interesting lesson in native coastal vegetation.

Take the paved trail from the parking lot to the lighthouse, where you can peer inside at the period furniture and imagine what life was like for the lighthouse keeper and his family at the turn of the century. Then check out the great views from the overlooks on the far side of the lighthouse. After this short tour pick up the paved road on the east side of the lighthouse, signed as Bayside Trail. Take the left fork, which is gravel, and wind gently downhill around Point Loma, occasionally tearing your eyes away from the view so you can read the interpretive signs. If you do, you'll learn all about coastal sage scrub and local and migrating birds. On every step of the trail the whole of San Diego Bay and the Pacific Ocean are yours to survey. You'll see huge navy ships sailing out to sea, flocks of seagulls following the fishing boats back into harbor, sailboats, jet skiers, and large offshore kelp beds. The trail ends 400 feet below the statue of Cabrillo where a sign says "Trail ends—Return by the same route." Darn. We had no interest in leaving.

Location: In Cabrillo National Monument; map J5, grid g9.

User groups: Hikers only. No dogs, horses, or mountain bikes. No wheelchair facilities.

Permits: No permits are required. A $5 day-use fee is charged per vehicle.

Maps: A free map/brochure of Cabrillo National Monument is available at the entrance kiosk or visitor center. Ask the USGS for a topographic map of the Point Loma area.

Directions: From Interstate 5 in San Diego take the Rosecrans Street/Highway 209 exit and drive south. Staying on Highway 209, you will turn right on Cañon Street and then left on Catalina Boulevard. The road ends at Cabrillo National Monument. The trail begins by the old lighthouse.

Contact: Cabrillo National Monument, 1800 Cabrillo Memorial Drive, San Diego, CA 92106; tel. (619) 557-5450.

5 Cabrillo Tide Pools

1.0 mi/0.5 hr

We love tide pools, and the ones at Cabrillo National Monument are some of the best in Southern California. You might want to stop in at the Cabrillo National Monument visitor center before you head straight for the tide pools, because the center has some great free handouts on how to explore the pools and identify the various creatures who live there. Even more important, you should check your tide table before you visit, or else your hike may be very, very short. A fenced trail leads along the bluff tops for a few hundred feet, but then you descend to the rocky beach and walk as far as you please. What will you see? Most likely you'll get a peek at mussels, crabs, abalone, barnacles, starfish, anemones, snails, and limpets. If you're lucky, you might see an octopus or a sea urchin. Is it wintertime? Why, we believe a passing gray whale just waved her flipper at you.

Location: In Cabrillo National Monument; map J5, grid g9.

User groups: Hikers and dogs. No horses or mountain bikes. No wheelchair facilities.

Permits: No permits are required. A $5 day-use fee is charged per vehicle.

Maps: A free map/brochure of Cabrillo National Monument is available at the entrance kiosk or visitor center. Ask the USGS for a topographic map of the Point Loma area.

Directions: From Interstate 5 in San Diego take the Rosecrans Street/Highway 209 exit and drive south. Staying on Highway 209, turn right on Cañon Street, left on Catalina Boulevard, and continue to the monument entrance. After paying the entrance fee at the kiosk take the right fork (immediately following the kiosk) that is signed as "Tide Pools Parking Area." Continue down the hill to the parking area.

Contact: Cabrillo National Monument, 1800 Cabrillo Memorial Drive, San Diego, CA 92106; tel. (619) 557-5450.

CHAPTER 16

THE LAST FEW YARDS OF THE
STONEWALL PEAK TRAIL

MAP J6

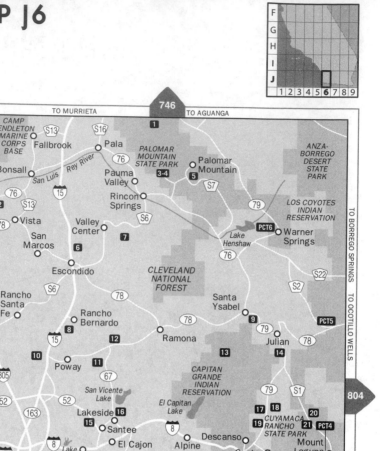

CAMP PENDLETON MARINE CORPS BASE
Fallbrook
Bonsall
Pala
Palomar Mountain
PALOMAR MOUNTAIN STATE PARK
Palomar Mountain
ANZA-BORREGO DESERT STATE PARK
San Luis Rey River
Pauma Valley
Vista
San Marcos
Valley Center
Rincon Springs
LOS COYOTES INDIAN RESERVATION
Warner Springs
Lake Henshaw
Escondido
CLEVELAND NATIONAL FOREST
Rancho Santa Fe
Rancho Bernardo
Santa Ysabel
Julian
Ramona
Poway
CAPITAN GRANDE INDIAN RESERVATION
San Vicente Lake
El Capitan Lake
Lakeside
Santee
El Cajon
Alpine
Descanso
Guatay
CUYAMACA RANCHO STATE PARK
Mount Laguna
Lake Murray
La Mesa
Coronado
National City
Jamul
CLEVELAND NATIONAL FOREST
Pine Valley
Laguna Junction 4,055 feet
Chula Vista
Barrett Lake
Lake Morena
Imperial Beach
Otay
Lower Otay Lake
Dulzura
Morena Village
Tecate Divide 4,140 feet
MANZANITA INDIAN RESERVATION
San Ysidro
Barrett Junction
Potrero
Campo
TIJUANA
CALIFORNIA MEXICO
Tecate
PACIFIC OCEAN
Rosarito

TO OCEANSIDE
TO DEL MAR
TO SAN DIEGO
TO BORREGO SPRINGS
TO OCOTILLO WELLS
TO BOULEVARD
TO LA RUMOROSA

776
804

© AVALON TRAVEL PUBLISHING, INC.

CHAPTER J6

1 Dripping Springs Trail. . 783
2 Guajome Lake Trail 784
3 Weir and Lower Doane
    Valley Loop 784
4 Boucher Trail and Scott's
    Cabin Loop 785
5 Observatory Trail 786
6 Jack Creek Nature Trail 786
7 Hellhole Canyon 787
8 Blue Sky Ecological
    Preserve 787
9 Inaja Memorial Trail . . . 788
10 Los Peñasquitos Canyon . 788
11 Sycamore Canyon
    Preserve 789
12 Mount Woodson 789
13 Cedar Creek Falls 790
14 Desert View and
    Canyon Oak Loop 790
15 Cowles Mountain 791
16 Silverwood Wildlife
    Sanctuary 792
17 Cuyamaca Peak Trail . . . 792

18 Stonewall Peak Trail . . . 793
19 Green Valley Falls 793
20 Garnet Peak 794
21 Lightning Ridge Trail . . 794
22 Cottonwood Creek Falls . 795
23 Desert View Nature
    Trail 795
24 Kitchen Creek Falls 796

Pacific Crest Trail
(PCT) Section Overview
PCT-1 Campo Border Patrol
    to Lake Morena Park . . 797
PCT-2 Lake Morena Park to
    Boulder Oaks Camp . . . 798
PCT-3 Boulder Oaks Camp to
    Sunrise Highway Trail . 799
PCT-4 Sunrise Highway Trail
    to Highway 78 Trail . . . 799
PCT-5 Highway 78 Trailhead
    to Warner Springs . . . 800
PCT-6 Warner Springs to
    Highway 74 801

1 Dripping Springs Trail

13.6 mi/2.0 days

At the very northern edge of San Diego County lies the Aqua Tibia Wilderness, a land of extreme summer heat, exposed slopes, no available water sources, and thick chaparral. The place appears suitable for only the most steadfast of hikers. Or so it seems. Actually, if you hike the Dripping Springs Trail in the spring, when the temperature is just right, the Aqua Tibia is a pastoral place with blooming shrubs and wildflowers, crystal-clear vistas, and flitting butterflies and bees. (Forget hiking in winter, though; these mountains are often covered in snow.) Trailhead elevation at Dripping Springs Campground is 1,600 feet, and the peak of Aqua Tibia Mountain is at 4,547 feet. The trail leaves the campground, crosses the rocky wash of Arroyo Seco Creek, and starts to climb. In the first three miles of trail you get views of Vail Lake to the north and the big mountains of Southern California—San Jacinto, San Gorgonio, and San Antonio (Baldy). Another mile passes and you can see the white dome of Palomar Observatory to the south. The chaparral gets taller as you go, and the trail gets steeper and narrower. When you finally near the peak of Aqua Tibia Mountain, you've climbed out of the chaparral and into oak woodland with a few scattered pines, which means—yes!—shade.

Location: In the Aqua Tibia Wilderness; map J6, grid a4.

User groups: Hikers, dogs, and horses. No mountain bikes. No wheelchair facilities.

Permits: A free wilderness permit is required for overnight stays and can be obtained at the Dripping Springs station near the campground or from the Palomar Ranger District at the address below. Day users should sign the register at the trailhead. A national forest recreation pass is required for each vehicle; fees are $5 for one day or $30 for a year.

Maps: For a map of Cleveland National Forest, send $6 to U.S. Forest Service, Map Sales, P.O. Box 587, Camino, CA 95709; tel. (530) 647-5390 or website: www.r5.fs.fed.us/visitorcenter. Ask the USGS for a topographic map of the Vail Lake area.

Directions: From Interstate 15 in Temecula take the Highway 79 east exit. Drive 10 miles east on Highway 79 to Dripping Springs Campground on the right. The trail begins at the south end of the campground.

Contact: Cleveland National Forest, Palomar Ranger District, 1634 Black Canyon Road, Ramona, CA 92065; tel. (760) 788-0250 or fax (760) 788-6130.

2 Guajome Lake Trail
2.0 mi/1.0 hr

As you drive into Guajome Regional Park a prominent sign reads, "No piñatas." Geez, don't these guys have a sense of humor? Guess not. Anyway, Guajome Regional Park is home to one of the richest riparian areas of any of San Diego County's parks. The big draw is a spring-fed lake and marsh, which have enticed 144 species of birds to visit the park. The waterways also entice frogs, which you will hear but probably not see. In fact, "Guajome" means "home of the frog." The park's main hiking trail leads from the parking lot and goes around mid-sized Guajome Lake, up to the park's wedding gazebo, and alongside Guajome Marsh. Equestrian trails also lead into the drier grassland and chaparral areas of the park, but most hikers stay near the water. An out-and-back trip will cover about two miles, and along the way you might see a few red-winged blackbirds or a white-faced ibis or even the rare least bell's vireo. Fishing is also popular in Guajome Lake, for bullheads, crappie, catfish, and sunfish.

Location: In Guajome Regional Park near Oceanside; map J6, grid b0.

User groups: Hikers, dogs, horses, and mountain bikes. No wheelchair facilities.

Permits: No permits are required. A $1 day-use fee is charged per vehicle.

Maps: Ask the USGS for a topographic map of the San Luis Rey area.

Directions: From Interstate 5 in Oceanside take the Mission Avenue and Highway 76 exit and drive east for seven miles to Guajome Lake Drive. Turn right (south) into the park entrance.

Contact: Guajome Regional Park, c/o San Diego County Parks and Recreation Department, 5201 Ruffin Road, Suite P, San Diego, CA 92123; tel. (858) 694-3049.

3 Weir and Lower Doane Valley Loop
3.0 mi/1.5 hrs

If you've never visited before, Palomar Mountain State Park is like a shock to your system—a good shock. At 5,500 feet in elevation the air is cool, the conifers are big, and suburban sprawl seems far, far away. We kept shaking our heads in disbelief at the Sierra Nevada-like feel of the place. A good introduction to the park is this loop hike on three trails: the Doane Valley Nature Trail, the Weir Trail, and the Lower Doane Valley Trail. From the parking area at Doane Pond (which is always busy with children learning to fish), head away from Doane Pond on the trail that crosses the park road. Start your walk on the Doane Valley NatureTrail and veer left onto the Weir Trail, following pretty Doane Creek under the shade of big pines, firs, and cedars. Cross the creek about one mile out (shortly after the left fork for the Baptist Trail), then follow the Lower Doane Valley Trail as it loops back around a meadow. You'll probably see deer and mountain quail and hear many birdcalls. You'll certainly see the evidence of resident woodpeckers in the big old trees. When the trail nears Doane Valley Campground, cross the creek again and make a sharp switchback to the right on the Doane Valley Nature Trail. The nature trail will close out your trip, bringing you back to the trailhead in .75 mile. As you pass the giant conifers and grassy meadows along the way, you will ask yourself again and again, "Is this really San Diego?"

Location: In Palomar Mountain State Park; map J6, grid b4.

User groups: Hikers only. No dogs, horses, or mountain bikes. No wheelchair facilities.

Permits: No permits are required. A $2 day-use fee is charged per vehicle.

Maps: A map of Palomar State Park is available for $1 at the entrance station or park headquarters. Ask the USGS for topographic maps of the Boucher Hill and Palomar Observatory areas.

Directions: From Interstate 15 north of Escondido, drive east on Highway 76 for 21 miles. Turn left (north) on Road S6/South Grade Road and drive 6.5 miles to the junction with Road S7. Turn left on Road S7 and drive three miles into the park. Drive past park headquarters, turn right, and drive to the parking area by Doane Pond and the school camp.

Contact: Palomar Mountain State Park, Palomar Mountain, CA 92060; tel. (760) 742-3462.

4 Boucher Trail and Scott's Cabin Loop

4.0 mi/2.0 hrs

You may be wowed by the view of Pauma Valley from the Boucher Lookout at elevation 5,438 feet, but start walking on the Boucher Trail and you'll be wowed even more. The trail descends from the lookout, passing meadows, oaks, dogwoods, and conifers, and dropping 600 feet as it crosses Nate Harrison Grade (a road) and heads for Cedar Grove Campground. The camp is well named; the cedars are huge and memorable here. You might want to check out the rope swing by the group camp. If not, bear right at the fork by the campground, walk a brief stretch on the camp road, and then cross the park road to pick up the Scott's Cabin Trail, which leads to the cabin site of an 1880s homesteader. Only the base of the cabin remains—it's a rather sad-looking pile of sticks and logs. From the site take the right fork to head back to park headquarters and the Silver Crest Picnic Area. Walk to your right on the park road for a few hundred yards until you can pick up the Boucher Trail once more and walk back to the lookout. Here the Boucher Trail is the narrow trail that runs between the legs of the driving loop to the lookout. What? You say you forgot your troubles along the way? That's what happens here at Palomar Mountain.

Location: In Palomar Mountain State Park; map J6, grid b4.

User groups: Hikers only. No dogs, horses, or mountain bikes. No wheelchair facilities.

Permits: No permits are required. A $2 day-use fee is charged per vehicle.

Maps: A map of Palomar State Park is available for $1 at the entrance station or park headquarters. Ask the USGS for topographic maps of the Boucher Hill and Palomar Observatory area.

Directions: From Interstate 15 north of Escondido drive east on Highway 76 for 21 miles. Turn left (north) on Road S6 (South Grade Road) and drive 6.5 miles to the junction with Road S7. Turn left on Road S7 and drive three miles into the park. Drive past park headquarters and bear left at the sign for Boucher Lookout. Park at the lookout and begin hiking on the Boucher Trail.

Contact: Palomar Mountain State Park, Palomar Mountain, CA 92060; tel. (760) 742-3462.

5 Observatory Trail
4.4 mi/2.5 hrs

The question: Is the Palomar Observatory as great as everybody says? The answer: Yes. And the hike to reach it is far better than the drive to reach it. Even if you have absolutely no interest in astronomy, the National Recreation Trail to Palomar Observatory is just plain fun to hike. From Observatory Campground the trail is an aerobic uphill climb, but on a well-graded, well-maintained trail with only a 600-foot elevation gain. The shade is dense from oaks and pines, and you'll find many giant-sized pine cones along the trail. At .5 mile you reach an overlook platform with a lovely view of Mendenhall Valley and then head back into the forest to climb some more. The last stretch of trail brings you out to the observatory parking lot, where you turn right, walk through the lot and past the museum, and head straight for the big white golf ball which is the 200-inch Hale telescope. If you like, hike up the couple flights of stairs to the telescope viewing area and learn all about how the thing works. Think about this: More than 100 billion galaxies like ours are within spotting range of the giant telescope.

Location: In Cleveland National Forest on Palomar Mountain; map J6, grid b5.

User groups: Hikers, dogs, horses, and mountain bikes. No wheelchair facilities.

Permits: No permits are required. A national forest recreation pass is required for each vehicle; fees are $5 for one day or $30 for a year.

Maps: For a map of Cleveland National Forest, send $6 to U.S. Forest Service, Map Sales, P.O. Box 587, Camino, CA 95709; tel. (530) 647-5390 or website: www.r5.fs.fed.us/visitorcenter. Ask the USGS for a topographic map of the Palomar Observatory area.

Directions: From Interstate 15 north of Escondido, drive east on Highway 76 for 21 miles. Turn left (north) on Road S6 (South Grade Road) and drive 6.5 miles to the junction with Road S7, and then continue north on Road S6 for three more miles to Observatory Campground on the right. Drive through the camp to the signed parking area for the amphitheater and trailhead.

Contact: Cleveland National Forest, Palomar Ranger District, 1634 Black Canyon Road, Ramona, CA 92065; tel. (760) 788-0250 or fax (760) 788-6130.

6 Jack Creek Nature Trail
1.0 mi/0.5 hr

If you are exceptionally lucky, it will be a rainy year in San Diego and you can see the waterfall flow along Jack Creek at Dixon Lake Recreation Area. We've only seen it trickle, but we've seen pictures of the 20-foot falls at flood, and it's quite beautiful. Nonetheless, a stroll on the .5-mile Jack Creek Nature Trail is good in any season, although best in winter and spring when the hills are green and the flowers in bloom. The trail begins by Dixon Lake's entrance station, traveling through a picnic area and along Jack Creek to the lake's edge. You can pick up an interpretive brochure at the trailhead or the park ranger station, or just march off boldly without one. Be on the alert: Many cute bunnies are likely to cross your path. (They are western cottontails, to be precise.) If the creek is flowing strong, be sure to take the right spur to the waterfall's base; otherwise just head straight for the lake. At the water's edge the trail connects to the Shoreline Trail and Grand View Trail, which is useful if you're in the mood to hike more. Many people choose instead to plunk a line in the water and see if they can catch a largemouth bass, rainbow trout, or catfish.

Location: In the Dixon Lake Recreation Area near Escondido; map J6, grid c2.

User groups: Hikers and dogs. No horses or mountain bikes. No wheelchair facilities.

Permits: No permits are required. A $1 day-use fee is charged per vehicle on weekends only.

Maps: Ask the USGS for a topographic map of the Valley Center area.

Directions: From Escondido drive north on

Interstate 15 and take the El Norte Parkway exit. Drive 3.1 miles east on El Norte Parkway, turn left (north) on La Honda Drive, and drive 1.3 miles to the Dixon Lake entrance on the right. The trailhead is located directly across from the park entrance. Park by the playground/picnic area to the right of the park entrance, signed as Hilltop Picnic Area.

Contact: Dixon Lake Ranger Station, 201 N. Broadway, Escondido, CA 92025; tel. (760) 741-4680.

7 Hellhole Canyon

3.0 mi/1.5 hrs

Hellhole Canyon Preserve seems a bit misnamed. We didn't think there was anything hellish about it, except maybe the heat on an August afternoon. The preserve takes up 1,700 acres on the west flank of Rodriguez Mountain and is bounded by Indian reservations to the north and south. The rocky land is covered in typical San Diego chaparral—redberry, manzanita, lilac, monkey flower—which means no shade, of course. Only five miles of trail have been built so far in the preserve, although more are in the works. In the meantime you can hike from the trailhead (behind the restrooms at the parking lot) and head downhill into the canyon. The main trail branches off to three different viewpoints, with a loop connecting the two on the right and the left one off by itself, making an out-and-back trip necessary. Take the right loop. As you walk you'll be surprised to find that the chaparral is often taller than you are, which creates a labyrinth effect. It's kind of fun, and the best part is the sense of solitude you get. One mile down the trail you'll reach Hell Creek, which runs with vigor in the wet season.

Location: In Hellhole Canyon Preserve; map J6, grid c3.

User groups: Hikers, dogs, horses, and mountain bikes. No wheelchair facilities.

Permits: No permits are required. Parking and access are free.

Maps: Ask the USGS for a topographic map of the Rodriguez Mountains area.

Directions: From Interstate 15 south of Temecula take Highway 76 east for 15 miles and turn right (south) on Road S6/Valley Center Road. Drive five miles and turn left on North Lake Wohlford Road. Drive two miles, and turn left on Paradise Mountain Road. Drive 3.3 miles to a T intersection, where you turn right on Los Hermanos Ranch Road and then immediately left on Kiavo Road. Drive .5 mile on Kiavo Road to the park entrance. Coming from Escondido and points south, take the Valley Parkway exit and drive northeast on Road S6 to Lake Wohlford Road. Take Lake Wohlford Road to Paradise Mountain Road and follow directions as above.

Contact: Hellhole Canyon Preserve, c/o San Diego County Parks and Recreation Department, 5201 Ruffin Road, Suite P, San Diego, CA 92123; tel. (858) 694-3049.

8 Blue Sky Ecological Preserve

4.0 mi/2.0 hrs

The Blue Sky Ecological Preserve provides habitat for several rare and threatened animal and plant species, including harried San Diego humans who desperately need a place to stop and smell the flowers. The preserve is good for the San Diego horned lizard, the Engelmann oaks, and for people who live in the Poway area. From the trailhead hike along the wide, flat fire road, ignoring the first two turnoffs. At the third junction turn right to pay a visit to Lake Poway. The lake is a fine place to catch catfish and trout (they get planted every two weeks) or a fine place to rent a rowboat and row your hiking partner around the lake. You can also hike the perimeter of the lake, which will add some climbing and descending to your basically flat route. Retrace your steps to the main preserve trail and head back to the trailhead for a four-mile round-trip. If you want to see more, continue on the main trail to the left fork for Lake

Ramona. So how do the flowers smell? Pretty good, we thought.

If you enjoy hiking with a naturalist, show up at Blue Sky Ecological Preserve on Saturday or Sunday at 9 a.m.; free guided hikes are offered every weekend. The trips are usually only a mile in length—just right for families.

Location: In the Blue Sky Ecological Preserve near Poway; map J6, grid d2.

User groups: Hikers, dogs, and horses. No mountain bikes. No wheelchair facilities.

Permits: No permits are required. Parking and access are free.

Maps: Ask the USGS for a topographic map of the Escondido area.

Directions: From Interstate 15 near Poway, drive north to the Rancho Bernardo Road exit. Drive east for 3.3 miles on Rancho Bernardo Road; the reserve is on the left, at the junction of Rancho Bernardo Road and Espola Road.

Contact: Blue Sky Ecological Preserve, tel. (858) 679-5469; San Diego County Parks and Recreation Department, 5201 Ruffin Road, Suite P, San Diego, CA 92123; tel. (858) 694-3049.

9 Inaja Memorial Trail
0.5 mi/0.5 hr

At 3,200 feet in elevation you can look down a long way into the steep canyon of the San Diego River. That's what you get here on the Inaja Memorial National Recreation Trail, a short but interesting trail that begins at the Inaja Picnic Area. There are steps built in places along the trail as the path undulates along the canyon edge amid various types of chaparral. If you pick up an interpretive brochure at the trailhead, you can learn about live oaks, scrub oaks, wild lilac, toyon, manzanita, and chamise, as well as the granitic rocks of this area. The trail's highlights are the views of both the Santa Ysabel Valley and the Volcan Mountains near Julian. The picnic area and trail have an interesting history: they were named to honor the 11 firefighters who lost their lives in the 60,000-acre Inaja forest fire of 1956.

Location: In Cleveland National Forest near Santa Ysabel; map J6, grid d7.

User groups: Hikers and dogs. No horses or mountain bikes. No wheelchair facilities except at the picnic area.

Permits: No permits are required. A national forest recreation pass is required for each vehicle; fees are $5 for one day or $30 for a year.

Maps: For a map of Cleveland National Forest, send $6 to U.S. Forest Service, Map Sales, P.O. Box 587, Camino, CA 95709; tel. (530) 647-5390 or website: www.r5.fs.fed.us/visitorcenter. Ask the USGS for a topographic map of the Santa Ysabel area.

Directions: From Julian drive northwest on Highway 78/79 for six miles (to one mile south of Santa Ysabel). The Inaja Picnic Area and Trailhead are on the south (left) side of the road.

Contact: Cleveland National Forest, Palomar Ranger District, 1634 Black Canyon Road, Ramona, CA 92065; tel. (760) 788-0250 or fax (760) 788-6130.

10 Los Peñasquitos Canyon
6.5 mi/3.0 hrs

If it's winter or spring and your thoughts are turning to love, there may be no better spot in San Diego for a first date than Los Peñasquitos Canyon Preserve. The trail that runs from one end of the canyon to the other is wide and flat, perfectly built for good conversation and maybe a little hand holding. If the cascades along the creek are flowing, you can find a big volcanic boulder to sit on and watch the reflections of the sky in the water. If not, there are numerous places where you could lay out a picnic under a spreading oak tree and sit and watch the birds fly past. Early in the year, the wildflowers bloom and the grasses become verdant. Can this much beauty be found so close to a large urban area? You bet. Although you can hike the trail through the canyon starting from either end, the eastern trailhead near Poway is preferred because the path is more shaded. As you wander, keep watching for mileage marker 3, because soon after it you'll see a hitching post and bike rack on the right, where you can head off trail and scramble down to the cascades on Los Peñasquitos Creek. Even when the stream is reduced to a trickle, the car-sized boulders in the creek are fascinating to look at.

Location: In Los Peñasquitos Canyon Preserve near Poway; map J6, grid e1.

User groups: Hikers, dogs, horses, and mountain bikes. No wheelchair facilities.

Permits: No permits are required. Parking and access are free.

Maps: Ask the USGS for a topographic map of the Poway area.

Directions: From Escondido drive south on Interstate 15 for 16 miles to the Mercy Road exit. Turn right (west) on Mercy Road and follow it for one mile, crossing Black Mountain Road, to the trailhead parking area.

Contact: Los Peñasquitos Canyon Preserve, c/o San Diego County Parks and Recreation Department, 5201 Ruffin Road, Suite P, San Diego, CA 92123; tel. (858) 694-3049.

11 Sycamore Canyon Preserve
2.5 mi/1.25 hrs

Are you looking for a good spot to watch the sun set, but you don't feel like braving the traffic to the beach? A trip to Sycamore Canyon Preserve could be just the ticket. The terrain is coastal sage scrub, chaparral, and oak woodland—no surprises here—but the path leads into beautiful canyons and offers wide vistas. The preserve's trails are well maintained and even have hand-painted signs with maps at major intersections. From the parking lot take the winding single-track trail through the chaparral, heading down through Martha's Grove (a group of old and lovely oak trees), and then heading out into the grasslands. Turn right on the fire road and then right again to loop back. Note that this is only one of many possible loops in the preserve, so if you want to hike longer, it's easy to add on a few miles. Also, although the preserve is popular with mountain bikers, the ones we met were extremely courteous and friendly to hikers.

Location: In Sycamore Canyon Preserve; map J6, grid e3.

User groups: Hikers, dogs, horses, and mountain bikes. No wheelchair facilities.

Permits: No permits are required. Parking and access are free.

Maps: Ask the USGS for a topographic map of the San Vicente Reservoir area.

Directions: From Poway drive east on Poway Road to Garden Road. Turn right, drive one mile on Garden Road, and turn right on Sycamore Canyon Road. Drive 2.5 miles to the road's end at a gate (the last 1.5 miles are dirt).

Contact: Sycamore Canyon Preserve, c/o San Diego County Parks and Recreation Department, 5201 Ruffin Road, Suite P, San Diego, CA 92123; tel. (858) 694-3049.

12 Mount Woodson
3.6 mi/2.0 hrs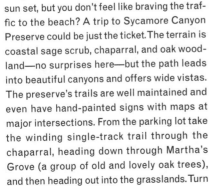

Mount Woodson is the neighborhood summit to climb for the thousands of people who live in the Poway, Scripps Ranch, and Rancho Bernardo areas. The light-colored, rocky mountain is always there in the background, looming over the suburbs below, a favorite playground of rock climbers from all over San Diego. If you've never seen Mount Woodson except from the bottom looking up, maybe it's time to lace up your hiking boots. The trail has a 1,500-foot elevation gain to reach the 2,894-foot peak, so you'll get in your workout for the day, but you won't be so wiped out that you can't enjoy the vistas or the fascinating giant boulders you'll pass along the trail. Hike on the path south of the fire station and then follow the paved Mount Woodson Road. You'll reach the top at 1.8 miles, where a ton of electronic equipment is in place. Wander around a bit on the ridge till you find the best spot to look out over the wide blue

Pacific and congratulate yourself for having bagged Mount Woodson's peak.

Location: Near Poway; map J6, grid e3.

User groups: Hikers only. No dogs, horses, or mountain bikes. No wheelchair facilities.

Permits: No permits are required. Parking and access are free.

Maps: Ask the USGS for a topographic map of the San Pasqual area.

Directions: From Poway drive east on Poway Road for 3.5 miles and turn north on Highway 67. Drive three miles to the Ramona CDF Fire Station on the left. The trail begins by the fire station, but you will have to park across the road.

Contact: City of Poway, Lake Poway Recreation Area, tel. (858) 679-4393.

13 Cedar Creek Falls

4.0 mi/2.0 hrs

Cedar Creek Falls is no secret among San Diego hikers since the trailhead is well signed and is an access point for the California Riding and Hiking Trail. But if you get up early on a winter or spring morning, you can probably be the first person at the waterfall and have it all to yourself for a while. Begin by hiking to the right and downhill on the wide fire road, enjoying good views of the far-off San Diego River Canyon, as well as colorful spring wildflowers on the slopes alongside the road. At 1.2 miles you'll reach an unsigned left fork, where you should bear left and hike up and over a small hill. On the far side you'll see three possible trail options; take the middle route for the most direct path to the falls. You'll come out upstream of the 100-foot free fall, at a series of clear pools under the shade of cottonwoods. Be very careful as you approach the lip of the waterfall; it has a sheer drop, and the granite is deadly slick. You cannot descend to the falls' base (in addition to being too dangerous, it's private property), but you can cautiously make your way around the side of the falls for the best possible view. Settle in at one of the upstream pools for sunning and

swimming. Note that although Cedar Creek flows year-round, the falls are most spectacular during San Diego's brief rainy season, so plan your trip accordingly.

Location: In Cleveland National Forest near Julian; map J6, grid e6.

User groups: Hikers, dogs, horses, and mountain bikes. No wheelchair facilities.

Permits: No permits are required. A national forest recreation pass is required for each vehicle; fees are $5 for one day or $30 for a year.

Maps: For a map of Cleveland National Forest, send $6 to U.S. Forest Service, Map Sales, P.O. Box 587, Camino, CA 95709; tel. (530) 647-5390 or website: www.r5.fs.fed.us/visitorcenter. Ask the USGS for a topographic map of the Santa Ysabel area.

Directions: From Julian drive two miles west on Highway 78/79 and turn left (south) on Pine Hills Road. In 1.5 miles bear right on Eagle Peak Road. In 1.4 miles bear right again, staying on Eagle Peak Road. Continue for eight miles on partly paved, partly dirt road to the signed Forest Service trailhead for the California Riding and Hiking Trail. The road gets rough after the first four miles, but it's usually suitable for a passenger car.

Contact: Cleveland National Forest, Palomar Ranger District, 1634 Black Canyon Road, Ramona, CA 92065; tel. (760) 788-0250 or fax (760) 788-6130.

14 Desert View and Canyon Oak Loop

3.5 mi/2.0 hrs

William Heise County Park is so pretty, so well run, and has such good hiking trails, we have to keep reminding ourselves that this is a county park and not a state park. We're not sure how they do it, but they really manage the park well, and it's clearly appreciated by the many campers and hikers who visit here regularly. The park is located near Julian at 4,000 feet in elevation, so the terrain is shady oak woodland with a few conifers mixed in—

the transition zone between valley and mountains. The black oaks display gorgeous colors in the fall. From the trailhead, start hiking through the oaks. You'll leave the Nature Trail to join the Canyon Oak Trail in .25 mile. Bear left on the loop, circling a lovely grove of ancient oaks, and then bear left on the Desert View Trail. The route is steep, but in .1 mile you reach an overlook, complete with a bench for resting on and a view of the Cuyamaca and Laguna Mountains and a sea of conifers. The trail continues upward for another .75 mile to a spur trail leading to a higher overlook—Glen's View. The vista here is largely obstructed by brush, but if you scramble as high as you can, you'll spy the Anza-Borrego Desert, the Salton Sea, and even the Pacific Ocean. A makeshift scope on top of a stone monument at Glen's View helps you identify all of San Diego County's best features. Hope you picked a clear day.

Location: In William Heise County Park near Julian; map J6, grid e8.

User groups: Hikers, horses, and mountain bikes. No dogs. No wheelchair facilities.

Permits: No permits are required. A $2 day-use fee is charged per vehicle.

Maps: A free map of William Heise County Park is available at the entrance station. Ask the USGS for a topographic map of the Julian area.

Directions: From Julian drive two miles west on Highway 78/79 turn left (south) on Pine Hills Road. Drive two miles, turn left on Frisius Drive, and drive two more miles. Frisius Drive turns into Heise Park Road and enters the park. From the park entrance kiosk continue straight on the park road and drive to near its end at the Area 1 group camp on the left (also called the Youth Area). Park above campsite 64 and then walk back down to the trailhead, signed as Nature Trail and Canyon Oak Trail.

Contact: William Heise County Park, c/o San Diego County Parks and Recreation Department, 5201 Ruffin Road, Suite P, San Diego, CA 92123; tel. (858) 694-3049.

15 Cowles Mountain
3.0 mi/1.5 hrs

There are tons of trails to hike (and bike and horseback ride) in Mission Trails Regional Park. The visitor center alone provides enough entertainment to fill an entire afternoon—it's a huge, architecturally unique building with state-of-the-art displays, and it's better designed than many museums. But if you can only hike one trail in the park, you might as well go for the summit of Cowles Mountain, a 1,591-foot peak with a 360-degree view of the city. They say Cowles Mountain is the highest point in San Diego, but they mean the city, not the county. Pick a cool day because the trail is sunny and exposed, with a 951-foot elevation gain to the summit. When you reach the top and you're looking out at the city below, think about the temporary state of all you survey compared to the rock you're standing on, which is nearly 150 million years old. Hmm.

Location: In Mission Trails Regional Park; map J6, grid f2.

User groups: Hikers, dogs, and horses. No mountain bikes. No wheelchair facilities.

Permits: No permits are required. Parking and access are free.

Maps: Ask the USGS for a topographic map of the La Mesa area.

Directions: From Interstate 15 south of Poway take Highway 52 east for seven miles until it ends. Turn right on Mission Gorge Road, drive 2.5 miles, and then turn left on Golfcrest Drive. Follow Golfcrest Drive to its intersection with Navajo Road, where the trailhead for Cowles Mountain Trailhead is located. If you wish to go to the park visitor center first to get hiking information, continue past Golfcrest Drive on Mission Gorge Road and then turn right at the park entrance.)

Contact: Mission Trails Regional Park, One Father Junipero Serra Trail, San Diego, CA 92119; tel. (619) 668-3275.

16 Silverwood Wildlife Sanctuary

1.5 mi/1.0 hr

The smartest thing you can do at the Silverwood Wildlife Sanctuary is show up on Sunday and take a guided walk with one of the Audubon Society's naturalists. These people know their stuff, and they tailor the walk to the ability of the people who attend. On the other hand, if you want your sweet solitude, you can wander around Silverwood on your own, although there won't be anybody around to tell you the difference between a wrentit and a bushtit. Seven miles of hiking trails lace the preserve, which is home to over 240 plant species and 160 bird species. Start by heading straight from the parking lot to the bird observation area, where in addition to watching birds, you can pick up a trail map. Follow the Cienaga Trail to the Chaparral, Sunset, and Circuit Trails, making a short and easy 1.5-mile loop.

Special note: The Silverwood Wildlife Sanctuary is open to the public only on Sundays from 9 a.m. to 4 p.m. Guided walks are available every Sunday at 10 a.m. and 1:30 p.m. The park is closed in August.

Location: In the Silverwood Wildlife Sanctuary near Lakeside; map J6, grid f3.

User groups: Hikers only. No dogs, horses, or mountain bikes. No wheelchair facilities.

Permits: Hikers must sign in at the trailhead register. Parking and access are free, but donations are gratefully accepted.

Maps: Ask the USGS for a topographic map of the San Vicente Reservoir area.

Directions: From Interstate 8 in San Diego drive east to Highway 67 near El Cajon. Drive north on Highway 67 to Lakeside, where you turn right on Mapleview Street. Drive a short distance, turn left on Ashwood Street, which becomes Wildcat Canyon Road, and drive 4.8 miles to 13003 Wildcat Canyon Road.

Contact: Silverwood Wildlife Sanctuary, 13003 Wildcat Canyon Road, Lakeside, CA 92040; tel. (619) 443-2998.

17 Cuyamaca Peak Trail

5.4 mi/3.0 hrs

A 6,512-foot mountain in San Diego? Yup, here it is. Cuyamaca Peak is the undisputed king of the peaks in Cuyamaca Rancho State Park, and it's just shy of being the tallest summit in the county. (Hot Springs Mountain near Warner Springs stands at 6,533 feet.) The main trail to the summit is a paved road closed to vehicle traffic. Luckily, many parts of the route are shaded by an assortment of hardwoods and conifers, or the pavement would be brutal on a hot day. Normally we avoid paved trails like the plague, but this one is a pleasant walk in the trees, as well as nicely graded, and provides hikers with first-class views. So what do you see when you get to the top of Cuyamaca? Just about everything surrounding San Diego—the ocean, the desert, Mexico, Mount San Jacinto, Mount San Gorgonio, Palomar Observatory, and the Salton Sea. It's sure to wow you. Our favorite spot wasn't exactly the peak, which had too many people, radio towers, and buildings on it, but a beautiful grassy clearing .5 mile below the peak, which looks out to the west. You'll know it when you see it. So what does Cuyamaca mean? Roughly, it's "place beyond the rain."

Location: In Cuyamaca Rancho State Park; map J6, grid f7.

User groups: Hikers, dogs, and horses. No mountain bikes. No wheelchair facilities.

Permits: No permits are required. A $2 day-use fee is charged per vehicle.

Maps: Maps of Cuyamaca Rancho State Park are available for a fee at the park visitor center or from Tom Harrison Cartography, tel. (415) 456-7940. Ask the USGS for a topographic map of the Cuyamaca area.

Directions: From San Diego drive east on Interstate 8 for 40 miles to the Highway 79 exit. Drive north on Highway 79 for 11 miles and then turn left (west) at the sign for Paso Picacho Campground. The trail begins on the south end of the campground, near site 37. Park at the picnic area parking lot.

Contact: Cuyamaca Rancho State Park, 12551 Highway 79, Descanso, CA 91916; tel. (760) 765-0755.

18 Stonewall Peak Trail
4.0 mi/2.0 hrs

Although slightly dwarfed by neighboring Cuyamaca Peak, Stonewall Peak is no slouch in the summit department: its peak stands at 5,730 feet in elevation. Stonewall Peak overlooks the site of the turn-of-the-century Stonewall Mine, as well as a large chunk of the Cuyamaca Mountains and Anza-Borrego Desert. The trail has only a 900-foot elevation gain and is remarkably well graded. About a million switchbacks whisk you to the summit, and about a million other hikers will likely join you on the trail, especially if it's a clear, not-too-warm day. But that's okay; everybody seems to be smiling as they ascend the well-graded path. The trail is mostly shaded by black oaks and incense cedars, but there are some sunny, exposed stretches, so bring your water bottle. The final 50 yards of trail are cut into an exposed stone ridge, with granite stair steps and a handrail keeping you from going over the edge. The view is grand, of course, taking in all of the park, Lake Cuyamaca, and the desert far to the east. Squint and you can see the Palomar Observatory, Mount San Gorgonio, and Mount San Jacinto.
Location: In Cuyamaca Rancho State Park; map J6, grid f8.
User groups: Hikers only. No dogs, horses, or mountain bikes. No wheelchair facilities.
Permits: No permits are required. A $2 day-use fee is charged per vehicle.
Maps: Maps of Cuyamaca Rancho State Park are available for a fee at the park visitor center or from Tom Harrison Cartography, tel. (415) 456-7940. Ask the USGS for a topographic map of the Cuyamaca area.
Directions: From San Diego drive east on Interstate 8 for 40 miles to the Highway 79 exit. Drive north on Highway 79 for 11 miles and look for Paso Picacho Campground on the left. The trail begins across the highway from the campground; turn into the camp entrance and park at the picnic area parking lot.
Contact: Cuyamaca Rancho State Park, 12551 Highway 79, Descanso, CA 91916; tel. (760) 765-0755.

19 Green Valley Falls
1.5 mi/1.0 hr

If it's a hot afternoon in Cuyamaca Rancho State Park, chances are good that you won't be in the mood for climbing Cuyamaca or Stonewall Peaks, above. But if you're looking for a walk with a good payoff on a warm day, the trip to Green Valley Falls should do the trick. From the picnic area parking lot at Green Valley Campground, follow the wide fire road along the Sweetwater River to the cutoff for the falls, then hike downhill to your left. By summer the river's cascades aren't terribly dramatic, but there are still many cool pools where you can soak your toes and wide granite ledges where you can lay out a towel and lounge around on the rocks.
Location: In Cuyamaca Rancho State Park; map J6, grid f7.
User groups: Hikers, horses, and mountain bikes. No dogs. No wheelchair facilities.
Permits: No permits are required. A $2 day-use fee is charged per vehicle.
Maps: Maps of Cuyamaca Rancho State Park are available for a fee at the park visitor center or from Tom Harrison Cartography, tel. (415) 456-7940. Ask the USGS for a topographic map of the Cuyamaca area.
Directions: From San Diego drive east on Interstate 8 for 40 miles to the Highway 79 exit. Drive north on Highway 79 for seven miles and turn left (west) at the sign for Green Valley Campground. Follow the signs to the picnic area. One sign points either straight ahead or to the left for the picnic area; continue straight to reach the trailhead.
Contact: Cuyamaca Rancho State Park, 12551 Highway 79, Descanso, CA 91916; tel. (760) 765-0755.

20 Garnet Peak

4.4 mi/2.5 hrs

The route to Garnet Peak begins on the Pacific Crest Trail at the Penny Pines Trailhead, where you can see the list of names of the good people who have donated funds to California's national forests for reforestation. Follow the well-graded PCT to the north (left), hiking along the edge of the pines. The trail has pleasantly little elevation gain, and it hugs the Laguna Mountain rim, offering nearly continual views of Storm Canyon and the Anza-Borrego Desert. You won't see any trail signs directing you to the peak. Ignore the first two right turnoffs at 1.5 miles out (they lead to expansive overlooks, but won't take you to the summit). Instead, turn right at the third right turnoff. The Garnet Peak Trail is rocky and uphill, but in less than a mile you reach the jagged, 5,900-foot summit. There you're rewarded with mind-boggling views of the Anza-Borrego Desert, Palomar Observatory, Mount San Jacinto and Mount San Gorgonio, the Laguna and Cuyamaca Mountains, and on and on. On a crisp January day we were able to spot snow-covered Mount Baldy as well, 90 miles to the northwest. Most remarkable is that the desert floor is 5,000 feet below you, and it appears to be straight down. If you enjoyed the views from the Desert View Nature Trail, below, this summit vista will blow your mind. Total elevation gain on the trail? A mere 500 feet. Judging by the popularity of this trail on the weekends, it might just be too easy.

Location: In the Laguna Mountain Recreation Area; map J6, grid f9.

User groups: Hikers, dogs, and horses. No mountain bikes. No wheelchair facilities.

Permits: No permits are required. A national forest recreation pass is required for each vehicle; fees are $5 for one day or $30 for a year.

Maps: A map of the Laguna Mountain Recreation Area is available for $1.25 from the Descanso Ranger District or the Laguna Mountain Visitor Center. For a map of Cleveland National Forest, send $6 to U.S. Forest Service, Map Sales, P.O. Box 587, Camino, CA 95709; tel. (530) 647-5390 or website: www.r5.fs.fed.us/visitorcenter. Ask the USGS for a topographic map of the Monument Peak area.

Directions: From Julian drive south on Highway 79 to the left fork for Road S1/Sunrise Scenic Byway. Bear left and drive south for about 12 miles to the Penny Pines Plantation between mile markers 27.5 and 27.0. Park along the road.

Contact: Cleveland National Forest, Descanso Ranger District, 3348 Alpine Boulevard, Alpine, CA 91901; tel. (619) 445-6235 or fax (619) 445-1753.

21 Lightning Ridge Trail

1.5 mi/1.0 hr

The Lightning Ridge Trail is one of the show-and-tell trails of the Laguna Mountain Recreation Area, where you can get up high and get a clear view of how beautiful and unusual this tall, cool mountain on the edge of the desert really is. The trail is easy enough for almost any hiker to accomplish, with only 250 feet of elevation gain. It begins at a small stone monument at Laguna Campground's amphitheater parking lot and follows the edge of a meadow, making several long, sweeping switchbacks uphill through pines and oaks. Kick a few pine cones as you walk. The trail tops out at a water tank at the top of the ridge. The cement tank is uninspiring, but the view is sweet: Laguna Meadow lies directly below, a beautiful, green expanse in spring. If you time your trip for after a good season of rain, you may see a rare sight: Little Laguna Lake in the middle of the meadow. This is the secret, vanishing lake of the Laguna Mountains.

What's the best time to hike this trail? Unquestionably it's winter or spring—by Memorial Day the meadow grasses are often dry and brown. If you're lucky, you can walk this trail on a clear winter day when it's covered with a few inches of snow.

Location: In the Laguna Mountain Recreation Area; map J6, grid f9.

User groups: Hikers, dogs, horses, and mountain bikes. No wheelchair facilities.

Permits: No permits are required. A national forest recreation pass is required for each vehicle; fees are $5 for one day or $30 for a year.

Maps: A map of the Laguna Mountain Recreation Area is available for $1.25 from the Descanso Ranger District or the Laguna Mountain Visitor Center. For a map of Cleveland National Forest, send $6 to U.S. Forest Service, Map Sales, P.O. Box 587, Camino, CA 95709; tel. (530) 647-5390 or website: www.r5.fs.fed.us/visitorcenter. Ask the USGS for a topographic map of the Monument Peak area.

Directions: From Julian drive south on Highway 79 to the left fork for Road S1/Sunrise Scenic Byway. Bear left and drive south for approximately 13 miles to Laguna Campground on the right, between mile markers 26.5 and 26.0. Turn right on the camp road and drive .75 mile to the amphitheater parking lot. Park there and then look for the small stone monument just beyond the restrooms on the northeast side of the parking lot. The trail begins there.

Contact: Cleveland National Forest, Descanso Ranger District, 3348 Alpine Boulevard, Alpine, CA 91901; tel. (619) 445-6235 or fax (619) 445-1753.

22 Cottonwood Creek Falls
2.0 mi/1.0 hr

If you don't have the time for the day hike to spectacular Kitchen Creek Falls, this shorter trip to nearby Cottonwood Creek Falls is a close second choice for scenic beauty. With only a one-mile downhill walk, you'll quickly be exploring the many small waterfalls and big pools along Cottonwood Creek or happily counting the bright pink flowers on the streamside cacti. The trail is unsigned at its start, and it usually appears overgrown with brush, but after about 100 yards the path widens and the downhill grade becomes less steep. When you reach the canyon bottom, which takes about 15 minutes, turn sharply left and walk alongside Cottonwood Creek, heading upstream. In just a few minutes you'll reach the first of several cascades, each about 12 feet high. Hike as far as you like, pick your favorite waterfall or pool, and have a seat alongside.

Location: In the Laguna Mountain Recreation Area; map J6, grid g8.

User groups: Hikers, dogs, horses, and mountain bikes. No wheelchair facilities.

Permits: No permits are required. A national forest recreation pass is required for each vehicle; fees are $5 for one day or $30 for a year.

Maps: A map of the Laguna Mountain Recreation Area is available for $1.25 from the Descanso Ranger District or the Laguna Mountain Visitor Center. For a map of Cleveland National Forest, send $6 to U.S. Forest Service, Map Sales, P.O. Box 587, Camino, CA 95709; tel. (530) 647-5390 or website: www.r5.fs.fed.us/visitorcenter. Ask the USGS for a topographic map of the Mount Laguna area.

Directions: From San Diego drive east on Interstate 8 for 47 miles to the Highway S1/Sunrise Scenic Byway turnoff. Drive north on Highway S1 for about two miles to the large pullout on the west side of the road (it has an obvious, graffiti-covered rock wall), between mile markers 15.0 and 15.5. Cross the road on foot and locate the unmarked trail at the north end of the guardrail.

Contact: Cleveland National Forest, Descanso Ranger District, 3348 Alpine Boulevard, Alpine, CA 91901; tel. (619) 445-6235 or fax (619) 445-1753.

23 Desert View Nature Trail
1.2–3.0 mi/1–2 hrs

Wow, what a view. If you've never stood on a conifer-covered mountain before and looked down on the vastness of the desert, your first time is something you'll always remember. That's what you get here on the Desert View Nature Trail, near the summit of Laguna Mountain. Start hiking from Burnt

Rancheria Campground, heading east to meet the Pacific Crest Trail. Turn north (left) on the PCT, hiking along the mountain rim. The trail hugs the rim, which is perched on the edge of Anza-Borrego Desert, providing fine views of the desert floor 4,000 feet below you. On a clear day you can see all the way to the Salton Sea, shimmering in the distance, and the odd-looking smokestacks of Plaster City. The trail continues north to the Desert View Picnic Area and returns via a loop through a shady forest of pines and oaks. When you reach a clearing .5 mile out, you'll find a water fountain with a plaque commemorating the Great Outdoors. Take the spur trail here for the best view of the day, heading east and uphill for a short distance. If you hike the nature trail loop only, you'll have a 1.2-mile round-trip, but most people get so captivated by the views that they wind up walking a bit farther on the Pacific Crest Trail to the north. It's so compelling, it's hard to stop.

Location: In the Laguna Mountain Recreation Area; map J6, grid g9.

User groups: Hikers, dogs, and horses. No mountain bikes. No wheelchair facilities.

Permits: No permits are required. A national forest recreation pass is required for each vehicle; fees are $5 for one day or $30 for a year.

Maps: A map of the Laguna Mountain Recreation Area is available for $1.25 from the Descanso Ranger District or the Laguna Mountain Visitor Center. For a map of Cleveland National Forest, send $6 to U.S. Forest Service, Map Sales, P.O. Box 587, Camino, CA 95709; tel. (530) 647-5390 or website: www.r5.fs .fed.us/visitorcenter. Ask the USGS for a topographic map of the Mount Laguna area.

Directions: From San Diego drive east on Interstate 8 for 47 miles to the Highway S1/Sunrise Scenic Byway turnoff. Drive north on Highway S1 for about 10 miles to Burnt Rancheria Campground on the right, between mile markers 22.5 and 23.0 (near the town of Mount Laguna). Park by the amphitheater at Burnt Rancheria Campground, where the trail begins.

Contact: Cleveland National Forest, Descanso Ranger District, 3348 Alpine Boulevard, Alpine, CA 91901; tel. (619) 445-6235 or fax (619) 445-1753.

24 Kitchen Creek Falls
4.5 mi/2.5 hrs

Kitchen Creek Falls is the most beautiful waterfall in San Diego, a visually stunning 150-foot drop that is hidden just a few hundred yards off the Pacific Crest Trail. Thousands of PCT hikers go right past it without even knowing it's there, although they may shake their heads and wonder where all those day-hikers are heading. The hike to reach the general vicinity of the falls is quite easy since it follows the well-graded Pacific Crest Trail from Boulder Oaks, which crosses underneath Interstate 8 and then climbs uphill. The total gain is only about 500 feet. The tricky part comes in finding the unmarked cutoff for Kitchen Creek Falls and then scrambling your way down steep slopes to reach its base. Here's how you do it: After 45 to 50 minutes of hiking, start looking carefully to your left for a narrow spur trail. You'll reach it at exactly two miles up, which for most people is about an hour of trail time. Turn left on the spur and hike a short distance to see if you're looking down on Kitchen Creek—a fairly flat stream with many good-looking pools. If you are, you're also right above the waterfall, and to reach it you must cut down the hillside on one of many use trails, heading downstream. (Keep the creek on your right; don't cross it.) Use great caution in getting to the waterfall's base—stay on the dirt trails and stay off the polished granite, even when it's dry. Get yourself safely to a spot where you can look up and admire the gorgeous falls, which are a series of tiered cascades that twist and turn over rounded ledges in the bedrock. Plan on staying a while.

Location: In Cleveland National Forest near Pine Valley; map J6, grid h9.

User groups: Hikers, dogs, and horses. No

mountain bikes. No wheelchair facilities.

Permits: No permits are required. A national forest recreation pass is required for each vehicle; fees are $5 for one day or $30 for a year.

Maps: For a map of Cleveland National Forest, send $6 to U.S. Forest Service, Map Sales, P.O. Box 587, Camino, CA 95709; tel. (530) 647-5390 or website: www.r5.fs.fed.us/visitorcenter. Ask the USGS for a topographic map of the Live Oak Springs area.

Directions: From San Diego drive east on Interstate 8 for 50 miles to the Buckman Springs Road turnoff. Drive south on the frontage road for 2.3 miles to the Boulder Oaks Store and Campground. Stay on the frontage road; do not turn onto Buckman Springs Road. Park across the road from the store at the signed trailhead for the Pacific Crest Trail.

Contact: Cleveland National Forest, Descanso Ranger District, 3348 Alpine Boulevard, Alpine, CA 91901; tel. (619) 445-6235 or fax (619) 445-1753.

PACIFIC CREST TRAIL (PCT) SECTION OVERVIEW
156.0 mi one way/15.0 days

Your heart will sound off like a bass drum on your first steps along this section of the Pacific Crest Trail—which extends from the Campo Border Station Trailhead north to the Highway 74 Trailhead—not from the terrain or grandeur, but rather from what these first steps along America's greatest hiking trail represent. It's an emotional impact that strikes nearly everybody. This is it, the PCT, from Mexico to Canada, 2,650 miles in all, traversing 37 wilderness areas and seven national parks, including some of the most breathtaking scenery anywhere in the world. The California section of the PCT spans 1,700 miles, and while only PCT through-hikers cover every mile, thousands of great day hikes and shorter backpacking expeditions are possible throughout much of the route. This first section features mountainous and high desert terrain that is both arid and hot. In summer lack of water and 100-degree temperatures can make it virtually impassable. PCT through-hikers start their journeys from late winter to spring, sometime between late February and late March, in order to minimize these problems. But instead of summer heat, they may find themselves stopping for two or three days at a time because of surprise rains, and in the higher elevations, snow. Regardless, this is better than setting out too late in the year and facing dried-up streams and springs, where you can go delirious wondering where your next drink of water will come from. For day hikes the best conditions are from November through April. Trail elevations within this section range from 3,000 feet to more than 6,000 feet.

Campo Border Patrol to Lake Morena Park
20.0 mi one way/2.0 days

Your first steps on the Pacific Crest Trail can be a profound moment, when you realize you can walk all the way from Mexico to Canada. A small wooden monument at the trailhead reads: "Southern Terminus Pacific Crest National Scenic Trail. Established by act of Congress on October 2, 1968. Mexico to Canada 2627 miles. 1988 A.D. Elevation 2915." There is a small trail register that everybody signs to mark the moment; then you take a deep breath, recognize what lies ahead, and start walking. You'll never forget it.

This first section is a good two-day pull, starting at the Mexico border and heading north 19 miles to your first supply point at a post office near Lake Morena County Park in Campo. Highlights include a climb up to Hauser Mountain, where you'll enter the Hauser Wilderness, California's smallest wilderness, and traverse one canyon after another, with the highest elevation at 3,400 feet. From here the trail drops down into Hauser Canyon, bottoming out at 2,320 feet. Most PCT hikers make their first night's

camp in this area, then climb out of the canyon on the following day and head back up to the ridge. After enjoying sweeping views of the Laguna Mountain you can push on to Lake Morena. A sidelight of this section, as well as others connecting to the north, is the adjacent mosaic of immigrant trails leading from Mexico into the United States, and the occasional surveillance of them—as well as the PCT—by the Border Patrol.

Location: From the Campo Border Patrol north to the trailhead parking area at Lake Morena south of Interstate 8; map J6, grid i8.

User groups: Hikers, dogs (except in national parks), and horses. No mountain bikes. No wheelchair facilities.

Permits: A wilderness permit is required for traveling through various wilderness and special-use areas the trail traverses. Contact the Cleveland National Forest, tel. (619) 445-6235, for a permit good for the length of your trip.

Maps: For an overall view of the trail route in this section, send $6 to U.S. Forest Service, Map Sales, P.O. Box 587, Camino, CA 95709; tel. (530) 647-5390 or website: www.r5.fs.fed.us/ visitorcenter. Ask for the Cleveland National Forest map. Ask the USGS for topographic maps of the Campo, Potrero, and Morena Reservoir areas.

Directions: To reach the Campo Trailhead from Highway 94 east of San Diego and south of Interstate 8, drive south on Forest Gate Road in the town of Campo to the U.S. Border Patrol Station; hikers are requested to check in here. The trailhead is located approximately 1.5 miles south of the station at the Mexican border. Specific directions will be given at the border patrol station. To reach the Lake Morena Trailhead from San Diego, drive approximately 53 miles east on Interstate 8. Drive south on County Road/Buckman Springs Road for five miles to Oak Drive. Turn right and follow the signs to the park. The PCT Trailhead is located at the corner of Lake Morena Road and Lakeshore Drive.

Contact: Cleveland National Forest, Descanso Ranger District, 3348 Alpine Boulevard, Alpine, CA 91901; tel. (619) 445-6235 or fax (619) 445-1753.

PCT-2 Lake Morena Park to Boulder Oaks Camp
6.0 mi one way/1.0 day

This six-mile hike is an easy jaunt north toward the Laguna Mountains, tracing along a ridge primarily amid chaparral. Looming north are the Lagunas, the first mountains PCT hikers will encounter (though the first genuine mountains are the San Gorgonios). Most are eager to cross this high desert country, make the first climb, and start getting the gigantic panoramic views for which the PCT is famous. The reason we included this short section as a separate segment is that it takes hikers near a U.S. Forest Service campground and the small Boulder Oaks Store, which is run by one of the nicest ladies on the planet; she let us fill up our canteens and sold us a few sodas before we set out for Kitchen Creek to see a hidden waterfall.

Location: From the trailhead parking area at Lake Morena south of Interstate 8 north to Boulder Oaks Camp near Interstate 8; map J6, grid h8.

User groups: Hikers, dogs (except in national parks), and horses. No mountain bikes. No wheelchair facilities.

Permits: A wilderness permit is required for traveling through various wilderness and special-use areas the trail traverses. Contact the Cleveland National Forest, tel. (619) 445-6235, for a permit good for the length of your trip.

Maps: For an overall view of the trail route in this section, send $6 to U.S. Forest Service, Map Sales, P.O. Box 587, Camino, CA 95709; tel. (530) 647-5390 or website: www.r5.fs.fed.us/ visitorcenter. Ask for the Cleveland National Forest map. Ask the USGS for topographic maps of the Morena Reservoir, Cameron Corners, and Mount Laguna areas.

Directions: To reach the Lake Morena Trailhead from San Diego, drive approximately 53 miles east on Interstate 8. Drive south on

County Road S1/Buckman Springs Road for five miles to Oak Drive. Turn right and follow the signs to the park. The PCT Trailhead is located at the corner of Lake Morena Road and Lakeshore Drive. To reach the Boulder Campground Trailhead from San Diego, drive approximately 53 miles east on Interstate 8. Drive south on County Road S1/Buckman Springs Road to Old Highway 80 and turn left. The Boulder Oaks Campground and the PCT Trailhead are located just off Old Highway 80.

Contact: Cleveland National Forest, Descanso Ranger District, 3348 Alpine Boulevard, Alpine, CA 91901; tel. (619) 445-6235 or fax (619) 445-1753.

PCT-3 Boulder Oaks Camp to Sunrise Highway Trail
22.0 mi one way/2.0 days

After paying your dues for a few days without being compensated with great views, you're ready to head up the trail into the Laguna Mountains and the beautiful panorama that comes with it. The trail departs from near the Boulder Oaks Campground, crosses beneath Highway 8 ("This is the PCT?" you'll wonder), then starts to climb, the first real climb of the hike, rising nearly 3,000 feet over the course of 14 miles in the Lagunas. In the process you'll hike above much of the scrub and be rewarded with long-distance views of the desert below. Sunsets can be stunningly dramatic and beautiful, with the colors changing minute by minute. In the spring the ceanothus blooms provide a lot of color on the climb up, and once you hit the 6,000-foot elevation mark, you'll find a sprinkling of oaks and pines. You end this segment by hiking on the Desert View Nature Trail, highlighted by a breathtaking view of the Anza-Borrego Desert directly below. Most hikers time this section so they arrive at the campground to spend the night.

Location: From the trailhead parking area at Boulder Oaks Campground near Interstate 8 north to the Sunrise Highway Trailhead near Horse Heaven Campground; map J6, grid h9.

User groups: Hikers, dogs (except in national parks), and horses. No mountain bikes. No wheelchair facilities.

Permits: A wilderness permit is required for traveling through various wilderness and special-use areas the trail traverses. Contact the Cleveland National Forest, tel. (619) 445-6235, for a permit good for the length of your trip.

Maps: For an overall view of the trail route in this section, send $6 to U.S. Forest Service, Map Sales, P.O. Box 587, Camino, CA 95709; tel. (530) 647-5390 or website: www.r5.fs.fed.us/visitorcenter. Ask for the Cleveland National Forest map. Ask the USGS for topographic maps of the Monument Peak, Cameron Corners, and Mount Laguna areas.

Directions: To reach the Boulder Oaks Campground Trailhead from San Diego, drive approximately 53 miles east on Interstate 8. Go south on County Road S1/Buckman Springs Road to Old Highway 80 and turn left. The Boulder Oaks Campground and the PCT Trailhead are located just off Old Highway 80. To reach the Sunrise Highway access from San Diego, drive approximately 50 miles east on Interstate 8 to the Laguna Junction exit. Go about 11 miles north on Sunrise Highway to the town of Mount Laguna. Drive two miles past Mount Laguna on Sunrise Highway/Laguna Mountain Road to the campground entrance and PCT access.

Contact: Cleveland National Forest, Descanso Ranger District, 3348 Alpine Boulevard, Alpine, CA 91901; tel. (619) 445-6235 or fax (619) 445-1753.

PCT-4 Sunrise Highway Trail to Highway 78 Trail
32.0 mi one way/3.0 days

Water becomes sparse on this section of trail, so prior to leaving the campground/trailhead make sure to contact the wilderness rangers to get updated on each of the most current reliable water supply points. That done, get ready to tromp, because this is where

PCT hikers start to really move. The PCT enters Cuyamaca Rancho State Park, and then drops and is routed into Oriflamme Canyon. When you rise out of the canyon and reach the rim, suddenly in front of you are 100 miles of high desert backed by the San Gorgonio Mountains. Here is where your wilderness skills, body condition, and knowledge of the land (and where the water is) become critical. Don't go on unless all three are first-rate. That done, plan a long-distance endurance test with surroundings so meager that in summer you'd be happy to drink water out of a hoof print.

Location: From the trailhead parking area near the Sunrise Highway Trailhead and Horse Heaven Campground to the Highway 78 Trailhead; map J6, grid f9.

User groups: Hikers, dogs (except in national parks), and horses. No mountain bikes. No wheelchair facilities.

Permits: A wilderness permit is required for traveling through various wilderness and special-use areas the trail traverses. Contact the Cleveland National Forest, tel. (619) 445-6235, for a permit good for the length of your trip.

Maps: For an overall view of the trail route in this section, send $6 to U.S. Forest Service, Map Sales, P.O. Box 587, Camino, CA 95709; tel. (530) 647-5390 or website: www.r5.fs.fed.us/visitorcenter. Ask for the Cleveland National Forest map. Ask the USGS for topographic maps of the Monument Peak, Cuyamaca Peak, Julian, and Earthquake Valley areas.

Directions: To reach the Sunrise Highway access from San Diego, drive approximately 50 miles east on Interstate 8 to the Laguna Junction exit. Go approximately 11 miles north on Sunrise Highway to the town of Mount Laguna. Drive two miles past Mount Laguna on Sunrise Highway/Laguna Mountain Road to the campground entrance and PCT access. To reach the Highway 78 Trailhead from Julian, head east on Highway 78 to the junction with County Road S2/Great Southern Overland Stage Route of 1849. The PCT crosses here near the Butterfield Stage Line commemorative marker.

Contact: Cleveland National Forest, Descanso Ranger District, 3348 Alpine Boulevard, Alpine, CA 91901; tel. (619) 445-6235 or fax (619) 445-1753.

PCT-5 Highway 78 Trailhead to Warner Springs

33.0 mi one way/3.0 days

Be done with it. That's the attitude most PCT through-hikers have about this section of trail. In late winter it's tolerable when temperatures are relatively mild and you calculate your water stops perfectly. Highlights are Barrel Spring (Water! Water!), lonely canyons, and occasional ridges with endless views of miles and miles of desert valleys backed by dry mountain peaks. For many years several sections of trail in this area were confusing, and many hikers either became lost or at least confused for a few hours. The new triangular PCT signs posted in the mid-1990s have done much to solve this frustration. As you near Warner Springs you're rewarded with a view of Lake Henshaw (is that water in there?), real live trees (mainly oaks), and even a small stream (yes, it really is water) in the final miles to your resupply point at Warner Springs Post Office.

Location: From the Highway 78 Trailhead to the Warner Springs Trailhead; map J6, grid d9.

User groups: Hikers, dogs, and horses. No mountain bikes. No wheelchair facilities.

Permits: A wilderness permit is required for traveling through various wilderness and special-use areas the trail traverses. Contact the Cleveland National Forest, tel. (619) 445-6235, for a permit good for the length of your trip.

Maps: For an overall view of the trail route in this section, send $6 to U.S. Forest Service, Map Sales, P.O. Box 587, Camino, CA 95709; tel. (530) 647-5390 or website: www.r5.fs.fed.us/visitorcenter. Ask for the Cleveland National Forest map. Ask the USGS for topographic maps of the Earthquake Valley, Julian, Ranchita, Hot Springs Mountain, and Warner Springs areas.

Directions: To reach the Highway 78 Trailhead from Julian, head east on Highway 78 to the junction with County Road S2/Great Southern Overland Stage Route of 1849. The PCT crosses here near the Butterfield Stage Line commemorative marker. To reach the Highway 79 Trailhead from Warner Springs, head west on Highway 79 for approximately one mile to mile marker 36.7 and a turnout parking area next to the highway. Hike back to the bridge and mile marker 36.6 for the PCT Trailhead.

Contact: Cleveland National Forest, Palomar Ranger District, 1634 Black Canyon Road, Ramona, CA 92065; tel. (760) 788-0250 or fax (760) 788-6130.

PCT-6 Warner Springs to Highway 74

43.0 mi one way/4.0 days

Here's the deal. We've met dozens of hikers en route from Mexico to Canada, and they all say the same thing: the most difficult sections of the PCT are the 30 miles out of Warner Springs, the Hat Creek Rim (in Lassen County), the Mojave, icy Forester Pass (north of Whitney), and Muir Pass (in high snow years). After leaving Warner Springs, you can face 28 miles without water. While we haven't hiked this particular section, PCT trail expert Ray Jardine says that in wet years, water can sometimes be discovered at about a half dozen spots along the way. Don't count on it, he also suggests. PCT through-hikers should have each of these spots mapped (location information is available from U.S. Forest Service wilderness experts). We have also met expert hikers who made the entire 28 miles without a resupply, though they resembled iguanas. The flora isn't much—mainly chaparral, cactus, and various scrub, the only plants that can live in such an inhospitable climate. The PCT feature point is a 2,500-foot climb near the top of Combs Peak (6,000 feet), where there's a fantastic turn-your-head-around view of desert, dry peaks, and your eventual destination, the San Gorgonio Mountains to the north. From here you drop into brush-beaten country, but then rise again to great lookouts over the course of a few days from Table, Bucksnort, and Lookout Mountains. If you have enough water, you might even enjoy it. Then again, maybe not.

Location: From the Warner Springs Trailhead to the Highway 74 Trailhead; map J6, grid b7.

User groups: Hikers, dogs, and horses. No mountain bikes. No wheelchair facilities.

Permits: A wilderness permit is required for traveling through various wilderness and special-use areas the trail traverses. Contact the Cleveland National Forest, tel. (619) 445-6235, for a permit good for the length of your trip.

Maps: For an overall view of the trail route in this section, send $6 for each map ordered to U.S. Forest Service, Map Sales, P.O. Box 587, Camino, CA 95709; tel. (530) 647-5390 or website: www.r5.fs.fed.us/visitorcenter. Ask for the Cleveland National Forest and San Bernardino National Forest maps. Ask the USGS for topographic maps of the Hot Springs Mountain, Warner Springs, Bucksnort Mountain, and Butterfly Peak areas.

Directions: To reach the Highway 9 Trailhead from Warner Springs, head west on Highway 79 for approximately one mile to mile marker 36.7 and a turnout parking area next to the highway. Hike back to the bridge and mile marker 36.6 for the PCT Trailhead. To reach the Highway 74 Trailhead from the town of Hemet, head east on Highway 74 to the intersection of Highway 74 and Highway 371/Cahuilla Road. The trailhead for the PCT is about one mile southeast on Highway 74 just west of the Santa Rosa Summit.

Contact: Cleveland National Forest, Descanso Ranger District, 3348 Alpine Boulevard, Alpine, CA 91901; tel. (619) 445-6235 or fax (619) 445-1753; San Bernardino National Forest, San Jacinto Ranger District, P.O. Box 518, 54270 Pinecrest, Idyllwild, CA 92549; tel. (909) 659-2117 or fax (909) 659-2107.

PCT CONTINUATION

To continue hiking along the Pacific Crest Trail, see chapter I6.

ONE OF SIX DISTINCT PALM GROVES IN
MOUNTAIN PALM SPRINGS CANYON

MAP J7

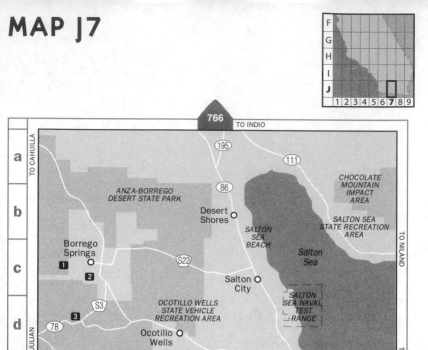

F G H I J
1 2 3 4 5 6 7 8 9

766 TO INDIO

195

111

a

TO CAHUILLA

ANZA-BORREGO
DESERT STATE PARK

86

CHOCOLATE
MOUNTAIN
IMPACT
AREA

b

Desert
Shores

SALTON
SEA
BEACH

SALTON SEA
STATE RECREATION
AREA

TO NILAND

Borrego
Springs

1

2

S22

Salton
Sea

c

Salton
City

S3

3

d

TO JULIAN

78

OCOTILLO WELLS
STATE VEHICLE
RECREATION AREA

Ocotillo
Wells

5

6

SALTON
SEA NAVAL
TEST
RANGE

78

TO BRAWLEY

e

782

4

ANZA-BORREGO
DESERT STATE PARK

Agua Caliente
Springs

86

812

f

Westmorland

Superstition
Mountain
759 feet

g

TO PINE VALLEY

S2

7

CARRIZO
IMPACT AREA
(CLOSED TO PUBLIC)

U.S. NAVAL AERIAL
GUNNERY RANGES
(CLOSED TO PUBLIC)

S30

MANZANITA
INDIAN
RESERVATION

Carrizo
Mountain
2,408 feet

Imperial

h

TO CAMPO

8

CAMPO
INDIAN
RESERVATION

Summit
4,350 feet

Ocotillo

S80

8

Plaster
City

Seely

EL CENTRO

Boulevard
Jacumba

Mountain Springs
Pass 3,241 feet

98

S29

i

TO TECATE, MEXICO

CALIFORNIA
MEXICO

Mount
Signal

TO CALEXICO

j

2

La Rumorosa

Colonia
Progreso

0 1 2 3 4 5 6 7 8 9

© AVALONTRAVEL PUBLISHING, INC.

CHAPTER J7

1. Borrego Palm Canyon
   Falls 805
2. Maidenhair Falls 805
3. Cactus Loop and
   Yaqui Well 806
4. Ghost Mountain Trail . . 806
5. Pictograph Trail 807
6. Elephant Trees 808
7. Mountain Palm Springs
   Canyon 808

1 Borrego Palm Canyon Falls
3.0 mi/1.5 hrs

The hike to Borrego Palm Canyon Falls is only 1.5 miles in length, but it feels like a trip from the desert to the tropics. You start out in a sandy, rocky, open plain, sweating it out with the cacti and ocotillo, and you end up in a shady oasis of fan palms, dipping your feet in the pool of a fern-covered waterfall. The trip begins on the Borrego Palm Canyon Trail from the state park campground, where you should top off your water bottles and start walking. If you pick up an interpretive brochure at the park visitor center, you can identify the array of desert plants that grow along the trail, including cheesebush, brittle-bush, catclaw (ouch!), and chuparosa. In .5 mile, when you pass interpretive post 20, you're suddenly surprised by the sight of hundreds of bright green, leafy palm trees up ahead. Borrego Palm Canyon is home to more than 800 mature native palms, the largest of over 25 groves in the park. It's one of the largest oases in the United States. Head toward the palms and in a few minutes you'll be nestled in their shade, listening to the desert wind rustle their fronds. Follow the trail a little farther and you'll reach a 15-foot waterfall that streams over giant boulders and forms a large, sandy pool tucked in among the palms. We saw many maidenhair ferns growing by the water's edge and a tiny hummingbird flitted about the scene. Ah, paradise.

Location: In Anza-Borrego Desert State Park near Borrego Springs; map J7, grid c0.

User groups: Hikers only. No dogs, horses, or mountain bikes. No wheelchair facilities.

Permits: No permits are required. A $2 day-use fee is charged per vehicle.

Maps: A free map of Anza-Borrego Desert State Park is available at the park visitor center. Ask the USGS for a topographic map of the Borrego Palm Canyon area.

Directions: From Julian drive east on Highway 78 for approximately 19 miles to Highway S3/Yaqui Pass Road. Turn left (north) on Highway S3/Yaqui Pass Road and drive 12 miles to Borrego Springs. Turn left on Highway S22/Palm Canyon Drive and drive one mile to the signed junction just before the park visitor center. Turn right and drive one mile to Borrego Palm Canyon Campground. The trailhead is at the west end.

Contact: Anza-Borrego Desert State Park, 200 Palm Canyon Drive, Borrego Springs, CA 92004; tel. (760) 767-5311; visitor center, tel. (760) 767-4205.

2 Maidenhair Falls
5.0 mi/3.0 hrs

If you have taken the hike to Borrego Palm Canyon Falls and found that it suited your taste for desert adventure, this trip to Maidenhair Falls is a more challenging path to a slightly bigger and more dramatic desert waterfall. Stop in at the park visitor center before you begin and pick up a handout with trail directions. Also remember to be prepared for a longer excursion in the desert (bring tons of extra water and cover your head with a light-colored hat). Your destination is a 20-foot waterfall with a walled backdrop of maidenhair ferns and mosses. The route to reach it travels from Highway S22 south of the visitor center into the mouth of Hellhole Canyon. Begin on the California Riding and Hiking Trail for the first 200 yards and turn right. You'll pass a few fan palms, a myriad of cacti, some odd-shaped rocks, and Native American grinding holes along the route. Cottonwoods grow in places along the stream. Maidenhair Falls is a bit tricky to find, tucked into a narrow canyon corner, but with luck, there will be enough water running in the stream to clue you in to its location.

Location: In Anza-Borrego Desert State Park near Hellhole Canyon; map J7, grid c1.

User groups: Hikers only. No dogs, horses, or mountain bikes. No wheelchair facilities.

Permits: No permits are required. A $2 day-use fee is charged per vehicle.

Maps: A free map of Anza-Borrego Desert State Park is available at the park visitor center. Ask the USGS for a topographic map of the Tubb Canyon area.

Directions: From Julian drive east on Highway 78 for approximately 19 miles to Highway S3/Yaqui Pass Road. Turn left (north) on Highway S3/Yaqui Pass Road and drive for 12 miles to Borrego Springs. Turn left on Highway S22/Palm Canyon Drive and drive one mile to the signed junction just before the park visitor center. Turn left and drive .75 mile to the large parking lot on the west side of the road.

Contact: Anza-Borrego Desert State Park, 200 Palm Canyon Drive, Borrego Springs, CA 92004; tel. (760) 767-5311; visitor center, tel. (760) 767-4205.

3 Cactus Loop and Yaqui Well
2.75 mi/1.5 hrs

The Cactus Loop and Yaqui Well Trails are two separate nature trails at Anza-Borrego Desert State Park, but since they're right beside each other, you might as well hike both. The Cactus Loop Trail is a .75-mile loop, and more hilly than you might expect from a nature trail. It shows off seven kinds of cacti, including barrel, hedge-

hog, fishhook, beavertail, and cholla, some as tall as six feet. Visitors often spot chuckwallas and other lizards scurrying among the spiny plants. The Yaqui Well Trail climbs for one mile among cacti, ocotillo, and cholla to a mesquite grove and then reaches sulfur-smelling Yaqui Well. In a small circle around this seep, a tremendous variety of greenery grows, including willows and mesquite, given life by the year-round presence of water. Desert birds show up here, particularly colorful hummingbirds. If you're in the mood for more desert education, drive five miles east of Tamarisk Grove to the short little loop trail at the Narrows. It's packed with a lot of geologic punch; you'll get a big lesson in geological processes, from faulting and landslides to erosion and earthquakes.

Location: In Anza-Borrego Desert State Park near Tamarisk Grove; map J7, grid d1.

User groups: Hikers only. No dogs, horses, or mountain bikes. No wheelchair facilities.

Permits: No permits are required. A $2 day-use fee is charged per vehicle.

Maps: A free map of Anza-Borrego Desert State Park is available at the park visitor center. Ask the USGS for a topographic map of the Borrego Sink area.

Directions: From Julian drive east on Highway 78 for 19 miles to Tamarisk Grove Campground at Road S3. The trailheads for the Cactus Loop and Yaqui Well Trails are opposite the camp entrance off Road S3.

Contact: Anza-Borrego Desert State Park, 200 Palm Canyon Drive, Borrego Springs, CA 92004; tel. (760) 767-5311; visitor center, tel. (760) 767-5311.

4 Ghost Mountain Trail
2.0 mi/1.0 hr

When most people imagine a life of living off the land, they instinctively think of doing so in a place where water is plentiful. Not so with Marshal South, who chose Ghost Mountain in Anza-Borrego Desert in the 1930s. South and his wife built an adobe home atop the mountain and lived there with their children for more than 15 years. The family tried to live simply, attempting to survive in the spartan style of early Native Americans. Sadly, South's wife eventually tired of the rugged desert life and her husband's odd idealism, and the family split up.

The Ghost Mountain Trail climbs through a series of switchbacks to the remains of the South homesite, which include a few partial walls, an old mattress frame, and some assorted cisterns and barrels used for storing precious water. The destination is worthwhile not just because the sight of it sparks your imagination, but also because of the lovely, 360-degree desert views you gain as you ascend Ghost Mountain. When you stand on the top on a clear, cool day, you can almost imagine why South chose this remote homesite.

Remember that Blair Valley and Ghost Mountain are higher in elevation than other parts of the park. Not only does this make them cooler spots for hiking, but it also means that a wide variety of desert plant life grows here. The ocotillos and yuccas put on a spectacular show in early spring.

Location: In Anza-Borrego Desert State Park near Blair Valley; map J7, grid e1.

User groups: Hikers only. No dogs, horses, or mountain bikes. No wheelchair facilities.

Permits: No permits are required. A $2 day-use fee is charged per vehicle.

Maps: A free map of Anza-Borrego Desert State Park is available at the park visitor center. Ask the USGS for a topographic map of the Earthquake Valley area.

Directions: From Julian drive east on Highway 78 for 12 miles to Road S2, turn south, and drive six miles to the left turnoff for Blair Valley Camp. Turn left (east), drive 1.4 miles on a dirt road, and then bear right at the fork. Drive another 1.6 miles, bear right again, and drive .5 mile to the Ghost Mountain/Marshal South Home Trailhead.

Contact: Anza-Borrego Desert State Park, 200 Palm Canyon Drive, Borrego Springs, CA 92004; tel. (760) 767-5311; visitor center, tel. (760) 767-4205.

5 Pictograph Trail
2.0 mi/1.0 hr

Although a Native American rock-art site is the destination of this trip, the Pictograph Trail comes with a bonus: an inspiring overlook of the Vallecito Mountains from the brink of a dry waterfall. It's a desert vista that's hard to forget. The path begins at the Pictograph Trailhead and wanders through huge granite boulders. First you head through a dry wash and then climb up a ridge. At .5 mile out you begin to descend. At .75 mile you'll find some pictographs, painted in red and yellow pigments by the nomadic Kumeyaay Indians. (Look for the pictographs on the side of a boulder on the right side of the canyon.) The slightly faded geometric designs were made with natural pigments and are estimated to be 2,000 years old. Continue farther on the trail, and the canyon narrows dramatically until its walls come together at the brink of a dry waterfall more than 150 feet tall. From its edge the panoramic view is stunning, both of the steep drop-off and the far-off mountains and valley.

Location: In Anza-Borrego Desert State Park near Blair Valley; map J7, grid e2.

User groups: Hikers only. No dogs, horses, or mountain bikes. No wheelchair facilities.

Permits: No permits are required. A $2 day-use fee is charged per vehicle.

Maps: A free map of Anza-Borrego Desert State Park is available at the park visitor center. Ask the USGS for a topographic map of the Earthquake Valley area.

Directions: From Julian drive east on Highway 78 for 12 miles to Road S2, turn south, and drive six miles to the left turnoff for Blair Valley Camp. Turn left (east), drive 1.4 miles on a dirt road, and then bear right at the fork. Drive another 1.6 miles and bear left at the next fork. In .25 mile bear left again. Continue two more miles to the end of the road at the Pictograph Trailhead.

Contact: Anza-Borrego Desert State Park, 200 Palm Canyon Drive, Borrego Springs, CA

92004; tel. (760) 767-5311; visitor center, tel. (760) 767-4205.

6 Elephant Trees

1.5 mi/1.0 hr

It's not just the odd-looking elephant tree that you get to see on this trail, but also many of the common flora of Anza-Borrego Desert—creosote bush, burroweed, indigo bush, barrel cactus, ocotillo, catclaw, cholla, smoke tree. . . . There's enough desert plant identification to do to keep you quizzing your hiking partner all day. But it's the elephant trees that steal the show, with the crinkled, folded "skin" on their trunks that looks somewhat elephant-like. The trees can grow to be 10 feet tall, which is huge by desert standards, and they are an odd patchwork of colors: yellowish bark, blue berries, and orange twigs. Their bark has a very evocative odor, something like a spicy air freshener. Don't expect to see a whole herd of elephant trees, however; this trail shows off only a few fine specimens. The best of the lot is near the end of the loop trail. Try to time your trip for early spring, when the ocotillos sprout brilliant red plumes and the pink sand verbenas bloom.

Location: In Anza-Borrego Desert State Park near Split Mountain; map J7, grid e4.

User groups: Hikers only. No dogs, horses, or mountain bikes. No wheelchair facilities.

Permits: No permits are required. A $2 day-use fee is charged per vehicle.

Maps: A free map of Anza-Borrego Desert State Park is available at the park visitor center. Ask the USGS for a topographic map of the Harper Canyon area.

Directions: From Julian drive east on Highway 78 for 35 miles to Ocotillo Wells. Turn south on Split Mountain Road and drive 5.8 miles to the right turnoff that is signed for Elephant Trees. Turn right and drive .8 mile on a dirt road to the trailhead.

Contact: Anza-Borrego Desert State Park, 200 Palm Canyon Drive, Borrego Springs, CA 92004; tel. (760) 767-5311; visitor center, tel. (760) 767-4205.

7 Mountain Palm Springs Canyon

2.6 mi/2.0 hrs

Although the groves of fan palms in Mountain Palm Springs Canyon are not as large as in Borrego Palm Canyon, they're still beautiful and popular with park visitors. The palm oases, fed by underground springs and shaded by the magnificent fan palms, create a haven for plants and wildlife, as well as for hikers looking for a cool and pleasant place to spend the day. Six distinct palm groves grow in Mountain Palm Springs Canyon, as well as occasional elephant trees; you can visit all of the groves in one walk. The trail doesn't look like much to start, just a rocky arroyo, but it gets more trail-like in short order. The first grove of trees, Pygmy Grove, has been burned. The second grove, Southwest Grove, is larger and prettier. Take the right fork just before you enter Southwest Grove and head uphill to an elephant tree and the one-mile path to the Surprise Canyon Grove. From Surprise Canyon you can turn left to see Palm Grove Bowl—it's a natural bowl that is ringed with more than 100 palm trees. Return to Surprise Canyon and loop back to your starting point, passing by North Grove on the way. Or retrace your steps to Southwest Grove and take the short spur to the southwest to see Torote Bowl. There are some good elephant tree specimens there. If you visit in early winter when the palms bear their fruit (dates), you may find so many birds singing in the palm trees that you can hardly hear yourself think. Look for the pretty hooded oriole in particular, which builds its nest on the underside of palm fronds.

Location: In Anza-Borrego Desert State Park near Bow Willow; map J7, grid g2.

User groups: Hikers only. No dogs, horses, or mountain bikes. No wheelchair facilities.

Permits: No permits are required. A $2 day-use fee is charged per vehicle.

Maps: A free map of Anza-Borrego Desert State Park is available at the park visitor center. Ask the USGS for a topographic map of the Sweeney Pass area.

Directions: From Julian drive east on Highway 78 for 12 miles to Road S2, turn south, and drive 29 miles to the Mountain Palm Springs Campground entrance road on the right. Turn right and drive straight for .6 mile (don't take any of the campsite turnoffs) to the parking area by a stone marker for Mountain Palm Springs Canyon.

Contact: Anza-Borrego Desert State Park, 200 Palm Canyon Drive, Borrego Springs, CA 92004; tel. (760) 767-5311; visitor center, tel. (760) 767-4205.

CHAPTER 18

At **228** feet below sea level, the Salton Sea is one of the lowest places in the United States.

MAP J8

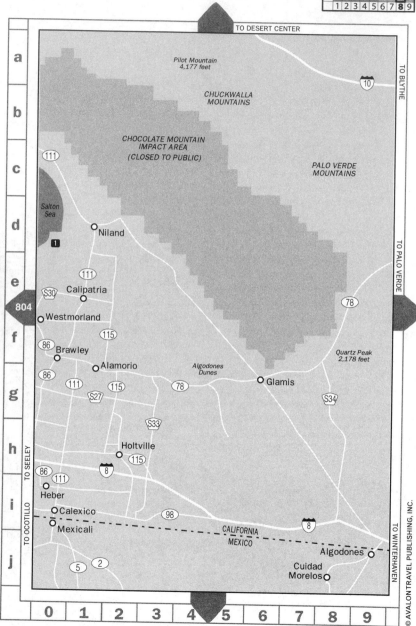

TO DESERT CENTER

TO BLYTHE

a

Pilot Mountain
4,177 feet

CHUCKWALLA
MOUNTAINS

b

CHOCOLATE MOUNTAIN
IMPACT AREA
(CLOSED TO PUBLIC)

PALO VERDE
MOUNTAINS

c

(111)

Salton
Sea

d

☐1

○ Niland

TO PALO VERDE

e

(S30)

(111)
Calipatria
○

804

○ Westmorland

(78)

f

(86)
○ Brawley

(115)

Quartz Peak
2,178 feet

g

(86)

(111)

○ Alamorio

(115)

Algodones
Dunes

(78)

○ Glamis

(S34)

(S27)

(S33)

h

○ Holtville

(115)

TO SEELEY

(8)

i

(86)
(111)

TO OCOTILLO

○ Heber

○ Calexico

(98)

(8)

TO WINTERHAVEN

j

○ Mexicali

CALIFORNIA
MEXICO

○ Algodones

(5) (2)

Cuidad
Morelos ○

0 1 2 3 4 5 6 7 8 9

CHAPTER J8

1 Salton Sea National
   Wildlife Refuge 813

1 Salton Sea National Wildlife Refuge

3.0 mi/1.5 hrs

If it's wintertime—anywhere from December to February—it's a good time to pay a visit to the Salton Sea National Wildlife Refuge, one of the lowest places in the United States at 228 feet below sea level. Winter is the only season when the area isn't blistering hot, and it's also the time that peak populations of birds are gathered at the refuge. The place has one hiking trail, called the Rock Hill Trail, which gets hiked by approximately 35,000 bird-watchers a year. From the observation platform behind the visitor center, the path heads out along a levee and then abruptly climbs to a hill above the Salton Sea. It's a great place to watch the pelicans dive and to shake your head in wonder at the immense size of the saline Salton Sea. It was formed from 1905 to 1907 when a series of man-made dams on the Colorado River burst their seams. The "sea" has become increasingly saline over the years due to agricultural runoff, evaporation, and the lack of a replenishing freshwater supply.

Although fish do not fare well in the changing waters of the Salton Sea, bird lovers find plenty to cheer about. In addition to seeing the plentiful waterfowl that spend the winter in the saltwater and freshwater marshes—geese of many kinds, mergansers, wigeons, and teals—hikers might spot an endangered species such as the Yuma clapper rail or peregrine falcon. Migrating snow geese and Ross geese are also big attractions along this trail. They are seen in great numbers every December.

Location: On the east shore of the Salton Sea near Calipatia; map J8, grid d0.

User groups: Hikers only. No dogs, horses, or mountain bikes. No wheelchair facilities.

Permits: No permits are required. Parking and access are free.

Maps: Ask the USGS for a topographic map of the Niland area.

Directions: From Indio drive south on Highway 111 for approximately 50 miles to the turnoff for Sinclair Road, which is four miles south of Niland. (If you reach Calipatria, you've gone too far.) Turn right on Sinclair Road and drive six miles to the Salton Sea National Wildlife Refuge visitor center, located at the intersection of Sinclair Road and Gentry Road.

Contact: Salton Sea National Wildlife Refuge, 906 W. Sinclair Road, Calipatria, CA 92233; tel. (760) 348-5278.

RESOURCE GUIDE

THE LANDSCAPE AROUND SELDEN PASS
IN JOHN MUIR WILDERNESS

RESOURCE GUIDE

National Forests

Many Forest Service trailheads are quite remote and have no drinking water. Parking and access are often free. For overnight use, campfire permits or wilderness permits are usually required. Dogs are permitted in national forests with no extra charge and no hassle. Always carry documentation of current vaccinations.

National Forest Adventure Pass

Angeles, Cleveland, Los Padres, and San Bernardino National Forests require an Adventure Pass for each parked vehicle. Daily passes cost $5; annual passes are available for $30. Adventure Passes can be purchased at national forest offices in Southern California and dozens of retail outlets and on-line vendors. The new charges are use fees, not entrance fees. Holders of Golden Age and Golden Access (not Golden Eagle) cards can purchase the Adventure Pass at a 50 percent discount at national forest offices only, or at retail outlets for the retail price. When you purchase an annual Adventure Pass, you can also buy up to three additional annual Adventure Passes for $5 per family vehicle. Major credit cards are accepted at most retail and on-line outlets, but not at Forest Service offices.

You will not need an Adventure Pass while traveling through these forests nor when you've paid other types of fees such as camping or ski pass fees. However, if you are camping in these forests and you leave the campground in your vehicle and park outside of the campground for recreation purposes, such as at a trailhead, day-use area, near a fishing stream, etc., you will need an Adventure Pass for your vehicle. You also need an Adventure Pass if camping at a no-fee campground. More information about the Adventure Pass program, including a listing of retail and on-line vendors, can be obtained by website: www.fsadventurepass.org.

There are additional charges (and rules) when climbing Mount Shasta or Mount Whitney, which are detailed in their respective zones in the book.

National Forest Maps

National Forest maps are among the best you can get for the price. They detail all backcountry streams, lakes, hiking trails, and logging roads for access. They cost $6, sometimes more for wilderness maps, and can be obtained in person at Forest Service offices, or by contacting U.S. Forest Service, Attn: Maps Sales, P.O. Box 587, Camino, CA 95709, tel. (530) 647-5390, fax (530) 647-5389, or website: www.r5.fs.fed.us/visitorcenter. Major credit cards are accepted if ordering by telephone.

Forest Service Information

Forest Service personnel are most helpful for obtaining camping or hiking trail information. Unless you are buying a map or Adventure Pass, it is advisable to phone to get the best service. For specific information on a national forest, contact the following offices:

USDA Forest Service
Pacific Southwest Region
1323 Club Drive
Vallejo, CA 94592
tel. (707) 562-USFS (707-562-8737)
website: www.r5.fs.fed.us

Angeles National Forest
701 N. Santa Anita Avenue
Arcadia, CA 91006
tel. (626) 574-1613
fax (626) 574-5233
website: www.r5.fs.fed.us/angeles

Cleveland National Forest
10845 Rancho Bernardo Road, #200
San Diego, CA 92127-2107
tel. (858) 674-2901
fax (858) 673-6192
website: www.r5.fs.fed.us/cleveland

Eldorado National Forest
100 Forni Road
Placerville, CA 95667
tel. (530) 622-5061
fax (530) 621-5297
website: www.r5.fs.fed.us/eldorado
or

Information Center
3070 Camino Heights Drive
Camino, CA 95709
tel. (530) 644-6048
fax (530) 295-5624

Humboldt-Toiyabe National Forest
1200 Franklin Way
Sparks, NV 89431

tel. (775) 355-5301
fax (775) 355-5399
website: www.fs.fed.us/htnf

Inyo National Forest
873 N. Main Street
Bishop, CA 93514
tel. (760) 873-2400
fax (760) 873-2458
website: www.r5.fs.fed.us/inyo

Klamath National Forest
1312 Fairlane Road
Yreka, CA 96097-9549
tel. (530) 842-6131
fax (530) 841-4571
website: www.r5.fs.fed.us/klamath

Lake Tahoe Basin Management Unit
870 Emerald Bay Road, Suite 1
South Lake Tahoe, CA 96150
tel. (530) 573-2600
website: www.r5.fs.fed.us/ltbmu

Lassen National Forest
2550 Riverside Drive
Susanville, CA 96130
tel. (530) 257-2151
fax (530) 252-6428
website: www.r5.fs.fed.us/lassen

Los Padres National Forest
6755 Hollister Avenue, Suite 150
Goleta, CA 93117
tel. (805) 968-6640
fax (805) 961-5729
website: www.r5.fs.fed.us/lospadres

Mendocino National Forest
825 N. Humboldt Avenue
Willows, CA 95988
tel. (530) 934-3316
fax (530) 934-7384
website: www.r5.fs.fed.us/mendocino

Modoc National Forest
800 W. 12th Street
Alturas, CA 96101
tel. (530) 233-5811
fax (530) 233-8709
website: www.r5.fs.fed.us/modoc

Plumas National Forest
P.O. Box 11500
159 Lawrence Street
Quincy, CA 95971
tel. (530) 283-2050
fax (530) 283-7746
website: www.r5.fs.fed.us/plumas

San Bernardino National Forest
1824 Commercenter Circle
San Bernardino, CA 92408-3430
tel. (909) 383-5588
fax (909) 383-5770
website: www.r5.fs.fed.us/san-bernardino

Sequoia National Forest
900 W. Grand Avenue
Porterville, CA 93257
tel. (559) 784-1500
fax (559) 781-4744
website: www.r5.fs.fed.us/sequoia

Shasta-Trinity National Forest
2400 Washington Avenue
Redding, CA 96001
tel. (530) 244-2978
fax (530) 242-2233
website: www.r5.fs.fed.us/shastatrinity

Sierra National Forest
1600 Tollhouse Road
Clovis, CA 93611
tel. (559) 297-0706
fax (559) 294-4809
website: www.r5.fs.fed.us/sierra

Six Rivers National Forest
1330 Bayshore Way
Eureka, CA 95501
tel. (707) 442-1721
fax (707) 442-9242
website: www.r5.fs.fed.us/sixrivers

Stanislaus National Forest
19777 Greenley Road
Sonora, CA 95370
tel. (209) 532-3671
fax (209) 533-1890
website: www.r5.fs.fed.us/stanislaus

Tahoe National Forest
631 Coyote Street
Nevada City, CA 95959
tel. (530) 265-4531
fax (530) 478-6109
website: www.r5.fs.fed.us.tahoe

State Parks

The California State Parks system provides many popular hiking trails in spectacular settings. For camping, reservations are often necessary during the summer months.

Due to fee reductions for camping, day use, tours, and boating, the state parks now provide about the best deal in camping in the country. Add-on fees for premium sites, peak season visitation, reservations, pets, extra vehicles, and boat launching have been eliminated at state parks. In addition, fees have been reduced for day use, museum and other tours, parking, boat mooring, swimming, pool use, and cabin rentals. You can now camp at a state park for as little as $1 per person per night at many walk-in or bike-in sites.

For general information about California State Parks, contact

California Department of Parks and Recreation
Office of Information
P.O. Box 942896
Sacramento, CA 94296
(916) 653-6995
website: www.parks.ca.gov

National Parks & Reservations

California's national parks are natural wonders, ranging from the spectacular yet crowded Yosemite Valley to the remote and rugged Lava Beds National Monument. Expect to pay a park entrance fee ranging from $5 to $20 per vehicle (Golden Eagle annual passes can be purchased). This entrance fee is valid for seven days. Various discounts are available for holders of Golden Age and Golden Access passports, including a 50 percent reduction of camping fees (group camps not included) and a waiver of park entrance fees.

National Park Service
Pacific West Region
600 Harrison Street, Suite 600
San Francisco, CA 94107-1372
tel. (415) 427-1304
fax (415) 427-1485
website: www.nps.gov

Cabrillo National Monument
1800 Cabrillo Memorial Drive
San Diego, CA 92106-3601
tel. (619) 557-5450
fax (619) 557-5469
website: www.nps.gov/cabr

Channel Islands National Park
1901 Spinnaker Drive
Ventura, CA 93001
tel. (805) 658-5730
fax (805) 658-5799
website: www.nps.gov/chis

Death Valley National Park
P.O. Box 579
Death Valley, CA 92328-0579
tel. (760) 786-2331
fax (760)786-3283
website: www.nps.gov/deva

Devils Postpile National
Monument
c/o Sequoia and Kings Canyon
National Parks
47050 Generals Highway
Three Rivers, CA 93271
tel. (559) 565-3341
website: www.nps.gov/depo

Golden Gate National Recreation
Area
Fort Mason, Building 201
San Francisco, CA 94123
tel. (415) 556-0560
website: www.nps.gov/goga

Joshua Tree National Park
74485 National Park Drive
29 Palms, CA 92277-3597
tel. (760) 367-5500
fax (760) 367-6392
website: www.nps.gov/jotr

Lassen Volcanic National Park
P.O. Box 100
Mineral, CA 96063-0100
tel. (530) 595-4444
website: www.nps.gov/lavo

Lava Beds National Monument
P.O. Box 867
Tulelake, CA 96134
tel. (530) 667-2282
website: www.nps.gov/labe

Pinnacles National Monument
5000 Highway 146
Paicines, CA 95043
tel. (831) 389-4485
website: www.nps.gov/pinn

Point Reyes National Seashore
Point Reyes Station, CA 94956-9799
tel. (415) 663-1092
fax (415) 663-8132
website: www.nps.gov/pore

Redwood National and State Parks
1111 2nd Street
Crescent City, CA 95531
tel. (707) 464-6101
website: www.nps.gov/redw

Santa Monica Mountains National
Recreation Area
401 W. Hillcrest Drive
Thousand Oaks, CA 91360
tel. (805) 370-2301
website: www.nps.gov/samo

Sequoia and Kings Canyon
National Parks
47050 Generals Highway
Three Rivers, CA 93271-9651
tel. (559) 565-3341
website: www.nps.gov/seki

Smith River National Recreation
Area
P.O. Box 228
Gasquet, CA 95543
tel. (707) 457-3131
fax (707) 457-3794

Whiskeytown-Shasta-Trinity
National Recreation Area
P.O. Box 188
Whiskeytown, CA 96095
tel. (530) 246-1225 or (530) 242-
3400
website: www.nps.gov/whis

Yosemite National Park
P.O. Box 577
Yosemite National Park, CA 95389
tel. (209) 372-0265 or (209) 372-
0200 for 24-hour recorded message
website: www.nps.gov/yose

Bureau of Land Management

Most of the areas managed by the BLM are primitive and in remote areas. Parking and access are usually free. Often there is also no fee charged for camping. Holders of Golden Age or Golden Access passports receive a 50 percent discount, except for group camps, at BLM fee campgrounds.

Bureau of Land Management
California State Office
2800 Cottage Way, Room W-1834
Sacramento, CA 95825-1886
tel. (916) 978-4400
website: www.ca.blm.gov

California Desert District Office
6221 Box Springs Boulevard
Riverside, CA 92507
tel. (909) 697-5200
fax (909) 697-5299
website: www.ca.blm.gov/cdd

Alturas Field Office
708 W. 12th Street
Alturas, CA 96101
tel. (530) 233-4666
fax (530) 233-5696
website: www.ca.blm.gov/alturas

Arcata Field Office
1695 Heindon Road
Arcata, CA 95521-4573
tel. (707) 825-2300
fax (707) 825-2301
website: www.ca.blm.gov/arcata

Bakersfield Field Office
3801 Pegasus Drive
Bakersfield, CA 93308
tel. (661) 391-6000
fax (661) 391-6040
website: www.ca.blm.gov/bakersfield

Barstow Field Office
2601 Barstow Road
Barstow, CA 92311
tel. (760) 252-6000
fax (760) 252-6099
website: www.ca.blm.gov/barstow

Bishop Field Office
785 N. Main Street, Suite E
Bishop, CA 93514-2471
tel. (760) 872-4881
fax (760) 872-2894
website: www.ca.blm.gov/bishop

Eagle Lake Field Office
2950 Riverside Drive
Susanville, CA 96130
tel. (530) 257-0456
fax (530) 257-4831
website: www.ca.blm.gov/eaglelake

El Centro Field Office
1661 S. 4th Street
El Centro, CA 92243
tel. (760) 337-4400
fax (760) 337-4490
website: www.ca.blm.gov/elcentro

Folsom Field Office
63 Natoma Street
Folsom, CA 95630
tel. (916) 985-4474
fax (916) 985-3259
website: www.ca.blm.gov/folsom

Palm Springs/South Coast Field
Office
690 W. Garnet Avenue
North Palm Springs, CA 92258
tel. (760) 251-4800
fax (760) 251-4899
website: ca.blm.gov/palmsprings

Redding Field Office
355 Hemsted Drive
Redding, CA 96002

tel. (530) 224-2100
fax (530) 224-2172
website: www.ca.blm.gov/redding

Ukiah Field Office
2550 N. State Street
Ukiah, CA 95482
tel. (707) 468-4000
fax (707) 468-4027
website: www.ca.blm.gov/ukiah

U.S. Army Corps of Engineers

Los Angeles District
911 Wilshire Boulevard/P.O. Box
532711
Los Angeles, CA 90053
tel. (213) 452-3908
fax (213) 452-4191
website: www.spl.usace.army.mil/

South Pacific Division/
San Francisco District
333 Market Street
San Francisco, CA 94105
tel. (415) 977-8272
website: www.spn.usace.army.mil/

Sacramento District
1325 J Street
Sacramento, CA 95814
tel. (916) 557-5100
website: www.spk.usace.army.mil/

State Forests

California Department of Forestry
and Fire Protection
Resource Management
P.O. Box 944246
Sacramento, CA 94244-2460
tel. (916) 653-5121
fax (916) 653-4171
website: www.fire.ca.gov

Jackson Demonstration State Forest
802 N. Main Street
Fort Bragg, CA 95437
tel. (707) 964-5674
fax (707) 964-0941

County/Regional Park Departments

Del Norte County Parks
840 9th Street, Suite 11
Crescent City, CA 95531
tel. (707) 464-7230
fax (707) 464-5824

East Bay Regional Park District
2950 Peralta Oaks Court
P.O. Box 5381
Oakland, CA 94605-0381
tel. (510) 635-0135
fax (510) 635-3478
website: www.ebparks.org

Humboldt County Parks
1106 2nd Street
Eureka, CA 95501
tel. (707) 445-7651
fax (707) 445-7409

Marin Municipal Water District
220 Nellen Avenue
Corte Madera, CA 94925
tel. (415) 945-1455
fax (415) 927-4953
website: www.marinwater.org

Midpeninsula Regional Open Space District
330 Distel Circle
Los Altos, CA 94022
tel. (650) 691-1200
fax (650) 691-0485
website: www.openspace.org

Pacific Gas and Electric Company
FERC/Land Projects
2730 Gateway Oaks, Suite 220
Sacramento, CA 95833
tel. (916) 386-5164
fax (916) 720-7044
website: www.pge.com/recreation

San Diego County Parks and Recreation Department
5201 Ruffin Road, Suite P
San Diego, CA 92123
tel. (858) 694-3049
fax (858) 495-5841
website:
www.co.san_diego.ca.us/parks

San Mateo County Parks and Recreation Department
455 County Center, 4th Floor
Redwood City, CA 94063-1646
tel. (650) 363-4020
fax (650) 599-1721
website: www.eparks.net

Santa Clara County Parks and Recreation
298 Garden Hill Drive
Los Gatos, CA 95032
tel. (408) 358-3741
fax (408) 358-3245
website: www.parkhere.org

State and Federal Offices

U.S. Fish and Wildlife Service
1849 C Street NW
Washington, DC 20240
website: www.fws.gov

U.S. Geological Survey
Branch of Information Services
P.O. Box 25286, Federal Center
Denver, CO 80225
tel. (888) ASK-USGS (888-275-
8747)
website: http://edc.usgs.gov/webglis

**California Department of Fish and
Game**
1416 9th Street, 12th Floor
Sacramento, CA 95814
tel. (916) 653-6420
fax (916) 653-1856
website: www.dfg.ca.gov

Information Services

**Lake County Visitor Information
Center**
875 Lakeport Boulevard
Lakeport, CA 95453
tel. (800) 525-3743 or (707) 263-
9544
fax (707) 263-9564
website: www.lakecounty.com

Mammoth Lakes Visitors Bureau
P.O. Box 48
Mammoth Lakes, CA 93546
tel. (800) 367-6572
fax (760) 934-7066
website: www.visitmammoth.com

The Nature Conservancy
201 Mission Street, 4th Floor
San Francisco, CA 94105
tel. (415) 777-0487
fax (415) 777-0244
website: www.tnccalifornia.org

**Shasta-Cascade Wonderland
Association**
1699 Highway 273
Anderson, CA 96007
tel. (800) 474-2782 or (530) 365-
7500
fax (530) 365-1258
website: www.shastacascade.org

Map Companies

Earthwalk Press
5432 La Jolla Hermosa Avenue
La Jolla, CA 92037
tel. (800) 828-MAPS (800-828-6277)

Map Center
2440 Bancroft Way
Berkeley, CA 94704
tel. (510) 841-6277
fax (510) 841-0858

Map Link
30 South La Patera Lane, Unit 5
Santa Barbara, CA 93117
tel. (805) 692-6777
fax (800) 627-7768
website: www.maplink.com

Olmstead Brothers Map Company
P.O. Box 5351
Berkeley, CA 94705
(510) 658-6534

Tom Harrison Maps
2 Falmouth Cove
San Rafael, CA 94901
tel./fax (800) 265-9090 or (415) 456-7940
website: www.tomharrisonmaps.com

U.S. Forest Service
Attn: Map Sales
P.O. Box 587
Camino, CA 95709
tel. (530) 647-5390
fax (530) 647-5389
website: r5.fs.fed.us/visitorcenter

U.S. Geological Survey
Branch of Information Services
P.O. Box 25286, Federal Center
Denver, CO 80225
tel. (888) ASK-USGS (888-275-8747) or (303) 202-4700
fax (303) 202-4693
website:
http://earthexplorer.usgs.gov

INDEX

A

Abalone Point: 77
Abbotts Lagoon Trail: 287
Adam and Eve Loop Trail: 609-610
Adams, Ansel: 458
Adam Tree: 609-610
Adventure Pass: 816
Aerial Tramway: 755-757
Afton Canyon: 687
Agassiz Tree: 411
Agate Beach: 77
Agave Trail: 325-326
Agnew Meadows: 565-566
Agnew Meadows Trailhead: 458
Agua Blanca Loop: 666
Agua Caliente Trail: 377
Agua Dulce: 677
Alabama Hills: 561, 563
Alambique Trail: 341
Alamere Creek: 298
Alameda Creek Quarries: 369
Alameda Creek Regional Trail: 369
Alamere Falls: 293
Alamere Falls Trail: 298-299
Alamo Trail: 362
Alcatraz Island: 325, 327, 328
Alder Creek Falls: 457
Alder Creek Trail: 207, 619
Alec Canyon and Contour Loop: 480
Alhambra Creek: 351
Alhambra Creek Trail: 353
Aliso Canyon Loop Trail: 653-654
Almaden Quicksilver County Park: 396
Almaden Valley: 393
Alphabet Lakes: 73
Alpine/Kent Lake Pump Trail: 299
Alpine Lake: 299
Alpine Meadows: 282
Alta Peak: 558-559
Alta Trail: 315, 556
Alum Rock City Park: 382
American River: 223
American River Canyon: 247
American River Parkway: 223-224
American River Trail: 233
Amos Alonzo Stagg Tree: 612
amphitheater: Mountain Theater 306-307

Ancient Bristlecone Pine Forest: 476
Anderson Dam: 398
Anderson Lake: 398
Anderson Peak: 247
Angeles Crest Highway: 741-742, 762-763
Angeles National Forest: 669, 677, 727, 741
Angel Falls: 513
Angel Island: 304, 319, 320, 327
Angora Lakes Resort: 260
Angora Lakes Trail: 259-260
Anniversary Trail: 375
Año Nuevo Lookout: 384-385
Año Nuevo State Reserve: 394
Año Nuevo Trail: 394
Ansel Adams Wilderness: 458, 467, 468, 470, 471, 513
Antelope Creek: 173
Antelope Valley: 674, 742
Antelope Valley Poppy Reserve Loop: 674
Antioch Bridge: 351
Antioch Pier: 351
Antler Point: 383
Anza-Borrego Desert: 791, 793, 794
Anza-Borrego Desert State Park: 805-809
April Trail Loop: 397
Aptos Canyon: 483
Aqua Tibia Wilderness: 783
Arboles Trailhead: 710
Arcata Marsh Trail: 78
Archery Fire Trail: 340
Arch Rock: 292
Arctic grayling: Bullpen Lake 228
Armstrong Redwoods: 209
Arrowhead Marsh: 356-357
Arroyo Flats: 365
Arroyo Seco Creek: 783
Arroyo Seco District: 727
Ash Camp: 122-123, 139-140
Asilomar Beach: 485
Asilomar Coast Trail: 485-486
Aspen Flat: 601
Aspen Grove Trail: 753-754
astronomy: Fremont Peak Trail 501
Audubon Canyon Ranch Trail: 304
Audubon Marsh: 378
Audubon Society tours: Arcata Marsh Trail 78; Silverwood Wildlife Sanctuary 792

avalanches: Sand Flat Trailhead 107
Azalea Trail: 522

B
Baboon Lakes: 532
Bachelor: 457
Backbone Trail: 708
Backbone Trail: 714
Back Ranch Fire Trail: 304
Baden-Powell, Lord: 725
Badwater: 635
Bailey Bridge: 541
Bailey Cove Loop Trail: 120
Baker Beach: 327
Balancing Rock: 253
Balch Park Nature Trail: 609
Balconies Caves: 501-502
Balconies Trail: 502
Bald Mountain Lookout: 620-621
Bald Mountain Loop: 218
Bald Mountain Trail: 393-394
Baldy Notch: 735
Baldy Peak Trail: 46
Banner Peak: 458, 470
Barker Dam Loop: 769-770
Barker Pass: 281-282
Barnabe Trail: 296
Barney Lake Trail: *see* Robinson Creek
   Trail 424-425
Barrel Spring: 800
Barrett Lake: 473-474
Barth, Emil: 306
Barth's Retreat: 306
Basin Falls: 480
Basin Peak: 240
Basket Dome: 447, 453, 454
Bass Lake: 293, 298, 513, 514
Battery Chamberlin: 327
Battery Crosby: 327
Bay Area Discovery Museum: 318
Bay Bridge: 336, 368
Baylands Catwalk: 342
Baylands Interpretive Center: 342
Baylands Trail: 342-343, 367
Bayside Trail: 778-779
Bay View Loop: 348
Bayview Loop and Trail: 484
Bay View Trail: 303-304, 484
Bayview Trail: 367
Beach Trail Loop: 778
Beacroft Trail: 233-234

BEARS
Buck Lake Trail: 42
Haypress Meadows Trailhead: 50
Kearsage Pass: 548-549
Lost Coast Trail: 80-81
Paradise Ridge: 599
Rancheria Falls: 427, 517

Beals Point: 223
Bear Canyon: 725-726
Bear Canyon Loop Trail: 739-740
Bear Gulch Caves: 503-504
Bear Gulch Trail: 341
Bear Hill: 553
Bear Lake: 423
Bear Lakes Loop: 189-190
Bear Mountain: 565
Bearpaw Meadow: 555
Bear Peak: 46
Bear River Falls: 230
Rancheria Falls 427, 517
Beartrap Mountain: 187
Bear Valley: 229, 240
Bear Valley Trail: 294-295
Bear Wallow Trailhead: 167-168
Beauty Lake: 262
Beck Lakes: 472
Belding's savannah sparrow: *see*
   savannah sparrow
Belgium Trail: 349
Belmont Creek: 337
Benbow Lake: 153
Ben Johnson Trail: 307
Ben Overturff Trail: 731-732
Benson Lake: 460
Berkeley Flats: 352
Berkeley Pier: 352
Berry Creek Falls: 387, 391
berry-picking: Tree of Heaven Trail 59
Bertha Peak: 750-751
best hikes: xvii-xxiii
Beyers Lake: 231
Bicentennial Bike Path: 315
Big Baldy: 547
Big Basin: 387, 390
Big Basin Redwoods: 382
Big Basin Redwoods State Park: 386
Big Bear Lake: 749, 750, 761
Big Bear Lake Trail: 112-113
Big Carson Creek: 298
Big Creek: 517

Big Falls: 583-584, 754
Big Falls Picnic Area: 755
Big Glass Mountain: 68
Big Hendy Grove Trail: 158
Bighorn Lake: 475
bighorn sheep: Crystal Canyon 692
Big Meadow: 625
Big Meadows: 545
Big Morongo Canyon Preserve: 767
Big Oak Trail: 177
Big Santa Anita Canyon: 727-728

Big Santa Anita Creek: 727
"Big Stump, The": 411
Big Stump Trail: 520
Big Sur River: 491, 492, 493
Big Sycamore Canyon Loop: 707
Big Trees Interpretive Trail: 238
Big Whitney Meadows: 608
Bird Island Overlook: 488
Bird Island Trail: 488
Bird Spring Pass: 678
Bishop Creek: 533

BIRD-WATCHING

Abbotts Lagoon Trail: 287
Afton Canyon: 687
Agave Trail: 325-326
Alder Creek Trail: 207, 619
Arcata Marsh Trail: 78
Arrowhead Marsh: 356-357
Asilomar Coast Trail: 485-486
Audubon Canyon Ranch Trail: 304
Baylands Catwalk: 342
Baylands Trail: 342-343, 367
Bayside Trail: 778-779
Bay View Trail: 303-304, 484
Bayview Trail: 367
Bicentennial Bike Path: 315
Bolsa Chica Ecological Reserve: 737
Cactus Loop: 806
Canyon Trail: 380, 495, 767
Captain Jack's Stronghold: 65
Carrizo Plains: 589-590
Chapman Creek Trail: 195
Charleston Slough: 376
Chester Marsh Trail: 499
China Wall Loop: 362
Coit Lake: 399-400, 401
Cottonwood Spring Oasis: 773
Deer Creek Trail: 176, 185-186
Desert View Trail: 755-756, 790-791
Donner Falls: 361
Dumbarton Pier: 368-369
East Bay Skyline National Trail: 352, 359, 370-372
Easton Canyon: 727
Elkhorn Slough South Marsh Loop: 484-485
El Moro Canyon and Ridge Loop: 738
Fish Slough: 531-532
Fortynine Palms Oasis: 770
Graham Pinery: 176
Guajome Lake Trail: 784
Guillemot Island: 488
Hawk Hill: 317-318

Janes Reservoir: 73
Juanita Lake Trail: 59-60
Kaweah Oaks Preserve: 593
Los Banos Wildlife Area: 499-500
Martinez Waterfront Park: 350-351
McGrath State Beach Nature Trail: 659-660
Mono Lake South Tufa Trail: 467
Moss Landing Wildlife Area Marsh Trail: 485
Mountain Palm Springs Canyon: 808-809
Oso Flaco Lake: 645
Owl Trail: 313-314
Palisades Trail: 215-216
Partington Point Trail: 495-496
Path of the Padres: 500-501
Pescadero Marsh: 378
Point Isabel Shoreline: 351-352
Ponderosa Vista Nature Trail: 751-752
Ravenswood Open Space Preserve: 341-342
Redwood Creek Trail: 36-37
Rock Hill Trail: 813
Salt Creek Interpretive Trail: 640
Salton Sea National Wildlife Refuge: 813
Sandy Wool Lake: 377
San Elijo Lagoon: 777
San Francisco Bay National Wildlife Refuge: 343, 368, 369
Satwiwa Loop Trail and Waterfall: 705-706
Shoreline Regional Park: 376-377
Shoreline Trail: 303, 304, 356, 367, 786
Silverwood Wildlife Sanctuary: 792
Soberanes Point Trail: 489-490
South Bay Nature Trail: 343
Spirit Lake Trail: 50-51
Sunnyvale Baylands: 377
Sunol Loop: 370
Tidelands Trail: 368
Vincent Tumamait Trail: 663-664
Waddell Creek Trail: 394-395
Weir and Lower Doane Valley Loop: 784-785
Winton Marsh Trail: 499

Bishop Creek's South Forth Canyon: 534
Bishop Lake: 535
Bishop Pass Trail: 534, 535
Bizz Johnson: 185
Black Butte: 271
Black Buttes: 231
Black Butte Trail: 105
Black Diamond Mines Regional Preserve: 353
black diamonds: Prospect Tunnel Loop 353-354
Black Mountain: 379, 621
Black Oak Picnic Area: 480
Black Rock Falls: 479
Black Rock Lake Trail: 163
Black Rock Mountain: 164
Black Wall Falls: see Black Wolf Falls
Black Wolf Falls: 606-607
Blackberry Springs: 585-586
Blackrock Mountain Trailhead: 615
Blair Valley: 807
BLM: see Bureau of Land Management
Bloody Canyon: 467
Blue Lake: 465, 532
Blue Lake Loop: 145-146
Blue Lakes Road: 279-280
Blue Nose Mountain: 187
Blue Point: 666
Blue Ridge Trail: 216-217
Blue Sky Ecological Preserve: 787-788
Bluff Cove: 716
Bluffs Trail: 492
Boat Taxi to Lake Aloha: 265-266
Bobcat Trail: 315
Bob Walker Ridge: 363
Bodega Bay: 285
Bodega Head Loop: 210-211
Bolam Creek: 105
Bolam Creek Trailhead: 105-106
Bolam Glacier: 106
Bolinas Lagoon: 297, 304
Bolinas Ridge: 207, 297
Bollinger Canyon: 355
Bolsa Chica Ecological Reserve: 737
Boney Peak: 708
Bon Tempe Shadyside Trail: 301
Boole Tree Loop: 519-520
Boomerang Lake: 262
Bootjack Loop: 307
Borel Hill Trail: 380-381
Borges Ranch Trailhead: 362

Borrego Palm Canyon Falls: 805
Bort Meadow: 359, 371
Bothe-Napa Valley State Park: 217
Bothin Marsh: 315
Boucher Trail: 785
Boulder Bay: 750
Boulder Creek: 419, 538
Boulder Lake: 419-420
Boulder Lake Trail: 92-93
Boulder Oaks Camp: 798-799
Boulder Peak: 461
boulders: Shasta Summit Trail 108-109
Bouquet Canyon: 677
Bouquet Reservoir: 677
Bowerman Meadows: 96
Box Lake: 529
Boyden Cave: 538
Boy Scout Tree Trail: 29-30
Brewer, William: 528
Brewer Creek: 105, 110
Brewer Creek Trailhead: 110-111
Bridalveil Creek: 449, 450-451, 453
Bridalveil Fall: 448, 449-450
Bridge Creek: 483
Bridge Creek Historic Site: 482
Briones Crest Loop: 353
Briones Peak: 353
Briones Regional Park: 353
Briones Reservoir: 349, 352
Briones-to-Mount Diablo Trail: 362
Brown Lake: 534-535
brown pelicans: Elkhorn Slough South Marsh Loop 484-485
Brownstone Mine: 531
Bruhel Point Tide Pools: 155
brussels sprouts: Old Landing Cove Trail 481
Bubbs Creek: 564
Buckeye Creek Trail: 424
Buckhorn Creek: 722
Buck Lake Trail: 42
Bucks Lake Wilderness: 195, 196
Bucks Summit: 196-197
Buena Vista Peak: 544
Bug Lake: 52
Bullards Bar Reservoir: 227
Bullards Bar Trail: 227-228
Bull Creek Flats: 81-82
Bull Lake: 535
Bullpen Lake: 228
Bull Run Lake: 275-276

Bumpass Hell Trail: 181-182
Bumpass Mountain: 181
Bunchgrass Trailhead: 131-132
Bureau of Land Management: 821-822
Burhardt Trail: 722
Burney Falls Trail: 128-129
Burney Mountain Summit: 129
Burnside Lake: 274-275
Burnt Lava Flow: 128
Burnt Monarch: 520
Burnt Ranch Falls: 93
Burst Rock: 423-424
Burton Creek Loop: 250
Burton Creek State Park: 250
Butano Canyon: 385
Butano Loop: 385-386
Butano State Parks: 382
Butcher Ranch Trail: 190-191
Butt Mountain: 198
Buzzards Roost Trail: 493

C
Cabin Gulch Lake: 52
Cabin Peak: 93
Cabin Trail: 488
Cabrillo, Juan Rodriguez: 695
Cabrillo Peak: 581
Cabrillo Tide Pools: 779
Cache Peak: 677-678
Cactus Loop: 806
Cahoon Gap: 560
Cahoon Meadow: 560
Cajon Pass: 762-763
Calabazas Creek: 377
Calaveras Big Trees State Park: 411
Calawee Cove Beach: 252
Calero Reservoir: 398
Caliche Forest: 695-696
California Falls: 438
California least terns: see least terns
California Riding and Hiking Trail: 769, 790
California's Watchable Wildlife: 177
California Tunnel Tree: 457
CalTrans Vista Point: 380
Cameron Meadow: 183
Camiaca Peak: 465
Camp Lake: 423
Campo Border Patrol: 797-798
Cañada de Pala Trail: 383, 384
Cannell Meadow National Recreation
    Trail: 627

canoeing: Abbotts Lagoon Trail 287;
    Estero de Limantour 289, 292; Lake
    Eleanor 425-426; South Bay Nature Trail
    343
Canyon Creek Lakes Trailhead: 97
Canyon Oak Loop: 790-791
Canyon Trail: 380, 495, 767
Canyon View Trail: 668
Caples Lake: 267, 268, 281
Captain Jack's Stronghold: 65
Cardiac Hill: 309
Cardinet Junction: 361
Caribou Lakes: 91
Caribou Lakes Trail: 91-92
Caribou Lake Trailhead: 137-138
Caribou Mountain: 184
Caribou Wilderness: 184
Carlon Falls: 427-428
Carmelo Meadow Trail: 488
Carmel River: 490
Carmel River Trail: 494
Carmel Valley: 490
Carquinez Strait: 350
Carrizo Plains: 589-590
Carr Lake: 231
Carson Canyon: 461
Carson Creek: 300
Carson Falls: 300-301
Carson-Iceberg Wilderness: 275, 415, 417,
    419, 461
Carson Pass: 279-281
Casa Vieja Meadow: 615-616
Cascade Falls: 255, 387
Cascade Lakes: 245
Cascades: 264
Castle Crags: 109
Castle Crags Wilderness: 122-123
Castle Lake: 115
Castle Lake Road: 115
Castle Peak: 240
Castle Rocks: 362, 548, 552, 553, 559
Castle Rock State Park: 389, 390
Castle Rock Trail: 750
Castro Valley: 370
Catalina Island: 714, 717-718
Cataract Falls: 299-300
Cathedral Cove: 701
Cathedral Lake: 255
Cathedral Lakes: 434, 459
Cathedral Peak: 434, 439, 440, 459
Cathedral Range: 436

Cattail Cove Picnic Area: 354
Cave Lake: 73-74
Cave Rocks: 370
caves: Bear Gulch Caves 503-504;
   Balconies Caves 501-502; Boyden Cave
   538; Hirz Bay Trail 120-121; Ice Caves
   Trail 127-128; Merrill Ice Cave 65-66; Old
   Landing Cove Trail 481; Packsaddle
   Cave Trail 622; Partington Point Trail
   495-496; see also interesting geology
Cecilville Road: 99
Cedar Creek: 664
Cedar Creek Falls: 790
Cedar Grove: 539, 542
Cedars Interpretive: 515-516
Center Hole: 328
Central House: 229
Century Lake: 710-711
Cerro Alto Loop: 580-581
Cerro Alto Summit: 579-580
Cerro Este: 370
Cerro Este Trail: 370
Chabot Regional Park: 371
Chalone Creek: 501
Chamberlain Creek Waterfall Trail: 157
Champion Lodgepole Pine: 749-750
Channel Islands: 646, 647, 652, 656, 666,
   695, 699-702
Chantry Flat: 727
Chaos Crags: 133
Chaparral Trail: 792
Chapman Creek Trail: 195
Chapman Trail: 735
charcoal kilns: Wildrose Peak Trail: 634-635
Charleston Slough: 376
Charmlee County Park: 709
Cherry Lake: 426
Cherry Valley: 716
Chester Marsh Trail: 499
Chicage Stump Trail: 518-519
Chickadee Trail: 340
Chickenfoot Lake: 529
Chicken Spring Lake: 608
Chief Lake: 565
Chihuahua Bowl: 606
Chilnualna Falls: 456
Chimney Peak Wilderness: 628
Chimney Rock: Little North Fork Trailhead
   51
Chimney Rock Lake: Little North Fork
   Trailhead 51

Chimney Rock Trail: 188, 290-291
Chimney Tree: 386
China Beach: 326
China Camp State Park: 303
China Cove: 488
China Wall Loop: 362
Chino Hills State Park: 736
Chiquito Basin Trail: 739
Chocolate Lakes: 535-536
Chumash Indians: 585, 653
Chumash Loop: 581
Chumash village: 699
Chumash Wilderness: 663
Church Dome: 621, 625
Cienaga Trail: 792
Cima Dome: 691
Cinder Cone Trail: 135-136
Circuit Trail: 792
clapper rails: Elkhorn Slough South
   Marsh Loop 484-485
Clark Fork: 419-420
Clark Fork Stanislaus River: 419
Clark Range: 432
Clear Creek: 44, 105
Clear Lake: 144-145; Little North Fork
   Trailhead 51
Clenaga Mirth: 537
Cleo's Bath: 422
Clicks Creek Trail: 613
Cliff House: 328
Cliff House Restaurant: 326
Clipper Valley: 692
Clouds Rest: 431, 432
Clover Creek: 560
Cloverleaf Lake: 475
Coachella Valley: 768
Coal Creek Open Space: 380
coal mining: Prospect Tunnel Loop 353-354
Coastal Trail (Fern Canyon/Ossagon
   Section): 35
Coastal Trail (Hidden Beach Section): 34-
   35
Coastal Trail (Last Chance Section): 32-33
Coastal Trail: 326, 327; Fort Barry 316-317;
   Fort Cronkhite 316
Coast Range: 444, 612
Coast Trail: 292-293, 298
Cobalt Lakes: 606
Codfish Creek Trail: 235-236
Codfish Falls: 235
Cogswell Marsh Loop: 364-365

Coit Lake: 399-400, 401
Cold Springs: 658
Cold Springs Nature Trail: 600
Coldstream Creek: 247
Coldwater Canyon: 714
College Rock: 516
Colonel McMenemy: 659
Columbia Point: 443
Columbia Rock: see Columbia Point
columnar-jointed rock: Devils Postpile 470
Columns of the Giants: 419
Combs Peak: 801
Condor Gulch and High Peaks Loop: 502-503
condors: Vincent Tumamait Trail 663-664
Cone Lake Trailhead: 136-137
Cone Peak Lookout Trail: 496
Congress Trail Loop: 556-557
Contra Loma Loop: 354
Converse Basin: 519
Convict Canyon: 475
Cooney Lake: 465
Cooper Cabin: 491
Cooper Canyon Falls: 722-723, 741
Copper Creek Trail: 542
copper mining: Black Wolf Falls 606-607;
    Moses Gulch Trail 611
Cora Lakes: 513
Corlieu Falls: 511
Cory Peak: 103
Cottonwood Meadows: 426
Cottonwood Canyon: 670
Cottonwood Creek Botanical Trail: 203
Cottonwood Creek Falls: 795
Cottonwood Lakes: 607-608
Cottonwood Pass: 608
Cottonwood Spring Oasis: 773
Cougar Crest Trail: 750-751
Cougar Ridge: 487
county park departments: 823
Covered Wagon Peak: 268
cow camp: Duck Lake 417-418
cow grazing: Taylor Lake Trail 52-53; Trail
    Creek Trail 88
Cowles Mountain: 791
Coyote-Hellyer County Park: 398
Coyote Hills Regional Park: 367, 369
Coyote Peak: 217-218
Coyote Peak Loop: 397
Coyote Point Trail: 336
Coyote Reservoir: 400

Coyote Spring Trail: 487
Coyote Trail: 363
Crab Cove: 356
Crabtree Trailhead: 423
Crags Trail: 116-117
Craig's Creek Trail: 30-31
Crater Meadows: 473
Crescent Meadow: 554, 555
Crest Trail: 347
Crissy Point: 328
Crooked Lakes: 230
Crown Memorial State Beach: 356
Crystal Basin: 261
Crystal Canyon: 692
Crystal Cove State Park: 738
Crystal Crag: 473
Crystal Creek: 603, 606
Crystal Lake: 605, 741
Crystal Lake Recreation Area: 732, 741
Crystal Lake Trail: 606
Crystal Range: 262
Crystal Springs Reservoir: 337
Crystal Springs Trail: 337, 692
Cuddihy Lakes: 50
Culbertson Lake: 228
"Cussin' Jim": 737
Cuyamaca Mountains: 791, 793, 794
Cuyamaca Peak Trail: 792-793
Cuyamaca Rancho State Park: 793, 800
Cuyler Harbor: 695
Cypress Grove: 487-488
Cypress Trailhead: 130-131

D

Dan Tunnel: 397
Dardanelle: 418-419
Dardanelle Resort: 418
Dardanelles: 417
Dardanelles Lake: 266-267
Darwin Falls: 634
Davenport Beach: 395
Davis Gulch Trail: 121-122
Davy Brown/Fir Canyon Trail: 652
Dawn Falls: 302-303
Deadfall Lakes Trail: 104-105
Dead Giant: 429, 556
Dead Giant Loop Trail: 521
Deadman Peak: 89
Deadwood Meadows: 625
Death Valley: 569-571
Death Valley National Park: 633-636, 639-641

Deep Creek: 762
Deep Creek Fishermen's Trail: 748-749
Deep Creek Hot Springs: 748
deepest canyon in the continental U.S.:
    Kings Canyon 539
Deep Hole: 175
Deer Creek: 566, 600
Deer Creek Trail: 176, 185-186
Deer Flat: 361, 395
Deer Lake: 95
Deer Lake Trail: 191-192
Deer Mountain: 60
Deer Park Lodge: 731
Deer Park Trail: 301-302
Deer Springs Junction: 757
Deer Springs Trail: 756, 758
deer: Captain Jack's Stronghold 65;
    Summit Lake Loop 134-135; Tehama
    Wildlife Area 173; Timber Mountain 69-
    70; White Deer Trail 483
Dees Peak: 89
Del Coyote Nature Trail: 398
Del Valle Regional Park: 405
Desert Tortoise Discovery Loop: 673-674
Desert View Nature Trail: 795-796
Desert View Trail: 755-756, 790-791
Desert Wash Trail: 767
Desolation Wilderness: 249, 251, 254, 256,
    261, 263, 264
Devils Backbone: 734
Devils Canyon Trail: 730
Devils Chair: 723-724
Devils Den Trail: 176-177
Devils Gulch: 448
Devils Kitchen: 198
Devils Kitchen Trail: 182
Devils Knob: 147
Devils Oven Lake: 245
Devils Peak: 245, 491
Devils Postpile: 470, 471, 473
Devils Postpile National Monument: 515,
    566
Devils Punchbowl: 42-43
Devils Punchbowl Loop: 723-724
Devils Slide: 513
Devils Slide Trail: 759-760
Dewey Point: 453
Diablo Canyon: 337
Diablo Range: 589
Diablo Summit Loop: see Mount Diablo
    Summit Loop

Diamond Crossing: 239
Diamond Lake: 95
Dicks Lake: 254, 281
Dillon Beach: 285
Dingleberry Lake: 532
Dinkey Lakes: 518
Dipsea Race: 309
Dipsea Trail: 309, 311
"Disney petroglyphs": 769
distances: xiii
Divine Meadow: 294
Dixon Lake Recreation Area: 786
D. L. Bliss State Park: 252, 253
Doane Pond: 784
Doane Valley Nature Trail: 784-785
Doe Flat Trail: 41-42
Doe Ridge/Goat Hill Trails: 386
Dog Lake: 437, 440-441
Dollar Lake: 755
dolphins: East Anacapa Island Loop Trail
    700-701
Dome Land Wilderness: 621, 625, 628
Dome Rock: 618, 620
Dominator: 716
Domingo Springs: 198-200
Don Castro Lake Loop: 365
Donkey Lake: 532
Donner Canyon Trail: 361-362
Donner Falls: 361
Donner Lake: 247
Donner Memorial State Park: 247
Donner Pass: 240, 282
Donner Trail: 361-362
Donohue Pass: 458
Dorothy Lake: 460, 475, 530
Doyle Springs: 611
Doyle Trail: 611-612
Drake Lake: 182
Drake Lake Trail: 182-183
Drakes Bay: 293, 294
Drakes Estero: 289, 291
Drakes Head: 289
Dripping Springs Trail: 783-784
Dry Creek Falls: see Shingle Falls
Dry Meadow Creek: 619
Duck Lake: 417-418
Dumbarton Bridge: 343, 367-368
Dumbarton Pier: 368-369
Duna Vista Trail: 584-585
dunes: Eureka Dunes 569
Durphy Creek Loop: 151-152

Dwarf Forest: 133
Dyerville Giant: 81

E

Eagle Creek Trail: 396
Eagle Falls: 253, 254
Eagle Lake: 254, 384
Eagle Lake Trail: 602-603
Eagle Meadow: 418-419
Eagle/Mosquito Trailhead: 601
Eagle Mountains: 773
Eagle Peak: 444
Eagle Rock: 712
Eagle Rock Loop: 382-383, 712
Eagle Sink Holes: 602
Eagle View: 554-555
East Anacapa Island Loop Trail: 700-701
East Bay Hills: 327
East Bay Municipal Utility District: 355
East Bay Regional Park District: 363, 406
East Bay Skyline National Trail: 352, 359, 370-372
East Camino Cielo: 653, 658
East Carson River Trail: 278
East Creek Loop: 146
East Cut Across Trail: 738
East Fork Bridge: 599-600
East Fork Coyote Creek: 401
East Fork Loop: 90
East Fork of Cold Springs: 657
East Fork San Gabriel River: 725
East Fort Baker: 318-319
East Lake: 425
Easton Canyon: 727
East Peak Mount Tamalpais: 307-308
East Ridge Loop: 358-359
East Ridge Trail: 210
East Snow Mountain: 166
Ebbetts Park: 276
Ebbetts Pass: 279, 458-459, 461-462
Echo Lake: 135, 265
Echo Lakes Resort: 265, 280-282
Ed R. Levin County Park: 377
Edison Catwalk: 659
Edison Lake: 565
Edith Lake: 475
8-Ball Trail: 227
El Camino Loop: 645-646
El Capitan Trail: 444
Elderberry Trail: 360
Eldridge Grade: 308-309

Elephant Back: 271, 279
Elephant Rock: 417
elephant seals: Año Nuevo Trail 394
Elephant Trees: 808
Elizabeth Lake: 436
elk: McClures Beach Trail 286-287; Muddy Hollow Loop 291-292; Tomales Point Trail 285-286
Elk Camp Ridge Trail: 28-29
Elkhorn Fault: 675
Elkhorn Slough: 485
Elkhorn Slough South Marsh Loop: 484-485
Ella Falls: 520
Ellis Peak: 249-250
El Moro Canyon and Ridge Loop: 738
El Paso Mountains: 673
El Sereno Open Space: 391
Elsie Roemer Bird Sanctuary: 356
Emerald Bay: 716-717
Emerald Bay Overlook: 252
Emerald Lake: 96, 557, 558
Emerald Lake Trail: 474
Emerald Lakes: 532
Emerald Point: 252
Emerson Trailhead: 145
Emigrant Lake: 268
Emigrant Pass: 247-248
Emigrant West Trail: 415
Emigrant Wilderness: 420, 423
Empire Landing Road Trail: 717-718
endangered bats: Bear Gulch Caves 503-504
endangered fish: Fish Slough 531-532
endangered plants: Santa Rosa Plateau Vernal Pools 740-741
endangered species: Blue Sky Ecological Preserve 787-788; Bolsa Chica Ecological Reserve 737; Elkhorn Slough South Marsh Loop 484-485; Fish Slough 531-532; McGrath State Beach Nature Trail 659-660; Salton Sea National Wildlife Refuge 813; Winton Marsh Trail 499
Engelmann oak: Blue Sky Ecological Preserve 787-788; Santa Rosa Plateau Vernal Pools 740-741
Ernie Maxwell Scenic Trail: 758-759
Escondido Falls: 711
Estero de Limantour: 289, 292
Estero Trail: 289

Etna Summit to Grider Creek: 54
Euchre Bar Trail: 231-232
Eureka Dunes: 569
Eureka Lake: 187
Eureka Peak: 769
Eureka Peak Loop: 187
Evelyn Lake: 435
Eve Tree: 609-610
Evolution Valley: 565
Ewoldsen Loop Trail: 495
Excelsior Mountain: 465

F
Fairview Dome: 439
Fallen Goliath: 543
Fallen Leaf Lake: 255-256, 259
Fallen Leaf Lake Trail: 257-258
Fallen Monarch: 522
Falls Loop Trail: 156-157
Falls Recreation Area: 754
False Gun Vista Point: 347-348
Fandango Pass: 74
Fannette Island: 252
Fantastic Lava Beds: 135
Farallon Islands: 326, 363
Farewell Gap: 606
Farewell Gap Trail: 601, 603
Father-of-the-Forest: 386
Feather Falls National Recreation Trail:
  186
Feather River: 197-198
federal offices: 823
Feely Lake: 229, 231
Fern Canyon Loop Trail: 35-36
Fern Canyon Trail: 157-158
Fern Lake Loop: 472-473
Fern Trail: 358, 490
Fife Creek: 210
Figueroa Mountain: 652
Figueroa Trail: 398
Fir Canyon Trail: 652
Fire Lane Trail: 293
First Dinkey Lake: 518
First Falls: 536
First Lake: 536-537
First Water Trail: 728
Fishbowls: 664
Fish Creek: 753
fish migration: Dumbarton Pier 368-369
Fish Slough: 531-532
Fish Trail: 399

Fissures: 452
Fitzgerald Marine Reserve: 336
5 Allens' Trail: 79-80
Five Brooks Trailhead: 295
Five Lakes: 248
Five Lakes Basin: 231
Five Lakes Creek: 239
Flat Iron Tree: 82
Flat Rock Point: 716
Fletcher Peak: 435
Floating Islands Lake: 255
Flower Lake: 549-550
Folsom Lake: 223
Folsom Lake State Recreation Area: 223
Forest of Nisene Marks State Park: 483
Forest Service: 817-818
Forest View Trail: 238
Forsee Creek Trailhead: 753
Fort Barry 316-317
Fort Cronkhite: 316
Fort Funston: 328
Fort Point: 328
Fort Scott Overlook: 327
Fortynine Palms Oasis: 770
Fossil Falls: 626-627
Founders Grove Nature Trail: 81
fountain water: Sand Flat Trailhead 107
Four-Mile Trail: 453
Fourth of July Lake: 270-271
Fourth of July Saddle: 271
Fowler Peak: 196-197
Fox Meadows: 545
Fox Trail: 314
Francis Lake Trail: 530
Franklin Canyon Park: 715
Franklin Lakes: 603-604
Franklin Ridge: 350
Franklin Ridge Loop Trail: 350
Frazier Falls Trail: 192
Freeman Creek Trail: 614
Fremont Peak Observatory: 501
Fremont Peak Trail: 501
French Hill Trail: 31
French Meadows Reservoir: 238-239
French Trail: 358
French Trail at Mammoth Pool: 515
Fresno Dome: 512
Frog Lake: 271-272
Frog Lakes: 465
Frog Pond Loop: 399
frogs: Guajome Lake Trail 784

FISHING

Agua Blanca Loop: 666
Antioch Bridge: 351
Antioch Pier: 351
Balch Park Nature Trail: 609
Berkeley Pier: 352
Blue Lake: 465, 532
Blue Lake Loop: 145-146
Brown Lake: 534-535
Buckeye Creek Trail: 424
Buck Lake Trail: 42
Bullards Bar Trail: 227-228
Bullpen Lake: 228
Cathedral Lakes: 434, 459
Cave Lake: 73-74
Charleston Slough: 376
Clark Fork: 419-420
Clear Lake: 144-145
Coit Lake: 399-400, 401
Cone Lake Trailhead: 136-137
Contra Loma Loop: 354
Cottonwood Lakes: 607-608
Culbertson Lake: 228
Cypress Trailhead: 130-131
Deep Creek Fishermen's Trail: 748-749
Deer Creek Trail: 176, 185-186
Devils Canyon Trail: 730
Domingo Springs: 198-200
Eagle Lake: 254, 384
East Lake: 425
Farewell Gap Trail: 601, 603
Golden Trout Wilderness: 608, 610, 613, 615, 616, 629
Green Lake: 425, 534-535
Guajome Lake Trail: 784
Gumboot Lake Trailhead: 114-115
Hartman Bar National Recreation Trail: 186-187
Hay Meadow Trail: 184-185
Hetch Hetchy Reservoir: 426, 427
Island Lake Trail: 45
Jack Creek Nature Trail: 786-787
Janes Reservoir: 73
Jenks Lake: 752-753
Juanita Lake Trail: 59-60
Lake Eleanor: 425-426

Lassen Volcanic National Park: 138-139, 198-200
Lewis Creek: 511
Lily Lake: 73-74
Little South Fork Lake Trail: 90-91
Loch Lomond Loop: 395-396
Lower Lola Montez Lake: 244
Lyell Canyon: 435, 436-437
Martinez Waterfront Park: 350-351
Matterhorn Canyon: 460
McCloud Nature Trail: 117-118
Medicine Lake Loop: 67
Mill Creek Falls Trailhead: 144-145
Mississippi Lake Trail: 400-401
Mumford Bar Trail: 232-233
Noble Lake: 276-277
North Arroyo Trail: 366-367
North Fork Kern River Trail: 619-620
Phoenix Lake Trail: 302
Pinecrest Lake National Recreation Trail: 422-423
Powell Lake: 423-424
Rancheria Trail: 174-175
Raymond Lake: 272-273
Relief Reservoir: 420-421
Rim Trail: 129
Sailor Flat Trail: 234-235
Salmon Creek Falls: 576, 624-625
Soberanes Point Trail: 489-490
Soup Spring Trailhead: 144
Spirit Lake Trail: 50-51
Spring Lake Trail: 217
Swift Creek Trail: 95
Tamarack Lakes: 530
Toad Lake Trail: 113
Trail Gulch: 88-89
Twin Lakes: 135, 261-262, 466, 516-517, 560-561
Tyee Lakes: 534
Upper Fisherman's Trail: 318
Upper Manzana Creek Trail: 651-652
Upper San Joaquin River: 470
West Lake: 425
Willow Creek: 197, 513-514
Yucca Point: 537-538
Zumwalt Meadow Loop: 541

Frypan Meadow: 538
Funeral Mountains: 639

G
Gabrielino Trail: 725-726, 727
Galena Creek: 611

Gardisky Lake: 442
Garfield-Hockett Trail: 598-599
Garin Peak: 365
Garin Regional Park: 365
Garland Ranch: 490
Garnet Lake: 458

Garnet Peak: 794
Garrapata State Park: 489
Garretson Point: 356
Gate, The: 109
Gavilan Mountains: 398
Gaviota Beach: 646
Gaviota Hot Springs: 646-647
Gaviota Overlook: 646
Gaviota Pass: 647
Gaviota Peak: 647
Gem Lake: 469
Gem Lakes: 529
General Creek: 250-251
General Grant Tree: 521-522
General Sherman Tree: 556, 612
George Lake: 516-517
George's Picnic Area: 483
Gerstle Cove: 208
Gertrude Lake: 262-263
Ghost Mountain Trail: 806-807
ghosts: Alcatraz Island 325; Thomas
    Wright Trail 66
Giant Forest: 553, 556
Giant Forest Village: 553
Giant Loop: 361-362
giant sequoias: Amos Alonzo Stagg Tree
    612; Forest View Trail 238; General Grant
    Tree 521-522; Mariposa Grove 457-458;
    Merced Grove 428; Muir Grove 547-548;
    Nelder Grove 512; Paradise Ridge 599;
    Redwood Mountain Loop 543-544; Trail
    of 100 Giants 616-617; Tuolumne Grove
    429
giant sequoia stumps: "Big Stump, The"
    411; Big Stump Trail 520; Boole Tree
    Loop 519-520; Chicago Stump Trail 518-
    519; Mark Twain Stump 520; Stump
    Beach Trail 208-209
Gibbs Lake Trail: 466-467
Gibson Beach: 488
Gibson Peak: 95
Gilbert Lake: 549
Gilliam Creek Trail: 209-210
Gill Trail: 402
Gilmore Lake: 256, 258, 259, 281
Glacier Lake: 231
Glacier Lodge: 536
Glacier Point: 450, 451, 453, 454
Glass Mountain: 69
Glen Alpine: 258
Glen Alpine Creek: 257

Glen Aulin: 437, 439, 460
Glenbrook Creek: 292
Glen Eden Trail: 158-159
Glen Pass: 564
Glen's View: 791
Goat Hill Trail: 384, 386
Goat Rock: 390
Goat Trail: 748
gold eagle nesting: Sunol Loop 370
Golden Canyon Interpretive Trail: 640-641
Golden Falls: 387, 391
Golden Gate Bridge: 311, 317, 318, 319, 320,
    326, 327-328, 363
Golden Gate Promenade: 328
Golden Gate Recreation Area: 297
Golden Trout Wilderness: 608, 610, 613,
    615, 616, 629
Gold Lakes Basin: 187, 189, 195
gold mines: Keane Wonder Mine Trail 639;
    Lost Horse Mine 772
Gold Rush sites: American River Trail 233;
    Euchre Bar Trail 231-232; Italian Bar Trail
    232; South Yuba Independence Trail 228
Goose Lake: 74
Gopherus agassizi: 673
Graham Pinery: 176
Graham Trail Loop: 357
"Grand Canyon of the Mojave": see Afton
    Canyon
Grand Canyon of the Tuolumne River: 430,
    460
Grand Sentinel: 541
Grandstand rock formation: 570
Grand View Trail: 786
Granite Chief Trail: 247-248
Granite Chief Wilderness: 239, 248, 249,
    281, 282
Granite Lake: 95, 273-274, 542
Granite Mountain: 691
Granite Point: 488
granite sculpture: Statue Lake 53
Grant County Park: 383, 384
Grant Lake: 383, 430
Grass Lake: 188, 527, 533
Grass Valley Loop: 359
Gray Butte: 109
Great Highway: 328
great-horned owls: Owl Trail 313-314
Great Mountain Lookout: 514-515
Great Sierra Mine: 441
Great Western Divide: 546, 547, 548, 552,

553, 559, 599, 608, 610, 620, 621
Green Butte: 111
Green Creek Trail: 425
Greenhorn Mountains: 623
Green Lake: 425, 534-535
Green Mountain: 93
Greenside Trail: 406
Greenstone Lake: 443
Green Valley Falls: 793
Green Valley Trail: 236-237
Grider Creek to Seiad Valley: 54-55
Gridley Trailhead: 665
Griffith Park: 715
Grizzly Flat Trail: 389
Grizzly Giant: 457
Grizzly Lake: 94-95
Grizzly Peak: 119
Grotto Trail: 707-708
Groundhog Meadow: 605
Grouse Falls: 237-238
Grouse Lake: 261
Grouse Ridge: 229
Grouse Ridge Trail (Sawmill to Eagle
   Lakes): 230
Grover Hot Springs State Park: 274, 277-
   278
Guadalupe Slough: 377
Guajome Lake Trail: 784
Gualala River: 207
guided walks/boat trips: Black Wolf Falls
   606-607; Blue Sky Ecological Preserve
   787-788; Caliche Forest and Point
   Bennett 695-696; Duna Vista and Two
   Waters Trails 584-585; Mitchell Caverns
   692; Path of the Padres 500-501;
   Pescadero Marsh 378; Sequoya
   Challenge 228; Silverwood Wildlife
   Sanctuary 792; South Bay Nature Trail
   343; Tidelands Trail 368
Guillemot Island: 488
gulls: Mono Lake South Tufa Trail 467
Gumboot Lake: 114
Gumboot Lake Trailhead: 114-115
Gunbarrel Trail: 32
Guy Fleming Loop Trail: 777-778

H
Hale telescope: 786
Half Dome: 363, 430, 432, 443, 447-448, 453,
   454
Half Dome Trail: 459

Half Moon Bay: 338, 339
Half Moon Bay State Parks Department:
   378
Half-Moon Meadow: 430
Halls Valley Loop: 383-384
Hamilton Lake: 555-556
Hammerhorn Mountain: 166
Hamms Gulch Trail: 376
Hanging Rock: 552
Hardin Butte: 66
Hare Creek: 575
Harkins Ridge Trail: 338-339
Hartman Bar National Recreation Trail:
   186-187
Hart Tree: 543
Harvey Peak: 165
Haskell Peak Trail: 193
Hastain Trail: 715
Hauser Wilderness: 797
Hawk Hill: 317-318
Hawkins Peak: 274
Hay Meadow Trail: 184-185
Haypress Creek: 194
Haypress Meadows Trailhead: 50
Hazelwood Nature Loop: 556
Headlands Loop: 207
Heart Lake: 529, 549
Heart Lake Trail: 115
Heart Rock Falls: 747
Heath Falls: 244-245
Heath Falls Overlook: 244
Heather Lake: 257, 281, 557, 558
Hecker Pass: 484
Heiser Lake: 275
Hell Creek: 787
Hell Hole: 239-240
Hellhole Canyon: 787
Hell Hole Reservoir: 239, 249
Hemlock Crossing: 513
Hemlock Lake: 261
Henry Cowell Redwoods State Park: 396
Henry W. Coe State Park: 399, 400, 401
Heritage Grove: 379
Hermit Falls: 728
heron rookery: Elkhorn Slough South
   Marsh Loop 484-485
Hetch Hetchy: 337, 425
Hetch Hetchy Reservoir: 426, 427
Hidden Springs Trailhead: 397
Hidden Trail: 492
Highland Trail: 395

High Marsh Trail: 305
High Peaks: 502-503
High Ridge: 585-586
High Ridge Loop: 365-366
High Sierra Trail: 554-556
High View Nature Trail: 767-768
Highway 44: 138-139
Highway 74: 760-761
Highway 75: 801
Highway 78 Trail: 799-801
Hi Grade National Recreation Trail: 74
Hill 1989: 667
Hills for Everyone Trail: 736
Hinckley Ridge: 483
Hirz Bay Trail: 120-121
historic sites: Bridge Creek Historic Site
    482; Cooper Cabin 491; Duck Lake 417-
    418; Potwisha to Hospital Rock 551
Hites Cove: 448
Hockett Trail: 599-600
Hoffman Channel: 352
Holcomb Valley: 751
Hollow Log: 6009
Holy Jim Falls: 737-738
Homer's Nose: 598
Honeymoon Lake: 531
Hoover Wilderness: 424, 443, 466
Horseshoe Loop: 473
Horseshoe Meadow: 607, 609
Horsetail Falls: 527
Horsetail Falls Vista: 264-265
Horse Trail Ridge National Recreation
    Trail: 87-88
Hospital Rock: 551
Hossack Meadow: 613
Hotel Creek Trail: 538, 539
Hotel Trail: 384
Hotlum Glacier: 106, 110
hot springs: Deep Creek Hot Springs 748;
    Gaviota Hot Springs 646-647; Grover
    Hot Springs State Park 274,277-278;
    Jordan Hot Springs 616
Hot Springs Canyon: 274
Hot Springs Creek Waterfall: 274
Howarth Park: 217
Huckleberry Loop Path: 357
Huckleberry Meadow Trail: 556
Huckleberry Preserve: 372
Huckleberry Trail: 420
Huddart Park: 337
Huddart Park Loop: 340

Humber Park: 759
Humboldt Redwoods State Park: 81, 83
Humboldt Summit: 197-198
Humboldt-Toiyabe National Forest: 460
Hummingbird Lake: 466
Hump Trail: 557
Huntington Lake: 516

I
Iceberg Meadow: 419
Ice Caves Trail: 127-128
Ice House Saddle: 735-736
Ides Cove National Recreation Trail: 165
Illilouette Fall: 455
Inaja Memorial Trail: 788
Independence Creek: 549
Independence Peak: 550
"Indian bathtubs": 610
Indian Joe Creek: 370
Indian Pools: 517-518
Indian Rock: 431
information services: 824
Inspiration Point: 308-309, 417, 448, 656,
    701
Inspiration Point Trail: 714
interpretive trails: Aliso Canyon Loop
    Trail 653-654; Balancing Rock 253;
    Bayside Trail 778-779; Big Trees
    Interpretive Trail 238; Blackberry
    Springs 585-586; Borrego Palm Canyon
    Falls 805; Burney Falls Trail 128-129;
    Burst Rock 423-424; Cabrillo Tide Pools
    779; Canyon Trail 380, 495, 767; Cedars
    Interpretive 515-516; Chester Marsh
    Trail 499; Cold Springs Nature Trail 600;
    Columns of the Giants 419; Cottonwood
    Creek Botanical Trail 203; Desert
    Tortoise Discovery Loop 673-674; East
    Anacapa Island Loop Trail 700-701;
    Golden Canyon Interpretive Trail 640-
    641; High View Nature Trail 767-768;
    Inaja Memorial Trail 788; Jack Creek
    Nature Trail 786-787; Kaweah Oaks
    Preserve 593; Lake of the Sky Trail 256-
    257; Myrtle Creek Trail 30; Painted Rock
    247, 589-590; Panoramic Point 522-523;
    Piño Alto Trail 652-653; Piñon Ridge
    Nature Trail 732-733; Ponderosa Vista
    Nature Trail 751-752; Rainbow Trail 256-
    257; Redwood Exhibit Trail 152; Redwood
    Loop 78-79, 386-387; Salt Creek

INTERESTING GEOLOGY

Afton Canyon: 687
Bailey Cove Loop Trail: 120
Balancing Rock: 253
Balconies Caves: 501-502
Bear Gulch Caves: 503-504
Bumpass Hell Trail: 181-182
Burnt Lava Flow: 128
Caliche Forest: 695-696
China Wall Loop: 362
Cinder Cone Trail: 135-136
Columns of the Giants: 419
Deer Creek Trail: 185-186
Devils Postpile: 470
Devils Punchbowl: 42-43, 723-724
Fossil Falls: 626-627
Glass Mountain: 69
Golden Canyon Interpretive Trail: 640-641
Hirz Bay Trail: 120-121
Homer's Nose: 598
Ice Caves Trail: 127-128
Inyo Craters: 469-470
Lembert Dome: 439-440
Medicine Lake Lava Flow: 67-68
Mitchell Caverns: 692
Moak Trail: 175-176
Mono Lake South Tufa Trail: 467
Mosaic Canyon: 633-634
Murray Canyon Trail: 772-773
Nobles Emigrant Trail:: 132-133
Packsaddle Cave Trail: 622
Palisades Trail: 215-216
Rainbow Basin: 683
Red Cliffs: 673
Round Top Loop Trail: 354-355
San Andreas Fault Trail: 379
Skull Rock Nature Trail: 771-772
Stevens Creek Nature Trail: 379-380
Trail of the Gargoyles: 420
Trona Pinnacles: 636
Vasquez Rocks County Park: 675
Whaleback, The: 60-61
Whitney Butte Trail: 65-66
Whitney Falls/Bolam Creek Trailhead: 105-106

Interpretive Trail 640; San Andreas Fault Trail 379; Sandy Wool Lake 377; San Elijo Lagoon 777; Shadow of the Giants 512; Sierra Discovery Trail 230-231; Skull Rock Nature Trail 771-772; Stevens Creek Nature Trail 379-380; Way of the Mono 514; Whispering Pines Trail 752; Wildwood Park Loop 710; Woodland

Trail 751
Inverness Ridge: 288, 293, 297
Inyo Craters: 469-470
Inyo Mountains: 608
Inyo National Forest: 458
Iron Horse Regional Trail: 360-361
Iron Mountain: 176, 472
Ishi Wilderness: 174
Island Lake: 229, 231, 261-262, 518
Island Lake Trail: 45
Islip Saddle: 733
Italian Bar Trail: 232
Italy Pass: 531

J
Jackass Creek National Recreation Trail: 621
Jackass Peak: 621
Jack Creek Nature Trail: 786-787
Jackrabbit Lake: 401
Jackson Flats Trail: 385
Jackson Meadow Reservoir: 240
Jacks Peak: 486
Jamison Lake: 188
Jamison Mine: 188
Janes Reservoir: 73
Jawbone Canyon Road: 677-679
Jedediah Mountain: 45
Jedediah Smith Memorial Trail: 223-224
Jenks Lake: 752-753
Jennie Lake: 545-546
Jennie Lakes Wilderness: 544
Jesuita Trail: 655
Jikoji Retreat: 382
JMT: see John Muir Trail
John Brooks Memorial Open Space: 337
John Jordan/Hossack Meadow Trail: 613
John Muir Loop: 446
John Muir Trail: xiii, 434, 435, 454, 459-460, 472, 512
John Muir Wilderness: 527-531, 532-535, 563, 564, 565, 607
Johnstone Trail: 288-289
Johnston Lake: 472
J. O. Pass Trail: 560
Jordan, John: 613
Jordan Hot Springs: 616
Jordan Peak Lookout: 612-613
Joshua Tree National Park: 767-772
Joshua trees: Red Cliffs 673; Ryan Mountain Trail 770-771; Saddleback

Joshua trees *(cont.)*
Butte 674-675; Teutonia Peak 691;
Warren Peak: 768-769
Juan Crespi Loop: 398
Juanita Lake Trail: 59-60
Julia Pfeiffer Burns State Park: 495
June Lake Loop: 468
June Mountain: 469
Juniper Canyon and High Peaks Loop: 502
Juniper Lake Loop: 183

K
Kaiser Peak: 516
Kaiser Wilderness: 516
Kangaroo Lake Trailhead: 103-104
Kaufmann Trail: 772
Kaweah Oaks Preserve: 593
Kaweah River Canyon: 548, 552, 599
kayaking: Abbotts Lagoon Trail 287;
Drakes Estero 289; Estero de Limantour
289, 292
Keane Wonder Mine Trail: 639
Keane Wonder Springs: 639-640
Kearsage Pass: 548-549
Kearsage Pass Trail: 549
Kelham Beach: 292
Keller Beach: 347
Kelly Cabin Lake: 400, 401
Kelsey Creek Trail: 48-49
Kelso dunes: 691-692
Kennedy Creek: 420
Kennedy Grove: 349
Kennedy Lake: 420, 421
Kennedy Meadows: 420, 628-629
Kenneth Lake: 530
Kent Dam Trail: 298
Kent Lake: 297, 299
Kern Canyon: 620
Kern Plateau: 621
Kern River: 613, 626
Kern River Basin: 615
Kern River Valley: 623, 624, 627
Kickapoo Waterfall: 89
King Crest Trail: 83
Kings Canyon: 538
Kings Canyon National Park: 520, 540, 541,
542, 548
Kings Canyon Overlook: 539
Kings Castle Trail: 47
King's Peak: 83
Kings River: 537, 564

Kinney Lakes: 277
Kirk Creek/Vicente Flat Trail: 575-576
Kitchen Creek: 798
Kitchen Creek Falls: 796-797
Klamath River: 59
Knapp, George: 654-655
Knapp's Castle: 653, 654
Knee Ridge: 249
Kratka Ridge: 741
Kreyenhagen Peak: 589
Kumeyaay Indians: 807

L
Lacey Mountain: 240
Lady Alice Tree: 609
Ladybug Falls: 597
Ladybug Trail: 597-598
Lafayette-Moraga Trail: 355
Laguna Loop Trail: 293-294
Laguna Meadow: 794
Laguna Mountains: 791, 794, 795, 798
Lagunitas Creek: 297, 298
Lagunitas Lake: 301
La Jolla Valley Loop: 706
Lake Aloha: 256, 259, 265-266, 281
Lake Alpine: 415, 417, 418
Lake Anna: 96
Lake Cachuma: 652, 655
Lake Casitas: 666
Lake Cleone Trail: 155-156
Lake Davis: 207
Lake Doris: 263-264
Lake Eleanor: 425-426
Lake Genevieve: 251, 475
Lake Isabella: 618, 623
Lake Lucille: 266
Lake Margaret: 268-269
Lake Margery: 266, 281
Lake Mary: 474
Lake Morena Park: 797-799
Lake of the Lone Indian: 565
Lake of the Sky Trail: 256-257
Lake of the Woods: 266
Lake Piru: 666
Lake Poway: 787
Lake Ralphine: 217
Lakes Basin Recreation Area: 188
Lakeshore Trail: 415, 417
Lake Sonoma: 208
Lakes Trail, The: 557-558, 559
Lake Sylvia: 260

Lake Tahoe: 246, 247, 249, 252, 253, 255, 256
Lake Thomas Edison: 564-566
Lake Trail: 218-219
Lakeview Trail: 507
Lake Virginia: 566
Lamarck Lake: 533
Lands End Trail: 326-327
La Purisima Mission: 645
largest privately owned sequoia: Stagg
  Tree 612
Las Zanjas Trail: 645-646
Las Zonas Trail: see Las Zanjas Trail
Lassen Peak: 68
Lassen Summit Trail: 133-134
Lassen Volcanic National Park: 138-139,
  198-200
Lassie: 752
Last Chance Range: 570
Las Trampas Creek: 355
Las Trampas Regional Wilderness: 360
Laurel Dell Loop: 304-305
Laurel Loop Trail: 349
Lava Beds National Monument: 68
least bell's vireo: Guajome Lake Trail 784
least terns: Bolsa Chica Ecological
  Reserve 737; Elkhorn Slough South
  Marsh Loop 484-485; McGrath State
  Beach Nature Trail 659-660
Leavitt Meadow: 422
Leavitt Peak: 460-461
LeConte Canyon: 564
LeConte Falls: 438
Leffingwell Landing: 579
Lembert Dome: 439-440
Leo Carrillo State Beach: 708
Lester Ranch: 695
Lewis Creek: 511
Lewis Creek Trail: 538-539
Lewis Falls: see Soldier Creek/Lewis Falls
Lexington Dam Trail: 392-393
Lexington Reservoir: 391, 392
Liberty Cap: 446, 460
Liebre Mountain: 669
Lightning Ridge Trail: 794-795
Lily Lake: 73-74; Little North Fork
  Trailhead 51
Lily Pond: 250-251
Lily Rock: 758
Lime Point: 319
Limekiln Falls: 575
Limekiln Trail: 575

limestone formations: Bailey Cove Loop
  Trail 120; Boyden Cave 538; Hirz Bay
  Trail 120-121; see also caves and
  interesting geology
Limestone Ridge: 90, 93
Lincoln Tree: 557
Lindsey Lakes Trail: 228-229
Lion Meadow: 521
Little Baldy: 548, 553
Little Buckskin Creeks: 239
Little Buttonwillow Lake: 500
Little Coyote Creek: 399
Little Crystal Lake:
Little Cull Canyon Reservoir: 364
Little Deer Creek: 553
Little Ed Davis Park: 668
Little Falls: 584
Little Hebe Crater Trail: 569-570
Little Jamison Falls: 188
Little Jimmy Trail: 733
Little Lakes Valley: 529-530
Little Mount Hoffman: 68-69
Little North Fork Trailhead: 51
Little Norway: 280
Little Pine Mountain: 654
Little Pothole Lake: 549
Little Red Mountain: 98
Little South Fork Lake Trail: 90-91
Little Yosemite: 370
Lizard Rock Trail: 710
Lloyd Meadows: 614, 615
Lobos Canyon: 699
Loch Leven Lake: 235, 533-534
Loch Lomond Loop: 395-396
Loch Lomond Reservoir: 395
Loch Trail: 395
Loma Prieta Epicenter: 482-483
Loma Prieta Grade Trail: 482
Lomas Cantadas: 371
Lompoc Valley: 647
London, Jack: 218-219
Lone Grave: 229
Lone Pine Creek: 561
Lone Pine Lake: 562-563
Long Canyon Trailhead: 95-96
Long Gulch Lake: 89
Long Lake: 529, 535
Long Meadow: 459, 559
Long Ridge Loop: 382
Long Ridge Open Space Preserve: 382
Long Valley: 756

Lookout Peak: 539-540
Lookout Point: 426-427
Lookout Point Loop Trail: 151
Lookout Rock: 196
Lopez Creek: 583
Lopez Lake: 584
Los Angeles: 714
Los Banos Creek Reservoir: 500
Los Banos Wildlife Area: 499-500
Los Cerritos Trail: 398
Los Gatos Creek: 392
Los Huecos Trail: 383
Los Osos Creek Trail: 581
Los Osos Oaks Reserve: 581-582
Los Padres National Forest: 647, 654, 663, 666
Los Peñasquitos Canyon: 788-789
Los Peñasquitos Marsh: 777
Los Piñetos Trail: 668
Lost Arrow Spire: 443
Lost Cabin Mine Trail: 270
Lost Coast Trail: 80-81, 154-155
Lost Creek Loop Trail: 379
Lost Horse Mine: 772
Lost Horse Valley: 770, 772
Lost Lake: 250
Lost Man Creek Trail: 36
Lost Palms Oasis: 773-774
Lost Trail: 376
Los Trancos Open Space Preserve: 379
Louis': 326
Lower Echo Lakes: 266
Lower Falls: 471
Lower Gaylor Lake: 435-436
Lower Hamilton Lake: 555
Lower Lola Montez Lake: 244
Lower McCloud Falls: 118
Lower Mill Creek: 175
Lower Morgan Lake: 529
Lower Pine Lake: 531
Lower Sardine Lake: 467
Lower Tent Meadow: 542
Lower Twin Lake: 262
Lower Velma Lake: 254
Lower Yosemite Fall: 444-445, 452
Luella Lake: 95
Lukens Lake: 429-430
Lunada Bay: 716
Lundy Lake Trailhead: 465-466
Lundy Pass: 466
Lupine Loop: 490

Lyell Canyon: 435, 436-437
Lyell Fork: 458
Lyndon Canyon: 391
Lyons Creek Trail: 260-261
Lyons Lake: 260

M
Mack Lake: 529
Madera Sugar Pine lumber flume: 511
Magee Trailhead: 130
Maggie Mountain: 612
Magic Forest Nature Trail: 714-715
Mahoney Ridge: 400
Maidenhair Falls: 805-806
Main Trail: 311-312
Malibu Creek: 710
Mammoth Lakes: 469, 471, 473
Mammoth Pool Reservoir: 515, 516
Manly Beacon: 641
Manter Meadow Loop: 625-626
Manzana Creek: 651
Manzanita and Azalea Loop: 522
Manzanita Lake Trail: 132
Manzanita Point: 480
map companies: 825
Maple Falls: 48, 482
maps: xiii-xiv; National Forest 816
Marble Falls: 550-551
Marble Fork Kaweah River Canyon: 553
Marble Mountain Rim: 47-48
Marble Mountains: 692
Marble Mountain wilderness: 51
Marie Lakes: 565
Marina Green: 328
Marin coast: 327
marine life: Bolsa Chica Ecological Reserve 737; Bruhel Point Tide Pools 155; Cabrillo Tide Pools 779; Fitzgerald Marine Reserve 336; McClures Beach Trail 286-287; McGrath State Beach Nature Trail 659-660; Mono Lake South Tufa Trail 467; Owl Trail 313-314
marine reserves: Gerstle Cove 208
Marine View Trail: 347
Marin Headlands: 314, 326
Mariposa Grove: 428, 457-458
Markleeville Peak: 274
Mark Twain Stump: 520
Marshall Beach Trail: 288
Marsh Lake: 529
Martha's Grove: 789

Martinez Fishing Pier: 351
Martinez Shoreline: 350-351
Martinez Waterfront Park: 350-351
Marvin Pass: 546
Mary Blaine Meadow: 89
M*A*S*H set: 710
Mason Station Trailhead: 185
Mastadon Peak: 773
Mather Pass: 564
Matlock Lake: 549-550
Matt Davis Trail: 310-311
Matterhorn Canyon: 460
Maud Lake: 263
May Lake: 431-432
McArthur-Burney Falls State Park: 139-140
McClendon Ford Trail: 31-32
McCloud Nature Trail: 117-118
McClures Beach Trail: 286-287
McClure Trail: 173
McCray Mountain: 210
McDonald Loop: 378-379
McGee Creek Trail: 527-528
McGrath State Beach Nature Trail: 659-660
McGuire: 238-239
McGurk Meadow: 450
McIntyre Rock: 613
McKay Creek: 421
McKinley Tree: 557
McMenemy Trail: 659
McPherson Peak Trail: 651
McWay Creek: 495
McWay Falls Overlook: 494-495
Meadow Brook: 449
Meadows Loop Trail: 341
Meadow Trail: 709-710
Medicine Lake Lava Flow: 67-68
Medicine Lake Loop: 67
Meeks Creek Trail to Rubicon Lake: 251
Mehrten Meadow: 559
Memorial County Park: 378, 388
Mendenhall Valley: 786
Merced Grove: 428
Merced River: 446, 460
mercury mines: Mine Hill Trail 396-397
Meridian Ridge: 361
Merrill Ice Cave: 65-66
Mesa Loop: 490
Mesa Trail: 710
Meteor Trail: 387-388
Methuselah Trail: 476

Methuselah Tree: 341
Meysan Lake: 563
Mezue Trail: 349
Michigan Bluff Trail: 237
Middle Deadfall: 104
Middle Falls Trail: 118-119
Middle Fork Eel River: 165
Middle Fork Feather River: 187, 195, 196
Middle Fork Kaweah River: 555
Middle Fork Trail: 551-552
Middle Gaylor Lake: 441-442
Middle Lake: 230
Middle Ridge Trail: 399
Middle Velma Lake: 281
Midpeninsula Regional open Space
   District: 393
Mildred Lake: 475
Milk Lake: 230, 231
Millard Falls: 726
Mill Creek: 184, 466
Mill Creek Canyon: 174
Mill Creek Falls Trailhead: 144-145
Mill Creek Lakes: 87
Mill Creek Picnic Area: 676, 742-743
Mill Creek Wash: 754, 755
Miller-Knox Regional Shoreline: 347
Miller Peak: 757
Mill Ox Loop: 385
Milton Creek: 240
Minalo Trail: 267-268
Minaret Falls: 471
Minaret Lake Trail: 471-472
Minarets: 470, 513
Mindego Ridge Trail: 381
Mine Hill Trail: 396-397
Mineral King: 602, 606
Mineral King Valley: 600, 601, 607
Mineral Lake: 601
Mineral Peak: 606
mineral springs: Keane Wonder Springs
   639-640; Soda Springs 601
Miner's Ridge: 601
mining cabins: Great Sierra Mine 441;
   Mono Pass 441; Moses Gulch Trail 611
Mirror Lake: 447
Mishe Mokwa and Backbone Loop: 708
Mission Creek: 655
Mission Peak: 369, 405
Mission Trails Regional Park: 791
Mississippi Lake Trail: 400-401
Mist and John Muir Loop: 446

Mist Falls: 541-542
Mist Trail: 445, 446, 454
Mitchell Canyon: 361
Mitchell Caverns: 692
Mitchell Peak: 546
Miwok Fire Trail: 303
Miwok Loop: 314
Moak Trail: 175-176
"Moguls, the": 376
Mojave Desert: 669, 674, 677, 768
Mojave National Preserve: 691
Mojave River: 748
Mokelumne Wilderness: 269, 279, 418, 461
Molera Beach: 491
Molera Point Trail: 491
Molera State Park Loop: 492
Monache Indians: 551
Monarch Creek: 605
Monarch Divide: 539
Monarch Lakes: 605-606
Mono Creek: 565
Mono Lake South Tufa Trail: 467
Mono Pass: 441, 528-529, 530
Monrovia Canyon: 731
Monrovia Canyon Falls: 730-731
Montaña de Oro Bluffs Trail: 582
Montaña de Oro State Park: 582
Monte Bello Open Space Preserve: 379
Montecito Overlook: 657
Monterey Bay: 381, 390, 396, 481, 484, 501
Monument Hamilton: 377
Monument Peak Trail: 377-378
Moonstone Beach: 579
Morgan Pass: 529
Morgan Territory Regional Preserve: 363
Morning Sun Trail: 315
Morongo Valley: 768
Moro Rock: 548, 552, 553-554
Morro Bay: 580
Morro Bay State Park: 581
Morro Creek: 580
Mosaic Canyon: 633-634
Moses Gulch Trail: 611
Moses Mountain: 612
Moses Spring Trail: 503
Mosquito Lakes: 275, 601-602
Moss Beach Distillery: 336
Moss Landing Wildlife Area Marsh Trail: 485
Mothball Fleet: 353, 361
Mother-of-the-Forest: 386

Mount Abel: 663
Mountain Home Demonstration State Park: 609, 610
Mountain Home Trail: 310
Mountain Palm Springs Canyon: 808-809
Mountain Theater: 306-307
mountain tunnel: Prospect Tunnel Loop 353-354
Mountain View Baylands: 367
Mountain Warfare Training Center: 422
Mount Allen: see Sandstone Peak
Mount Baden-Powell: 725, 729, 741
Mount Baldwin: 527
Mount Baldy: 734-735, 794
Mount Banner: 513
Mount Barcroft: 475
Mount Conness: 437
Mount Crocker: 527
Mount Dana: 440
Mount Diablo: 304, 336, 350, 353, 354, 361, 362, 363, 381
Mount Diablo Summit Loop: 362-363
Mount Eddy: 104, 123
Mount El Sereno: 391
Mount Elwell: 187, 189
Mount Elwell Trail: 189
Mount Emerson: 533
Mount Etna: 196
Mount Gibbs: 440
Mount Gibraltar: 196
Mount Gleason: 676, 677
Mount Goddard: 516, 522-523
Mount Goode: 535
Mount Hamilton: 383-384, 393
Mount Harwood: 734
Mount Hawkins: 733
Mount Hillyer: 729-730
Mount Hoffman: 432
Mount Hollywood: 715-716
Mount Hutchings: 542
Mount Islip: 733-734
Mount Jenkins: 628
Mount Lamarack: 533
Mount Lassen: 109
Mount Livermore: 320-321
Mount Madonna County Park: 483, 484
Mount Mallory: 563
Mount Pacifico: 729, 742
Mount Pinos: 663
Mount Pleasant: 197
Mount Ritter: 513, 516

Mount Round Top: 269, 354, 372
Mount St. Helena: 304
Mount St. Helena Trail: 215
Mount San Antonio: *see* Mount Baldy
Mount San Gorgonio: 750, 752, 755, 767, 792, 793, 794
Mount San Jacinto: 768, 769, 773, 792, 793, 794
Mount Shasta: *see also* Shasta
Mount Stewart: 553
Mount Tallac: 258
Mount Tallac from Tallac Trailhead: 255-256
Mount Tallac Loop Glen Alpine Trailhead: 258-259
Mount Tam: *see* Mount Tamalpais
Mount Tamalpais: 299, 300, 304, 306, 309, 310, 348, 350
Mount Tamalpais State Park: 307
Mount Thompson: 532, 535
Mount Umunhum: 393
Mount Waterman: 722, 723
Mount Whitney: 459, 555, 620, 628-629, 635, 678, 741
Mount Whitney Trail: 562
Mount Williamson: 724
Mount Wittenberg: 293, 294
Mount Wittenberg Loop: 294
Mount Woodson: 789-790
Mud Creek Falls: 111
Muddy Hollow Loop: 291-292
Muir Beach Overlook: 313
Muir Grove: 547-548
Muir Pass: 564
Muir Woods: 309
Muir Woods National Monument: 307
Mule Bridge Trailhead: 52
mule deer: Canyon Trail 767; Captain Jack's Stronghold 65; Timber Gap Trail 604-605
Mule Peak Lookout: 617
Mumbo Basin: 123-124
Mumford Bar Trail: 232-233
Murietta, Joaquin: 406
Murietta Falls Trail: 406-407
Murray Canyon Trail: 772-773
Musch Trail: 712
Mussel Rock: 328
Mussel Rocks: 77
Mustang Pond: 401
Myrtle Creek Trail: 30
Mystery Lake: 518

N
Napa Valley: 215
Natalie Coffine Greene Park: 302
national forests: 816
national parks: 819-820
National Recreation Trail: 589
"nation's Christmas tree, the": 581-582
Native American grinding bowls: 363
natural spring: Old Ski Bowl Trailhead 111-112
nature centers: Devils Punchbowl 723-724; Easton Canyon 727; Placerita Canyon County Park 668
Nature Conservancy: McCloud Nature Trail 117-118; Potato Harbor Trail 700
nature preserves: Blue Sky Ecological Preserve 787-788; Carrizo Plains 589-590; Kaweah Oaks Preserve 593; Red Cliffs Natural Preserve 673; Silverwood Wildlife Sanctuary 792
nature walks: *see* guided walks
Needles Lookout: 615
Nelder Grove: 457, 512
Nelson Creek: 613
nesting: peregrine falcons 215-216
Nevada Fall: 446, 453, 460
New River: 89
New River Divide Trail: 93-94
New River Trailhead: 89-90
New York Creek: 233
New York Mountains: 691
Niche, The: 513
Nicholas Flat Trail: 708-709
Nidever Canyon: 695
night herons: Agave Trail 325-326
Niles Community Park: 369
Nimitz Way: 352-353
Niña Mora Overlook Trail: 692
Ninemile Creek: 615
Nobe Young Falls: 617-618
Noble Lake: 276-277
Nobles Emigrant Trail: 132-133
Nojoqui Falls: 647-648
Nordhoff Peak: 665-666
North Arroyo Trail: 366-367
North Dome: 430-431, 443, 541
Northern California Hikes: 24-476
North Fork American River: 233, 236, 245
North Fork Beegum Trailhead: 98
North Fork Coffee Creek: 89
North Fork Feather River: 197

North Fork Kern River Trail: 619-620
North Fork of Big Pine Canyon: 536
North Gate: 105
North Gate Trailhead: 106-107
North Grove: 808
North Grove Loop: 411, 521
North Knee: 308
North Marsh: 367
North Pond Trail: 378
North Ridge/Sunset Trail: 320-321
North Ridge Trail: 489
North Shore Trail: 487
North Stove Mountain: 198
North Tepee Trail: 710
North Yolla Bolly Mountain: 164

O

Oak Tree Trail: 366, 741
Oak View Trail: 581
Oats Peak: 582-583
Observatory Trail: 786
obsidian: Glass Mountain 69
Ocean Beach Esplanade: 328-329
Ocean Lake: 293
Ocean Overlook: 709-710
Ocean View Summit: 388
Ocean View Trail: 312
"Octopus Trees:" 77
Odell Lake: 466
Ohlone Trail: 397
Ohlone Wilderness Trail: 405
Ojai Valley: 665, 666
Old Boney Trail: 705
Old Cove Landing Trail: see Old Landing
    Cove Trail
oldest documented living tree:
    Methuselah Tree 476
Old Greyback: 755
Old Haul Road: 156
Old Landing Cove Trail: 481
Old Pinnacles Trail: 502
Old Ski Bowl Trailhead: 111-112
Olema Creek: 295
Olema Valley: 295-296, 297
Ollason Peak: 486-487
Olmo Fire Trail: 386
Olmsted Brothers Map Company: 307
Omega Overlook: 229
One Mile Lake: 50
Onion Meadow Peak: 617
Opal Creek: 386, 388

Orestimba Valley: 401
Orestimba Wilderness: 400, 402
Oriflamme Canyon: 800
O'Rourke's Bench: 305, 306
Osborne Hill: 415-416
O'Shaughnessy Dam: 427
Oso Canyon: 653
Oso Creek: 654
Oso Flaco Lake: 645
Osprey Lake: 52
Ostrander Lake: 450, 451
Overlook Loop: 168-169
Overlook Trail: 539, 707
Overturff, Ben: 731
Owens River Valley: 531
Owens Valley: 475
Owl Canyon: 683
owls: Owl Trail 313-314
Owl Trail: 313-314

P

Pacheco Canyon: 402
Pacheco Trail: 401
Pacific Crest Trail: xiii, 53-55, 98-99, 122-
    124, 138-140, 195-199, 247, 278-282, 458-
    462, 564-566, 608, 627-629, 669-670; 675-
    679, 722, 724, 741-743, 750, 760-763, 794,
    796, 797-801
Pacific Flyway: 737
Packer Lake: 194
Packsaddle Cave: 624
Packsaddle Cave Trail: 622
Painted Dunes: 135
Painted Rock: 247, 589-590
Paiute Indians: 627
Palace Hotel Tree: 411
Pala Seca Trail: 383
Palisade Creek Trail: 244-245
Palisade Glacier: 537
Palisade Lakes: 564
Palisades Trail: 215-216
Palmer's Point: 77
Palm Grove Bowl: 808
Palm Springs Aerial Tramway: see Aerial
    Tramway
palm tree groves: Borrego Palm Canyon
    Falls 805; Fortynine Palms Oasis 770;
    Lost Palms Oasis 773-774; Mountain
    Palm Springs Canyon 808-809; North
    Grove 808; Palm Grove Bowl 808; Pymgy
    Grove 808; Southwest Grove 808;

Surprise Canyon Grove 808
Palo Alto Golf Course: 342
Palomarin Trailhead: 293, 298
Palomar Mountain: 785
Palomar Observatory: 783, 792, 794
Palos Verdes Estates Shoreline Preserve: 716
Panamint Mountains: 641
Panamint Valley: 635
Panorama Trail: 454-455, 492
Panoramic Highway: 310
Panoramic Highway Trail: see Ocean View Trail
Panoramic Point: 522-523
Panther Creek: 551-552
Panther Gap: 558
Panther Gap Loop: 559-560
Panther Meadows: 109-110
Pantoll Ranger Station and Trailhead: 307
Pantoll Trailhead: 307
Papes Place: 175
Papoose Lake: 565
Paradise Creek Trail: 552-553
Paradise Lake: 240, 401
Paradise Lake Trail: 46-47
Paradise Ridge: 599
Paradise Valley: 541
Parker Creek: 468
Parker Lake Trail: 468
Park Ridge Fire Lookout: 522
Park Ridge Lookout: 522-523
Park Ridge Trail: 581
Parson's Lodge: 437, 439
Partington Point Trail: 495-496
Path of the Padres: 500-501
Patricia Lake: 184
Patrick's Point: 77
Patterson Lake: 147
Pauley Creek Trail: 191
Pauma Valley: 785
PCT: see Pacific Crest Trail
Peacock Gap Trail: 304
Peak Trail: 369-370, 489
Pear Lake: 557
Pelican Lake: 293, 298
pelicans: Bicentennial Bike Path 315;
    Bolsa Chica Ecological Reserve 737;
    Elkhorn Slough South Marsh Loop 484-485; Partington Point Trail 495-496
Pena Trail: 398
Penitencia Creek: 382

Penner Lake: 229-230
Pepperdine Trailhead: 143
Peppermint Creek Fals: 618-619
peregrine falcons: Salton Sea National Wildlife Refuge 813
Perimeter Road: 319-320
Pescadero Marsh: 378
Peters Dam: 298
petroglyphs: Barker Dam Loop 769-770;
    Fish Slough 531-532; Fossil Falls 626-627
Pettyjohn Basin: 163
Pfeiffer Big Sur State Park: 493
Pfeiffer Falls and Valley View Loop: 492
Pfeiffer Ridge: 493
Phoenix Lake Trail: 302
pictographs: Painted Rock 589-590;
    Pictograph Trail 807-808; Potwisha to Hospital Rock 551
Pictograph Trail: 807-808
Piedra Blanca: 664-665
Piedras Blancas Lighthouse: 580
Pigeon Springs: 739
Pillar Point: 337-338
Pillar Point Harbor: 339
Pilot Knob Trail: 301
Pilot Peak: 196
Pinchot Pass: 564
Pine Canyon: 669
Pine Creek: 73
Pine Creek Canyon: 531
Pine Creek Trailhead: 143-144
Pinecrest Lake National Recreation Trail: 422-423
Pine Flat: 627
Pine Gulch Creek: 295
Pine Mountain: 300-301
Pine Ridge: 399
Pine Trail: 396
Pine Valley: 493-494
Pinnacles National Monument: 501, 502, 503
Piño Alto Trail: 652-653
Piñon Ridge Nature Trail: 732-733
Pioneer Basin: 530
pioneer cabins: Duck Lake 417-418;
    McGurk Meadow 450
Pioneer Trail: 229
Pioneer Trail Loop: 153-154
Pioneer Tree Trail: 297
Piru Creek: 664
Pismo Dunes: 585

Pismo Dunes Natural Preserve: 645
Piute Crags: 533
Piute Lake: 533
Placerita Canyon County Park: 668
Placerita Creek Waterfall: 668-669
Plasse's Resort: 267
Pleasanton Ridge Regional Park: 366
Pleasant Valley: 770, 772
Plumas National Forest: 187
Pohono Trail: 448, 453-454
Point Bennett: 695-696
Point Bonita Lighthouse: 317
Point Conception: 647
Point Isabel Shoreline: 351-352
Point Lobos Perimeter: 488
Point Lobos State Reserve: 487
Point Loma: 778
Point Mugu State Park: 705, 706, 707
Point Pinole: 348
Point Reyes Hostel: 292
Point Reyes Lighthouse: 289
Point Reyes National Seashore: 286, 287,
    289-296, 326
Point Richmond: 347
Point Sur Light Station: 492
Pole Corral Gap: 98
Polly Dome: 433
Ponderosa Vista Nature Trail: 751-752
Poop Out Pass: 545
Poore Lake: 422
Poppy Hill: 741
Porcupine Creek Trailhead: 431
Porter Picnic Area: 483
Port Hueneme: 701
Portola Redwood State Park: 378, 388
Portola Valley: 375
Potato Harbor Trail: 700
Pothole Trail: 666
Potter Pass: 516
Potwisha: 551
Powderhorn Trail: 239-240
Powell Lake: 423-424
predators: Palisades Trail 215-216
Preston Peak: 43, 44-45
Priest Rock Trail: 393
Princeton Harbor: 338
Prospect Peak Trail: 136
Prospect Tunnel Loop: 353-354
Providence Mountains: 691
Pulgas Water Temple: 337
pupfish: Salt Creek Interpretive Trail 640

pure water: Castle Lake 115
Purisima Creek Redwoods: 338-339
Purple Lake: 566
Pymgy Grove: 808
Pyramid Canyon: 687
Pyramid Peak: 260

QR

Quarry Trail: 581
Queen Valley: 770, 772
Racetrack Valley: 570
Rae Lakes: 564
rafting: North Fork Kern River Trail 619-620
Railroad Canyon: 278
railroads: see "Rails to Trails"
"Rails to Trails": Bizz Johnson 185; Iron
    Horse Regional Trail 360-361; Old Haul
    Road 156
Rainbow Basin: 683
Rainbow Falls Trail: 471
Rainbow Mountain: 603, 606
Rainbow Trail: 256-257
Ralston Lake: 266
Ralston Peak: 265
Rancheria Falls: 427, 517
Rancheria Trail: 174-175
Rancho del Oso: 391, 394
Ranger Lakes: 561
raptors: Hawk Hill 317-318; Palisades Trail
    215-216
ratings: xii-xiii
Rattlesnake Canyon: 656-657
Rattlesnake Lake: 90, 93-94
Ravenswood Open Space Preserve: 341-
    342
Ray Miller Trailhead: 706
Raymond Lake: 272-273
Razorback Ridge Trail: 376
Razor Point: 778
Rebel Ridge Trail: 227
Red and White Mountain: 527
Red Cathedral: 640
Red Cliffs: 673
Red Cone Loop: 473
Red Contes: 566
Red Fir Meadow: 559
Red Hill: 46
Redinger Lake: 515
Redrock Beach: 313
Red Rock Canyon State Park: 673
Red Rock Falls: 511

Reds Meadows: 458
Reds Meadows Resort: 471
Red Star Ridge: 239
Red Tahquitz: 756
Redwood Canyon: 542-543
Redwood Creek: 358
Redwood Creek Trail: 36-37
Redwood Crossing: 610
Redwood Exhibit Trail: 152
Redwood Loop: 78-79, 386-387
Redwood Mountain Loop: 543-544
Redwood National Park: 32-37
Redwood Regional Park: 358, 371
Redwood Trail: 310, 339-340
Redwood Trail Loop: 217-218
regional park departments: 823
Relief Reservoir: 420-421
reservations: national parks 819-820
Reynold Wilderness: 279
Ribbon Fall: 449
Richard Road's Trail: 340
Richardson Bay: 315
Richardson Lake: 281
Ridge Loop Trail: 365
Ridgeline Trail: 366
Ridge Trail: 391-392
Rift Zone Trail: 295
Rim Loop Trail: 77
Rim Trail: 129
Rincon Trail: 623-624
Rising Sun Loop Trail: 711-712
Ritter Peak: 458, 470
River Trail: 396, 470, 492, 540; see also
    Wrights Valley Trail
Road's End: 540, 541
Roaring River Falls: 540
Robert Louis Stevenson State Park: 216
Roberts Regional Recreation Area: 357
Robinson Creek Trail: 424-425
Robinson Lake: 550
Rockbound Pass: 263-264
Rockhouse Basin: 626
Rock Creek: 529
Rock Creek Canyon Trailhead: 530
Rock Hill Trail: 813
Rockhouse Basin: 628
Rock Lake: 189, 228
Rock Lake: 518
Rock Pool: 710-711
Rock Springs Trail: 305-306
Rocks Road/Cerro Este Trail: 370

RARE PLANTS

Blue Sky Ecological Preserve: 787-788
Eureka Dunes: 569
Guy Fleming Loop Trail: 777-778
Huckleberry Loop Path: 357
Razor Point and Beach Trail Loop: 778
Santa Rosa Plateau Vernal Pools: 740-741

Rocky Point: 77, 716
Rocky Point Trail: 312-313
Rocky Ridge: 405, 406, 488-489
Rocky Ridge Loop: 360
Rodeo Beach: 316
Rodeo Lagoon: 316
Rodeo Valley: 316
Rodeo Valley Trail: 315
Rodriguez Mountain: 787
rolling boulders: Shasta Summit Trail 108-
    109
Rooster Comb: 401
Rooster Comb Loop: 401-402
Root Creek Trail: 116
Rosalie Lake: 458
Rose Peak: 405
Rose Valley Falls: 665
Rose Valley Recreation Area: 664
Round Lake: 231, 266-267
Round Lake Trailhead: 193
Round Top Geologic Area: 271
Round Top Loop Trail: 354-355
Round Top Summit: 270
Round Valley: 609
Round Valley Trail: 756
rowing: Blue Sky Ecological Preserve 787-
    788
Rubicon and Lighthouse Loop: 252
Rubicon Lake: 251
Rubicon Point: 252
Rubicon River: 239
Rubicon Trail: 252-253
Ruby Lake: 530-531
ruins: Chihuahua Mine 606; Knapp's
    Castle 653, 654
Rush Creek: 468
Rush Creek Canyon: 228
Russ City Park Double Loop: 79
Russian Ridge Open Space Preserve: 380-
    381
Russian Wilderness: 88, 99
Ruwau and Chocolate Lakes Loop: 535-536
Ryan Mountain Trail: 770-771

S

Sabrina Basin Trail: 532
Saddleback Butte: 674-675
Saddlebag Lake: 466
Saddlebag Lake Loop: 442-443
Saddlerock Lake: 535
Sailor Flat Trail: 234-235
St. Joseph's Hill Trail: 392
Saline Valley: 570
Salmon Creek Falls: 576, 624-625
Salt Creek Interpretive Trail: 640
salt flats: Saline Valley 570
salt marshes: Elkhorn Slough South
    Marsh Loop 484-485
Salt Point State Park: 208
Salton Sea: 773, 791, 792
Salton Sea National Wildlife Refuge: 813
Samuel P. Taylor State Park: 296
San Andreas Fault: 295, 723, 734
San Andreas Fault Trail: 379
San Benito County: 393
San Bernardino National Forest: 753, 761
Sanborn Creek: 389
Sanborn-Skyline County Park: 389
San Cristobel Tunnel: 397
Sand Dunes: 633
Sand Flat Trailhead: 107
sandhill cranes: Carrizo Plains 589-590;
    Los Banos Wildlife Area 499-500
Sand Hill Trail: 488
San Diego horned lizard: Blue Sky
    Ecological Preserve 787-788
Sand Point Overlook: 483
Sandstone Peak: 708
Sandy Wool Lake: 377
San Elijo Lagoon: 777
San Felipe Creek: 384
San Francisco: 304, 317, 319, 325, 327, 368,
    369
San Francisco Bay: 304, 315, 319, 326, 327,
    328, 348, 349, 375
San Francisco Bay National Wildlife
    Refuge: 343, 368, 369
San Francisco Fish and Game Refuge: 337
San Francisquito Canyon: 677
San Francisquito Canyon Road: 668
San Francisquito Creek: 343, 376
San Gabriel Canyon: 733
San Gabriel Mountains: 674, 721, 723, 724,
    732
San Gabriel Wilderness: 730, 741, 762

San Gorgonio Pass: 760-762, 768
San Gorgonio Wilderness: 753
San Jacinto Mountains: 759
San Jacinto Pass: 760
San Jacinto Peak: 756-757
San Jacinto State Park and Wilderness:
    756
San Joaquin Delta: 350
San Joaquin River: 351, 515, 565
San Joaquin Valley: 589
San Juan Canyon: 739
San Juan Loop Trail: 739
San Leandro Bay: 356
San Leandro Reservoir: 358
San Lorenzo Creek: 365
San Lorenzo River: 390-391, 396
San Luis National Wildlife Refuge: 499
San Mateo Bridge: 336, 368
San Mateo Canyon Wilderness: 739, 740
San Miguel Island: 695
San Pablo Bay: 304, 348, 349
San Pablo Reservoir: 349, 352
San Pablo Ridge: 349, 372
San Pablo Ridge Loop: 348-349
San Rafael Wilderness: 651, 652
Santa Barbara Island: 701
Santa Catalina Island Conservancy: 717
Santa Clara Estuary: 659
Santa Clara Tree: 386
Santa Clara Valley: 377, 382, 383, 389, 392,
    397
Santa Clarita Valley: 667
Santa Cruz: 396
Santa Cruz Island: 700
Santa Cruz Mountains: 338, 369, 382, 395,
    479, 484
Santa Cruz Trail: 654
Santa Lucia Mountains: 490, 493, 501, 580
Santa Lucia Wilderness: 583, 585
Santa Monica Mountains: 706, 707, 708,
    709, 714
Santa Monica Mountains Conservancy:
    668
Santa Monica Mountains National
    Recreation Area: 711
Santa Paula Canyon: 667
Santa Paula Creek: 667
Santa Paula Peak: 667-668
Santa Rosa Island: 699
Santa Rosa Plateau Vernal Pools: 740-741
Santa Teresa County Park: 397

Santa Ynez Canyon: 712-713
Santa Ynez Mountains: 652
Santa Ynez Recreation Area: 654
Santa Ynez Valley: 652
Santa Ysabel Valley: 788
San Ysidro Canyon: 659
San Ysidro Trail: 658-659
Sapphire Lake: 96
Saratoga Gap: 380
Saratoga Gap Loop: 389
Saratoga Gap Trail: 390
Sardine Falls: 421-422
Sardine Lake: 194
Satwiwa Loop Trail and Waterfall: 705-706
Satwiwa Native American Indian Culture
    Center: 705
savannah sparrow: Bolsa Chica
    Ecological Reserve 737; McGrath State
    Beach Nature Trail 659-660
Sawmill Lake: 230
Sawmill Mountain: 663
Sawpit Canyon: 731
Sawtooth Peak: 605
Sawtooth Ridge: 91, 425, 600
Sawtooth Trailhead: 604
Scenic Cliffs Preserve: 673
Schonchin Butte Trail: 66-67
Schoolhouse Creek: 209
Schulman Grove: 476
Scorpion Canyon: 700
Scott Mountain: 99, 123-124
Scott's Cabin Loop: 785
Sculptured Beach: 292
Seafoam Trail: 349
Sea Lion Point Trail: 487
Sea Lion Rocks: 487
sea lions: East Anacapa Island Loop Trail
    700-701; Pillar Point 337-338; Partington
    Point Trail 495-496
Seal Rock: 328
seal-watching: Lake Cleone Trail 155-156;
    Old Landing Cove Trail 481; Point
    Bennett 695-696; Sea Lion Point Trail 487
Second Dinkey Lake: 518
Second Falls: 536
Second Lake: 536-537
Secret Lake: 422
Seeley Creek Trail: 747-748
Seiad Valley: 55
Sentinel Dome: 451-452, 453
"sequedar": 616

Sequoia: see also Sequoya
Sequoia Creek: 520
Sequoia Crest: 612
Sequoia Lake Overlook: 521
Sequoia National Forest: 521, 678
Sequoia National Park: 538, 540
Sequoia Trail: 378, 388-389
Sequoya: see also Sequoia
Sequoya Challenge: 228
Serpentine Trail: 398-399
Settlers Loop Trail: 152-153
7-Ball Trail: 227
Seven Falls: 655-656
Seven Pines Trail: 757-758
Shackleford Creek Trail: 49-50
Shadow Cliffs Lake: 366
Shadow Lake: 251, 458
Shadow Lake Trail: 134
Shadow of the Giants: 512
shark migration: Dumbarton Pier 368-369
Shasta Summit Trail: 108-109
Shaver Lake: 516
Sheep Camp Trail: 337
Sheep Creek: 540
Sheep Mountain Wilderness: 741, 763
Shell Mountain: 545
Shell Tree: 388
Sherman Pass Vista: 620
Sherman Peak Trail: 620
Sherman Tree: 557
Sherrold Lake: 461
Sherwin Creek: 474
Shingle Falls: 223
Shinn Pond: 369
Shipwreck Trail: 716
Shoreline Loop Trail: 364
Shoreline Regional Park: 376-377
Shoreline Trail: 303, 304, 356, 367, 786
Shotgun Lake: 230
Showers Lake: 272, 281
Sibley Preserve: 354, 371, 372

SEQUOIA GROVES

Freeman Creek Trail: 614
Garfield Grove: 598-599
General Grant Tree: 521-522
Mariposa Grove: 457-458
Merced Grove: 428
Nelder Grove: 512
Trail of 100 Giants: 616-617
Tuolumne Grove: 429

Sierra Azul Loop: 393
Sierra Azul Open Space Preserve: 393
Sierra Azul Range: 392
Sierra Buttes: 191, 195
Sierra Buttes Trail: 194
Sierra-Callahan: 113-114
Sierra Discovery Trail: 230-231
Sierra National Forest: 457, 565
Sierra Pelona Ridge: 677
Sierra Vista National Scenic Byway: 513
Sierra Wilderness: 629
Signal Peak Loop Trail: 701-702
Siligo Peak: 95
Silliman Creek: 560
Silliman Crest: 546, 548
Silver Creek: 263, 611
Silver Falls: 387, 391
Silver Lake Trail: 468-469
silver mining: Chihuahua Mine 606; Keane
    Wonder Mine Trail 639
Silver Moccasin Trail: 722, 729-730

Silver Pass: 565
Silver Peak: 247
Silverwood Lake: 762
Silverwood Wildlife Sanctuary: 792
Sir Francis Drake Trail: 291
Sirretta Peak: 625
Siskiyou Wilderness: 41-43
Skillman Flat: 229
Skinner Ridge Trail to Devils Peak: 491
Skull Rock: 713
Skull Rock Nature Trail: 771-772
Sky High Lakes: 49
Skyline Boulevard: 338, 339, 340, 389
Skyline Gate: 371
Skyline Nature Trail Loop: 486
Skyline Ridge: 340, 389
Skyline Ridge Trail: 381
Skyline-to-Sea Trail: 387, 390-391
Skyline Trail: 340-341
Skylonda: 341
Sky Meadows: 474

SHORT HIKES

Amos Alonzo Stagg Tree: 612
Antelope Valley Poppy Reserve Loop: 674
Antioch Pier: 351
Arcata Marsh Trail: 78
Audubon Canyon Ranch Trail: 304
Bald Mountain Trail: 393-394
Bayside Trail: 778-779
Berkeley Pier: 352
Big Falls: 583-584, 754
Big Hendy Grove Trail: 158
Big Trees Interpretive Trail: 238
Black Wolf Falls: 606-607
Bodega Head Loop: 210-211
Bridalveil Fall: 448, 449-450
Cabrillo Tide Pools: 779
Canyon View Trail: 668
Cascade Falls: 255, 387
Cave Lake: 73-74
Cecilville Road: 99
Cedars Interpretive: 515-516
Chamberlain Creek Waterfall Trail: 157
Chester Marsh Trail: 499
Chicage Stump Trail: 518-519
Chimney Rock Trail: 188, 290-291
Columns of the Giants: 419
Contra Loma Loop: 354
Cottonwood Creek Botanical Trail: 203
Coyote Point Trail: 336
Devils Punchbowl Loop: 723-724

Don Castro Lake Loop: 365
East Peak Mount Tamalpais: 307-308
Elephant Trees: 808
Emerald Lake Trail: 474
Fern Canyon Loop Trail: 35-36
Fitzgerald Marine Reserve: 336
5 Allens' Trail: 79-80
Founders Grove Nature Trail: 81
Frazier Falls Trail: 192
Fremont Peak Trail: 501
Frog Pond Loop: 399
General Grant Tree: 521-522
Glacier Point: 450, 451, 453, 454
Golden Canyon Interpretive Trail: 640-641
Graham Trail Loop: 357
Grizzly Peak: 119
Guy Fleming Loop Trail: 777-778
Hawk Hill: 317-318
Headlands Loop: 207
Hi Grade National Recreation Trail: 74
Inaja Memorial Trail: 788
Indian Pools: 517-518
Inyo Craters: 469-470
Knapp's Castle: 653, 654
Lake of the Sky Trail: 256-257
Lake Trail: 218-219
Lexington Dam Trail: 392-393
Lily Lake: 73-74
Lookout Point Loop Trail: 151

Sky Trail: 490
Slate Mountain: 612, 614, 618
Slick Rock: 417
Slide Ranch: 313
Smith, James T.: 737
Smith Lake: 189, 261
Smith Meadows: 426
Smuggler's Cove: 700
Snag Lake: 183
Snivley's Ridge Trail: 490
Snow Mountain: 216
Snyder Trail: 653
Soberanes Canyon Loop: 488-489
Soberanes Point Trail: 489-490
Sobrante Ridge Trail: 350
Soda Gulch Trail: 338
Soda Lake: 589
Soda Spring: 437
Soda Springs: 601
Soldier Creek/Lewis Falls: 732
Soldier Creek Trail: 732

Soldier Meadows: 198
Soldier Ridge Trail: 166
Soldiers Trails: 553
Solomon Peak: 166
Solstice Canyon: 711
Solstice Road: 711-712
Sonoma Creek: 218
Sonora Pass: 460-462
Soup Spring Trailhead: 144
South Bay: 336, 340, 342
South Bay marsh: 343
South Bay Nature Trail: 343
South Beach Trail: 289-290
South Fork Bishop Creek Canyon: 534
South Fork Kings River: 540, 541
South Fork Merced River Trail: 448
South Fork National Recreation Trail: 97-98
South Fork Stanislaus River: 422
South Grove Loop: 411
South Kelsey Trail: 33

SHORT HIKES (cont.)

Lost Man Creek Trail: 36
Lower Yosemite Fall: 444-445, 452
Lukens Lake: 429-430
Magic Forest Nature Trail: 714-715
May Lake: 431-432
McClures Beach Trail: 286-287
McGrath State Beach Nature Trail: 659-660
Middle Falls Trail: 118-119
Millard Falls: 726
Mill Creek Falls Trailhead: 144-145
Morning Sun Trail: 315
Mosaic Canyon: 633-634
Mount Diablo Summit Loop: 362-363
Mount Wittenberg Loop: 294
Mud Creek Falls: 111
Nobe Young Falls: 617-618
Nojoqui Falls: 647-648
North Arroyo Trail: 366-367
North Grove Loop: 411, 521
Peppermint Creek Fals: 618-619
Piño Alto Trail: 652-653
Point Bonita Lighthouse: 317
Point Isabel Shoreline: 351-352
Ponderosa Vista Nature Trail: 751-752
Rainbow Falls Trail: 471
Rainbow Trail: 256-257
Redwood Exhibit Trail: 152
Redwood Trail: 310, 339-340
Roaring River Falls: 540

Robinson Lake: 550
Rocky Point Trail: 312-313
Rose Valley Falls: 665
Round Lake Trailhead: 193
Rubicon and Lighthouse Loop: 252
Salt Creek Interpretive Trail: 640
San Andreas Fault Trail: 379
San Juan Loop Trail: 739
Scott Mountain: 99, 123-124
Sea Lion Point Trail: 487
Seeley Creek Trail: 747-748
Sequoia Trail: 378, 388-389
Serpentine Trail: 398-399
Shadow Lake Trail: 134
Shadow of the Giants: 512
Shoreline Loop Trail: 364
Skull Rock Nature Trail: 771-772
Soup Spring Trailhead: 144
South Beach Trail: 289-290
Trail of 100 Giants: 616-617
Trona Pinnacles: 636
Upper Fisherman's Trail: 318
Uvas Park Waterfall Loop: 479-480
Vikingsholm: 253-254
Way of the Mono: 514
Whispering Pines Trail: 752
Winton Marsh Trail: 499
Woodland Trail: 751
Zumwalt Meadow Loop: 541

STEEP/ROUGH TRAILS

Alder Creek Falls: 457
Alec Canyon and Contour Loop: 480
Aliso Canyon Loop Trail: 653-654
Alta Peak: 558-559
Audubon Canyon Ranch Trail: 304
Balconies Caves: 501-502
Bay View Trail: 303-304, 484
Bayview Trail: 367
Beacroft Trail: 233-234
Bertha Peak: 750-751
Big Baldy: 547
Big Bear Lake Trail: 112-113
Black Butte Trail: 105
Boulder Lake: 419-420
Brewer Creek Trailhead: 110-111
Bunchgrass Trailhead: 131-132
Butano Loop: 385-386
Cannell Meadow National Recreation Trail:
  627
Castle Rock Trail: 750
Cedar Creek Falls: 790
Cerro Alto Summit: 579-580
Chamberlain Creek Waterfall Trail: 157
Chilnualna Falls: 456
Cinder Cone Trail: 135-136
Clouds Rest: 431, 432
Coit Lake: 399-400, 401
Condor Gulch and High Peaks Loop: 502-503
Cone Peak Lookout Trail: 496
Convict Canyon: 475
Copper Creek Trail: 542
Cougar Crest Trail: 750-751
Crags Trail: 116-117
Crystal Lake Trail: 606
Dardanelle: 418-419
Deep Creek Fishermen's Trail: 748-749
Deer Park Trail: 301-302
Deer Springs Trail: 756, 758
Desert View Trail: 755-756, 790-791
Devils Canyon Trail: 730
Dipsea Trail: 309, 311
Dripping Springs Trail: 783-784
Durphy Creek Loop: 151-152
Eagle Meadow: 418-419
East Ridge Loop: 358-359
Elizabeth Lake: 436
Ellis Peak: 249-250
Emerson Trailhead: 145
Escondido Falls: 711
Euchre Bar Trail: 231-232
Eureka Peak: 769
Ewoldsen Loop Trail: 495
False Gun Vista Point: 347-348

Fern Lake Loop: 472-473
Fowler Peak: 196-197
Gardisky Lake: 442
Garfield-Hockett Trail: 598-599
Gaviota Peak: 647
George Lake: 516-517
Giant Loop: 361-362
Gilmore Lake: 256, 258, 259, 281
Glass Mountain: 69
Granite Lake: 95, 273-274, 542
Great Mountain Lookout: 514-515
Grizzly Lake: 94-95
Half Dome: 363, 430, 432, 443, 447-448, 453,
  454
Harkins Ridge Trail: 338-339
Huckleberry Loop Path: 357
Ice House Saddle: 735-736
Illilouette Fall: 455
Inspiration Point: 308-309, 417, 448, 656, 701
Italian Bar Trail: 232
Jennie Lake: 545-546
Jordan Hot Springs: 616
Juniper Canyon and High Peaks Loop: 502
Kaiser Peak: 516
Kangaroo Lake Trailhead: 103-104
Keane Wonder Mine Trail: 639
Kitchen Creek Falls: 796-797
Las Zanjas Trail: 645-646
Lembert Dome: 439-440
Lewis Creek Trail: 538-539
Little North Fork Trailhead: 51
Little South Fork Lake Trail: 90-91
Loch Leven Lake: 235, 533-534
Long Canyon Trailhead: 95-96
Long Ridge Loop: 382
Lookout Peak: 539-540
Lost Coast Trail: 154-155
Lost Palms Oasis: 773-774
Magee Trailhead: 130
Manzanita and Azalea Loop: 522
Marble Falls: 550-551
Mastadon Peak: 773
McPherson Peak Trail: 651
Meadows Loop Trail: 341
Meysan Lake: 563
Middle Fork Trail: 551-552
Mississippi Lake Trail: 400-401
Mist and John Muir Loop: 446
Mist Trail: 445, 446, 454
Mitchell Peak: 546
Monarch Lakes: 605-606
Mono Pass: 441, 528-529, 530
Montecito Overlook: 657

STEEP/ROUGH TRAILS (cont.)

Monument Peak Trail: 377-378
Morning Sun Trail: 315
Moro Rock: 548, 552, 553-554
Mosquito Lakes: 275, 601-602
Mount Baden-Powell: 725, 729, 741
Mount Baldy: 734-735, 794
Mount Hoffman: 432
Mount St. Helena Trail: 215
Mount Tallac Loop Glen Alpine Trailhead: 258-259
Mount Whitney Trail: 562
Murietta Falls Trail: 406-407
Nevada Fall: 446, 453, 460
Niche, The: 513
Nicholas Flat Trail: 708-709
Nimitz Way: 352-353
Nordhoff Peak: 665-666
North Dome: 430-431, 443, 541
Observatory Trail: 786
Ocean View Trail: 312
Ollacon Peak: 486-487
Ostrander Lake: 450, 451
Overlook Loop: 168-169
Palisade Creek Trail: 244-245
Palisade Glacier: 537
Palisades Trail: 215-216
Paradise Ridge: 599
Peak Trail: 369-370, 489
Peppermint Creek Fals: 618-619
Poore Lake: 422
Pothole Trail: 666
Powderhorn Trail: 239-240
Preston Peak: 43, 44-45
Priest Rock Trail: 393
Prospect Peak Trail: 136
Relief Reservoir: 420-421
Robinson Lake: 550
Rocky Ridge Loop: 360
Rooster Comb Loop: 401-402
Round Top Summit: 270
Ruby Lake: 530-531
Russ City Park Double Loop: 79
Ruwau and Chocolate Lakes Loop: 535-536
Saddleback Butte: 674-675
Sailor Flat Trail: 234-235
St. Joseph's Hill Trail: 392
Salmon Creek Falls: 576, 624-625
Sand Flat Trailhead: 107
Santa Paula Peak: 667-668
San Ysidro Trail: 658-659
Schonchin Butte Trail: 66-67
Seven Pines Trail: 757-758

Shasta Summit Trail: 108-109
Shipwreck Trail: 716
Sierra-Callahan: 113-114
Silver Lake Trail: 468-469
Sirretta Peak: 625
Skinner Ridge Trail to Devils Peak: 491
Slate Mountain: 612, 614, 618
Snivley's Ridge Trail: 490
Snyder Trail: 653
Soldier Ridge Trail: 166
Stuart Fork Trailhead: 96
Summit Trail: 146-147, 320, 388, 614
Swift Creek Trail: 95
Table Mountain Trail: 173-174
Taft Point and the Fissures: 452, 453
Tamarack Lakes: 530
Tamarack Lake Trailhead: 116
Telescope Peak Trail: 635-636
Ten Lakes/Grant Lakes: 430
Timber Gap Trail: 604-605
Toumey Grove Trail: 154
Trail Creek Trail: 88
Twin Lakes: 135, 261-262, 466, 516-517, 560-561
Ubehebe Peak: 570-571
Upper Fisherman's Trail: 318
Upper Jamison Trail: 188
Upper Yosemite Fall: 443-444, 452
Valencia Peak: 582-583
Valentine Lake Trailhead: 474-475
Virginia Lakes Trail: 465
Vivian Creek Falls: 755
Walker Lake Trailhead: 467-468
Warren Peak: 143, 768-769
Watchtower: 557, 558
Waterfall Loop: 490
Waterwheel Falls: 438-439
West Fork Cold Springs: 658
West Ridge and Aptos Creek Loop: 483
Whaler's Knoll: 487-488
Whiskey Flat Trail: 621-622
White Chief Mine Trail: 604
Whitney Falls/Bolam Creek Trailhead: 105-106
Whitney Portal National Recreation Trail: 561-562
Whittemore Gulch: 339
Wildrose Peak Trail: 634-635
Winnemucca Lake Loop: 270
Woodchuck Basin to Wheeler Lake: 418
Yost Lake Trail: 469
Young Lakes Loop: 437-438

South Lake Trailhead: 208
South Lake: 518, 535
South Marsh Loop Trail: 485
South Plateau Trail: 488
South Ridge Loop: 736-737
South Ridge Trail: 759
South San Francisco Bay: 365
South Shore Trail: 488
South Sierra Wilderness: 621
Southwest Grove: 808
South Yolla Bolly Mountain: 165
South Yuba Independence Trail: 228
Spanish Mountain: 519
Spanish Ridge Trail: 82
Spearhead Lake: 535
Spencer Meadow Trail: 184
Spengler Trail: 353
Spicer Meadow Reservoir: 417
Spirit Lake Trail: 50-51
Split Rock: 620, 708
Springboard Trail: 406
Spring Creek: 601
Spring Lake Trail: 217
Spring Trail: 492
Spring Valley Trail: 369
spring water: Old Ski Bowl Trailhead 111-112
Spruce Creek Trail: 576
Squatter's Cabin: 556
Squaw Creek: 267
Squaw Lake: 565
Squaw Peak: 147
Squaw Valley: 282
Stafford Mountain: 187, 196
Stagg Tree: 612
Stairstep Falls: 296
Stanford Point: 448-449
Stanislaus National Forest: 427-428
Stanislaus River: 420
Stapelveldt Trail: 307
Star Mine: 354
state forests: 822
Stateline Lookout: 246-247
state offices: 823
state parks: 819
Statue Lake: 53
Steamboat Canyon: 239
Steelhead Lake: 527-528
Steep Ravine Canyon: 309
Steep Ravine Trail: 311
Stevens Creek Nature Trail: 379-380

Stevenson, Rovert Louis: 487
Stevens Trail: 236
Stewartsville Trail: 354
Stillwater Cove: 209
Stinson Beach: 310
Stockoff Creek Loop: 209
Stonebridge: 359
Stone Ridge Trail: 575
Stonewall Mine: 793
Stonewall Peak Trail: 793
Stoney Creek Trail: see Stony Creek Trail
Stony Creek Trail: 28
Stony Ridge Lake: 249
Storm Canyon: 794
Stout Grove Trail: 29
Stream Trail Loop: 358
Stuart Fork Trailhead: 96
Stump Beach Trail: 208-209
Sturtevant Falls: 7272
Sugarloaf Mountain: 166
Sugarloaf Ridge State Park: 218
Sugar Pine Point State Park: 250
Sugar Pine Reservoir: 237
Suicide Rock: 758
Suisun Bay: 353, 360
Suki Goldman Nature Center: 715
Summit Lake: 95, 246, 465
Summit Lake Loop: 134-135
Summit Meadow: 540
Summit National Recreation Trail: 614
Summit Rock Loop: 389-390
Summit Springs Trail: 340
Summit Trail: 146-147, 320, 388, 614
Summit Valley Trail: 33-34
Sunday Peak Trail: 623vws
Sunnyvale Baylands: 377
Sunol Loop: 370
Sunol-Ohlone Regional Wilderness: 406
Sunol Regional Wilderness: 370
Sunrise Highway Trail: 799-800
Sunrise Lakes: 432, 433
Sunset Rock: 563
Sunset Trail: 320-321, 520-521, 792
Surprise Canyon Grove: 808
Surprise Valley: 74
Susan River Canyon: 185
Susanville Railroad Depot: 185
Susie Lake: 256, 257, 281
suspension bridge: Point Bonita Lighthouse 317
Sutil Island: 702

Sutro Baths: 326
Sutter Buttes: 216
Swanson Creek: 479
Swede Lake: 518
Sweetwater River: 793
Swift Creek Trail: 95
Switzer Falls: 725
Sycamore Canyon Falls: 705
Sycamore Canyon Preserve: 789
Sycamore Canyon Trail: 705
Syd Cabin Ridge Trail: 164

T

Table Mountain: 617
Table Mountain Trail: 173-174
Tadpole Creek: 233
Taft Point and the Fissures: 452, 453
Tahoe National Forest: 191
Tahquitz Peak: 756, 758, 759-760
Tallac Point: 256
Tallac Trailhead: 255
tallest lodgepole pine: 749-750
tallest sand dunes in California: Eureka
    Dunes 569
tallest waterfall in North America: Upper
    Yosemite Fall 443-444
Tall Trees Trail: 37
Tamarack Lake: 266
Tamarack Lakes: 530
Tamarack Lake Trailhead: 116
Tamarack Trailhead: 131
Tamarisk Grove: 806
Tan Bark Trails: 495-496
Tangerine Falls: 658
Taylor Creek Marsh: 256
Taylor Dome: 625
Taylor Lake Trail: 52-53
Tehachapi Mountains: 670, 674
Tehachapi Pass: 670, 677-678
Tehachapis: 612
Tehama Wildlife Area: 173
Telegraph Canyon: 736-737
Telegraph Peak: 735
Telescope Peak Trail: 635-636
Temescal Canyon and Ridge Trail: 713
Tenaja Falls: 740
Tenaya Canyon: 431, 432, 433, 459
Tenaya Canyon Loop: 447
Tenaya Creek: 447
Tenaya Lake: 432, 433-434
Ten Lakes/Grant Lakes: 430

Tennessee Valley: 314-315
Teutonia Peak: 691
Tharp, Hale: 554
Tharp's Log: 554
Thermalito Trail: 366
Thimble Peak: 268
Thomas Aquinas College: 667
Thomas Wright Trail: 66
Thompson Peak: 94
Thompson Ridge: 532
Thornton Beach: 328
Thousand Island Lake: 458, 470
Three Brothers: 444
Three Graces: 457
Three Lakes: 197
Three Points: 669-670, 741-743
Thunder Mountain: 735
Tidelands Trail: 368
tide pools: Cabrillo Tide Pools 779
Tilden Regional Park: 372
Tiltill Creek: 427
Timber Gap Trail: 604-605
Timber Mountain: 69-70, 735
times: xiii
Tinker Knob: 247
Tioga Pass: 441
Tioga Peak: 442
TJ/Barrett Lake Trail; 473-474
Toad Lake Trail: 113
Toiyabe National Forest: 274
Tokopah Falls: 560
Tokopah Valley: 557, 558
Tomales Bay: 288
Tomales Bay State Park: 288
Tomales Point Trail: 285-286
Tomhead Saddle Loop: 163-164
Topanga State Park: 712, 713
Toro County Park: 486
Torote Bowl: 808
Torrey pines: Guy Fleming Loop Trail 777-
    778; Razor Point and Beach Trail Loop
    778
Torrey Pines State Reserve: 778
Torrey Pines Trail: 699-700
Toumey Grove Trail: 154
Tourist Club: 310
Towsley Canyon: 668
Trail Camp Loop: 390
Trail Canyon Falls: 721
Trail Canyon Trail: 721-722
Trail Creek Trail: 88

Trail Crest: 564
Trail Gulch: 88-89
Trail Gulch Lake: 89
trail names: xiii
Trail of 100 Giants: 616-617
Trail of the Gargoyles: 420
Trail Pass: 608-609, 629
Trail Peak: 609
Trans Preserve Trail: 741
Treasure Island: 487
Tree of Heaven Trail: 59
TreePeople: 714
Tresidder Peak: 459
tricolored blackbird: Winton Marsh Trail
   499
Trinidad Head: 77
Trinity Alps: 87
Trinity Divide: 116
Trinity River: 89
Triple Falls: 480
Trona Pinnacles: 636
Tropical Terrace: 711
Tsurai Loop: 77-78
Tubatulabal Indians: 623
Tub Flat: 610
Tueeulala Falls: 426
Tufa Falls: 601, 603
tufa formations: Fossil Falls 626-627;
   Mono Lake South Tufa Trail 467; Trona
   Pinnacles 636
Tularcitos/Agua Caliente Trail: 377
Tulare Peak: 603
Tule Elk State Reserve: 593
Tule River: 610
Tule River Valley: 617
Tully Hole: 566
Tumamait, Vincent: 663
tunnel: White Chief Mine Trail 604
Tunnel Log: 543
Tunnel Trail: 503
Tuolumne Falls: 438, 439, 460
Tuolumne Grove: 429
Tuolumne Meadows: 427, 435, 440, 458-461
Tuolumne River: 427
Tuoski Trail: 585
Turkey Ridge: 585
Turner Creek: 491
20 Lakes Basin: 442, 466
Twin Lakes: 135, 261-262, 466, 516-517, 560-
   561
Twin Oaks Trail: 481

Twin Peaks: 247
Two Harbors: 716-717
Two Harbors Visitor Services: 717
Two Lakes Trail: 301
Two Waters Trail: 584-585
Tyee Lakes: 534
Tyler Lake: 262-263

UV
Ubehebe Crater: 569
Ubehebe Peak: 570-571
Unal Trail: 623
Unicorn Peak: 436, 439, 440
Union Lake Trail: 92
Union Valley Reservoir: 194
unusual rock: Marble Mountain 47-48;
   Statue Lake 53
Upper Angora Lake: 260
Upper Echo Lakes: 266
Upper Falls: 480
Upper Fisherman's Trail: 318
Upper Gaylor Lake: 441-442
Upper Hamilton Lake: 555
Upper Horse Meadow: 466
Upper Jamison Trail: 188
Upper Manzana Creek Trail: 651-652
Upper Morgan Lake: 529
Upper Pine Lake: 531
Upper San Joaquin River: 470
Upper Soda Springs Trailhead: 470-471
Upper Stevens Creek County Park: 389
Upper Velma Lake: 254, 281
Upper Yosemite Fall: 443-444, 452
U.S. Army Corps of Engineers: 822
Uvas Park: 480
Uvas Park Waterfall Loop: 479-480
Vail Lake: 783
Valencia Peak: 582-583
Valentine Lake Trailhead: 474-475
Vallecito Mountains: 807
Vallecitos Trail: 398
Valle Vista Staging Area: 355
Valley View Trail: 493
Van Dusen Canyon Road: 761-762
Vasquez Rocks County Park: 675, 676—677
Velma Lakes: 254-255
Velvet Peak: 683
Ventana Wilderness: 492, 496
Vernal Fall: 445, 453, 460
vernal pools: Santa Rosa Plateau Vernal
   Pools 740-741

VIEWS

Aerial Tramway: 755-757
Agave Trail: 325-326
Agnew Meadows Trailhead: 458
Alamere Falls Trail: 298-299
Alder Creek Falls: 457
Alec Canyon and Contour Loop: 480
Aliso Canyon Loop Trail: 653-654
Alta Peak: 558-559
Angora Lakes Trail: 259-260
Anniversary Trail: 375
Asilomar Coast Trail: 485-486
Aspen Grove Trail: 753-754
Bald Mountain Loop: 218
Bayside Trail: 778-779
Bay View Loop: 348, 484
Bay View Trail: 303-304, 484
Bayview Trail: 367
Bear Canyon Loop Trail: 739-740
Berry Creek Falls: 387, 391
Bertha Peak: 750-751
Big Baldy: 547
Bizz Johnson: 185
Blue Lake: 465, 532
Bodega Head Loop: 210-211
Bolinas Ridge: 207, 297
Boole Tree Loop: 519-520
Borel Hill Trail: 380-381
Bort Meadow: 359, 371
Boucher Trail: 785
Bridalveil Fall: 448, 449-450
Briones Crest Loop: 353
Buena Vista Peak: 544
Burney Falls Trail: 128-129
Burney Mountain Summit: 129
Burst Rock: 423-424
Butano Loop: 385-386
Buzzards Roost Trail: 493
Cabrillo Peak: 581
Cannell Meadow National Recreation Trail: 627
Canyon View Trail: 668
Caribou Lakes Trail: 91-92
Carson Falls: 300-301
Cascade Falls: 255, 387
Castle Lake Road: 115
Castle Rock Trail: 750
Cathedral Lakes: 434, 459
Cedar Creek Falls: 790
Cerro Alto Summit: 579-580
Chilnualna Falls: 456
Chimney Rock Trail: 188, 290-291
China Cove: 488
Cinder Cone Trail: 135-136
Coal Creek Open Space: 380

Coastal Trail: 326, 327; Fort Barry 316-317;
    Fort Cronkhite 316
Coast Trail: 292-293, 298
Cold Springs Nature Trail: 600
Columbia Point: 443
Condor Gulch and High Peaks Loop: 502-503
Cone Peak Lookout Trail: 496
Copper Creek Trail: 542
Cottonwood Pass: 608
Cowles Mountain: 791
Coyote Peak Loop: 397
Coyote Point Trail: 336
Crags Trail: 116-117
Crystal Lake Trail: 606
Cuyamaca Peak Trail: 792-793
Cypress Grove: 487-488
Davenport Beach: 395
Deadfall Lakes Trail: 104-105
Deer Park Trail: 301-302
Deer Springs Trail: 756, 758
Desert View Nature Trail: 795-796
Desert View Trail: 755-756, 790-791
Devils Punchbowl Loop: 723-724
Dog Lake: 437, 440-441
Dome Rock: 618, 620
Donner Falls: 361
Dorothy Lake: 460, 475, 530
Dripping Springs Trail: 783-784
Dumbarton Bridge: 343, 367-368
Duna Vista Trail: 584-585
Eagle Creek Trail: 396
Eagle Lake Trail: 602-603
Eagle Peak: 444
Eagle Rock Loop: 382-383, 712
East Anacapa Island Loop Trail: 700-701
East Ridge Loop: 358-359
Empire Landing Road Trail: 717-718
Eureka Peak: 769
Ewoldsen Loop Trail: 495
False Gun Vista Point: 347-348
Farewell Gap Trail: 601, 603
Feather Falls National Recreation Trail: 186
Fern Lake Loop: 472-473
Fishbowls: 664
Forest View Trail: 238
Fort Cronkhite: 316
Four-Mile Trail: 453
Fourth of July Saddle: 271
Fowler Peak: 196-197
Franklin Lakes: 603-604
Fremont Peak Trail: 501
Fresno Dome: 512
Gardisky Lake: 442

(continues on next page)

VIEWS *(cont.)*

Garfield-Hockett Trail: 598-599
Garnet Peak: 794
Gaviota Peak: 647
George Lake: 516-517
Ghost Mountain Trail: 806-807
Giant Loop: 361-362
Golden Canyon Interpretive Trail: 640-641
Golden Gate Bridge: 311, 317, 318, 319, 320, 326, 327-328, 363
Great Mountain Lookout: 514-515
Grizzly Lake: 94-95
Grizzly Peak: 119
Grouse Falls: 237-238
Gumboot Lake Trailhead: 114-115
Guy Fleming Loop Trail: 777-778
Half Dome: 363, 430, 432, 443, 447-448, 453, 454
Hastain Trail: 715
Hawk Hill: 317-318
Haypress Meadows Trailhead: 50
Headlands Loop: 207
Heath Falls Overlook: 244
Heather Lake: 257, 281, 557, 558
High Ridge Loop: 365-366
High Sierra Trail: 554-556
High View Nature Trail: 767-768
Ice House Saddle: 735-736
Inaja Memorial Trail: 788
Inspiration Point: 308-309, 417, 448, 656, 701
Inspiration Point Trail: 714
Jacks Peak: 486
Jenks Lake: 752-753
Jennie Lake: 545-546
Jordan Peak Lookout: 612-613
Juan Crespi Loop: 398
Kaiser Peak: 516
Kangaroo Lake Trailhead: 103-104
Keane Wonder Mine Trail: 639
Kearsage Pass: 548-549
Kearsage Pass Trail: 549
King Crest Trail: 83
Kings Canyon Overlook: 539
Kings Castle Trail: 47
Knapp's Castle: 653, 654
Kreyenhagen Peak: 589
Lake of the Sky Trail: 256-257
Lakeshore Trail: 415, 417
Lakes Trail, The: 557-558, 559
Lands End Trail: 326-327
Las Zanjas Trail: 645-646
Lassen Summit Trail: 133-134
Leffingwell Landing: 579
Lembert Dome: 439-440
Lightning Ridge Trail: 794-795

Little Baldy: 548, 553
Little Crystal Lake:
Little Falls: 584
Little Lakes Valley: 529-530
Little Mount Hoffman: 68-69
Loch Leven Lake: 235, 533-534
Loch Lomond Loop: 395-396
Lone Pine Lake: 562-563
Long Ridge Loop: 382
Lookout Peak: 539-540
Lookout Point: 426-427
Lost Coast Trail: 154-155
Lost Horse Mine: 772
Lost Palms Oasis: 773-774
Lower Gaylor Lake: 435-436
Marble Mountain Rim: 47-48
Mastadon Peak: 773
Matt Davis Trail: 310-311
Matterhorn Canyon: 460
McClures Beach Trail: 286-287
McGurk Meadow: 450
McMenemy Trail: 659
McWay Falls Overlook: 494-495
Middle Fork Trail: 551-552
Mishe Mokwa and Backbone Loop: 708
Mist Falls: 541-542
Mitchell Peak: 546
Miwok Loop: 314
Molera Point Trail: 491
Molera State Park Loop: 492
Monarch Lakes: 605-606
Mono Pass: 441, 528-529, 530
Monrovia Canyon Falls: 730-731
Montaña de Oro Bluffs Trail: 582
Montecito Overlook: 657
Morning Sun Trail: 315
Moro Rock: 548, 552, 553-554
Mosaic Canyon: 633-634
Mosquito Lakes: 275, 601-602
Mount Baden-Powell: 725, 729, 741
Mount Baldy: 734-735, 794
Mount Diablo Summit Loop: 362-363
Mount Islip: 733-734
Mount Tallac from Tallac Trailhead: 255-256
Mount Tallac Loop Glen Alpine Trailhead: 258-259
Mount Waterman: 722, 723
Mount Whitney Trail: 562
Mount Williamson: 724
Mount Wittenberg Loop: 294
Mount Woodson: 789-790
Mud Creek Falls: 111
Mule Peak Lookout: 617
Mumford Bar Trail: 232-233

VIEWS (cont.)

Murietta Falls Trail: 406-407
Needles Lookout: 615
Niche, The: 513
Nicholas Flat Trail: 708-709
Nimitz Way: 352-353
Nojoqui Falls: 647-648
Nordhoff Peak: 665-666
North Dome: 430-431, 443, 541
North Fork of Big Pine Canyon: 536
North Gate Trailhead: 106-107
North Ridge/Sunset Trail: 320-321
Oats Peak: 582-583
Ocean Overlook: 709-710
Old Landing Cove Trail: 481
Ollason Peak: 486-487
Omega Overlook: 229
Osborne Hill: 415-416
Palisade Creek Trail: 244-245
Palisades Trail: 215-216
Panorama Trail: 454-455, 492
Panoramic Point: 522-523
Panther Creek: 551-552
Paradise Ridge: 599
Parker Lake Trail: 468
Park Ridge Lookout: 522-523
Partington Point Trail: 495-496
Peak Trail: 369-370, 489
Penner Lake: 229-230
Peppermint Creek Fals: 618-619
Perimeter Road: 319-320
Pictograph Trail: 807-808
Piño Alto Trail: 652-653
Piñon Ridge Nature Trail: 732-733
Pioneer Trail: 229
Pohono Trail: 448, 453-454
Point Bonita Lighthouse: 317
Point Isabel Shoreline: 351-352
Ponderosa Vista Nature Trail: 751-752
Pothole Trail: 666
Preston Peak: 43, 44-45
Prospect Peak Trail: 136
Rainbow Falls Trail: 471
Rainbow Trail: 256-257
Rattlesnake Canyon: 656-657
Razor Point: 778
Red Cliffs: 673
Redwood Mountain Loop: 543-544
Relief Reservoir: 420-421
Ridgeline Trail: 366
Ridge Trail: 391-392
Rim Loop Trail: 77
Rim Trail: 129
Robinson Lake: 550
Rocky Point Trail: 312-313
Rocky Ridge: 405, 406, 488-489
Rocky Ridge Loop: 360
Rooster Comb Loop: 401-402
Round Top Summit: 270
Round Valley Trail: 756
Rubicon and Lighthouse Loop: 252
Ruby Lake: 530-531
Ruwau and Chocolate Lakes Loop: 535-536
Ryan Mountain Trail: 770-771
Saddleback Butte: 674-675
Saddlebag Lake Loop: 442-443
Sailor Flat Trail: 234-235
St. Joseph's Hill Trail: 392
San Andreas Fault: 295, 723, 734
Sand Flat Trailhead: 107
San Jacinto Peak: 756-757
San Juan Loop Trail: 739
Santa Cruz Trail: 654
Santa Paula Peak: 667-668
Schonchin Butte Trail: 66-67
Sea Lion Point Trail: 487
Seeley Creek Trail: 747-748
Settlers Loop Trail: 152-153
Shasta Summit Trail: 108-109
Sherman Peak Trail: 620
Shipwreck Trail: 716
Shoreline Trail: 303, 304, 356, 367, 786
Showers Lake: 272, 281
Sierra Buttes Trail: 194
Signal Peak Loop Trail: 701-702
Silver Pass: 565
Sir Francis Drake Trail: 291
Sirretta Peak: 625
Skinner Ridge Trail to Devils Peak: 491
Skyline Nature Trail Loop: 486
Skyline-to-Sea Trail: 387, 390-391
Slate Mountain: 612, 614, 618
Snivley's Ridge Trail: 490
Snyder Trail: 653
Soberanes Point Trail: 489-490
Stanford Point: 448-449
Stateline Lookout: 246-247
Steep Ravine Trail: 311
Stevens Trail: 236
Stonewall Peak Trail: 793
Stump Beach Trail: 208-209
Suicide Rock: 758
Summit Rock Loop: 389-390
Sunrise Lakes: 432, 433
Sycamore Canyon Preserve: 789
Tahquitz Peak: 756, 758, 759-760
Tan Bark Trails: 495-496
Telescope Peak Trail: 635-636

(continues on next page)

VIEWS (cont.)

Temescal Canyon and Ridge Trail: 713
Ten Lakes/Grant Lakes: 430
Tennessee Valley: 314-315
Teutonia Peak: 691
Tidelands Trail: 368
Tomales Point Trail: 285-286
Toumey Grove Trail: 154
Trail Camp Loop: 390
Trail Canyon Trail: 721-722
Trail Creek Trail: 88
Tsurai Loop: 77-78
Twin Lakes: 135, 261-262, 466, 516-517, 560-561
Ubehebe Peak: 570-571
Upper Gaylor Lake: 441-442
Upper Jamison Trail: 188
Valencia Peak: 582-583
Vetter Mountain Lookout: 729
Vikingsholm: 253-254
Vincent Tumamait Trail: 663-664

Vista Point: 227, 318
Warren Peak: 143, 768-769
Watchtower: 557, 558
Way of the Mono: 514
West Fork Cold Springs: 658
West Ridge and Aptos Creek Loop: 483
Whaler's Knoll: 487-488
White Chief Mine Trail: 604
Whitney Falls/Bolam Creek Trailhead: 105-106
Whitney Portal: 564-565
Whittemore Gulch: 339
Wilder Ridge and Zane Grey Trails: 481-482
Wildrose Peak Trail: 634-635
Willow Creek: 197, 513-514
Winnemucca Lake Loop: 270
Woodland Trail: 751
Yellow Bluff Trail: 319
Young Lakes Loop: 437-438
Yucca Point: 537-538
Zumwalt Meadow Loop: 541

Vetter Mountain Lookout: 729
Vicente Flat Trail: see Kirk Creek/Vicente Flat Trail
Vidette Meadow: 564
Vikingsholm: 253-254
Vikingsholm Castle: 252
Vincent Gap: 725
Vincent Tumamait Trail: 663-664
Virginia Canyon: 465
Virginia Lakes Trail: 465
Vista Peak: 365
Vista Point: 227, 318
Vivian Creek Trail: 755
Vogelsang Loop: 434-435
Volcanic Tableland: 475
Volcan Mountains: 788
volcano: Mount Round Top 354
Vollmer Peak: 372
Volvon Loop Trail/Bob Walker Ridge: 363-364

WX

Waddell Creek: 388, 390
Waddell Creek Trail: 394-395
Walker Lake Trailhead: 467-468
Walker, Bob: 363
Walker Pass: 628, 678-679
walk-through tree: Tuolumne Grove 429
Wapama Falls: 426

Ward Creek: 248-249
Ward Peak: 282
Warner Springs: 800-801
Warren Lake: 245-246
Warren Peak: 143, 768-769
Warrior Lake: 565
Washington Tree: 556
Watchtower: 557, 558
Waterdog Lake Trail: 337
"Waterfall House": 494
Waterfall Loop: 490
Waterfall Loop Trail: 166-167; see also Uvas Park Waterfall Loop
Waterfall Trail: 668
Waterfowl Tour Route: 499
Waterman Gap: 390
Waters Gulch Overlook: 119-120
water slides: Alder Creek 619; Bear Canyon 725-726; Gabrielino Trail 725-726
Waterwheel Falls: 438-439
Watson Monument: 248
Waugh Lake: 469
Wawona Dome: 456
Wawona Meadow Loop: 455-456
Wawona Tunnel: 453
Wawona Tunnel Trailhead: 448
Way of the Mono: 514
Weaver Lake: 544-545
Webb Creek: 311

WATERFALLS

Alamere Falls: 293
Alamere Falls Trail: 298-299
Alder Creek Falls: 457
Angel Falls: 513
Barnabe Trail: 296
Basin Falls: 480
Berry Creek Falls: 387, 391
Big Falls: 583-584, 754
Big Santa Anita Canyon: 727-728
Black Rock Falls: 479
Black Wolf Falls: 606-607
Borrego Palm Canyon Falls: 805
Bridalveil Fall: 448, 449-450
Burney Falls Trail: 128-129
Burnt Ranch Falls: 93
California Falls: 438
Canyon Creek Lakes Trailhead: 97
Carlon Falls: 427-428
Carson Falls: 300-301
Cascade Falls: 255, 387
Cataract Falls: 299-300
Cedar Creek Falls: 790
Chamberlain Creek Waterfall Trail: 157
Chilnualna Falls: 456
Coast Trail: 292-293, 298
Codfish Creek Trail: 235-236
Codfish Falls: 235
Cooper Canyon Falls: 722-723, 741
Corlieu Falls: 511
Cottonwood Creek Falls: 795
Crystal Creek: 603, 606
Darwin Falls: 634
Dawn Falls: 302-303
Deep Creek Fishermen's Trail: 748-749
Devils Canyon Trail: 730
Devils Postpile: 470, 471, 473
Devils Slide: 513
Donner Falls: 361
Doyle Trail: 611-612
Eagle Falls: 253, 254
East Fork Bridge: 599-600
Easton Canyon: 727
Ella Falls: 520
Escondido Falls: 711
Falls Loop Trail: 156-157
Farewell Gap Trail: 601, 603
Feather Falls National Recreation Trail: 186
First Falls: 536
First Water Trail: 728
Franklin Lakes: 603-604
Frazier Falls Trail: 192
Gabrielino Trail: 725-726, 727
Golden Falls: 387, 391

Greenstone Lake: 443
Green Valley Falls: 793
Grizzly Lake: 94-95
Grotto Trail: 707-708
Grouse Falls: 237-238
Heart Rock Falls: 747
Heather Lake: 257, 281, 557, 558
Hermit Falls: 728
Hetch Hetchy Reservoir: 426, 427
Holy Jim Falls: 737-738
Horsetail Falls: 527
Hot Springs Creek Waterfall: 274
Jack Creek Nature Trail: 786-787
Kearsage Pass: 548-549
Kickapoo Waterfall: 89
Kitchen Creek: 798
Kitchen Creek Falls: 796-797
Ladybug Falls: 597
Laurel Dell Loop: 304-305
LeConte Falls: 438
Lewis Creek: 511
Limekiln Falls: 575
Little Falls: 584
Little South Fork Lake Trail: 90-91
Lookout Point: 426-427
Los Peñasquitos Canyon: 788-789
Lower Falls: 471
Lower McCloud Falls: 118
Lower Yosemite Fall: 444-445, 452
Lundy Lake Trailhead: 465-466
Maidenhair Falls: 805-806
Maple Falls: 48, 482
Marble Falls: 550-551
McArthur-Burney Falls State Park: 139-140
McGee Creek Trail: 527-528
McWay Falls Overlook: 494-495
Middle Falls Trail: 118-119
Millard Falls: 726
Mill Creek Falls Trailhead: 144-145
Minaret Falls: 471
Mist Falls: 541-542
Monrovia Canyon Falls: 730-731
Mud Creek Falls: 111
Murietta Falls Trail: 406-407
Murray Canyon Trail: 772-773
Nevada Fall: 446, 453, 460
Nobe Young Falls: 617-618
Nojoqui Falls: 647-648
Peppermint Creek Falls: 618-619
Pfeiffer Falls and Valley View Loop: 492
Pine Valley: 493-494
Placerita Creek Waterfall: 668-669
Rainbow Falls Trail: 471

(continues on next page)

WATERFALLS (cont.)

Rancheria Falls: 427, 517
Red Rock Falls: 511
Ribbon Fall: 449
Rincon Trail: 623-624
Roaring River Falls: 540
Rose Valley Falls: 665
Salmon Creek Falls: 576, 624-625
San Andreas Fault: 295, 723, 734
San Juan Loop Trail: 739
Santa Paula Creek: 667
Santa Ynez Canyon: 712-713
San Ysidro Trail: 658-659
Sardine Falls: 421-422
Satwiwa Loop Trail and Waterfall: 705-706
Second Falls: 536
Seeley Creek Trail: 747-748
Seven Falls: 655-656
Silver Falls: 387, 391
Skyline-to-Sea Trail: 387, 390-391
Soldier Creek/Lewis Falls: 732
Solstice Road: 711-712
South Yuba Independence Trail: 228
Sunol Loop: 370
Sunset Trail: 320-321, 520-521, 792
Susie Lake: 256, 257, 281
Switzer Falls: 725
Sycamore Canyon Falls: 705
Tangerine Falls: 658

Temescal Canyon and Ridge Trail: 713
Tenaja Falls: 740
Tokopah Falls: 560
Trail Canyon Falls: 721
Triples Falls: 480
Tueeulala Falls: 426
Tufa Falls: 601, 603
Tuolumne Falls: 438, 439, 460
Upper Falls: 480
Upper Yosemite Fall: 443-444, 452
Uvas Park Waterfall Loop: 479-480
Vernal Fall: 445, 453, 460
Vikingsholm: 253-254
Vivian Creek Falls: 755
Wapama Falls: 426
Waterfall Loop: 490
Waterfall Loop Trail: 166-167; see also Uvas Park Waterfall Loop
Waterwheel Falls: 438-439
West Fork Cold Springs: 658
White Chief Mine Trail: 604
Whitney Falls/Bolam Creek Trailhead: 105-106
Wilderness Falls: 44
Wild Plum Loop/Haypress Creek: 194-195
Wildwood Park Loop: 710
Willow Creek: 197, 513-514
Wolf Creek Trail: 277-278

Wedding Rock: 77
Weir and Lower Doane Valley Loop: 784-785
Wellman Divide: 756
Werder Picnic Area: 340
west Delta: 353
Western Divide: 564
Western Mono Indians: 514, 515
Western States Trail: 248
Western States Trail/McGuire: 238-239
Western States Trail/Michigan Bluff: 237
West Fork Cold Springs: 658
West Lake: 425
West Ridge and Aptos Creek Loop: 483
West Snow Mountain: 166, 168
West Walker River: 422
West Walker-Sonora Emigrant Trail: 423
Whaleback, The: 60-61
Whale Peak: 489
Whale Rock Reservoir: 580
Whaler's Knoll: 487-488
wheelchair access: xiii

Wheeler Lake: 418
Whiskey Flat Trail: 621-622
Whispering Pines Trail: 752
whistling swans: Alder Creek Trail 207
White Chief: 601
White Chief Mine Trail: 604
White Cloud: 229
White Creek Lake: 90

WHALE-WATCHING

Bodega Head Loop: 210-211
Cabrillo Tide Pools: 779
Headlands Loop: 207
Lake Cleone Trail: 155-156
Leffingwell Landing: 579
McWay Falls Overlook: 494-495
Nicholas Flat Trail: 708-709
Partington Point Trail: 495-496
Rim Loop Trail: 77
Rocky Point Trail: 312-313
Soberanes Point Trail: 489-490
Willow Creek Overlook: 708

WILDFLOWERS

Alder Creek Falls: 457
Aliso Canyon Loop Trail: 653-654
Alta Peak: 558-559
Antelope Valley Poppy Reserve Loop: 674
Aspen Grove Trail: 753-754
Azalea Trail: 522
Bear Canyon Loop Trail: 739-740
Bear Lake: 423
Big Falls: 583-584, 754
Blue Sky Ecological Preserve: 787-788
Bort Meadow: 359, 371
Brewer Creek Trailhead: 110-111
Bridalveil Creek: 449, 450-451, 453
Buckeye Creek Trail: 424
Cabrillo Peak: 581
Camp Lake: 423
Carrizo Plains: 589-590
Casa Vieja Meadow: 615-616
Cave Lake: 73-74
Clenaga Mirth: 537
Codfish Creek Trail: 235-236
Coit Lake: 399-400, 401
Cold Springs Nature Trail: 600
Cottonwood Creek Falls: 795
Cottonwood Lakes: 607-608
Deer Park Trail: 301-302
Desert Tortoise Discovery Loop: 673-674
Dinkey Lakes: 518
Dripping Springs Trail: 783-784
Duna Vista Trail: 584-585
East Anacapa Island Loop Trail: 700-701
Echo Lake: 135, 265
Elephant Trees: 808
Freeman Creek Trail: 614
Fresno Dome: 512
Frog Lake: 271-272
Frypan Meadow: 538
Gaviota Overlook: 646
George Lake: 516-517
Ghost Mountain Trail: 806-807
Giant Loop: 361-362
Green Creek Trail: 425
Green Lake: 425, 534-535
Guy Fleming Loop Trail: 777-778
Headlands Loop: 207
High Sierra Trail: 554-556
Hites Cove: 448
Indian Pools: 517-518
Johnstone Trail: 288-289
Kearsage Pass: 548-549

Kelsey Creek Trail: 48-49
Kelso dunes: 691-692
La Jolla Valley Loop: 706
Lakeview Trail: 507
Lewis Creek: 511
Lily Lake: 73-74
Lookout Point: 426-427
Los Peñasquitos Canyon: 788-789
Lupine Loop: 490
Lyons Creek Trail: 260-261
Manzanita and Azalea Loop: 522
Marble Falls: 550-551
Marble Mountain Rim: 47-48
Meadow Trail: 709-710
Mesa Loop: 490
Mill Ox Loop: 385
Mine Hill Trail: 396-397
Mississippi Lake Trail: 400-401
Molera State Park Loop: 492
Montaña de Oro State Park: 582
Muddy Hollow Loop: 291-292
Muir Grove: 547-548
North Fork Kern River Trail: 619-620
North Fork of Big Pine Canyon: 536
Paradise Creek Trail: 552-553
Path of the Padres: 500-501
Pauley Creek Trail: 191
Pfeiffer Falls and Valley View Loop: 492
Rancheria Falls: 427, 517
Rattlesnake Canyon: 656-657
Rim Loop Trail: 77
Round Valley Trail: 756
Santa Paula Canyon: 667
Seven Falls: 655-656
Signal Peak Loop Trail: 701-702
Skyline-to-Sea Trail: 387, 390-391
Soberanes Canyon Loop: 488-489
Solstice Road: 711-712
Stevens Trail: 236
Sugarloaf Ridge State Park: 218
Summit Valley Trail: 33-34
Sunset Trail: 320-321, 520-521, 792
Timber Gap Trail: 604-605
Tokopah Falls: 560
Twin Lakes: 135, 261-262, 466, 516-517, 560-561
Waddell Creek Trail: 394-395
Waterfall Loop: 490
Wawona Meadow Loop: 455-456
White Chief Mine Trail: 604
Winnemucca Lake: 269-270

WILDLIFE VIEWING

Afton Canyon: 687
Año Nuevo Trail: 394
Baylands Trail: 342-343, 367
Buck Lake Trail: 42
Canyon Trail: 380, 495, 767
Captain Jack's Stronghold: 65
Chapman Creek Trail: 195
Charleston Slough: 376
Coit Lake: 399-400, 401
Cottonwood Spring Oasis: 773
Crystal Springs Trail: 337, 692
Deer Creek Trail: 176, 185-186
Desert Tortoise Discovery Loop: 673-674
Donner Falls: 361
Dumbarton Pier: 368-369
East Bay Skyline National Trail: 352, 359, 370-372
Empire Landing Road Trail: 717-718
Graham Pinery: 176
Groundhog Meadow: 605
Hastain Trail: 715
Hotel Trail: 384
Janes Reservoir: 73
Marble Mountain Rim: 47-48
Matterhorn Canyon: 460
McClures Beach Trail: 286-287
McClure Trail: 173

Mount Wittenberg Loop: 294
Muddy Hollow Loop: 291-292
Partington Point Trail: 495-496
Pauley Creek Trail: 191
Pillar Point: 337-338
Piñon Ridge Nature Trail: 732-733
Point Bennett: 695-696
Redwood Creek Trail: 36-37
Satwiwa Loop Trail and Waterfall: 705-706
Sea Lion Point Trail: 487
Soberanes Point Trail: 489-490
South Bay Nature Trail: 343
South Lake Trailhead: 208
Spirit Lake Trail: 50-51
Summit Lake Loop: 134-135
Sunnyvale Baylands: 377
Tehama Wildlife Area: 173
Timber Mountain: 69-70, 735
Tokopah Falls: 560
Tomales Point Trail: 285-286
Tule Elk State Reserve: 593
Unal Trail: 623
Waddell Creek Trail: 394-395
Weir and Lower Doane Valley Loop: 784-785
White Deer Trail: 483-484
Wildwood Park Loop: 710

White Deer Trail: 483-484
White Dome: 621
Whitemore Gulch Trail: 338
White Mountain: 437
White Mountain Peak Trail: 475-476
White Mountains: 531, 561, 635
White Rock Lake: 240
Whitney Butte: 65-66
Whitney Butte Trail: 65-66
Whitney Falls/Bolam Creek Trailhead: 105-106
Whitney Portal: 564-565
Whitney Portal National Recreation Trail: 561-562
Whitney Range: 621
Whittemore Gulch: 339
Wildcat Camp: 292-293
Wildcat Canyon: 297
Wildcat Canyon Regional Park: 348, 372
Wildcat Creek Trail: 349
Wildcat Lake: 293
Wildcat Peak: 352
Wilderness Falls: 44

Wilder Ranch Picnic Area: 668
Wilder Ridge and Zane Grey Trails: 481-482
Wildlife Dune Area: 27-28
Wild Plum Loop/Haypress Creek: 194-195
Wildrose Peak Trail: 634-635
Wildwood Park Loop: 710
William Heise County Park: 790
Williams Grove Trail: 83
Williams Gulch: 406
Willow Creek: 197, 513-514
Willow Creek Overlook: 708
Willow Crest: 401
Willow Springs Road: 670
Willow Trail: 767
Will Rogers State Historic Park: 714
Wilmer Lake: 460
Wilsonia: 522
windsurfing: Davenport Beach 395
Windy Cliffs: 538
Windy Gap Trail: 733-734
Windy Hill Loop: 375-376
Windy Point Trailhead: 167

Winnemucca Lake: 269-270
Winnemucca Lake Loop: 270
Winona Mill Site: 773
Winton Marsh Trail: 499
Wishon Fork Tule River: 61, 610, 612
Wittenberg Trail: 585
Wolf Creek Gap: 461
Wolf Creek Meadows: 278
Wolf Creek Trail: 277-278
Wolf Ridge: 316
Wolverton's Rock: 560
Wolverton Trailhead: 557, 559
Wonderland of Rocks: 769, 770
Wood Canyon Trail: 707
Woodchuck Basin to Wheeler Lake: 418
Woodlands Loop Trail: 153
Woodland Trail: 751
Woods Lake: 269-270
Woods Trail: 348
world's tallest tree: 37
Wotan's Throne: 564
Wrights Lakes: 260
Wrights Valley Trail: 165-166
Wunderlich Park: 340-341

YZ
Yaqui Well: 806
Yellow Bluff: 319

Yellow Bluff Trail: 319
Yokut Indians: 500
Yolla Bolly Wilderness: 163-164
Yosemite Falls: 453
Yosemite Falls Trail: 431
Yosemite Lodge: 454
Yosemite National Park: 425, 427, 428, 429,
    442
Yosemite Point: 443
Yosemite Valley: 363, 431, 432, 443, 448, 454,
    459-460
Yost Creek/Fern Lake Trailhead: 469
Yost Lake Trail: 469
Yost Meadows Trail: 469
Young Lakes Loop: 437-438
Youngs Valley Trail: 43
Yuba River: 196, 240
Yuba River Canyon: 228
Yucca Point: 537-538
Yucca Valley: 767
Yuma clapper rail: Salton Sea National
    Wildlife Refuge 813
Yurok Loop: 34
Zabriskie Point: 641
Zane Grey Trail: 481-482
Zuma Beach: 709
Zumwalt Meadow Loop: 541

ABOUT THE AUTHORS

Tom Stienstra has made it his life's work to explore the West—hiking, camping, fishing, and boating—searching for the best of the great outdoors and writing about it. Tom is married and lives with his family in Northern California.

For this book, he was responsible for the San Francisco Bay Area and chapters A to E, except D4 and E4, and for the entire length of the Pacific Crest Trail. To accomplish this, he has hiked over 20,000 miles.

Tom Stienstra is the outdoors writer for the *San Francisco Chronicle*, which distributes his column on the New York Times News Service, and associate editor for *Western Outdoor News*. He has twice been named National Outdoor Writer of the Year (newspaper division) by the Outdoor Writers Association of America, and four times named California Outdoor Writer of the Year. You can visit Tom's website at www.TomStienstra.com. His books are the best-selling guidebooks in America:

California Camping
Calfornia Hiking (with Ann Marie Brown)
California Wildlife, The Practical Guide
California Fishing
Pacific Northwest Camping
California Recreational Lakes & Rivers
Tom Stienstra's Outdoor Getaway Guide
Easy Camping in Northern California
Epic Trips of the West: Tom Stienstra's 10 Best
California Boating and Water Sports
Sunshine Jobs: Career Opportunities Working Outdoors

Author of eight outdoor guidebooks with Avalon Travel Publishing, **Ann Marie Brown** is a hiker extraordinaire. Each year she hikes more than 1,500 miles, exclusively on California trails. She was raised in Southern California and attended Pomona College, at the foot of the San Gabriel Mountains. She holds a master's degree in journalism from Stanford University, and teaches courses in

kinesiology at San Francisco State University. For this book she was responsible for Southern California, Central California, and chapters D4 and E4. Ann Marie Brown's outdoor guidebooks with Avalon Travel Publishing include

California Waterfalls
Day-Hiking California's National Parks
Easy Hiking in Northern California
Easy Hiking in Southern California
Easy Biking in Northern California
Easy Camping in Southern California
101 Great Hikes of the San Francisco Bay Area

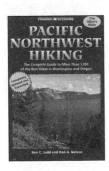

FOR TRAVELERS WITH SPECIAL INTERESTS

GUIDES

The 100 Best Small Art Towns in America • Asia in New York City
The Big Book of Adventure Travel • Cities to Go
Cross-Country Ski Vacations • Gene Kilgore's Ranch Vacations
Great American Motorcycle Tours • Healing Centers and Retreats
Indian America • Into the Heart of Jerusalem
The People's Guide to Mexico • The Practical Nomad
Saddle Up! • Staying Healthy in Asia, Africa, and Latin America
Steppin' Out • Travel Unlimited • Understanding Europeans
Watch It Made in the U.S.A. • The Way of the Traveler
Work Worldwide • The World Awaits
The Top Retirement Havens • Yoga Vacations

SERIES

Adventures in Nature
The Dog Lover's Companion
Kidding Around
Live Well

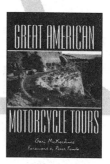

MOON HANDBOOKS

provide comprehensive coverage of a region's arts, history, land, people, and social issues in addition to detailed practical listings for accommodations, food, outdoor recreation, and entertainment. Moon Handbooks allow complete immersion in a region's culture—ideal for travelers who want to combine sightseeing with insight for an extraordinary travel experience.

USA

Alaska-Yukon • Arizona • Big Island of Hawaii • Boston
Coastal California • Colorado • Connecticut • Georgia
Grand Canyon • Hawaii • Honolulu-Waikiki • Idaho • Kauai
Los Angeles • Maine • Massachusetts • Maui • Michigan
Montana • Nevada • New Hampshire • New Mexico
New York City • New York State • North Carolina
Northern California • Ohio • Oregon • Pennsylvania
San Francisco • Santa Fe-Taos • Silicon Valley
South Carolina • Southern California • Tahoe • Tennessee
Texas • Utah • Virginia • Washington • Wisconsin
Wyoming • Yellowstone-Grand Teton

INTERNATIONAL

Alberta and the Northwest Territories • Archaeological Mexico
Atlantic Canada • Australia • Baja • Bangkok • Bali • Belize
British Columbia • Cabo • Canadian Rockies • Cancún
Caribbean Vacations • Colonial Mexico • Costa Rica • Cuba
Dominican Republic • Ecuador • Fiji • Havana • Honduras
Hong Kong • Indonesia • Jamaica • Mexico City • Mexico
Micronesia • The Moon • Nepal • New Zealand • Northern Mexico
Oaxaca • Pacific Mexico • Pakistan • Philippines • Puerto Vallarta
Singapore • South Korea • South Pacific • Southeast Asia • Tahiti
Thailand • Tonga-Samoa • Vancouver • Vietnam, Cambodia and Laos
Virgin Islands • Yucatán Peninsula

www.moon.com

www.travelmatters.com

User-friendly, informative, and fun: Because travel *matters*.

Visit our newly launched web site and explore the variety of titles and travel information available online, featuring an interactive *Road Trip USA* exhibit.

also check out:

www.ricksteves.com

The Rick Steves web site is bursting with information to boost your travel I.Q. and liven up your European adventure.

www.foghorn.com

Visit the Foghorn Outdoors web site for more information on the premier source of U.S. outdoor recreation guides.

www.moon.com

The Moon Handbooks web site offers interesting information and practical advice that ensure an extraordinary travel experience.

U.S.~METRIC CONVERSION

1 inch = 2.54 centimeters (cm)
1 foot = .3048 meters (m)
1 yard = 0.914 meters
1 mile = 1.6093 kilometers (km)
1 km = .6214 miles
1 fathom = 1.8288 m
1 chain = 20.1168 m
1 furlong = 201.168 m
1 acre = .4047 hectares
1 sq km = 100 hectares
1 sq mile = 2.59 square km
1 ounce = 28.35 grams
1 pound = .4536 kilograms
1 short ton = .90718 metric ton
1 short ton = 2000 pounds
1 long ton = 1.016 metric tons
1 long ton = 2240 pounds
1 metric ton = 1000 kilograms
1 quart = .94635 liters
1 US gallon = 3.7854 liters
1 Imperial gallon = 4.5459 liters
1 nautical mile = 1.852 km

To compute celsius temperatures, subtract 32 from Fahrenheit and divide by 1.8. To go the other way, multiply celsius by 1.8 and add 32.

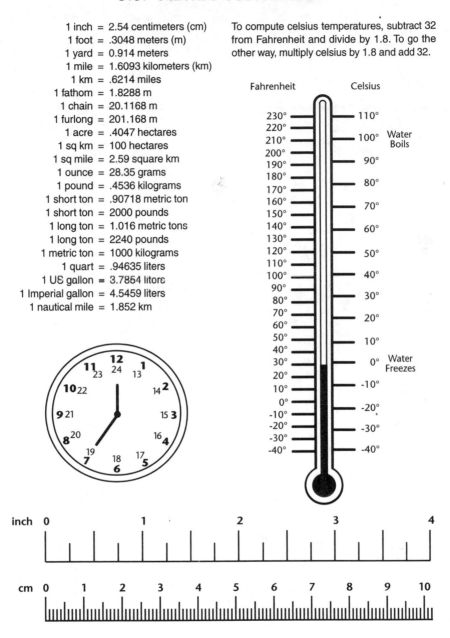

CALIFORNIA INDEX MAP

NORTHERN CALIFORNIA

CENTRAL CALIFORNIA

SOUTHERN CALIFORNIA

Crescent City
Yreka
Newell
Mount Shasta
Alturas
Eureka
Redding
Red Bluff
Susanville
Fort Bragg
Chico
Point Arena
Cloverdale
Yuba City
Grass Valley
SACRAMENTO
Auburn
Santa Rosa
South Lake Tahoe
Placerville
SAN FRANCISCO
Oakland
Stockton
Sonora
Mantec
Lee Vining
Yosemite
SAN JOSE
Mammoth Lakes
Santa Cruz
Merced
Bishop
Monterey
Salinas
Big Sur
Fresno
Visalia
Lone Pine
Furnace Creek Ranch
San Simeon
Kettleman City
Death Valley Junction
San Luis Obispo
BAKERSFIELD
Santa Maria
Wheeler Ridge
Mojave
Barstow
Baker
SANTA BARBARA
Ventura
Palmdale
Needles
San Bernardino
LOS ANGELES
Santa Ana
Palm Springs
Long Beach
Oceanside
Blythe
Escondido
Salton City
SAN DIEGO
El Centro
Yuma

MAPS

NORTHERN CALIFORNIA

MAP A0 26
MAP A1 40
MAP A2 58
MAP A3 64
MAP A4 72
MAP B0 76
MAP B1 86
MAP B2 102
MAP B3 126
MAP B4 142
MAP C0 150
MAP C1 162
MAP C2 172
MAP C3 180
MAP C4 202
MAP D0 206
MAP D1 214
MAP D2 222
MAP D3 226
MAP D4 242
MAP E1-Marin 284
MAP E1-San Francisco 324
MAP E1-East Bay 346
MAP E1-South Bay 374
MAP E2 404
MAP E3 410
MAP E4 414
MAP E5 464

CENTRAL CALIFORNIA

MAP F1 478
MAP F2 498
MAP F3 506
MAP F4 510
MAP F5 526
MAP F6 568
MAP G1 574
MAP G2 578
MAP G3 588
MAP G4 592
MAP G5 596
MAP G6 632
MAP G7 638
MAP H2 644
MAP H3 650
MAP H4 662
MAP H5 672
MAP H6 682
MAP H7 686
MAP H8 690

SOUTHERN CALIFORNIA

MAP I2 694
MAP I3 698
MAP I4 704
MAP I5 720
MAP I6 746
MAP I7 766
MAP J5 776
MAP J6 782
MAP J7 804
MAP J8 812

Will you have enough stories to tell your grandchildren?

Yahoo! Travel

Do You Yahoo!?